ILLUSTRATED DICTIONARY OF

TROPICAL FISHES

Hans Frey

Distributed in the U.S. by T.F.H. Publications, Inc., 211 West Sylvania Avenue, P.O. Box 427, Neptune, N.J. 07753; in England by T.F.H. (Gt. Britain) Ltd., 13 Nutley Lane, Reigate, Surrey; in Canada to the book store and library trade by Beaverbooks, 953 Dillingham Road, Pickering, Ontario L1W 1Z7; in Canada to the pet trade by Rolf C. Hagen Ltd., 3225 Sartelon Street, Montreal 382, Quebec; in Southeast Asia by Y.W. Ong, 9 Lorong 36 Geylang, Singapore 14; in Australia and the South Pacific by Pet Imports Pty. Ltd., P.O. Box 149, Brookvale 2100, N.S.W., Australia; in South Africa by Valiant Publishers (Pty.) Ltd., P.O. Box 78236, Sandton City, 2146, South Africa; Published by T.F.H. Publications, Inc., Ltd., The British Crown Colony of Hong Kong.

FOREWORD BY THE PUBLISHER

In 1958 and 1959 over 18,000 copies of "Das Aquarium von A bis Z" were sold in the Communist part of Germany. So remarkable was this sales report, that we immediately negotiated through 'irregular' channels for a copy to see for ourselves what kind of fish book could possibly win such unanimous acceptance. The book was a dictionary of aquarium terms . . . the title literally translated means "The Aquarium from A to Z." The original German edition had few photos, mostly old line drawings. All of the photos that now make up the "Illustrated Dictionary of Tropical Fish" were added after translation.

The book itself has a very international flavor. It was written by Hans Frey, editor of the East German aquarium and terrarium magazine. The translation was done by Dr. A. Viggo W. Schultz, Professor of Languages in Porto Alegre, Brazil, brother of the world famous Harald Schultz, tropical fish writer, photographer and explorer. Many of the photos were taken by G. J. M. Timmerman in Amsterdam, Holland, as well as by myself in Jersey City and in Brazil, Africa and Malaya.

For years American and British aquarists have envied the meticulous works published in the German language on their favorite subject . . . tropical fish. It has long been my personal ambition to take the best of these foreign books, translate it into English, illustrate it properly, print it on the best paper available, and offer it to English-reading hobbyists everywhere. When Mr. Frey, the author, saw the first "dummy" copy of this book, tears came to his eyes and he muttered . . . "It is surely a dream come true."

I hope that the more than a thousand illustrations of fishes, plants and snails, helps you to identify many rare fishes, as well as to help you understand terms that appear in magazines and other books. The translation job was immense and took two full years of devoted effort. The author and the translator join me in dedicating this book to

HARALD SCHULTZ

for all he has done for the hobby.

HERBERT R. AXELROD, PH.D.

April 10, 1961

NOTE TO THE READER

This book has been literally translated from the German and rephrased only as far as it might lead to a misunderstanding by the reader. The author has freely utilized abbreviations and to the novice aquarist some of these might be misleading. SD appears frequently and means "sex differences." The letters A, D, V, P usually refer to the anal, dorsal, ventral and pelvic fins respectively. Other abbreviations are more obvious.

The publisher takes quite opposite views on certain taxonomic decisions and the nomenclature of most of the fishes is that of the original author. It is the objective of the publisher to present as complete and acceptable a book as possible without destroying the style which has made this book so popular in the original German language.

A.: Abbreviation for the anal fin.
Aaron's Rod Plants—see ARACEA
abbreviata: shortened, abbreviated.
— *Polycentropsis*
abbreviations: In scientific literature certain terms and Latin names are often not written out, but abbreviated. These abbreviations follow definite rules. Certain fins and bones are internationally identified by letters. For instance, the dorsal fin is identified D. There is no period placed after D, so that it will not be mistaken for the abbreviation of a generic name of a fish or plant. Scientific names may also be abbreviated to one letter for the generic name, for instance the name *Aphyosemion* may be referred to as *A*. The name *Aphyosemion bivittatum bivittatum* could thus be abbreviated *A.b. bivittatum*, with the first two names abbreviated and the third name written out. It would also be possible to write out the first name and the third name, abbreviating only the second. This method might be used where similarly abbreviated names could be confused.
abdomen: The belly.

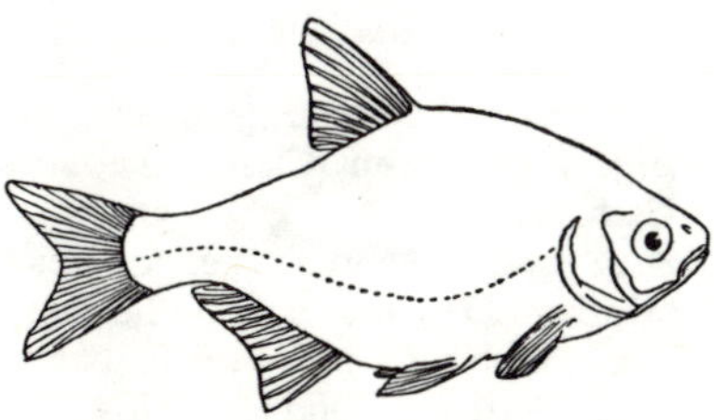

Abramis - Type of the genus

Abramis: Generic name derived from the French, describing the Bream. A Carp-like fish which occurs in more or less large schools, belonging to the family of Carp-like fishes, or *Cyprinidae*.
FORM: Elongated to high-backed, greatly compressed laterally, with a keeled belly. The mouth is turned downward, with no barbels.
COLOR: Very shiny scales, called "Whitefish" in certain regions.
RANGE: Standing or slowly flowing waters of Europe and northern Asia, usually near the shore or near the bottom.
CARE: The numerous species are only possible to keep in the home aquarium while very young, because of their size. May be kept as described under the keyword *Cyprinodontidae*.

Abramites microcephalus

Abramites: Similar to *Abramis* (Bream-like); a South American Characin-like fish of the family of Headstanders or *Anostomidae*. Small fishes which usually travel in small schools, which may be recognized by their compressed bodies, wavy markings on the back and a tiny, pointed head. There is an adipose fin. *Abramites* is a so-called "Headstander" which prefers to stay near the bottom, where it searches for food. Its method of reproduction is unknown.

— microcephalus (Norman): Marbled Headstander, Norman's Headstander.
BODY SHAPE: As given in the description of the genus. D 10 A 13. Length up to 2¾ inches.
COLORS: On a yellowish to reddish brown background there are some irregular wavy bands and spots. Very nicely colored.
RANGE: Amazon region and the Guianas.

CARE AND BREEDING: They prefer aquaria with well-established plants and a number of hiding-places, also a good amount of open swimming space, and a layer of mulm on the bottom. An omnivorous eater, especially fond of worms, red larvae and detritus, but also require a certain amount of vegetable substances in their diet. Breeding is unknown.

Acanthocephalus, enlarged

Acanthocephala: With spines on the head.

Class of the genus of tube-worms or *Nemathelminthes*. The Scratchers, which give rise to the Scratcher Diseases, live in the intestines of fishes, where they attach themselves by means of a snout which is ringed with hooks. Nourishment is taken through the skin, and robbed from the intestine. When they propagate, there is a change of hosts. In the aquarium they are often introduced with *Gammarus*, on which they appear as red streaks or spots on the upper side of the back. Most of all *Gammarus* from swampy waters seem to harbor these worms. The genera *Pomphorhynchus* and *Polymorphus* are usually found in aquarium fishes.

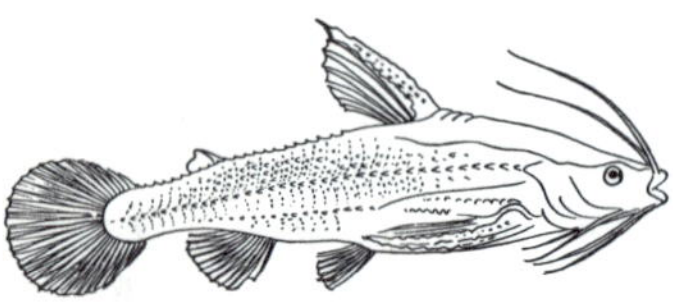

Acanthodoras, type of the genus

Acanthodoras: With lance and thorns.

A popular genus of Catfishes of the group of Spiny Catfishes or *Doradidae*. These are very short and somewhat plump fishes, whose bodies as well as the fins are covered with many spines. The powerful spines of the pectoral fins can cause painful and slowly healing wounds if the fish is handled carelessly. There is an adipose fin. The sides are armored with bony plates which begin about the start of the dorsal fin. The flatly compressed head has a wide mouth opening. Gills are armed with many tiny bristly teeth. There are 3 pairs of barbels.

During the day they bury themselves in the sand. They are shy of sunlight and do not become active until twilight and at night. The only thing we know about their breeding is that some species exercise care of the young and build a nest.

Acanthodoras spinosissimus

— spinosissimus Eigenmann & Eigenmann: Spiny Catfish, Talking Catfish.

BODY SHAPE: As in the general description. D I/5, A I/11. The pectoral fins have a powerful first ray. The flattened body attains its greatest breadth at the start of the pectoral fins. Attains a length of about 6 inches.

COLOR: Dark brown, marbled, with whitish patches and bands. There are no known outward sex differences.

RANGE: Middle Amazon region.

CARE: They like an aquarium which is not too brightly lighted, and affords opportunities for hiding. A soft bottom is preferable. Live foods which are not too big should be given, and it is picked up off the bottom. Easily kept; nothing is known about their breeding.

Acanthophthalmus: Thorn-Eye. A genus of Loaches or *Cobitidae*. These small, elongated fishes possess a cylindrical body which is covered with tiny scales. The eyes are small and are covered with a transparent skin, which protects this bottom-dwelling fish from injury. Under the eyes is an erectible spine.

Their life habits resemble those of the European Loaches. The *A.* species like clean, clear and not too fresh water, with a soft bottom which has a layer of mulm, best duplicated in the aquarium by a layer of boiled peat-moss. Hiding-places should also be provided. Avoid the use of sharp sand, because they like to dig and could injure themselves. Water which is rich in infusoria or foul is not tolerated. As they like darkness, they do not become active until dusk and then swim up and down the glass with snake-like motions. Food can consist of small live foods which stay near the bottom, and also any scraps of dried food which are left behind by the other fish. They are also fond of lying jammed among the plants, where their markings show very plainly. Almost all importations include a few individuals which are uniformly light or dark. Colors vary greatly in the different species. The often used names of many of the known species are in many cases incorrect, according to Fraser-Brunner. It is, however, possible that some species and subspecies are one and the same species and develop different color patterns over their wide range.

None of the species has been successfully bred. According to Vogt, they spawn with bowed

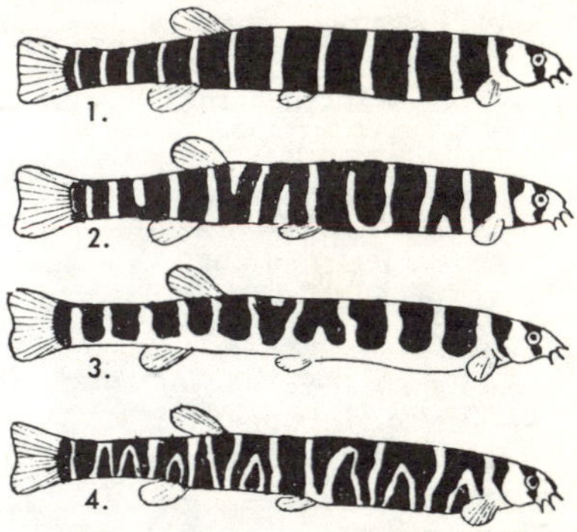

Acanthophthalmus species: 1. A. kuhlii kuhlii, 2. A. kuhlii sumatranus, 3. A. semicinctus, 4. A. shelfordi.

bodies pressed tightly together and whirling around with ever rising speed. Eggs which were reddish-brown were produced, but never brought to hatch. Temperature varied from 75° to 85° F. According to Dr. Axelrod, these fish build a bubble-nest.

— kuhlii kuhlii Cuvier & Valenciennes: The Coolie Loach.

BODY SHAPE: As described for the genus. The slightly developed fins show D9 and A6-8. Head is small and rounded, and the undershot mouth is surrounded by 3 pairs of barbels. Gill-slits are very short.

COLOR: On a light background there are regular, brownish-black bands, which extend to the belly.

RANGE: Thailand and some parts of India.

— kuhlii sumatranus Fraser-Brunner:

BODY SHAPE: Same as given for *A. kuhlii kuhlii.*

COLOR: This subspecies differs from the main species by having irregular markings, which like those of *A. k. kuhlii* reach to the belly, but they are irregular and may be broken up.

RANGE: Indonesia, especially in

small swampy waters of the island of Sumatra.

— **semicinctus** Fraser-Brunner: Half-Banded Loach.

Very similar to the preceding species, also in care. Difference is in the vertical markings, which only extend halfway down the sides. Length to 4 inches.

RANGE: Malaya and Sumatra.

— **shelfordi** Popda:

BODY SHAPE: Like the others. D6, A5.

COLORS: This species has vertical markings coming down from the back, and others coming up from the belly.

RANGE: Borneo.

CARE AND BREEDING: As described for the genus.

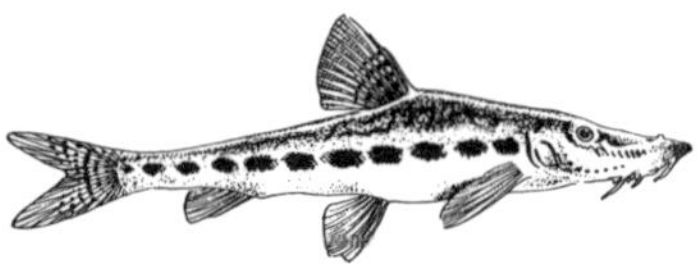

Acanthopsis choirorhynchus

Underside of the mouth

Acanthopsis: Thorn Eye.

Genus of Loaches or *Cobitidae*. Living habits and care are the same as those described for *Acanthophthalmus*.

— **choirorhynchus:** Bleeker.

BODY SHAPE: Similar to *Acanthophthalmus*. Scales are better developed; D 12-13, A 7-9. The skin-covered eyes lie high on the elongated head. The spines under the eyes are erectible and double-pointed. The small, underslung mouth has a fringed underlip and 3 pairs of barbels, and the nasal openings are extended. Scales are very small. Length to 7 inches.

COLOR: On a brownish background there are rows of dark-brown spots, which extend across the back.

RANGE: Southeastern Asia, occurring only in fresh water.

CARE: see NOEMACHEILUS.

Acara: *Aequidens*.

— **Blue:** *Aequidens pulcher*.

— **True:** *Aequidens thayeri*.

Acari: Mites; *Chelicerata*.

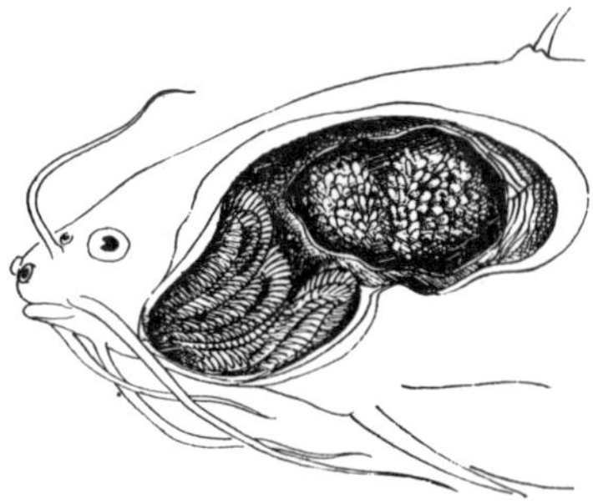

Accessory breathing organs of a Catfish

accessory breathing: An additional method of breathing besides the intake of oxygen through the gills, which in some cases makes the gills dispensable. As substitute organs there is usually either a sac through the walls of which a great deal of blood flows, or sac-like folds in addition to the gills or the intestines, or special, lung-like bags. Accessory breathing has in many cases been developed in such fishes that inhabit waters which are poor in oxygen content or have a muddy bottom (see BREATHING). Fishes which possess accessory breathing organs must as a rule make use of their gills if the oxygen content of the water is rich enough. BADER makes reference that his many species of armored Catfishes come up for air no matter what the oxygen content of the water is. More important than the oxygen content of the water is the activity of the fish. At times of excitement many more trips for air are made than under normal conditions. Catfishes which were shipped in a thermos flask which was filled with water to the top suffocated, while other fishes under similar conditions survived without any trouble.

acclimation: see ADAPTATION.

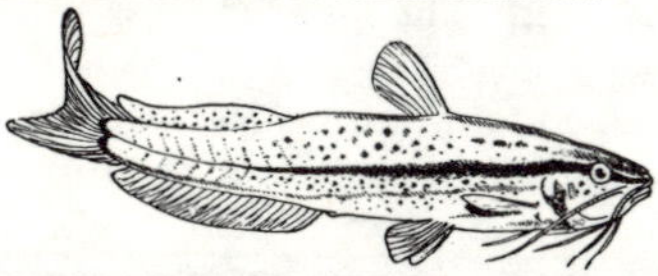

Acentronichthys leptos

Acentronichthys: Fish without spines.

A South American Catfish genus of the family *Pimelodidae*, with an elongated and supple body, relatively long and narrow head with small eyes, wide, undershot mouth with 3 pairs of barbels. The tiny teeth are placed in closely-spaced rows. The skin is totally naked. One species is sometimes imported: *A. leptos*.

Acerina: Pointed.

Genus of true Perches or *Percidae*, which occur throughout Northern and Central Europe, Siberia and the Danube region. They are small and medium-sized fishes with a cone-shaped head and large, highly-placed eyes and spiny gill-plates. The double dorsal fin is joined at the point between the spiny and soft rays.

Acerina cernua

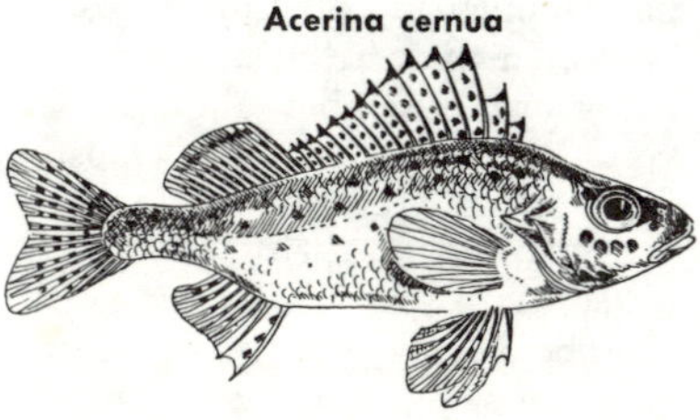

— cernua Linné:

BODY FORM: As described for the genus. D XII-XIV/11-14; A II/5-6. The scales are moderately large. Length to 6 inches.

COLOR: Dirty green with dark spots, light underneath.

RANGE: This species is found mostly in the mouths of streams, sometimes entering brackish water.

CARE: This is a predatory species, which likes to stay near the bottom. Here it feeds on all sorts of bottom life, and has made itself unpopular among fishermen by stealing eggs of game species. The eggs are laid in clumps and strings on rocky bottoms and among plants, and there is no parental care. In the aquarium this species is quite easy to keep, if given a good amount of space and clear, oxygen-rich but not too fresh water. The best plants are the oxygenators, preferably *Anacharis*, *Myriophyllum* or Willowmoss. Additional oxygenation is also required. The bottom may be covered with pebbles and rocks.

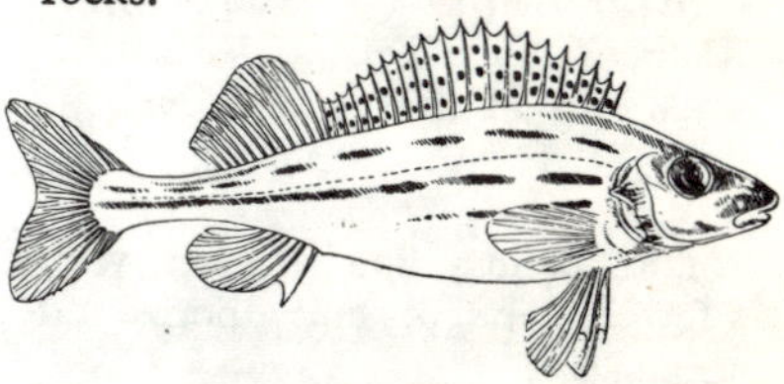

Acerina schraetzer

— schraetzer Linné:

BODY FORM: A very elongated fish with an almost spindle-shaped body. D XVII-XIX/12-13; A II/6-7. The scales are relatively small, and the mouth is partly underslung. Length to 10 inches.

COLOR: Lemon yellow with black, partly broken horizontal stripes.

RANGE: In the Danube region, one of the few Danube Perches.

CARE: A predatory species which

prefers a sandy or pebbly bottom. Sometimes kept in the aquarium, but somewhat sensitive and not recommended for any but experienced aquarists.

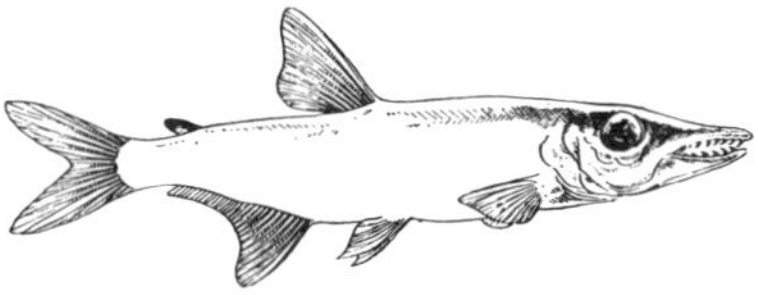

Acestrorhynchus - type of the genus

Acestrorhynchus: Pointed snout, referring to the pike-like shape of the snout.

A genus of South American predatory fishes of the family *Characidae*. These are definite predators, with an elongated, very muscular body which is only slightly compressed. The belly is rounded, and the short dorsal and large anal fins are set well back. The adipose fin is small, and there is a lateral line. Body and head are covered with tiny scales. The wide mouth has many more or less small, sometimes hooked teeth.

— microlepis (Schomburgk): Robber or Pike Tetra.

FORM: As in the general description. D 11; A 28-33, length to 30 cm.

COLOR: Solid yellowish green with a few darker spots and a horizontal stripe.

RANGE: Eastern tropical South America from British Guiana in the north to Rio de Janeiro in the south. Plentiful in the entire area, traveling in large schools while young, singly when older.

CARE: The imported specimens proved to be, perhaps because of damage to the intestinal tract, not very adaptable to keeping. This species accepts only living foods, preferably fish. Keeping them requires an aquarium which is large enough for their large size and does not have too high a temperature; best kept at 76°. Not as yet bred, spawning habits unknown.

acicularis: Needle-shaped (leaves). — *Heleocharis*.

acidity: pH, hydrogen ion concentration.

Acilius: Name of a Roman family. Genus of diving beetles or *Dytiscidae*. Body egg-shaped and flattened. The sucking pads of the males have larger sucking-discs at the bottom. Hind feet with two irregular claws, one of them movable. The very plentiful, free-swimming larvae have swimming bristles on both body segments, and two caudal threads at the end of the body.

— sulcatus Linne: Furrowed Swimmer.

Most common species of the genus. Length 15-16 mm. Belly black with yellow spots. Back with a yellow edge, flat in the male, furrowed in the female. Drop eggs into the water while swimming.

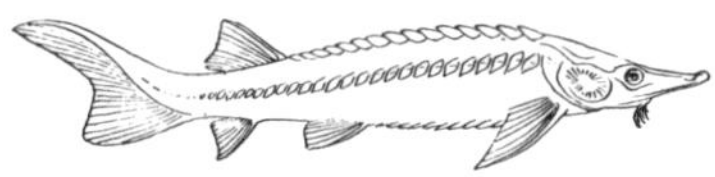

Acipenseridae - type of the Sturgeons

Acipenseridae: Sturgeons. Family of the order *Chondrostei*.

The Sturgeon-like fishes were very numerously represented in the middle geological ages. The skeleton is incompletely boned, and the skull cartilaginous. The back is almost spineless, and there are no completely developed backbones. In their inner structure the Sturgeons resemble the Sharks very closely. They are mostly fishes which are slender and elongated in form, their skin partly naked, and partly covered with rhomboid bony plates. The mouth is underslung, the gills turned back, and the mouth may be folded out, with four comb-like lined-up barbels, which are used in searching for food.

The Sturgeons are mostly inhabitants of the northern temperate zones, where they are found in large rivers and at times in the ocean. They are very interesting captives, which are hardly adaptable for the home aquarium, while they are excellent show specimens in larger public aquaria.

Acorus: With a sour flavor.
Genus of marsh plants of the reed family *Araceae*. Occurs in the temperate zone of East Asia, and one species (*A. calamus*) introduced into Europe, where it has long grown wild. Marsh plants, which are found on the flat banks of ponds and lakes, sometimes completely on land. The leaves which touch the ground are grasslike and sword-shaped and at the base are sheathed, and in places also wavy. Hardy, with a creeping root-stock, from which propagation is accomplished by splitting and sprouting. The tiny blossoms are massed on a node, on a short stem at the base of the leaves.

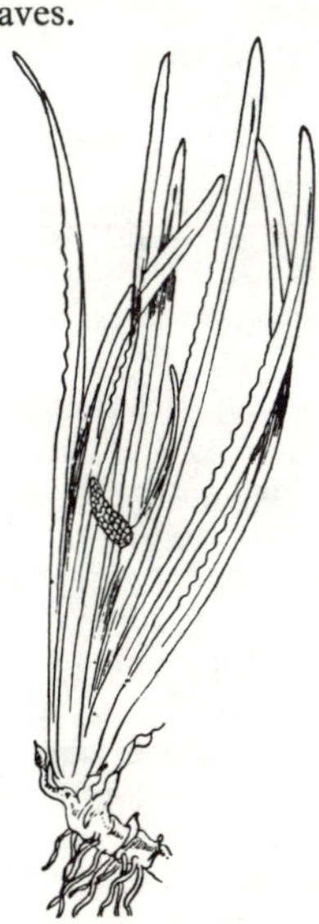

Acorus calamus

calamus Linne: German Ginger.
This species comes originally from East Asia, but has been introduced as a medicinal plant almost all over the world and has grown wild everywhere. It attains a height of 150 cm, is very hardy and has a root-stock up to 1¼ inches thick. The leaves are easily distinguishable from other similar plants by their wavy edge. The aromatic root is used for medicine and cosmetics.

A. calamus is not adaptable for the home aquarium, but is very good for open pools. Here it requires a very fertile bottom, which should be deep enough for the roots.

— gramineus Solander: Rush, Japanese Rush.
This delicate little species, which appears in several varieties, comes from East Asia, where it appears in calm waters in the temperate zone. Here it grows in swampy places, sometimes also in dry spots, but in the aquarium it can be grown completely submerged. The "species" offered in the trade, *A. japonicus*, *A. intermedius*, *A. pusillus*, are all varieties of this species, even a garden variety with pretty leaves. Most of them may reach a length of 50 cm, and the *pusillus* variety remains very much smaller. The hard, bright green to dark green leaves are narrow, grasslike and pointed. They are arranged fan-wise on the creeping root-stock.

The species, with all its varieties, is very hardy and easily kept, and can be kept in a cold as well as a moderately heated home aquarium. Naturally it is also suited to the swamp aquarium. For a bottom soil one uses unwashed sand, with a little clay added. These species do not root readily, and should be anchored at first with glass rods.

Acorus gramineus

Propagation is accomplished by breaking up of the root-stock. The plants grow very slowly, still more slowly if they are in too dark a location, even if their light requirements are not particularly high. The temperature should average 65 to 68°. It can also sink lower, but these plants are sometimes somewhat sensitive to higher temperatures. Water characteristics are not particularly important otherwise.

The plants are very decorative and their bristling fan-shaped leaves give an unusual note in aquarium decoration.

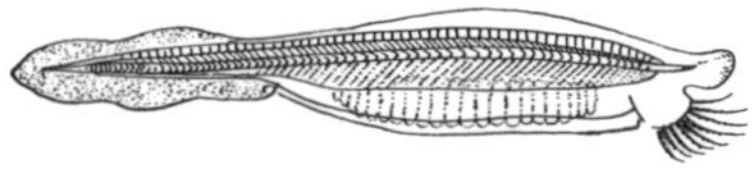

Acrania - type of the Lancetfishes

Acrania: Without a skull (Lancetfishes).
Fishlike ancestor of the true fishes, which can be considered the link between the tunicates and the vertebrates (see VERTEBRATA). They are identified by the presence of an unjointed spinal cord (see CHORDA DORSALIS), and the absence of a skull. The spine resembles a series of bubbles. The position of the heart is taken up by a pulsating horizontal tube, the front arm is developed into a receptacle for the gills. The sensory organs are very simple structures. There seems to be a balancing organ. The position of the eyes is taken by a mass of pigment-cells which would only be capable of receiving light and dark impressions through the skin. The after end carries a fin-like skin edging, and paired joint-masses are absent. The transparent Lancetfishes, which attain a length of almost 3 inches, live buried in the sand. Their nourishment is stirred up and into the oral opening by a circle of hairs, which surrounds the oral opening. There are several species known, of which *Brachiostoma lanceolatum* (*Amphioxus lanceolatus*) is the best-known. They are found principally in warm waters, but also in the North Sea. They are absent in eastern waters.

Acriflavine (Trypaflavin): see REMEDIES, HEALING BATHS.

activated charcoal: see FILTER, FILTRATION.

aculeatus: Spiny.
— *Gasterosteus.*

acuticeps: Pointed head.
— *Geophagus.*

acutidens: With pointed teeth.
— *Phenacogrammus.*

acutifolius: With pointed leaves.
— *Potamogeton.*

acutirostre: With a pointed snout.
— *Ctenopoma.*

adaptation, accommodation:
1. ACCLIMATIZATION: Individual adaptation of live things to changed conditions of life, especially to changes of climate. The aptitude to adapt is different, according to species. Even within the same species may be found individuals and strains with greater or lesser adaptability. Also in aquarium plants and fishes one often finds an adaptation to conditions which

often diverge strongly from the natural ones. The degree of adaptability makes care and breeding easier. The often nearly overwhelming difficulties with freshly imported tropical fishes may be based on the following facts:

(a) the respective species is closely specialized and hard to adapt, its natural conditions of life being unknown to the aquarist;

(b) by chance they happened to be unadaptable specimens of an otherwise adaptable species which have been imported.

Adaptation. Upper fish has become adapted to top-feeding, and the lower to bottom-feeding.

If the natural conditions of life become known, they can be copied, and thus even specialized species may be induced to reproduce (Neon Tetras, many of the egg-laying Tooth Carp, etc.). If the species is imported more frequently later on, and in greater numbers, among the many fish one will find specimens that are more adaptable and which will proceed to multiply in the aquarium. Furthermore it is often only the first breeding which is difficult, and later on breeding succeeds with greater frequency. This may be explained by the fact that there are single more adaptable individuals among the brood, which of course will reproduce preferentially and transmit their favorable degree of adaptability hereditarily. This probably was the case with *Pterophyllum*. It is difficult to decide how far a real adaptation to life in the aquarium becomes as a consequence of hereditary changes in body structure and functions among aquarium fishes. It will probably occur from time to time, but so far one can hardly speak of exact observations.

2. GENETIC: Historically one defines as adaptation in general any step of the accommodation of living things to changed conditions of life. The sum total of such steps is the genetic-historic development.

3. The adaptation to already existing but not completed resultants of development, according to which a living thing makes adjustments in body structure and functions to the demands posed by certain ambient world conditions. The degree of adaptation is often astonishing, such as e.g. the body structure of fishes as related to their dwelling place, the disposition of colors for the purpose of "camouflage", the development of certain parts of the body for the gathering of food, etc. Similar conditions do not necessarily call forth similar phenomena of adaptation, there is e.g. the survival in quick-flowing waters by means of the strongly developed muscles of the Trout, and by means of a sucking apparatus in Catfishes. On the other hand they may cause similar results even in species which are not related to each other (see CONVERGENCE). Converseley, adaptation is the cause of the demands on life of the organisms. Thus e.g. the Mud-Skipper (*Periophthalmus*) is adapted to living in the tidal zones of tropical coasts with their changing water level and salt content. For this reason it needs shallow water with a piece of dry land, an addition of sea water, and tropical warmth in air and water, even in captivity.

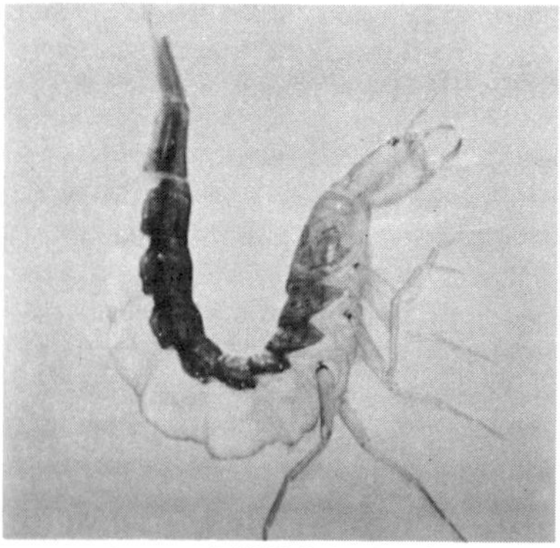

Larva of Whirligig Beetle

Underside of Dytiscus

Water Beetles attacking fish

Adephaga (Predatory Beetles): Suborder of the order of Beetles or *Coleoptera*, with numerous families, of which the Diving Beetles, *Dytiscidae*, and the Whirligigs, *Gyrinidae* would be of interest to the aquarist.

adhesive organs of alevins: Glands of more or less complex construction which may be located at greatly varying spots on the head, exuding a sticky secretion upon touching firm objects, which fastens the young fry while in a larval stage. In species which exert specialized care for their young, for instance in the mouths of the parents, or in nests, the adhesive organs may be absent. Instead of adhesive organs Bubble Nest Builders sometimes have oil containers which keep the alevins at the surface. A forcible displacement of the young fry from their adhering bases, for instance, by means of a water current or by too strong aeration, may harm them or cause them to die.

adloffi: After the man's name.
— *Cynolebias.*

adulteration of fauna: Falsifying the fauna that is native to a certain region by releasing species which so far did not live there. Due to the frequently harmful effects of such measures, adulteration of fauna is usually strictly forbidden.

Adventitious plant

adventitious plant parts: Roots, sprouts, buds, etc., which develop from the fully developed plant and not from vegetation points.

aeneus: Bronze.
— *Corydorus.*

Aequidens: With teeth of equal length.
Genus of the family of Cichlids

or *Cichlidae*, with a very high, laterally compressed body, large head and steep, in some cases knobby forehead line. The eyes are quite large. The vertical fins are slightly to strongly pointed or elongated in the males, but the caudal fin is rounded.

The genus is scattered all over South America; belongs to the most peaceful of the family, with the exception of the Dwarf Cichlids. Some species do not dig a great deal and do not disturb the plants. Care, spawning and breeding is the same as that for the other Cichlids (see CICHLIDAE).

— **curviceps** (Ahl): Spotted Cichlid.

FORM: As given in the general description, oval outline, forehead strongly arched. D XV/7, A III/7. Scales quite large. Length 3 inches, females somewhat smaller.

COLOR: The dark edged, bluish to whitish gleaming scales are on a greenish background. On the gill-plates and the pretty fins there are many highlights. Sex differences are sometimes slight, the dorsal and anal fins of the male are more pointed, and besides they also show a more lively color at spawning time.

RANGE: Amazon region, but not in Peru. In quiet, not too deep spots, and also in places where there is a slight current.

CARE AND BREEDING: As with most of the Cichlid species (see CICHLIDAE). The species is relatively peaceful and may be kept in the community aquarium, but it is not well to place them with lively fishes. They do not dig very much; plants are undisturbed, especially if there is plenty of room. It is important to provide sufficient retreats. An occasional change of about ⅓ of the water is recommended, as they are very apt to become diseased in old water. Temperature 74 to 76°.

The holes for fry are often dug at the base of plants, and it is possible that now and then a leaf could be bitten off. For breeding 82 to 86°

Aequidens latifrons

— **latifrons** (Steindachner): Blue-Spot Cichlid.

FORM: As given in the general description. Forehead very wide, with age somewhat bumped. D XIV/9, A III/8, scales large. Length about 6 inches, mature at half that size.

COLOR: Overall impression is bluish green, with wine-red rows of dots and gleaming streaks or dots on the sides, gill-covers and fins. Vertical fins are wine-red at the base. Sexual differences sometimes slight, dorsal fin of the male and the anal fin are drawn out longer, and besides the female has a different spawning coloration.

RANGE: From the Magdalena River to Panama in the north, in standing or slowly flowing waters, also in swamps or ponds.

CARE AND BREEDING: Similar to *A. curviceps*, somewhat less peaceful but not as active a digger. However there are individual differences to be found. Temperature 74 to 77°, for spawning 76 to 80°, lowest possible temperature 61°.

— **maronii** (Steindachner): Maroni Cichlid.

FORM: As described for the genus, but the body is particularly short and high, which impression is heightened by the powerfully developed fins. The forehead line is steep, the body is laterally very compressed. D XV/10-12, A III/9-11; scales are very large. Length in the aquarium up to 4 inches.

COLOR: Basic color yellowish to reddish, with dark blotches and stripes, of which a round dark spot stands out in the upper half of the body. Each scale has a dark spot. The species is not very colorful, but nevertheless is very attractive. Sex differences are only slight.

Aequidens maronii

RANGE: Guiana, in streams, slowly flowing brooks and still waters.

CARE: This is one of the most peaceful of all Cichlids, which digs very little and does not disturb plants. However, an occasional plant which is loose to begin with could be dislodged when they spawn. Exceptionally peaceful toward other fishes, even the smallest, if a large enough aquarium is given them.

BREEDING: As with all Cichlids, somewhat difficult to spawn. For unknown reason some pairs will not care for their broods, in spite of the fact that they spawn willingly. It is advisable with such pairs to raise the fry without parental care. Good parents however are very interesting and tend their young until they are 6 months old. Temperatures 74 to 76°, for breeding 79 to 82°, minimum temperature 68°.

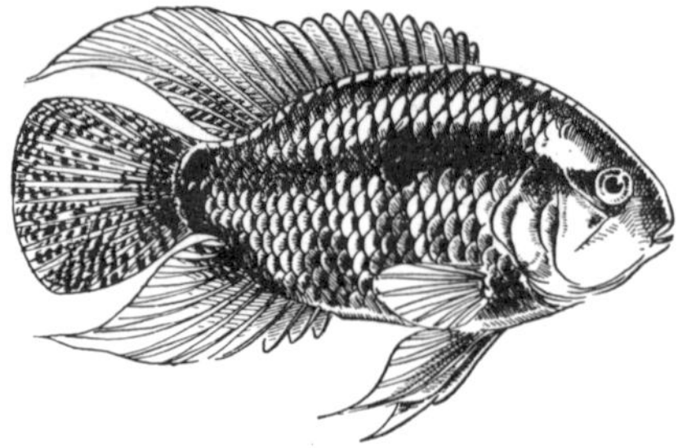

Aequidens portalegrensis

— portalegrensis (Hensel): Striped Cichlid.

FORM: As described for the genus. D XIV-XVI/9-11, A III/8-10. The scales are comparatively large.

COLOR: On a reddish-brown background with a bluish-green sheen and dark bands and patches. Fins greenish and marbled dark. In the middle of the body and at the caudal base there is a dark patch, with the latter surrounded by gleaming dots. The vertical fins with the exception of the caudal fin of the male are very pointed, and the colors are brighter. Length in the aquarium up to 6 inches.

RANGE: Brazil, to Rio Uruguay in the south, especially in still, calm places with slowly flowing or standing water.

CARE AND BREEDING: This species digs more than the others and is also not as peaceful. This is especially true of young but mature pairs. Plants should be placed in pots and covered with stones at the roots. Otherwise the species is not touchy, above all they do not require a great deal of heat. 62 to 68° is sufficient in the Winter, otherwise 72 to 75°. For breeding, 75 to 78°.

— tetramerus (Heckel): Green Shimmer Cichlid.

FORM: As described for the genus. This species resembles *A. portalegrensis* greatly. D XIII-XV/9-11, A III/8-10; large scales. Length in

CARE AND BREEDING: Younger specimens are relatively peaceful, but later they become progressively nasty. Temperatures 75 to 78°, for breeding 82 to 86°. They are not very prolific, but breed like the others.

— thayeri (Steindachner): True Acara.

FORM: Bodily structure very similar to *A. portalegrensis.* D XV/7, A III/7. Length in the aquarium about 4½ inches.

COLOR: Not very attractively colored. Dorsal and anal fins of the male are drawn out to threads.

RANGE: In calm and shallow pools of the flowing and still waters of the Amazon region.

Aequidens tetramerus

the aquarium to 4½ inches.

COLOR: Olive to brown ground color with black patches under the eyes, in the middle of the body and at the caudal base, the last being surrounded with a gold edge. Sides of the head greenish with glowing blue dots and streaks. Dorsal and anal fins in the males are somewhat elongated.

RANGE: Northern South America southward to the Parana region in the south, here especially in quiet, calm and sheltered places in flowing waters, also in forest brooks and overflowed swamps.

aeration: Technical aid which can make the care and breeding of fishes in aquaria much easier. Initially it should be pointed out

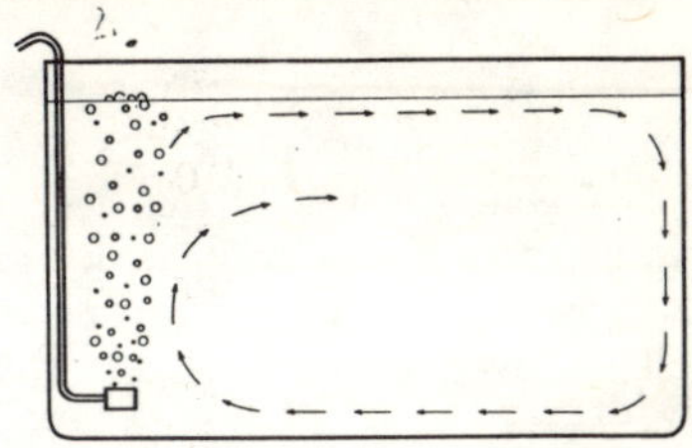

Circulation caused by flow of air

that a tank which is normally stocked with fishes and plants does not need special aeration, since in such aquaria generally the production of oxygen suffices to satisfy the needs of animals and plants. This, however, only happens if the aquarist really is moderate in all things, and if he knows how to adapt the population with the seasonal rhythm. In many cases, though, a trustworthy aeration proves really to be necessary, and even indispensable. Aquarists who believe they are able to do without it should still provide for it in their installations and keep an aerator in reserve for cases of need. Lack of oxygen as an exceptional condition may appear in many instances which even the most careful fancier cannot always avoid. It sets in as a permanent condition if the aquarium does not contain enough plants, if its location is too dark, not permitting the plants to effect the right amount of assimilation,

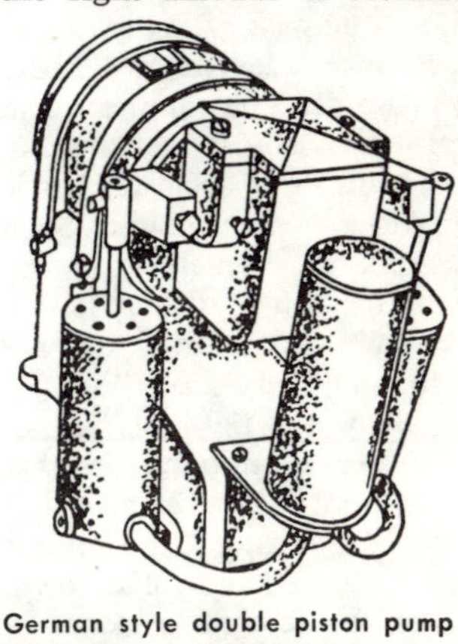

German style double piston pump

or if it is overstocked with fishes or understocked with plants. Breeding itself generally causes the need to keep more fishes in a tank than correspond to its real capacity, unless one wants to be content with rearing only a few of the fry.

Besides supplying oxygen, aeration may still fulfill other, secondary functions, e.g. an even mixing of all warmth layers of the water in case of artificial heating, especially in big and tall tanks, destruction or prevention of the so-called 'oil' films, and sometimes even removal of too large quantities of oxygen, when the tanks are exposed to too intense sunlight.

Strongly heated tanks always contain less oxygen than less-heated or cold-water aquaria, but for this one has also to consider that as a rule tropical fishes need less oxygen than cold-water ones, so that the smaller oxygen content of the tropical aquarium may not be used as an unconditional reason for the need to aerate. To the contrary, it is just in the cold water aquarium that strong aeration is needed, especially in summer, in order to supply the great demand for oxygen of our native cold water fishes and others from similar climates.

Aerators may be of many different systems, adapted to many different needs. The simplest form of aerator is based on the system of expelling air from a closed bottle by admitting water dripwise. Such Drip Aerators, which may be sufficient for simple demands, are easy to build. Sometimes they are even found ready-made in pet shops. However, the pressure of such devices is minute, so that they only work if the water level of the tank is low, and if the aerator stone has little friction of its own. For this choose aerator stones of

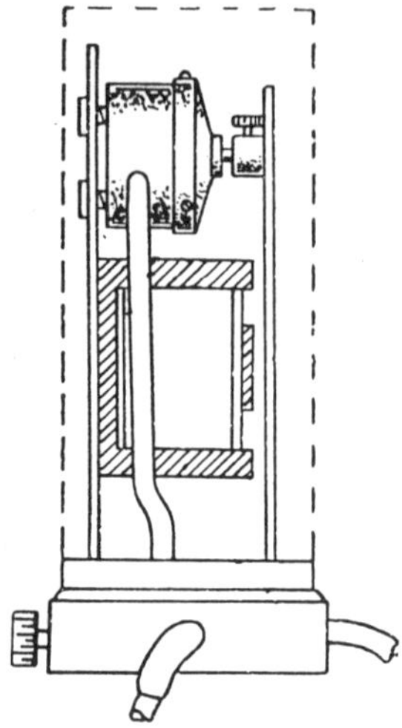

Diagram of vibrator pump

porous silica, provided they are not too fine-grained. Another simple aeration, which today is hardly ever found in use, functions with the aid of an air tank, which is filled by means of an air (tire) pump. Such tanks must always be equipped with a pressure gauge and a reduction valve in order to make sure that the air flows out evenly. Also the inner tube of an automobile tire may do the same service in case of need. Such aerators, too, are made only for simple demands, especially since pumping them full consumes time and is laborious.

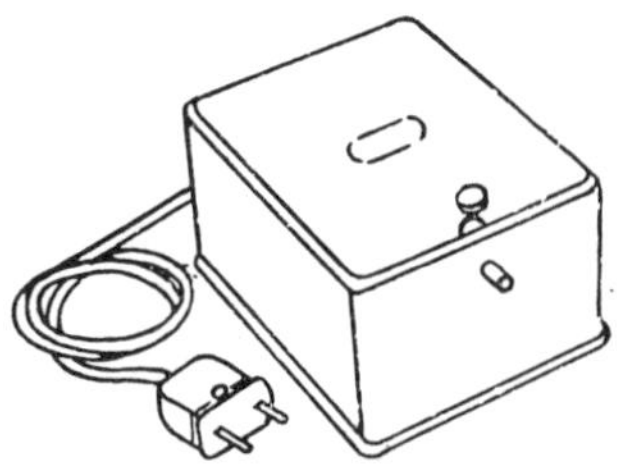

Vibrator pump

Very efficient and economic to operate are water pressure aerators, which are connected with the water pipes of the domestic tap system. Even an extremely small amount of water is sufficient to move the piston which pumps the admitted air to the aquarium. Such aerators are best installed in the kitchen of the house, above the water pipe, with an air duct of sufficient length laid to the aquaria. The air duct may be made of lead pipes or something similar. Modern water pressure aerators are completely noiseless, and need no surveillance if solidly mounted. More expensive in operation, but equally commendable are electric aerators, of which several systems are offered for sale. If you have just a few aquaria, you will be able to manage with a membrane aerator, which works on the Summer principle (Wagner's hammer). They are not always noiseless, and their output is not very large.

If you have a greater number of aquaria, or if you intend to enlarge your installations, it will be better to reckon with this enlargement beforehand and to get a more productive machine. Such aerators are found in sufficient numbers of models, which work on different principles. We have no space in this book to give specific advice as to the choice of these.

The air ducts may be made of rubber hose, or of lead, glass, or plastic pipes. In the tanks themselves the best would be to use glass tubes bent to shape, or, better still, plastic ones, as these are unbreakable. Glass tubes may be bent in the flame of a Bunsen burner, plastic ones in hot water. In order to avoid pinching the tubes in at the bending sites, fill them with fine-grained sand before heating them. Distributing the air to the different working sites (aerator stones, filters), demands some experience. You will have to reckon with the fact that filters always use up much more air than simple aeration, so that small pumps (membrane aerators) as a rule are unable to supply both simultaneously. Distribution and adjustment of the air flow is generally either done with air valves (flow meters), or with hose clamps. For larger pumps it is advisable to place an air tank with valves between pump and aquaria, in order to achieve an even flow of air. Furthermore you will have to pay attention to the fact that most motors have to produce a minimum output in order to avoid harming their mechanisms.

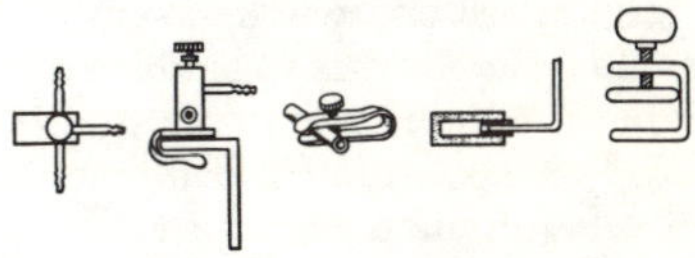

Types of clamps and valves

In some cases it is advisable to let part of the compressed air escape without using it. Sometimes it happens that sudden stops of certain aeration systems are followed by siphoning water back from the aquarium with subsequent flooding of floors or pumps. This is best avoided by placing the aerator higher than the water level of the aquarium.

In cases where this is impossible, Denk advises the intermission of an automatic check valve—similar to the valve of an automotive inner tube—somewhere in the air duct shortly before it enters the aquarium. Naturally such a valve has to be installed in a manner that will not obstruct the free flow of air, but will still prevent water from being siphoned back.

The best aerator stones, which are finding ever-increasing acceptance, are those made of silica or of porous earthenware, as they are very long-lasting. If in time they get obstructed, it is easy to clean them in hot water or over a gas flame. When you connect your aerator stones, take care to check that the air really flows through them and does not escape in great bubbles near the connecting site, as sometimes happens.

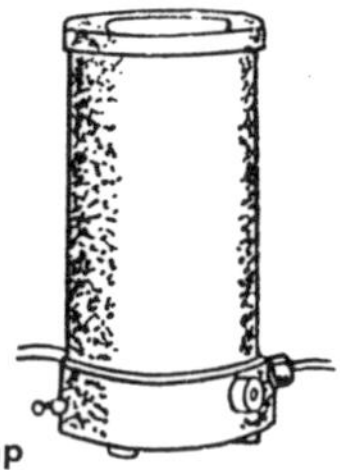

Cylindrical vibrator pump

The question whether aeration should be large or small bubbled has found a definite reply in the studies of KRAMER. The commonly-defended opinion that the value of aeration consists in gradually bringing all layers of the water to the surface—where real oxygenation occurs—has already been disproved by FINCK (1922), who showed clearly that this 'turnover' effect is only of secondary value.

Indeed, it is nearly exclusively the passage of atmospheric air by means of aeration which enriches the water significantly with oxygen. For this fine-bubbled aeration is preferable, as this provides the larger surface of the bubbles with reference to the surrounding water.

Mathematically we find the following results: An air bubble of one cubic inch capacity has a surface of 4.8 square inches. 10 air bubbles totalling a capacity of one cubic inch have 10.4 square inches of surface. 100 air bubbles with a total of 1 cubic in. have 22.5 sq. in. of surface. Based on this calculation of the effectiveness of the different manners of dividing air, KRAMER reaches the following results:—

2.5 gals./hour of air increase the oxygen contents of 25 gals. of water by:

1.5 mg. per liter with coarse aeration;

2.2 mg. per liter with medium-sized aeration;

3.3 mg. per liter with fine aeration.

Coarse aeration may indeed yield useful effects much quicker, e.g., if the fishes are in danger, but it uses up much more air. This consumption is biggest when the air bubbles escape directly from the tip of the tubulation. This explains the high air consumption of the different kinds of filters, which generally make it uneconomical, if you believe you can connect simultaneous aeration with the filter (see FILTRATION).

aerator stones: see AERATION.

aerial leaves: Leaves of aquatic plants that rise above the surface of the water.

afer: African.

— *Notopterus.*

affinis: Similar, related.

— *Aphyocharax.*

— *Cambarus.*

— *Creatochanes.*

— *Gambusia.*

— *Leporinus.*

affinis holbrooki: After the man's name.

— *Gambusia.*

Africa. Second largest continent, covering with its islands about 30 million square kilometers. A very little-indented continent, poor in bays, peninsulas and natural harbors. On the whole quite flat, lacking almost entirely in mountain ranges and deep valleys. Only a few outlying islands. Almost a third of the continent is desert, where the waters have no outlet to the sea. In the Sahara and Kalahari the river beds carry water only after the rare rainfalls. There are springs and accumulations of water in the oases.

AFRICA
FRANCE
SPAIN
PORTUGAL
POLAND
UKRAINIAN S.S.R.
HUNGARY
RUMANIA
YUGOSLAVIA
BULGARIA
GREECE
TURKEY
BLACK SEA
MEDITERRANEAN SEA
Bay of Biscay
Adriatic Sea
MOROCCO
ALGERIA
SOUTHERN TERRITORIES
TUNISIA
LIBYA
TRIPOLITANIA
CYRENAICA
FEZZAN
UNITED ARAB REPUBLIC
EGYPT
U.A.R. SYRIA
LEBANON
ISRAEL
JORDAN
ARAB FEDERATION
IRAQ
SAUDI ARABIA
KUWAIT
YEMEN
ADEN PROT.
RED SEA
SUDAN
ETHIOPIA
ERITREA
FR. SOM'LD.
SOMALILAND PROT.
KENYA
UGANDA
TANGANYIKA (Br. Trust Terr.)
ZANZIBAR PROT.
BELGIAN CONGO
RUANDA-URUNDI
FRENCH EQUATORIAL AFRICA
TCHAD
OUBANGUI CHARI
GABON
MOYEN CONGO
CAMEROUN (Fr. Trust Terr.)
NIGERIA
DAHOMEY
TOGO
GHANA
IVORY COAST
LIBERIA
FR. GUINEA
SENEGAL
FRENCH WEST AFRICA
MAURITANIA
SUDAN
UPPER VOLTA
NIGER
SP. W. AFRICA
Gulf of Guinea
SP. GUINEA
ANGOLA
FED. OF RHODESIA & NYASALAND
N. RHODESIA
NYASALAND PROT.
SO. RHODESIA
MOZAMBIQUE
Mozambique Channel
MADAGASCAR
SOUTH WEST AFRICA
BECHUANALAND PROTECTORATE
TRANSVAAL
SWAZI LD.
ORANGE FREE STATE
BASUTO LD.
NATAL
CAPE OF GOOD HOPE
UNION OF SOUTH AFRICA
C. of Good Hope
Ascension I. (Br.)
St. Helena I. (Br.)
Tristan da Cunha
TROPIC OF CAPRICORN
SOUTH ATLANTIC

Rivers of central Sudan have their mouths in Lake Chad, where the waters evaporate. The large streams come from the interior of the continent, in many cases breaking through the edges of the highlands of interior Africa.

The river which carries the most water in Africa is the Congo, 4650 km long, and the longest is the Nile with 6671 km. The Nile makes possible in its valley at the edge of the Sahara the existence of human settlements. Next in importance is the Niger with 4160 km, whose mouth is in the upper coast of Guinea, the Zambesi with 2660 km, the Oranje with 1860 km, the Kubango with 1800 km, and the Limpopo with a length of 1600 km. In the East African valleys, which lie in highly volcanic regions, some deep lakes have formed (Tanganyika, Nyassa), while Lake Nyassa fills a more shallow hollow. These lakes are the habitat of many species of Cichlids, many of them mouthbreeders, principally of the genus *Tilapia.*

Climatically almost all of Africa belongs to the tropics. Along the Equator there is much precipitation at all times of the year, with the exception of the highlands of East Africa. The most important region for the collection of aquarium fishes at present is the tropical coastal strip from the Congo mouth in the south to the Senegal in the north, which is about 50 to 300 km wide. Here we find temperatures which vary little from day to day and at all times of the year, 76 to 78°. In the regions which are further from the Equator the dry periods of the Winter are somewhat more pronounced. Average rainfall: more than 1500 mm, in places several thousand (by comparison, Munich, as one of the wettest cities in Europe has 930 mm). In the damp Equatorial regions, in parts of the East African coast and on the coast of Guinea we find always-green rain-forests. In this zone there are also places with less precipitation, and here there is an exchange of summery rain with winter dry periods. The typical landscape here are separate trees or groups of trees in plains of tall grass, the savannahs. The dry seasons lengthen as one travels toward the south or toward the north. At the same time the savannahs gradually change to steppes, then dry steppes, semi-deserts and finally deserts. The Sahara and the Namib Deserts in Southwestern Africa are almost totally devoid of rain. The southern Cape territory and the northern slope of the Atlas Mountains belong to the sub-tropic regions of Winter rains, with Mediterranean flora.

The water characteristics of the river mouth territories are often extraordinarily complicated, which causes the fish life in the coastal region to be subjected to strong changes. A similar situation exists in the areas which have definite dry periods. Many African fishes are therefore able to withstand extreme changes in their surroundings, whether it be in the salt content of the water, other water characteristics, temperatures or a sharp drop in oxygen content. The *Aphyosemion* species are examples of fishes which have adapted to the waters of the rain-forests which are very rich in humic acid.

According to LADIGES the following is a review of the ecological reports from the most important waters of the continent:

In the vicinity of the coasts, in the bays and river-mouths, characterized by a mangrove-jungle and a change in the salinity of the water, we find certain Tooth-Carps (*Aplocheilichthys*, *Epiplatys*) and

Cichlids (*Tilapia*, *Hemichromis* and *Pelmatochromis*). In the small waters of the rain-forest near the coast which are rich in absorbed humic acid, and at times also contain quantities of salt water, we find many *Aphyosemion* species, as well as some species of *Epiplatys*. In the creeks which carry completely fresh water and are tributaries of the larger stream systems, which for the most part run through bush forests and savannahs with trees, there are, as well, many representatives of the Tooth-Carps and Cichlids, as well as Characins, for example *Alestes* (*Bryconalestes chaperi*), various Barb species, the Butterfly-Fish (*Pantodon*) and the Nandid *Polycentropsis abbreviata*. In the water-holes for the settlements, in the small clear-flowing forest brooks, there are Lamp-Eyes, *Aplocheilichthys macrophthalmus* and *A. flavipinnis*. In the papyrus-swamps of the Nile region, the muddy middle stretches of the West African streams, outside of the zone where there is a salt water influx, in the shore waters of Lake Victoria and Lake Chad we find Lungfishes, *Polypterus*, Mormyrids, Climbing Fish (*Ctenopoma*), Snakeheads, Knife Fishes, Catfishes and Barbs, and in the large lakes mostly Cichlids, especially *Tilapia*.

The continent, as far as general observations have shown, is not particularly rich in aquatic plants. The waters in the tropical rain-forests of the coastal region are mostly free of underwater vegetation. North Africa has an aquatic flora very similar to that of southern Europe.

African big-scale Characin, the: see ARNOLDICHTHYS SPILOPTERUS.

African Climbing Fishes, the: see CTENOPOMA; Bush Fishes.

African Lizardfish: see PROTOPTERUS ANNECTENS.

African Tetra, the: see NANNAETHIOPS UNITAENIATUS.

African-Three Spot Barb, the: see BARBUS TRISPILUS.

Afronandus: Genus of the family of Nandids, which were found in one species in the course of a collecting expedition in West Africa by SHELJUZHKO. With this was added another genus to the then well-known genus *Polycentropsis*. The species was named *Afronandus sheljuzhkoi* by MEINKEN. They were found in a small brook with a very muddy bottom near Abidjan. The fish are 1¼ to 1½ inches in length, with a somewhat elongated form, with large eyes, mouth at the end of the head and scales on the head. There is no lateral line.

Agassiz, Louis: Zoologist, 1807 (Switzerland) to 1873 (USA). Known for his comprehensive works on the natural history of fossil and living fishes.

agassizi: After the well-known zoologist Agassiz.
— *Ambassis*.
— *Apistogramma*.
— *Corydoras*.

agilis: Agile, lively.
— *Rasbora*.

aggregate conditions: Solid, liquid or gassy condition of a substance, for instance with water as ice, flowing water or water vapor.

Agnathi: Without gills.
Class of the order of Vertebrates which in contrast to other members of the order do not yet have gills and for this reason occupy a special place. This takes in only one group of fish-like, ancient creatures of the Silurian Period which today would be considered eel-like, and could not yet be considered true fishes. They occupy a place more to themselves alongside of these. There is only one class: the *Marsipobranchii*, with the order of Roundmouths or *Cyclostomata*.

Agonostomus - type of the genus

Agonostomus: Referring to the structure of the mouth.

Genus of the family of *Atherinidae*, with a very slender, laterally strongly compressed body. The head is small, and the mouth is equipped with strong lips. The members of this genus, like the others of the family *Atherinidae*, have two distinct dorsal fins, the first with spiny rays, and the second possessing only one spiny and several soft rays. The scales are relatively large.

— monticola (Bancroft):

FORM: As described for the genus. The straight or somewhat down-turned mouth is split very little, but still has powerful lips. D_1IV, D_2 I/8, with the first dorsal fin set about in the middle of the body, A II/10. Length can approximate 10 inches.

COLOR: Gleaming yellowish, with a metallic greenish sheen above, plain silvery toward the belly, where there are a few washed-out dark patches toward the rear. Fins are reddish, the rays of the first dorsal fin almost black. No known outward sex differences.

RANGE: Throughout Central America, also in Mexico and the West Indies. Here the species is found in fresh water as well as in brackish water, but it prefers the small, fast-flowing mountain brooks.

CARE: As this is an active and speedy swimmer, large tanks with a great deal of open space are a necessity; these must be well covered, because these are good jumpers. Water must be clear and rich in oxygen. Temperatures should average about 75°. Omnivorous, and not at all particular where food is concerned, and will eat anything from small fishes to dried foods. Not yet bred.

Agrion: see ODONATA, Dragonfly.

Ahl, Ernst: German ichthyologist. Born 1898 in Berlin, reported missing in the Second World War. For years Director of the Ichthyological and Herpetological Division of the Zoological Museum in Berlin. From 1927-1934 he was Editor of the magazine "Das Aquarium." With J. P. Arnold he wrote the well-known standard reference work on aquarium fishes "Fremdlandische Süsswasserfische (1936)."

albifrons: With a white forehead.

— *Stenarchus.*

albinism: Absence of black pigmentation, or partial absence of color due to the absence of pigment cells, a condition which is capable of being inherited or being passed on to future generations (see COLOR IRREGULARITIES). Albinistic forms (albinos) are found in many fish species.

albinistic, albinotic: Colorless because of albinism.

albolineatus: With white stripes or lines.

— *Brachydanio.*

albonubes: White cloud (referring to White Cloud Mountain in Canton).

— *Tanichthys.*

Alburnus: Whitefish.

Genus of school fishes of the family of Carplike Fishes or *Cyprinidae.* With an elongated form and a short dorsal fin and somewhat longer anal fin.

Alburnus lucidus

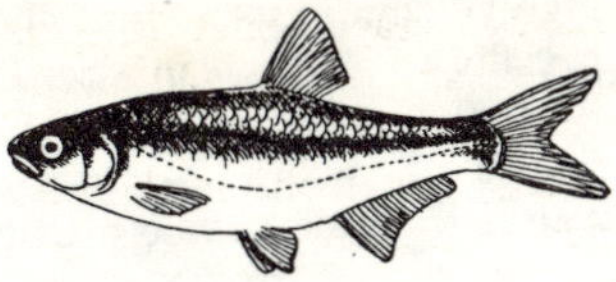

Alburnus bipunctatus

— **alburnus:** see ALBURNUS LUCIDUS.

— **bipunctatus** Linné: A school fish which is very similar to the preceding species and comes from clear, fast-flowing streams in South and West Germany, rare in other places.

— **lucidus** Heckel.

FORM: Body elongated, somewhat variable depending upon location from which taken. Mouth turned steeply upwards. D II, A 20; scales very silvery, loosen very easily. The guanin crystals which give the scales their sparkle are extracted commercially. There are two rows of pharyngial teeth, some of which are hooked. Length at least 8 inches.

COLOR: Very silvery sides, fins tinted a light brown.

RANGE: Europe from the Volga River to France, also in brackish waters along the Baltic Sea, and in schools in lakes and streams.

CARE: Small specimens may be kept like the other Cyprinids; room is required for swimming and oxygen. Temperatures should not exceed 65°. Will eat any food, including algae. Excellent jumpers. They spawn in schools in calm waters, with a considerable amount of splashing.

Aldrovanda: After the Italian botanist U. Aldrovandi.

Genus of carnivorous aquatic plants of the family of Sundews or *Droseraceae*.

— **vesiculosa** Linné: Bladderwort. A rootless floating aquatic plant, with leaves which are used as traps. Supplements its nourishment with small crustaceans, etc. Soft water and good lighting are beneficial. In the absence of animal nourishment the plant remains small. Forms winter buds, which may be kept through the winter months in a jar of water which is not permitted to freeze. Widely scattered over Europe, eastern Asia, Japan, India and Australia. Occurs in still, peaty waters. The plant is very rare, and for this reason should be protected. For this reason it is not advisable to collect it, and furthermore it is a poor aquarium plant.

Aldrovanda vesiculosa. At the right is a magnified view of one of the food traps.

Alestes: see BRYCONALESTES.

Alestidi: Related to the Tetra family or *Characidae*, a group which is native to tropical Africa. The following genera are (according to Hoedeman) interesting to the aquarist: *Bryconalestes*, *Micralestes*, *Arnoldichthys*, *Alestopetersius* and *Phenacogrammus*. These are on the average small and medium-sized school fishes with an attractive silvery sheen and relatively large scales.

Alestopetersius: Genus of the family of Characins or *Characidae*, sub-family *Alestidi*.

— **hilgendorfi** (Boulenger): Rarely imported species from the Congo region. Has the same requirements as *Phenacogrammus interruptus*. A number of sub-species are spread over tropical West Africa. They are

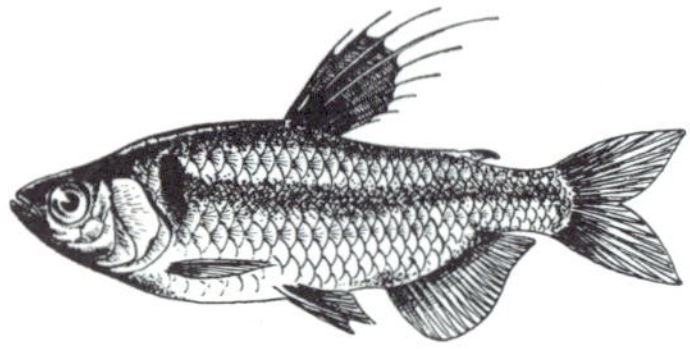

Alestopetersius hilgendorfi

school fishes with an attractive silver gleam, a more or less distinct shoulder-spot and dark fins. The dorsal fin rays of the males extend beyond the edge of the fin. Length about 4 inches. Spawning habits unknown, but are probably the same as *Phenacogrammus interruptus*.

Alfaridi: Division of the sub-family of livebearing toothcarps or *Poeciliinae*. The under edge of the caudal base is compressed very thin and unusually scaled, which distinguishes this division. Body is relatively high in structure. Gonopodium is of the simplest structure, without any appendages or hooks. Fish's diet is mostly vegetarian.

Genera: *Alfaro, Furcipenis.*

Alfaro: After the zoologist Dr. Alfaro.

Genus of livebearing toothcarps of the sub-family *Poeciliinae*, division *Alfaridi*. The leaf-like thin underedge of the caudal base looks like a very wide anal fin. Care and breeding, see POECILIINAE.

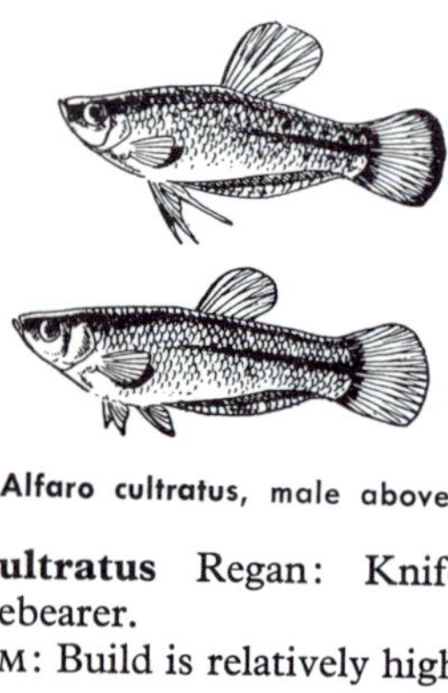

Alfaro cultratus, male above

cultratus Regan: Knifetailed Livebearer.

FORM: Build is relatively high, very highly compressed laterally, especially in the caudal base. D 7-9, A 9-10. Length, male 1½ inches, female 2½ inches. In their native waters they may attain a length of 3½ inches.

COLOR: Yellowish, with a light blue shimmer.

RANGE: Small bodies of water in Costa Rica and Panama.

CARE AND BREEDING: As given in the description of the sub-family (see POECILIINAE). A very active swimmer, also somewhat quarrelsome. A carnivorous feeder, resembling the genus *Gambusia* in this respect. Requires some heat, about 75°, also enjoying higher temperatures.

So far this species has been seldom imported and has found no great distribution. Not very productive; the females remain fertile for a long time, but the number of tiny, delicate but very active fry is small. They grow very rapidly.

A related species from the Amazon region, which has also disappeared from the ranks of aquarium fishes is *Alfaro amazonas* Regan, which resembles this species greatly.

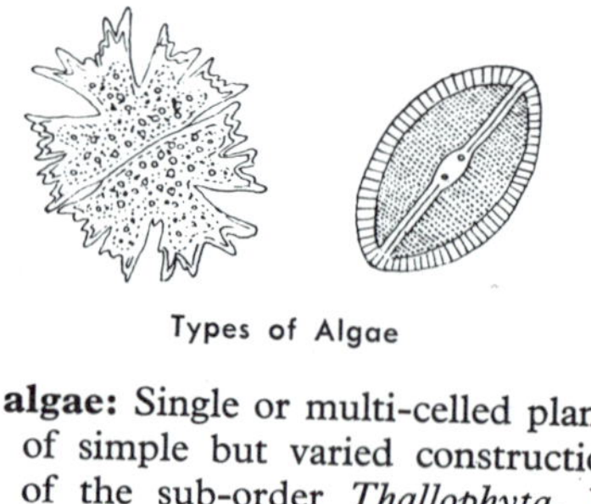

Types of Algae

algae: Single or multi-celled plants of simple but varied construction of the sub-order *Thallophyta*. In fresh water they usually consist of threadlike or small to microscopically tiny forms. The body of the multi-celled forms is known as the thallus, and can take on complicated forms, including a stem and leaf-like structures. Multiplication may be performed sexually or asexually.

Algae represent the beginning of the development of organisms, some also making small inroads into the animal kingdom. In some groups the cells have no nucleus, but in others have one or more nuclei. The classes of algae can be split up as follows:

1. Blue or split algae (see CYANOPHYCEAE), which as a rule are included with the split plants (see SCHIZOPHYTA).

2. Flagellates (see FLAGELLATA), which could also be included with the protozoans.

3. Green algae (see CHLOROPHYCEAE).

4. Yoke algae (see CONJUGATAE).

5. Diatoms (see DIATOMEAE).

6. Dim light growths (see CHARACEAE), also grouped with CHAROPHYTA (which see).

There are also those which are of no interest to the fresh-water aquarist, the red algae (*Rhodophyceae*) and the brown algae *Phaeophyceae* of the ocean.

Algae have a great significance in the aquarium. Some kinds are used for food by fishes, and also their fry. Bundles of algae are often the hiding places for many food organisms for fry nourishment. Thread algae are also a valuable spawning medium for many fishes. Nevertheless algae can also be a nuisance, sometimes harmful. There are few remedies for algae control. Aquarium hobbyists usually identify algae by their color and composition as brown algae, green algae, and thread algae. This division is of course not valid botanically.

algae, eradication of: The annoying mass development of algae in the aquarium makes many particular methods of eradication necessary.

The damage resulting from a mass appearance of algae, especially the ill-famed blue algae, by raising the pH value (see BIOGENIC DECALCIFICATION and CALCIFICATION) can be considerable. Besides, the growth of algae hinders the growth of higher plant life, and may even cause plants to die. Not rare also are mechanical damages to fishes by thread algae. However there are seldom cases of disease which can be traced to the invasion of skin or gills by algae.

The eradication of blue algae is not always simple. Most important is the determination of the biological factors which cause its appearance, which should be sought as too great a hardness in the water, too much sunlight or too great an accumulation of wastes on the bottom and on the plants. It is advisable to eradicate an invasion of blue algae in its first stages. The measures may be mechanical (scraping it off and siphoning it out), but the better measure is to change the biological conditions in the affected aquarium. Another good remedy is the introduction of algae-eating fishes, for example *Xiphophorus* (*Platypoecilus*) *variatus*, which keep picking on the algae and never leave it alone. STERBA recommends sprinkling in iron filings. It must be especially cautioned not to leave any decaying food particles on the bottom.

STETTLER states that all methods so far recommended are useless or even harmful. Eradication can only be accomplished by the creation of healthy water conditions. Stettler also refers to the researches of Boas, who says that the appearance of blue algae can be traced to a scarcity of borium in the water, without answering the question of whether or not the introduction of borium alone would cause blue algae to die. He sums up his findings on the conquest of blue algae as follows:

The most healthy, clean and oxygen-rich water by means of:

(a) a rich planting of the higher water-plants, to reduce dissolved organic wastes;

(b) sufficient light (natural or artificial) to make possible a rich plant growth;

(c) a moderate fish population, as conditions permit;

(d) the addition of 100 cc 3% boric acid solution for each 100 liters of aquarium water.

In conclusion BRUNNER warns against the thoughtless use of boric acid. So the dosage recommended by STETTLER is a possible overdose. However there should be no poisonous reaction on the higher plants, but continuous use in an aquarium which has a fish population should be accompanied with some care, because in a higher concentration boric acid is stored in the body. Above all nitrogenous fertilizing tablets or nutritive salts should be used very sparingly when boric acid is present. BRUNNER recommends the use of a peat filter along with the boric acid treatment.

Green algae, usually a soft, fluffy layer on glass sides and plants, is as a rule harmless. If they get the upper hand, they can be removed by scraping the sides with a cleaner. The layer which covers the plants is best conquered by darkening considerably, or at the same time introducing algae-eating fishes. However they do not tolerate a very soft and acid water.

Thread algae, inasmuch as they are shorter-lasting species, are eradicated in the same way as green algae. The longer-lasting species like the very similar yoke-algae, can be rolled up on a rough wooden stick and pulled out. This is not always easy, as sometimes the higher plant life is also pulled out.

algae diseases: Diseases of the epidermis brought out by parasitic algae, particularly the Coral Fish Disease and the *Oodinium* disease.

Alisma: Ancient Greek name for the Frog Spoon, an aquatic plant. Genus of aquatic or swamp plants of the family *Alismataceae.* The species of this genus develop partly in the juvenile stage or in deep water, partly also permanent ribbon-shaped underwater leaves. The aerial leaves which appear in the forms which grow in the swamps are as a rule lanceolate to broadly oval and more or less pointed. The leaves are rooted in the ground. Blossoms almost always appear above the surface, where they form a many-branched, somewhat loose and pyramid-shaped panicle. Flowers are white to reddish.

Alisma graminifolium lanceolatum plantago-aquatica

— plantago-aquatica Linné: Common Frog Spoon.
This well-known species is distributed as the other cosmopolitan species. It attains a height of 32 inches. The rhizome is knobby; the spoon-shaped and sometimes very broad leaves are bottom-

standing. The many branched blossom stalk sometimes attains a height of 40 inches and more. The blossoms are white or light pink. The species is adapted only to outside locations. Here it grows well and is very decorative. In the open it is very abundant on the shores of all sorts of waters.

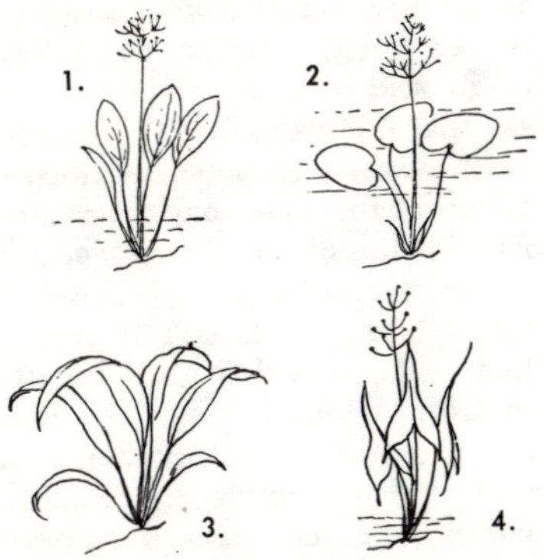

1. Alisma 2. Caldesia 3. Echinodorus 4. Sagittaria

— **graminifolium** Erhardt: Grass-leaved Frog Spoon.

GENERAL INFORMATION: A desirable cold-water plant, which may be cultivated submerged in several forms.

FORM: The species is very variable and shows various ways of growing. It is very hardy. The rhizome is knobby. There are a number of submerged forms, which develop leaves 6 inches to 40 inches long and up to ½ inch wide, ribbon-shaped leaves. With this form the blossom panicle as a rule reaches above the surface, and only one small form also has this submerged.

RANGE: In standing or slowly flowing bodies of water in Europe, North Africa, Asia Minor and the West Indies.

CULTIVATION: The submerged forms are very well adapted to the cold-water aquarium and give little difficulty. These plants like plenty of sunlight. With good bright light the ribbon-shaped leaves do not even stop growing in the winter. Under suitable conditions they get quite large and grow rapidly. They particularly like a rich bottom, and at least they should be kept in unwashed sand, otherwise they would take too much room.

— **lanceolatum** Withering: Lancet-leaved Frog Spoon.

This species is not suited to the home aquarium, because it cannot be kept submerged. It is very similar to the common Frog Spoon, but has somewhat narrower leaves. It is especially apt to be found on the shores of bodies of water where the soil is alkaline. This species is relatively scarce.

Alismataceae: Plants similar to the Frog Spoon.

Family of aquatic and bog plants of the class of single seed-leaved plants or *Monocotyledoneae*, which includes some genera which are more or less valuable to the aquarist: *Alisma*, *Caldesia*, *Damasonium*, *Elisma*, *Echinodorus* and *Sagittaria*.

GENERAL INFORMATION: Some of the genera in this family include very popular aquarium plants, and belong to the basic plants for this use.

FORM: Most of the genera of this family are bog plants, which either have submerged leaves at certain seasons and later become surface plants, or in a few cases are definite underwater plants. Most of them are hardy. From the rhizome which as a rule is buried in the bottom soil, which in some cases takes the form of an onion-like bulb, spring the bottom-anchored leaves. These are usually fully edged and often are on more or less long stems. Leaf forms are varied; there are ribbon-shaped, lanceolate, heart-shaped and arrow-shaped ones. Usually the leaves which appear first (the primary leaves) are formed differently than the leaves which follow, the real leaves. Leaves may also vary greatly depending on their location. Also the position of the blossoms varies with the different genera. Either they grow from a long stem above the surface of the water or they remain entirely submerged. The single blossoms have three divisions. Blossoms form ears, clusters or panicles on a single stem. As a rule there are three petals, which are white, yellowish or reddish in color. Pollination is performed by insects or by the wind.

RANGE: There are about 75 species in the temperate, subtropical and tropical zones of the earth.

CULTIVATION: For the care of the different species, see the individual headings. They usually multiply by sprouting or by runners, but seldom by seeds. Many of the blossoming plants kept in the home aquarium do not develop seeds, and besides the vegetative multiplication is simpler as a rule.

alismoides: Similar to the Frog Spoon.
— *Ottelia.*

alkaline: Pertaining to the nature of alkalis.

Alkalinity: The absence of sodium carbonates and sodium hydroxides, a normal condition in the aquarium; the measuring unit for the contents of the water in calcium and magnesium carbonates. Depending on the quantity of these carbonates contained in the water, one may add acid to alkaline reacting water without making the pH value turn acid. The water remains alkaline, the acid being neutralized. The water becomes neutral only after the whole carbon dioxide contained in the carbonates is dislocated, and thereafter it finally turns acid.

Calcium and magnesium carbonates in water absorb all excessive acids until they themselves are used up. Therefore water with carbonate hardness can never react in an acid way. In such cases we say that the water is well buffered.

Measuring is done by mixing 100 cc of the water under test with 2 or 3 drops of methyl orange, after which it generally shows a yellow color. Now one adds 1/10 normal hydrochloric acid from a burette, in drops, while shaking same, until the color just turns orange from yellow. The number of cc of 1/10 normal hydrochloric acid measures the alkalinity. Multiplying the results by 2.8, one finds the carbonate hardness (CH).

alkalinity: The ability to combat acid action.

Alligator Fishes: see LEPISOSTEIDAE.

aloides: Similar to aloes.
— *Stratiotes.*

alpinus: Occurring in the Alps.
— *Potamogeton.*

Alternate: Plant members, leaves, or flowers, which stand alternately on different places of the stems.

alternifolia: With varying leaves.
— *Ludwigia.*

altior: High in build.
— *Rasborichthys.*

amarus: Bitter.
— *Rhodeus.*

Amazon, Amazon River: Largest river in South America, one of the greatest river systems of the world, which has a tremendously varied fish population, and is one of the most important sources for our aquarium fishes. The Amazon

results from a union of the Maranon and Ucayali Rivers, which originate in the Peruvian Andes Mountains. It is 3400 miles in length, of which about 2600 miles is navigable. Oceangoing vessels may travel upstream as far as Manaos, a distance of 1000 miles. The region with its tributaries and feeder streams covers about 4 million square miles, approximately two-thirds the area of Europe. Many of the more than 200 larger tributary streams are longer than the Rhine. At its mouth the river is about 150 miles wide. The Island of Marajo which lies here is larger than Lower Saxony. At a normal level, the Amazon flows 120,000 cubic meters per second, as compared to the Rhine, which delivers 2330. Because the drop along its main stretches is very light, tides from the ocean may be felt as far as 600 miles inland. In the lower reaches the tides may vary up to about 20 feet, more at times. At the city of Santarem the river is almost 10 miles wide, and in its middle reaches it is divided into many tributary streams, which enclose a mass of islands so large that they cannot be spanned with the eye. In the rainy season, which has its greatest influence on the tributary streams and lasts approximately from November to July, the water may in extreme cases rise to a depth of about 50 feet. Then the tremendous Amazon overflows its banks and forms a sea which the eye can scarcely span in many cases, which has given it the name of "The River Sea." On these huge flooded regions the greatest part of the lush vegetation dies. Only the tops of the trees show as tiny islands rising out of the flood.

The main stream runs almost parallel to the Equator. Here very high humidity and temperatures prevail. The yearly average temperature in Manaos, for example, is about 80°. Temperature changes are very light, between 2° and 4°. The yearly average humidity is about 80%. The Amazon Basin, a widespread valley, has been determined by its geological properties to have been originally a huge fresh-water lake which emptied into the Pacific Ocean. After the Andes Mountains formed, the outflow to the Pacific was blocked, and the lake emptied into the Atlantic. This lake was eventually washed out by the almost ceaseless rains and periodic floods. The Andes Mountains, being young geologically and getting heavy downpours, add ingredients to the waters. In this way it can be explained that the streams which originate here, and the main stream itself, are very clouded. However this suspended matter could scarcely influence the main character of the river. Its water is very clean chemically, almost approaching distilled water in its purity in some places. If this is true of the main stream, it is still more true of the feeder streams, which come from the granite and gneiss of the hills and low mountains of the regions to the north and south of the river. These areas add very little mineral matter to the water, which is perfectly clear in many tributary streams.

The center of this region is covered by a dense jungle. This also has little influence on the water, because the decaying vegetation is removed by the regular floods. Because of this the soil is enriched very little with humic acid, however in places the streams are discolored, such as the Rio Negro. According to the researches of Sioli three types of water and landscape may be distinguished:

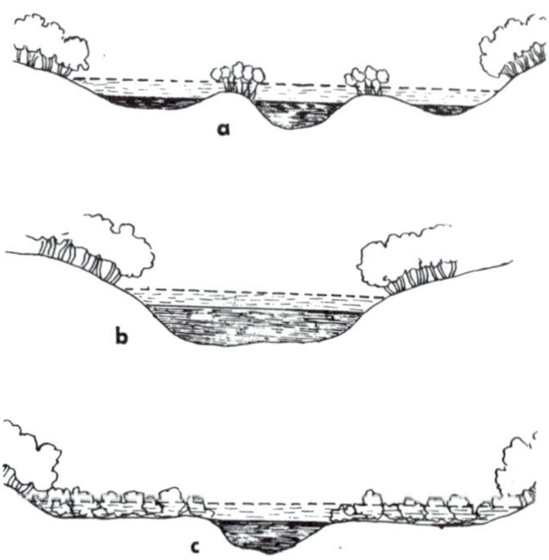

Types of shore regions

1. In the White Water Region, in which the main stream is included, there are inorganic infiltrations from the Andes Mountains which cause a whitish discoloration. At the middle height of the water, both sides have a swampy shore region. As far as the stream reaches, there are no impassable jungles, but there are mangrove growths; Type (a).

2. In the Black Water Region the forests, thickets and underbrush is flooded for weeks at a time. The decaying vegetable matter, which is later swept away, stains the usually clear water a dark brown; Type (c).

3. In the Clear Water Region one finds neither influxes from the tributaries nor introduced humus

products. Even at highest water levels the savannahs, forests and jungle growth through which the river flows do not become flooded; Type (b).

These water types of course all have their specialized flora and fauna. Unfortunately because of the widespread nature of these regions and the difficulties which hinder a study in all places, the real life in these waters is little known. There are always only few observations, which cannot be made general. SIOLI and BRAUN have made observations of the small life in several places. As a result it was found that supposedly conditions for lower life in many of these waters is very unfavorable. This was especially true of waters where there was a strong influx of humus. Molluscs, that is snails and mussels, are found in quantity only in places where there was a certain amount of calcium in the bottom soil. Of the small life which inhabits the larger and smaller bodies of water, a search during the dry season yielded *Chironomus* larvae, dragonfly larvae, tube worms, various mosquito larvae, leeches, water mites, mayfly larvae and small crustaceans. Here there are more copepods than *Daphnia*. There are no more exact observations to record. Suffice it to say that during the dry season plankton life is very scarce, becoming much more plentiful at the beginning of the rainy season. This increase in plankton occurrence coincides with the start of the breeding season. For details about fish fauna see SOUTH AMERICA.

Amazon Swordplant, Giant: *Echinodorus paniculatus.*

Amazon Swordplant, Narrow-leaved: *Echinodorus brevipedicellatus.*

Amazon Dwarf Cichlid: *Apistogramma pertense.*

Amazon Dwarf Swordplant: *Echinodorus intermedius.*

Ambassidae: Retired family of Glassfishes. At present grouped with the *Centropomidae.*

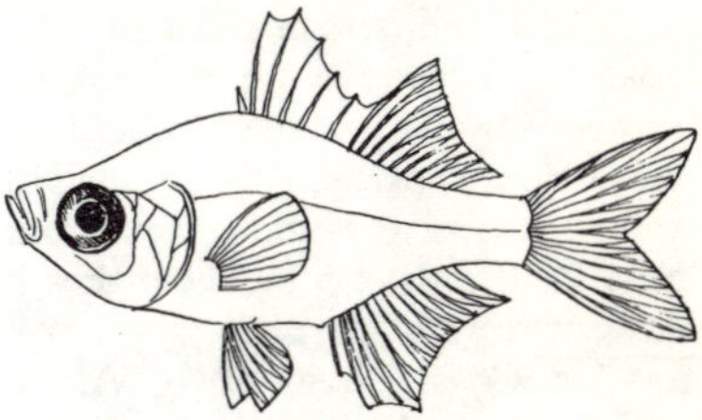

Ambassis - type of the genus

Ambassis: Worthless as food (Glassfish).

Genus of the family *Centropomidae*, previously designated as the individual family *Ambassidae.* The body is elongate to high, dented in at the forehead and more or less glassily transparent. The dorsal fin is in two parts. Another name for this genus is *Chanda.*

— agassizi Steindachner: Australian Glassfish.

FORM: As given in the general description, but longer in the body than the other species. The mouth is tilted upwards. D_1 VII, D_2 I/8, A II/8. The scales are delicate. Length to 1½ inches.

COLORATION: Body color brassy with varied indistinct patches, the fins darkly banded and edged. The male has brighter colors, and the female shows a more rounded swimbladder and is deeper toward the anal opening.

RANGE: Freshwater and brackish streams of East Australia.

CARE AND BREEDING: Care as given for *A. lala*, but this species does not require as much heat. Usually 72 to 75° suffices, over the winter months 68°, never below 61°, for breeding 75 to 78°. This species lives peacefully with the others and is somewhat shy if kept alone. A dark background and toplight shows off the colors particularly well. Probably has never been successfully bred.

— **commersoni** Cuvier & Valenciennes: Commerson's Glassfish.

FORM: This species differs from the former by a slightly different coloration, especially by the bright yellow fins of the males with dark tips. Its length of 5 inches makes it considerably bigger.

RANGE: Coastal regions of Africa and northern Australia.

CARE AND BREEDING: Like the above species, but because of their size larger quarters are required. Imported specimens often require the addition of salt or sea water to the aquarium water. Breeding, which has been successfully accomplished, is like *A. lala.*

Ambassis lala

— **lala** (Hamilton-Buchanan): Indian Glassfish.

FORM The very short and high-backed body is very much compressed laterally. The forehead is deeply indented in older specimens. The mouth is pointed and turned sharply upward, and the under jaw juts forward slightly. D_1 VII, D_2 12-15, A III/14-17. Scales are very small. In nature they are said to attain a length of $2\frac{3}{4}$ inches, but specimens kept in the aquarium remain considerably smaller.

COLOR: The delicate and transparent body gleams golden when reflecting light, the females somewhat more silvery. The fins are yellowish to faintly red, and with the males the soft dorsal rays and anal rays are beautifully edged with sky blue.

RANGE: Northern India to Burma, well distributed and plentiful. Is especially also found in clear fresh water.

CARE AND BREEDING: If this species is provided with an old established tank, they become very lively and friendly. It is advisable to show their colors to the best advantage by providing a dark background and a dark bottom, and placing the aquarium in such a position that the light falls on it. Temperature 65 to 76°; some sunlight adds to their well-being.

The Glassfish is best appreciated with its own kind, but may also be kept with other small and peaceful fishes. It goes without saying that these should not be too active. At first they are always a bit shy. They spend much of their time near the bottom, where the hiding-places may be easily reached, but in time they become tamer. They should be fed living foods of not too large size. Adding salt to the water is not necessary.

Breeding temperatures 75 to 78° and higher. The male dances around the female with beautiful, even movements, at which time his golden gleam is especially intense. The spawning site is selected some days previous by the male and guarded against all intruders. The little fellows can be very scrappy at such times. The actual mating takes place in a side-by-side position among the roots of a floating plant (such as the Water Sprite *Ceratopteris*) and almost stand on their tails. The female may even lie on her back. With a quivering motion there are 4 to 6 eggs expelled each time and swished into the plant roots, where they hang immediately. This procedure is repeated until about 100 to 120 eggs have been released. As the fry are very small, it is advisable to drop the height of the water 4 to 6 inches. The parents do not usually eat their eggs or fry, still it would be advantageous to remove them. Fry hatch after about 24 hours and remain anchored for two to 4 days afterward until they become free-swimming. At this time they are about 2½ millimeters long. They remain in a dense school at the light side near the bottom.

The main difficulty lies in the provision of a proper food for the very tiny but greedy youngsters. Nourishment with infusoria is not sufficient, and the food question is very much argued. According to one way of thinking, they will only take *Diaptomus* larvae, but other sources say all *Copepod nauplii*, but never rotifers. If they do not get the proper food, they starve in 2 to 4 days. They must be surrounded by food, this must be renewed daily. In their growing tank a light aeration will circulate the water and distribute the food throughout the entire tank. It is also advantageous to build up a terrace toward the light side to provide a shallow area where the young fry and food will congregate. If these precautions are taken, the fry are not delicate. They are even very well able to withstand a certain amount of foulness in the water and changes in temperature. If the pair is separated after being taken out and well fed, they will be ready to spawn again in about three weeks. With larger specimens a drop in temperature to 67° will certainly do no harm. A recommended method for keeping glassfish healthy is the addition of table salt to the water, especially if they keep folding their fins.

— nana Hamilton-Buchanan: Elongated Glassfish.

This species is of a very elongated form and grows to a length of 4¼ inches. Native to upper India and Burma, near the coastal regions. Care and breeding like *A. lala*.

— ranga Hamilton-Buchanan: Red-Finned Glassfish.

The species is very similar to *A. lala*. It is however a fresh-water fish, which attains a length of 1¾ inches. Native to upper India, Burma and Malaya. Care and breeding as with *A. lala*.

ambient world: The totality of all external factors which influence a live being. The ambient world determines the possibilities of life of the organisms, and thus also their distribution on earth, showing decisively in the shaping and development of all live beings. Its study (ecology), gains ever more importance also in aquaristics, as far as it is related to the natural conditions of the ambient world of animals and plants that are kept in aquaria. The ambient world influences the organisms either by attracting them, that is by granting them favorable conditions of life, or by repelling them, denying them such conditions. Further to this it changes organisms totally. This shaping influence is not only being exerted at present, but has been in action since the appearance of life on earth. At the beginning, and under special circumstances it created the primary conditions for the process of life, and then this process in itself, and has been active since then as the moving force of tribal and individual development. There are three main factors which aim at this effect:

1. The selective action of the factors of the ambient world, which either encourages organisms and certain qualities, or else represses them (natural selection).

2. The direct influence of the ambient world factors on the organism through its whole metabolism (which does not mean feeding only), through which development is guided over firm paths, attuned to the ambient world.

3. The steady change of the conditions of the ambient world, which ever anew forces the organisms to adapt to it, to adapt, so that selections always find new points of application.

Thus the adaptation to the ambient world takes place under its direct influence. This does not define, however, in which direction adaptation takes place in a species in its details. Moreover, this is, at least in part, determined by the possibilities of development inherent to any live being. Thus, for instance, fishes of quite different build and manner of living inhabit the same surroundings, such as, e.g. a swift-flowing mountain brook. There we find the predatory Trout, which defies the current with its strong muscles, the peaceable Minnow, which prefers quiet bights (thus at the same time searching for a different surrounding), the fish-like Lamprey, which is able to suck fast to rocks and the like and thus to resist the current, the Bullhead which even without a swimming bladder keeps up by clinging to the bottom in a way with its flat belly and its large pectorals, etc.

This single condition of the ambient world, the current, did definitely not act in a standardizing manner on the live beings which have to fight it. Only the totality of all the factors within a biotopical region cause the creation of types that are similar without needing to be closely related to each other. The factors of the ambient world in water are hugely manifold. It is difficult to form a relatively complete idea of them. If this is achieved even in rough strokes only, each type of water still has its numerous special sub-regions in which the total conditions change in many ways and even differ completely from one place to the other (see Biotope).

However, one can recognize certain basic traits, which permit listing the main conditions of the ambient world. We differentiate:

1. The major factors.
2. The minor factors.

The major factors include:

(a) the geographical data, on which depend the climate and the daily and seasonal rhythms;

(b) the geological data, which include the surface conditions of the soil (lowlands, plains, mountains, etc.), the composition of the geological strata, especially of those of the surface, and the distribution of the waters.

The settling of the major areas of the globe with animals and plants depends on these two factors.

Based on the major factors, the minor factors include all closely limited inanimate (abiotic) and animate (biotic) factors of a live being's special ambience or biotope.

For fishes, as water-dwellers, water stands out decisively as the determinating vital element. In aquaristics it took some time until it was understood that water is not a standardized, abstract definition. On the contrary, by its physical qualities, and by its capacity to dissolve substances, it is subject to substantial changes, which on their part result from a dependence on the major factors mentioned above. The geographical data or situation determines the water temperatures and their average values and fluctuations, the supply of new water which generally varies according to the season, the degree of evaporation or of freezing, and, linked to all this also the fluctuations of the water level, the daily and seasonal rhythms of lighting, of the prevailing winds and wind directions, the atmospheric pressure, etc.

On the geological data depend: the general character of the water, that is, whether it is a river, a swamp, a lake, a brook, a pond, etc., furthermore its depth and consequently the water pressure, the water's motion, the degree of permeability to light which depends on the bottom soil and on the loamy deposits, its chemical composition, meaning its contents in dissolved substances such as salts, trace elements, gases, etc. Further influenced by plants, this also determinates the natural reaction of the water (pH value). This lists most of the immediate abiotic factors of the ambient world, to which fishes are subject in a more or less strong way, but to which on the other hand they are also adapted.

The settling with organisms in its totality forms the animate factors. In the order of importance these are:

(a) The plant population, both of its surroundings, and of the water itself. The plants that grow on the shores of a body of water often decide on the distribution of lights and shadows, especially in the tropics, and thus on the growth of aquatic plants, furthermore on the contents of humic acids in the water due to floating leaves and wood. The aquatic plants themselves are of decisive influence of the varying pH values and on the biogenous calcification and decalcification (see these) caused by assimilation (see this) and dissimilation, furthermore the circulation and exchange of gases. Besides this the plant stands may represent dwelling places or shelters, they may play a role as spawning substrata, and may, in rare cases, even compete for food (carnivorous plants): in some cases also plants appear as enemies, either as parasites (*Ichthyosporidium*), as a direct danger (thread algae with reference to young fry), or through the excessive production of gases (oxygen).

(b) The animal population. Here we mention primarily the members of the same species, which either form tribal societies (swarms, schools, groups), or which establish relationships as sexual partners, but may also be competitors for food or enemies, even if this latter case happens only to a very small extent. The quantity of individuals of the same species may be decisive for the food situation in a body of water and thus for individual development (surviving rogues among Pike and Trout, runts among Whitefish, Sticklebacks, etc., in closed waters). The animal population also includes the neighbors, that is the masses of all animals which are neither members of the same species nor enemies, at the maximum being competitors for food to a certain extent. This includes many aquatic insects and their larvae, snails and other lower animals, etc. Sometimes a fish establishes a closer relationship with such neighbors with a more or less understandable mutual usefulness (symbiosis) for aim, e.g. the Bitterling and the mussel, the Coral-Fish and the anemone. Other animals, especially fishes, are competitors for food to a high degree, needing the same nutrition. The enemies are manifold. They range from unicellular organisms to man. The relationship to enemies on one hand, to preys on the other, strongly determines the life of fishes. Finally we still have to mention the animal parasites and disease germs. The quota of reproduction of a fish species generally depends on enemies and parasites.

In a closed vital space (closed does not mean shut off!) the organisms which live in it form a society, in which each has its place established by its functions and necessities of life, its manner of feeding, the number of its enemies and competitors, etc., etc. They are all mutually interrelated, forming a pattern, and compensate for each other to a certain point (see BIOLOGICAL EQUILIBRIUM). A body of water can only offer the amount of vital possibilities, which the totality of factors can offer a single organism.

The fishes also correspond to their natural ambient world in construction and function (see: ACCOMMODATION), and are accommodated to it. It has to be pointed out beforehand, however, that in nature there are no rigid limits. Therefore we find numerous transitions, and the motile fish may migrate to other areas or be scattered to them. Anyway, conversely we may conclude roughly on the natural ambient world of a fish from its build and functions (see BODY SHAPE OF FISHES).

There are accommodations of many kinds, general ones as well as specialized ones. It is impossible to list them all even approximately. For example the muscular shape, or the slender spindle shape, in fins, the whole body construction of fishes, the design of the fins as steering organs, etc. are adaptations to a physical state of water, in this case to the current. Also the sensory organs are adapted to the special demands of the waters. Many fishes need certain temperatures, possess some very special manner of acquiring food, or are accommodated to drying out, to scarcity of oxygen, etc., etc. These accommodations are more or less hereditary, that is, they are characteristics of a species, or of a whole group of similar fishes. They may be rigid, but also plastic, lasting, or linked to certain phases of age. Thus, the types of adaptabilities to variable conditions of the ambient world are variable, often even within the same species, since there are tribes that are more adaptable than others, or less so. Many species have a closely limited vital ambience, for instance the Carps of the genus *Cynolebias*, others have a wide one, as the Sticklebacks. Such observations may be made in any fish species. Therefore one should never forget that in aquaristics most species have a certain latitude in the individual capacity of adaptation, which makes it possible to keep the fishes, and to induce them to reproduce, even under somewhat differing circumstances. Summing up, it has to be said once more that all mentioned factors never appear alone; none ever stands separate!

In aquaristics the study of the natural ambient world of animals and plants as a basis for their natural, biologically correct care, is gaining more and more importance.

Ambloplites: With a dull armament

(referring to the rounded spines in the dorsal fin).
Genus of the family of Sunfishes or *Centrarchidae*.

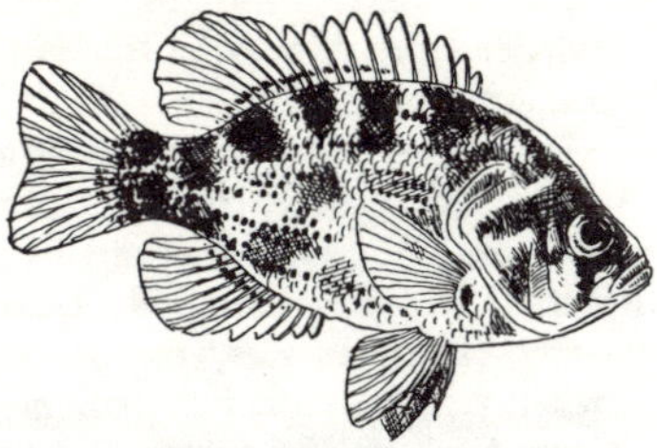

Ambloplites rupestris

— rupestris (Rafinesque) Rock Bass.
FORM: Moderately elongated, laterally compressed. D X-XI/10-12, A V-VII/9-11. Wild specimens attain a length of 10 inches, aquarium specimens 4 to 4¾ inches.
COLOR: On a grayish background there are a number of dark, marbled markings. The males have somewhat brighter colors, with dark pectoral fins.
RANGE: Northern USA and southern Canada, particularly in the Mississippi River and its tributaries. The species likes clear and cool water with a rocky bottom, where they prefer to lie among the stones and roots near the shore.
CARE AND BREEDING: As with *Centrarchus*. They accept only live foods, especially small fishes. They are shy and retiring, but also quarrelsome and nasty, even with bigger fishes. They like to lie hidden in retreats.

Amblydoras: Short, spiny Catfish.
South American genus of the family of spiny Catfishes or *Doradidae*. Strongly armored fishes, whose sides are equipped with many bony plates which frequently have many spines on their surface. The body is relatively short and compressed, tapering off strongly toward the end of the caudal base and heavily plated toward the front. The pectoral fins are equipped with strong spines, and the other fins are small with a short adipose fin. The genus is distinguished from the similar genus *Acanthodoras* by the different formation of the first dorsal ray, which is equipped with little hooks in *Acanthodoras*, and not in *Amblydoras*.

— hancockii Cuvier & Valenciennes:
FORM: As described for the genus. D I/6, A I/11. The first spine in the dorsal fin is not saw-edged, but furrowed with square furrows. The spines of the pectoral fins are very long and have saw-toothed edges. There are three pairs of barbels. Length to 6 inches.

Amblydoras hancockii

COLOR: Basic color fawn, with irregular black markings and ivory edges. On the white belly of the male there are many dark spots, which are much smaller in number in the female.
RANGE: Amazon region to Peru, also in Bolivia and Guiana. The species is found only in fresh water.
CARE AND BREEDING: Above all, this Catfish likes a soft bottom, in which it often buries itself until only the front part of the head and eyes show. Temperature 72 to 78°. The fish is omnivorous, sucking in its food and rarely taking a more active part in capturing it.

Capable of producing grunting and purring sounds, which are emitted by moving the pectoral fins, but the exact mechanics of the thing are not known. Breeding them in the aquarium has not yet been accomplished, but both parents are supposed to build a nest and guard the eggs and fry. During courtship the male "rides" on top of the female.

Amblyopsidae: With dull vision, blind (blind fishes).
Family of the Order *Microcyprini*. These are slender, probably livebearing fishes from North America, which are partly inhabitants of cave waters and as such are without pigmentation and blind. Some species are however native to surface waters and possess normally developed eyes and a pigmented skin. The fishes of this group, as far as the cave-dwelling species are concerned, are interesting aquarium objects, which until a short time ago were not at all available to aquarists, because they refused all nourishment offered them.

Of the two genera the *Amblyopsis* comes from the caves in the Ohio region and *Chlorogaster* from the surface waters in the southern USA. *Amblyopsis speleatus* DeKay gets to be 5 inches long and is almost completely colorless except for a yellowish to pink tint. The eyes are completely absent. As with many other cave-dwellers the sense of taste is extraordinarily well developed.

Amblypharyngodon: With dull pharyngeal teeth.
Genus of the family *Cyprinidae*. The body is slender, laterally compressed and the head somewhat flattened. The mouth is at the end of the head, with a sharply upturned angle. There are no barbels. The genus is distinguished from the closely-related *Rasbora* genus by the larger mouth and the smaller scales. The lateral line is incomplete. The genus consists of about 8 known species which have a range over upper India and Burma. Care as with the *Rasbora* species, and breeding has not yet been successfully accomplished with any of the species.

Amblystegium: Swamp Mosses.
Genus of leafy mosses of the suborder *Bryophyta*, family *Amblysteriaceae*.

— riparium Linné: Feathermoss.
A delicate, bright-green moss which may be found as a terrestrial form. It has an outer resemblance to the Willowmosses, but is considerably finer and after prolonged culture in the aquarium often becomes as thin as a thread. For the aquarium the best are plants from small, shallow bodies of water, ditches, etc. Here we have the best assurance that they will tolerate higher temperatures. One should never use the entire clumps which are lifted out of the water. It is better to take a few of the green shoots from the ends and make a little bundle by tying them together and fastening them between stones or roots or anchoring them with plant needles of glass to the bottom. Tight balls, which also contain dead plants, decay easily. Feathermoss likes bright light, but a too strong sunlight should be avoided. They grow well enough with artificial light, and keep growing through the winter.

Feathermoss can be placed loose in Cichlid tanks, where it remains freeswimming for a longer time, allowing the fish activities and still allowing for some decorative plant life.

Ambulia: see LIMNOPHILA.

Ameiuridae: Family of North American Catfishes of the suborder *Siluroidea* represented by the genera *Ameiurus* and *Ictalurus*.

Ameiurus: With an abbreviated tail.
Genus of North American Catfishes of the family *Ameiuridae*, with a single species, *A. nebulosus*, which in the last decades has been

introduced into European waters.

— nebulosus Rafinesque:

FORM: Rounded body shape, laterally compressed toward the rear, broad in the head and flattened. D I/6, A I/20-22; adipose fin is present. Of the 8 middle-sized barbels 4 are like a comb on the underjaw. Length to 18 inches.

COLOR: Grayish-brown to black with a greenish shimmer and light-colored belly. Ripe females are heavier.

RANGE: In standing and slowly flowing waters of North America. Has been introduced into Germany and become numerous.

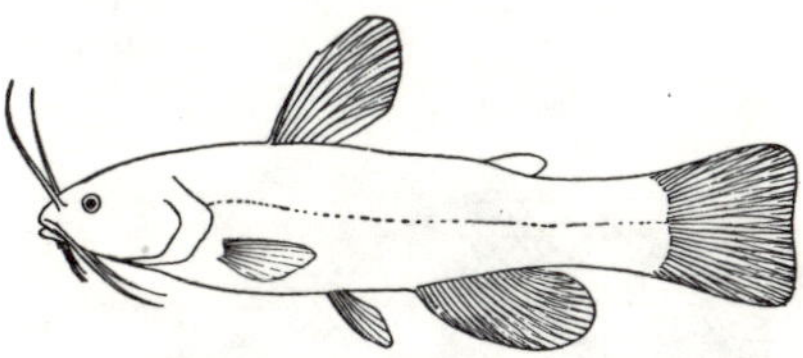

Ameiurus nebulosus

CARE AND BREEDING: A very pleasing aquarium fish, which likes to remain hidden and actually is nocturnal, but takes well to life in the aquarium. It combs the bottom with the help of its barbels for food, but can also eat swimming food, and requires a great deal of nourishment. The Catfish may become very active at times, but requires a number of hiding-places for its well-being; these may consist of rocks, roots or clumps of plants. It is a cold-water fish which does not require aeration, because it is capable of intestinal breathing. Breeding them may be possible in large aquaria. The male takes care of the young. Many scientific tests have been made in the field of hearing with Catfish.

America: see NORTH AMERICA; see SOUTH AMERICA, also CENTRAL AMERICA and WEST INDIES.

American Flagfish: see JORDANELLA FLORIDAE.

American Knife Fishes: see GYMNOTIDAE.

American Shiner: see NOTROPIS LUTRENSIS.

Amia calva, young

Amia calva Linné: Mudfish.

The North American Mudfish is the only representative of the family *Amiidae* in the order PROTOSPONDYLI (which see).

FORM: The body is elongated, in front almost cylindrical in diameter, toward the rear slightly compressed. Scales are small and thin, the bones of the head are covered with an enamel, and the throat is protected by a bony plate. The very long dorsal fin, which imparts a forward motion by a certain waviness, has a musculature of its own, with the help of which each individual ray can be moved. The anal fin is considerably shorter. Length to 24 inches.

COLOR: Darkly marbled on a brownish background. The male has a dark spot, ringed reddish, on his caudal base.

RANGE: North America, in the Mississippi and also in large lakes. Here it prefers standing or sluggish waters and shallow, weedy spots.

CARE AND BREEDING: A distinctly predatory species with powerful jaws, suited especially for large show aquaria. Here it keeps quite well, adapting easily to being fed with pieces of raw meat and making no demands on the oxygen supply because of its accessory breathing organs. Temperature

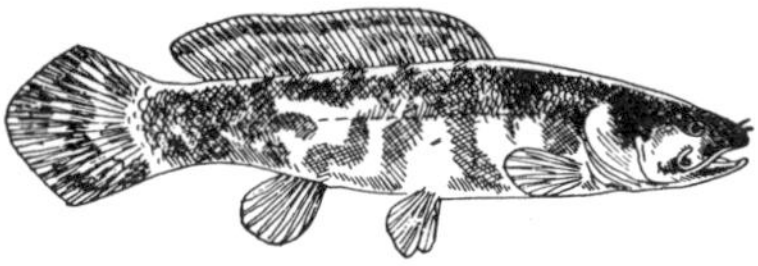

Amia calva, adult

should not fall below 40°, and the fish already becomes attractive at a temperature of 58°. It feels best at a temperature of 65 to 68°. Breeding them in the aquarium has not yet been accomplished, but they have spawned in open pools. The eggs are placed in a nest of plant leaves and guarded by the male.

amitosis: Cell division without previous loosening of the cell nuclei in chromosomes (see CELL DIVISION).

Amoeba: A microscopic animal which does not possess a stiff body covering and is capable of changing its form while moving (see RHIZOPODA).

amphiacanthoides: Like the *Amphiacanthus*, a plant-eating fish from the Pacific Ocean.

— Uaru: A South American Cichlid.

amphibian: Leading an aquatic as well as a terrestrial existence.

Amphipoda: With feet on both sides.

Order of *Crustacea* of the class of higher *Crustacea* or *Malacostraca*. Mostly sea inhabitants, but with several fresh-water representatives. They are small to medium-sized ringed crabs with a laterally compressed body and a head which is clearly separated. There are gills on the breastbone. The first three abdominal rings have three pairs of swimmerets, and the last three rings are provided with hopping feet. The crabs can propel themselves with good speed with jerks of their muscular after sections of the body, but they are also capable of a slow, gliding motion.

The order is divided into four sub-orders. Of the fresh-water species, the best-known is the native *Gammarus pulex pulex*.

amplexicaulis: Going around the stem.

— Bacopa.

Ampullarius: A vessel with a wide belly (Apple Snails).

A genus of large fresh-water snails of the family *Architaenioglossa* with globular, covered shells. The breathing space is divided into a gill-space and a lung. As a result these creatures can live for some time out of water. The apple snails are attractive snails with sometimes nicely striped shells. The foot is wide. On the head there are two lip feelers and two very long main feelers, at whose base are the eyes, on stems.

Ampullarius, laying eggs

Coming from tropical South America, all species are somewhat partial to heat. At temperatures under 68° they become sluggish and bury themselves in the bottom. They are very greedy, and therefore must be fed by themselves on lettuce, bits of plants, dry food and meat. Aquatic plants cannot be kept with them.

The eggs are laid in grape-like bunches above the surface of the water. As they develop they become more transparent. The young snails hatch in 2 to 6 weeks depending upon temperature and roll into the water.

Anabantidae: Climbing Perches. Family of tropical fresh-water fishes pertaining to the sub-order of the *Anabantoidea*, which are characterized by possessing the

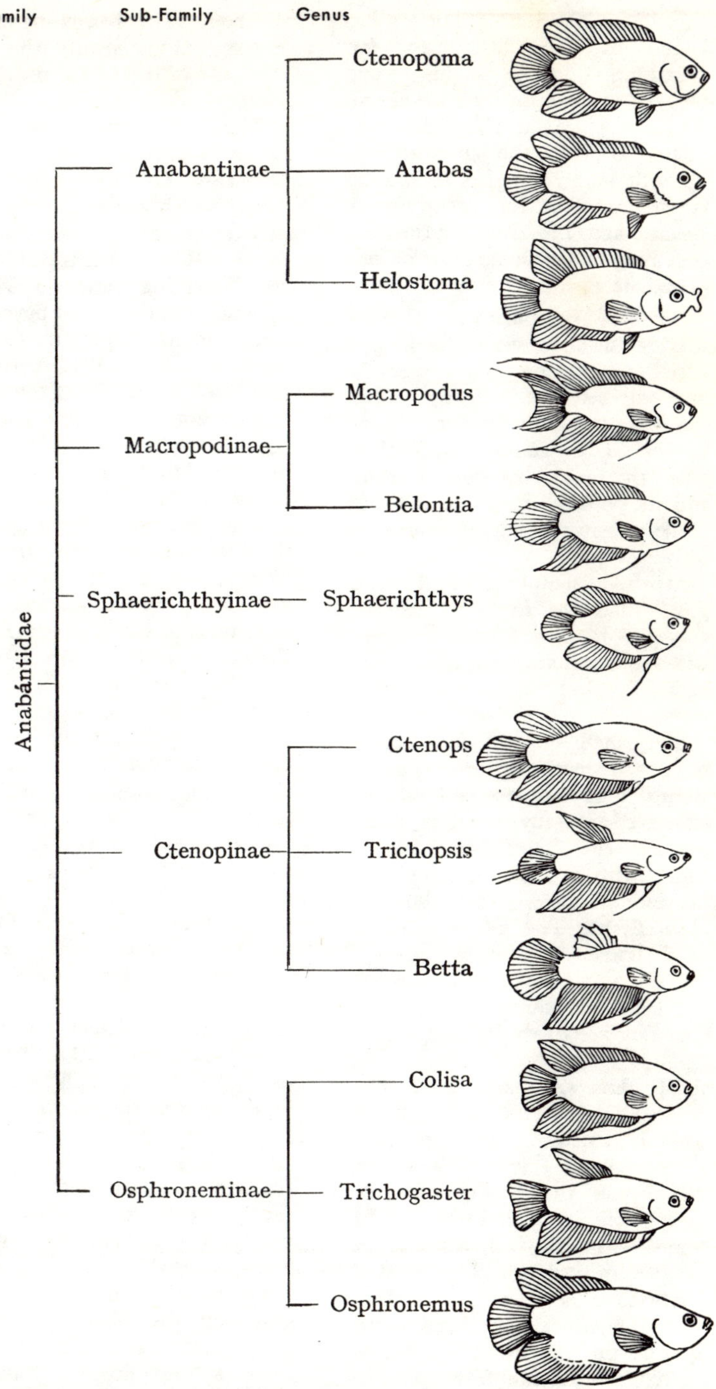
Family
Sub-Family
Genus
Anabantidae
Anabantinae
Ctenopoma
Anabas
Helostoma
Macropodinae
Macropodus
Belontia
Sphaerichthyinae
Sphaerichthys
Ctenopinae
Ctenops
Trichopsis
Betta
Osphroneminae
Colisa
Trichogaster
Osphronemus

so-called labyrinth. The gills, which often are insufficient for breathing, are aided by this organ. Oxygen is taken in by gulping air at the surface. If the fishes are unable to do so, the labyrinth fills up with water, and they drown. It is true, however, that according to species and age this labyrinthine breathing may become more or less pronounced.

Some of the species are able to survive out of the water for longer periods, while only one species is able to leave it actively. This species, the Climbing Perch, pertaining to the genus *Anabas*, has given the family both its scientific and its popular name. In case its home waters dry out, it is able to travel overland.

Most Anabantids still find living possibilities even in waters that are very poor in oxygen, but, of course, without restricting to these biologically unfavorable dwelling places.

The members of the family possess a more or less flexible, elongated to compact body shape, and are generally strongly compressed laterally. The snout is short, with a tilted and not very big mouth opening. The lips are often fleshy. The gill opening is very narrow. The moderately-sized, comb-shaped scales cover the head and throat. Dorsal and anal fins are often divided into a long part with hard rays, and a short part with soft ones. The ventrals insert on the breast, being strongly extended, and on some species changed into threads. In these cases they contain mainly taste buds. The lateral line may be complete, interrupted, vestigial, or completely lacking. The ventral cavity is very spacious. It extends to the root of the tail and is supported by ribs throughout. The anus is located toward the front part of the body. The swimming bladder is long, filling nearly the whole rear part of the body, and is two-lobed.

The family ranges over Southeast Asia, Indonesia, and Africa. It comprises exclusively fresh-water fishes, which are limited to bodies of fresh water even on the island systems. They never travel into the sea. Excepting the genus *Anabas*, they are never diffused beyond the Great Sunda Isles, but the Gourami has been artificially spread for economic reasons. It is remarkable that except in the central part of the Nile no Anabantids are found in East Africa, the family being restricted only to West Africa. Similar to what happens also with the Nandids, the cause of this is found in the fact that towards the end of the Cretacean and at the beginning of the Tertiary Era the Eastern part of Africa was flooded by the sea for a long time.

In general the needs of the Climbing Perches are modest, if one does not count the need for warmth of most species. Since they very often are colorful, and exert very interesting care for their spawn, they belong among the most highly valued aquarium fishes. Take special care to have the tanks well covered! Being air breathers, the fishes are sensitive to the intake of too cool external air. With insufficient cover they are apt to contract "colds." Furthermore many species like to jump, especially if disturbed while caring for their spawn.

With regard to food the fishes are very undemanding. They may nearly be considered omnivores, as, besides live foods, they willingly take nearly all kinds of prepared foods as well. In part they also graze off the plant and animal growths in the aquarium. However, some species are anything but peaceful. They may act quite brutally toward many other fishes, especially, however, toward members of their same species or toward the opposite sex. Strutting males are especially aggressive.

Breeding them is easy, except for a few special cases. Some of the species simply spawn beneath the surface after an embrace that is typical for all species, but without paying further attention to the eggs. Other species exert the otherwise usual building of bubble nests only temporarily, or hardly at all. Apparently there are divergences in the manner of behaving even within the same species. Some fighting fishes, which probably live in running waters, do not build bubble nests, but are mouthbreeders, exhibiting an interesting ceremony of transmitting the eggs.

By far the greatest number of species build a nest of foam bubbles near the surface, the texture of which is reinforced by an outer coat of oral cavity secretion. The nest, which generally is erected next to floating plants or to other objects which offer support, is partly permeated with algae and parts of plants. The biological significance of the bubble nest has been the subject of discussions for a long time. Even on this date its aim has not yet been completely explained. One may suppose that its main end is to keep eggs and alevins together. The construction is carried out more or less industriously by the male, and is again and again improved and completed. In this there are not only differentiations deriving from the different species, but also individual gradations. After very pretty mating games and after in part displaying the most effulgent pageantry of colors, the fishes spawn beneath the nest, the male closely embracing the female and overturning her under pressure. During this act some eggs are released and fertilized. The eggs of some species, which are very rich in oil, rise to the surface, while those of others sink slowly to the bottom. The male collects them, takes them to the bubble nest, and imbeds them in the foam. Often this is done by both sexes. After the spawning it is advisable to remove the female.

It is necessary to set up the aquarium at a vibration-free location, as otherwise the nest runs the risk of being destroyed by the fluctuations of the water surface. The spawn is watched by the male. The fact that the upper bubbles burst, new ones being always added at the bottom, causes the eggs to be ever deeper imbedded in the nest and finally to become visible at the surface. The fry, which hatch as undeveloped larvae, are watched and kept together by the male until they grow big enough to swim. At first they return to the nest by means of whirling motions and in a vertical position, if perchance they sink from it. After a few days they change to a horizontal manner of swimming, and begin to swarm out from then on. The male impulse to care for the brood disappears when the father is no more able to keep the fry together. At this moment he should be removed as from then on he starts to prey on the brood. The young of species which build insufficient nests or none at all possess an adhesive apparatus on the head, while the fry of other species are equipped on both sides of the body with so-called "oil sacs" which keep the fish at the surface and which are gradually absorbed together with the yolk sac.

The very small alevins need great quantities of infusoria during their first days after free swimming.

In amateur breedings, where big broods are not so important, these are best produced in the aquarium itself. For this the tank should stand at a sunny location and be well grown with algae. After 5-7 days the fry take the finest dust food as additives, as well as moderate quantities of dry food, egg yolk, mashed enchytrae, and mashed daphnia. The temperature should be kept as constant as possible, and the water height should be kept at 4″ to 6″. For big broods it is advisable to keep up a fine-bubbled aeration during the first weeks, as the respiratory labyrinth develops only after 3-4 weeks. Young fish that grow quickly should be removed from time to time.

The best-known genera, which may be found under this general group are the following: *Anabas, Betta, Belontia, Ctenopoma, Ctenops, Colisa, Helostoma, Macropodus, Osphronemus, Sphaerichthys, Trichogaster*, and *Trichopsis*.

Anabantoidea: Suborder of so-called "labyrinth" fishes, pertaining to the order of the Perch-shaped Fishes or *Percomorphi*, with two families, the Climbing Perches or *Anabantidae*, and the Pike Heads or *Luciocephalidae*.

Formerly they were classed together with the Snake-Head Fishes or *Ophiocephalidae*, in the suborder of the *Labyrinthici*, but had to be set apart from the latter due to their diverging body shape. Even the supposedly connecting and common feature, the labyrinth organ, a cavity above the gill arches used for breathing, is shaped so diversely in the two mentioned groups, that it does not warrant their being placed together in systematics. All *A.* are tropical or sub-tropical fresh water fishes, which range over Southeast and East Asia, the Indo-Australian insular system except Australia and New Zealand, and parts of Africa.

Anabas: The Climber.

Genus pertaining to the family of the Climbing Perches or ANABANTIDAE (see these), which has lent its name to the family despite the fact that only the members of this genus are able to leave the water. Even the African relatives, which are close to the genus *Anabas*, are not, or no more, able to do so. The species pertaining to the genus *Anabas* are fishes of Perch-like shape, the dorsal fin of which is as long as or longer than the anal. The opercles are strongly toothed; the pectorals are especially vigorous and stiff. The jaws and some other oral bones are well equipped with teeth.

— testudineus (Bloch): The Climbing Perch.

SHAPE: As per description of genus. A quite rugged and vigorous fish, with rather parallel, straight dorsal and ventral outlines. The mouth is terminal. D XVI-XIX/7-10, A IX-XI/8-11. The scales are big. Length up to 10″.

COLOR: Solid colored olive green to gray brown. The dorsal and anal fins of older males are bigger than those of females, the anal fin of the males being slightly pointed.

RANGE: All of Southeastern Asia, from India to South China and the Philippines. There the Climbing Perch lives in slowly-flowing and standing waters, swamps, and rice paddies, but it is found temporarily also in ponds which are drying out and in brackish water.

CARE AND BREEDING: This fish is remarkable for the fact that it is able to stay out of the water for long periods of time, as well as for being able to move on dry land by means of its spiny gill covers and its fins. In case of need it can even climb over small gradients. This peculiarity has early spread the fame of this fish, so that it was said

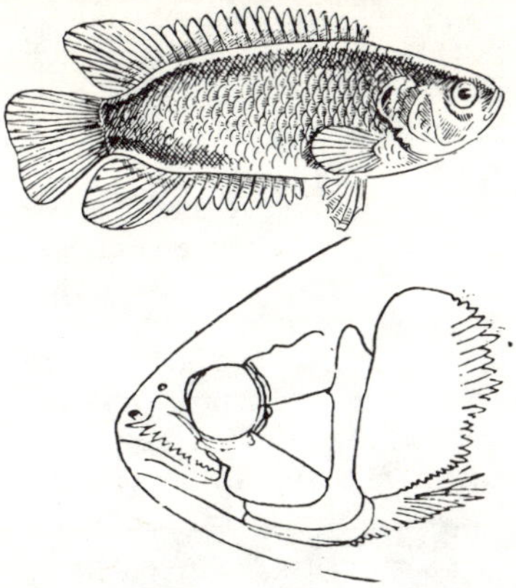

Anabas testudineus. Below is a detailed view of the head, showing spines on the operculum. (After Berg).

to be typical of the whole genus, despite the fact that it is the only species possessing this specialization.

The species is quite abundant in its home region, but has not been able to find its place in the indoor aquarium due to its simple coloring and to its viciousness. Notwithstanding this, it presents an interesting object to study. The fish try to leave the tanks at night, for which reason these should be well covered. They do not need a great deal of warmth. Average temperature amounts to 54 degrees F, but they feel better at temperatures up to 86 degrees F. They thrive well in the aquarium, but are vicious, especially toward each other. Up to lengths of 3″ they may be fed normal foods, but after this feeding becomes difficult, inasmuch as the fish become very voracious, and will accept only big and varied live foods. Occasionally they also need plant food.

For breeding especially spacious tanks with low water level are needed, as the fish reproduce only in very big tanks. Spawning takes place under close embraces, in a manner similar to that of all other species of the family, near the surface. They exert no care for the spawn.

Anablepinae: Four-Eyes.

Sub-family of live bearing fishes pertaining to the order of the MICROCYPRINI (see these) family of the Tooth Carps or CYPRINODONTIDAE (see these). Peculiar fishes, characterized by the wide head, the blunt snout with the transverse mouth, and the fleshy lips, especially, though, by the peculiar construction of the eyes. These insert high up in the head, and protrude over same. Cornea and pupil are divided horizontally into two halves by means of a strangulation of the conjunctiva, so that the fishes are able to see equally well above and below the water. This is related to their manner of living. They dwell in muddy coastal regions of tropical South America. When ebb tide sets in, they remain on dry land in great numbers. In the water they swim skimming along the surface, so that their divided eyes can see both above and below the water surface with their halves. It is further remarkable that mating can be achieved only from the right or only from the left, as both males and females possess unilaterally disposed sexual organs. Regular copulation takes place among these fishes.

Anableps tetrophthalmus

Especially well-known is the Four-Eye, *Anableps tetrophthalmus*, which has its home from the coasts of Central America down to Brazil. It reaches lengths over 12″. Very good for show aquaria, but difficult to keep for longer periods.

analagous: Similar, exerting similar functions.

analysis: Dissection of a complete whole into its simple component parts. In aquaristics, e.g., we make analyses of waters in order to check on what substances are contained in them.

anatomy: The science which studies the inner structure of live beings by dissecting them; also the inner structure of live beings in itself.

ancient fins: see PALAEOPTERYGII.

Ancistrus: With barbed hooks.

American genus pertaining to the family of the armored Catfishes or LORICARIIDAE (see these). Fishes whose body is covered with a great number of bony plates of complex structure. They differ from the very similar genus *Plecostomus* especially by the structure of the opercles. The front part of the body is flattened, the rear showing an angular section. Dorsal and pectorals are rather big. The blunt snout is equipped with many short, densely-disposed and sometimes-ramified tentacles.

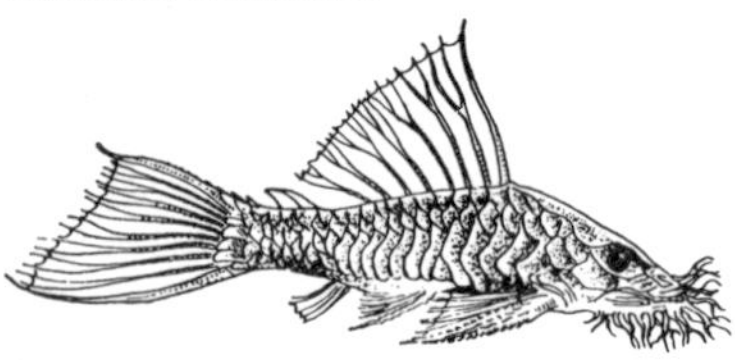

Ancistrus cirrhosus

— cirrhosus (Cuvier and Valenciennes): The Bristle-Mouth.

SHAPE: As per description of genus. D I/7, A I/4. The dorsal fin is very high, the pectorals possess a strong spine, the adipose fin too is supported by a spine. Length up to 5½″.

RANGE: Eastern South America, in the Amazon River system, in the Rio Paraguay, in Guiana, and on Trinidad. The species inhabits waters of different kinds, and is also found in brackish water.

CARE AND BREEDING: Like most Catfishes, it requires not too brightly lighted tanks with hiding caves which it leaves only at twilight or during night time. The species comes from more or less strongly flowing waters. Therefore it prefers clean, oxygen-rich water, at 72-75 degrees F. According to origin an eventual addition of salt may be necessary. Food consists of small bottom-dwelling animals as well as algae. Breeding in the aquarium has not yet been achieved.

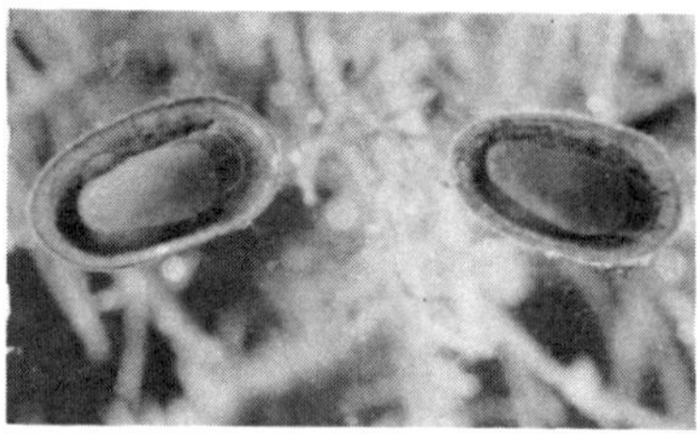

Ancylus

Ancylus: Cap Snails.

Genus pertaining to the sub-class of the Lung Snails or PULMONATA (see these), order of the *Basommatophora*. The shell is not spiralled, the rather high tip is tilted backwards, so that the whole looks like a cap. The very broad foot plate permits the snails, which live in very fast-flowing waters, to cling to their supports. In the aquarium the Cap Snails are not very enduring, and besides this they like to hide from sight. Small Cap Snails measuring up to 3/32″ are often found on the glass panes.

Angel Fish, the: see PTEROPHYLLUM.

Angiospermae: Plants with covered seeds.

Sub-division of the Flowering Plants or *Phanerogamae*, characterized by the fact that the seeds are enclosed in a fruit knot. They are divided into *Monocotyledonae* and *Dicotyledonae*.

angolensis: Coming from Angola.
— *Clarias*.

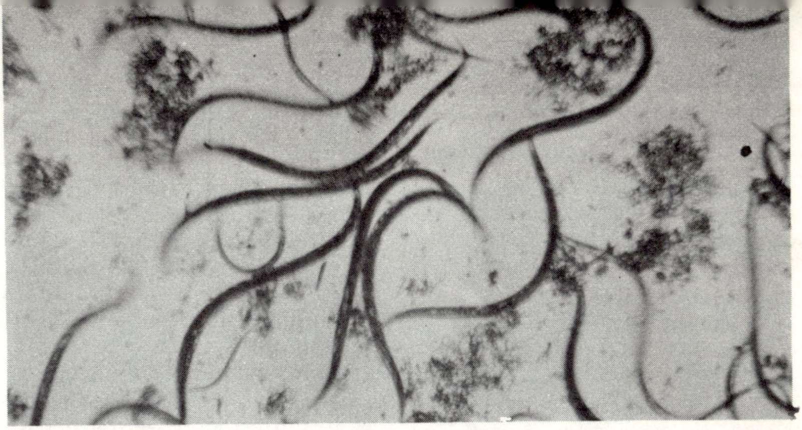

Anguilulla, Micro Worms.

Anguilla: Eels.
Genus pertaining to the family of the Real Eels or *Anguillidae*, of the order of the *Apodes*.

— vulgaris Linné: The Eel.
SHAPE: A fish of snake-like shape and round body section. The rear half is bordered by a connected fin seam; no ventral fins are present. The gill slits are vertical and very narrow.
RANGE: Europe, in standing and flowing waters which are connected with the Atlantic Ocean, but completely absent in the affluents of the Black Sea. It lives in waters of all kinds and is partly even introduced in same for economic reasons.
CARE AND BREEDING: A very predatory fish that lives within the bottom and leads a predominantly nocturnal life. Only young specimens, measuring from 2¾″ to 4″, are fit for the indoor aquarium. For a time they are quite interesting, but with time they become boring due to their hidden manner of living.

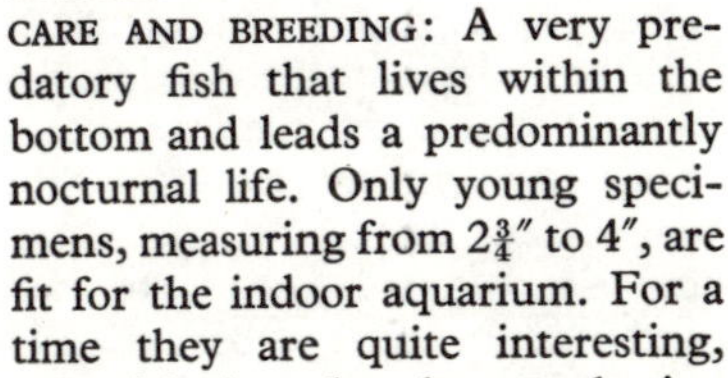

Anguilla vulgaris

Eels require a large, hard water tank, with fine sand and hiding places. Plants should only be used in loose strands. They are omnivorous and prefer live foods. For spawning they enact a remarkable migration which leads them to the Atlantic Southeast of the Bermudas (the Sargasso Sea, Nares Deep) after maturing in fresh water. After having spawned in the greater depths at that site, the old specimens die, while the alevins swim back to their home waters in order to grow up in fresh water.

anguillaris: Eel-shaped.
— *Clarias.*
— *Plotosus.*

Anguilliformes: Eel-shaped ones. Name for the Eel-like or *Apodes* proposed by Goodrich.

Anguillula: Micro-Worm; see TURBATRIX.

annectens: Connected, put together.
— *Pelmatochromis.*

Annelides: Ring Worms.
Group of worms pertaining to the tribal group *Articulata.* The body is composed of a number of externally distinguishable rings (segments), the intermediate skin of which extends into the body cavity and divides this into chambers. The number of rings is indeterminate. In some groups the externally visible rings do not indicate

the really present number of body cavity segments.

The mouth opening is found behind the first body ring on the belly. The front part of the intestine is often protractable like a trunk. Oscules may be present or not. The intestine is straight and ends at a certain segment. Most species possess a closed system of blood vessels. Locomotion is generally achieved by means of stiff bristles, which either insert on the foot stubs which belong to each body segment, or else simply in the skin. Only the Leeches, and still with one exception, have no bristles.

The classes which are of special interest to aquarists are the *Clitellata* with the order of the Scarce-Bristles or OLIGOCHAETA (see these), and the Leeches or *Hirudinae.*

Anodonta

Anodonta: Pond Mussels.
Genus pertaining to the family of the river Mussels or UNIONACEAE (see these) with three species coming from flowing or standing waters. The shell is generally oval shaped, however very changeable, according to living place, so that even the expert often finds it difficult to tell the different species apart. The Pond Mussels reach sizes of up to 8″, and live more or less deeply hidden in the mud through which they roam in search of food.

anomala: Anomalous, abnormal. — *Nannacara.*

anomalus: Anomalous, abnormal. — *Nannostomus:* see NANNOSTOMUS BECKFORDI.

Anopheles: Malaria mosquitoes; see NEMATOCERA.

Anoptichthys: Fish without eyes. Genus of blind Mexican cave fishes pertaining to the family of the Characins or *Characidae.* The genus with its single species, which has developed a few local varieties with minute differentiations, originates from a cave region near San Luis Potosi, in Mexico. Within times that are recent with regard to Earth's history it has developed from the species *Astyanax fasciatus,* which is found in the waters of the surface of the same region.

In general the body shape resembles that of the original form, but life in the caves and the different demands connected with it have caused certain divergences to appear. The fishes are characterized by the skin, which is completely pigmentless in the adult stage, and by the eyes, which are retrogressed into tiny nodules. Under a light which falls on them one notices unclear, slightly shiny bands on the sides, into which greater numbers of sensory cells are imbedded.

The Cave Fish are very interesting from a scientific point of view, since in them one can watch the different stages of the development of a species under the influence of a specific ambient world. In this one should especially notice that the alterations in body structure and in the manner of behavior that result from the lack of use of an organ are more or less fixed hereditarily. However, it is not the lack of eyes as such that is transmitted hereditarily, but the process of development back of the eyes. Specimens of the most advanced stages do not attain vision even in youth and after reproducing in the aquarium for many generations have not attained it yet.

Anoptichthys jordani

— **jordani** Hubbs and Innes: The Blind Cave Fish.

SHAPE: The body shape is the same as that of *Astyanax fasciatus* and *A. mexicanus*. Length up to $3\frac{1}{8}$″.

RANGE: Mexico, the caves near San Luis Potosi.

COLOR: Pigmentless, in youth with an indicated diamond-shaped spot on the tail-root; whitish yellow to pink, with shiny silvery parts. The male is slenderer and remains smaller.

CARE AND BREEDING: The fish move very freely, but in a manner noticeably different from seeing ones. They avoid obstacles in time without touching them. Swimming is a restless gliding, as if finding their way by touch, while orientation is achieved by perceptions of current, which have their cause in especially strong waving motions of the tail, which exceed the intensity of the motions necessary for swimming. The disturbance of the water produced by this is reflected by the surroundings, received by the system of the surface nerves, and results in a sensory perception. A strong sensitivity toward fish of the same species has been observed. When put together with fishes of other species, the Cave Fish become unsure and collides. Probably the chemical senses too are extraordinarily developed. It is an admissible supposition that in the caves the fish have to cover great distances in search of food. At least the fish glide restlessly over the bottom of the aquarium while searching for nourishment. During the first stages of development the alevins (of the specimens that have progressed to the final stages of adaptation) still possess small eyes in the form of vestiges, which later are re-adsorbed. LUELING made the observation, however, that they cannot distinguish their food optically. Live and moving food is only gobbled up after direct contact with the body. For this the fry snap towards the site of contact, often missing their aim. Furthermore, simple stimuli of motion, caused by edible animals, sometimes trigger snapping motions. If on the other hand the prey swims by at a distance from where there is neither contact nor sufficient nearness for its motion still to be detected, the alevins do not react even if the food animal is still within their visual field. LUELING and MEDER have also done extensive research into the reproduction of the species. The fish are egg scatterers, which immediately prey on the spawn that sinks to the bottom. Probably in adaptation to the conditions prevailing in the caves, the temperature plays only a minor role. Even fry were still completely motile at 55-59 degrees F. In one case the pairs spawned at 64-68 degrees F, in another case at above 75 degrees F, pH value (according to LUELING) 7.2-7.3, hardness DH 8.40.

Before spawning the fish rooted along the body with violent movements, probably in order to establish mutual contact. In this they possibly set up "odor marks", as the male consecutively visits all spots the female has touched. The behavior differs completely from that of the closely related *Astyanax fasciatus*, *A. mexicanus* and others. LUELING tried to mate male *Astyanax bimaculatus* with female *Anoptichthys*, but these were unable to react visibly to the excited males. This is one reason why in nature hybridizing between the two species should be impossible.

During the act of spawning the pairs rushed to the surface, close together, pressing together with rocking and trembling motions. According to the observations of LUELING, the eggs were released exclusively in the presence of males, while other parties observed that the laying of eggs was also effected without the presence of any males, a storing of the male semen by the female having been verified. According to these reports, several spawnings of fertile eggs took place after only one mating.

The Blind Cave Fish likes clear water, but makes no demands as to its composition. It may be kept at room temperatures. It is advisable to set up the tanks under muted light. Spawning takes place in absolute darkness. The parents have to be removed immediately, as they prey intensely on their spawn. The fry hatch on the third or fourth day, and become free-swimming from the 6-7th day on. If well fed, they grow quickly and may be ready to propagate after 3-4 months.

Anostomidae: Head-standers.
Family of Characin-like, South American fishes pertaining to the sub-order of the *Cyprinoidea*. This is a group of fishes which are especially characterized by their peculiar position (head standing). All species are more or less small. They possess a small mouth, often equipped with fleshy or wrinkly lips. The fishes are able to rasp off animal and plant growths with their teeth, which insert on the lips. They always show adipose fins. Some of the species possess accessory respiration.

The following genera are mentioned under the respective entries: *Abramites, Anostomus, Chilodus, Curimatopsis, Curimatus, Leporinus,* and *Prochilodus*.

Anostomus: With supraterminal mouth.
South American genus of Characin-like fishes pertaining to the family of the Head-Standers or *Anostomidae*.

Anostomus anostomus

Some of these moderately-sized fishes possess a nearly spindle-shaped body, of cylindrical appearance, and in part they may be lightly compressed. The upper surface of the head is slightly flattened. The lips are thick and wrinkled. The front openings of the nasal pit are extended in the shape of tubes. The supraterminal mouth is set with weak teeth. Apparently the position of the mouth disagrees with the manner in which the fish live, near the bottom. In fact, it is this position of the mouth which permits them to graze off growths despite their body position. The Headstanders leave this tilted position of the body only temporarily, under excitement, or when hungry or frightened. Not all of the approximately 20 known species can be considered pronounced head-standers.

— anostomus Linné:
SHAPE: As per description of genus. D 11-12, A 10. The scales are of

moderate size.
COLOR: Three dark-brown longitudinal stripes on ochre-yellow base. The whole body is covered

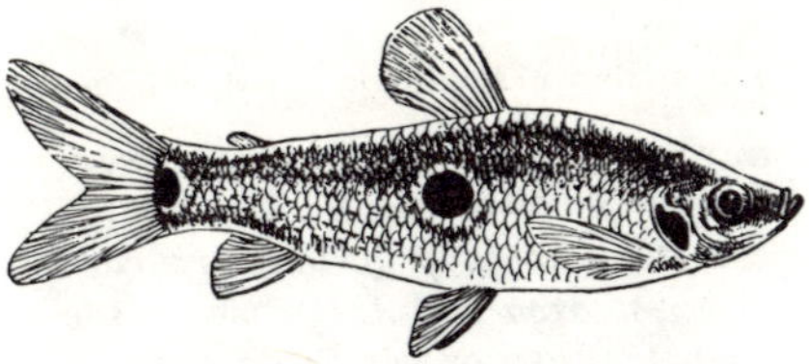

Anostomus trimaculatus

with a red tint, the fin bases being a vigorous red.
RANGE: Guiana and the Amazon basin from Manaus up. The species is also found in those tributary waters which show biologically unfavorable conditions of life and which temporarily dry up nearly totally. They are considered quite rare, especially as they probably are hard to find in their densely overgrown home waters, which furthermore are difficult of access.
CARE AND BREEDING: The fish like to swim with their heads down among plants that grow up vertically. They need sufficient open space as temporarily they may become very lively. In general they are considered peaceful and quiet, but sometimes it may happen that bigger specimens chase other fishes. *A. anostomus* take all kinds of bottom foods, but have to turn on their backs in order to eat food that has sunk to the bottom, as the supraterminal mouth does not permit another position of the body. If they do not find sufficient algae to eat, the Headstanders will also attack other soft plants.

Anostraca: Shell-less ones.
Class of crustaceans which is characterized by the fact that its members have no shells, but possess bodies that are distinctly articulated into head, breast, and abdomen. They are of elongated shape. The reticulate eyes are paired and sit on stalks. The little crustaceans are restlessly in motion, the 11—less frequently 17-19—pairs of legs beating ceaselessly and rhythmically. This movement simultaneously helps nutrition, as it sifts out the food and sweeps it into the mouth opening which is located between the legs. *A.* generally live in waters that dry up temporarily. The eggs of some species need a dry period in order to be able to develop. The animals appear suddenly after the melting of the snow or after rainfalls. Of the different species and genera we shall mention here only the Hand-Head, *Chirocephalus grubei* Dyb, and the genuine Gill-Foot, *Branchipus schaefferi* Fisch. These two species show up at different times of the year (in Germany); *Chirocephalus* from March to June, *Branchipus* from May to September. In part they are very prettily colored animals, which swim around very actively, upside down, and know how to escape lightning-quickly from eventual attempts at catching them. They spawn fertilized eggs. The males are easily identified by their remarkable, often antler-like ramified forehead lobes. The eggs pass through their first stage of development in a breast bag at the tip of the trunk. Then they fall out and go into a rest period. The nauplius resulting from this appears only a few days after the beginning of the flooding.

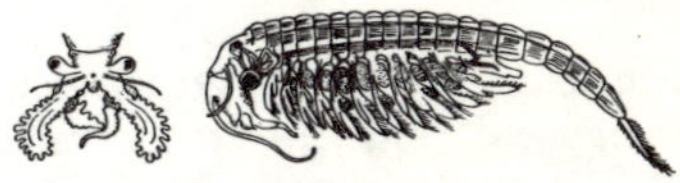

Anostraca. Detail of head

Another member of this class which is of interest to the aquarist is the Fairy, or Brine Shrimp, *Artemia salina*. It is one of the few species found in salty inland waters, while all other species live in fresh water.

All *A.* are interesting to keep, but demand a certain skill on the part of the fancier. The summer forms resist better than those of the cold seasons.

ansorgei: After the English collector, Dr. Ansorge.
— *Neolebias.*
— *Phractolaemus.*

antagonism among plants: An often seen, apparent or real, mutual suppression among aquatic plants. It is also found among terrestrial plants, but is very difficult to prove in the aquarium. Real antagonism is based on the secretion of certain growth-inhibiting substances by various plants, which act repressingly on the growth of neighboring plants or even kill them. The presence of antagonisms in the aquarium has not yet been fully proven. The impression of the existence of antagonisms may also originate from the fact that the need for food of one plant is greater than that of another, or that the vital conditions in an aquarium are not equally good for all plants. The experiments of LEWER could not prove the existence of antagonisms. He proved, e.g., that the hostility between Vallisnerias and Cryptocorynes is only apparent, and that the two species simply present basically different demands on life, for which reason they cannot thrive side by side.

antennae: Feelers of crustaceans, myriapods, and insects, divided into articulations. They have developed from the front limbs, and are the carriers of several sensory organs, especially of the senses of smell and touch, but many antennae simultaneously fulfill functions of locomotion.

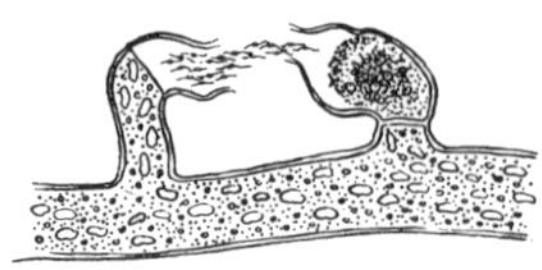

Antheridium of **Vaucheria** at left, enlarged

antheridium: The male sexual organ of lower plants. It produces great numbers of germinating cells (*spermatozoa*), which penetrate the female organ or *archegonium.*

antibiotics: Organic products coming from vegetable micro-organisms (algae, lichens, fungi, bacteria), which, even if present in very small quantities only, inhibit the growth of other micro-organisms. The antibiotics have reached great significance in medicine. Lately experiments have been made by aquarists with antibiotics as a means of fighting diseases, of furthering growth, etc. So far the experiments have seldom led to positive results.

antipyretica: Against fever.
— *Fontinalis.*

Anubias, type of the genus

Anubias: After the Egyptian divinity of the Nether World, *Anubis.* The name indicates that the plants grow in dark waters (Spear Leaf).

Genus of West African swamp plants pertaining to the family of the Aaron's Rod plants or *Araceae*. Perennial, amphibious, the root-stock is generally strongly ramified. The long-stemmed leaves are lanceolate, spear, arrow, or heart shaped. The monosexual flowers consist of a pestle-shaped inflorescence, which is surrounded by a more or less fleshy flower sheath. The fruits are berry-like. Twelve known species, which grow in swamps, on the banks of rivers, especially in tropical rain forests, and at other shady spots. They are quite sensitive and adequate only for swamp aquaria and moist-warm terraria. The bottom soil, old clay mixed with coarse sand, should be at least 4″ high. Temperature of air and water 77-86 degrees F, in winter 64-68 degrees F. Reproduction through division of the root stock.

Apeltes: The scale-less one.

Genus of North American Sticklebacks pertaining to the family of the GASTEROSTEIDAE (see this), similar to the European genus *Gasterosteus*, un-armored, the back equipped with four spines which are a little tilted laterally.

Aphaniops: Similar to *Aphanius*. Genus pertaining to the family of the Tooth Carps or *Cyprinodontidae*, sub-family of the *Cyprinodontinae*, differing from the closely related genus *Aphanius* by the small number of rays in the dorsal fin and by the structure of the anal.

— *dispar* Rueppell: The Mother-of-Pearl Carp.

SHAPE: The body, which looks rather short and vigorous, is compressed laterally, the upper side of the head is flattened, the mouth opening is small and tilted upwards. D 8-9, A 10, both fins inserting far back. The scales are quite small. Length, males up to $3\frac{1}{8}$″, females up to $2\frac{3}{4}$″.

COLOR: The species is very variable, besides this the sexes are very differently colored. The male has shiny silver-colored longitudinal stripes on a blue-gray base, the female is much less vivid, with dark longitudinal stripes on the flanks. The fins of the males are considerably bigger.

RANGE: Asia Minor and the coastal waters around the Red Sea and the Arabian Sea to Northwestern India. It seems that lately the species is also spreading further into the Mediterranean region. It is found in fresh as well as in brackish and salt water.

CARE AND BREEDING: The species is very rugged and deserves greater popularity. It is lively, even if a little quarrelsome, but otherwise quite easily kept. It is advisable to offer the fish tanks with plenty of hiding places in the form of dense plant growths. A small admixture of salt is favorable, especially for imported specimens, but in time the fish also adapt to pure fresh water. Temperature 60-77 degrees F, preferably 70-75 degrees F.

For breeding the fish should be well fed, as otherwise there will be no development of eggs. The act of spawning takes place on the roots of floating plants, each egg being fertilized separately. The fry hatch after 10-14 days. Generally they stay near the surface and take all kinds of dust-sized live and dry foods. They are easy to rear and grow quickly, but are quite short-lived.

Aphanius: From 'aphano', living hidden, invisibly.

Genus pertaining to the family of the Tooth Carps or *Cyprinodontidae*, sub-family of the *Cyprinodontinae*. Notably differentiated from the closely-related North American genus *Cyprinodon* by a number of body peculiarities. All *A.* like a well-illuminated, sunny location, but are quite insensitive to fluctuations of temperature. They may be kept at room temperature. Do not use too small tanks as the fish are very lively and a little quarrelsome. Above all one should provide for sufficient hiding places. All species are grateful for an addition of salt to the water. The relatively big eggs are 'hidden' singly among bolsters of algae. Well-fed fish hardly ever prey on them. The fry hatch in quite varying lengths of time. They are relatively easy to rear with dust-sized live and dry foods, but breeding them should not be done by impatient people. The genus comprises a series of species, of which in this book we shall describe only the two best-known ones.

—iberus (Valenciennes): The Spanish Tooth Carp.

SHAPE: A species of somewhat compact build, compressed laterally, the fins inserting far back. D 9-10, A 9-10. Length: males 2⅜", females 3⅛".

COLOR: The males with 15 luminous light-blue cross stripes on blue base, the females completely different, much simpler in color.

RANGE: Spain and the highlands of Algeria, generally in fresh water.

CARE AND BREEDING: The species is very lively and hardy, but unfit for communities as it is a little vicious, especially towards smaller fishes. Besides algae it eats mainly live foods. The need for warmth is not great. Temperatures between 59 and 77 degrees F, mean temperature may sink as low as 50 degrees F. Breeding takes place as per description of genus. The very big eggs are spawned among plants near the surface.

— sophiae (Heckel): The Persian Tooth-Carp.

SHAPE: Similar to the previous species, but a little smaller and shorter. D 10, A 9-10.

COLOR: An especially beautiful

Aphanius sophiae

aquarium fish. The male is dark brown, during the spawning period nearly dark blue, with light dots and spots, the fins light edged. The female light brown with a darker spot design.

RANGE: In fresh and brackish waters, but also in the sea around Asia Minor.

CARE AND BREEDING: As described for the previous species and for the genus. This species too eats mainly live food, which must be rich since otherwise there will be no development of spawn. Despite the fact that it is possible to keep them also in fresh water, the fish are livelier with an admixture of salt. They spawn in plant thickets after violent chasing. The glassily-transparent and big eggs are laid among algae, etc. The fry hatch after 10 days at 75 degrees F. The parents should be removed after spawning. Temperatures should be held between 60 and 86 degrees F, the best being 72-75 degrees F. The species requires much sun.

Aphyocharax: Small *Charax* (another genus of Characins).

South American genus pertaining to the family of the Characins or *Characidae*. Small and slender school fishes of the open water, of even, elongated build. An adipose fin is present. About 20 known species, which nearly all are strongly silver-colored and show

Aphyocharax axelrodi

different delicate tints under reflecting light. The fins of some species are totally colored with a vivid red, or vivid red at the bases. Keep them in large schools in not too small tanks which offer the fish space for swimming. They like sunlight. They are egg scatterers, which also spawn in schools after vigorous chasing. After spawning the parents should be removed as they prey heavily on their own spawn. Rearing the young with very fine dry and live foods is easy. In this book we describe only one species, as all resemble each other strongly.

— **rubropinnis** Pappenheim: The Blood-Fin.

SHAPE: As per description of genus. D 9-10, A 20-21. Length up to 1¾″.

COLOR: Strongly greenish silvery with dark red fins. The male is more slender, possessing small hooks on the anal fin (invisible to the naked eye), which easily get caught in the net when netting the fish from a tank.

Aphyocharax rubropinnis

RANGE: Argentina, in the La Plata system.

CARE AND BREEDING: As per description of genus. A very lively and peaceful school fish which poses no special demands as to temperature. Notwithstanding this, it is mostly lively at 75-77 degrees F. At low temperatures, which may sink down to 50 degrees F they become sluggish. Spawning takes place in the morning hours. The 300-500 glass-clear and very small eggs are scattered freely. At 77-79 degrees F the fry hatch after 30 hours and hang directly from the surface or from near it. They grow very quickly and may already be able to reproduce after 6 months.

Aphyocypris: Small Carp.

Genus of Carp-like school fishes pertaining to the family of the CYPRINIDAE (see these), with one species. The reason for them to be classed as a genus is doubtful.

— **pooni** Lin Shu Yen: The Venus Fish.

Closely related to the species *Tanichthys albonubes*, differing from this only by a minute difference in the color of the fins.

ORIGIN: South China.

Aphyosemion: Small fish with flag.

Genus of Tooth Carps pertaining to the sub-family of the egg-laying Tooth Carps or *Cyrpinodontinae*. Originating from tropical West Africa, where it is widespread with many species and sub-species which are very difficult to differentiate from each other. The body is slender, nearly cylindrical in the front part, a little flattened on the upper portion of the head, more strongly compressed at the caudal peduncle. The mouth opening is wide and slanted obliquely upwards, the lower jaw protruding.

The body shape is a little similar to that of the Pike. It is difficult to describe these very colorful fishes, and for this reason we shall not try depicting the colors of each species, excepting some very simple general remarks, as the reader would still be unable to form an idea of the appearance of the fish. In all cases the males differ from the generally plainly-colored females by their more striking colors and the richer development of the fins. The tail fin of the males is often indented in three parts, and often single fin rays are extended in the shape of threads. In some species the females too are a little more vividly colored, as for instance in *A. bivittatum*, but they are always weaker in color than the males. Some of the species of *A.* like to stay near the bottom, or in the central reaches of the water, while others are surface fishes. Too intensive lighting, as well as too high temperatures, are unadvisable, as they are apt to shorten considerably their already short span of life. All species of *A.* are forms that have adapted to life in dark waters in tropical rain forests, with strongly changing water conditions. Some are also found in very small puddles of water which may dry up at any time.

They are vigorous eaters. Daphnia and cyclops are eaten only in case of need, the bigger species scarcely taking notice of them. Preferred food: small fishes, enchytrae, tubifex, mosquito larvae of all kinds, and earthworms. If you want to induce the fish to spawn, rinse all food in netting, in order to avoid the development of infusoria as far as possible. It is preferable to feed frequently, rather than to feed too richly. Most species find it difficult to withstand dirtying of the water.

The water must be relatively free of bacteria and infusoria. Uneasiness is immediately shown by closing the fins; then the fishes become prone to all diseases. Generally speaking, all species like soft water with a slightly acid pH value, and containing humic acid. If such water cannot be obtained, MEDER advises an addition of about ½ oz. of kitchen salt per 10 quarts of water, which inhibits the development of bacteria. TUSCHE recommends the use of the purest possible salt. With the admixture of salt, filtering and occasional changes of water become unnecessary.

Unfortunately the special care and measures needed for breeding the *A.* species have led the fishes to have become rare in planted aquaria. As a rule they are seen only in bare whole-glass tanks or in breeding jars. This fact has restricted breeding them considerably. Their full beauty, however, is only shown in tanks that are rich in plants and other decorations, with a dark bottom and low water level. The best is to cover the bottom with boiled peat moss, filtering the water over peat as well.

The species of *A.* permit a general division into two groups, of which one is relatively peaceful while the other is predatory and vicious. While for instance *A. coeruleum* attacks and chases all fishes, in the peaceful species generally only the members of the same species attack each other. If two males of the same species meet, they approach with distended gill covers and spread fins, and may come to vicious fights in which the ornamental fins are apt to be torn. Such lacerations generally do not regenerate! Other species of *A.* which share the same tank are scarcely noticed. This circumstance should be considered when stocking the aquarium, and for this reason one should always provide for dense planting.

In nature reproduction is probably simultaneous with the start of the rainy period, during which the temperatures are lower. For this reason the breeding temperatures should not be too high; higher degrees of warmth generally inhibit the development of the spawn. The act of spawning is preceded by beautiful mating games. Fins and gill covers are spread. The male woos the female with vivacious motions. Females which are not yet ready to spawn may be chased too rapidly and may suffer serious wounds. With the bottom-spawners the male presses the female down near the bottom, with the plant spawners near the bunches of plants, etc., the bodies being pressed closely together. Under violent trembling, an egg is expelled, caught in the distended anal fin of the male, fertilized, and thrown into the mulm or a plant thicket with a strong stroke of the tail fin. Generally the act of spawning takes place in the morning, in the first months of the year. The eggs go through a more or less long period of development, and are sensitive to light. In nature they resist even a temporary dryness, during which the fry, protected by the egg shells, weather this unfavorable period within the damp bottom of the ponds. When floods fill the waters up again, the young burst their shells. Since they immediately get a rich supply of food, they grow up very quickly and become mature for spawning within a few months, before the beginning of the new dry period. MEDER has made some research on this.

Lodged in a disinfectant solution (Acriflavine), the unhatched fry were unable to burst the egg shells. The microscope showed the very slowly-beating heart, and a sluggish circulation of blood; that is, a state of rest with a minimum of metabolism. When the water was changed and some dry food was thrown on it, there was soon a slight clouding, and the next day the egg shells were destroyed and the alevins hatched. It seems that some unicellular organisms act as 'obstetricians'.

For breeding the plant spawning species, of which *A. bivittatum* is typical, TUSCHE gives the following instructions, which are abridged here: The occasional breeder places bundles of thread algae or nylon mops at sparsely planted spots in the aquarium. Those who want to achieve better results should take a small whole-glass tank and fill it with rain water up to a height of 2″ or more. Add ½ oz. of kitchen salt per 10 qts. of such water, but do it 3-4 days before setting the fish up for breeding. Then the pair is put in for 3-4 weeks. During this time the fish may be fed sparingly with rinsed enchytrae or tubifex. As spawning substratum use thread algae, feather moss, or nylon mops. The latter are especially advisable, as they are completely sterile. The tank is placed on a dark base, the sides covered with light-green tissue paper in order to create a subdued lighting. The spawnings begin immediately after introducing the fish in the tank. The spawn is expelled while still soft, and hardens after being in the water. The sticky eggs hang singly or in small numbers from threads, but conglomerations of them get fungused easily. Six to ten eggs daily are laid, after longer separation also thirty to forty, according to size and state of nutrition of the parents. Each evening, under lamplight, one should gather the eggs. They are put into shallow dishes filled with some of the breeding water with an admixture of 1/10 gram of Acriflavine per 10 qts. of water. The dishes are set up at dark spots, keeping the temperature the most even possible (water immersion). The fry hatch after 12-20 days, are siphoned from the dish by means of small glass tubes, and are carefully transferred to a bigger all-glass tank with soft water at the same temperature. From this point on rearing them is relatively easy. During the first week they are fed infusoria or smallest dust-sized foods, the sizes of which are increased gradually. If you want to feed chopped enchytrae, these have to be rinsed. The fry are a little shy, and sometimes they are hard to find.

The bottom-spawning species too should best be allowed to spawn in all-glass tanks. The composition of the water is the same as that for the group of plant spawners. MEDER advises the use of sea sand as bottom covering, since it has rounded edges. Also ground filter coal, sifted through a sieve with a mesh of .02″, carefully washed, may do very well, according to MEDER. After spawning, the eggs, with the adhering filter coal, remain in the sieve. For *A. arnoldi* TUSCHE recommends a thick covering of mulm and feather moss on the bottom, which is kept fixed there by means of little glass tubes or rods. After the act of spawning, which lasts for about an hour for this species, the 10-30 eggs are shaken out of the moss. They collect on the bottom, are siphoned off with the mulm, and sifted out. The parents do not become disturbed by these handlings if they are done with sufficient care.

The eggs of the bottom-spawners are also kept in dishes. Their treatment is more difficult, though, since the period of hatching may last 4-6 weeks, in winter even up to 12 weeks. The best temperatures are found between 71-75 degrees F, higher warmth retards the development of the eggs or halts it completely. Infertile, that is white, eggs should be separated every day. The completely developed eggs, recognizable by the shiny, golden eyes of the fry that are enclosed in the shells, are transferred to other dishes filled half with rain water, half with tap water. Scatter as much artificial food on the surface as you can hold between thumb and index finger. The fry that do not hatch immediately are transferred to another dish and receive the same treatment again on the next day.

If you collect the harvest of eggs of several days in the same dish, you will have to consider the different periods of development, which furthermore may differ for the individual eggs.

— **arnoldi** (Boulenger): Arnold's Lyre Tail.

SHAPE: As per description of genus. D 15-16, A 15-17. The tail-fin of the male is trilobate, the outer rays being filiform and extended. Also the female's tail fin is somewhat arched on the outer edge. The scales are relatively big. Length about 2½″, the male generally remaining a little smaller.

COLOR: The species varies very strongly in coloration. A point that, according to TUSCHE, makes things especially difficult, is that the females of the species hardly differ, but are specialized to the extent that they only produce fertile eggs

Aphyosemion arnoldi

with males of their own species.
RANGE: The region of the Niger delta, in swamps, ditches, and other small bodies of water.
CARE AND BREEDING: In its behavior the species resembles *A. coeruleum*, and, like this, it is vicious, voracious, and robust. Therefore they are best kept alone, especially as several males together will not keep the peace. Temperature 68-75 degrees F. It is true that at higher degrees of temperature the fish are more vivacious, but they are also less healthy and shorter-lived.

The eggs are generally laid into the bottom, but sometimes also on the roots of plants, or on bundles of plants near the bottom. During one spawning period, which lasts for about 4 weeks, a total of about 150-200 eggs may be spawned. At about 68-75 degrees F, their period of development lasts about 32 days. For this one should use the methods mentioned in the description of the genus.

Aphyosemion australe

— **australe** (Rachow): The Lyre Tail.
SHAPE: As per description of genus. D 11-13, A 13-15; the vertical fins of the males are pointed, the tail fin is trilobate. Length up to 2⅜″.
COLOR: One of the most beautiful species, which is especially remarkable for the porcelain-white tips of the fins of the males.
RANGE: The region around Gabon, in West Africa.
CARE AND BREEDING: A completely peaceful and lovely fish, which is best kept in company with similar species of *A*. Temperature 72-75 degrees F, but withstanding temporary lower temperatures. For breeding proceed as indicated for "plant spawners" in the description of the genus.

Aphyosemion bivittatum bivittatum

— **bivittatum bivittatum** (Loennberg): The Red Lyre Tail.
This species is typical for a whole series of sub-species, where it is not yet clear whether they are entitled to be considered as separate species.
SHAPE: As per description of genus. D 11-13, A 13-14. The scales are relatively big. The tail fin is trilobate. Length up to 2¾″.
COLOR: A very colorful species, but which varies strongly, the subspecies differing considerably from one another. The common characteristic of all is the more or less visible longitudinal band design.
RANGE: In swamps and small bodies of water in West Africa, from Cameroon to the mouth of the Niger. There the fish often appear in small schools.
CARE AND BREEDING: As per description of the genus. The species is quite vivacious and remains mainly in the lower and central reaches of the water. Temperature for breeding may amount to about 75-77 degrees F. The male chases very strongly. The relatively big, initially glass-clear, later slightly yellow eggs are spawned near the bottom among plants or roots, where they adhere. Each spawning period lasts for about 8-12 days,

producing a total of 60 to 80 eggs. The females re-ripen after three weeks, so that they may be set up for spawning again. In general one cannot consider the parents spawn eaters. The spawn, the hatching of which is handled as narrated for 'plant spawners' in the description of the genus, at first grow rather slowly with rich feeding, but recover lost time with advancing age. After 10-12 weeks it is already possible to recognize the sexes; at the age of 4-6 months they become sexually mature. It is advisable, however not to set the young fish up for spawning before they are nine months old, in order to avoid lesions.

— **bivittatum multicolor** (Meinken):
SHAPE: Similar to the original form, D 10, A 13. Length: males 2″, females 1⅝″.
COLOR: Except for the coloration and fin shape, only slightly different from the original form.
RANGE: Nigeria, interior of Lagos.
CARE AND BREEDING: As given for *A. bivittatum bivittatum.*

— **bivittatum loennbergi** (Boulenger):
SHAPE: Similar to the original form. D 10, A 12. Length: females 2″, males 1¾″.
COLOR: This sub-species differs from the original form only very slightly in color and structure of the fins.
RANGE: Nigeria, the hinterlands of Lagos.
CARE AND BREEDING: As described for *A. bivittatum bivittatum* and for the genus.

— **bivittatum splendopleuris** (Meinken):
This species differs from the original form only in color. Length up to 2⅜″.
ORIGIN: Cameroon.

— **calabaricus** Ahl:
SHAPE: As per description of genus. D 9-11, A 14-15. The tail fin is not

Aphyosemion calabaricus

trilobed nor extended. Length 2⅜″, the male remaining a little smaller.
COLOR: A very splendidly colored species, in which steel-blue hues predominate. The female is characterized by a black spot on the upper edge of the caudal peduncle.
RANGE: Caught in the hinterlands of Calabar.
CARE AND BREEDING: As described for *A. b. bivittatum* and for the genus. The species likes to jump. Normal temperature may amount to 70-73 degrees F, for wintering 64-68 degrees F, for breeding 75-79 degrees F. The fry eat dust-sized food immediately after hatching.

Aphyosemion calliurum calliurum

— **calliurum calliurum** (Boulenger): The Red-Chinned Panchax.
SHAPE: As per description of genus. D 9-10, A 12-13. The tail fin of the male is trilobate, the vertical fins are extended into threads. Length up to 2¾″.
COLOR: A beautiful, but variable, species, of which there are some sub-species.
RANGE: Tropical West Africa, relatively abundant.

CARE AND BREEDING: As described for *A. b. bivittatum* and for the genus. The fish like to stay near the bottom and avoid sunlight. Each spawning period lasts about 2-3 weeks, a daily average of about 20 eggs being laid.

Aphyosemion cameronense

— **cameronense** (Boulenger): Differing from many other species of *A.* this relatively simply-colored species has no forked tail fin. Length up to 2⅜″.

ORIGIN: From Cameroon to the Congo.

The species has not been able to find its place in the aquarium.

— **coeruleum** (Boulenger):

SHAPE: As per description of genus. A relatively big and vigorous species, which sometimes may look a little awkward. D 15-16, A 16-18. The front part of the anal fin of the male is a little longer. The tail fin is trilobate, some of the fin rays, both of the tail and of the anal fin, being extended beyond the fin edge. The scales are relatively big. Length up to 5″.

COLOR: Color, as a rule a more or less intense blue-green to blue-violet, changes strongly according to geographical origin, surroundings, and mood of the fish.

RANGE: Equatorial West Africa. The species is found in quietly flowing and standing waters, especially small ones, probably also in those which on occasion dry up totally or in part. Like many members of the genus, they are adapted to changing conditions of the water.

CARE AND BREEDING: As per description of genus. The fish are bottom spawners and need roomy tanks in accordance with their size. Too much light is not advisable, but they appreciate occasional, muted sunlight. For a bottom soil use very fine sand and a layer of wrung-out peat mulm. Planting should be dense in some spots, so that the female may hide from the male, who chases roughly. The most favorable temperature lies around 68-73 degrees F, lowest temperature 61 degrees F. The fish should not be kept too warm, as thus they become even shorter-lived than usual. An addition of kitchen salt is desirable, but not necessary. The species is voracious, vicious, and predatory. It attacks fishes of smaller size, and even ones of its own size, too, and seems to need fish food for its well-being. Afford them varied, robust live foods, but do not feed them too richly. Breeding takes place in the manner described for the 'bottom spawners' of the genus.

Aphyosemion coeruleum

— **cognatum** Meinken:

SHAPE: As per description of genus. The body is rather rounded, but the dorsal outline a little flattened and nearly straight. D 8-9, A 13-14. Only the fins of the male are slightly pointed. As compared

Aphyosemion cognatum

with those of other species of the genus, the scales of *A. cognatum* are a little smaller. Length up to 2⅜″.

COLOR: The all-over hue is reddish with red dots.

RANGE: The region of the lower Congo.

CARE AND BREEDING: As described for *A. b. bivittatum* and the genus. Temperature 73-77 degrees F, also for breeding, lowest temperature 68 degrees F. The beginning of the spawning period coincides with the first months of Spring, and lasts to the end of June. In this interim 200-250 eggs may be spawned. It is advisable from time to time to substitute the spawning male with a well rested one, as one of them alone is unable to fertilize all the eggs of a whole spawning period. The fry should be sorted out and separated according to size, as the larger specimens will attack the smaller ones. They are relatively dark in color.

Aphyosemion filamentosum

— **filamentosum** Meinken:

SHAPE: As per description of genus. D 13, A 14. Some of the rays of the anal and tail fins of the males are considerably extended. Length: males up to 2¼″, females around 1¼″.

RANGE: Tropical West Africa, around Togo.

CARE AND BREEDING: As described for *A. b. bivittatum* and for the genus.

— **gardneri** (Boulenger):

SHAPE: As per description of genus. D 13, A 15. The tail fin of the male is only a little trilobate. Length: males around 2⅜″, females around 1¼″.

Aphyosemion gardneri

RANGE: Tropical West Africa.

CARE AND BREEDING: As per description of genus. Excepting one report, by MEINKEN, all others describe the species as vicious and quarrelsome, so that it seems unfit for keeping in communities. The fish like to stay in the middle reaches of the water, and like strong light. They may be kept quite cool, around 68 degrees F, and the temperature should by no means exceed 73 degrees F. *A. gardneri* are bottom spawners. Breeding takes place as described in the description of the genus. MEDER had them spawn in rinsed peat moss, drew off the water above the peat down to a level of only a few inches, and let the remainder dry up. The peat moss was kept moist, though. After six weeks he filled the tank up again with soft water. The hatching fry immediately ate freshly hatched baby brine shrimp. The males drive vigorously.

— **gulare** (Boulenger): The Gularis.

SHAPE: As per description of genus. D 15-16, A 16-18. The tail fin is trilobate. Length, in its home waters around 3¾″, in the aquarium up to about 2¾″.

COLOR: An impressively colored species, on which yellow and red hues predominate.

RANGE: Cameroon and the Niger delta. Rather rare in the same range as *A. coeruleum*.

Aphyosemion gulare

CARE AND BREEDING: As described for *A. coeruleum* and for the genus.

— **meinkeni** Myers: Meinken's *Aphyosemion*.

SHAPE: As per description of the genus. D 12, A 14. The fins are not extended into points even on males. Length up to 2⅜″.

RANGE: Tropical West Africa.

CARE AND BREEDING: As described for *A. b. bivittatum* and for the genus.

— **roloffi** Ahl: Named to honor E. Roloff.

SHAPE: As per description of genus. D 12-13, A 14-15. The tail fin is not extended, not even on males, but slightly rounded. Length: males 2″, the females remaining a little smaller.

RANGE: Tropical West Africa. Found in a cool spring-fed brook in the Sierra Leone region.

CARE AND BREEDING: As described for *A. b. bivittatum* and for the genus.

— **schoutedeni** (Boulenger): This species became known as *A. singa*, but there is no species with that name.

Aphyosemion schoutedeni

SHAPE: As per description of genus, but a little more cylinder-shaped, little compressed laterally in the front part, somewhat more so towards the rear. The dorsal outline is nearly straight. D 8, A 14. The tail fin is trilobate, but not markedly so. Length about 1¾″, the female remaining a little smaller.

COLOR: A beautiful, delicately bluish color. Resembles *A. cognatum*.

RANGE: The Belgian Congo.

CARE AND BREEDING: As described for *A. b. bivittatum* and for the genus. The species is rather shy and remains among plants or in other hiding places if under too intense light, which it does not like. They become livelier towards the evening. The fish should not be kept too warm, 68-73 degrees F being entirely sufficient. *A. schoutedeni* also eat artificial foods, but one should always consider that they take food from the bottom unwillingly. They like to stay in the upper reaches of the water. The spawn is not especially sensitive to light.

— **singa** (Boulenger): see A. SCHOUTEDENI.

— **sjoestedti** Loennberg: The Golden Pheasant.

SHAPE: As per description of genus,

Aphyosemion sjoestedti

nearly cylindrically round, the front end of the body especially robust. The vigorous caudal peduncle is slightly compressed laterally. D 17-19, A 17-19. Length up to 4″.

COLOR: Very vividly colored, like almost all the species of *Aphyosemion;* the upper part of the body a brassy to reddish golden yellow, the lower part a luminous steel to navy blue. The body colors extend also to the fins. The tail fin is three-colored, the central rays of the anal of the male are extended. The female is less brightly colored.

RANGE: In the coastal waters of Guinea and Cameroon.

CARE AND BREEDING: This very aggressive and robust species feels especially well in densely planted tanks with a dark bottom and soft, acid water. Breeding does not differ from that of the other species of *A.* that are bottom-spawners, but the eggs often incubate for up to 9 months. During this time they naturally are exposed to many dangers. Notwithstanding this, breeding them is not especially difficult.

— **vexillifer** (Meinken):

SHAPE: As per description of the genus. D 9, A 14. Length up to 2½″, the female remaining a little smaller.

The species originates from Tropical West Africa and resembles *A. bivittatum bivittatum* in care and breeding.

Apistogramma: With unreliable lateral line.

Genus pertaining to the family of the Cichlids or *Cichlidae,* which is restricted to South America in its range. According to LADIGES and others, most species should be found in the region of the upper courses of the rivers, in sunny, narrow, shallow waters with soft bottom.

The body is more or less elongated and of small size in all cases. The genus is included among the so-called 'Dwarf Cichlids,' a group of Cichlids composed of several genera, not representing a systematic unit. It is probable that in time science will have to subdivide the genus, since it congregates species which probably should belong to different genera (a so-called 'collective' genus). It is difficult to list common characteristics for the different species.

The aquarist will find them most interesting in the field of behavior, especially in reproduction. In accordance with their size, most species of *Apistogramma* are relatively peaceable, especially in comparison to their bigger relatives. They root and dig little or not at all, since as a rule they breed in caves, and they spare the plants. Care for the brood takes place in the manner that is typical for the non-mouthbreeding Cichlids. It is best to offer the fish not too small tanks, with many hiding caves, dense planting, and, in order to bring out the full beauty of their colors, incident light. According to present experience they like the softest possible water, even if not all species are equally exigent to this. The eggs are spawned as in a closed cluster, partly on rocks, in case of need also on leaves, partly under the roof or on the walls of caves. During the care for the brood the fish tend to be very sensitive to disturbances. Therefore it is best to screen off the tank with thin paper or something similar until the fry become free-swimming. At first the hatching fry are lodged in hiding places which are very inaccessible, keeping out of sight until they complete their development. They show up after 10-12 days under the care of one or both of the parents. It is mainly the females of this genus who care for the young, the males doing this only exceptionally. During the breeding period the behavior of all species of *A.* is very fetching. For this reason they represent excellent material for the study of animal psychology. Breeding them is not always simple. Besides the factors of water, warmth and food, mating also depends on the choice of pairs that are adaptable to each other. For this it is best to rear a number of young specimens, letting the pairs mate according to preference. Rearing the fry, which are fed during the first week, is not difficult. Right from the beginning they take finely ground food, enchytrae sifted through a piece of cloth, egg yolk,. micro-worms, and baby brine shrimp. If there are sufficient hiding places available and if the breeding tank is sufficiently big, several pairs will be able to breed and rear their young simultaneously.

— agassizi (Steindachner): Agassiz' Dwarf Cichlid.

SHAPE: As per description of genus. The body of this species is elongated and at times it looks peculiarly stiff due to the dorsal outline being nearly straight. The ventral contour of the male may sometimes be a little bent inwards. The lateral line is only weakly developed. D XV-XVI/6-7, A III/6. The scales are relatively big. The vertical fins of the male are a little pointed. Length: males 2⅜"-3⅛", females 1⅝"-2⅜".

COLOR: The species varies in color according to origin, but as a rule the males are blue-gray to blue-

Apistogramma agassizi

green with luminous shiny dots and a broad black horizontal stripe on the sides. The female shows pronounced mating colors, becoming vivid yellow with deep black spots. Under certain circumstances the female may be very similar to the male. Then it shows even the typical male colors in the tail fin.

RANGE: The system of the Amazon River, including the central tributaries, as well as the upper course of the Parana and Paraguay Rivers.

CARE AND BREEDING: As per description of the genus. In general the species may be considered moderately peaceable, but at certain times both sexes may become quite aggressive, the female especially so during the care for the brood. However, serious fights rarely take place. Temperatures 72-75 degrees F, no lower than 68 degrees F, for breeding 77-82 degrees F. The species is a little sensitive to changes of water and to chemicals in the water. This should be given special consideration when treating eventual diseases or when preparing artificial breeding water. They like soft, slightly acidified water. Breeding does not always succeed. The care for the brood is almost exclusively exerted by the female, but the male is generally tolerated near the breeding site.

— **borelli** (Regan): Borelli's Dwarf Cichlid.
A very beautiful species which was imported only once and has become extinct again in the aquarium.

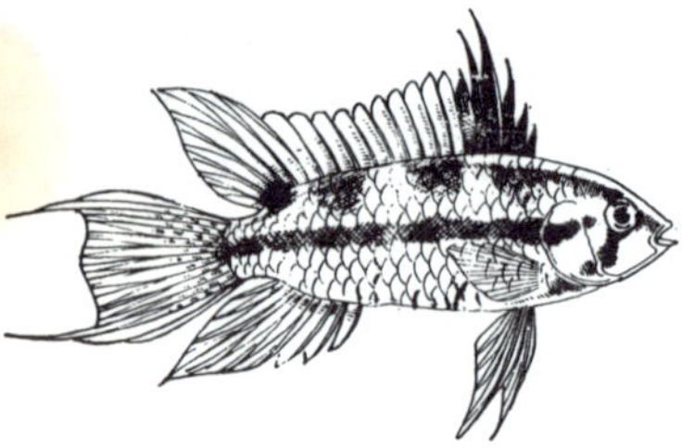

Apistogramma cacatuoides

— **cacatuoides** Hoedeman: The Cockatoo.
SHAPE: As per description of genus, the body elongated and nearly cylindrical. Only slightly compressed laterally. D XV/5, A III/7. Length around 2¼″, the female remaining a little smaller.
COLOR: Over the olive brown basic coloring extends a dark horizontal band and from the eye to the edge of the gill cover there is a vertical dark stripe. A dark spot is found at the base of the soft dorsal fin. All fins are slightly bluish to greenish. The first rays of the dorsal are extended and of a dark color. The less brightly colored female lacks these extensions.
RANGE: Surinam and British Guiana.
CARE AND BREEDING: In part like *A. agassizi*, but the care for the brood resembles more that of *A. ramirezi*. The fish reached Europe under the popular name *Apistogramma* 'U2'.

— **commbrae** (Regan):
The name of this species originates from a misunderstanding of the site where they were first found

Apistogramma commbrae

and should really be '*corumbae*'.
SHAPE: As per description of genus, the body rather short as compared to *A. agassizi*, could be called elongated-oval, and is compressed laterally. The number of fin rays is not always the same, being generally D XVI/5-6, and A III/6-7. Length up to 2″.
COLOR: Strongly variable, in general yellowish-brown with a band design and dots, on the sides a series of black spots. The female is smaller and usually less colorful. Sometimes, however, the sexes are difficult to tell apart. During the breeding period the color changes to an intense yellow.
RANGE: The upper course of the Parana and Paraguay Rivers.
CARE AND BREEDING: As per description of the genus. The species likes seasoned tanks with old water, of which, however, one has to change a part from time to time. Temperatures 68-72 degrees F, for breeding 77-82 degrees F, lowest temperatures 59-62 degrees F.

— **ornatipinnis** Ahl: The Beautiful-Finned Dwarf Cichlid.
SHAPE: As per description of the genus, the body elongated-oval, strongly compressed laterally. D XV/7-8, A III/6. The outer edge of the tail fin is slightly curved inwardly, the outer rays being a little extended, the same happening with the first rays of the ventral. The scales are relatively big, the lateral line is interrupted. Length:

males $2\frac{3}{4}''$, females 2″.
COLOR: Brownish base with darker spots and faint bands, shiny stripes on the opercles and two rows of shiny spots along the flanks. The fins show very beautiful colors and designs. The female remains a little smaller and is more simply colored.
RANGE: British Guiana, especially in secondary waters, among plants and vegetable deposits.
CARE AND BREEDING: The species seems to require much warmth, 75-77 degrees F are adequate, for breeding 77-82 degrees F, lowest 73 degrees F.

Apistogramma ortmanni

— ortmanni (Eigenmann): Ortmann's Dwarf Cichlid.
The species resembles *A. commbrae*, but is more demanding with regard to the warmth of the water. Little known up to this date. It originates from sources similar to those of the previously described species. According to NEUBAUHR breeding is similar to that of *A. reitzigi*.

Apistogramma pertense

— pertense (Haseman): The Yellow Dwarf Cichlid.
SHAPE: As per description of the genus, the body elongated-oval, somewhat compressed laterally. The lateral line is interrupted and incomplete. D XV/6, A III/6-7.
LENGTH: Males $2\frac{1}{4}''$, females $1\frac{3}{4}''$.
COLOR: In general gray-brown with a very variable design which is formed by cross bands, one horizontal band, and more or less noticeable dark spots. On the sides of the head of the male one sees shiny dots and dashes. During the breeding period the colors change over into an intense orange yellow.
RANGE: The central Amazon River, and also in the Tapajoz River, everywhere, especially in the secondary waters of the big rivers.
CARE AND BREEDING: As per description of the genus.

— pleurotaenia (Regan): The Checkered Dwarf Cichlid.
SHAPE: As per description of the genus, the body elongated-oval, strongly compressed laterally. D XVI/6, A IV/5. The dorsal fin is quite high. Ventral, anal, and dorsal fins are extended into long points. Length: males 3″, females $2\frac{1}{2}''$.

Apistogramma pleurotaenia

COLOR: Yellowish to brownish base with darker cross and horizontal bands, which sometimes form a checkered design. During the spawning period the female takes on a yellowish color.
RANGE: South America, from the Amazon to the La Plata.

CARE AND BREEDING: As per description of the genus. The demands as to temperature may change according to origin; in general 68-72 degrees F, for breeding 73-77 degrees F. The species roots a little more than the other species of the genus.

— **ramirezi** Myers and Harry: The Butterfly Dwarf Cichlid.

SHAPE: The body of this species looks relatively high, especially due to the high dorsal fin, which is generally carried erect. Strongly compressed laterally. The head is short, the snout rounded and blunt, the mouth opening very small and terminal. The forehead contour arches steeply upwards. D XIV-XVI/9, A III/8. On both sexes—especially on the males, though—the fin web of the 2nd, 3rd, and 4th spines of the dorsal may be extended into very thin points, which look like horse-hair. These extensions are of different lengths and may reach 1¼″ on some of the males. Under excitement they are stiffly distended together with the whole fin.

COLORS: The species shows remarkable, very delicate colorings, of which especially several rows of turquoise blue dots on the sides and the fins stand out. At times the sexes are difficult to differentiate, as there are only minute differences in coloring. During the breeding period the female possesses a carmine-red dot on both sides. Sometimes one cannot even differentiate the sexes based on the behavior of the fish, as the females often act like males. However, the observant aquarist will generally be clearly able to tell them apart after a certain period of observation. Shortly before the act of spawning the female shows a short genital papilla.

RANGE: Western tributaries of the central Orinoco, no exact data being

Apistogramma ramirezi

known on the exact locations where found however.

CARE AND BREEDING: The species is very charming, colorful, and of butterfly-like vivacity. It is unpretentious and peaceable, but shortlived and prone to diseases. Temperatures 72-75 degrees F, for breeding 77-86 degrees F. Direct sunlight enhances their well-being. Generally they accept only live foods of smaller sizes.

The behavior of the species is quite interesting. They like to take over and hold a certain site, defending it, in a stance that is slightly tilted downwards, and with spread fins, by making sorties against the invader from their hiding places. During this many fights develop, but always harmless ones. Both sexes show a vivid interest in the brood, the spawn being watched alternately. The species likes soft water, but has already been bred with medium degrees of hardness.

The divergence in behavior from the other species of *Apistogramma* is remarkable. It seems that the species was erroneously included in the genus for which reason lately there has been a proposition to classify it in a new genus, *Microgeophagus*. It could at least represent a transitional form.

— **reitzigi** Ahl: Reitzig's, or the Yellow Dwarf Cichlid.

SHAPE: As per description of the genus. The body is moderately

Apistogramma reitzigi

elongated, laterally compressed. D XVI/5, A III/5. The dorsal fin of the males is very high. The scales are relatively big.

LENGTH: Males up to $3\frac{1}{4}''$, females up to $1\frac{5}{8}''$.

COLOR: The male is gray-blue with a luminously yellow throat and breast, especially during the spawning period; at this time the female takes on an intense yellowish to reddish color.

RANGE: The central part of the Rio Parguay.

CARE AND BREEDING: As per description of the genus. They are the species of *A.* which is easiest to breed. Their behavior was comprehensively studied by VOGT and offers an interesting example of the single phases of behavior of Cichlids, the etiquette observed, and the relationship between the phenomena of coloring and behavior.

Aplocheilichthys: Fish with simple lips.

African genus pertaining to the sub-family of the egg-laying Tooth Carps or CYPRINODONTINAE (see these). Here we have an instance of surface fishes which possess an elongated build and are only slightly compressed laterally in front, being more so toward the rear. The mouth opening is slanted obliquely upwards. The head is flattened on the upper side, the eyes are very big. It is not improbable that the luminous eyes, like the luminous spots of other Tooth Carps and of young Archer Fish, function as bait for flying insects, which probably represent the main food of the genus in free nature. The fins insert far towards the rear. In their habitat the fishes are mainly found in the waters of the rain jungles of tropical Africa, where as a rule they appear in schools closely beneath the surface. They also travel over into the region of the river mouths, the mangrove swamps, and thus into brackish water.

All species like sunlit tanks which, besides good planting, offer sufficient space for swimming around, especially near the surface. It is advisable to set up the tanks in a manner that the light plays on the fish, as only thus their delicate colors and the big shiny eyes can be fully appreciated. They are undemanding as to food, needing live foods mainly however, especially those kinds which hang from the surface. *A.* are lively, generally peaceable, pets. For breeding use tanks standing in sunny places and with low water levels. Ripeness for spawning in the females is easily recognized by the eggs which shine through. The act of spawning takes place in plant thickets, generally under the morning sun and near the surface. The relatively large eggs are expelled singly and hang from plants, etc. on little threads. The hatching fry look like tadpoles, and keep closely beneath the surface. Their food, too, is taken exclusively there. For this reason one should keep the water level as low as possible. Furthermore it is advisable to put in finely bubbling aeration on the light side, thus avoiding the development of oily films on the surface of this side, where the fry like to stay. They do not grow very quickly, and the genus is not very productive.

— **flavipinnis** Meinken: The Yellow-Finned Panchax.

SHAPE: As per description of the genus. D 6-7, A 13-14. The scales are relatively big. Length, a scarce 1¼″.

COLOR: Metallic greenish to shiny silver, the fins lemon yellow. The male shows more intense colors and is slenderer, besides this its dorsal and anal fins end in points.

RANGE: In small flowing waters of tropical West Africa, especially in the region around Lagos, swimming in schools in the current beneath the surface.

CARE AND BREEDING: As per description of the genus. Considering their small size, the tanks may be relatively small. Artificial food is taken unwillingly. Temperatures 68-72 degrees F, lowest 63 degrees F, for breeding 72-74 degrees F.

The fish originate from jungle regions, where they live in flowing waters. For this reason it is advisable not to keep them too warm, as otherwise they become prone to diseases. The act of spawning takes place in plant thickets after stormy chasing, the pairs pressing close together. The parents pay scarcely any attention to the eggs. The fry hatch after 4-8 days and should at first be fed minute quantities of watered egg yolk or of the finest dry foods. Only after they are 10-12 days old do they take very fine dust-sized food and start growing more quickly. They become full-grown at the age of 12-15 months.

— **macrophthalmus** Meinken: The Lamp Eye.

SHAPE: Very similar to the previously-described species, and as per description of the genus. D 7, A 11. The fins a little bigger than those of the previous species. Length 1⅜″ to 1⅝″.

COLOR: Intensely brass-colored with a greenish tint, the fins yellow to orange-colored with reddish seams. Furthermore the vertical fins end in points, the female is paler in color.

Aplocheilichthys macrophthalmus

RANGE: In the same region as the preceding species.

CARE AND BREEDING: As described for the genus and the preceding species, but the fry are harder to rear.

— **myersi:** The Humming-Bird Panchax.

SHAPE: As per description of the genus. The smallest of all species of *A.* that have been imported so far. Length: males up to 1⅛″, females up to ⅞″.

COLOR: The sides of the body a luminous blue-green, with a narrow yellowish zone. The vertical fins are yellowish-green, the upper edge of the dorsal fin of the male being black-tinted, furthermore arched in the shape of a sickle.

ORIGIN: Smaller bodies of fresh water on the Gold Coast.

CARE AND BREEDING: As per description of the genus. The marvelous colors become especially outstanding when the fish are kept in schools. The eggs, which are spawned among fine-feathered plants, should be gathered. According to E. KOCH the fry hatch after 12 days at 75 degrees F. It is impossible to rear the fry without having infusoria available for them. Their growth is very slow, and the fish become sexually mature at the age of 7 months.

— spilauchena (Dumeril): The Spotted-Neck Panchax.

SHAPE: As per description of the genus, but more vigorous than the previous species. Length up to $2\frac{3}{8}''$ and more.

COLOR: Yellowish-green base at the extremity of the body with shiny silvery cross stripes. Above the pectoral fins a luminous, blue-green spot. The fins lemon yellow, The male is more vividly colored.

RANGE: In the region of the river mouths and of the mangrove swamps in tropical West Africa, especially near the Ivory Coast. The manner of living resembles that of the other species of the genus.

CARE AND BREEDING: The species is very lively and likes to swim, needing much space near the surface. According to the present observations, the fish seem quite frail in pure fresh water, for which reason an addition of kitchen salt (1-2 tablespoons per $2\frac{1}{2}$ gals of water) is advisable. In contradiction to the two previously-described species, this one needs quite some warmth. 82-86 degrees F should be adequate. According to a report from 'Wasserspiegel', Hannover, one should collect the rugged-shelled eggs from the spawning substratum into special nursery jars. There the fry hatch after about 12-14 days at 77 degrees F at a low water level. They are described as very sensitive to chemical changes. At a hardness of 1-2 degrees they hatch within 14 days, at one of 5-8 degrees only after 3-4 weeks. The first food one should give them are freshly-hatched brine shrimp, which are put into the stream of a finely bubbling aeration. After 3 weeks the fry take finely-chopped Grindal worms, which one should first put into a dish with water for 1-2 hours in order to get waterlogged.

Aplocheilus: With simple lips. Genus of Southeast Asiatic Tooth Carps, pertaining to the sub-family of the egg-laying Tooth Carps or *Cyprinodontinae*.

More or less small fishes of very pike-like shape and, at least in part, a predatory manner of living. But also the large species attack only smaller fishes. As a rule they are pronounced surface fishes, which like to lie among floating plants, ambushing insects that fly onto the water and catching them by jumping after them. They are marked by a strongly shiny spot on the crown of the head, which has earned them their Malayan name 'Tin-Heads'. This spot probably functions as a lure for aerial insects. It is remarkable that in darkness this spot is covered by layers of black pigment. Since all of them are skilled jumpers, it is necessary to keep the tanks covered without leaving any openings, especially since the fish are able to hit even the narrowest clefts. They need vigorous live foods, but will occasionally also take artificial food.

The body is elongated, flattened from above, of nearly circular cross section in front, strongly compressed laterally towards the rear. Especially the head is flattened with a very wide and supraterminal mouth opening and a somewhat protuberant lower jaw. All species appreciate well-illuminated, densely-planted tanks, where they are able to find hiding places. They like sunlight and also warmth. The eggs are spawned singly on plants, up to about ten units a day. They are rather big and not very numerous, so that in general the different species cannot be called very productive. The fry hatch after 12 to 14 days and immediately take finest dust-sized foods. They grow very quickly, especially those of the bigger species.

— **blockii** (Arnold): The Dwarf, or Green Panchax.

SHAPE: As per description of the genus. D 7, A 15. Length up to 2″, the female a little smaller.

COLOR: Blue-greenish base with rows of red and shiny golden dots, the fins yellow with red and green dots. The female is plainer in color and has more rounded fins.

RANGE: India, the region around Madras.

Aplocheilus blockii

CARE AND BREEDING: As per description of the genus. Because of its minute size this species may be kept in smaller containers. They are a little frail and it is advisable to keep them in pairs. The fish do not stay exclusively near the surface, but generally only when disturbed by other, lively, fishes. The eggs may be gathered and transferred to special hatching dishes. Anyway, rearing the young is not as easy as for the larger species. Temperatures 72-79 degrees F.

— **dayi** (Steindachner): *A. lineatus dayi.*

SHAPE: As per description of genus. D 6-7, A 15. Length 3″ to $3\frac{1}{2}$″.

COLOR: This species possesses a quite delicate coloring consisting of blue or greenish shiny hues. The females have rounded fins and at times show strongly outstanding cross bands.

ORIGIN: Ceylon.

CARE AND BREEDING: As per des-

Aplocheilus dayi

cription of the genus. The species is rather rugged and robust. It needs substantial live foods, especially aquatic insects. The eggs are 2 mm. in size, and the fry grow up very quickly.

— **lineatus** (Cuvier and Valenciennes): The Panchax Lineatus.

SHAPE: As per description of the genus. A very robust fish, the biggest of the genus. D 8-9, A 15-17. Length up to 4″.

COLOR: The male is very prettily colored, with many rows of shiny green and golden dots, which also extend on to the red fins. The female is considerably simpler, with several dark cross bands at the body extremity, but very fetching in its colors too.

Aplocheilus lineatus

RANGE: Along the Eastern coast of India, and also in Ceylon, where the species is found in waters of all kinds, but mainly in sunlit and calm small waters. It is very highly appreciated as an exterminator of mosquitoes.

CARE AND BREEDING: As per description of the genus. Older specimens need somewhat larger tanks. If insufficiently fed, this fish may become quite predatory. It needs quantities of live foods, especially mosquito larvae, and the larvae of aquatic insects.

— **panchax** (Hamilton-Buchanan): The Blue Panchax.

SHAPE: The typical species of the genus, which shows different colors according to origin. D 7-8, A 15-16. Length $2\frac{3}{8}''$ to $3\frac{1}{8}''$.

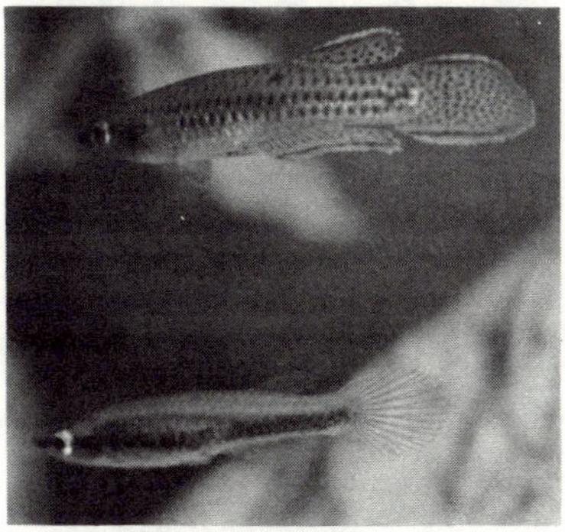

Aplocheilus panchax

COLOR: Bluish base with rows of red dots on the male, the fins with pretty red and black seams. The female is a little plainer in color.

RANGE: The whole of India and Indo-China, partly also on the Indonesian islands, in ponds and smaller waters, also in brackish water. The species is quite frequent everywhere.

CARE AND BREEDING: As per description of the genus.

— **panchax dorsomarginatus** Klausewitz:

A sub-species, discovered and imported in 1957 by Roloff, which differs from the original form mainly by the big, luminous-green spots on the opercles, and on most of the fins. The basic color of the body is a light gray-brown to vigorous red. Based on the actually existing systematic descriptions of the species *A. panchax*, KLAUSEWITZ defends the opinion that in it we find a widely distributed circle of forms which consist of a series of geographically limited sub-species, the differentiating characters of which are to be sought in their colors.

ROLOFF observed and caught this sub-species on the Southern peninsula of Thailand, and verified that they differ considerably from the specimens coming from the center of the range of the species. None of the fish were longer than $2\frac{3}{8}''$.

Apodes: Without feet (fins).

Order of Eel-shaped fishes with 18 families, including the genuine Eels (*Anguillidae*), with ANGUILLA (see this), and the Morays (*Muraenidae*).

apogon: Without barbels.

— *Cyclocheilichthys.*

Aponogeton: The name is vague, perhaps an imitation of the name of the genus *Potamogeton* (Water Ears).

Only genus pertaining to the family of the Water Ears or *Aponogetonaceae* (see these). Shape, range, and cultivation are described under that entry.

— **bernierianus** (Decaisne): Bernier's Water Ear.

GENERALITIES: A rare species which grows only submerged.

SHAPE: As per description of the family. The light to bright green leaves are elongated linear to lanceolate. The 2-4 long nervures to the right and the left of the central rib are connected by cross veins. In part the leaf tissue is lacking. The leaves may reach lengths of up to 8″, and widths of $1\frac{5}{8}''$. They grow up from the bottom on stems 2-8″ long, coming from a nearly spherical root stock, which has a diameter of ⅜″ to 1¼″. The stem of the inflorescence rises above the water surface, and may be divided two to six-fold. The small flowers are white to pink.

RANGE: In calm, standing or slowly flowing waters of the islands of Madagascar and Nossi-Bé, especially at spots which are overshadowed by marginal plants.

CULTIVATION: As per description of the family. According to WENDT the species should not be planted in too rich soil, and should preferably stand in a shadowy location. No great demands are made as to temperature; in summer 68-72 degrees F will suffice and may be raised to 77 degrees F during the blooming period. From November to February, the plants should enjoy a rest pause at 64-68 degrees F.

— **crispus** Thunberg: The Ruffled Sword Plant.

GENERALITIES: One of the best-known species, which is, however, rarely found in commerce as a pure strain, but only in hybridizations with *A. undulatus.*

SHAPE: As per description of the family. The very tender, light to bright green leaves are linear to lanceolate, and generally more or less provided with small ripples on the edges. Lengths may reach up to 10-16″, widths 1″ to 2″. Often the rippled leaf edges are finely crinkled on their part too. The leaf insertion on the stem is generally rounded, sometimes also heart-shaped. There are 3-4 longitudinal nervures on both sides of the central rib, which are interconnected as usual. Leaf tissue is always present. The root stock is bulbous and rounded, $\frac{5}{16}$″ to $2\frac{3}{16}$″ in diameter. The inflorescence is not ramified, the flowers are white to yellowish.

RANGE: In shallow, calm, and clear waters of the Isle of Ceylon.

CULTIVATION: As per description of the family. This species does not necessarily require soft water to thrive, and is not very sensitive to direct sunlight. But one should avoid excessive illumination anyway, as this always represents the danger of having the plants overgrown with algae. If the bottom is poor in nutritional substances, the leaves remain thin and frail, becoming darker and more robust with an addition of clay.

— **distachyus** Linné:

GENERALITIES: This species is hardly fit for the indoors aquarium, but it is very good for the outdoor tank. It develops almost exclusively floating leaves.

SHAPE: The floating leaves have a leather-like shine and are a little rounded off at both ends. They may be 1¼″ to 10″ long, and ⅝″ to 2¾″ wide. To the right and left of the central rib they show 3-4 longitudinal nervures which are connected by cross veins.

COLOR: Light to vigorous green, with single brownish spots. From the root bulb, which reaches a diameter of 1¼″, grow bottom-standing leaf stems which may reach lengths of up to 5′ depending on the depth of the water. The inflorescence, divided in two, the simple ears of which may grow 2⅜″ long, carries the white and pink single flowers. Some beautiful, large-flowered garden strains have been grown from this species.

RANGE: In standing and flowing waters of South Africa. The species has run wild in Southern France, parting from garden ponds.

CULTIVATION: In its home country the plant is adapted to periodical times of rest, when it withdraws down to the bulb. The same happens in garden ponds where it should be well covered in Autumn in order to protect the bulbs against frosts. Little demands are made as to temperature. In winter one may keep the plants within the house, at temperatures of 41-50 degrees F, if they receive some sunlight.

— **elongatus** F. Mueller: The Elongated Sword Plant.

GENERALITIES: A very beautiful plant for medium-sized tanks, which grows mainly submerged leaves, excepting some occasional floating leaves.

SHAPE: As per description of the family. The very delicate, bright-green submerged leaves may reach lengths of 8-12″ and widths of 1⅛″-2″. To both sides of the central rib one finds 2-4 longitudinal nervures which, as usual, are connected by cross veins. The lanceolate floating leaves attain lengths of 4¾″ to 6″. The root bulb shows diameters of ¾″ to 1″. The simple inflorescence grows to lengths of 3⅛″. The flowers are white.

RANGE: In the shallow inlets of flowing waters in North and East Australia.

CULTIVATION: As per description of the family. The species grows rapidly and during its vegetative period it develops many leaves in quick succession. During summer it withstands a temperature of 72-77 degrees F, which may slowly go down to 62-64 degrees F in winter. From February on, the temperature may be gradually raised again. The species likes soft and moderately acid water. A semi-shaded location, with occasional, but never too intense sunlight, is advisable. It thrives best under overhead light.

— **fenestralis** (Poiret): The Madagascar Lace Plant.

GENERALITIES: The most difficult of all *Aponogetons*, the cultivation of which demands very special skill. It grows only submerged.

SHAPE: As per description of family. The elongated, oval leaves, which are blunt or slightly pointed at the extremities, reach lengths of up to 12″, widths of 2⅜″ to 3⅛″, and stand on stems which grow 4-8″ long. The leaf tissue between the nervures and the cross veins is always totally absent, so that the whole leaf resembles a net or a sieve. The root stock, which lies flat within the bottom, is elongatedly cylindrical and may attain a thickness of about ¾″ with a length of 4-5″. The stem of the inflorescence, which divides into 2-3 ears, each of which reaches a length of 2″-2¾″, carries the fragrant, yellowish-white flowers.

RANGE: In shady, slowly-flowing waters of the Island of Madagascar, generally at depths of 20″-32″.

CULTIVATION: As per description of the family. According to WENDT the plant is best kept in clear, soft, slightly acid water, which should be renewed frequently as the plant is sensitive to old water. Otherwise it easily gets stunted, growing young leaves with a whitish color instead of a reddish one. It is best cultivated under a northern exposure, but even there one has to dampen the light if the location is too well-illuminated. The species thrives under muted light which may temporarily even change to complete darkness. The bottom sand should by no means have any admixtures of earth. The Lace Plant is extremely sensitive to the development of algae furthered by this. If algae should show up in the tank, the best will be to stock same with algae-eating fishes. The plants do not tolerate high degrees of warmth. In summer 64-72 degrees F are sufficient, in winter 59-64 degrees F. After developing runners the root stock may be divided, but the pieces should never be shorter than ¾″ each, states WENDT. Besides this manner of reproducing, it is also possible to grow the plants from seeds, which develop after artificial pollination. But such seedlings are hard to rear, as they have to receive a change of water of the same composition at least once a week.

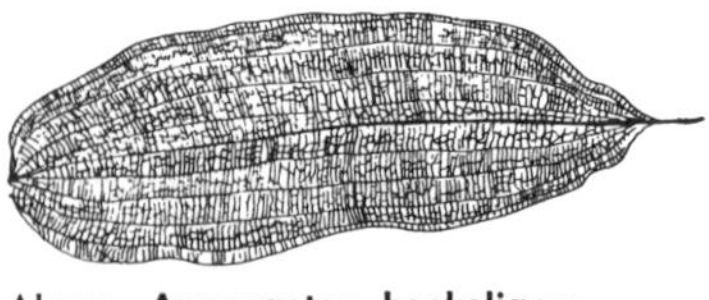

Above: Aponogeton henkelianus

Below: Aponogeton fenestralis

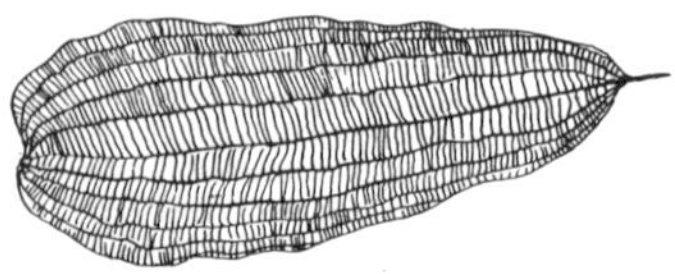

— **henkelianus** Falkenberg and Baum: Henkel's Lace Plant.
This species is very similar to the preceding one, but it is a little more irregular, showing even smaller perforations. The rhizome is not cylindrical but has the shape of an egg. The species is hardly cultivated by anyone any more.

— **leptostachyus** E. Meyer: The Frail-Leaved Sword Plant.
Of all *Aponogetons*, this is the one that should be recommended least, as it develops only floating leaves, and has to go through a rest period in a state of half-dryness every year. It originates from the desert regions of East and South Africa, where it grows in shallow watering places that remain dry for longer periods.

— **ulvaceus** Baker: The Ulva-leaved Water Ear.
GENERALITIES: A very big and beautiful species, which grows exclusively submerged, and is remarkable for its wavy leaves.
SHAPE: As per description of the genus. The pretty, light-green and

Aponogeton ulvaceus

very delicate leaves are broadly ribbon-shaped and reach lengths of 8-14″ at widths of 1¼″ to 3⅛″. They stand on stems that are 10-12″ high. The leaves are remarkable for often being wavy in their entire width, to the central rib. To the right and left of this we find 2-6 longitudinal nervures which are connected in the usual way. The leaf tissue is always present. The rhizome is rounded and bulbous, with a diameter of ⅜″ to 1¼″. The inflorescence shows two ears each of which may be 2⅜″ to 3⅛″ long. The flowers are pale to golden yellow.
RANGE: In the inlets of calm and clear waters on Madagascar.
CULTIVATION: As per description of the family. Some specimens of this species do not always demand soft water. Apparently their origin plays a role in this. Since the plants grow very big, they can only be used in roomy tanks, but look very ornamental in these. Also this species should receive a winter rest period at 64-68 degrees F. Reproduction is easily achieved by means of seeds. The bulb is not divisible.

— **undulatus** Roxburgh: The Wavy Water Ear.
GENERALITIES: A species which is good for small tanks, but which unfortunately is only rarely found pure in commerce, being generally cross-bred with *A. crispus*.

SHAPE: As per description of family. The light to vivid green, but not especially delicate, leaves may grow $4\frac{3}{4}''$ to 6″ long, and $1\frac{1}{4}''$ to 2″ wide. They are lanceolate, a little blunted at the base, and slightly pointed at the tip. The leaf edge is not curled, but shows a weak waviness. On both sides of the central rib we see two longitudinal nervures, which are interconnected in the usual way.

Aponogeton undulatus

Leaf tissue is always present. The bulb is round and attains a diameter of 1″. The one-eared inflorescence carries the little white flowers on the $1\frac{1}{8}''$ to $1\frac{5}{8}''$ long ear.
RANGE: In standing and slowly-flowing, shallow waters in India.
CULTIVATION: The species does not grow very quickly, and is difficult to induce to flower. The pure species, which is hard to find, however, needs only little space, due to its small size.

Aponogetonaceae: Water Ear, or Sword Plant.

Family pertaining to the class of the single-germinating leaved plants or *Monocotyledoneae,* with the only genus *Aponogeton* and about 27 known species. The family is scattered over Africa, Madagascar, parts of Australia and South East Asia, New Guinea, and Indonesia. The existence of further species in Mexico and in Korea has not yet been confirmed. One species is found in Southern France, having run wild there.

The *A.* are perennial plants, submerged or with floating leaves, possessing a well-developed rhizome. The submerged leaves are always elongated. Often the primary leaves differ considerably from the secondary ones, especially the floating ones. The longitudinal nervures are interconnected by cross veins, forming a grille-like design. This is often especially stressed by the fact that the intervening leaf tissue may be totally or partly absent. As a rule the submerged leaves are more or less strongly wavy. The floating leaves are more rugged, smooth-edged, and generally not curly or wavy. Leaves and inflorescences grow up from the bottom. The inflorescences rise above the surface on a correspondingly long stem, and carry one or more ears. The placement of the small flowers is variable. Their usual colors are white, light yellow, reddish, or a delicate violet. Fertilization takes place through self-pollinization. It may also be done artificially.

The *A.* are very beautiful aquarium plants. It is true, however, that they are a little touchy and demand skill and adaptability on the part of the fancier. As a rule they should not be cultivated at even temperatures the year over, but need a wintering rest at 64-68 degrees F, if one wants them to achieve full growth again the next year. During the blooming period the temperature may be raised to

77 degrees F or more. Most species prefer soft, slightly acid water, especially since this is easier to keep free of algae. The delicate, submerged leaves are especially sensitive to infestations with algae and to getting covered with mulm. According to WENDT the bottom soil should consist of one part weathered clay to seven parts sand, with an admixture of a little charcoal. A further addition of clay, in case of increasing growth, may be effected by pressing clay pellets, $\frac{3}{8}''$ to $\frac{3}{4}''$ in diameter, into the bottom sand. Avoid adding earth or dirt as they contain decay germs and may encourage the development of algae. The rhizome should be buried in the soil at a depth equal to its diameter, the vegetative insertion, the so-called 'eye' being placed in an upward position. WENDT also gives instructions as to the reproduction. Accordingly, the development of seeds is best achieved after artificial pollination with the aid of a fine paint brush. The flowers should be protected against drafts of air and drying by means of a close-fitting cover glass. Artificial pollination should be effected the moment the yellow pollen begins to fall down when shaken. It should be repeated several times, during the 10-14 days of the blooming period, as the little flowers open only gradually. The fertile ear sinks down to the water level and has then to be bound in thin gauze in order not to lose its seeds. One may also cut off the ear, putting it into a water-filled dish that floats in the aquarium. After ripening, the fruits come off and float on the water surface for one or two days. After dissolving the meaty part of the fruit, the seed is freed. If the sowing out is not to be done immediately, the seeds may be kept for some time in cooler water at 59-61 degrees F. Seeding is done in shallow dishes with low water level, at 68-77 degrees F. After the first very small leaves and roots have developed, the plants are transferred to a nursery jar, containing one inch of bottom soil made up of sand and clay, mixed with boiled peat moss or with the mulm of decayed willow leaves. Plant the seedlings very carefully. For this purpose one presses the blunt end of a pencil into the smoothed surface, putting in a seed without covering it. Then carefully fill in water to a height of about $\frac{3}{8}''$, preferably drip-wise. Germination takes place very quickly at 68-77 degrees F. The water level is increased to accommodate the increasing growth. After the little plants have become sufficiently strong, they may be transferred to their eventual location.

Aquaristics: The study, care, and breeding of aquatic animals and plants in the aquarium, done on a scientific basis, but without losing its esthetic and refreshing value for the biologically interested layman. Because of the fact that today aquaristics has spread to wide strata of the populations of all countries of the world, it is a good medium for diffusing biological knowledge in an easily understood form to the general public, as well as to supply science with numerous explanations of the phenomena of life under water. For this reason connections have been established between aquaristics and the corresponding branches of science for a long time.

Aquaristics plays an important role in this cooperation in the following fields: Classification. of the species of the native and foreign aquatic fauna and flora; breeding of animals and plants; fish diseases; practical methods for keeping animals and plants; ecology; and ethology (the science of behavior).

Called "Bionomic Ichthyology" by Dr. Leonard P. Schultz.

aquarium: From Latin *aqua*, water. 1. Container made of glass, or with glass walls, which permits watching easily and for prolonged periods of time aquatic animals and plants which inhabit it, as well as their care and breeding. In this one generally strives for an esthetic effect as well as for the most perfect possible imitation of nature.

The name aquarium was first used by the English naturalist Henry Gosse, in 1853, and acquired importance very quickly all over the world. During the hundred-odd years which have transpired since then, the aquarium has undergone a series of changes in shape and motivations. Having originally—around 1856—been intended as a parlor ornament for instructive watching of the live beings of our home waters, as was stated by Rossmaessler (see this entry) at that time, the fishes at first taking only a secondary place, with time much has changed in the stocking of the aquarium. Always to a greater extent have foreign fishes and plants, especially small fishes from the tropics and the sub-tropics (ornamental fishes), taken the place of our native live species. As a consequence of the strong interest resulting from this, the care for the aquarium has ever more changed from a simple hobby to scientific aquaristics.

Today we differentiate the following types of aquaria:

(a) according to the manner of construction:
the all-glass aquarium, and
the frame aquarium;

(b) according to the origin of the animals and plants from:
inland waters or from the sea,
the fresh water aquarium, and
the sea or salt water aquarium;

(c) according to the temperature of the water, which is a dependent upon the origin and vital demands of animals and plants;
the cold water aquarium, and
the warm water aquarium.

The most frequent form with reference to stocking it with living things is the community tank, in which different species of plants and animals are assembled, either according to the whim of the hobbyist, or else according to geographic or biological points of view. Generally in this one anticipates no breeding. The biotopical aquarium, under which heading one should also include the paludarium or SWAMP AQUARIUM (see

Aquarium, atop a well-designed cabinet

this), assembles only animals and plants with the same or with similar vital needs. The landscape (aquascape) aquarium tries further to pay attention to zoogeographic or phytogeographic points of view.

The breeding of aquarium fishes is effected in the BREEDING TANK (see this). Of course, the mentioned kinds of tanks are extremely interrelated. However, for all of them the following demands, which one has to make of an efficiently organized aquarium, are valid:

(a) The aquarium should appeal to the sense of beauty of its viewers.

(b) The aquarium should imitate certain natural conditions to which animals and plants are adapted, to the maximum extent.

(c) The aquarium should teach hobbyists and viewers to know life in nature.

Life in the aquarium for longer periods of time is made possible by adequate measures of care, and a healthy relationship is created and maintained between animal and plant, through which a sort of 'biological equilibrium' is established. For this one needs an effective location, installation, and care for the aquarium. For this the aquarist avails himself of technical accessories, which may make his work considerably easier, and which in part are indispensable.

2. A public show installation, generally as an addition to zoological gardens, installed in special buildings, used to instruct the public about life in water, and simultaneously serving scientific purposes.

aquarium cement: A special black cement for filling out the putty joints in frame aquaria, which is used in liquid state. Such cements must be guaranteed to be free of poison. One cannot caution aquarists sufficiently against the use of cements of impure or unknown composition. Cementing should always be done after the aquarium has been in use for some time and after the putty has hardened sufficiently, as otherwise the cement will come loose easily due to the settling of the panes, or else it is dissolved by the oil contents of the putty.

Aquatica: Living in water.
— *Argyroneta.*
— *Cabomba.*

aquatic insects: see HEXAPODA, INSECTS.

aquatic plants and their care: Aquatic plants are important in the aquarium for many reasons; keeping an aquarium without them is unthinkable. Only their presence makes possible a biological condition which permits the well-being of the fishes within the closely limited water container. Together with the biological value we have, of course, the esthetic one. This is no less important.

The ornamental effect of plants will further one of the most important aims of aquaristics, that of offering pleasure and relaxation, if it is not pure utility which necessitated the installation of the tank. This alone is a sufficient reason why more attention should be paid to the efficient and loving care of the plants than is generally done. Fully developed aquarium plants are beautiful. They enhance the colors of the fishes and at the same time induce them fully to develop their natural behavior through the differentiated surroundings which may be created with their aid. Aquarium plants are indispensable for many species of fishes insofar as dense stands offer them the necessary hiding places into which they may retire, either because they pursue a hidden manner of living, or else to escape a too strong pursuit of males or tormentors. Especially young fishes seek such hiding places and may spend their first period of development there nearly unmolested.

For numerous species, plants are the natural spawning substratum. Frequently, among the so-called egg-scatterers, the act of spawning takes place in plant thickets. Others, the so-called egg hangers, stick the eggs to the plants one by one. Fishes that care for their spawn need parts of plants to build their nests, or spawn on large leaves. Numerous micro-organisms settle on plants, serving in their part as nourishment for fish fry which thus find their food waiting as soon as they hatch.

The biological value of plants, however, reposes in the irreplaceable interrelationship between them and the animals. Above all it is the circulation of gases necessary for the life of both parts, conditioned by breathing, and assimilation, which makes plants indispensable. The production of oxygen, of which some plants are capable to a larger, other to a lesser degree, cannot be replaced even by the best aeration, especially since plants simultaneously assimilate the excesses of carbon dioxide, and also make use of other organic and inorganic substances. the accumulation of which in the aquarium is undesirable. In order to thrive, plants need some basic factors which shall be discussed as follows:

1. LIGHT. The fact that assimilation (photosynthesis) is achieved with the aid of light leads to the conclusion that one can never pay too much attention to the conditions of lighting. Indeed the needs of plants in this are diverse, but nearly all the plants we keep in our aquaria require sufficient light in order to thrive. Also plants of which one knows that they will also grow under less lighting, Cryptocorynes for instance, are thankful for larger amounts of illumination. Only very few plants, the very sensitive Madagascar Lace Plant for example, visibly prefer darker locations. In general submerged (meaning, under-water) plants need less light, especially sunlight, than emerged swamp plants. These need sunlight above all if they are expected to bloom. Also plants that float on the surface need more intense illumination. At the same time these screen off too intense lighting from the submerged plants. Our domestic water plants are adapted to 15-18 hours of daylight during their principal vegetative period. In murkier winter, however, they recede or die, even if we offer them sufficient lighting. Contrarily, tropical plants are adapted to a shorter day, which lasts exactly 12 hours along the Equator. One should consider this especially if one wants to make such plants bloom. For growing, however, they also withstand longer periods of light. In winter, when daylight often lasts for comparatively only a few hours, one has to help them to thrive with artificial lighting. It should by no means be supposed that tropical and subtropical plants always present special needs as to the intensity of light. It is a well-known fact that in the hot regions of the globe, if there is sufficient rainfall, plants compete with each other for places in the best-lit spots. Many of them have to make do with half-shade or shade, possibly even with twilight. Of course this does not mean that such plants would not be grateful for stronger illumination. Too-strong incidence of light unfortunately favors the development of the noxious algae. Consequently one may partly be forced to deprive aquatic plants of the benefits of sunlight in order to prevent the

harmful, for some plants even lethal, consequences of too intense proliferation of algae. Combating algae, and the location of the AQUARIUM (see this) have to receive special attention for this reason. However, faulty locations may be compensated to a great extent with artificial lighting.

Besides its duration and intensity, the angle of incidence of the light has great influence on the growth of water plants. Light from above is the most favorable for the plants. It is thus that they are illuminated, for instance in hatcheries, where they are cultivated in hot-houses and in cement or wooden tanks. Unfortunately the consequence of this is that under the changed conditions of the aquarium they are not able to develop well. In most cases light from above is rather difficult to obtain in the home aquarium, unless one can light artificially from above. Lateral artificial lighting is not advisable for longer durations, for physiological reasons to plants and animals, since such light does not correspond to the natural adaptation of the living beings. The most favorable angle of incidence of the light has to be found experimentally. In bigger installations it generally is impossible to satisfy all demands. It is astounding, however, how strongly an often insignificant change of location may affect the thriving of aquatic plants. The hard-to-control obstacles which may hinder the growth of plants also include the different permeabilities to light of window panes and of the aquarium glass itself.

2. THE BOTTOM SOIL. The bottom soil in itself has already been discussed under its own entry. Naturally it is very important for the development of the aquatic plants. The natural conditions of the soil cannot be duplicated in the aquarium with its restricted conditions. The attempts to use soils similar to the natural ones in the aquarium have always again led to failures. It is advisable to choose a bottom soil which is able to offer the plants the necessary hold for their roots, and to add sufficient food substances of which only minute quantities often suffice. In general a bottom soil consisting of sand, mixed with clay in the lower layers, is completely sufficient. WENDT advises a mixture made up of more or less coarse sand and clay for nearly all plants, especially for the home aquarium. The food substances contained in this are sufficient not only for the plants that root in the soil, but it also supplies them in the water. Thus also the plants that draw their food from the water profit from this mixture. Only the fact that most of the rooted plants also feed additionally from the water makes it understandable at all that the relatively minute food contents of the soil are able to suffice.

Exigent plants, above all those we do not want to disturb while cleaning, etc., may be cultivated in pots. This has the added advantage that one does not have to provide the whole tank with a heavy bottom soil in case one or the other plant should need it.

A richer bottom soil may be created by changing the mixture. In normal cases this should be 1/3 sand, 1/3 clay, and 1/3 well-rinsed sphagnum. The sphagnum, or peat moss, serves to loosen the mixture. The plant pots should conform to the manner of growing of the respective plants. Plants that grow runners need shallow and correspondingly spacious pots or dishes, for plants without runners, smaller pots will do. It is important that they are neither too big nor too small, corresponding to the expected size of the plants. Often the pots are shaped in a manner that permits placing them in corners. The only building material that is to be considered for plant pots is porous baked (pottery) clay, and any glazings hinder growth. The bottom should be provided with holes in order to permit sufficient circulation. This ir itself is very important. One should pay attention to the fact that the sand around the pots is not packed too densely. The best is to use only coarse gravel or to set the pots in a loose packing of sphagnum. The loosening of the soil in general too, should receive more attention. Too thin sand, especially if further mixed with clay, forms a solid layer, impermeable to water and air, in which the roots of plants rot. Therefore it is advisable to spread a first layer of coarse gravel, hazel-nut-sized or a little smaller, on the bottom of the aquarium. If you want to use a bottom filter, put it into this layer. Thus a current of water is drawn through the soil, which brings food substances to the plants and restricts stoppages of the bottom soil. Put the usual bottom covering over this layer. Internal filters which are imbedded into too thin and firm sand, harm the plants more than they benefit them by developing foci or decay due to the stopping of the mulm and by killing the bacterial flora.

All substances used for the bottom soil should be air-dried as much as possible, and stored under the influence of winter cold for some time. Choose sand of a quite coarse grain, if nothing different has been advised specifically. Also gravel the grains of which measure .08 to .12″ is quite good. This coarse grain has the advantage that due to its permeability to water the plants are induced to grow roots. If you use dry sand instead of river sand or gravel, this must be well washed and air-dried for a longer time. Clay which may be added to the sand as a complement, must be soft and well-aged. The best for this is clay from old, dismantled brick buildings. From clay diggings one can only use the upper layer, about 1″ thick, which is found immediately under the layer of common dirt. It is advisable to store the clay protected from rain for a few months. Then it may be finely mashed and mixed with the sand at any time. Light and bottom soil are two factors which complement each other, and which have to be attuned to each other. It is wrong, for instance, to try to increase insufficient growth which stems from ineffective lighting by enriching the bottom soil. Plants that do not assimilate enough due to weak light, simply cannot take in the food substances of the soil.

3. The Water. The water and the bottom soil are also in a close mutual relationship. The characteristics of the water are very important for many aquatic plants, as in nature the flora of a body of water depends on this in the first place. In addition to suspended matter which influence it, this composition depends also on the bottom soil. Many tropical plants are adapted to soft water, slightly acid due to dissolved humic acids. Thus their vital necessities coincide with those of many tropical fishes. For such plants one may use artificially prepared water. Also the presence of hard-to-control trace elements in the bottom soil may be important for growth. Domestic plants generally prefer harder water with stronger calcium content.

4. The Temperature. The demands as to warmth have been given

in detail for each plant in the descriptions of the genera and the species. In general even tropical plants need lower temperatures than is commonly supposed. Anyway, the need for warmth has to be respected for plants as much as for fishes. Domestic plants and those of the temperate zones can only be kept in the cold water aquarium. At too high temperatures, generally from 68 degrees F on, they become stringy and pale, or dissolve.

The choice of plants, their distribution in the aquarium, and the manner of planting them, has been fully discussed under the entry "Planting." Summing up, we conclude that a topsy-turvy mixture of plants finds its limitation in their diverse demands on life. Therefore one has to choose them in a similar manner to the choosing of congenial fishes, that is, by looking at their living conditions. Also the possibility of an eventual antagonism has to be considered.

aquatic plants, nutrition and fertilizing: Aquatic plants which live submerged or which float on the surface differ essentially in the manner of feeding from terrestrial plants, while emerged swamp plants which just root in ground covered with water are similar to them. Genuine aquatic plants receive their nutritional substances from the water. This intake is in part effected through the leaves, in part through the roots, and in part through both. In general one may draw conclusions as to the manner of feeding from the design of the roots. Very thin, single roots, without many ramifications, generally serve only for anchoring in the bottom. In this case feeding is done through the leaves. Vigorous, richly branched roots lead to the conclusion that the respective plants are supplied with nourishment from the soil. All aquatic plants, however, draw oxygen and carbon dioxide by means of the leaves. Based on the manner of feeding, one may establish the following groups:

1. Aquatic plants which feed almost exclusively through the roots. These include *Cryptocorynes*, Water Nuts (*Trapa*), Water Aloes (*Stratiotes*), *Marsilea*, and *Acorus*. They need a rich bottom soil, with a high percentage of clay. Never use dung-fertilized soil, or similar substances, as they foul the water.

2. Aquatic plants which feed partly through the leaves, partly through the roots. These generally show frail and transparent leaves, which seldom are finely divided, however, thriving in unwashed sand, that contains a slight admixture of clay. Among these belong: *Echinodorus*, *Sagittaria*, *Vallisneria*, *Aponogeton*, *Cabomba*.

3. Aquatic and floating plants which feed nearly exclusively through the leaves. These are delicate, often finely feathered, frequently with thin, delicate thread roots. The finely divided leaves possess a very large surface in order to leave free the greatest possible leaf area for feeding and assimilation. They include, among others, Milfoils (*Myriophyllum*), *Elodea*, *Limnophila*, perhaps also *Cabomba*, Horn Wort (*Ceratophyllum*), Crystal Wort (*Riccia*), *Salvinia*. For this kind of plants unwashed, and even washed sand is sufficient. In part they grow free-floating. It must be considered however, that a bottom soil rich in nourishment, sends dissolved nutritive substances also to these plants.

The growth of plants always depends on the nutritional substance which is rarest, even if the other ones are sufficiently available. (Law of the minima). For feeding all plants need minerals, nutritive salts, etc., such as e.g., calcium, chlorine, sulphur, phosphorus, potassium, iron. The lack of these substances is noticed through stoppages in growth. A whitish coloration of the leaves (lack of chlorophyll) sometimes is a sign of a lack of iron. Insufficiency of carbon dioxide, which may occur in tanks that are over-stocked with plants, is shown by stunted growth. It may easily be remedied by occasionally adding pure sparkling water to the aquarium. For this add one fifth bottle per week per 100 qts. The development of chlorophyll may be increased by adding small quantities (1 gram per 20 qts. of water) of sulphate of iron and of magnesium. A good fertilizer is found in ammonium nitrate, which also may be added to the aquarium water in the above-mentioned quantities at intervals of one to four weeks. According to WAGNER one may also keep plants satisfactorily in a feeding solution. This is composed as follows:

1 qt. distilled water
15 grams ammonium phosphate
15 grams potassium nitrate
15 grams sodium nitrate
40 grams ammonium sulphate

Add 2 drops of this solution to every 5 qts. of water.

According to WENDT plants may efficiently be fertilized with clay pellets stuck into the sand. For this, shape pellets of moist clay, drying them in the sun or on a kitchen range. Then they are taken with the fingers and stuck into the bottom soil near the plants so that the sand covers them. If you work quickly, the pellets will not dissolve and cloud the water.

Commercial fertilizer pills and solutions contain fertilizing salts of different compositions and concentrations. Testing them has to be left to the aquarist. Make it a rule, though, always to proceed in accordance with the instructions for use.

aquaticum: Aquatic, living in water. — *Orontium.*

aquaticus: Aquatic, living in water. — *Asellus.*

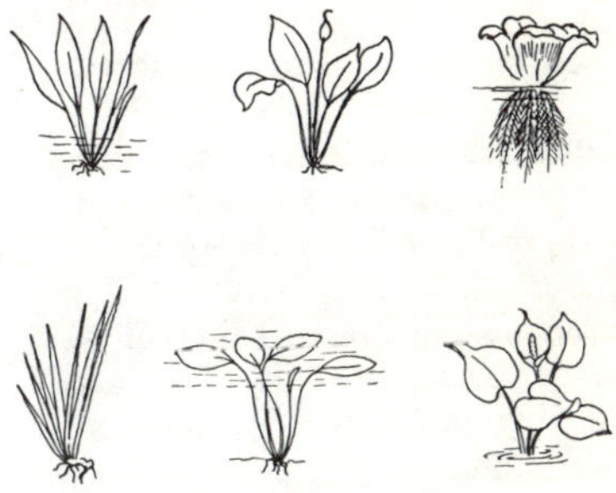

Araceae: 1. Anubias 2. Cryptocoryne 3. Pistia 4. Acorus 5. Orontium 6. Calla

Araceae: Aaron's Rod Plants. Family of terrestrial, paludic, and aquatic plants pertaining to the class of the single-germinating-leaved plants or *Monocotyledoneae*, with very great multitudes of shapes and manners of living. More than 1,800 species are known, which are spread mainly over the tropical and sub-tropical regions.

For the aquarium we have to give special consideration to the representatives of the two genera, *Acorus* and *Cryptocoryne*, which enjoy great popularity.

Further genera: *Anubias*, *Calla*, *Orontium*, *Pistia*.

Archegoniateae: Phylum of flowerless plants or *Cryptogamae*, which is sub-divided into two sub-phyla, the Mosses or *Bryophyta*, and the Ferns or *Pteridophyta*.

The *A.* are characterized by their sequence of generations. One generation develops spores in an asexual way. The resulting sexual generation possesses male and female sexual organs. The fertilized egg cells on their part give origin to asexual, spore-bearing plants.

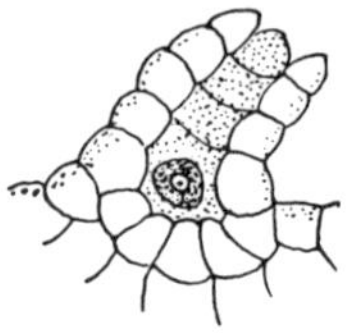

Archegonium of a fern; cross-section, enlarged

Archegonium: Female sexual organ of Mosses and Ferns, which in each case produces only one egg cell.

Archer Fishes: see TOXOTES.

Architaenioglossa: Tribe of Lid Snails pertaining to the sub-class of the Front Gills or *Prosobranchia*, comprising among others the European Paludic Lid Snail (see VIVIPARUS), and the tropical Mystery Snails: *Ampullarius*, and *Marisa*.

arcuatus: Arched, vaulted.
— *Corydoras.*

argenteus: Silver-colored.
— *Curimatus.*

Argentinian Cabomba: see CABOMBA AUSTRALIS.

Argentinian Elodea: see ELODEA DENSA.

argentoventer: With silver-colored belly.
— *Ctenopoma.*

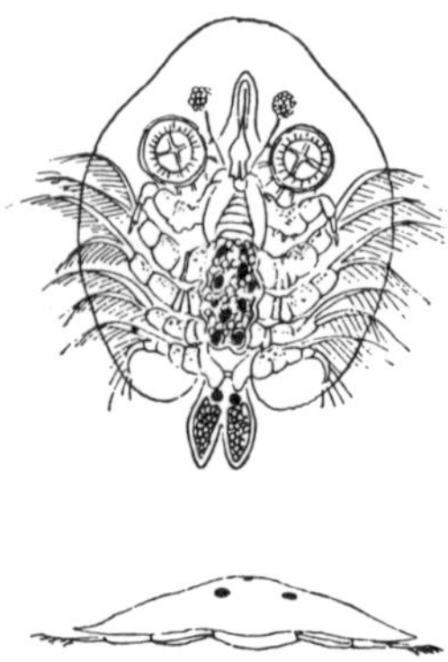

Drawing of **Argulus**. Above, view of underside. Below, front view. Enlarged.

Argulus: Carp Lice.
Genus belonging to the family of the *Argulidae*, class of the BRANCHIURA (see this), with several species. The $\frac{1}{4}''$ to $\frac{1}{2}''$ long crustaceans possess a disc-shaped anterior part of the body and a stunted, two-lobed rear part. The mouth articulators consist of stinging bristles, sucking discs, and a protractable trunk.

The Carp Lice live as parasites on fishes of all kinds. Some of the species are specialized on certain fishes, many of them, however, are also found on other cold-blooded aquatic animals. They are able to leave their hosts, especially during the period of reproduction, and to swim freely in the water. The eggs are not carried in sacs, but scattered freely. Up to the fourth change of skin the cyclops-like nauplii swim free, and only from then on the parasitic manner of living develops together with the sucking organs.

According to HERTER, at first the fish do not 'know' the little crustaceans which swim free in the water, and snap them up, the subsequent behavior being differentiated individually and locally.

Sticklebacks, e.g., generally spit them out immediately, Crucians and Tenches eat them if very hungry, while Minnows swallow them without hesitation. It is also interesting to notice that the free-swimming Carp Louse, swims always at the same height above the bottom of the water in which it has the best chance of meeting a fish. When they appear in numbers the crustaceans can cause considerable damage, especially on small fishes. In the aquarium they are often brought in together with live foods coming from ponds. At the spots where they suck on fishes develop blood-shot, crater-shaped depressions, due to repeated stinging and to the incessant motion of the legs of the parasites; secondarily the wounds may also be attacked by *Saprolegnia* (Fungus) and other disease germs.

To fight the infestation, one takes the fish out of the water, picking off the parasites with tweezers, or pushing them off with a paint brush, during which they generally come free from the skin of their own accord. The sucking wounds should be treated with vaseline.

An especially well-known species is *Argulus foliaceus* Linné.

argus: Cowherd of Greek legend, who was supposed to have one hundred eyes scattered all over his body. In our case the name refers to the spot design of the fish.

— *Scatophagus*.

Argyroneta: The silver spinning one.

— aquatica Linné: Water Spider. European water spider belonging to the order of the real spiders, family of the *Agelenidae*. The species is completely adapted to life in water. It is a fact that it is bound to breathe air through its respiratory organs, but it makes the constant stay under water possible by building one or more diving

Argyroneta aquatica

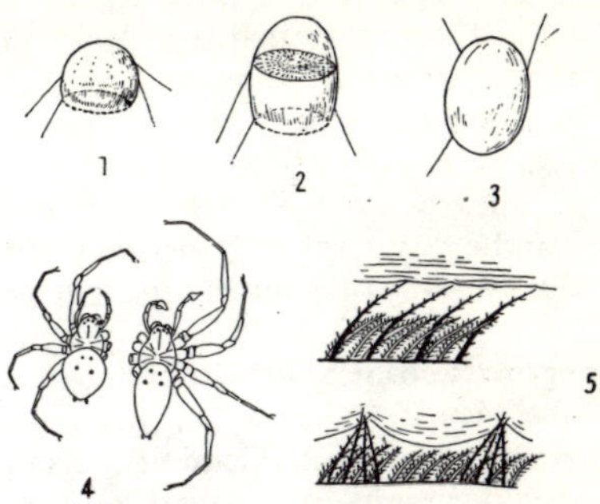

Argyroneta aquatica. 1. Living bell 2. Breeding bell 3. Winter bell 4. Left, female, right, male 5. Above, healthy hairs, below, diseased hairs.

bells. These bells are completely air and water-tight. The spider fills them with air, taken at the surface by means of the hairy abdomen and released within the bells. The spider generally hangs its web among aquatic plants, but sometimes it also covers a root cave or something similar with web fibres, filling it with air. It builds several bells for lasting sojourns, wintering, changing skin, and for its brood. The male stays only in a web tube. Parting from the bell the spiders sally forth on predatory raids. Their food consists of insect larvae, aquatic insects, etc. The male with its body length of $\frac{5}{8}''$ is bigger than the female. The sexes leave each other unscathed and one spider never attacks another one. Therefore several specimens may be kept together in the same tank.

The Water Spider possesses the most complete spinning apparatus of all spiders. By means of its structure of two kinds of hairs it is able to keep the air it needs for living, as well as to prevent getting wet. Disease of the hairy covering therefore, always has the death of the spider as consequence.

The eggs are spawned into a special breeding bell and spun in there. The young spiders go through the first stages of life in this bell.

The Water Spider lives in standing waters with dense plant growth. It is an interesting pet in the aquarium.

argyrotaenia: Silver-striped.
— *Rasbora.*

aripirangensis: Coming from Areia Piranha, an island on the lower Amazon.
— *Nannostomus beckfordi.*

Armored Catfish: see CALLICHTHYS CALLICHTHYS; PLECOSTOMUS PLECOSTOMUS.

Armored Catfish, Speckled: see CORYDORAS PALEATUS.

Armored Catfishes: see CORYDORINAE.

Armored Catfishes: see LORICARIIDAE.

Arnold, Johann Paul: Well-known German aquarist, who has contributed very much to the cooperation between science in general and aquaristics. Born Oct. 1, 1869 in Thuringia, deceased on July 1, 1952. Being a merchant by trade, his hobby led him to meet in the city of Hamburg many seafaring people through whose hands went the greatest number of imported aquarium fishes at those times. Arnold reported in words and illustrations on these new imports, creating extensive connections with experts, to whom he sent the imported specimens for classification. We are indebted to Arnold for numerous new discoveries, many of which bear his name. Together with Ernst Ahl he wrote 'Die Fremdlandische Susswasserfische' (The Foreign Fresh-Water Fishes), in 1936. This work had been considered a standard book of reference in the field of the description of aquaristically important small fishes, until the Axelrod books came out 16 years later.

Arnoldi: After the German aquarist J. P. Arnold.
— *Aphyosemion.*
— *Cheirodon.*
— *Cichlasoma.*
— *Copeina.*
— *Pelmatochromis.*

Arnoldichthys: Arnold's fish, after J. P. Arnold.
African genus pertaining to the family of the Characins or *Characidae* (see these). They are vivacious, strongly silver-colored school fishes, which possess a complete lateral line. Dorsal and anal fin insert far towards the back. Only one known species.

— spilopterus (Boulenger): The Big-Scaled African Characin.
SHAPE: The body of this species is elongated and strongly compressed laterally, looking a little squat in all. The mouth opening is big. D 12, A 14. The scales are quite big and very shiny.
COLOR: Bluish to greenish shiny silvery base with a pretty band design, a vivid red iris, and a deep-black light-edged spot on the dorsal fin. The male is more vividly colored, and besides this it possesses a band design on the anal fin.
RANGE: Tropical West Africa.
CARE AND BREEDING: The species needs roomy, well-covered tanks, as it swims very swiftly and likes to jump. They need warmth: 75-82 degrees F are advisable, at least 72 degrees F. Breeding has not yet been successful.

arrhiza: Rootless.
— *Wolffia.*

Arrow Beaks: see MASTOCEMBELIDAE.

Arrow Grass: see SAGITTARIA.

Artemia salina Linné: The Brine Shrimp.
A Gill Foot pertaining to the class of the *Anostraca*, which is present in all the bigger salt lakes and waters

of the whole world. The greater part of the Brine Shrimp eggs which are offered commercially come from the Great Salt Lake, in the State of Utah, U.S.A. It is peculiar that, despite its need for salt, this species is not found in the oceans. In certain places the Brine Shrimp is found in such numbers that it becomes of value as a source of food.

The Shrimp grow to lengths of $\frac{5}{8}''$. The head is short, the trunk divided into fifteen segments. The pairs of oared feet attached to these serve the double purpose of locomotion and of feeding. The sexual organs are located in the appendix of the body. Brine Shrimp are a pale pink to red color, which grow stronger depending on the concentration of the salt in the water. Also the body size and shape depend on this concentration to a great extent. Reproduction generally occurs through parthenogenesis. Males are relatively rare. The eggs can be shipped as fish food in glass jars, and keep for years. They measure about 1/5 mm, may be kept for years if dry, are very hard-shelled, and do not swell. In order to get them to hatch, prepare a solution of kitchen salt with about two oz. of salt per quart of water. Then scatter a quantity of the eggs on the surface of the water, according to need and to the size of the tank. It is good to keep the eggs from spreading by means of a food ring, as they easily wander out of the water at the edges, especially if the tank is not placed in a commotionless location. They do not hatch outside the water. Never use metallic vessels as containers for the salt solution, but always those made of glass, stoneware, or enameled ware. If you are in constant need of very small-sized food, it is advisable to set up only a small quantity of eggs daily, since the nauplii are relatively big and grow very quickly. It is advisable to afford them a weak aeration. Warmth speeds up the hatching: at 63-66 degrees F it lasts 40-50 hours, while at 82-86 degrees F the nauplii come out after only 20-24 hours.

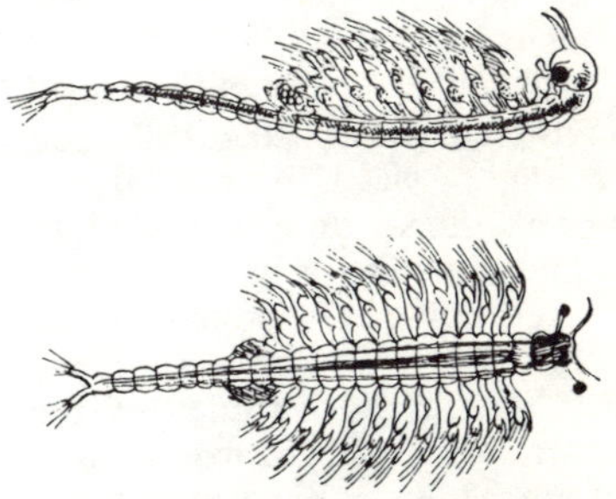

Brine Shrimp, **Artemia salina.** Above, side view, below, view from above.

It is possible to breed Brine Shrimp at home. DAHLKE supplies the following short instructions, supplemented by his own experience: Fill a salt water-resistant dish made of one of the above-mentioned materials with the solution of kitchen salt and place it in the sunlight or at a well-illuminated spot. At the beginning the water should be stirred up frequently, in order to avoid settling of the salt then a consequent formation of a stronger concentration near the bottom. The most favorable water height is about $2\frac{3}{8}''$. The warmer the water, the quicker the hatching and growth of the shrimp. The temperature should be kept above 68 degrees F. Water that evaporates can always be replaced with fresh water. After a strong growth of algae has developed, hang some strongly ramified twigs into the water, in order to offer the algae still more points of support. Then either put in a quantity of Brine

Shrimp eggs, or else some full-grown Brine Shrimp. Algae, especially floating algae, represent the main food. If no algae develop, for instance in winter, the Shrimp may also be fed dust-sized artificial foods. When doing this, however, be especially careful not to foul the water by over-feeding. If no algae develop, put in a weak aeration.

It is advisable to gather a small provision of the eggs that collect on the edge of water in order always to be able to set up new broods. In summer breeding may be effected in bigger containers located out-of-doors. This will always supply a great number of Shrimps of the most varied sizes. The nauplii have a drop-shaped look, possess strong rowing arms, and are about .02″ long. Since they are very hungry for light, they collect at the best illuminated spot of the container. In order to use them as food, draw them off with a hose and pass them through a small-meshed sieve dipping them quickly in fresh water before feeding them to the fishes. In fresh water the nauplii and adult shrimp live only for a few hours. Therefore be careful never to feed more than will be eaten by the fishes within a short time.

Arthropoda: Articulated Feet. Great phylum of invertebrate animals which comprise about 80% of the world of animals. It is characterized by an articulated body, divided into segments. The limbs and other body appendages too are articulated. The body is enclosed within a firm outer skeleton of chitin, which often forms an armor by means of generous deposits of calcium. The different parts of the chitin skeleton are connected by articulatory skins. Since the chitin skeleton cannot grow simultaneously with the animal, from time to time changes of

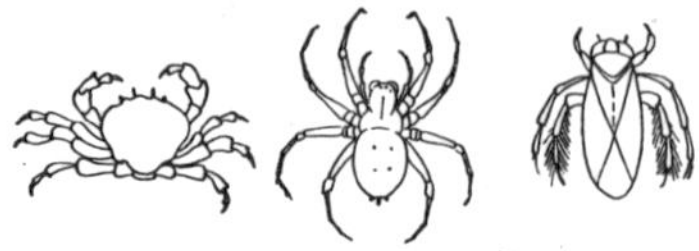

Arthropoda: 1. Crustacea 2. Chelicerata 3. Hexapoda

skin become necessary, or else growth takes place exclusively during the larval period. The Arthropods possess a so-called 'rope-ladder' nerve system. The dorsal blood vessel impels the blood by means of pumping motions into the abdominal cavity, where it flows out freely from the vessel, being drawn in again by other vessels.

Three sub-phyla: the Crustaceans or *Crustacea*, the Spiders or *Chelicerata*, and in the Insects or *Hexapoda*.

artificial and dry foods: Foods that play an important role in aquaristics as an auxiliary alimentation. Generally artificial foods are inadequate to replace natural foods, either alive or dead, but good commercial foods may be of value for certain species as they contain the components necessary for building up the body. If served alternately with live foods, the artificial foods may render good services. One should avoid, though, feeding them exclusively over longer periods.

The most natural dry food is constituted by dried *Daphnia* and other small crustaceans, which one spreads on gauze frames on hot summer days so that they are exposed to the burning sun while simultaneously the air has access to them. If drying is done in an oven, the process is similar, but one should take care not to let the *Daphnia* burn. Quickly processed, sun-dried *Daphnia* are richest in food value and nearly odorless. If given in commensurate quantities, this kind of food is willingly taken by most fishes. It is not considered an especially rich food, though, but in winter, when much food without hard bulk is given (*Tubifex*, *Enchytrae*, etc.) the shells constitute a welcome stimulus for digestion.

In order to afford also a vegetable diet in winter to fishes who need it, it is advisable to pulverize some lettuce, mixing it with the other foods. Lettuce powder may eventually also render good services in the development of infusoria in the aquarium.

Commercial foods are of varying qualities. Always be careful to buy a product of a well-known brand. The composition of these foods, made from the meat of frogs or bivalves with an admixture of vegetable juices, vitamin preparations, egg yolk, etc., may turn them into highly valuable foods for our aquarium fishes.

When feeding artificial or dry foods, always proceed sparingly, as otherwise the water may easily become clouded, permitting the development of bacteria and infusoria which are difficult to remove again. Too great quantities of artificial food may furthermore lead to digestive disturbances of the fishes.

Asellus aquaticus (Linné): Water Sow Bug.
German aquatic Sow Bug pertaining to the family of the *Asellidae* order of the Sow Bugs or *Isopoda*. An Arthropod that lives on the bottom or among plants, ⅜″ to ¾″ long, found mainly in standing waters, but also in slowly-flowing ones. Apparently the *A.* are sluggish, but they may become very agile in case of danger. They feed mainly on decaying vegetable matter. In case the ditches where they live dry out, they dig into the mud. *A.* are found the year over,

Asellus aquaticus

also in plant bundles, as e.g. in *Fontinalis*, under the ice. The males are bigger than the females.

A. spawn up to 100 eggs, which are carried around in a brood sac. The young swarm out after 3-6 weeks, and look very similar to the adult animals. Aquatic Sow Bugs are an excellent food for bigger fishes which like hardy food. However, they may be transmitters of the so-called Scratcher Disease, being hosts to Scratchers (see ACANTOCEPHALA).

Asia: The greatest of the continents, strongly divided, which comprises about 16,500,000 square miles. The border between Asia and Europe has more of a historical value than a geographical one. The greatest distance from west to east amounts to about 6,000 miles, the one from north to south about 7,500 miles. The continent is connected with Africa by the Isthmus of Suez. It is separated from America by the Bering Strait, which is about 60 miles wide, and which furthermore is closed by ice during a great part of the year. Asia is in a certain relationship to Australia by means of the bridge of islands formed by the Malayan Archipelago. One fourth of the total area of the continents is made up of islands and peninsulas, two thirds of the whole region are mountain systems, which comprise the highest elevations on earth. The huge manifoldness of the geographical divisions and the great extension of the continent cause the corresponding diversity of climatic conditions and of the world of animals and plants.

Map of Southern and Southeastern Asia

Northern Asia (Siberia) is covered nearly exclusively by a gigantic extension of coniferous woods, the Taiga. There we find very short, but warm summers with sufficient moisture which in part originates from the thawing of the permanently frozen soil. The great rivers flow toward the Polar Sea. Towards the South the region changes gradually—or due to high mountain systems, quickly—into the Central Asian belt of deserts and plains. Northern Asia is very rich in edible fishes of all kinds, especially Salmonids and Coregons. The fauna of small fishes corresponds more or less to that of East and Central Europe. The dry and cold region of Central Asia can hardly be called significant from an ichthyological point of view.

West Asia (Asia Minor) possesses a dry vernal period. The winter rains fall in the region of the bordering mountains without reaching the inner part of the highlands. In the western coastal regions of Asia Minor we find a pronouncedly Mediterranean vegetation. The region is poor in flowing waters, of which the Euphrates and the Tigris are the biggest ones. As far as aquarium fishes are concerned, in this part we find either Tooth Carps in smaller numbers, with a great adaptability to extreme water conditions and to greater admixtures or salt, or else Cichlids which stem over from the African Continent.

To the contrary, South and South-East Asia are very rich in small fishes of all kinds. This includes the region called Monsoon

Asia, on the edge of the great mountain walls, in the south and south-east of the continent to the island groups in the Pacific and the Indian Oceans. The climate is conditioned by the dry, hibernal, and, in Northern China, very cold land winds, and the vernal, very warm and moist, sea winds (monsoons). The sub-tropical or tropical warmth, together with rich precipitations in summer, on the islands also in winter, create a very lush vegetation. In the tropical regions extensive stretches are covered with always green rain jungles, which in spots are substituted by quick-growing bamboo woods. Typical of this region are the wet fields (rice paddies) favored by the climate. The great rivers here are those flowing waters of Asia which are richest in volume.

Ecological examinations and reports on the fish fauna are available of single regions of tropical South Asia, especially from the outskirts of Singapore, from Java, Malaya, Ceylon, and Sumatra, which were summed up by LADIGES. Climatically the mentioned regions belong to the country of the East Indian-Australian Monsoons. They are characterized by periodical rainfalls, even temperatures with only minute fluctuations during the year, and strong southwest, or northwest winds. In part of the region there are very considerable precipitations which may attain 40″ to 80″ per year, especially in the western part of the Malayan Archipelago. The rain periods are influenced by the geographical position and the surface division of the different regions.

Despite the evenness of the seasons, however, one can separate periods of fruitfulness from those of recession in the whole region, similar to what we know more pronouncedly in the temperate zones. These are caused especially by the times of increased precipitation, in which, due to the general rise of the water levels, much decaying organic matter is swept into the waters. During this period, when the world of micro-organisms also develops especially well, we have the spawning period of many fishes. However, it is very difficult to establish a general norm, as the conditions are misleadingly manifold. The world of fishes, of which naturally mainly aquaristically important small fishes were studied, in general shows to be very adaptable. Thus many species of fishes are found under the most variable conditions. However, certain types of water offer possibilities of living only to certain species, e.g., shallow, over-heated, oxygen-poor, flooded zones harbour only Anabantids. But this does not mean that for this reason these species are found only in waters of this kind. These are just their minimum living conditions.

To follow we are giving a description of the countries separately:

CEYLON: Considerable differences in altitude, different conditions of temperature, and very differing precipitations (from 40 to nearly 150 inches) create very many-sided water conditions. The world of fishes resembles that of India. Thus of the 30 Cyprinids of Ceylon, 20 are also found in India.

SUMATRA: A typical landscape of the world of the Indonesian islands. It is characterized by the chain of mountains on the west coast, from which the waters run off as short mountain waters, while they form water-rich rivers on the other side. There we find a very many sided aquatic picture. LADIGES describes a typical swamp site near the town of Medan: "The waters were thickly matted with plants, roots, decaying parts of plants, and showed only few open spots. The terrestrial plants—trees, bushes, grasses, and ferns—threw dense shadows on the water. At an air temperature of 90 degrees F, the water measured only 84 degrees F. The muddy soil was soft and contained iron. A subsequent analysis of the water showed a total hardness of 2.4 degrees DH. Besides the Harlequin, other species of *Rasbora*, as well as *Barbus lateristriga*, *Barbus binotatus*, *Laubuca laubuca*, and *Brachydanio albolineatus* were found in the open water spaces. The Banded Barbs diminished correspondingly in numbers. At the surface one met Half-Beaks (*Hemirhamphodon*). The number of young fishes was especially great. In the plant thickets was found quite a different fish community, consisting especially of Anabantids and Snake-Heads. Especially *Trichogaster leeri* seemed to prefer this type of location. Besides these there were Nandids, Spiny Eels and Cobitids, and in lesser numbers also the big Gouramis, *Helostoma* and *Osphronemus*. In a quickly-flowing creek, with deeply shaded, completely opaque water, we found mainly Banded Barbs, in spots also small schools of *Rasbora maculata*. Smaller, artificially-built ponds, densely grown with submerged plants, harbored Banded Barbs, Gouramis, *Sphaerichthys*, *Osphromenoides*, and the Pike-Head *Luciocephalus*. The latter, however, seems to prefer flood regions with grassy areas." In a body of water studied by MARSACK the principal subaquatic plants that were found were *Blyxa*, *Sagittaria sinensis*, and *Cryptocorynes*. In the stands of *Cryptocoryne* of the bights dwelled especially the young of *Rasbora heteromorpha*, while the adult specimens were found more frequently in open water near the surface. The body of water held clear water at temperatures varying from 77 to 102 degrees F. It was shadowed and possessed a gravelly bottom. Quite different was the fish community in the mountain waters. In the zone of the high mountains numerous falls limit the advance of many species of fishes. In the penetrable parts, especially in the hill country of Java, BUSCHKIEL caught the Mouthbreeder Fighting Fish, *Betta picta*, at an altitude of 4200 ft., a little lower the Croaking Gourami, *Trichopsis vittatus*, and the Blue Gourami, *Trichogaster trichopterus*.

Betta taeniata was found in minute, clay-yellow puddles near settlements, where the the daylight temperature measured 98 degrees F, falling at least 18 degrees below this measurement during the night.

SCHMIDT examined a series of waters on Sumatra with the aid of native fish catchers. All of them showed surprisingly soft, slightly acid water, and were colored brownish by the plant parts they contained.

In a swift-flowing creek with a depth of 20″-30″, clear brownish water, and a clay-sand bottom, at about 9:00 A.M. he measured a hardness of .5 DH and a pH value of 5.9. There he found Banded Barbs, *Betta picta* in greater numbers, Pike-heads, and schools of several species of *Rasbora*. In the undergrowth near the banks also the Croaking Gourami, *Trichopsis vittatus*, was found. The natives use the bigger Anabantids, e.g. Gouramis, Kissing Gouramis, Mosaic Gouramis, as well as Barbs, Snake-Heads, and Cichlids of the genus *Tilapia*, imported from Africa, as food fishes.

In a slowly-flowing, muddy creek with similar conditions, the bottom of which was covered with decaying twigs and leaves, *Cryptocoryne griffithi* was found at shadowy spots. Near the surface there were Half-Beak Pikes, as well as very small alevins of an unknown species of *Rasbora*. Furthermore *Sphaerichthys osphromenoides*, some unknown fresh-water *Sphaerichthys*, Spiny Eels (*Mastocembalus*), *Betta picta*, and *Trichopsis vittatus* were caught. Many other bodies of water showed similar aspects. In the flood regions lived greater swarms of the Glass Catfish, *Cryptopterus bicirrhis*.

A plant that was similar to *Cryptocoryne* grew in a quick-flowing jungle creek with the same water conditions, near Palembang. In the subdued light plants with moss-green leaves, red on the underside, grew densely together. At a better illuminated spot stands of the same plant were found again, but this time the leaves were green on both sides.

Near huts on stilts major numbers of *Trichopsis*, *Betta*, *Sphaerichthys*, and *Trichogaster leeri* were found in the clay-muddy waters, soiled by domestic refuse.

The comprehensive findings on the waters yielded the following values:

(a) low hardness of the water: DH 0.3 to 0.5

(b) acid water, enriched with humus substances, with pH values of 5.8-6.2

(c) High temperature: 82-86 degrees F.

The air over the waters is saturated with moisture and very warm.

HERMS examined a series of creeks in Siam. In a creek, at the lower rung of a cataract, among coarse-grained gravely rocks, he found *Rasbora lateristriata*, *Danio* (*Brachydanio*) *pulcher*, further up *Puntius* (*Barbus*) *binotatus*, and a great number of Gudgeons of many species. Furthermore the creek was inhabited by *Cyprinids* of the genus *Garra*, with a sucking disc on the underside, as well as some Snake-Heads. In other creeks he found *Barilius intrafasciatus*, *Rasbora lateristriata*, *Puntius binotatus*, and other Barbs and Gudgeons. The interesting Trunk Gudgeon *Acanthopsis*, and minute tadpole-like Catfishes of the genus *Akysis* completed the picture. A greater river, in the north of the country harbored in its bights species of *Barilius*, *Rasborins*, Fringe-Lipped Sharks of the genus *Labeo*, Trunk Gudgeons, and others. In flowing waters also some species of *Botia* were found representing the Gudgeons.

A special community of life is also harbored in the artificially created rice paddies of South-East Asia, as well as in drainage ditches which lead through the settlements, of which too HERMS gives a description. The ditches in the coastal zone, which already come under the influence of the tides, harbor as a main form the ring Gobies (*Brachygobius*) as well as other Gobies and Carps, such as e.g. *Oryzias javanicus*. This zone gives way into the pronounced mangrove coast with its typical species of fishes, the Mud Skippers, Gobies, Argus Fishes, etc. The fishes in these regions feed preponderantly on the larvae of *Chironomus* and of other mosquitoes, flying insects, and, whenever they can catch them, on smaller fishes. In his compilation LADIGES remarks several times that the available studies do not permit generally valid conclusions on the general conditions of the water, even if naturally many waters coincide with the described types. During the daytime the pH values fluctuate considerably due to the soft, hardly buffered waters especially where the waters are strongly overgrown with plants.

Despite the fact that many of the wild fishes need acid pH values in order to reproduce, this is not always the case, however. BÜSCHKIEL remarks that for instance the best fish ponds of Java show pH values within the alkaline range, between 7.5 and 8.5, similar to those of our own commercial ponds, respectively conditioned to this artificially. Doubtlessly in slightly acid waters it is not a question of the pH value in itself, but one of the nature of the acidifiers which produce the acidity. The studies made up to this date seem to show that degrees of hardness above 6 degrees are unfavorable for aquarium fishes coming from these regions.

Aspro: The Danube Perches. Genus pertaining to the family of the real Perches or *Percidae*.

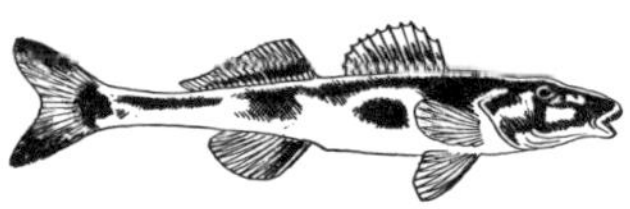

Aspro streber

— **streber** Sieb: The Streber.
SHAPE: The body long and spindle shaped, flat and broad on the upper side, the caudal peduncle round. The mouth is subterminal. Length up to 7″.
COLOR: Yellow-brown base with black slanting cross stripes.
RANGE: A deep-water Perch of the Danube and its tributaries.
CARE: This rare fish may be kept temporarily in the aquarium, under special care.

— **zingel** Linné: The Zingel.
SHAPE: A bottom Perch of elongated build, flattened above. The head is triangular, the mouth subterminal. Length up to 20″.
COLOR: Brownish-yellow base with indistinct dark bands and spots.
RANGE: Only in the Danube and its tributaries. Rare.

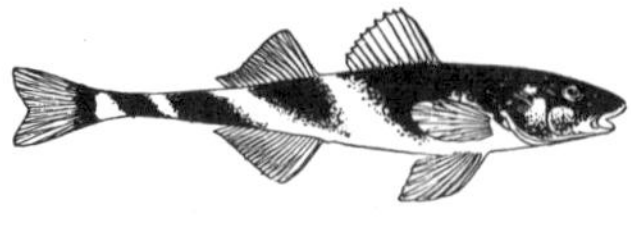

Aspro zingel

CARE: A predator which lives on the bottom. An interesting pet, of which smaller specimens may be kept temporarily in the aquarium. It needs much oxygen and thus demands either strong aeration or, better still, flowing water. It does not like intense light and becomes lively only towards the evening.

assimilation: Elaboration of factors of the ambient world through the organism. Especially the intake of foreign, inorganic substances and their transformation into organic matters, equal or similar to those of the body. In green plants especially the transformation of carbon dioxide and water into starch and other substances (photosynthesis) by aid of sunlight and the greenness of the leaves (chlorophyll).

The activity of assimilation of plants is important in the aquarium, since these exude oxygen as a final product, which on its part is necessary for the metabolism of animals. It must be the aim of the aquarist to regulate the relationship between animals and plants in a manner that the production of oxygen corresponds to the demands of the animals, and that the carbon dioxide eliminated by these may be absorbed by the plants. Therefore the fundamental rule has to be: No over-stocking with plants, but also no excess of fishes!

If they do not receive sufficient light, the green plants stop assimilating. They only breathe, using up oxygen like animals. Therefore one has to pay attention to locating the aquarium in a manner that it either receives sunlight, or else that it may be illuminated additionally. On many plants, such as, for instance, *Vallisneria*, *Elodea*, etc., the produced oxygen is visible under sunlight as a thin chain of small air bubbles.

Only green plants (and therefore not the not-green fungi) are able to effect assimilation. Only they can transform inorganic substances into organic ones. They are autotrophic in their feeding. All animals, including man, are forced to acquire the substances that are elaborated by the plants, either by direct intake, or else over indirect ways. Their existence is based on the presence of plants, they are heterotrophic.

association: 1. The living in communities of plants and animals, of the same or of different species. The large-sized living regions, including those of the waters, comprise numerous smaller living sites or biotopes (see this) which under certain conditions harbor a typical community of animals and plants, attuned to the place. These in their association form an interdependent vital community (biozenosis).

2. The combination of a sensorial impression with a trace of memory in the brain, from which results an act influenced by same. It combines an innate manner of reacting with experiences which are retained in the brain by the memory. There is an association for instance, when the sight of some food awakens the memory of its bad taste, thus subduing the natural snapping reaction. This shows that the animal has learned to choose its food according to tastiness. The presence of association is very easy to verify in aquarium fishes. Science tests the extent of possible associations by means of attempts at training.

Astacidae: River Crustaceans.

Family of higher Crustaceans pertaining to the sub-order of the pincer-bearing Crustaceans or *Reptantia*. They are characterized by the fact that the first pair of legs always carries large pincers, while the second and third pairs show smaller ones. One of the two front pincers is bigger and more awkward than the other one, equipped with a few strong prongs on the cutting side, and is used to hold and smash the prey. The other one is slimmer, and set with toothlets and sensorial hairs on the inside. It is with its aid that the Crustacean searches for food. A great number of species are sea dwellers. For the fresh-water aquarium one should only consider the River Crustacean, *Astacus fluviatilis*, the American River Crab, *Cambarus affinis*, and lately also the Galician Swamp Crab, *Astacus leptodactylus*.

Astacus fluviatilis (Linné): The River Crab.

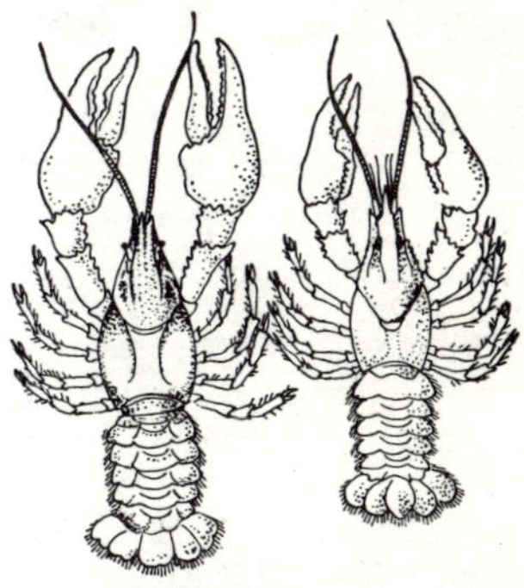

Left: **Astacus fluviatilis,** right, **Cambarus affinis**

A higher Crustacean pertaining to the family of the River Crabs or *Astacidae* (see this). The armoring is nearly complete, the great head and breast piece ends in a point. Length 6″ to 10″, the female remaining a little smaller. Colors differ according to origin, brownish to greenish, often also spotted.

The River Crab was widely diffused over Europe until it receded strongly due to a Crab disease. It dwells in standing and flowing waters with hiding places, especially ones with overhanging banks and a soft bottom. The 'Rock Crab', which lives in swiftly-flowing mountain brooks, is hardly fit for keeping in the aquarium. The changes of skin, necessary for growth, take place eight times a year on younger specimens, one to two times on older ones. For this they do not only throw off the outer armor, but even internal organs are involved, so that a shedding is laborsome and dangerous for the crustacean. After this process, which lasts for several hours, the animal becomes quite sensitive and, as a 'soft-shelled crab', it is defenseless for several days.

During this time it remains hidden. The calcium necessary for building the armor is mainly taken directly from the water.

For food the crabs take frogs, insect larvae, small fishes, earthworms, but also calcium-supplying plants and decaying organic substances. The 200-300 eggs, spawned in fall, hang from the swimming feet of the female until next spring. The young crabs, which hatch at that time, are still carried around for some time more, clinging to the swimming feet. The River Crab is an interesting inmate of the aquarium, which may live for years in captivity. The tank should be well covered as the animals like to roam at night. They demand plenty of space, soft sand as bottom covering, and rock and root structures as hiding places. These structures may also protrude above the surface. Strong aeration is advisable.

asterifrons: With a star on the forehead.

— *Astrodoras.*

Astrodoras: Star Doras.

Genus of Catfishes pertaining to the family of the Spiny Catfishes or DORADIDAE (see these), with strongly armored body, of which each plate is additionally equipped with spines and thorns. The intermediate and lower jaws show narrow ribbons of very fine teeth. There are three pairs of barbels.

— asterifrons Heckel: The Helmeted Catfish.

SHAPE: As per description of genus, otherwise very similar to the genus *Acanthodoras.* Dorsal and ventral fins carry a strong spine each. D I/6, A 10-11. Length up to 4⅜″.

COLOR: Gray base with many dark spots and bands. The upper whisker threads are ringed with white.

RANGE: The region of the central Amazon River.

CARE AND BREEDING: A hardy Catfish, which likes to live hidden, though, and which, becoming active during twilight and at night, prefers tanks placed in dark locations. It likes to amble around on the bottom and digs itself in temporarily. As food it takes everything that is not too big to be swallowed. However, live bottom foods are preferred. In darkly-located aquaria the species becomes relatively lively. Harmless toward other fishes. Temperature 72-75 degrees F. Breeding in the aquarium has not yet been achieved. It is known that related species care for their brood, building regular nests out of parts of plants.

Astronotus: With a star-like design.

South American genus pertaining to the family of the Cichlids or *Cichlidae,* with relatively high, laterally compressed body, big head, and big eyes. Care and breeding is similar to that of the other non-mouthbreeding Cichlids. Only few species are known.

Astronotus ocellatus, adult

Astronotus ocellatus, young

— ocellatus (Cuvier): The Oscar. SHAPE: As per description of genus. The elongated oval body is relatively high, especially at an advanced age. The fish looks very powerful. The mouth opening is very big and the eyes insert very high. D XII-XIV/19-21, A III/15-16. All vertical fins are rounded off, the pectorals are very big. Length, also in the aquarium, 10″, but able to reproduce from 4″ on. COLOR: The species is remarkable for the fact that the different stages of age show completely different colors, small specimens, $1\frac{1}{8}''$ to $1\frac{5}{8}''$ long, resembling Coral Fish. Specimens that have just matured sexually show beautiful irregular yellowish band designs and spots on olive-drab to brownish base, which also go over onto the fins, furthermore an outstanding light-edged spot on the caudal peduncle. It is said that the male reportedly shows three black dots at the base of the spiny dorsal fin.
RANGE: In the secondary waters of the great rivers in central South America, especially at spots with large amounts of wood in the water.
CARE AND BREEDING: As described for *Cichlidae* (see these). The species roots strongly and is voracious and pronouncedly predatory, especially when fully grown. Because of its persistence it is able to hunt down even the swiftest fishes. As compared to other fishes, it shows marked individual differences in behavior. In general, however, *A. ocellatus* may be kept in communities with fishes of the same size, especially if sufficient space is available. Temperatures 72-77 degrees F, for breeding 79-82 degrees F, lowest temperature 60 degrees F.

Astyanax: From Greek mythology. A genus very rich in species, belonging to the family of the Characins or CHARACIDAE (see these), which is spread over South and Central America and reaches even into the U.S.A. They are school fishes with a silvery shine, coming from open and flowing waters. All species are rugged, undemanding, and very motile. Care and breeding as described for *Hemigrammus caudovittatus*.

Astyanax bimaculatus

— **bimaculatus:** A very hardy species which attains a length of 6″. It originates from Eastern South America, from Colombia to the La Plata. Shiny silver with a diamond-shaped spot on the root of the tail, and a weak golden sheen. The species requires warmth and becomes lively only at temperatures from 73 to 82 degrees F, and if it has plenty of space.

Astyanax fasciatus fasciatus

— **fasciatus fasciatus** Cuvier: A little bigger than the preceding species, with many sub-species which live in Central and South America. Length up to 7″.

Astyanax fasciatus mexicanus

— **fasciatus mexicanus** (Filippi): The only species of Characins whose range reaches into the South of the U.S.A. Probably the original form of the Blind Cave Fish, *Anoptichthys jordani*.

Atherinidae: Ear Fishes.
Family pertaining to the sub-order of the MUGILOIDEA (see this). School fishes from tropical and sub-tropical regions, which mostly dwell in the parts of the sea that are near the coast, having in part migrated into fresh water and adapted there. As far as the species from fresh water are concerned, they are small fishes, of elongated, laterally compressed build throughout. They are characterized by having a second, separate dorsal fin, which is characteristic of the whole order. The first dorsal possesses 3-8 spines, which, however, are not especially stiff.

Of the numerous genera, so far aquarium fishes have been imported from the following four (which see): AUSTROMENIDIA, TELMATERINA, PSEUDOMUGIL, and MELANOTAENIA.

atpar.
— *Oxygaster.*

atracaudatus: With black tail fin.
— *Gephyrocharax.*

atratulus: Blackish.
— *Rhinichthys.*

atrizona: Black-belted.
— *Quintana.*

Auchenoglanis, type of the genus

Auchenoglanis: Catfish with bone plates on the neck.
African genus of Catfishes pertaining to the family of the *Bagridae*.

— **occidentalis** (Cuvier and Valenciennes):
SHAPE: A Catfish of compact body structure, the body surface of which is covered with a resistant and strongly mucous skin. The head is flattened from above, the forehead outline falling roof-like from the insertion of the dorsal fin towards the snout. The head is covered

with small elevations and prongs. The terminal, relatively small mouth opening is edged by thick and fleshy lips. The species possesses three pairs of barbels. D I/7, A 10-12. Like that of all Bagrids, the adipose fin is especially big. Dorsal and pectorals possess strong spines, which may be kept erect by locking articulations, and with which the fish are able to cause dangerous and hard-to-heal lacerations if handled carelessly. Length up to 20″.

COLOR: Brownish with darker, rounded spots. SD are not known.

RANGE: The species is quite common in the most widely varying waters of tropical Africa, especially in the upper Nile.

CARE AND BREEDING: Like most Catfishes, the members of this species are also nocturnal fishes, which avoid light, and therefore like a darkly located tank with hiding places. Only at twilight do they become lively, and then they are very predatory. They should be fed generously with live foods which agree with their size. Temperatures 75-79 degrees F. The species has not yet been bred in the aquarium.

auratus: Gold-colored, golden.

— *Carassius gibelio.*

aureum: Golden.

— *Cichlasoma.*

— auriculata: With little ears; referring to the shape of the leaves.

— *Salvinia.*

autitus: With ears; refers to the dark extensions of the gill covers.

— *Lepomis.*

australe: Southern.

— *Aphyosemion.*

— *Geophagus.*

Australia: Comprising about three million square miles, the smallest continent, basically a big island which is surrounded on all sides by the Indian or the Pacific Oceans. The coasts are not greatly broken

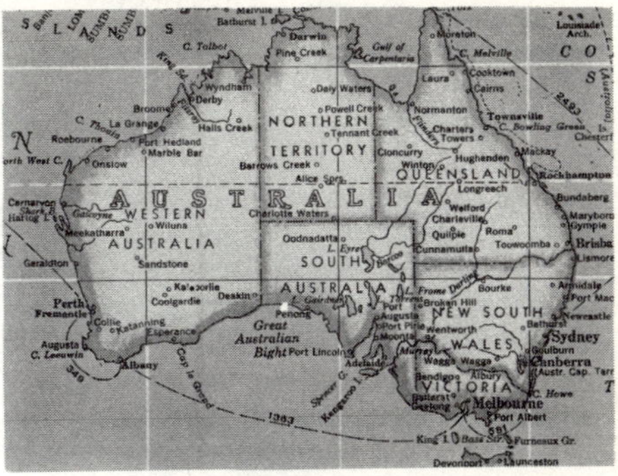

Map of Australia

up. Only few peninsulas and islands exist, of which Tasmania is the biggest. In the east and south-east there is mountainous country with the character of a medium-high system of mountains. (The Australian Alps). To the west of this extense are plains, crossed in the south by Murray and the Darling, the biggest rivers of Australia. To the west the plains connect with a huge, dry plateau which shows an average height of 1300 feet. On this there are numerous salt lakes and salt swamps. In the north and the north-east Australia possesses a moist-hot tropical climate. In the east, south-east, and south-west a moderately warm one. The interior is very hot and dry.

In the internal waters of the continent as a rule we find fishes that have a relationship with the sea, or are immigrated sea dwellers which have adapted to fresh water. It is a known fact that the Australian fauna in general is very ancient. For this reason we find also among the fishes forms such as e.g., the well-known Australian Lung-Fish, *Neoceratodes forsteri*, as well as representatives of the peculiar family of the *Osteoglossidae*, which are numbered among the *Isospondyli* and are found in the coastal rivers in parts of Queensland.

The fish which the English-speaking inhabitants call Australian Minnow, and which takes the place of our Trout, belongs to the family of the *Galaxiidae*, also fresh water fishes, which in part are very colorful. It is remarkable that all the relatives of this group are restricted to the southern tips of the continents of South America, Africa, and Australia, as well as to Tasmania and New Zealand. They could possibly be classed as left-overs of the fauna of a formerly unified southern continent. All other fishes of Australia visibly derive from sea fishes. Here we find representatives of the Mucus Fishes (*Blenniidae*), the Gudgeons (*Gobiidae*)—of which *Mogurnda mogurnda* has become well-known —the Glass Perches (*Ambassis*), the Ear Fishes (*Atherinidae*) with the two species *Melanotaenia nigrans* and *M. maccullochi*, and some others which it would not pay to mention here. Like everywhere else, also in Australia we find Catfishes.

RUDEL found the Australian Rainbow Fish, *Melanotaenia nigrans*, in all kinds of waters around Brisbane, where the fish stayed in open water in rather big schools. If disturbed they vanished immediately among the dense aquatic plants. He mentions the sub-aquatic flora as quite numerous, listing representatives of the following genera: *Hydrilla*, *Vallisneria*, *Nitella*, *Myriophyllum*, Spawn Worts, Horn Worts, *Ottelia*, and *Marsilea*. He describes the water, especially that of the creeks, as quite hard, in part also cloudy with a strong development of algae.

Australian Glass Perch, the: see AMBASSIS AGASSIZI.

Australian Sleeper Gudgeon, the: see CARASSIOPS COMPRESSUS.

Australian Spotted Gudgeon, the: see MOGURNDA MOGURNDA.

australis: Southern.

— *Cabomba*.

Austromenidia: Silver Fish from the South.

South American genus of rather big fishes belonging to the family of the Ear Fishes or *Atherinidae* (see these). They are fishes of the open water, of elongated shape which is little compressed laterally, and, like all members of the family, they possess two separate dorsal fins, located at a distance from each other. The mouth cleft is very big, the snout long and pointed, the upper jaw extendable. Jaws, palate, and wing bone are equipped with teeth. The scales are relatively small. Something especially remarkable is the glassy translucency of the body.

The genus is found in the coastal waters and the river mouths of Chile, Peru, and Argentina, but very little is known regarding its manner of living. Despite the fact that the fish are also found in brackish water with quite small salt contents, they are hardly fit for keeping in the fresh-water aquarium. It has been proved, however, that they can be quite rugged and enduring.

autochtonous: The quality of live beings originating from a certain region, that is, which have not immigrated to it.

autotrophic: The quality which permits live beings to feed by transforming inorganic substances into organic ones, incorporating them in their body, such as happens especially with green plants.

autumn mortality: An often observed occurrence through which in late fall major losses of aquarium fishes take place. It is probably derived from the fact that the days, growing shorter, carry a radical change in the biological occurrences within the aquarium. The plants have only a short span of daylight in which to assimilate, and this upsets the gaseous economy. The world of micro-organisms changes its behaviour. In most cases also a deep change in the manner of feeding of fishes takes place. Animals and plants urgently need a rest after the biological climaxes or reproduction.

The best remedy against autumn deaths is a decrease in fish population, with a simultaneous weeding out of surplus plants, a gradual lowering of the temperature, and a moderate, but variegated nutrition. As long as it is possible to catch foods in free nature, this source of alimentation should be exploited.

The use of artificial illumination will help to avoid many of the circumstances which formerly led to autumn mortality.

autumn tasks: see Care of the Aquarium.

Axelrod, Herbert Richard: Born 1927, the most prolific author on aquaristic subjects and the world's leading authority on tropical fishes. Taught first course on tropical fishes at New York University; wrote many major works on aquarium fishes with Dr. Leonard P. Schultz, William Vorderwinkler and others. Collected many new fishes from Africa and South America as well as Asia. Axelrod received Ph.D. from NYU in biostatistics. Publisher of 'Tropical Fish Hobbyist' magazine; 'Tropische Fische'. Has works published in English, German, Spanish and French languages. Several fishes have been named in his honor: *Cheirodon axelrodi* (The Cardinal Tetra); *Aphyocharax axelrodi* (Red-tailed *Pristella*) and *Symphysodon aequifasciata axelrodi* (The Discus Fish). Presently living in America.

axillary: Pertaining to blossoms, etc., which grow from the axil of a plant, i.e., the spot where a leaf stem meets the main stem.

Axillary blossom

aymonieri: After a personal name. — *Gyrinocheilus*.

Azolla: Moss Ferns.

Genus of tropical and sub-tropical floating plants belonging to the family of the Floating Ferns or *Salviniaceae*, the small leaves of which are superimposed like scales or shingles.

— caroliniana Wildenow: The Carolinian Water Fern.

GENERALITIES: A very pretty floating plant, but which can only be used sparingly in the indoors aquarium.

SHAPE: The small, gray-green leaves stand in a double row along the multiple-ramified axis, being superimposed like roofing shingles. On the underside one finds numerous long and threadlike roots. Size of the plants up to 10″.

RANGE: Tropical and sub-tropical America. The species was set out in Southern Germany and in Southern France, where it is found wild in spots with especially favorable conditions.

CULTIVATION: The plants thrive best with moist, warm air, a well-illuminated location, not too hard water (up to about 10° DH), and a water temperature of 64-77° F. Cultivation is especially favorable if effected under the open sky. There the little plants strike root in shallow spots near the banks and proliferate strongly. In the indoor aquarium, however, they are rather difficult to keep, weaken easily, and

Azolla caroliniana

frequently die completely during winter. They can be wintered in shallow covered dishes at 55-59° F, at a well illuminated location, keeping them on moist mud only.

— **filiculoides** Lamarck: The Fern-like Moss Fern.

A species which is spread over South America and has grown wild in several regions of Europe. It resists winter in mild regions. In the Andes it is found up to a height of 16,000 feet. The plants need plenty of fresh air, for which reason they frequently do not thrive well in covered tanks. Under the open sky they proliferate still more luxuriantly than the previous species. This Moss Fern is strongly ramified and the branches may grow quite distant from each other.

— **azurea:** Sky blue, azure.

— *Eichhornia.*

background of the aquarium: see INSTALLATION.

Backswimmer: see HYDROCORYSAE.

Back-Swimming Congo Catfish, the: see SYNODONTIS NIGRIVENTRIS.

Bacopa: After the native name (Fat Leaves).

Genus of swamp plants belonging to the family of the SCROPHULARIACEAE (see these).

The different species of *Bacopa* are swamp plants with a relatively sturdy stem which looks a little stiff, possessing whole-edged, crossed fat shiny leaves. They bloom only when living emerged. The little white to violet flowers insert in the angles of the leaves.

They are hardy plants which may be cultivated submergedly in the indoor aquarium, but also in the swamp aquarium or under the open sky. Their demands as to temperature are only small, it being best to keep them at 64-68° F, as at higher degrees of warmth they degenerate easily. In summer they withstand more intense sunlight, especially outdoors. In the indoor aquarium use clean sand with an admixture of some clay as a bottom ground, while outdoors one may use the usual mixture. There are no special demands as to the composition of the water, but it seems that the plants bloom more easily in soft water. According to WENDT, wintering is effected as a swamp plant in a flower pot which is to place it in an empty, covered aquarium. Since the plants find difficulty in blooming and to develop seeds in the indoor aquarium, multiplication in this is effected by means of easily growing planted twigs.

— **amplexicaulis** (Pursch): Wettstein.

SHAPE: As per description of genus. The stiff stems, which grow upwards but creep in shallow waters, break easily. The whole-edged, crossed-inserting, oval to rounded leaves are fleshy and colored a pretty, shiny green. They surround the stem at its base. All leaves are slightly arched, older ones bend a little downward. The stem is finely fluted and equipped with downy hairs on the underside, and so also are the leaves. The plants reach heights of up to two feet.

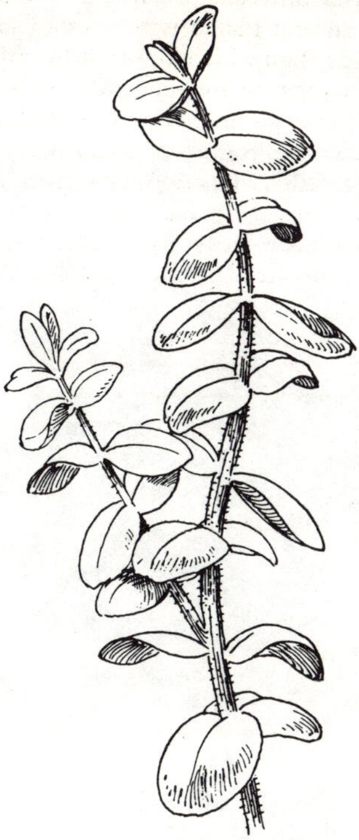

Bacopa amplexicaulis

The blue- sometimes also violet-tinted flowers insert in the angles of the leaves of emerged plants. Submergedly cultivated specimens do not bloom. *B. amplexicaulis* gives off a faint aromatic fragrance.

RANGE: Southern and central U.S.A., in swampy regions, especially on the banks of shallow waters.

CULTIVATION: As per description of genus.

— **monniera** (Linné): Wettstein. This species resembles the preceding one very much, but differs from it by the fact that stems and leaves are hairless, besides the fact that the leaves are smaller. The flowers of the emerged plants are white to light blue. Its home countries are the tropics and subtropics of Africa, Asia, America, and Australia. Possibly the species is also found in Southern Europe. Cultivation is similar to that of the preceding species, but the plants withstand a little more warmth.

bacteria: Microscopically small live beings, which lack a real nucleus, chromosomes, and chlorophyll which are peculiar to green plants. They are able to move, many species possess permanent or temporary flagelli, with the aid of which they achieve locomotion. Since bacteria possess no chlorophyll, they are unable to feed in the manner of plants, but have to effect

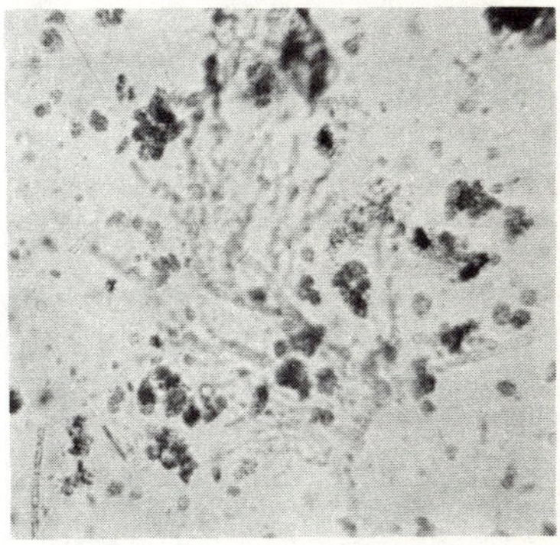

Colony of bacteria, greatly magnified

their metabolism of building and food substances in a different way. In general they decompose organic matter. Some species (nitrate, iron, sulphur, bacteria, etc.), oxydize inorganic substances. Nearly all bacteria are parasites or live on decaying matter. Through their capability to decompose organic substances and thus to make them usable for plants, they are also important in the aquarium.

As so-called 'bottom' bacteria they settle in the bottom soil and work up the settling mulm. The decomposed substances are either bound chemically, or else incorporated into the body economy of plants. This biological process, however, stops if the mulm collects in the aquarium in such great quantities that water can no more circulate within the bottom soil. This leads to disturbances in the bacterial economy of the soil, and to extensive processes of putrefaction, as well as to stoppages. In most cases the aquarist will set up peat filters, but these are unable to take over the work of the bacteria, but will, contrarily, trap bacteria which thus are removed from the aquarium. Generally the hobbyist makes use of the bacteria in keeping up the biological balance in his aquarium in an unconscious way by endeavoring to balance all factors as far as possible.

bacterial and virus diseases of fishes: Among the diseases caused by bacteria and viruses count among others the following, which may be found under the respective entries:
FURUNCULOSIS, INFECTIOUS DROPSY, INFLAMMATION OF THE SWIMMING BLADDER, FIN ROT, FISH TUBERCULOSIS, THE *Lymphocycstis* DISEASE, BOILS and SWELLINGS (in part).

Bade, Emil: Author of the well-known book 'Das Suesswasser-aquarium' (The Fresh Water Aquarium), which for a long time was considered one of the most important descriptions in the whole field of aquaristics, and which found broad dissemination in a total of five printings. Special importance is given to the world of small live beings. With regard to aquarium fishes the book became obsolete very soon, since the great number of imports no longer permitted comprehensive reports. Bade himself illustrated his book with pictures which in part are excellent.

Badis: After the native name.
Genus of Indian Perches pertaining to the family of the Nandids or *Nandidae* (see these), which possesses an elongated body, slightly compressed laterally, diverging from the usual family type. The only known species is very variable, and divided into several local types, according to its broad distribution. The fish are peaceful, with some exceptions. They like to rest among rocks and roots in a typical position.

Badis badis

— badis (Hamilton-Buchanan): The Badis.
SHAPE: As per description of the genus. The relatively low body has a slightly arched back, and the belly region of the male is a little drawn-in. Head and mouth opening are quite small. D XVI-XVIII/6-10, A III/6-8. Length up to $3\frac{1}{4}''$, the female remaining a little smaller.
COLOR: The many color variations do not permit a color description. In general the males possess reddish cross bands composed of spots on a dark-blue to blackish base. However, these vanish during the spawning period, giving place to a uniform color. Each scale is bordered by a dark edge. The dorsal fin carries differently colored length bands in which a beautiful, luminous blue-green predominates. The female is considerably simpler in color, and besides this she is easily differentiated by her fuller belly.

RANGE: India and Indo-China.

CARE AND BREEDING: The species is hardy and relatively peaceable, despite the fact that little, generally harmless fights are fought with each other or with other fishes. Older males, however, especially rogues, may sometimes be quite vicious and aggressive. The Badis will remain contented with smaller tanks, appreciates dense stands of plants, and especially likes sufficient hiding places among rocks and roots. It also likes to hide in coconut shells. To state that the fish are monotonous is an injustice done them. They are indeed a little quiet, but show themselves quite often after having become domesticated, especially if several pairs live together in the same tank. The species needs warmth. For keeping it one needs 68-77° F, which may be raised to 82-86° F for breeding. Only live foods are eaten.

The Badis is a cave breeder. Spawning takes place after very remarkable mating games with a close embrace within the cave which was previously chosen and defended by the male. The total of 40-100 eggs are stuck to the walls or the roof of the breeding cave, sometimes also on the underside of broad-leaved aquatic plants, and are watched by the male. The initially very small fry hatch within 48-60 hours, according to temperature. At first they feed on infusoria, which they find in sufficient quantities in big and well-planted tanks. When growing up, they switch over to dust-sized live foods. Even if at first their growth is quite slow, they catch up quickly as soon as they are able to conquer bigger-sized foods. The female may be removed immediately after spawning, the male after the swarming-out of the fry. If the breeding tank is sufficiently big and offers sufficient possibilities for hiding, the young may even be reared in the presence of the parents.

— **badis siamensis** Klausewitz: A sub-species discovered by ROLOFF and imported in 1957, which was captured in a small body of water on Phuket Island, in the Bengal Gulf, and which differs considerably in some of its characteristics from the original form. D XV-XVI/8-10, A III/7. Length probably about 2⅜″-2¾″. This sub-species is also very variable in color. On a red-brown base we find 6-7 rows of dots, the color of which changes from brick red to black. Dorsal angle, upper part of the head, and insertions of the fins show dark spots. Under excitement the male turns nearly blue-black. The female is simpler in color, but at times is difficult to differentiate from the male, except for her shape.

Care and breeding are similar to those of the original type. Similar to this, also the Siamese Badis leads a hidden life. Roloff was not able to bring more than one pair back to Germany, but he succeeded in breeding them, so that we may count upon the preservation of this new fish. Reproduction and the method employed for breeding correspond to those of *Badis badis*.

Bagridae: African and Asiatic family of Catfishes belonging to the sub-order of the SILUROIDEA (see these), which possesses a moderately elongated build and a completely naked skin. The dorsal fin inserts relatively near the front end. An adipose fin is always present, and on nearly all species disproportionately big. The fish possess 3-4 pairs of barbels; the jaws are always equipped with teeth. The big and independent swimming bladder is well developed. The genus is found exclusively in fresh water.

The family comprises about 13

genera, among others AUCHENOGLANIS (see this), SPERATA (see this), and LEIOCASSIS (see this), with numerous species.

Baldner, Leonhard: 1612-1694. Fisherman from Strasbourg who was one of the first to keep fishes and plants in glass containers for purposes of observation. He reports on this in a 'Bird, Fish, and Animal Book' published in 1666.

Banded Barb, the: see BARBUS FASCIOLATUS.

Banded Barbs: 1. **Barbus tetrazona** 2. **Barbus partipentazona** 3. **Barbus pentazona** 4. **Barbus hexazona.**

Banded Barbs: A group of small fishes belonging to the family of the Carp-like or *Cyprinidae*, genus *Barbus*. The several species are very similar and are only unreliably differentiated externally by the number and disposition of the black transverse bands. In the case of many banded Barbs which today are still being considered as different species, we are probably only considering local varieties of the same species.

Banded Cichlid, the: see CICHLASOMA SEVERUM.

Banded Cynolebias: see CYNOLEBIAS ADLOFFI.

Banded Cyprinodont: see LEPORINUS FASCIATUS.

Banded Fundulus, the: see FUNDULUS CINGULATUS.

Banded Jewel Fish, the: see HEMICHROMIS FASCIATUS.

Banded Limia, the: see LIMIA VITTATA.

Banded Panchax: see EPIPLATYS FASCIOLATA.

Banded Shiner, the: see NOTROPIS HYPSELOPTERUS.

Banded-Tail Limia, the: see LIMIA CAUDOFASCIATA.

Banjo Catfishes: see BUNOCEPHALIDAE.

Banner Cichlid, the: see CICHLASOMA FESTIVUM.

Banner Tetra, the: see HEMIGRAMMUS ULREYI.

barbatulus: With a small barbel.
— *Noemacheilus.*

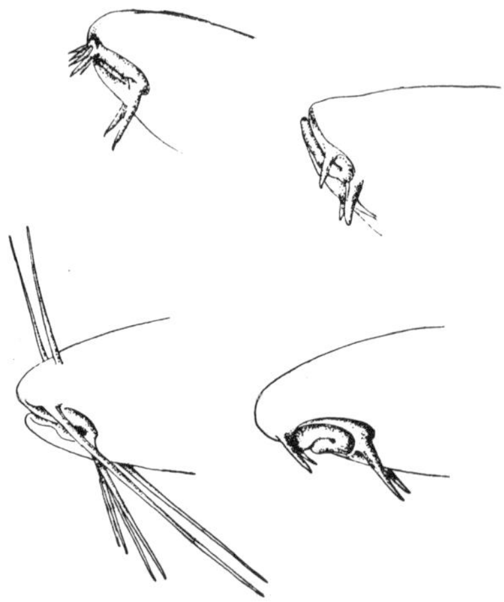

Barbels: 1. a Loach species 2. a Carp 3. a Catfish 4. the River Barb

barbels: Fish whiskers. Appendages of the head, especially of the mouth region, which may possess cartilaginous or bony supporting tissues. Barbels are either moved passively, while opening the mouth, or else actively by means of muscles which swing them in and out. They carry taste buds. It is especially the bottom dwellers among fishes who are characterized by the presence of barbels, which make it easier for them to search for food.

barberi: After the collector, Dr. Barbero.
— *Mimagoniates.*

Barb-like fishes: A term for a group of small, tropical and sub-tropical Carp-like fishes which resemble the Barbs, particularly the genera *Rasbora*, *Danio* (*Brachydanio*) and *Esomus*.

Barbs: see BARBUS (PUNTIUS).

Barbus (Puntius): With barbels. A genus of small, medium-sized, or big fishes, belonging to the family of the Carp-like or CYPRINIDAE (see these). The genus is very rich in species and is not yet completely clear as to its position in systematics.

The genus was established by CUVIER in 1817. For its basic type it depended on the River Barb, which up to then had been called *Cyprinus barbus*. Later on the genus was divided into several genera, since the number of River Barb-like fishes had grown to an extent where the original genus had gotten out of control and many of the newly classified fishes differed completely from the type of the River Barb. In doing this, the genus *Puntius* was also established. Unfortunately the type for this new genus was a fish without barbels, so that now the lack of barbels was taken as a characteristic of the genus. Later on it was discovered that many of the species classified under the genus *Puntius* possessed barbels anyway. The type according to which HAMILTON-BUCHANAN established the genus name in 1822 was *P. puntio*. A new proposition made by Dr. L. P. Schultz is based fundamentally on BLEEKER (1863) who established three subgenera for the genus *Puntius*, viz. *Puntius* (*Puntius*), *Puntius* (*Barbodes*), and *Puntius* (*Capoeta*), the main differentiation of which is the number of barbels. According to SCHULTZ the division would be the following:

Puntius: without barbels
Capoeta: With two barbels
Barbodes: With four barbels.

Whether the inclusion of the number of barbels as a differentiating character holds water, cannot be said as yet.

Due to the resulting lack of clearness, we have desired to follow the practice of many authors, describing all Barb-like fishes within the genus *Barbus*, despite the recommendation of the Committee for Nomenclature to use the name of the genus *Puntius* for some of these species.

The genus comprises mostly school fishes of more or less elongated body structure, generally with strong lateral compression. The scales are generally rather big and often possess a strong silvery polish. Barbels are present or may be lacking. The first rays of the dorsal and anal fins are not articulated. The genus is distributed over Europe, Africa, and Asia. Not including the European River Barb, *Barbus fluviatilis* Agassiz, of which only smaller specimens would fit the indoor aquarium, the genus musters a great number of small and very small fishes, especially from the tropical and sub-tropical regions of Asia and Africa. These fishes are peaceable, and sprightly, skillful swimmers. Since many species come from flowing waters of the plains and the mountains, they may, in part, be quite undemanding as to the warmth of the water; but it is impossible to make any statements of general validity on this. All, or most species like sunlight and sufficient space for swimming and playing, as well as dense planting which offers occasional hiding places. What was said regarding the manner of keeping the Carps in general, under the heading CYPRINIDAE (see this), is also valid for the Barbs. There is hardly a case in which breeding any of the

Barbs offers difficulties worth mentioning even if one or the other species needs a somewhat more careful treatment than the majority.

Most species are so-called egg scatterers. Only a few hang their eggs from leaves of aquatic plants. The most favorable period for breeding is early spring. In nature the pairs separate from the school, in the aquarium one should generally mate one spawn-ripe female to two males, but in part it is also advisable to put together simple pairs. The males fight lively, but generally harmless encounters. Frequently too, they defend a certain place in the aquarium, which the fish seek for short rest periods. The mating games are very interesting. The males woo the females with vivacious, somewhat dancing movements, spread their fins open, and vibrate them in a peculiar manner. Sometimes they nearly stand on their heads, or it comes to a kind of fin beat, during which the pair remains in one place for a short time. Often, too, the males muzzle their female partners in the region of the genital opening. Temporarily the mating games are substituted by violent chasing, in which sometimes very high speeds of swimming are reached.

The act of spawning generally takes place under the morning sun. It is preceded by a number of false matings. Then suddenly a male shoots forth from the chase to the side of the female. Some short contacts take place, as a rule among plants, but sometimes also in open water. With a sudden, violent motion, in which the fish frequently repel each other, or whirl around each other, the eggs are expelled and fertilized. These are scattered far by the violent movement of the water, and stick to plants if they have a mucilaginous shell, or sink to the bottom. Generally the eggs are the size of a grain of millet. Each mating releases 20-30 of them, to a total of several hundred, depending on species, size, and age. The complete act of spawning may last several hours. After it the parents should be removed immediately, since they prey actively on the spawn. One may also feed some enchytrae during the spawning. The spawn should be protected by special measures. It is especially advisable to cover the bottom with rough gravel over which one spreads a layer of fine-feathered plants, weighted down with little glass tubes.

The fry hatch after about 30 hours and hang as glass-clear little dashes about $\frac{3}{16}''$ long from panes, plants, and other firm objects for another 24-36 hours. After a few days they become free-swimming and go out in search of food. To begin with, offer them infusoria, moistened egg yolk, and very fine artificial foods. After a few days, depending on growth, go over to dust-fine food and artificial foods of corresponding grain in addition. If well-fed they will take sifted Cyclops after two weeks, normal food of relative size after three weeks.

Barbus binotatus

— **binotatus** (Cuvier and Valenciennes): The Sooty Barb.
SHAPE: As per description of genus, the body slender and elongated, the terminal mouth with four barbels. D 12, A 8. Length, in its

home waters, about 7″, in the aquarium 4″ to $4\frac{3}{4}$″.
COLOR: Shiny silver with single black spots and dots on the sides, showing a reddish hue when excited.
RANGE: In ponds, rivers, and lakes, from the Malayan Islands up to the Philippines, quite frequent everywhere.
CARE AND BREEDING: As per description of the genus. Needs some warmth.

— **callipterus** Boulenger: The Pretty-Finned Barb.
SHAPE: As per description of the genus, the body slender and elongated, strongly compressed laterally. The terminal mouth is equipped with four barbels. D 11, A 8. Length up to $3\frac{1}{2}$″.
COLOR: Brownish to greenish with strong silvery sheen, each scale with a brown edge and a dark spot at the base. The fins are reddish, on the dorsal a deep black spot. The upper half of the iris is a vivid red.
RANGE: In brooks and rivers of West Africa, from Cameroon to the Niger.
CARE AND BREEDING: As per description of the genus. No need for warmth. Temperature 68-72° F, lowest 64°F. It seems that the species has not yet been bred.

— **camptacanthus** (Bleeker): The African Red-Finned Barb.
SHAPE: As per description of the genus, slender and elongated, with an arched dorsal outline. The mouth is a little subterminal and carries four barbels. D 11, A 8. Length, in its home waters up to $6\frac{1}{4}$″, in the aquarium up to $4\frac{3}{4}$″.
COLOR: Shiny silver with a yellow-green hue, added to which sometimes come a weak horizontal band and further, indistinct, band-shaped designs. The fins of the male are red, those of the female yellow. During the spawning period the slimmer male shows a grainy rash on the sides of the head.
RANGE: A species which is quite frequent in West Africa, found in ponds and quietly-flowing waters from the Congo to the Niger.
CARE AND BREEDING: As per description of the genus, but especially needing much warmth. Normal temperature 75-82° F, but becoming quite sluggish at 75° F, lowest temperature 72° F. Probably not yet bred.

— **chola** (Hamilton-Buchanan): The Swamp Barb.
SHAPE: As per description of the genus, the laterally compressed body looks quite compact. Head and mouth are small, the mouth opening is slanted upwards and carries one pair of barbels. D 11, A 7. Length, in its home waters $5\frac{1}{8}$″ to $5\frac{7}{8}$″, in the aquarium up to 4″.
COLOR: A strong silvery sheen with a greenish-gray hue. A big red spot on the gill covers. The fins are yellowish to reddish, the dorsal is black at the base. The root of the tail fin shows a black spot as well. During the spawning period the males shows a reddish hue, being generally slimmer.
RANGE: The species is quite frequent in all kinds of waters, even rice paddies, of East India and Burma.

Barbus chola

CARE AND BREEDING: As per description of the genus. The species may be kept at room temperature. The tank should be well-covered, as the fish like to jump. Breeding resembles that of the Rosy Barb.

— **conchonius** (Hamilton-Buchanan): The Rosy Barb.

SHAPE: As per description of the genus. The body of the male is elongated and slender, that of the female a little higher-backed and fuller. The species possesses no barbels. D 10, A 7-8. Length, in its home waters up to 6″, in the aquarium exceptionally up to 3⅛″.

COLOR: A strong silvery sheen with vivid moss-green back and a black spot on the caudal peduncle. During the spawning period the male becomes an imposing red with a deep-black dorsal fin.

Barbus conchonius

RANGE: In standing and slowly-flowing waters of Northern India, quite frequent everywhere.

CARE AND BREEDING: As per description of the genus. The Rosy Barb is one of the hardiest tropicals. It needs no warmth. To keep it, 64-72° F are sufficient, for breeding 70-73° F, lowest temperature may amount to 52-60° F, but here the fish become sluggish and colorless. They may be kept at room temperature. Like all Barbs, the Rosy Barb is omnivorous and likes to eat some vegetable food occasionally. Breeding them can be achieved even in outdoor pools.

Barbus cumingii

— **cumingii** (Guenther): Cuming's Barb.

SHAPE: As per description of the genus. The body is strongly compressed laterally, but not overly elongated. The mouth is slightly subterminal, and carries no barbels. D 11, A 8. Length up to 2″.

COLOR: On a shiny yellowish base each scale carries a dark spot at the base. The fins are a pretty yellow to reddish with a thin dash design. The male is slimmer and more vividly colored.

RANGE: In some forest brooks in the mountains on Ceylon. Relatively rare.

CARE AND BREEDING: As per description of the genus. The species is very likeable and vivacious, the males are very playful and fight little jealous encounters with each other. They are said to need warmth, 72-75° F, for breeding 75-81° F, lowest 68° F. The fish like a not-too-well illuminated location, if possible a semi-shaded one, and a dark, mulm or peat covered bottom. In order to enhance their well-being it is advisable to give them frequent partial changes of the water. Breeding is not very easy, as not all pairs mate. Besides this, the fry may be a little sensitive and frail. If possible, use soft water for breeding.

— **dunckeri** Ahl: Duncker's Barb.

SHAPE: As per description of the genus, in part a little high-backed,

Barbus dunckeri

but varying in shape. Possibly the species is identical with B. EVERETTI (see this). It possesses two pairs of barbels. D 12, A 8. Length, in its home country up to 12″, in the aquarium up to 6″.

RANGE: Malacca, Singapore, and Borneo. Nowhere frequent.

CARE AND BREEDING: As per description of the genus. Because of its size, it should be kept in big tanks. The species needs warmth, 75-77° F, for breeding up to 86° F, are adequate. At 72° F the fish already show marked discomfort. The species seems to become prone to diseases if kept in old water. Therefore it is advisable to effect frequent partial changes of water. They are omnivores, but need rich and vigorous food. Sexual maturity already sets in at a length of 4″. It is remarkable that the spawn-ripe females often behave like males. The chasing is started by the female, and later continued by the male. The eggs are spawned at shadowy spots among plants. It seems that the fry are sensitive to fluctuations in temperature. Therefore it is advisable to keep the warmth constantly at about 79° F. The changes of water, indicated for the adults, should also be made for the alevins, as soon as these have grown to a length of about ¾″. The young grow quickly, but considering the size to which they have to grow, they become able to reproduce only after they are two years old.

— **everetti** Boulenger: The Clown Barb.

This species is very similar to the preceding one, even if it seems to remain a little smaller and is perhaps a little slimmer. Differently from *B. dunckeri* it shows no vertical stripes which start from the back. Possibly *B. dunckeri* is identical with *B. everetti*—in this case both would have to be called *B. everetti*

Barbus everetti

Boulenger. It is also possible, however, that both species could be sub-species of still another species.

— **fasciatus** Bleeker: The Striped, or Zebra, Barb.

SHAPE: As per description of the genus. The body contour is elongated and diamond-shaped; the head is pointed, no barbels are

Barbus fasciatus

present. D 11, A 8-9. Length, in its home country up to 6″, in the aquarium up to 4″.

COLOR: Yellowish-gray-silvery base with four dark horizontal stripes, the vertical fins slightly reddish. The male is slimmer, a little smaller, and more highly colored.

RANGE: Not exactly known, probably mostly in Malaya. In standing and flowing waters. Not rare.

CARE AND BREEDING: As per description of the genus. Breeding is not easy, and has only lately been achieved to a greater extent. The water should be soft and slightly acid, temperature 72-75° F, for breeding 77-79° F. If kept alone, the fish easily becomes shy.

— **fasciolatus** Guenther:

SHAPE: As per description of the genus, very slender, and strongly compressed laterally. The small, subterminal mouth carries two pairs of barbels. D 11, A 8. Length up to $2\frac{3}{4}$″.

Barbus fasciolatus

COLOR: The sides have a blue-green hue with 12-13 bars, which are only occasionally visible. The fins are brownish, the iris is big and black. The male is slimmer.

RANGE: Angola.

CARE AND BREEDING: As per description of the genus. The species is considered quarrelsome and jealous of its food. It needs warmth: 73-75° F, for breeding probably more. Spawning them, however, has not yet been achieved.

— **fluviatilis** Agassiz: The River Barb.

SHAPE: As per description of the genus, but coinciding only slightly with most members of the *Barbus-Puntius* group which are known to the aquarist. The body is elongated, the belly contour straight. The subterminal, thick-lipped mouth carries two pairs of barbels. D 11, A 8. The scales are rather small. Length up to 26″.

COLOR: Uniformly brownish-green with light belly.

RANGE: Europe, North of the Alps, from Roumania to France. At the bottom of slow-flowing waters, often living together in schools. During daytime the fish remain in the current, going out after food at night.

CARE AND BREEDING: Only small specimens are for the indoor aquarium, otherwise to be kept only in bigger exhibition tanks. Young Barbs are very pleasing and lively. They like to stay in the median reaches of the water, being sensitive to sunlight and needing cool water, as they require much oxygen. Food is taken especially from the bottom.

— **gambiensis** Svensson: The Gambian Barb.

SHAPE: As per description of the genus. Rather elongated fish with a pointed snout. Barbels are present. Length $3\frac{1}{8}$″-4″.

COLOR: Greenish to bluish-silvery base with a black-brown horizontal band. During the spawning period the male shows a reddish hue.

RANGE: The Gambia River, in a region where the influx of the tides creates strongly changing conditions of the water.

CARE AND BREEDING: As per description of the genus. A vivacious species, which roots little, peaceable and fit for communities with other active fishes. However, it needs quite some warmth, 75-

82° F should be adequate. Breeding has already been achieved, taking place as for most Barbs. The very small eggs are not adhesive and sink to the bottom.

— **gelius** (Hamilton-Buchanan): The Golden Dwarf Barb.

SHAPE: As per description of the genus; quite slender and elongated, the female a little higher-bodied. No barbels or only stunted ones. D 10-11, A 8. Length 1¾″, the male remaining a little smaller.

Barbus gelius

COLOR: Greenish to golden shiny, translucent and with irregular dark spot designs. The male possesses a copper-colored spot on the middle of the body and is slimmer.

RANGE: In waters of all kinds in India. They stay mostly in small schools near the banks or among plant thickets. The species is rare.

CARE AND BREEDING: As per description of the genus. The fish are vivacious, peaceful, and root little. It is advisable to offer them not too old water, and a dark bottom. Small demands are made as to temperature, 64-72° F is sufficient, lowest 61° F. According to present experiences, the species degenerates easily, the descendancy getting always smaller and finally losing its ability to reproduce. Therefore one has to be careful to get only a good stock of breeders. The eggs are stuck to the underside of broad-leaved plants. The parents hardly ever prey on them. The act of spawning is said to be very violent. At too high temperatures, many eggs get fungused; in all the species cannot be called productive.

Barbus hexazona

— **hexazona** Weber and De Beaufort: The Tiger Barb.

SHAPE: As per description of the genus. Compared to other banded Barbs, the body is a little more elongated, laterally compressed. D 12, A 8. Length $2\frac{3}{16}$″.

COLOR: On dirty golden-yellow to reddish-yellow base six cross bands extend from the back to the belly edge. The vertical fins are reddish at the base. The female is more compact. Possibly this is a local variety of *B. pentazona.*

RANGE: In standing and slowly-flowing waters of the great Sunda Island.

CARE AND BREEDING: As per description of the genus. This likeable fish is not easy to keep. Soft and slightly acid water should contribute to its well-being. Nothing is known about breeding it.

— **holotaenia** Boulenger: The Full-Striped Barb.

SHAPE: As per description of the genus. The subterminal mouth carries two pairs of barbels. D 11-12, A 8. Length up to 5″.

COLOR: Greenish to strong silvery sheen, and a blue-black stripe along the sides. The vertical fins are reddish to red, the dorsal fin with

Barbus holotaenia

a black tip.

RANGE: From Cameroon to the Congo region. Appears in schools in flowing waters.

CARE AND BREEDING: As per description of the genus. The species requires much warmth and does not feel well at temperatures below 68° F. Breeding has not yet been achieved.

— **hulstaerti** Poll: The Butterfly Barb.

SHAPE: Small, dainty species of vivacious motility. Body elongated. Head small, mouth rounded, with two barbels. The lateral line is difficult to see. D 10, A 8. Length about $1\frac{5}{8}''$.

COLOR: Shiny red-brown to coppery base, which fades into a yellowish-white hue towards the belly, with three jet-black spots on the sides of the body. Fins yellowish, dorsal, anal, and ventral fins with vivid black designs. The female is plumper with transparent fins, the shoulder spot rounded, while it is comma-shaped on the male.

Barbus hulstaerti

RANGE: The region of the lower Congo.

CARE AND BREEDING: A vivacious, hardy species, which likes company, as long as this is composed of peaceful companions of the same size. The species poses no special demands as to food, taking all kinds of live and artificial foods. Closer reports on the vital demands and reproduction are still lacking, but they can hardly differ from those of similar small Barbs.

— **lateristriga** Valenciennes: The T-Barb.

As per description of the genus. The species resembles *B. dunckeri*, but is higher-backed. It possesses four barbels. Length, in its home country 7″, in the aquarium up to $4\frac{3}{4}''$.

Barbus lateristriga

RANGE: Southeast Asia, parts of Indonesia. The population shows several divergences which have to be evaluated as sub-species.

COLOR: A very variable species. Dirty-pale-gray base, green back, orange-colored belly with remarkable blue black spots, and a stripe of the same color from the tail base to the middle of the body. The male is more slender and more vividly colored, the red hue in the dorsal fin being stronger.

— **lineatus** Duncker: see BARBUS FASCIATUS.

— nigrofasciatus Guenther: The Black Ruby Barb.

SHAPE: As per description of the genus. The fish are relatively high, especially with increasing age. No barbels are present. D 11, A 7-8. The dorsal fin is quite high and fan-shaped when spread. Length up to $2\frac{5}{8}''$, the male remaining a little smaller.

COLOR: Yellowish-gray with 4 to 5 indistinct, dark or black bars. The snout is reddish on both sexes. During the spawning period the bars of the male become deep black and run together in the rear part of the body, so that this may be totally covered. The front part becomes a shiny, glowing, carmine red, the vertical fins and the ventrals taking on a deep black color.

RANGE: In the brooks of mountain woods on Ceylon. There the fish appear in small schools, especially in calm, shadowy inlets, set with plants.

Barbus nigrofasciatus

CARE AND BREEDING: As per description of the genus. The species likes not-too-small well-planted tanks with a little sunlight, but especially half shade which results from covering the surface with floating plants. If kept under unfavorable conditions, the fish become pale and shy. A dark, peaty bottom enhances the colors. Temperatures 68-72° F, for breeding 75-82° F, lowest 68° F. This Barb is not considered very productive. The male needs a rest pause between the spawning periods.

— oligolepis (Bleeker): The Checker Barb.

SHAPE: As per description of the genus. The female is a little higher-backed than the male. The barbels are stunted or very small. D 11, A 8. Length up to 2″.

Barbus oligolepis

COLOR: Yellow-brown base with many light-reflecting spots and irregular black dots which are found especially at the base of the very big scales. The fins are yellow, those of the males in part brick-red with black edges.

RANGE: The Great Sunda Islands, especially on Sumatra, in small swarms in the quiet inlets of flowing waters.

CARE AND BREEDING: As per description of the genus. The species is vivacious, peaceable, and likes subdued sunlight. Besides live and dry foods they also eat plenty of soft algae, especially searching the bottom for food. Temperatures 68-75° F, for breeding 75-79° F, lowest 64° F.

— paludinosus Peters: The Swamp Barb.

SHAPE: As per description of the genus; very slender and elongated, the dorsal contour a little more arched than the ventral one. The subterminal mouth carries two pairs of barbels. D 11-12, A 8. Length up to 12″.

COLOR: Shiny greenish silver with a dark spot on the caudal peduncle. The fins are reddish to red.

RANGE: In waters of all kinds in Tunis, Morocco, and Algiers, not rare anywhere.

CARE AND BREEDING: As per description of the genus. The species is hardly adapted for the indoor aquarium. It is quite rugged and likes to root in the ground. The fish pose no demands as to temperature, which may sink to the freezing point without harming them.

So far nothing is known of the manner of breeding them, but there could hardly be any deviation in this.

— partipentazona Fowler: The Banded Barb.

SHAPE: As per description of the genus. The body is relatively high, especially with increasing age, and strongly compressed laterally. The small mouth carries a short barbel on each side. D 11, A 8. Length up to 2″.

Barbus partipentazona

COLOR: Shiny yellow base with four full black vertical bars and one partial one. Each scale with a brownish edge which becomes shiny depending on the angle of incidence of the light. Most fins are red at the base, those of the male being more intensely colored. This species belongs to the group of banded Barbs, which are hard to differentiate and possibly are no more than local forms of a few species. They could eventually be counted as sub-species of *B. tetrazona*.

RANGE: The Malayan Peninsula.

CARE AND BREEDING: As per description of the genus. Very remarkably and strikingly colored, always lively, school fish of very likeable behavior. They are playful, but have the reputation of being a little quarrelsome. It seems that they are quite prone to attacks of *Ichthyosporidium* (*Ichthyophonus*), especially if kept in old water. Therefore it is advisable to effect frequent changes of part of the water. Temperatures 68-79° F, for breeding 79-83° F, lowest 64° F.

— pentazona (Fowler): The Five-Banded Barb.

This species is very similar to the preceding one and differs from it only by the number and position of the bands and by the number of barbels (two pairs). Origin: Singapore, Malaya, and Borneo, especially in the waters of the lowlands. Quite rare everywhere.

CARE AND BREEDING: As described for the preceding species.

— phutunio (Hamilton-Buchanan): The Dwarf, or Pygmy, Barb.

SHAPE: As per description of the genus. The body is relatively high-backed, moderately compressed laterally. No barbels are present. The mouth is small. D 10-11, A 8. Length, in its home country up to $3\frac{1}{8}$″, in the aquarium as a rule no more than 2″.

COLOR: Silvery with five indistinct, changeable bluish cross bands. The fins are reddish, the ventral of the male being reddish too, while that of the female is yellowish. The male is slimmer.

RANGE: In ponds, rice paddies, and small bodies of water in India and Ceylon. The species is not rare anywhere.

CARE AND BREEDING: As per description of the genus. The Pygmy Barb is hardy, lively, peaceful, and is best kept in communities of its own kind. It feels best in schools

Barbus phutunio

and becomes shy if kept alone, preferring to remain among plants in this case. The males are a little quarrelsome toward one another. Give them old water, with additions of fresh water from time to time. Temperatures 68-75° F, for breeding 75-79° F, lowest 60° F.

— **roloffi** (Klausewitz): Described as *Puntius roloffi* by Klausewitz in 1957.

SHAPE: Small, elongated, dorsal and ventral contours equally arched. The scales rather big. Small barbels. D 11, A 8. Length about $1\frac{1}{4}''$.

COLOR: Silvery base, which may show a temporary golden sheen. Dark, crescent-shaped spots stand out clearly on each scale. A dark spot is on the caudal peduncle. Fins are transparent to yellowish or reddish. The male remains a little smaller and has red ventral fins.

Barbus roloffi

RANGE: Thailand, caught near Patalung.

CARE AND BREEDING: A peaceful, not too lively species, which seems to get on best if kept in communities of its own kind. Despite their not being pronounced bottom fish, they like to stay near the bottom. The eggs are stuck to the underside of aquatic plants while swimming upside down. They are relatively big, numbering from 50 to 70 from adult females. The young hatch within 24 hours at 75-79° F. At first they hang from plants and glass panes, becoming free-swimming after five days. Raising them presents no difficulties, since they eat nauplii of brine shrimp right from the beginning. ROLOFF, who also was the first to import the species in 1957, has succeeded in breeding them.

— **'schuberti':** The Gold Barb. A name without scientific value for a selectively bred xanthoristic form of *Barbus semifasciolatus*.

Barbus semifasciolatus

— **semifasciolatus** Guenther: The Half-Banded Barb.

SHAPE: As per description of the genus. Has an elongated and rugged-looking body. Barbels small and stunted. D 11, A 7-8. Length up to 4″, the male remaining a little smaller.

COLOR: Greenish to bronze-colored base with 6-7 irregularly spaced black cross stripes. The belly part of the male is orange-colored during the spawning period.

The fins are yellowish to pale reddish. The male shows more vivid colors and is slimmer.

RANGE: Southeastern China.

CARE AND BREEDING: As per description of the genus. Temperatures 68-75° F, for breeding 73-75° F, lowest 63° F. The species is very productive; the fry grow very quickly.

— **setivimensis** Cuvier and Valenciennes:

A North African species which can hardly be considered for the indoor aquarium. It is very similar to *B. paludinosus.*

— **stigma** (Cuvier and Valenciennes): The Dotted Barb.

SHAPE: As per description of the genus. Of elongated build, with slightly arched back, compressed laterally. The mouth cleft is tilted obliquely upwards. No barbels are present. D 11-12, A 8. Length in its home country up to 8″, in the aquarium hardly above 3-4″.

COLOR: Shiny silver color with a few darker spots, the fins reddish. The male is slimmer.

RANGE: In waters of all kinds in India and Indo-China, common everywhere.

CARE AND BREEDING: As per description of the genus. The species may be kept at room temperature. They root strongly. As yet nothing is known about breeding them.

— **stoliczkai** Day: Stoliczka's Barb, the Sun-Spot Barb.

SHAPE: As per description of genus moderately elongated, increasing in height with age, compressed laterally. The small mouth carries no barbels. D 10-11, A 7. Length up to $2\frac{3}{8}$″.

COLOR: Shiny silver with a big, gold-bordered black spot on the caudal peduncle and a similar streak above the pectorals. The male possesses a very beautifully designed, red dorsal fin. Possibly this is a sub-species of *Barbus*

Barbus stoliczkai

ticto.

RANGE: In flowing waters of Burma.

CARE AND BREEDING: As per description of the genus. Temperature 68-75° F, for breeding 75-79° F.

— **terio** (Hamilton-Buchanan): The One-Spot Barb.

SHAPE: As per description of the genus. Elongated, dorsal and ventral contours equally arched, compressed laterally. The mouth cleft is slanted obliquely upwards. Barbels are lacking. D 11, A 7. Length up to $3\frac{1}{8}$″.

COLOR: Similar to *B. conchonius,* but not so intensely red, and distinctly differentiated from it by two spots above the anal fin. The male is more slender and becomes dark red on the belly during the spawning period.

RANGE: In waters of all kinds in Bengal, also in rice paddies. A quite common fish.

CARE AND BREEDING: As per description of the genus. Temperatures not below 61° F.

— **tetrazona** (Bleeker): The Sumatran Tiger Barb.

SHAPE: As per description of the genus and of the other banded barbs.

COLOR: Similar to *B. partipentazona,* but with four bars.

CARE AND BREEDING: As per description of the genus and of *B. partipentazona.* Also this species is not always easy to breed. It requires soft water, as in hard water the eggs do not develop well.

Barbus tetrazona

In general also this banded Barb is sensitive to fouling of the water. Its water should not be too fresh nor too old.

All banded Barbs are best kept in schools of their own kind. If put in communities with slower fishes, they prove to be too active and quarrelsome. Furthermore they like to nip the fins of other fishes.

This species is probably the original form of a series of subspecies.

— **ticto** (Hamilton-Buchanan): The Two-Spot Barb.

SHAPE: As per description of the genus. Of moderately elongated build, dorsal and ventral contours equally arched, compressed laterally. The obliquely rising mouth cleft carries no barbels. D 11, A 7. Length up to 3½″.

Barbus ticto

COLOR: Silvery-gray with a round, gold-edged, black spot on the caudal peduncle. Above the pectorals is a gold-edged stripe, which is located higher up than the eye. During the spawning period the male shows a brownish-red sheen.

RANGE: In waters of all kinds, especially flowing ones, of India and Ceylon.

CARE AND BREEDING: As per description of the genus, especially like *B. conchonius*.

— **titteya** (Deraniyagala): The Cherry Barb.

SHAPE: As per description of the genus. Very elongated and only moderately compressed laterally. The dorsal contour is more strongly arched than the ventral one. The subterminal mouth carries one pair of barbels. D 19, A 9. Length up to 2⅛″.

Barbus titteya

COLOR: Reddish-yellow base with a horizontal stripe covered by a lighter band, which in turn is bordered on the upper side by the darker back. The fins are yellowish, those of the male more reddish, and reddish prevails in the overall coloring of this sex.

RANGE: In shaded brooks and small rivers of the plains on the Island of Ceylon.

CARE AND BREEDING: As per description of the genus. The species likes not-too-intensely lit, old established, planted tanks, which should show a dark bottom in order to enhance its colors. Besides hiding places one should also offer them plenty of room for swimming and exercising. It is advisable to keep the species in company with their own kind, as generally they keep apart from other fishes. Toward one another the fish are a little 'jealous' and quarrelsome. Vanquished specimens take on female colors. The species needs some warmth. Temperatures, 73-77° F, for breeding 77-79° F, lowest 64° F. For breeding, set them up in pairs as several males together disturb each other mutually. The eggs are usually eliminated singly, at the maximum three, near broad-leaved plants, where they immediately remain hanging from a threadlet. The act of spawning lasts for a few hours. During the pauses between one spawning and the next one, it is advisable to feed enchytrae to the fish. The parents are spawn eaters. The rather quick-growing fry lead a hidden existence. Breeding is not simple, but the species may be considered productive.

— **trispilus** (Bleeker): The African Three-Spot Barb.

A West African Barb, shiny silver-colored with three black spots, which has not yet been able to win a place in the aquarium. Care similar to that for *B. camptacanthus*.

Barbus unitaeniatus

— **unitaeniatus** (Guenther): The Red-Finned Barb.

SHAPE: As per description of the genus, slender, compressed laterally. The sub-terminal mouth carries two pairs of barbels. D 11, A 8 Length $3\frac{1}{4}''$.

COLOR: Intense mother-of-pearl with a black horizontal stripe. The male is slimmer.

RANGE: South Africa, from Angola to Natal.

CARE AND BREEDING: As per description of the genus: The species needs much warmth. Manner of reproducing is unknown.

— **usambarae** Lönnberg: The Usambara Barb.

SHAPE: As per description of the genus, compressed laterally. The terminal mouth carries two pairs of barbels. D 10, A 8. Length up to $3\frac{1}{4}''$.

COLOR: Gray-brown-silver with a dark horizontal stripe that is light-bordered above and below.

RANGE: In swift-flowing waters of the coastal regions of East Africa.

CARE AND BREEDING: As per description of the genus. The species does not need much warmth, lowest temperature may amount to 50-54° F, but for breeding—which so far has not yet succeeded—they probably need temperatures above 68° F.

— **vittatus** Day:

SHAPE: As per description of the genus; of elongated build, the female a little higher than the male. The small, terminal mouth carries no barbels. D 10, A 7. Length up to $2\frac{3}{8}''$.

COLOR: Yellowish-green with a strong silvery glitter, the scales darker at the base. The fins are yellowish, at the front part of the dorsal fin a slanting, blackish stripe. The male is slimmer and a little smaller.

RANGE: In waters of all kinds, from India to Ceylon, also in rice paddies. The species is quite frequent everywhere.

CARE AND BREEDING: As per description of the genus.

— **werneri** Boulenger: Werner's Barb.

SHAPE: As per description of genus.

Slender, laterally compressed, the body of the female a little higher-backed than that of the male. The terminal mouth carries two pairs of barbels. D 10-11, A 8. Length up to 4″.

COLOR: Silvery, with bluish sheen.

RANGE: From Egypt to tropical East Africa.

CARE AND BREEDING: As per description of the genus. Bred only occasionally so far.

— **zelleri** Ahl: Zeller's Barb.

SHAPE: As per description of the genus. The body is moderately elongated, and looks quite rugged, especially that of older specimens. The dorsal contour is strongly arched. The nearly terminal mouth is equipped with two pairs of barbels. D 10, A 6. Length up to 2¾″. It is quite possible that this is a sub-species of *B. lateristriga*, which it resembles in color.

According to KLAUSEWITZ, *B. zelleri* is only an immature form of *B. lateristriga*. The name *B. zelleri* should be counted as a synonym only, without being valid.

RANGE: In clear, swiftly-flowing brooks with gravely bottoms in Indo-China.

CARE AND BREEDING: As described for the genus and for *B. lateristriga*.

Barilius: After the native name. Genus of small, Barb-like fishes belonging to the family of the Carp-like or *Cyprinidae* (see these), very closely related to *Danio* and *Rasbora*, The body is slender, generally moderately compressed laterally. The mouth cleft is very big and the eyes insert high. The genus is distributed over the whole of South East Asia to Africa, with several species.

— **christyi** (Boulenger): The Gold Mouth.

SHAPE: As per description of the genus; very slender. The ventral contour is more strongly arched than the dorsal one. D 10, A 16.

Barilius christyi

The scales are relatively small. Length up to about 4″.

COLOR: Bluish to greenish silvery, with 8-16 indistinct, dark, incomplete bars on the sides. The fins are reddish. On the snout a remarkable, red-golden spot.

CARE AND BREEDING: As described for CYPRINIDAE (see this). The fish like to assemble in loosely-connected schools, below the surface or in the central reaches of the water. They are very lively swimmers which like to jump and do this very well. For this reason the tanks should be well covered. The fish take any kind of food, but dislike picking it from the bottom, as for this they have to turn on their sides. Temperature 72-75° F. Possibly the species has lately been bred.

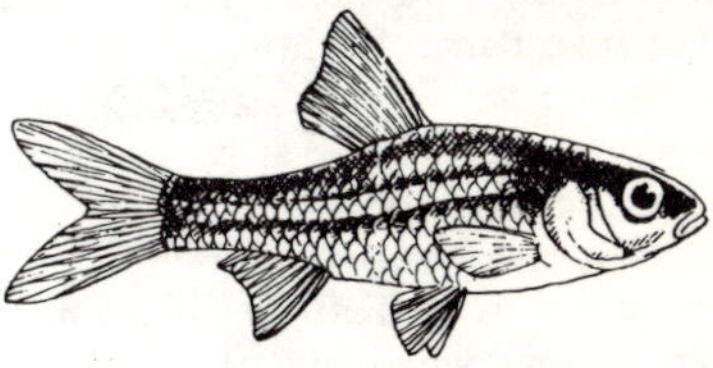

Barilius neglectus

— **neglectus** Stiler: The Japanese Barb.

SHAPE: As per description of the genus. D 10, A 11.

COLOR: On brownish-green base a silver-white horizontal stripe, bordered in dark above and below. The male is more vividly colored and possesses a bigger dorsal fin.

CARE AND BREEDING: As described for *Cyprinidae* and Barbs.

The species likes not-too-small, densely-planted tanks with sufficient sunlight and a dark bottom, near which they like to stay. They may be kept at room temperature, 72-75° F being sufficient for breeding.

base: Lower part of a body or of a body part, on which other parts are built.

Basic Biogenetic Law, the: Rule, established by Ernst HAECKEL, according to which in the individual development (development of the ovum and of the embryo) the development of the species is repeated in large strokes—strongly abridged—for instance, the unicellular phase, the coelenetratum phase in the development of the germinating leaf, the transitory presence of gill openings on the embryos of mammals, etc. The BBL may be of significance for establishing genetic-historical relationships.

Batrachus: Frog.
— *Clarias.*

Beaked Pike: see HEMIRHAMPHIDAE.

Beaked Tetras: see PHAGO.

beccabunga: Latinization of the German name 'Bachbunge'.
— *Veronica.*

beckettii: Named after Beckett, the discoverer of the plant.
— *Cryptocoryne.*

behavior of fishes: By behavior of an animal we define the form of its reaction to the stimuli of the ambient world, resulting from hereditary dispositions and from its own experience, as well as its typical manner of carrying out its vital functions. Behavior, like the whole physiology with which it is closely connected, is the product of genetic-historical development. No animal is free in its behavior, being bound to a certain manner of reacting by its body design, its organs, and its senses. The manifestations of life take place 'in preordained paths'. The behavior is as typical of an animal species as all its other qualities and characteristics. The differentiation from other species also is more or less great in this, depending on relatedness. Certain basic manners of behaving are common to the major groups of animals, such as e.g., the strokes of the fins, which are found in nearly all fishes.

Behavior composes of a number of parts (components), all of which are intertwined. For this reason it often is difficult to understand the causes of animal behavior in their particulars. The following (which see) may have a part in them: REFLEXES, TAXIES, and INSTINCTS, to which one has to add TRAINING based on individual experience. While in lower animals the simple reflexes and taxies predominate, higher up the always greater instinct is added which so strongly rules the curriculum vitae of insects, for instance, in vertebrates these 'automatic manifestations of life' are more and more influenced by individual experience, depending on the degree of development. As attempts at training have shown, this is already true to a certain extent in fishes. Basically it has to be stated that animal behavior reposes on bases that are totally different from those of man. Therefore it is wrong to ascribe human motivations to animals and to 'humanize' them. When watching the often extremely pragmatical behavior of fishes, which looks as if it were completely reasoned out—for instance, in the care for the spawn—one easily reaches this erroneous estimate. It can only lead to inexact conclusions, however.

The scientific study of animal behavior is called ETHOLOGY, being a branch of animal psychology.

Especially Cichlids are appropriate for ethological studies, as they carry out many vital functions (defense of individual range, care for spawn, etc.), which do not appear with the same perfection in other fishes. *Apistogramma reitzigi* may be used as an example with which to illustrate the aspects of behavior of a Cichlid species (VOGT). Let us suppose that the young fishes have just matured sexually. At first there will be fights for the supremacy (fights for the 'pecking order') among the males. These fights always are carried out with the same movements and in the same sequence of hostile acts. We are able to divide the whole course of the fight into two parts: making impressions (bluffing) and real fighting. The following listing shows the sequence of movements in a fight between two males:

Lying on the side
Spreading the fins
Stroke of the tail fin
Opening the gill covers } Impressing phase
Ramming stroke
Pulling mouth } Fight.

If a fish interrupts the tourney before the pulling of mouths, it is considered the loser and is run off by the winner. If both contenders show about equal strength, the fight goes through all phases to the pulling of mouths. The fish which weakens first and is vanquished by the stronger one, is run off from the winner's range.

Toward females the male at first behaves as if they were other males for while the female is not sexually mature she is considered an enemy. Only with the beginning of the inclination to spawn the females start to behave differently, so that now the males may start wooing them.

It is interesting to notice that the female only symbolizes the submission which is a condition for successful mating, if it should prove to be physically stronger than the male. Contrariwise, only in Dwarf Cichlids, which possess a maternal family system with exclusive care for the spawn by the female, the generally stronger male may respect the female.

During the care for the spawn, the fry react to certain colors and movements of the caring fish. While still very small, they sink motionless to the bottom when warned, collecting again near the mother, or swimming free, only after certain signals are given. The female does not have any idea about the number of young, and does not notice it if the school grows smaller. As soon, however, as it sees an alevin which has left the swarm, it goes to fetch it back.

These signals, which lead the fish to exert certain actions, are called triggers. Since fishes are 'eye' animals, triggers are of an optical nature. It is for this reason that spawn-caring fishes show striking colors, in which black often plays an important part. It is remarkable that all these motions are valid for one species only or, in case they are found in many kinds of fishes, that only the partner of the same species responds to them. This applies also to the fighting behavior. Fishes of other species are attacked without any previous protocol. It is true that there are also deviations from this rule, in which relatedness, and therefore resemblance of motions, generally plays an important part.

belizanus: After a Mexican geographical name.
— *Belonesox.*

bellica: Warlike, belligerent.
— *Betta.*

bellotti: After the Italian zoologist Bellott.
— *Cynolebias.*

belly fin: Ventral fin.

Belonesox: A Pike which resembles the Horn Pike, *Belone.*
Genus of Tooth Carps belonging to the sub-family of the Live Bearing Tooth Carps or POECILIINAE (see this), of Pike-like shape and predatory manner of living. The only species of this genus is said to have become nearly extinct in its home country, due to unbiological measures of fighting mosquitoes.

— **belizanus** Kner: The Pike Top Minnow.
SHAPE: The elongated body is little compressed laterally and nearly cylindrical in the fore part. The extraordinarily long head is flattened from above. The big mouth opening possesses remarkably big jaws, which are a little curved, and equipped with long, pointed teeth. D 8-10, A 10-12, both fins inserting far back. The scales are small. Length: males up to $4\frac{3}{4}''$, females up to 8″.
COLOR: On a brownish to brassy body a few rows of dark spots, which, however, may be absent. On the base of the tail fin a round, black, light-bordered spot.
RANGE: The species is found in shallow, standing or slowly-flowing waters, even under the most unfavorable biological conditions, in the secondary waters of rivers, lagoons with brackish water, muddy and swampy pools with reed on the banks, etc. It is distributed over the whole of Central America, Southern Mexico in the North to Nicaragua in the South. Clear waters are avoided whenever possible.
CARE AND BREEDING: In adulthood this species has a pronouncedly Pike-like manner of living. While the young fish still live in schools, the older specimens segregate. They are very voracious and need rich and vigorous live food, which for full-grown specimens consists especially of fishes. Sparing and irregular feeding results very unfavorably in breeding. Towards each other the fish are very pugnacious. Especially the bigger females are very vicious and do not let the males court them. For this reason copulation takes place in a sudden approach of the male. It is advisable to keep the pairs apart and to put them together only for mating, especially if the males are much smaller than the females. These have to be well fed before being mated, as otherwise they will attack the males.

Belonesox belizanus

In order to feel well the species requires higher temperatures, which may amount to 86 degrees F. A weak admixture of salt may act favorably. Very prolific in breeding. After a pregnancy of 4-6 weeks, large females produce litters of 100 or more fry which at birth already measure $1''$-$1\frac{1}{8}''$. If sufficiently and richly fed, they grow very quickly.

Belontia: After the native name Belontya.
Genus belonging to the family of the Climbing Perches or *Anabantidae* closely related to the genus *Macropodus.*

— **signata** (Guenther): The Comb Tail.

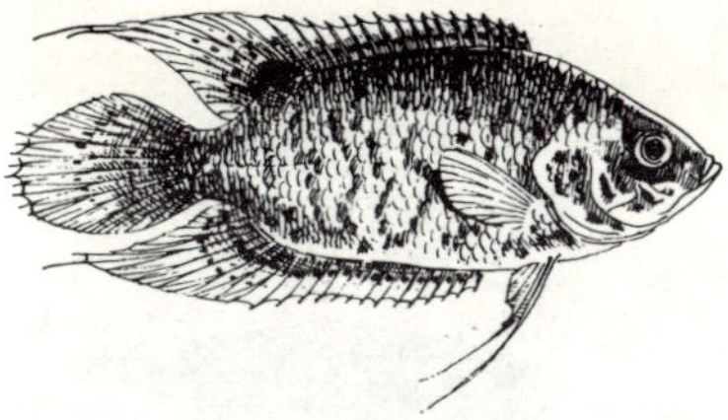

Belontia signata

SHAPE: Rather compact and high-backed, strongly compressed laterally. Superficially considered, it strongly resembles a Cichlid. D XVI-XVIII/7-10, A XIV-XVII/9-12. Dorsal and anal fin, as well as the central rays of the caudal fin of the male are extended in thread shape, and also the first ray of the ventrals is considerably elongated. Length up to about 4¾″.

COLOR: Greenish-brown to dirty brick-red, with only occasionally visible, dim cross bars. At the base of the soft part of the dorsal there is a black spot. The female is smaller, less colored, and possesses only slightly extended fin rays.

RANGE: In standing waters of Ceylon. The species is shy and remains hidden.

CARE AND BREEDING: As per description of the family and of *Macropodus*. Very pugnacious and vicious. Requires plenty of warmth.

beni: After the Rio Beni, in South America.
— *Creagrutus*.

benthal: The bottom region of waters, living space of the Benthos.

benthos: Collective name for all organisms which live on the bottom of waters and which may either be firmly located (sessile), or mobile.

bentosi: After a geographical name.
— *Hyphessobrycon callistus*.

Berg, L. S.: Prominent Soviet naturalist and ichthyologist, member of the Soviet Academy of Sciences. Especially well-known for his work on the genetic history and the systematics of fishes. His main work in this field is the 'System of Fossile and Living Fishes and Fish-like Animals' (1955).

bernieranus: After the botanist Bernier.
— *Aponogeton*.

Bernier's Aponogeton: see APONOGETON BERNIERANUS.

Betta: After the native name.
Genus of Fighting Fishes belonging to the family of the Climbing Perches or ANABANTIDAE (see this). Slender, partly very supple fishes, with short dorsal and long anal fins. The ventrals show one hard and five soft rays, the first ones of the soft rays often being strongly elongated. There is no lateral line.

The genus is distributed with several species over Indo-China, Malaya, and Indonesia, where in part it is found in swampy, warm, and richly-vegetated waters of the plains, in part, however, also at quiet spots in mountain brooks and streams. Reproduction is the same as described for the family (see ANABANTIDAE). Some divergences in the usual care for the brood are pointed out in the description of the different species.

— **bellica** Sauvage: The Red-Brown Fighting Fish.

SHAPE: As per description of the genus. Very slender, elongated, and supple. D I/10, A II/30-32. Length up to 4″.

COLOR: Not very colorful: brown, with gleaming-green bordered scales, the fins brownish-red with green reticulations. The male is more vividly colored.

RANGE: Malaya.

CARE AND BREEDING: As per description of the genus. The species has shown to be sluggish and frail in the aquarium, so that it does not seem suitable for keeping. Temperatures 77-86 degrees F. Reproduction is reported to be similar to that of *Betta splendens*. Only rarely imported.

— **brederi** Myers: The Mouth-Breeding Betta.

This species resembles *Betta bellica* very greatly, but is more compact. At times it shows indistinct cross bars. Length up to $3\frac{1}{2}''$.

ORIGIN: Johore.

The fish are mouth-breeders, with the male keeping the spawn in its mouth.

— **fasciata** Regan: The Striped Betta.

SHAPE: As per description of the genus, very similar to the preceding species, but still slimmer and nearly cylindrical. Length about 4″.

COLOR: Velvet blue with vivid green rows of dots. During the spawning period the male is very colorful, the female sometimes showing indistinct cross bars.

RANGE: In nearly dark-brown colored swamp waters on Sumatra.

CARE AND BREEDING: As per description of genus. Reproduction is said to be similar to that of *Betta splendens*.

— **picta** (Valenciennes): The Javanese Fighting Fish.

SHAPE: As per description of genus, small and relatively short. D I/6, A III/19. Length about $2\frac{1}{4}''$.

COLOR: Brownish, with only occasionally visible length stripes and irregular brown spots. The anal fin of the male is blue edged.

RANGE: The great Sunda Islands, at heights up to 5000 feet.

CARE AND BREEDING: As per description of the genus. The species does not need much warmth, withstanding temperatures down to 59 degrees F, despite the fact that higher temperatures up to 86 degrees F are preferred. Reproduction may often present interesting aspects.

BUSCHKIEL observed that before the act of spawning the female pulled off swabs of algae, out of which

Betta picta

she shaped little balls in her mouth and spat them out in front of the mouth of the male. In all, the female showed to be very active and chased the male until finally the spawn was released near the bottom. During this there were embraces similar to those of *Betta splendens*. At each mating only a few eggs were laid, which fell into the spoonlike arched anal fin of the male, were taken from there by the female, and spat out again in front of the male some minutes later, being then taken into the mouth of the male. Eggs which fell to the bottom during the act of spawning, or which were not snapped up by the male, were picked up by the female and offered to the male once more. Thereafter he stood with distended head among the plants, breathing quickly and having the female near him as guardian.

— **pugnax** (Cantor): The Big Mouth-Breeding Betta.

SHAPE: As per description of genus, relatively short and sturdy. D I/8-9, A II/26. Length up to about 4″.

COLOR: Quite changeable, basically brown, sometimes with a horizontal band or several cross stripes, temporarily also with rows of gleaming green dots. When excited, the throat and ventrals become metallic blue-green, and so does the edge of the anal. The male is more intensely colored.

RANGE: Malaya and Penang Island.

CARE AND BREEDING: Younger specimens of this species are quite lively and like to jump; with increasing age they become quite lazy. It seems that their life span is only short. The fish like warmth, 72-77 degrees F, higher for breeding, and plenty of sunlight. Adult specimens need rich live foods, especially insect larvae. Artificial foods are taken only occasionally. Reproduction resembles that of *Betta picta*, but the fry remain in the mouth of the male for only two days after hatching. Thereafter they come out and are already free-swimming. It is reported that the parents scarcely ever prey on them.

— **splendens** Regan: The Siamese Fighting Fish.

SHAPE: As per description of the genus, but not excessively elongated. D I/8-9, A II-IV/21-24. Length up to 2⅜″, the female a little shorter.

Betta splendens

COLOR: The color of the original form varies greatly, according to origin. Generally a dark-brown base with rows of gleaming green dots. The fins are red with shiny green or blue reticulations, the ventrals a vivid red with blue-white tips. These colors may pale completely. The artificially-bred strains are remarkable for very long fins and gleaming colors. The female is considerably simpler in color and possesses shorter fins. It is always recognizable by a short, but noticeable genital papilla.

RANGE: Singapore, Malaya, and Indo-China, in standing and slowly-flowing small waters with swampy bottom.

CARE AND BREEDING: As per description of the family. One of the most beautiful ornamental fishes, which is especially charming through its pageantry of colors when excited, and its impressive poses for fighting and mating. Opercles and gill skin may be widely distended. The species needs much warmth and feels best at 82-90 degrees F, but is otherwise completely undemanding. It is content with small containers, despite the fact that greater space is advantageous, likes dense planting, sunlight, floating plants, algae, and a dark, peaty bottom soil. It eats all kinds of foods as long as it is of a proper size.

Tank-raised forms are the so-called Veil-Tail Fighting Fish, which are remarkable for the magnificent development of their fins and for the beautiful colors which cover the entire body. Among aquarists there is a white strain known under the Latin name *B. sp. var. cambodia*. This name has no scientific value, but is simply a commercial designation. There are many color sports of this strain. The life-span of the Veil-Tail Fighting Fish is shorter still than is the case with the original form. They are most beautiful at the age of 4-12 months, after this they age quickly and become sluggish. Since they too show the belligerence of the original form, it is only possible to keep them in pairs. If you value flawless fins, you will keep the males alone anyway. Among the progeny one finds many throwbacks to the short-finned, simple forms. Only a part of the spawn develops the ornamental fins. Rear the best young males in small jars, with not-too-rich food. In Thailand people stage public beauty contests or fights with these fish, these shows being taxed by the government.

bichir: Two-handed (referring to the hand-shaped pectoral fins).
— *Polypterus.*

bicirrhis: Two-threaded, referring to the barbels.
— *Cryptopterus.*

bifasciatus: With two stripes.
— *Hyphessobrycon.*

Big-Scaled Characin, the: see HOLLANDICHTHYS MULTIFASCIATUS.

Big-Scaled Rasbora, the: see RASBORA PAUCISQUAMIS.

Big-Spotted Pike, the: see EPIPLATYS MACROSTIGMA.

bimaculata: Two-spotted.
— *Lebiasina.*

bimaculatum:
— *Cichlasoma.*

bimaculatus: Two-spotted.
— *Astyanax.*
— *Hemichromis.*
— *Pseudoxiphophorus.*

binotatus: Two-spotted.
— *Barbus.*

biocellatum: With two ocellated spots.
— *Cichlasoma.*

Biogenous decalcification and calcification: Biogenous calcification and decalcification are parts of the circulation of substances in water, which is extraordinarily complex. Among water and all its components, climatic influences, the bottom, the plants, the animals, etc. exists an intimate mutual interaction.

Under the influence of light in all plant-stocked waters there is a rhythmic exchange of substances which is based on the assimilation (see this) of the plants. During this the free carbon dioxide dissolved in the water is taken in by the plants. After this is used up, carbon is taken from bicarbonates (bicarbonate of calcium), which too are dissolved in the water. Thus a simple carbonate of calcium is de-

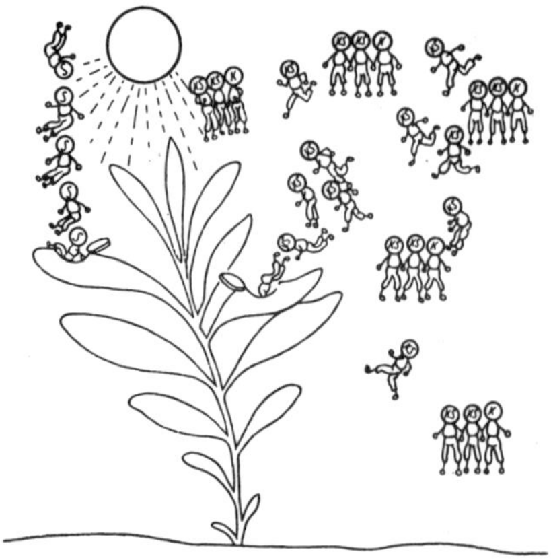

Biogenous decalcification — In daylight the plants assimilate. Under the influence of light they draw from the water the free carbon dioxide KS and give off oxygen S.

Biogenous decalcification — The free carbon dioxide is used up. Now part of the carbon dioxide KS is taken from the dissolved calcium bicarbonate KS - KS - K. The rest is simple calcium carbonate KS-K, which is insoluble and settles to the bottom.

Biogenous calcification — At night the plant only breathes. It takes in oxygen S and gives off carbon dioxide KS. This reacts with the undissolved simple calcium carbonate KS-K, forming calcium bicarbonate KS - KS - K, which again dissolves in water.

Biogenous calcification — Further carbon dioxide is given off. Since there are no more possibilities of reacting, this remains as free dissolved carbon dioxide in the water.

veloped in the water, precipitating and settling on plants, the bottom, etc. This process is called biogenous decalcification. Through this using up of the carbon dioxide by the plants, the pH value rises into the alkaline range. Thus the bicarbonates are a kind of reserve, on to which the plants fall back when the water-dissolved free carbon dioxide, which in part stems from the respiration of fishes, is insufficient.

At night, or under insufficient light, the process is reversed. The plants breathe and release carbon dioxide like animals. This reacts with the deposits of simple calcium carbonate ($CaCO_3$), forming calcium bicarbonate ($Ca(HCO_3)2$), which now dissolves in water again. Through the excess of carbon dioxide the pH value sinks down again into the acid range. This explains why in planted waters the pH values generally are lower in the morning than in the evening.

The smaller the body of water is, the stronger become these periodical changes. In this sense we have to consider an aquarium as a small body of water. The smaller it is, the more it is influenced by external factors, such as temperature, light, etc. Add to this that the complete factors, such as calcium contents of the water, duration of illumination, numerical ratio of fishes and plants, etc. may be changed at will by the aquarist. All these changes may have more or less comprehensive chemical sequels.

Biological equilibrium: The state of a body of water in which a community of animals and plants in mutual interdependence finds favorable conditions for living and preserving the species. It makes provision for the physical and chemical adequacy of the water, for the correct numerical ratio of neighbors, fellow specimens, enemies, and food, so that none of these factors surpasses its quota significantly. Thus, e.g., in such a body of water predatory fishes and peaceful ones maintain an equilibrium. If for some reason it would come to a preponderance of predators, the peaceful fishes would by and by become extinct by having been eaten or by the absence of the devoured fry, but at the end also the predators would lose their basis for living and their numbers too would recede. Similarly a body of water can only give permanent shelter to as many peaceful fishes as it can feed, that is, for which it holds plankton, mosquito larvae, etc. If external factors dampen one or the other internal factor, furthering others, this will lead to an initial proliferation of the latter, and as a final consequence to a re-establishment of the equilibrium. The B.E. is never a firm, unchangeable state, but is in permanent fluctuation.

In an aquarium we cannot speak of a 'biological', that is, a self-adjusting state of equilibrium. If an aquarium were left to itself, it would certainly establish a B.E. in time, but would then be unable to offer living conditions to most of our fishes. Indeed the aquarist endeavors to maintain a certain equilibrium, but in most cases one cannot speak of a natural situation as one category of live beings is favored, the other subdues, according to the wishes of the fancier. For this the aquarist uses several artificial means. In consequence the community in an aquarium is generally very one-sided and rarely resembles the manifoldness of natural waters.

biology: The science of life. A collective name for all branches of natural science, which are concerned with live beings and their vital manifestations. It includes, among others, Zoology, Botany, Anatomy, Morphology, Physiology, Ethology, Ecology, and General Biology (the science of cells, the biology of heredity, the science of genetics, etc.)

Mastering biological ideas is a must for the aquarist who wants to keep in step with the latest developments of science.

Biology of the reproduction of fishes: It must be considered a merit of aquaristics that the processes of reproduction of many native and exotic fishes have become known, down to their smallest details. The fact that many aquarium fishes can be induced to propagate with relatively simple means has contributed much to the popularity of the aquarium hobby.

Like everywhere else, also in the kingdom of fishes the aim of reproduction is that of maintaining the stock of the different species. This goal may be considered reached if of the progeny of the parents one male and one female in turn become able to reproduce and to produce descendants.

The process of reproduction must be considered as an adaptation to the specific conditions of the surroundings, and depends on these being influenced and shaped by them. Reproduction takes place almost always in water. Only in very rare cases the eggs are spawned out of it, during a very short space of time, as happens with the Splashing Tetra, for example. This means that all fishes are true water dwellers, even those which have adapted to short sojourns on land.

The reproduction of fishes is exclusively sexual, and fishes always are bisexual. The sexual products are generated in special sexual organs (see this), if certain conditions for this are fulfilled. As a rule they keep up a more or less sharply defined spawning period. In addition to changes in behavior, frequently there are also external signs which permit recognizing a fish which is ripe for spawning. The females increase considerably in girth, due to the developing spawn. The males often show specially striking spawning colors, or show other characters of rutting, for instance, a whitish rash on parts of the body. Furthermore the external, secondary sexual characters become more marked during the spawning period. These include enlarged or extended fins, color characteristics, differences in size, etc.

The act of spawning takes place under all kinds of circumstances. As a rule mating (see this) in pairs is the climax of the spawning process, but in some cases mating is substituted by a 'collective marriage', or else insemination takes place by introduction of the spermatozoans into the female body long before the act of spawning itself.

In general fishes lay unfertilized eggs, fertilization taking place in open water through the spermatozoans which are released simultaneously by the males. Only rarely fecundation is anticipated, the eggs remaining within the body of the mother, which they leave in an apparent birth after having completed their development.

The number of eggs, their size, and the quota of destruction form a firm, balanced ratio. Since eggs and alevins are sensitive, and defenseless to the dangers and harms of their surroundings, they have to be protected against total extermination through special measures. For this there are two distinct possibilities; either the progeny is produced in such great numbers that the prospects are that at least a few specimens will reach reproduction on their part, despite the fact that they are left to themselves, or else the parents protect their progeny against the dangers of the ambient world by means of acts of care for the brood.

While, as stated above, in the first of the two cases the number of eggs has to be enormous, it may be quite less for fishes that care for their brood. But also in these cases where no pronounced brood care is exerted, we can already see clearly that there are certain measures of provision, by the fact that eggs are lodged in sites which offer good possibilities of development and which also warrant such conditions for the hatching fry. Many species of fishes effect long migrations for this, which in part may have originated from the far-off alterations of shape of the surface of the earth. Frequently these migrations lead to the source regions of rivers, but in some cases also to internal lakes or to the sea.

There are not only the great migrations, however, which are explained by reproduction; this applies also to smaller wanderings, and even to changes of biotope within the same body of water. Many species rise to the surface, coming from the depths, others, to the contrary, seek the bottom. In most cases fishes which want to spawn go to the shallow parts of the water, to flooded regions, etc. Generally these biotopes show conditions that differ completely from the habitual dwelling places of the adult fishes. Small spawning migrations and changes of biotope generally are conditioned by the chemical and physical properties of the water in the new biotope, on which depends the presence of the necessary food organisms. Spawning migrations and trips of small or very small extent doubtlessly are quite more frequent than is generally supposed. The fact that in most cases these are not known to the breeder explains many difficulties and lacks of success in breeding aquarium fishes. These special con-

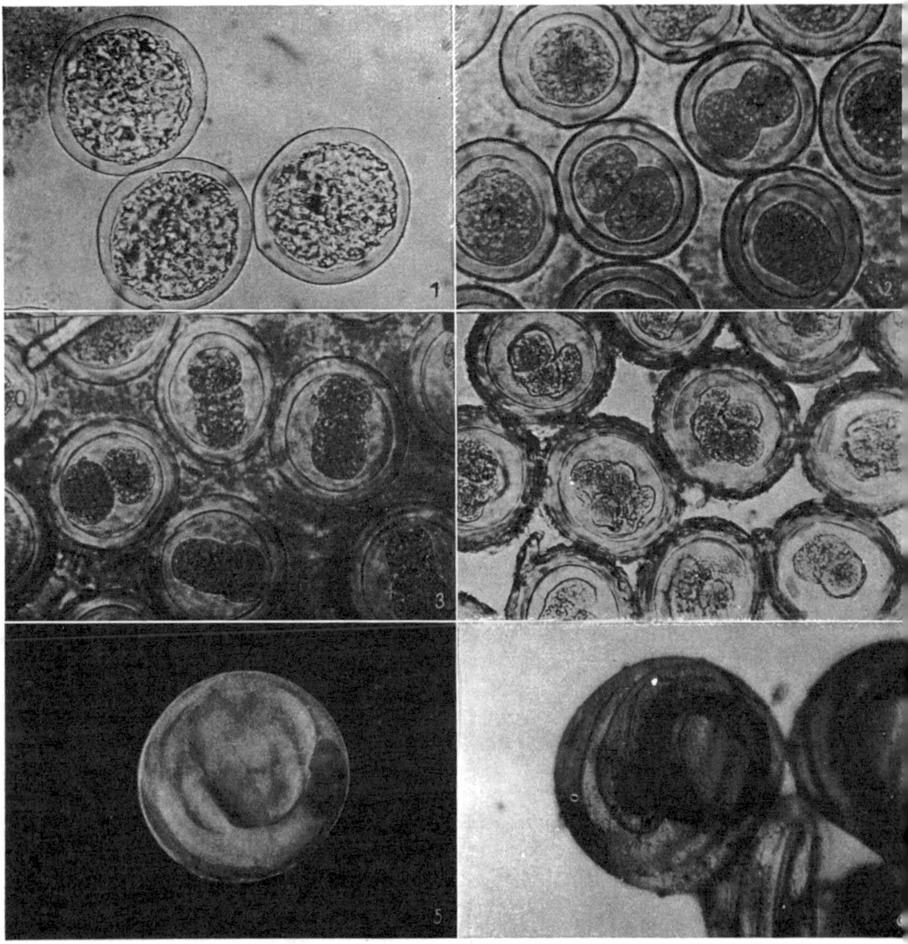

Biology of Reproduction 1 — enlarged - 1. Unfecundated eggs of thread worms (Nematodes) - 2. Fecundated eggs, during the first strangulation - 3. Same, strangulation progressed - 4. Same, after several strangulations - 5. Egg of **Leucaspius delineatus**, after 36 hours - 6. Same, after 48 hours.

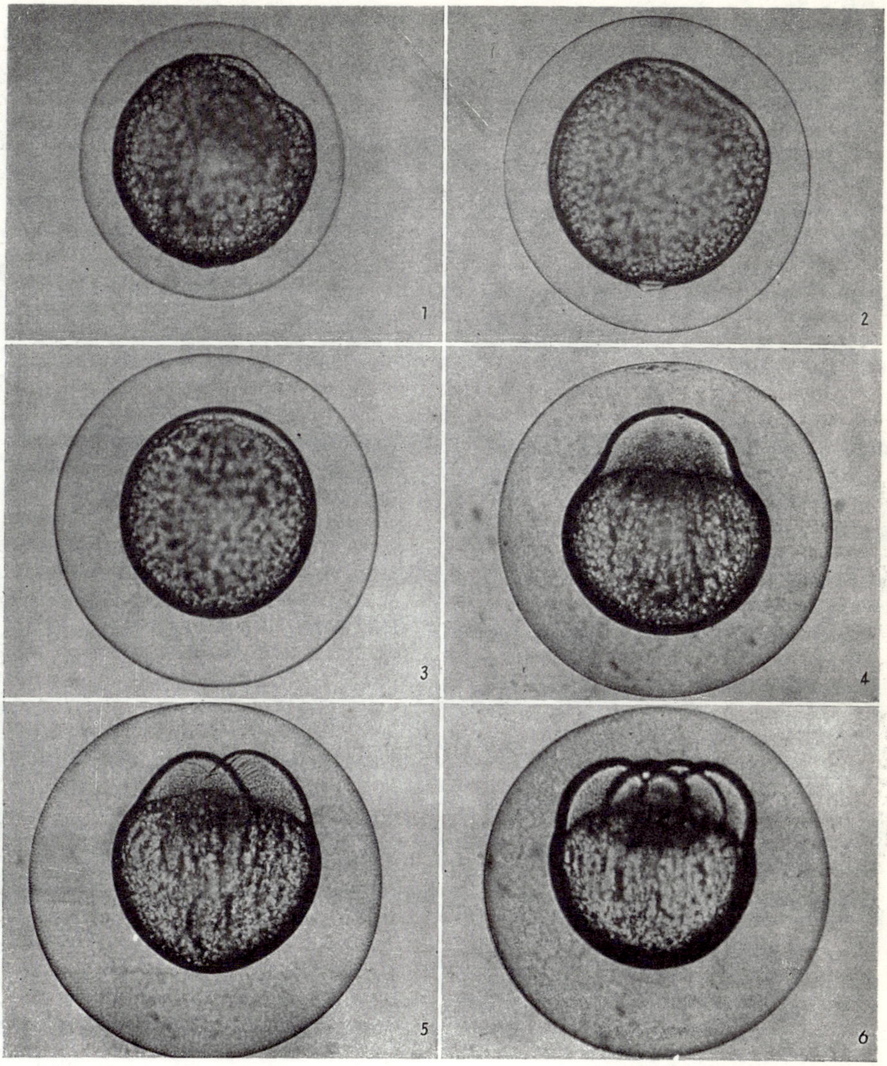

Biology of Reproduction 2 — 1. An egg, shortly after laying and insemination - 2. The perivitelline space enlarges through the admission of water - 3. The egg itself is rounded through currents of the plasma, and the germinal disc is clearly visible - 4. Immediately before the first furrowing the germinal disc is a cap - 5. The germinal disc furrows and two blastomers result (2-cell stage) - 6. A further furrowing creates the 4-cell stage.

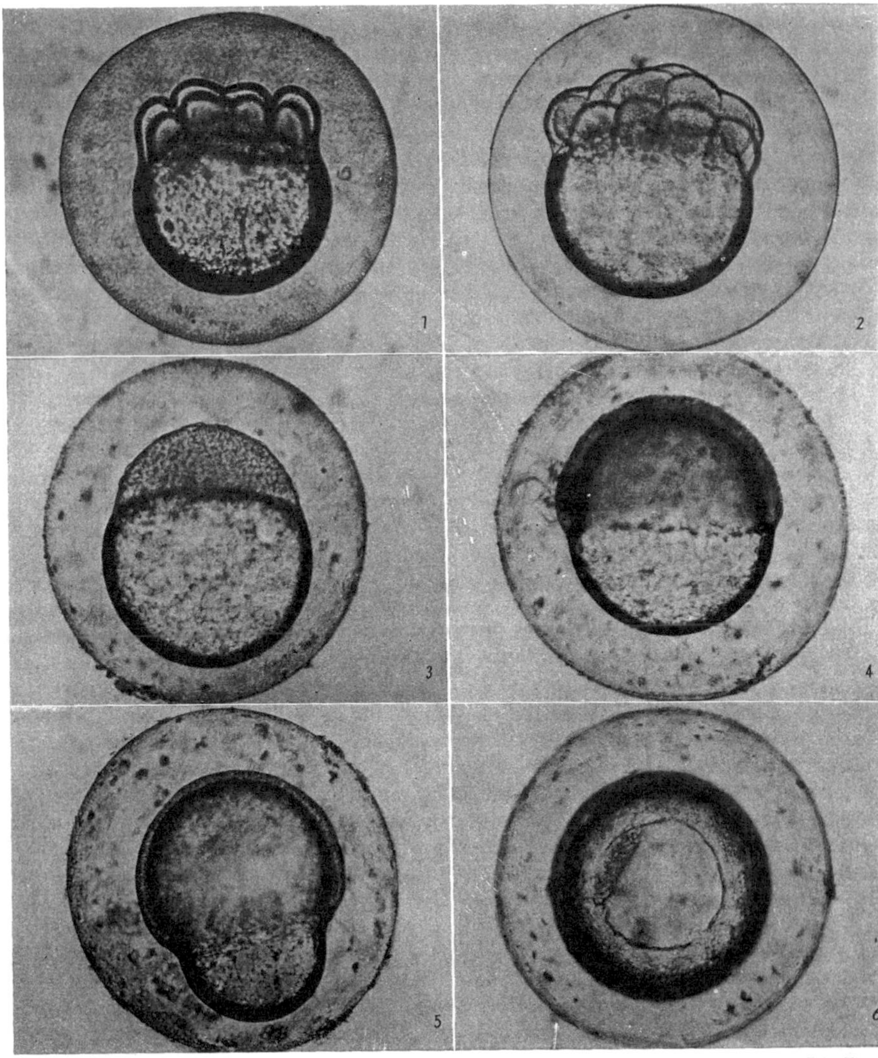

Foto: Knaack

Biology of Reproduction 3 — 1. 8-cell stage - 2. 32-cell stage - 3. Further strangulations cause the cells to increase in number and decrease in size, developing a multiple-cell stage - 4. The cell cap, which rests on the yolk, begins to grow around this - 5. This compresses the yolk, and a yolk protuberance develops - 6. With a frontal view (vegetative pole), one sees the concentric growth around the yolk.

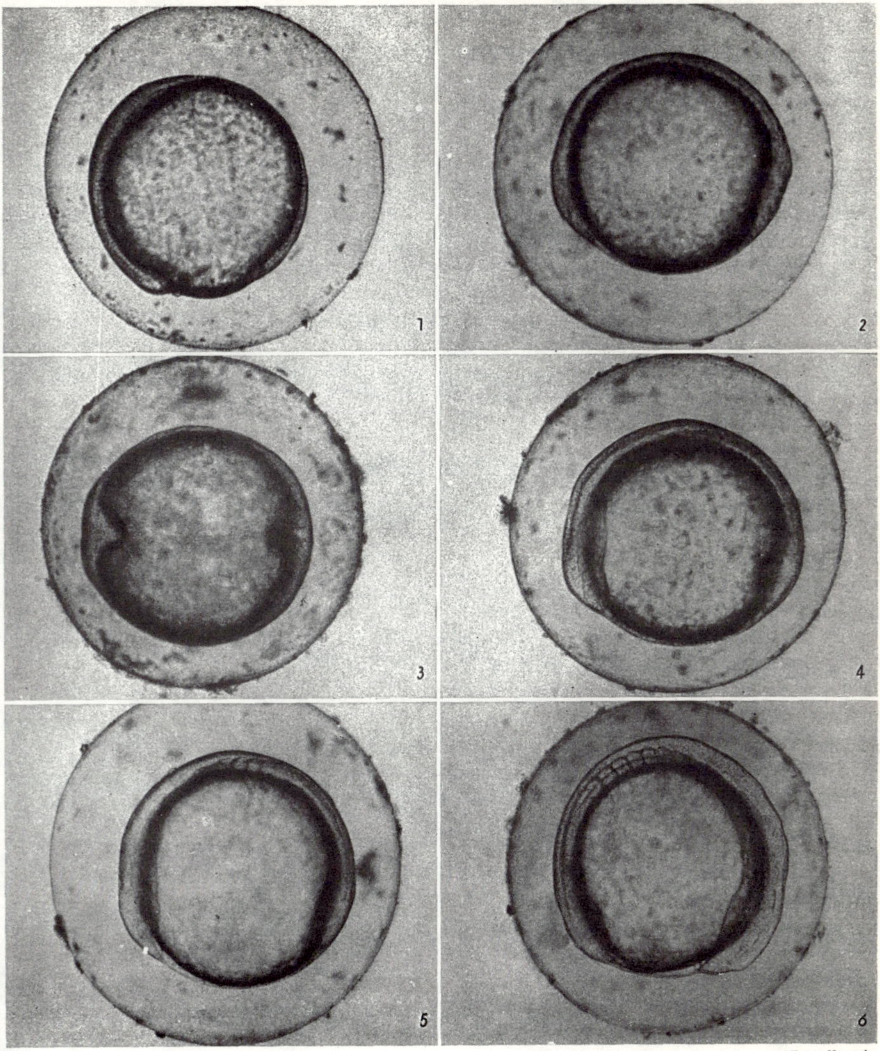

Foto: Knaack

Biology of Reproduction 4 — 1. The growth around the yolk is almost completed, only the primitive mouth is not yet closed - 2. Optical section shows a clearly visible germinal ring, and to the right the marginal head - 3. Frontal view shows a wedge-shaped incision in the yolk at this stage - 4. The tips of the head and tail grow toward each other - 5. A little later the first primitive segments increase rapidly, the eye bubble being weakly indicated on the right.

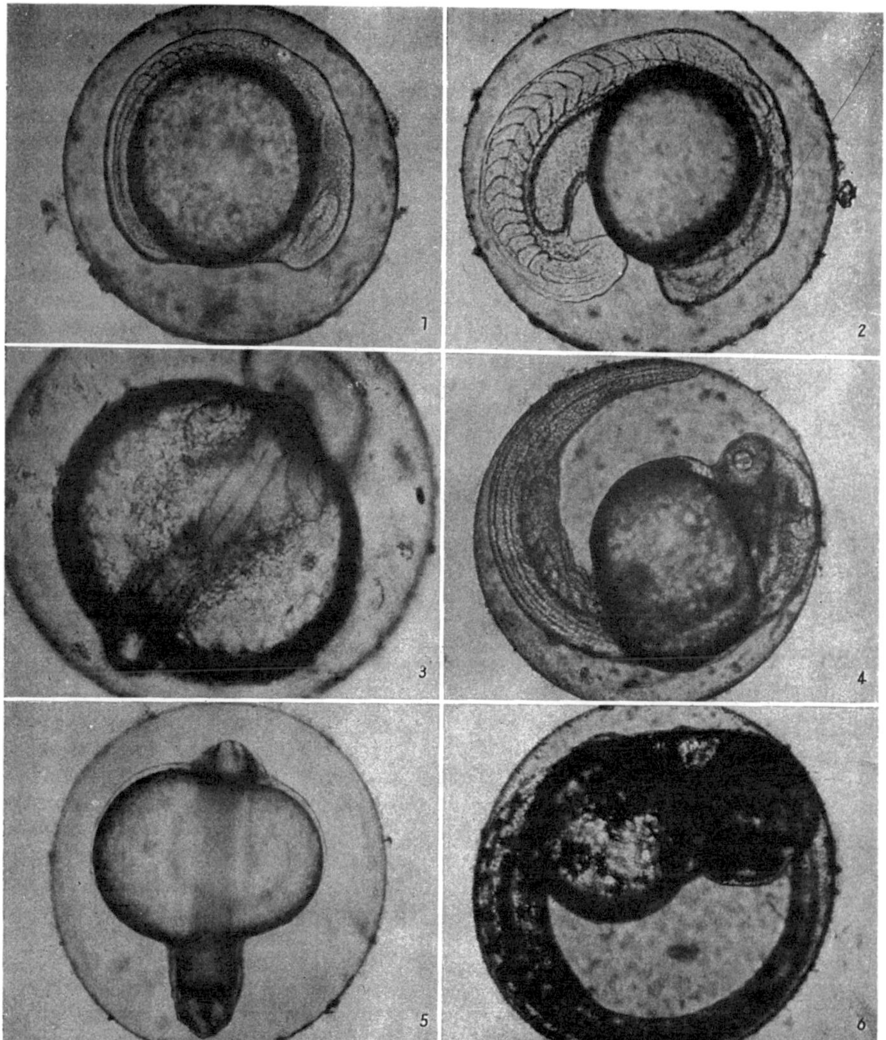

Biology of Reproduction 5 — 1. The number of primitive segments has further increased, and the developing eye-bubble is clearly visible - 2. The tip of the tail has lifted up from the yolk. The ear-bubble is located directly above the yolk - 3. A frontal view shows the head with the eyes. The embryos make contracting motions - 4. The embryo grows gradually and continually, head and tail tips push against the egg membrane - 5. In this stage of development the embryos frequently change their position - 6. An embryo shortly before hatching, body and yolk covered with melanospores, eye-dot stage.

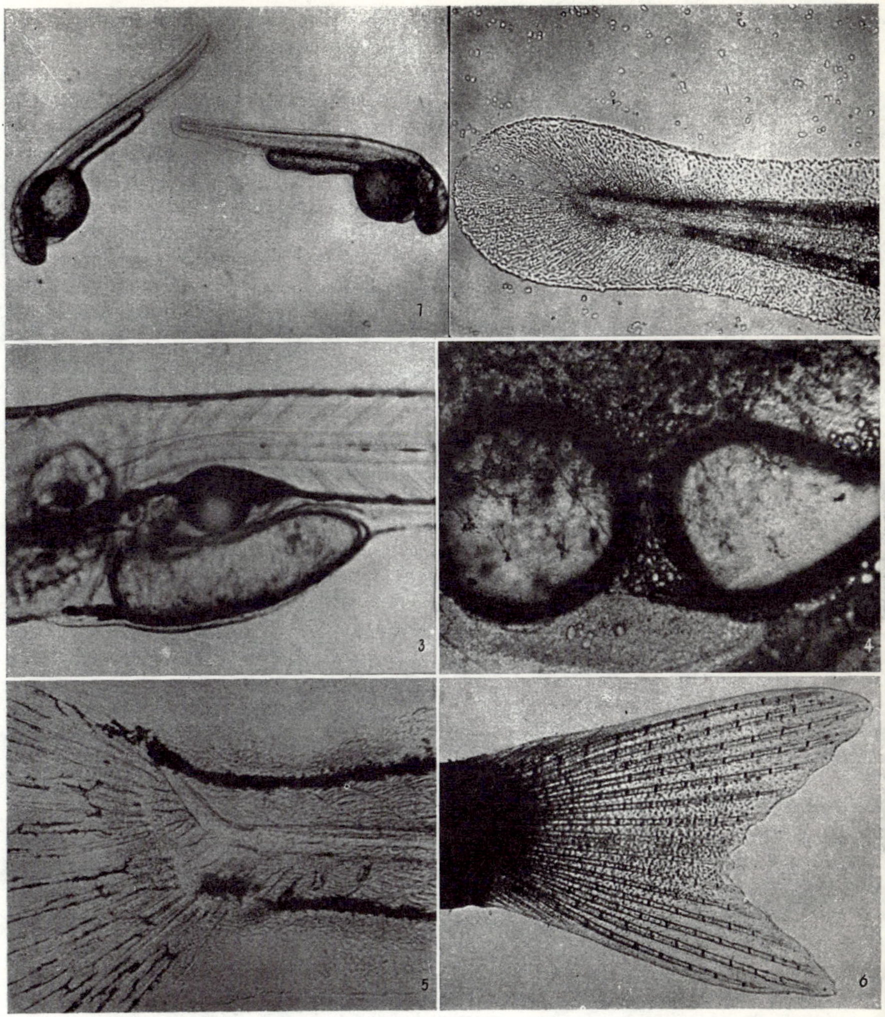

Biology of Reproduction 6 — 1. Freshly-hatched alevins lying on their sides - 2. Two days have elapsed; the fin seam at the tip of the tail grows a little indented (homocercal stage) - 3. After the yolk sac contents have been consumed the fry have to fill their swimming bladders with air. At first the bladder is round - 4. A second bladder develops later on through protraction toward the head. Both are connected by a narrow canal - 5. The tip of the chorda bends upwards and the hypuralia show fin rays (heterocercal stage) - 6. Fully developed tail fin.

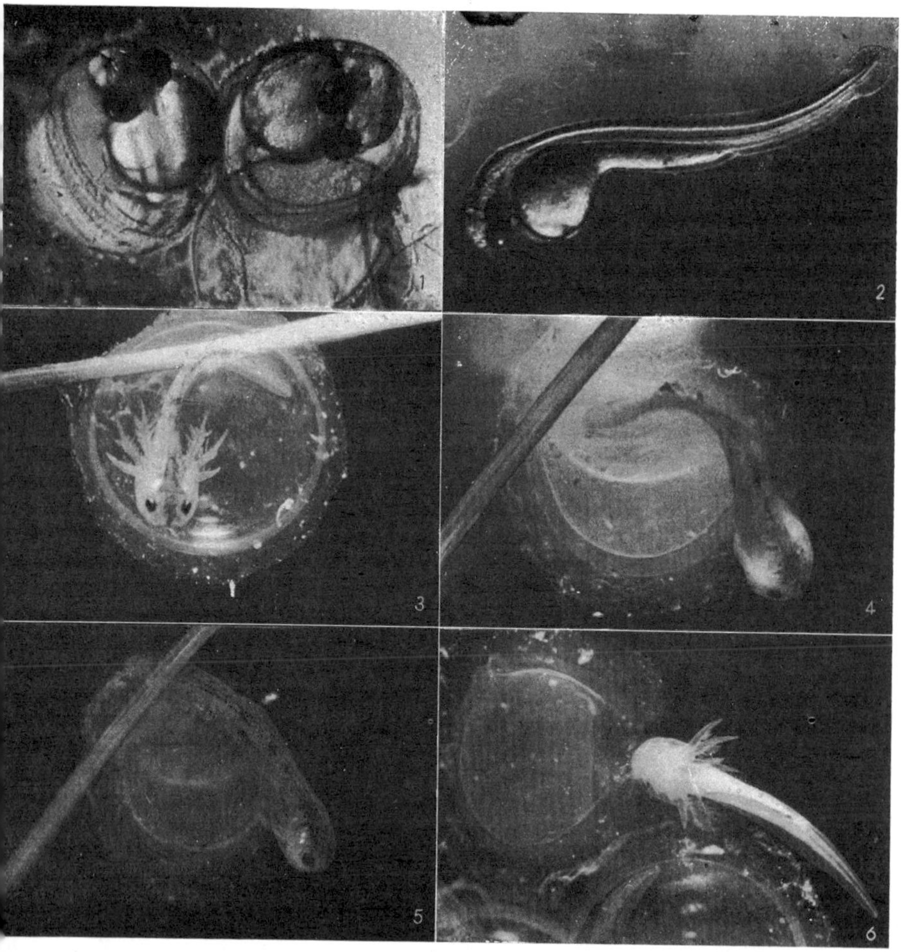

Foto: 1–2 Helmert, 3–6 Knaack

Biology of Reproduction 7 — 1. Fry of **Leucaspius delineatus** within the egg shell, shortly before hatching - 2. Larva, immediately after leaving the egg - 3. Young Axolotl makes lively efforts to burst the egg membrane - 4. The larva has contrived to establish an opening and forces its head through - 5. The very sticky membrane permits only slow hatching, in jolts - 6. Often the sticky membrane still adheres to the larva for some time.

ditions of the spawning site can only be imitated in the aquarium if their basic particulars are known. And it is just in this that we still lack quite some knowledge.

The huge expenditure of energy made in reproduction, which in some cases even leads to the death of the parents, makes it clear that the process of propagation cannot be a permanent phenomenon. Therefore it is bound to certain seasons of the year, in which optimum vital conditions prevail. In these periods the fishes find available everything that leads to the development of the sexual products, to the creation of maturity for spawning, and finally to the development of the alevins. In some cases the spawning periods come at the end of such optimum periods, which in this case are used to accumulate the necessary reserves of strength. Frequently the eggs go through a rest period, or the development of eggs and fry is so extended that they catch up with the beginning of the next optimal seasons.

For this reason the spawning periods do not have to be the same for all species of fishes, but conform to their special demands on life. Thus trout and other salmonids, for instance, are pronounced winter spawners, since the warmer months, with their greater availability of nourishment, have to be set aside for the accumulation of reserves of strength.

In the temperate zones it is mainly Spring with its increasing warmth, its influx of greater quantities of water after hibernal stagnation, and the resulting abundance of nutritional organisms, into which fall the spawning periods of our native fishes. In the tropics and subtropics it is the rain periods in which the reproduction of many species of fishes takes place, while the dry periods, with their scarcity of rains, are times of rest. It is extremely important that the breeder of aquarium fishes observe the resulting rhythm of reproduction, in the interest of the health of his breeding stock. He should therefore always keep regular rest periods in the breeding activities.

Factors which may determine beginning of spawning periods of fishes are: the seasonal changes in climate, the influx of larger quantities of rain or melting waters, increased sun radiation and consequent rise of temperatures, but sometimes also a lowering of the warmth, the sudden availability of great numbers of food organisms, significant changes in the chemical and physical properties of the water, etc. These factors, the listing of which does not lay claim to being complete, influence the fishes singly or collectively and trigger increased metabolism, which also includes the activity of the sexual glands.

The influence of the activity of these glands does not only lead to the development of certain external characteristics, but also to significant changes in the behavior and manner of living of fishes.

The intake of nourishment during reproduction recedes to a great degree, or is even completely stopped. Predators become 'peaceable', and on the other hand quite gregarious fishes may become rather bellicose when defending their breeding sites. Frequently all caution is put aside, contrary to the usual habits. In their migrations the fishes are dominated by the impulse to reach a certain goal. Frequently a greater gregariousness is noticed and under certain conditions fish schools of huge dimensions are formed. On the other hand schools of otherwise gregariously living fishes dispel totally or according to sexes, and isolated specimens, e.g. male Sticklebacks or Cichlids, settle and defend certain territories as breeding sites. At the end of the migratory routes isolated specimens separate in pairs from the school, or else spawning communities are formed in which frequently no pronounced mating is observed.

The so-called egg scatterers (see this) release their sexual products in open water, for which the females often swim above the males so that the eggs have to pass through the semen-saturated layers while sinking to the bottom. Quite frequently spawning is done in very shallow water, sometimes over gravel or pebbles, the friction with the bottom soil easing the release of the sexual products. During this sometimes the fishes dig real spawning beds with their violent movements. Other species seek the plant thickets of the shore regions in order to spawn there. The eggs either ripple to the bottom, or else they are equipped with a special adhesive cover, sticking to plants, respectively to grains of sand or gravel on the bottom.

In many cases, too, the site where the eggs will remain to the moment of hatching is not left to chance, each egg being concealed in a hiding place, for instance, by opening holes in bundles of algae with the snout, each hole harboring one egg. The so-called bottom-spawners (see this) bury their eggs within the soil. For this they dig regular holes, placing the eggs in them one by one. Frequently the bottom is roiled up by means of violent strokes of the tail fin, so that it covers the spawn after settling.

The egg hangers or anchorers (see this) stick their spawn to a firm substratum. This manner of disposing of the eggs does not have to be followed by further care for the brood. Quite often the spawn is left to itself. More frequently, however, this is followed by lasting care for the brood.

While the egg scatterers often relegate paired spawning in favor of 'mass matings', for the bottom spawners and the egg anchorers the rule is a pronounced pairing off. Eggs of fishes quite often are laid with a sticky cover, an adhesive device, or a mucous belt. Also the hatching fry may be equipped with such an adhesive device, until they reach the point of becoming free-swimming. This may be unnecessary if the eggs are hidden or hatched in rock or root caves, or in nests built of plant parts or bubbles. No general rule can be given for this.

Active care for the brood (see this) is not rare among fishes, and there prevails great variety in this. The measure of caring for the brood may differ considerably in intensity or duration, as well as in manner, or the difference may also be found in which of the parents exerts them. Watching brood-caring fishes is one of the most charming experiences in aquaristics. In this there are all gradations, from simple fanning of the eggs, to intense guarding the swarm of fry for weeks on end.

Before spawning brood-caring fishes nearly always settle a certain territory, a range, the size of which corresponds to an innate conception, and defend this breeding site against strange trespassers of any kinds. Even if outside the spawning period they live gregariously, during the time in which they care for their brood they leave the community—or at least the one partner which takes charge of the brood leaves it. As a rule in nature fishes of the same species generally respect the borders of such breeding sites. Only in our small aquaria, in which such borders overlap, the fishes fight violent battles, which may go to the extent that one of the contenders is killed.

According to duration, the manners of caring for the brood may be divided as follows:

(a) Watching the spawn to the point of hatching;

(b) Watching the spawn and the fry to the point of free-swimming;

(c) Watching the spawn and the fry beyond the point of free-swimming.

When breeding is done in the aquarium, the processes of reproduction may be subject to certain changes and divergences from those in free nature, resulting from the changed conditions in the aquarium.

In aquaria the fish which is ready to spawn frequently does not have the possibility of free choice of its mate. This circumstance may be relieved if the fishes are kept in greater communities, and if the breeder selects those specimens which seem to find each other spontaneously. Furthermore there is no possibility of seeking certain spawning areas. The installation of the breeding tank, and the 'conditioning for breeding' represents a certain substitute for the changes of location which occur in free nature. Often, too the breeding stock is compelled to reproduce incessantly and the natural breeding periods are not respected. However, rest periods are easy to observe in the aquarium by separating the sexes, which frequently corresponds exactly to the conditions in nature, or this may be done by changing temperatures, conditions of the water, or conditions of feeding.

The experienced breeder will endeavor not to generalize his breeding procedures too much, but to pay attention to the natural diversity of the processes of reproduction.

biotope: The living site, i.e., the region in nature which offers the necessary vital conditions to groups or communities of different living beings. For this, alive and dead nature, even the smallest section of the landscape, must always be considered as a whole. The unity of all factors—those which make life possible as well as the living beings themselves—is comprehensive. If one wants to characterize an animal or plant with exactitude, one should not only describe its shape and behavior, but one has also to know and to consider the respective ambience. Without this the being cannot be fully grasped as an organism. It is this which in part causes the changes (degeneration) in aquarium fishes after a more or less long period of keeping them captive. Biotopes never are uniform conceptions. If, for instance, we consider a bigger pool as such, it will always be divisible into smaller biotopes, despite the fact that as a whole it offers possibilities of life to a multifaceted community of living beings. We can even consider as such biotopes the depth zones, the central open reaches of water, the surface, the region of the submerged weeds, the zone of the reed stands, and the shallow, sun-warmed inlets (see AMBIENT WORLD).

biotopic aquarium: An aquarium in which—based on the most exact knowledge that is possible—an attempt has been made to attain a far-reaching imitation of the living and dead factors of a natural biotope (see this). However, to begin with, we have to realize that in the aquarium there is no such thing as the creation of a real biotope, and that we can never reach more than a rough similarity to all natural con-

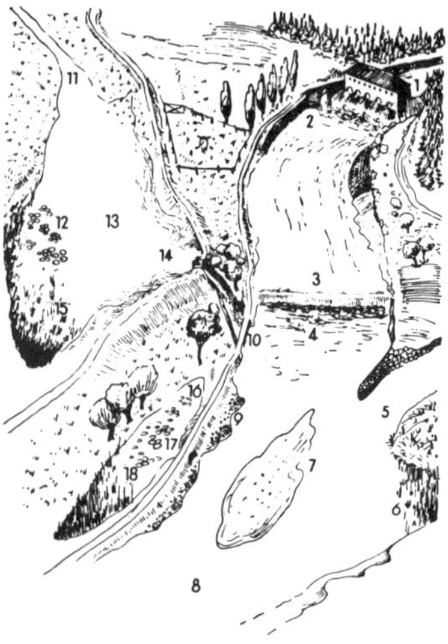

A small indication of the varied biotopes. At 1 the river leaves the mountains. The fish-ladders 2 enable migrating fishes to wander up-river. At 3 the water is dammed up, nearly standing still and deep, then it falls over the dam at 4. A different set of conditions prevails at drainage ditch 10. At 7 there is a sand bank. Here there are shallow and warm spots, unlike 5, where cool mountain water enters. At 6 a shallow inlet with rushes gives refuge to small life. At 9 there is a swift current, and at 8 there are eddies. The bottom is soft and muddy at 16, at 17 the water lilies form a shady cover, and at 18 all sorts of small life proliferates. This pool overflows periodically into the river at 17, especially in the spring, when many fishes spawn there. The fry leave here in autumn. The lake above shows a tributary at 11, open water at 13 and 14, a spot for water lilies at 12 and reeds at 15.

ditions. For an aquarium is an artificial, artificially maintained structure, even if it is subject to natural laws. Anyway, in most cases this rough imitation is already sufficient to induce most plants to satisfactory growth and most tropical fishes to an extensively natural behavior. At present we may consider the biotopic aquarium as that form of aquarium which best corresponds to the vital demands in care and breeding of the fishes.

A great many ambient factors can hardly or not at all be reproduced in the aquarium. This becomes quite clear if one considers the view of the ambient world in all its details. This includes, for instance, the always too small space, to which the motile fish is bound for the duration of its captivity, the currents and motion of the water, the whole micro-mechanism of chemistry in a body of water, the alternations of the weather conditions, the incidence of light, which in the aquarium always comes from many sides contrary to natural conditions, fluctuations of the water level or of the composition of the water, the presence of enemies or competitors for food, free choice of food and the hunt for nourishment, free choice of animal communities, etc. Some of these factors may be imitated in a rough way. But these imitations always depend upon the knowledge and skill of the fancier, often even upon his whim. Under all circumstances, though, one factor remains, which WAHLERT has pointed out and which is of extreme significance. The aquarium fish never has a free choice of the dwelling place which it likes. It cannot congregate in schools or in communities, and it cannot carry out the migrations demanded by its vital rhythm. To the contrary, it must accept the vital conditions which are offered by the hobbyist, and it reacts accordingly. It is evident that this entails certain changes which have to be considered phenomena of adaptation (see this) to the conditions of the aquarium. This initial consideration is necessary in order to limit the existing possibilities of building a biotopic aquarium. This should, of course, not be sufficient cause to give up the attempt to shape the aquarium as naturally as possible. In copying a certain biotope externally the fancier has, as a rule, to depend upon his own imagination. However, in our native nature we find many patterns which can be imitated just for this aim. It would be completely wrong to neglect the external shaping of the subaquatic landscape, as is often done, due to the circumstance that here are to a greater extent the internal factors anyway, which are of importance. Also the biologically correct aquarium should be as beautiful as possible, for its main aim is to grant joy to mankind for whose pleasure tropical fishes are caught after all. Beyond this it is in no way true, as people so often state, that decorating with plants, rocks, roots, reed stems, etc. must disturb the fish or is of no importance to it. Not considering the fact that we are completely unable to grasp possible 'perceptional phenomena' in fishes, it should be certain that all species of fishes which are not pronounced open water dwellers need the thicket of plants, the stone or root cave, the reed stand, etc., according to their vital demands, for their well-being. Doubtlessly, though, it is correct that the so-called inner factors, such as, for instance, composition of the water, temperature, rhythm, light, food, composition of the fish community, and choice of sexual partners, are much more significant. For this reason attention to the probable vital conditions and to the ambient world demanded by the species belongs among the duties of the serious aquarist. With regard to this we have to state, however, that our knowledge in this field is minute. We know very little about the internal vital phenomena in our own domestic waters, and much less about those in tropical and subtropical ones. A small part of them only is known to us from small investigations, which have been published now and then in the technical press and which have been compiled and completed with his own observations by LADIGES in his work 'Der Fish in der Landschaft' (The Fish within the Landscape). On the other hand, with sufficient caution they may be deduced from the body shape and the behavior of the fishes. If these do not lead to any conclusions, one has to make tests for the freshly imported species based on the experience gleaned from similar species.

According to what has been stated above, it is obvious that when setting up a biotopic aquarium one has to inquire less into the geographic origin of the respective fishes, plants, or other live beings of the water, than into their probable vital demands. Setting it up from geographic points of view may also lead to a biotopic aquarium, but it does not have to be installed in accordance with these points of view. The geographic point of view is more or less insignificant if it takes into account only great concepts such as for instance continents, countries, or whole regions. Type names such as Asiatic, or South American tank, may, under certain circumstances, not have any meaning, since there we are talking of regions of great extent with the most different climatic conditions, which show a very variegated fauna and flora in the different climates. It is true, however, that in exhibitions, or in pet shops, where the intent is to show animals and plants according to geographic origin, consideration for the geographic connections is not completely avoidable.

Bishop, the: see BRACHYRAPHIS EPISCOPI.

bitaeniatus: With two stripes. — *Chaetobranchopsis.*

A pair of Bitterlings in spawning position over a fresh-water mussel.

Bitterling, the: see RHODEUS AMARUS.

Bitterling Barb, the: see BARBUS TITTEYA.

Bivalvia: Shell Fishes.

Class belonging to the phylum of the Molluscs or MOLLUSCA (see this), with only slightly articulated body and without separate head. The shell consists of two valves which are composed of calcium carbonate plus an organic substance. At the back the shells inter-grip by means of a system of teeth and alveoles, and are hinged by a tough, elastic band. Closing is effected through strong muscles. On the inside the shells are generally lined with a layer of mother-of-pearl. The shells connect with the mantle leaves, which enclose the gills. In spots their edges are grown together, but they always leave a passage for the foot, and some openings which partially serve to admit food and breathing water, in part to eject the waste products of the body and the sexual products. The paired gills consist of two leaves each, with tender lamellae, in which also the eggs ripen.

The foot of the shell-fish is broad and tongue-shaped. It lends the animals only little motility, when they draw ahead in a jolting manner, $\frac{3}{8}''$ to $\frac{3}{4}''$ at a time, that is, they do not push. The Triangular Shellfish *Dreissena* is the only fresh-water shellfish which from a certain age on fastens to a substratum by means of threads. The sensory organs are scattered over the whole body. Near the mouth opening and on the mantle we find the organs of touch, on the belly side the hearing bubbles, especially near the foot. On the edge of the mantle sit the relatively well-developed eyes, but these may also be lacking totally. Near the breathing tube an olfactory ledge is found, which serves to check on the quality of the breathing water.

Nearly all shellfishes are heterosexual, only a few species being hermaphrodites. Most of them are oviparous, but a few are live-bearers. Sometimes there is even a kind of care for the spawn, the eggs going through their development within the gill space. Nearly all shellfishes pass through a larval stage. The larva already possesses the rudiments of the later-developing shell, together with a special swimming organ, which is re-adsorbed in the metamorphosis. The larvae of many fresh-water shellfishes live parasitically within the skin and the gills of fishes, and cause external symptoms which are similar to those of *Ichthyophthirius.*

It hardly pays to keep shell-fish in the aquarium, unless kept in separate tanks for a certain time in order to study their manner of living, or else as an indispensable means for breeding Bitterlings. Quite pretty in the fresh water aquarium, however, is the Triangular Shellfish (*Dreissenia*), which, due to its manner of feeding, causes a pronounced filtering action. This book brings more detailed descriptions of the River Shellfishes or UNIONIDAE (see these), and of the Triangular Shellfishes or DREISSENIA (see these).

bivittatum: With two bands. — *Aphyosemionbivittatum*.

Black-Banded Limia, the: see LIMIA NIGROFASCIATA.

Black-Banded Sunfish, the: see MESOGONSITIUS CHAETODON.

Black-Barred Livebearer, the: see QUINTANA ATRIZONA.

Black-Eyed Tetra, the: see PHENACOGASTER SUBORBITALIS.

Black-Nosed Dace, the: see RHINICHTHYS ATRATULUS ATRATULUS.

Black-Ringed Tetra, the: see LEPORINUS AFFINIS.

Black Ruby Barb, the: see BARBUS (PUNTIUS) NIGROFASCIATUS.

Black-Spotted Medaka, the: see ORYZIAS MELASTIGMA.

Black-Tailed Tetra, the: see HEMIGRAMMUS MARGINATUS.

Black Tetra, the: see GYMNOCORYMBUS TERNETZI.

Black-Throated Tilapia, the: see TILAPIA GUINASANA.

black water: The water of many jungle waters which are fed by rainfalls, and for this reason are very soft, showing a more or less strong acid reaction. Many tropical fishes are adapted to such waters and reproduce in them. Black water may be prepared artificially to some extent by filtering soft water (rain water, soft spring water, distilled, and artificially softened and de-salted water) through peat moss (see PEAT MOSS FILTRATION).

Blackamoor, the: see GYMNOCORYMBUS TERNETZI.

blackening of bottom sand: The blackening of sand may be ascribed to many causes. Reaction products from badly insulated metallic bottoms, inadequate or harmful cements may lead to it. Too thin, densely packed sand, which possibly even contains clay, and in which the circulation of the water is imperfect or even impossible, is especially prone to getting black. The accumulation of detritus in bottom soil where the plants show insufficient capacity of adsorption, e.g. around an inefficiently established gravel filter, also permits the development of black, evil-smelling spots in the bottom. No plant can thrive permanently in such soils, since the decay also attacks its roots. In all cases the first thing to do is to find and remove the cause. The old sand should be discarded, and the new bottom soil should be packed loosely, e.g. by first putting in a layer of coarse gravel and spreading the thinner layers on this. If a gravel filter is used, its suction opening should stand within the layer of coarse gravel, generating a subterranean current which is of advantage for the growth of plants and precludes the blackening of the sand (see BOTTOM SOIL; BACTERIA).

Bleak, the: see ALBURNUS LUCIDUS.

Bleeker, Pieter: Dutch physician and ichthyologist. Born July 10, 1819, died January 24, 1878. Physician in the service of the Dutch East India Army, stationed on Java. During 18 years he studied, collected, and described the fishes in the Dutch colonial regions. With the 'Atlas of East Indian Fishes' he created the first effective survey of the fish fauna of these regions. Many new discoveries are attributed to this man.

Blind Cave Fish, the: see ANOPTICHTHYS JORDANI.

Bloch, Markus Eleser: German physician and ichthyologist. Born 1723 in Ansbach, died 1799. Practising medicine in Berlin for many years, he turned early to the study of fishes, to which later on he devoted his full time. At the age of 56 he began to write a compendium of all known fish species, which in its first part, the Ökonomische Naturgeschichte der Fische Deutschlands' (Economic Natural History of the Fishes of Germany) was an excellent scientific work, the impact of which on ichthyology is felt to this day. The nine-volumed second part, the 'Naturgeschichte der Ausländischen Fische' (Natural History of Foreign Fishes) has to be considered a lesser success.

blockii: Honoring Captain Block, from Hamburg.

— *Aplocheilus.*

Bloodfin, the: *Aphyocharax rubropinnis.*

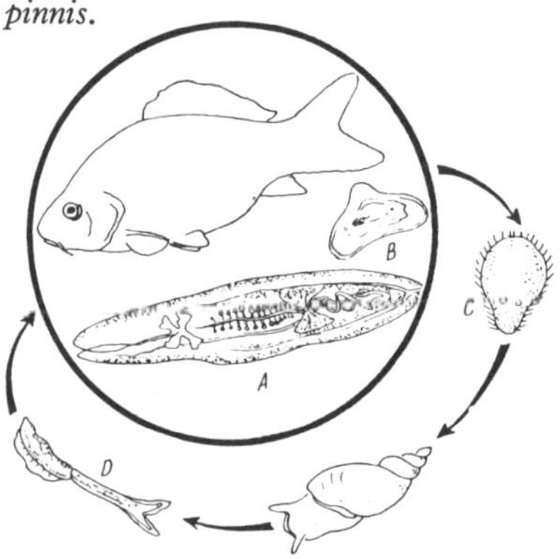

Cycle of **Sanguinicola inermis** (after Schaeperclaus): A, mature worm in blood of the fish lays eggs B. Larvae C develop into cercarii D within aquatic snails.

Blood Worm Disease: A disease transmitted through snails, caused by the immature forms of the Blood Worm *Sanguinicola inermis* Plehn, which at a certain phase leaves the snails and settles on fishes.

They then penetrate the fish through skin and gills, where they develop into sexually mature worms, about .4″ long. The eggs, laid by them in great numbers, are swept into all kinds of vessels by the blood and may cause obstructions (thromboses) which may become lethal. Especially the young fry are endangered. Therefore it is advisable not to put fresh water snails together with fishes immediately after catching them, but to keep them in quarantine for several weeks.

Blowfish, the: see TETRAODON FLUVIATILIS.

blue algae: see CYANOPHYCEAE.

Blue Badis, the: see BADIS BADIS.

Blue Corydoras, the: see CORYDORAS NATTERERI.

Blue Cynolebias, the: see CYNOLEBIAS BELOTTI.

Bluefin Top Minnow, the: see CHRIOPEOPS GOODEI.

Blue Gambusia, the: see GAMBUSIA PUNCTATA.

Blue Gourami, the: see TRICHOGASTER TRICHOPTERUS SUMATRANUS.

Blue Gularis, the: see APHYOSEMION COERULEUM.

Blue-Lipped Tilapia, the: see TILAPIA VORAX.

Blue Loach, the: see BOTIA MODESTA.

Blue Tetra, the: see MIMAGONIATES MICROLEPIS.

Blyxa: The flowing one.

Genus of aquatic plants belonging to the family of the Frogbit Plants or HYDROCHARITACEAE.

— **echinosperma** (Clarke) Maximowics: The Indian Blyxa.

GENERALITIES: A very beautiful and ornamental subaquatic plant.

SHAPE: This annual, submergedly-growing aquatic plant possesses narrow leaves which end in a very thin point, forming dense rosettes which total 40 to 100 leaves. The thin-fibred roots are very numerous. The flowers stand on a long stalk in the leaf insertions.

RANGE: In a few regions of India, at the shallow spots of calm or slowly-flowing waters.

CULTIVATION: The cultivation of this beautiful plant suffers the harmful influence of the fact that

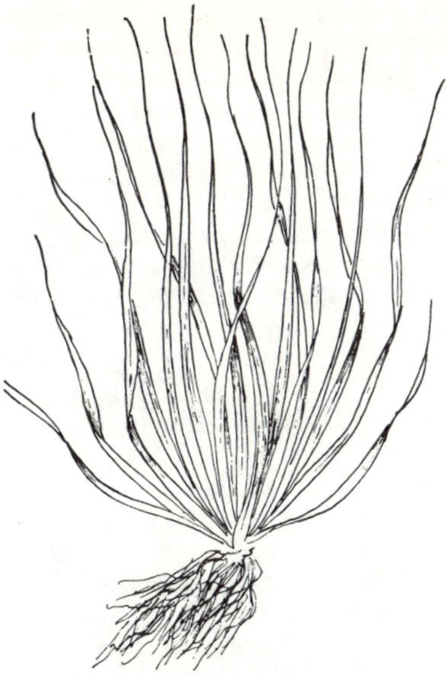

Blyxa echinosperma

it is an annual and has to be regrown from seeds every year. Planting them is effected as described for VALLISNERIA (see this). Under favorable conditions, which include soft water, a temperature of 68-77 degrees F, occasional irradiation with sunlight, and a bottom composed of sand mixed with weathered clay, the plant thrives.

boddaerti: After the Dutch naturalist Boddaert.
— *Boleophthalmus*.

body shape of fishes: The shape of fishes is determined by the construction of their skeleton, muscles, and fins, and represents the result of an adaptation to certain conditions of living during the course of the history of genetics of the species. On the other hand it prescribes for many fishes, especially the highly specialized ones, their place of living. Together with the functions of the organs, and with the behavior, it supplies the basis for the life demands of fishes.

For most fishes the spindle shape of the body is typical, especially so if they are adapted to moving more or less rapidly. Therefore the body, either looked at from all sides, or at least from a certain angle, is an equally pointed and converging wedge, intended to cut through the water and to overcome its resistance with the least expenditure of strength. The most ideally spindle-shaped bodies are therefore found either in fast-swimming fishes, or else in those which have continually to fight a strong current, as for instance in many Cyprinids, Coregons, Trout, and others. Fishes that move relatively slowly in the water, and which live temporarily among stones, plants, roots, etc., may have a high-backed body, strongly compressed laterally. On open water fishes, the fins often are very small, with exception of the frequently strongly developed pectorals, while they may be lengthened or enlarged on fishes that live in hiding places. Both shapes permit many intermediate forms. Among the Characins one finds open water forms with disc-like shapes and a sharp keel. On the other hand just fishes of the plant thickets may be acutely spindle-shaped. This body shape facilitates their remaining both between plants and obstacles, and in open water. Fishes that live near, or at, the bottom of the water, diverge considerably from the normal fish shape, or even lack it totally. Many times the body is compressed from above. The maximum development of this is seen on Flatfishes (Soles, Flounders, etc.), in which the entire construction of the body suffers a peculiar dislocation.

Other fishes, mostly species that live at or near the bottom, possess a worm or snake-shaped body, or even a band-shaped one. There are many transitions among all body

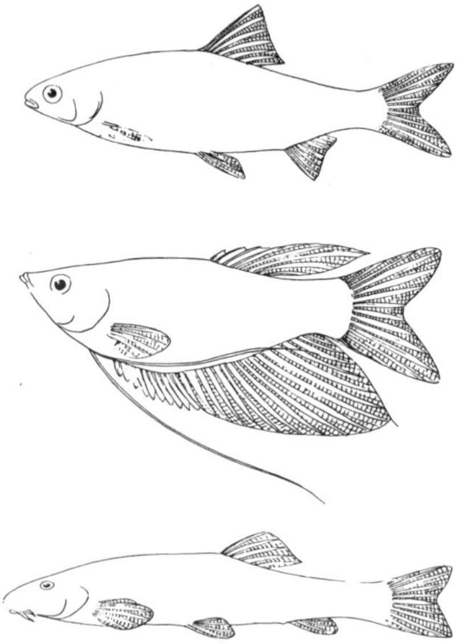

Body Shape of Fishes — top: A fast-swimming fish from open water; center: A fish from regions rich in plant life; bottom: A bottom fish.

shapes. Therefore it is impossible to establish firm and generalized rules. In no case can the body shape serve to establish relationships. Thus very similar shapes are often found in species that are not related at all (see CONVERGENCE), as for instance on the African and South American Knife Fishes. On the other hand members of the same, cosely-related group, often differ considerably from each other. Consider, for instance, the shapes of the Cichlid family, ranging from *Crenicichla* to *Pterophyllum*. Often the body shape may afford points of reference among very closely related species, say within one genus.

The body of fishes permits distinguishing externally the following parts: head, trunk, tail, and fins. Their relations of size to one another are variable. The head begins at the tip of the snout and ends internally at the extension of the occipital, respectively externally at the gill cleft. To measure the length of the head, one should state up to which of the two final points the measuring was done. The trunk is measured from the gill opening to the anus, but this is not always possible as in some fish groups (Knife Fishes, etc.) the anus is placed far toward the fore end. The remainder of the body constitutes the TAIL. The length of a fish is either measured as TOTAL LENGTH (including the tail fin), or else as BODY LENGTH (without the tail fin). The EYES are generally placed laterally, closer to the tip of the snout than to the gill cleft. On flat heads compressed down from above, the eyes generally are located very high, in some cases directed straight upwards, on the upper side of the head. The space from eye to eye, over the head, is called WIDTH OF THE FOREHEAD (intraorbital space, intraorbital width); along the throat it is called suborbital space. The diameter of the eyes, and their position, are important aids for the taxonomist in classifying the several species. Within the region of the snout are the NOSTRILS and the MOUTH. The latter may be of many shapes. The mouth opening may be narrow or wide, in some cases reaching back to the rear edge of the head. According to the position of the mouth opening, we speak of supraterminal, terminal, and subterminal mouths. This may be of many shapes. Sometimes it is tube-shaped, extendable, or adapted to sucking. The mouth opening is often framed by lip folds or LIPS, and frequently one finds BARBELS, which function as organs of taste.

On the rear part of the head one finds the GILLS, serving for breathing purposes, which are protected externally by the GILL COVERS. These generally consist of two

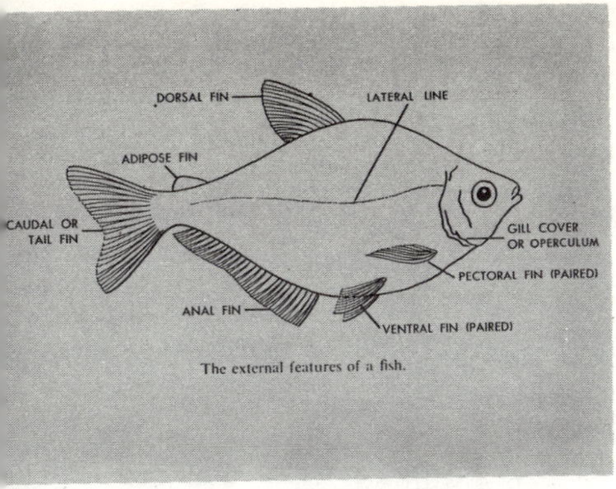

Body structure of a fish

main parts, the main cover or operculum, followed by the secondary cover or sub-operculum. After bathing the gills, the water taken in for breathing is expelled through the GILL OPENING, which sometimes is developed as a hole, a small slit, or, as a rule, a somewhat longer cleft. The edges of the opercles are surrounded by skin seams which serve the purpose of better closing off the gill opening. These gill skins may grow together with the underside of the head, at the so-called ISTHMUS, or else they may remain free. All this may constitute, among others, a characteristic with which to distinguish between related species or genera of fishes. The region of the isthmus is also called THROAT, while the name of the upper side of the head is the FOREHEAD and the region of the occipital is the NECK. The trunk is divided into BACK, FLANKS (or sides), and BELLY. The region shortly below and behind the gill covers, where the pectoral fins insert, is the BREAST. The trunk finally goes over into the TAIL. Between dorsal and anal fin generally exists a free part of the tail called CAUDAL PEDUNCLE. The FINS (see these) are more closely described under their own entry.

A comprehensive description of the main groups of fishes is given below, but one has to remark expressly that between all of them there are transitions, and furthermore that many species of fishes are accustomed to change their usual haunts.

(a) OPEN WATER FISHES. Fishes that remain mainly in the middle and upper strata of open water where there are no plants. The body of the species which live in quick-flowing waters is generally constructed in the shape of a torpedo, i.e., the usual spindle shape shows a rounded cross section through strong development of the muscles, as happens, for instance, with Trout. The fins generally are not overly developed, so as not to offer too much resistance to the water. Colors generally are not especially strong, and one often finds silver color or weak shiny colors disposed in horizontal bands. The open water fishes of calmer waters possess elongated bodies, compressed laterally, the cross section of which is an elongated oval. In most cases too the fins are not overly developed, but here we already see enlargements of fins, not only of the pectorals, but of other fins too. Furthermore here we find transition forms to fishes which really often stay in open waters, but temporarily change their place of living, and therefore belong to the next group.

(b) FISHES OF CLOSED WATERS. Fishes that remain temporarily or definitely among plant thickets, clefts, dead woods, etc. in the middle or upper strata. The body is often compact and flattened laterally. This flattening may be overly developed among the dwellers among plants, especially reeds. Life among many-clefted rocks, too, calls for a flattened body. The fins may be greatly enlarged. Often too the body is very supple, as is the case with some Anabantids, or it may be strongly specialized, as happens with Knife Fishes, which swim forward and backward with the same ease. At times also a puncheon-like shape is found, as e.g., in the Characin-like fishes of the *Hemiodontidae* family.

(c) FISHES OF THE BOTTOM ZONE. Fishes that live near, on, or in the bottom.

(aa) *Fishes from near the bottom* as a rule remain in the immediate vicinity of the bottom, where they hunt for food, without which the group could be clearly differentiated from the fishes of other regions. In most cases the ventral contour is straight, and the dorsal one more arched. The paired fins are moved towards the sides. The mouth opening is subterminal, and one often finds barbels or extendable lips.

(ab) Fishes that *lie directly on the ground* often have a more clearly flattened underside, the body not rarely being also flattened from above. The paired fins, too, are distinctly moved to the sides, and the pectorals may in some cases be used for creeping or "walking". Furthermore the mouth or the whole underside may be adapted to fixation by sucking, as for instance, is the case with some Catfishes which live among the pebbles of rapid mountain brooks. The eyes of this group of fishes often are small, sometimes protected by a special lid of skin. As a rule there are barbels.

(ac) Fishes that *dig in into the bottom* show the strongest specialization. The fins often are partly retrogressed, and the body is worm-shaped or has the shape of a ribbon. The colors of this group are often cloudily blended, re-

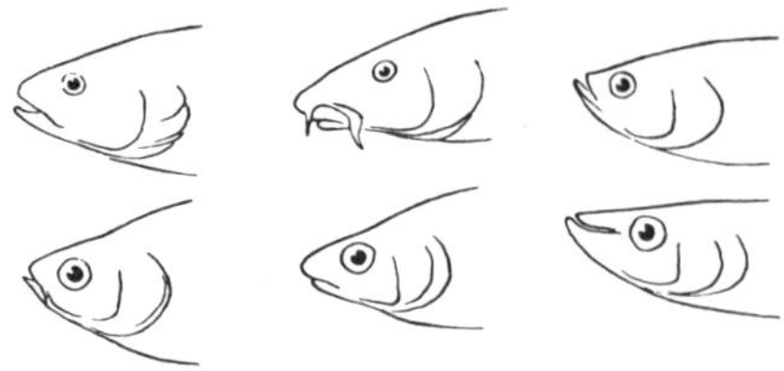

Mouth structure of fishes—left: terminal; center: subterminal; right: supraterminal.

markably spotted, or uniformly dark.

(d) FISHES OF THE SURFACE. Fishes that are found immediately below the surface either in open or in planted waters. The construction of the body is characterized by a strong flattening of the back, which is nearly straightlined. The most especially developed dorsal fin inserts far back. Some species have very strongly developed pectorals, which may lift the fish out of the water in long leaps over the surface. A well-known specimen of this group is the Butterfly fish, *Pantodon buchholzi*, as well as the different species of the Hatchet Fishes, *Gasteropelecidae*, the Flying Barbs of the genus *Esomus*, and others. The mouth generally is supraterminal, meaning that the mouth opening is directed sharply upwards.

Surface fishes naturally have a distinct relationship to the air space above the water surface, both in their manner of feeding and in their manner of reproducing.

Some species, e.g., the *Aplocheilus* Tooth Carps, *Toxotes* the Archer Fish, and others, possess one or more shiny spots on the crown of the body, which are dependent upon light and may possibly serve to attract prey.

boils of fishes: Boil diseases of fishes are those illnesses caused by unicellular sporozoans, which show externally through boils located in the conjunctive or the muscular tissue. In open nature pronounced boils appear on Barbs, Coregons, Shiners, Smelts, and Sticklebacks. They can probably also be carried into the aquarium and transmitted to other fishes. Since the reproduction of the sporozoans is extremely prolific, even smaller boils may contain some billions of spores. Therefore all fishes with boils should be segregated from the community. All stocks of fishes in which even one specimen diseased with boils is noticed have to be considered under suspicion of the disease. In cases of stronger incidence, destroy the suspicious and diseased fishes, since attempts at cure are hopeless. The tank should be disinfected with a 1% solution of Chloramine, and sand and plants should be discarded. The Boil Diseases probably include the so-called Neon Disease (see PLISTOPHORA), despite the fact that it is not characterized by boils.

Boleophthalmus: Throwing eye. Genus belonging to the family of the Gudgeons or *Gobiidae*, subfamily of the PERIOPHTHALMINAE (see this). The range is restricted exclusively to South East Asia. The body is elongated, slightly compressed laterally, more so at the rear end than in front. With two dorsal fins, of which the foremost is supported by a few stiff rays, while the second, soft one is very much elongated. The eyes insert on the upper side of the head and may be moved to all sides. The shovel-shaped pectoral fins which are fastened to a strong muscle, may be moved like legs, while the ventrals are joined into a clinging disk.

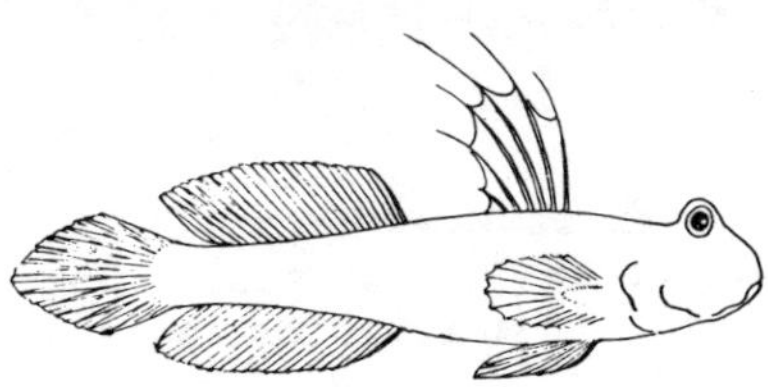

Boleophthalmus — type of the genus

— **boddaerti** (Pallas): The Pop-Eye.

SHAPE: As per description of the genus. D_1 V, D_2 24-25, A 24. The hard rays of the first dorsal fin are greatly extended and reach beyond the edge of the fin. The scales are very small. The swimming bladder also is very small.

COLOR: Gray-brown base with 6-7 indistinct blackish cross bands, and spots. Older specimens show numerous little, luminous light-blue spots on body and fins.

RANGE: The coasts of East and South East Asia, in the same biotopes as the other members of the sub-family. The species also migrates to pure fresh water, and it is reported that it does not live as much amphibiously as the members of the genus *Periophthalmus*.

CARE AND BREEDING: As described for the sub-family PERIOPHTHALMINAE (see this). Breeding in the aquarium has not yet been achieved. Nothing is known about the reproduction of the Pop-Eyes.

Bony Fishes, the: see OSTEICHTHYES.

borelli: After the collector, Dr. Borelli.

— *Apistogramma.*

Bosmina: Trunk-Bearing Crustaceans.

Genus pertaining to the tribe of the *Anomopoda*, which differs from the other Water Fleas by their long first antenna and the trunk, which is firmly attached to the head. The little crustaceans live as plankton in the open water of bigger ponds and lakes, and are subject to an annual cycle of changes in shape.

Bosmina are a much-liked baby food. It is true, however, that some breeders have had to observe that

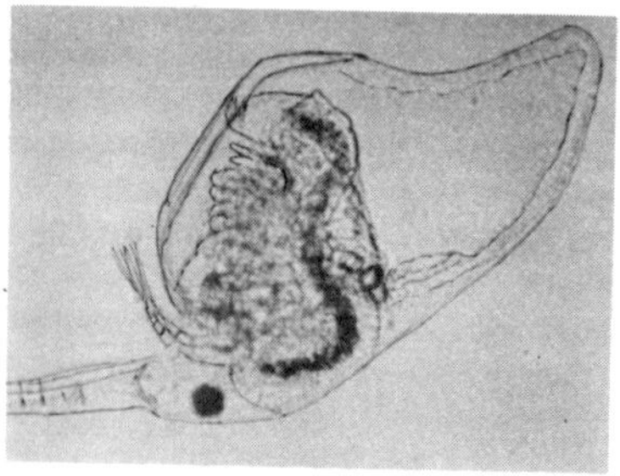

Bosmina

at certain periods they are so hard-shelled that the fry cannot eat them. This may depend on ecological conditions. Frequently other micro-organisms, such as *Rotatoria*, and baby *Daphnia*, are mistaken for *Bosmina* and fed to the fish as such.

Botia: Meaning of the name is unknown.

Genus pertaining to the family of the Loaches or COBITIDAE (see this), the members of which differ strongly from the other Loaches, both in body shape and, generally, also in the manner of living. The body is elongated, plump, and compressed laterally, the dorsal outline being arched while the ventral one remains nearly straight. Generally the caudal peduncle is very high. The long and pointed head possesses a terminally extended mouth, equipped with a long upper lip and 3-4 pairs of barbels. The eyes insert high in the head, the sub-ocular thorn being two-pronged and erectable. The swimming bladder is enclosed in a bony capsule. The scales are regressed to a great degree.

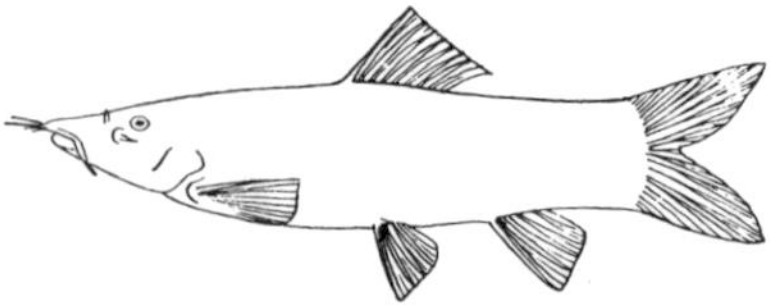

Botia, type of the species

All species of *Botia* are school fishes, which easily become vicious if kept alone. When keeping them, do not let the fact that the Loaches often live in muddy water mislead you to keep them in mulmy tanks. Nearly all species of the genus like clear, oxygen-rich, not-too-warm water, and a clean gravel bottom. Besides this they like to make use of hiding caves. If no caves are available, they dig protective holes beneath rocks or other ornamental objects, where they stay, with only the extended upper lip visible, in wait for food. In nature they probably like to swim head-on against the current. Hiding places made of shallowly-set, empty coconut shells have proved to be especially efficient. Temperatures should not exceed 77 degrees F. Specimens that are kept alone frequently become vicious. For this reason try to keep them in greater communities of their own species. If you keep only 2 or 3 fish together, it may happen that the strongest one annoys the others to death. At such occasions whole pieces of skin are torn off the vanquished.

Botia horae

— **horae** H. M. Smith:

SHAPE: As per description of the genus; Dorsal and ventral contours especially flatly arched, the caudal peduncle very high.

COLOR: Greenish to bluish base with an always even stripe on the dorsal ridge, which turns downwards at the tail root. On the sides three or four black cross bars, which are very variable and may also vanish completely. SD unknown.

RANGE: Indo-China (Thailand).

CARE AND BREEDING: As per description of the genus. No particulars known.

— **hymenophysa** (Bleeker): The Tiger Loach.

SHAPE: As per description of the genus. D 13-15, A 8. Three pairs of barbels. Length, in its home country up to 12″, in the aquarium only up to 6″ (?).

COLOR: Strongly variable. Greenish and yellow with narrow, brownish or bluish cross bands, which often run together. The fins are yellowish to orange-colored, the dorsal showing blue spots.

RANGE: In flowing waters of Indo-China, Malaya, and Indonesia, in freshwater only.

Botia hymenophysa

CARE AND BREEDING: As per description of the genus. The fish, which become lively only at twilight, may temporarily be very vivacious. Then they swim up and down the glass panes very quickly and whirl up the bottom sand. The species needs some warmth, but 72-77 degrees F are sufficient. They eat all kinds of live and dry foods.

— **lohachata** Chandhuri: The Reticulated Loach.

SHAPE: As per description of the genus. D 10-11, A 6-7. The dorsal fin inserts exactly on the center of the body. The two-pointed, erectable under-eye thorn is tilted backwards. The very small scales are imbedded deep in the skin. Length: unknown.

COLOR: The color is highly variable, possibly caused by geographic races. On silver-gray base, which may show a yellowish tinge, one finds several cross bars, which fork on the upper half of the body and run beyond the dorsal ridge. The bands may be darker on the edges than in the middle.

RANGE: East Pakistan, in standing and slowly-flowing waters, even the smallest puddles.

CARE AND BREEDING: As per description of the genus. Likes to remain in schools of its own species. Clear, oxygenated water at about 77 degrees F or more promotes their well-being, but also lower temperatures are easily withstood. The species eats live and dry foods of all kinds, also from the surface, to do which they turn on their backs. Bottom food is dug out from the soil. Digging into the bottom has not been observed, but the fish have been seen to lie flat on the bottom (BADER).

— **lucas-bahi** Fowler:

SHAPE: As per description of the genus. The body is elongated and strongly compressed laterally. The species possesses 6 pairs of barbels. Length about $3\frac{1}{8}$″.

COLOR: Reddish to bluish-brown base with 10-15 more or less clearly

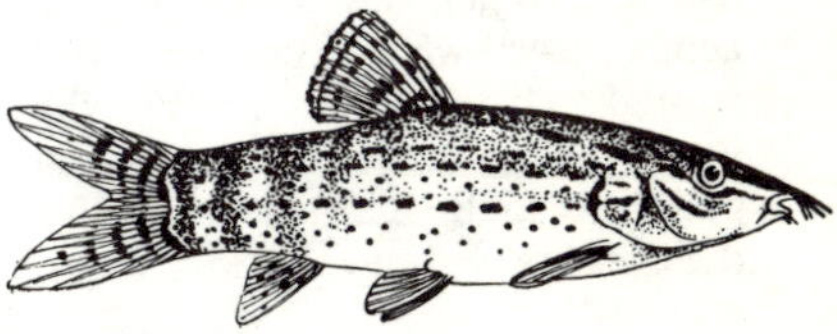

Botia lucas-bahi

visible cross bars. On the belly region and the sides we see variable numbers of black dots.

RANGE: In flowing waters of Thailand.

CARE AND BREEDING: As per description of the genus. This species is more peaceful and less quarrelsome than the other species of *Botia*.

Botia macracantha

— **macracantha** (Bleeker): The Clown Loach.

CARE AND BREEDING: As per description of the genus, with four pairs of barbels. The real length is not exactly known, the greatest length of captured specimens being about 6″.

COLOR: Golden to reddish yellow with three deep black cross bands. Fins brick red.

RANGE: Sumatra, Borneo, and the other Sunda Islands.

CARE AND BREEDING: As per description of the genus. This species likes to show up also in the daytime, swimming up and down excitedly at the glass panes. It likes to join the schools of Banded Barbs.

— **modesta** (Bleeker): The Blue Loach.

SHAPE: As per description of the genus, somewhat compact, but strongly flattened laterally; the ventral contour arched, the caudal peduncle high. The thorns below the eyes are well developed. Length up to 10″.

COLOR: The basic coloring is a beautiful green-blue to blue, the

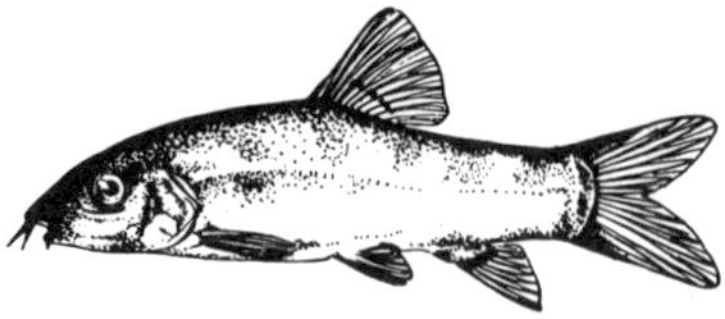

Botia modesta

tail fin yellowish to red. Young specimens show some cross bands, older ones have a weakly indicated, often missing, spot on the root of the tail fin.

RANGE: In flowing waters of Indo-China.

CARE AND BREEDING: As per description of the genus. This species may turn out to be very vicious and annoy even big Cichlids. They are skilled swimmers, but like to stay hidden in caves.

bottom heating: see HEATING.

bottom nettle, the: see HYDRILLA VERTICILLATA.

bottom soil: The bottom soil within an aquarium is one of the factors which may be of decisive importance for the well-being of plants and fishes. For many years the use of the most different kinds of bottom soil was a matter of much controversy, which, however, never has found a general solution. The choice of the bottom soil depends basically on whether the hobbyist gives preference to his fishes, or to his plants, or both.

In general, the bottom soil will be perfectly sufficient if it consists of a layer of not-too-thin, still a little clay-bearing sand, which is covered by a stratum of clean, washed gravel. Any experiments with this may lead to disturbances of the biological processes in the aquarium.

The biology of the bottom soil represents part of the total biology of the aquarium. Generally, however, the aquarist does not consider the bottom soil as a biological unit. It is only by the blackening of the sand that he becomes aware that something is out of order. The interstices between the single grains of sand are filled with water. In this develops a kind of life which is important to the whole household of the aquarium. Soil bacteria, algae, and unicellulars give the soil its special characteristics. The main activity of the soil bacteria consists in decomposing the collecting substances that sink down, and thus to make them usable for the plants. New water, which should always be in circulation in the soil, prepares good vital conditions for the bacteria, simultaneously removing the collecting decomposed products. It is in this that we find the value of well-functioning under gravel filters (see FILTERS, FILTRATION).

The thinner-grained the bottom soil is, the harder it becomes for the circulation in it to keep up its steady flow. Therefore it is no wonder that in such soils black spots appear much more quickly than in the more penetrable coarse gravel bottoms. Also metal compounds which penetrate the sand, coming from badly-isolated aquarium bottoms, are able to disturb the life within the bottom soïl in its functions, or even to kill it completely. For this reason too fine sand furthers the development of decay spots and of poisonous gases. If you keep species of fishes which lie on the bottom, or which dig into it, you will in any case be forced to use soft, round-cornered sand. In such cases you should try to prevent eventual harmful consequences by previously putting in a layer of coarser sand, which is then covered by the fine sand. Little-washed sand with some clay contents is perfectly sufficient for most aquatic plants (see CARE FOR AQUATIC PLANTS). If you keep fishes that demand soft water, give special care to see that your sand contains little or no hardeners, since these will harden the water quickly again. Pure quartz sand or gravel are the best in such cases. Traces of hardening substances may be removed with the aid of a 1% solution of Muriatic Acid, in which the sand is rinsed for some hours (do not use metallic containers!). They can be considered removed when the solution over a soil sample remains acid after intensive washing. Many species of fishes, especially Cyprinids, Gudgeons, and Catfishes, like to root in the soil. In this case the upper layer must be rinsed until completely clean, respectively, the decaying mulm must be siphoned off frequently. In order to favor the vital habits of these species it may be advisable to create an artificial layer of mulm above the soil, by spreading finely disfibred, boiled and squeezed-out peat moss in a ½″ to 1″ high layer over the sand. (Be careful not to let it form lumps, as these might later on obstruct the siphoning hose.) Of course this layer has to be replaced from time to time.

In general terms it may be stated that a dark bottom soil enhances the vividness of the color of the fishes, while they become paler over a light-colored bottom. In order to achieve the desired effect, spread a thin layer of split basalt gravel over the bottom, but remember that basalt always will look a little cold, while peat moss creates a more natural impression.

For strongly rooting fishes (Cichlids) use coarse sand, which has to be so well-washed that it will no more cloud any water. Since this generally excludes the use of subaquatic plants, in order to achieve an ornamental effect, and to meet the fishes' need for hiding and breeding sites, one may use different means, such as rocks, roots, or floating plants with strong development of roots (*Pistia*, etc.).

In the breeding tank it will often be necessary to desist totally from using any bottom soil.

bottom spawners: A small group of fishes, especially egg-laying Tooth Carps of the genera *Aphyosemion*, *Cynolebias*, *Pterolebias*, and *Nothobranchius*, which imbed their eggs into the soil of the waters where they live, from where these develop into fry, generally after a rest period. This manner of reproduction represents an adaptation to waters which dry up or vanish periodically.

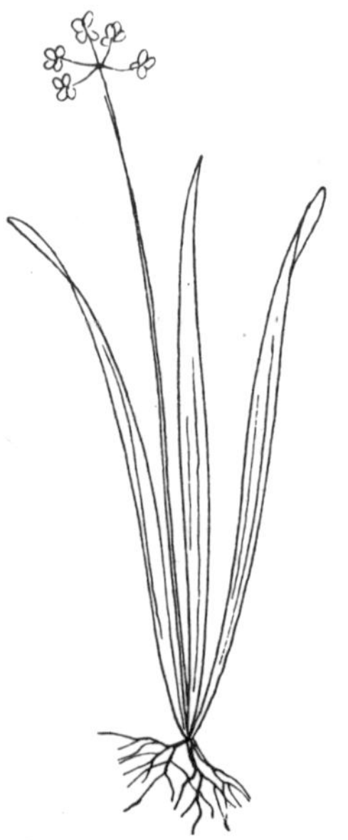

A bottom-standing plant

bottom-standing: Parts of plants that grow upwards directly from the root.

Boulenger, Georges Albert: Belgian ichthyologist, one of the greatest experts on the world of fishes in general, to whom the aquarium hobby owes much. Born 1858. Successor of the celebrated aquarist Albert Guenther, who soon recognized his talent and called him to London in 1881, where he gradually took over Guenther's tasks. Boulenger became Guenther's successor as Director of the Ichthyological Department of the British Museum. Boulenger performed enormous labors within this field, following in the tracks of Guenther's achievements, and did intensive research, especially on the world of fishes of Equatorial Africa.

Brachydanio: Short Danio.

Sub-genus of small, Carp-like school fishes, pertaining to the family of the CYPRINIDAE (see this), genus DANIO (see this). Of slender, elongated build, more or less compressed laterally, the belly rounded. The small mouth is slanted obliquely upwards, showing barbels, which, however, are partially stunted. The lateral line is incomplete, or totally absent, and always runs below the central axis of the body. It is advisable not to choose too small tanks for them, and to keep the fishes in bigger schools. The school of fish of their own kind is their vital element. But all species are also fit for living in communities with other swift-swimming fishes. Care and breeding as described for CYPRINIDAE (see this). For breeding use several males per spawn-ripe female. The act of spawning generally takes place under the morning sun.

— albolineatus (Blyth): The Pearl Danio.

SHAPE: As per description of the genus. The upper jaw carries two shorter and two long barbels. D 9, A 16. The lateral line is incomplete. Length up to $2\frac{3}{8}''$.

COLOR: With a blue-green to violet sheen and a wine-red horizontal stripe from the center of the body to the tail fin. The male is slimmer and more vividly colored.

Brachydanio albolineatus

RANGE: In brooks and rivers in Indo-China, Malaya, and Sumatra.
CARE AND BREEDING: As per description of the sub-genus. Temperatures: 68-73 degrees F, for breeding 75 degrees F, lowest 64 degrees F.

Brachydanio nigrofasciatus

— nigrofasciatus (Day): The Spotted Danio.
SHAPE: As per description of the sub-genus. An especially small and dainty species, which formerly was known as *B. analipunctatus.* One pair of barbels in the angle of the mouth. D 9, A 13. Length, males up to $1\frac{1}{2}''$, females up to $1\frac{3}{4}''$.
COLOR: Yellowish-white base with a blue-black horizontal band and parallel rows of dots above and below it, which in part run into one another, and of which the lower row is bigger-sized on females.
RANGE: Northern Indo-China.
CARE AND BREEDING: As per description of the sub-genus, but needing a little more warmth, and not as easy to breed as the other species.

— rerio (Hamilton-Buchanan): The Zebra Danio.
SHAPE: As per description of the sub-genus, only little compressed laterally. On the upper jaw two shorter and two longer barbels. D 9, A 15-16. Length $2''$-$2\frac{3}{8}''$.

Brachydanio rerio

COLOR: The base is silvery, on the males often golden, with several luminously blue to blue-black horizontal stripes, which also appear on the fins. The male is slimmer.
RANGE: Waters in the region of the East coast of India.
CARE AND BREEDING: As per description of the sub-genus. Temperatures: 64-70 degrees F, for breeding up to 75 degrees F, lowest 61 degrees F.

Brachygobius: Short Gobio or Gudgeon (Dwarf Gudgeons).
Genus of small tropical fishes belonging to the family of the Gobies or GOBIIDAE (see this), with compact, cylindrical body, which is a little more compressed laterally

only toward the rear end. The head is short. The first of the two dorsal fins shows only hard rays.

— **doriae** (Guenther): The Bumblebee Fish.

SHAPE: As per description of the genus. The species strongly resembles *B. nunus*, but it is its big head which is especially remarkable. Length: $\frac{3}{4}''$-1″.

Brachygobius doriae

COLOR: Brownish cross bars and spots on dirty-yellow base. As compared to *B. nunus* the cross bars take up more space than the yellow interstices. During the spawning period the female is noticeably more fuller-bodied.

RANGE: Borneo and the Malayan Archipelago.

CARE AND BREEDING: As described for *B. nunus*. This species also likes possibilities for hiding and should preferably be kept alone.

Brachygobius nunus

— **nunus** (Hamilton-Buchanan):

SHAPE: As per description of the genus. The species is identical with *B. xanthozona*. Several rows of small teeth on the jaws of the terminal mouth.

Length up to $1\frac{5}{8}''$.

COLOR: Yellowish base with four dark, often blurred, cross bands of different widths. The male is more brightly colored, the female plumper.

RANGE: In very small waters, canals, road ditches, etc. in India and Indo-China, as well as on the Sunda Islands. The species lives especially in brackish water and in biologically unfavorable ones.

CARE AND BREEDING: This species is not adapted for keeping in communities. If kept alone in smaller tanks, however, it is very fetching and interesting. Like those of most Gobies, the ventrals are united into an adhering disk, with which the fish are able to cling to rocks, glass panes, etc. for hours. Occasionally, though, especially while feeding, they become quite lively. Since this fish originates from the zone of brackish waters, it is advisable to offer it an admixture of kitchen salt (one heaping tablespoon per four gallons of water) or of sea water. Planting the aquarium is superfluous, but the fish like hiding places made of rocks and roots.

PINTER, who bred the species, reports that the approximately 150 eggs were stuck to the underside of a rock in a hiding cave, and that they were watched by the male. In soft water, disinfected with a little methylene blue, and at a temperature of 86 degrees F, the first fry hatched after 48 hours, the last ones only after 5 days. They needed another 48 hours to become free-swimming. At this moment they were 4 mm. long, lived for another two days from their yolk sacs, and were then reared on dust-sized live food. After a month they began to change colors, and were nearly full-grown when 6 months old.

— **xanthozona:** see B. NUNUS.

Brachyraphis: With short thorn (gonopodium).

Genus of Tooth Carps belonging to the sub-family of the Live Bearing Tooth Carps or POECILIINAE (see this), closely related to the genus *Gambusia*.

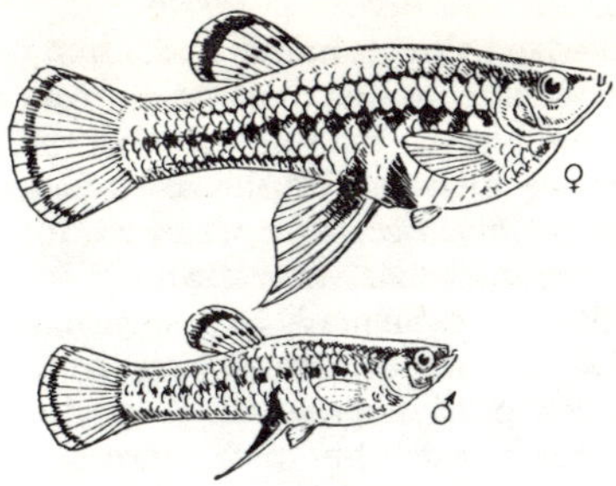

Brachyraphis episcopi

— **episcopi** (Steindachner): The Bishop.
SHAPE: This quite dainty species possesses a relatively big gonopodium. The mouth opening is remarkably wide. D 8-9, A 10. Length: males a scant 1⅛″, females up to 2″.
COLOR: Yellowish base with some faint, red horizontal stripes and several dark cross lines. The fins of the males are partly orange-colored.
RANGE: In all kinds of waters, ditches, ponds, inlets and outer tributaries of the bigger bodies of water of Panama.
CARE AND BREEDING: As per description of the sub-family (see POECILIINAE). The species requires much warmth. If possible, do not keep the temperature below 75 degrees F for any long periods of time. Live food of adequate size are preferred, artificial ones are taken only in case of need. The fry, which at first seem to grow up normally, do not reach the size of the imported specimens and remain extremely sensitive. For this reason the species has not yet been able to find its place in our aquaria.

Brachyura: Short-Tailed Crustaceans, Crabs.
Division of the sub-order of the Claw-bearing Crustaeans or REPTANTIA (see this), of compact body and with a short tail which folds back under the head-and-breast piece. Often one of the two claws is bigger than the other one, both being developed in different ways. Most Crabs run sideways. On land they move quite rapidly. Many of them live in the tidal zones awaiting the return of the flood tide in puddles or buried in the sand. Some species have adapted totally to living on dry land. From the eggs of the ocean forms hatches a planktonic-living larva, which turns into a completed Crab after several changes of skin. The only species that may be kept in the fresh-water aquarium is ERIOCHEIR SINENSIS (see this), an interesting transitional form of an ocean Crab which can spend its whole life in fresh water.

brackish water: The mixture of salt and fresh water resulting from the meeting of waters of both species, for instance, in river mouths and lagoons which are connected with the sea and have an influx of fresh water. The brackish water region possesses a world of live beings of its own, which generally is very versatile.

Branchipus schaefferi: see ANOSTRACA.

Branchiura: Class of parasitical lower Crustaceans belonging to the phylum of the Crustaceans or CRUSTACEA (see this), of which the Carp-lice (see ARGULUS) are of interest to aquarists.

branneri: After the collector, Dr. Branner.
— *Micropoecilia.*

Branner's Livebearer: see MICROPOECILIA BRANNERI.

brasiliense: Coming from Brazil, Brazilian.
— *Myriophyllum.*

brasiliensis: Coming from Brazil, Brazilian.
— *Geophagus.*

Brass Rasbora, the: see RASBORA MEINKENI.

Brazilian Dirt Eater, the: see GEOPHAGUS BRASILIENSIS.

Bream: see ABRAMIS.

Bream Characin, the: see ABRAMITES MICROCEPHALUS.

breast fin: Pectoral fin.

brederi: After a personal name.
— *Betta.*

breeding: In aquaristics "breeding" means the obtaining through adequate measures of healthy, vigorous offspring which correspond to the prototype of a species, or to an artificial selective aim. Successful breeding may be proof of correct keeping and should be considered the climax of keeping fishes in the aquarium, due to the biological observations it makes possible, and due to the joy and contentment it affords the fancier. It is only in reproduction that the fish unfolds its complete nature. Many biological problems which make aquaristics interesting, appear only when breeding.

We differentiate two aims of breeding:

(a) NATURAL BREEDING, the purpose of which is to make domestic and tropical fishes reproduce by maintaining the best possible preservation of their natural characteristics; and

(b) ARTIFICIAL BREEDING, which endeavors to breed color and shape mutants from existing strains which can be used for this.

Both efforts are justified side by side. The often raised objection that artificial breeding is tampering with Nature, based on "human conceit that wants to improve upon Nature" could as well apply to other fields of improving breeds, for instance, to the gardener who breeds beautiful garden plants from simple wild forms. Breeding is done both by amateur hobbyists and by professional breeders. Both deserve their praise in the development of aquaristics, and often the distinctions between the two groups overlap. The objections which are so often raised against "mass breeding" partially miss the scope of the question, as this is needed to supply the great demand for aquarium fishes. Only the irresponsible "production" of aquarium fishes, without considering hereditary or sanitary conditions of the resulting fishes has to be rejected.

The breeder has to acquire the most comprehensive knowledge of the species of fishes he wants to breed. He has to know their vital necessities or must be able to draw conclusions on their probable exigencies from his experience with similar species, should they be unknown. He must also be aware that he has a great responsibility towards the fishes he keeps, and that this should stand above all other interests. To this he must add a good amount of adaptability, which is difficult to learn—if it can be learned at all—and which is born from his love of Nature and for his pets. Harmonizing all these qualities makes the skilled breeder.

Contrary to what happens in plant culture, up to this date adequate points of view have hardly been able to assert themselves in animal breeding, and scarcely at all in aquaristics. It is true that already from a utilitarian point of view most breeders keep their stocks as free of disease as possible, but relatively few pay attention to the simplest rules of animal breeding. Thus it is no wonder if after a more or less long period the stocks show certain signs of degeneration, and that then the cry is raised for "new imports to freshen up the blood".

Generally the damages observed in our aquarium fishes, for instance, dwarf growths, malformations, changes in shape and color, decreases in fertility, etc. are laid at the door of INBREEDING (see this). To this we would like to comment that inbreeding, on the contrary, is an indispensable aid in fixing good strains if breeding is done conscientiously. As a rule it is wrong care, together with faulty selection and the unknown furthering of undesirable traits that lead to a decline of fish stocks. The breeder who succeeds in spawning an import starts generally with an extremely small number of specimens, often with only one pair. If possible, he uses the entire offspring for breeding again, or else he sells it without considering its condition, in order to take advantage of the favorable moment of novelty. However, also with less rare, but good-selling species, frequently not the least attempts at selection are made, which could only begin, anyway, if the breeder reared the fishes to a certain size or, better still, to the point of sexual maturity. On the contrary, it is the general mispractice to sell the fry at an age when judging them as to quality is not yet possible at all. The custom of removing the spawn from parents that care insufficiently for it, and to rear the young separately, may lead to the development of strains that care insufficiently. The constant inbreeding of brother-and-sister pairs, which is the rule for aquarium fishes, may lead to the union of bad hereditary factors, and to the development of whole races which show these characteristics, if no control and selection are exerted. This might explain the proneness of whole stocks of Neon Tetras to the *Plistophora* disease.

A change in this can only be achieved by planned breeding. The breeder should have a clear idea of the ends he wants to attain. He himself must create a kind of breeding standard according to what he wants to obtain. As a minimum, though, the breeder should show the ambition to breed the healthiest and most typical fishes.

A primary condition for obtaining good descendencies is the choice of good breeding specimens. Naturally these have to be healthy. They should not suffer from infections, nor from hereditary diseases. The presence of acquired damages, for instance, parts of fins that have been bitten off, is unimportant, as long as it does not impair any vital functions. Of decisive importance for the choice of the breeder specimens is doubtlessly the external impression they cause, which may disclose a lot of information. One should not be too cautious in this, however. If it is the case of preserving a rare imported species, for instance, certain methods of breeding permit the ulterior removal of certain errors that stem from faulty parents. One has always to consider, that the good qualities of a tribe are not decided by the looks of single pairs, but by the hereditary image of the whole stock. Specimens with obvious hereditary defects—shortening of the skull, for instance, will, of course, hardly lead to enjoyable final results.

It is always advisable to choose one's breeders from a school of fishes of the same species. The alert fancier or buyer will soon develop an eye for the fishes which are flawless. Hereditary defects are not visible if they exist hidden (recessively). In this you will have to trust to your luck, if the seller can or will give no information. In general one should make it a rule to rear one's own breeders by buying a number of young fishes and keeping them together to the time of sexual maturity. To buy 'guaranteed matched pairs' is fraught with certain dangers, since a breeder of fishes would hardly part with such as long as he is interested in breeding them himself.

The breeding stock should be as typical of the species as possible, and also flawless in shape and color, as well as young and vigorous, but not too young. Naturally it will be one's own wishes and ideas that will decide in this. If, for instance, one makes demands with a view to human ideas of beauty, let us say that on cross-striped fishes like *Collisa lalia* the cross stripes be regular and undivided, this is included in the choice. Also the demands for especially shiny and luminous colors, or for long, flowing fins, for peacefulness toward other fishes, for willingness to care for the brood, or for the disposition to procreate, are based on human ideas. Inversely, the idea of excluding from breeding those specimens that are especially vicious, this peculiarity exceeding what is typical of the species, is dictated by aquaristic considerations as well. Everywhere in breeding conscious or unconscious selections are made that favor keeping the fishes in the aquarium, turning them into domestic animals, that is, domesticating them. There is no such thing as objective selection for breeding.

A further premise for successful breeding is the careful attention paid to the vital demands of the fishes. Reproduction can only be achieved under conditions that are optimum for the species. Therefore we often hear the demand for natural keeping. What this means is explained in the entry 'ambient world' (see this). The surrounding factors listed there may be summed up into a few main factors of the ambient world, the observance of which generally is sufficient to incite our aquarium fishes to reproduce. The outer picture of the aquarium is less important for breeding than these factors. They include:

(a) THE WATER (see this), its composition, hardness, pH value, contents of salts and other additives, its state of motion (imitated in the aquarium by aeration or filtration), and the height of the water level.

(b) THE TEMPERATURE (see this), in which not only its level, but also its fluctuations and constancy may be of importance.

(c) THE BOTTOM SOIL (see this).

(d) THE LIGHTING (see this) of the aquarium, e.g. sunlight, the daily rhythm.

(e) THE LOCATION OF THE AQUARIUM (see this), for instance, protection against disturbances, commotions, etc.

(f) THE PLANTING (see this), its distribution and density, as well as its usefulness as spawning substratum.

(g) FEEDING (see this), which is especially important and which needs exact planning and thought.

(h) THE CHOICE of harmonizing pairs of breeders, and of the fish community.

Naturally all breeding aquaria have to be kept strictly free of pests. As such we have to mention: snails, worms, aquatic insects, micro-crustaceans, hydras, and an excess of unicellulars. The eggs and fry of many tropicals are especially sensitive to just the latter. Therefore the hobbyist has to endeavor to keep the water for such species as free as possible of infusoria. Very soft water with a slightly acid pH value retards the development of bacteria and unicellulars, or prevents it completely. Furthermore breeding fishes have to be protected against all disturbances. One should eventually glue transparent paper on the aquarium in order to avoid these.

The manner of living of a species decides whether the breeders should be set up alone for breeding, or in communities. No general rules can be given as to this. In some cases one has also to take special measures to accustom the sexes to each other, for instance, by separating them with glass panes. The set-up of the breeding aquarium (see this) is a consequence of the manner of living of the fishes, and of the end at which one aims in breeding. If possible, the sexes should be kept separated until they reach their full development. Nothing is more detrimental than premature mating. The fishes should, therefore, be completely mature. This is true not only for live-bearing Tooth Carps, but for all fishes. Furthermore obeying this principle has the added advantage that one can grade the matured specimens as to their breeding qualities. A frequently-seen error, too, is that people induce fishes to reproduce constantly without pauses. Tropical fishes also have their spawning periods and need to rest in the interim.

When rearing the young one has to consider that their vital needs may be different from those of their parents. This may affect the water, warmth, etc., but always the food (see YOUNG FRY). As a principle one should never rear more fry than one can feed, lodge, and dispose of. The use of methods that aim at mass breeding is only warranted if there is a real demand for the produced specimens. Otherwise one should restrict to happenstance breeding which places less strain on quantity than on quality and on biological observation. For aquaristics in general it is better to breed many species in good quality, than to mass-produce a few of them at the cost of good quality.

Furthermore one should also consider that too great numbers of fry, reared in insufficiently large containers hinder each others' growth. The strong accumulation of organic waste products, the acute competition for food, and other still unexplained reasons retard their development. This is seen, for instance, in those species that are remarkable for their ornamental fins. Sail-fin Mollies, e.g. seem to develop the high dorsal better if kept solitary. It is also senseless to want to force the growth of so called 'runts', that is weak and valueless specimens.

Summing up: in natural breeding it is necessary to work toward a quality breeding and to breed only the best, healthiest and most vigorous fishes, typical of their species, by means of correct selection and control. The hereditary inclinations have to be led to their full development by optimum conditions learned from nature.

Artificial breeding can only succeed when it starts with species which are appropriate for it.

The first aim has to be the isolation of hereditarily firm strains, that is strains that show one or more desirable qualities in full development constantly through all generations. When hereditary firmness has been reached, the otherwise quite difficult problems of the breeder become easier, and these stocks may also be reproduced as pure lines in greater quantities, naturally under constant control.

In order to obtain such stocks (races) it is necessary at first to establish a certain breeding aim and to act accordingly. From the descendants one always selects and reproduces those specimens which correspond most closely to the breeding aim. Of course in this one has to take special steps in order to prevent premature or undesirable matings. This includes, for instance, exact keeping of records, separate rearing of sexes and generations, controlled matings. Breeding is done exclusively through inbreeding. Desirable qualities may be crossed in from strange strains. Inbreeding between brothers and sisters, and eventual re-crossing with parents may cause the desired qualities to appear, even when they are inherited in a hidden, recessive state. One has to notice that many of these qualities are inherited by only one of the sexes. Thus in the Guppy, for instance, certain ornamental characteristics are passed on exclusively through the female, even if they show visibly only on the male. Some qualities act dominantly, others recessively. A comprehensive discussion of all these questions would not be possible in this book. Breeding on a scientific basis is still recent in aquaristics and the observations that are available up to this date are too uncertain to permit publishing them comprehensively. Therefore it is advisable to follow up the corresponding information in aquaristic literature.

breeding tanks: Aquaria that are set up exclusively for breeding, with a view to rearing the greatest possible number of young. A biotopic aquarium, e.g. in which fishes reproduce occasionally, could not be called a breeding tank for this reason.

According to the needs of each case, one sometimes chooses very large, sometimes very small tanks for breeding purposes. In the latter case the tanks serve only as mating tanks, while the fry later on are reared in special nursery tanks.

The water level of the breeding tank in general has to be kept as low as possible. A bottom soil is not always necessary, and sometimes even harmful. Often a covering of the bottom with bigger gravel stones, glass grilles, sphagnum, or, in the case of bottom-spawners, with fine sand, will be sufficient. Tanks without a bottom covering should be set on heat-preserving bases (paper or felt), in order to prevent cooling of the bottom area on which eggs or fry repose.

Planting is restricted to the necessary minimum. Put in only those plants that are used as a spawning substratum or as hiding places. They may also be replaced by artificial means, such as, for instance, green nylon mops. The composition of the water depends on the requirements of the fish species, and so does temperature.

The location of the breeding tank has to be carefully planned. Some species of fishes need sunlight, others shun it. One has also to consider that all handling has to be convenient, such as, for instance, inserting separating panes, catching the parents for removal after spawning, etc. This is especially important when the tanks are located on stands, in heating cases, etc.

Brehm, Alfred Edmund: 1829-1884. Well-known zoologist and explorer. Among other things, founder of the Berlin (Germany) Aquarium, and author of the famous popularized zoological work 'Brehm's Tierleben'. Among others, he edited the second edition of Rossmaessler's 'Das Suesswasser-Aquarium' (The Freshwater aquarium). Brehm wrote his very readable books following the spirit of his time, which tended strongly to humanize animals.

brevipedicellatus: With short flower stalk.
— *Echinodorus.*

brevis: Short.
— *Pyrrhulina.*
— *Rachovia.*

Brine Shrimp, the: see ARTEMIA

SALINA.

Bristle-Mouth, the: see ANCISTRUS CIRRHOSUS.

Broad-Finned Mollie, the: see MOLLIENISIA LATIPINNA.

Broad-Leaved Sagittaria, the: see SAGITTARIA PLATYPHYLLA.

Broad-Striped Characin, the: see NEOLEBIAS ANSORGEI.

broccae: After a personal name. — *Phoxinopsis*.

Brochis, type of the genus

Brochis: Sling, referring to the structure of the barbels.

South American genus belonging to the sub-family of the CORYDORADINAE (see this), within the family of the Armored Catfishes or *Callichthyidae*, which differs from the closely-related genus *Corydoras* by its armored snout and higher body, which is also more compressed laterally. The fishes possess accessory breathing organs.

— **coeruleus** Cope: The Emerald Brochis.

SHAPE: The body is compact and relatively high, the head big. D I/10, A I/6-7. The adipose fin is supported by a hard spine. Length up to 3¼″.

COLOR: Brownish-green to vivid emerald green, sometimes with spot designs, the belly ochre-yellow.

RANGE: Tropical South America.

CARE AND BREEDING: Keep them like the species of *Corydoras*. Absolutely peaceful towards smaller fishes. While coming up for air, the fish often stick their whole heads out of the water. Breeding has not yet been successful.

Bronze Corydoras, the: see CORYDORAS AENEUS.

Bronze Girardinus, the: see GIRARDINUS METALLICUS.

brood care: The more or less intensive watching and guarding of spawn and fry by both parents or by only one of them, as also exerted by many aquarium fishes. Care for brood pertains to the innate, that is hereditary, behavior of the fishes, and can therefore suffer only marginal influences by experiences in life, for which reason it generally is extremely difficult to change. Partially aquarium fishes continue to exert their hereditary care for their brood for generations even in the aquarium, despite the fact that many of the primary conditions have ceased to exist, thus making the care for the brood meaningless. It is impossible to assert whether a certain slackness in the care for the brood found among aquarium fishes represents a phenomenon of adaptation to these changed conditions, or whether it is based on individual disposition and would also have happened in their natural state.

The simplest case of care for brood consists of fanning water over the spawn by means of body movements, of keeping the eggs clean, and perhaps of protecting them against very small enemies. Often, too, the hatched fry are aided through the difficult period of development immediately after hatching (continuation of embryonal development outside the egg shell). In especially highly developed cases of care for a brood the fry are watched and guarded for weeks, even after being fully developed. The specific manner of caring for the brood that is peculiar to it, is typical of the species—it may coincide in general terms for whole groups, but it may also differ completely even for closely related species. Care for the brood includes certain individual acts, such as choice of the breeding site, cleaning it, building of nests, typical movements of body or fins in order to create a current in the water, movements with which to inform the fry of dangers or food, etc. According to which one of the two parents exerts the care for the brood, we speak of paternal, maternal, or parental families. Parental and maternal families keep together for much longer times. The paternal family generally dissolves soon.

Brook Lamprey, the: see PETROMYZON PLANERI.

Brook Shrimp, the: see GAMMARUS PULEX.

Brown Gourami, the: see SPHAERICHTHYS OSPHROMENOIDES.

Brown Pencilfish, the: see NANNOSTOMUS BECKFORDI ARIPIRANGENSIS.

Brown Rivulus, the: see RIVULUS CYLINDRACEUS.

Bruening, Christian: Famous German aquarist. Born November 5, 1861. Teacher in Hamburg, early in contact with importing mariners. In 1897 co-founder of the 'Salvinia' society in Hamburg. 1914-1916 chairman of the first Federation of German Aquarium Societies. From 1911 to 1921 editor of the '*Wochenschrift fuer Aquarien- und Terrarienkunde*'. Author of the well-known '*Ichthyologisches Handlexikon*' (Handy Ichthyological Dictionary), a first attempt at writing a book on the (then) known aquarium fishes in the form of a dictionary.

Brycon: Biter, teeth gnasher.

South American genus of Characins pertaining to the family of the CHARACIDAE (see this). Big to medium-sized fishes of elongated, oval body structure, strongly compressed laterally, especially toward the rear end of the body. The

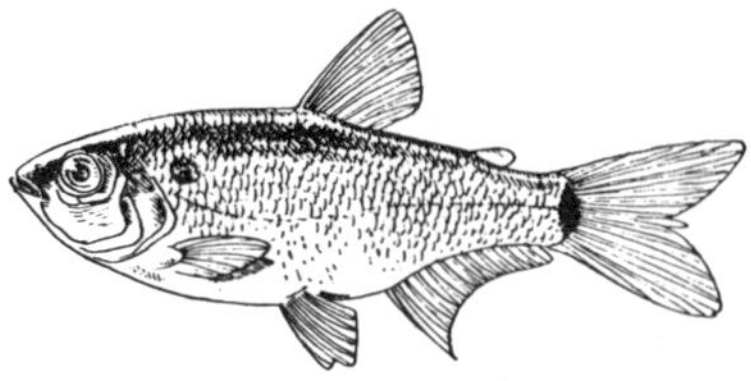

Brycon, type of the genus

anal fin is longer than the dorsal. Widely scattered over South America, from the La Plata in the South to Guatemala in the North, with more than 35 species.

— falcatus Mueller and Troschel: SHAPE: As per description of the genus. The wide mouth is terminal D 11, A 18-19. The edge of the anal fin is arched in crescent shape. The fish carry an adipose fin. The scales are very small. Length up to 10″. COLOR: Uniformly silver colored. RANGE: Guiana.

CARE AND BREEDING: So far the species is little known. It has rarely been imported as, due to its simple color, it offers little enticement for keeping it in the aquarium. Give it a roomy tank with sufficient central space for swimming around. The need for warmth is not very great, 64-73° F being sufficient. Since the fish are quite predatory, they should never be kept in communities with smaller fishes. Breeding has not yet succeeded.

Bryconalestes: From Greek: 'the miller', referring to its teeth.

African genus of Characins pertaining to the family of the CHARACIDAE (see this), with about 12 known species. These are slender, very elongated, laterally compressed school fishes, with a rounded belly edge. The intermediate jaws are equipped with just a few, but strong teeth. The lateral line is complete and slightly arched. The fish always show an adipose fin. The mouth opening is relatively big.

The fishes need spacious, well-covered tanks since they are lively swimmers and jumpers. In general they need some warmth. So far breeding seems not to have been achieved for any of the species.

— chaperi Sauvage: The Green Characin.

SHAPE: As per description of the genus. D 9, A 16-18. Length up to 3½″. The fundamental hue is green with a strong glitter, the fins are slightly reddish. The stripe on the caudal peduncle runs exactly along the center of this, which helps us to differentiate even young specimens from *B. longipinnis*.

RANGE: Africa, from the Gold Coast to Cameroon, especially in flowing waters.

CARE AND BREEDING: The tank has to be chosen according to the size of the fish. Besides sufficient plants, they should have sufficient space for swimming around. A plant covering on the surface may help to dampen the inclinations to jump shown by this species. But even if this is present, the aquaria should always be kept well covered. Breeding unknown.

— longipinnis (Guenther): The Long-Finned Characin.

SHAPE: As per description of genus. Young specimens are even more elongated than older ones. D 10, A 21-23. The males are rather big. Length up to 4¾″.

COLOR: A very shiny silver color, the eyes with a luminous red iris, on the lower part of the caudal peduncle a short, deep-black band which continues on the tail fin. The fins of the males are partly reddish, those of the females being yellowish. The dorsal of the male is extended.

RANGE: In flowing waters of West Africa.

CARE AND BREEDING: As per description of the genus.

Bryophyta: Mosses.

Sub-division of the ARCHEGONIATAE (see this), which includes only few aquatic plants. Mosses generally live on dry land, only few species having adapted to life in water. They lack true roots, in place of which they show only root-like cell threads, so-called rhizoids. Important to aquaristics are the families of the RICCIACEAE (see this) or Crystal Worts, and the FONTINALACEAE (see this) or Spring Mosses, as well as the Feather Moss AMBLYSTEGIUM (see this), and the Java Moss VESICULARIA DUBYANA (see this).

Bryozoa: Moss Animals.

Class of aquatic animals that form colonies and belong to the phylum of the *Tentaculata*. In the aquarium they are noticed as ramified, slightly brown formations, which often settle on glass panes and on plants. They adhere to a substratrum and form long-stretched tube systems, from which the real animals protrude with long, double-horseshoe shaped crowns of cilia, which they pull back lightning-quick when touched. The crown of cilia sweeps in the animals' food, which consists of algae and detritus. A well-known species is *Plumatella repens*. Each individual consists of two parts: the tube-shaped housing the walls of which are made firm by inclusions of chitin or of calcareous substances, the second part being the so-called polypid.

The *Bryozoans* show a very interesting manner of reproduction, being hermaphroditical and autofecundate. The eggs develop within the body of the specimens into a ciliate larva which, being made up of up to twenty individuals, already constitutes a colony. This swarms around for some hours, settling down firmly thereafter. Besides this there is also an asexual reproduction through budding, which

Bryozoa colony

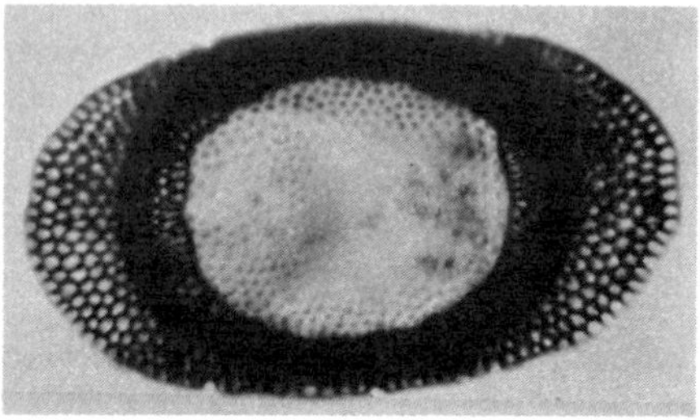

Statoblast of a Bryozoan, Plumatella

represents the general rule. From time to time they develop permanent germ-cells, which are called statoblasts, inside their bodies. These cling to the feathers of waterfowl by means of a crown of hooklets and are disseminated in this manner. They are able to withstand frosts and droughts.

Despite the fact that externally the *B.* are extremely similar to minute *Hydras*, they are absolutely harmless in the aquarium.

Bubble Snails: see PHYSIDAE.

Bubbly Water Trap, the: see ALDROVANDA VESICULOSA.

buchholzi: After the German naturalist Buchholz.

— *Pantodon.*

bulk substances in fish food: Chitin shells and hard components of the food of fishes, which have no nutritional value in themselves, but which nevertheless contribute considerably to the utilization of the food by giving work to and stimulating the digestive organs. When feeding permanently with rich, soft foodstuffs (e.g. artificial food, *enchytrae*, etc.), the lack of these causes digestive disturbances and tends toward overfattening of the fishes.

Bumblebee Fish, the: see BRACHYGOBIUS DORIAE.

Bunocephalidae: Banjo Catfishes. Family pertaining to the sub-order of the Catfish-like Fishes or SILUROIDEA (see this), with completely naked skin. The body is short and compact, especially wide and flattened at the head and shoulder belt.

The family is found exclusively in fresh waters of the north-east of South America, with about 10 known species.

Genera, among others, BUNOCEPHALUS (see this).

Bunocephalus: With humped head.

South American genus belonging to the family of the Banjo Catfishes or BUNOCEPHALIDAE (see this), characterized by the remarkably thick head, the narrow rear part of the body, and the completely naked skin. Head and sides carry rows of little warts.

— **kneri** Steindachner: The Banjo Catfish.

SHAPE: As per description of the genus. The mouth is terminal to slightly subterminal, with three pairs of barbels, the eyes are very small. Length up to 8″.

COLOR: Light-colored base with irregular, darker mottlings. The species is very variable, besides which it possibly might only be a sub-species of *B. bicolor* Steindachner, or even identical with same.

RANGE: From the Amazon region to the La Plata.

CARE AND BREEDING: This is one of the species of Catfishes which like to dig themselves in. For this reason the bottom of their tank should be soft and sparsely planted, but the aquarium should contain plenty of hiding places among roots, etc. The tanks should be in accordance with the size of the fish, but should never be too small. Being a twilight fish, the Banjo only leaves its hiding place at twilight when it becomes relatively lively. The fish is not considered as greatly in need of warmth, 68-72° F may be sufficient. Food, preferably small bottom-dwelling animals, is taken from the bottom. So far the species has not been bred in captivity.

butis: After the native name. — *Eleotris*.

Butomaceae: Very variably-shaped, perennial swamp and aquatic plants, which either possess robust root-stocks which creep in the soil, or else short, compact, vertical ones, and occasionally also thin, richly-ramified roots. The leaves are bottom-standing, rising steeply, very variably shaped, or, in one case, there are oval to round, submerged, floating, or aerial leaves which stand on long, creeping stems. The flowers are hermaphroditic, generally in umbellated inflorescences. Scattered over all continents, but each species limited to a definite region.

Genera: BUTOMUS, LIMNOCHARIS, HYDROCLEIS (see these).

Butomus: Genus belonging to the family of the BUTOMACEAE (see this). *Butomus umbellatus* Linné, the Water-Gladiolus, is a pretty, beautifully blooming, perennial swamp plant with a thick rhizome which creeps horizontally in the soil. The bottom-standing, lineal, unstemmed leaves, which are a little fluted on the upper side, grow even submerged if the water is deep enough, but the plant does not bloom under such circumstances. Not favorable for the indoor aquarium, but very beautiful for the outdoor tank or pool.

Butomus umbellatus

butterflies: see LEPIDOPTERA.

Butterfly Barb, the: see BARBUS (PUNTIUS) HULSTAERTI.

Butterfly Cichlid: see APISTOGRAMMA RAMIREZI.

Butterfly Fish, the: see PANTODON BUCHHOLZI.

Butterfly Fishes: see PANTODONTIDAE.

C.: Abbreviation for Caudal Fin (tail).

Cabomba: After an Indian name. Genus of very beautiful subaquatic plants belonging to the family of the Water Lilies or NYMPHACEAE (see this). They are perennial plants, with finely-feathered leaves, which possess more or less ramified stems and soft, dense roots. During the blooming period the upper tips of the stems develop Water Lily-like floating leaves over which the white or yellow flowers rise above the surface. Adapting to the water level, the plants may grow very long. The submerged leaves, the

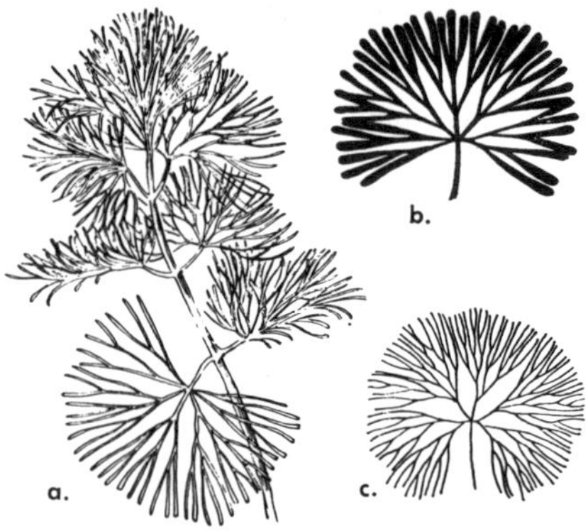

Cabomba a. Type of the genus b. C. caroliniana c. C. aquatica

contour of which is circular, stand paired opposite around the stem.

All species of *Cabomba* are beautiful, but quite sensitive plants, which demand loving care. The bottom soil should be mixed from coarse sand and weathered clay in a proportion of 1:1, the plants are very sensitive to disturbance of all kinds, for which reason they should not be kept in tanks with fishes which are very lively or which disturb them unnecessarily in any other manner. Furthermore they should only be transplanted when it becomes unavoidable. The fine-feathered and delicate leaves should be protected against dirt and infestations by algae. Mulm likes to settle in the leaf feathers and impedes them from breathing and assimilating.

Reproduction in the aquarium can only be achieved by planting twigs, for which the long shoots are cut off and stuck into the soil where they put out roots very quickly.

— **aquatica** Aublet:

SHAPE: As per description of the genus. The species has very finely-feathered leaves.

RANGE: In small waters and flood puddles of the rivers from Southern Mexico to Central Brazil.

CULTIVATION: As per description of the genus. The plants need soft water not above 6 DH. For this reason the danger of infestation with algae, to which it is very sensitive, is smaller. Therefore it should not be exposed to too intense sunlight. Temperatures around 77° F, in winter not below 64° F.

— **australis** Spegazzini: The Argentinian Cabomba.

GENERALITIES: This beautiful and relatively hardy species is especially adequate for semi-warm aquaria.

SHAPE: As per description of the genus. The species resembles *C. caroliniana*, but differs from this by its smaller leaves, which are more finely-feathered, differing also by the reddish tips of the shoots. The stems, the underside of the floating leaves, and the flower stems feel slippery to the touch. In contrast to *C. caroliniana*, the flower stems may be slightly thickened.

RANGE: Argentina, Uruguay, and Chile.

CULTIVATION: As per description of the genus. The species does not need very much warmth. In summer 64-72° F will be sufficient, while in winter it needs a rest period at 46-50° F. If the plants are kept too warm in winter, they grow stunted and finally die. It is best to hibernate them at room temperature.

— **caroliniana** A. Gray: Carolinian Fanwort.

SHAPE: As per description of the genus. The leaves are not quite as finely divided, but a little broader. There is a sub-species (*C.c. var. pulcherrima*) with reddish leaves, but which only keeps this color under intense lighting from above.

RANGE: In nearly the same regions as *C. aquatica*, but its range goes a little farther north and south than the former.

CULTIVATION: As per description

of the genus. The plant may be kept at 64-72° F in summer and at 59-64° F in winter.

cacatuoides: Cockatoo-like, after the spines of the dorsal fin, which look like a feather crest.
— *Apistogramma.*

calabaricus: From the Calabar Coast, in West Africa.
— *Aphyosemion.*

Calamoichthys: Finlet Eels.
Genus belonging to the family of the Finlet Fishes or POLYPTERIDAE (see this). Eel-shaped fishes, which possess diamond-shaped, enamel-covered fins. The mouth opening is very broad. Jaws and palate are covered with small comb teeth. Two nasal openings, the front one equipped with a tentacle, on each side of the snout. The fish possess a lateral line. Each of the dorsal fins is equipped with only one articulated ray, and there are no ventrals. The swimming bladder is connected with the oesophagus and is used as an accessory breathing organ. The best-known species is *C. calabaricus.*

— calabaricus (J. A. Smith): The Finlet Eel.
SHAPE: As per description of the genus. D divided into 7-13 individual fins, A 9-14 rays. Length about 14″.
COLOR: Shiny yellowish to greenish without any special design. The male has 12-14, the female 9-12 rays in the anal fin. During the spawning period the anal of the male grows thick.
CARE AND BREEDING: The Finlet Eels are predators which only eat moving live foods. They glide snake-like like all Eels, but are also able to 'run' along the bottom by means of the pectoral fins. It is true that they are twilight and nocturnal fish, but will also show themselves in the aquarium after they are duly domesticated. In their home country they bury themselves in the mud in case of drought, and

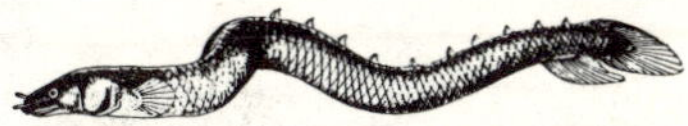

Calamoichthys calabaricus

are also able to leave their home waters in case of need. The fish need warmth, 73-82° F being advisable. Nothing is known about their reproduction.

calamus: see ACORUS.

Calanoidea: Order belonging to the class of the Rowing Feet or COPEPODA (see this), which among others includes the well-known genus *Diaptomus.* The representatives of this order form an important source of food for whales and fishes, being generally found floating free in water, in big swarms. In contrast with many members of the order *Cyclopoidea* (which belong to the same class), the *Calanoidea* are harmless.

Caldesia: After the Italian botanist Caldesi.
Plant genus belonging to the family of the Frog Spoons or ALISMATACEAE (see this).

— parnassifolia (Bassi) Parlatore: The Heart-Leaf Frog Spoon.
A perennial swamp plant, scattered over Central Europe, South Asia, Northern Australia, and Madagascar, being found in standing waters of all kinds. The primary leaves are ribbon-shaped, up to 12″ long, remain submerged, and are very sensitive. These are followed by simple floating leaves, which finally are substituted by the heart-shaped, final floating leaves. These show 5-15 nervures on the underside. The inflorescence rises above the surface with 3-6 verticils of flowers. The plant is sometimes offered commercially as a species of *Echinodorus* or of *Sagittaria.* When cultivated indoors, instead of flowers on the flower stems there

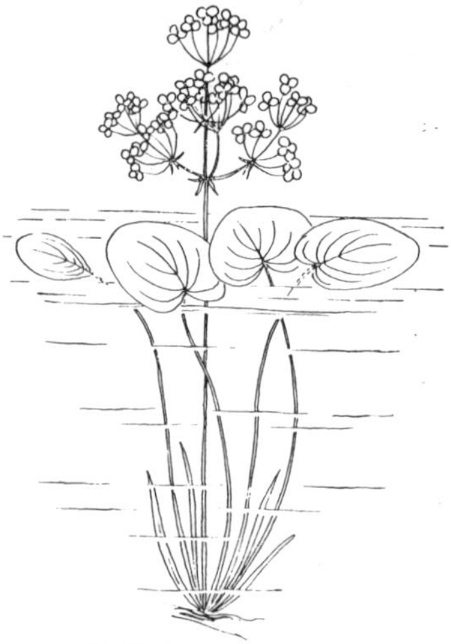

Caldesia parnassifolia

grow leaf buds which fall off in autumn and may be used to get the plants to reproduce.

Calla palustris Linné: The Swamp Calla.

A pretty swamp plant, belonging to the family of the Aaron's Rod Plants or ARACEAE (see this), scattered over the temperate regions of Europe, Siberia, East Asia, and North America. It possesses vividly green, heart-shaped leaves, and a typical flower sheath which is green

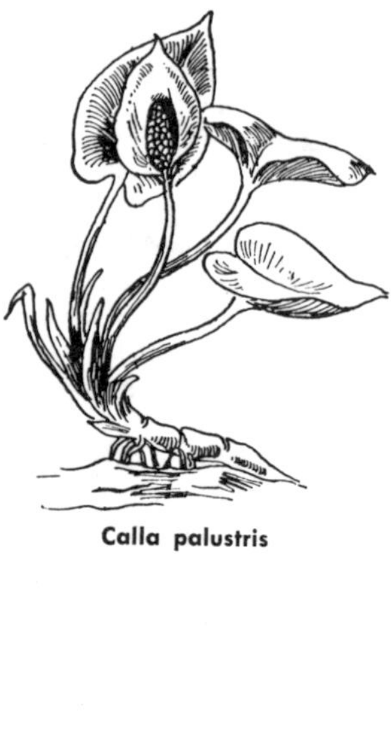

Calla palustris

on the outside and white on the inside. It is adequate for the outdoor pools only, and even in this only for the edges, since the depth of the water in which it stands should not exceed 2″. Reproduction through division of the root stock. The red berries are poisonous! Found on moors, in great ponds, and in swamps.

Callichthyidae: Callused Catfishes. Family belonging to the sub-order of the Catfish-like or SILUROIDEA (see this). These Catfishes are characterized by strong armor, which consists of two big rows of bony plates, the edges of each plate overlapping with the next one. The adipose fin is supported by a strong bony fin ray. The small, subterminal mouth carries one pair of barbels on the upper jaw and one or two pairs on the lower one. The jaws are either equipped with weak teeth, or else toothless. The swimming bladder which is covered by a bony casing, is divided in two. Callused Catfishes have accessory breathing which makes use of the intestine as an auxiliary organ. All the species live in fresh water in tropical or sub-tropical South America, coming from slowly-flowing or standing waters, puddles,

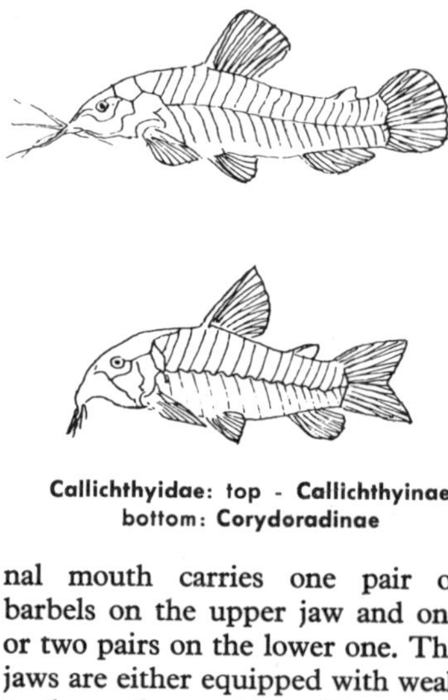

Callichthyidae: top - Callichthyinae
bottom: Corydoradinae

ditches, etc. Some species are able to migrate over land in case of drought, "walking" by means of the strong spines of the pectoral fins. The family is divided into two sub-families, the CALLICHTHYINAE (see this), and the CORYDORADINAE (see this).

Callichthyinae: Sub-family belonging to the family of the CALLICHTHYIDAE (see this), comprising the three genera CASCADURA, HOPLOSTERNUM (see this), and CALLICHTHYS (see this), of which so far only representatives of the latter two have been kept in the aquarium. The fishes live in rivers with muddy bottoms which do not flow too swiftly, in flood regions, swamps, etc. From time to time they come to the surface in order to get fresh air, since they are equipped with internal accessory respiration. They are able to move quite nimbly on land. This motion is interrupted by occasional rest periods after about 25″ have been covered. While doing this the fish often emit grating noises.

Some species are known to build nests from parts of plants which they cement together with an oral secretion which hardens gradually. The completed nest is kept at the surface by means of air bubbles gathered beneath it. The male is the builder of the nest and does not permit any females near it while building it. After the nest is ready, mating takes place outside it. In every mating a number of eggs is spawned into the ventral fins which are folded into a purse, fertilized there, and transferred to the nest by the female, which turns on its back to do so. The male puts foam bubbles around the eggs in the nest, and guards them. Every complete spawning yields several hundreds of eggs.

callichthys: Callused Catfish. — *Callichthys*.

Callichthys: South American genus pertaining to the Callused Catfishes or *Callichthyidae*, sub-family of the CALLICHTHYINAE (see this).

This genus differs from the other genera of the family by the manner in which the bone plates are interconnected. The body is a little elongated, but looks stout. The dorsal contour rises slightly at first, while the ventral one remains nearly straight. The head is broad, the upper jaws are toothless, the lower jaws being equipped with minute teeth, but only on the sides. The flanks are armored, while the belly is covered with a leathery skin, and the back is unarmored.

Callichthys callichthys

— **callichthys** (Linné): The Callused Catfish.

SHAPE: As per description of the genus. One pair of barbels on the upper jaws, and another one on the lower ones. The side plates number 26-29 for the upper row, and 25-28 for the lower one. D I/6, A I/5-6. The dorsal fin is positioned near the head, the well-developed adipose very far towards the tail. Length up to 7″.

COLOR: Gray to brown, without any designs. The male is a little more intensely colored, and the spines of his pectorals are a little thicker than those of the female.

RANGE: South America, East of the Andes, in quiet, fresh waters with muddy bottom.

CARE AND BREEDING: As per description of the genus and of the sub-family. This relatively lively species resembles the members of the genus *Corydoras*. It is hardy, but prefers live foods, which it takes from the bottom. Bigger specimens are reported to eat small fishes. No demands are made as to temperature: 64-72° F generally being sufficient. It seems that so far breeding has not succeeded fully. The only one to report more extensively on it some decades ago was SHELJUZHKO, of Kiev, Russia. His data agree with what so far is known about the reproduction of the Callused Catfish. The male guarded the eggs in a bubble nest. The fry grew very quickly. After three weeks they had already reached a length of $\frac{5}{8}''$-$\frac{3}{4}''$. They did indeed look like Catfishes, but showed no resemblance at all to their parents.

callipterus: With beautiful fins.
— *Barbus.*

callistus: With beautiful sail (fin).
— *Hyphessobrycon callistus.*

Callitrichaceae: Water Star Plants. *C.* are perennial plants. The delicate, light-green leaves are disposed oppositely around the stem. They are strongly ramified and form dense mats. The leaves are narrowly lineal, and many species form flat, round rosettes at the surface. The white flowers rise above the surface of the water. Generally the different species are quite hardy. They remain green even in winter, but need a rest period at quite low temperatures. Plants from flowing waters, especially from those of mountain regions, are inadequate for keeping in aquaria. Furthermore it is advisable not to put these frail plants into tanks with too active fishes. Sand mixed with some clay is a sufficient bottom soil. For transfer to the aquarium, take the plant bundles with their whole roots from the bottom of the water. They will simply

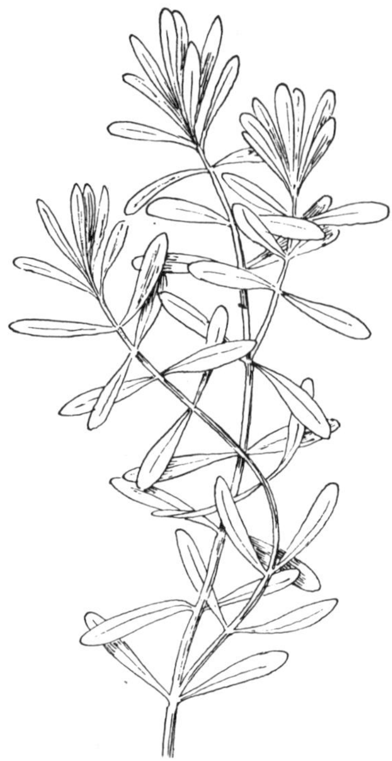

Callitriche autumnalis

continue growing there. In the aquarium reproduction is achieved exclusively through planted twigs. Generalizing, we have to state that most Water Stars are rather hard to keep in the aquarium, due to their sensitiveness to higher temperatures. If you are able to get your plants from shallow and warmer standing waters, it will be especially the Pond Water Star, *Callitriche stagnalis* Scopoli, or the Autumnal Water Star, *Callitriche autumnalis* Linné, which you will like best for keeping in your tanks.

callitrichoides: Similar to *Callitriche.*
— *Elodea.*

calliurum: With a beautiful tail.
— *Aphyosemion calliurum.*

callolepis: With beautiful scales.
— *Copeina.*

calva: With a bald head.
— *Amia.*

Cambarus affinis: The American River Crayfish.
Species belonging to the family of the River Crayfishes or ASTACIDAE (see this), which is a native North American, but was introduced in Germany in order to replenish the ranks of edible Crayfishes, since the native German ones had been decimated by a Crustacean disease. Today it is nearly the exclusive inhabitant of the North and Central German waters. The species diverges from the European River Crayfish, *Astacus fluviatilis*, by its smaller size, its more delicate body structure, and its smaller pincers. For information on the manner of keeping this species in the aquarium, see ASTACUS FLUVIATILIS.

cameronense: Coming from Cameroon.
— *Aphyosemion.*

Campanulaceae: Blue-Bell Plants.
Family belonging to the class of the Double-Germinating-Leaved Plants or DICOTYLEDONEAE (see this), with more than 1100 known species which are distributed mainly over the temperate and subtropical regions. Of this group only the genus LOBELIA (see this) has supplied aquarium plants.

camptacanthus: With bent back.
— *Barbus.*

canadensis: Canadian, coming from Canada.
— *Elodea.*

Canadian water pest: see ELODEA CANADENSIS.

Candelabrum plant: see CHARA.

Candelabrum plants: see CHARACEAE.

Cap Snails: see ANCYLUS.

carapo: After the native name.
— *Gymnotus.*

Carassiops: Similar to Carassius, the Crucian.
Genus belonging to the family of the Sleeper Gudgeons or ELEOTRIDAE (see this), the body of which is slightly higher than that of the other members of the family, and compressed laterally. Furthermore head and back are rounded, and not flat like that of the other Eleotrids. The relatively small mouth opening is slanted upwards. The fish possess two dorsal fins.

— **compressus** (Kraft): The Australian Sleeper Gudgeon.
SHAPE: As per description of the genus. D_1 VI-VII, D_2 I/9-10, A I/10-11. Length up to 6″.
COLOR: The species is very variable. Generally the males show designs composed of red dots and dashes on bluish-green base, and red stripes on the opercles, also showing a luminous blue spot at the insertion of the pectorals. Also the fins are very beautifully colored. During the spawning season the colors probably become considerably more vigorous. The female generally is a little paler.
RANGE: The coastal regions of Eastern Australia.
CARE AND BREEDING: This species needs big-sized tanks with good planting, fine-grained bottom soil, and rocks disposed as hiding places. Temperature 72-77° F. Despite not being pronouncedly predatory, the species prefers robust live foods, especially fishes. The fish are quite long-lived in the aquarium. There are reports on breedings in the indoors aquarium in Australia, but no particulars are known on this.

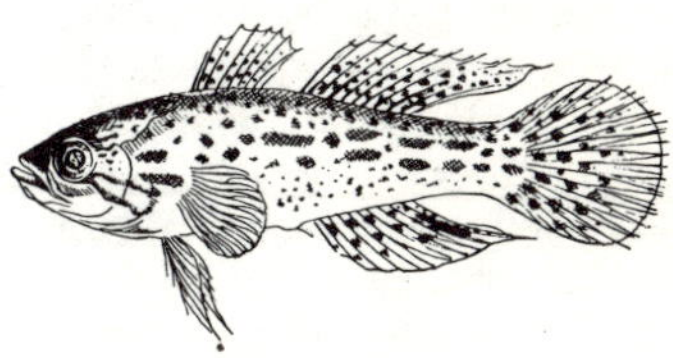

Carassiops compressus

Carassius: Derived from a Classical Greek fish name.

Genus of Carp-like fishes pertaining to the family of the CYPRINIDAE (see this). According to nutrition they are moderately elongated to high-bodied. Easily differentiated from the Carp and others by the fact that they have no barbels.

— auratus gibelio Bloch: The Gold Fish.

SHAPE: D 3/17, A 2/5-7. The species is similar to the preceding one, differing from it in some minute details in scales, fins, and colors. RANGE: In the same regions as *C. carassius*, but going East to the Amur. It is the original form of our Gold Fish.

The Gold Fish is a xanthoristic strain of *C. auratus gibelio*, which represents long years of selective breeding by the Chinese, and imported to Europe about 200 years ago as the first exotic ornamental fish. Initially it was generally kept in the so-called Goldfish Bowls. Today it has to a wide extent been displaced by other ornamental fishes, so that now it is only rarely found in the aquarium. However, the Gold Fish continues to be seen frequently in garden ponds, where it stands out due to its colors. The golden colorings may differ in hue, and there are also white and natural-colored specimens, as well as those that show differently colored spots.

The Chinese knew the Gold Fish already more than 1000 years ago, and kept it in porcelain bowls or in garden ponds. In the course of the centuries many color and shape strains were developed in China, and also in Japan, where the fish reached coming from China. The first Gold Fish came to England in the year 1691. At about the same period—probably together with Chinese porcelain—they arrived also in Portugal spreading to the other countries from this starting point. They have even grown wild in some places. While the simpler forms of Gold Fish have become relatively cheap due to mass breeding, choice specimens of the different strains are still today considered expensive luxuries. This holds especially true for the Asiatic countries.

Among others, we find the following artificially bred strains in commerce:

The Comet: A simple form of Gold fish, but with the fins more or less enlarged.

Shubunkin: Similar to the Comet, but the generally scaleless body beautifully colored (red, blue, black, white, yellow, spotted).

Veiltail: The strain which has moved farthest from the original form, both in shape and fins. Doubtlessly the most beautiful of the strains. Despite the fact that today it no more enjoys the same popularity as 30 or 40 years ago, it cannot be denied that an aquarium with high-grade veiltails has a high esthetic value. There are certain breeding norms for body structure and fins, which determine the value of the fish. The body should be as compact and rounded as possible, the tail fin longer than the body, with two pairs of veils, which should be separated in the middle. The big dorsal fin must be carried held high, and the other fins too must be long and harmoniously developed. There may be scales present or not. Many color hues are possible, even spotted ones (Tiger Veiltails).

One needs biggish tanks if the fish are to show their real beauty. Set them up as you would do it for the Common Gold Fish, but without rocks or sharp-edged objects on which the fish could tear their fins. Breeding is achieved in the same manner as for the Gold

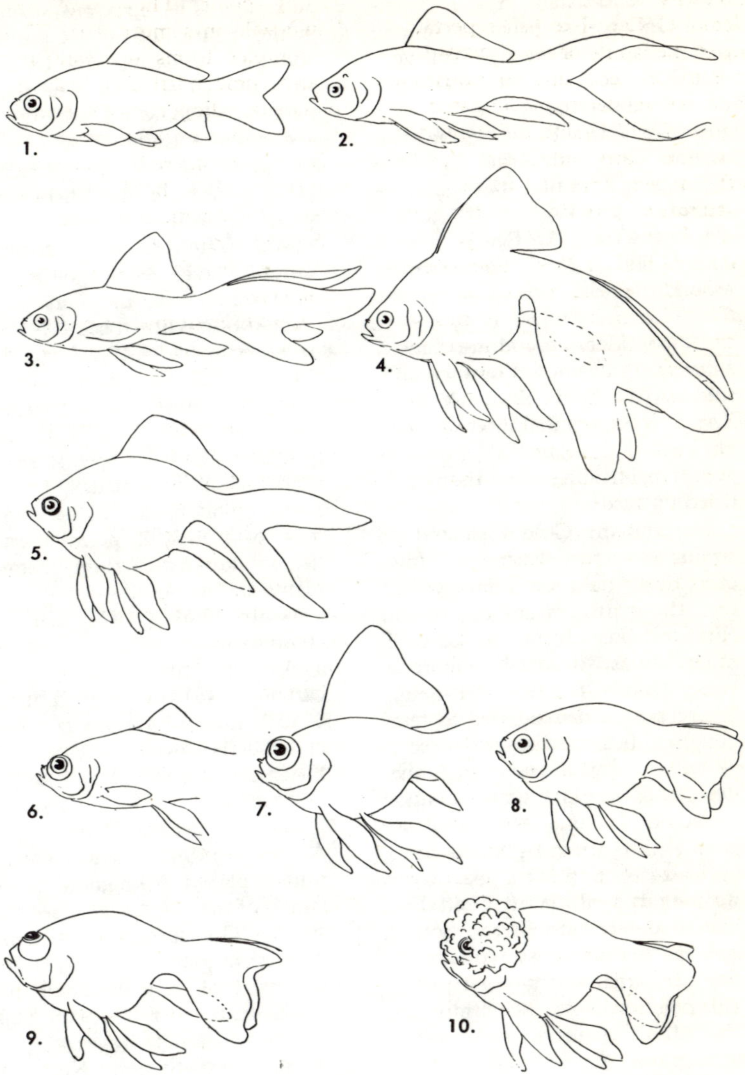

Common Goldfish types — 1. Common 2. Comet 3. Fantail 4. Veiltail (Ryukin) 5. Nymph 6. Telescope 7. Telescope Veiltail 8. Eggfish 9. Celestial 10. Lionhead.

Fish. The growing fry must be subject to constant careful selection. Only a few specimens among the numerous progeny—but very valuable ones, at that—reach the demanded standards.

The Egg Fish: Body egg-shaped, without dorsal fin, the fins little developed, double—but short—tail fin.

The Lion Head: An Egg Fish with sponge-like skin excrescences around the head.

The Telescope Fish: The eyes protrude considerably and are slanted sideways or upward. Commercially sold also as the Telescope-Veiltail.

The Sky-Gazer: The body shaped like that of the Egg Fish, but with greatly protruding eyes, the pupils tilted upwards.

Keeping the Gold Fish and its strains is extremely simple. However, this should not induce you to feed the worthless ant pupae (ant eggs) or bread crumbs. Like all other fishes, it needs vigorous, varied foods for its well-being. There are no demands as to temperature, but the fish feel best at 57-68° F. If possible avoid higher degrees of warmth. Good aeration is advisable. As bottom cover choose thin, round-grained sand, at least for a thick upper layer, washing it well, as all Gold Fish like to dig around in the bottom soil. For the same reason do not use fine-feathered, easily-soiled plants. All plants should be firmly anchored, the planting site covered with gravel.

They can be bred in bigger indoor aquaria, but this is generally done in outdoor tanks. The fish should hibernate cold, in order to give them a real rest period. This should be observed especially for the bred strains. SD: the anus of the male is lightly dented in, that of the female arches outwards. In spring the males show a knotty rash on the opercles and on the insertion of the pectorals. The eggs are scattered in the manner of most Cyprinids, after violent chasing. The fry hatch after about one week. For rearing them see CYPRINIDAE.

— **carassius** Linné: The Crucian.
SHAPE: D 3/17-19, A 3/7. Length up to about 8″. Yellowish-brown to shiny greenish.
RANGE: The temperate zones of Europe and Asia, going East approximately to the Lena River.
CARE AND BREEDING: see CYPRINUS.

carbon dioxide CO_2: A colorless, slightly acid, gas which does not burn, and causes harm to animal organisms if inhaled in large quantities. It is of special significance to all live beings, for, exhaled by animals and serving as food to plants, it permits establishing an equilibrium between plants and animals.

carbonic acid HCO_3: Chemical combination resulting as a weak acid from the introduction of carbon dioxide in water. The salts of carbonic acid are the carbonates and bicarbonates. See BIOGENETIC DECALCIFICATION; HARDNESS OF WATER.

Cardamine lyrata: Bunge.
A very beautiful and delicate cold water plant, belonging to the family of the CRUCIFERAE (see this).
SHAPE: The species is perennial. The stems rise up vertically from the creeping and ramified rootstock, and generally carry small, rounded, alternate leaves.
RANGE: East Siberia, North and East China, Japan, in places that are similar to those where we find our Pennywort, growing both submergedly and emergedly.
CULTIVATION: The plant is nearly always cultivated submergedly in the aquarium, but does not bloom under such circumstances. Coarse sand mixed with clay is a sufficient bottom soil. Too high degrees of

Cardamine lyrata

warmth easily make it degenerate. Reproduction is achieved by dividing the root stock, or by planting twigs which put out roots quickly. It does well under the open sky and may be cultivated as a swamp plant with success. Protect the plant against snails, as these like to eat the delicate leaves. *C. lyrata* likes a well-lighted location and needs sunlight and temperatures between 59-68° F for blooming. The plants grow bigger in soft water.

Cardinal Lobelia: see LOBELIA CARDINALIS.

cardinalis: Red like a cardinal's hat.
— *Hyphessobrycon.*
— *Lobelia.*

Carnegiella: Dimunitive, honoring Miss M. Carnegie.

Genus of Hatchet Fishes belonging to the family of the GASTEROPELECIDAE (see this). It diverges from the other members of the family by the shape of its teeth. There is no adipose fin.

— **marthae** Myers: The Pygmy Hatchet Fish.

A very small and delicate species with the typical body shape of all Hatchet Fishes. Length up to about $1\frac{3}{8}''$.

COLOR: A simple shiny silver.

ORIGIN: Calmly-flowing, partly-planted waters of the Amazon and the Orinoco region.

Keep them at 72-82° F. The species likes shadows. Reproduction unknown.

— **myersi** Fernandez-Ypez: Myers' Hatchet Fish.

The smallest and most elongated species of this genus, which reaches a length of about $\frac{7}{8}''$. It is shiny-silvery with weakly indicated little bluish-black dots on the belly region.

ORIGIN: Peru, caught in a creek near Yurimaguas. Temperature 72-82° F. Reproduction unknown.

— **strigata** (Guenther): The Striped Hatchet Fish.

SHAPE: As per description of the genus (see GASTEROPELECIDAE). Also this species is quite slender. D 10, A 25-30. The lateral line is incomplete, or completely lacking. Length up to $1\frac{3}{4}''$.

COLOR: Shiny silvery to yellowish base with irregular dark stripes and designs.

RANGE: Guiana and the Central and Lower Amazon, also in coastal regions. The species generally lives in small jungle creeks and the outer waters of rivers, especially near plant thickets.

CARE AND BREEDING: Despite being a surface fish, this pretty species often remains among plants in the central reaches of the water. To show it at its best, it needs sufficient space for swimming around, especially near the surface. The fish are peaceful, adequate for communities, and long-lived, liking sunlight. Nutrition poses no problem, dry foods are taken willingly, but have to float on the surface. Occasionally they will also take food from the bottom, for which the fish take on an oblique position. In free nature their food probably consists of flying insects. Their water should be clear, maintaining a temperature of 75-86° F. KLUGE has lately succeeded in breeding the species, having verified the report of INNES according to which the males dance flutteringly around the females. The small eggs are spawned with the pair lying side by side, 1-4 eggs per act of spawning, into fine-feathered plants. The parents prey on the spawn. Rearing is similar to that of most other Characins. Having obtained 36 fry, KLUGE gave proof that the species is breedable.

carnivorous plants: Group of partly unrelated plants which have developed the ability to trap insects and other small animals, dissolving them and feeding on their proteins by means of a digestive process. In case of lack of adequate animal nourishment they are also able to feed in the manner which is conventional for plants, but the additional trapping of animals is necessary as an adaptation to soils which are poor in nitrogen, or to other unfavorable conditions. Important for aquaristics are UTRICULARIA (see this), and ALDROVANDA (see this).

Carolinian Water Fern: see AZOLLA CAROLINIANA.

caroliniana: Carolinian, coming from Carolina.

— *Azolla.*

— *Cabomba.*

Carp, the: see CYPRINUS CARPIO.

Carps, the: see CYPRINIDAE.

carpio: The fruit, the harvest.

— *Cyprinus.*

Carp-like: see CYPRINOIDEA.

Carp louse: see ARGULUS.

Cartilaginous Ganoids, the: see CHONDROSTEI.

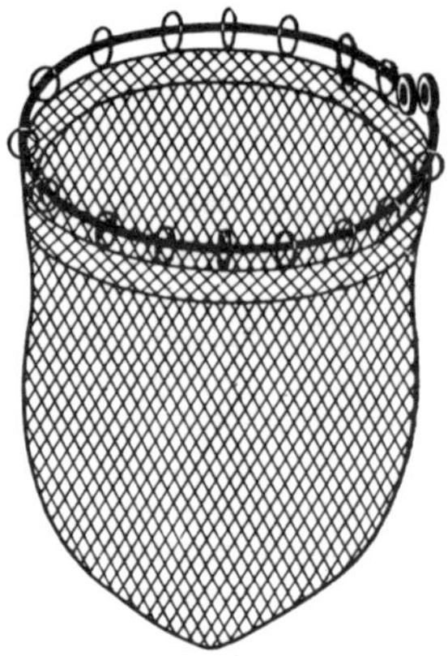

Plankton net

catching food: The method of catching food depends on the food animals you want to catch. In order to trap unicellulars, rotatoria, and larval forms of micro-crustaceans, you will need food nets (see this) of especially fine mesh. Since these are only slightly permeable to water, they can only be handled by pulling the net up vertically through the water and taking it out slowly while the water runs off. Rinse the net in your transportation can and repeat the procedure until your needs are supplied. This is the case especially with meshes of 150 microns or less. All these small-meshed nets clog up easily. Therefore they have to be washed (but not boiled), in detergent periodically. All coarser meshes from about 200 microns up, especially nets used for micro-crustaceans, may be handled in the usual way by drawing them back and forth through the water.

It is not unimportant, however, how this is done. Simple movements that come and go in the same direction will only push the micro-crustaceans away from the catching site. Therefore draw your net in a figure-8 movement, with-

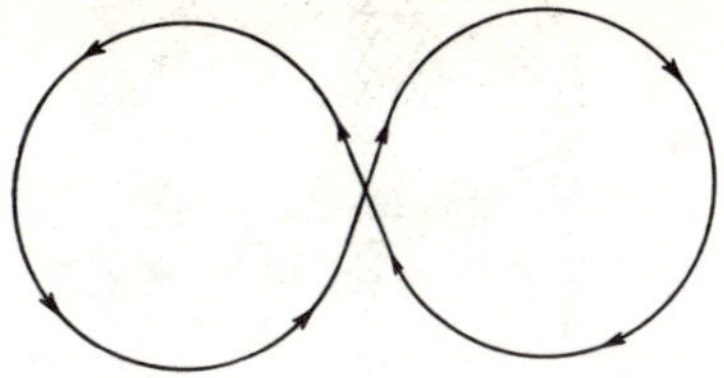

Best way of moving net to catch food.

out pressure in the curves, but with strong pressure in the straight parts of the line. This creates an eddy which tends to suck ever-increasing numbers of food animals into its range. When trapping plankton or micro-crustaceans, pay attention to the direction of light and wind (see DAPHNIA AS FOOD). Experience with regard to the dwelling sites of food animals differs for each body of water. Never lose heart too quickly if the catch is unsuccessful at one spot. Try another place! It may also happen that your first nettings show little luck, and that success comes gradually after the animals have collected at the catching site or after they have been whirled up from the bottom.

Black Mosquito Larvae (*Culex* and others) have the bad habit of disappearing when you approach the water and dip in your net. In this case dip in the net and wait until they return to the surface for breathing. Only then will you be able to catch them in greater numbers. The net for this should be coarse-meshed, the same going for white mosquito larvae (*Corethra*). These are nimble and can only be caught by quick, sudden strokes of coarse-meshed nets.

Larger insect larvae, which are preferred by predatory fishes, are best caught singly with a coarse-meshed net. *Amphipoda* and *Isopoda* are always found in greater numbers on bundles of plants and algae, or on submerged leaves, etc., from where they may be shaken or washed out. They may also be caught drawing a coarse-meshed net through the plants, if this is done against the current of flowing waters. Red Mosquito larvae (*Chironomus*) and Tubifex are best taken home in the mud in which they live, washing them out from this as described under the respective entries.

catching pipe: Glass implement in the shape of a smoking pipe which, together with a net, is very useful for catching aquarium fishes from tanks.

Used especially for transferring fry from one tank to another.

Catfish, the: see AMEIURUS NEBULOSUS.

Catfish-like: see SILUROIDEA.

Caudo, the: see PHALLOCEROS CAUDOMACULATUS.

caudofasciata: Striped on the tail.
— *Limia.*

caudomaculatus: Spotted on the tail.
— *Phalloceros.*

caudovittatus: With band on the tail.
— *Hemigrammus.*

Cave Fish, the Blind: see ANOPTICHTHYS JORDANI.

Cave Fishes: The fauna of caves is very peculiar. In them one finds lower animals, as for instance, spiders, insects, crustaceans, but also fishes and reptiles. The world of fishes is composed of species belonging to different families, which have more or less adapted to life in subterranean waters. They go gradually from normal construction of the body to total blindness and absence of pigments. Life in darkness in many cases has caused a regression of pigments and light-sensitive organs. No light-emitting organs are found. According to LADIGES this is explained by the fact that the caves we know are still rather new developments with reference to the history of the

Earth for which the time for developing special light-emitting organs has not yet been sufficient. None of the cave-dwelling fish species is without relationship to the fishes of normal waters from which they originate. Cave-fishes are known from many regions of the earth. According to HUBBS, in the cave waters of Yucatan, besides the Blind Cave Fish, others are found which have not undergone any alteration. The cave-dwelling sub-species of *Cichlasoma urophthalmus*, to the contrary, shows an increase in the eye size.

celebensis: From Celebes.
— *Oryzias*.

Celebes Medaka, the: see ORYZIAS CELEBENSIS.

Celebes Rainbow Fish, the: see TELMATHERINA LADIGESI.

cell: Live formation made up of a mixture of viscous substances containing protein (see PROTOPLASM) which is either surrounded by a skin, or else by a bordering layer of protoplasm. The intimate structure is more or less complex. Of especial importance within the cell is the presence of one or more bubble-shaped bodies, the nuclei.

The vital functions of a cell are extremely manifold, in unicellulars often much more so than in multicellulars, due to the lack of specialization. These functions, however, are characteristic for the activities of all cells, and consist of the metabolism of substances and energies, reactions to stimuli, and changes of shape. In multicellular organisms, which may consist of from several units to various billions of cells, a division of labor is reached, which causes the multiformity of these organisms. The cell is not the exclusive bearer of life, as there is also non-cellular live matter.

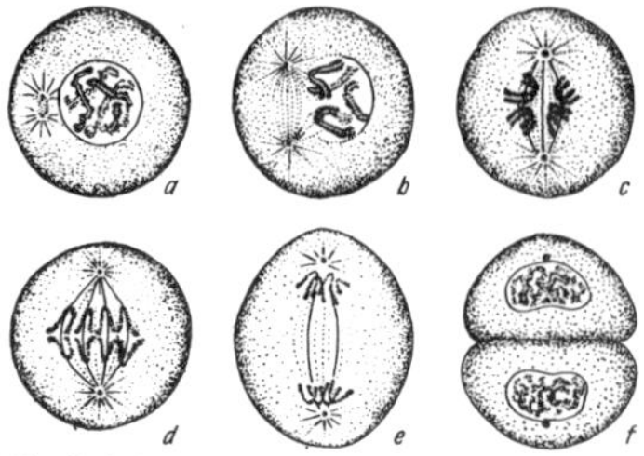

Cell division stages, from the formation of chromosomes in the nucleus to the formation of two separate cells about to split.

Probably the first live beings on earth were only simple little lumps of protein which, as characteristics of their being alive, possessed simple metabolism and the faculty of reproducing. Characteristic for cells are also certain cell substances, the so-called nuclear acids, which, above all, exert a decisive importance on the development of body substances and on reproduction. In the most primitive forms of life, for instance, in bacteria, they are distributed throughout the plasm, in the higher ones they are found in the nucleus, especially in the CHROMOSOMES (see these).

The multicellular organisms have developed from unicellular ones. According to the basic biogenetical law (see this), established by Ernst HAECKEL, they therefore pass through a unicellular stage also in their individual development. From this, through planned division, results the cell state, the cells, however, not being closed to each other, but having a lively interrelationship. Therefore the whole multicellular organism has to be considered as an ingeniously co-operating whole, considering the division of labor of the specialized cells which are attuned to each other. The multiplication of cells, which in multicellular organisms generally shows in the form of growth, takes place through cellular division (see this). In this an ingenious process causes an equal distribution of the cellular mass to the newly forming cells.

Cellophane-Plant, the: see ECHINODORUS ROSTRATUS.

cellular division: Any process of growth is preceded by cellular division, for growing means multiplication, respectively enlargement of the body cells. The simplest form of cellular division is that of strangling the cell in two (*amitosis*).

A more complex cellular division is that in which also the nucleus divides. This process (*mitosis*) is preceded by some changes in the nucleus. At first the chromosomes (see these), which are invisible in the resting nucleus, become visible. In this phase a microscopic cut looks as if one had cut through a skein of wool and were now seeing the wool ends cut at random (*prophasis*). Slowly the long-threaded chromosomes contract until they become shorter and thicker, and thus more clearly visible. In the second phase (*prometaphasis*) the nuclear plasm gives origin to a nuclear axis, which causes the impression as if the chromosomes were tied to threads. Then the chromosomes, which are always composed of two equal parts, range themselves on the equatorial plain in a nuclear or equatorial plate (*metaphasis*). Now the chromosomes, after splitting lengthwise, migrate to the poles in equal parts, that is, one half goes to the upper pole, the other half to the lower one (*anaphasis*). Thus now each pole possesses an equal group of chromosomes. These draw together and form new rest nuclei at the poles, while the nuclear axis dissolves (*telophasis*). Simultaneously a new wall develops between the two new nuclei, so that one cell has turned into two, which both show the same number of chromosomes.

Another type of division, the maturity division (*meiosis*) sets in when the purpose is that of developing germinating cells (see these), that is semen or ova. Since two cells unite in the conjugation of such sexual cells, the number of chromosomes must previously be reduced in half (*division of reduction*). If this were not the case, and if, for instance, two cells with 20 chromosomes each mated, the resulting new cell would have 40 chromosomes, and in the subsequent generations the number of chromosomes would always double. In order to prevent this, and to keep the number of chromosomes constant, the simple division described above is followed by a further one in which always pairs of chromosomes migrate to the poles, so that each pole finally receives only half the usual number of them.

In all, this manner gives origin to four new cells coming from one, of which each possesses only half the usual set of chromosomes, in our above-given example therefore only 10. When mating, the male and the female germinating cells each contribute with their own number of them, so that at the end the normal set of 20 chromosomes is re-formed.

celluloid: Transparent, flexible compound of cellulose with an admixture of camphor, which is used in aquaristics for the manufacture of filters, etc., due to its insolubility in water, and due to the ease with which it is worked. It has the advantage over glass of being unbreakable. The query whether celluloid could act harmfully can be answered by stating that the introduction of minute quantities of camphor into the aquarium water is not completely impossible, but that so far no one has been able to prove that this caused any harm. Celluloid accessories may therefore safely be used in aquaristics.

Central America: Bridge of land connecting North and South

America, which as to fauna belongs either to NORTH AMERICA (see this), or to SOUTH AMERICA (see this).

Centrarchidae: Sunfishes.
Family belonging to the sub-order of the Perch-like Fishes or PERCOIDEA (see this), with about 12-14 genera, which originates from North America. The Sunfishes live mainly in standing or flowing, clear waters with rocky or gravelly bottom. They are found almost exclusively in fresh water, and only a few species live in brackish water.

Sunfishes are small to medium-sized fishes, more or less compressed laterally, whose shape should be termed as being high. This impression of relatively great body height is still further enhanced by the often rather big dorsal fins, which are carried erect. The mouth is terminal, the small teeth being disposed in ribbons. Cheeks, gill covers, and body are completely covered with scales. As a rule the scales are round, less frequently they are comb scales, respectively transitional forms between round and comb-shaped ones. A lateral line is nearly always present. The dorsal fin is composed of two parts which are connected.

All Sunfishes are very striking and beautifully-colored fishes, the colors of which may change according to age, mood, and surroundings.

External SD are generally hard to verify. All species are pronounced meat eaters, which scorn artificial foods of all kinds. Some of the species may be classified as predators. Nearly all *C.* are interesting inmates for aquaria, which deserve greater distribution due to their small demands as to water temperature. However, one or the other species is not as insensitive to warmth as the common run of cold water fishes, a fact that is explained by the latitude of their origin. Sunfishes demand medium-sized to big tanks, depending on species and individual body length, furthermore clear, clean water, and hiding places among rocks, roots, or plants. Most species are not difficult to breed, but some of them can only be bred in outdoor ponds due to their size. As a rule the male cares for the brood by digging a shallow pit in the sand and watching and fanning the eggs placed in this. Only few species care for the fry after hatching.

The following of the genera are important for aquaristics, and may be found under the respective entries: AMBLOPLITES, APOMOTIS, CENTRARCHUS, ELASSOMA, ENNEACANTHUS, LEPOMIS, MESOGONISTIUS, and MICROPTERUS.

Centrarchus: Refers to the spiny anal fin.
Genus of Sunfishes belonging to the family of the CENTRARCHIDAE (see this).

— macropterus Lacépede: The Peacock Sunfish.
SHAPE: As per description of the family. The oval, laterally strongly compressed body looks especially tall due to the steeply rising fins. D XI-XII/12-14, A VI-VIII/13-15. Length: in nature up to $6\frac{1}{4}''$, in the aquarium $4\frac{3}{4}''$, but already ready to reproduce at $3\frac{1}{8}''$.
COLOR: Shiny greenish to brownish base with irregular dark bands and spots. During youth a peacock's eye appears clearly on the base of the soft part of the dorsal, disappearing almost completely later on, together with the pretty design on the body. SD are minute, the female being a little plumper during the spawning period.
RANGE: The East of the U.S.A., to the Mississippi region in the West, North to about Illinois, and South to Florida. The species is not rare anywhere.

Centrarchus macropterus

CARE AND BREEDING: A very interesting cold water fish which, if feeling well, stays much in open water with its fins spread. It is relatively lively, and may be considered peaceful towards other fishes. Temperatures between 46-77° F. Despite the fact that the fish is not very shy, the tank should not be densely planted as otherwise it likes to retire among the plants, becoming a little timid.

Use well-washed, not-too-coarse gravel for the upper layer of the bottom, in order to avoid clouding of the water during the spawning period, when the fish build pits. Breeding is possible in spacious tanks, and, of course, also in open air installations. The spawning period is in April/May, beginning with a water temperature of about 68° F. The preparations take place with very pretty games of bluffing and of wooing. The male digs a shallow pit at the foot of plants. The female takes little or no part in this. The real mating, during which the pair circle each other quickly in the pit, is preceded by a couple of mock matings. A total of 200-400 eggs is spawned in 4-6 acts of mating. After spawning the female should be removed, as it is the male alone who cares for the brood. The fry hatch after 24-36 hours, are fanned out of the pit by the male, hang for another 3-4 days from plants and the like, and become free-swimming after this. Rearing them is a little difficult, because the fry stay near the bottom and do not like to swim. After having weathered the first day, though, they grow very quickly. Change part of the water from time to time.

Centropomidae: Family belonging to the sub-order of the Perchlike fishes of PERCOIDEA (see this), comprising small and large fishes, the range of distribution of which reaches from the Persian Gulf to Australia on one side, and to China on the other. The fishes are inhabitants of the coastal regions around the Indian and the Pacific Oceans, being found in river mouths, tidal zones, and the sea. However, many species have adapted totally to life in fresh water, and some of them are able to live both in fresh and in salt water. The only genus of the family which is known in aquaristics (and which comprises only two genera), is that of the Glass Perches AMBASSIS (see this), which formerly lent its name to a family of its own (*Ambassidae*).

cephalothorax: Head-and-breast armor of Arthropods.

Ceratophyllaceae: Horn Worts. Family of sub-aquatic plants pertaining to the class of the DICOTYLEDONEAE (see this). The Horn Worts are perennial, brittle plants, which possess no roots. The leaves, which are manifoldly divided, more or less hard, and equipped with small thorns, form verticils around the stem. With the beginning of Winter the European members of the family develop closely-growing leaf shoots, which come off and sink to the bottom as winter-buds. These may be collected, wintered in cold water, and used in spring for reproducing the plants.

The two European species are quite undemanding aquarium plants. They may either be anchored to the bottom with glass needles, or else they may be cultivated free floating. If the shoots grow too long, they may be shortened by cutting off the lower ends. Cutting off the tips of the shoots is a little unreliable, as then they may not always continue growing. While the European species recede, the tropical ones, which however are rarely seen in aquaria, go on growing the year round. Propagation of thc plants always takes place by division.

Ceratophyllum: Horn-leaf.

Genus of perennial sub-aquatic plants belonging to the family of the Horn-Wort plants or CERATOPHYLLACEAE (see this), with several species, of which the two that are found in Europe are cosmopolitan, and are much appreciated for cultivation in the aquarium.

— **demersum** Linné: Coarse Horn Wort.

A quite common species, which is distributed over nearly the whole world.

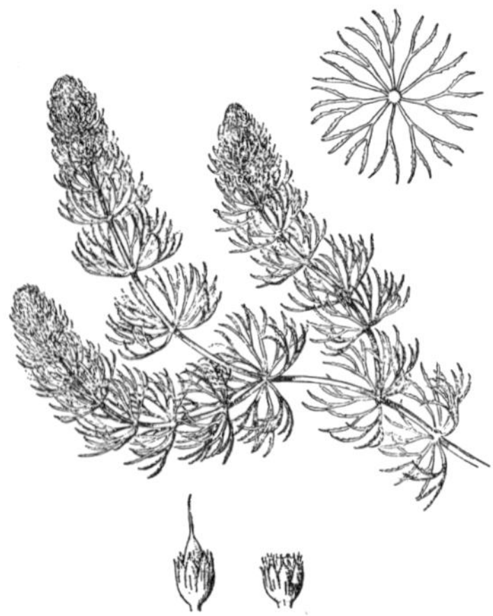

Ceratophyllum demersum

Brittle, richly ramified, and rugged plants, the leaves of which are equipped with small thorns. The very small and unassuming flowers grow in the leaf insertions, but the plants hardly ever bloom. Cultivation as per description of the family. Specimens native from the Temperate Zones tolerate little warmth. They are hungry for light, but should not be exposed to too much sunshine, as this may lead to infestations with algae.

— **submersum:** Smooth Hornwort.

Similar to the preceding species, but thinner and more delicate. This species too is distributed widely, but it is less common.

Ceratopteris: Horn Fern.

Genus of ferns that live amphibiously, pertaining to the family of the PARKERIACEAE (see this), with only one, very variable species, diffused over the tropics in nearly all the world.

— **thalictroides** (Linné): Brongniart (Water Sprite).

GENERALITIES: A very highly valued plant for the warm water aquarium, which may be cultivated submergedly, as a swamp plant, or as a floating one.

SHAPE: This fern, whose soft and sensitive leaves are bottomstanding, varies strongly in shape. The delicate, light-green leaves may be big-surfaced, with slightly or deeply indented edges, lobate, or very finely divided. It is typical for the dry-land forms that the leaf tissues recedes nearly down to the main nervures, which gives the leaves an antler-like look. The plants is found in dry-land forms with aerial leaves of several shapes, in shallow water as a semi-emerged form, in deep water as a submerged form with large-lobed or finely-divided leaves, or else as a floating form. There are many transitions between the different forms. The plant is able to adapt to all kinds of manners of living. If cultivated in favorable locations, it grows to heights of up to 18″. The root balls are fine-feathered and richly ramified.

RANGE: In the tropics of nearly the whole globe. The fern lives in all kinds of waters, but prefers swamp regions with periodically changing water levels, since these satisfy its vital demands best.

CULTIVATION: The species demands very well illuminated locations, with (not excessive) sunshine and sufficient warmth, preferably not below 77° F. Since the plants are able to grow very big under good care, one has to consider their growth beforehand when planting them in the aquaria. Pure sand bottom does not lead them to become very strong. The best is coarse sand with an admixture of weathered clay (1/3 to 1/2). Soft water is desirable. To thrive floating ferns need slightly tilted cover panes, in order to avoid drippings of precipitated water on the leaves.

Multiplication is simple. Just cut off the buds that develop everywhere on the edges of the leaves after they have developed sufficient roots, and plant them or treat them as floating plants. When winter comes most specimens usually die, since the fern generally is annual. Only the buds withstand winter as swamp plants, preferably in shallow dishes in well-illuminated locations and with temperatures of about 64-68° F.

A very commendable aquarium plant. The fine-feathered form is called Sumatran Water Sprite.

cerci: Appendages on the abdomen of insects and their larvae, generally of thread-like shape. They should not be taken for tracheal gills of insect larvae which live in water.

cernua: Overhanging, tipping the head.

— *Acerina.*

Cestodes: Tape Worms.

Class pertaining to the phylum of the Flat Worms or PLATHELMINTHES (see this), which live exclusively as intestinal parasites.

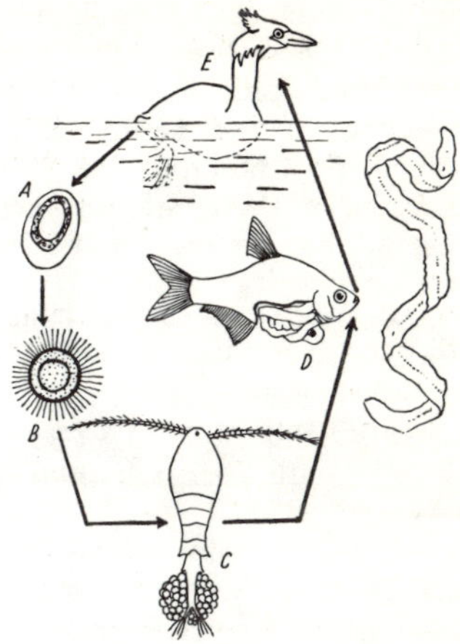

Cestodes — Tapeworms. Development of Ligula intestinalis — A. egg B. ciliate larva C. intermediate host, Diaptomus D. intermediate host, fish E. final host, bird.

C. are generally found inside vertebrates where they absorb the liquefied intestinal food of the host through their skins. Their own intestine is completely stunted. The body is long-stretched and ribbon-shaped as a rule. The head, which has sucking openings or a crown of hooks or both, in order to hold fast to the wall of the host's intestine, is visible as a small swelling at the tip of the body. Generally the body itself is divided into sections. The rear sections drop off from the body and are eliminated in the feces of the host, where they decay, freeing eggs or embryos.

Tape worms generally need several intermediate hosts, which serve as food to each other and to the final host. These may be small crustaceans, fishes, or other animals.

For information on fish diseases caused by Tape Worms, see the entry: TAPE WORM DISEASES OF FISHES.

Ceylon Barb, the: see BARBUS CUMINGII.

Chaetobranchopsis: Similar to the genus *Chaetobranchius*.

South American genus of fishes belonging to the family of the Cichlids or CICHLIDAE (see this), possessing a short, strongly compressed, relatively high body with a large head.

— bitaeniatus Ahl: The Golden Cichlid.

SHAPE: As per description of the genus; D XV-XVI/11, A VI/14-16; the scales rather large. Length up to 4¾″.

COLOR: Shiny yellow-gray-golden, each scale edged, the fish with two darker length stripes. The fins are ornamented with vivid red designs. SD unknown.

RANGE: The system of the Amazon River.

CARE AND BREEDING: The species is quite peaceful. It needs much warmth, 77-86° F should be advisable. Breeding has not yet succeeded.

chaetodon: After a similar-looking family of salt water fishes.

— *Mesogonistius.*

chalceus: Brazen, copper-colored.

— *Tetragonopterus.*

Chalceus: Refers to the strong luster of the scales; literally 'the coppersmith'.

South American genus of Characins belonging to the family of the CHARACIDAE (see this). Lively school fishes of elongated build, with a remarkable gleam of the scales.

— macrolepidotus Cuvier: The Slim Tetra.

SHAPE: The body is elongated, the upper and lower body contours being evenly arched. The head is a little flattened from above. The vigorously toothed mouth is terminal. D 12, A 11-12. The scales are very large. An adipose fin is present. Length up to 10″.

COLOR: The strong silvery glitter shows reddish and violet hues, the

Chalceus macrolepidotus

fins are reddish. SD unknown.

RANGE: Guiana.

CARE AND BREEDING: The species is very lively and likes to jump. The fish like company of their own kind. 75° F should be a commensurate temperature. Being vigorous eaters, they should be offered rich and vigorous food. Breeding has not yet succeeded.

Chalcinus: The brassy one.

Genus of South American Characins pertaining to the family of the CHARACIDAE (see this), of elongated build, strongly compressed laterally. The front part of the belly is arched in a curve, and shows a sharp edge in front of, and to the rear of the ventral fins. The scales are very large. The mouth opening is of moderate size, the lower lip being remarkable for its fleshy thickening. On the sides of the mouth opening we see some kind of whisker threads, especially on young specimens.

Jaws and intermediate jaws are equipped with teeth. The complete lateral line at first forms a down curve, going along the central line of the body thereafter. An adipose fin is present. The dorsal inserts far to the rear, and the central rays of the caudal are extended into a lobate dark tip. The anal is quite long. The pectorals are large and crescent-shaped.

— elongatus (Guenther): The Goiter Characin.

SHAPE: As per description of the genus. D 11, A 27-31. Length up to about 8″.

COLOR: Shiny silver with weak darker spots and a faded, narrow horizontal band which ends in the central tip of the tail fin. SD are not completely clear, but the darker designs are probably more accentuated on the males.

RANGE: The Amazon region and parts of the Orinoco, from Guiana in the North to the Plate River in the South.

CARE AND BREEDING: A rarely-imported species. Being a lively and swift-swimming school fish, it needs large tanks with plenty of room for swimming. Plenty of sunshine and temperatures around 77° F are desirable. The nourishment of the fish consists mainly of live foods, aquatic insects, flying food, and also small fishes. Otherwise the fish are quite hardy and long-lived in the aquarium. Reproduction unknown.

Chanchito, the: see CICHLASOMA FACETUM.

Chanda: An older name for the genus AMBASSIS (see this). HAMILTON formulated the genus *Chanda* in 1822, but his type specimen had already been classified as *Leiognathus* in 1802. In 1828 CUVIER and VALENCIENNES established the genus *Ambassis*, including seven of Hamilton's species in it. Today both the names *Chanda* and *Ambassis* are used for the same genus. In this book we mention the different species under *Ambassis*.

change of hosts: The feature, typical of many parasites, not to conclude their development on or in one host only, but to search out several, often completely different living beings for this.

Channa: Genus belonging to the family of the Snake-Head Fishes or OPHIOCEPHALIDAE (see this).

Chaperi: After the French collector Chaper.

— *Bryconalestes.*

— *Epiplatys.*

Chara foetida

Chara: The meaning of the name is not completely clear; perhaps from the Greek 'Charax'—Post, pole.

Genus pertaining to the family of the Candelabrum plants or CHARACEAE (see this).

— **foetida** A. Braun: The Stinking Candelabrum.

A slightly stiff, monoecian, gray-green plant which is distributed over the whole globe. It is found especially in small ditches, ponds, peat holes, and the inlets of greater bodies of water. *C. foetida* grows up to heights of 16″. The dense verticils stand around the stems at great distances, the fecundating organs inserting singly or in pairs in the leaf angles. Generally perennial. For cultivation and propagation see the entry: *Characeae.* May be used as spawning substratum if crusting has not progressed too far. Disagreeable odor.

— **fragilis** Desvaux: The Frail Candelabrum.
A very brittle plant which grows up to 12″ high, resembling the preceding one but evergreen and with a less strong odor. Distributed over the whole globe, also in brackish water and in the Baltic Sea. The leaves carry no spines. Monoecian, and generally perennial. Commercially offered for a long time. Tolerates higher temperatures.

Characeae: Candelabrum or Candlestick Plants.
Highly developed algae without roots or with thin root threads. Verticillated, needle-shaped 'leaves' are grouped around the main stem at some distance from each other, making the plant look like a many-armed candelabrum or candlestick. Generally a little frail, more or less covered with a crust. Sexual reproduction through seminal and egg cells which, after uniting, form a zygote which comes off from the plant. The new plant develops from this after a winter rest. The *C.* are monoceian, the fruit organs stand singly or in small groups within the leaf verticils. Reproduction in the aquarium is vegetative or through the seeding of spores. Genetically the family is very ancient.

Genera which are of importance for the aquarist: CHARA (see this), and NITELLA (see this).

Characidae: Characins.
Family belonging to the sub-order of the Carp-like fishes or CYPRINOIDEA (see this). A great group of fishes which is distributed over Africa, South America, and Central America, being represented in our aquaria by many species. The family lives in all kinds of waters in the tropics and the sub-tropics, and has developed well-differentiated types of shape, which justify the formulation of a series of sub-families.

Considering the manifold shapes of the Characins, it is impossible to isolate a typical standard shape. There never are barbels. The teeth are well developed. Many species show a skinny, generally unsupported, more or less long skin fold, the adipose fin. This is often mentioned as the characteristic of the Characins, but it may also be lacking. Of the many sub-families we shall mention only the SERRASALMINAE (see this), the GLANDULOCAUDINAE (see this) and the PYRRHULININAE (see this), as they show special peculiarities in their manner of living or in body structure. The members of the other sub-families are simply mentioned as genera of the whole family in this book.

The majority of the Characins are skilled swimmers which live in schools in open, partly even in flowing waters, but do not avoid the plant-stocked water regions either. The family includes inhabitants of all kinds of biotopes. The species of the surface and those of the middle reaches show the well-known glitter of the scales. Vigorous colors are rare in nearly all species, or else they concentrate on single parts of the body in the form of luminous dots or dashes. The body shape varies from that of a puncheon to that of a disc. Throat and the front part of the belly often are vaulted outwards, so that the front part of the body looks heavier. Furthermore the sharp edge of the belly is often equipped with saw-like rows of scales. Generally the fins are relatively small, and only one or the other species has them enlarged and extended into points. Most Characins like sunshine, clear water, and rich plantings, but with sufficient space for swimming

The genera of the family **Characidae** from **Acestrorhynchus** through **Hemibrycon**

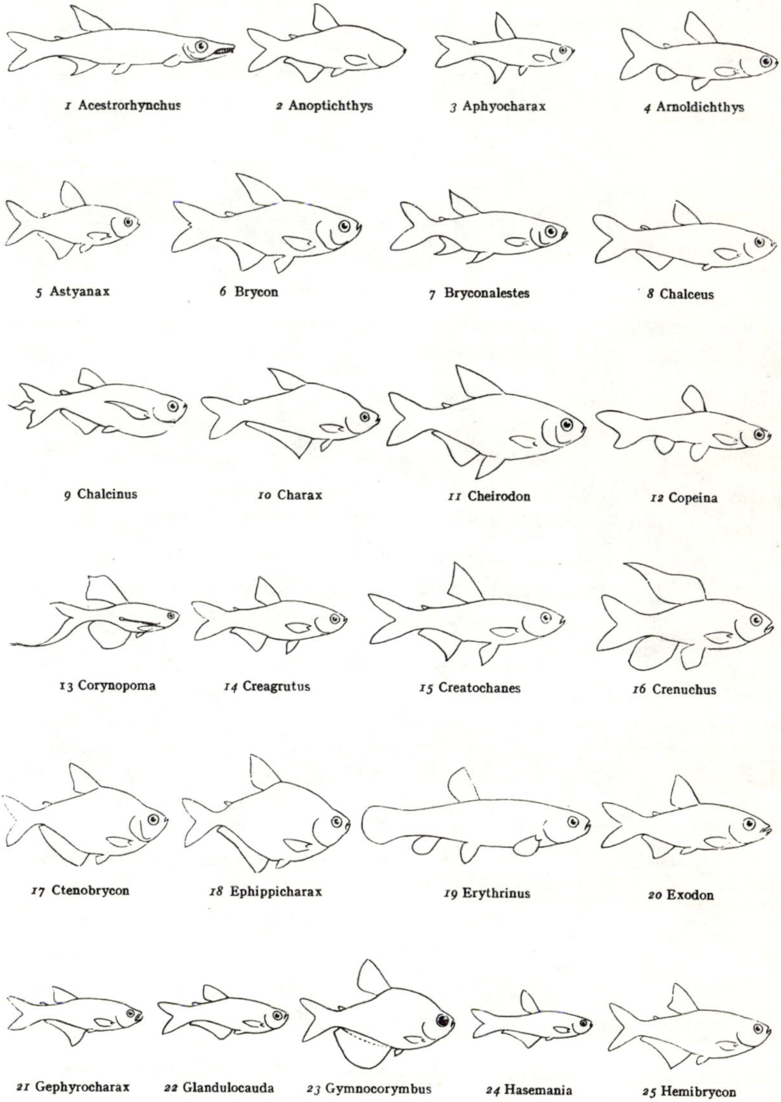

The genera of the family **Characidae** from **Hemigrammus** through **Thayeria**

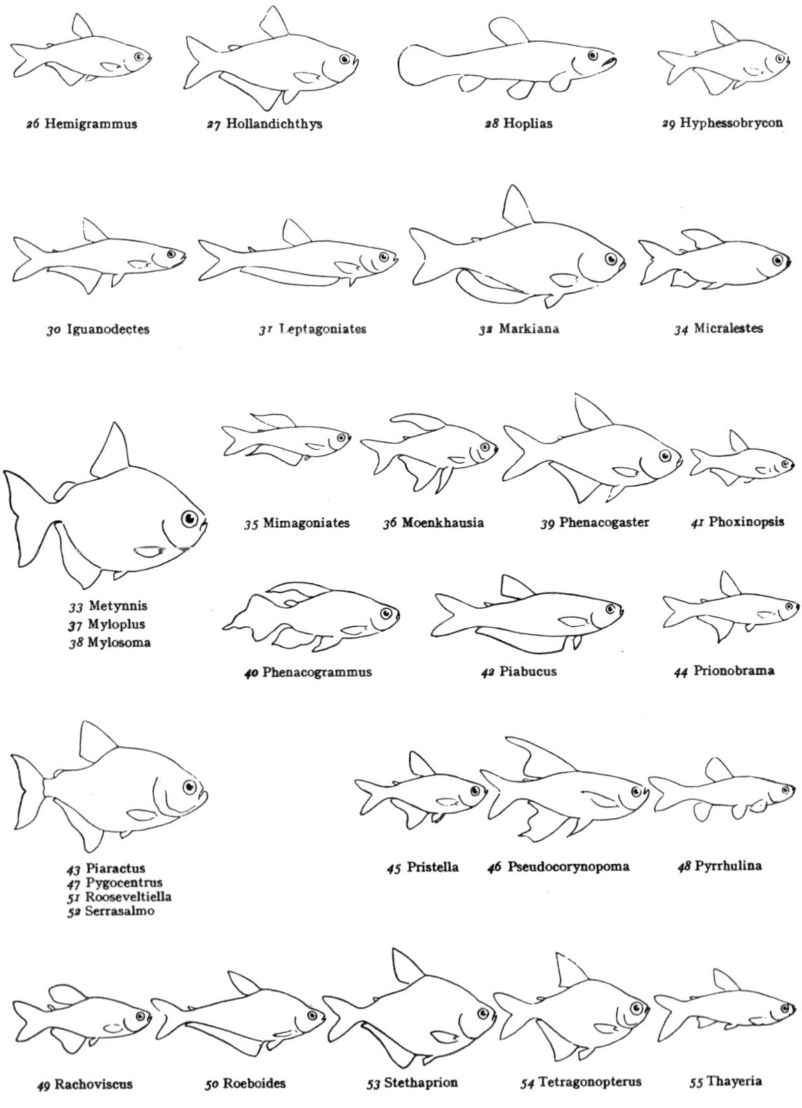

around. Dark bottoms enhance their colors (a layer of basalt gravel). All types of feeding are represented, from the plant eater, to the predator. Most species are very hardy, and will accept dry foods besides the live ones. Despite their tropical and sub-tropical origin, many species do not need excessive warmth. Generally they are peaceful, and only rarely do their fights end up with torn fins.

Some of the species, however, know very well how to use their teeth, and are even counted among the most ferocious predators of fresh water. Breeding is sometimes quite easy, but in part also pronouncedly difficult. More details on the care of each of the genera are found under the respective entries, which may be looked up in accordance with the following listing:

Anoptichthys
Aphyocharax
Arnoldichthys
Astyanax
Brycon
Bryconalestes
Chalcinus
Chalceus
Charax
Cheirodon
Copeina
Corynopoma
Creagrutus
Creatochanes
Crenuchus
Ctenobrycon
Ephippicharax
Erythrinus
Exodon
Gephyrocharax
Glandulocauda.
Gymnocorymbus
Hasemania
Hemibrycon
Hemigrammus
Hollandichthys
Hoplias
Iguanodectes
Leptagoniates
Markiana
Metynnis
Micralestes
Mimagoniates
Moenkhausia
Myloplus
Mylosoma
Phenacogaster
Phenacogrammus
Phoxinopsis
Piabucus
Piaractus
Prionobrama
Pristella
Pseudocorynopoma
Pygocentrus
Pyrrhulina
Rachoviscus
Roeboides
Rooseveltiella
Serrasalmo
Stethaprion
Tetragonopterus
Thayeria

Characidium: Derived from the name of the genus *Charax*.

South American genus of Characin-like fishes pertaining to the family of the Half-Teeth or HEMIODONTIDAE (see this). All species are small and peaceful fishes of more or less elongated body structure. The dorsal fin inserts well to the front; an adipose fin is present. The outer rays of the pectorals are thickened. Upper and intermediate jaws each show a row of three-pronged teeth.

The *Characidium* species inhabit flowing waters and are mainly found on sand banks or in courses of water which have a stony or gravelly bottom. There they stay near the bottom, hunting for nourishment and swimming with jolting motions. Nutrition consists of bottom foods. When spawn-ripeness sets in, the females become rather unruly. The act of spawning takes place near the bottom, in open water, but also among stands of plants. A total of 150 eggs is spawned during the repeated matings. The quite small fry hatch within 30-40 hours and become free-swimming after about three days. Thereafter they grow relatively quickly, and are already ¾″ long when one month old.

— **fasciatum** Reinhardt: The Darter Characin.

SHAPE: As per description of the genus; the back a little arched; the terminal mouth with its opening slightly tilted down. D 11, A 7-8. Length up to 4″.

COLOR: On brownish base is a variable design which consists of one length stripe with 10-12 cross stripes. The better developed fins of the males are yellow hued.

RANGE: Eastern South America, from the Orinoco to the La Plata.

CARE AND BREEDING: As per description of the genus. The species is lively, hardy, and quite long-

Characidium fasciatum

lived. It needs roomy aquaria, with hiding places which are defended against the other inhabitants of the community tank. Temperature: 64-79° F.

Characidium rachovii

— **rachovii** Regan: Rachow's Darter Characin.

SHAPE: As per description of the genus, but a little more compact than the preceding species. D 13-15, A 8-9. Length up to 2½″.

COLOR: Brownish base with a darker horizontal stripe, the rear half of the body with dark spots and a reddish sheen, the fins yellowish with brownish dots. The male is more vividly colored.

RANGE: Southeastern Brazil.

CARE AND BREEDING: As per description of the genus.

Characins, Tetras: see CHARACIDAE.

Charax: The pointed stake, referring to the teeth. South American genus of Characins pertaining to the family of the *Characidae* (see this). A typical genus, the name of which was applied to the whole family.

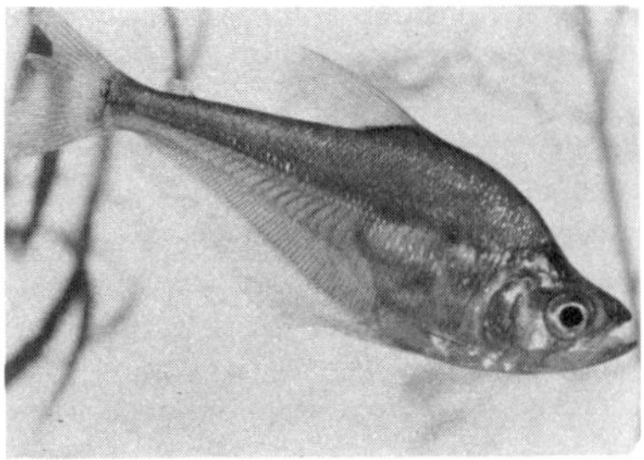

Charax gibbosus

— **gibbosus** (Linné): The Humpbacked Characin.

SHAPE: The elongated, laterally compressed body shows a remarkable arched back and an indented forehead contour. The mouth opening slants obliquely upwards. D 11, A 28-29. The scales are very small. Length up to 6″.

COLOR: Shiny brownish-silvery base with a great number of greenish glittering lights, a dark shoulder spot, and yellowish to brownish fins. The male is slimmer and more intensely colored during the spawning period.

RANGE: Guiana, and the regions of the lower and central Amazon as well as the Rio Paraguay.

CARE AND BREEDING: The species is not very motile and likes to stand quietly among plants. Its appearance makes the fish seem predatory, but it is completely harmless. *Ch. gibbosus* is an omnivore which also eats delicate plant foods and hunts for nourishment in a slightly tilted position. It needs spacious tanks, since it seems that breeding can only be achieved with plenty of room. Temperature around 77° F. Reproduction takes place in the manner of most other Characins, but breeding is not very simple.

The fish are egg scatterers. The extremely small fry hatch after about 30 hours, are very voracious, and need very small live food. Since it is difficult to have this permanently available, many alevins die of starvation.

Charophyta: Section pertaining to the sub-phylum of the Flowerless plants or CRYPTOGAMAE (see this), of the members of which only the family of the Candelabrum Plants or CHARACEAE (see this) is of significance to the aquarium. The *C.* are distributed over the whole globe and live in all kinds of bodies of water. They are found even in the coastal regions and in brackish or salt water. All plants of this group are brittle, and they are always multicellular, growing to lengths which go from a few inches to three feet. Frequently they are richly articulated, developing lateral shoots disposed in verticils around the main stem and which erroneously are called leaves. Partly they grow thin threads of cells, the rhizomes, with which the plants fasten to the bottom. Reproduction is either vegetative, by means of lateral shoots, or else sexually through fecundated egg cells.

Checker Barb, the: see BARBUS OLIGOLEPIS.

Cheirodon: Hand-shaped Teeth. South and Central American genus of Characins pertaining to the family of the CHARACIDAE (see this), closely related to the Tetragonopterids, from which it differs only by its less developed teeth. An adipose fin is present.

Single rays of the anal and pectoral fins of the males are equipped with hooklets. The lateral line is uncomplete. Nearly all species are small, simply-colored, silvery fishes. Care and breeding as described for HEMIGRAMMUS (see this). The genus comprises about 12 known species.

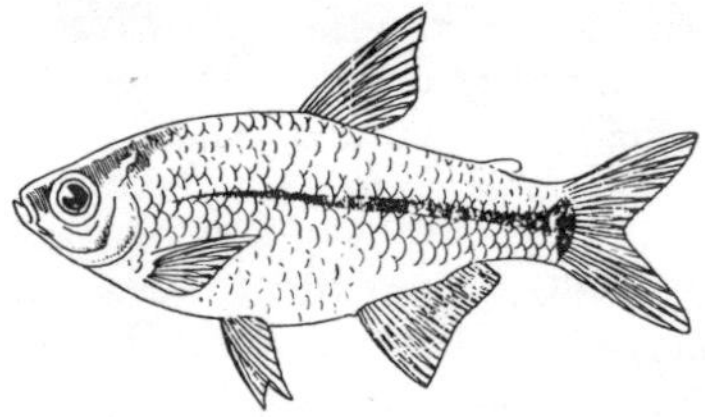

Cheirodon, type of the genus

— arnoldi Boulenger: From Mexico and Central America. Length up to 3½″. Vicious and voracious.

— axelrodi Schultz: Cardinal Tetra.

SHAPE: Very similar to the Neon Tetra, *Hyphessobrycon innesi*, likewise slender and elongated, slightly compressed laterally. D 11, A 19. Length about 1¼″.

COLOR: A luminous green stripe extends from the upper edge of the eye to a point below the adipose fin. On the lower side it is bordered by a wide red band which goes from the caudal peduncle to the tip of the snout, being closed off on the upper side by a brownish, blood-red back. The iris is a luminous green. The colorless dorsal and anal fins have a narrow white seam at the front edge. The female is a little more plump.

RANGE: The few specimens of this recently imported species probably originate from one of the northern affluents of the Amazon, the Rio Negro.

Cheirodon axelrodi

CARE AND BREEDING: Discovered and imported only a few years ago, so that only relatively few reports are available as to its breeding up to this date (1958). ROLOFF and others have bred them. Spawning and raising the fry is similar to that of *H. innesi*.

There was much confusion over the scientific name of this fish at first. Myers and Weitzman named it *Hyphessobrycon cardinalis* at almost the same time that Schultz named it *Cheirodon axelrodi*. The latter name was eventually accepted, and is now official.

Data on the origin of the Cardinal Tetra is a bit inexact up to this date. Their existence in the Rio Negro may be considered as certain, even if such statements have only relative value considering the great length of the river, which is over 600 miles. Apparently the ranges of the two species *H. innesi* and this species are unrelated as far as our present knowledge permits an opinion.

— **interruptus** Jenyns:

SHAPE: As per description of the genus. D 11-12, A 17-24. Length up to $2\frac{3}{8}''$.

COLOR: Shiny silver with a dark spot on the caudal peduncle, the fins reddish. The anal fin of the male is considerably better developed.

RANGE: Southeastern Brazil and Uruguay.

CARE AND BREEDING: As described for HEMIGRAMMUS (see this). The species is omnivorous and needs plenty of live food above all. It likes sunshine at 68-77° F. The act of spawning generally takes place under the morning sun, close to the surface, the numerous eggs being scattered far around. The parents are avid spawn-eaters. The very small fry hatch after about 36 hours, become free-swimming after another three days, and are very voracious. They grow very quickly if their need for nourishment is satisfied.

— **leuciscus** Ahl:

An unassuming, Shiner-like species from the Parana and the La Plata. Length up to $3\frac{1}{8}''$. Keep them at room temperature.

— **piaba** Luetken:

D11, A 19-27. Length up to $1\frac{3}{4}''$. Mouth small, terminal. The anal fin of the male is strongly bulged out. Base of the tail fin slightly reddish, otherwise simply silver-colored.

ORIGIN: Eastern South America.

A hardy species. MT 64° F. Prefers live foods, however.

Chela: After the native name.

Genus of Carp-like school fishes belonging to the family of the CYPRINIDAE (see this).

— **oxygastroides** (Bleeker): The Glass Barb.

SHAPE: The species has an elongated, laterally compressed body structure. The dorsal contour is nearly straight, while the belly edge arches outwards to the insertion of the anal fin with a sharp bow. D 9, A 31-35, the latter long and low. The species has no barbels. Length up to 8″.

COLOR: The glassily translucent body glitters silvery under incoming light, with a thin horizontal stripe on the center of the sides, and another one on the lower edge of the caudal peduncle. The male is slimmer and more delicate.

RANGE: In all kinds of standing and flowing waters in Indo-China and Indonesia. The fish appear in schools which may also be mixed with other Cyprinids and are common everywhere.

CARE AND BREEDING: This hardy, peaceful, and lively school fish needs sufficiently long tanks with space for swimming. Being a surface fish it takes its food preferably from there, accepting all kinds of live and artificial foods. Breeding has not yet succeeded.

Chelicerata: Spiders.

Sub-phylum pertaining to the phylum of the ARTHROPODA (see this), the body of which consists of two main segments: the head-and-trunk segment (cephalothorax), and the abdomen. The cephalothorax carries six pairs of limbs, of which four pairs are used for locomotion, and two pairs for nutrition. The abdomen has no legs. The eyes are located on the front edge of the cephalothorax. Breathing is done through fan or tube-shaped tracheae. The fan-shaped tracheae rest within the abdomen (tracheal lungs), where their fan-like leaves are bathed by the blood. The tubular tracheae resemble the respiratory organs of insects. The body of spiders is richly equipped with organs of touch, especially in the jaw antennae and the body hairs. A sense that is especially well developed is that of concussion.

Generally the *Ch.* are land dwellers, and only a few water spiders and *Acari* have adapted to aquatic life. Most of them live as predators, and are equipped with poison glands. Some of them, however, especially the *Acari*, are parasites. A number of members of this group feeds on all kinds of vegetable and other decaying substances.

Of the numerous orders of the sub-phylum, the aquarist is especially interested in the Real Spiders (*Aracneae*), which include the well-known Aquatic Spider (see ARGYRONETA AQUATICA), and the Aquatic *Acari* or HYDRACARINA (see this), which, however, do not represent a systematic unit as such.

chemical processes in water: see WATER.

chevalieri: After a personal name. — *Epiplatys.*

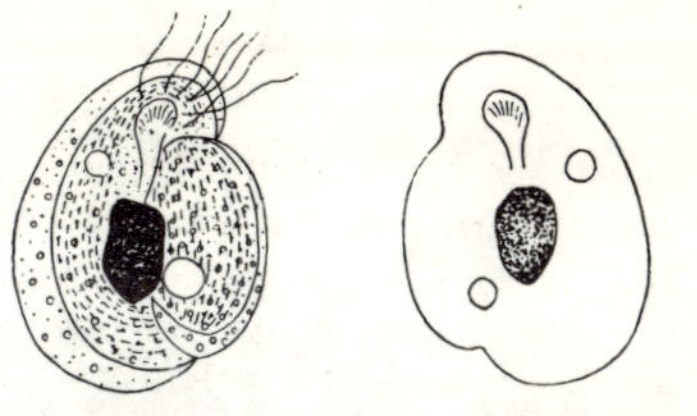

Chilodon (ella) cyprini, enlarged, after Schaeperclaus. Left, ventral view; right, dorsal view.

Chilodon (Ella): Unicellular causers of skin discolorations on fishes, pertaining to the Ciliates (see SKIN DISCOLORATIONS, INFECTIOUS).

The genus comprises a number of species, of which, however, the larger part is rather doubtful and might possibly be identical with *Chilodon(ella) cyprini.* The species is adaptable, and is found on fresh water fishes of all kinds, including even tadpoles. Infection with *Ch.* must always be preceded by weakening of the fish. Generally the fish becomes infected through direct transmission.

Chilodus: With teeth on the lips.

South American genus of Characin-like fishes pertaining to the family of the Head-Standers or ANOSTOMIDAE (see this), of elongated build, with slightly arched back and rounded belly edge, otherwise strongly compressed laterally. The scales are quite big; the lateral line is complete; an adipose fin is present. The mouth is small and terminal; the jaws are equipped with small teeth in the region of the lips. The last gill arch is changed into an accessory respiratory organ. The fishes often take on the head-down position that is typical of the Head-Standers. Only one known species.

— punctatus Mueller and Troschel: The Spotted Head-Stander.

SHAPE: As per description of the genus; D 11, A 12-13. Length, a little over $2\frac{3}{4}''$.

COLOR: Silvery glitter, brownish to

Chilodus punctatus

greenish base with a dark, temporarily disappearing length band, and a dark spot at the base of each scale. SD are not completely clear, the male probably being a little slimmer.

RANGE: Northeastern South America, in swamps and biologically unfavorable waters, quite rare, or at least hard to find.

CARE AND BREEDING: The species is harmless and may be kept in company with other quiet fishes of which it hardly takes notice. It is advisable to offer the fish tanks with dense spots of vertically-growing plants, such as, for instance, Vallisnerias. The species likes some warmth. Temperatures 68-82° F. Otherwise it is quite hardy and takes all kinds of bottom foods, preferring decaying vegetable matter. Nourishment is taken in the typical head-standing stance. Only occasionally do they swim horizontally, for instance, when disturbed, or during the mating games. Breeding has already been achieved.

chinensis: Chinese, from China. — *Macropodus.*

Chirocephalus grubei: see ANOSTRACA.

chitin: The substance from which the armor of arthropods is made. It contains nitrogen, and is very resistant to acids and alkalis.

chloramine: see HEALING BATHS.

chlorine: Greenish-yellow, pungent-smelling gas, which acts corrosively on mucous tissues. It combines with hydrogen into colorless hydrochloric acid (this in turn dissolves in water), and with metals into chlorides, as for instance, with sodium into sodium chloride (kitchen salt). Due to its disinfecting qualities, chlorine is added to the water of water mains, for which reason fresh tap water may sometimes become dangerous to aquarium fishes, whose gills it corrodes. This harm may result both from the free chlorine dissolved in the water and from the developing hypochloric and hydrochloric acids. Cold water retains more free chlorine gas than warm water, but it is nearly completely eliminated if the water is left standing for a few days. For this reason it is advisable never to stock an aquarium with fishes immediately after setting it up. Also water that is intended for keeping live fish foods should be left standing in open containers for at least one day.

Testing the presence of chlorine in tap water is easily done, by mixing 100 c.c. with 3 c.c. of a solution of iodine amylum (10 grams of soluble amylum dissolved in a liter of boiling water, and mixed with 10 grams of potassium iodide and 0.3 grams of mercury iodide in order to stabilize it). If chlorine is present, the solution turns blue.

Chlorine may be removed to a great extent in a simple way when filling up with water. For this connect a garden hose to a tap and press its outlet together. The resulting sharp, thinly-divided jet causes the chlorine to escape, as you will soon notice by its smell. The most efficient means of eliminating chlorine is by filtration through activated carbon (Hydraffin carbon). This carbon traps free chlorine.

Chlorophyceae: Green Algae. Group belonging to the sub-

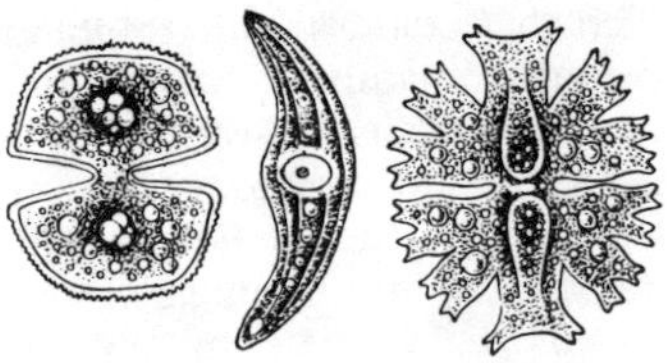

Several forms of **Chlorophyceae**

phylum of the Flowerless Plants or CRYPTOGAMAE (see this). *C.* are single to multi-cellular plants, with a vivid green color. They live either planktically, or firmly located, in fresh and salt water.

In well-lighted waters they form dense pads on any kind of substratum, which may be more or less long-threaded, according to species. Such coverings may be harmful to aquatic plants, as they tend to stop the activities of breathing and of assimilation. Some of the species also live outside water, for instance, on rock walls, the weather side of trees, and in the soil. Some *C.* form lichens by living symbiotically with lichen fungi, others still live on other algae, on fishes and crustaceans, even in animal furs. Others still, the Zoochlorelles, live in symbiosis with Infusòria or multicellular animals, such as for instance, certain fresh-water Hydras. The parasitic algae nest within the cells, or in the cellular interstices of other plants. Worth special notice are the Net Algae (see HYDRODICTYACEAE).

Propagation takes place through simple cell division, by means of free, motile spores, or sexually through the fusion of two ciliate, sexually-differentiated cells, the always motile male cell, and the sometimes non-motile female cell.

Many species belong among the live beings of the plankton, and live either singly or in loose cell-associations. They are often called Ornamental Algae, due to their beautiful shape. Besides the adult, real planktic algae, in plankton we also find the temporarily motile zoo-spores of other algae, which sometimes may show a red 'eye' spot.

The light green film on glass panes of aquaria generally consists of unicellular Green Algae, or of Tube Algae (*Siphonales*), which form cotton-like covers of ramified threadlets. Less agreeable are the so-called Thread Algae. The threads consist of a series of single cells, which may also be ramified. To these we have to add the Tube Algae of the genus *Cladophora*, and Curly Algae of the genus *Ulothrix*, the latter consisting of un-ramified and single strands of Algae. These may be very long, so that even bigger fishes may get tangled in the maze of Thread Algae. On the other hand, balls of Thread Algae form a good spawning substratum for egg-laying Tooth Carps and other fishes. For conquering Green Algae see FIGHTING ALGAE.

chlorophyl: Leaf green, a pigment in the CHLOROPLASTS (see this) of green plants, which serves ASSIMILATION (see this).

chloroplasts: Round, generally green, bodies, which are found in vegetable cells, and through which assimilation of carbon dioxide takes place. Their inside is of very complex composition, consisting of chlorophyll, proteins, and lipoids.

Chlorosis: Green-sickness. A sickness which also attacks aquatic plants in the aquarium, being caused by lack of iron salts.

choanes: Connective passages between the nasal cavity and the throat, which generally are not found in fishes, and are developed only by a few groups, which generally show signs of transition into Batracheans (see CROSSOPTERYGII).

Choanichthyes: Synonym for the Tassel Fins or CROSSOPTERYGII (see this) which also include the Lung Fishes or DIPNEUSTI (see this).

Chocolate Cichlid, the: see CICHLASOMA CORYPHAENOIDES.

Chocolate Gourami, the: see SPHAERICHTHYS OSPHROMENOIDES.

choirorhynchus: With a pig's snout.

— *Acanthopsis.*

chola: After the native name.

— *Barbus.*

Chondrostei: Cartilaginous Ganoids.

Order belonging to the *Acipenseridae*, of the sub-class of the Ancient Fins or PALEOPTERYGII (see this).

They are ancient fishes with incomplete ossified axial skeleton and cartilaginous head. The jaws are incomplete, the body is naked or covered with diamond-shaped scale plates, respectively with ossified skin cells, which frequently cover only spots or are disposed in rows. Partly the swimming bladder shows an open air passage which ends in the throat. The ancestors of this group, which lived during the Middle Age of Earth, in part had a totally ossified skeleton (see ACIPENSERIDAE, STURGEONS).

Chorda dorsalis: Back String.

Body formation characteristic of the second highest group within the animal kingdom, which is found in the ancestors of the vertebrates, in modern times in the *Tunicata* and the *Acrania*, and in the higher vertebrates during the embryonal stage at least. The chorda is the simplest form of an articulated, axial skeleton. In vertebrates, which include most fishes, during the embryonal development it becomes enclosed within arch to ring-shaped cartilaginous bone pads, which reduce it more and more until finally it is totally displaced and substituted by the spinal column.

The *Ch. d.* has given its name to the whole phylum of the *Chordata*, which also includes the vertebrates.

Chordata: Phylum of animals with a chorda dorsalis, characterized by permanent or temporary possession of such a chorda. The phylum comprises all higher animals.

Chriopeops: Similar to the fish *Chriope.*

North American genus belonging to the sub-family of the egg-laying Tooth Carps or CYPRINODONTINAE (see this), with slender, nearly cylindrical body, and terminal mouth. Dorsal and anal fins insert relatively near the head and are shaped similar to a fan.

— goodei (Jordan): The Blue-Fin Top Minnow.

SHAPE: As per description of the genus. D 9-12. A 9-11. Length: 1½″-2″.

COLOR: Greenish-yellow base with reticulate edges on the scales and a nearly black zig-zag length stripe to which sometimes is added another one on the caudal peduncle. The males show a copper-red spot at the base of the tail, the tail fin being carmine-red, the other fins being striped with beautiful colors. The male is more vividly colored and has bigger fins.

RANGE: Shallow spots of standing or slowly flowing waters in the South of the U.S.A.

CARE AND BREEDING: For its well-being this species needs not-too-small tanks, since it is quite lively. At times it is a little quarrelsome towards specimens of its own kind as well as to other fishes, which makes it necessary to provide for hiding places among rocks and roots. The fish seems a little sensitive to new water. They should not be kept too warm, 54-61° F being sufficient for wintering, otherwise 60-68°, for breeding 68-75° F. Too high temperatures make them prone to diseases. Nourishment consists mainly of live foods of adequate size, while dry food is taken only in

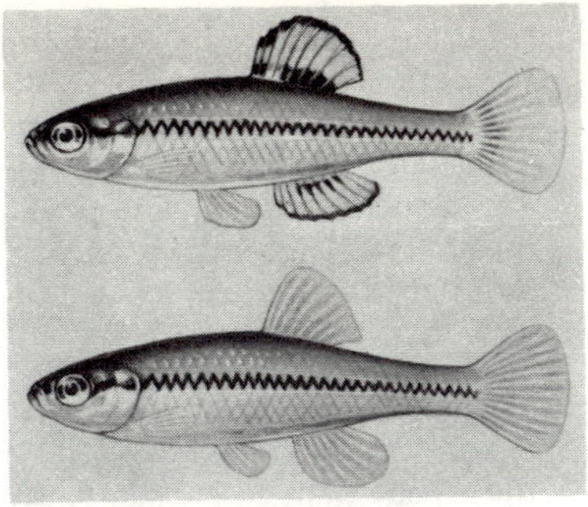

Chriopeops goodei, male above

case of necessity.

The act of spawning and the manner of breeding resemble those of the APHYOSEMIONS (see this). The rather big, yellowish eggs, which hang from a short thread, are spawned after charming mating games, among fine-feathered plants, generally near the surface, in daily batches of 3-5. Each spawning period lasts for about 5 weeks, after which the fish rest for 6-8 weeks. During the spawning periods they should be fed white worms or Tubifex. Avoid feeding Cyclops at any cost. The fry hatch after two weeks at 66-68° F, but after only one week at 72° F. Under too high temperatures many eggs remain sterile. It is advisable to feed the parents abundantly, as they prey strongly on their own spawn. The hatching fry keep beneath the surface and may easily be gathered and transferred to special tanks.

christyi: After a personal name.
— *Barilius.*

chromatophores: Color carriers of plants and animals, in the former known as chloroplasts. In animals *C.* are cells in the skin containing coloring substances. In fishes the *C.* are able to distend or to contract very quickly, which causes the changes of color.

chromosomes: Nucleus loops. Loop or rod-shaped formations which play an important role in the processes of fecundation. The *C.* are always found in pairs, of which only one set remains before fecundation and after a double process of division (see DIVISION OF REDUCTION). Since both the male and the female nucleus contribute with one such simple set each, they become paired again after completed fecundation. The *C.* are the main carriers of nucleine acids, which are found compressed within the cell nucleus, and are significant in the command of the processes of reproduction and of heredity. Their number and shape is different for the different live beings, but alike within the same species.

Chrosomus: With colored body. Genus of North American school fishes pertaining to the family of the Carplike fishes or CYPRINIDAE (see this), of elongated, slightly compressed body.

— erythrogaster (Rafinesque): Red-Bellied Dace.

SHAPE: As per description of the genus, relatively vigorous-looking, similar to the European Minnow. D 7, A 7-8. The scales are very small. Length up to $3\frac{1}{8}''$.

COLOR: With a large golden band along the sides, which is fringed above and below with black stripes, belly and throat vivid red. The male is slimmer and more intensely colored than the female and shows a rash during the spawning period.

RANGE: In clear, especially in flowing waters of the Northern and Central U.S.A., as a rule in small schools.

CARE AND BREEDING: This lively school fish likes big and long tanks with plenty of space for swimming. It is an undemanding omnivore, but should not be kept warm as otherwise it becomes prone to diseases. It is advisable to winter the fish in unheated, frost-free rooms. Breeding in the aquarium seems not to have succeeded as yet, but probably it resembles that of the other Cyprinids.

chrysotaenia: With golden band. — *Rasbora.*

chrysotus: Golden, gilded. — *Fundulus.*

Chub, the: see ACERINA CERNUA.

Cichla: Ancient name of a Perch-like fish.

Genus belonging to the family of the Cichlids or CICHLIDAE (see this), the name of which has been used for the whole family. Compared to the other Cichlids, though, the body is more Perch-like, strongly compressed laterally, with a relatively small head. The spiny part of the dorsal fin is distinctly set-off from the soft part, so that we could really speak of two separate dorsals. The scales are small.

— **ocellaris** (Bloch and Schneider): The Eye-Spot Cichlid.

SHAPE: As per description of the genus; D_1 XIII-XV, D_2 I/16, A III/10. Length up to 24″.

COLOR: The species is very variable, according to origin and age. In general shiny gray-greenish with occasionally noticeable cross bands and a length band. On the basis of the tail fin a dark, light-edged eye spot. Half-grown specimens look best. SD unknown.

RANGE: In standing and slowly-flowing waters of South America, especially in swampy and well-planted secondary waters of rivers. The species is also found in brackish water in river mouths. It is a much appreciated food fish in its home country.

CARE AND BREEDING: Only smaller specimens are fit for the indoor aquarium, otherwise only for the show tank. The fish are very predatory; furthermore they need oxygen and warmth. Temperatures of 73-77° F are adequate, lowest 68° F. The fish do not attack plants. Breeding has not yet succeeded.

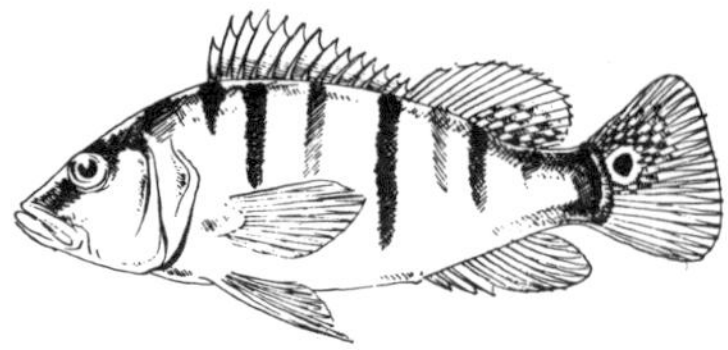

Cichla ocellaris

Cichlasoma: With body like Cichla. South American genus belonging to the family of the Cichlids or CICHLIDAE (see this), which is distributed over the tropical and sub-tropical regions of Central and South America. The body is more or less oval-elongated, the head big, the eyes large and vivacious. Generally the fins are of moderate height, dorsal and anal fins of the males commonly being a little pointed. In behavior they generally are real Cichlids, which root in the soil and are more or less quarrelsome towards their own species as well as toward other fishes, but showing a very interesting behavior. As for all Cichlids, the size of the tank influences their peaceful behavior. In very large tanks the fish drop many of their less appreciated traits. Care and Breeding as described for CICHLIDAE (see this).

— **arnoldi** Ahl: The Black Cichlid.

SHAPE: As per description of genus; D XV/11, A V/9. Length over 4″.

COLOR: Brownish base with dark dashes on the opercles and some spots at the insertions of the dorsal and caudal fins. The fins gray with blackish band designs, the tail fin edged with black. SD unknown.

RANGE: The Amazon River system.

CARE AND BREEDING: As per description of family. So far only a few specimens have been imported, but these are reported to be vicious, especially towards each other. They need warmth, 77-82° F, at least 68° F are advisable. Not yet bred.

— **aureum** (Guenther): The Golden Cichlid.

SHAPE: As per description of genus, the head rather pointed, the forehead contour a little indented, the eyes especially big. D XV-XVIII/9-12, A VI-VIII/7-8. All fins quite big, especially the pectorals. The tail fin is curved inward. Length, in the aquarium 4″-5″.

COLOR: Shiny golden with luminous greenish dots and a blue-black spot on the opercles. All fins very pretty, the dorsal edged with a vivid red. Dorsal and anal of the male are greatly extended.

RANGE: In densely-planted, standing or flowing waters of Guatemala and Southern Mexico.

CARE AND BREEDING: As described for CICHLIDAE (see this). The species is considered relatively peaceful, but unfortunately it has only rarely been imported, and has again disappeared from the market. Temperatures 72-77° F, for breeding 75-79° F.

— **bimaculatum** Linné: The Two-Spotted Cichlid.

SHAPE: As per description of the genus, but of somewhat higher build than the other species, especially the forehead contour rising in a steep curve to the insertion of the dorsal fin. D XIV-XVI/9-11, A IV/8-9. The tail fin is rounded, pectorals and ventrals are especially large. Length up to 8″.

COLOR: Brownish to bluish with dark band and spot designs. The dorsal and anal fins of the males are extended into points.

RANGE: Northern South America, in the region of the Amazon River, in the Rio Grande, and on Trinidad, but not in the Magdalena River. The species is found in standing and flowing waters with a muddy bottom and avoids clear water.

CARE AND BREEDING: As described for CICHLIDAE (see this), relatively

Cichlasoma bimaculatum

peaceful and needing little warmth. Temperatures 64-72° F, for breeding 75-77° F, lowest 59° F.

— **biocellatum:** Regan: The Jack Dempsey.

SHAPE: As per description of the genus, but the body a little more elongated, with rather straight dorsal and ventral contours and indented forehead. The fish looks strong and robust. D XVIII/9, A VIII/8. Length up to 8″. The female remains a little smaller.

COLOR: Dark blue-black or dark-brown base with luminous blue-green dots on gill covers, fins, and on each scale. The male has pointed dorsal and anal fins, the female distinctly differentiated by paler coloring and a band design, a dark spot, surrounded by shiny golden dots often standing out on the middle of the body.

RANGE: The region of the Amazon River, up to Costa Rica and Guatemala in the North.

CARE AND BREEDING: As described for CICHLIDAE (see this). A real Cichlid; very beautiful, but often

Cichlasoma biocellatum

extremely vicious and strongly rooting, hardy and long-lived. Temperatures 72-75° F, for breeding 77-82° F, lowest 50-54° F.

— **coryphaenoides** (Heckel): The Chocolate Cichlid.
Body oval-elongated, laterally compressed, the head big and quite pointed. D XVI/12-13, A VI-VII/9-11. Brownish base with some band and spot designs. Originates from the Amazon region. A little-

Cichlasoma coryphaenoides

appreciated, vicious, unseeming Cichlid which needs some warmth. Attempts at breeding miscarry due to the quarrelsome nature of the sexes.

— **crassa** Steindachner:
Of relatively high build, the forehead line rises steeply and is strongly indented on older specimens. D XVI-XVII/12, A VII/9-10. Length up to 8″. The ventrals of the male are considerably longer.
ORIGIN: The central Amazon region. Not yet bred.

Cichlasoma cutteri

— **cutteri** Fowler: Cutter's Cichlid.
SHAPE: As per description of genus. D XVIII-XIX/10, A IX/8. Length up to $4\frac{1}{8}$″.
COLOR: Greenish with 7-8 irregular, zebra-like, blackish cross bands and a spot on the tail root. The iris is a luminous blue-green, the fins of the male a dark wine-red. The female is a little paler in all its colors.
RANGE: Honduras.
CARE AND BREEDING: As described for CICHLIDAE (see this), but one of the prettiest Cichlids, which does not root much, sparing the plants, among which it likes to establish its spawning pit. However, the males fight a little more gallantly during the spawning season. Temperature 72-75° F, for breeding 79-82° F, lowest 64° F.

— **facetum** (Jenyns): The Chanchito.
SHAPE: As per description of the genus, not very strongly compressed laterally, the back slightly arched, the forehead rising steeply, a little indented above the eyes on older specimens. D XV-XVII/9-11, A VIII/7-9. The tail fin is rounded and fan-shaped, the pectorals are rather big. Length: may grow to over 12″, generally remaining smaller in the aquarium, and is already sexually mature at $3\frac{1}{4}$″.
COLOR: Strongly variable, according to mood and surroundings, as a rule with more or less visible cross bands on gray-yellowish base, the fins transparent or brownish red. During the spawning period the colors become much more intense, so that then the fish may be quite beautiful. The sexes are hard to differentiate, often only by the differently-shaped genital papilla. The eyes of the male show a red iris.
RANGE: In standing and flowing waters of Southern Brazil, Northern Argentina, and Uruguay. The fish are found especially in the secondary waters of the large

Cichlasoma facetum

rivers, both in fresh and in brackish water.

CARE AND BREEDING: As described for CICHLIDAE (see this). For a long time this was the best-known and best-liked Cichlid. It is considered 'intelligent', but roots strongly and is bellicose. Due to its hardy nature and ruggedness it may be kept in outdoor tanks, and may even be bred there in especially warm and favorable summers. Temperatures, 72-75° F, for breeding, 75-81° F, lowest 54° F.

— **fenestratum** (Guenther): The Window Cichlid.

A little-kept, unseeming, and vicious species.

ORIGIN: Mexico, in standing and flowing, densely-planted waters.

— **festivum** (Heckel):

SHAPE: As per description of genus, but differing strongly from the other species in type. The body broadens considerably towards the rear, beginning at the big and pointed head. It is strongly compressed laterally, and somewhat telescoped into itself, especially with advancing age. The throat, with the small, terminal mouth, recedes more and more, while the forehead contour advances. D XIV-XVI/10-12, A VIII-IX/10-12. Dorsal and anal fins are pointed, those of the males being extended into threads; the tail fin rounded in the shape of a fan; the second rays of the ventrals are strongly extended and reach to the center of the anal, when turned back. Length up to 6″, the female remaining a little smaller.

COLOR: Like all Cichlids, this species too is quite variable. In general yellowish-gray to green, with a dark band from the point of the snout to the upper tip of the dorsal fin. Above the band the color generally is darker. Temporary cross bands composed of connected spots appear on the sides. On the caudal peduncle we see a dark, light-edged spot. The male is more stately, with more pointed fins, its blue-green throat standing out remarkably. The only absolutely sure sexual differentiation, however, is to be sought in the differently-shaped genital papillae.

Cichlasoma festivum

RANGE: From Guiana in the North to the Plate River in the South, also in the river systems of the Amazon and the Paraguay. There the species is found in slowly-flowing waters, which are well-stocked with plants, twigs and rocks, also in flood regions and together with *Pterophyllum* (Angelfish). One of the commonest Cichlids of South America.

CARE AND BREEDING: One of the most peculiar Cichlids, which, due to its size, needs space and is best kept in richly-planted tanks with hiding places among roots and rocks. If it lacks these conditions, it easily becomes a little shy. *C. festivum* needs plenty of oxygen and is a little sensitive to chemicals in the water and to soiled water. It needs vegetable food, sometimes attacking the young tips of valuable plants. Experience shows that it spares Water Sprites and Cryptocorynes. Its need for vegetable nourishment may be sated with boiled and rinsed oat flakes. Breeding is not always simple, as it depends on mated pairs; otherwise it resembles that of the pit-spawning Cichlids.

— **hellabrunni** Ladiges: The Emerald Cichlid.

SHAPE: As per description of the genus; compressed laterally; quite elongated in youth, but growing higher-backed with age. Old specimens possess a protruding pad of fat on the forehead. D XV-XVI/9-12, A VI-VII/7-8. Length up to 12″. During youth the back is moss to emerald green. The sides and the head are rust to brick red. With age this color displaces the green hues nearly completely. A narrow, black horizontal stripe goes from the tail root to the head, but it is not always present. Two more or less distinct black spots are found on the caudal peduncle and the middle of the body. The SD are only minute, the female showing a larger genital papilla during the spawning period.

RANGE: In larger bodies of waters of the Amazon region and the Guianas.

CARE AND BREEDING: As described for the pit-spawning Cichlids (see CICHLIDAE). A robust, beautifully-colored species of Cichlid, which needs large tanks. Temperature 68-75° F, lowest 64° F.

— **meeki** (Brind): The Firemouth Cichlid.

SHAPE: As per description of the genus, rather high, strongly compressed laterally. The species is

Cichlasoma meeki

characterized by its steeply-rising forehead contour, its straight belly line, and the disproportionately big head. Under excitement they lower the bottom of the mouth like a goiter. D XV-XVI/9-10, A VIII-IX/7-9. The fins are relatively high, the caudal fin slightly arched in, the outer rays of the vertical fins of the males are either strongly pointed or extended. The crescent-shaped pectorals are quite big. Length up to 4″, in very big tanks even more, the females remaining a little smaller.

COLOR: Greenish-violet, with dark-edged, weakly luminous scales and dark, temporarily vanishing band designs. A dark spot on the opercles is edged with greenish gold. Throat and breast are a vivid red, the iris a luminous green. The SD are only minute; the female may temporarily show the same colors as the male. During the spawning period the throat of the female becomes temporarily whitish with a green hue, the same color being seen also on the gill flaps.

RANGE: Guatemala, Southern Mexico.

CARE AND BREEDING: As described for all pit-spawning Cichlids (see CICHLIDAE). One of the most beautiful and interesting species. The fish are relatively peaceful and rarely attack plants if these are sufficiently hard and well-rooted. There are individual differences in this, though. Temperature, 72-75° F, for breeding 75-79° F.

Cichlasoma nigrofasciatum

— **nigrofasciatum** (Guenther): The Convict Cichlid.
SHAPE: As per description of the genus; resembles *C. cutteri*; D XVII-XVIII/8-9, A VII-X/6-8. Length up to 4″.
COLOR: Silver-gray base with 8-9 variable, sometimes deep-black cross bands, which are placed like convicts' stripes. The vertical fins in part show a luminous metallic green. The male is more vividly colored, generally also a little bigger. The female occasionally shows a coral red spot on the sides.
RANGE: In the lakes Amatillan and Atitlan, in Guatemala.
CARE AND BREEDING: As described for all pit-spawning Cichlids (see CICHLIDAE). Temperature 75-79° F, lowest 59° F. A very commendable species.

— **octofasciatum** (Regan): The Eight-Banded Cichlid.
A very beautifully-colored, but vicious and bellicose species from flowing and standing waters of Central America, also from natural wells. Resembles *C. biocellatum* very much.

— **salvini** (Gunther): Salvin's Cichlid.
A very beautifully-colored species, with a peculiar design on the upper half of the body. Rarely imported so far, and not yet bred.
ORIGIN: Southern Mexico, Guatemala, and Honduras, in lakes and rivers. Vicious and bellicose.

— **severum** (Heckel): The Banded Cichlid.
SHAPE: As per description of the genus, but especially high. The forehead line rises steeply, the belly contour is flat. D XVI-XVII/13-14, A VII-VIII/12-14. Length over 8″.
COLOR: Young specimens show 8-9 dark cross bands on yellowish to greenish base which vanish gradually later on. At the bases of the soft parts of dorsal and anal fins each a dark spot, light-edged and connected with each other by a dark cross band. The iris is blood-red. The males have drawn-out and pointed fins and become occasionally more vivid in color.
RANGE: All over Northern South America, except in the Magdalena River.
CARE AND BREEDING: As described for all pit-spawning Cichlids (see CICHLIDAE). Despite its lack of bright color the species is quite noteworthy. Temperature, 73-77° F, for breeding 77-82° F, lowest 70° F.

— **tetracanthus** (Cuvier and Valenciennes): The Cuban Cichlid.
SHAPE: As per description of the genus, but relatively slender and with very large and pointed head. D XV-XVI/10-12, A IV/8-10. Length up to 8″, but ready to spawn after reaching 4″.
COLOR: The species is extraordinarily variable. Generally it shows a great number of darkly shining dot and dash designs on yellowish to whitish base, the whole coloring being noted for its constant changes. The SD are minute, the dorsal and anal fins of the males being slightly pointed. The two sexes are similar in color in a large extent.
RANGE: In standing and flowing bodies of water on Cuba and Barbados, both in fresh and brackish water.
CARE AND BREEDING: As described for all pit-spawning Cichlids (see

Cichlasoma tetracanthus

CICHLIDAE); a very beautiful, but vicious and bellicose species. Temperature, 80-86° F, lowest 72° F.

Cichlidae: Cichlids.

Family belonging to the sub-order of the Perch-like Fishes or PERCOIDEA (see this). Similar to the Perches, but differing clearly from these by the structure of the throat bones and by the presence of only one olfactory pit on each side of the head. Small to medium-sized, generally beautifully-colored freshwater fishes. Distributed from India (including Ceylon) through Africa (including Madagascar and Asia Minor) to America from Texas in the North to Uruguay in the South. Very rich in number of species in tropical and sub-tropical Africa, especially on the West Coast and in the large East African lakes. India is represented by one species only, the remainder originating mainly from tropical and sub-tropical South America. Body shape varies from a Pike-like to a disc-shaped structure. Most species are moderately high and elongated, the head being large, often with vaulted or indented forehead contour and big and vivacious eyes, the mouth opening often with strongly developed lips. The scales are rather big, generally comb-shaped. The dorsal fin shows a long, hard part, plus a shorter, soft one, both being fused together. The anal fin generally contains three hard spines and a large soft part. The ventrals face to the front, generally with one or two spines and 5 soft rays. The lateral line usually interrupts in the middle of the body.

Most Cichlid species are predators, which need varied, robust live foods, some species eating vegetable food additionally or predominantly. Individual characters are quite strongly pronounced. Behavior is always very interesting. Many species become tame towards their caretaker. The C. might hold a preferential place in aquaristics if this were not opposed by many of their traits, a great number of species being quite bellicose and vicious. It is related to defense of range and to care for the brood that most Cichlids root strongly in the soil and will not tolerate plants in the aquarium. Notwithstanding this, however, they are advisable as aquarium fishes.

A well-set-up Cichlid aquarium is able to compete with any other kind of tank in beauty. It is an interesting fact that the space factor bears so great influence on the behavior of Cichlids, and that many of the less desirable traits only develop under the influence of the (generally too small) indoor aquarium. Specimens that are kept in very large tanks (exhibition aquaria), behave in a completely different manner and prove to be relatively peaceful and absolutely not unfriendly. Among C. prevail laws of division of the territory and also of the relationship of property in the common vital space, that are similar to those observed among the Sticklebacks.

Nearly all species, excepting a few dwarf forms, demand very spacious tanks, measuring about 40″ or more in length. The more space you are able to offer the fishes, the better will be the ex-

Cichlidae — Types of Cichlid genera

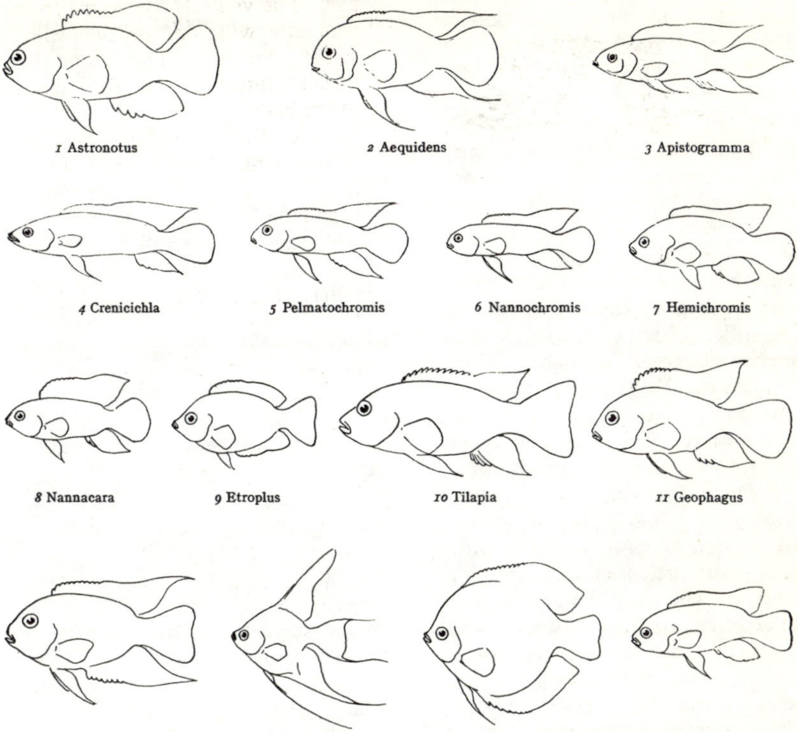

1 Astronotus — *2* Aequidens — *3* Apistogramma — *4* Crenicichla — *5* Pelmatochromis — *6* Nannochromis — *7* Hemichromis — *8* Nannacara — *9* Etroplus — *10* Tilapia — *11* Geophagus — *12* Cichlasoma — *13* Pterophyllum — *14* Symphysodon — *15* Haplochromis

perience you have with them. For your bottom soil choose not-too-thin gravel, which should be rinsed completely clean. In spots it may also alternate with thinner sand, in order to give the bottom covering some variety. Use some larger rocks and vigorous roots to build a sort of aquascape, so that the fish may have some hiding caves.

When doing this, pay attention to the fact that your handiwork should stand on firm foundations and can not be overturned by rooting beneath it. It should always stand directly on the bottom of the tank itself, and never on the sand. Some hardier plants, planted in flower pots and covered with gravel or stones should be placed in corners of difficult access, where the fish cannot deploy fully anyway. The pots might be hidden from the viewer's eyes by flat stones or something along this line. If you have sufficient room, have the decoration lead over to a shallower part of the tank, into which you may plant young willow twigs, which will soon send their whitish or reddish root tips into the tank. The roots of *Monstera* will serve a similar purpose if planted in the aquarium. Furthermore you may also place balls of Feather Moss (Amblystegium) loosely in the tank; they spread out on the bottom and make the whole set-up look more natural. A covering of floating ferns on the surface, too, may contribute considerably to achieve this effect. Besides this you will nearly always need effective aeration and filtration.

Most Cichlids pose no special demands as to the composition of the water. A great number of them do not need much warmth either, despite the fact that many species need temperatures between 70 and 75° F, due to their tropical origin, and sometimes even more for breeding. As nourishment serve them variegated live foods, such as mosquito larvae, aquatic insects and their larvae, tadpoles, earthworms, and in case of need also Daphnia. Most Cichlids show a special preference for small fishes.

The arrival of the act of spawning announces itself by enhanced colors of the fishes, violent fights, and sometimes by the robust wooing which now begins. C. are very choosy in the selection of mates, and generally close a sort of lifetime 'marriage', or at least a 'mating marriage' of very long duration. Shortly before the act of spawning itself, the chosen spawning site is picked and fanned clean with mouth and fins, besides being fiercely defended against all other inhabitants of the aquarium. It is now that the fishes become more quarrelsome in indoor tanks with too little space than in very roomy ones. They pick violently on other, weaker fishes, and also on unattached males and females, the fights being apt in many cases to end with the death of one of the contenders. Fishes that have grown up together from youth on, generally behave more peaceably towards each other, but in any case the onset of the spawning period makes caution advisable.

Adult fishes that are strangers to each other, even if they are of different sexes, may only be made acquainted through a separating pane of glass (which is removed shortly before spawning) or not at all. It may also happen that pairs which have lived peaceably together for months suddenly get involved in vicious fights and have to be separated. Such quarrels usually take place temporarily during the care for the spawn. Many Cichlids place their spawn on rocks, plants, roots, etc., caring for it very self-sacrificingly. The eggs are kept in a constant current of water created by fanning motions the parents execute with fins and body, infertile eggs being picked out, and the fish defending the breeding sites against any disturbances. As a rule there is a certain division of labor in this, one of the pair paying more attention to the eggs, while the other one is concerned with guarding the breeding site. The fry, which hatch after 48-72 hours, at first are not yet fully developed. While they are still absorbing the yolk sac, the caring parent moves them from the breeding site with its mouth and transfers them to a previously-dug pit, which frequently is located in such a hidden manner, that the aquarist only notices the presence of the fry after they have come to the stage of free-swimming. After another 4-6 days the young show up as a dense school, accompanied by their parents, keeping close to the bottom as a rule. The parents lead, guard, and take the school to feeding sites, bedding it down in the pit at night. The fry are instinctively attuned to certain colors of the parents, as well as to the motions with which these direct the swarm. The care for the brood may last 6 or 8 weeks and ends when preparations for a new brood begin.

Among Cichlids which maintain parental families, it sometimes happens that two females spawn together, one of them taking the part of the male as if it were a real one. When doing so this female too gets rid of her spawn. Despite the fact that these unfertilized eggs soon become fungused, it may happen that the two fishes continue living together as a 'pair'. For this reason it sometimes is hard for the aquarist to know whether his pair of Cichlids really are a male and female, or whether he has two females. Therefore, if several spawnings become successively fungused, it will be advisable to exchange one of the specimens for another, new one. For this the best to exchange is that which acts like a male.

The manner of propagating of the mouth-breeding Cichlids diverges from this. These spawn their eggs in shallow pits, one of the parents taking them into its mouth where they hatch. Even the hatched and already-swimming alevins find protection in the mouth for still some time. The oral cavity of the mouth-breeders is enlarged in a sack-shape for this. The swimming young continue returning to the parental mouth for some time. This manner of care for the brood permits very interesting studies on the behavior of fishes (see MOUTH-BREEDERS). The fry are voracious and grow very quickly. Since they are already quite big at the moment of free-swimming, the infusoria stage in nutrition may be by-passed. Feeding with dust-sized foods, eventually also additions of auxiliary foods (egg yolk, mashed White Worms and Daphnia, etc.) may now begin immediately. Since it is generally difficult to sell Cichlid young, it is advisable for the Cichlid breeder simultaneously to keep other kinds of predatory fishes, for which the growing alevins will represent a welcome additional nourishment.

The Dwarf Cichlids, which too care for their brood in the described way, but which differ a little in behavior from the other Cichlids, hold a special place. They do not root in the gravel and they spare the plants, and in most cases it is the mother which cares for the brood (see MATERNAL FAMILY).

Nearly all Cichlids are characterized by the ability quickly and radically to change their colors and designs, according to age, surroundings, and state of greater or lesser excitement. Besides this, frequently certain situations in life are connected with typical colorations.

So far no divisions have been made within this family, which is so rich in species. It is extremely difficult to find constant characteristics for this, based on their genetic history. HOEDEMAN has lately made an attempt to suggest such a division. The origin of the Cichlids is probably to be found in the Cretacean era, that is, at the time when Asia, Africa, and South America still were one connected continent. Probably they originated from salt water fishes, the ancestors of the Pomacentridae (a family of Perch-like sea fishes), which to this date are closely related to the Cichlidae. Presumably the members of the Indian genus Etroplus, with their semi-maritime manner of living, are relics of these form of development.

Probably the separation of the African and South American continents took place when the Cichlids had already specialized, so that today we find representative members with common characteristics in both regions. During the long eons since this separation, however, the fishes have continued specializing to a large extent.

According to HOEDEMAN, the family should be divided as follows:

ASIAN	AFRICAN
genera	
Sub-family ETROPLINAE:	
Etroplus	*Paretroplus* (from Madagascar)

AFRICAN	AMERICAN
Sub-family TILAPIINAE:	
Tilapia	*Crenicichla*
Neotilapia	*Cichlasoma*
Parachromis	*Herichthys*
Chilochromis	*Petenia*
Pelmatochromis	*Uaru*
genera	
Nannochromis	*Paraneetroplus*
Heterochromis	*Neetroplus*
	Herotilapia
	Pterophyllum
	Symphysodon
	Astronotus
	Aequidens
	Geophagus
	Apistogramma
	Nannacara
	Acaronia
Sub-family HAPLOCHROMINAE	
Haplochromis	*Cichla*
Hemichromis	

Cichlids: see CICHLIDAE.

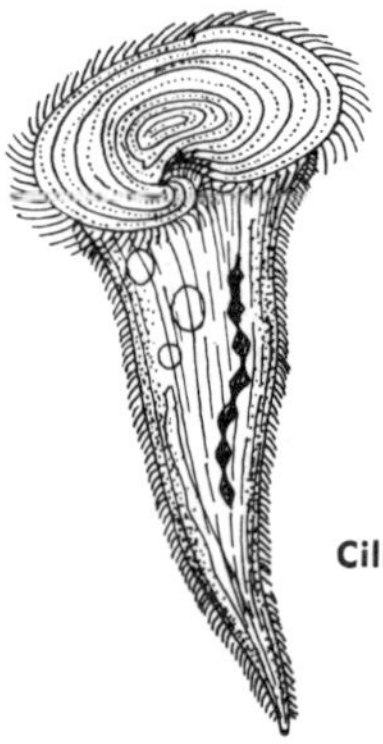

Ciliata, showing cilia

cilia: Small whip hairs which are used for locomotion or feeding, and which are found on all kinds of organisms, especially unicellulars.

ciliata: With eye-lashes.
— *Cryptocoryne.*

Ciliata: Infusoria.

Tribe of unicellular animals pertaining to the division of the *Cytoidea.*

The *C.* are the most highly developed of the Cytoids. They are of highly differentiated shapes, and many of their species seem like multicellulars. The whole body, or part of it, is covered with numerous motile cilia, which exert a rhythmical, synchronized rowing motion. These cilia serve the two purposes of locomotion and feeding. Each specimen has two nuclei, a macronucleus for metabolism, and a micronucleus which probably regulates reproduction. Infusoria react very quickly to stimuli, but so far it is not yet clear whether they have a special nerve organism or not. A great many species are bacteriophages (or bacteria eaters), which for this reason live in waters containing decaying parts of plants and consequently bacteria. They develop quickly and in great numbers in infusions (vegetable decoctions), which gave origin to the name infusoria. The tribe is sub-divided into two classes: *Euciliata* and *Suctoria.* According to the type of their cilia the *Euciliata* are divided into four orders: *Holotricha, Spirotricha, Peritricha*, and *Chonotricha.*

The *Holotricha* include, among others, the well-known Slipper Infusoria of the genus PARAMECIUM (see this), the predatory Nose Infusoria (*Didinium nasatum*), and the fish-killer ICHTHYOPHTHIRIUS (see this).

Also the order of the *Spirotricha* contains some very well-known species, such as, for instance, the Trumpet Infusoria (*Stentor*), and the peculiar Clam Infusoria (*Stylonichia mytilus*), which runs quickly along the bottom by means of the few, but strong, cilia which are located on its belly.

The order *Peritricha* includes the beautiful Bell Infusoria of the genus *Vorticella*, which form dense, whitish colonies—visible even to the naked eye—on plants, etc. These micro-organisms are able to retract their bell-shaped upper structures very quickly by means of a foot which may be coiled up in a spiral. Also Daphnia and similar animals may carry Bell Infusoria on them, while the 'Hydra Louse' *Trichodina* moves quickly on freshwater Hydras.

The class of the *Suctoria* is composed exclusively of predatory species, which suck up the internal juices of other infusoria by means of one or more sucking tubes.

cingulatus: Banded as if with a belt. — *Fundulus*.

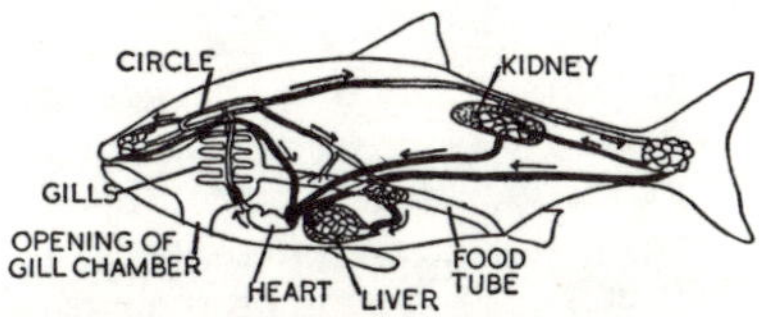

Diagram of a fish's circulatory organs

circulatory organs of fishes Fishes have a "simple" blood circulatory system. The heart lies under the gill openings ahead of the shoulder girdle in a heart sac, which is separated from the belly cavity by a wall of tissue. It consists of three chambers: the *Sinus venosus*, in which the venous blood from the body is accumulated, the antechamber and the real heart chamber. Only this has a strong, muscular wall. The return flow of the blood which has been driven from the chamber is prevented from returning by a pair of valves.

Only the heart of the Lungfishes (*Dipneusti*) is more highly developed. With all the other bony fishes the blood is pumped by the action of the heart chamber from the antechamber and passed by the large gill artery through the gills. In the gills there are a number of paired branches of smaller arteries which branch into the gills. With some fishes which have accessory breathing organs, part of the blood also is diverted into these organs. In the gills or other breathing organs the blood is laden with oxygen, and is then passed into the main artery, which runs along the back, and from this is distributed throughout the entire body. After all body parts and organs have been provided in this manner with blood which is rich in oxygen, the smaller blood vessels unite again and deliver into the sinus. The oval, nucleate blood corpuscles have a diameter of 0.005-0.025 mm (see BREATHING, BREATHING ORGANS).

cirrhosus: Fringed. — *Ancistrus*.

Citharinidae: African Characins. Family of Characin-like fishes belonging to the sub-order of the Carp-like or CYPRINOIDEA (see this). Of short to elongated body structure, partly almost spindle-shaped, more or less compressed laterally. Most of the genera are completely peaceful, one genus (*Phago*) being pronouncedly predatory. Genera, among others: NANNEATHIOPS (see this), NEOLEBIAS (see this), DISTICHODUS (see this), and PHAGO (see this).

Cladistia: Order of very ancient fishes pertaining to the sub-class of the Ancient Fins or PALAEOPTERYGII (see this), characterized by the fact that the dorsal fin is divided into many small and independent finlets. The diamond-shaped scales are covered with a hard layer of enamel (*Chondrostei*). Only one family: the POLYPTERIDAE (see this).

Cladocera: Fish Food Crustaceans. Sub-order of lower Crustaceans belonging to the order of the *Onychura*, class of the PHYLLOPODA (see this). The body is generally enclosed within two shells and little articulated. Two lateral eyes, which on the final, completely-developed form fuse into one unpaired eye. Frequently a secondary eye is

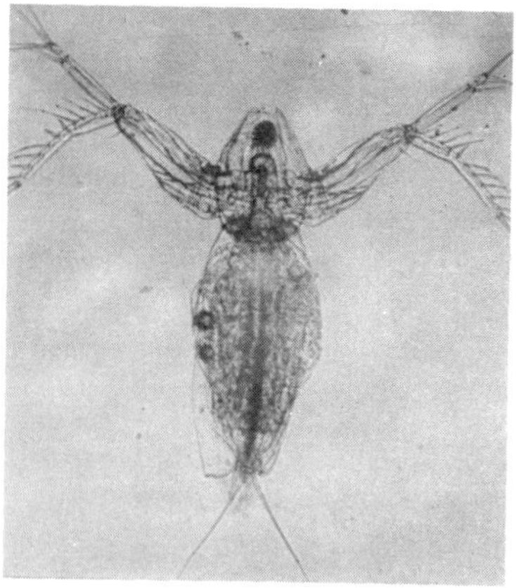

Bythotrephes longimanus

found below this. Only on the *Bosminae* or Trunk Crustaceans the first pair of antennae is strongly developed, while the second pair, which is used for locomotion, is robust on all species. The 4-6 pairs of pectoral legs are only used to acquire nourishment, and form a filtering system on most species. Only those of the few predatory forms are changed into a trapping and catching device. The shape of the *C.* changes considerably according to their surroundings and to the season of the year (*Cyclomorphosis*). Reproduction follows a peculiar cycle of generations. The hibernated eggs, which are able to withstand drought and cold, give origin to females exclusively. In most *Cladocera* the subsequent eggs of these develop without fecundation (*parthenogenesis*) within the breeding space on the back of the crustaceans, which is enclosed within a second shell.

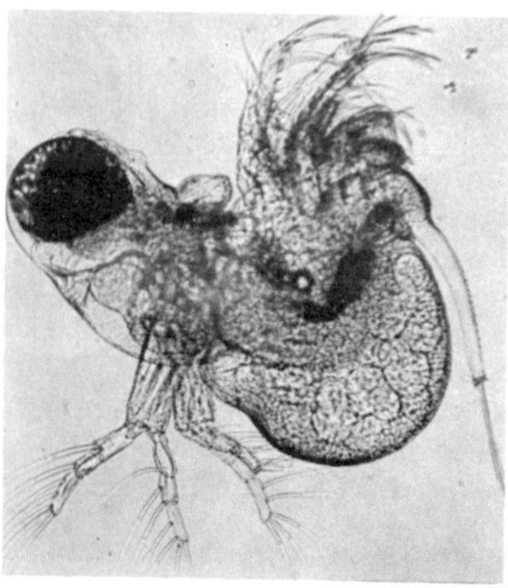

Polyphemus pediculus, with eggs in brood-pouch

Development takes place very quickly at high temperatures. The newly-born females still struggle and kick for some time within the breeding space, but soon leave it. After this the mother changes her skin and sets up a new batch of eggs for hatching. On adult specimens the eggs may number 50 to 100 units. The young on their part begin developing eggs after only a few days. This leads to the well-known mass reproduction in the warm season, in which the descendants of one female may be calculated at about 30 millions. Over-population, which soon sets in, leads to lack of food and to phenomena of degeneration. Consequently the development of spawn recedes. A similar process takes place when the water dries up, a fact to which the *C.* are well adapted. Now males are produced which fecundate their mother generation. Therefore the permanent eggs are fertile eggs, which are thrown off with part of the back carapace as a covering. These eggs may rest dry for long periods, insuring the survival of the species even under the most unfavorable conditions. They are carried to all possible kinds of water sticking to the feathers of water fowl, to flying insects, etc.

Cladocera are an extremely important fish food.

In all there are four tribes, the members of which partly live on or among aquatic plants, at the surface of the waters, in mud, and (in smaller numbers of species, but in great masses of individuals) as plankton. To do this, most species do not float, but have to keep in constant motion. This book describes the following of the many genera: DAPHNIA (see this), BOSMINAE (see this), POLYPHEMUS (see this), and LEPTODORA (see this).

Clam Flower: see PISTIA STRATIOTES.

clams, mussels: see BIVALVIA.

clarias: Meaning unknown.

— *Pimelodus.*

Clarias, type of the genus

Clarias: Genus of Catfishes belonging to the family of the Gill Sac Catfishes or CLARIIDAE (see this).

— angolensis Steindachner: The Angola Catfish.

SHAPE: As per description of the family. D 70-82, A 55-63; no adipose fin. Length up to 14″.

COLOR: Uniformly greenish to brass colored. SD unknown.

RANGE: West and Central Africa, especially in fresh, but also in brackish water, always over muddy bottom.

CARE AND BREEDING: Likes darkly-located, densely-planted tanks. A predatory twilight and nocturnal fish. Eats only live food. Older specimens take earthworms, small fishes, clam meat. Not yet bred.

— anguillaris Linné:

Body structure like that of the other species. D 65-76, A 53-62. Length up to 30″. SD unknown.

ORIGIN: The Nile, Lake Tsad, exclusively in fresh water.

— batrachus (Linne): The Frog Catfish.

Body structure like that of the other species. D 62-76, A 45-58. Length up to 20″. Gray-blue with lighter spots, fins green with red edges. The male slimmer, more vivid in color, the genital papilla longer and more pointed than that of the female.

ORIGIN: All of South East Asia, up to Hongkong in the North.

— dumerilii Steindachner:

Body structure like that of the other species. D 66-72, A 49-55. Length up to 10″. Brownish with dark mottlings.

ORIGIN: Angola, Old Calabar, in standing and slowly-flowing waters with muddy bottom.

— lazera Cuvier and Valenciennes:

Body structure like that of the other species. D 62-82, A 50-65. Length up to $4\frac{3}{4}$″. Uniformly brownish to blue gray.

ORIGIN: Syria, furthermore in the Nile, and West Africa from Senegal to the Niger.

Clariidae: Gill Sac Catfishes.

Family of Catfishes belonging to the sub-order of the Catfishlike or SILUROIDEA (see this), distributed over Africa, Asia Minor, and Southeastern Asia. Catfishes of elongated shape, with broad, flattened head and terminal mouth around which they carry four pairs of barbels.

The front part of the body is little compressed laterally, but the rear part is strongly so and nearly ribbon shaped. The small teeth sit in ribbons on the jaws and on the ploughshare bone. The generally long dorsal fin begins shortly behind the head; the anal too is very long; the ventral cavity is short as compared to the total length of the fish. The body is naked, and covered with a leathery mucous skin. All fins are without spines. An adipose fin may be present or lacking. The Gill Sac Catfishes are inhabitants of biologically very unfavorable waters, which they are able to leave for hours and even days. During dry periods they come out on land at night to go hunting for food, while they bury in the mud during daytime. They are able to cover greater distances on these hunting trips, due to having an accessory breathing organ, which lies within the body cavity as a shorter or longer respiratory sac, extending especially along the sides of the spinal column. This respiratory sac either encloses the gills, or else thin, cauliflower-like ramifications of the gill arches which lead to the sac. The *C.* are twilight and nocturnal fishes, but absolutely not shy in the aquarium, where they show themselves freely even in daytime. With snaking movements they swim unceasingly along the bottom, hunting out food with their barbels. Some species utter sounds if disturbed while out of the water. These sounds are produced by pressing air out of the respiratory organ. They like dimly illuminated tanks with soft bottoms and shadowy hiding places. All species are very voracious and predatory.

Genera: CLARIAS (see this), HETEROPNEUSTES (see this), and GYMNALLABES (see this).

Clay Groundling, the: see ELEOTRIS LEBRETONIS.

Climbing Perch, the: see ANABAS TESTUDINEUS.

Climbing Perches, the: see ANABANTIDAE.

cloudiness of water: Clouding of water may have several causes. Freshly installed tanks often cloud over during the first days, due to a proliferation of bacteria and unicellulars, which disappear again after some days with the establishing of a certain equilibrium. A cloudiness which comes from carelessness while filling in water (roiling with bottom particles) settles automatically after some days. The clouding components are then held on the bottom by micro-organisms, especially algae, etc. Strongly rooting fishes too can of course roil the water. In this case it is advisable to thicken the clear-washed covering layer, for which one preferably uses coarse gravel which the fishes cannot budge. Cloudiness which originates from careless overfeeding with artificial foods is very difficult to counteract. The best is to extract this with a filter. It may become the reason for a secondary clouding by infusoria. This is best fought by overstocking with daphnia. Certain prepared foods, as well as oat flakes, which are liked by plant-eating fishes, often cloud the water with a delayed action in spite of great care and pre-treatments, due to the fact that the clouding substances return to the water in the excrements of the fishes. In such cases it is advisable to stop using these foods and to switch over to live foods with simultaneous filtration. The most dangerous are cloudings which result from the development of metallic salts due to insufficient insulation of the aquarium frame. These cloudings, which cause poisonings of fishes and plants, are generally accompanied by foul odors. A poor grade of cement and poor workmanship, too, give rise to cloudings. In such cases the only thing to do is to clean out the whole aquarium and to remedy the causes of failure.

cloudy water: see CLOUDINESS.

Clown Loach, the: see BOTIA MACRACANTHA.

Clupeiformes: Herring-shaped fishes: see ISOSPONDYLI. Designation for the Herring Fishes or *Isospondyli* formulated by BERG in

1940.

New in this is that on one hand BERG has excluded the Nile Pikes as a separate order (*Mormyriformes*); on the other hand, however, considering the inclusion of the Pike Fishes justifiable, mentioning them as a sub-order (*Esocoidea*), while at present they constitute an order of their own (*Haplochromi*).

Cnesterodon: With teeth like razors.

Genus of live-bearing Tooth Carps belonging to the sub-family of the POECILIINAE (see this).

— decemmaculatus (Jenyns): The Ten-Spot.

SHAPE: Delicate, very elongated body, especially the males. Head and forepart of the body compressed horizontally, the rear end compressed laterally. Moderately large, up-slanted mouth opening; very large gonopodium with a peculiar, bent tip. Length: males 1″, females 1⅜″.

COLOR: Brownish to yellowish-drab, with bluish to violet hues, and 8-11 comma spots on the caudal peduncle.

RANGE: Southern South America.

CARE AND BREEDING: Despite its small size, a robust and long-lived fish which withstands low water temperatures, nearly down to the freezing point, but also warmths up to 77° F and more. About 20, quite quick-growing fry per litter. One of the first live-bearing Tooth Carps to be imported (1902).

Cobitidae: Loaches.

Family of highly specialized fresh water fishes belonging to the sub-order of the CYPRINOIDEA (see this) or Carp-like, with a great range in Europe, Asia, Abyssinia, and Western Indonesia. Predominantly bottom fishes, which in part also live in rapidly-flowing mountain waters.

The small to moderately-large fishes have a more or less elongated, or even worm-shaped body. Frequently they are only little compressed laterally, the head being a little flattened from above. The skin is mucous, and the cycloid scales which are imbedded in it range from small to stunted. The mouth is generally subterminal and protractable. The mouth opening is surrounded by thick lips with three or more pairs of barbels. The lateral line is interrupted or lacking totally. The double-compartmented swimming bladder is enclosed within a bone capsule with its front part, while the rear part is stunted and sometimes even reduced to nothing but vestiges. Many *C.* are famed for their sensitiveness to changes in atmospheric pressure, which is due to the special structure of the swimming bladders. The intestine is used as an additional (accessory) respiratory organ. To a certain extent this enables many species to live in oxygen-poor waters or to bury themselves in mud in case of long-lasting droughts. The fins are relatively small. The eyes are frequently covered with a protective skin lid. Near them we find a simple or two-pronged thorn (eye thorn), which some species are able to erect and with which the fishes are able to hurt enemies.

Many of the Groundlings or Loaches are excellent aquarium fishes. Despite the fact that many species lead a hidden life and cloud the aquarium by their constant rooting in the soil, they are all very interesting. The fishes are also able to bury themselves completely in the soil. Some tropical species also swim more or less freely. Feeding them is not difficult. Live or dead foods are taken from the bottom, where the fishes search them out with their barbels. The olfactory sense is very pronounced. The fish often chew regularly through the bottom, bigger bites being broken up in the mouth and the detritus being expelled through the gill covers. So far breeding in the indoor aquarium has succeeded only very rarely and only with a few species, these achievements as a rule having been achieved by pure chance.

Genera, among others: COBITIS (see this), NOEMACHEILUS (see this), MISGURNUS (see this), BOTIA (see this), ACANTOPHTHALMUS (see this), ACANTHOPSIS (see this), and *Lepidocephalus*.

Cobitis: The Classical Greek name of this fish.

Genus belonging to the family of the Loaches or COBITIDAE (see this).

— taenia Linné: The Stone-Grig or Suck-Stone.

SHAPE: Elongated body, compressed laterally, flat on the underside. D 8-10, A 7-9; scales very small, partially lacking. The mouth is subterminal, provided with thick, fleshy lips and three pairs of barbels. The fins are small. The eye thorn is erectable and double-pronged. The gill slit is narrow and small. The pointed pharyngeal teeth stand in one row. Length up to $4\frac{3}{8}''$.

COLOR: Pale yellow with several rows of irregular dots along the body. The second ray of the pectoral fins of the males is thickened.

RANGE: Europe, Northern Asia, North Africa, in flowing and standing, clear fresh waters.

CARE AND BREEDING: Twilight and nocturnal fish, which remain buried in the sand during day-time. They avoid direct sunshine. Equip the tank with fine-grained, clear-washed sand and hiding places. The species is sensitive to lack of oxygen, using its intestinal breathing only in cases of extreme need.

Cobitis taenia

Nourishment consists of live bottom foods, but also of vegetable matter and organic detritus. Difficult to keep, and thus far hardly ever bred in the aquarium. To our knowledge breeding has succeeded only once. The fish spawned at a temperature of 61° F in shallow water among the roots of floating plants. The fry hatched after four days and were not hard to rear.

Cockatoo Cichlid, the: see APISTOGRAMMA CACATUOIDES.

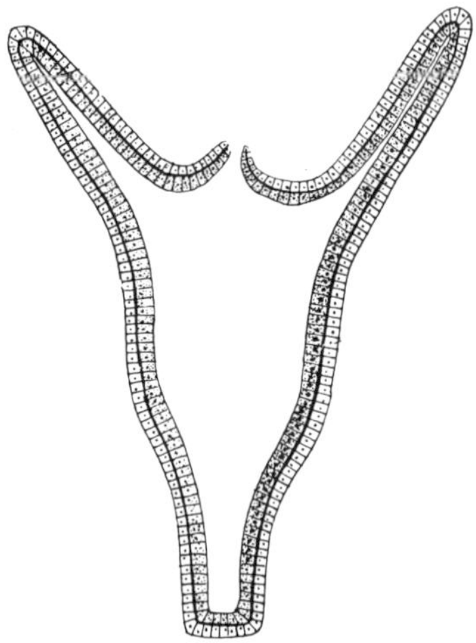

Diagram of Coeleneterata

Coelenterata: Sub-division of invertebrates, more or less simply built, differing from the sponges by the presence of real tissue and organs. Basically the body walls consist of two layers of cells, the outer, ectoderm, with muscle fibres, sensorial cells, nerves, and weapons of attack (relatively of defense), and the inner, entoderm, which assimilates nourishment. Both layers enclose a simple hollow space. Between them lies a thin skin, richly equipped with nerve cells, the 'supporting lamella'. The whole is completed by undifferentiated cells from which any kind of body cells may be developed in case of need. This is the reason why the *C.* have such a strongly developed power of regeneration. Nearly all of them are equipped with nettle cells, very complex structures, which generally are used for defense or in order to acquire food. Most *Coelenterata* live in the sea, with very complex forms. In fresh water they are represented exlucsively by the order HYDROIDEA (see this). The members of the genus MICROHYDRA (see this) develop a special medusa form.

coeruleum: Blue.
— *Aphyosemion.*

coeruleus: Blue.
— *Brochis.*

cognatum: Related, akin.
— *Aphyosemion.*

cold water aquarium: Aquarium that needs no artificial heating and may be set up in an unheated room summer and winter, as long as it is protected against frost. The cold water aquarium is used to keep domestic animals and plants, as well as those of the temperate zones of other continents.

Cold Water Haplochilus, the: see ORYZIAS LATIPES.

Coleoptera: Beetles, Scarabs.
Order pertaining to the sub-phylum of the Insects or HEXAPODA (see this), characterized by the freely articulated head, the equally well-differentiated breast segment, and by the fore-wings, which generally are changed into hard wing-covers. The Coleopterans possess robust oral organs, generally masticatory ones, and well-developed faceted eyes. They go through a complete metamorphosis.

Water Bugs are adapted to life in water, not only as larvae, but also as fully developed insects. This adaptation is least developed in the HYDROPHILIDAE (see this), and best in the DYTISCIDAE (see this). The following genera are of interest for the aquarium: among the Predatory Beetles (see ADEPHAGA), the Swimming Beetles (see DYTISCIDAE), and the Tumble Bugs (see GYRINIDAE), among the Glutton Beetles (see POLYPHAGA), the HYDROPHILIDAE (see this).

Colisa: After the native name.
Genus of Gouramis belonging to the family of the Climbing Perches or ANABANTIDAE (see this), the body of which is round-elongated and strongly compressed laterally. The dorsal fin is as long as the anal, the second ray of the ventrals has grown into a long, thread-like formation, which is the seat of taste buds.

— fasciata (Bloch and Schneider): The Giant Gourami.
SHAPE: As per description of the genus; a relatively big species. The small mouth possesses thick, fleshy lips. D XV-XVII/9-14, A XV-XVIII/14-19; the scales relatively large. The length may reach 4¾", the female remaining a little smaller as a rule.
COLOR: Reddish to brownish base, with blue-green cross stripes, which slant toward the rear. Opercles, breast, and belly a luminous blue-green; the fins a pretty color. The female is simpler in color. Dorsal and anal fins are rounded.
RANGE: From India to Burma. Due to its large range, the species varies greatly.
CARE AND BREEDING: Like all other Gouramis, this species too shows a certain timidity and shyness, which is especially noticed in freshly set-

up and too-well-illuminated tanks. Domesticated specimens are quite lively; the males may become a little quarrelsome during the spawning period. Due to their size, the fish demand spacious tanks, which should be well-planted and must offer sufficient hiding places for the female. The species likes some warmth and is best kept at 75-82° F. During the spawning period the temperature may rise to 86° F. On the other hand the fish also tolerates an occasional lowering down to 59° F. They are omnivorous, but need rich and variegated nourishment. The male builds a very big bubble nest, which is supported by floating plants. For more details see ANABANTIDAE.

Colisa labiosa

— **labiosa** (Day): The Thick-Lipped Gourami.

SHAPE: As per description of the genus. A little smaller than the previous species, but often mistaken for it. The small, terminal mouth is located beneath a remarkable thickening which results from a puffing up of the skin above the upper jaw in sexually mature specimens, especially males. D XV-XVIII/8-10, A XVI-XVIII/17-20. Length up to 4″.

COLOR: Shiny greenish base with irregular, slanted reddish cross bands, which stand out more clearly at the rear end of the body. The green basic color is often covered with a darker horizontal band on the middle of the body. Under excitement throat and belly become dark violet with gray-white designs, the fins beautifully colored. The female is much simpler in color, its dark length stripe generally standing out more clearly; the dorsal fin is rounded.

RANGE: Indo-China.

CARE AND BREEDING: As described for the preceding species and for the family.

Colisa lalia

— **lalia** Hamilton-Buchanan: The Dwarf Gourami.

SHAPE: As per description of the genus; the smallest and shortest of the species. D XV-XVIII/7-10, A XVII-XVIII/13-17. Length up to $2\frac{3}{8}$″, the female generally remaining a little smaller.

COLOR: One of the most beautiful of all tropicals. Shiny blue-green base with slanting, vivid red cross bars, the fins shiny blue and green with red dots and seams. The female is much paler in color.

RANGE: India.

CARE AND BREEDING: As per description of the genus. The species is a little shy. It likes smaller, sundrenched tanks, with plenty of algae. The bubble nest is built incorporating algae and loose parts of plants; it is small but high and firm.

In general the species may be considered hardy and peaceful, but the male is a little bellicose during the spawning period. The fish need much warmth, 75-81° F, for breeding up to 90° F.

Colisa Disease, the: see OODINIUM.

color malformations: Divergences from the natural coloring of fishes, which, even if not directly fatal, must at least be considered malformations.

These changes in color generally are based on the absence, or on the preponderance, of some of the pigments. Thus, for instance, certain disturbances which are caused by internal diseases, eye defects, lesions, upsettings of metabolism, and other not yet explained hurts, may produce a sudden development of black pigment cells. Such phenomena generally have nothing to do with the normal changeability of the melanophores of fishes. SCHAEPERCLAUS differentiates between melanosis conditioned by the surroundings, and hereditary melanosis, which is comparable to other hereditary changes of color.

According to their hue, these changes of color are called melanism (black coloring), xanthorism (golden coloring), albinism (partial or total absence of all chromatophores), and alampy (inability to develop glitter crystals—see GUANIN).

In most of these cases we face mutations which are recessively (in a covered manner) hereditary, and which may be fixed by selective cross breeding. Besides this many of the changes of color are subject to occasional alterations in the course of growth and life. Thus it frequently happens that Black Mollies are not born purely black, and acquire this color later on. The same may happen with Gold Fish, while albinos sometimes develop melanophores later on, or fishes with alampy grow guanin crystals. Changes in color cannot be called diseases. Therefore SCHAEPERCLAUS proposes to call them 'color malformations'.

Of value for science are the cases of excessive accumulation of pigments in connection with malignant, cancerous swellings found in hybrids of the species of *Xiphophorus*, which have been studied by BREIDER, GORDON, HAEUSSER, and KOSSWIG. We shall not discuss the particulars of the problem, but the solution to the question has been advanced a large step by the aid of just an aquarist. BREIDER states about this: 'Our findings have brought the first proof that the development of cancer may be a question of heredity, insofar as a hereditary proneness is a primary condition fot the action of a cancer trigger. The cancer trigger itself may be of hereditary nature or not . . . Aquarists may claim the merit of having supplied an essential contribution to the solution of these problems, which are of such huge import for genetics, medicine, and mankind in general'.

colors of fishes: Fishes are counted among the most colorful animals, especially the tropical species being extremely manifold in colors and designs. This beauty is one of the main reasons why they are so much appreciated in the aquarium.

The seats of the pigments are relatively large cells in the dermis, of irregular, ramified shape, containing the pigment inside themselves in the form of grainlets or droplets (CHROMATOPHORES, see this). The black, blue-black, and blackish-brown pigments (melamines) are of grainy structure, while the red to yellow ones (lipochromes) are liquid. It is peculiar that there are absolutely no green or blue pigments, despite the fact that just

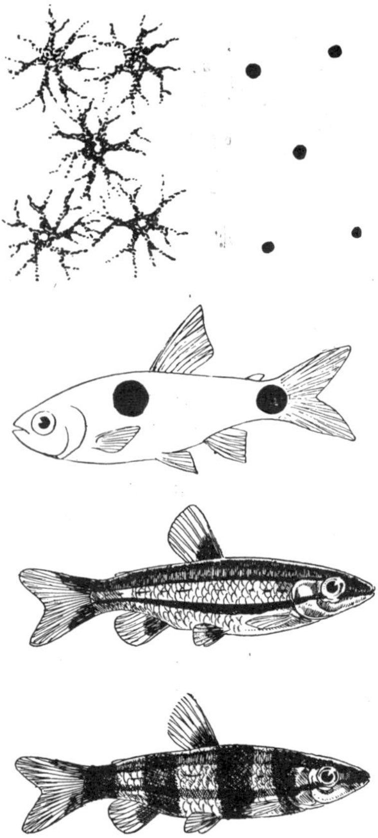

Fish Coloration. Above: color cells in the skin, opened on the left and closed on the right. Middle: signal marking of a school fish (**Exodon**). Below: day colors of **Nannostomus trifasciatus**. **Bottom**: night colors of the same fish.

these colors are very frequently seen on fishes. These are created by an association of the other colors with shiny crystals, and by shining through the upper layers of the dermis, which look yellow due to inlays of fat. Especially the black chromatophores contribute to this. Genuine coloring, produced by pigments, should not be confused with the, generally delicately-hued, metallic glitter of fishes. This results from the fact that mirroring GUANIN (see this) crystals, imbedded more or less deeply in the second layer of the dermis are caused to shine up by light reflexes. This explains the fact that many fishes seem colored only under incident light, while in light that shines through they only show the hues which depend on the direct action of the chromatophores. The delicately hued reflexes rise especially when the guanin crystals lie very near the surface. If they lie deeper below the scales, where they form the silver layer (*argenteum*), they either produce the silvery glitter of many fishes, or, if they are covered by color cells, the beautiful luminous colors which we admire on Neon Tetras, for instance.

The development of color cells probably depends to a large degree on light. This may be the reason why the bellies of fishes which lie on the bottom very often are nearly colorless. Cave fishes too have a pigment-less skin. Furthermore fishes have the ability to adapt to their surroundings in color and design. Changes in color take place by distension or contraction of the pigment in the chromatophores. This may take over the whole surface of the fish, which may pale in case of discomfort, or may conversely increase the intensity of its colors when excited. Furthermore the change of colors may affect only special parts of the body, so that colors and designs change only at these spots. Depending on which color tones distend or contract, marked changes in color may result, a fact which is known from many aquarium fishes. The change of colors may take place very quickly—sometimes in no more than a few seconds—or it may extend over hours and days. External influences, such as low temperatures, lack of oxygen, sudden fright, etc., may also cause these changes, as well as diseases, one-sided feeding, discomforts or well-being, and especially excitement. It is of special biological significance that many fishes are to a large extent able to adapt to their surroundings in color and design. This is especially true for the designs, for instance, dots, spots, stripes, bands, etc. But also colors as such may play a part.

Experience shows that most fishes look much more colorful if they live over a dark bottom or background, while they pale if the bottom is light-colored or the tank placed in a too-well illuminated location. Some fishes possess this adaptability to an especially high degree, which happens, for instance, with Soles. In general the colors stand out more intensely in dark waters. Fishes which come from such waters often possess colors which are disposed in luminous (that is, strongly reflecting) signals. This happens especially with school fishes from jungle waters. Excitement frequently causes strong changes of color. Quite often certain colorings and designs are conditioned by certain phases of behavior.

While certain fishes have nearly permanently even 'mating colors'—for instance the Rosy Barb—others may show different colorations for each stage of the spawning period. Thus most Dwarf Cichlids, for instance, have special colors of fright, bluffing, mating, spawning, and breeding. As a rule the males are more intensely colored than the females. Frequently the prettier colors are also allied to special peculiarities of the body, for instance ornamental fins. This differentiation may go so far, that it is difficult to recognize that the sexes belong to the same species, as for instance, happens with some egg-laying Tooth Carps. In some rare cases it may be the female which is more intensely colored, especially if it takes a very active part in caring for the brood, or if it does this alone.

Protective coloration of **Cottus gobio**

Quite a number of fishes also shows a change of colors in states of rest. Thus some Half-Beaks (see HEMIODONTIDAE), have a pronounced night color. While during the day-time the colors essentially show as length stripes, at night they are substituted by very dark cross bands.

Most fishes are also differently colored in the different stages of age. Young fishes rarely have the full coloring of their parents. Frequently the different phases of growth are characterized by special colorings.

The biological significance of colors and designs has to be evaluated in different manners. Often the colors represent phenomena of adaptation in one or the other sense. Frequently they serve to identify their bearers to a certain point with their surroundings. It is in this sense that we have to understand the darker back of most fishes, the lighter belly of the free-swimming species, the silvery glitter of the fishes of open waters, the spotted back of the bottom-dwellers, the cross stripes of many inhabitants of the plant regions, or the dark, cloudy designs of the shore-dwellers. Even very striking colors may serve a function of

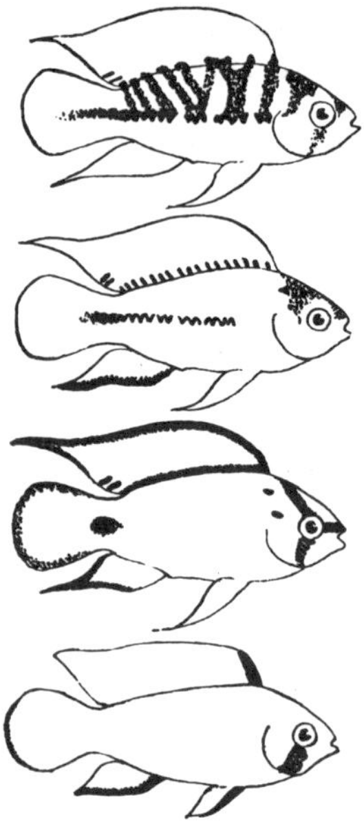

Diagram of color phases in **Apistogramma reitzigi.** Top to bottom: fright colors, threatening colors, courting colors of males. Bottom: Courting colors of a female (after Vogt)

defense and camouflage under certain circumstances. Flashy colors may also be colors of warning, if their bearer has some quality which is disagreeable to attackers. In this sense we have also to mention the bluffing colors of fighting males. Also in wooing the intensity of the then-appearing 'mating colors' seems to play an important part. It is possible, however, that many of these colorings go beyond the biological needs, it being especially uncertain whether the colors act on the wooed females in the sense of 'sexual selection'. At least in part colors must also be evaluated as signs of enhanced vitality (increased metabolism). We have to consider very especially, that all colors may cause quite different impressions in their native waters from those they cause in the aquarium with its completely changed conditions of lighting.

Some striking colors and designs seem to be of importance in the care for the brood. Presumably many fry of brood-caring species have an innate idea of the signal colors of their parents. Such colors may be, for instance: strong black spots on light base, contrasting colors on the lower half, etc. Also the luminous reflex colors and remarkable spots of many tropical school fishes are of importance for keeping the school together.

As a rule the color mechanism is put in motion by transmissions from the eye to the central nerve system. This happens especially in the phenomena of adaptation to certain surroundings. Frequently, however, there are other stimuli, routed over other organs, which influence the coloring. The colors of excitement, especially mating colors, seem to be triggered by an increased output of hormones.

color sense of fishes: Considering the biological significance that colors ought to have for fishes, it must be supposed that most fishes possess a more or less strongly developed color sense. Despite this consideration, however, the question has been vigorously disputed for a long time. The experiments of V. FRISCH and others, though, have proved undeniably that the color sight of fishes coincides with that of man to a large extent. An important role in this was played by numerous careful attempts at training. These led to the conclusion that at least the fishes which received training really see colors in the same way as they appear to our eyes as long as there are no special conditions of the water (roilings, shadowings, great depths) which could weaken or change their effect. It is interesting to notice that in water many colors are seen as hues of gray, similar to those shown on black-and-white photographs.

coloratus: Colored.
— *Potamogeton.*

Colossoma nigripinnis: see PIARACTUS NIGRIPINNIS.

Comb Tail, the: see BELONTIA SIGNATA.

commbrae: Mutilated from Corumbae, after the town of Corumba, on the Paraguay River.
— *Apistogramma.*

commersoni: After the French naturalist Commerson.
— *Ambassis.*
— *Plecostomus.*

Commerson's Glass Perch: see AMBASSIS COMMERSONI.

Common Frogspoon: see ALISMA PLANTAGO-AQUATICA.

Common Puffer: see TETRAODON CUTCUTIA.

Community tank: A form of aquarium in which different animal species, mostly fishes, are kept together. Generally the C.T. is found wherever fishes are kept for a purely ornamental purpose. Basically nothing can be said against keeping several species together, but unfortunately this is often done indiscriminately, so that a C.T. may have to be considered quite unbiological. The widely-spread preference of today for this manner of keeping fishes can only hinder real aquarists, whose main aim is the observation of the animal in its natural behavior. Only the earnest endeavor of the keeper to create such surroundings for his pets can lead them to show their natural behavior. In the C.T., though, where fishes are put together arbitrarily, they often enough repel each other, and furthermore in most cases it will be impossible to do justice to the different exigencies of life that become apparent.

For this reason one should only put together such fishes (or other aquatic animals) which have equal or similar living conditions, that is, which occur under equal conditions in nature or of which, in case they come from the same geographical origin, one is led to believe that also in nature they are found together. Whenever possible, though, one should proceed most cautiously, keeping in mind that the individual species-aquarium, in which one keeps fish of one species only (in schools, groups, or singly, according to habits and needs of living), permits a much more exact biological observation. For this reason with time the individual species-tank turns out to be more interesting and preferable to the C.T.

compressus: Compressed.
— *Aponogeton.*
— *Carassiops.*

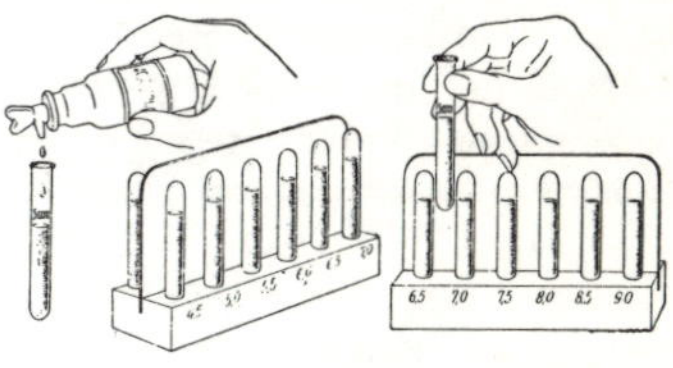

A pH testing kit

concentration of hydrogen ions (pH value): The pH value of water shows the natural reaction of same, that is, whether the water is acid, neutral, or alkaline. In aquaristics we watch the pH value when breeding certain tropical fishes and aquatic plants. However, the pH value is no quantity in itself having to be considered in its relationship to other factors, especially to the HARDNESS OF WATER (see this). The pH value is not a constant factor, being subject to constant fluctuations due to the influences of the weather, the influx of water, the deposits of substances, and especially to assimilation (see BIOGENOUS CALCIFICATION and DE-CALCIFICATION). These fluctuations are the stronger, the smaller the contents of the water of dissolved calcium and magnesium compounds, since these are able to equalize strong acids and bases, especially to react with fluctuations in carbon dioxide which may appear, that is to 'buffer' them. Since calcium and magnesium salts are decisive for the hardness of water, this means at the same time that pH value and hardness are closely intertwined factors. The natural reaction of water is indicated by the weight of its contents of:

(a) free, negative hydroxyl ions;
(b) free, positive, hydrogen ions.

A series of numbers from 1 to 14 gives the weight of the ions of hydrogen (H^+) in a liter of water at 20°C (68° F). The weight of the negative hydroxyl ions (OH^-), which is not mentioned, is in the corresponding inverse ratio. A liter of water at 68° F contains:

	H^+	OH^-
pH 1	1/10 grs.	1/10 000 000 000 000 grs.
pH 2	1/100 grs.	1/1 000 000 000 000 grs.
pH 3	1/1000 grs.	1/100 000 000 000 grs.
pH 4	1/10 000 grs.	1/10 000 000 000 grs.
pH 5	1/100 000 grs.	1/1 000 000 000 grs.
pH 6	1/1 000 000 grs.	1/100 000 000 grs.
pH 7	1/10 000 000 grs.	1/10 000 000 grs.
pH 8	1/100 000 000 grs.	1/1 000 000 grs.
pH 9	1/1 000 000 000 grs.	1/100 000 grs.
pH 10	1/10 000 000 000 grs.	1/10 000 grs.
pH 11	1/100 000 000 000 grs.	1/1 000 grs.
pH 12	1/1 000 000 000 000 grs.	1/100 grs.
pH 13	1/10 000 000 000 000 grs.	1/10 grs.
pH 14	1/100 000 000 000 000 grs.	1 gr.

Therefore the hydrogen ions and the hydroxyl ions balance at pH 7 in neutral water. In this case the weight of both is $\frac{1}{10{,}000{,}000}$ grs. that is a number '1' with 7 zeros, for short 10^7 grs. Consequently, only the denominator of the series is mentioned. Furthermore, it is always the weight of the hydrogen ions that is given. The tables show that there are very considerable differences between the individual numbers of the pH series, so that even small displacements of the pH value may exert great influence on the live beings that are found in water.

The difference in water conditions between the temperate zones and the tropics and subtropics has already been discussed under the entry HARDNESS OF WATER (see this). These special conditions have as a consequence that in the temperate zones the pH value is kept more evenly at the neutral point, due to the buffering of the carbonates, than happens in the tropics. Accordingly, domestic aquatic plants and animals generally are adapted to neutral or alkaline pH values, while many tropical ones are accommodated to pH values with major fluctuations and which often incline towards the acid range.

A constant pH value—reached by acidifying the tanks with the only inorganic acids which may be used, hydrochloric acid, sulphuric acid, or phosphoric acid—can only be kept up over a period of time in tanks without bottom soil or plants. The most favorable for doing this is phosphoric acid. Use 1/10 grs. of phosphoric acid in 10 ltrs (about 2½ gals.) of water and add the solution to the water until reaching the desired pH value. The water should first stand for 3-4 days after treatment before using it. Natural conditions are imitated by filtering with peat moss (SPHAGNUM—see this), with which one can reach a weak acidification of very soft water. Also decoctions made from sphagum or tree barks (especially thin barks of oak, willow, or alder) may affect an acidification. It is wrong to blame all failures in breeding on the chemical composition of the water, as also a great number of other factors play a big part. This includes, for instance, the correct mating of pairs, the keeping of definite spawning periods and periods of rest, varied feeding, etc. The experience of the latest years has shown that the influence of the pH value on animals and plants is still hazy to a great extent, and that so far no definite assertions may be made.

The measuring of the pH value in aquaristics may be made with inexpensive and easy-to-handle instruments. Among these we count the color-scale indicators. Measurings with pH papers generally are too inexact, if done by laymen, and have to be excluded for this reason. Liquid indicators are better. Some drops of a solution that changes to certain colors at certain pH values, are put into a standardized test tube, the liquid that is to be measured is added, filling the tube up to the mark, the whole is shaken, and compared with a printed or liquid color scale.

conchonius: After the native name. — *Barbus*.

concolor: Uniformly colored. — *Macropodus opercularis*.

Congo Tetra, the: see PHENACOGRAMMUS INTERRUPTUS.

Conjugatae: Yoke Algae.

The *C.* are single or multi-cellular forms of fresh-water ALGAE (see this), partly of very charming shape. There is only one nucleus in each cell. Being Thread Algae, they are not as firm and taut as the corresponding Green Algae. They may become obnoxious, however, when they hinder the growth of plants with their cotton-like coverings. Some *C.* prefer water that reacts acidly, and consequently they are found in peat waters. Among the most beautiful shapes we find some that look like crosses, moons, little stars, etc. The placement of the chlorophyll in the species that develop threads is peculiar. It appears in spirally wound bands. The name of the *C.* derives from the sexual reproduction (conjugation) of many of the species. For this two algae threads lie alongside each other, each cell sending a small extension toward its neighbor. These fuse and form what is called a yoke bow, across which the cellular contents of one cell migrate into the other one. Both nuclei fuse together and form a zygote. After the empty cell dies, these zygotes come out, settle down after a short wandering period, and develop new threads. This kind of reproduction is unique among algae. Besides it, however, many *C.* also show asexual and sexual reproduction in the conventional manner of the other algae.

conjugation: Fertilization of ciliates by temporary juxtaposition of two individuals and subsequent exchange of nuclei. *C.* also happens in the world of plants, in certain algae, the Conjugates.

conjunctive tissue: Body tissue which surrounds, keeps together, and supports the internal organs. It contains the vessels and lymph ducts; bones, tendons, blood, and blood vessels have developed from conjunctive tissue.

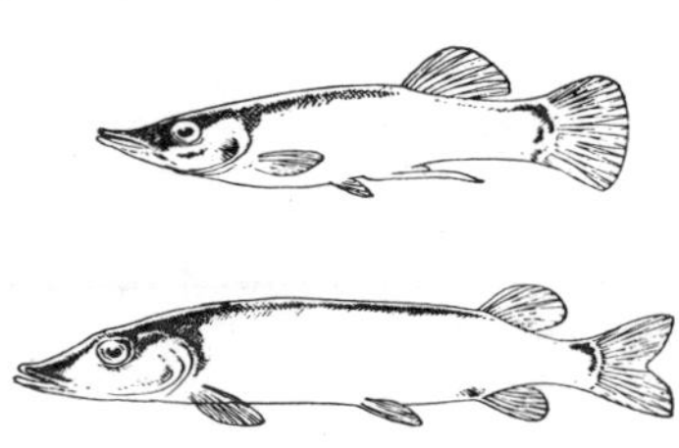

Convergence. Pike types in two unrelated species with similar feeding habits.

convergence: Similarity of external characteristics and behavior developed in otherwise widely separated live beings. It consists of the fact that similar conditions of living may call forth similar organs and manners of behavior. An example of this is the typical "pike" shape of both the Pike (*Esox lucius*), and the live-bearing Pike Top Minnow (*Belonesox belizanus*).

Convict Cichlid, the: see CICHLASOMA NIGROFASCIATUM.

Cope, Edward D.: Noted American paleontologist and ichthyologist. Born 7-28-1840, died 1896. Classified more than half of all the fishes of the Southern U.S.A., and many South American species. Many fishes were named in his honor.

Copeina: After the American zoologist Cope.

South American genus of fishes belonging to the family of the Characins or CHARACIDAE (see this).

— arnoldi Regan: The Splash Tetra.

SHAPE: Of elongated, very slender, laterally only moderately compressed build; D 10, A 11, The scales are very large. The dorsal fin is placed far toward the rear; the fins of the male are strongly developed and curved. Length up to 3⅛", the female remaining a little smaller.

COLOR: Reddish-brown with silvery sheen, sometimes an indistinct, temporarily zig-zag-shaped band on the middle of the body, besides this a dark design which results from the edged scales. The fins are yellowish with red tips, on the dorsal a black, light-fringed spot.

RANGE: In the region of the Amazon and the Rio Para, especially in plant-thick secondary waters of the rivers.

CARE AND BREEDING: The species is peaceful, vivacious, and gregarious, being also very long-lived and un-

Copeina arnoldi

demanding as to nourishment. The fish are omnivorous, but need varied fare, liking to jump after flying insects. For this reason the tanks should be very well covered. Temperatures 75-82° F, lowest 64° F. Reproduction is remarkable. The fish spawn out of the water on overhanging leaves of land plants, in the aquarium on the cover glass is case of need, or else on side panes or other make-shift anchorages. The coming of the act of spawning is announced by marked restlessness of the male, which evidently is looking for a good spawning site. When the female is ripe to spawn, it seeks the male and both go to the chosen place, swimming side by side. There they rise to the surface while touching very closely. After a short pause both jump out of the water and stick to the chosen spot. According to the report at hand it seems that the male always takes only the right or only the left side of the female, this choice being individual. After a few seconds the fish fall back into the water, generally not together. Many false matings take place in this manner, only the last leaps constituting real matings during which the fish hang 50-220 eggs on the spawning site in a total of 5-12 leaps. The male cares for the brood by remaining near the spawn, showing up beneath it from time to time and splashing the eggs with water by means of strong strokes of the tail fin. This process is repeated every 20-30 minutes, up to the moment when the fry hatch after 36 hours, being washed down into the aquarium by the splashed water. Rearing the young is then done as with those of most other Characins, and is not overly difficult. It is advisable to remove the parents after hatching.

— **callolepis** Regan: The Beautiful-Scale Characin.

SHAPE: The body is slender, only moderately compressed laterally, the dorsal contour nearly straight. D 10, A 11. The scales are very big. Length up to $2\frac{3}{8}''$, the female remaining a little smaller.

COLOR: Gray-greenish base, each scale with a dark edge and provided with a dark-red spot at the insertion.

RANGE: The region of the lower Amazon.

CARE AND BREEDING: The species is a little sensitive and needs warmth. For breeding give it up to 86° F. The fish need spacious, well-illuminated tanks stocked with broad-leaved plants. The act of spawning takes place on the upper leaves of such tanks, but without sticking the eggs, which may number up to 200 on them. These are spawned after violent chasing while the fish lie closely pressed together on the leaf, the male

Copeina callolepis

catching the released eggs in its folded anal fin, from where they fall to the bottom. The fry hatch after 36 hours and hang from sides and plants, generally near the surface, for another two days. Being very small, at first they need very small-sized food, but already take sifted daphnia after 10-14 days.

— **guttata** (Steindachner): The Red-Spotted Copeina.

SHAPE: This species differs from the two previous ones by its more robust-looking and trout-like body structure. The head is a little flattened on the upper side, laterally the fish are only moderately compressed. D 10, A 12; the scales are rather big. In the aquarium the species grows to lengths of 6″, but it is reported that no specimens of that size are found in nature.

Copeina guttata

COLOR: A blue-greenish sheen, the males with a bright red dot on the insertion of each scale, the fins yellowish to brick-red.

RANGE: In well-planted secondary waters of the central Amazon River.

CARE AND BREEDING: The species is hardy and long-lived, very peaceful and adequate for community tanks. Unfortunately many specimens are very shy. The fish like to leap. Temperatures 73-77° F, lowest 64° F. The act of spawning takes place in a pit dug by the male in the sand, after violent chasing.

During this the fish lie side by side, the male slipping its anal fin beneath the genital opening of the female. Depending on size, the pair spawns 100-250 eggs, in several matings, for which the male cares by fanning them. The fry, which hatch after 30-50 hours, are a little sensitive to fluctuations in temperature. Since the broods from larger specimens are very numerous, efficient aeration is advisable. The alevins are very small, but grow quickly if they are fed with plenty of very small-sized live foods. The parents are ripe to spawn again after 3-4 weeks.

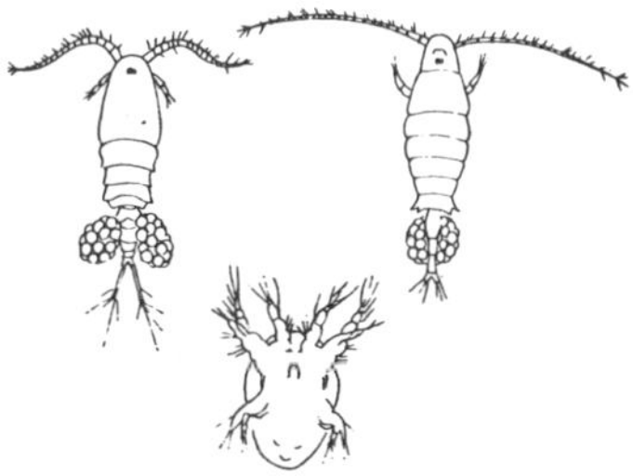

Copepoda, enlarged. Top, left: Cyclopoidea—right: Calanoidea—below: type of nauplius.

copepoda: Rowing Feet.

Class of micro-crustaceans belonging to the sub-phylum of the CRUSTACEA (see this). A group which is very rich in forms, with over 1000 small, in part even microscopically small, species. The *C.* are cosmopolitan, generally living free in the sea, a smaller number also in fresh water. Some groups live parasitically. The non-parasitical *C.* generally show three body divisions, the head-and-breast section, the trunk, and the abdomen. The body is distinctly divided into 10-11 segments. The head and breast segments of those forms which live planktically are grown firmly together, while those of the forms which live in the shore regions are movable independently. In some cases there may also be no trunk at all. The abdomen ends in two forked bristles. The head-and-breast section carries two pairs of antennae and two pairs of jaw feet, while the trunk shows the same number of pairs of rowing feet as it has segments (generally five). On the center of the head segment sits an unpaired eye spot. The first antennae of *Cyclops* are shorter, while those of *Diaptomi,* for instance, are longer, the body fluid keeping them stiff. These antennae are used as floating organs. The antennae carry sensorial bristles, being used by the males as gripping organs with which to hold the females, besides this. The pectoral legs are used both for locomotion and for anchoring fast to places or to sweep in nourishment. This is also helped by a trapping device located near the second antennae, which vibrates up to 3000 times per minute. *Diaptomus* possesses a heart, while in *Cyclops* the pulsating intestine provides for the circulation of the fluids.

Most species are built in the shape of a pestle. The size is relatively smaller for the floating forms. Commonly the color of these is glassy-gray, while that of the shore and pond forms frequently is brown to red. The frequently-noticed green coloring stems from abundantly consumed algae food, the red coloration being produced by droplets of oil from floating algae. Red specimens have considerable contents of carotine besides this. The bundles of eggs show different colorings. Nourishment generally consists of floating algae, infusoria and detritus, but many *C.* also eat dead higher animals and even attack weakened live ones.

The Copepods are heterosexual. Their manner of reproducing is quite interesting. It is well adapted to the changeable conditions of small bodies of water. As a rule the females are recognized by the little 'egg sac', of which *Cyclops* carries two, *Diaptomus* one at the rear of the trunk. These consist of a cluster of eggs which is held together by a jelly-like substance. Fecundations takes place before the extrusion of the eggs, the male attaching itself to the female and sticking spermatophores (see this) near its genital opening, the contents of which are freed after swelling up. The sperms penetrate the body of the female. The eggs of the planktic forms number 2-10, those of the others 20-50 units.

The larvae (nauplii), which hatch from the eggs are completely different from the adult animals, and only reach the shape of these after completing a total of 12 changes of skin. Those nauplii which hatch in Autumn need 7 months to reach sexual maturity, while Summer broods develop much quicker. The periods of greatest reproduction happen in Winter and Spring, so that in Summer one sees nearly all young specimens. On the other hand reproduction also takes place in the warm season in small and shallow bodies of water which dry out in Summer. Before the water dries up, thick-shelled eggs are produced, which are able to withstand the heat while buried in mud. Some specimens also hibernate by means of permanent eggs, while others do so hidden in mud; under certain conditions full-grown *Cyclops* also develop cysts as permanent spores. The planktic forms of *C.* of the fresh water are an important fish food and their nauplii are indispensable as nourishment for fish fry. They are easier to keep handy than *Cladocera*, since *Copepoda* are considerably more robust and long-lived.

The following of the fresh-water

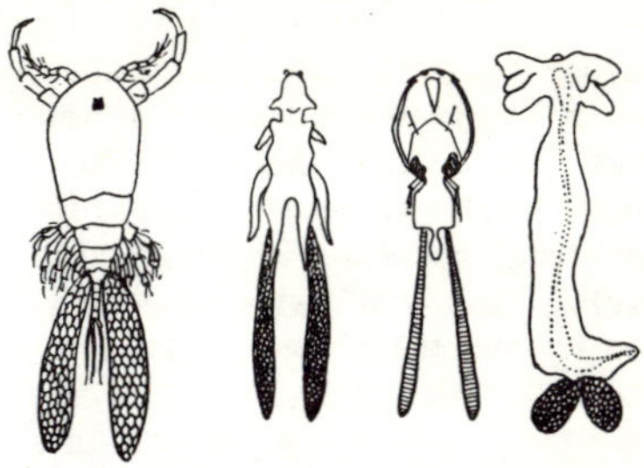

Parasitic **Copepoda.** Left to right: **Ergasilus, Chondracanthus, Caligus, Lernaea.**

forms are of main interest for the aquarist: CYCLOPOIDEA (see this), and CALANOIDEA (see this). The different species of the genera are practically alike from the outside, that differentiating them is a task that should be left to experts.

Copepoda diseases: Harm to fishes caused by parasitic COPEPODA (see this). The attack is in the first place directed against the gills and the adjacent regions, in some cases also against the skin and fins. Partly, however, the parasites also penetrate deeply into the body of the fishes. The group of parasitical *Copepoda* is extremely rich in shapes. A small number of them may still be recognized externally as *C.*, but generally they have changed their shape in adaptation to their manner of living, so that it is no more easy to recognize them as Copepods. The harm caused by these parasites generally takes effect by hindering the fishes from breathing, feeding on the epithelial and mucous cells, and by the fact that the attacked spots are secondarily infected with fungus (*Saprolegnia*). Due to the restricted respiration the body can no more be fed sufficiently, which makes the fishes become extremely lean, and finally causes them to die. The extent of the harm depends on a series of factors, such as the number of parasites as compared with the size of the host, for instance. So far *Ergasilus sieboldi*, which is the main parasite of this kind on food fishes, has not been observed in aquaria. *Lernaea cyprinacea*, one of the Copepods with a very changed shape, however, has already made its appearance in the aquarium. In general terms, though, it may be stated that *Copepoda* Diseases do not play a significant part for aquarium fishes. Attempts at cure have not yet led to certain results.

Copper Characin, the: see HASEMANIA MELANURA.

copulation: Introduction of the spermatozoans into the female body in order to achieve FECUNDATION (see this) with the aid of special organs. In fishes real copulations only take place in special cases, such as, for instance, to a limited extent among certain live bearers. Many of the fishes pertaining to this group possess a fin, generally the anal one, developed into a copulating organ. Notwithstanding this, only a few species present true copulation, and for other species it is not yet clear whether it happens or not. Generally the spermatozoa are brought near the female sexual opening with the aid of the organ—called gonopodium in the *Poeciliinae*—where they are sucked in.

Coral Fish Disease: Epidemic disease of Coral fish and other salt water fishes from tropical regions, the causer of which belongs to the same genus *Oodinium*, one of the unicellular algae, as the causer of the well-known velvet disease. The germs especially attack the gills. High temperatures only help to spread the disease farther. The cycle of development resembles that of *ichthyophthirius*.

cordata: Heart-shaped.
— *Cryptocoryne*.

Corixidae: see HYDROCORYSAE, water bugs.

Corumba Dwarf Cichlid, the: see APISTOGRAMMA COMMBRAE.

corydoradinae: Armored Catfishes.
Sub-family belonging to the family of the CALLICHTHYIDAE (see this). A group of Catfishes which is very rich in species, harmonizes strongly in body shape, and is well-liked in aquaristics. Often they are considered 'the scavengers of the aquarium', but they really deserve a better appreciation due to their likeable behavior. The idea that the fishes live exclusively on organic detritus, as is so frequently supposed, is erroneous. To the contrary, the hobbyist who decides to breed them had better provide for plenty of bottom food. They are especially good at pulling up tubifex which have buried in the soil. Of the numerous species so far only a few have been bred in the aquarium. They do not care for their brood, but their mating is very interesting.

Genera, among others: CORYDORAS (see this), *Aspidoras*, and BROCHIS (see this).

Corydoras: With helmet and spear. South American genus pertaining to the family of the *Callichthyidae*, sub-family of the CORYDORADINAE (see this), which differs from the other genera of the family by its unarmored back. The body is pestle-shaped, the dorsal outline strongly arched, the ventral contour straight. In general the fishes are of very short build.

They inhabit waters of all kinds and are able to live even under very unfavorable biological conditions, due to their intestinal respiration. Not all species are as rugged and long-lived as the well-known Peppered Corydoras, *C. paleatus*. In nature they are found both in flowing and in standing waters, especially at shallow spots with muddy bottom. The Armored Catfishes are quite undemanding in many respects. However, their needs of warmth differ specifically, and fluctuate for freshly imported specimens according to geographic origin. KNAACK, for instance, re-reports that he found living Corydoras in the mud of an outdoor pool covered with an 8″ layer of ice in January. This shows that at least some of the species seem to be little sensitive with regard to temperature. *Corydoras paleatus*, for instance, still spawns at temperatures which are no more adequate for other fishes from the same geographic latitudes. For this reason we should try to find out whether the Corydoras in our aquaria are not being kept too warm.

All species like plenty of hiding places. But they also like to lie on rocks, roots, etc. *C.* are absolutely not discriminating with regard to nourishment. They eat all kinds of live foods, especially ones they can take from the bottom. Daphnia too, however, are not refused, if these move near the bottom, as often happens. To what extent they feed on detritus is open to discussion, but this manner of feeding is complementary at best.

Up to very recent times there still was a series of uncertainties as to reproduction, especially regarding the process of fecundation. So far a number of species of *C.* could not be induced to spawn in the aquarium. PINTER points out that one will possibly have to consider certain spawning periods during which attempts at breeding have the best chance of success. Probably this happens in the period between August and March. The fact that *C. paleatus*, as well as its spawn and fry, is very insensitive, should not lead to the conclusion that other species do not need considerably more loving care. The manner of reproducing seems to be largely the same for all species. Set them up for breeding in spacious, densely-planted tanks, with new, clean, and clear water. The hardness of the water is unimportant, but it seems that harder waters are preferred. It is possible to induce the Armored Catfishes to reproduce not only in set-up aquaria, but even in all-glass tanks with less water.

For setting them up, calculate 3-4 males per female. Despite their awkward shape the fishes are quite lively and ardent during the spawning period. When spawn ripeness approaches, the female cleans the spot she deems fit as a spawning site with her mouth. The mating games of the males are interrupted by the fact that the female approaches one of them lightning-quick and—according to the opinion that prevailed so far—sucks fast to it. This so-called 'sucking fast' remained undisputed for a long time. Lately the experiments of KNAACK, documented with photographs, have shown that in fact it is the male who holds the female by pinching her barbels against his belly with his pectorals. With this Knaack seems also to have explained the so-far disputed process of fecundation. As is known, during each mating 2-4 eggs are laid into a pouch formed by the ventral fins of the male. So far it had not become clear when and how the eggs were fecundated. Thus, among others there was the supposition that the female picks up the sperms with her mouth, sending them to the rear through the gill openings along the body by means of violent respiratory motions until they reach the eggs in the male's ventral pouch. KNAACK has also demonstrated the impossibility of this by means of dyes. He verified that the sperm of

Corydoras is able to live longer than that of other fishes. The water around the mating pair is full of it, even if not in very large proportions. The small number of spermatozoans released by one male might perhaps explain why one female spawns with several males. After the eggs are fecundated, the female anchors them on the previously-cleaned spot.

Here is an attempt to make a systematic division of the genus *Corydoras* (according to GERY):

A. The *paleatus* group
  1. *C. paleatus* (Jenyns)
  2. *C. punctatus* (Bloch)
    (a) *C. punctatus acutus* (Cope)
    (b) *C. punctatus leopardus* Myers —possibly identical with *C.p. julii.*
    (c) *C. punctatus julii* (Steindachner)
    (d) *C. funelli* Fraser-Brunner
    (e) *C. reticulatus* Fraser-Brunner
  3. *C. melanistius* (Regan)
    (a) *C. brevirostris* Fraser-Brunner (?)
    (b) *C. longirostris* Fraser-Brunner (?)
  4. *C. agassizi* (Steindachner)
  5. *C. undulatus* (Regan)

B. The *aeneus* group
  1. *C. aeneus* (Gill)
    (a) *C. aeneus nattereri* (Steindachner)
  2. *C. metae*
    (a) *C. metae arcuatus* (Elwin)
    (b) *C. metae myersi* (Miranda-Riberro)
    (c) *C. metae 'auratus'* (?)
  3. *C. elegans* (Steindachner)
  4. *C. barbatus, C. macropterus, C. treitlii, C. trilineatus* are rarer species which have appeared occasionally in importations.

C. The *hastatus* group
  1. *C. hastatus* Eigenmann and Eigenmann
    (a) *C. hastatus australe* Eigenmann and Ward.

Corydoras aeneus

— **aeneus** Gill: The Bronze Catfish.

SHAPE: As per description of the genus. D I/7-8, A I/6-7. The dorsal fin is relatively large, the adipose fin is supported by a spine. The pectorals are provided with a strong spine each, and the tail fin is deeply forked. Upper scale plates: 21-23, lower ones: 19-21. The belly is covered with a tough leathery skin. Two pairs of barbels. Length up to 2¾″.

COLOR: Brownish base, with an irregular shiny dark-green horizontal spot, which stands out especially above the pectorals. The dorsal fin of the males is higher and more pointed, the female is plumper.

RANGE: Found in nearly all of South America, down to the La Plata region in the South, also on Trinidad Island, with many local strains.

CARE AND BREEDING: As per description of genus. The needs for warmth of the species differ according to geographic origin. Breeding as described for *C. paleatus*. PINTER supposes that leading the sperms to the eggs within the fin pouch is unnecessary, considering the violent motions during the mating. The eggs may number about 300. At 77° F the fry hatched on the fifth day and sank to the bottom, while the empty egg shells continued clinging to the spawning site. The yolk sac was consumed during the first days, and the alevins soon started to eat dust-sized foods and micro-worms. Sexual maturity was reached after about 12 months.

— **agassizii** Steindachner:
SHAPE: As per description of the genus, but especially high-backed and short. The head very large. D I/7, A I/6-7. Upper armor plates: 23, lower ones: 21. Length up to $2\frac{1}{2}''$.

Corydoras agassizi

COLOR: Yellowish-white base with brownish spots, leaving a narrow, lighter-colored stripe in the middle open. SD probably similar to those of the preceding species.
RANGE: The Amazon region, Western Brazil.
CARE AND BREEDING: As per description of the genus. Probably breeding has not yet been successful.

— **arcuatus** Elwin: The Streamlined Corydoras.
SHAPE: As per description of the genus. D I/7, A I/6. Upper armor plates: 21-23, lower ones 19-20. Length up to $1\frac{3}{4}''$.

Corydoras arcuatus

COLOR: Yellowish-gray to whitish with a deep-black band which runs along the upper edge of the body. SD probably similar to those of *C. paleatus*.
RANGE: The river system of the Amazon.
CARE AND BREEDING: As per description of the genus. Like most *Corydoras*, the species likes to live in small groups. Quite lively. Probably breeding has not yet succeeded.

— **barbatus** (Quoy and Gaimard): The Bristly Corydoras.
SHAPE: As per description of the genus, but a little bigger and more elongated than the other species. D I/7-8, A I/6-7. Upper armor plates 24-27, lower ones 22-23. Three pairs of barbels. Length up to over 4″.

Corydoras barbatus

COLOR: Shiny metallic base with remarkable black bands and spots. The male carries stiff bristles on both sides of the snout; besides which its pectorals and dorsal are more strongly developed.
RANGE: Southeastern Brazil.
CARE AND BREEDING: As per description of the genus. The species is said to need some warmth. 75-79° F should be adequate. The fish like to bury themselves in the soil, for which reason it is advisable to cover the bottom with fine-grained, well-washed sand or with squeezed

peat mulm. Breeding seems not to have succeeded so far.

— **elegans** Steindachner.

SHAPE: As per description of the genus. D I/7, A I/6-7. The adipose fin is supported, as in all species. The first rays of dorsal, anal, pectoral, and ventral fins show numerous, up-tilted hooklets. Upper armor plates 21-22, lower ones 20. Length up to $2\frac{3}{8}''$. The breast and belly regions strongly armored.

COLOR: Olive-brown with darker spots. The male probably has a more intense design on the dorsal fin and is smaller than the female.

RANGE: The central region of the Amazon.

CARE AND BREEDING: As per description of the genus. No particulars known. Breeding seems not to have succeeded as yet.

— **hastatus hastatus** Eigenmann and Eigenmann: The Dwarf or Pygmy Catfish.

Corydoras hastatus

SHAPE: The species differs a little from the other species of the genus in body structure. For this reason many authors include it in a special genus: *Microdoras*. The fish are very small, look quite graceful, and like to stay in the middle reaches of the community tank, where they swim around in schools. At a first, superficial glance they resemble Characins, such as, for instance, those of the genus *Hemigrammus*. D I/7-8, A I/6-7. Armor plates: upper 22, lower 20. Length up to $1\frac{3}{8}''$.

COLOR: Greenish to yellowish, slightly transparent, with a deep-black horizontal band which ends on the caudal peduncle in a diamond-shaped spot which is edged with a lighter color above and below. The male is smaller and more slender, its dorsal fin being more pointed. However, the sexes can only be clearly differentiated during the spawning period.

RANGE: Known only from a few places in the Amazon region.

CARE AND BREEDING: As per description of genus. The species will also live in smaller tanks. It prefers clear water at 79-82° F and a bottom covering of thin mulm. Nourishment, especially small-sized live foods, is captured while swimming free. The few and small eggs are anchored to a support after mating, like those of all Corydoras. The relatively big fry hatch after 6-9 days.

— **leopardus** Myers: see *C. punctatus julii*.

— **melanistius melanistius** Regan: The Spotted Catfish.

SHAPE: As per description of the genus. D I/7, A I/6. Upper armor plates 21-23, lower ones 19-20. There are several sub-species of this species. Length up to $2\frac{3}{8}''$.

COLOR: Light-colored base with numerous dark dots, the eye crossed by a darker band, below the dorsal fin a crescent-shaped dark spot which also goes over on the fin.

Corydoras melanistius melanistius

RANGE: Northern South America.
CARE AND BREEDING: As per description of the genus. So far no particulars are known, but the species probably needs a little more warmth. Breeding has probably not yet been achieved.

Corydoras nattereri

— **nattereri** Steindachner: The Blue Corydoras.
This species originates from Eastern Brazil. Particulars are lacking so far. According to HOLLY it was bred once in the Berlin (Germany) Aquarium, but the process was not observed in its minutiae. D I/7, A I/5-7. The body especially pudgy. Upper armor plates 21-23, lower ones 20-21. Length up to 2⅜″.
— **paleatus** (Jenyns): The Peppered Catfish.
SHAPE: As per description of the genus. D I/7-8, A I/6. Upper armor plates 22-24, lower ones 20-22. Length up to 3″.
COLOR: Shiny greenish to brownish base with dark mottlings and dots.

Corydoras paleatus

The male is slimmer and more graceful, its dorsal fin being higher and more pointed than that of the female.
RANGE: Southeastern South America to the La Plata region.
CARE AND BREEDING: As per description of the genus. This is the species that is most common in the aquarium, and which probably is typical for the manner of living and reproducing of all other species.
— **punctatus julii** (Steindachner): The Leopard Corydoras.
SHAPE: As per description of the genus. D I/7, A I/6. Upper armor plates 22, lower ones 21. Length up to 2⅜″.

Corydoras punctatus julii

COLOR: Light-gray base with beautiful dark mottlings and spots, on the center of the body a dark, light-edged horizontal band. The male is slimmer and more graceful.
RANGE: Eastern and Northeastern Brazil.
CARE AND BREEDING: As per description of the genus. The species is reported to need some warmth. 72-79° F should be adequate. Breeding seems not to have succeeded as yet.

— **punctatus punctatus** (Bloch): The Head-Stripe Corydoras.
This species is typical for a series of sub-species. D I/7, A I/6. Upper armor plates 22-24, lower ones 20-21. Length up to 2¼″. Distributed all over Northeastern and Eastern South America.

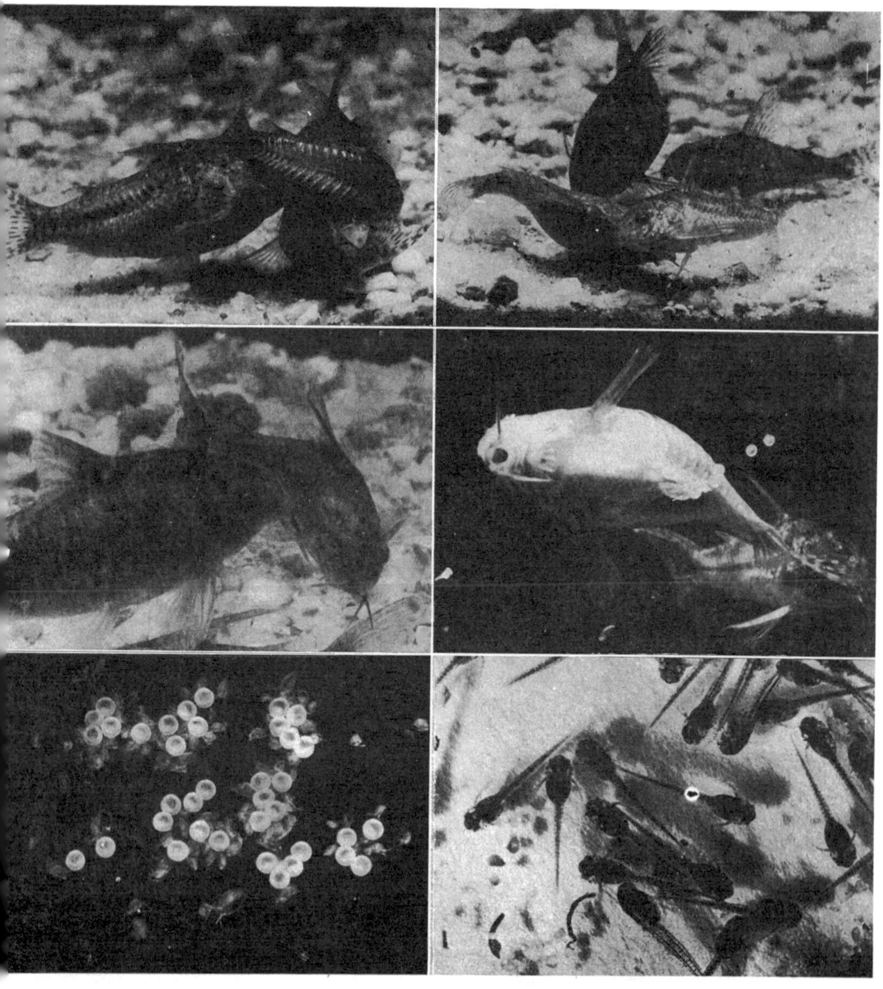

Foto: Knaack

Spawning **Corydoras paleatus** — 1. The males crowd each other for a position across the mouth of the female - 2. One of the males has attained the proper position - 3. The male clasps the female's barbels firmly with his pectoral fins. The eggs are then released into the pocket formed by the female's ventral fins and the male's sperm passes freely into the water - 4. The female sticks the fertile eggs on the glass side - 5. The eggs, surrounded by **Daphnia** - 6. The hatched fry, enlarged.

Corydoras rabauti

— rabauti La Monte: *C. myersi* (Rabaut's Corydoras).
The species is very similar to *C. arcuatus*, but the dark horizontal band does not go through the eyes beginning in front of the dorsal fin. Length 1¾″. According to INNES there are some differences in reproduction between this species and *C. paleatus*. During the mating the male 'rides' on the head of the female, after which the pair lie down on the bottom side by side. Probably it is at this moment that the eggs are fecundated. They hatch after 6-7 days. PINTER describes this Catfish as a pronounced school fish. It needs quite some warmth.

— schultzei Holly: The Golden-Striped Corydoras.
SHAPE: As per description of the genus. D I/7, A I/6. Upper armor plates 24, lower ones 21-22. Length up to 2⅝″.
COLOR: Head and back dark brown, below this a shiny golden stripe, bordered below with a dark-green to black surface. No SD in coloring, the female being a little larger and fuller-bodied.
RANGE: The Amazon region, in small and very small waters.
CARE AND BREEDING: As per description of the genus. The species has been repeatedly bred recently (1957). Reproduction as for *C. paleatus*. HAFNER observed that also the males of this species held the barbels of the females with their pectorals. This Catfish lives in a pronouncedly gregarious manner, in small groups.

Corynopoma: With pestle-shaped extension of the opercles.
Genus of South American Characins belonging to the family of the CHARACIDAE (see this), sub-family of the GLANDULOCAUDINAE (see this). This sub-family is characterized by the fact that the sexes are differentiated by marked sexual features (sexual dimorphism). Stored fecundation takes place, which enables the females to spawn fertile eggs without the presence of males. The genus comprises two species, of which so far only one has been imported.

— riisei Gill: The Sword-Tailed Characin.
SHAPE: A quite elongated fish with nearly straight back, while the central contour arches to the insertion of the anal fin. The upper side is a little flattened, the sides moderately compressed. The male has a long, spoon-shaped extension of the opercles, which may be spread during the mating games. Furthermore it shows some fused-together scales at the lower edge of the caudal peduncle, which form a pouch-like structure. D 9-11, A 24-30; all fins of the male are enlarged and lobately extended. The tail fin is deeply cleft, the lower lobe extended and drawn out into threads. The scales are relatively small. Length: males up to 2¾″, females up to 2⅛″.
COLOR: Transparent, under incident light glittering metallic silvery, with a narrow dark length stripe. Under excitement the 'spoon extension' becomes black-edged. The fins are simple in color. The tail fin of the male shows a white and yellow lower seam. SD can be deduced from the description above. There is a bred xanthoristic form of this species.
RANGE: Northern South America,

Corynopoma riisei

probably in the whole Orinoco region, also on Trinidad Island.

CARE AND BREEDING: This lively species makes no demands on the hobbyist. They are extremely skilled swimmers and generally peaceful towards other fishes. The fish feel best at 75-79° F, for hibernation 70-73° being sufficient, lowest 59° F. Sunlight and clear water enhance their wellbeing. *C. riisei* are omnivores which eat all kinds of smaller-sized live and prepared foods.

Breeding is not difficult. The males are extremely vivacious during the mating games, swim in the most peculiar stances, erecting their gill cover extensions and fins stiffly. Probably it is while this happens that fecundation takes place, the particulars of the process not having been fully explained as yet. BREIDER, who examined spawn-ripe females, found spermatophores among the eggs; these spermatophores may also be stored in the oviduct. The process is similar to that known from the live-bearing Tooth Carps. The female places the eggs on broad-leaved plants, generally on the underside of them, turning on her back for spawning. Thus the presence of a male while spawning becomes superfluous. The fry hatch after 24-36 hours, become free-swimming after another 3 days, and may be raised in the manner that is usual for most egg-scattering Characins.

coryphaenoides: Similar to *Coryphaena*, a fish of the high seas. — *Cichlasoma.*

cosmopolitan: Citizen of the world. Such species of animals or plants which are found all over the world.

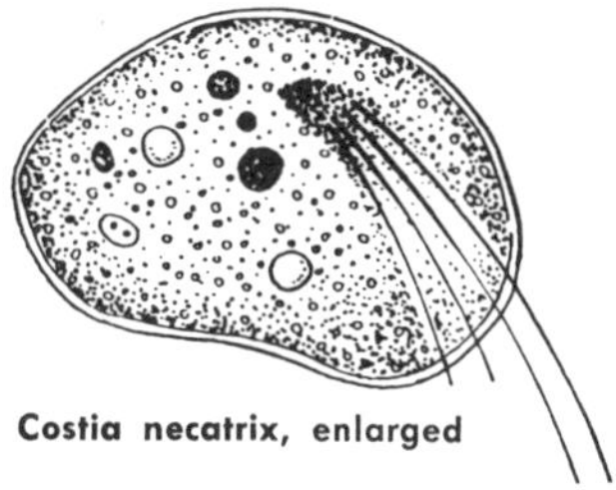

Costia necatrix, enlarged

Costia: Genus of Flagellates, which lives parasitically on the epidermis and on the gill epithelium of fishes. The species *C. necatrix*, together with other parasites, calls forth the symptoms of the contagious SKIN DISCOLORATION.

Cottidae: Family belonging to the order of the Armored Cheeks or SCLEROPAREI (see this). The family is characterized by the fact that the first, spiny dorsal fin is not as long as the second, soft one. There are no hard rays in the anal fin. Their main range is the Northern Seas, and only a few species are found in fresh water. There are no *C.* at all in the tropics.

Genera, a.o.: *Cottus.*

Cottus: Big Head.

Genus belonging to the family of the COTTIDAE (see this).

— gobio Linné: The Bull-Head.

SHAPE: Round, pestle-shaped, with thick, flattened head in which the eyes insert very high. The lateral line is complete. The fish lacks a swimming bladder. D_1 VIII-IX, D_2 13-19, A 10-15. No scales. Length up to 8″.

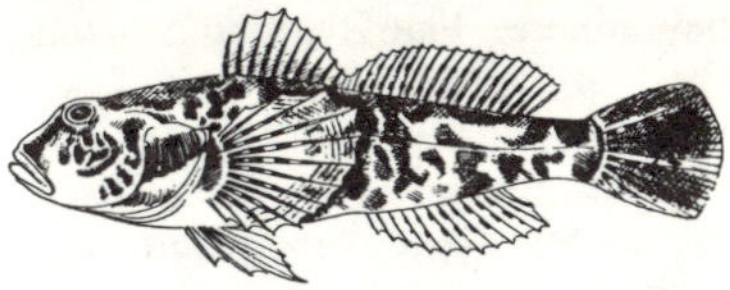

Cottus gobio

COLOR: Dark mottled on brownish base.
RANGE: Europe, generally in the region west of the Elbe, one or the other specimen also east of that river. As a rule, however, to the east the species is substituted by the Colored-Fin Bull-Head *C. poecilopsis* Heckel. The Bull-Head lives in swift-flowing brooks, especially in the trout region, furthermore in clear lakes and clear waters of the plains which are a little less fast-flowing.
CARE AND BREEDING: The species is a great predator on spawn, which may cause losses in Trout streams. In these it generally lives hidden beneath rocks. With good care and sufficient aeration and filtration Bull-Heads may also be kept for longer periods in aquaria, especially if they come from lowlands waters. They need hiding caves among rocks, and a bottom soil of clear, coarse-grained gravel. The fish eat only live foods. After domestication they will also eat meat, if this is moved in order to cause the impression of being alive.

Breeding in the aquarium is not impossible, if the necessary measures are taken. The 100-300 eggs are spawned in pits or caves and guarded by the male.

cover glass, cover glass supports: Aquaria should be kept covered for many reasons. It serves the end of avoiding losses of fishes that might jump out, as well as avoiding excessive dust falling on the water surface, creating a layer of moist-warm (charged) air which is a necessity for many tropical fishes which breathe atmospheric air accessorily and for some tropical plants which need this for their survival. In order not to restrict light from above, it is advisable to choose a cover of glass.

For this, one has to reckon with the fact that glass always filters light and changes its composition. Whenever possible, the cover pane should be placed in a tilted position, so that deposits of precipitated water, which is harmful to many floating plants, may run off. Cut the openings for those accessories which protrude over the aquarium frame as small as possible.

On all-glass aquaria the cover glass is either laid on the rim, or else placed on corks which have first been slitted in order to permit sticking them on the rim of the glass.

If the cover supports are to be anchored firmly to the frame of the tank, it is good advice not to make them of materials that rust or otherwise are able to contaminate the precipitated water. The best ones are made of oak, anchored to the frame—which is drilled through for this—by means of stainless bolts.

MUELLER advocates the use of a rubber strip, which is loosely stuck on the frame or else glued to it with a universal adhesive. Pet shops offer cover supports of different makes and systems, of which those made of plastic deserve special mention.

crabs: see CRUSTACEA.

crassa: Fat, thick.
— *Cichlasoma.*

crassiceps: Thick-headed.
— *Rachoviscus.*

crassipes: Thick-footed.
— *Eichhornia.*

Creagrutus: Meat-tearer, referring to its teeth.

South American genus belonging

to the family of the Characins or CHARACIDAE (see this), comprising generally small fishes of elongated build. These are only slightly compressed laterally. The lateral line is complete. The head is only small. An adipose fin is present. The genus comprises about ten known species.

— **beni** Eigenmann: The Gold-Striped Characin.

SHAPE: As per description of the genus, moderately compressed laterally. D 10, A 11-13; the scales are very small. Length up to 3¼″.

COLOR: Shiny greenish with black, gold-edged length band. The dorsal fin shows a black and red spot, tail and anal fin with red seams. The species is strongly variable, the female frequently being prettier in color than the male.

RANGE: Probably distributed over a large region, but known as coming from the upper Amazon and the rivers that come from the Andes. The species is also reported from the state of Para (Brazil) and the lower Amazon.

CARE AND BREEDING: A species that is very lively, but said to be occasionally a little bellicose. Despite their awe-inspiring scientific name, the fish are harmless and may be kept in communities with other peaceful fishes. *C. beni* likes to stay in the lower reaches of the water. It prefers dense planting, with possibilities occasionally to withdraw into the thickets. Naturally it also needs sufficient room for swimming. The fish are omnivorous, eating all kinds of smaller live and prepared foods. They need some warmth: 75-82° F are most favorable, lowest 68° F. The process of fecundation has not yet been explained. Similar to *Corynopoma*, it takes place before the act of spawning. Therefore the male may be removed from the tank before the female spawns. The approximately 50 eggs are laid among fine-leaved plants, where they adhere. The fry, which hatch after 24-36 hours, become free-swimming after another three days and are not hard to rear. They search for their food near the bottom and are not discriminating. It is said that the species eats even flat-worms.

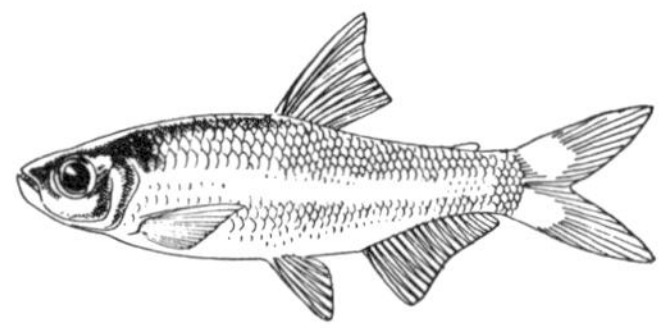

Creatochanes, type of the genus

Creatochanes: Refers to the large, very dilatable mouth with tongue. South American genus belonging to the family of the Characins or CHARACIDAE (see this), of elongated build and more or less compressed body. The lateral line is complete and runs below the center of the body. An adipose fin is present. All species are distinctly carnivorous and of predatory behavior. About five known species.

— **affinis** (Guenther):

SHAPE: As per description of the genus. Especially remarkable for the large mouth opening, which is equipped with many teeth. D 11, A 26-29. Length about 4¾″.

COLOR: Shiny silver with a black band on the tail root and an adjacent yellow spot on the tail fin. The male is a little more robustly built than the female, besides this the lobes of its tail fin are a little more pointed.

RANGE: Eastern tropical South America.

CARE AND BREEDING: The species is considered predatory and is very vicious, not only toward strange fishes, but also against their own species. The fish are huge eaters, which demand robust live foods, especially occasional small fishes. Since they need some warmth, a temperature of 77° F should be favorable. They are not sensitive to occasional low temperatures, however. Being lively swimmers, they prefer large and long tanks. Breeding has not yet been successful.

— caudomaculatus Guenther: This species resembles the preceding one in looks and manner of living. It originates from South America east of the Andes down to the La Plata. Temperatures: 59-77° F. Reproduction unknown.

Crenicichla: From Latin 'crena'-notch, referring to the structure of the gills; and *Cichla*—another genus of Cichlids.

Genus belonging to the family of the Cichlids or CICHLIDAE (see this), with very elongated, Pike-shaped body, long and evenly high dorsal fin, pointed head, and great mouth opening, which is strongly set with teeth.

The species live in a predatory manner. They like to remain in hiding places, ambushing prey, which they catch in quick pounces in the manner of Pikes. Preferentially they eat fishes of adequate size, or, if these should be unavailable, earthworms, insect larvae, tadpoles, etc. The tanks should be covered, since the fishes are excellent jumpers. Reproduction and breeding take place as described for all pit-spawning Cichlids (see CICHLIDAE), with the difference that the male alone of *Crenicichla* exerts the care for the brood. The fish are very bellicose among themselves. SCHROEDER has observed that the female of *C. lepidota* is very active in wooing the male, and keeps up this activity during the care for the brood, similar to what happens with *Pelmatochromis kribensis*. The parents keep the peace excellently with each other.

— dorsiocellata Haseman: The Two-Spot Pike Cichlid.

SHAPE: As per description of genus. D XX-XXIII/10-13, A III/8. Length up to 8″.

COLOR: Bluish base with variable band design. On the dorsal fin a red-edged eye spot. The fins are quite beautifully colored.

RANGE: The region of the central Amazon and of the Rio Parahyba.

CARE AND BREEDING: As per description of the genus. The species has only rarely been imported; it has probably never been bred in the aquarium.

— lepidota (Heckel): The Pike Cichlid.

SHAPE: As per description of genus. D XVII-XVIII/13-14, A III/8. Length up to 8″.

Crenicichla lepidota

COLOR: This species contains many color sports which are difficult to differentiate. In general gray-green with a black horizontal band, from which cross bands start towards the back. At the base or at the upper edge of the tail fin a black golden-yellow edged spot. The dorsal fin is very beautifully colored. The soft rays of the dorsal and anal of the female may be a little longer, the female being a little more vividly colored than the male.

RANGE: In standing or slowly-flowing waters of tropical South America, from the Amazon to the Plate River.

CARE AND BREEDING: As per description of the genus. The species is commendable for the Cichlid specialist and for the exhibition aquarium. Unfortunately it has not become popular. It needs warmth: 75-81° F, for breeding up to 86° F. lowest 70° F. According to INNES the male keeps the fry closely together, fugitives being devoured.

— **saxatilis** (Linné): The Ring-

Crenicichla saxatilis

Tailed Pike Cichlid.

This species resembles the two previously-mentioned ones in body shape and manner of living. It originates from tropical South America and Trinidad. The fish is not especially colorful.

Crenuchus: Ruler of the fountain. South American genus belonging to the family of the Characins or CHARACIDAE (see this), with only one species. This diverges externally from the usual type of Characin. The body is compact, strongly compressed laterally. The lateral line is only slightly developed. An adipose fin is present. Intermediate and lower jaws are equipped with three-pronged teeth disposed in ribbons.

— **spilurus** Guenther: The Sailfin Characin.

SHAPE: As per description of the genus. D 17-18, A 11. From the second or third year of age on the dorsal and anal fins of the males develop very strongly so that especially the middle parts of these fins are extended into lobes. Length a little over $2\frac{3}{8}''$.

COLOR: Reddish-brown base with a

Crenuchus spilurus

dark band, seamed above with shiny gold, along the sides. The upper half of the iris is blood red. The male is larger and more vividly colored.

RANGE: So far found only in British Guiana and the region of the central Amazon.

CARE AND BREEDING: The species has the reputation of being a little predatory, but it is less vicious than is commonly supposed, and even pronouncedly peaceful towards fishes of its own size. It needs densely-planted, not-too-small tanks, which afford the fish hiding places. Without such facilities it may become pronouncedly timid. Nourishment consists exclusively of live foods of all kinds, especially small fishes being preferred. Breeding seems not to have succeeded so far, despite the fact that spawning has already been observed. The eggs were stuck to leaves or rocks. No particulars are known.

crispus: Curly, curled.

— *Aponogeton.*

Croaking Gourami, the: see TRICHOPSIS VITTATUS.

Croaking Spiny Catfish, the: see AMBLYDORAS HANCOCKI.

crossbreeding: Sexual conjugation of live beings of different races, species, or genera, the result of which is called a 'hybrid'.

Crossopterygii: Tassel Fins. Sub-class of ancient fishes belonging to the class of the Bone Fishes or OSTEICHTHYES (see this), which includes the Lung Fishes of the order DINPEUSTI (see this).

Crow's Foot Plants: see RANUNCULACEAE.

Crucian, the: see CARASSIUS CARASSIUS.

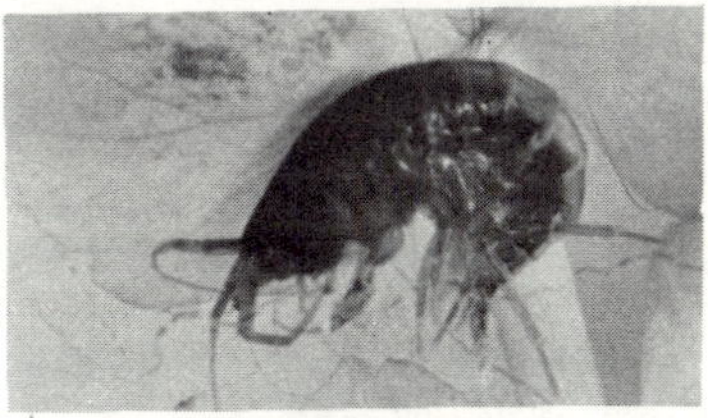

Fresh-water Crustacean

Crustacea: Crustaceans. Sub-phylum belonging to the phylum of the Arthropods or ATHROPODA (see this), which differs from the other members of the phylum among others by the structure of the respiratory organs. Generally the *C.* are water dwellers, which absorb air for breathing either through the whole surface of the body, or else through special gills. The few groups which have adapted to life on dry land, for instance, the *Aselli* and a few crabs, possess respiratory organs of gill-like character notwithstanding this. Nearly all Crustaceans have more than four pairs of legs. Also in this they differ from the Insects, which have three pairs, and from the Spiders, which have four pairs of these. In nearly all cases two pairs of antennae are found in front of the mouth opening. The body is covered by a shell of chitin, which on many *C.* turns into an armor reinforced with inclusions of calcium. This fact has given the animals their name, *Crustacea*—animals with a shell or crust.

The shell has to fit progressive growth, and for this reason it has to be substituted periodically by means of changes of skin. The skin below the armor contains numerous changeable color cells, which often permit the great capacity for color adaptation that Crustaceans possess. The manner of functioning of these is ruled by hormones. The segments are developed in a very widely differentiated manner. Some of them are grown together, such as, for instance, the head and breast section (see CEPHALOTHORAX). The limbs are so-called split feet, which are forked from the third articulation on, with only few exceptions. The jaws are formed by body appendages. Upper and lower jaws generally are paired and move against each other when chewing. Frequently also the limbs of the cephalothorax are transformed into auxiliary jaws, and serve to touch, hold, and transport nourishment. The walking feet are not forked, and sometimes end in strong pincers. The abdominal legs are used for swimming and are often absent on lower Crustaceans. The nerve system is of the 'rope ladder' type which is frequent in lower animals, with a nerve center in the abdominal medulla. In part the sensory organs are highly developed. The eyes are either simple or reticulately composite, and frequently they are not paired. The hearing sense has been the subject of discussions, but often there are organs of the sense of equilibrium, the equilibrium bubbles, present. The digestive organ frequently has the shape of a short, straight barrel. Many of the higher, and also some lower Crustaceans eat nearly exclusively animal food. Vegetarian species possess a longer intestine. The spacious stomach is often equipped with lasts and teeth on the inside; it is moved by special muscles and serves a masticatory organ. A kind of liver that is found within the C. is not only a glandular organ, but takes active part in digestion. The circulatory organs are developed in very varied shapes. The lower forms frequently show simple, pulsating dorsal vessels, while the *Cladocera* possess small, barrel-shaped hearts. High Crustaceans on their part have a quite complex system of blood vessels, which, however, is not completely closed. Generally the blood liquid is colorless.

C. are heterosexual with exception of a few stationary or parasitical forms. As a rule they go through a larval stage, the lower Crustaceans often even as nauplii. These are oval, possess only a single eye, and initially only three pairs of limbs.

The sub-phylum is divided into nine classes, of which the following are of interest for aquaristics: Leaf-footed Crustaceans or PHYLLOPODA (see this), Clam Crustaceans or OSTRACODA (see this), Shell-less ones or ANOSTRACA (see this), Rowing-footed Crustaceans or COPEPODA (see this), Gill-Tailed Crustaceans or BRANCHIURA (see this), and the Higher Crustaceans or MALACOSTRACA (see this).

crustacean diseases of fishes: Diseases caused by crustaceans are not very frequent among aquarium fishes. Sometimes carp lice (*Argulus*) are introduced together with the food, but these are only able to cause major harm in case of carelessness or lack of attention on the part of the fancier, as they are relatively easy to combat.

So far there are only occasional reports on *Copepoda* becoming parasitic on aquarium fishes.

Crustaceans, Higher: see MALACOSTRACA.

Crustaceans, Ten-footed: see DECAPODA.

Cryptocoryne: With concealed androecium, referring to the inflorescence.

Genus of swamp plants pertaining to the family of the Aaron's Rod Plants or ARACEAE (see this), widely distributed over Southeast Asia, with 46 known species. The plants possess a robust root stock, which creeps within the soil, able to ramify many times and to grow many runners. The bottomstanding leaves stand on more or less long stems and are linear to cordiform or oviform. They are always whole-edged, but sometimes they show a slight curliness at the edges. The upper face is light to dark-green, sometimes with a brownish sheen or a spot design, on the underside often going over into reddish or with reddish veins. The leaves of emerged plants are tougher, and those of some species even diverge from the shape of the submerged ones. The inflorescence is typical, consisting of a series of distinctly differentiated parts. From the bottom up they are the following:

1. the floral peduncle;
2. the kettle-shaped, enlarged central piece, in which we find the floral organs;
3. the long tube of the floral spathe;
4. the vividly colored spathe blade.

The latter is what most strikes the eye of the viewer and is therefore generally taken for the real flower. Many *C.* bloom only if cultivated emergedly, others however, flower even if kept submerged. For this the spathe blade often rises above the water surface, but sometimes it also remains below it. Fecundation takes place through self-pollination or by means of small insects, which are lured by the colored blade and creep down into the kettle. The seeds are partly reported to start germinating already within the fruit knot, which makes the plants 'live-bearing'. All Cryptororynes are of tropical origin, and need sufficiently high tem-

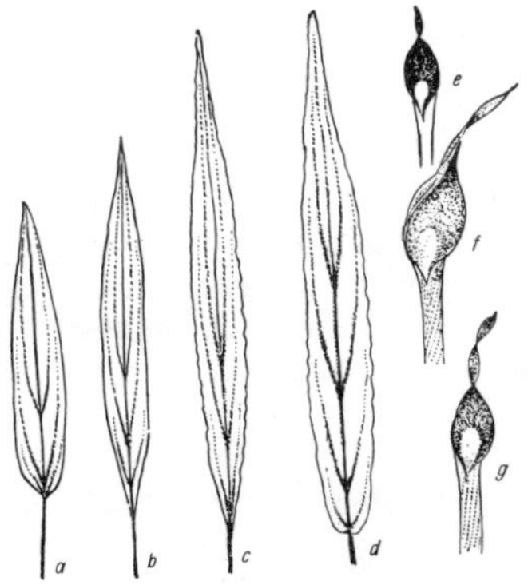

Differences in Cryptocorynes—after Wendt Cryptocoryne nevillii, broad-leaved form—a. leaf - e. blossom - b. narrow-leaved form—C. undulata - c. leaf - f. blossom —C. willisii - d. leaf - g. blossom.

peratures for this reason. They may be cultivated submergedly or emergedly. Coarse, clay-mixed sand is a satisfactory bottom soil. The plants should not be transplanted or disturbed more than the absolutely necessary minimum, as they are sensitive to this and generally find difficulties in striking roots again, often even not continuing to grow after such disturbance. It is reported that they like a heated bottom soil. This should be sufficiently deep to afford the roots sufficient space to grow fast, meaning $2\frac{3}{8}''$-$3\frac{1}{4}''$ for smaller specimens, 4″ and more for larger ones. The plants only proceed to grow emergedly if the water level is lowered gradually, the *C.* being able to accompany this decrease.

Distinguishing Features of Some Cryptocorynes (According to WENDT)

	C. beckettii	*C. nevillii*	*C. undulata*	*C. willisii*
LEAF STEM	reddish brown	green	reddish brown	reddish brown
SHAPE OF LEAF	elongated-oval to lanceolate	narrow-lanceolate to lanceolate	narrow-lanceolate	narrow-lanceolate
LEAF BASE	rounded to wedge-shaped, often unsymmetrical	going over into leaf, or rounded to wedge-shaped	going over into leaf	rounded to wedge-shaped
LEAF LENGTH	$2\frac{3}{8}''$-6″	1″-4″	4″-7″	4″-8″
LEAF EDGE	smooth or faintly curled	smooth	with small curls	with small curls
COLOR OF LEAVES				
(a) Upper face	Olive to brownish green, sometimes with dark spots	grass green	luminous green with slanted dark stripes	luminous green with slanted dark stripes
(b) Underside	reddish	dim green	reddish	reddish
SPATHE BLADE				
(a) Shape	lanceolate with short, twisted tip	lanceolate with short, twisted tip	lanceolate with short, twisted tip	lanceolate with short, twisted tip
(b) Color, inside	yellowish with broad red ring	blackish purple	pale green with narrow dark-green ring	pale brown to pale red-brown

Reproduction in the aquarium nearly always takes place by means of runners, which may be cut off after some time. Only the lately-imported *C. ciliata* is reported to grow small seed plants even in the aquarium. Most species make no special demands as to lighting, but nearly all thrive better under a more intense illumination and with occasional sunlight. Take care, however, to protect the plants against infestations with algae, as these choke the *C.* when accumulating on the leaves. Soft, slightly acid water favors their growth, and too hard water kills the plants. For so-far-unexplained reasons the *C.* are occasionally attacked by some typical diseases, which sometimes are erroneously lumped together under the name of 'Cryptocoryne Disease'. Such diseases may show as glassy spots in the leaf tissues with subsequent opening of holes and a quick, often total, decay of the plant. Probably there is more than one cause. One is led to suppose that the primary cause is to be sought in the unbiological, exclusively submerged, cultivation and in the propagation through runners.

— **beckettii** Thwaites:

GENERALITIES: Up to a recent date this species was erroneously called *C. ciliata.*

SHAPE: As per description of the genus. The elongated and pointed leaves are somewhat curled on the edges, slightly undulated at the leaf insertion, sometimes also folded along their full length. The underside is nearly always touched with red, the upper side brownish-green with a faint, silky sheen. If kept submerged, the species blooms only rarely. The spathe blade is greenish-yellow with a dark red ring.

RANGE: Ceylon, in swampy terrains, at or in the water, growing both emerged and submerged.

CULTIVATION: As per description of the genus. The species also grows in denser shadows, despite the fact that sunlight favors its growth. Temperatures between 68 and 86° F. 75° F being best. Despite the fact that soft water is the more favorable, vegetation may still be sufficient in moderately hard water.

— **ciliata** (Roxburgh):

GENERALITIES: The real *C. ciliata* was re-imported only lately. The species which up to now was known as *C. ciliata* is really *C. beckettii*, and the species which was called *C. beckettii* received the name *C. undulata.*

SHAPE: The leaves are narrowly to broadly lanceolate, often blunted at the tip, lighter on the underside than the light green of the upper surface, which on emerged specimens becomes dark green. Spathe blade is yellow in the center, purple-red on the edges, and equipped with fringes.

RANGE: India, Malaya, and the Sunda Islands, in the same sites as the preceding species, also in brackish water.

CULTIVATION: As per description of the genus. Reproduction takes place through runners, but also through young plants which are 'live-born' after self-pollination.

— **cordata** Griffith:

GENERALITIES: It is not easy for the aquarist to differentiate this species from *C. griffithii.*

SHAPE: As per description of the genus. A large, broad-leaved species. The leaves are heart-shaped near the base, slightly pointed at the tip. The upper face is dark-green, the underside sometimes reddish. The spathe blade is purple, yellow towards the inside, and the yellow color may sometimes spread over the whole blade.

CULTIVATION: As per description

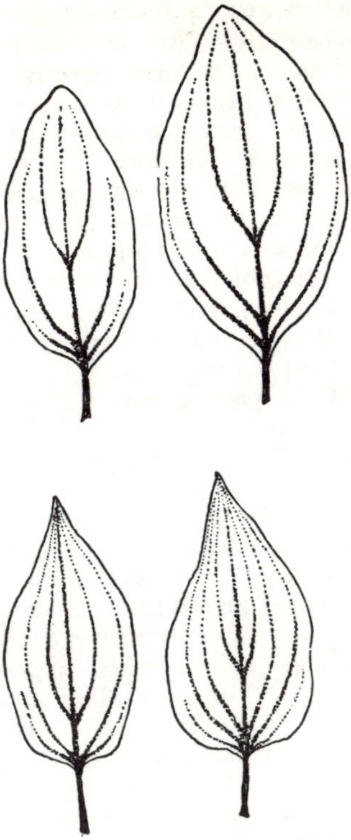

C. cordata and C. griffithii—top: leaf and veining of C. cordata—bottom: C. griffithii. Below: blossom of C. cordata — bottom: C. griffithii

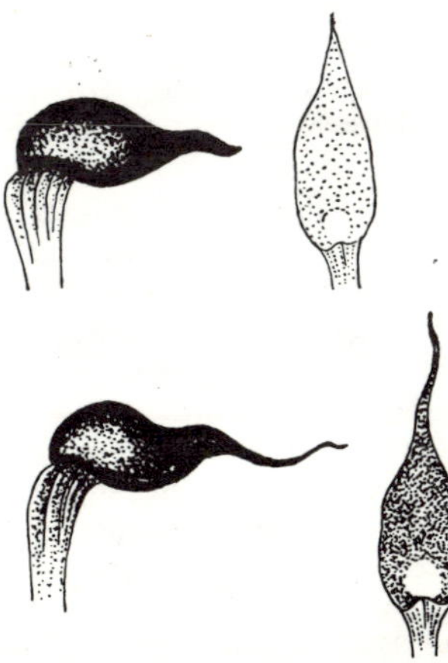

of the genus. Reproduction only through runners.

— **griffithii** Schott:

GENERALITIES: Hard to differentiate from the preceding species. Possesses more distinctly visible leaf nervures, tougher leaves, and a more blunted leaf tip.

SHAPE: As per description of the genus. The color of the spathe blade resembles that of the preceding species and represents no differential character. It ends in a narrow lappet, however.

RANGE: Indonesia and Malaya, found in the same locations as the other species.

CULTIVATION: As per description of the genus. The species blooms more often when submerged than the previously described one, even at low temperatures. Reproduction through runners.

— **haerteliana** Jacobsen:

GENERALITIES: The most prolific and best-growing of all Cryptocorynes.

SHAPE: As per description of the genus. The elongated leaves are dark-green with a silky sheen and lighter-colored nervures, the underside reddish to vivid red. There are two forms of growth, one with leaves that grow up vertically, another one with horizontal leaves. The spathe blade is dark red and very long-tailed, the stem being spirally wound.

RANGE: Origin unknown.

CULTIVATION: This is the species which needs the least light of all Cryptocorynes. Due to its strong growing of runners it may cover the whole bottom area of the tank.

— **lutea** Alston:

GENERALITIES: A species which was imported in 1954 and has not yet found any great acceptance.

SHAPE: As per description of the genus. From about $\frac{3}{8}''$ on the rhizomes rise the elongated-oval to oval leaves on stems that grow up to 6″ long. The leaves themselves may become $4\frac{3}{4}$″ long and $1\frac{5}{8}$″ wide. The point is slightly blunted, the leaf base wedge-shaped, the leaf edge smooth in the upper part, slightly curled towards the base, less frequently serrated. Often the edge is bent upwards.

COLOR: Vivid green, pale green on the underside, reddish when young. The 4-5 leaf nervures, which run along both sides of the central rib, stand out strongly on the underside and show a bright red color. The spathe blade is greenish yellow; its edge is bent inwards.

RANGE: Ceylon.

CULTIVATION: As per description of the genus. Reproduction through runners is not satisfactory. According to WENDT the best way is to let the rhizomes float until they develop young plants at the internodes.

— **nevillii** Trimen:

GENERALITIES: The species develops two local varieties, of which the broad-leaved one is being offered commercially under the name of *C. willisii*, which, however, is not valid for the species.

SHAPE: The smallest of the species. The lanceolate, slightly arched leaves are of different widths, light to dark green, and a little tough. The spathe blade is blackish purple.

RANGE: Ceylon.

CULTIVATION: As per description of the genus. The species grows very slowly. It should not be put in too dark locations. Blooms rarely.

— **retrospiralis** (Roxburgh) Fischer:

GENERALITIES: A species which is very similar to *C. spiralis*, but which is a little larger.

SHAPE: As described for *C. spiralis*, but with the rhizome growing $\frac{3}{8}$″ thick, the leaves up to 12″ and $\frac{3}{16}$″ to $\frac{5}{8}$″ wide. Differing from *C. spiralis*, the spathe blade is turned along its whole length in the shape of an open spiral.

RANGE: India, and parts of the Malayan Peninsula. It is reported that the species is not found on Ceylon.

CULTIVATION: No particulars known.

— **spiralis** (Retzius) Fischer:

GENERALITIES: A species that has recently appeared on the market, and which differs considerably from the others.

SHAPE: The narrowly linear or lanceolate leaves, which may become 4″-6″ long and $\frac{3}{8}$″-$\frac{1}{2}$″ wide, stand on 2″-4″ long stems and grow up from the 4-5 mm. thick rhizome. They are pointed at both ends, the basis going over into the leaf nearly imperceptibly. The inflorescence stands on a very short peduncle; the spathe tube grows approximately $3\frac{1}{8}$″-4″ long. The spathe blade is purple inside, greenish-white on the outside, its edges being thinly serrated. It is remarkable that its lower part forms an open spiral, closing completely, in ever-tightening spirals, on the upper part.

RANGE: India and Ceylon, also in parts of the Malayan Peninsula.

CULTIVATION: As per description of the genus, no particulars being known so far, however.

— **undulata** Wendt:

GENERALITIES: This species was at first known as *C. beckettii*, later as *C. pseudo-beckettii*.

SHAPE: The narrow-lanceolate, rather long-stemmed, leaves, which are green with dark slanted lines, are curled on the edges. Spathe blade greenish.

RANGE: Ceylon.

CULTIVATION: As per description of the genus. The species grows very slowly. It blooms when emerged. Reproduction only through runners.

— **willisii** Engler:

GENERALITIES: The species is very similar to *C. undulata*.
SHAPE: The narrow-lanceolate leaves are shiny green to olive green on the upper face. They grow up to 8″ long and 1″ wide, differing distinctly from *C. undulata* by the fact that the base of the leaves does not go over into the leaves, but is distinctly separated. The leaf edges show small curls. The spathe blade is pale brown to pale reddish-brown. The species is considered very willing to bloom. According to WENDT it is more frequently cultivated than *C. undulata*, for which it is often mistaken.
RANGE: Ceylon.
CULTIVATION: As described for the genus and for *C. undulata*.

Cryptogamae: Flowerless plants, part of the kingdom of plants. The following divisions are of interest to the aquarist: SCHIZOPHYTAE (see this), which include the Blue Algae, CHLOROPHYCEAE (see this), with the Green Algae, CHAROPHYTA (see this), with the family of the *Characeae* or Candelabrum Plants, ARCHEGONIATAE (see this) with the Mosses or *Bryophyta*, and the PTERIDOPHYTA (see this) or Ferns.

Cryptopterus: With hidden fin (refers to the small or lacking dorsal fin).
Southeastern Asian genus pertaining to the family of the Glass Catfishes or SCHILBEIDAE (see this), of elongated, and laterally strongly compressed build, the body of which is completely naked and glassily transparent. The terminal mouth is equipped with very small teeth. At the edge of the upper jaw stands one pair of barbels. Contrary to what is the case with most other Catfishes, the *C.* species are pronounced daylight fishes, which are very lively and motile. They live in schools and stay mainly in the central reaches of the water.

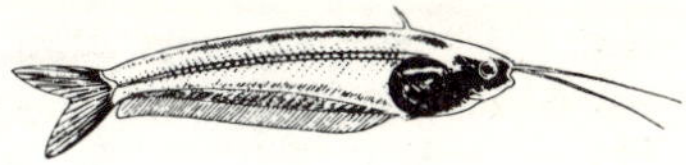

Cryptopterus bicirrhis

— bicirrhis (Cuvier and Valenciennes): The Indian Glass Catfish.
SHAPE: As per description of the genus. The dorsal fin consists of only one very small ray, the A 53-70. No adipose fin. Length up to 4″.
COLOR: Gray-greenish to yellowish, strongly glittering and transparent, sometimes with a violet spot above the pectorals. SD unknown.
RANGE: Thailand and Indonesia, exclusively in fresh water.
CARE AND BREEDING: The species needs some warmth and is best kept at 77° F or more, lowest 68° F. It feels especially well in densely-planted tanks with open space in the middle. No special demands are made as to nourishment, but small live foods are preferred. Not yet bred.

— macrocephalus (Bleeker): The East Indian Catfish.
SHAPE: As per description of the genus. The dorsal fin is only rudimentary. On the upper jaw there are two long whiskers, and one stunted pair beneath the mouth. The species is reported to reach lengths of $4\frac{3}{8}$″ in its home waters.
COLOR: Not completely as transparent as the preceding species. Yellowish with three blackish horizontal stripes or mottlings. SD unknown.
CARE AND BREEDING: The species needs warmth, temperatures up to 86° F. It likes variegated live foods. The fish are peaceful toward other fishes of their own size. According to DACHSEL they do not seem to be as intensely gregarious as the preceding species. *C. macrocephalus* occasionally stay alone among

plants. While swimming, which is aided by wavy motions of the long anal fin, the body takes on a slightly tilted stance. Frequently the fish lie on the bottom among plants as if dead, sometimes even on their sides. If touched they swim away frightened.

crystalwort plants: see RICCIACEAE.

Ctenobrycon: Brycon (a Characin species) with comb-shaped scales. South American genus belonging to the family of the Characins or CHARACIDAE (see this), with quite high, laterally compressed body. The anal fin is very long; an adipose fin is present. Diverging from the related kinds, the fishes possess ctenoid scales.

— spilurus (Valenciennes): The Silver Tetra.

SHAPE: As per description of the genus. D 11, A 41-45. The scales are relatively small. Length $2\frac{3}{4}$"-$3\frac{1}{4}$".

COLOR: Intensely silver-colored with a bluish hue, occasionally with a faded shoulder spot and a greenish-gleaming horizontal band, which is not always visible, though, and ends in a blue-black spot on the caudal peduncle. The male is slimmer and more elongated, its anal fin reddish.

RANGE: Coastal waters of Northern South America.

CARE AND BREEDING: This pretty species is extremely lively and motile, even if sometimes a little bellicose towards smaller fishes. Keep it in long tanks with sufficient room for swimming and exercising. The fish need clear water for their well-being. No special demands are made as to temperature: 68-77° F are sufficient, lowest 64° F.

Being omnivorous, the fish eat all kinds of live and artificial foods. Breeding is not difficult and resembles that of all other egg-

Ctenobrycon spilurus

scattering Characins. The mating games are especially beautiful, the pairs whirling around each other and chasing violently, partly near the surface. The species is very prolific. They may spawn 600-2000 eggs, which are scattered all around in the water. The fry hatch after 50-70 hours, become free-swimming after 3-4 days, and are easy to rear.

ctenoid scales: Scales with a more or less deeply toothed edge, also called comb scales (see SKIN, and SKIN ORGANS).

Ctenopoma: With a comb on the (gill) cover.

African genus belonging to the family of the Climbing Perches or ANABANTIDAE (see this). Fishes of compact to moderately elongated body shape, which in part are able to move very nimbly. The dorsal fin is longer than the anal. Both head and body are covered with scales. The upper and lower body contours are relatively evenly arched. At a first glance many species look like Nandids. The mouth opening is moderately large, the gill covers are a little serrated on the edges. The respiratory labyrinth is not very strongly developed. LADIGES points out that the name 'Climbing Perches' for the members of this genus is a little misleading despite the fact that they are closely related to the genus *Anabas*. These fishes have either lost the ability to leave the water,

Symphysodon aequifasciata haraldi, the famous Blue Discus.
Photo by Dr. H. R. Axelrod

1. and 2. **Cryptocoryne nevillii** - 3. **Cryptocoryne beckettii** - 4. **Cryptocoryne undulata**
5. **Cryptocoryne cordata** - 6. **Cryptocoryne haerteliana.**

Top left: Stickleback male, breeding colors at left, normal colors at right; center group: **Barbus nigrofasciatus** above and **Barbus conchonius**, normal colors at left and breeding colors at right; bottom group: **Hemichromis fasciatus**, normal colors above and breeding colors below; right: female **Nannacara anomala** in normal colors above, and breeding colors below.

1. **Vallisneria spiralis tortifolia**, the Corkscrew Vallisneria - 2. **Vallisneria spiralis**, the Common Vallisneria - 3. **Elodea canadensis**, the Canadian Anacharis - 4. **Elodea minor**, the Dwarf Anacharis - 5. **Elodea densa**, the Dense-Leaved Anacharis - 6. **Hydrilla verticillata** - 7. **Lagarosiphon muscoides**, the Curly Anacharis.

Cichlidae (Cichlids)

1. **Cichlasoma tetracanthus**, the Cuban Cichlid - 2. upper, **Apistogramma reitzigi**, male - 2. lower, the same, female - 3. **Geophagus jurupari** - 4. **Pterophyllum scalare**, The Angel Fish - 5. **Geophagus gymnogenys** - 6. **Symphysodon discus**, the Discus - 7. **Astronotus ocellatus**, the Oscar - 8. **Geophagus acuticeps** - 9. left, **Apistogramma agassizi**, Agassiz's Dwarf Cichlid, male - 9. right, the same, female.

Cyprinodontidae (Tooth Carps) - Sub-Family **Cyprinodontinae** (Egglaying Tooth Carps) - **Amblyopsidae** (Blind Fishes).

1. **Aphyosemion calabaricus** - 2. **Aphyosemion calliurum calliurum**, female below - 3. **Aphyosemion schoutedeni** - 4. **Nothobranchius rachovi** - 5. **Nothobranchius guentheri** - 6. **Pterolebias longipinnis** - 7. Cynolebias bellottii - 8. **Rivulus strigatus** - 9. **Cynolebias nigripinnis** - 10. **Rivulus ocellatus** - 11. **Rivulus harti** - 12. **Rivulus santensis** - 13. **Aplocheilichthys spilauchena** - 14. **Aplocheilichthys macrophthalmus** - 15. **Rivulus urophthalmus** - 16. **Cynolebias (Cynopoecilus) melanotaenia** - 17. **Rivulus cylindraceus** - 18. **Chologaster cornutus** - 19. **Oryzias javanicus** - 20. **Amblyopsis speleus.**

1. **Ceratopteris thalicroides**, floating form - 2. same, rooted form - 3. **Marsilea**, type of the genus - 4. **Ceratopteris thalicroides**, fine-leaved form - 5. type of Quillwort, **Pillularia** - 6. **Azolla caroliniana** - 7. **Salvinia auriculata.**

Symphysodon discus Heckel, the true Discus.

Photo by Dr. E. Schmidt

Ctenopoma acutirostre

or else they have never had it. For this reason L. proposed the name 'Bush Fishes'.

— **acutirostre** Pellegrini: The Leopard Bush Fish.

A Bush Fish which lately has often been imported, and which reaches a length of about 4″. The species shows a striking, irregular spot design on reddish to yellow-brown base. No particulars are known on the manner of living.

— **argentoventer** (Schreitmueller and Ahl): The Silver Bush Fish.

SHAPE: As per description of genus; relatively elongated and strongly compressed laterally. The lateral line is interrupted. D XVI/10, A IX/10. The scales are relatively large. Length up to 6″.

COLOR: Silvery grey, younger males with two shiny golden bands on the sides.

CARE AND BREEDING: This predatory species is absolutely unfit for the community tank. It needs robust live food, in which fishes play an important part, but probably also takes vegetable nourishment additionally. The fish need warmth, 82-86° F being most favorable, lowest 68° F. They are very sensitive to lower temperatures. *C. argentoventer* like hiding places among rocks and roots. The eggs are spawned in open water, while embracing, and float to the surface due to their oil content.

— **fasciolatum** (Boulenger): The Banded Bush Fish.

SHAPE: As per description of the genus, but of relatively high build. D XVI/8-9, A X/9-11. Length up to $3\frac{1}{8}$″.

COLOR: With up to ten dark cross bands on yellow-gray base, and a luminously blue spot on the opercles. The coloring gives the species a certain resemblance to *Macropodus opercularis*. The female is dimmer in color.

RANGE: Tropical West Africa, especially in the Congo region.

CARE AND BREEDING: The species is long-lived, but not very peaceful. Even if it cannot be said to be a pronounced predator, it needs robust live foods, especially small fishes. The fish need warmth: 77-82° F, lowest 72° F. Breeding has not yet succeeded. The fish become especially bellicose during the mating season.

— **nanum** Guenther:

SHAPE: Of somewhat elongated build; possibly identical with *C. fasciolatum*. D XVI/7, A X/10.

COLOR: Blue-gray to yellowish base with 8-9 more or less distinct cross bands, which also enter the fins.

RANGE: The Congo region.

CARE AND BREEDING: As for the other Bush Fishes. The species builds bubble nests.

— **oxyrhynchus** Boulenger: The Peacock-Eye Bush Fish.

SHAPE: As per description of the genus. With increasing age the fishes become quite high-backed. The head is pointed. They should be considered grown-up after reaching a length of 4″. Like those of many Nandids, the soft parts of the dorsal and anal fins are wholly or nearly transparent.

COLOR: Very strikingly and changeably colored, with dark brown mottlings on a yellow-brown base.

RANGE: Imported from the Belgian Congo in 1952.

CARE AND BREEDING: The species is not predatory, being an eater of micro-organisms. It needs warmth and feels best at 82-86° F. LADIGES informs us on their reproduction. The very small eggs were spawned in great numbers after intense chasing and floated along the surface. No care for the brood was exerted. The light-shy fry hatched after 3-4 days at 82-86° F.

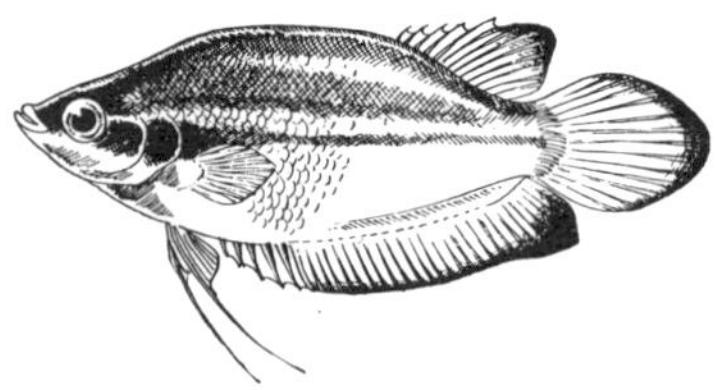

Ctenops nobilis

Ctenops: Refers to the teeth on the sub-ocular bone.
Southeast Asian genus belonging to the family of the Climbing Perches or ANABANTIDAE (see this), characterized by their very short dorsal fin. The lateral line is only slightly indicated or totally missing. The present genus formerly included some species which now belong to the genus TRICHOPSIS (see this). A rarely-imported species from India is *Ctenops nobilis*.

Cuban Cichlid, the: see CICHLASOMA TETRACANTHUS.

Cubanichthys: Fish from Cuba.
Genus belonging to the sub-family of the egg-laying Tooth Carps or CYPRINODONTIDAE (see this), characterized by the relatively short build and by the dorsal and anal fins which insert exactly over the center of the body.

— cubensis (Eigenmann): The Cuban Killie.
SHAPE: As per description of the genus; small, but quite robust-looking. D 11-12, A 10-11. Length, $1\frac{3}{8}''$-$1\frac{5}{8}''$.
COLOR: Shiny golden base with dark-blue length stripes. The male is much more colorful and slimmer.
RANGE: In small, shallow, and weed-grown waters on Cuba.
CARE AND BREEDING: The species is peaceful and quite hardy. Small tanks at sunny locations and with temperatures of 72-77° F will suffice. As nourishment all kinds of live and artificial foods are eaten, and also algae as well. The act of spawning takes place among fine-feathered plants after violent chasing, but it seems that the process has not yet been fully explained. The observation, photographed by INNES, according to which the eggs are carried around as a bundle hanging from a thread for some time, is contradicted by others who deny this. The eggs are quite small and glass-clear. The fry hatch only after 10-12 days. Since they too are rather small, at first feeding them turns out to be a little difficult, at least up to the point when they become able to eat dust-sized micro-crustaceans. The number of eggs is very small. This is the reason why rearing 40-50 young is considered a success. Furthermore it is reported that the females predominate among the fry.

cubensis: Cuban, coming from Cuba.
— *Cubanichthys.*

cultratus: Knife-shaped.
— *Alfaro.*

cumingii: After the collector Cuming.
— *Barbus.*

Cuming's Barb: see BARBUS CUMINGII.

cupanus: After a geographic name.
— *Macropodus.*

cupanus dayi: After Sir Francis Day.
— *Macropodus.*

Curimatopsis: Similar to *Curimatus.*
South American genus of Characin-like fishes, belonging to the family of the Headstanders or ANOSTOMI-

DAE (see this). Small, toothless fishes, the lower jaw of which instead of teeth is equipped with a thin sharp ridge. Besides this the genus differs from the other, closely-related genera by the possession of a long tongue. The small, terminal mouth slants slightly upwards. The species are egg-scatterers. Care and breeding resembles that of most egg-scattering Characins.

— saladensis Meincken: The Rose-Colored Curimatopsis.

SHAPE: As per description of the genus, moderately elongated and compressed laterally. D 11, A 9. Length up to $2\frac{3}{8}$″.

COLOR: Shiny silvery with blue to greenish sheen and a dark spot on the caudal eduncle. The male glitters more and its fins possess a slight hue. Besides this the caudal peduncle of adult males is much higher.

RANGE: The region of the Rio Salado, in Argentina.

CARE AND BREEDING: As described for the genus and for CHARACIDAE (see this). This hardy and peaceful species is especially suited for the community tank, since it becomes a little shy if kept alone. They are omnivorous, eating all kinds of live and artificial foods, especially from the bottom. Temperatures, 68-73° F, for breeding 77° F.

Curimatus: After the native name. South America genus of Characin-like fishes pertaining to the family of the Headstanders or ANOSTOMIDAE (see this), widely distributed over the whole of South America, up to Panama. The elongated body, which is only little compressed laterally, looks quite robust. The adipose fin is always well developed. The lateral line is complete. The mouth is small, without lips or teeth, but possesses a thin and sharp ridge on the lower jaw with which the fishes rasp off algae and similar food. The species are inhabitants of standing and slowly-flowing waters, where they search the bottom for decaying bits of plants and for micro-organisms that live in the mud. About 50 known species.

— argenteus Gill:

SHAPE: As per description of the genus. D 10-11, A 8-9. Length up to 6″.

COLOR: Shiny silver with dark spot on the tail root and reddish fins. SD cannot be given with exactitude.

RANGE: Trinidad, Venezuela, and Colombia.

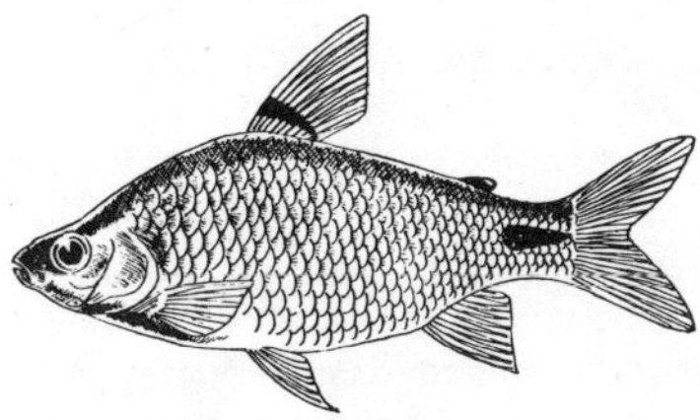

Curimatus argenteus

CARE AND BREEDING: The species needs large tanks with space for swimming. It is advisable to give them well-washed bottom soil, since the fish are incessantly rooting through the bottom. Reproduction corresponds to that of most egg-scattering Characins (see CHARACIDAE).

curviceps: With curved head.

— *Aequidens.*

cutcutia: After the native name.

— *Tetraodon.*

cutteri: After a personal name.

— *Cichlasoma.*

Cutter's Cichlid: see CICHLASOMA CUTTERI.

Cuvier, George de: 1769-1832. Famed zoologist, who, among other things, has also presented ichthyological works. Cuvier was the author of the first effective systematic division of the kingdom of animals, according to bone structure. He still taught the immutability of the species, however, trying to explain the change of forms within the animal world by the supposition that great catastrophes on earth had caused the extinction of many live beings, after which a new creation and new settling had taken place.

cyanellus: Blue-green, diminutive form of the word.
— *Lepomis.*

cyanoguttatum: Blue-dotted.
— *Herichthys.*

cyanophyceae (Blue Algae): Algae belonging to the class of the SCHIZOPHYTA (see this). Quickly-proliferating algae, very obnoxious in the aquarium, which form blue-green colored carpets, covering bottom, walls, and plants with an evil-smelling veil. Since many Blue Algae exude a jelly-like substance used in their reproduction, they are also called Smear Algae. The blue-green coloring originates from phycocyane, a dye-stuff or pigment.

Blue Algae possess no real cellular nucleus, but only a nucleoid thickening of the plasma, which probably exerts the nuclear functions. Chlorophyll and other pigments are located in the outer layer of the cell. The inside of the cell is colorless, Their color is not always blue-green, as there are also olive-green, yellowish, reddish, and light violet hues. Furthermore coloring may also change according to age or to incidence of light.

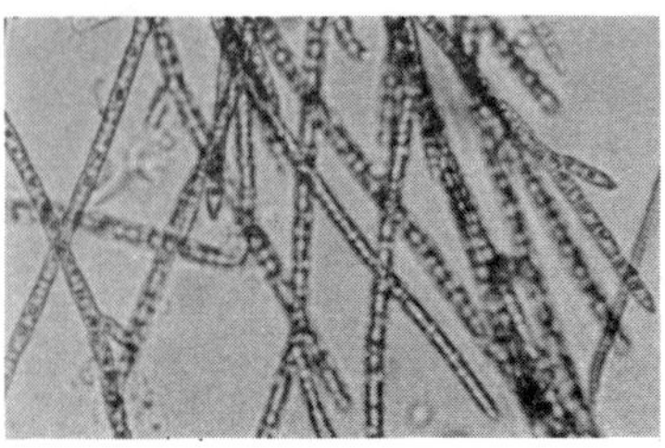

Chains of **Anabaena**

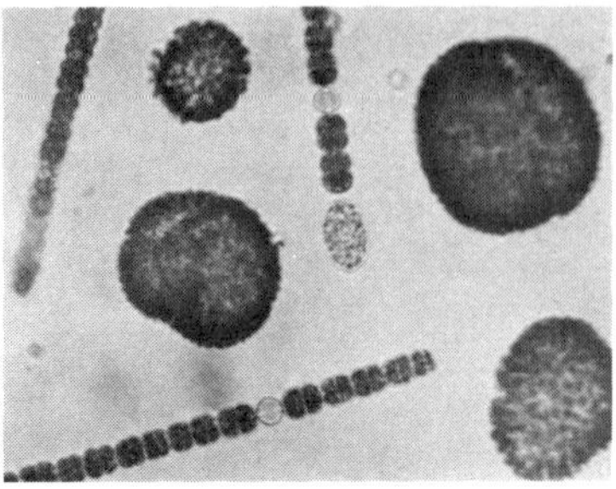

Coelosphaerium naegelianum

Reproduction takes place through cellular division. So far it has not been possible to verify sexual reproduction too. Many species develop spores, while many others propagate through fragmentation of the cells. Single cells may become encysted, thus becoming able to withstand droughts and cold. They are practically omnipresent, which explains their presence in aquaria despite the greatest caution in preventing them.

On means of destroying Blue Algae, see the entry FIGHTING ALGAE.

Cyclochaeta: see TRICHODINA.

Cyclocheilichthys: Fish with round lips.
Indian genus pertaining to the family of the Carp-like or CYPRINIDAE (see this), of quite compact body build and high, arched back. The slightly subterminal mouth carries no barbels.

— **apogon** (Cuvier and Valenciennes): The Indian River Barb.
SHAPE: As per description of the genus. D 12, A 8-9. The scales are relatively large. The species is reported to attain lengths of up to 20″.
COLOR: Greenish mother-of-pearl, each scale with a dark dot. One black spot behind the opercles, and another one on the tail root. The fins are a slightly -brownish hue.
RANGE: One of the most valued edible fishes of Indo-China, Malaya and the Sunda Islands, which lives

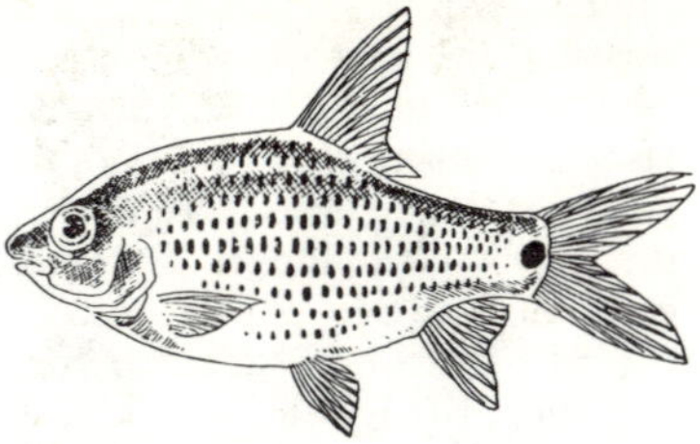

Cyclocheilichthys apogon

mainly in flowing water.

CARE AND BREEDING: In general this large species fits only into the exhibition aquarium. It is peaceful, quiet, and remains hidden among plants, but needs sufficient room for swimming. The fish are omnivorous and like also to eat organic detritus from the bottom. They need warmth: 75-79° F, lowest 68° F. Breeding has not yet succeeded.

cycloid scales: Scales with round, unarticulated edge, also called round scales. See SKIN and SKIN ORGANS.

Cyclopoidea: Order of lower Crustaceans belonging to the Class of the Rowing-Footed Crustaceans or COPEPODA (see this), with a great number of species in salt and fresh water, which can only be exactly differentiated by experts. The two pairs of antennae are un-forked, the second antennae of the males being built as gripping organs for holding the female. Respiration takes place through the skin. The circulation of the body fluids is activated by the intestine.

The *C.* swim in short, hopping, curved jumps. They are frequently seen resting on all kinds of firm objects. Nourishment, which consists of decaying organic residues, micro-organisms, etc., is usually caught and transferred to the oral device. It also happens, however, that the *C.* settle on bigger animals, chewing on them. In such cases they may become dangerous to fish fry in the aquarium.

For information on their reproduction see the entry COPEPODA.

C. are excellent fish food, especially during the winter months, when they are found in great numbers beneath the ice. Their nauplii of which great numbers already show up in early Spring, forming the main part of what is called dust-sized food, are especially good for rearing young fry in the aquarium. Be cautious, however, in their use, as uneaten nauplii, which are quicker to grow than the alevins, may become dangerous to them. Therefore make it a rule never to feed more nauplii than are eaten at once. Full-grown *Cyclopoidea* should never be put into indoor aquaria, as they frustrate any attempts at breeding if there in sufficient numbers.

Cyclops: Genus of lower Crustaceans pertaining to the order of the CYCLOPOIDEA (see this).

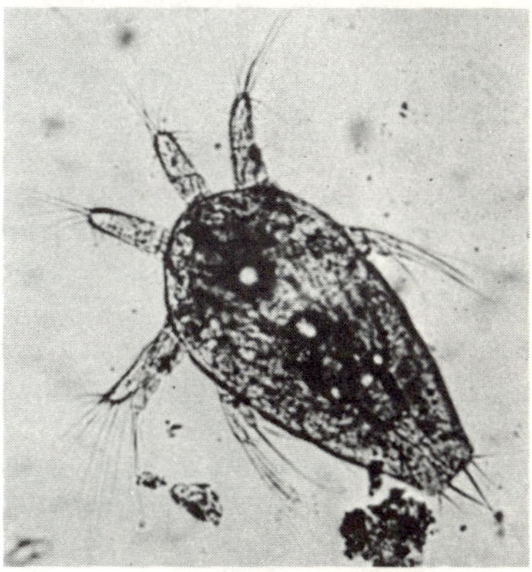

Cyclops nauplius

Cyclostomata: (Round Mouths). Order of fish-like aquatic animals belonging to the super-class of the Jawless Ones or AGNATHI (see this), characterized by their worm-shaped, elongated body. They have no paired fins, instead of which a narrow fin fringe runs from the back around the tail to the anus. The skeleton is purely cartilaginous and incompletely developed, the axial skeleton still consisting mainly of the chorda. The brain capsule is incomplete, and there are no jaw arches. The lips of the circle-shaped sucking mouth are equipped with teeth.

The order comprises several sub-orders, of which that of the *Petromyzoidea*, with the only family of the PETROMYZONIDAE (see this) is discussed in this book.

cylindraceus: Cylindrical, cylinder-shaped.
— *Rivulus.*

Cynolebias: Dog Lebias, Lebias being the ancient name of a fish species.
Genus of South American Tooth Carps belonging to the sub-family of the egg-laying Tooth Carps or CYPRINODONTINAE (see this). Fishes of somewhat compact, pestle-shaped build. The mouth is relatively large, and strongly studded with teeth. The vertical fins are very long, the number of fin rays differing for the two sexes. The tail fin is big and fan-shaped. The pectorals, too, are large, and can be moved in a peculiar, 'paddling' way like those of the Dog Fishes. The sexes differ strongly in coloring, too.

Cynolebias are very peculiar fishes whose manner of reproducing represents an adaptation to periodically dry waters. In part they are fishes of the Argentinian grass plains, the Pampas, where the waters dry up completely during the hot season, from December to January, while the winterly rainfalls from May to September fill them up again. The eggs are imbedded within the bottom mud, and withstand the drought there. The fry show up immediately after the first rain showers, and become sexually mature within 6-8 weeks. The complete life span generally lasts no longer than 6-8 months. One does not succeed in keeping the fishes alive longer than this even with the best of care. According to MEDER, the fishes become ever more tired, swim stumblingly, and show clear signs of senescence, especially the males. Therefore the aquarist should buy his specimens as young as possible.

THOMAS caught the fishes in water holes of different depths, the characters of which differed by the fact that the shallow ones contained clay, while the deeper ones showed a dark, slate-gray hue. The adaptability of the fishes was shown by the fact that those from the darker holes were more intensely colored. No plants were found in any of the holes. Of micro-organisms they contained *Cladocera* and mosquito larvae. TH. verified that only few fishes lived in each water hole, which leads one to suppose that there is considerable cannibalism during the period of growth among the Cynolebias. All species are very voracious, due to the fact that they need huge quantities of nourishment for their quick growth. For this reason there is the necessity for robust live foods in great quantities. The voraciousness is still increased during the spawning period and is the basis for the enormous sexual production.

C. like sunlight, with changeable temperatures from 64-72° F, which under solar radiation may rise still higher, sinking down again thereafter. LADIGES found water temperatures of 46° F in the home country of the fishes in June and July. During this time there are frequent nocturnal frosts. Everyday temperatures, as well as breeding temperatures, should therefore not be kept too high, 64-68° F being sufficient. It may be advisable, though, gradually to raise the temperature for the eggs up to 77° F, according to the conditions which prevail in their native habitat.

The fishes are best kept in tanks with soft, peaty bottoms, under certain conditions even refraining from using plants. Instead of these perhaps a root decoration might be built. The sexes should be kept separate until they are ripe for spawning, as otherwise the fishes keep spawning continually, and breeding becomes unsuccessful. According to MEDER, several males may be kept together in larger tanks, provided there are sufficient hiding places. However, two males only should never be kept together alone, as then they fight like Siamese Fighting Fish. The fishes are lively, pugnacious, and especially vicious during the spawning period.

ROHRBACH bred *C. bellotti* in sterilized pond mud. The act of spawning took place at 64° F. After it the temperature was raised to 77° F within 14 days and the water was siphoned off down to the bottom. Evaporation made the bottom still drier. After 30 days the tank was replenished with water again to a level of 4″. The first fry appeared after 24 hours. 80% of these were normally developed, the rest being unable to swim. Hatching the alevins in dishes did not succeed. MEDER has still perfected this method of breeding. He bred the fish in water of 3 DH, to which he added a heaped tea-spoon of kitchen salt per 2½ gallons. The eggs, which were spawned in Perlon (Nylon) mops, 20-50 per day were picked up and mixed in an emulsion of loess which had previously been strained through a fine-meshed brass sieve. This loess mud was placed in shallow dishes, about ⅜″ high, which stood open at a temperature of 73-77° F until the loess began cracking and fissuring. Thereafter the dishes were covered. MEDER points out that in completely dry loess no eggs develop. Evaporation, too, should take place slowly, as otherwise the loess becomes too dense and suffocates the eggs. Soft water was poured in after several weeks of rest. The first fry already showed up 1-2 hours later. With this method, which simpler than that of ROHRBACH, MEDER too obtained 80% of normal alevins.

Furthermore MEDER observed that the fully-developed fry are able to remain in moist loess for months without hatching. He raises the question, how long this 'vernal sleep' may last.

If the transition to drying out is too quick, the fecundated eggs do not develop at first, but rest, no one knows for how long, as 'germs'. Rearing the young is not considered difficult. With sufficient live food, the fish are nearly grown up within 8 weeks.

— **adloffi** Ahl: The Banded Cynolebias.

SHAPE: As per description of the genus, strongly compressed laterally. D: males 22-23, females 19; A: males 26-27, females 25. Length about 2″.

COLOR: The male metallic blue-green during the spawning period,

Cynolebias adloffi

with 9-14 black cross bands, the female mud-colored with darker dots and bands.
RANGE: In watering places and flood regions of Southeastern Brazil.
CARE AND BREEDING: As described for genus.

Cynolebias bellotti

— **bellotti** Steindachner: The Argentine Pearl Fish.
SHAPE: As per description of the genus. D: males 21-24, females 16-19; A: males 26-30, females 22-26. Length up to 2¾″, the female smaller.
COLOR: During the spawning period the male is greenish to navy blue with numerous luminous spots on body and fins. The female is clay yellow with brown spot designs.
CARE AND BREEDING: As per description of the genus.

— **melanotaenia** (Regan): The Fighting Gaucho.
SHAPE: As per description of the genus, however the number of fin rays does not diverge for the sexes. Of elongated build, slightly compressed laterally. D 16-18, A 17-20. Length about 2″.
COLOR: Brownish base with carmine red length bands and gleaming green dots. The fins of the males partly with extended rays. The female is paler in colors.
RANGE: In small waters of Southeastern Brazil.
CARE AND BREEDING: A very motile and pugnacious species, which likes

Cynolebias melanotaenia

to stay near the surface and reminds one of the different species of *Rivulus* in its behavior. Do not offer them too high degrees of warmth, as this shortens their life span, about 68° F is sufficient. The fish spawn on surface plants, but it seems that rearing the fry has not yet succeeded. This species, which so far has been seldom imported, has not been able to survive in the aquarium. Possibly the specimens that came in were too old.

— **nigripinnis** Regan: The Black-Finned Cynolebias.
SHAPE: As per description of the genus. The smallest of the species. Length up to 2″, the female remaining smaller.
COLOR: During the spawning period the male dark-blue with blue-black fins, dorsal and anal fins with whitish seam, gleaming white dots on body and fins. The female is clay-yellow with brown dots and spots.
RANGE: Rio Parana.
CARE AND BREEDING: As described for the genus. KAHNAU reports that the eggs did not hatch if left in water. Development started only after they were kept moist, so that 105-130 days elapsed until the fry hatched.

Cynopoecilus: South American genus belonging to the sub-family of the egg-laying Tooth Carps or CYPRINODONTINAE (see this), which was voided by Myers. Today the species of this genus are included

Spawning **Cynolebias nigripinnis** — Top, left: the male approaches the female, right, with outspread fins. Top, right: the male, right, keeps in front of the female with waving motions of the body. Center, left: the pair presses closely together over the bottom. Center, right: the male digs into the soft bottom, followed by the female. Bottom, left: spawning completed, the male is the first to emerge. Bottom, right: a little later the female's head emerges.

among the *Cynolebias*, but presently (1958) this measure is being actively disputed by many parties due to morphological, physiological, and ethological peculiarities.

Cyperaceae: Reed or Cyprus Grasses.

Family of swamp plants pertaining to the class of the MONOCOTYLEDONEAE (see this), which is distributed over the whole globe with about 3000 known species. The plants are perennial, grass-like, and grow runners. Their external shapes vary very much, due to the fact that they are found in the most different kinds of biotopes.

In this book we mention the following genera: HELEOCHARIS (see this), and CYPERUS (see this).

Cyperus: From the island of Cyprus.

The genus of the Cyprus Grasses, belonging to the family of the *Cyperaceae*, comprises tall, perennial swamp plants which possess false leaves which are disposed in the shape of palm leaves. The rhizome is short and thick. The real foliage leaves sit at the bottom part of the stalks, are completely stunted, and dry up. Stalk and false leaves are stiff, possess a dark green color, and their edges feel a little coarse to the touch. The flower ears bud from the axillae of the false leaves.

Reproduction takes place through division of the root stock, or through old leaf verticils, or parts of the same, which are stuck into wet sand or put in water. From these develop young plants, which may be planted in pots. They may also develop baby plants instead of flowers on robust old specimens especially in moist-warm air. All species of *C.* like water levels of about 4″. WENDT advises that the bottom soil be made up of coarse sand mixed with a little old clay, in case of cultivation in pots a mixture of sand, clay, and humus, with an admixture of some fertilized loam and peat.

The two following species are most commonly cultivated: *Cyperus alternifolius* Linné, the Alternate-Leaved Cyprus Grass, from Madagascar, Mauritius, and Reunion, which has found wide distribution as a supplier of raffia; and *Cyperus gracilis* R. Brown, the Gracile Cyprus Grass, from Australia and New Caledonia.

Both speces have only a limited use for the indoor aquarium. The best is to cultivate them in moist-warm air in the paludarium, as in house air they easily dry up, even if frequently moistened. Both species may be summered out-of-doors.

Cyprinidae: Carp Fishes.

Family of Carp Fishes pertaining to the sub-order of the Carp-like or CYPRINOIDEA (see this).

This family, which is very abundant in species, is very strongly represented in Europe and Asia, but also in Africa and North America with a number of species. On the other hand it is originally absent in South America, Australia and the neighboring island groups, and Madagascar, excepting those species which have been imported for economic reasons. Being different from the Characins, the *C.* show no real teeth, but only horny throat teeth, which are important for the differentiation of the genera. The throat teeth chew against a palatal plate.

Generally the body structure is elongated-round to oval, but frequently also slender, with small fins and often with large scales. The mouth is often protractable, and in many cases it carries one or more pairs of barbels. Many *C.*, the so-called White or Silver Fishes, possess a striking glitter of the scales.

The Carps are found in nearly

The genera of the family Cyprinidae

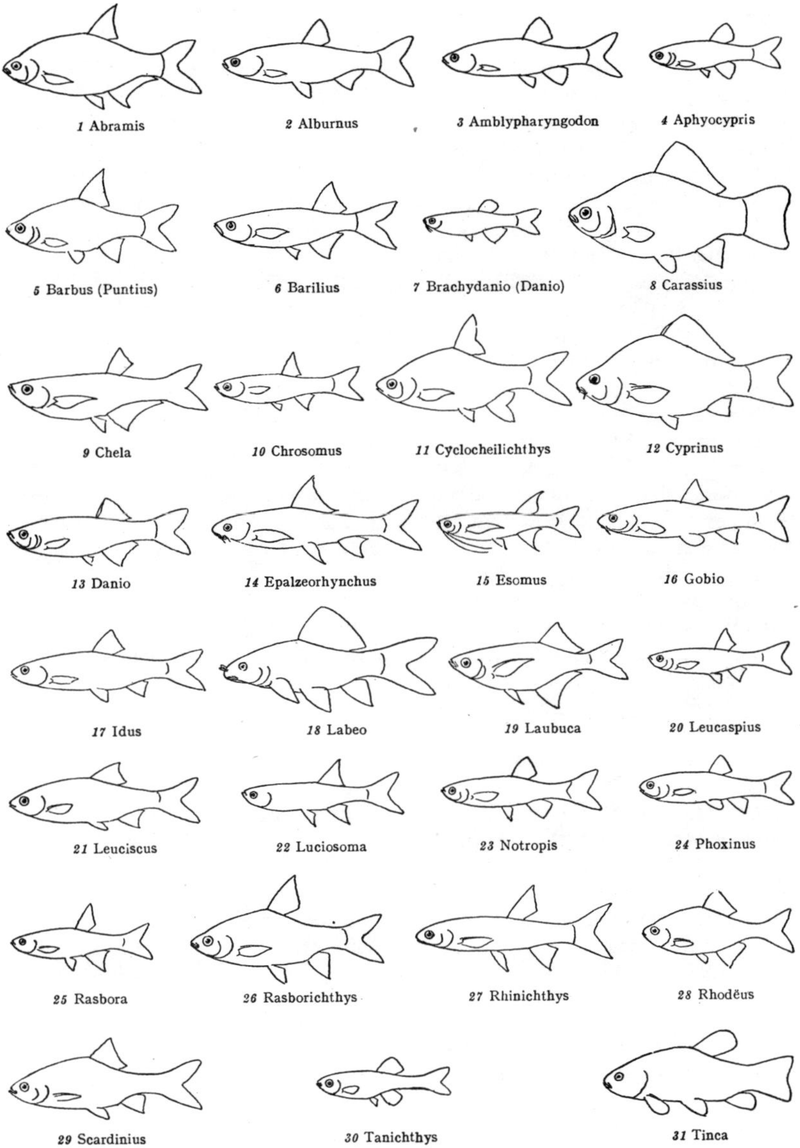

all kinds and regions of waters, except those of the high mountains. Many species like standing or slowly-flowing waters with soft bottom, which they search for nourishment with their 'trunk' and barbels. Others are inhabitants of more or less swiftly-flowing streams and prefer gravelly bottoms.

The peculiarity that the *C.* root in the soil may be counted against them in aquaristics. As a rule, however, most species are easy to keep, hardy, and peaceful. Predatory fishes are very rare within the family. Most species like to live gregariously or in larger schools. Therefore they generally are advisable for keeping in communities. When doing so, however, pay attention to putting them in with other equally lively fishes. Some of the species like to nibble on the fins of other fishes. A dark bottom enhances their colors.

It is advisable to cover the bottom with split basalt gravel, which has the added advantage of protecting the water against the disagreeable cloudings caused by rooting in the soil. This may be mixed with some coarse gravel of a lighter hue, as basalt alone looks somewhat dead. Fine-feathered plants, such as *Cabomba*, *Myriophyllum*, and *Limnophila*, cannot be kept in the same tanks with rooting species, as the whirled-up mulm smothers them. The demands as to light, water warmth, and water composition vary. One cannot give any generally-valid rules for these.

Besides live and artificial foods, the Carps also eat vegetable fare, which in part seems to be a primary condition for their well-being.

Tropical regions of Asia harbor many species which are excellent pets for the fancier's aquarium due to their minute size, pretty coloring, hardiness, and ease to breed. Breeding may generally be considered easy. Most species are egg scatterers, which spawn their eggs in open water or among plants after violent chasing. Only rarely are the eggs anchored to plants or other firm objects. Care for the brood is only found in exceptional cases, such as the European *Leucaspius delineatus*, and the Bitterling. The parents generally are vicious spawn robbers, and should therefore be removed immediately after spawning in order to protect the eggs against their preying. In order further to protect these, put stones, plant pads, breeding traps, etc. on the bottom, and especially into the corners of your tanks. Plants should be weighted down with little glass tubes in order to keep them on the bottom. The average time for the hatching of eggs is 24-48 hours. After this time the alevins generally hang for some few days more from glass panes, plants, etc., being visible as thin and glassily transparent little dashes, which soon thereafter become free-swimming. From this moment on they have to be fed with very small-sized live foods, partly infusoria, partly rotatoria, etc. Usually you may offer the dust-sized artificial or accessory foods (mashed White Worms, egg yolk, etc.) in small quantities as an addition.

Of the many genera, the following may be found in this book under the respective entries:

Abramis	*Labeo*
Alburnus	*Laubuca*
Amblypharyngodon	*Leucaspius*
Aphyocypris	*Leuciscus*
Barbus	*Luciosoma*
Barilius	*Notropis*
Brachydanio	*Oxygaster*
Carassius	*Phoxinus*
Chela	(*Puntius*)
Chrosomus	*Rasbora*
Cyclocheilichthys	*Rasborichthys*
Cyprinus	*Rhinichthys*
Danio	*Rhodeus*

Epalzeorhynchus *Scardinius*
Esomus *Tanichthys*
Gobio *Tinca*
Idus

Cyprinodon: Tooth Carp.
Genus of North American Tooth Carps belonging to the sub-family of the egg-laying Tooth Carps or CYPRINODONTINAE (see this).

— variegatus (Lacepede): The Sheepshead Minnow.
SHAPE: The species is of short build and looks quite robust, especially older specimens are quite high-backed. The mouth is terminal to supraterminal, D 9-11, A 9-11; the scales relatively large. Length: males up to $3\frac{1}{8}''$, females up to $2\frac{3}{8}''$.
COLOR: The species may show quite variegated colors, according to geographic origin. Generally it is shiny blue with darker cross bands and many luminous dots. The underside is orange-colored. The fins, too, are very prettily colored. The females are considerably simpler in color.
RANGE: In all kinds of smaller waters of Northern Mexico and the South of the U.S.A., but also in Cuba. The species lives mainly in waters near the sea coast, in fresh, brackish, and salt water.

Cyprinodon variegatus

CARE AND BREEDING: This fish is rather hard to keep, since it is only with difficulty that it adapts to the conditions in the aquarium. Wild specimens should initially receive an admixture of 25% of salt water, or a strongish addition of kitchen salt. Since plants hardly will resist this condition, hiding places have to be provided for by other means. At first the fish are timid and sensitive to disturbance. They are able to hide for a considerable time completely buried in sand. Therefore it is advisable to cover the bottom with a layer of peat mulm. After domestication, however, the fish become lively, bellicose, and vicious. They need plenty of live food, preferring small fishes. With regard to temperature they are hardy, 68-72° F being sufficient for breeding, while the lowest may be 50° F. A sunlit location is favorable, especially if you want to achieve success in breeding. The Sheepshead Minnow is not difficult to breed. If it is well fed, the fish spawns nearly unceasingly. The male is a very violent suitor and does not show any gentleness at all. This gives importance to hiding places into which the female may retire. The numerous eggs are spawned one by one, preferably into thick bushes or plants, algae, etc. The fry hatch after 8-12 days. They are voracious and grow quickly, devouring those of their brothers and sisters which are retarded in growth. Therefore the young have to be graded as to size. They may already become able to reproduce at the age of five months.

Cyprinodontidae: Tooth Carps.
Family belonging to the order of the Small Carps or MICROCYPRINI (see this), which has risen to special importance in aquaristics. In systematics it was sometimes placed close to the Cyprinids, sometimes close to the Pikes, both connections being shown in their English name, as well as in their scientific denomination. With reference to genetic history, though, the *C.* are doubtless higher developed than both mentioned groups.

The range of the family coincides

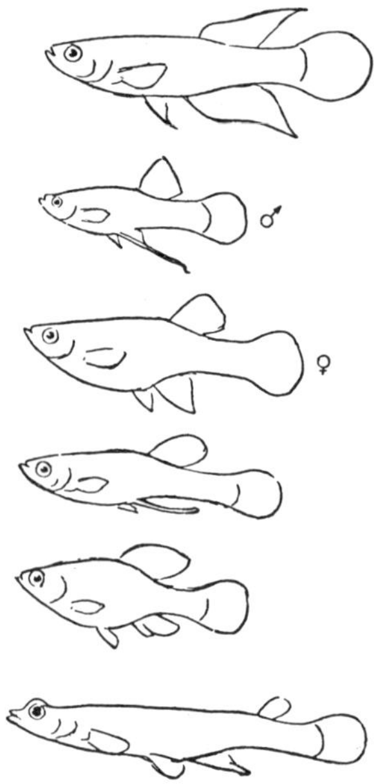

Cyprinodontidae — types of the genera. Top to bottom: Egglaying Toothcarps, Livebearing Toothcarps (Poeciliinae), male above, female below, **Jenynsiinae** male, **Goodeinae** male, **Anableps** male.

with that of the order *Microcyprini*. They avoid the temperate zones nearly completely, and populate waters of all kinds, especially fresh water, but are also found in brackish ones, and, to a small extent, even in the ocean. All *C.* are small or very small fishes, including species which may be considered the smallest of all vertebrates. Very few of the presently known 400 species reach lengths of $4\frac{3}{4}''$ and up to 6″.

The body of the Tooth Carps is more or less elongated, and only in few cases relatively compact to very compact. Generally it is flattened on the head, and more or less compressed laterally towards the rear. The mouth opening is small to relatively large. They never carry barbels. The jaws are equipped with teeth. The upper jaw is only slightly, or not at all, movable, the intermediate jaw is more or less protractable. The fishes never have lateral lines.

The family is divided into the following sub-families: the egg-laying Tooth Carps or CYPRINODONTINAE (see this), the live-bearing Tooth Carps or POECILIINAE (see this), the JENYNSIINAE (see this), the GOODEINAE (see this), and the Four-Eyes or ANABLEPINAE (see this).

Cyprinodontinae: Egg-laying Tooth Carps.

Sub-family belonging to the family of the Tooth Carps or CYPRINODONTIDAE (see this). The species are excellent aquarium fishes, some of which are counted among the most colorful of all tropicals. The scales are relatively large. Some species lack the lateral line; but to compensate for this they often show a strong concentration of nerve tips at the head. Some species have no swimming bladder. All egg-laying Tooth Carps are small to medium-sized fishes, partly of Pike-like shape and predatory manner of living, but this should absolutely not be considered as the general rule. They are advisable for keeping in the aquarium, despite the fact that nearly all of them are not fishes for beginners, and even less for keeping in communities. In their home countries they dwell in the most varied kinds of waters, generally in great numbers. Many species are very shortlived, a shortcoming which generally is still increased if they are kept in heated tanks. All these Tooth Carps need rich and robust live foods, in keeping with their sizes. They relish mosquito larvae especially, being noted in their home

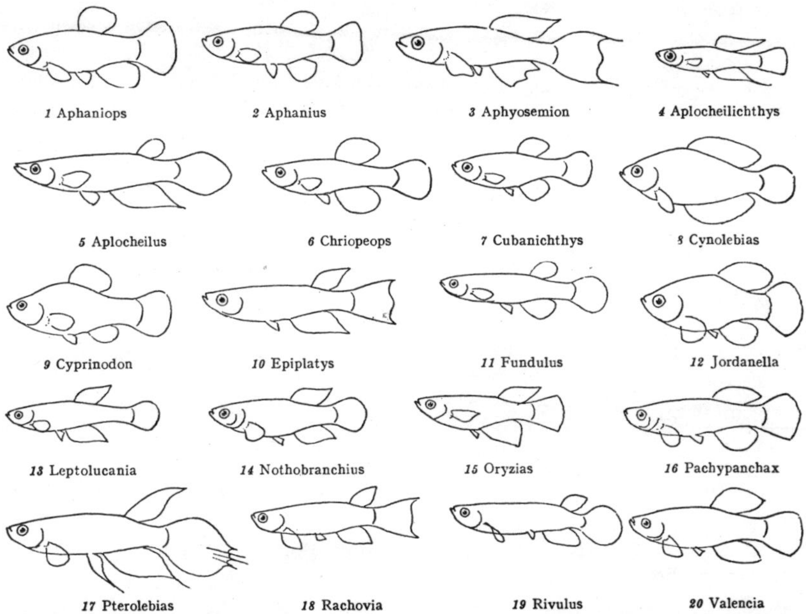

countries as destroyers of these. Additionally they also eat some kinds of good artificial foods. Some of them need algae occasionally for their well-being. Nothing comprehensive may be stated about their character traits, as there are peaceful species as well as bellicose and vicious ones. For keeping them one has to consider that many species like well-planted tanks with hiding places, and, as far as surface types are concerned, a good covering of floating plants. If kept in bare, all-glass tanks, as has become usual, the fishes are unable to develop fully. An overall dark character of the tank enhances their colors. Notwithstanding this, most species like sunlight, at least occasionally, even if otherwise they keep in dark hiding places, and only a few shun sunlight completely. The larger species need plenty of space, but their needs are not excessive as compared with the swift-swimming fishes of other families.

Temperatures should generally be handled with care. Many species do not tolerate high degrees of warmth, and others are short-lived with warmth further shortening their span of life. However, some of the surface fishes among them like to lie in the burning sun.

With exception of *Jordanella floridae*, which exerts an indifferent care for its brood, the egg-laying Tooth Carps are egg hangers and bottom spawners, which do not pay any attention to their spawn. Many species prey on eggs and fry. In most cases breeding demands a certain amount of experience, thought, and luck.

The following of the genera are described in this book, and may be found under the respective entries:

Aphaniops
Aphanius
Aphyosemion
Aplocheilichthys
Aplocheilus
Chriopeops
Cubanichthys
Cynolebias
Cyprinodon
Epiplatys
Fundulus
Jordanella
Leptolucania
Nothobranchius
Oryzias
Pachypanchax
Profundulus
Pterolebias
Rachovia
Rivulus
Valencia

The genera of the family **Cyprinoidea**

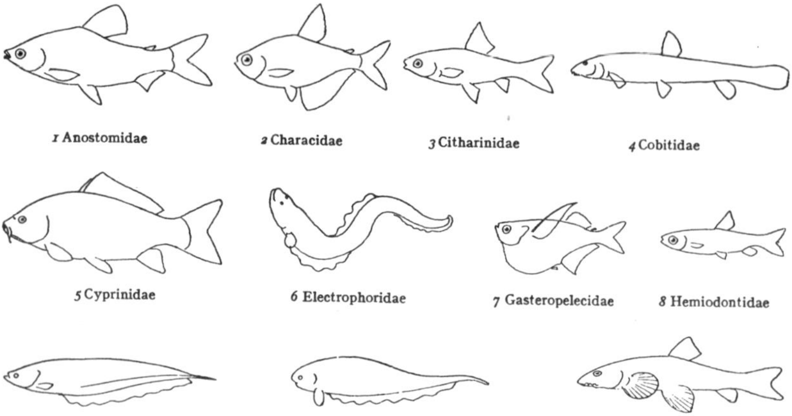

Cyprinoidea: Carp-Like Fishes. Sub-order belonging to the order of the OSTARIOPHYSI (see this), a group which is rich in families and is distributed over nearly the whole globe, with exception of Australia and Madagascar, to which countries, however, some of the members have been imported for economic reasons. Due to their wide distribution, they have developed differentiated forms, which in systematics have given origin to orders or sub-orders of their own. Thus BERG, for instance, considers Characins, Knife Fishes, Carps, and Catfishes as sub-orders with equal rights. Despite the fact that this makes the system easier to understand, his opinion has not been able to win recognition. HOEDEMAN recently established three sub-orders: the Carps, the Characins, and the Catfishes. He includes the Knife Fishes in the sub-order of the Characins. In the systematics of this book we follow the 'Zoological Record' and advise the reader to make his own choice between the systematics of HOEDEMAN and those of BERG. The body of the Carp-like Fishes is generally covered with scales, rarely naked, and the head is never scaly. Barbels are seen on the families of the Loaches, the Carps, the Carp Loaches, and the *Gyrinocheilidae.* These families possess no jaw teeth. In compensation their throat bones are equipped with horny formations, which exert the functions of teeth. The Characins and some other families, however, possess real teeth. The mouth of some of the families is proctractable. The intestine may be developed as an accessory respiratory organ, enabling the fishes to stay in waters that are very poor in oxygen by making use of atmospheric air. This happens especially with the Loaches, but also with some Characins and related groups.

The sub-order is divided into 14 families: Headstanders or ANOSTOMIDAE (see this), CATOSTOMIDAE, Characins or CHARACIDAE (see this), African Characins or CITHARINIDAE (see this), Loaches or COBITIDAE (see this), Carps or CYPRINIDAE (see this), Knife Eels or ELECTROPHORIDAE (see this), Hatchet Bellies or GASTEROPELECIDAE (see this), Knife Fishes or GYMNOTIDAE (see this), Sucker Loaches or GYRINOCHEILIDAE (see this), Half-Teeth or

HEMIODONTIDAE (see this), Carp Loaches or HOMALOPTERIDAE (see this), RHAMPHICHTHYIDAE, and Sea Cow Fishes or STERNARCHIDAE (see this).

Cyprinus: After the Greek goddess of fertility, from Cyprus island. Genus of real Carps, belonging to the family of the Carp-like Fishes or CYPRINIDAE (see this). Little elongated to high fishes, only little compressed laterally, and wide-backed. The mouth is terminal and strongly protractable, with four barbels on the upper jaw. The throat teeth form three rows. The front edges of the dorsal and anal fins show strong rays, serrated toward the rear. Only smaller specimens are fit for the indoor aquarium.

— carpio Linné: The Carp.

SHAPE: As per description of the genus. The species is the original form of a number of bred varieties, which differ strongly in shape and scales. The most important of these forms are the Leather, the Mirror, and the Scale Carp, which on their part diverge according to the different schools of breeding. D 20-26, A 8-9. The scales are relatively large, but on some of the bred forms they may stand isolated or may even be totally absent. Length up to more than 40″.

RANGE: The original home country of the Carp is the temperate regions of Central Asia and Eastern Europe. Only rarely are wild specimens found in the Danube, others generally being pond Carps which have run wild.

CARE AND BREEDING: As described for *Cyprinidae*. Carps like to root and investigate the bottom for nourishment. Consider this when setting up the tank for them! Breeding Carps in the aquarium is impossible.

Cyprus Grasses: see CYPERACEAE.

cyst: Resistant cover, developed by some lower animals, with the aid of which they are able to a large extent to isolate from the ambient world, and eventually to remain in an extended state of rest.

D.: Abbreviation for dorsal fin.

Dactylogyrus: Genus of sucker worms (Trematodes), the members of which live parasitically on the gills, less frequently on the epidermis of fishes. A group which is very rich in species which differentiates from the closely-related *Gyrodactylus* by the fact that it possesses a four-lobed head with four black eyes and, contrary to what happens with the others, is less frequently found on the epidermis than *Gyrodactylus*. They attack mainly young fry and fishes weakened by other causes. Isolated parasites on healthy fishes generally are not permitted to develop and therefore harmless. Generally the different species of the genus are specific for the fishes, that is, they specialize on certain species of fishes. To what extent they are transmissible to tropical fishes has not been yet fully verified. See SKIN DISCOLORATIONS and GILL DISEASES.

Dactylogyrus, enlarged

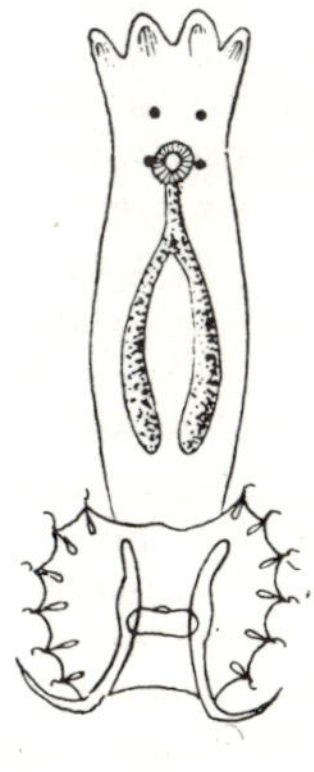

Dageti: After a personal name.
— *Epiplatys.*

Damasonium: Old name for *Alisma.*

Genus pertaining to the family of the Frogbit Plants or ALISMATACEAE (see this). Swamp plants with band-shaped, submerged primary leaves and secondary floating leaves. Scarcely fit for the indoor aquarium.

daniconius: After the native name.
— *Rasbora.*

danio: From 'dhani', the name in a Hindu dialect.

Genus of school fishes belonging to the family of the Carp Fishes or CYPRINIDAE (see this), of elongated, slender to compact body structure, strongly compressed laterally. The lateral line is complete; barbels may be present, absent, or stunted. The Danios are lively and of peaceful nature, very well adapted for keeping in communities. They eat all live and dry foods that are appropriate to their size. For breeding the fishes need large tanks and an addition of new water. The act of spawning, generally begun by the female, takes place under the morning sun after violent chasing. The courtships may be very graceful and pleasing. In these we see above all fin beatings and turning around each other crosswise. Sometimes spawning is done while the male shortly embraces the female. The pairs meet within the school. They are very productive, but one has to take measures to protect the eggs from the parents.

Many authors mention a genus *Brachydanio*, but this should be evaluated as a sub-genus only, as the characteristics which are considered as determinative for it are not even well defined. Therefore some authors write, for instance, the name of the Zebra Danio as *Danio* (*Brachydanio*) *rerio*. The species which belong to the sub-genus *Brachydanio* are still mentioned under the respective entry in this book.

— devario Hamilton-Buchanan:
SHAPE: As per description of the genus, but not very elongated. Especially older specimens and females are relatively compact. D 12-15, A 15-19. Length up to $3\frac{1}{8}''$.

Danio devario

COLOR: Shiny bluish to greenish violet silvery with some bluish horizontal bands on the rear of the body, which dissolve into faded cross bands towards the front. The male is slimmer and more vividly colored.
RANGE: Quite frequent in standing or flowing clear waters of India.
CARE AND BREEDING: As per description of the genus, 70-75° F, for breeding up to 82° F.

— malabaricus (Jerdon): The Giant Danio.
SHAPE: As per description of the genus, very slender and elongated, sharply compressed laterally. The supraterminal mouth carries one pair of barbels, while a further pair is only stunted or may be lacking completely. The lateral line forms a slight curve. D 12-15, A 15-19. Length, in its home waters up to 6″, in the aquarium up to 4″.
COLOR: On yellowish to orange-colored base several steel blue horizontal stripes which dissolve behind the opercles to form short cross stripes. The male is slimmer and more highly colored, its horizontal stripes reaching into the

Danio malabaricus

upper lobe of the tail fin, while those of the female run straight.

RANGE: Quite common in clear, flowing or standing waters of the West Coast of India and on Ceylon.

CARE AND BREEDING: As per description of the genus.

danricus: After the native name. — *Esomus.*

daphnia: see DAPHNIDAE.

Daphnia: see CLADOCERA.

— dried: see ARTIFICIAL FOODS.

Daphnia as food: *Daphnia* are an excellent live food for nearly all species of aquarium fishes. They may be caught with appropriate nets from April to October, sometimes there are sufficient quantities even in winter, under the ice. For biological reasons (see CLADOCERA), they show up in such huge quantities in summer, that they form grey-green to red swaths beneath the water surface. When catching them pay attention to the direction of the wind. The wind sweeps the *Daphnia* to one side, or into a corner, and they are found in the lee of overhanging banks. When feeding them to your fishes, be careful not to transfer *D.* directly from cold to warm water, as otherwise they will die very quickly. For smaller quantities, which are eaten immediately, this may not have any significance, but larger remainders are left to rot, and soon spoil the water. In fact, you should never feed too many *Daphnia* at once, it being preferable to feed several times a day, especially in summer. Greater numbers of *Daphnia* consume considerable oxygen, and once the equilibrium in an aquarium is disturbed, it is hard to correct it again.

Daphnia will keep for several days even in summer if kept in larger containers at places which are cool and not too exposed to intense sunlight. Never use zinc or other metallic containers to keep them in, always preferring enamel ware, ceramic, or glass bowls instead of these.

Make it a rule to leave the water standing for at least one day, in order to enrich it with oxygen by means of aeration and also to evaporate the chlorine which generally is contained in tap water. The chlorine contents of newly drawn tap water are apt to kill freshly introduced *Daphnia.* Furthermore make sure that the temperature of the water is the same as that of the water in which the crustaceans were transported. A great difference too may endanger your whole catch.

Dead *Daphnia* should immediately be siphoned off, this operation being repeated on the bottom of the aquarium every day. Beginners frequently commit the mistake of catching too many of them, killing many of the crustaceans through lack of oxygen already on the way home. For this too, moderation is the supreme law and preferable to senseless wasting of resources. The best manner of transporting *Daphnia* is not in water-filled containers, but on frames (see CATCHING FOOD). Furthermore one should never feed them to the fishes directly from the transport container, but should let them stand for a couple of hours in order to be able to form

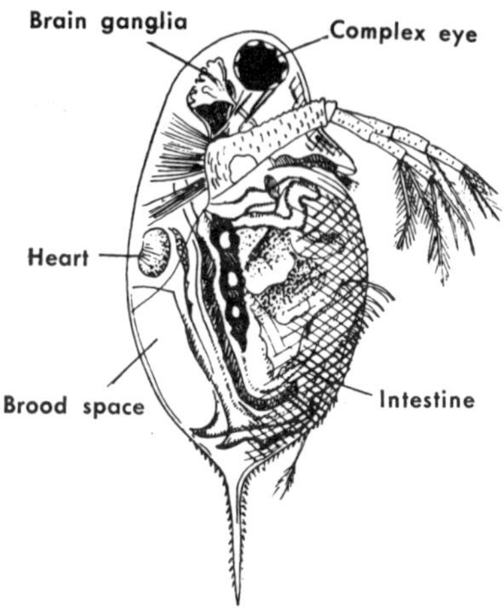

Daphnia, enlarged diagram

a general idea of what one is really bringing home, as well as to let dead specimens sink and to kill parasites and their young which may eventually be mixed up with the *Daphnia*. For the same reason do not catch the food allotment of your fishes with a net, but syphon it off carefully with a hose, straining it through a fine-meshed net or sieve. Thus you will always be enabled to serve your fishes clean food. Rain barrels in gardens, or other containers of corresponding size, offer good conditions for storing, if kept in cool, frost-free rooms. If you have such containers available, it will be perfectly possible for you to breed the needed *Daphnia* for a normal fancier's outfit at home. For this set up several wooden tubs, water barrels cut in half, well-insulated metallic containers, or similar, with a capacity for about 12 gallons each. Take care to keep the water level low, but the surface as large as possible. Put a handful of old, weathered (never fresh) sheep, cow, pigeon, or chicken manure in each tank. Then leave the whole thing standing for approximately a fortnight. After this time add a small quantity of baking yeast to the water. Furthermore you may also pour in some blood or meat water, about one quart per container. After some more days put in the *Daphnia*. Be conservative. Excesses only kill the *Daphnia* for lack of oxygen and spoil the water. Besides yeast and blood water, your *Daphnia* may also be fed on milk (two tablespoons per tub). After the water has been eaten 'clear', feeding should be renewed. If you proceed in this manner, you will have sufficient *Daphnia* even in winter.

Daphnidae:

Family of the *Daphnia* within the order of the CLADOCERA (see this) in the stricter sense of the word, with many European genera, which represent the greater number of the food animals known as *Daphnia*. The Large *Daphnia* (*Daphnia magna*) reaches $\frac{1}{4}''$ in diameter. The Common *Daphnia* (*Daphnia pulex*), which is hard to differentiate from *Daphnia magna*, remains a little smaller. Both species live mainly in somewhat stagnant waters with a rich flora of algae (village ponds with fowls). The Long-Spined *Daphnia* (*Daphnia longispina*) with its very variegated shapes, inhabits greater ponds and lakes. It possesses a long shell spine. The Helmeted *Daphnia* (*Daphnia cucullata*) changes its shape with the seasons. This species too inhabits greater lakes.

Besides these and other species, which should be considered as belonging to the zoo-plankton, some others are specialized in a different manner of living. Thus, for instance the Horned *Daphnia* (*Scapholeberis mucronata*) runs along the underside of the water surface. Besides other peculiarities in its structure, it possesses a forehead spine, which changes according to its sur-

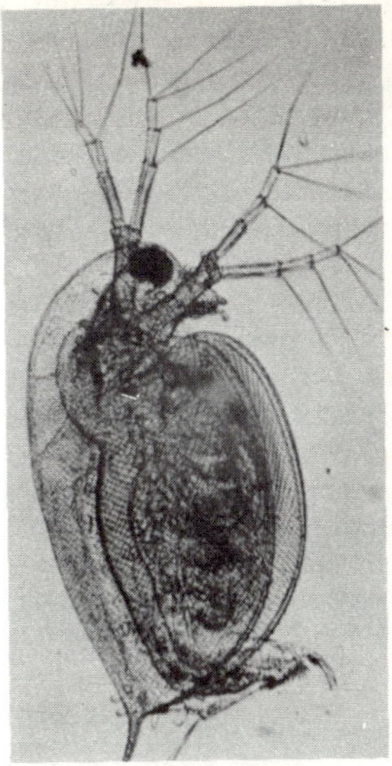

Daphnia magna

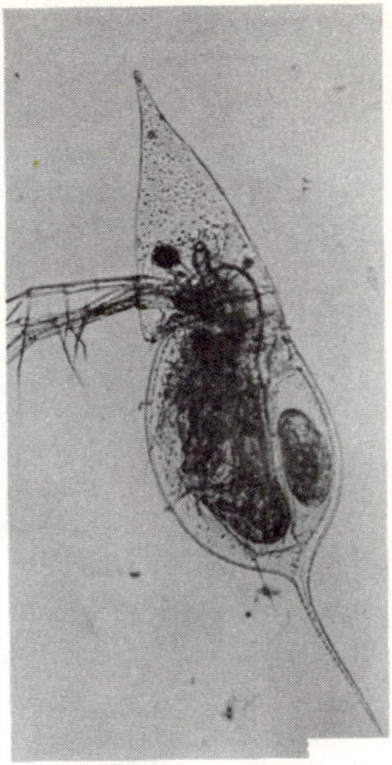

Daphnia cucullata

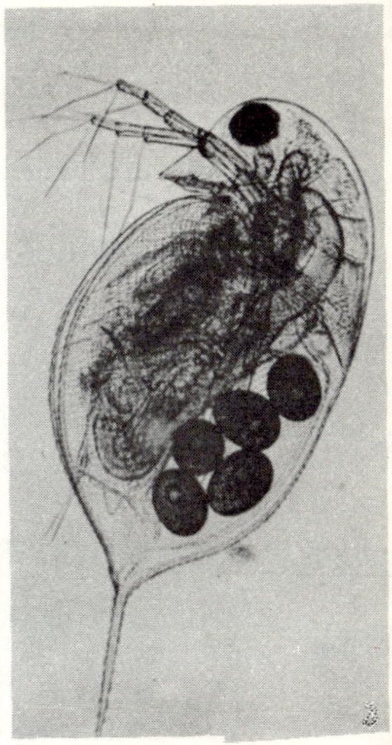

Daphnia longispina

roundings and to the season. Other species still, such as, for instance, the Flathead (*Simocephalus vetulus*), live among plants. *D.* move by beating their richly bristled second pair of antennae, which causes their spurt-like jumping. They feed on unicellular algae, unicellular animals, and detritus.

Darter Characin, the: see CHARACIDIUM FASCIATUM.

— Rachow's: see CHARACIDIUM RACHOVI.

Darwin, Charles Robert: 1809-1882. Famous English naturalist, who above all holds an important part in the rise of modern Natural History through his works on genetic-historical development. His best-known work is 'The Origin of Species by means of Natural Selection'.

Darwin's description of the genetic-historical phenomena is part of the basic biological knowledge even in our days (see ORIGIN OF THE SPECIES).

Dawn Tetra, the: see HYPHESSOBRYCON EOS.

day-flies: see EPHEMERIDA.

dayi: Honoring the name of Sir Francis Day (1829-1889).

— *Aplocheilus.*

— *Macropodus cupanus.*

debauwi debauwi: After a personal name.

— *Eutropiellus.*

Decapoda: Ten-Legged Crustaceans.

Order of crustaceans pertaining to the class of the MALACOSTRACA (see this), which possess a hard calcified shell and eyes on stalks. Of the 16 limbs on the breast segment, ten are used as walking legs, while the front pairs are transformed into pincers. The head and breast pieces are enclosed within a hard shell. The lateral wings of the shell form large respiratory caves, into which protrude the gills, which are located on the pectoral legs. The long abdomen of the pincer crustaceans may be used for locomotion, while that of the crabs is less developed or even stunted. Two sub-orders: the Shrimps or NATANTIA (see this), and the Pincer Crustaceans or REPTANTIA (see this).

decemmaculatus: With ten spots.
— *Cnesterodon.*

delineatus: With (lateral) line.
— *Leucaspius.*

demersum: Submerged.
— *Ceratophyllum.*

densa: Dense, thick.
— *Elodea.*

Dense-Leaved Anacharis: see ELODEA DENSA.

densus: Thick, dense.
— *Potamogeton.*

dentatus: With teeth, serrated.
— *Piabucus.*

Dermogenys: With skin jaws (half-beaks).

Genus belonging to the family of the Half-Beak Pikes or HEMIRHAMPHIDAE (see this). The body is elongated, only slightly compressed laterally. The 'beak' always carries a thin protruding skin fold on both sides. The lower jaw carries very small pointed teeth only opposite the intermediate jaw. The dorsal fin is shorter than the anal, and begins to the rear of the insertion of this. The first rays of the anal of the male are transformed into a fecundating organ, which, however, is not as perfect as that of the live-bearing Tooth Carps. All fins are small. The scales are medium-sized and come off easily. The indistinct lateral line runs along the lower half of the body. The Half-Beaks are pronounced surface fishes, which like to remain among floating plants or to swim in schools in the open water below the surface. They are widely distributed over South Eastern Asia and are very common in waters of all kinds, both fresh and brackish ones.

In nature they eat mainly flying food, for which the 'beak' is specialized. When catching it, the immovable lower jaw is placed below the prey, and the lifted movable jaw is closed on it, so that the whole device acts as a trap. The fish like to jump after insects, but do not scorn vegetable food, especially algae. In captivity, natural, varied food is one of the most important factors. Only *Daphnia* and dry foods are not conducive to healthy offspring. Whenever possible, they should be supplemented with small insects, such as Fruit Flies (*Drosophila*), grasshoppers, ants, etc.

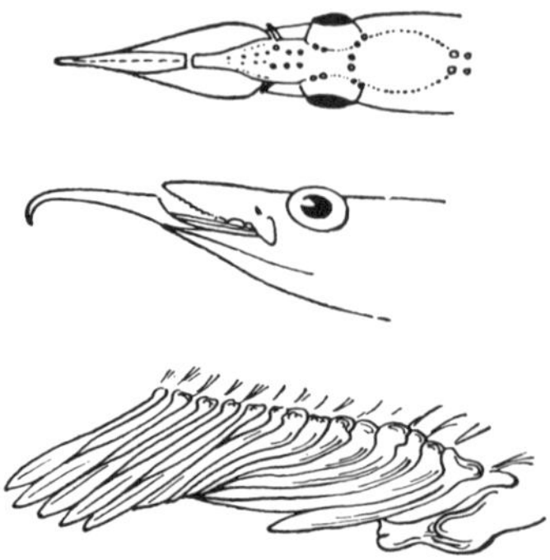

Dermogenys pusillus — top and center: head from above, and from the side; bottom: anal fin of a male.

Freshly imported and moved fishes may be quite timid. Therefore domestication should take place cautiously, as otherwise the fishes may hurt their lower jaws, which do not regenerate. Give imported specimens an admixture of sea water or of kitchen salt (one teaspoon of salt per 5 quarts of water). The Half-Beaks need warmth, 77-86° F are optimum, at lower temperatures they soon become sluggish. Otherwise, though, they are very lively. The males, which are smaller than the females, are quite bellicose and quarrelsome among themselves, stalking around each other with open mouth and erected opercles. The fights, in which the fishes only try to cause an impression, nearly always end harmlessly.

The males are constantly trying to mate. For this they swim below the female, with the mouth near her genital opening, the body slanted slightly downwards. Then they suddenly stand on their heads in order to come close to the females, with their anal fins bent a little inwards. This is accompanied by violent strokes of the tail fin.

Depending on the state of nutrition and on temperature, pregnancy lasts for 28-30 days, but longer periods too have been reported. The females should be kept alone in small densely-planted tanks with low water levels before having their litters. The great number of fry incapacitated in swimming which often occur are exclusively caused by unnatural manners of feeding, according to SAUER. Such unsatisfactory litters may to a large extent be avoided if the fishes get insects as food. KOCH obtained optimum results, feeding nest larvae of Anabantids (Paradise Fish, Siamese Fighting Fish), which he bred for this expressly.

The fry are generally born at night. Larger and older females may bear up to 25 baby fish. At the moment of birth they are scarcely ⅜″ long and do not yet possess the extended jaw, which develops only after a few weeks. Rearing them demands some care. After the jaws are fully developed, the young fishes will have to receive insects as food. The metamorphosis of the sexes takes place after 8-9 weeks.

— **pusillus** van Hasselt: The Half-Beak.

SHAPE: As per description of the genus. D 9-10, A 14. Dorsal and anal fins insert far to the rear. Length: females over 2¾″, the males remaining a little smaller.

COLOR: Yellow-brown, transparent, with a metallic gleam. The fins are very slightly tinted. The anal of the male is transformed into a sexual organ.

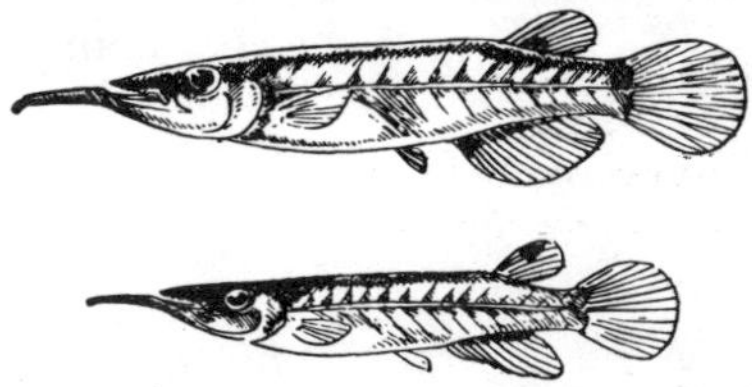

Dermogenys pusillus, male below

RANGE: Indonesia, Malaya, Indo-China; in all kinds of waters, also brackish ones; common everywhere.

CARE AND BREEDING: As per description of the genus.

— **sumatranus** (Bleeker): The Sumatran Half-Beak.

SHAPE: As per description of the genus. D 9-10, A 15. A little smaller than the previous species. Length around 2¾″.

COLOR: Similar to the other species, but with a narrow horizontal band.

RANGE: Singapore, Sumatra, Borneo. Especially in flowing waters, generally in fresh water, less frequently in brackish ones.

CARE AND BREEDING: As per description of genus.

detritus: Small-sized floating or sinking substances of organic origin, generally decaying parts of animal or vegetable tissue, which are found in water, and which serve wholly or in part as nourishment for many species of fishes. Detritus are the main component of the so-called mulm.

devario: Fish with decreasing color in places.

— *Danio.*

Diamond Perch, the: see ENNEACANTHUS OBESUS.

Diaptomus: Genus of lower crustaceans belonging to the order of the *Calanoidea*, class of the COPEPODA

Diatomeae: Silicon Algae.

Order belonging to the class of the ALGAE (see this), often erroneously called Brown Algae by the aquarist, due to their color. *D.* form brown films on glasses, rocks, and plants in the aquarium, especially under unfavorable, weak illumination.

They are microscopically small, unicellular plants, which occasionally unite to form loose threads or chains, feeding in the manner of green plants, but their chlorophyll is covered by brownish pigments which gives them their coloration. The cell walls are permeated with silicon, becoming glassily transparent and consisting of two box-like inter-gripping halves. These shells are of a miraculously accurate structure and differ for the different species. Raised and recessed spots, stripes, ribs, etc. form the finest ornaments, which are of great beauty and of manifold shapes. Despite the small size of the shells, their structure is of the greatest precision. The shells are practically indestructible. Silicon algea, which in bygone eras of earth's history died in unimaginable numbers and times, have contributed much to the development of the terrestrial crust. The layers of diatomaceous soil, which often are many yards thick, consist of such shells. This process continues up to date in the seas. *D.* are present in any body of water, playing an important part as one of the main components of PLANKTON (see this). Thanks to their ability to originate fats as the final product of assimilation, they are of outstanding economic significance.

We differentiate two groups according to their manner of living: the *D.* of the bottom, and those of the plankton. The former make their home in shallow waters, settling on firm foundations, while the latter live floating free in the upper, still illuminated layers of fresh waters and of the sea. Many of the bottom forms are motile. Their peculiar, spurting manner of moving is caused by plasm currents, based on the principles of thrust, along a perforated seam which runs along the shell. Reproduction is effected by division, the new cell taking along the bottom of the silicon box. Both halves now build new half-shells, so that the mother cell retains its original size, while the descendant becomes correspondingly smaller. When new divisions occur, the diminution naturally progresses correspondingly, until a minimum size is reached which can no more be passed. At this point the minimized cell throws off its shell, in some species after exchanging sexual cells (gametes). The plasma body, which now is called an auxospore, swells to a multiple of its circumference and develops to the maximum size of the species after going through a transitory change.

In darkly located aquaria the Silicon Algae form films on plants, firm objects of all kinds, etc. They are able to harm the growth of higher plants by preventing their activities of breathing and of assimilation. They may also show up in better-illuminated tanks, however, if the water is enriched with decay substances, and, as it seems, also after a simple softening of waters with high degrees of hardness with any of the commercial softeners.

Dicotyledoneae: Plants with two germinating leaves.

Class of flowering plants with two, rarely more than two, germinating leaves. In cases where they apparently possess only one such leaf, this only means that the other one is stunted.

This class includes the following families which in part are described

under the respective entries:
Water Lily Plants or NYMPHACEAE.
Horn Worts or CERATOPHYLLACEAE.
Crows-Foot Plants or RANUNCULACEAE.
CRUCIFERAE.
Sun-Dew Plants or DROSERACEAE.
Water Star Plants or CALLITRICHACEAE.
ELATINACEAE.
Water Nut Plants or HYDROCARYACEAE.
Night Candle Plants or OENOTHERACEAE.
Sea Berry Plants or HALORRHAGACEAE.
HIPPURIDACEAE.
PRIMULACEAE.
Gentian Plants or GENTIANACEAE.
Fox Glove Plants or SCROPHULARIACEAE.
Water Tube Plants or LENTIBURIACEAE.
Blue-Bell Plants or CAMAPANULACEAE.

Difflugia: see TESTACEA, shell-bearing amoebae.

digestive ailments of fishes: Ailments of the digestive system which are not of a parasitic nature. Digestive diseases are particularly apt to occur when there is a long-extended, one-sided nourishment or where there is a sudden change in feeding methods. They are best prevented by a proper, varied diet. Healing is usually much more difficult.

The most common result of improper feeding is a fattening of the internal organs. This is not usually found with younger fishes, but is a typical sign of fully-grown, older fishes. Fattening is one of the most frequent causes of death and can be a secondary cause of other diseases. Cramped quarters, one-sided and often too generous feedings and constant high temperatures lead to a high adipose development. Most commonly attacked is the belly cavity with the intestines, ovaries, kidneys and the liver. Liver degeneration is the most common result of fattening. The organs become incapable of functioning. Fishes which have become fat are therefore not usable for breeding. One of the most common infectious diseases which occurs frequently after fattening, is INFECTIOUS DROPSY.

Stomach and intestinal inflammations are often the result of one-sided nourishment. These often take place in the winter when substitutes are sometimes given for the better foods, and these may have a deficiency in roughage. In many cases it is also overlooked that some fishes require a supplemented vegetable diet.

digestive organs of fishes: Organs which mainly serve to alter the food substances which are taken in. Comprehensively they are the following: The *mouth opening* leads to the spacious *throat cavity*. Without a clear delineation the muscular *oesophagus* leads to the *stomach* which is completely absent, however, in some groups of fishes. This is connected with a short tightening to the *small intestine*, which reaches nearly to the *anus*.

The *mouth* is located at the front end of the body. It is either tilted upwards (supraterminal), forward (terminal), or downward (subterminal). In exceptional cases, for instance, on Sucker Catfishes, it may also be found on the underside of the body, displaced a little towards the rear. On predatory fishes which feed mainly on other fishes, it is large and widely cleft, while on omnivores and eaters of plankton or of micro-organisms it is small and narrow. In certain cases it is also designed for sucking, or else it is protractable like an elephant's trunk, to permit rummaging through the mud.

In many cases the *oral cavity* is more or less strongly equipped with *teeth*, which may be developed in many shapes. Rows of teeth may be found on the upper jaw, the intermediate jaw, the palatal bone, the lower jaw, or on all possible bones connected with the oral cavity.

Cyprinids show tooth-like bony plates on the palatal bones. After wearing out, the teeth generally are renewed. There are pointed or cone-shaped fangs, comb, brush, or velvet teeth, broad, flat grinding teeth, and others. Only few fishes are completely toothless. Strong teeth are not an absolute feature of the predatory character of the fish. Thus many peaceful fishes, for instance, possess impressive rows of teeth. The gripping teeth of predators are tilted towards the rear in order to hold the prey and also in order to aid in swallowing it. Eaters of micro-organisms and of plants often possess *food traps*, which serve to keep the gills free of food, while expelling excessive water. On the bottom of the oral cavity one finds the small, scarcely movable tongue, which is supported by a tongue bone. The throat cavity, which lies behind this, is interrupted by the gill openings. The real digestive system consists of oesophagus, stomach, and intestinal tract. The oesophagus is short and narrow. The stomach, which is lacking in Carps, is very muscular in its front part and developed as a masticating organ. It is often followed by one or more *blind sacs*. The *intestine* runs through the body with several windings and turnings. That of meat eaters is short and straight, in vegetarians, however, it may be very long and spirally wound. Within the gut lies the mucosa, in folds, while real villi appear only rarely. The rectum is very short. The anus is located near the end of the trunk. In rare cases it is more or less dislocated towards the throat. The rectum either discharges directly outward, else, for instance, in Lung Fishes, it ends in a *cloaca* together with the urinary and sexual openings.

Digestive juices are mainly supplied by the *pancreas*. We find pituitary glands in the whole digestive tract, from the mouth to the anus, and in the stomach, also acid-generating cells. Pepsin is not only produced in the stomach, but also in the intestine. The liver is always big and rich in fat. Its function consists, among others, also in developing the gall, important in the digestion of fats, for which as a rule there is a special gall bladder. The *kidneys*, which generally lie close to the spinal column, serve to eliminate wastes from the body. Their products go through the *urinary bladder* to the *urinary duct*. The outlets of the kidneys discharge behind the anus, generally together with those of the sexual products, into the *urogenital papilla*.

Digestive organs of a fish

dimorphism: Differences in the shapes of live beings of the same species which may appear in individual development during the STAGES OF AGE (see this), or in METAMORPHOSIS (see this). It is called sexual dimorphism when male and female of a species differ

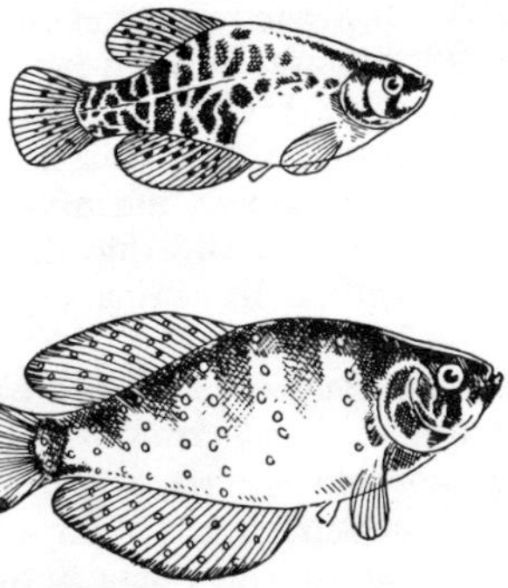

Sexual dimorphism in *Cynolebias bellotti*, showing the difference in size and number of fin-rays between the male, below, and the female, above.

by essential and visible secondary sexual characters, respectively, when they show different body structures.

Dinobrycon: Armored Moss.
Genus belonging to the tribe of the Flagellates or FLAGELLATA (see this), order of the Colored Monads or *Chrysomonadina*. The Armored Mosses form ramified colonies, in which each cell cup sits with its bottom on the preceding one, thus forming more or less ramified settlements.

diotic: Two-housed. Plants of which the one carries only male flowers, the other one only female ones.

Diplozoon: Double Animals.
Genus of gill parasites belonging to the class of the Sucker Worms or TREMATODES (see this). Remarkable for the fact that always two sexually mature animals are grown crosswise together.

Dipneusti: Lung Fishes.
A very ancient order pertaining to the class of the Bony Fishes of *Osteichthyes*, sub-class of the Tassel Fins or CROSSOPTERYGII (see this), of more or less elongated, salamander-like body structure. Special features are the cartilaginous, only partly ossified skeleton, the *Chorda dorsalis* which is permanently present, and the scaly body, which is a specially fish-like feature. The body is slightly compressed laterally to cylindrical, the gill arches are little or not at all developed, the unpaired fins form an uninterrupted seam around the greater part of the body. Paired limbs are present, but not always in the shape of fins. If there are fins, these are supported by horny rays. Contrary to what happens with nearly all other fishes, the paired nostrils are each connected with the mouth by means of nasal passages (choanes).

The Lung Fishes breathe through gills and lungs. The latter corresponds to the swimming bladder of the other fishes, being paired or unpaired, and showing an internal subdivision into chambers. The development of the circulatory organs too is adapted to the double form of respiration, lungs and gills being supplied with blood separately. A stomach is present, the intestine is short and straight. Most Lung Fishes go through a larval stage, that is, their development includes a metamorphosis. The larvae possess bunched outer gills on both sides of the head, and an adhering organ beneath it. The Australian Lung Fish *Neoceratodus* is an exception to this.

The order divides into two families, the *Ceratodontidae*, with *Neoceratodus*, and the *Lepidosirenidae*.

Dipnoi: Lung Fishes, see CROSSOPTERYGII.

Disc Tetra: see MYLEINAE.

— Spotted: see METYNNIS MACULATUS.

— Roosevelt's: see METYNNIS ROOSEVELTI.

— Schreitmueller's: see METYNNIS SCHREITMUELLERI.

— Black-Finned: see PIARACTUS NIGRIPINNIS.

discus: Disc.
— *Symphysodon*.

diseases of fishes: Aquarium fishes are very prone to the danger of getting sick. Inadequate keeping, too-late diagnosis of incipient diseases, transferring from tank to tank, and the frequently too-dense population in confined spaces, aid the insurgence of, and contamination with, diseases.

According to their causes two main groups of diseases may be found:

(a) parasitic ones, and
(b) non-parasitic ones.

Sometimes the two groups are difficult to distinguish, since they may overlap, one being the cause of the other, and at times several different diseases may show up on the same fish.

Most maladies are produced by PARASITES (see these). In spite of the fact that the number of these is relatively large, healthy fishes possess strong natural defenses, which may still be strengthened by measures taken by the hobbyist, but may also be weakened by the same. The sole presence of parasites or disease germs in itself generally is not sufficient cause for the eruption of a disease. To the contrary, one or the other germ is probably always present without causing noticeable harm. This is always the case where there exists a certain condition of equilibrium between host and parasite, warranting a normal course of life. Frequently too the host, in this case the fish, is stronger than the parasite and neutralizes it through its general defenses, in most cases by encysting it. Only if the fish, due to some special circumstance, proves to be weaker, can it be vanquished by the germ. These conditions may always dislocate one way or the other.

Inadequate, insufficient, or overabundant, qualitatively poor, or one-sided food, and the consequent symptoms of starving, may lead to a weakening of resistance (see RESISTANCE) of the fishes. The condition of the water, i.e. the components dissolved in it, and its temperature, are of decisive importance too. Add to this also pH values, conditions of gases, and chemical changes. Also other inadequate manners of keeping, for instance, too small tanks, poor care, inharmonious species as members of the community, etc. play a certain part. To this one has, of course, still to add all rough mechanical influences, wounds, etc.

Furthermore conditions may set in which are especially favorable to the parasite, so that its combativity is heightened and its latency (state of repose) is nullified. Therefore the point is always to increase the natural resistance of fishes. But even the most careful hobbyist is not totally protected against his fishes becoming ill.

When breeding, use only healthy, normally shaped fish with normal behavior, in order to develop resistant strains. In case of mass attacks of disease the remaining specimens either have acquired a high degree of immunity (see this), or else they are naturally resistant. Such fishes are best for building up healthy and resistant strains, as resistance may be passed on hereditarily.

Non-parasitic diseases may either be brought forth by external causes, being therefore conditioned by the surroundings, or else they may be of internal, especially hereditary, nature. All harm caused by water, food, and mechanical influences have to be classified among the diseases caused by external influences.

Fish diseases can only be fought effectively after the respective causes have been detected. There are no panaceas which will fight all diseases. Whenever such medicines

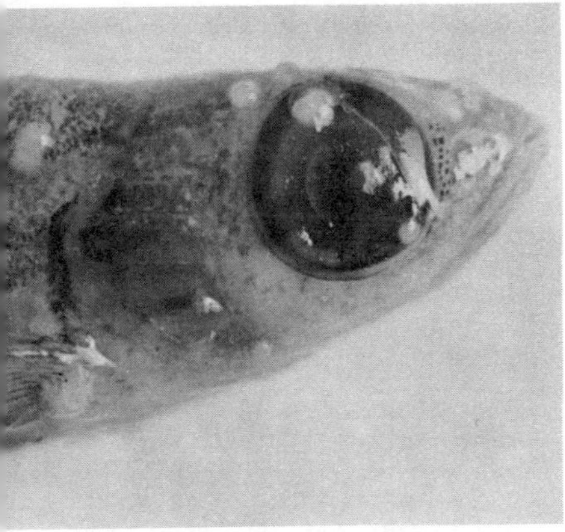

Ichthyophthirius patches, slightly enlarged

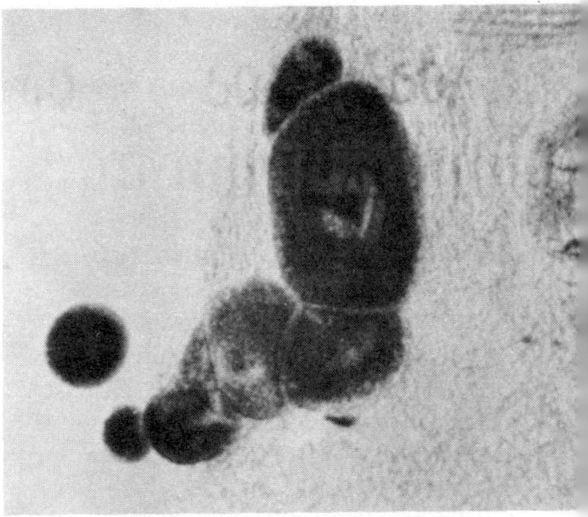

Smear from the skin of an ichthyophthirius-infected fish, showing the parasite in several stages.

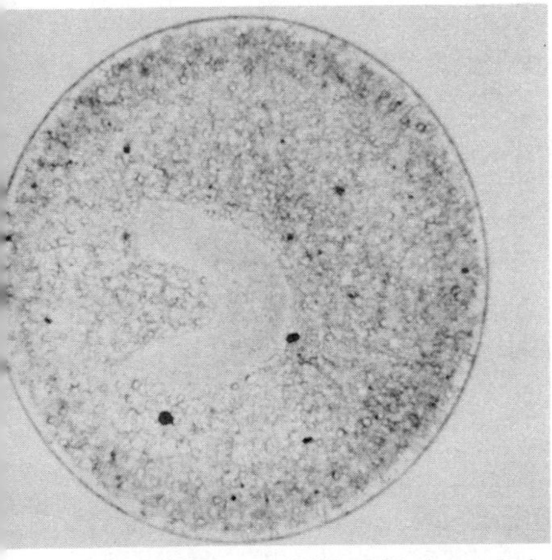

Ichthyophthirius multifiliis with its typical curved nucleus, highly magnified.

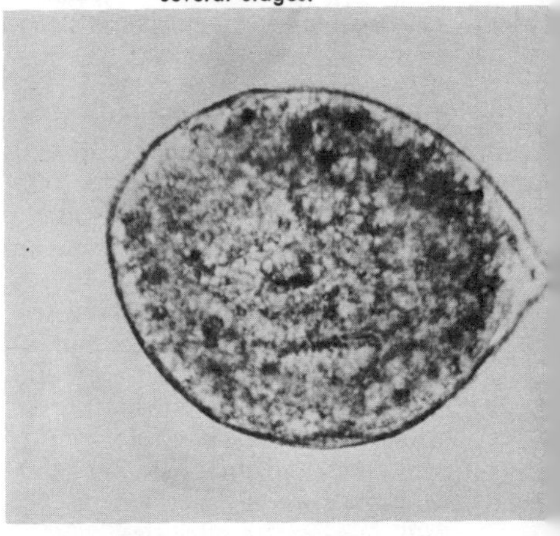

A spore of the parasite, highly magnified

Dropsy, with the scales beginning to stand out

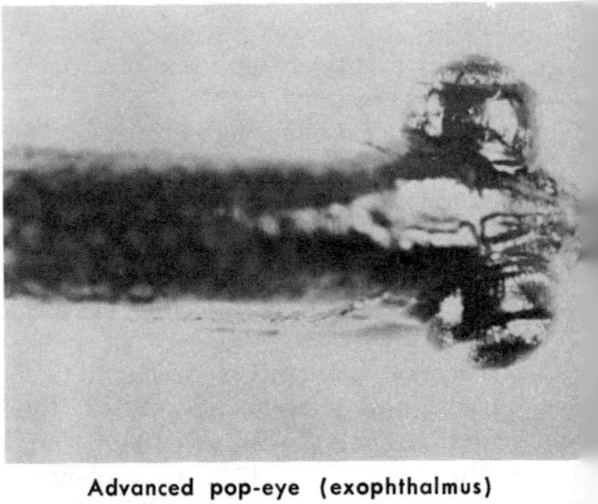

Advanced pop-eye (exophthalmus)

are offered, they are humbugs. The diagnosis of diseases is possible through the observation of the symptoms, the anatomical changes of the body, the divergence of functions, and the changes in behavior, but the species of the disease cannot always be determined externally. Thus, for instance, a creeping poisoning can hardly be differentiated in its manifestations from an internal, parasitic disease. Add to this that the latent stage of certain parasitic diseases does not permit one to point out a fish as an infection carrier from a purely external point of view. Internal tests, which frequently are the only ones capable of bringing light into the matter, generally can hardly be effected by the aquarist. They have to be left to the institutes or the observation posts of the federations.

Each species of fish has its typical way and manner of moving, which the observant hobbyists become able to distinguish within a short time. Therefore they will be able to conclude from this general behavior whether their fishes are well off or not. Of course one has to be acquainted with the whole curriculum vitae of the fish, but its manifestations of vigor and well-being are as a rule clearly recognizable. Divergences from the usual manner of living may be signs of a more or less advanced illness. The decrease in appetite is nearly always ominous. One should therefore observe one's fishes very closely while feeding them. Lively fishes become less active, surface fishes seek the bottom, and bottom fishes come to the surface. Noticeable shyness, motionless positions in unusual postures, in corners or between firm objects, closing of the fins, gulping air at the surface while permanently swimming in circles, shimmying or jumpy movements, sinking to the ground with subsequent fruitless efforts to rise again—all these may be signs of disease. Glued-together fins, especially tails and pectorals, are a sign of an attack by external parasites.

"Scratching" on firm objects, when noticeably repeated, may reveal the presence of gill or skin parasites. The sinking-down, mentioned above, with constant endeavors to reach the surface, may also derive from a disease of the swim bladder. If, contrary to their usual custom, the fishes squat on the ground, possibly a constipation due to one-sided feeding is the cause. The same phenomenon may be seen if the aquarium is heated from the bottom up and fishes needing warmth lie down on the heating element or the warmed spot, as Black Mollies like to do. Cramped, winding motions may indicate a discomfort from internal causes. Lightning-quick, nervous, running-to-and-fro at the least provocation, possibly accompanied by subsequent spasms and lying on the side, are nearly always symptoms of water contamination, which may have varied causes. Unrest, cramps, staggering movements, forced breathing, and lying on the back are signs of an extensive poisoning. Certain internal diseases also show through the fact that the fishes are no more able to keep a horizontal position, the tail pointing upwards. Also certain changes on the surface of the body permit conclusions as to diseases. Frequently such cases show through changes in color and design. Sick fishes often are pale, with the normal colorations disappearing and abnormal ones setting in. Diseases under strong pain or other stimuli may also cause intensification of the colors and make the fish very vividly colored. If the coloration remains continually dark, an eye disease may be the cause. Blinding of one eye generally leads to the darkening of one part of the body, while everything else remains normally colored. Many species, for instance, *Pterophyllum*, may occasionally show little dark spots, irregularly scattered, which are caused by the larvae of a leech. This phenomenon has no further harmful sequel.

Scale protrusion is always hazardous. Even observation through a simple magnifying glass generally shows that the scales have been dislocated from their normal position through water deposits in the epidermis. Often too the skin shows white discolorations, which at first may be seen very clearly on the fish if observed against the light, and later on they are easily noticed on the body surface. These cloudy-white, veil-like films are called skin discolorations, and may result from various causes.

A dangerous, even if not incurable disease, is the attack of *Ichtyophthirius*. Its presence is shown by irregularly placed white nodules, which at first are rather minute, but later grow in size reaching diameters of up to 1 mm. It is a fact, though, that the larvae of pond clams, parasitizing on the skin, may bring forth a similar phenomenon. If the attack is not very intensive, it causes no further harm. If the little knots are yellowish-gray, looking like grains of sand scattered over the fish, one is facing the so-called Colisa-parasite, *Oodinium*. Bloody spots beneath the skin are signs of the presence of vegetable or animal parasites. Quite frequently we also observe boils which sometimes break open. They may have different causes, being often a symptom of the presence of the untreatable *Ichthyosporidium* disease.

Bite wounds on fishes are whitish as a rule. Frequently, like all other lesions, they are the point of penetration for the so-called fungus infection (*Saprolegnia*). This may incide at any possible place on the body, in consequence of other diseases. On Tooth-Carps it likes to fasten at the region of the mouth, but also the cornea of the eye may be infested.

Sticking out of the gill covers too is always a sign of danger, especially if the gills that protrude over the edges have lost their delicately red coloration. If they are yellowish-white and swollen, or if they show yellowish, often bloody, spots, visible under a magnifying glass, gill parasites are the cause. Danger of suffocation is indicated by dark red gills as well as desperate efforts of the fish to get air at the surface. Suffocated fishes often have their mouths wide open and the gill covers sticking out strongly. Strongly protruding eyes may have different causes, often being secondary symptoms of internal diseases or of eye parasites. Sometimes this is even a sign of contamination of the water by excesses of excreta (old water). A sucked-in belly is always a symptom of an advanced internal disease. The aquarist generally calls this phenomenon 'tuberculosis', but it may have quite a number of causes. It never is a consequence of faulty feeding, unless a prolonged famine should have given rise to an internal disease. The real tuberculosis generally is a sign of external parasites. Intestinal parasites show up quite frequently in fishes. They may show their presence by a swollen lumpy, body, or by bumps on the sides. If, though, the body is swollen evenly, especially in the belly region, and shows protruding scales, this points to the dangerous *dropsy*.

Besides the points of view shown on the synopsis, fish diseases may be considered under the following headings:

1. PARASITIC FISH DISEASES:
   Diseases caused by crustaceans—ones caused by worms—protozoan-caused diseases—fungus diseases.
2. NON-PARASITIC DISEASES CONDITIONED BY THE WAY OF LIVING:
   Harm caused by water and gases—poisonings—metabolism diseases—roe-binding—lesions and wounds caused by non-parasitic live beings—mechanical lesions.
3. NON-PARASITIC DISEASES, CONDITIONED HEREDITARILY:
   Cripplings—malformations of coloring—boils and swellings.

For the treatment of fish diseases see the different entries and the entry TREATMENTS.

In general, the following basic precepts may be accepted:

1. An ounce of prevention is better than a pound of cure.

2. Always keep your fishes under favorable conditions, and care for them conscientiously. Healthy fishes have more resistance to diseases of all kinds.

3. Always keep newly purchased fishes under observation for some time (2 to 4 weeks) in a special tank (quarantine aquarium). Even without showing external symptoms they may be infection carriers.

4. Never take foods from ponds stocked with fishes. Waters empty of fish populations cannot contain 'professional' parasites.

5. Let foods stand for a while before offering them to fishes, and always draw off the required portion from the middle of the container by means of a hose. Disease germs and marauders sometimes cling to the bottom or the side walls. Furthermore the free-swimming spores and swarms of parasites die off within a few days or hours if they do not find a host.

6. Pay attention to the careful insulation of all metallic parts of the aquarium. Metal salts, putty components, inadequate paints, and inadequate cements may be causes of mass mortality.

7. Avoid sudden fluctuations in temperature and unnecessary changes of water.

8. When aerating, take care that no noxious gases are pumped into the water (furnace smoke, steam from heaters, factory smog, insect killers, excessive tobacco smoke, etc.).

9. If the whole fish population of a tank is ill, preferably take radical measures, which means destruction of fishes and plants, discarding the sand, and subsequent disinfection of the aquarium and all its gadgets with a solution of permanganate of potassium.

10. Immediately remove fishes that show symptoms of illness, before they infect others.

dispar: Different-looking (the sexes).
— *Aphaniops.*
— *Fundulus.*

dissimilation: The opposite of ASSIMILATION (see this). The decomposition of carbohydrates and fats to produce energy.

distachyus: Two-eared.
— *Aponogeton.*

Distichodus: With two rows of teeth.
African genus of Characin-like fishes belonging to the family of the CITHARINIDAE (see this), of quite robust-looking structure, with thick-lipped mouth. An adipose fin is present. The fishes eat mainly vegetable food. About 18 known species.

— noboli Boulenger:
SHAPE: As per description of the genus. The mouth is small and terminal. D 20, A 16. Length up to $3\frac{1}{8}''$.
COLOR: Shiny silver with red fins.

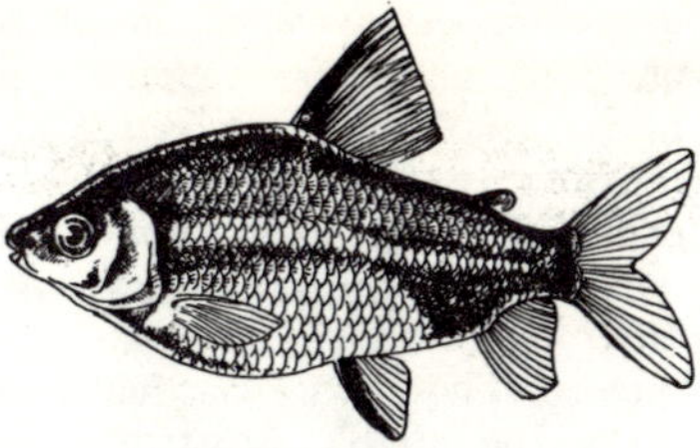

Distichodus noboli

SD are not yet fully known, but the female is probably fuller and more robust.

RANGE: The Congo region.

CARE AND BREEDING: A peaceful species, which is relatively quiet and swims in short spurts, often with the head tilted to the bottom, while the fins vibrate unceasingly. The fish like to play but may occasionally become a little timid, retiring into hiding places. They feel at a disadvantage if kept together with much livelier fishes. Dense planting is desirable. *D. noboli* needs plenty of vegetable food. This should be taken into consideration when choosing the plants for its tank, as well as when feeding it. According to present experience, vegetarian fishes hardly ever touch Water Ferns (*Ceratopteris*). Furthermore they like to pick their food from the bottom. No particulars are known about reproduction.

distilled water: Water that has been made chemically completely pure by evaporation (distillation), and which is important in aquaristics as a basic material with which to prepare breeding waters (see WATER).

division of reduction: Maturity division of the GERMINATING CELLS (see these), in which the set of chromosomes is reduced to half in quantity and quality.

Dogfish, the Hungarian: see UMBRA KRAMERI.

dolichoptera: With long wings (fins).

— *Xenocara.*

dolloi: After the Belgian zoologist Dollo.

— *Tilapia.*

dominant: Predominant. Designation for hereditary dispositions, which cover others during the embryonal development, thus appearing alone externally.

dominicensis: From the Island of Dominica.

— *Gambusia.*

Doradidae: Spiny Catfishes.
Family of Catfishes belonging to the sub-order of the SILUROIDEA (see this), among others, with the following genera: ACANTHODORAS (see this), AMBLYDORAS (see this), ASTRODORAS (see this), *Doras*, and TRACHYCORYSTES (see this).

doriae: After the Italian zoologist G. Doria.

— *Brachygobius.*

— *Pseudocorynopoma.*

dorni: After Richard Dorn, the New York aquarist.

— *Rivulus.*

dorsal: The fin on top of the back of fishes.

dorsalis: Referring to the striking color of the dorsal fin.

— *Epiplatys.*

dorsimaculatus: With spotted dorsal fin.

— *Barbus.*

dorsiocellata: With eye (spot) on the dorsal fin.

— *Crenicichla.*

— *Rasbora.*

dortmanna: After the Dutch botanist Dortmann.

— *Lobelia.*

Double-Row Water Ear: see APONOGETON DISTACHYUS.

double-sexed blossoms: Blossoms in which both the male and female organs are united.

Dragon Fin, the: see PSEUDOCORYNOPOMA DORIAE.

Dragonflies: see ODONATA.

Dreissenacea: Triangular or Zebra Clams.

Family of bivalves belonging to the sub-order of the *Heterodonta*, which includes the well-known Triangular or Zebra Clam, *Dreissensa polymorpha* Pallas. This has a shape which is similar to that of the Salt-Water Mussel, and differs from all other fresh-water clams by a byssus gland and by its manner of living. In summer the small, 3-4 mm. long clams sit spun fast to plants and other firm objects, in great numbers. In winter they withdraw into deeper water. They come from the Caspian and the Caucasian Seas, having migrated to Germany during the last 100 years, but today they are found in nearly all European waters. Initially they always appear in great numbers and are thus able to displace all other vivalves, being able, besides this, to cause harm to technical installations, which they obstruct. Later they reach normal numerical proportions. The species is able to survive out of the water for weeks. It is easier to keep in aquaria than any other clam, and enjoys the fame of exerting a strong filtering action.

dropsy of fishes: Dropsy of the ventral cavity. Dangerous, infectious disease which especially during the last years has taken on greater importance, being extraordinarily harmful to commercial breeding of fishes. It is caused by the aquatic bacterium *Pseudomonas punctata f. ascitae*. This bacterium is normally harmless and present everywhere. The symptoms of D. consist in a sponge-like, swollen body—especially the belly swelling strongly—scale protrusion, and pop-eyes (exophthalmus). These symptoms may differ to a large extent, as the disease appears in different shapes. Thus it may, for instance, come to the formation of boils, to malformations of the skeleton, to bodily decay, or extensive inflammations on body and fins. Generally an initial condition for infection is a previous weakening due to inexpert care, especially to one-sided feeding, which may bring over-fattening of the liver as a consequence. The disease can hardly be said to be curable. SCHAEPERCLAUS prescribes the following measures for combating it:

1. Immediate removal of fishes that are infected with D.
2. Avoidance of introducing the germ by fishes that are acute carriers of D.
3. Careful keeping, especially avoidance of disturbances of the metabolism, of degeneration of the liver and of other connected diseases, which often are the predecessors of *punctata* infestation.
4. Introduction of bacteriophages (Bacteria eaters), *Phagus punctata*, which are able to dissolve *Ps. punctata*.
5. Complete disinfection of infected tanks before re-stocking.

Feeding with bacteriophages (as outlined under 4) is possible without difficulties, and should promise results. However, in aquaristics it has not yet been approved.

Droseraceae: Sun Dew Plants. Family belonging to the class of the DICOTYLEDONEAE (see this). Generally perennial land or swamp plants which are carnivorous (insect eaters) and equipped with special trapping devices. The leaves are equipped with glands on the upper face, more or less hairy, and generally equipped with long lashes on the edges. The glands secrete a sticky, digestive liquid. The highly excitable leaves act as insect traps, commonly together with the lashes. About 87 known species, among which the well-known Sun Dew, but only few aquatic plants. In this book only *Aldrovanda* is mentioned of these.

Drosophila: see FRUIT FLIES.

drummondii: After a personal name.

— *Marsilea.*

dry food: see ARTIFICIAL FOOD.

dubyana:

— *Vesicularia.*

dumerilii: After the French ichthyologist Duméril.

— *Clarias.*

Duncker, Georg: 1870-1953. Noted German ichthyologist, famous for his contributions to the systematics of fishes.

dunckeri: After the German zoologist, Dr. Duncker.

— *Barbus.*

duriventris: With hard belly.

— *Mylosoma.*

dust food, powdered food: This is a heading under which the aquarist mentions collectively a great number of very different micro-organisms, which have only their minute size in common. Since they often are no bigger than the largest unicellulars, they represent one of the most important baby foods for young FRY (see these). Dust food is generally composed of *Rotatoria*, nauplii of *Cyclops*, and baby forms of *Daphnia*. The unicellulars (Infusoria) are not included in Dust foods.

Many species of fishes eat dust foods from their first free-swimming day on, others, however, only after going through the infusoria stage, which generally lasts for about a week.

Dwarf Barb, the: see BARBUS (PUNTIUS) PHUTUNIO.

Dwarf Carps: see MICROCYPRINI.

Dwarf Catfish, the: see CORYDORAS HASTATUS HASTATUS.

Dwarf Cichlid, the: see APISTOGRAMMA AGASSIZI.

— borelli's: see APISTOGRAMMA BORELLII.

— Checkered, the: see APISTOGRAMMA PLEUROTAENIA.

— Ortmann's: see APISTOGRAMMA ORTMANNI.

— Pretty-Finned, the: see APISTOGRAMMA ORNATIPINNIS.

— Pretty, the: see NANNACARA TAENIA.

— Reitzig's: see APISTOGRAMMA REITZIGI.

— Shiny, the: see NANNACARA ANOMALA.

Dwarf-Dragonfin, the: see CORYNOPOMA RIISEI.

Dwarf Gourami, the: see COLISA LALIA.

Dwarf Gourami, the Croaking: see TRICHOPSIS PUMILUS.

Dwarf Hatchet Fish, the: see CARNEGIELLA MARTHAE.

Dwarf Limia, the: see LIMIA HETERANDRIA.

Dwarf Panchax, the: see APLOCHEILUS BLOCKII.

Dwarf Pencilfish, the: see NANNOSTOMUS MARGINATUS.

Dwarf Rasbora, the: see RASBORA MACULATA.

Dytiscidae: Whirligig Beetles. Family of water beetles of the suborder of predatory beetles or ADEPHAGA (which see). Beetles of various sizes, where the forelegs of the males are converted to sucking-discs. The feelers are threadlike; the hind legs are flatly compressed, provided with hairs and developed into swimming legs. The larvae are elongated and pointed at both ends. On the head, which carries four-jointed feelers, there are 6 tiny eyes on each side. The upper jaw is sickle-shaped, hollow and perforated just before the point. The last body ring has two hairy breathing-tubes. The larvae have long legs, each with five joints.

Among others, genera include *Dytiscus, Cybister, Acilius, Hydaticus* and *Colymbetes*.

The species of the genus *Dytiscus*, the yellow-edged or whirligig beetles, have an elongate oval body, which is flatly arched. The sucking discs of the male are round, the

Dytiscus, larva at left, beetle at right

wing-cases smooth, while those of the female are furrowed. The larvae possess dense swimming-bristles on both the last body segments, further back two tail-threads with swimming-bristles. The best-known species is *Dytiscus marginalis* L. It is an active, lively swimming beetle which loves sun and warmth and is very well suited to a life in the water. The adult insects, but especially the larvae are predators which, because of their size may be considered to be among the most dangerous of the lower aquatic creatures of our native waters. The larvae are ravenous. The adult insect not only attacks lower animals but also attacks larger sick fishes, attaching itself to them and eating large holes in their bodies. The method of nourishment of the larvae is unique. They sink their sickle-shaped jaws into their prey—insect larvae, salamander eggs, salamanders, tadpoles, small fishes, etc.—and inject a blackish digestive juice which makes the body parts so fluid that they can be sucked in by the larva (exterior digestion).

Besides the digestive juices there is also a poisonous substance introduced which paralyses the prey. Copulation of the beetles is accomplished by the male attaching himself by his sucking discs to the furrowed wing-cases of the female. Egg-laying takes place in April, the eggs being pushed into plant-stems by an ovipostor spike. Two to three weeks later the larvae hatch from the eggs; after development they leave the water and pass their pupal stage on land. This pupal stage lasts about 3 weeks. Larvae which pass into the pupal stage in late autumn do not develop into beetles until the following spring.

Breathing is accomplished by larvae and adult beetles by the intake of atmospheric air, which is carried by the beetles under their wing-cases. At night the beetles often leave their native waters. When threatened a burning fluid is released by the glands in the head and body. In the aquarium these beetles make interesting inhabitants, but of course it is understood that they cannot be kept with any other creatures which one wants to keep alive.

The *Cybister* species are not as common in Europe. More numerous are the *Acilius* species, of which the most common is *Acilius sulcatus* L. which is often considered a young whirligig beetle. This error is a result of a mistaken impression that many aquarists have that an insect can grow once it has reached its adult stage. In contrast to the other, the underside of this beetle is black where the other is brown, sometimes with yellow spots. The female releases the eggs into the water while swimming. The larvae are sometimes plentiful and are caught along with *Daphnia*. This beetle is not quite as dangerous as the whirligig beetle, and is relished as food by the larger fishes.

Earthworms: see LUMBRICIDAE.

eatonii: After the British botanist Eaton.

— *Sagittaria*.

Echinodorus: Porcupine-tube, because of the spiny fruits (Sword

Plants).
Genus of aquatic and swamp plants pertaining to the family of the Frog Spoon Plants or ALIMATACEAE (see this). The species which are cultivated in the aquarium, known as Sword Plants, enjoy great popularity. They are in fact swamp plants, which in nature grow above the water surface, but in aquaria they are generally cultivated submerged.

Sword Plants generally have a short and compact root stock, from which the smaller species develop runners. Reproduction of the larger species generally takes place by the budding of young, so-called adventive, plants from the long inflorescences, instead of blooms. These may be pushed down to the bottom and anchored with pieces of glass; after striking roots, they may be cut off. Submerged plants generally do not develop flowers nor seeds.

The species of *Echinodorus* are perennial. The more or less grass-like, lineal or lanceolate leaves either sit on the root stock, or else they are bottom-standing on more or less long stems. Sometimes they are vaulted in width and curved crescent-like along the length. During the stages of growth the leaves may change shapes. This is determined especially by external circumstances. Thus they may, for instance, vary from a narrow lanceolate type to a broad spoon shape. If the larger species are cultivated as paludal plants, the flower stems rise high above the surface with their loose verticils of blooms, and may reach heights of over 3 ft. Cultivation is described specifically for each species, as it may diverge strongly from one to the next.

— **brevipedicellatum** (O. Kuntze) Buchenau: The Narrow-Leaf Amazon Sword Plant.

GENERALITIES: The species, which is not common in aquaria, was formerly known as *E. tenellus*, but this turned out to be the name of another species.

SHAPE: As per description of the genus. The lanceolate, pointed leaves are, as a rule, slightly arched, and generally also a little vaulted over the width. Their stems are 2″-6″ long. The robust leaf nervures ramify from the base in part, and in part a little higher up from the central rib. The peduncle of the inflorescence of emerged plants, with its cluster-shaped flower verticils, rises up to over 25″ above the water surface. Submergedly cultivated specimens generally develop adventive plants instead of blooming.

RANGE: Brazil.

CULTIVATION: This beautiful stately plant thrives in bottom soil consisting of a mixture of coarse sand with plenty of weathered clay. In order to develop completely, however, it needs spacious tanks. The water should not be too hard, if possible; filtering soft water through peat is especially advantageous. Light, but not excessive sunlight, is advisable. On bleak days the plants should receive accessory illumination. The temperature should be kept between 64 and 86° F, the best being around 68-77° F. The species remains relatively small if kept too cool.

— **grandiflorus** (Chamisso and Schlechtendahl) Micheli: The Big-Flowered Sword Plant.

GENERALITIES: This species can only be kept in swamp aquaria or in outdoor tanks.

SHAPE: The large leaves are leathery, broadly oval, with a blunted tip. The inflorescence may grow up to 60″ high.

RANGE: South America, down to Patagonia, in swamp lands, on moist shores, etc.

CULTIVATION: This stately swamp plant grows best in large, spacious paludaria. It needs solid bottom soils containing clay. Reproduction takes place through seeds, which may be kept in dry storage for from one to two years.

— **intermedius** Grisebach: The Dwarf Amazon Sword Plant.

GENERALITIES: A quick-growing, smaller species, which is often sold under a wrong name. It differs completely from *E. brevipedicellatus.* Its runners run along the bottom, while *E. brevipedicellatum* develops the well-known adventive plants, which strive upwards.

SHAPE: The submerged form is very variable, according to location, lighting, etc. The bottom-standing leaves are quite frail, lanceolate to narrowly elliptical, their bases following a little down along the stem. The tip is blunt to pointed. The plant grows 2″ to 6″ high. It develops numerous runners and does not bloom submerged.

RANGE: South America and Cuba, especially Brazil. No particulars are known about its habitat, but it is probably found in the same sites as the other species, that is mainly in paludal territories.

CULTIVATION: The species is especially adequate for warm water aquaria, in, which, under favorable conditions, it may overrun the whole bottom. Unwashed sand with an admixture of weathered clay will suffice as bottom soil. Light bears special influence on its growth. Well-illuminated and sunnily placed specimens often grow low rosettes, while in shadowed locations the leaves become larger and broader. Specimens which stand in quite dark places grow especially high if they receive temporary additional artificial illumination. Trimming the runners in time results in quite robust and bushy plants. Temperatures of 77-86° F have proved to be especially favorable. Growth begins to stop at temperatures below 68° F, and halts completely at still lower temperatures, and without that this kills the plants. The species does not demand any special compositions of water and probably thrives in any degree of water hardness, reacting to all changes by modifying its growth, however.

— **longistylus** Buchenau: The Long-Shafted Sword Plant.

GENERALITIES: A swamp plant which may also be cultivated submerged and is especially good for large aquaria, paludaria, and open-air ponds.

SHAPE: As per description of the genus. The elliptical to elongated-elliptical leaves may grow up to 9″ long and sit on stalks up to 20″ high.

RANGE: Brazil, in the same type of locations as the European Frog Spoon (see ALISMA).

CULTIVATION: A hardy and robust plant. In the open-air pond it grows in the usual soil mixture, while indoors coarse sand, mixed with clay is good in order to avoid excessive spreading. In summer it needs 68-77° F, but should be wintered at 60-64° F. The leaves like to grow above the surface of the water. The species likes soft water, and is especially grateful for sunlight. Unfortunately reproduction is a little difficult. The development of seeds is very rare. Very infrequently robust specimens grow new plants, which may be separated from the original specimen.

— **martii** Micheli.

GENERALITIES: A species of *E.* which was imported recently and, so far, is only rarely cultivated in our aquaria.

SHAPE: As per description of the genus. The leaves are lanceolate, and may attain lengths of 12″-20″, with widths of $1\frac{1}{8}$″-$2\frac{3}{8}$″. They have blunt tips and slightly wavy or curly edges. The stalks, with lengths of 2″-4″, are very short.

RANGE: Brazil.

CULTIVATION: A large plant, which is especially adequate for spacious tanks. It likes temperatures between 72 and 86° F and soft water. Reproduction as usual through adventive plants.

— **paniculatus** Micheli: The Giant Amazon Sword Plant.

GENERALITIES: The largest of all Sword Plants, which differs from *E. brevipedicellatus* mainly by the fact that all nervures part from the base of the leaf.

SHAPE: As described for *E. brevipedicellatus* and the genus. Leaves lanceolate, pointed at both ends, and running a little down the stalk at the base. Sometimes they may also be slightly arched, reaching a length of up to 20″, without counting the stalk. Submerged specimens rarely produce flowers, developing adventive plants instead of these.

RANGE: Widely diffused over South America, amphibious on shores, or more or less submerged.

CULTIVATION: As described for *E. brevipedicellatus*.

— **radicans** (Nutall) Engelmann: The Water Plantain.

GENERALITIES: The species is adequate for large aquaria and paludaria.

SHAPE: The broad, oval leaves grow up to 8″ long, and the plants up to 25″ if conditions are favorable. The long-pediculated inflorescence, which generally only develops adventive plants, if kept submerged, may become very tall when emerged and carries loose verticils with white flowers. The plants always strive to grow above the water surface.

RANGE: The Southern U.S.A. and Mexico, in the usual locations of the Sword Plants.

CULTIVATION: The plants grow submerged and emerged, but need plenty of space. In the indoors aquarium it is best to keep them in lean sand bottoms, as otherwise they easily grow too big. They like a well-illuminated location and temperatures of 68-77° F. Reproduction either takes place through adventive plants, or else through seeds. Older specimens may be trimmed to size. Sometimes the root-stock produces off-springs.

— **ranunculoides** Linné: Engelmann:

GENERALITIES: The only European species of *Echinodorus*, which is rarely offered in pet shops, being sold as *E. radicans* when found there.

SHAPE: The species shows a large number of sub-species, which differ in growth. These different shapes often intereact. Submerged specimens develop ribbon-shaped leaves, after these also floating leaves on thin stalks, rarely growing inflorescences. However, if these are produced, they rise above the surface when completely developed. The flowers stand in umbellae, being white or reddish. In the aquarium the inflorescences generally produce adventive plants.

RANGE: Europe, North Africa, and the Canary Islands, rare in Germany; in the same locations as the Frog Spoon Plants.

CULTIVATION: The plants are hardy and are good to keep in cold water tanks. Water level, lighting and temperature exert great influence on the development of the different shapes of leaves. Reproduction takes place through adventive plants, runners and seeds. The submerged forms grow in the aquarium even in winter.

— **rostratus** (Nutall) Engelmann: The Cellophane Plant.

A very-recently imported plant, which possesses very variable leaf shapes. The leaves vary from narrow-linear shapes to long-stalked cordiform (heart-shaped) ones, which are especially frail and transparent. If kept submerged, the inflorescence develops adventive plants. The species is distributed as a swamp plant over the Central and Southern U.S.A., Central America, and the West Indies. Cultivation is said to be difficult. RAMSHORST advises that the bottom soil should be mixed with peat, but the plants may also grow in pure sand if the water contains sufficient nutritive substances. Soft water is favorable; the pH value may amount to 6 or 7. Temperatures between 68-77° F. Like all *E.*, this species also probably likes a rest period. The plants grow especially large if they receive sufficient light.

The species develops no runners. Reproduction is best obtained with young plants which grow from the inflorescence. Young buds occasionally also grow directly from the root stock of older specimens.

— **tenellus** (Martius) Buchenau: The Junior Amazon Sword Plant.

GENERALITIES: The name of this species was at first erroneously applied to *E. brevipedicellatus.*

SHAPE: The plants may appear both as cold and as warm water forms. In our aquaria it is probably the latter which is more frequent. They rarely grow taller than 4″, the under-water leaves being of grass-like shape. The tropical perennial form grows up to $1\frac{1}{8}''$ to $1\frac{5}{8}''$ at the maximum in aquaria. Only emergedly growing plants develop inflorescences.

RANGE: The species is distributed over the whole American Continent. Due to its great range it appears both as an annual, cold-water form, and as a perennial warm-water one. It is found at shallow shores with soft bottom.

CULTIVATION: The plants need a well-lighted location, and temperatures not below 68° F for the tropical form. The bottom should be soft and contain an admixture of peat. Under favorable conditions the Junior Sword Plant may spread quickly, forming a rug-like lawn on the bottom of the tank. Reproduction takes place through runners.

echinosperma: Porcupine-seeded. — *Blyxa.*

echinospora: Porcupine-spored. — *Isoetes.*

ecology: The science of the relationship of live beings with their live and dead surroundings.

ectoparasites: Parasites which live on the surface of the body of the host.

Eel: see ANGUILLA VULGARIS.

Eel-shaped: see ANGUILLIFORMES.

egg, development of: The egg is the female GERMINAL CELL (see this), which is developed within the ovary of female animals. After a complex process of maturation and division (see DIVISION OF REDUCTION), the egg is ready to be fecundated. Generally maturity lasts only for a short time. Completely mature eggs are more or less nutritionally enriched, generally spherical formations of different sizes and colors, which are enclosed within membranes.

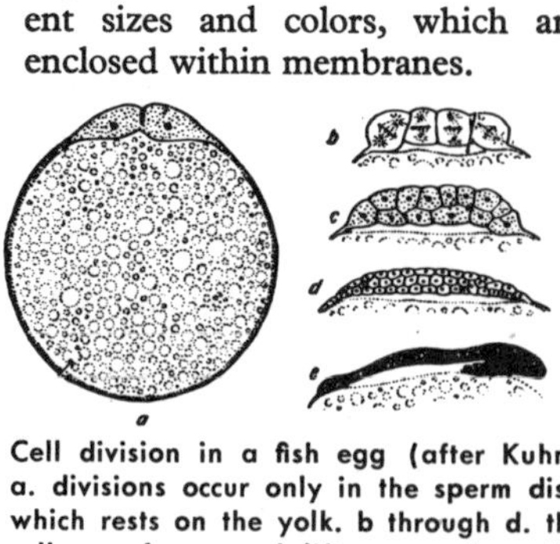

Cell division in a fish egg (after Kuhn) a. divisions occur only in the sperm disc, which rests on the yolk. b through d. the cell cap forms and lifts away from the yolk, forming a furrow. e. the cell cap grows in and forms the first cell layers, ectoderm, entoderm and mesoderm.

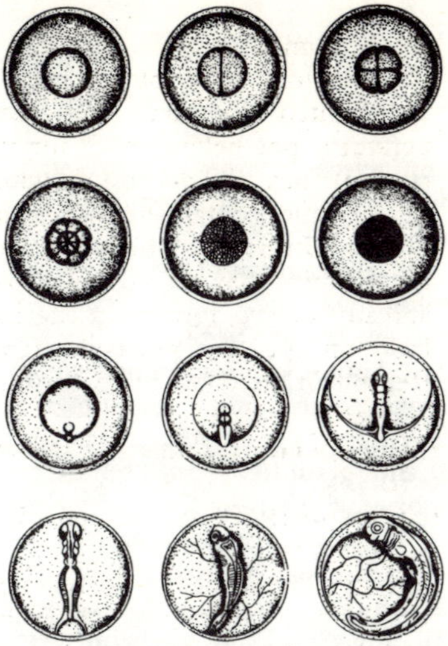

Egg development (after Sterba). The cell begins as a cap on the yolk, then divides progressively to the stage where the fry can be seen in the last diagram.

The eggs of water-dwelling animals, which pursue reproduction in the water itself, and which are our main interest in this book, are either spawned freely into the water, hung on firm objects of all kinds, or hidden in spots which favor development (for instance in the bottom soil). Among fishes fecundation, respectively insemination, takes place almost exclusively at the moment when the eggs leave the mother's body. A short time after being extruded, the eggs swell up and therefore become unable to admit semen threads. Generally there is no hard shell. Instead of this they usually are covered by an externally sticky, sometimes even double, skin or membrane, and frequently further imbedded in a jelly-like substance, if they belong to aquatic animals. Often they are also carried around by one of the two parents, or else they may be lodged in special cocoons. Many animal species take protective measures, which on one hand favor the development of the egg, on the other protect it against harm coming from its surroundings. (See: CARE FOR BROOD). If there are no such protective measures, commonly the number of eggs is very large to compensate for this fact. The development of the eggs generally begins immediately after the fecundation, but it may sometimes be retarded for a certain period of time in adaptation to special conditions of the ambient world. Development of the egg ends after varying periods with the production of a baby animal, which generally is not yet completely developed and has to pass through other phases of growth after leaving the egg shell, before it resembles its parents.

The development of the egg takes place after an innate plan, which is similar within the major groups of animals, however with the particulars being specifically different for each species. In this book we do not have the necessary space to discuss the development of eggs in general, and shall therefore restrict ourselves to the eggs of Bony Fishes.

The total output of eggs produced by a fish in one period is called spawn. The eggs of Bony Fishes are generally extruded from the female's ovary into free water (after passing through the ventral cavity in some special cases, but through the oviduct in general). For this reason as a rule they develop outside the female body. Only in a few, special cases—among live-bearing fishes, or those which subsequently keep the eggs in their mouths (mouthbreeders)—they remain within the body of the mother until the embryo is completely developed. But even in these cases the process of development is the same as for all other Bony Fishes.

Development may be very quick, but it may also be delayed due to external factors. In most cases low temperatures retard, and high temperatures accelerate development, but in some cases exactly the contrary is what happens. The eggs of certain fishes need a certain rest period before developing, or even develop only after having had such a pause. The average time for developing them is 12-72 hours, but in some cases this may last several weeks or months.

The eggs of Bony Fishes are abundantly endowed with yolk. Consequently the furrowing, which sets in after fecundation, does not include the whole egg, but just the germinal region or germinal disc. This is visible microscopically as a flat cap on the egg yolk. Furrowing is divided into three phases:

1. Simple multiplication of the cells by division of the cap into 2, 4, 8, 16, 32, or more cells of the same kind, forming regular tissues, the edges of which sit on the yolk, but the center of which is raised and forms a hollow space underneath it.

2. Differentiation of the cells, which leads to the development of the primitive vestiges of organs, and to the final completion of the organs themselves. During this the cells of the germinal disc remain in constant contact with the egg yolk, which supplies them with the necessary substances from which the cells are built.

The germinal disc turns inward at the spot where later on the tip of the embryo's tail will locate. Now there originate two layers: the outer germinal leaf (ectoderm) externally, and the inner germinal leaf (entoderm) internally. These are later on joined by a further, intermediate layer: the mesoderm. Each of these layers has to perform its specific task in the construction of the embryo. The ectoderm serves to make the skin with its glands and appendages, the nerve system, and the sensorial organs, the entoderm builds the greater part of the intestine with its glands, and the mesoderm gives origin to the conjunctive tissues, skeleton, muscles, excretory organs, heart, and circulatory system.

3. Development of the embryonal beginnings and of the embryo. The embryonal beginnings consist of a knob-like thickening, which elongates gradually, standing out increasingly from the remainder of the germinal disc, the extra-embryonal germinal region. Now the different primitive organs develop further, simultaneously with the central nerve system, the eyes, the muscles, the skeleton, etc. Meanwhile also the extra-embryonal germinal region continues to grow, but remains flat, with only the edges rising as a bulge. It spreads gradually over the yolk, possibly by growing, but possibly also by simply being drawn out by the plasm layer of the yolk. At the end of the process only a hole beneath the tail end of the embryo remains free, and finally this too is closed.

Meanwhile the development of the embryo also has continued. Gill arches and openings, aural bubbles as vestiges of a later growing ear labyrinth, and other beginnings of organs become visible. Soon the tail lifts from its resting place, already edged all around with a little fin seam which goes nearly around the whole body of the hatching fish, excepting only a small portion of the front end. Finally the head too lifts up from the yolk, but this continues to be connected with the embryo by many blood vessels as a yolk sac. This makes possible a further period of development outside the burst egg membrane.

The development of most Bony Fishes is not ended with what is called 'hatching'. It is now followed by a larval stage, while a number of body organs complete their full development.

egg hangers: Fishes which hang their sticky eggs on to firm objects (stones, plants, etc.). Many egg hangers, such as Cichlids for instance, exercise spawn-care. Others lay their eggs out of sight, for instance, the underside of broad-leaved plants, without paying further attention to them, as for instance *Rasbora heteromorpha.* Egg hangers are found in many fish families, even in those where the greater part are EGG SCATTERERS (see these). (See BIOLOGY OF THE REPRODUCTION OF FISHES).

egg-laying Tooth Carps: see CYPRINODONTINAE.

egg scatterers: The great number of fishes which release their sexual products free in water and leave fecundation and development to chance. Egg-scatterers are, for instance, most Cyprinids (see CYPRINIDAE) and Characins (see CHARACIDAE), but in most other groups of fishes as well we find egg-scattering species (see REPRODUCTION; BIOLOGY OF REPRODUCTION OF FISHES).

Egyptian Mouthbreeder, the: see HAPLOCHROMIS STRIGIGENA.

Eichhornia: Water Hyacinths.
Genus of perennial plants belonging to the family of the PONTEDERIACEAE (see this). Tropical plants which grow submerged, as well as rooted down semi-emerged, and floating free as surface plants. The emerged and floating specimens have oval to spherical leaf stalks which are more or less filled with air and of a sponge-like internal texture. From these grow the beautiful, luscious-green, generally heart-shaped leaves. The inflorescence forms an ear with 6-20 blooms, very large, light-gray to light violet, hyacinth-like, densely-placed flowers. The Eichhornias are only restrictedly adequate for the indoor aquarium, but they grow quite well in warm and sunlighted paludaria. They need plenty of light, sun, and moist warmth at 77-86° F. If kept cooler than this, the plants remain smaller and more compact.

— azurea (Swartz) Kunth: The Azure-Blue Water Hyacinth.
GENERALITIES: The species which blooms most easily and which may be cultivated as a sub-aquatic plant, as least occasionally.
SHAPE: As per description of the genus. The submerged form diverges totally from the emerged one. Temporarily the lineal, light-green leaves stand opposite on a robust stem, from the articulations of which frequently part thin roots. The strong, ramified rhizome creeps within the soil. The leaves of the emerged plants are long-stemmed, and nearly without swollen leaf stalks if they grow in shallow water. The emerged plant is most willing to bloom. The flowers are light-blue, with a yellow spot in the calyx.
RANGE: Tropical and sub-tropical America, on the shores of the waters, either rooted down in the soil, or floating.
CULTIVATION: The submerged form loses its lower leaves easily, but may be wintered submerged, while wintering emerged specimens presents some difficulties. Submerged plants may be induced to propagate by cutting them off at half their height before they reach the surface and then planting the twin in the soil. Emerged forms reproduce by division of the creeping rhizome. The species is most adequate for moist-warm paludaria. It needs very well lighted locations, especially sunlight. If kept submerged it also grows well under artificial light.

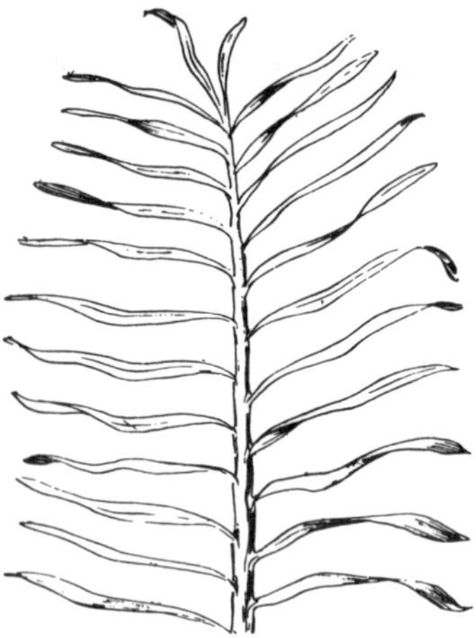

Eichhornia azurea

The plant needs warmth, and even the air above it should be moist and warm. Temperatures between 72 and 95° F.

— **crassipes** (martius) Solms: Water Hyacinth.

GENERALITIES: The species is generally cultivated as a floating plant but may also strike root. It is not quite as willing to bloom as the preceding one.

SHAPE: The heart-shaped, shiny light-green leaves stand in rosettes on more or less thickened stems. The leaf-stems are filled with a sponge-like tissue, which keeps the plants floating at the surface. The long, bushy roots are blackish-blue and very finely divided. They are very dense and grow into the mud if the water level is low. The flower stalk grows up to a height of 16″, the flowers being a delicate blue to light violet with a yellow center.

RANGE: The tropical regions of the entire globe. Seen everywhere as an obnoxious weed, which forms dense rugs on the banks and shores of rivers and other waters, being apt to overgrow the whole surface from shore to shore to a point where navigation is hindered. When the waters are low the plants often strike root in the mud, where they remain until a flood lifts them out and carries them off as floating islands.

Eichhornia crassipes

CULTIVATION: The species needs much light, and moist, warm air at 68-86° F. It does not keep well in the indoor aquarium, but does very well in well-lighted, moist-warm paludaria, where it may reach the bottom in order to send down its roots. In warm summers it may also be cultivated out-of-doors, where the plants become more compact and the leaf stems rounder. If you desire that your plants flower, you should avoid the development of sinkers, as these use up the strength of the specimens. Wintering may be effected as floating forms in artificially lighted aquaria. Besides this they may also be wintered emerged on sphagnum in flower pots, or in covered all-glass tanks at 60-68° F.

Eigenmann, Carl H. 1863-1927: Noted American ichthyologist of German extraction, married to ichthyologist Rosa Smith. Famous for his work on cave fishes in Kentucky and other American states.

Collaborating with his pupil John D. Haseman, he became one of the foremost experts on the South American fish fauna. Of especial worth are his writings on the world of fishes of the Guianas and Colombia, as well as his comprehensive description of American Characins. He died as a victim of his efforts as an explorer in tropical countries.

Eigenmannia virescens (Valenciennes): The Green Knife.

South American Knife Fish, belonging to the family of the Sea Cow Fishes or *Sternarchidae*.

SHAPE: Elongated and pestle-shaped. No dorsal fin. The caudal peduncle is extended in the shape of a whip. The anal fin is very long, with 240 rays, and promotes swimming by means of wavy movements. Length up to 18″.

COLOR: Greenish-bronze base with several horizontal and cross stripes. Very variable. SD unknown.

CARE AND BREEDING: Keep them in spacious, densely-planted tanks, which should not be too well lighted. They are shy nocturnal fishes, quarrelsome and very voracious, eating only vigorous live foods. Temperatures 72-79° F. Not yet bred.

Eigenmannia virescens

Eight-Banded Cichlid: *Cichlasoma octofasciata.*

eimekei: After the German importer Eimeke.

— *Pterophyllum* scalare.

einthoveni: After the Dutch physician, Dr. Einthoven.

— *Rasbora.*

Elassoma: Small body.

Genus belonging to the family of the Sunfishes or CENTRARCHIDAE (see this), originating from the Southern part of the U.S.A., of which so far only one species has found acceptance in the aquarium.

— evergladei Jordan: The Pygmy Sunfish.

SHAPE: Of relatively elongated body, compressed laterally. All fins are beautifully rounded in the shape of fans. D IV/9-10, A III/5. The mouth is very small and slightly tilted upwards. Length about $1\frac{1}{4}$″.

COLOR: Outside the spawning period both sexes are brownish with darker spots and cross bands. During the spawning period or under special excitement the males become blue-black with darker bands and luminous spots on body and fins. The female is plainer in colors and is recognizable by its rounded belly.

RANGE: In the swampy jungles of the Everglades, a restricted region in the State of Florida, U.S.A.

CARE AND BREEDING: The hardiness of this small species has made it an appreciated aquarium fish. The fish are able to live in small tanks, but develop better in larger ones, where they become more interesting and lively. This becomes especially noticeable when many pairs are kept together. The males fight harmless encounters, during which they show a beautiful display of the fins. The fish like dense growths of fine-feathered plants among which they may find hiding places, but stay also in open water in front of these plants. They do

Elassoma evergladei, male above

not need high temperatures, 59-72° F being amply sufficient. The Pygmy Sunfish, like all Sunfishes, prefers live foods, which however must be commensurate with its own small size. Artificial foods are eaten only rarely, and in case of need. Breeding is possible even with several pairs kept together. The eggs are scattered helter-skelter among plants after very pretty mating games. They exert no care for the brood, but generally the fish do not prey on eggs or alevins. The fry hatch after 2-6 days at 59-77° F, hanging as thin little dashes from panes and plants for another 1-2 days. After this they become free-swimming, but like to hide near the bottom. The baby fish need smallest-sized live foods from the first day of feeding on, and grow quite quickly if well fed. The differences between the sexes become noticeable already within 10-12 weeks, the young being able to reproduce when 3-4 months old. In large, densely-planted tanks there will always be numerous young growing up in the presence of older specimens.

Elassomatidae: Pygmy Sunfishes. A former family taken from the sub-order of the Perch-like fishes or *Percoidea*. Very small fishes of somewhat elongated body, with small, terminal mouths and strong teeth. The dorsal fin is very clearly divided in two, the spiny and the soft parts being connected. The only genus is *Elassoma*.

Elatinaceae: Annual or perennial swamp plants, found as submerged, semi-emerged, or land plants on occasionally flooded shores. As a rule they have creeping stems from which the little leaves and ramifications grow vertically up. Cultivated in aquaria only submerged. Genus: *Elatine*.

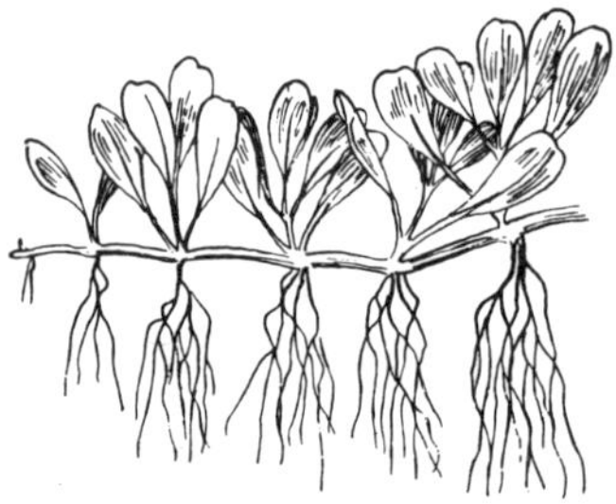

Elatine, type of the genus

Elatine: From Greek 'elate', the fir-tree.

Genus belonging to the family of the ELATINACEAE (see this).

— macropoda Gussone: The Big-footed Elatine.

SHAPE: The species is perennial. The spatula-shaped leaves with rounded tips are opposite, 4-17 mm. long and 1-3 mm wide. The much-ramified stem creeps along the bottom; the roots are very long. The plain little flowers grow only on emerged plants.

RANGE: France, Spain, North Africa, Malta, and Sicily. Nurseries sell a cultivated form of the species as '*forma submersa*'.

CULTIVATION: Unwashed sand with an admixture of old clay is a satisfactory bottom soil. The plants require quiet while taking root, and should not be disturbed by fishes. In order to have them spread over the whole bottom, distribute them well while planting. Reproduction takes place through division of the stem. The species likes light and sun. There are no stringent demands as to water temperatures. 64-70° F should prove to be the most favorable.

elationoides: Fir-like.
— *Myriophyllum.*

electric heating: see HEATING THE AQUARIUM.

Electric Catfish, the: *Malapterurus electricus.*

Electric Eel, the: *Electrophorus electricus.*

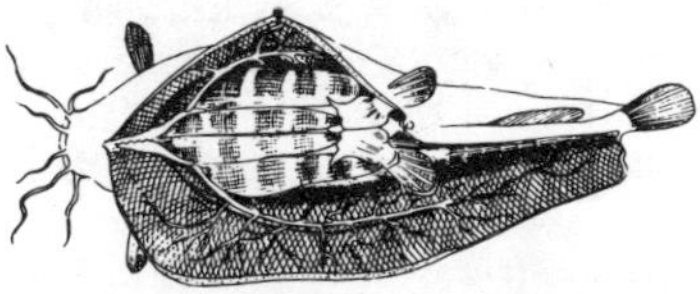

Electric organs of a Catfish, showing how the nerves and blood vessels are in a spongy tissue.

electric organs of fishes: Organs found in fishes with the aid of which electricity may be generated and released. Such organs generally originate from cross-striped muscles or, in the Electric Catfish (*Malapterurus electricus*) from transformed skin glands. In the Electric Roach they are located right and left between the gills and the pectoral fins, in the Electric Eel there is an upper and a lower pair of electric organs along the tail. On Mormyrids the location is the same as for the Electric Eels, while the Electric Catfish is completely wrapped up in its transformed skin glands as in a cape. The structure of the electric organs on the different species is largely the same. Generally they are little plates placed alongside or on top of one another, so that they form columns, each plate being surrounded by a sheath of conjunctive tissue, nerves, and blood vessels. While in repose the tension in the organs is hardly worth mentioning. Under excitement the side which is connected with the nerves receives a negative charge, and the opposite side a positive one. The total voltage depends on the number of plates. Thus one column of the Electric Eel (*Electrophorus*) contains about 6000 plates and is able to raise the tension to about 800 volts. Compared to this the output of the Electric Catfish (*Malapterurus*), which shows 500 plates and yields about 50 volts, is rather weak. The discharge is very quick, taking place in a few thousandths of a second. COATES has made extensive experiments with Electric Eels. These showed that the blind or nearly blind fish has small protuberances on the head which work together with the electric organ at the end of the body. While swimming around the fish sends out weak electric pulsations, which are reflected by its prey and are received back by the sensorial buds on the head. After the Eel has approached its prize in this manner, it paralyzes it with a strong shock and is then able to seize it effortlessly. It was also proved that the Electric Eel loses its faculties if the 'receptor' organs are covered with an insulating substance which does not permit the passage of the current.

electricus: Electric.
— *Electrophorus.*
— *Malapterurus.*

Electrophoridae: Knife Eels. Family belonging to the sub-order of the Carp-like Fishes or CYPRINOIDEA (see this), which are remarkable for possessing electric organs. The fishes resemble Eels, but have a long anal fin the manner of moving of which shows their relatedness to the Knife Fishes. Besides the anal fin there are only pectorals, the tail fin being obscure. Genus: *Electrophorus.*

Electrophorus: Bearer of electricity.

Genus of Eel-shaped fishes pertaining to the family of the Knife Eels or *Electrophoridae.*

— **electricus** Linné: The Electric Eel.

GENERALITIES: A very interesting fish, fit for larger exhibition aquaria only, which, however, represents a main attraction in these.

SHAPE: The long-stretched, eel-shaped body is covered with a mucous skin. The mouth opening is very large. The anal fin shows 350 rays. Length up to 7 ft.

COLOR: Brown young specimens with dark mottlings, throat and belly orange-red. SD unknown.

RANGE: Guiana, and the lower and central Amazon region.

CARE AND BREEDING: The Electric Eels are bellicose, vicious, and extremely voracious nocturnal and twilight fishes which eat exclusively live foods. The electric organ acts like a radar in their hunts for food, but it is also able to distribute strong electric shocks. The Electric Eels need spacious, densely-planted tanks with soft water and soft bottom. In order to make them feel well they need 77-82° F. Not yet bred in the aquarium.

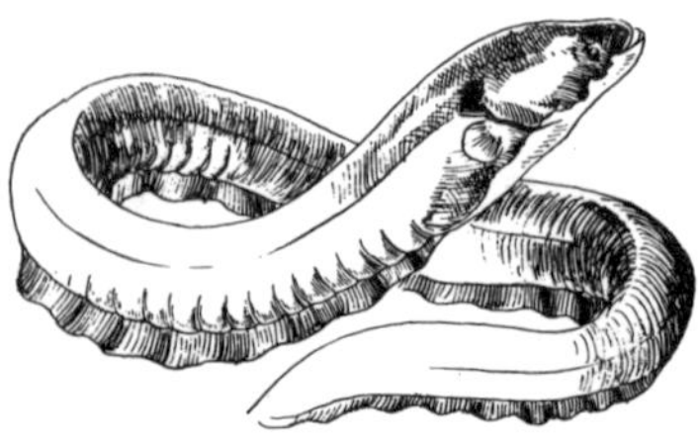

Electrophorus electricus

elegans: Elegant, nice, tasteful.

— *Corydoras.*

— *Pterolebias.*

— *Rasbora.*

— *Steatogenes.*

Eleotridae: Sleeper Gudgeons.

Family of bottom fishes belonging to the sub-order of the Gudgeon-like Fishes or GOBIOIDEA (see this). Fishes with two dorsal fins, the first of which is supported by bony spines, while the second one consists of one body spine and additional soft rays. The ventral fins insert on the throat and are not grown together in the middle like those of most Gobies. The pectorals are normally developed and possess no arm-like base. The eyes are not protractile. Only those of some sand-dwelling species protrude a little.

The Sleeper Gudgeons are found in the seas, as well as in fresh and brackish waters of the tropical and sub-tropical regions from Africa to Australia. Genera, among others, as follows: *Carassiops, Dormitator, Hypseleotris, Mogurnda,* and *Eleotris.*

Eleotris: Name of a Nile fish, mentioned by Aristotle without being specified.

Genus belonging to the family of the Sleeper Gudgeons or *Eleotridae,* of elongated, cylinder-shaped body, which is slightly compressed towards the rear. The head is large, broad, and generally a little flattened. The big mouth cleft is studded with numerous small, but very pointed, teeth. As a rule the lower jaw is a little protuberant. The pupil of the eyes has a greenish or pale-gray gleam, which gives the eyes a slightly 'dead' look.

— **africana** Steindachner: The African Sleeper Gudgeon.

SHAPE: As per description of the genus and family. D_1 VI, D_2 I/10, A I/8-9. Length up to about 6″.

COLOR: Gray-brown with dark spot and band design. SD are not known.

CARE AND BREEDING: As described for the next species.

— **butis** Hamilton-Buchanan: The Pointed-Head Gudgeon.

Eleotris butis

SHAPE: As per description of the genus. D_1 VI, D_2 I/8, A I/8. Length up to 5⅛″.

COLOR: Very variable, generally yellowish-brown with rows of darker dots and mottlings. SD unknown.

RANGE: Along the coast of the Indian Ocean, from Australia to East Africa, especially in brackish and salt water. The species is reported to go only unwillingly into fresh water.

CARE AND BREEDING: A very hardy and rugged fish which cannot be kept together with other fishes due to its predatory manner of living. It likes spacious tanks with soft sand bottom and hiding caves built of rocks. Imported specimens should at first receive a stronger admixture of kitchen salt, or what is still better, their water should be blended with sea water in a ratio of 2:1. Experience shows, though, that it is possible to accustom them to fresh water gradually. Their great need for oxygen makes good aeration compulsory. Only with twilight do the fish become lively, coming out of hiding in order to hunt for prey. Nourishment consists of vigorous live foods, especially of small fishes. Temperatures, 64-79° F. Breeding has not yet succeeded.

— **lebretonis** Steindachner: The Clay Gudgeon.

SHAPE: As per description of genus, but the head less pointed. D_1 VII-VIII, D_2 I/8-9, A I/9-10. Length up to 4¾″.

COLOR: Yellow-brown base with a dark horizontal band which is composed of dots, and a few irregular designs. Throat and belly become orange-red during the spawning period. The rear rays of the second dorsal of the males are extended, the free rim of the anal is seamed in white, the rays of this fin too being extended. The ventrals of the males are pointed.

RANGE: In quiet waters of tropical West Africa, generally in fresh waters but also in brackish ones.

CARE AND BREEDING: The species is best kept in densely-planted tanks with hiding caves and bottom of fine-grained sand, at low water levels. Imported specimens are domesticated with an admixture of sea water of 5% or with a small addition of kitchen salt. They are easily accustomed to fresh water at any time. Despite the fact that in general the species may be said to be long-lived and hardy, it needs some warmth, 68-75° F, for breeding 75-79° F. Feeding this fish demands robust live foods.

Breeding has already succeeded several times. The act of spawning took place near the bottom, the eggs being spawned among fine-feathered plants. The parents prey heavily on the spawn. Rearing the young with very small-sized live foods is reported to be easy.

— **marmorata** Bleeker: The Marble Gudgeon.

SHAPE: As per description of genus. The very large eyes protrude a little from their sockets. D_1 VI, D_2 I/8, A I/8. Length up to 4¾″.

COLOR: Very beautifully colored, even if considerably variable. The basic color is greenish to pink, the lower half of the body with clearly marked dark-brown spots and bands, which also ornament the fins. The second dorsal and the anal fins of the males are strongly developed, the genital papilla being conical, while that of the female is tubular.

RANGE: In standing and slowly-

Eleotris marmorata

flowing fresh waters of Malaya and the Great Sunda Islands.

CARE AND BREEDING: As described for *E. lebretonis*. The species likes to bury itself in the sand leaving only its eyes visible, and is a nocturnal predator like the other species of the genus. Temperatures, 79-82° F, lowest 72° F. Breeding has not yet succeeded.

— **melanosoma** Bleeker: The Black-Belly Gudgeon.

A species from the Sunda Islands, which very much resembles the preceding one. The back is yellow-brown, the sides are black-brown with luminous stripes and dots. Care is similar to that of the preceding species.

— **pleurops** Boulenger: The Niger Gudgeon.

SHAPE: As per description of the genus; a little more compact and shorter than the other species; quite strongly compressed laterally. Length around 4″.

COLOR: Uniformly brown, sometimes also with faded spots.

RANGE: In mangrove swamps and lagoons of the Niger Delta, almost exclusively in brackish water.

CARE AND BREEDING: As described for *E. butis*. The species is said to be able to get accustomed to fresh water.

— **procephalus** Cuvier and Valenciennes: The Snake-Head Gudgeon.

SHAPE: As per description of the genus. The head, which is equipped with peculiar pores and pits, reminds one a little of the Snake-Head Fishes. D_1VI, D_2 I/8-10, A I/17. Length up to 9″.

COLOR: Brownish-red with horizontal rows of small dots and brown band designs. SD are not known.

RANGE: The coastal regions of Southeast Asia, also on Madagascar and the Seychelles, in the sea and in brackish water. The species shows several local strains.

CARE AND BREEDING: No particulars are known so far. Care probably resembles that of *E. butis*.

— **vittata** Dumeril: The Senegal Gudgeon.

SHAPE: As per description of the genus. D_1 VI, D_2 I/8, A I/8. Length up to 9″.

COLOR: Brownish with pleasing dark designs on the sides of the body and the fins. The male is more vividly colored, its second dorsal fin being higher.

RANGE: Tropical West Africa, from the Senegal to the Congo. The species lives mainly in fresh waters, but is also found in brackish ones.

CARE AND BREEDING: Care as for *E. lebretonis* and *E. marmorata*. Temperatures, 79-82° F, lowest 72° F. This species is livelier than the other Sleeper Gudgeons, being relatively vivacious also during the day. Breeding has not yet succeeded.

Elisma: Derived from *Alisma*.

Genus belonging to the family of the Frog Spoon Plants or *Alismataceae*.

— **natans** Linné: The Floating Frog Spoon.

GENERALITIES: A submerged cold-water plant, which is adequate for smaller to medium-sized aquaria.

SHAPE: This perennial species has narrow, ribbon-shaped leaves which grow 12″ to 16″ long and $\frac{1}{16}$″ to $\frac{1}{4}$″ wide, tapering gradually into points. It sends out numerous runners, the connecting vine of which is thin like a thread. The floating inflorescences on their long peduncles rise just a little above the water surface. The flowers are white. If the water levels are very high, the plants develop very small submerged leaves only, while in shallow water they also grow floating leaves.

RANGE: Central Europe, from Southern Sweden to Northern Spain, including the central, European part of the U.S.S.R. Commonly the species lives in standing waters and is also found in the moors.

CULTIVATION: If the submerged leaves receive sufficient light, they continue vegetating even in winter. In summer the plants grow quickly and reproduce abundantly through runners. Sand with an admixture of some clay and peat is a sufficient bottom soil. If placed in sunlit locations it also blooms in the aquarium.

Elodea: Swamp dweller.

Genus of sub-aquatic plants pertaining to the family of the Frogbit Plants or *Hydrocharitaceae*.

The genus comprises very useful and hardy aquarium plants, which are much appreciated as good suppliers of oxygen. Sometimes they are also sold under the names of *Helodea*, or *Anacharis*.

The Elodeas have only simply-growing, thread-shaped roots. These are only weakly anchored to the soil, and the plants may also be cultivated free-floating. Stems and leaves are very frail, generally a fresh green. The stems may be richly ramified. The leaves insert around the stem in verticils of three or five. Often they are slightly wavy or curved, narrow, and with one nervure.

Frequently importers have received only male, or only female specimens of the generally separately sexed plants. Fecundation takes place in the manner which is peculiar to the *Hydrocharitaecae*. The male flowers either fall off and float up to the surface, or else they are carried up on their long peduncles.

The Elodeas are very hardy plants, which draw their nourishment directly from the water, and which possess a very strong capacity of assimilation. They propagate by simple division, each segment of the stem being able to develop into a new plant. All species like plenty of light and sun.

— **callitrichoides** (Richard) Caspary: The Chilean Anacharis.

GENERALITIES: The species is adequate for cold water aquaria, and especially for outdoors tanks.

SHAPE: As per description of the genus. The leaves form a triple verticil. The female flowers insert at a height on the upper segments which just permits them to reach the surface with the crown and the scars of the stylus, floating there.

RANGE: Argentina and Chile, in clear waters, especially also in the high mountains.

— **canadensis** Michaux: The Canadian Anacharis.

GENERALITIES: A very hardy and easily-kept species for the cold water tanks.

Elodea canadensis

SHAPE: As per description of the genus. The species is very small-leaved, but quite robust. The leaves stand in verticils of 3-5, the leaf rims being thinly serrated, and the leaf tips slightly blunted. In Europe nearly exclusively dioecian females plants are found, while in America there also are hermaphroditic ones.
RANGE: Originally from Canada and the U.S.A. Found today in great areas of the whole globe after having run wild.
CULTIVATION: This hardy species grows best in cold or moderately warm water. It is quick-growing, but easily gets a little thin in the indoor aquarium.

— **densa** (Plancon) Caspary: The Argentinian Anacharis.
GENERALITIES: One of the most beautiful species, which grows very rich and dense shoots with long leaves if it receives favorable conditions. Such plants reach the market as *E. d. longifolia*.

Elodea densa

SHAPE: The pretty lush-green leaves stand more or less densely around the stem, in verticils of 3 to 5 each. Sometimes they are a little curly or arched. In Europe we see only male specimens of this dioecian plant. The male flowers do not come off, but grow up to the surface on a thin peduncle.
RANGE: Tropical and sub-tropical South America.
CULTIVATION: Like all species of *Elodea*, but needs and tolerates more warmth.

elongatus: Elongated, extended.
— *Aponogeton.*
— *Chalcinus.*

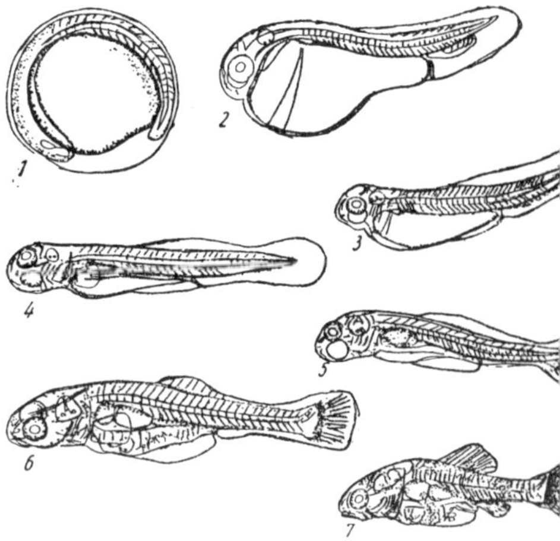

Development of **Barbus tetrazona** — 1. egg shortly before hatching. 2. Fry, 1 day, 4 hours old. 3. 2 days, 5 hours old. 4. 3 days, 12 hours old. 5. 5days, ½ hour old. 6. 7 days, 9½ hours old. 7. 11 days, 6½ hours old.

embryo: Young organism within the egg shell or the mother's body, which develops from the egg cell. Not yet completely developed larval stages of many fishes also may be called embryos in a broader sense of the word, even after having burst out of the egg, but before free-swimming.

Emerald Cichlid, the: *Cichlasoma hellabrunni.*

Emerald Panchax, the: *Epiplatys ornatus.*

emerged: This definition applies to aquatic plants which grow partly or totally above the surface of the water.

emissions of sound: Emissions of sound are not all too rare in fishes. It is true that generally they do not have too great an importance, having a certain biological significance, though, in certain species. Emissions of sound may originate from friction of parts of the skeleton, or from the expelling of air from the swimming bladder or from the respiratory organs. They are well-known in quite a number of salt-water fishes, but are also found in some fresh-water ones. Among aquarium fishes there are especially the species of Catfishes which emit such sounds when frightened, especially if taken out of the water. Also the Anabantids may sometimes give forth quite distinctly audible sounds, especially during the excitement of mating. Well-known for this are both Croaking Gouramis of the genus *Trichopsis*, but also other species, as for instance, the Pearl (or Mosaic) Gourami, *Trichogaster leeri*, may produce sounds by expelling air from the respiratory organs.

Enchytraeidae: Family of worms pertaining to the order of the Scarce-bristled Ones or *Oligochaeta.*

Enchytraeus: White Worms.

Genus belonging to the family of the *Enchytraeidae.* Soil-dwelling worms which enjoy great importance in aquaristics, both as winter and as complementary food, due to being easy to breed and to their great nutritional value. All species are hermaphroditic. Fecundation takes place with two specimens lying closely together, while they secrete a mucus which keeps them united until the mating has been completed. The eggs are spawned in somewhat transparent cocoons, through which they are dimly visible.

Tweezers for removing worms

Breeding is done in wooden boxes with well-fitting lids. Fill such boxes to ¾ of their height with a 1:1 mixture of good garden loam and peat, with forest humus, or other loose, non-crusting soils which are free of chemical fertilizers. Soil that contains clay, or that come from too-fatty dung heaps should never be used. It is always advisable to give the dirt an admixture of peat. Leave a small pit open in the center of the box, in which to place the food mash, and cover it with a small piece of glass. Feeding is done with a stiff mash of oat flakes to which you may add a dash of sugar or a blob of margarine. You may also feed the worms with other soft food left-overs, mashed potatoes, for instance. Put the breeding stock of worms into the pit, spread the food mash over them, and cover the whole with the piece of glass. Then leave your breeders alone for about three weeks, while keeping the loam always slightly moist. In order to grant the worms sufficient time in which to reproduce, it will be best to set up several boxes, rotating weekly for fish food.

Feeding the worms to the fishes is easy. A few days after feeding the worms, these collect in great numbers beneath the glass and may easily be taken out with tweezers. If the dirt does not drop off from them, take a small portion of the

White Worms, put them in the cover of a preserve jar, and place them on a warm base. This will make the worms assemble and ball together at the surface.

Spiders and cockroaches which settle in the box may be left undisturbed since they exterminate obnoxious mites.

Infestations with mites often are difficult to avoid. Greater numbers of them show up especially if feeding is excessive. Therefore you should make it a point to feed more frequently, but sparingly each time. Remember, though, that the worms should never go foodless for longer periods of time. In order to combat the mites it is advisable to dip a rag in coal oil and to place it in a corner of the box. Springtails, which also like to appear, can be blown away from time to time, while you tilt the box on one side. Furthermore you may immerse the whole box in water, and the mites and springtails will float away on the surface. However, both only compete for food with the White Worms, and cause no further harm.

Partial renewing of the earth within the box may be effected by exposing it to intense sunlight with the cover opened. The worms will withdraw from the clodding upper layer to the bottom. Then you may lift off the upper crust and replace it with fresh soil. Generally this is followed by a strong increase in the reproduction of the worms. Be cautious when feeding your fishes with *E.* The worms are very nutritive and may lead to overfattening if served in excessive quantities. This may also lead to sterility and loss of color for the fishes. They are very commendable as a food complement, however, especially in winter, when nothing else is available.

— **albus:** The White Worm.
White Worms differ from the subsequent species by their size as well as by their insensitivity as to temperature. You may breed them in winter at room temperature, and they withstand occasional cold spells easily, as long as they are not subject to frosts. The species is commonly found in dung heaps, especially near decaying turnips. Specimens found in such spots may be used as fish food, but should never be placed in breeding boxes, as it is reported that wild specimens attack those which already live in boxes.

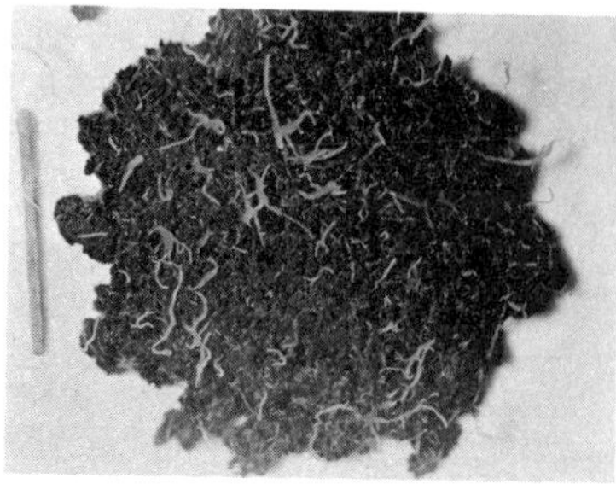

Enchytraeus albus culture

— **buccholzi** (Vejdovsky): Micro Worms.
Close relatives of the preceding species, but of lesser size and greater need for warmth. They are best kept at 64-75° F, and stop reproducing at 57° F. Adult worms, though, tolerate occasional lowerings of the temperature down to the freezing point.

Reproduction is quicker and more abundant than for *E. albus*, but the worms need more attention. It is best to control the temperature periodically with a thermometer. Micro Worms are a good food for baby fishes.

Enneacanthus: The Nine-spined One.
Genus belonging to the family of the Sunfishes or *Centrarchidae*, of short and high body structure, which might be called nearly oval,

strongly compressed laterally. The cone-shaped teeth cover even the palate.

— obesus (Girard):

SHAPE: As per description of the genus. D VIII-X/10-12, A III-IV/8-11. A few rows of scales on the opercles. Length, in its home waters up to 4″; ready to reproduce in the aquarium when 2″-2⅜″ long.

COLOR: The reddish-brown body is sprinkled with a great number of luminous green and golden dots, especially during the spawning period. SD may sometimes become minute; in general the male is more vividly colored and its vertical fins are more strongly developed.

RANGE: The whole East of the U.S.A., from Florida in the South to near the Great Lakes in the North. The species lives in clear waters of secondary waters of rivers and lakes, especially in spots where dense plant thickets offer possibilities for hiding.

CARE AND BREEDING: A very beautiful and valued cold water fish. It is quiet, peaceful and sensitive to disturbance. Its special susceptibility to becoming frightened makes it prone to spasms, which sometimes become lethal. *E. obesus* should be kept in sufficiently large, well planted tanks, are best placed in communities of their own species, and should never live together with very lively fishes. They like clear, clean, well aerated water with occasional sunlight. Avoid excessive sunshine, however. There are no special demands as to water temperature, but this should never be permanently lower than 50-54° F. On the other hand, though, it is unfavorable to winter the fish too warm, as this makes them prone to diseases and hard to breed the next year. Like all Sunfishes the species generally eats only live foods, taking artificial ones only occasionally and unwillingly. Considering that the fishes bury themselves if scared, you should choose a very soft and well-rounded sand for the bottom cover. The spawning period comes between May and September. When the temperature rises to 64-68° F, the male shows the SD strikingly. The eggs are either spawned on fine-feathered plants, or in a pit previously dug by the male, in case there should not be sufficient plants available. The female is not pursued. On the contrary, when she is ripe for spawning, she comes to the spawning site where the male awaits her of his own accord. The mating games are very interesting and graceful. While spawning the male swims a little behind the head of the female and, with quick movement of his fins, he scatters the eggs over the plants. The spawning site is watched by the male. The fry hatch after 2-4 days, and the male watches them superficially for another 7 days while they hang from plants. After this it is best to remove the male. The water should be no deeper than 6″. At first the babies eat infusoria, and after a few days dust-size live foods as well as complementary foods, such as mashed White Worms, etc. They grow slowly, even if well fed, and reach sexual maturity only after two years. It is advisable periodically to grade and to separate them according to size, as bigger fry attack smaller ones. *E. obesus* may also be bred in the outdoor tank and in warm ponds. Severe winters, however, always kill it.

Entomostraca: Lower Crustaceans.
Former class of crustaceans which today is voided and distributed in a different manner.

entoparasite: Parasite which lives

within the organs or the body of a host.

environment: Collective term for all the external factors which influence the existence of a living being. The environment controls the possibilities for life of the organisms and with it their distribution on the Earth and is the deciding factor in its structure and development. Its study (ecology) is becoming increasingly important in aquarium keeping, because it concerns the natural environmental factors of the animal and plant life in the aquarium. The environment influences the organisms either that they are attracted by good living conditions or repelled when they are bad. This causes a change in its entirety of the organisms. This influence toward change is not only effective at the present time, but has been taking place since the beginning of life on Earth. At first there were certain requirements for life and finally these were preferred and became a motivating factor in evolutionary development. There are three factors which govern these results:

1. The selective results of environmental factors, which either encourages or discourages the organisms and certain of their properties (natural selection).

2. The direct influence of the affecting environmental conditions on the collective metabolism (by this we mean more than nourishment) whereby development is guided into certain courses, governed by environment.

3. The lasting changes in environmental factors which forces all organisms constantly to adapt themselves to the changes, causing selection to seek constantly for new values.

Adaptability to environment fulfills itself therefore under its direct influence. However there is nothing said about what direction this adaptability takes with an individual species. This is much more, at least partially governed in each living thing by its own developmental possibilities. In this way, for instance, the same biotope may be occupied by fishes of highly varied construction and manners of living, for example a fast-flowing brook in the mountains. Here we find the predatory Trout, which can conquer the rapid flow with its muscular body; also the peaceful Elritze, which prefers the quieter pools (thereby seeking a different biotope), the fish-like Lamprey which can attach itself to stones or other firm objects and thereby withstand the current, and the Darter, which has no air-bladder but can fasten itself to the bottom by its flat underside and large pectoral fins, etc.

The one environmental factor, namely the current, has not affected the life which fights it uniformly. Only the uniformity of all factors in a living range can result in similar types, without them necessarily being related. The environmental factors in bodies of water are greatly varied. It is difficult to comprehend them completely. Even if they are roughly similar, each individual body of water has countless characteristics which make it different in many ways, in some ways radically. .

There are however some basic things to recognize, which can lead us to find the most important environmental factors. They can be recognized thus:

1. The major factors.
2. The minor factors.

The major factors include:

(a) the geographical influences, with which are connected the climate and rhythm of the length of days and the time of year.

(b) the geological influences, in

which the ground relief (lowland, level and highland), the composition of the geological strata, particularly the surface stratum, and the distribution of the water should be considered.

Both of these factors are the deciding issues in the many-sided population of the Earth's surface with plant and animal life.

To the minor factors we must figure the major factors of all uninhabited (abiotic) and more narrowly defined inhabited (biotic) factors in their special environment, the biotope of a living thing.

For fishes as water inhabitants, the water comes to the foreground as the deciding life element. In aquarium-keeping it took some time to understand generally that water is no single abstract thing. It is by its physical qualities and its capability of dissolving matter liable to undergo widespread variations, which would make it dependent upon the above mentioned major factors. Its geographical location would determine: the water temperatures, its average height and variations, the different additions of fresh water, the degree of evaporation or freezing, and connected with all this the variations in water level, the seasonal rhythm of lighting, prevailing wind directions, barometric pressures, etc.

The geological properties would depend upon the following: the general character of the body of water, that is, if it is a river, swamp, brook, pond, etc. and besides the water depth and with it water pressure, water movement, the transparency of the water, governed by the bottom and the amount of suspended matter, its chemical composition, namely its content of dissolved substances, salts, trace elements, gases, etc. These influences, together with the plant life, govern the natural reaction (pH value) of the water. This shows most of the abiotic environmental factors. The fish are more or less strongly opposed to these, or on the other hand have adapted themselves to them.

The population with organic life gives us the living factors. They may be named as follows: (a) the *plant life* in the surrounding territory and in the water itself. The plant life along the banks is largely responsible, especially in the tropics, for the distribution of light and shadow and by this the growth of aquatic plants, and to a lesser extent the contents of humic acid in the water by an influx of leaves and wood particles. The aquatic plants themselves are a governing factor in the variations in pH value, and by their assimilation and dissimilation the biogenic decalcification and calcification, and to a lesser extent the circulation and exchange of gases. The plant thickets can also be a harbor or hiding-place, they can play a part as a spawning medium and in a few cases (carnivorous plants) may be rivals for food. Here and there plant life may become an enemy, either as a parasite (*Ichthyosporidium*), as a direct enemy (such as young fry becoming entangled in thread algae) or by an overproduction of gases (oxygen);

(b) The *animal life*. Here we must consider the species which either form communities of their own kind (schools) or sexual partnerships, which could also become rivals for food or enemies, which might rarely be the case. The amount of the same species can govern the nourishment conditions in a body of water and thereby their individual development; (left-over individuals among Pikes and Trout, runts among Breams and Sticklebacks, etc. in a closed body of water). With the animal population we must also include the neighbors, that is all life which is neither of the same species nor enemy, but to a certain extent offers competition for food. Here we may include many aquatic insects and their larvae, snails, etc. Now and then a fish may establish a closer connection with such neighbors for the purpose of a common usefulness (symbiosis), for example the Bitterling and the mussel, or the Clownfish and the Anemone. Other animal life, especially fishes, are to a great extent food competitors, which consume the same nourishment. The enemies are manifold. They range from one-celled animalcules to human beings. Their relation to their enemies, and on the other side their prey, governs the life of a fish very greatly. Finally there are animal parasites and disease carriers. The fish population is usually dependent upon the amount of enemies and parasites.

In an enclosed space (enclosed but not closed) the inhabitants living therein form a community, in which each takes its place, which is governed by living requirements and functions, the manner of feeding, the number of enemies which occur, competitors, etc., etc. These all have different requirements, and build a community which holds itself in a biological balance. A body of water can supply only as much in the way of living possibilities as the separate factors permit.

Also the fish life is suited to its natural environment, having become adapted to it. It should be said in advance, however, that in Nature there are no distinct borders. There are many transitions and the fish may seek other biotopes or be driven into them. However we can determine to a great extent a fish's environment by its body form and functions.

There are adaptations of many sorts, general and special. It is impossible to enumerate them except in a general manner. Adaptations to the physical conditions of the water, for example to currents, are shown by a muscular or spindle-shaped body, and finally by the entire structure of the fish, the fins as driving organs, etc. The sensory organs are also adapted to the special conditions in the water. Many fishes require certain temperatures, a certain type of nourishment or they possess a special way of getting their nourishment, or are adapted to drying out, oxygen scarcity, etc., etc. These adaptations are of a hereditary nature, and are the means of identifying a species or entire group of similar fishes. They can be rigid, but also elastic, permanent or only applicable to certain stages of development. Therefore the capability of adaptation to varying environmental conditions changes, often even within one species, which could give rise to adaptable strains. Many species are confined to only a very close living space, such as the *Cynolebias* species, and others a very wide one, for example the Sticklebacks. Such observations can be made with each individual fish species. The aquarist must never forget that most species have a certain innate width of their individual adaptability, and it is possible to keep fishes in somewhat unfavorable conditions and even get them to propagate.

To sum up it must be reiterated that of all the named factors, none ever exist by themselves. For the aquarist, the provision of a natural environment for fishes and plants forms the basis for a natural, biologically correct care of his aquarium inhabitants.

eos: Sunrise Pink.
— *Hyphessobrycon.*

Epalzeorhynchus: With strong snout.

Southeast Asian genus of Barb-like fishes belonging to the family of the Carp-like fishes or CYPRINIDAE (see this). Fishes of very slender and laterally compressed shape, with subterminal mouth, far-protruding snout, and two pairs of barbels.

— kallopterus (Bleeker): The Trunk Barb.

SHAPE: As per description of the genus, the body nearly cylindrical. D 11, A 7; the scales relatively large. The fins are well developed. The dorsal fin is arched like a crescent, the tail fin is indented. Length, in their home country 5½″, in the aquarium up to 4″.

COLOR: A broad, black band along the body, rimmed above by a golden zone, and a beautiful design on the reddish fins. SD are not yet known.

RANGE: Sumatra, Borneo, Java, rarely imported up to this date.

Epalzeorhynchus kallopterus

CARE AND BREEDING: A very pleasing and peaceful fish, which sometimes likes to lie on the bottom or on plants, propped up on its pectoral fins, partly, however, likes to swim very nimbly. It needs not-too-small tanks, richly-planted and with a soft bottom. The fish graze off growths and organic detritus from the bottom with their mouths which are surrounded by fringe-like excrescences. They are omnivorous, behaving peacefully toward even the smallest fishes. *E. kallopterus* needs some warmth, 73-82° F being most favorable, but this may occasionally drop a little lower.

Manner of reproducing is not yet known.

Ephemerida: Dayflies.

Order belonging to the phylum of the Insects or HEXAPODA (see this). Frail, very short-lived insects, the existence of which as imagos (completed insects) lasts only a few days or even hours and is dedicated to reproduction exclusively. Small to medium-sized, unassumingly colored insects, with two pairs of richly-veined wings. Their special characteristic feature are the long, articulated tail bristles (cerci). The eggs are spawned in water. From these hatch larvae, called nymphs, which initially are very small. They are equipped with tracheal gills and also possess several tail bristles which are characteristic for them. Partly they live on detritus and algae, in part they prey on other small animals. Kept in the aquarium, they frequently attack small fish fry. Development into a completed imago is attained in 20 or more changes of skin. Duration of this development differs for the different species and may last from one to three years.

Curiously the metamorphosis includes successive changes of skin from each of which results a winged insect, but only the last one is able to propagate, and dances through the air on fair summer days or evenings, in great numbers.

Among others we mention: the Common Dayfly, *Ephemera vulgata*, and *Polymitarcis virgo*, the nymphs of which live in great numbers in

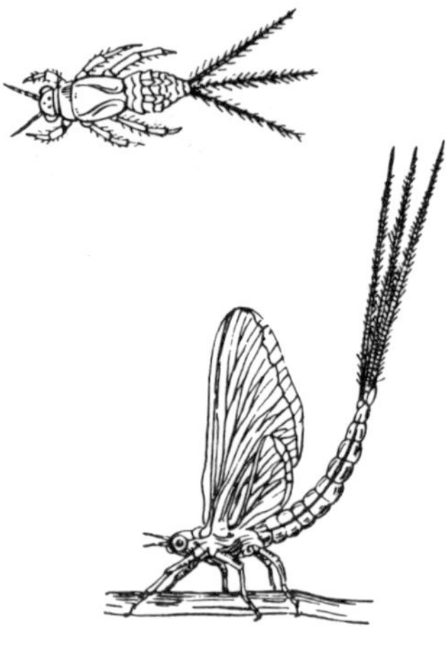

Larval and adult form of **Ephemerida**

the muddy bottoms of rivers. All dayflies and their larvae represent an excellent fish food, which in some regions is even sold dried as a winter food.

Ephippicharax: South American genus belonging to the family of the Characins or *Characidae,* of disc-like shape. The lateral line is complete. The anal fin is very long; an adipose fin is present; in front of the dorsal fin is a short spine.

Ephippicharax orbicularis

— orbicularis (Cuvier and Valenciennes): The Silver Dollar.

SHAPE: As per description of the genus. D 11-12, A 30-36. Length up to 4¾″.

COLOR: Shiny silvery to coppery, with a greenish or violet gleam. Beneath the adipose fin a striking, luminous spot, furthermore two faded shoulder spots. The females are a little smaller.

RANGE: The East of tropical South America.

CARE AND BREEDING: As per description of the family. This very active species needs larger tanks, which should not be too densely planted, but should be kept well covered. The fish are omnivorous, requiring vegetable foods besides their rich live foods. Temperatures between 64 and 75° F, for breeding a little higher, lowest 59° F. Spawning takes place in open water, near the surface, with lively splashing. Rearing the numerous fry is not difficult.

ephippium: Saddle.
Protective cover of the permanent or winter eggs of *Daphnia,* of brownish to blackish color, which is developed within the incubating space of the females and sits on their backs like a saddle. The E. contains the permanent eggs.

Epicyrtus microlepis: see ROEBOIDES MICROLEPIS.

epidermis: The outer layer of the skin.

Epiplatys: (Fish) with broad back. African genus of Tooth Carps pertaining to the sub-family of the egg-laying Tooth Carps or CYPRINODONTINAE (see this), with elongated body, strongly flattened from above, wide, supraterminal mouth, and a dorsal fin which inserts far towards the rear. The shape has something of that of the Pikes. They are more or less surface fishes, partly of predatory nature, but adult specimens of several species do not stay exclusively at the surface, especially if they are not disturbed. Most species need not too small tanks, with well-planted lateral spaces and covers of floating plants. There they like to remain in the central reaches of the water, among plants, ambushing prey. This is captured in sallies like those of the Pikes. Furthermore all species like to jump after flying insects. Nourishment consists of robust live foods of all kinds, especially insects and their larvae, or small fishes. Artificial foods are only taken in case of absolute need and reluctantly.

Not all species tolerate sunlight, and you should provide for at least some shadowed spots, by having some floating plants on the surface of the water. The water height should not be excessive. Dark bottoms enhance their colors. For breeding it is advisable to locate the tanks in not too well lighted spots. Spawn and fry should be protected against too intense sunlight. Spawning generally takes place in the morning, among surface plants or in dense thickets of fine-feathered sub-aquatic plants. The males drive very violently. Either remove the parents after spawning, or else take out the plant bundles with the eggs and transfer them to special breeding tanks. The fry generally hatch after 10-14 days. Rearing them is not all too difficult.

— **chaperi** (Sauvage): The Fire-Mouth Panchax.

SHAPE: As per description of the genus. The front part nearly cylindrical, more compressed toward the rear. D 7-8, A 14-15. The scales are relatively large. Length up to 2⅜″, the female remaining a little smaller.

COLOR: Greenish to bluish base with the scales dark-rimmed. On the rear part of the body are four vertical black bands, which in part also cover the anal fin. The male has a brick-red throat and pretty yellow fins with black edges. The rear of its anal fin is pointed, and the lower rays of the tail fin are black and a little extended. The female does not show these characteristics.

Epiplatys chaperi

RANGE: In shallow puddles with plenty of plants, in West Africa.

CARE AND BREEDING: As per description of the genus. The smallest and most peaceful of the *Epiplatys*. They are not shy at all, and very commendable for keeping in community tanks. Temperature, 70-73° F, for breeding 75-79° F, lowest 61° F. The males fight very active encounters in order to cause an impression. Also the mating games, during which the opercles are spread out, are very pretty. The eggs are hung from plants, the pair swimming alongside each other. Since the number of eggs is very small, it is advisable to use several females to each male. Each spawning period lasts for several weeks. Therefore it will be good to place bundles of fine-feathered plants or nylon mops in the mating tank, and periodically to transfer these with the eggs to a nursery tank. The fry hatch after 8-10 days. They are ⅝″ long, stay near the surface, and are immediately able to eat dust-sized food. Since their growth is not regular, they should occasionally be separated according to sizes. The alevins grow quickly and after about 8 weeks you will be able to sex them.

— **chevalieri** (Pellegrini):

SHAPE: As per description of the genus. D 9, A 15 (?). Length about 2⅜″, sometimes more.

Epiplatys chevalieri

COLOR: Emerald base with wine-red rows of dots, which are a little slanted and join to form band designs on the lower half of the body. Wine-red designs, dashes, and dots on gill covers and fins, the latter yellowish to greenish white. Sometimes the female shows a dark horizontal band along the middle of the body; the male is more colored, with pointed fins, the caudal fin extended into points above and below.

RANGE: The central course of the Congo.

CARE AND BREEDING: As per description of the genus. A somewhat predatory species. Breeding as described for the genus. Not pronounced spawn eaters.

— **dageti** Poll.

SHAPE: As per description of the genus. A slightly compact-looking species. D 7, A 12 (?). Possibly a sub-species or a local strain of *E. chaperi*.

COLOR: Similar to *E. chaperi*, but with less black in the fins. The caudal of both sexes is egg-shaped and ends in a central point.

RANGE: The Gold Coast.

CARE AND BREEDING: As described for *E. chaperi*.

— **fasciolatus** (Guenther): The Banded Panchax.

SHAPE: As per description of the genus. D 11, A8. Scales relatively large. Length up to 3⅛″.

COLOR: Olive drab base with 9 narrow, dark cross bands, the male with a carmine red spot on the base of each scale, and with many luminous green dots. The yellow-green fins are dotted and rimmed with red. The female is simpler in color, her anal fin is rounded.

RANGE: The coastal regions of tropical West Africa and also in the Upper Nile.

CARE AND BREEDING: As per description of the genus. A large and predatory species. It is sensitive to changes of water. Imported specimens should receive an admixture of 10% of sea water or a small quantity of kitchen salt (one heaped tea spoon per 5 quarts). Temperatures 70-73° F, for breeding 75-77° F.

The male is very vicious during the spawning period, for which reason the sexes should be kept separate, especially if the female is not yet ripe for spawning. The breeding tank should not be placed under direct sunlight, as the eggs do not tolerate solar radiation. The fry like to remain among surface plants, from which they may be ladled off with a spoon and transferred to a nursery tank. From the first day on they are able to eat small live foods and grow quickly but unevenly, so that periodically they have to be graded as to size. If they are well fed the color change of the sexes begins within 4-5 weeks.

— **grahami** (Boulenger): Graham's Panchax.

A very pretty, but rarely imported species from South Nigeria. Length up to 2⅜″. Brownish base with rows of red dots and faded oblique cross stripes. The fins are greenish to bluish. The female is simpler in color. Otherwise as per description of the genus.

— **longiventralis** (Boulenger): The Red-Spotted Panchax.
Very similar to the previous species, coming from South Nigeria and Cameroon. The male shows especially long ventral fins.

— **macrostigma** (Boulenger): The Green or Big-Dotted Panchax.
SHAPE: As per description of the genus. D 8-9, A 15-16. Length around $2\frac{3}{8}''$, the female remaining a little smaller.
COLOR: Luminous blue-green base with wine-red dots, which often fuse together. Fins yellow-green with wine-red dots and dashes. The female is simpler in color.
RANGE: The region of the Congo mouth.
CARE AND BREEDING: As per description of the genus. The species likes soft, old water, a dark bottom, and hiding places. It needs no excessive warmth, 68-72° F being sufficient, for breeding a little more.

Epiplatys macrostigma

— **marnoi** (Steindachner).
SHAPE: As per description of the genus; one of the smaller species. Length probably about $1\frac{3}{8}''$-2″. D 8, A 14 (?). The caudal fin of both sexes is rounded.
COLOR: Olive drab base with a dark-brown horizontal band composed of spots, and numerous red dots on the sides of the body and the opercles. Fins violet to bluish, with red rims. The male is bigger and more intensely colored.
RANGE: The Upper and the Central Nile.
CARE AND BREEDING: Not yet known.

— **ornatus** Ahl: The Emerald Panchax.
SHAPE: As per description of the genus. Very similar to *E. macrostigma.* D 9, A 16. Length up to $2\frac{3}{8}''$.
COLOR: On a gleaming greenish base each scale with a red dot at the base and a luminous light-green rim. The female is simpler in colors and has rounded fins.
RANGE: Tropical West Africa, probably Cameroon.
CARE AND BREEDING: As per description of genus. Temperature 72-77° F, temporarily also a little lower, for breeding 77-81° F. The very small fry have to be fed carefully with auxiliary foods (mashed White Worms, egg yolk, etc.) during the first days after hatching. Only after one week do they begin to eat very small-sized live foods. Later they grow up very quickly, and become able to reproduce when only 7-8 months old. The species is not considered very fertile.

— **sexfasciatus** Gill: The Six-Banded Panchax.
SHAPE: As per description of the genus. D 10-12, A 15-17. Length up to $4\frac{3}{8}''$.
COLOR: Olive-green-golden gleaming base with dark-red rimmed scales. The lower lips and the gill covers are luminous blue green, and the lower half of the body is decorated with six slightly-slanting cross bands. The female is simpler in color, its cross bands are light on a darker base, the fins rounded.
RANGE: Coastal waters in tropical West Africa, from Liberia to the mouth of the Congo.
CARE AND BREEDING: As per description of the genus. The species is especially fond of sunlight.

Epiplatys sexfasciatus

Temperatures 72-75° F, for breeding 75-79° F.

— **sheljuzhkoi** Poll: The Spotted Epiplatys.

SHAPE: As per description of the genus. A relatively compact-looking species. Length 2⅜″-2¾″. D 11, A 16.

COLOR: Rows of red-brown dots on brownish to greenish base, the back brown-red. Fins greenish with reddish dots. According to MEDER aquarium-bred specimens are said to differ considerably from imported ones. The female shows a few dark cross bands on the rear half of the body. D and A. of the male are pointed.

RANGE: Tropical West Africa (the Ivory Coast), in ditches, ponds, etc.

CARE AND BREEDING: Surface fish, which likes to jump after insects, but eats other robust live foods too, for instance, tubifex, mosquito larvae, etc. Very voracious. Kept alone or in communities of their own species, the fish like to swim in the middle reaches of the water. 72-75° F, for breeding up to 77° F. According to HEGER it is advisable to keep the pairs separated until the female shows pronounced ripeness for spawning. Each male may be mated to two females. The glass-clear spawn is released among fine-

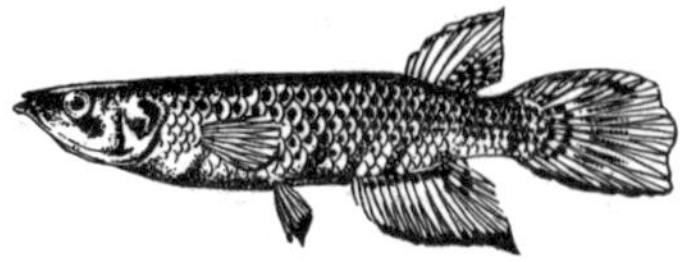

Epiplatys sheljuzhkoi

feathered plants or near the bottom. Development takes 8-9 days. The fry hide near the surface, the parents hardly ever preying on them. It is advisable to remove the breeders. Feed them *Cyclops* nauplii. The young are quick-growing.

episcopi: The bishop's.
— *Brachyrhaphis.*

epithelium: Connected body tissue which covers the surface of the organs, respectively lines the cavities of the inside of the body. E. may consist of one or more layers. In its multiple-layered form it is called SKIN.

eques: From Latin 'equus'—horse; probably horse-faced.
— *Nannobrycon.*

Equisetaceae: Shave Grasses.
Family belonging to the sub-order of the Ferns or *Pteridophyta.* Perennial land or swamp plants with long, very ramified rhizomes, growing roots at all knots and creeping in the bottom. The leaves are stunted, their assimilatory functions being performed by stems and branches. The small, scallop-shaped leaves grow in verticils around every knot, and are telescoped with the internodes.

Only one genus of water-dwelling species, which grow amphibiously in swamps or more or less deep water. They are unfit for the aquarium but very pleasing if cultivated in small groups in open air pools.

Eriocheir sinensis (Milne-Edwards): The Woolly-Handed Crab.
Square crab belonging to the

family of the *Grapsidae*, a South East Asian group of short-tailed Crustaceans or *Brachyura*. It probably was brought into Europe decades ago (before 1912), coming from China, presumably in its larval stage, within the ballast of freighters. It is supposable that this happened repeatedly during longer periods of time, and in great numbers.

The body of *E. sinensis* grows up to $3\frac{1}{2}''$ in width and is nearly square; The pincers of the male are covered with a dense wooly fur. The crabs are olive-green with darker spots. Due to their strong migratory urge, they have become scattered over the fresh water regions of large parts of Europe where they have in part become severe pests.

The crabs spawn in brackish waters. From the numerous eggs hatch larvae which live as plankton and metamorphose into adult specimens after several changes of skin. Especially the females wander upriver and away from the coast in migrations that may take several years, overcoming all kinds of obstacles and reaching all kinds of waters. To reach Dresden (on the Elbe), coming from the coast, they migrate for 3-4 years. The crabs start their return trip after becoming full-grown, for which they remain especially in the middle of the rivers, mating after they reach the river mouths. From there the females swim still on in order to spawn in the sea. The Woolly-Handed Crab is omnivorous, eating vegetable matter, clams, snails, and rarely also young fishes. Their main damage is caused by their digging of holes in dams and embankments, as well as by destroying nets and fishing traps. In case of massed attack the destruction may be considerable. Measures to fight them have been taken in several ways, but only with partial success.

Eriocheir sinensis, plankton form at left

Keep them in spacious tanks, at low water heights, with a corner of firm land built of rocks which should simultaneously offer possibilities for hiding, Since the crabs are nimble and strong climbers, the tank should be well covered and the lid weighted down. Feed them with vegetable matter (aquatic plants, lettuce, etc.), earthworms, snails, insect larvae, etc.

Erythrinus: Small reddish (fish). South American genus of Characins belonging to the family of the *Characidae*, of very elongated, cylindrical shape, with broad back and flattened head. As a rule the large mouth is tilted upwards, and the swimming bladder is developed into an accessory respiratory organ.

— **erythrinus** (Bloch and Schneider).

SHAPE: As per description of the genus; D 10-12, A 9-12; the scales relatively large. Length up to 8″.

COLOR: Greenish base with very pretty dark spots, stripes, and bands, and a gleaming spot on the opercles. The dorsal fin of the male is considerably bigger, its ventrals are of remarkable length.

RANGE: All over Eastern South America, from Guiana in the north to Rio de Janeiro in the south.

CARE AND BREEDING: This predatory species, which likes to remain hidden among plants near the bottom, needs spacious tanks with hiding places. Towards the evening it becomes livelier and goes hunting for prey, which consists of robust live foods, such as aquatic insects, and especially small fishes. The species is peaceful toward fishes of its own size, however. Keeping it is rather difficult, due to its great voracity, which can hardly ever be satisfied. Up to a length of 4″, growth is rather quick, slowing up after this size. Breeding in the aquarium has not yet succeeded.

erythrogaster: Red-bellied.
— *Chrosomus.*

erythrophthalmus: Red-eyed.
— *Scardinius.*

erythrozonus: Red-striped.
— *Hemigrammus.*

erythrurus: Red-tailed.
— *Hyphessobrycon.*
— *Labeo.*

Esocidae: Pikes.

Family belonging to the order of the Pikelike Fishes of *Haplomi*, with quite original structural characteristics. The swimming bladder has an open connection with the oesophagus. Bony rays in the fins are sparsely developed or absent, the fins insert far to the rear. Genera, among others: *Esox*. Distributed over the fresh waters of the Northern Hemisphere.

Esomus: With long body.

Genus of South Asian fishes pertaining to the family of the Carplike fishes of CYPRINIDAE (see this). The body is elongated, strongly compressed laterally, the dorsal contour nearly straight. The mouth is small, its opening tilted obliquely upwards. The dorsal fin inserts far towards the rear, ventrals and pectorals are highly developed, the latter extended in the shape of wings. One pair of short, and one of long barbels. The genus is distributed over India and Indo-China with 15 known species.

All of them are lively school fishes, which generally live near the surface. The tanks for them should be as long as possible, with plenty of space for swimming and exercising, and dense planting on the sides. The schools are rather loosely formed, one or the other fish separating occasionally from them and remaining among the plants in a typical position, flipping its fins. The males especially like to defend a certain individual range. All species like sunlight, but also shadows into which they may withdraw occasionally. The fishes are omnivores, and may be quite voracious and like varied fare. Surface food is preferred. For breeding, which is similar to that of all *Cyprinidae*, preferably use a freshly set-up tank with new water and fine-feathered plants in bundles, also on the bottom and in corners. If the weather is sunny, put in the male in the morning, the spawn-ripe female the next day, in the evening. The act of spawning generally takes place very early, under the morning sun, after lively chasing, the male circling the female with nimble swimming motions and erected barbels. The 30-50 glass-clear, small eggs of each spawning, totalling about 700 for one period from a robust female—are spawned within 60-90 minutes. The parents should be removed after spawning, as especially the females prey strongly on the eggs. Rearing the fry, which generally keep close to the surface, is easy. The water height should not be above 8″. The alevins are very quick-growing. Some specimens may be able to reproduce after only 12-15 weeks.

— **danricus** (Hamilton-Buchanan): The Flying Barb.

SHAPE: As per description of the genus. D 8, A 8. Length, in its home waters up to $5\frac{1}{2}$″, in the aquarium up to $3\frac{1}{8}$″.

COLOR: Brownish, with a faded red-brown horizontal band, which disappears with progressing age and is rimmed on the upper side with a lighter color. A shiny silver and violet gleam under incident light.

Esomus danricus

The male is smaller and more slender.

RANGE: In small, standing or flowing waters of all kinds, also in rice paddies, of India, Ceylon, and possibly also Malaya. As a rule the fish appear in small schools.

CARE AND BREEDING: As per description of the genus, vivacious, long-lived, and hardy. Temperature 72-75° F, for breeding 75-79° F, lowest 64° F.

— **lineatus** Ahl: The Striped Flying Barb.

Body shape like that of the preceding species. Length up to 3⅛″, the male a little smaller and slimmer. Gray-greenish base with blackish horizontal stripe, lighter-edged above.

ORIGIN: Indo-China, the mouth of the Ganges. A less-known species which hardly differs from *E. danricus*.

Esomus malayensis

— **malayensis** (Mandée): The Malayan Flying Barb.

SHAPE: As per description of the genus. Length: in its home country over 4″, in the aquarium up to 3⅛″.

COLOR: Shiny silver with deep-black, gold-rimmed spot on the tail root. The male more slender and smaller.

RANGE: Indo-China, Malaya, in flowing and standing waters, also in rice paddies.

CARE AND BREEDING: As per description of the genus. Temperatures 68-77° F, for breeding 77-82° F.

Esox: Genus belonging to the family of the Pikes or *Esocidae*. The snout juts far out, in the shape of a duck's bill. On the palate and the plow-share bone several rows of strong comb-teeth, one row each on the lower and the intermediate jaw. Some of these teeth are developed into long fangs. Undivided, long swimming bladder. Scales small, firmly inserted, also on cheeks and tail fin. Jaws and gill system very dilatable. Only a few species.

— **lucius** Linné: The Pike.

SHAPE: Robust, elongated, very muscular build, torpedo-shaped. Lateral line interrupted. D 20-23, A 16-18, scales 110-130. Length up to 52″.

COLOR: The color is very variable, according to location. Greenish to bronze, with darker greenish-brown spots, bands, etc.

RANGE: Europe, Northern Asia, North America, only in fresh water, especially in the reed stands of the shores.

CARE AND BREEDING: A predator which remains skulking among plants. Nourishment consists exclusively of fishes, which are captured in quick and sudden lunges. Only during this do the fish develop greater speeds, as otherwise the Pike is no enduring swimmer. The spawning period falls into Feb-

Esox lucius

ruary/April. The eggs are spawned on flooded meadows, which the Pikes visit in local migrations, partly when they are still covered with ice. At a length of about 12″ the fish become sexually mature. They are not breedable in the aquarium. However, it is very interesting to hatch Pike spawn in your pools.

Pikes need spacious pools, in which they may grow up without having to consider their size. Offer them hiding places among roots, plants, and reeds, as well as clear water, rich in oxygen, and, if possible no more than 64° F. Very small Pikes will be satisfied with insect larvae and earthworms, bigger ones have to have fishes.

ethology: Science of behavior. The part of animal psychology which studies the causes and processes of animal behavior. Of importance in aquaristics, since ethology gives the aquarist better information on the behavior of fishes, and on the other hand because he himself may supply valuable data to science through his observations.

Etroplus: With armed belly. The only Indian genus belonging to the family of the *Cichlidae*. Few species, of which so far only two have been imported. According to HOEDEMAN, the members of the genus represent relicts of the transitional forms from which the Cichlids have developed. Consequently they are mainly inhabitants of coastal zones, brackish waters, and river mouths, despite the fact that some species are found in fresh water. The body is high, strongly compressed laterally, the forehead contour rising steeply, dorsal and anal fins are long and rather low. Cichlids which do not root much, and do not disturb plants even during their spawning period, unless they need vegetable food. Rather peaceful towards fishes of their own size, even those of their own species, but in this there are individual differences.

CARE AND BREEDING: See CICHLIDAE.

— **maculatus** (Bloch): The Orange Chromide.

SHAPE: As per description of the genus; the body height increases with age. The large and active eyes are slightly oval. D XVII-XX/8-10, A XII-XV/8-10. The caudal fin is fan-shaped, slightly bent inward on the free edge. The mouth opening protrudes slightly in the shape of a snout. Length up to $3\frac{1}{8}$″.

COLOR: Shiny light-yellow with orange-colored belly and throat, and cloudy, more or less distinct, blue-black spots on the lower half of the body. A big blue-black spot on the center of the body, which is light-edged, generally remains invisible. A red dot on the base of each scale. The fins are yellowish, the anal with a black seam, the ventrals deep black. SD are occasionally quite insignificant. In general the female remains a little smaller, and sometimes it is a little paler in color.

RANGE: In fresh and brackish water along the coast of India, 60 miles and more inland, also on Ceylon.

CARE AND BREEDING: As per des-

Etroplus maculatus

cription of the genus. The species is a little sensitive to changes of water, especially young specimens sometimes which die without apparent reason. It seems that occasional changes in the percentage of salt of their water increase their well-being. In case of lack of food—sometimes also in other cases—the fish eat tender shoots of plants, giving special preference to the Indian Water Star (*Hygrophila*), while Water Sprite (*Ceratopteris*) seems to be avoided. Use harder plants, for instance, *Cryptocoryne* to stock your tanks. The species needs warmth: 72-75° F, for breeding 77-86° F, lowest 68° F.

Etroplus suratensis

— suratensis (Bloch): The Striped Chromide.

SHAPE: Body high, head relatively small, D XVIII-XIX/14-15, A XII-XIII/11-12. Length, in its home country up to 16″.

COLOR: Strongly changing in color with age, younger specimens with dark cross bands, older ones with more or less marked luminous spots. Basic color greenish to purple-red.

RANGE: In brackish and salt water along the coast of India and Ceylon. A purely salt and brackish water fish, which does not feel well in fresh water.

CARE AND BREEDING: Not yet bred. Especially adapted for larger marine aquaria.

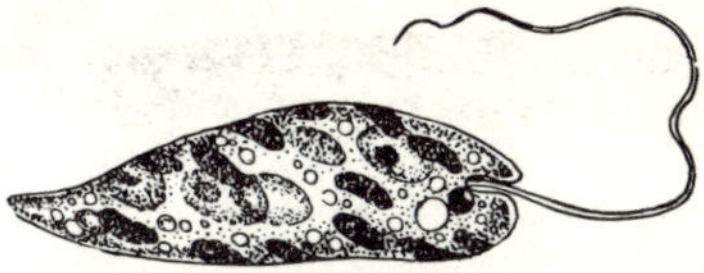

Euglena

Euglena: Genus belonging to the tribe of the *Flagellata* order *Euglenoidea*. The best-known species is *E. viridis*. It carries a simple flagellum, which is extended out in front. The body is spindle-shaped, on the middle a star-shaped, green chromatophore, at the base of the flagellum a red 'eye' spot. The peculiar, spiralling manner of swimming by turning around its own axis is remarkable. They are able to turn shallow puddles of water green if they inhabit them in great numbers (green water). The species appears mainly in stagnant waters. Another species, *E. sanguinea*, is colored a vivid red and is the cause of the so-called 'lakes of blood'.

Europe: A continent which geographically is nearly united with Asia, but which takes a separate position with regard to colonization and historical development. Being the Western peninsula of Asia (Eurasia), it is related to that continent in geological formations, climate, and world of plants, as far as the Asian temperate and Northern regions are concerned. The continent is characterized by its relatively small size (about 4 million square miles), by its strong articulation into peninsulae and islands, and by its strong penetrability through seas and parts of seas. Numerous high and median mountain systems.

Beginning in Northern Germany there are deep plains which connect with the Siberian Taigo through the Russian plateau. Numerous navigable rivers, which often are connected by canals, and of which the Volga is the longest with 2210 miles. Through the proximity of the sea and the influence of the Gulf Stream, the climate is relatively mild, especially in Western and Central Europe. Southern Europe shows hot, partly dry summers (Mediterranean climate). Eastern Europe has strong contrasts between warm, dry summers and cold snowy winters. In the extreme north prevails a polar climate, and in the region of the lower Volga desert or steppe climate. The world of fishes of Eastern and Northern Europe is related in many aspects to that of Central Europe, which in part also includes that of Western and Southern Europe. Notwithstanding this, the fish waters of Eastern Europe are characterized by the fact that they have remained more natural and primitive, and that consequently they harbor a fish fauna which in number of species and individuals by far surpasses that of Central Europe.

The landscape in Central Europe has been changed considerably by human settling, which is especially dense in that part, and through restless agricultural and industrial exploitations this landscape, influenced and re-shaped by man, includes also the inland waters. These are characterized by flowing waters which to a large extent have been regulated and tamed by dams, locks, and gradings, and by many artificially built, or at least humanly influenced, standing waters. Add to this the soiling of the waters by influxes of industrial wastes, which still more diminish the fish fauna gradually from year to year.

Notwithstanding this we can still today classify the waters according to the main fish species which live in them.

euryhaline fishes: Fishes which are independent of the salt content of waters, impervious to changes, for instance, the Sticklebacks.

eurythermic fishes: Fishes which tolerate great fluctuations of temperature without suffering harm.

Eutropiellus: Diminutive of *Eutropius*.

African genus belonging to the family of the Glass Catfishes or *Schilbeidae*, characterized by the very small dorsal fin and the absence of frontal barbels on the lower jaw. The anal fin is very long. The body is very frail and glassily transparent. Catfishes that live gregariously, it being a vital need for them to be connected with the school. They are daylight fishes which swim against currents in moderately flowing waters. Extremely skilled swimmers.

— debauwi debauwi Boulenger.

SHAPE: Elongated, very delicate and sinuous body. D 5, A 37-40 (?). The adipose fin is very small. The dorsal is immediately to the rear of the pectorals. No scales.

COLOR: Brownish to yellowish base with a dark horizontal band below the back and another one on the middle of the body. The subspecies *E. d. vittatus* shows a more silvery basic color on which the horizontal bands stand out more clearly.

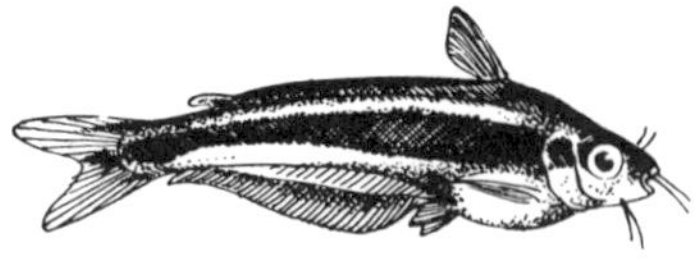

Eutropiellus debauwi debauwi

RANGE: *E. d. debauwi*, the Congo region; *E. d. vittatus*, Cameroon.

CARE AND BREEDING: This Catfish can only be kept in communities of four or more specimens of its own kind. Kept isolated it dies quickly. No special demands as to composition of water. 64-77° F. Nourishment consists of small live foods, which are caught while free-swimming. So far little is known about reproduction. According to American reports the eggs are scattered among plants.

Eutropius: The well-fed one.

African genus of Catfishes pertaining to the family of the *Siluridae.*

— niloticus (Rueppell).

SHAPE: The front part quite high, compressed laterally, and covered with a mucous skin. Lateral line distinctly visible. D I/5-6, inserting far to the front, A IV-V/49-64. Mouth slightly subterminal, with four pairs of whisker threads, which are very short. Length up to 16″.

COLOR: Uniformly greenish to brownish. SD unknown.

RANGE: The river system of the Nile, furthermore in West African rivers from the Senegal to the Ogowe, in fresh water only.

CARE AND BREEDING: A twilight and nocturnal fish, which likes dark locations. Only smaller specimens are fit for the indoor aquarium, otherwise for the exhibition aquarium. Likes warmth, 79-86° F, lowest 72° F. Eats only live foods, but is not discriminating. Not yet bred.

everetti: After the scientist-collector Everett.

— *Barbus.*

evergladei: After the swampy jungles of Florida, the Everglades.

— *Elassoma.*

evolution of fishes: The fishes of today are only a fraction of the forms which have inhabited our planet in the course of its history. They alone have developed from several millions of years ago until today, while many other forms of life have died out.

Scientific taxonomy of the fishes

Ancient fishes.

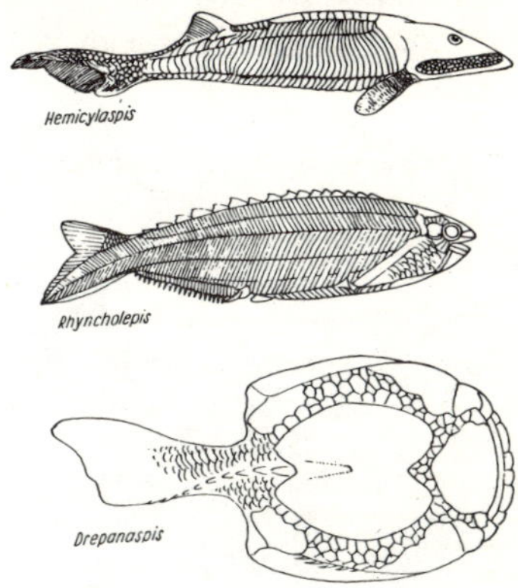

Above: **Hemicylapsis** - center: **Rhyncholepis** - below: **Drepanaspis.**

now living is only possible to comprehend in its entirety with a knowledge of evolutionary development, because the present-day relationships are based on it. Most of our knowledge of past evolutionary forms are based on fossil deposits. The first impressions and remains of fishes are found in the Middle and Upper Silurian Age Previous deposit distributions show no fossil remains, possibly because the more primitive forms had too few solid body parts. The first fishes may have developed from forms which were closely related to the Tunicates (*Tunicata*) and the Lancetfishes (*Acrania*).

The earliest fish fossils already show such a strong specialization that previous periods of development can be assured. In the Silurian Age we find the representatives of the Jawless Fishes (*Agnathi*). These are the fish-like, primitive vertebrates whose jaws were set in muscular sacs, which led to their being referred to as Sac-Jawed Fishes (*Marsipobranchi*). They possessed neither jaw-bones nor gills, and their direct descendants might be today's Round-Mouthed Fishes (*Cyclostomata*). Those which re-

Fish evolution.

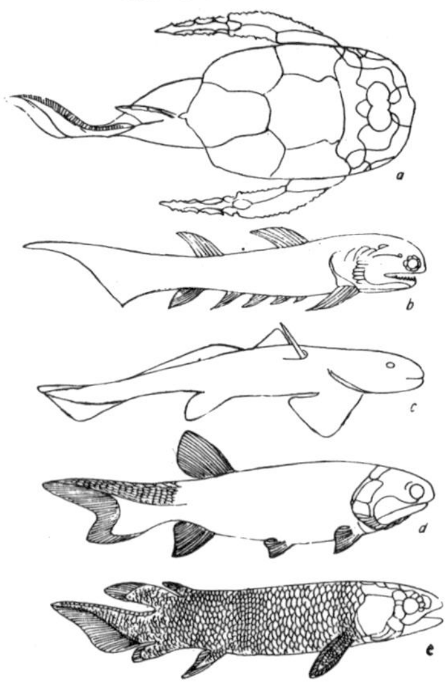

evolution. a. **Bothriolepis**, an ancient fish. b. **Climatius**, a cartilaginous fish which preceded the Sharks. c. **Helodus**, a more advanced form from a later time. d. **Phanerosteon**, ancestor of the Sturgeons and other bony fishes. e. Tassel-Fin, ancestor of today's Lungfishes.

mained to us were covered with bony plates, of which some were very well preserved. This does not mean that there were not others where there was not as much armor or none at all, of which we would have no fossils.

Still more heavily armored kinds are found in the Devonian and Carboniferous Ages: the Armored Fishes or *Placodermata*. These already belong to the true fishes, because here we find jawbones; probably they also possessed paired limbs. From these it is possible that the present-day Sharks (*Selachii*) evolved. These fishes were of varying sizes, and giant forms are also known. The length of time which they already had been developing is evidenced by the multitude of forms and widely varied manners of living. Only very few remains of these ancient Sharks remain to us. Mostly these consist of teeth, some of which have a length of 6 inches. These must have been very large creatures.

The Cartilaginous Fishes of today can be traced to the middle of the Triassic Age. They may have occurred already in the Carboniferous and the Permian Ages, and the later found fossils differ scarcely at all from the forms living today.

The Bony Fishes developed very early, and the branching off to the later Cartilaginous Fishes is scarcely distinguishable. Probably both were derived from common ancestors. The first slight traces of Bony Fishes are found in the Devonian Age. If we separate the Bony Fishes according to their finnage into the Ancient Fins (*Paleopterygii*), the Tassel Fins (*Crossopterygii*) and the New Fins (*Neopterygii*), then we have only a small group of the Ancient Fins left, although they were very numerous in the middle ages of the world's development. Most of them have become extinct. These included members of families which could be considered the original forms of the Bony Fishes. They were predatory by nature, spindle-shaped and had highly developed teeth. At the beginning of the Triassic Age we find the ancestors of the present-day Sturgeon-like Fishes (*Acipenseridae*). It is remarkable that these enamel-scaled fishes possessed a bony skeleton at that time. Descendants of the Ancient Fins are found today in Africa with the *Polypteridae*.

The Tassel-Finned Fishes, which are perhaps covered by the *Choanichthyes*, were formerly a widely distributed group of fishes. Today there are only a few forms. This group is further important because it has probably given rise to the

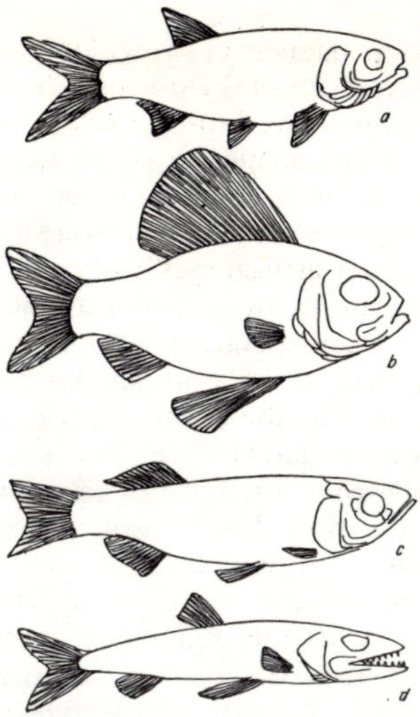

Fish evolution. a. **Anaethalion,** ancestor of the Herrings. b. **Ctenothrissa,** one of the first bony fishes. c. **Thaumaturus,** a Salmon-like fish of the Jurassic Age. d. **Euryphelis,** a predatory Pike-like fish from the end of the Jurassic Age.

terrestrial vertebrates. The structure of the skull and the paired fins gives indications of certain characteristics of the primitive lizards. One order of the Tassel-Fins has recently achieved fame when the *Latimeria*, which had been considered extinct and which was reconstructed from fossils, was brought up alive from the ocean depths a few years ago. It was found that scientists, working with only a few fossils, had given an accurate representation of this species.

Another order of the Tassel-Fins, the Lungfishes or *Dipneusti*, were also widely distributed in former times, while today there are only a few representatives.

The New Fins or *Neopterygii* alone have developed fully until the present time and encompass the main part of all living fishes with about 20,000 known species. Their existence can be traced from the Permian Age. The oldest, mostly extinct forms are still found today in the Bowfin (*Amia*) and the Alligator Gars (*Lepisosteus*).

From the Permian Age on more and more of our modern forms came into being. In the Jurassic Age there were found Herring-like Fishes, which became always more widespread in the chalk deposits. From these there developed the Eels (*Apodes*) and besides the Bony Fishes, of which there are numerous orders today, the most recent being the Perch-like Fishes or *Perciformes*.

evolution, theory of: Today a generally accepted bit of knowledge which was once a revolutionary controversy, it teaches that all forms of life evolved from simple prototypes by gradual changes over great periods of time. This theory was first propounded by the Frenchman Jean Lamarck, but was actually introduced by the Englishman Charles Darwin. Jean Lamarck gave the reasons for evolutionary changes rather primitively as making it possible to conform with ecological changes (that the use or disuse of an organ causes development or atrophy of that organ in an individual). Darwin pointed out that natural selection of the fittest was the underlying cause in evolutionary changes, and that individuals all varied somewhat. In this way, for example, we might find certain individuals among surface-feeding fish where the mouth opening is directed more upwards than the others. Their progeny might find that their mouths gave them an advantage over their fellows, and they and their progeny would survive the others, being better equipped to get their nourishment.

These hereditary changes (mutations) although only slight, could eventually lead to separate genera. The conditions which would lead to eventually forming a new genus are therefore more or less haphazard. Newer findings could lead to a greater understanding at this point, however. It is unlikely that the purely haphazard mutations alone sufficed to make the complicated changes in form and environmental adaptations in the evolution of flora and fauna. Many cannot be explained by Darwin's theory alone. For example, the change from the genus *Astyanax* to the Blind Cave Fish *Anoptichthys* can be seen in a fixed degenerative process in the eyes from the newly hatched fry to the adult fish, so we cannot call this a 'mutation,' but a process brought about by extreme conditions, which has become hereditary. There must therefore be other influences besides natural selection which could lead to the complicated changes in form and function. In particular there is the innate tendency to develop progressively, and for the separate genera to take their own directions according to their development. The adaptation to similar conditions can therefore be very different. Were this not so, it would not be possible to explain the species, and all would end with a few highly-developed forms. Development is therefore more than adaptation. Moreover an organism doubtless lives by the never-ending stream of energy given off by the absorbed intake, which upholds its balance and permits it to maintain itself in its surroundings. So it has been said for example that modifications which are brought on by a change in environment can take place in a reverse manner when the reason for these modifications cease. Over a number of generations, it would be possible by experiment to gradually provide a duplication of original conditions, and it would then be possible to span great periods of time and fix such modifications as existed then.

Even if Darwin's theories should be superseded by newer developments brought about by a general advance in scientific knowledge, we will always consider his teachings as paving the way.

excitement: A series of changes within the plasma which are triggered by an external stimulus or by hormones, and which become visible externally by a reaction which is characterized by increased vitality. For this a sensorial impression is transmitted to the central by the nerve system, and this on its part releases a certain reflex. In fishes the external signs may, for instance, be: changes of color, erection of fins and opercles, unrest, increased bellicosity, extrusion of the genital papilla, etc.

Exodon: Fish with teeth that slant outwards.

South American genus belonging to the family of the Characins or *Characidae,* with only one known species. An elongated, but robust-looking fish with a big mouth studded with strong teeth. An adipose fin is present.

— **paradoxus** Mueller and Troschel.

SHAPE: As per description of the genus; D 10-12, A 19-22; the scales are relatively big. Length up to 6″.

COLOR: Two remarkable, big, dark spots on the body sides on shiny silvery and slightly greenish to gleaming base. The male has reddish-hued fins. One of the most beautiful Characins.

RANGE: In partly shadowed waters of Guiana.

CARE AND BREEDING: This predatory and not very peaceful species is rarely found in aquaria, due to the fact that it is very hard to catch in open water.

It needs spacious, spotwise densely-planted tanks with hiding

Exodon paradoxus

places and occasional sunlight. Temperature should amount to about 77° F, but it seems that the fish is not sensitive to temporary cooling. It demands vegetable fare besides robust live foods which latter include big larvae of aquatic insects and small fishes. Reproduction seems to take place in the manner of most Characins. It is reported that the relatively large eggs are released in small numbers.

exoleta: Grown out (from the water ?).
— *Utricularia.*

exophthalmy: Pop-eyes of fishes, see EYE DISEASES.

extremities: Body appendages, limbs. Parts added to the animal body, which either serve for locomotion, or else specialize for other functions, for instance, as antennae, jaws, pincers, etc.

eye diseases: Diseases of the eyes are quite frequent on aquarium fishes. They either show through a protrusion of the whole ocular globe (*Exophthalmia*), or by a clouding of the lens, which may be unilateral or bilateral, to complete blindness.

Pop-eye, or exophthalmus

EXOPHTHALMY may result from the accumulation of feces and urine in the water. Certain species of fishes, for instance some Cichlids, are sensitive to too old water, and show strongly protruding eyes as a result. But this may also be a result of dropsy, fish tuberculosis or *Ichthyosporidium* (*Ichthyophonus*), or it may be caused by parasitic worms and their larvae, or even by the accumulation of gas bubbles in the eye socket.

CLOUDING and DESTRUCTION of the eyes either of the lens, or of the whole ocular surface, may have different causes. Chemicals in the water, poisonings, mechanically caused wounds, may originate this symptom. The Archer Fish, *Toxotes jaculatrix*, with the slightest cause shows a clouding of the vitreous body which may become quite dangerous. Worm cataract, caused by parasitic worms or their larvae, may lead to the total destruction of the eye.

At present most eye diseases are still incurable, but many fishes are able to exist for longer periods blinded or half-blinded in the aquarium if the primary illness does not prove to be lethal.

MECHANICAL LESIONS of the eyes may lead to a whitish clouding of the cornea, even after healing. Bite wounds with complete destruction of the eye ball may result in the death of the injured specimens. Especially Cichlids and Anabantids are inclined to hurt each other's eyes in fights. A wounded cornea is prone to attacks by *Saprolegnia* (fungus), which often forms a bushy covering. These fungi adhere very firmly to the surface. They may subsequently cause considerable harm to the eye, or destroy it, even if the lesion in itself was not very severe.

Try to destroy the Saprolegnia by painting the infected eye with a 2% solution of silver nitrate! This measure should be repeated several times. After each time put the fish immediately into a 1% solution of kitchen salt, in order to neutralize the action of the silver nitrate before it attacks the eye itself.

Eye-spot Rasbora, the: see RASBORA DORSIOCELLATA.

eyes of fishes: see SENSORY ORGANS.

facetum: Pretty, handsome.
— *Cichlasoma.*

Fahak, the—*Tetraodon fahaka.*

fahaka: After the Egyptian name.
— *Tetraodon fahaka.*

falcatus: sickle-shaped.
— *Brycon.*

False Swordtail, the: see PSEUDOXIPHOPHORUS BIMACULATUS.

Fanwort: see CABOMBA CAROLINIANA.

fasciata: Striped, banded.
— *Colisa.*
— *Pristolepis.*

fasciatum: Striped, banded.
— *Characidium.*

fasciatus: Striped, banded.
— *Anostomus.*
— *Astyanax.*
— *Barbus.*
— *Hemichromis.*
— *Leporinus.*

fasciolatum: Narrow-banded.
— *Ctenopoma.*

fasciolatus: Narrow-banded.
— *Barbus.*
— *Epiplatys.*

Fat-leaf: see BACOPA.

fauna: The world of animals.

fauna falsification: Falsification of the animal world in a particular area by the introduction of species which were not previously found there. Because of the damaging influences which are often the result of such actions, fauna falsification is usually forbidden by law.

feather moss: see AMBLYSTEGIUM.

Featherfin, the: see HEMIGRAMMUS UNILINEATUS.

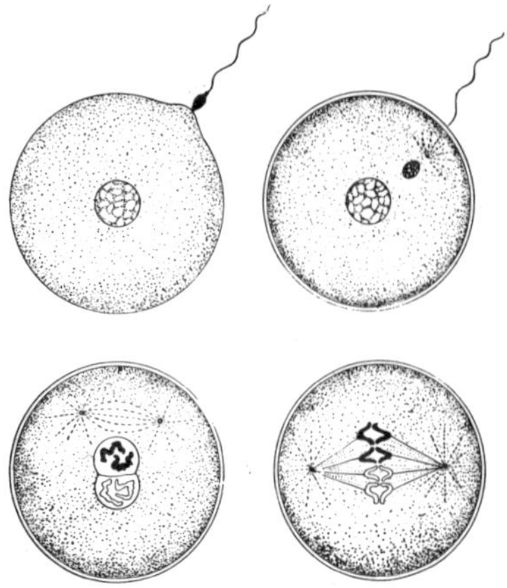

Fecundation (after Kuhn) — Top, left: Sperm comes in contact with the egg, forming a mound. Top, right: Head and intermediate body of the sperm force themselves in. Bottom, left: The male and female protonucleus have each developed two chromosomes. Bottom, right: First phase of the divisional development has begun.

fecundation: The union of two sexually differentiated cells or gametes and of their nuclei into a new organism, which in multicellular organisms parts from a unicellular stage, the zygote, serving as a starting point of development. As a rule fecundation serves the purpose of combining the hereditary characteristics of two individuals, and that of starting the development of the female egg cells. From this develops a new individual, which, despite its individual differences, corresponds to the general plan of the species, if there is no question of crossbreeding different species. It is only a condition for sexual reproduction, not for reproduction in all cases.

In multicellular organisms the gametes are always of different shape. The resting egg is searched out by the motile sperm cells. After insemination only the head and the so-called intermediate part of the sperm cell penetrate the egg cell, while the tail, which serves only the purpose of locomotion, is discarded. After penetration the head swells up into a nucleus with a nuclear structure, which fuses with the female nucleus in order to form a zygotic nucleus. This is the sign that fertilization has been completed.

The process of fecundation is triggered by the complex co-operation of special fecundating substances, the gamones. Thus in fish for instance, both the egg cells and the sperm cells secrete several active substances, which diffuse quickly in water, and which have to fulfill very differing functions. In part they attract the sperm and aid their motility, extending their capability of fecundating, in part, depending on the phase of the fecundation, they have a paralyzing or lethal effect on them. The aim of sexual differentiation and therefore of fecundation, is possibly to be sought in the development of polar tensions in the individual, out of which—at least in part—comes the impulse for further development.

In animals, as a rule, fecundation takes place during mating.

fenestralis: With window-like design.
— *Aponogeton.*

fenestratum: With window design, fenestrated.
— *Cichlasoma.*

ferment: Active substance which aids metabolism, but without being decomposed itself. A catalyst.

ferns: see PTERIDOPHYTA.

festivum: Festive, pretty.
— *Cichlasoma.*

Fighting Fish: see BETTA.

filamentosum: filamented, with filament-like appendages.
— *Aphyosemion.*

filiculoides: Fern-like.
— *Azolla.*

filiformis: Filiform, thread-shaped.
— *Potamogeton.*
— *Sagittaria.*

filigera: Bearing threads; refers to the extended rays of the anal fin.
— *Prionobrama.*

filters, filtration: A valuable aid in keeping aquaria in a clean state, and to introduce substances into it the presence of which are desirable for aquaristic reasons. A number of filters have been developed during the last years, all of which work aided by aeration, and which therefore have to be connected to the air system. Since generally the consumption of air is rather high, makeshift aerators (drip aerators, automobile inner tubes, pressure tanks) are inadequate.

Effective filtration can keep water crystal clear and odorless. Depending on the method you use, you may achieve the following:

1. Ridding the water of coarse, floating, undissolved dirt particles, eventually also of micro-organisms (unicellulars, bacteria, etc.);

2. Cleaning the water as above, plus ridding it of dissolved organic waste products or foreign matter.

Simple *mechanical filtration* as needed under 1 is easily attained by making the water pass through glass wool, gravel, and sand.

The simplest form of such a filter is a glass bell, open on the underside and filled with nylon wool, placed on the bottom. A current of

Diagram of an outside filter

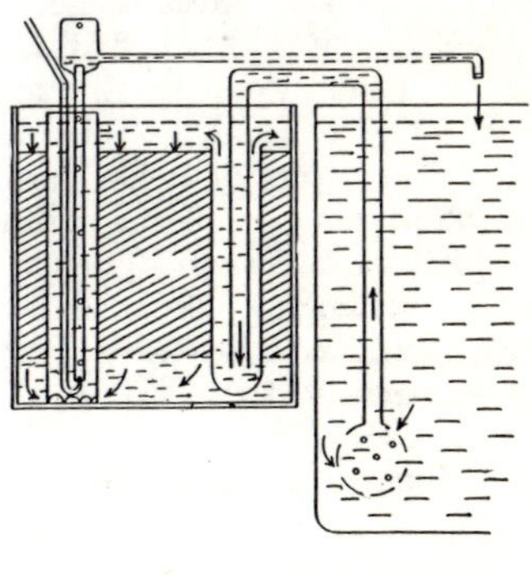

water is swept upwards by air bubbles through a riser tube stuck on the upper end of the bell and connected to an air pump. The draft created by this draws particles of mulm into the bell, where they are trapped by the wool, while the cleaned water is discharged at the upper end. It is advisable to set up such filters on a flat piece of glass, so that they may be withdrawn from the aquarium together with it when you want to clean them. After renewing the packing, the filter is again ready to work.

A second form of inside filter is the so-called *under-gravel filter*. For this you bury a similarly-built bell in the bottom soil, connecting it with the air duct too. The resulting wake draws the mulm particles into the bottom soil enriching it with nutritive substances. It is important that the filtering bell be placed within a layer of very coarse, permeable gravel, which must cover the whole bottom, with the finer-grained sand placed only on top of it. Such under-gravel filters are especially useful in tanks which are abundantly stocked with plants which draw their main nourishment from the soil (*Cryptocoryne*, *Echinodorus*, *Sagittaria*, etc.). Coarse dirt particles will hardly be completely removable by this kind of filtration. Both described types do NOT remove dissolved components and micro-organisms. A very effective mechanical filtration is attained if the water is made to pass through several layers of sand, gravel, and intermediate layers of nylon yarn. Such filters may be placed inside the aquarium as described, or outside it as hanging filters. Since their cleaning power may be very large—especially if the size of the filter is commensurate with the water contents of the aquarium—the withdrawal of part of the mulm particles may also act restrainingly on the growth of micro-organisms and plants. The combination of mechanical filtration and of absorption of water-dissolved waste substances, as demanded under point 2, goes still farther in the coal filter. This is done by placing a corresponding amount of activated coal (2 lbs. per 25 gallon of water) in the filter, and running the water through it after having it passed through a preliminary filter for mechanical purification. The best-known for this is the scientifically-approved Hydraffine-Aquarium-Coal, developed by KRAMER, which has recognized powers of absorption for the following: dissolved organic waste products of animal metabolism, certain gases for instance swamp gas (methane) and chlorine, as well as paints. How far other animal charcoal will serve the same purpose, where hydraffine coal is not available, has to be left to experience. The effectiveness of this activated carbon is based on the fact that in each of its particles there are innumerable very thin channels, which greatly enlarge the surface and considerably increase the force of attraction created by surface tension. According to FINK, the force of attraction is negligible for substances with small molecular weight, which include the substances that feed plants (chlorides, sulphides, nitrates, and nitrites), while organic waste products with greater molecular weight—like those resulting from metabolism or from the decay of organic matter—are attracted and absorbed to a high degree. Indeed, the urine of fishes, which is a growth-inhibiting poison, is also absorbed, but the development of nitrates, in which this substance plays a part, is so quick, that only part of the amount of urine released by the fishes can be removed. Therefore not even coal filtering can restrict the accumulation of nitrates, but at least this is considerably delayed.

Carbon filters may be installed both as inside or as outside filters. In both cases the principle is the same. The best results seem to come from outside filters, for which a small tank, filled with the necessary filter packing and supplied with a filtering tube, is hung outside the aquarium in a wire basket. An overflow pipe guarantees that the water level remains the same in aquarium and filter. From the top down, the packing consists of a layer of glass wool, perhaps some fine-grained gravel or sand, which is separated from the carbon by another layer of wool. Then follows a thick layer of filter carbon, which on its part is separated from the subsequent layer of coarse gravel by glass wool. The water which flows in from the aquarium is at first purified mechanically in the upper layer, being freed of dissolved soilings in the layer of coal, and collecting in the clear water chamber, from which it penetrates the riser tube and is conveyed back to the aquarium by the air pump. Inside filters may be simpler in construction.

It has to be stated, however, that the small filters which one frequently finds in pet shops are adequate only for small tanks. All filters must be watched, having to be cleaned occasionally. Simple gravel or sand filters are rinsed out. Exhausted filter carbon cannot be reactivated. As an average, calculate that the carbon (2 lbs. per 25 gallons of water stocked with plenty of fishes) may be used continuously for about 60 days. Since filtration, however, is only used in case of need and for a few hours or days at a time, the real life span of the carbon may be calculated as being much longer. Before putting in the coal, it should be well rinsed and boiled, in order to expel any air trapped inside it. Packing should be done by pressing down with a piece of wood each of the about $\frac{1}{2}''$ thick layers, in order to prevent the development of direct passageways.

It is a sure sign that the coal works flawlessly if methylene blue, dissolved in the water and sent through it, is absorbed, the water flowing out clean, which is best checked by placing a white china dish under it.

Depending on the dirt in your tank, you may eventually have to clean your primary filters more frequently. Badly cleaned filters represent a great danger to the aquarium, as they may release poisonous decay substances in great amounts. According to FRIESEN, filters are of little value as aerating devices, especially if they are full of accumulated dirt. The accumulations in filters consume much oxygen, and the water only finds a chance to absorb oxygen during the short course of the return, which makes the measurable results minute. Since the air bubbles which rise in filters always have to be large, their surface of contact with the water is only small.

In order to modify water, filters may also be filled with other packings, for instance split basalt gravel, which is said to supply trace elements that are beneficial to animals and plants, or with peat. Thanks to the suggestion of MEDER, it is especially the peat filter which lately enjoys great favor both for outside and for inside installations.

fin destruction: The manner in which the fins are carried usually represents an infallible sign of the health condition of fishes. Healthy fishes generally carry their fins spread, depending on the specific behavior of the species. In this case the fins should not show any milky rims, nor be stuck together. If the fishes begin to close their fins, especially the caudal, and if they start to move them in quick jerks, this shows that for some reason they are uncomfortable. Fin destruction may naturally also result from fights between the fishes, but these generally are of a more harmless nature, so that they heal more or less completely.

Also lesions of other origins generally heal quickly. Harm resulting from bad conditions of the water, either through excessive increases in the pH values, or through metal poisoning (caused for instance by the development of metal poisons in badly insulated tanks), are considerably more dangerous. But these too may heal again, if the destruction has not progressed too far and if the causes are removed. Such lesions may also progress into 'tail rot' which is caused by bacteria. Furthermore fin lesions may be signs of other diseases which also attack the fins, for instance *Ichthyophthirius*, Skin Discoloration, *Ichthyosporidium*, and Infectious Dropsy.

final host: That host of parasites which change hosts, on or in which these parasites reproduce.

Finlet Eels: see CALAMOICHTHYS.

Finlet Fishes: see POLYPTERIDAE.

Finlet Pikes: see POLYPTERUS.

fins: External organs of water-dwelling animals, which are used for locomotion, steering, and maintenance of equilibrium. The fins of fishes have a more or less well developed supporting skeleton. The unpaired fins rest on fin supports which in Bony Fishes are anchored deep within the body and are loosely in touch with the spiny extensions of the spinal column,

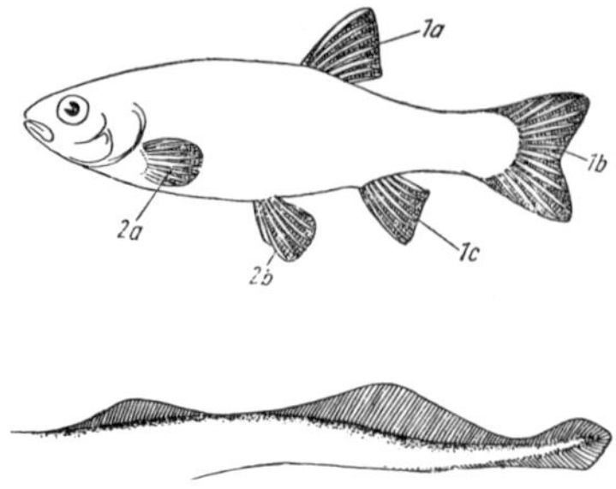

Fins. 1a. dorsal fin, 1b. caudal fin, 1c. anal fin, 2a. pectoral fins, 2b. ventral fins. Below, the simple finnage of a Lamprey.

while the paired ones sit on carriers of bone or of cartilage. The pectorals are connected with the shoulder belt, while the ventrals simply lean on a long bone which is deeply inserted within the muscles, but which may also be in touch with the shoulder belt if the fins are located on the breast or on the throat.

The unpaired fins are also called vertical fins. They are:

1. The dorsal fin (D), which may also consist of two separate parts (for instance on Perches), or even of three such parts (for instance on Codfishes). In this case the parts are represented as follows: D_1, D_2, D_3.
2. The anal fin (A).
3. The tail or caudal fin (C).

Some groups of fishes still add a skin flap located between dorsal and tail fin, the so-called fleshy dorsal or adipose fin, which may sometimes be without support, but in part also (for instance on many Catfishes) supported by a spine.

The paired fins are:

1. The ventral or belly fins (V).
2. The pectoral or breast fins (P).

The fins of Cartilage Fishes are supported by horny rays, those of Bony Fishes by hard or soft ones.

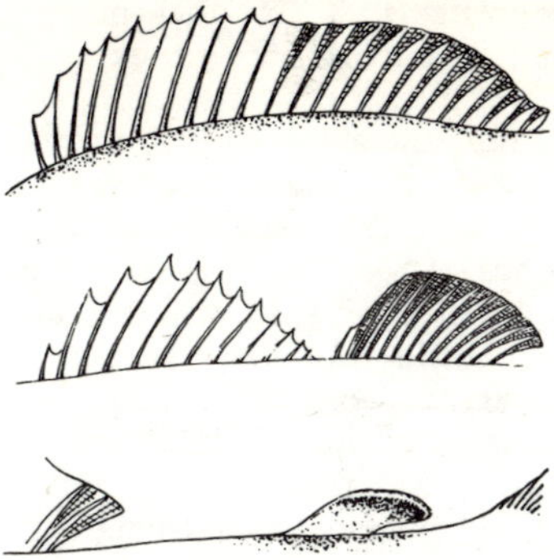

Top, dorsal fin of a Cichlid, with the spiny rays in front and the soft rays behind. Center, dorsal fins of a Perch, spiny rays in front and soft rays behind. Below, adipose fin.

The soft rays may be simple, but also articulated or ramified.

The spines or hard rays are always unarticulated and not ramified. The number of fin rays is important for the identification of the fish species. For this it is usual to express their numbers of rays in formulas in which for the paired fins only the number of rays of one fin is mentioned. In general only the formula of the dorsal and anal fins is given. It is usual to mention the hard rays in Roman numerals, while the soft ones are given in Arabic figures. A fin formula may, for instance, look as follows: D 7-8, A 25-26. This means that the species shows 7 or 8 soft rays in the dorsal fin, and 25 or 26 of them in the anal. Sometimes, however, it may prove necessary to mention the unarticulated soft rays separately. Then the formula may look as follows: D 3/8-9, A 2/9-10. This means that the respective species shows three unarticulated soft rays and 8 or 9 articulated ones in the dorsal, while they number 2, respectively 9 or 10 in the anal.

If hard and soft rays are united in one fin, the resulting formula may be as follows: D XV-XVI/9-

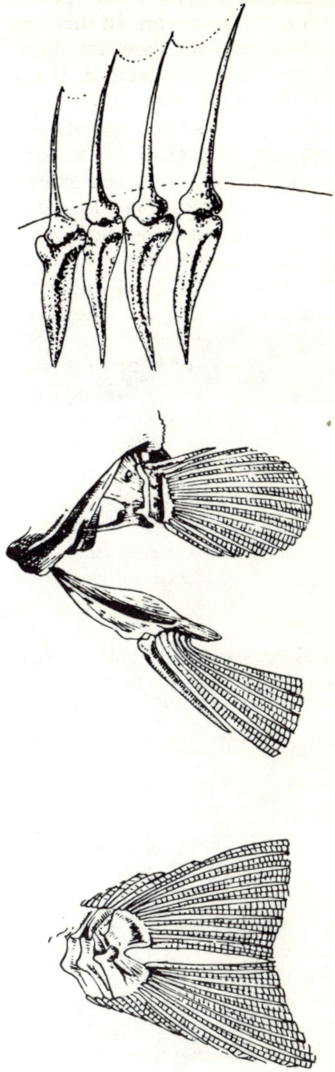

Above, fin rays are anchored in bony sockets deep in the musculature. Center, pectoral and ventral fins of a Perch are connected with a bony girdle. Below, caudal fin of a Perch.

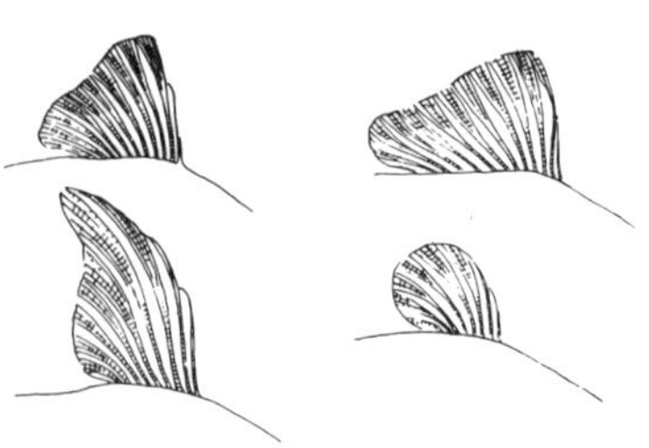

Forms of soft-rayed dorsal fins

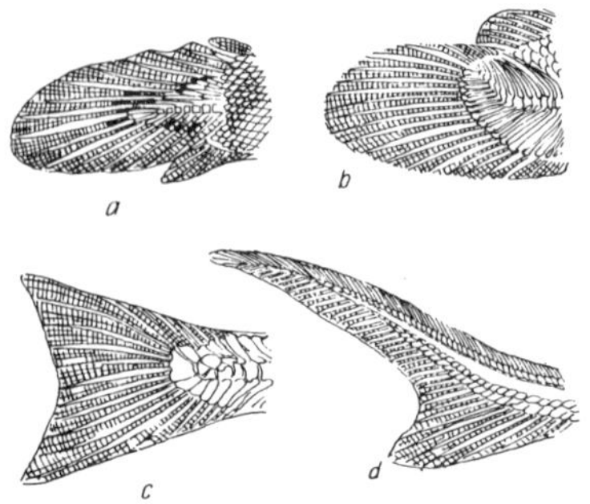

Forms of caudal fins: a. totally symmetrical, b. and c. outwardly symmetrical, but inwardly of an uneven structure. d. inwardly and outwardly unsymmetrical (after Zittel).

10, A III/7. This signifies that the dorsal contains 15 or 16 hard rays and 9 or 10 soft ones, while in the anal the count is 3 and 7 respectively.

For a dorsal consisting of two parts the formula may look as follows: D_1 X, D_2 12, A IV/11, which means that the first dorsal is composed of 10 hard rays, the second one of 12 soft ones, and the anal of 4 hard and 11 soft rays.

In some species of fishes, such as certain Catfishes, armored cheeks, etc. the hard rays may be developed into strong and sharp spines or stings, which have a pronouncedly poisonous action. In some cases, for instance in Sticklebacks, the spines are equipped with locking articulations, so that they may be carried erected without expenditure of muscular strength.

Fins generally serve the purpose of locomotion, however sometimes they are also used as auxiliary organs of reproduction, serving as means of wooing, to clasp and hold the female, as purses to receive sexual products, or else they are transformed into fecundating organs. Frequently the male sex is marked by especially striking, enlarged fins, or fin veils (ornament fins).

Firemouth, the: see CICHLASOMA MEEKI.

Firemouth Panchax, the: see EPIPLATYS CHAPERI.

Fishes (*Pisces*): Group of vertebrates which is no more accepted as such in modern systematics. This science includes them within the super-class of the jawed animals (*Gnathostomata*) as two classes, the Cartilaginous Fishes or *Chondrichthys*, and the Bony Fishes or *Osteichthys*.

The fishes have developed from simple chordates, like all other higher vertebrates. The preponderant majority of fishes are adapted to life in water. This fact is characterized by the limbs which are developed into fins, often with further unpaired fins. Besides this, the scale-covered body, which however may also be covered with skin teeth or bone plates, may also be naked. Breathing generally takes place through gills; in some isolated cases other organs may be used for accessory respiration.

The heart generally is of simple structure, consisting of auricle and ventricle and pumping the venous blood. Fishes are of changeable temperature. The body shape of fishes generally is that of a more or less compressed spindle, since this shape is the most fit for overcoming the high friction of water. It is the result of adaptation to certain surroundings which acquired over long eras, is the basis for the present vital needs of the different kinds of fishes. The spindle shape may be more or less altered, in certain cases it has even been abandoned completely. The connections between body shape, manner of living, and the ambient (changing) world are clearly visible.

The body shape depends on the skeleton, the muscle system, and the fins. The skin of fishes is mucous, and contains the different skin organs which are typical of fishes. The respiratory organs, gills, the circulatory system, the digestive organs, the nerve system, the sensory organs, and the sexual organs of fishes are described under the respective entries.

Fish Leech: see PISCICOLA.

Fish Louse: see ARGULUS.

fish tuberculosis: Nodule diseases of fishes, caused by rod-shaped bacteria of the genus *Mycobacterium*, one of the most dangerous diseases of aquarium fishes. The symptoms are: unwillingness to eat, followed by emaciation, milky discoloration of the skin, paling of colors and later loss of scales, skin lesions which are visible as blood spots and open sores, exophthalmy, and fin lesions marked by the decay of the outer parts of the fin rays. Under the microscope the internal organs show to be infested with numerous nodules (SCHOLZ-KLINKE).

The course of the malady is very slow. The germs can only be detected through microscopic tests. The bacteria of fish tuberculosis are not infectious to warm-blooded animals, since the best temperatures for their growth lie between 64 and 75 degrees F (according to SCHAPERCLAUS between 77 and 86 degrees F), while they die at 100 degrees F. Otherwise they are very similar to the tuberculosis germs of warm-blooded beings. According to SCHOLZ-KLINKE, this too is a consequence of wrong care, like many fish diseases which appear epidemically. For this reason it is quite difficult to cure. Under normal conditions the natural defenses of the fish are sufficient to isolate the germs. Under bad conditions the proneness increases. Sources of danger may be found in inefficient care, insufficient illumination (especially lack of ultra-violet rays) one-sided feeding, and excessive crowding with fishes. Evenly high temperatures favor its development, fluctuations seem to restrict it. Changes of temperature, however, do not represent an effective manner of combating the disease. Killing the bacteria with remedies seems hardly feasible at present. Certain modern drugs, sulphonamides for instance may eventually promise success, but they are expensive and have to be reserved therefore for human medicine. The best prevention is keeping the fishes under favorable conditions.

Five-Banded Barb, the: see BARBUS PENTAZONA.

Flag Cichlid: see CICHLASOMA FESTIVUM.

Flag Tetra: see HEMIGRAMMUS ULREYI.

Flag Tetra, the: HYPHESSOBRYCON HETERORHABDUS.

Flagellata: Phylum of unicellulars or protozoans, which stands halfway between animals and plants, and is characterized by the possession of special organs of locomotion, the lashes (flagellae). These are motile plasm threads, tilted forward while swimming, which may be found singly or in numbers. In some cases one flagellum may extend backwards. The flagella are anchored to a basal bubble, which is either connected with the cell nucleus, or else with a special flagellar nucleus.

Furthermore we often find a red spot, the so-called 'eye spot' (stigma) which might perhaps be the seat of a sense of light. *Flagellata* often show vivid colors, caused by imbedded green, yellow, brown, or red chromatophores (pigment carriers). The cell body is of relatively simple structure. Only the fresh water forms have a pulsating vacuole. If chromatophores are present, nutrition is autotrophic in the manner of plants, otherwise it is heterotrophic like that of animals. Thus even closely related forms often show differentiated manners of feeding, and some species are able to go over from one manner to the other, if forced to do so. For this reason the *F.* are considered very primitive unicellulars, which still stand on the border between animals and plants. Reproduction takes place either asexually through simple longitudinal division, or sexually through fusion with subsequent division. Unfavorable conditions may be weathered by developing a water-proof cover (cyst). Well-known genera: *Dinobryon*, *Euglena*, *Volvox*, and *Costia*, which is a noted fish killer.

F. are always bound to water. Some live in fresh water, others in the sea, but they are found practically everywhere. The kinds of *F.* which live in a body of water permit conclusions as to the fitness of said water for drinking and aquarium use. A number of *F.* are dangerous parasites, for instance the germs which cause sleeping sickness, the tse-tse cattle plague, and many kinds of boils.

Flagellata

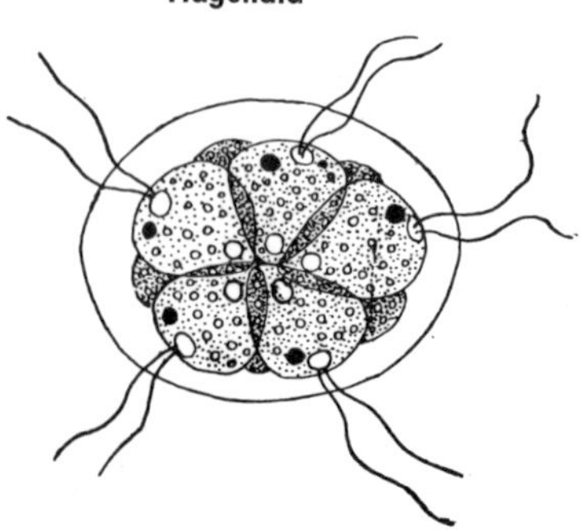

flagellates: see FLAGELLATA.
flammeus: Flaming, burning.
— *Hyphessobrycon.*
Flatfishes: see HETEROSOMATA.
Flatworms: see PLATYHELMINTHES.
flava: Yellow, blönde.
— *Limnocharis.*
flavipinnis: With yellow fins.
— *Aplocheilichthys.*
flea crustaceans: see AMPHIPODA.
fleshy dorsal (fin): see ADIPOSE FIN.
flexilis: Flexible, pliable.
— *Nitella.*
— *Otocinclus.*
flora: The world of plants.
floridae: From Florida (U.S.A.).
— *Jordanella.*
Flounder: see TRINECTES.
flowerless plants: see CRYPTOGAMAE.
flower stalk: The part of a plant which carries the blossoms and forms no leaves, also does not develop vegetatively.
fluitans: Floating, roving (on the water).
— *Riccia.*
fluviatilis: Of the river.
— *Astacus.*
— *Barbus.*
— *Gobio.*
— *Perca.*
— *Petromyzon.*
— *Tetraodon.*
Flying Barbs: see ESOMUS.
flying food: Edible animals, generally air-borne insects and other arthropods, which live close to the water surface and are caught by the fishes by means of jumps or when falling directly upon the surface of the water.
foetida: Stinking, fetid.
— *Chara.*

Fontinalaceae: Willow Mosses. Family of aquatic mosses belonging to the section of the Moss Plants or *Bryophyta*. Highly variable plants which are distributed over large areas of the globe, especially the cold and temperate zones. Instead of roots, they show ramified threads, called rhizoids. The small, scale-like leaves, which are of different shapes, possess no central rib and are yellowish, different hues of green, or reddish to brown. The *F.* are dioecian. The spore cysts sit on short peduncles, are surrounded by leaves, and are equipped with a cover. Only one species, which has several local forms, is commonly cultivated in the aquarium.

Fontinalis: Living in springs. Genus pertaining to the family of the Willow Mosses or *Fontinalaceae*, with one species adaptable for the cold water aquarium.

Fontinalis antipyretica

— antipyretica (Linné): Willow Moss: An aquatic moss rich in shapes, which is distributed over Europe, Siberia, North America, and North Africa. In these regions it is found anchored to rocks in clear, standing or flowing waters. Only the expert is able to differentiate the many local forms. The only fact important to the aquarist is that the plants he intends to cultivate should not stem from cold, swift-flowing brooks, as these hardly ever acclimatize. The plants grow to a length of 16″-20″, form dense bushes, and vary more or less, according to origin.

Willow Moss is very long-lived in cold water aquaria if the temperature does not rise excessively above 64 degrees F and if the plants come from standing and shallow, warmer waters. The collecting site may be an indication on how to cultivate the plants. It is advisable to transfer the moss with its substratum to the aquarium. Otherwise they may be anchored to the bottom by means of glass needles or stuck between rocks. Willow Moss is a valued spawning substratum.

food, feeding: For information on the importance of efficient feeding, see NUTRITION, FEEDING FISHES, and the entries which describe the different kinds of food and food animals: PROTOZOA, ROTATORIA, COPEPODA, CLADOCERA, DAPHNIA, ISOPODA, AMPHIPODA, ENCHYTRAEUS, NEMATOCERA, DROSOPHILA, LUMBRICIDAE, TUBIFEX, MICROWORMS, ARTIFICIAL (PREPARED), and DRY FOODS.

These entries point out the different species of food animals, their significance as fish foods, the manner of keeping them and of feeding them, generally preceded by considerations on the respective systematic group.

The general theme, put forth under the entry NUTRITION, will once more be resumed here, with a special view to aquaristics.

Each species of fishes has its own, innate manner of acquiring nourishment. In free nature it hunts for the food that yields the best results to it, while in captivity it depends on the nourishment supplied by its owner. If the aquarist values the health of his fishes, and if he wants them to behave in the manner that is peculiar to their species, and also to reproduce, he has to study their food necessities. Only after it has become clear whether he can obtain the necessary foods or not, should he decide on what species to keep in his tanks. It is useless, for instance, to try to 'domesticate' predators to eating dried foods for reasons of convenience. If you are unable to supply the live foods they need, better refrain from keeping them in your tanks.

It is especially harmful and detrimental if the fishes are fed the same kinds of food animals and artificial foods for longer periods. Each food has its own, specific nutritional substances, and you can only satisfy the needs of your pets by alternating their kinds of food. The hobbyist should always consider that inadequate feeding is the first prerequisite for many diseases. Disease germs, which normally are present everywhere, can generally only develop their harmful activities after the organism of the fish is weakened and has become less resistant through this. Therefore let us once more repeat the commandments of good feeding which have already been mentioned elsewhere in this book:

1. Feed according to the needs of your fishes, and not according to your own whims.

2. Alternate the foods, and make use of all possibilities the seasons offer you for this.

3. Do not overfeed—but do not feed too sparingly either. If possible feed several times a day. Watch your fishes in order to see whether they eat willingly or not.

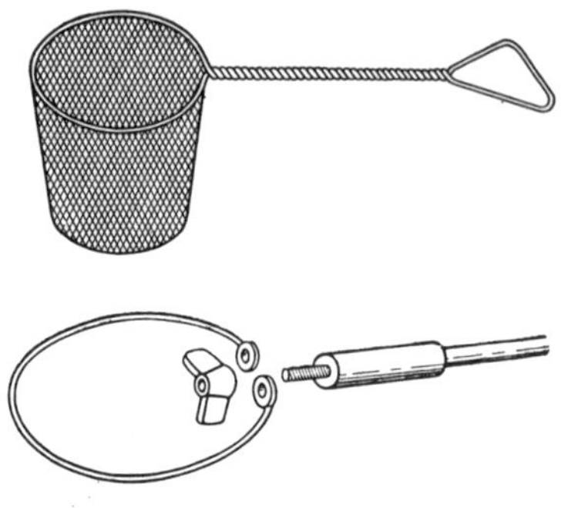

Above: small hand net; below: frame for a collapsible food net.

food nets: Nets of different shapes, which are stuck on a pole and used for catching food animals. The simplest manner of building them is by fixing a simple wire support with a piece of a ladies' stocking tied to it. In addition to this there are all kinds of net structures. The net pole should preferably be of bamboo, as this is solid and non-rotting, and simultaneously very light-weight. A length of 8 feet should generally suffice for the pole. Too long or too short rods are generally difficult to handle. The pole should be cut in two and equipped with two brass pieces in order to make it collapsible like a fishing rod. Rods made of aluminum tubing, too, have proved to be very efficient. The net support should be made in a manner that will permit taking it off from the rod, and also so that the net fabric may be taken from it. Collapsible supports are easier to carry. Do not make the diameter of the net support too large nor too small, 8″ to 12″ is sufficient. The larger of the two diameters permits larger catches, if the water depth is sufficient. In shallower waters, though, the smaller net will prove easier to handle. Whenever possible, use non-rusting metallic parts.

The net itself should preferably not be attached to the support directly, since there it does not dry well or is eaten away by rusting net supporting bows, and then it easily gets torn due to lack of motility. Therefore it is advisable to sew metallic rings to the upper rim of the net, so that you may slip them over the net bow. These can move freely there, permitting the net to conform to the changing conditions of the water current while in use without getting torn. When cutting the fabric with which to sew the net, avoid giving this a pointed tip, as in such tips the food animals easily get crushed. Experience shows that the bottom of the net should best be flat and spacious. The net bag should not be too short, nor too long, as in the latter case the net becomes unmanageable for turning around. The best rule is to build the net with a ratio of 2:3 between its upper diameter and its depth.

As a fabric you may use any kind of non-swelling, permeable cloth. Fine-meshed linen, as we often see it as a make-shift fabric on the nets of children, is hardly adequate, unless used for dust-sized foods. The best is silk bolting cloth (as used in flour and grist mills), which is long-lasting, permeable to water and swells little. Lately also fine-meshed nylon fabrics have shown up, which seem to be of great advantage as compared to other cloths.

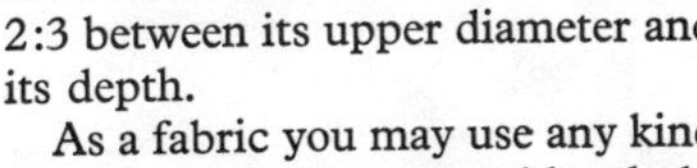

Small kitchen-type strainer

food strainers: Sieves of different meshes, with wooden or metallic frames, which permit grading food as to sizes, used either as assembled

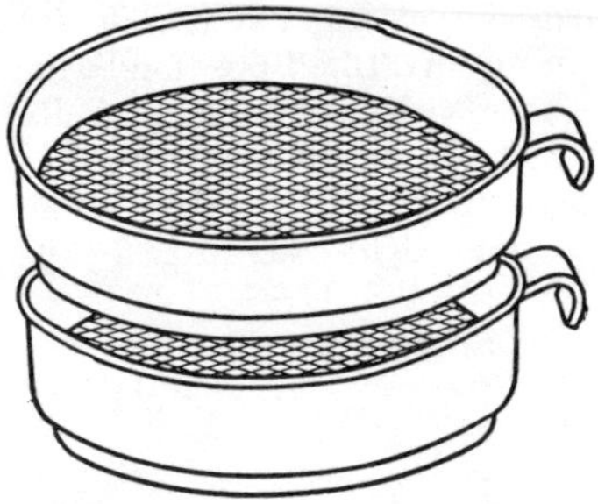

Frame sieve, for grading foods by size

sets or singly. Brass mesh is preferable for reasons of durability. Grading foods for the different uses is extremely important.

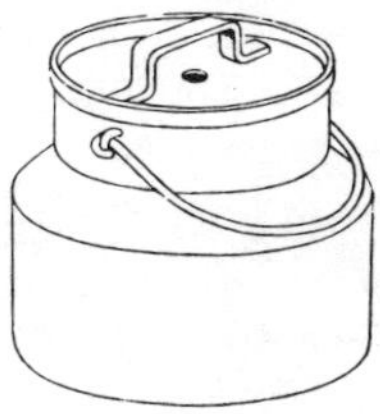

Food transportation can

food transportation: Transporting live foods may be done in different ways, depending on the kind of food. Transporting crustaceans in water-filled cans over long routes and under heat has proved not to be very advisable. It is much better to carry them on little frames. Such wooden frames are covered with silk bolting cloth (as used in flour mills) or with small-meshed brass wire netting, and may be placed in a transportation box with drawers. When catching food, moisten the frames, drip the food on them, and float them on the water so that the small crustaceans may spread evenly over their area. In order to avoid floating away of the frames, anchor them to the shore with a string. After having filled all frames in this way, take them out of the water and stand them up in a tilted position against a tree or wall or something similar, so that the excess water may run off completely. The food should look quite light-colored and dry—

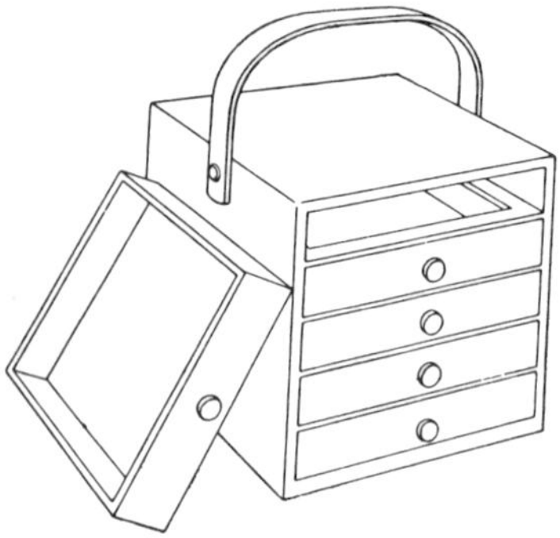

Food transportation frame

take your time while letting the water drip out! When transferring to the storage tanks you have previously prepared at home, take care that the water temperature is the same as the air temperature. Do not use too cool water on hot summer days! Small crustaceans that sink to the bottom should immediately be fed to the fishes, or put to dry. Most other live foods (insect larvae etc.) may also be transported moist in this way.

formosa: Pretty, beautiful.
— *Heterandria.*

forsteri: After M. Forster, discoverer of the species.
— *Neoceratodus.*

fossilis: Dug up (from the mud); by analogy also: ancient.
— *Heteropneustes.*
— *Misgurnus.*

fossils: Prints and petrified remainders of animals and plants which lived in former geological eras, representing an important means with which to form an idea of the development of life on earth.

Four-Banded Barb, the: see BARBUS (PUNTIUS) TETRAZONA.

Four-Eyed Fish: see ANABLEPIDAE.

Four Leaf Clover: see MARSILEA.

fragilis: Brittle, frail.
— *Chara.*

frame aquarium: Aquaria with a welded frame made of angle iron, steel, aluminium, or plastics, with riveted metallic or putty fixed glass or slate bottoms, and sides of glass panes puttied in from the inside. It has the advantages over the all-glass aquarium of being more rugged, less subject to breakage, and the possibility of using flawless panes, which is more advantageous in observing the kept animals and plants. It is important, though, to employ harmless materials, which should be handled in a proper and professional way. The

A frame aquarium on a useful stand

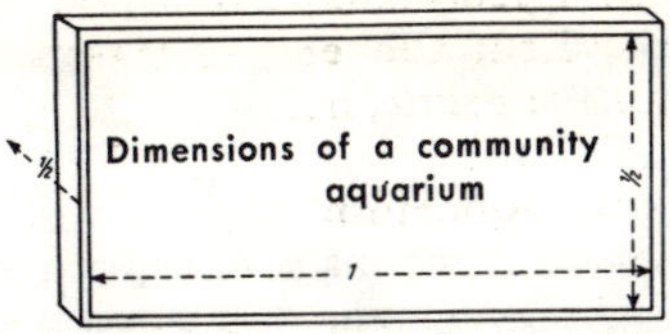

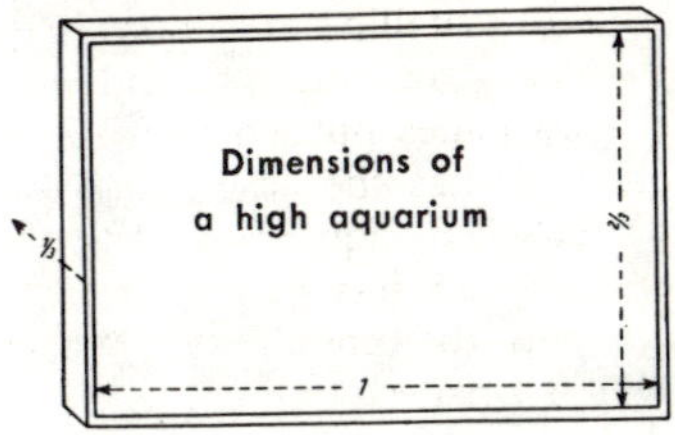

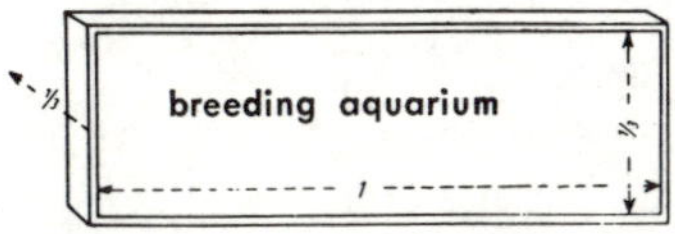

time and trouble put into the building of the tank hardly pay for themselves in the end. If one does not have sufficient know-how and skill, it would be advisable to entrust the work to a professional. The point has to be stressed, though, that not every tinsmith knows how to build a good aquarium frame, nor can every glazier put in the panes exactly as it should be done. This too requires a certain measure of special experience.

When buying ready-made frame aquaria, pay attention to their good quality and make sure that the interior part is well insulated. Especially do not accept an uncoated metallic bottom. Defects resulting from bad materials or poor workmanship are hard or impossible to correct later on. It is especially important to use exclusively steel pieces that are new and free from rust. Pay especial attention to the squaring of the workmanship. Tanks with welded length pieces are more resistant and nicer than riveted ones, which were used formerly. The welding spots should be carefully filed off and ground flat. For very big tanks, with lengths of 60″ and more, it is advisable to reinforce the upper and lower frames by means of steel strips, and also to put steel bars across the bottom. Thickness of frame steel and bottom plate depend upon the size of the tank. The bottom plate should be riveted in from the inside, cutting it to size with .04″ less than the inner measurements of the frame. Before riveting, all single parts (frame and bottom plate) should be carefully cleaned of iron filings and rust. This may be done with steel brushes or abrasive cloth, but best results are obtained with a sanding jet. Then one drills and countersinks the

Battery of aquaria on a high stand

rivet holes in plate and frame. Take care that the rivets sit tight. They should not be flattened too much. If you want to do something very special, paint the space between plate and frame with a red-lead varnish before riveting. Then one rivets in the cover holders, if such are included in the planning. For these, though, only stainless materials should be chosen. Cut the supporting surfaces as narrow as possible, or, for the moment, drill holes only, into which, later, bolt the cover holder of oak. Now drill holes on the right and left for the air ducts (¼″), and, if you want to putty in a glass bottom, make two or more holes of ⅛″ diameter in the bottom plate. If the holes in the bottom are too small, they are useless, as in case of an eventual breakage they will not permit passage of the water, and thus they will hinder you from seeing that there has been an infiltration between the glass bottom and the bottom plate.

It is hard to give general directions as to the most useful sizes of aquaria. They depend upon the purpose for which the tank is built, space on hand, etc. One might perhaps accept the following norms as serving the purpose:

Large frame aquarium on a cabinet stand. Note convenient drawer and decorative shelves underneath.

COMPARATIVE TABLES OF THICKNESSES FOR ANGLE STEEL AND BOTTOM PLATES

Size of tank			Angle Steel	Bottom Plate
Length	*Width*	*Height*		
20″	10″	10″	5/8″- 5/8″- 1/8″	BWG 16 to 15
24″	10″	12″	5/8″- 5/8″- 1/8″	BWG 16 to 15
24″	12″	16″	5/8″- 5/8″- 1/8″	BWG 16 to 14
32″	12″	12″	3/4″- 3/4″- 1/8″	BWG 14 to 12
32″	12″	16″	3/4″- 3/4″- 1/8″	BWG 13 to 12
32″	16″	18″	1″ -1″ - 3/16″	BWG 12
40″	16″	16″	1″ -1″ - 3/16″	BWG 12 to 11
40″	14″	16″	1″ -1″ - 3/16″	BWG 12 to 11
40″	16″	24″	1 3/16″-1 3/16″-3/16″	BWG 11
48″	20″	20″	1 3/16″-1 3/16″-3/16″	BWG 10
60″	24″	32″	1 3/4″ -1 3/4″ - 3/8″	BWG 6
80″	20″	40″	3 1/8″ -3 1/8″ - 3/8″	3/8″

(*a*) *Community and ornamental tanks.* Width and height scarcely or exactly ½ of the length, for instance:

Length	Width	Height
40″	16″	20″
24″	10″	12″
16″	8″	8″

(*b*) *Special tanks for big, high fish and plants of corresponding size.* Width ⅓, height at least ½, better still ⅔, of length, for instance:

Length	Width	Height
40″	14″	24″

(*c*) *Breeding tanks.* Width ⅓ to ½ of length, height ⅓ or less of length, for instance:

Length	Width	Height
40″	14″	10″
24″	10″	8″
16″	8″	7″

As a rule it is better to choose the sizes a little on the ample side than on the scant one. Even small fishes develop better in bigger containers in which it is easier to keep up a certain balance of biological factors. For breeding purposes a tank can never be too big.

free-swimming: (a) The point after hatching, in the development of fish fry, when the remainder of the egg yolk has been consumed, the eating system and the digestive organs have developed fully, and the larva, which up to this moment hang from a thread fixed on its head or was under parental care, being unable to swim, takes on a horizontal stance and begins to swim. Free-swimming is generally preceded by filling the swimming bladder with air at the surface. Many fishes which care for their brood stop this care at the moment of free-swimming.

(*b*) The independent swimming of most fishes, as opposed to the jumping, hopping, snaking, or creeping swimming motions of some bottom-dwelling fishes.

fresh water: As opposed to aged water, any water which is free of organic matter, coming from springs, tap-water or well-water, as well as freshly fallen rain-water. Where the old water which is laden with waste products could still promote growth and photosynthesis, fresh water has a tendency to stimulate them. Notwithstanding the fact that requirements differ, it is always well from time to time to replace some of the overaged water with fresh water.

fresh water Medusae: see MICROHYDRA.

fresh water Hydras: see HYDROIDEA.

fresh water sponges: see SPONGILLIDAE.

friedrichsthali: After an Austrian collector.

— *Cichlasoma.*

fright substances: Chemical secreta of fishes that live in schools, which are significant for the existence of the school. According to the observations of FRISCH Minnows showed a fright reaction after about half a minute when an injured school-fellow was set into the aquarium. It then was days until the old tameness returned. So far these fright substances, which are chemicals eliminated by the skin of wounded specimens, have been observed in Cyprinids that live in schools. Their biological significance rests in the advantage the school enjoys in case of a predatory attack, when a wounded school-fellow warns the remainder in this way. A striking fact is linking of the fright substance to a spot, which causes the school to avoid the said place for a long time thereafter.

fringe-lips: see LABEO.

Frogbit: see HYDROCHARIS MORSUS RANAE.

— South American: see LIMNOBIUM STOLONIFERUM.

Frogbits: see HYDROCHARITACEAE.

Frog Catfish: see CLARIAS BATRACHUS.

Frog Spoon: see ALISMA, ECHINODORUS.

Frog Spoon plants: see ALISMATACEAE.

front gills: see PROSOBRANCHIA.

fruit-flies as fish food: Fruit-flies are small flies, about 2 to 4 mm in length, belonging to the family of the *Drosophilidae*. For feeding one has to consider especially *Drosophila fasciata* (formerly *melanogaster*) as from this a stump-winged form that is unable to fly and therefore very adequate for feeding in the aquarium has been bred. Insect food is of great importance for the feeding of aquarium fishes, especially in winter. The flying *Drosophila*, which herpetologists like to use as nourishment for their pets, is hardly proper for aquaristics, as it is difficult to keep it on the surface of the water. In the larder such flies are unwelcome guests. However, it is perfectly possible to breed the stump-winged form pure, but one has to avoid carefully that no normal fruit-flies enter the culture.

For breeding set up a number of preserve jars, which should be kept in a heated room at about 68-72 degrees F. Cover the mouths of the jars with linen or with fine gauze. Put a food mash into the jars to a height of about $\frac{5}{8}$-$\frac{3}{4}$″, the mash being in a state of sour fermentation. This feeding ground must always be moist, and special attention has to be paid to this. Not even the surface should start getting dry. JAHN offers the following recipe for the food substratum: a fruit mash of pears, tomatoes, plums or the like is stirred to stiffness with wheat bran and cooked. After cooling off add a bean-sized piece of baking yeast or sprinkle some commercial yeast preparation on it. After fermentation has started, add the breeder flies. (The rear end of the male is blunter than that of the female).

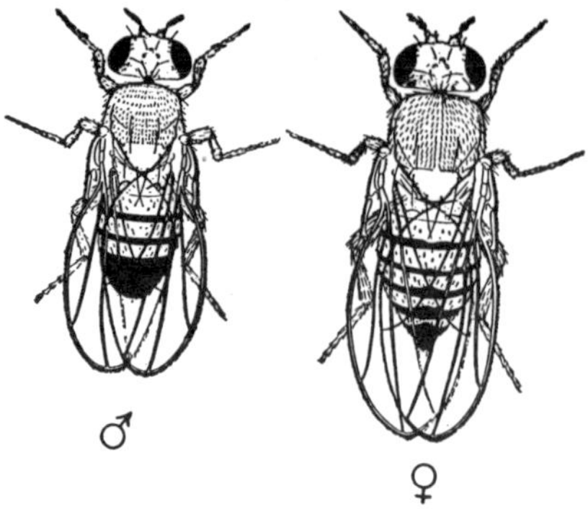

Drosophila, winged variety; male left, female right

In order to offer the grubs an opportunity to change into chrysalises, put some folded cellulose into the jars. After sufficient chrysalises have developed, let the feeding mash dry out and feed the freshly hatched flies to your fishes. Meanwhile breeding continues in the other jars. Temperatures below 68 degrees F delay hatching.

The flies may be shaken without difficulty onto the water surface from the jars with the dry substratum by knocking on the containers. Nearly all fishes take them willingly, especially, however, surface fishes which are used to flying foods.

Full-Striped Barb, the: see BARBUS (PUNTIUS) HOLOTAENIA.

functional aquaristics: A manner of keeping fishes advocated by MEDER, which only considers the chief functions of the fish, without paying attention to the impression the aquarium causes on mankind. Functional aquaristics rejects the ornamental tank. Doubtless this manner of keeping aquaria permits a number of achievements which are impossible in the normally set-up ornamental tank. Functional aquaristics is indeed adequate and excellent for all experiments with closely defined, scientific aims. However, the thesis defended by MEDER is that aquarists have a duty towards their fishes to keep them in this manner.

fundulus: Collective name, usually used in amateur circles, for groups of egg-laying Tooth Carps, without value in systematics. (See CYPRINODONTINAE).

Fundulus: Of the bottom.

Genus of North American Tooth Carps belonging to the sub-family of the egg-laying Tooth Carps or *Cyprinodontinae*, of *Rivulus*-like structure, but more compressed laterally than that genus. Head broad, dentition in the form of a narrow ribbon composed of several rows of pointed toothlets. The vertical fins insert far toward the rear, the mouth is large and terminal to supraterminal. Despite the name of the genus, most species cannot be considered pronounced bottom fishes. They like to stay in the central and upper reaches of the water. Like many of their African relatives, the *F.* too probably come from shallow waters, where the differences in depth are insignificant. Due to their geographic origin, many of the species do not need much warmth, and may be considered hardy also in other respects. So far they have not been able to find all the popularity they deserve, despite the fact that their colors are very pleasing. The sexes show very diverse colorings. Care and breeding takes place as described for *Aphyosemion*.

— **chrysotus** (Guenther): The Golden Ear.

SHAPE: As per description of the genus, the body is relatively short. D 8-9, A 10-11; the scales relatively large. Length up to 2¾″.

COLOR: Greenish base with numerous red or shiny golden dots, the female paler in color. This species also presents a color strain with black dapplings.

Fundulus chrysotus, male below

RANGE: In shallow waters near the coast of the Southern U.S.A.

CARE AND BREEDING: As per description of the genus. The species likes not-too-small, sunlit tanks, needing a little more warmth than the other species of the genus; 73-77 degrees F the most favorable, for breeding also a little more, lowest 68 degrees F. Excepting the spawning period, during which the males become a little bellicose, the species may be kept in communities with other fishes without any danger. Breeding is not difficult, the Golden Ear is very willing to spawn. Each spawning period, during which a total of about 20 eggs is laid, lasts about one week. The spawn is released among algae or fine-feathered plants after violent chasing. From there it may be collected daily with an eye-dropper, and transferred to a nursery tank. At 80 degrees F the fry hatch within 8-10 days. They are about ⅜″ long and sprinkled with numerous silvery spots. Due to their rather large size, they need infusoria food only for a short time and already go over to dust-sized foods after a few days.

— **cingulatus** Cuvier and Valenciennes: The Belted Fundulus.

Very similar in body structure to the preceding species. D 7-8, A 9-10. Length about $2\frac{3}{4}''$. Gleaming blue base and red belly with rows of scarlet dots, red cross bands and red fins. The female very simply colored.

Care and breeding as for the previous species.

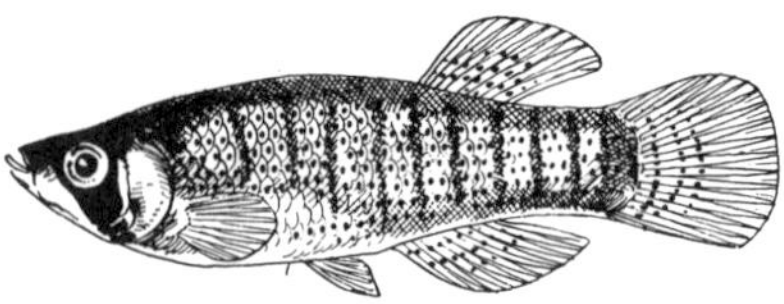

Fundulus dispar

— **dispar** (Agassiz): The Star-Head Top Minnow.

SHAPE: As per description of the genus; D 7-8, A 9-10; length up to about $2\frac{3}{8}''$. The species has a gleaming spot on top of the head, similar to that found on the species of *Aplocheilus*. It is a pronounced surface fish.

COLOR: Reddish to greenish base with rows of brown dots, the male with indistinct cross bands. Both sexes show a dark band across the eye. The female is simpler in color.

RANGE: The Southeast of the U.S.A., in standing and flowing waters.

CARE AND BREEDING: As described for *F. chrysotus*, but does not require as much warmth: 68 degrees F, for breeding a little more, lowest 54 degrees F; may be kept at room temperature.

Fundulus heteroclitus

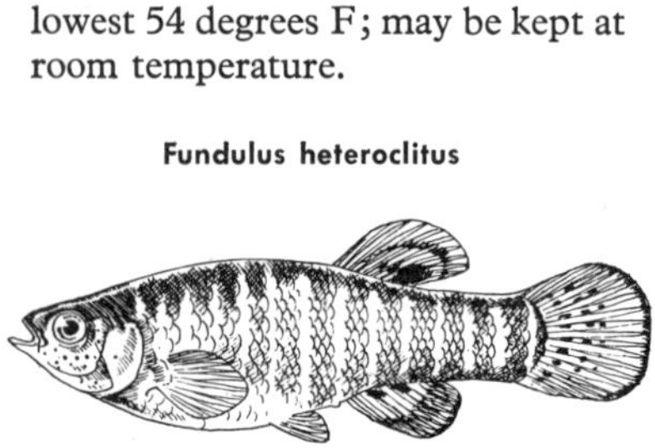

— **heteroclitus** (Linné): The Common or Zebra Killie.

SHAPE: As per description of the genus; highly variable in shape, fins, and color, according to geographic origin. D 11-13, A 10-12. Length up to about $4\frac{3}{4}''$.

COLOR: Brownish base with 12-13 gleaming cross bands. The female is simpler in color.

RANGE: In coastal waters of the whole East of the U.S.A., also on the Bermudas, rarely found in fresh water, but generally in brackish or salt water.

CARE AND BREEDING: As described for the genus and for *F. chrysotus*. *F. heteroclitus* is especially long-lived and hardy. At first it needs a strong admixture of salt, as far as imported specimens are concerned, but becomes gradually adjusted to fresh water. It needs absolutely no warmth, to the contrary, temperatures over 68-72 degrees F make it prone to diseases. Lower temperatures, down to 50 degrees F are tolerated without difficulties. When breeding, take care to get a quite big and robust female, as the male chases very actively.

— **majalis** (Walbaum): The May Killie.

SHAPE: A rather elongated species. D 12-13, A 10-11. Length up to 6″, the male smaller.

COLOR: Metallic-gleaming, brownish base, the male with cross bands, the female with horizontal stripes.

RANGE: The East of the U.S.A., from Canada to Florida.

CARE AND BREEDING: An admixture of 10% sea water is advisable. Very robust and long-lived, may also be kept in unheated aquaria at room temperature. Breeding has only succeeded in open-air ponds and concrete pools so far.

— **notatus** (Rafinesque):

SHAPE: Rather long and slender; D 9-10, A 11-12. Length about $3\frac{1}{8}''$, the northern specimens remaining smaller.

COLOR: The upper part of the body dark olive-drab, the lower part yellowish-white, both regions separated by a black horizontal band, the males crossed by many stripes, the females simpler in color.
RANGE: The East of the U.S.A., in standing and slowly-flowing waters.
CARE AND BREEDING: Care as for *F. chrysotus*. Breeding has not yet succeeded. A pronounced surface fish which too shows a gleaming spot on top of the head.

— **sciadicus** (Cope): The Plains Top Minnow.
SHAPE: As per description of genus. D 10-12, A 12-14. Length about $3\frac{1}{8}''$-$3\frac{1}{2}''$.
COLOR: Shiny bluish-green, a white line on top of the back, the vertical fins of the male red rimmed.
RANGE: In fresh waters of the Central U.S.A., especially in the river system of the Mississippi, there mainly in the upper and median courses of the rivers.
CARE AND BREEDING: As per description of the genus. Temperatures: 72-75 degrees F. During the spawning period the temperature should not sink below 68 degrees F, but when wintering a rest period of 6-8 weeks at 59 degrees F is advisable. The fish are not very prolific breeders. The few, quite big fry hatch after 8 days and should be reared as described for *F. chrysotus*. They eat prepared foods in addition to dust-sized live foods right from the beginning.

fungus diseases: Diseases caused by parasitic fungi, among which the *Ichthyosporidium* (*Ichthyophonus*) disease counts as the most dangerous. The contagion with *Saprolegnia* is a secondary consequence of other diseases or of damage where there remain open wounds.

furunculosis: A disease of fishes, especially Salmonids, caused by bacteria, which also appears on aquarium fishes and which is characterized by sores. Despite its name, the malady has nothing to do with human furunculosis. The sores may differ in number and character. Their seat is within the muscles, the skin being only sympathetically attained, but breakthroughs to the surface are possible. *F.* seems to be rare in the aquarium. Infections may be avoided by granting your fishes favorable living conditions, even if the bacteria are already present in your pets, as the disease only manifests itself after debilitation. Infected specimens should be destroyed, and tanks, plants, and accessories disinfected. Isolate and watch all other fishes.

galilaea: Coming from Galilea.
— *Tilapia.*

gambiensis: After the Gambia River in Africa.
— *Barbus.*

Gambusia: A ridiculous nothing. Species of livebearing Tooth Carps of the Sub-Family *Poeciliinae*, which is primarily carnivorous. The body is elongated and slightly compressed laterally, especially in the females, and the head flattened. There are about 12 known species.

— **affinis affinis** (Baird & Girard).

Gambusia affinis affinis. Note how much smaller the upper fish (male) is from the lower (female).

Gambusia affinis holbrooki, male below

— **affinis holbrooki** (Girard): Holbrook's Gambusia.

SHAPE: As in the description for the genus, quite slender; D 8-9, A 10-11.

LENGTH: Males 1⅜", females 2½ to 2¾".

COLOR: Shiny olive-green, a slanted black line through the eye. The fins show small dark spots. Often there are specimens with a black mottling, usually males but sometimes also females. Formerly *G. affinis* and *G. holbrooki* were considered two species, but according to INNES they are only local forms of the same species. The males are smaller, and the females larger, otherwise as with all *Poeciliinae*.

RANGE: *G. affinis affinis:* southwest Texas; *G. affinis holbrooki:* southeastern states of the U.S.A.

CARE AND BREEDING: The species was once one of the best-known livebearers. It had earned above all a certain fame as a consumer of the larvae of the malaria mosquito, and for this reason was transplanted in many tropical and subtropical lands. It is very adaptable and not at all sensitive to temperature changes. The best temperatures lie between 65 and 69° F. Breeding can also be accomplished in outdoor pools. All sorts of small foods are taken, especially that of an animal nature. Supplementary nourishment with algae is beneficial. Their tanks should be heavily planted, because due to their quarrelsome nature some hiding-places are necessary. The young are sometimes somewhat sensitive, and the breeding of this species has proven to be somewhat problematical.

— **dominicensis** Regan: Dominican Gambusia.

SHAPE: As described for the genus, somewhat compressed in shape. D 9, A 10-11.

LENGTH: Males 1 inch, females 2½ inches.

COLOR: Brownish-gray background with small black spots, also on the fins, and a line through the eyes. Along the side there is a narrow black horizontal stripe.

RANGE: Haiti and Cuba.

CARE AND BREEDING: The species is undemanding and hardy, but requires some warmth: 76-82° F is advisable. They have proven themselves to be very quarrelsome, and the pregnant females are especially nasty toward the males. Each brood amounts to about 15 youngsters, which nevertheless grow very rapidly.

— **nicaraguensis** Gunther: Nicaraguan Gambusia.

Body is somewhat more high-backed and strongly compressed laterally. D 6-8, A 11. Length: males a little over 1", females 2". Uniformly grayish-green with rows of dark patches in the upper half of the body.

RANGE: Atlantic side of Central America from southern Mexico to Panama. Equally at home in fresh as in brackish water. Care as for the other species.

— **patruelis** Baird & Girard: Silvery Gambusia.

Very similar to *G. affinis*, occurring

in the southern United States. Possibly only a local form.

— **punctata** Poey: Spotted Gambusia.

FORM: Elongated but powerful in build, with a particularly high caudal base; gonopodium relatively short. Length: males 1″, females $3\frac{1}{8}$″.

COLOR: Bluish-gray background with rows of reddish-brown dots. Body and fins gleam light blue, dorsal and anal fins of the male with a red border.

RANGE: Cuba, where it abounds, especially in the environs of Havana.

Gambusia punctata, male below

CARE AND BREEDING: Typical of the genus, also one of the most satisfying, hardy and undemanding of all the species. Sometimes accepts dried food very willingly. Breeding is easy, 70-75° F. Broods are as high as 30, and in contrast to most other Gambusias all usually survive. Grows very rapidly with sufficient heat. Sexes can be distinguished when $1\frac{1}{8}$″ long.

— **yucatana** Regan: Yucatan Gambusia.

Elongated, slender form. D 7-9, A 10-11.

LENGTH: Males $2\frac{1}{4}$″, females 3″. Darker rows of spots on a grayish-green background.

RANGE: Yucatan and Mexico.

CARE: As for the other species. Requires warmth. Also very quarrelsome. 12-20 very fast-growing youngsters.

gametes: Germ cells which are differentiated sexually, such as egg cells and sperm cells. (Egg cells: macrogametes; sperm cells: microgametes.)

Gammarus pulex pulex L.: Brook shrimp.

Native shrimp of the family *Gammaridae*, order *Amphipoda*. A very numerous species, 15 to 20 mm. in length. Lives in clear standing and especially flowing waters. Remains on the bottom among stones, twigs and plants, but does not care for muddy bottoms. Nourishment is principally composed of bits of decaying vegetable or animal matter, but they can also be predatory. Moves by crawling or swimming. Considerable speed in swimming is attained, either on the side or on the back. They hibernate by burying themselves in the bottom, appearing on warm days at times. After they leave the brood-pouch, the young are guarded for a time by the mother, who permits them to seek shelter between her legs when danger threatens. Brook shrimp are eagerly sought as food by the larger fishes. They can be the carriers of parasitic fish-worms, the so-called "scratchers" *Acanthocephala*.

Gammarus

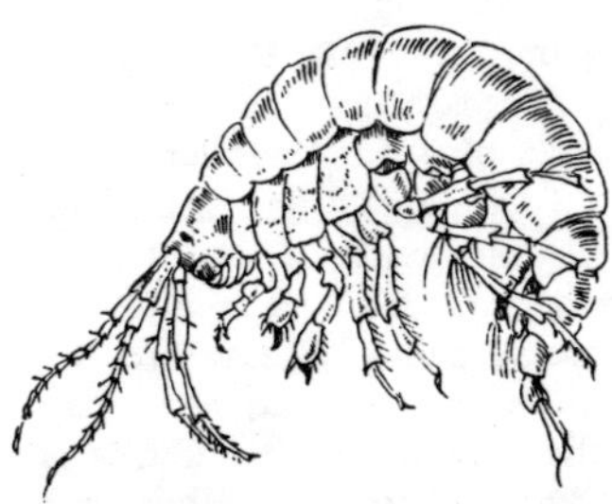

gamones: Fertilizing agents, chemical substances which regulate fertilization.

ganoin: Enamel layer on the sides of ganoid fishes, such as the Sturgeons.

gardneri: After a personal name. — *Aphyosemion.*

Garnet Tetra: see HEMIGRAMMUS PULCHER.

gas-bubble disease: Appearance of gas-bubbles under the skin, in blood-vessels, etc., which results in the tearing of tissues, shredding of fins and eye disorders, which can result in death. This is usually caused by the blocking of the blood-vessels with gas bubbles (gas embolism). Gas-bubble disease is caused by a sudden change in gas pressure, such as "when the total pressure of the dissolved oxygen in the blood is higher than the dissolved gases in the water which is being breathed" (SCHAPERCLAUS). Such pressure changes can occur if for instance fishes are placed in a tank with fresh water which has been under high pressure. The fish regulates itself with outward and inward breathing (cell breathing). As the gas pressure in such water drops very quickly (by disposing of the excess air in the form of bubbles) the fish cannot readjust itself as quickly. The result is the formation of bubbles on or in the body. A similar thing may take place if a tank is heavily planted and algae-infested and placed in too strong sunlight. By assimilation of the plants a strong oversaturation of oxygen may take place with a resulting increase in gas pressure, which can also drop suddenly. In the open, dangerous situations may be encountered by a fish which swims from a region of high pressure into one where the pressure is low. The aquarist may draw the conclusion that if this is avoidable, a change of fishes into fresh tap water or into intense sunlight, especially in a heavily planted aquarium, should be avoided.

Gasteropelecidae: Family of the Hatchetfishes, of the sub-order *Cyprinoidea.* These are Characin-like fishes from the South American tropics which have an unusual body shape. The relatively high form is characterized by a straight back line and a deeply bowed and forward bent ventral edge, which in its lower portion is set with sharp-cornered scales. The skeleton has undergone considerable changes from the typical form for the family. The Hatchetfishes are greatly compressed laterally. The mouth is moderately wide to small, the gills usually carry teeth, and the jaws are toothless. The full horizontal line drops off at the region of the pectoral fins. The dorsal fin is set far back, an adipose fin exists but is missing with some, and the anal fin is very long; the caudal fin is deeply forked, and the ventrals are remarkably small. Particularly outstanding are the powerful, wing-like, elongated pectoral fins.

The Hatchetfishes are pronounced surface-dwellers, and when faced with danger or for other reasons, can lift themselves half out of the water and glide along the surface. This motion is made possible by quick beats of the pectoral fins. Some species can even leave the water for short stretches, landing on their side after the end of the leaps and falling back into the water. The muscles which are required for such actions

Gasteropelecidae, type of the genus; left, front view.

are extraordinarily powerful and account for up to $\frac{1}{4}$ the total body weight. The family consists of few genera and is distributed from Panama in the north to the La Plata in the south. Here we find them in the tributary streams, above all in the mouths, where they remain in the open water near beds of plants. Breeding of most species is unknown. Genera: *Gasteropelecus*, *Carnegiella*, *Thoracocharax* and *Pterodiscus*.

Gasteropelecus: Keeled belly.
South American species of Characin-like fishes of the family *Gasteropelecidae*, which also leads to the somewhat shaky genus of *Pterodiscus*. There are two known species and several sub-species.

— sternicla (Linné): Silver Hatchetfish.
FORM: As given for the family. D 10-11, A 31-34. Length about $2\frac{3}{8}$".

Gasteropelecus sternicla

COLOR: Shiny silver with a narrow, dark horizontal stripe. Base of the anal fin is dark, and there is a dark patch at the base of the dorsal fin. Sex differences are not known.
RANGE: Tropical South America from Guiana to central Brazil, west to eastern Peru.
CARE AND BREEDING: As given in the family description. Likes sunny aquaria with ample free space for swimming, especially near the surface. Requires warmth, 76-82° F, at least 70°. Tank must be well covered! Leave enough room between the glass cover and the water surface. Water level should not be too low. They are fond of jumping. Feeding with the usual foods, but flying foods and those which stay near the surface are particularly relished, while those at the bottom are unwillingly accepted. A very active species, which requires careful handling.

Gasterosteidae: Family of the Sticklebacks, of the order *Thoracostei*.
Fishes of a very elongated form; body is naked or armored with more or less complete rows of bony plates. Four comb-shaped gills. The forward portion of the dorsal fin ends in a number of strong,

Spawning Sticklebacks — 1. The male smears the secretion over the nest entrance - 2. The male nudges the head of the female - 3. The female follows the male, touching the spine on his back - 4. The male shows her the nest entrance - 5. The female has slipped into the nest and spawned - 6. Brood care by the male begins.

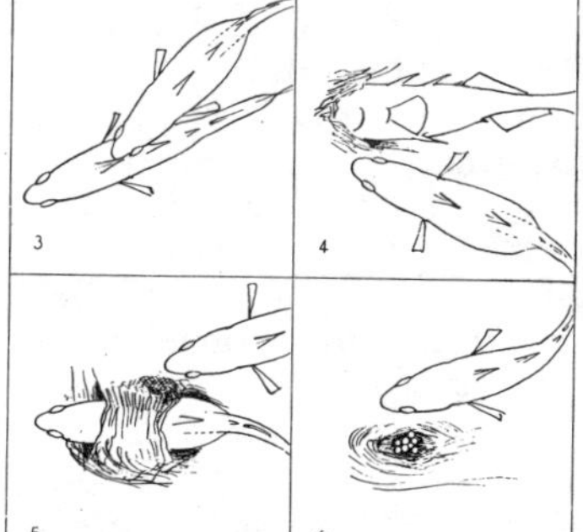

individual spines. Range is limited to the Northern Hemisphere, partly in fresh water and partly in salt water, also migrating from one to the other. A group of fishes whose evolutionary background is not completely clear.

Gasterosteus: Sticklebacks.

Genus of the family *Gasterosteidae*, of elongated, spindle-shaped build and 3, 9 or more dorsal spines as well as a pair of sturdy ventral spines, which evolved from the ventral fins. Besides there is a short spike before the anal fin. On the Three-Spined Stickleback, the third spine is nothing but a short spike in front of the dorsal fin. The body is naked or covered with more or less complete rows of bony plates.

Distributed over Europe, northern Asia and North America, (there also with another genus, *Apeltes*.

The Sticklebacks are very interesting aquarium inhabitants. They are lively, quarrelsome, beautifully colored at spawning time and possess a high degree of intelligence. Their behavior is remarkable in every way, particularly the brood care which is exercised by the male (paternal family). For this purpose the males construct nests from plant pieces and guard the eggs laid there and the hatched young. After they leave the nest the fry are herded for a few more days.

It is best to keep them in a tank which is not too small, even if they can adapt to a smaller tank. Only in a larger tank is it possible to keep several pairs together and observe the individual characteristics of the creatures. There have been numbers of highly informative experiments made on Stickleback behavior (WUNDER), which resulted in the finding that their coloration is coupled with certain phases of behavior and that males who were guarding broods respected each other's territories, when enough space was at hand which corresponded to their instinctive conception of what their requirements were.

— aculeatus Linné: Three-Spined Stickleback.

FORM: As described for the genus, D III/10-12, A I/8. Sides may be armored with more or less complete bony plates, but may also be almost naked. There are up to 5 subspecies, distinguished by the form of armoring. Length $2\frac{1}{2}''$ and more, depending upon local conditions.
COLOR: Silvery with dark gray-green patches, very variable. At spawning time, the male has a bright red belly and brilliant green back. The female is fuller in body, and younger specimens are sometimes difficult to distinguish.

Gasterosteus aculeatus — various forms of armor.

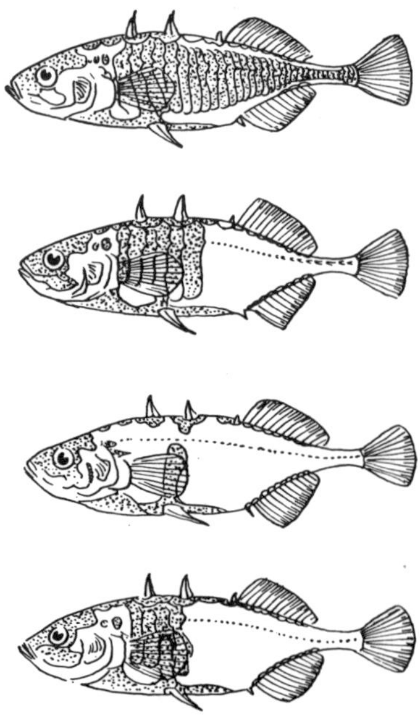

RANGE: Europe, northern Asia and North America. Lately this species has been found in the Danube and the Mediterranean area, probably introduced in these places. Found in all sorts of waters, some of which are not inhabited by any other fish life, also in brackish and marine waters.

CARE AND BREEDING: As given for the genus. An undemanding cold-water fish, which does not require a great deal of oxygen. It can also withstand temporary temperature rises to 68° F. It has been found advisable to plant the light side and the corners of the aquarium densely and thereby to provide retreats. All sorts of food are accepted, but living foods are distinctly preferred. Some individuals do not care at all for dry foods. Breeding is simple, and the young may be raised with very fine live foods, also helping out with microworms in addition.

It is advisable to keep several females to each male, so that the nests may be properly filled with eggs. The ripe females are easily recognized by their bulging bellies. After spawning females should be separated, while the male is taken out only after brood care is fully completed, namely, when the fry begin to scatter.

Gasterosteus pungitius

— **pungitius** Linné: Nine-Spined Stickleback.

FORM: As described for the genus. D IX-XI/11, A I/9-11. The body is naked, with only a few little bony plates covering the caudal base. Length up to 2¼″.

COLOR: Dark brownish, belly light except during spawning time, when the bellies of the males become velvety black.

RANGE: Northern Europe. Unknown in southern Europe.

CARE AND BREEDING: As for the previous species, but the nest hangs freely among the plants. These fish battle furiously to protect their territories.

Gastropoda: With foot on the belly (snails).

Class of the family of *Mollusca* which is distinguished by a fleshy foot, a scarcely separated head with mouth opening, eyes and feelers. The foot is flattened on the bottom and forms a creeping sole, which affords locomotion by muscular contractions and the release of slimy substances. On the back there is a circular mantle which forms the snail-shell. The internal organs are protected by a tough sac which is protected by the mantle and shell. Looking at it from the point, the shell is usually coiled spirally to the right, but also at times to the left. The shell form is highly varied. It is composed of several layers, which are separated from the mantle. The calcium required for its structure is extracted from the vegetable nourishment. The lid which is sometimes present is connected to the body of the snail, and not to the shell. It closes the shell when the snail retreats into it. When moving forward the fore part of the sole exudes a slime on which the foot can creep easily with an undulatory motion. The skin is rich in slime glands. In some species breathing is accomplished solely through the skin, but usually there are accessory breathing organs in the mantle cavity, which in the aquatic snails are composed partly of gills and partly of lungs. There is a heart and circulatory system. The "feelers" which are located on the head serve principally as organs of smell. The eyes lie either in the skin or at the ends of the feeler-shaped extensions. They are sometimes highly developed, and the surrounding skin is also sensitive to light. Small bubbles serve as balancing organs. There are also well-developed brain ganglia and a nervous system.

A particularly remarkable organ is the rasping tongue (radula) which picks up the nourishment, masticates it and prepares it for the intestine. This is built in a varied manner, depending upon the type of nourishment on which the animal feeds. The intestinal tract is highly articulated. Most snails are hermaphrodites. The simple sperm gland forms both eggs and sperm threads. The eggs are often very large, and in fresh-water snails they are frequently imbedded in a slimy substance. Some snails are livebearing. Classification is made according to their breathing organs in this order: Front Gills (*Prosobranchia*), Lung Snails (*Pulmonata*), and Back Gills (*Ophistobranchia*), of which there are no fresh-water representatives.

The many kinds of aquatic snails are suited partly for the aquarium of native species, and those coming from the tropics are also suited to the warm-water aquarium. Native snails do not last long in the latter type of aquarium. For the native aquarium it is best to choose specimens which occur in warm, standing waters in which there is no fish life. It pays to keep snails in special tanks. Wild snails, that is, snails from local waters should not be kept with fishes, because there is the possibility that they might be disease carriers. For community aquaria in which it is desired to keep snails, only those which were aquarium-bred should be chosen. It is a mistake to consider them "the scavengers of the aquarium." The amount of waste substances which they eat is relatively small and does not compensate for the excrement which is left by them. Besides, snails can be very prolific and they may become a nuisance, being very difficult to eradicate completely.

Snails should never be allowed in the breeding aquarium, because they eat the eggs even of brood-protecting fishes which cannot always drive them off.

gathering (**collecting**) **trips:** The aquaristic name of hydrological field trips, which for decades single persons, clubs, and scientific groups have been undertaking.

Even before the birth of aquaristics scientists and interested laymen explored domestic waters in order to get acquainted with their live beings as well as with their conditions of life. A result of this exploring and collecting activity was the need that arose also to take animals and plants home in order to study them closely in water-filled containers.

Therefore AQUARISTICS (see this) has a not unimportant ancestor in hydrology, as far as this is concerned with biological and ecological questions. Still in the times of E. A. ROSSMAESSLER the gathering trip, the excursion, was a preliminary to keeping aquaria at all, for the animals and plants that would be harbored in the aquarium had first to be collected in free nature. It is evident that the aquarist of those times was simultaneously a terrarist and cultivated a considerably closer relationship to his native nature, than is the case with his modern successor.

Only the ever-increasing displacement from the aquarium of native organisms in favor of foreign, mainly tropical and sub-tropical fishes and plants decreased the significance of the gathering ttip. The interest aroused by the constantly new imported fishes and plants from tropical waters, their richness in shapes and colors, and the biological problems that were posed in connection with their care and breeding, forced the love for the native nature ever more into the background, with time even creating a certain disdain towards it and its friends who continued to make it their hobby.

For decades the 'native aquarium' was at low par, and even today it does not enjoy the same appreciation as the tropical aquarium. Temporarily it seemed as if the aquarist only showed interest in native nature for utilitarian reasons. He only went 'gathering' when he had to provide food for his fishes and their brood. Anyway, this thread that linked the fancier to his native waters was still strong enough not to disrupt this connection totally. Animals and plants that were caught in the net together with the live foods, just challenged one to keep and observe them.

It is a special merit of the clubs and federations, that the interest for the open nature not only did not lag, but that with time the different yearly field trips became tradition, forming an indispensable part of the yearly program. It is true that here and there the real character of the field trip as a studying jaunt had to relinquish its place to a kind of family picnic, but with time a certain method of effecting real excursions has developed. With these young aquarists have a chance to acquire their first knowledge of the world of animals and plants, which otherwise would not be available to them. The study of the different spots in a body of water, of the behavior of animals in their native haunts, of the natural harmony of all factors of nature, which becomes visible under learned leadership, all this could only further aquaristics in general, and it is no accident that the lately increasing understanding of the ecological relations has on its part again given considerable impulse to the interest in the phenomena in our native waters.

The genuine, useful gathering trip needs extensive planning. At first one has to choose the waters which are to be visited during the year. With regard to this it should be said that it is more educational to choose certain destinations ever again, for instance, to visit them in different seasons of the year. It is only in this way that a body of water will disclose all its secrets depending on the climatic data to the observer. Only through comparisons that extend over longer periods of time is it possible to gather clear ideas on its special peculiarities, on the haunts of certain animals and plants, as well as on their changing seasonal dwelling places, their reproductive cycles, and on many other things.

In case permission is needed to enter the intended locations, this should be secured in advance. This is especially true for fenced sites as well as for waters that are being economically exploited (fish ponds, etc.), or for localities that are protected by law. It is always advisable to gather extensive information on the legislation that protects nature before starting on a gathering trip, in order to avoid clashes with persons in charge of surveillance, and even to avoid unknowing transgressions of the law.

Also the equipment necessary for a field trip should be chosen in a previous discussion with all participants, in order to avoid that certain accessories be brought in duplicate or triplicate, while others are simply forgotten by everybody. It would be useful to divide the participants into several groups, for instance the group of the watchers, which may be outfitted with field glasses and photographic equipment, the group of the catchers, which is the only one entitled to catch animals and plants, the evaluating group, which distributes the collected animals and plants into viewing glasses and transportation containers that have been brought along, and which at the end of the collecting activity, when all participants have returned to the place of reunion, proceeds to give a scientific evaluation of the yields. Such a division precludes that all participants start catching and collecting right from the beginning, which could not happen without considerable muddying and roiling of the water, and without frightening away the animals one wants to watch or to catch. Wrong and undisciplined behavior on the spot may endanger the final results of the gathering trip.

The equipment should consist of the following accessories:

1. Catching Equipment. Big and small-meshed nets with collapsible rods; short hand nets with big mesh; throwing nets for plankton; catching bells of glass; fishing rods and reels (Permit!).

2. Transporting Equipment. Glass tubes (empty aspirin tubes, etc.) with stoppers or screw caps; preserve jars with screw caps (if possible in expressly made protective boxes of wood); transportation cans; watertight plastic bags; food frames, tin, or plastic, boxes and cans with air vents for insects and similar animals.

3. Watching and Observation Equipment. Microscope in carrying case; measuring instruments for pH value, hardness of water, temperature, and atmospheric pressure within transporting container, simple magnifying lenses; a small instrument kit for field trips; viewing containers (small, portable aquaria, jars, and dishes); sieves of different-sized meshes; anesthetics for small animals; preserving fluid.

4. Auxiliary Equipment. Maps; compass; sketching block and colored pencils; literature (traveling guide, and classifying books); photographic equipment; field glasses; string; thread and needles; safety pins; spirits of ammonia for insect bites; penknife; lunch.

5. Clothing. Clothing should be practical and in accordance with the season of the year, and should very specially permit walking on the side without being bound to roads and paths. Especially important: swimming trunks and rubber boots, at least for the catchers. Avoid 'Sunday clothes' as they will only get spoiled.

A gathering trip and a social family picnic are two absolutely different things, which should not intermingle. The circle of participants in the former should be composed only of those people who are interested in serious studies of the waters. One cannot, of course, object to the presence of children and relations, if these behave in accordance with the pursuits of the trip. In general, though it is more advisable to stage special trips for the children, on which these go alone, except for the presence of an expert and adult guide. The presence of trained experts should be especially stressed.

Behavior in the field is, of course, dependent on the aims of the gathering trip. It is self-evident that all buildings which were erected for the conservation and economical use of the waters, for instance, dams, locks, dikes, etc. deserve the most careful handling on the part of the members of the excursion. Loud conversations, shouting, singing, etc. should be avoided. All unnecessary disturbances to the animal world should be avoided. It is clear that no animals or plants that are protected by law should be caught or gathered, respectively, that this should only be done if a special permit has been secured, and then exclusively as far as it serves the aims of the trip. Camping sites should be restored to the same apparently untouched state in which they were encountered.

The evaluation of the trip's yield is best effected on the spot, at least in part. As far as this is possible, sketches, photographs, and scientific preparations should already be made or preserved on the site. Animals and plants should only be carried to the extent as this is demanded by the purpose of the trip, which, of course, may also be that of collecting materials for lectures or exhibitions. One should always remember, though, that any unnecessary removal of animals and plants from their native habitat always depletes our landscape which needs protection anyway.

The evaluation of the trip is of the utmost importance. If it is done in an expert way, especially if the results are recorded in writing and with illustrations, this will permit comparing them with the yields of future trips. Therefore special attention should be paid to the keeping of records.

Summing up, it may be said that the gathering trip is an important means of educating to the feeling of genuine love for one's country, to acquire a better knowledge of the species that compose our native nature, to demonstrate biological, and especially ecological connections, as well as a necessary counter-weight against the preponderant tinkering with exotic animals and plants which is otherwise essential of modern aquaristics.

Gaucho, The Fighting: see CYNOLEBIAS (or CYNOPOECILUS) MELANOTAENIA.

gelius: After a native name.
— *Barbus*.

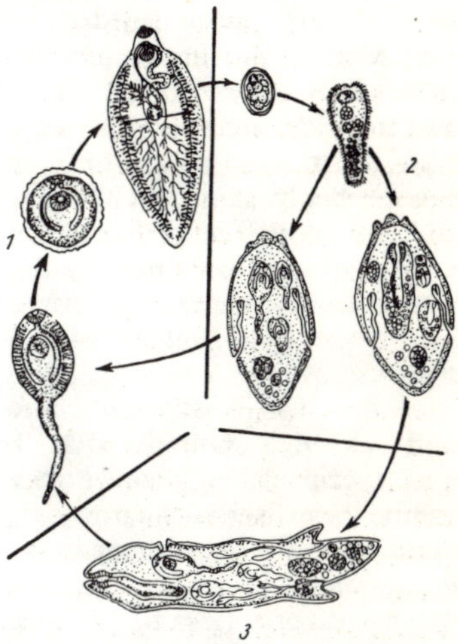

Generational change—development cycle of the Liver Leech—1. double-sexed first generation - 2. single-sexed second generation - 3. single-sexed third generation

generational change: The more or less regular cycle in some forms of animal or vegetable beings of the reproductive manner and often also in the structure. Frequently the change is from sexual to asexual propagation which we find with some plants and animals, for instance the single and double sexed propagation of water fleas, etc.

genetic history of fishes: The fishes of today are only a fraction of the forms which have populated our planet in the course of its history. Only they, however, have gone through their development up to this date, through millions of years, while many phyla and lateral branches have become extinct.

The scientific SYTEMATICS (see this) of the fishes presently living can only be completely understood with a knowledge of their genetic development, since it is built up on the relationships that become evident in this. Most enlightenment about the past forms of development is gleaned from excavations (fossils). The first imprints and remainders of fishes and parts of fishes are found in stratified rocks of the Median and upper Silurian (see TIME TABLE). From the previous, still older layers no fossils are left to us, since the more primitive forms probably possessed too few firm body parts. The first fishes in these early times had probably developed from shapes that were close to today's *Tunicata* and *Acrania*.

The first fish fossils that were found already showed such a strong specialization, that we may presume the existence of a previous, longish period of development. In the Silurian we find representatives of the jawless ones (*Agnathi*). These are fish-like primitive vertebrates, the gills of which were located in muscle purses, for which reason they are called the Purse Gills (*Marsipobranchi*). They lacked both jaws and gill arches. Their direct descendants could be today's Round Mouths (*Cyclostomata*). Those that were transmitted to us were clad in bone armors, of which there are some quite well-preserved ones in existence. Of course this does not preclude that in those times also unarmored or less armored forms may have lived, of which no fossils could be preserved, however.

Still more strongly armored species appear in the Devonian and the Lower Carboniferous: The Armored Fishes or *Placodermata*. These already belong among the genuine fishes, for in them we find jaw bones; presumably they also already possessed paired members. From this tribe should derive today's Sharks (*Selachii*). These fishes were of different sizes, and giant forms of them are known. How long the period of development lasted is shown by the manifoldness of the forms, and by their presumably very differentiated manner of living. Of these Primitive Sharks, the ancestors of our Cartilaginous Fishes, however, only minute remains are preserved. Generally they are teeth, of which some show lengths of 6″. Therefore they must have been considerably large animals.

The Cartilaginous Fishes which live today may be accompanied down to the beginning of Earth's Middle Age (Triassic). Probably, though, they already originated in the Carboniferous and the Permian, as the fossils from later ages hardly differ from the species that live in our times.

Bony Fishes too developed very early, so that one may hardly suppose a derivation from cartilage fish forms. It is probable that both tribes spring from the same root. The first, minute traces of Bony Fishes are found in the Lower Devonian. If we divide the Bony Fishes according to their fins into Ancient Fins (*Palaeopterygii*), Tassel Fins (*Crossopterygii*), and New Fins (*Neopterygii*), the Ancient Fins, which were very strongly represented during Earth's Middle Age now form an only small group. Most have become extinct. Among these we find also the members of families which may be considered as the forms which have given origin to the Bony Fishes.

They were predators, of spindle-shaped body, which possessed very strongly developed teeth. At the beginning of Earth's Middle Age, the Triassic, we find the predecessors of the Sturgeon-like (*Acipenseridae*). It is peculiar to note that these Ganoids at that time still had a bony skeleton. From the first *Palaeopterygii* derive also the *Polypteridae* which still live in Africa up to this date.

The Tassel Fins which more or less coincide with the systematic unit of the *Choanichthyes* were formerly a widely distributed group of fishes too. Today they are only represented by a few surviving forms. This group is important as it was probably from it that the branching off of terrestrial vertebrates took place. The construction of the skull and of the paired fins permits the observation of certain relationships with primitive amphibians. An order of the Tassel Fins has very lately reached fame through the fact that the Tassel Fin *Latimeria*, which was supposed extinct and had been reconstructed from fossils, was fished up alive a few years ago from the deep seas. By this it was shown that science had created an absolutely correct image of this species, based only on sparse fossil findings.

A further order of the Tassel Fins, the Lung Fishes or *Dipneusti* also was strongly represented formerly, while today there are only a few species left.

Only the New-Fins or *Neopterygii* have continued developing completely up to modern times, and comprise the greater number of all living fishes, with about 20,000 known species. Their origin should be supposed as coming from the End of the Ancient Age of Earth, the Permian. Of the most primitive, generally extinct forms of this group, today only the Bald Pikes (*Amia*), and the Gars (*Lepisosteus*) survive.

genetics: The science which deals with heredity and hereditary influences.

Gentianaceae: The Gentians.
Family of the sub-order *Dicotyledonidae*, mostly annual or perennial plants, which are widespread all over the world with about 800 species. Of those which live in the swamps or in the water there are only a few kept in the aquarium, of which the genus *Nymphoides* is described.

Gentian plants: see GENTIANACEAE.

genus: Group in taxonomic division in which a larger or smaller number of species are gathered which are of the same evolutionary origin and largely resemble each other in body structure and functions. The generic·name is capitalized in scientific literature, for example *Cyprinus*, the genus of the true Carps.

Geophagus: Dirt-eater, from the Greek and carried over into the Brazilian name "pappaterra."
South American genus of the family *Cichlidae*. The body is quite high, strongly compressed laterally and often with a pointed head and large, lively eyes. All species require large quarters because of their size. Their tanks should be arranged like those for the other Cichlids. Active diggers, which gives rise to their name "dirt-eaters." The bottom is diligently searched for anything edible. Some species exercise parental care in the manner of most South American Cichlids, some are mouthbreeders and some take the fry into their mouth when danger threatens. In the aquarium the observations made in their native waters cannot always be duplicated. Distributed all over South America as far south as the La Plata region.

— acuticeps Heckel:
FORM: As described for the genus. An elongated oval head, strongly compressed at the sides, relatively high in structure, especially in front. The forehead line rises steeply up to the beginning of the dorsal fin, but the belly line is quite flat. The large head is distinguished by a large mouth, because of the

length of the pointed snout. D XII-XIV/11-12, A III/7-8. The caudal fin has an almost straight outer edge which is only slightly indented; the pectoral fins are very large and the ventral fins considerably elongated. Dorsal and anal fins of the males are elongated at the points. Length up to 10 inches, but is already able to reproduce at 3″ to 4″.

COLOR: Greenish background with three black spots; scales at the bottom are silvery, and the sides of the head have green streaks and dots. Fins are greenish to brownish, the elongated ventral fins yellow. Females have somewhat less color.

RANGE: Quiet waters of the Amazon region, especially near the shore among rocks, roots and other hiding-places.

CARE AND BREEDING: As given in the description for the genus. One of the most active diggers among the Cichlids; very attractive in large aquaria with a number of hiding-places. Breeding is like that of the other digging Cichlids.

— **australe** Eigenmann:
Similar to the preceding species. The forehead line rises quite steeply, but the back falls toward the caudal base a little more abruptly than in the other. D XII-XIV/10-11, A III/8. Ventral fins not elongated. Length to 6″.

RANGE: La Plata near Buenos Aires, in fresh and brackish water. A little-known and seldom-kept species. Lowest temperature 55° F.

— **brasiliense** Quoy & Gaimard:
FORM: As described for the genus. The forehead, which is indented somewhat in older specimens, rises sharply; in younger specimens the head is more pointed. D XIV-XVI/10-13, A II/8-9. Dorsal and caudal fins are relatively large. Length to 11″, but in captivity is capable of reproducing at a size of 2¾″.

COLOR: Yellow to reddish-brown background with variable bars and numerous gleaming bluish-green dots on the sides of the head, sides and fins. Sex differences are slight; dorsal and anal fins are more pointed in the males.

RANGE: East coast of Brazil to the La Plata region in the south, found in fresh as well as brackish water. The species seems to prefer waters with a rocky bottom.

Geophagus brasiliense

CARE AND BREEDING: As given under *Cichlidae* and in the description for the genus. Very quarrelsome, pugnacious and vigorous rooters, which do not need a great amount of warmth. They may be kept at room temperature, and for breeding a temperature of 74-76° F is sufficient. Lowest temperature 50° F. According to present information, however, breeding in the aquarium has not so far been successful. In native waters the parents are said to take the young into the mouth when danger threatens.

— **gymnogenys** Hensel:
FORM: As described for the genus, but a little more elongated than the other species. The forehead line, especially with older specimens, is heavily indented. D XIII-XIV/10-11, A III/8-9. Ventral and caudal fins very large, dorsal, anal and ventral fins of the males are elongated at the points. Length over 12 inches, in the aquarium usually to 8 inches, but already

capable of reproducing at 3 inches.
COLOR: Brownish background with large, luminous green dots and streaks on the head, sides and fins. The female when not spawning is somewhat paler as a rule, but at the same time is often more intensely colored than the male. At such times the sexes can only be told by the differently formed genital papillae.
RANGE: In quiet waters of southeastern Brazil to the La Plata region in the south, also in tributary streams of the large rivers, particularly near the shore.
CARE AND BREEDING: As under CICHLIDAE and in the description for the genus. This species is a true Cichlid, digs vigorously and is pugnacious and nasty. No particular temperatures are specified, but the lowest may be near 50° F. The observation by HASEMAN that the female takes the young in her mouth to protect them has not been confirmed in the aquarium as yet.

Geophagus jurupari

— **jurupari:**
FORM: As described for the genus, but with a very pointed head, a gradually rising forehead, flat belly and large undershot mouth. The eyes are particularly large and lively. D XV-XVI/9-10, A III/6-7. The stiff dorsal rays are distinctly separated in the high dorsal fin and the tail is short. Length 9″, in the aquarium up to 6″.
COLOR: Yellowish background with a black stripe from the gill cover to the caudal base. At the sides of the head there are alternate light brown and light yellow bars, the fins have light yellow spots, and at the base of the scales there is often a gleaming green dot. Dorsal, anal and ventral fins of the male are elongated at the points.
RANGE: Northeastern South America, from the Amazon region to Guiana, especially in waters which have sandy bottoms.
CARE AND BREEDING: A very unusual Cichlid, which best earns the name "dirt-eater." Traveling in small schools, they "chew" through the bottom, separating the inedible substances and pushing them out through the gill-covers. In spite of their fierce appearance, this species can be described as very peaceful, perhaps the most peaceful of the genus. Here we already have an indication of this by the fact that the narrow mouth can only permit the entry of small foods. If plants are placed in sheltered spots, they will not be damaged even while the fish are spawning. This species, in contrast to the others, requires warmth. Lowest temperature is around 68°, and 76-82° F are required for spawning. In its parental care this fish represents a link between the Cichlids that dig holes and the mouthbreeding species, as the young are only occasionally taken into the mouth. The time in which this may happen may cover up to 4 weeks.

— **surinamensis** Bloch:
FORM: As given for the genus; body is quite high, the large head has a wavy and sharply rising forehead, which is somewhat dented under the eyes. The mouth opening is very big, and the belly line flat. D XVII-XIX/11-13, A III/7. The pectoral and ventral fins are very large. Length to 10″.
COLOR: Brownish-red background with a large black spot in the middle

of the body and a bar through the eye. The breast is reddish, and on the sides of the body are found blue horizontal stripes and yellow patches, in addition to many rows of green or blue gleaming dots. The fins are red with blue between the rays. Dorsal, anal and ventral fins of the males are pointed.

RANGE: Standing or slowly flowing waters of northeastern South America, from the Amazon region to Guiana. They like permanent territories among pieces of wood or stones.

CARE AND BREEDING: As given for the other Cichlids and in the description for the genus. This species is quarrelsome, pugnacious and digs a great deal. The observation by Eigenmann, who caught one with young in its mouth, have not been confirmed in the aquarium.

Gephyrocharax: Bridging-over *Charax*; because it represents an intermediate form (bridge) between two genera.

A South and Central American genus belonging to the family of the *Characidae*, with an elongated, laterally compressed body. The lateral line is complete. The dorsal fin is located far to the rear. An adipose fin is present. The genus includes the sub-family of the *Glandulocaudinae*, which among other things is noted for the fact that in most of its species an internal fertilization takes place before the actual act of spawning. The eggs are then either stuck to plants, or scattered among these where they generally stick, in the absence of the male.

— **atracaudatus** (Meek and Hildebrand): The Platinum Tetra.

SHAPE: As per description of the genus. D 9-10, A 26-33. Length up to $2\frac{3}{8}''$.

COLOR: Bluish-green base with whitish band that has a sky-blue lower edge. The caudal fin has a

Gephyrocharax atracaudatus

strongly luminous light dot with black upper and lower edges. Another luminous green-blue dot is found on the root of the caudal fin. The slimmer male has more intense colors, and its anal fin is more strongly developed.

RANGE: Panama, in clear waters of all kinds.

CARE AND BREEDING: As per description of the genus. Since this fish is very vivacious and likes to swim in schools with other fishes, a roomy tank with plenty of free space is advisable. Plant growth should not be too dense. The fish are peaceful, even if at times they have harmless little spats with fishes of the same or similar species. Average temperature around 75° F, for breeding 80° F. The females are relatively pugnacious during the breeding period, while the males are absolutely peaceful. During the mating period they do curious little dances, the climax of which consists in that they stand upright, with the heads up. They execute wavy motions which give the impression of being slightly crampy. These peculiar happenings may perhaps be related to insemination. The male takes no part in the actual act of spawning. The female glues her eggs to fine-feathered plants. The young, which hatch after 30-36 hours, need another three days to become free-swimming. Up to that time they move by sliding on plants and other firm objects. They grow rather quickly and, if well-fed, are able to reach a length of 1½″ within 3 months.

— **valencia** Eigenmann.

D 9, A 30-32. Length up to 2″. Bright silvery blue with white rays in the dorsal fin. The males have a lobed anal fin, the females a full one.

ORIGIN: Lake Valencia in Venezuela.

Care and breeding are the same as for the previous species. The female sticks the eggs on the underside of broad-leaved plants by means of her oviduct. Insemination sufficient for several spawnings (?).

germinal cells: Cells developed within the sexual organs and which serve for reproduction. In animal, as well as in many plant organisms, as a rule the germinal cells are differentiated into egg cell, or ovum, and sperm cell. The stationary, generally not self-moving, feminine egg cell, rich in plasma, is searched out by the strongly motile, generally plasma-poor, male sperm cells. These are equipped with whip-threads (flagelli) for locomotion. Germinal cells are of manifold types as to size and shape, so that also for this reason unchosen unions of germinal cells of different species become impossible. In order to cause fecundation, the sperm cells have to penetrate the ovum cells after these have reached a definite stage of maturity. This maturation takes place on one hand in the ovum, in substance, through the accumulation of carbohydrates, proteins and fats in the epithelium of the female sexual organs, on the other hand in both egg and sperm cell, through a necessary internal preparation, which attains especially the cell nucleus.

Giant Danio, the: see DANIO MALABARICUS.

Giant Gourami, the: see COLISA FASCIATA.

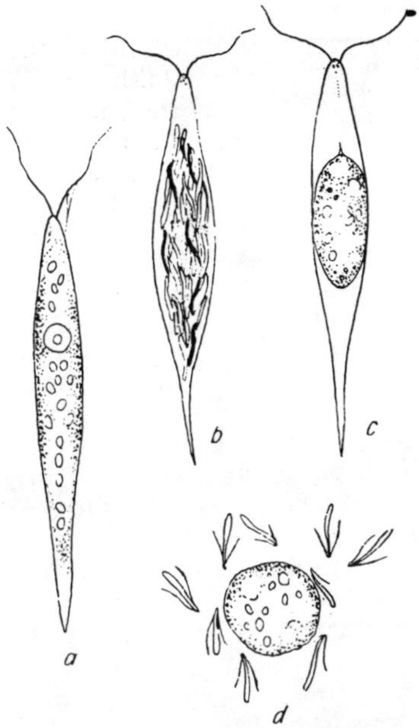

Simple germinal cell division of a flagellate - a. Vegetative individual - b. A male individual development ends with a multiple number of spermatozoa - c. The female development ends with only one egg cell - d. Fertilization follows. After Pascher, modified and enlarged.

gibba: Humpback.

— *Lemna.*

gibbosus: Humpbacked.

— *Charax.*

— *Lepomis.*

Giant Loach, the: *Brachygobius anurus.*

Giant Water Star: see NOMAPHILA STRICTA.

gigantea: The giant sized.

— *Vallisneria.*

Gill Bag Catfish, the: see HETEROPNEUSTES FOSSILIS.

gill diseases of fishes: Diseases of the gills may be caused by irritation (acids, bases, chlorine, chronic lack of oxygen), or through attacks by parasites.

Corrosion through chemical components of the water is indicated by the destruction of the gill epithelium, which appears especially at the tips of the little gill blades. Often a secondary fungus attack is its immediate consequence. If the harm caused is not too extensive, cures may be obtained by remedying the causes. Corrosion through chlorine may occur especially through the use of fresh tap water.

Gill parasites may be brought in together with live foods that come from waters populated with fishes. Also snails, which are hosts of several stages of development of the Blood worm (*Sanguinicola*) may be spreaders of gill parasites. An attack of sporozoa, unicellular parasites with a complex development, shows, among others, by spherical white cysts on the gills. If this happens, we have a species belonging to the genus *Myxobolus*. Semi-spherical white cysts, which occur mainly on Perches, Pikes, and some other fishes, indicate an attack by *Henneguya sporospermica*. The cysts of some of the species of *Myxobolus* may also take the shape of a grain of rice.

These kinds of diseases are incurable, and therefore very dangerous. Fish populations with stronger incidences, meaning, with many nodules on the gills, should be destroyed completely. Plants, sand, and snails, should be discarded. The tank and all accessories should be disinfected for 24 hours in a wine-red solution of potassium permanganate, or in a 2%-solution of Lysol. After this the tank should, of course, be well rinsed.

A bluish-white discoloration of the gills may be caused by an attack of the slimy Skin Disease (see SKIN DISCOLORATION). In this one has to mention especially the peculiar double beast *Diplozoon*. If in the destruction of the epithelium light spots are found on the gills, and, under the microscope, worm eggs, a blood worm disease is present.

To prevent gill diseases it is especially necessary to pay attention to the origin of foods, snails, and plants brought into the aquarium from free nature. If there is no other possibility of gathering food, at least it should be left standing for some hours. Furthermore, snails from free waters have no place in the home aquarium.

Gill, Theodore Nicholas: American zoologist who dedicated a great part of his life to ichthyological research. Born March 21, 1830 in New York, N.Y., died September 25, 1914.

Since 1897 Gill was the president of the American Society for the Furthering of Sciences. He, devoted his attention especially to questions of nomenclature and systematics.

gills: see RESPIRATORY ORGANS OF FISHES.

Girardinus: After the American zoologist Girard.

Genus of tooth carps pertaining to the sub-family of the live bearing tooth carps or *Poeciliinae*, with only one species. Closely related to the genus *Gambusia*.

— metallicus Poey: The Girardinus.

SHAPE: Elongated, slightly compressed laterally, with the caudal peduncle rather high. The big mouth opening is directed upwards. D 9-10, A 10-12.

LENGTH: Males up to 2″, females over $2\frac{5}{8}$″.

COLOR: Metallic-yellowish base with a series of short, shiny-black, slightly curved lateral stripes. The sexes are similar in color. SD as described for all *Poeciliinae*.

RANGE: In all kinds of waters on Cuba, even those that are directly connected with the sea. The species is quite abundant everywhere.

CARE AND BREEDING: A hardy species, but needs warmth, feeling

Girardinus metallicus

best around 77° F. They are omnivorous, and their diet includes even soft algae. After reaching a length of about 1⅜″ the female is already ready to breed. Pregnancy lasts a little over 4 weeks, the period being shorter or longer according to conditions of warmth, food, and sunshine, which latter the species loves very much. The number of young varies from 20 to 50. They grow very quickly.

Glandulocauda: With gland at the caudal peduncle.

South American genus pertaining to the family of the Characins or *Characidae*, sub-family of the *Glandulocaudinae*. The species of this genus are of a more or less elongated shape, laterally compressed. The dorsal fin inserts a little behind the middle of the body, and the adipose fin is well-developed. The lateral line is incomplete. The fish have accessory respiration seated in a cavity above the gills. Besides this the males have a glandulous pocket, formed of scales, at the insertion of the tail fin, which probably is significant in fecundation.

— inequalis Eigenmann: The Croaking Tetra.

SHAPE: As described for the genus. D 10, A 27-33. Length: males up to 2⅜″, females up to 1¾″.

COLOR: Metallic blue to green and silvery bright, with a vivid red upper edge of the eye, and quite prettily colored fins. The male is livelier in its colors, and its fins are more strongly developed.

RANGE: Southeastern Brazil.

CARE AND BREEDING: This pretty species is lively, peaceful, and endures the aquarium well, although, considering its activity, the tanks for it should not be too small. No special requirements are made as to temperature. 65-72° F are sufficient. For breeding give them about 75° F. It seems that higher temperatures are harmful for them. Atmospheric air is taken in in lightning-quick advances to the surface, while the used-up air is expelled through the gill covers. This causes a relatively audible noise, heard frequently especially during the pretty mating play of the males. It is probably during these plays that insemination occurs. The male executes very vivacious, quivering motions. The real act of spawning follows later, without participation of the male. The female generally glues the eggs to the underside of broad-leaved plants, obviously preferring leaves that are located near the surface. The eggs, about .045″ in diameter, numbering about 70, hatch after 36 to 48 hours. The fry continue hanging from plants and glass sides for another two days before they become free-swimming. They need much food, but grow quickly so that after 3 to 4 months they may already be able to propagate.

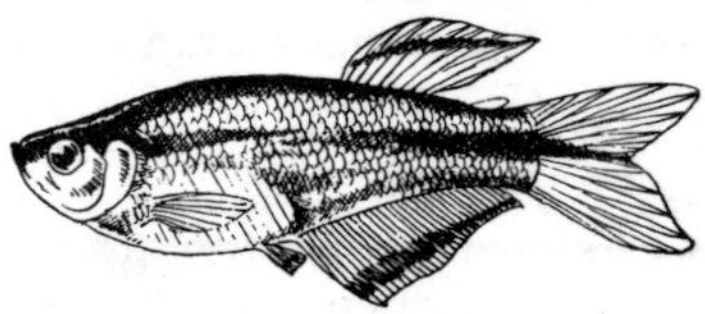

Glandulocauda inequalis

Glandulocaudinae: Sub-family belonging to the family of the Characins or *Characidae*, all of small size and elongated body shape, more or less compressed laterally. The dorsal fin inserts far back, and the pectorals often are big and sickle-shaped. The males often have grotesquely developed fins, a peculiar formation of opercle or of certain scales, and at the base of the tail fin a pocket or bag-like formation of glands. The tail fin is often split down to the caudal peduncle. The *G.* are noteworthy in their method of procreation in that the insemination in most species occurs before the act of spawning itself and may be sufficient for several layings (stored insemination). During the act of mating the females receive several batches of semen in a manner as yet unexplained. Genera, among others: *Corynopoma*, *Gephyrocharax*, *Glandulocauda*, *Mimagoniates*, and *Pseudocorynopoma*.

Glass Barb, the: see CHELA OXYGASTROIDES.

Glass Crabs: see LEPTODORIDAE.

Glass Catfish, the African: see PHYSAILIA PELLUCIDA.

Glass Catfish, the East Indian: see CRYPTOPTERUS MACROCEPHALUS.

Glass Catfish, the Indian: see CRYPTOPTERUS BICIRRHIS.

Glass Characin, the Small-Scaled: see ROEBOIDES GUATEMALENSIS.

glass cleaner: Accessory for cleaning the inner surface of aquarium glass, usually consisting of a handle with attached clamp which holds a razor blade or sponge.

Glass Fish, the: see AMBASSIS LALA.

Glass Fishes: A glass-like transparency in aquatic beings is not rare. In fresh water animals it is often found in unicellulars and micro-organisms that lead a planktic life, furthermore in many fish larvae and freshly hatched young

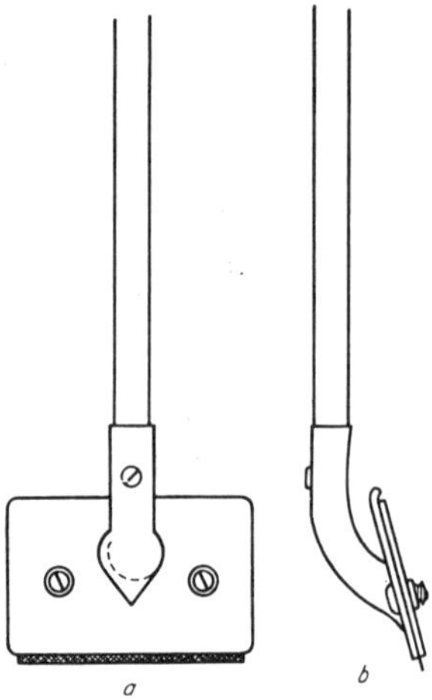

Glass cleaner which holds a razor blade. a. Top view. b. Side view.

in the first stages of development. But also many full-grown fishes, especially the smaller species, may be more or less transparent so that with back lighting one can clearly see the dorsal spine and some organs. This transparency is to be explained by a scantness of pigments on a body that in itself is flatly compressed. Sometimes one still finds concentrations of pigments on certain limited spots of the body, especially the eyes. Whenever colors appear, they are very delicate and pure reflex colors, which originate from refraction of the light that incides on the scales.

glass panes and their thickness: see GLAZING THE AQUARIUM.

Glass Perches: see AMBASSIS.

Glass Tetra, the: see MOENKHAUSIA OLIGOLEPIS.

glass, thickness of: see GLAZING.

glass wool: Spun glass which, due to its density and inertia to water has found manifold uses in aquaristics, especially in filters. Opposed to its use though, recently—and probably justly—objections have been raised as one cannot disprove possible harm to the skin and gills of fishes caused by dispersed splinters. It is advisable to use nylon or perlon threads, or fabrics, instead of glass wool.

glazing the frame aquarium: Glazing the aquarium deserves the maximum attention, and should always be done by an expert, who is also experienced in glazing aquaria. Work efficiently done may save much chagrin, especially since a perfectly glazed aquarium is protected to a great extent against the development of poisonous metal salts.

The thickness of the panes must correspond to the size of the tank. It is calculated according to length and height, especially the latter. The thickness that should be used may be seen from the tables given below. For insulating the bottom it is best to use a pane of common glass, which is cemented on the metallic bottom, while for smaller tanks generally a simple glass bottom is used. The sides and the back may be made of common glass of good quality, while the front pane should be of plate-glass, if possible. The panes should be perfect, without blemishes or inclusions. If possible, one should always use glasses without strong color hues. The cut edges of big panes should be slightly ground in order to minimize the danger of breakages, which start from smallest fissures on the edges.

The cementing of the glasses too should be done by an expert. Badly cemented tanks are sources of constant vexation, since the defects caused by this (leakages, penetration of water between metallic and glass bottom—eventually also poisonings that result from this) are very hard to repair. It is foolish to economize in this. The panes have to be cut exactly to size. Tanks with glass bottoms are glazed in the following order: bottom, length panes, lateral panes. The bottom glass should fit exactly, less an all-around free space $\frac{1}{8}''$ wide. The measurements of the length panes result from the inner length of the tank (less $\frac{1}{8}''$ on each side), and the inner height (less thickness of the bottom pane plus $\frac{1}{8}''$ putty plus $\frac{1}{8}''$ upper edge). The measurements of the lateral panes, since they are placed on the bottom glass like the length panes, and also between these, are calculated as follows: inner length of sides (less the thickness of the front and back length panes plus $\frac{1}{8}''$ free space for cement on each side) and inner length of the sides (less thickness of the bottom pane plus $\frac{1}{8}''$ thickness of cement and $\frac{1}{8}''$ upper edge).

Tanks without glass bottom are glazed in the following sequence: length panes—lateral panes. We deduce the calculations from the ones given above simply by leaving out the thickness of the bottom pane and of the cement, or putty, in the heights.

When cementing, or puttying, it is advisable to include cork discs of the thickness of a match-stick in the putty at distances of 8″ from each other, in order to decrease the tension. Otherwise it may happen that quite long panes bend too strongly in the middle and break.

Putty Recipes:

2 lbs. of good common putty.
1 tablespoon linseed oil.
Red lead until the cement turns an intense red color.

2 lbs. pure varnish putty.
1 table-spoon red lead.
Sufficient sifted whitening to avoid doughiness of the cement, respectively to avoid breaking.

The mixtures should be well kneaded and worked while still warm, if possible.

Sterba points out that in aquarium putty one should only use

THICKNESS OF THE GLASS PANES OF AQUARIA

Length of tank	12″	16″	20″	24″	28″	32″	36″	40/44″	44/48″	48/60″
Height	12″	12″	12″	12″	12″	12″	12″	12″	12″	12″
Min. thickness of pane	7/64″	9/64″	5/32″	11/64″	11/64″	11/64″	3/16″	1/4″	9/32″	23/64″
Height	16″	16″	16″	16″	16″	16″	16″	16″	16″	16″
Min. thickness of pane	9/64″	11/64″	13/64″	7/32″	15/64″	1/4″	17/64″	9/32″	9/32″	23/64″
Height	20″	20″	20″	20″	20″	20″	20″	20″	20″	20″
Min. thickness of pane	11/64″	13/64″	15/64″	17/64″	9/32″	5/16″	21/64″	11/32″	23/64″	7/16″
Height		24″	24″	24″	24″	24″	24″	24″	24″	24″
Min. thickness of pane		15/64″	17/64″	19/64″	11/32″	3/8″	25/64″	27/64″	29/64″	15/32″
Height		28″	28″	28″	28″	28″	28″	28″	28″	28″
Min. thickness of pane		17/64″	19/64″	21/64″	23/64″	13/32″	7/16″	31/64″	33/64″	35/64″
Height		32″	32″	32″	32″	32″	32″	32″	32″	32″
Min. thickness of pane		19/64″	27/64″	11/32″	3/8″	7/16″	31/64″	35/64″	15/32″	41/64″

varnish that has aged for years, and never fresh. Furthermore it is his opinion that the use of red lead is superfluous in well-insulated and carefully glazed tanks. According to him, pure varnish putty remains soft on the inside, developing an outer, hard crust.

According to MUELLER in order to manufacture a non-decaying putty one needs only completely dry, powdered whitening and vegetable oil dehydrated by boiling. The whitening is kneaded with the oil until the dough does not stick to the hands. After this the putty should rest for at least one day, so that oil and whitening may combine well. This putty may be stored for long times.

When puttying, it is important to exert moderate pressure on the edges of the panes while working them into the putty, which has previously been placed in sausage-shaped pieces on the frame. The holes in the bottom plate should not be stopped up.

After the glazing, fill the aquarium with water to the upper edge and let it stand for several days, possibly with repeated changes of water. Leaking spots should be repaired during this period. Painting is only done after the tank has proven to be water-proof.

Glochidia: Shellfish larvae, see UNIONIDAE.

Glossiphoniidae: Flat Leeches. Family belonging to the superfamily of the Trunk Leeches or *Rhynchobdellodea.* Small leeches with a flattened body, which swim little or not at all, but live clinging to stones or plants. They suck on cold-blooded vertebrates, and sometimes even on molluscs or worms. They include, among others:

Hemiclepis marginata (Mueller), which is about 1⅛″ long, with a greenish to brownish color with yellow dots. *H. m.* cares for its young, the mother providing them with fresh water by means of wavy motion of her body. A still smaller species, which reaches only 3/16″ to ⅜″ in length, is *Helopdella stagnalis* (L.). Of this species the mother carries the eggs on her body.

Glowlight Tetra: see HEMIGRAMMUS ERYTHROZONUS.

Glugea-disease of fishes: A disease caused by the microsporidium *Glugea pseudotumefasciens* Pflugfelder, symptoms of which resemble those of *Ichthyosporidium.* Consequently the disease was only recognized as such in 1952. The parasite attacks especially the conjunctive tissues, causing relatively big nodules in the most diverse organs, even pop-eye and boil-like sores may appear. So far no cure is known. Diseased fish should be destroyed immediately.

Gnathobdellodea: Jaw Leeches. Super-family pertaining to the order of the *Archaetobdellae*, with two families: the *Hirudinidae* and the *Haemadipsidae*. To the *Hirudinidae* family belong, as the best-known species, the medicinal leech, *Hirudo medicinales*, and the Horse Leech, *Haemopis sanguisuga*.

Gnathonemus: With threads on jaw.
Genus pertaining to the family of the Nile Pikes or *Mormyridae*.

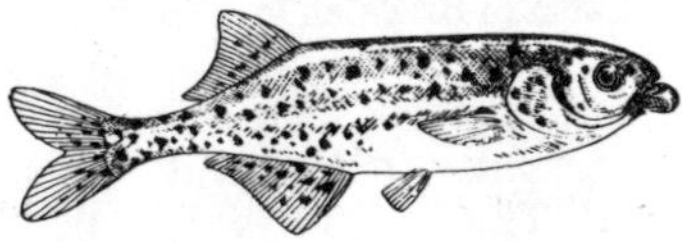

Gnathonemus macrolepidotus

— macrolepidotus Peters:
SHAPE: Fish of elongated construction, with arched brows and rounded appendix on lower jaw. D 23-25, A 28-32. Length about 10″.
COLOR: Darkish brown with numerous black specks.
RANGE: In dark and muddy waters in East Africa.
CARE AND BREEDING: This nocturnal species needs roomy tanks with hiding places made of stones and roots, and a dark, soft bottom. The water level should be low, and the temperature should be kept between 72 and 83° F. Manner of procreation is unknown.

— petersii Guenther:
In early youth an attractively colored species, coming from tropical West Africa, from the Niger and Congo Rivers. Length up to 9″. Care as described for previous species.

Gnathonemus petersii

Gnathostomata: Jawed Animals. Sub-class of the Vertebrates, which opposes with its bigger number the jawless animals or *Agnathi*. Comprises, among others, also the fishes (*Pisces*), which in systematics, though, do not appear as such any more, but are divided into two classes: the cartilaginous fishes or *Chondrichthyes*, and the bony fishes or *Osteichthyes*.

gnats, mosquitoes: see NEMATOCERA.

Gobiidae: Family of mostly small species belonging to the sub-order of the *Gobioidea*. They differ from the closely related family of the *Eleotridae* especially by the construction and position of the ventral fins. In the *Gobiidae* these are grown together at the basis and form a sucking plate with the aid of which the fishes are able to stick onto objects. This may be considered as an adaptation to their special surroundings, for they come mainly from the surf zone or from quick-moving waters. All representatives of the genus live in brackish or salt waters, but some species migrate occasionally to fresh water. It is always advisable to add some salt to the aquarium water, even in the case of the *Brachygobius* species. As food they willingly take worms besides insects and other live foods. Dry foods are always scorned.

For aquaristics two sub-families are significant: The *Gobiinae* themselves, and the *Periophthalminae.* The latter are noticeable for their high-inserted eyes and the leg-like pectorals, which are lacking in the *Gobiinae.*

The sub-family *Gobiinae* comprises mainly the genera *Gobius, Stigmatogobius,* and *Brachygobius.*

Gobio: Genus belonging to the family of the Carp or *Cyprinidae.* Elongated bottom fishes from the shore zones, which live especially in waters with sandy or gravelly bottom. In the corners of the mouth two barbels are found. The eyes are inserted high. The hooklike gullet teeth form two rows. The scales are big; the dorsal fin has no stiff or saw-like rays.

— fluviatilis Cuvier.

SHAPE: As per description of the genus. The body has a rounded cross-section, slightly compressed in the rear part. The mouth is subterminal. Length up to 6″.

COLOR: Gray-brownish base with irregular bluish-black dots. The male has bigger pectorals and, during the spawning period, shows a spawning rash.

RANGE: In many parts of Europe and Northern Asia, in flowing waters and clear lakes.

CARE AND BREEDING: The fish live in schools and like to remain near the bottom straining against the current. They are omnivorous, taking all kinds of live and dry foods. Mating time is from May to June. The 1000 to 3000 eggs are laid in lumps on stones and aquatic plants.

Gobio fluviatilis

To keep this species one has to have not too small containers. Clear water, strong aeration, and cleanly washed gravel on the bottom are musts. Spawning them in the aquarium has been accomplished. The rearing of the young was similar to that of all Cyprinids.

gobio: Relates to the Goby-like looks of the fish.

— *Cottus.*

Gobioidea: Sub-order belonging to the order of the Perch-shaped or *Percomorphi,* which has its home especially on the coast of the Southern seas. The *G.* are a group which is very rich in species, numbering about 900 of these. Most of them live in the sea, a small number also in brackish and fresh water.

All *Gobioidea* have two separate dorsal fins, the first of which has hard spines, the second one soft ones. The tail fin is rounded or pointed, never forked. The ventrals stand on the breast, and are often joined together into a sucking plate. The body is more or less elongated, sometimes thickened and pestle-like at the head. Scales may exist or not. They show both comb-like and round scales. In most cases the swimming bladder is absent.

Of the many families of this sub-order our interest goes especially to the *Gobiidae* and the *Eleotridae.*

Gobius sadanundio: see STIGMATOGOBIUS SADANUNDIO.

Gold Band Characin, the: see CREAGRUTUS BENI.

Gold Fish, the: see CARASSIUS AURATUS GIBELIO.

goldfish bell: Unnatural container for the keeping of goldfish, possibly an imitation of certain Chinese containers, which are much roomier though. Because of the narrow neck, the goldfish bell did not permit planting and hindered the exchange of gases, forcing the fish

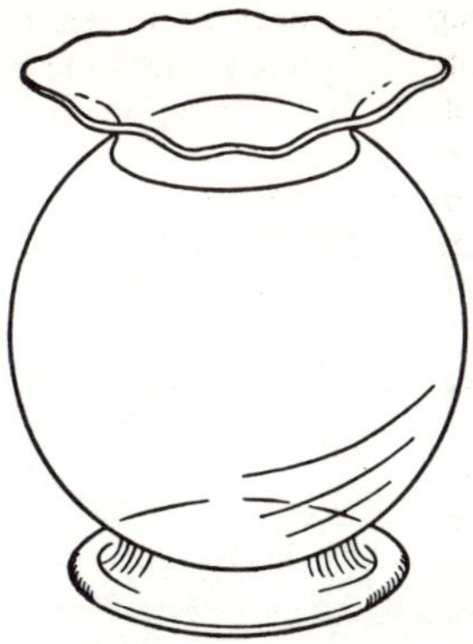

Old-fashioned goldfish bowl

kept therein to take the oxygen necessary for their breathing at the surface in a painful position of the body.

Gold Ring Puffer, the: see TETRAODON MBU.

Gold Stripe Rasbora, the: see RASBORA TAENIATA.

Golden Cichlid, the: see CHAETOBRANCHOPSIS BITAENIATUS.

Golden Cichlid, the: see CICHLASOMA AUREUM.

Golden Ear, Golden Pestle: see ORONTIUM AQUATICUM.

Golden-Eyed Dwarf Cichlid, the: see NANNACARA ANOMALA.

Golden Line Rasbora, the: see RASBORA LEPTOSOMA.

Golden Pencil Fish, the: see NANNOSTOMUS BECKFORDI.

Golden Pheasant Gularis, the: see APHYOSEMION SJOESTEDTI.

Golden (or Green) Rivulus, the: see RIVULUS UROPHTHALMUS.

gonad: Germ cell.

gonopodium: Mating organ of the live bearing tooth carps pertaining to the sub-families of the *Poeciliinae*, *Jenynsiinae*, and *Goodeinae*, developed on the male fishes by a transformation of the anal fin, and which serves to bring near to, or to introduce into, the female sexual opening the spermatozoa, which generally are joined into bundles.

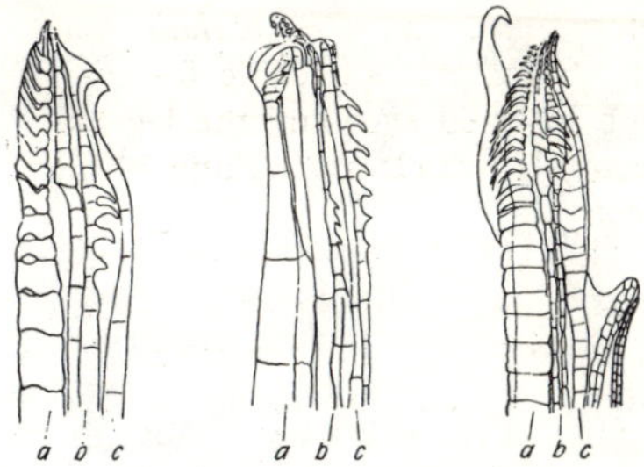

Gonopodium of several **Poeciliinae.** a. First ray of the converted anal fin. b. Second ray. c. Third ray.

The intimate structure of the gonopodium is generally very differentiated and is used to establish the systematical division of the sub-families as it permits binding conclusions as to the relationships of the different species.

Goodea: Genus of live bearing tooth carps belonging to the sub-family of the *Goodeinae*.

— atripinnis Jordan: A species coming from Central Mexico and only rarely imported. Greenish base with dark-edged fins and rows of dark dots. Length of the females up to 3⅜″, while generally the male is a little smaller. 67-74° F suffices for keeping this species. Procreation corresponds in general terms to that of the other live bearing tooth carps. For each litter, though, a new insemination is necessary. The gonopodium is of very simple construction.

Goodea atripinnis, male at left

goodei: After the American ichthyologist Goode.

— *Chriopeops*.

Goodeinae: Sub-family of live bearing tooth carps pertaining to the family of the tooth carps or *Cyprinodontidae*, noted by the fact that in the males the transformation of the anal fin into a gonopodium is only partly accomplished. Only the first rays are joined together, while otherwise the fin remains unchanged. Probably each procreation period depends upon a new mating. The species *Goodea*, probably the only one of this family, is limited in its range to a narrow area of Central America.

goramy: After the native name.
— *Osphronemus*.

Gourami: see OSPHRONEMUS GORAMY.
— Blue, the: see TRICHOGASTER TRICHOPTERUS (SUMATRANUS).
— Chocolate, the: see SPAERICHTHYS OSPHROMENOIDES.
— Croaking, the: see TRICHOPSIS VITTATUS.
— Dwarf, the: see COLISA LABIOSA.
— Giant, the: see COLISA FASCIATA.
— Kissing, the: see HELOSTOMA TEMMINCKI.
— Opaline, the: see TRICHOGASTER TRICHOPTERUS.
— Pearl or Mosaic, the: see TRICHOGASTER LEERI.
— Silver, the: see TRICHOGASTER MICROLEPIS.
— Snake-Skinned, the: see TRICHOGASTER PECTORALIS.
— Thick-Lipped, the: see COLISA LABIOSA.
— Three-Spot, the: see TRICHOGASTER TRICHOPTERUS.

Gracile Ambulia, the: see LIMNOPHILA GRATIOLOIDES.

Gracile Dwarf Cichlid, the: see NANNACARA TAENIA.

Gracile Pencilfish, the: see NANNOSTOMUS MARGINATUS.

gracilis: Gracile, delicate, slender, graceful.
— *Hyphessobrycon:* see HEMIGRAMMUS ERYTHROZONUS.
— *Nitella.*
— *Pimelodella.*

graminea: Grass-like.
— *Sagittaria.*

Gramineae: Grasses.
Numerous family of plants belonging to the class of the *Monocotyledoneae*. As a rule they are perennial herbs, more rarely bushes. The stalks are provided with knots at regular intervals. The leaves, which are lodged in sheaths, are alternate. The flowers are mostly hermaphroditic, less frequently monosexual, and form panicled or ear-like stands. The family comprises no real aquarium plants. For warm swamp aquaria one may use some species of the Sugar-cane group (*Sacharum*), or Rice (*Oryzia*), furthermore in open air pools Reed (*Phragmites*), Manna Grass (*Glyceria*), and Dwarf Bamboo (*Bambuso nana*).

gramineus: Grass-like.
— *Acorus.*
— *Potamogeton.*

graminifolium: With grass-like leaves.
— *Alisma.*

grandiflorus: With great flowers.
— *Echinodorus.*

Grass Leaved Frog Spoon, the: see ALISMA GRAMINIFOLIUM.

Grasses: see GRAMINEAE.

gratioloides: Of delicate aspect.
— *Limnophila.*

Green Characin, the: see BRYCONALESTES CHAPERI.

Green Panchax, the: see APLOCHEILUS BLOCKII.

green water: see FIGHTING ALGAE. OXYGEN.

gregarious instinct: School instinct—the need of many fishes for gregariousness, pertaining to the hereditary aspects of their species, which shows already in larvae and young fry, and is also significant for the behavior of full-grown specimens.

griemi: After a surname.
— *Hyphessobrycon.*

griffithii: After the Botanist Griffith.
— *Cryptocoryne.*

Grindal Worms: see ENCHYTRAEUS.

grislagine.
— *Leuciscus.*

Groundling, the: see GOBIO FLUVIATILIS.

growths: As growths we consider algae or firmly located unicellular animals which settle on aquatic plants, rocks, etc. Growths are needed as food by many fishes, such as, for instance, Live-Bearing Tooth Carps and Headstanders. Besides grazing off algae, the intake of animal micro-organisms connected with this also plays an important part.

Guanin crystals

guanin, guanin crystals: An excretion product that is deposited as a shiny metallic, crystalline layer in the skin, iris, swimming bladder, and some other spots of the body of fishes. The crystals have a strong refractory action on light and produce the silvery sheen on fishes, as well as the glow-colors when combined with other pigments.

guatemalensis: Coming from Guatemala.
— *Roeboides.*

Guenther, Albert C. L. G., 1830-1914. Well-known ichthyologist of German origin who, after having written a paper on the fishes of the Neckar River (1855), was called to the British Museum in London. From there he published in 1859-1870 the eight-volumed "Catalogue of Fishes" which described 8525 species. Later appeared a comprehensive presentation of the whole science of ichthyology (1880) which was published under the title "Handbook of Ichthyology". G. was active at the British Museum for over 39 years.

guentheri: After the ichthyologist Albert C. Guenther.
— *Nothobranchius.*
— *Pelmatochromis.*

Guenther's Cichlid: see PELMATOCHROMIS GUENTHERI.

Guinasana: From Lake Guinas, in South West Africa.
— *Tilapia.*

Guinea Cichlid, the: see TILAPIA GUINEENSIS.

gulare: Notable for its throat.
— *Aphyosmemion.*

Gullet Leeches: *Pharyngobdellodea.*

Guppy: Popular name for *Lebistes reticulatus,* which formerly was called *Girardinus guppyi,* after the Englishman Guppy, who brought the first fish of this species to England.

guttata: Drop-shaped.
— *Copeina.*

Gymnallabes: With naked spot on the cheek.
African genus belonging to the family of the Gill-Sac Catfishes or *Clariidae,* with only one species. The body is long and Eel-shaped. The head is small and flattened, and carries four pairs of barbels. The skin is naked and mucous. The vertical fins, which are very elongated, are connected to each other, and form an uninterrupted edge around the rear part of the body. The teeth are very thin and stand together in ribbons. The species *G. typus* Guenther comes from West Africa. During the daytime they are very lively, but like a shadowy tank with sufficient roots and stones to serve them as hiding places. The fish come to the surface

Gymnallabes typus

in order to breathe and to expel the used-up air in big bubbles. They are harmless and live on worms, etc. which hide in the soil. 68-75° F gives sufficient warmth.

Gymnarchus: Naked anus, as the anal fin is lacking.

Genus pertaining to the family of the *Mormyridae* or Nile Pikes, which, contrary to the other representatives of the family, are eel-like. They lack ventral, anal, and caudal fins. Motion is achieved by moving the body and by waves that run along the dorsal fin. The genus might eventually be considered as the independent family of the *Gymnarchidae*.

The peculiar manner of reproduction of *Gymnarchus niloticus* has become well-known. This species builds floating nests from parts of plants in shallow waters. The male defends eggs and young aggressively. The fry hatch after about 8 days, and leave the nest after another 10 days. During their time in the nest, the larvae show long red gill threads and an elongated yolk sac. They unceasingly move in an endeavor to come to the surface in order to fill their swimming bladders.

Gymnocorymbus: With naked crown of the head.

South American genus belonging to the family of the Characins or *Characidae*.

— ternetzi (Boulenger): The Black Tetra, or The Blackamoor.

SHAPE: A rather high fish, the body height of which still increases, especially in older specimens. They may then look a little hunchbacked. D 11-12, A 40-42. Length up to

Gymnocorymbus ternetzi

$2\frac{3}{8}$″.

COLOR: Gray-green silvery base with several black transverse bands over the body. The rear part, dorsal, adipose, and anal fins of younger specimens are deep black, later only gray in several shades. The tail fin lobes of the males are distinctly white, and generally the male sex remains smaller and more delicate.

RANGE: Upper Paraguay River.

CARE AND BREEDING: The species loves sunny locations and tanks with clear water. Since they like to assemble into bigger schools, it is advisable to keep them in roomy tanks, together with swift-swimming fishes. They feel especially well at higher degrees of warmth. 74-77° F are adequate, and may be increased to 83° F for spawning. On the other hand they are not too sensitive to lower temperatures. The species is lively, peaceful, and eats all kinds of live and dry foods of corresponding size. The 600-800 eggs are expelled into the free water. The fry, which hatch after about 48 hours, are easy to rear, in the manner of most Characins.

gymnogenys: With naked gill covers or opercles.

— *Geophagus*.

Gymnotidae: With naked back.

A family of South American Knife Fishes pertaining to the sub-order of the CYPRINOIDEA (see these) with elongated, partly eel-like shapes of body, which should not be mistaken for the Knife Fishes of the ancient hemisphere, which belong to the family of the *Notopteridae*. The body is naked or covered with tiny scales. The front part is rather high, tapering to a point in the rear, where often a whip-like tip appears. The head is small, and the eyes tiny. The mouth opening is narrow, provided with many weak teeth. The anus is located near the throat. The dorsal fin is totally absent or consists of one only thread. The anal fin is very long and comprises nearly the whole lower side. Motion is achieved through wavy movements of the anal fin and is peculiarly gliding, with the same agility forward or backward. The swimming bladder consists of two parts joined together by a duct.

Only smaller specimens of Knife Fish are advisable for the home aquarium, but they are very impressive in public aquaria. They lead a retiring, often even nocturnal life, but when they finally come forward, they cause a sensation by their manner of swimming. The fish are shy and suspicious. Older specimens are especially hard to catch. Food consists of good-sized live foods. With proper care they may be hardy and long-lived. Genera, among others, *Gymnotus*.

Gymnotus carapo Linné: American or Striped Knife Fish.
South American Knife Fish belonging to the family of the *Gymnotidae*. Body shape as per description of the family. The anal fin shows 200-260 rays. All other fins are absent with exception of the small pectorals. Length up to 24″. A lighter base is covered with many cross stripes, listing a little forward. The species originates from tropical and sub-tropical South America down to the La

Gymnotus carapo

Plata in the South. Care as per description of the family. Very vicious.

Gyrinidae: Swimming in circles. Tumble bugs.
Family of water bugs of the order of the Beetles or *Coleoptera*. The family generally is known even to the superficial observer as the small beetles cut figures on the water surface like skaters. Their body is excellently adapted to their manner of life. It is boat-shaped and its surface is water-repellent. The two rearmost pairs of legs are enlarged to the shape of fins, while the first pair is used to catch food or for the male to hold the female during mating. The composite eyes are divided in the middle and disposed in order to permit seeing above and below the water surface. The beetles can swim submerged in a straight line, due to an extended steering gear, while on the surface they can only move in the well-known arcs. In case of danger they dive lightning-quick from the surface, but have to cling to firm objects due to the water-shedding qualities of their bodies, as otherwise they are impelled upwards. All tumble bugs are good fliers. They hibernate under water clinging to plants or in hiding places. The eggs are anchored in rows on plants by the end of May. The predatory larvae live at the bottom, have poison glands, but have no external digestion like, for instance, the larvae of *Dytiscus marginalis*. The family ranges especially in the Tropics. Anyway, some species are also found in Central Europe, of which the well-known tumble bug, *Gyrinus natator* L. is the most

common.

Gyrinocheilidae: Family of small fresh water fishes belonging to the sub-order of the Carplike or *Cyprinoidea* which differ from the real *Cyprinidae* by a series of peculiarities. Similar to certain Sucker Catfishes, the mouth is transformed into a sucking disc which enables the fish not only to hold their own in swift-flowing waters, but also to follow their quest for food, rasping off the growth of algae which grows on fixed objects of all kinds. Simultaneously the respiratory apparatus has suffered a transformation by which the fish, even with the sucking mouth attached firmly to its anchorage, may cover their need for oxygen without the breathing water passing through the oral cavity. In this the sucking apparatus of the *G.* is more perfect than that of the Armored Catfishes of the genus *Plecostomus*, as in these the breathing water flows in through a thin cleft between lip edge and base.

The family comprises only the genus *Gyrinocheilus*, which has its home in India with only a few species.

Gyrinocheilus: Indian genus belonging to the family of the *Gyrinocheilidae*. Of the few species of the genus up to this date only one has been imported from Thailand.

— aymonieri H. M. Smith:

SHAPE: Elongated body, only slightly compressed laterally. Back slightly vaulted, rising in an arch to the insertion of the dorsal fin, belly side flat and wide. Insertion of the dorsal in the first third of total length; D 11-12. Intake and outlet of breath occur while sucked fast, by aid of a skin extension of the gill cover edge and a funnel shaped opening at the upper end of the gill cover. Through this is created a breathing stream that is directed mainly backward and which possibly aids the sucking aptitude of the fish. Length not exactly known, probably a little over 8″.

COLOR: Strongly changing in the different stages of age. Brownish with light belly. At the dorsal ridge and on the flanks a row of dark spots, the latter of which may flow together into an irregular band.

RANGE: Thailand, especially in swiftly flowing, clear waters, but also in slow streams of the plains, ponds, and ditches. They appear periodically in great numbers.

CARE AND BREEDING: A harmless and very hardy fish, which may become useful in the aquarium, especially through its manner of feeding. Food consist mainly of algae and other growths which are grazed off water plants and glass panes with the utmost speed and thoroughness. Additionally, in case of insufficient quantities of algae, the fish will also take dry foods, small live foods, and boiled spinach and lettuce. Rasping off alimentation may be done in any posture of the body, and is done with the utmost speed and intensity. When this happens, one can observe very well the quick motion of the opercles. Due to the little-developed swimming bladder, general motion is jumpy and hasty.

No special demands are made as to composition of water. Apparently not even aeration is needed. Notwithstanding this, the species should do especially well in oxygen-rich water. Sun and warmth are desirable, especially the former, to further the growth of algae. Temperatures around 77° F. The method of spawning is unknown.

Gyrodactilus: With curved hook. Genus belonging to the class of the flukes or Trematodes. Small worms 0.5 to 1.00 mm in length, with a double-tipped head and without eyes. Reproduction is effected without change of generations, not through eggs, but by giving birth to live young. Often the daughter worm remains in her mother's body and produces grandchildren and great-grandchildren therein. A characteristic of the true Trematodes is the big sucking-disc with a crown of chitin hooks, by means of which they claw into the epidermis of the fish, destroying it. Where they attack in numbers, which may occur especially after a previous weakening of the host, the parasites also penetrate into the gills. A few specimens are often found even on healthy fishes, not rarely together with *Costia* and other skin parasites. When attacking in numbers, one may detect them against the light with the naked eye.

habitus: External appearance or shape.

Haeckel, Ernst, 1834-1919. German naturalist who has contributed much to the publicizing of Darwin's theory of evolution. He became known, amongst other things, through the basic biogenetic law discovered by him. Haeckel was a champion of materialism based on the history of genetics. Best known is his work of popularized science 'Die Weltraetsel' (The Riddle of the World).

Haemopis sanguisuga L. The Horse Leech.

The genus *Haemopis* belongs to the super-family of the *Gnathobdellodea*. The Horse Leech, which reaches lengths of 4″ to 6″, is not as flat in construction as its close relative, the Medicinal Leech. Its color is nearly black with yellow edges. It is not a blood sucker, but swallows its prey which consists of worms, insect larvae, etc. This leech is very voracious. It likes to leave the water. Eggs are laid at damp spots on the margins, where the mother Leeches also dig in.

Haertel, Hermann. Well-known German aquarist, importer, and breeder of ornamental fishes, to whom we owe many first spawnings and new imports. Born 1869, he died on January 30th, 1955. From very minute beginnings, Haertel developed a fish hatchery in Dresden which is known far beyond the German borders.

haerteliana: After Haertel, the German importer of the plant.
— *Cryptocoryne.*

Half-Banded Barb, the: see BARBUS SEMIFASCIOLATUS.

Half-Beaks, the: see HEMIRHAMPHIDAE.

Half-Beaks, Live Bearing: see DERMOGENYS.

Half-Stripe Characin, the: see HEMIODUS SEMITAENIATUS.

Halorrhagaceae: Sea Berry Plants. One-year or perennial water, swamp, or land plants, found all over the world, showing the most diversified shapes. For keeping in the aquarium only the Milfoil genera *Proserpinaca* and *Myriophyllum* are of interest.

hancockii: After the English naturalist M. J. Hancock.
— *Amblydoras.*

Haplochromis: Unassuming Chromide (Cichlid).

African genus of mouth-breeders belonging to the family of the Cichlids. Small fishes of elongated body build with a relatively short dorsal fin. The females show a bag-like swollen throat.

The members of the genus are vivacious, often pugnacious fishes, whose care for their spawn belongs among the most notable manner of reproducing. In spite of the fact that these fishes will make do with smaller containers, it is advisable to afford them plenty of room, well-planted and with many roots or stones for hiding places. For feeding they preferentially take strong live foods, such as mosquito larvae and similar.

PETERS made conclusive experiments with mouth-breeders on the instinctive behavior of fishes, which proved that newly hatched alevins have an innate idea of the looks of their mother.

For spawning the male digs shallow holes in the sand by means of twisting motions of the body, generally at the foot of plants. The female follows the male into the pit for spawning, after the games of wooing. In this both animals move along the edge of the pit, one behind the other, after which the eggs are spawned, fertilized, and taken up into the mouth of the female.

The number of eggs depends on the age and state of nutrition of the female. It may vary from 15 to 100. The male should be removed after the act of spawning, as it continues to woo and pester the female actively. At first the mother fish goes into hiding, but returns to the open water within a few days.

Eggs and alevins develop within the throat sac of the mother. There are unconfirmed reports according to which the male cares for the spawn. In these cases its throat sac, deviating from the normal, becomes a little more enlarged than in normal males.

During the hatching period the female moves about very little. Her breathing has become difficult. According to most reports no intake of food occurs during this time, but it seems that this is not always the case. The colors are pale. The fish is very shy. Looking against the light, one can observe the happenings within the throat sac rather well. Eggs and hatched young from time to time are shifted around by violent chewing motions. Hatching time is about 10 to 11 days. The more the young develop, the more the throat sac swells. During the last days the female is unable to close her mouth. Before releasing the litter from her mouth—at this moment the fry are already able to swim freely—the female seeks a protected place and makes sure there is no danger by typical abrupt movements. In case of danger the female lures her freed young back by means of characteristic motions, which, among others, seem to consist of lifting and dropping the dorsal fin, for which the body is turned towards the greatest number of young. This is repeated at certain times of the day, about sundown. The alevins generally seek the mouth of their mother spontaneously. Those which do not react to her motions, or have gone too far away, are gathered up by force. After a few days they seek to emancipate themselves from the motherly care. Besides this they no longer find sufficient space in her throat sac.

Rearing the young is easy. From the first day on they eat finely sifted live foods and grow quickly.

— **desfontanesi** Boulenger:

SHAPE: As per description of the genus. The species reaches a length of 6″. The male remains a little shorter.

COLOR: Brownish to greenish, with a mother-of-pearl lustre when the light incides, evanescent bands, and a blue-black gold-edged spot on the gill covers. During the mating period the male becomes a vivid dark blue, while the female generally is somewhat paler.

RANGE: The species is widely distributed in North Africa where, according to WERNER it is found in artesian wells, water holes in oases, subterranean rivers, as well as in the Nile and lakes of Lower Egypt.

CARE AND BREEDING: As per description given for the genus. KIRCHSHOFER gives a very informative description of the free life of these fish, which permits one to draw conclusions on the other species belonging to the genus. He found the fish in Central Tunisia in the water holes of oases which were very shallow but always kept water and were inter-connected. Here they live in great schools in the middle of a rich fauna. Their behavior may be compared in many points with that of our Stickleback. Outside the mating period the fish swim around in big schools, but at spawning time the males settle in distinct territories, while young fish and the females keep up the previous manner of living. The territories, in the middle of which the male digs a pit, have a diameter of 3 to 5 feet, and are all of approximately the same size. In the part of the ponds where there is vegetation, the territories are smaller than in the open parts. The males respect one another's homesteads and repel invading neighbors, often only by assuming threatening poses at the border. The females, ripe for spawning, approach in loose formations, and are actively wooed, for which the males show gala colors. Mating then takes place in the pit, in the known manner. The females do not mate with one male only, but swim from pit to pit. Assuredly there also occur mock-matings. Later on the females with their eggs retire into the stands of aquatic plants and into the cross channels. The smaller breeding schools of the young fish later coordinate into bigger federations. Fish pertaining to the same school generally are of the same size and probably of the same age too.

— **multicolor** (Hilgendorf): The Egyptian Mouthbreeder.

SHAPE: As per description of the genus. D XIV-XV/8-10, A III/8-9. Length up to approximately $6\frac{3}{8}''$, the females sometimes a little

Haplochromis multicolor

longer.

COLOR: With incident light the fish have a metallic gloss. Each fin has a glossy edge. The gill covers show a blue-black, light-edged spot. The fins carry rows of shiny dots. The anal fin of the male has an orange-red tip. The female has simpler colors.

RANGE: All of East Africa, from the Nile Delta to the great Central African lakes in the South.

CARE AND BREEDING: As per description given for the genus. The species does not need excessive warmth. 68-74° F are sufficient. For spawning raise the temperature to 75-78° F. Lowest 64° F. Also with this species it is advisable to choose pairs for mating from young fish that have been reared together. During the mating period, the male may woo the female very ardently, so that it is advisable to separate him from her by means of a pane of glass in order to protect her until she is ripe for spawning.

— **philander dispersus** Trewavas. A sub-species of the not yet imported species *H. philander* (Weber) which in most cases has been described erroneously as *H. moffati*. Even the sub-species itself shows many color sports, which may besides this vary in size ($2\frac{3}{4}''$ to

$4\frac{5}{16}$"). It ranges all over Southern Africa. Care and breeding should correspond to that of the other species of the genus.

Haplomi: Pike-like.

Order belonging to the sub-class of the new fins or *Neopterygii*, comprising the two families: Pikes or *Esocidae* and Dog Fishes or *Umbridae*.

According to BERG (1940) the sub-order should be included with the Herring-shaped (*Clupeiformes*), as the Pikes and these seem to descend from the same stem and have great similarities in body build.

hardness of water: The capacity of water, caused by dissolved calcium and magnesium compounds, to agglutinate a greater or smaller quantity of soap components when reacting with soap, before it begins to foam with the excedents. According to the degree of hardness, the skin feels soft and slippery when washing with soap, or rough and hard. Soft water contains few, hard water many of the mentioned compounds. The terrous-alkaline metals calcium and magnesium react chemically with carbon dioxide. They form what chemists call carbonates. These are difficult to dissolve in water, and for this reason they would be meaningless for the hardness of water if they did not possess the property of attracting further parts of carbon dioxide when there is an excess of this in the water, and thus to form the easily soluble double carbonates, the bicarbonates. The formula therefore reads:

Simple carbonates (hard to dissolve) + carbon dioxide = easily soluble. Carbon dioxide is incorporated by rain water—which in itself is soft and resembles distilled water—while oozing into the humic layer of the soil. In subsequent layers it meets salts of calcium or magnesium, these react in part with the carbon dioxide dissolved in the water, and turn this hard. The water then collects at the proper spots and comes forth again as spring water, or else it is lifted out from wells. Thus the development of hard water depends in part on its own contents of carbon dioxide, in part on the calcium or magnesium contents of the soil.

Since the bicarbonates originate only after an additional admission of carbon dioxide, they will revert to hard-to-dissolve carbonates if they lose carbon dioxide again. This may happen, for instance, when there are aquatic plants in the water, which during the day, under the influence of sunlight, assimilate and thus use up much carbon dioxide. This process is called BIOGENOUS DECALCIFICATION. Something similar takes place when water is boiled. Since boiling water retains gases with difficulty, the free carbon dioxide, and that which forms the bicarbonates, is expelled. Only the difficult-to-dissolve, simple carbonates remain, which precipitate on the walls of the container (boiler fur). Through this the water becomes softer. While cooling, the reverse may happen again, the water attracting carbon dioxide from the air. Since the hardness conditioned by bicarbonates of calcium and/or magnesium is liable to be a transitory phenomenon, it is called TRANSITORY (TEMPORARY) HARDNESS. However, the hardness of water is conditioned by still other factors, that is compounds of calcium and magnesium which are formed with the aid of nitric, sulphuric, and hydrochloric acids. This hardness cannot be altered by biological means nor by boiling. The hardness caused by them is called the PERMANENT HARDNESS. Both together are the TOTAL HARDNESS.

Cyprinidae (Carplike)

1. **Carassius carassius** - 2. **Cyprinus carpio,** Scaled Carp - 3. **Gobio fluviatilis** - 4. **Cyprinus carpio,** Mirror Carp - 5. **Tinca vulgaris,** the Tench - 6. **Barbus fluviatilis,** the River Barb - 7. **Phoxinus laevis,** the Elritze - 8. **Leuciscus rutilus** - 9. **Rhodeus amarus,** the Bitterling - 10. **Leucaspius delineatus** - 11. **Alburnus lucidus** - 12. **Idus melanotus,** the Ide or Orfe.

Hemiodontidae (Half-Teeth) - Anostomidae (Headstanders)

1. Nannobrycon eques eques - 2. Nannostomus beckfordi beckfordi - 3. Nannostomus marginatus marginatus, the Dwarf Pencil Fish - 4. Nannostomus beckfordi aripirangensis - 5. Anostomus anostomus - 6. Nannostomus trifasciatus - 7. Hemiodus semitaeniatus - 8. Characidium rachovii - 9. Leporinus fasciatus - 10. Abramites micorcephalus - 11. Curimatopsis saladensis - 12. Chilodus punctatus, the Spotted Headstander - 13. Prochilodus insignis.

1. **Aequidens maronii**, the Keyhole Cichlid - 2. **Aequidens latifrons**, the Blue Acara - 3. **Aequidens tetramerus**, the Saddle Cichlid - 4. **Herichthys cyanoguttatus**, the Texas Cichlid - 5. **Hemichromis bimaculatus**, the Jewel Fish - 6. **Crenicichla saxatalis**, the Pike Cichlid - 7. **Hemichromis fasciatus** - 8. **Uaru amphiacanthoides** - 9. **Tilapia mossambica natalensis** - 10. **Nannochromis nudiceps** - 11. **Pelmatochromis kribensis** - 12. **Haplochromis multicolor**, the Egyptian Mouthbreeder.

Cyprinodontidae (Tooth-Carps) - Sub-Family **Poeciliinae** (Livebearing Tooth-Carps)

Ia through Ie **Lebistes reticulatus**, the Guppy, male forms - If Female - 2. **Limia melanogaster** - 3. **Limia vittata** - 4. **Limia nigrofasciata**, the Humpbacked Limia - 5. **Xiphophorus (Platypoecilus) maculatus**, the Platy or Moon - 6. **Xiphophorus variatus**, the Sunset Platy - 7. **Xiphophorus montezumae**, the Montezuma Swordtail - 8. Hybrids of Platies and Swordtails - 9. **Xiphophorus helleri**, the Swordtail, several bred forms 10 **Xiphophorus** helleri, original form.

1. **Danio devario** - 2. **Chela oxygastroides** - 3. **Barilius christyi**, the Coppernose - 4. **Danio malabaricus**, the Giant Danio - 5. **Danio (Brachydanio) nigrofasciatus**, the Spotted Danio - 6. **Danio (Brachydanio) albolineatus**, the Pearl Danio - 7. **Danio (Brachydanio) rerio**, the Zebra Danio - 8. **Rhinichthys atratulus atratulus**, the Black-Nosed Dace - 9. **Chrosomus erythrogaster** - 10. **Epalzeorhynchus kallopterus** - 11. **Esomus malayensis**, the Malayan Flying Barb - 12. **Tanichthys albonubes**, the White Cloud Mountain Fish - 13. **Rasbora pauciperforata** - 14. **Esomus danricus**, the Flying Barb - 15. **Rasbora heteromorpha**, the Harlequin - 16. **Rasbora elegans** - 17. **Rasbora trilineata**, the Scissortail - 18. **Rasbora daniconius** - 19. **Labeo erythrurus** - 20. **Rasbora maculata**, the Dwarf Rasbora - 21. **Labeo bicolor**, the Red-Tailed Shark - 22. **Acanthophthalmus semicinctus**, the Half-Banded Loach - 23. **Misgurnus Fossilis**, the Weather Fish - 24. **Rasbora urophthalma** - 25. **Noemacheilus barbatulus** - 26. **Acanthophthalmus kuhlii kuhlii**, the Coolie Loach - 27. **Rasbora vateriflora** - 28. **Cobitis taenia** - 29. **Botia hymenophysa** - 30. **Rasbora dorsiocellata** - 31. **Botia macracantha**, the Clown Loach.

1. **Cichlasoma festivum**, the Flag Cichlid - 2. **Cichlasoma meeki**, the Firemouth - 3. **Cichlasoma nigrofasciatum**, the Convict Cichlid - 4. **Cichlasoma severum**, the Banded Cichlid - 5. **Cichlasoma biocellatum**, the Jack Dempsey - 6. **Etroplus maculatus**, the Orange Chromide - 7. left, **Nannacara anomala**, the Golden-Eyed Dwarf Cichlid, female - 7. right, the same, male - 8. **Cichlasoma facetum**, the Chanchito - 9. **Apistogramma ramirezi**, Ramirez's Dwarf Cichlid.

Characidae (Tetras) - **Citharinidae** (African Tetras) - **Gasteropelecidae** (Hatchet Fishes)

1. **Metynnis schreitmuelleri** - 2. **Chalceus macrolepidotus** - 3. **Neolebias ansorgei** - 4. **Metynnis roosevelti** - 5. **Rooseveltiella nattereri** - 6. **Myloplus schultzei** - 7. **Chalcinus elongatus** - 8. **Nannaethiops unitaeniatus**, the African Tetra - 9. **Carnegiella strigata**, the Marbled Hatchet Fish - 10. **Gasteropelecus sternicla**, the Silver Hatchet Fish - 11. **Nannaethiops tritaeniatus**, the Three-Striped African Tetra - 12. **Phago loricatus.**

Cyprinidae (Carplike)

1. **Barbus binotatus**, the Two-Spot Barb - 2. **Barbus callipterus** - 3. **Barbus chola**, the Swamp Barb - 4. **Barbus cumingii**, Cuming's Barb - 5. **Barbus fasciatus**, the Striped Barb - 6. **Barbus conchonius**, the Rosy Barb - 7. **Barbus everetti**, the Clown Barb - 8. **Barbus titteya**, the Cherry Barb - 9. **Barbus phutunio**, the Dwarf Barb - 10. **Barbus fasciolatus**, the Banded Barb - 11. **Barbus gelius**, the Pygmy Barb - 12. **Barbus oligolepis**, the Checkered Barb - 13. **Barbus holotaenia** - 14. **Barbus nigrofasciatus**, the Black Ruby Barb - 15. **Barbus tetrazona**, the Tiger Barb - 16. **Barbus semifasciolatus**, the Half-Banded Barb - 7. **Barbus terio** - 18. **Barbus lateristriga**, the T-Barb - 19. **Barbus schuberti**, a bred form of **Barbus semifasciolatus**, the Golden Barb - 20. **Laubuca laubuca** - 21. **Barbus ticto** - 22. **Barbus stoliczkanus**, Stoliczka's Barb.

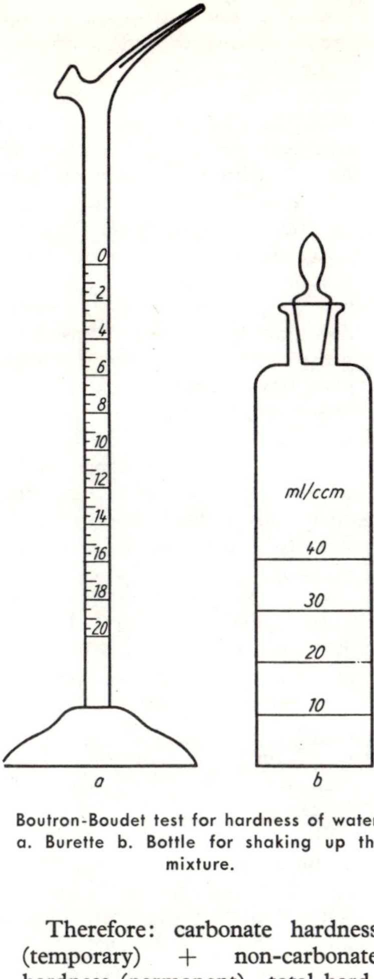

Boutron-Boudet test for hardness of water. a. Burette b. Bottle for shaking up the mixture.

Therefore: carbonate hardness (temporary) + non-carbonate hardness (permanent) = total hardness.

In practical aquaristics, only the total hardness is measured. The measuring unit used in Germany is the German hardness (DH). From it result the following tables of evaluation:

0-4° DH—very soft water
4-8° DH—soft water
8-12° DH—medium-hard water
12-18° DH—hard water
18-30° DH—very hard water
30° DH and over—extraordinarily hard water.

Since the total hardness, however, is conditioned by different chemical compounds, each with a different influence on the organisms that live in the water, this means that at first the measuring of the degree of hardness does not represent too great an accomplishment. At the maximum it permits checking whether the water is soft enough for a certain finality. Two waters may, for instance, both show 12° DH, but may be quite different in their composition notwithstanding this. Therefore, when testing water it is necessary at least to find the three factors: carbonate hardness, total hardness and, derived from the former, non-carbonate hardness.

For testing its hardness, water is at first neutralized in an agitating flask by adding bicarbonate, or acid, whatever the case. In order to make the test, one needs an agitating flask with a scale divided up to 40 cubic centimetres, a burette with a hardness scale, and a soap solution, prepared faultlessly according to the method of BOUTRON-BOUDET. Pour 40 c.c. of the prepared water into the agitating flask. Then add the soap solution drop by drop, while constantly shaking the flask, until a small-bubbled foam appears which no longer crackles when held to the ear. Then read the quantity of soap solution used to reach this point, which will at the same time indicate the German hardness (DH). For waters below 2° DH, calculate with an error of up to 10%, for those between 2 and 15°, up to 5%. To achieve greater exactitude it is advisable to mix waters that probably will assay at over 10° DH with distilled water. Up to 15 degrees of hardness, the agitating flask is filled only up to the 20 c.c. mark, at even greater hardnesses only up to 10 c.c., while the remaining space is filled up with distilled water to completion of the 40 c.c. mark. In the former case the result is multiplied by 2, in the second by 4.

Thus the total hardness is found as the initial step. But testing also the temporary, or carbonate, hardness may be of importance too. For this one needs a burette with a capacity of 10 or 25 c.c., an Erlenmeyer flask holding 300 c.c., $\frac{1}{2}$ liter of 1/10 normal hydrochloric acid, and a 0.1% of the indicator Methyl-Orange. 100 c.c. of the water under test are mixed with 2-3 drops of the methyl-orange solution in the Erlenmeyer flask. Now drip the 1/10 normal hydrochloric acid solution from the burette into the Erlenmayer flask until the initially yellow preparation turns orange-colored. While dripping the acid into them, the materials have to be constantly shaken. The number of c.c. of 1/10 normal hydrochloric acid immediately show the capacity of reacting with ACIDS (see this), which, multiplied by 2.8, yields the carbonate hardness. Deducting this carbonate hardness from the total hardness, we have the permanent hardness as final result.

For the aquarist it is important to know that there may exist fundamental differences between the conditions in our domestic waters and many tropical and sub-tropical ones with regard to hardness.

The water economy of the Temperate Zones is conditioned by a quantitatively relatively insignificant circulation. This means that the precipitations, which as an average are not very strong, find time in great part to ooze into the soil, there enriching themselves with carbon dioxide and secondarily with hardeners. Since furthermore the hardeners, especially calcium, hold a great share in the geological development, from this results that the major part of our domestic waters is placed within the hard range. Since also the pH value of water depends on its hardness, that is, on its faculty of buffering, the pH values of pronounced plains and moors lie nearly exclusively within the neutral range. Dislocations, if any, generally occur towards the alkaline side. In the Temperate Zones the water organisms have adapted to these conditions. Therefore domestic fishes and plants have nearly all to be kept in harder waters with neutral pH values if one wants them to thrive. It is a firmly established rule in domestic commercial breeding, that harder waters are more 'fertile' than soft ones. This is true not only with regard to stimulating fishes to reproduce, but especially with reference to the development of the micro-organisms, unicellulars to micro-crustaceans, necessary to rear the alevins. By the way, also in the tropics commercial breeders of food fishes appreciate harder waters for the same reason (BUSCHKIEL, On Food Fish Waters in Java).

In the Sub-Tropics and the Tropics (generalizing) conditions often are quite different. The best-watered regions of these zones of the globe are simultaneously the main fish regions. There the water economy is conditioned by the very quick circulations of the water, which is significant with regard to quantities. The rain precipitations are great masses of water which are not polluted chemically, and nearly equal to distilled water. These waters often cannot really penetrate the soil and flow away in numerous water courses, respectively stem up in standing waters of all kinds, among which swamps and flooded regions play a big part. In the regions where a pronounced rain period alternates with a dry period

—which is not always completely 'dry'—there may occur seasonal changes in the composition of the water, the consequence of which is a greater adaptability of the organism.

If the surface water in the Tropics is already soft for the reasons given above, one has to add to this that vast regions, for instance, Ceylon and parts of Indonesia, the territory from Indochina to the spurs of the Himalayas, including the mountain system itself, show only small percentages of calcium. In Africa the Congo and the Niger, in South America the Amazon and the Rio de la Plata flow through chalky mountains only with their short upper courses. The hardeners carried along from there are only minute as compared to the precipitations and to the total length and water masses of these rivers. From this we conclude that soft water has to be advantageous for keeping many tropical and subtropical fishes, and that it often is a 'must' for successfully breeding them. This does not mean, however, that all species make the same demands. Furthermore, adaptability is so great, that they will also accept other water conditions. Many species may also originate from waters the composition of which resembles ours. A sample of this large adaptability is the Neon Tetra, which at first could only be bred in regions with very soft, natural water, or else in artificially prepared water, but which today (according to LADIGES) can also be induced to spawn and procreate in harder waters.

The soft waters of the tropical regions probably are very poor in bacteria and unicellular organisms. According to SIOLI, the following bacteria were counted in the Amazon region, at pH values of 5.8 to 6.7:

at 1° DH—8 bacteria in 1 c.c. of water
at 8° DH—2700 bacteria in 1 c.c. of water
at 15° DH 60,000 bacteria in 1 c.c. of water

This may possibly explain why the eggs and fry of certain tropicals seem sensitive to attacks by bacteria and unicellulars, it being perfectly possible, however, that such attacks are only secondary symptoms, preceded by chemical damage. It is an established fact, though, that the fry of certain species of fishes succumb to certain species of unicellular protozoans when these appear in numbers. It seems sure that small water hardness acts repressively on the development of micro-organisms. The Biology of Commercial Fisheries considers such water as 'barren'. Besides this also the tanning substances, which are dissolved in great quantities in tropical waters, seem to act toward this end. Possibly even the calcium salts in harder water act on the process of fertilization itself, when one makes attempts at breeding. It is known that the process of fertilization is steered by chemical substances which might be prevented from acting on fishes adapted to soft water that is poor in calcium, when the water contains a too large proportion of hardeners.

Summing up, we have to state that, when keeping tropical plants and fishes, the use of soft water will be advantageous. Especially for imported specimens and their first progenies, such water often is a primary condition for life and reproduction. On the other hand, those species which can successfully be bred in our harder water, and which have gradually adapted to our local conditions, should be bred in the locally available water.

Harlequin, the: see RASBORA HE-

TEROMORPHA.

harti: After a surname.

— *Rivulus.*

Hasemania: After the American scientific collector Haseman. South American genus belonging to the family of the Characins or *Characidae*, with about four known species.

— melanura Ellis: The Copper Characin.

The species is generally known as *H. marginata*. Perhaps *H. marginata* Meinken may be a local variety of *H. melanura*. Maybe there even is a relationship with *Hemigrammus nanus*.

SHAPE: Delicate, slender, flattened laterally. D 11, A 16. Length up to 2″.

COLOR: The male generally has a coppery gloss with a blue-black band to the caudal peduncle and whitish fin tips. The female is silver-colored and fuller-bodied.

RANGE: Southeastern Brazil.

CARE AND BREEDING: The species likes clear water at 68-77° F, for spawning a little higher. They are vivacious and peaceful, but need room for exercising, and also hiding places among plants. They take all kinds of food, as long as it corresponds to their size. Spawning is not difficult. Mating is done in pairs, the act of spawning itself after stormy wooing among plants. The species is not considered very productive, the number of eggs totalling 150-200. The fry hatch after 30-40 hours. During the first few days they are a little small, and quite sensitive.

hastatus: Refers to a lance-shaped spot on the sides of the body.

— *Corydoras.*

Hatchet Belly, Hatchet Fish: see GASTEROPELECUS STERNICLA.

— Spotted, the: see THORACOCHARAX MACULATUS.

— Striped, the: see CARNEGIELLA STRIGATA.

Hatchet Fishes: Several genera of so-called 'flying fishes' pertaining to the family of the *Gasteropelecidae*. Considering their strongly differentiated body structure, as well as the fact that this is harmonized within the group, they were separated from the *Characidae* or true Characins as a special family. The Hatchet Fishes are widely distributed over South America. They are able to move by gliding along the water surface by means of their wing-like, enlarged pectoral fins, and even to take off in a kind of flight for short stretches. This manner of locomotion should not be considered as true flying. See GASTEROPELECIDAE.

Head and Tail Light, the: see HEMIGRAMMUS OCELLIFER.

Headstanders, the: see ANOSTOMIDAE.

hearing in fishes: see "SENSORY ORGANS" and "SENSORY FUNCTIONS."

heating: Heating a tropical aquarium is indispensable. Even in summer, during occasional cool spells, one cannot always keep the temperature at the necessary levels. One or the other species of fishes is quite adaptable, but there is a difference between an occasional decrease in temperature to the permitted minimum, or whether such a sub-temperature holds on for days and weeks. Tropical and sub-tropical fishes can by no means be "hardened." To the contrary, each fish is adapted to certain temperatures. For this reason, if for some reason or other one does not want to heat the aquarium, one should refrain from keeping species that need warmth. Generally speaking, it is favorable to the well-being of our exotic fishes if one can get organized to afford them all necessary temperatures between 68 and 86° F. With a greater number of aquaria it will not always be possible to pay strict attention to the needs of warmth of every species of fishes, but one should get used to giving more importance to this factor. By no means should the fancier govern his behavior by a single scheme, perhaps keeping the fishes too cool out of a false sense of economy, or perhaps overheating them due to a wrong evaluation of their need for warmth. The demands are very diversified. There are species of fishes originating from the regions around the Equator which just for spawning do not need all too high degrees of warmth as their mating time falls into the cooler rain period, and which may feel better at móderate degrees of temperature due to coming from shady waters in the woods. With such species it may happen that their span of life is considerably shortened because of the increased metabolism caused by high temperatures. On the other hand fish from the same latitude may show very high demands as to their water's warmth. As an average one may place the minimum temperatures at about 68° F. For wintering generally 68-72° F will prove sufficient. The medium temperature for summer lies around 72-75° F, and for spawning most tropicals and sub-tropicals require 75-79° F or more. Exceptions in both directions, up and down, are not rare. All these special demands are pointed out for every case in the descriptions of families, genera, and species given in this book. At too low temperatures the fishes lose color, become sluggish, or remain at the bottom or among plants with closed fins. The consequences of such errors in keeping may be detrimental to the health to an extent that the fishes often are unable to recover at all. Fish that are kept too cold (sometimes also specimens that are kept under too much heat) become prone to di-

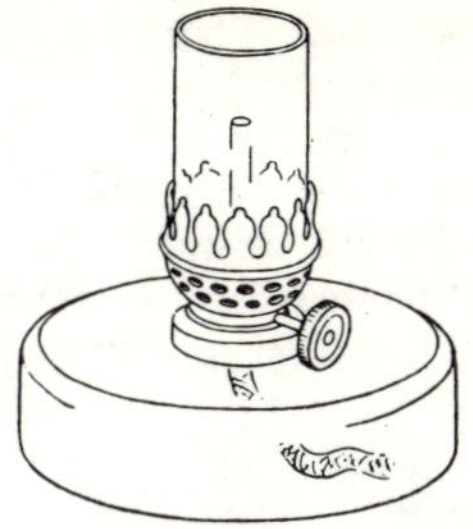

Kerosene heating lamp

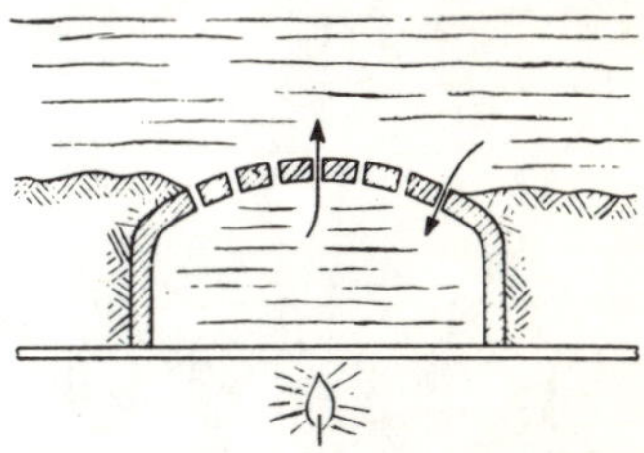

Heating dome inside the aquarium

Simple electric heater in a glass tube

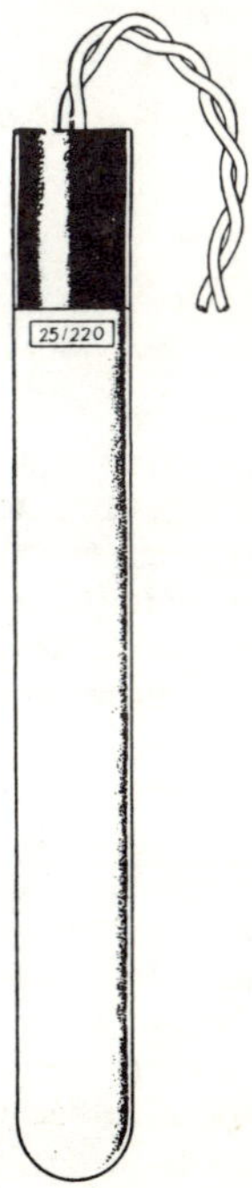

seases of all kinds. There is nothing to be said against a decline of temperature within the yearly or daily rhythm, if it keeps within bounds. To the contrary, fluctuations in temperature correspond more to the natural conditions than

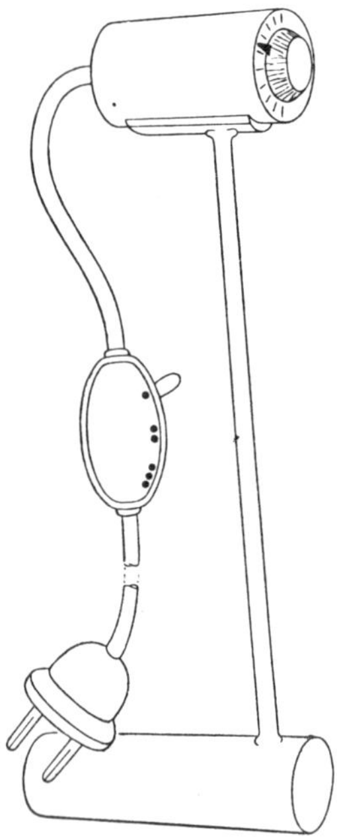

Electric heater with adjustable switch and adjustable thermostat

a constant degree of warmth. Above all one should observe that nearly all animals and plants need a seasonal resting pause. In our latitudes it is advisable to extend this over the period of less availability of foods, therefore from November to February.

Native fishes and foreign cold water fishes need such a rest by all means. They may winter in an occasionally heated but frostless room, where temperatures should not sink below 39° F. In summer the water warmth should not exceed an average of 68° F, which of course does not mean that the fish cannot withstand an occasional higher temperature. But then the aeration should be intensified, and such heating should not be kept up indefinitely.

The formerly used 'bottom heating' with oil, paraffin, or coal oil lamps, coke or illuminating gas, has been more and more displaced by electrical heating. For bottom heating the source of warmth is put beneath the aquarium. It acts on sand and water through warming the bottom plate. Disadvantages are to be found in the condensation which often appears, the complicated servicing, and the duty of careful supervision which may never be neglected with this kind of heating. Small lamps, especially built for aquaristic purposes are today nearly completely discontinued by all manufacturers, but one still finds lamps on the market that will do for this aim. First of all make absolutely sure that they are explosion-proof. If you use the so-called heating cases, use much care in their manufacture. They should be lined with heat-resistant material (asbestos), and have sufficient aeration holes. These cases are open at the top, and correspond in size to the aquarium to be heated. When lighting up, pay attention to the fact that the flame increases after heating up the wick cylinder. Therefore regulate it as small as possible at the beginning. Of very safe operation, and absolutely odorless, are paraffin lamps. All-glass tanks are set into correspondingly sized tin cans with low edges bent upwards and filled with sand. However, this manner of heating all-glass containers cannot be considered as absolutely safe, especially if the glasses are of high value. Where the open flame hits the bottom of the tin, solder on a square piece of tinplate in order to

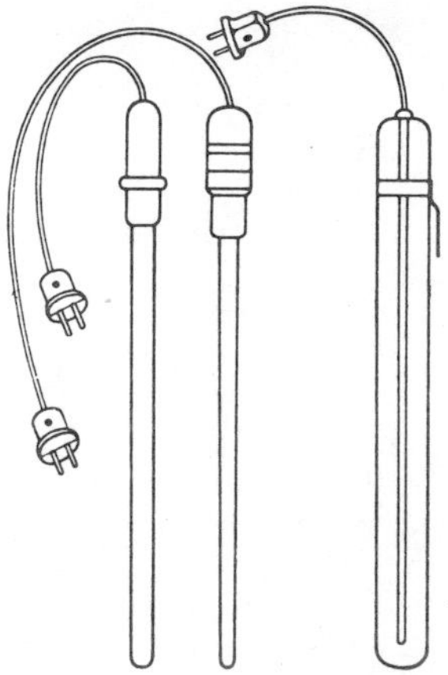

Immersion heaters

prevent the fire from burning through. STERBA recommends riveting on a piece of asbestos. The distance between the flame and the bottom should measure $1\frac{5}{8}''$ to $2''$ with the wick fully raised. A flame that touches the bottom, soots.

Gas heating is still advisable in our days, especially where electric heating is unobtainable. It is preferable to all the previously mentioned kinds of heating. Use safety burners for this, as these generally protect the flame against going out or, if that should happen anyway, automatically shut off the gas outlet. Besides this, they should always be made by a reliable gas technician.

A too strong heat applied to the aquarium bottom is detrimental to some plants. Protection against this is obtained by inserting a heating bell in the tank. This also aids to a better distribution of the introduced heat. Such bells are put exactly above the source of heat on the bare bottom of the tank. The circulation holes give passage to a continuous stream of warmed water, without unnecessary losses of heating warmth into the bottom ground. Occasionally a small in-

TABLES OF NEEDED HEATER OUTPUTS, IN WATTS

(Values for normally glazed, well-covered tanks, according to Nedl)

Contents of tank in quarts	Desired heating capacity in degrees F above room temperature														
	2	4	6	8	10	12	14	16	18	20	22	24	26	28	30
	= Needed heating performance in Watts														
10	2	5	7	9	11	13	16	18	20	22	24	27	29	31	33
20	4	8	12	16	20	24	28	32	35	39	44	47	51	55	59
30	6	11	16	22	28	33	38	44	49	55	60	66	71	77	82
40	7	14	20	27	34	40	47	54	60	67	74	80	87	93	100
50	8	16	23	31	39	47	54	62	69	77	85	93	100	108	115
60	9	18	26	34	42	51	59	68	76	85	93	102	110	119	128
70	9	18	28	37	46	55	64	73	82	91	101	110	119	128	137
80	10	19	29	38	48	57	67	77	86	96	105	115	124	134	144
90	10	20	30	40	50	59	69	79	89	98	108	118	128	138	148
100	10	20	30	40	50	60	70	80	90	100	110	120	130	140	150

These tables are especially advantageous for calculating the optimum heat output of a stage heater. The shown values, though, represent data only gathered in practical observation, so that one has to count upon divergences according to local conditions. The tables furthermore show that big tanks from the point of view of the technique of heating are more advisable than small ones. They do not follow the fluctuations of room temperature to the same degree as small ones.

verted flower pot with an enlarged vent may serve the same purpose.

Even when heating electrically it is always advisable to keep some oil lamps in reserve, so that in case of an eventual failure of current one may be able to save valuable young fry and fishes.

Bottom heating is adequate only for frame aquaria. For all-glass tanks it may only be used restrictedly. The bottom of frame aquaria in such cases should not be insulated by a glass pane.

Greater hatcheries resort to heating the room by keeping the hatching rooms constantly at the required average temperature. Auxiliary electrical heating is used only in special cases. This type of heating is generally uneconomical for the amateur fancier.

Electrical heating is preferable to all other systems. If well-built, it is relatively free of danger, cheap, and reliable, needs little supervision and may be left alone even during longer absences if adjusted correctly. In most cases the heating elements are hung up in the aquarium. There are the most varied systems. The simplest form is the so-called salt heater in which electrical current is made to pass through a salt solution. Take two carbon rods out of an old flashlight battery and solder their metal caps to the two respective wires of an electric cord. Introduce the rods into a U-shaped glass tube full of salt solution covering them half-way up. In order to prevent the carbon rods from sliding deeper into the salt, thread the wires through perforated rubber stoppers, which at the same time will close off the glass tube. Besides the electric cord also stick a $\frac{1}{16}''$ diameter glass tube through the stoppers in order to afford escape to the originating steam. You will have to find out the

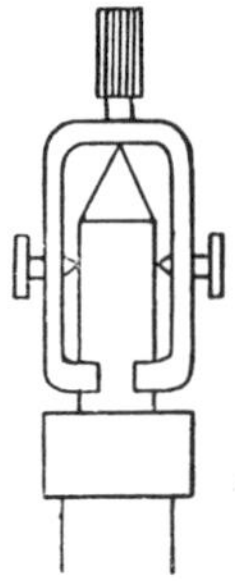

Adjustable magnet for a contact thermometer

strength of the concentration of salt by trial and error, as the intensity of the produced heat is affected by it. A weak, but constant, heating is better than one able to raise the temperatures suddenly, and which for this same reason needs constant watching. Therefore do not make the concentration too strong. It is advisable at first to check the heat output in a special container. Prepare the salt solution outside the glass tube, before filling it in. Salt heaters work only on alternating current.

Relay

Most heaters, though, work with a spiral heating resistor or some other glowing element. They may be used with both A.C. and D.C. The spiral is imbedded in fine sand in a glass or porcelain tube, or else a heating element is imbedded in metal cases of various shapes. All these heaters are quite rugged and therefore cheap at a long range. The expert may want to make them himself, otherwise they may be purchased at any pet shop. Before making the purchase, insist on trying out the instruments. For smaller tanks simple glass tubes in the shape of test tubes will do. They are available in different sizes, according to output. For bigger tanks preferably choose the so-called boot-heaters, bent at a 90° angle, in which the heating element itself lies on the bottom, so that the warmth rises upwards from below. In all these cases one has, of course, to consider the greater or smaller roominess of the aquarium. If it consists of a simple tube, the heating element should hang vertically in the tank whenever possible. Boot heaters should rest on the bottom, masked by stones and the like. The neck of heaters, which generally is caulked water-tight with a cement, should protrude a little over the water surface, and should be located in a manner that no condensation water from the cover plate drops on it. The heaters in themselves are very rugged. As a rule, when they spoil prematurely, this is due to the fact that the cement is a little permeable and water or moisture get into the insulating sand through it. Generally the instruments consume 1-120 watts of current; wattage and voltage should be shown on their specification. The disadvantage of these simple heaters is that they cannot be adjusted gradually. Therefore it is difficult to adapt them to the ever-changing demands, since the output required does not only conform to the quantity of water to be heated, but also to the ambient temperature of the room in which the aquarium stands.

Quite better are heaters with a stage-graduation by means of which one can obtain a three-stage heating the steps of which are expressed by the consumption of current, for instance 10-20-40 watts, or 25-50-100 watts, etc. With such we are enabled to make the intensity of heating conform with changing situations. Better still are heaters which can be set to a certain temperature and then keep the water constantly at that level of warmth, the heater disconnecting automatically whenever the temperature limit is overstepped.

The same purpose is served by the thermostat which functions in connection with a contact thermometer. This too automatically disconnects the source of heat at a certain temperature. For one tank only a simple, non-stage graduated heater will suffice, since the thermostat does the setting. If several aquaria are connected to the thermostat, one has to use staged heaters for the tanks that are connected up with the system in case these should not be of the same size as the main one in which the controlling thermostat hangs. Installations of this kind have the disadvantage of being a little more expensive. Furthermore it is to be pointed out in justice that the constantly equal temperature is unbiological. Undoubtedly this is often the case, but the advantage for the caretaker, which consists in that he may leave the installation without surveillance for greater lapses of time, is so great, that a great many hobbyists decide for this type of heating installation in spite of all that may be said against them.

Furthermore it is always possible to provide for a sinking temperature during night time by means of a daily adjustment. To be sure, in such cases one has to have a thermostat with magnetic readjustment.

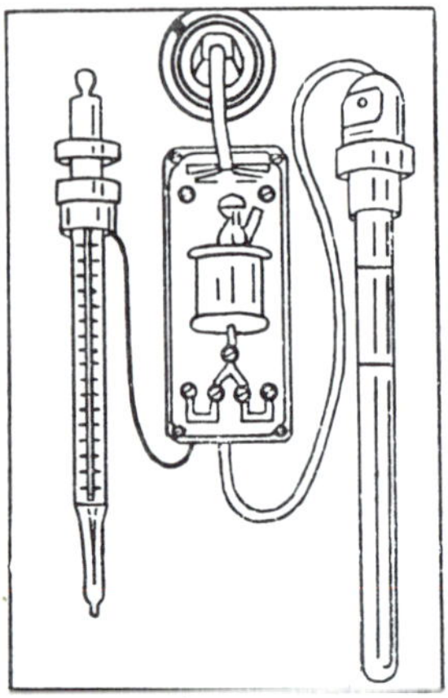

Heater with thermostatic control and relay

Whenever possible, one may insulate the tanks against loss of heat by lining back, sides, and bottom with a material that is a poor conductor of heat (paper, cardboard, glass wool). The best possibilities for doing this exist if the tank or tanks are kept within a wooden frame, or if they are set up within a heating case. Heating cases are closed boxes with sides and a door made of glass, which permit good distribution of the warmth and diminish the cost of heating. They are indispensable especially for the specialized breeder who for his work needs many breeding containers and minute tanks which are difficult to heat.

Heleocharis: Swamp beauty.
Genus belonging to the family of the Cyprus grasses or *Cyperaceae.*

—acicularis (Linné) Needle Grass: A hardy, enduring plant, distributed all over Europe, Asia, Australia, and North and South America, found especially on the banks of standing waters. The stiff, needle-like leaves, which originate from a creeping system of roots, afford good protection to the spawn of egg-scattering fishes which eat their own eggs. A satisfactory growing medium is represented by unwashed sand. The plants look best when standing together in bunches. If they meet favorable conditions, they may cover the whole bottom with a thick lawn. Multiplication is achieved through divisions of the root system. They need light and

Heleocharis acicularis

sun. Domestic specimens may be kept at room temperature. Tropical ones (from gardening establishments) need 77-86° F. No special demands are made as to composition of water.

Helicidae: Family belonging to the sub-class of the *Pulmonata* or Lung Snails. Mostly land animals of which only the genus *Succinea* (Amber Snails) is found in fresh water. They are amphibious snails, living on the shores of waters.

Heliozoa: Class belonging to the tribe of the root-footers or *Rhyzopoda*. The pseudopods of the *H.*, which live mostly as plankton, irradiate to all sides and are relatively rigid in consequence of an imbedded axil rod. The body often is protected by a more or less complex external skeleton. Without significance in the aquarium, but often of beautiful striking shape.

Helisoma nigricans Spix: A small saucer-snail from Brazil which lives in warm water and reaches a scant $\frac{3}{4}''$ but generally keeps below this size. A red form of this species, little pigmented, is offered commercially. This snail is hardy but cannot withstand low temperatures. 68-77° F are needed.

helleri: After a surname.

— *Xiphophorus.*

Helmeted Catfish, the: see ASTRODORAS ASTERIFRONS.

Helodea: see ELODEA.

Helostoma: Relates to the thick, distinctly set-off lips.

Southeast Asian genus belonging to the family of the Climbing Perches or *Anabantidae* with only one species. The dorsal fin is longer than the anal, and the spines of the hard part of these fins are distinctly differentiated from each other. The mouth in itself is narrow, but the thick, fleshy lips may be extended far out. They are provided with rows of thin, thickly grouped little teeth. In spite of the fact that the *H.* are much liked food fishes in their native habitat, knowledge about their manner of living is scant. They like to graze off the growths on plants and solid objects with the aid of their lip-toothlets. Besides this they dip up water by means of strong movements of the lips, and sift out the food particles contained in same.

Whenever they take live food, it has to be uncommonly small as they are unable to swallow bigger bites. Fish of 2″ to $2\frac{3}{8}''$ in length are still pronounced fine food eaters. Only after outgrowing this size they will also take Cyclops, and small Daphnia, but even the intake of bigger mosquito larvae causes difficulties. If several fish are kept together, they show the peculiarity of joining their tipped-up lips. It is a curious sight, indeed, to see them endeavouring to fit their pairs of lips exactly on one another.

— **temmincki** Cuvier and Valenciennes: The Kissing Gourami.

SHAPE: Relatively high, in the whole nearly egg shaped, strongly compressed laterally. The mouth is terminal. D XVI-XVIII/13-16, A XII-XV/17-19. Length up to 12″.

COLOR: Yellowish to greenish base with several dark length stripes, conforming to the body contours, which in part overlap onto the fins. The species presents a semi-albinoid form which shows up only out of captive spawnings. In the

Helostoma temmincki

mostly smaller specimens kept in aquaria the SD are scarcely discernible. After reaching lengths of 4″ to 5″, the males are reported to be a little fuller-bodied, the females of the normally colored variety showing more intense designs.

RANGE: Central India and Indonesia.

CARE AND BREEDING: Of this species, which grows very big, only the smaller specimens are of a size fit to be kept in the home aquarium, while the bigger ones prove very effective in greater public aquaria. They need warmth and feel best at 77° F or more. The need for food is very great, and, if well-fed, they grow very quickly. Sometimes it is rather hard, though, to keep small specimens during the winter time, due to lack of the proper food. In spite of the fact that at times they chase other fishes, the species may be safely termed as absolutely peaceful. They have already been bred in the home aquarium. No bubble nests are built. Instead of this the eggs and fry swim freely at the surface, kept up by oil deposits. The young are rather big. Nothing is known about correct feeding to rear them.

Hemibrycon: Half *Brycon* (another genus of *Characins*).

South American belonging to the family of the *Characidae*. Small fishes that differ from the closely related genus *Creagrutus* only by the number and position of the teeth. An adipose fin is present. About 15 species are known.

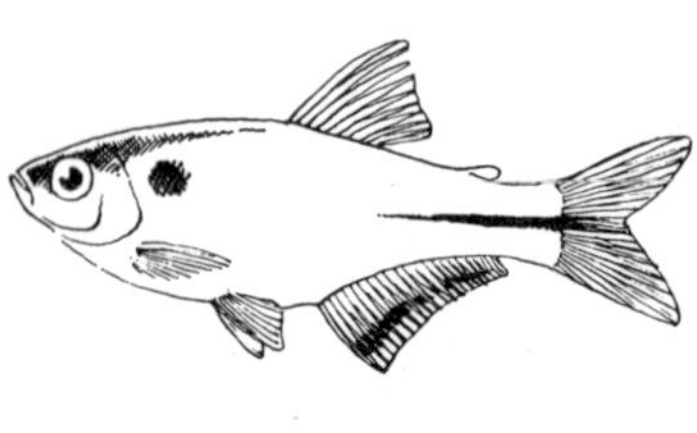

Hemibrycon, type of the genus

— guppyi (Regan): The Short Head Characin.

SHAPE: As per description of the genus; relatively elongated and laterally compressed. The mouth is supraterminal. D 10; A 28-32. Length about 4″.

COLOR: Yellowish-green with a silvery gloss and a bronzed-yellow horizontal stripe which changes to a blackish color at the caudal peduncle.

RANGE: In clear brooks with gravel bottom in Venezuela and on Trinidad.

CARE AND BREEDING: This species has rarely been imported and therefore is scarcely known. They are said to be rugged and hardy, but to need warmth. It seems that there are no special demands as to food. Spawning has not been achieved so far, but breeding should correspond to that of most other Characins.

Hemichromis: Half Chromide, not totally corresponding to type.

Genus of African Cichlids, closely related to *Haplochromis*. Fish of slender, elongated body, with a low, long dorsal fin and long ventrals which end in points, especially those of the males. On the gill cover is a dark, light-rimmed round spot. Vicious, pugnacious, and very active diggers. For Care and Breeding see CICHLIDAE. Up to this date two species have been imported.

RANGE: North, Central, and West Africa.

— bimaculatus Gill: The Jewel Fish.

SHAPE: As per description of the genus, with dorsal and ventral contours very equally arched. The forehead is a little indented above the eyes. D XIII-XV/9-13, A III/7-9. The ventrals, strongly extended in the second and third rays, are located on the breast. The vertical fins are rounded. Length: in nature up to 8″, in captivity up

Hemichromis bimaculatus

to 5″, but ready to propagate after reaching 3⅛″ to 4″.

COLOR: May change a little, according to origin. Ochre color base which, in case of some excitement, may flush with a glowing red shade, rows of blue-green luminous spots, which transit onto the fins. Color is no reliable sexual characteristic. During the mating time the female may appear even more intensely colored than the male. The sexes may be correctly told apart only during the mating period, by the different construction of their genital papillae.

RANGE: From North Africa to the South of the African Continent. Due to the very wide range, there is a series of local varieties.

CARE AND BREEDING: As described for Cichlids. During the spawning season this is one of the most beautiful Cichlids. At the same time, though, they often are extraordinarily vicious and dig very actively.

— **fasciatus** Peters: The Banded Jewel Fish.

SHAPE: As per description of the genus, but with pointed head, and pike-like elongated body. The mouth opening is very big and the forehead line slightly indented. With growing age the body becomes somewhat higher. D XII-XVI/11-13, A III/8-10. All vertical fins are rounded. Length in the aquarium up to 6″, ready to propagate at 3⅛″.

COLOR: Brass colored, the upper sides copper green, the lower sides glowing red during the mating period. The scales of the fore part of the body are edged with red. On the flanks are five blue-black dots which sometimes change into length and cross bands. The SD are scarcely noticeable in the colors, and only the differentiated genital papillae yield a reliable way of distinguishing the sexes.

RANGE: In waters of all kinds, even brackish ones, in tropical West Africa, found abundantly from Senegal to the Congo.

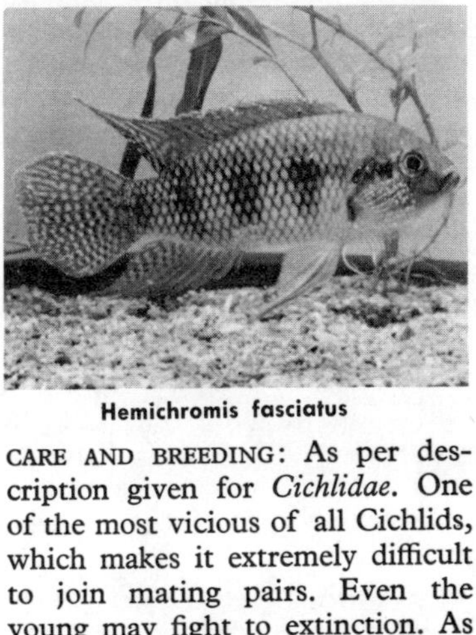

Hemichromis fasciatus

CARE AND BREEDING: As per description given for *Cichlidae*. One of the most vicious of all Cichlids, which makes it extremely difficult to join mating pairs. Even the young may fight to extinction. As for all Cichlids, also for this species behavior depends much on the size of the available room.

Hemigrammus: With half side line.

South American genus belonging to the family of the Characins or *Characidae*. Small, vivacious school fish of elongated to moderately high build, somewhat compressed laterally. The mouth opening is moderately big, with numerous, very small teeth. An adipose fin exists. The side-line is incomplete. The root of the tail fin shows scales. A genus, rich in species, which in its manner of propagating is typical for most Characins. According to size, the fish need more or less roomy tanks, which may be well-planted on the edges and on the side from where the light comes, but should have plenty of open space in the middle. All of the species are rather peaceful fishes, well fit for keeping in the community tank. They take all live or dry foods corresponding to their sizes, and generally are not too exacting with reference to warmth.

For breeding, cover the bottom and corners of the aquarium with bundles of feathery-leaved plants, such as, for instance, thread algae, *Nitella*, *Myriophyllum*, Willowmoss (*Fontinalis*), etc. Nylon yarn too will do. Add 50% fresh water to the tank and raise the temperature to the value given for spawning. Then put in the breeders, either as a pair, or else two males to one female. If they are nearing maturity to spawn, they begin to chase each other, which generally is started by the female. Spawning often occurs under the morning sun. The fish press through the maze of plants, side by side, expelling a total of several hundreds of eggs in many matings of 12 to 15 eggs each. The parents show great eagerness to eat their own eggs and should be removed. Depending on the degree of warmth, the fry hatch within 24 to 40 hours. Thereafter they still hang for 3 to 4 days from the glass panes, etc. consuming the yolk sac, after which they become free-swimming. Now they will take finest plankton, rotatoria, etc., and additionally also the smallest dry foods. After 8 to 10 days, they generally already are able to eat very small Cyclops. The different species of *H.* generally have no special demands as to the composition of water.

—**caudovittatus** Ahl: The Buenos Aires Tetra.

SHAPE: As per description of the genus. D 11, A 26-27. Length up to 4″.

COLOR: Silvery, with a lozenge-shaped spot at the caudal peduncle, edged in light color. The vertical fins are red on the males, lighter on the females. The females are a little bigger, and more full-bodied.

RANGE: The La Plata region around Buenos Aires.

CARE AND BREEDING: As per description given for the genus. Very hardy, lively, and easy to breed. The fish are omnivorous, and like to eat the tender shoots of plants. For this reason it is advisable to use only very hard aquatic plants. No special demands are made as to temperature, 68-72° F, for breeding 75° F, being sufficient. Lowest 59° F. Occasionally the fish become very quarrelsome. Therefore they should be kept only in very roomy containers where they have sufficient space for swimming. Breeding them is easy. At each spawning 500 or more eggs are laid. For mating put two males with each female.

Hemigrammus caudovittatus

Hemigrammus erythrozonus

— **erythrozonus** Durbin: The Glow Light Tetra.

Formerly this species has been known as *Hyphessobrycon gracilis*.

SHAPE: As per description of the genus. Quite elongated, with the dorsal contour sometimes more arched than the ventral one. Especially the males occasionally show a somewhat pinched-in belly. D 11, A 17-22. Length up to $1\frac{5}{8}''$.

COLOR: Gray-brown base with a glowing red horizontal stripe which goes from the eye to the caudal peduncle, sometimes even reaching over onto the tail. The male is slimmer and there is a difference of construction in the translucent swimming bladder.

RANGE: In the jungle waters of Northeastern South America.

CARE AND BREEDING: As per description given for the genus. The species needs some warmth. 75° F is adequate. Increase this a little for breeding. Procreation is rather similar to that of the Neon Tetra (*Hyphessobrycon innesi*). The breeding tank, preferably an all-glass aquarium, should be kept clean and free of infusoria. The species seems not to present all too high demands as to soft water, as happens with the Neon Tetra. Only fully developed and spawn ripe specimens should be used for breeding purposes. The roe in the female is easily noticed when seen against the light. Spawning occurs after very pretty mating games in plant mazes, where the fish lie on their sides or even on their backs. After spawning the parents should be taken out, and the tank should be somewhat darkened. The fry hatch after about 24 hours and need another 4 days before becoming free-swimming. Rearing them demands solicitude, but is not overly difficult.

— **marginatus** Ellis: The Black Tail Tetra.

SHAPE: As per description of the genus. D 11, A 20. Length up to 2″.

COLOR: Silvery with a dark stripe, light-edged on the upper part, along the flanks. The tail fin has a nice bow design. The male is livelier, his white fin tips are more intensely colored, and besides this he is slimmer.

RANGE: From Venezuela to Northern Argentina.

CARE AND BREEDING: As per description given for the genus. The species has already been bred, but no particulars are known.

— **nanus** (Reinhardt): The Silver-Tipped Tetra.

A very recently imported species which reminds one a little of *Hasemania*. It is not clear whether these two species are not only varieties of the same species. Very

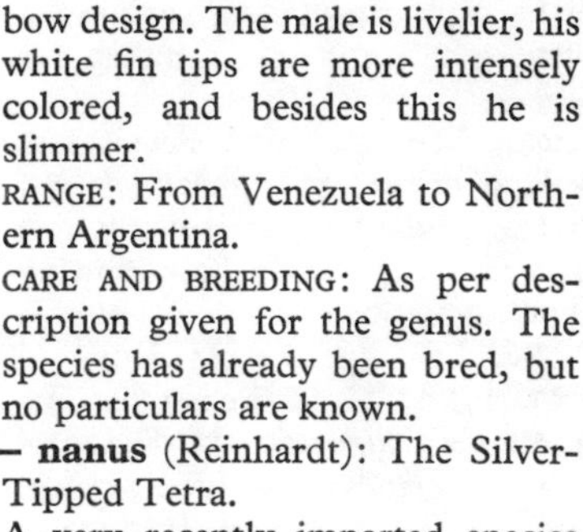

Hemigrammus nanus

pretty, slender, and lively fish, the males brownish red with white fin tips. Bred for the first time by PINTER. The fry are very small.

Hemigrammus ocellifer

— **ocellifer** (Steindachner): The Head-and-Tail-Light.

SHAPE: As per description of the genus. D 10-11, A 22-28. Length up to 2⅜″, the male remaining a little smaller and slimmer than the female.

COLOR: Gray-greenish silver gloss with a cross-shaped black design on the caudal peduncle, over which is placed a golden-yellow glowing spot. Sometimes a similar spot is found at the upper edge of the gill covers. The iris of the eye too is a luminous yellow and red. The male is more slender than the female, and a little smaller. According to KOEHLER even while still small the males are easily recognized by the thickened first fin rays.

RANGE: From the Guianas to the Amazon region.

CARE AND BREEDING: As per description given for genus. The species loves warmth without being excessively sensitive to occasional fluctuations in temperature, though. 73-80° F are advisable. Lowest 68° F. For spawning put two males together with each female.

— **pulcher** Ladiges: The Pretty Tetra, or, The Garnet Tetra.

SHAPE: As per description of the genus. The body is relatively high, strongly compressed laterally. Length up to 2″.

COLOR: The sides have a reddish to greenish gloss, with a yellow-greenish luminous spot on the shoulder and a short, wide, black band on the caudal peduncle, which may be lined with a vivid golden yellow at the upper and lower edges.

RANGE: In the Peruvian region of the Upper Amazon.

CARE AND BREEDING: As described for the genus, but the species is not as lively as many other members of the genus. The colors stand out especially well against a dark background. Breeding is difficult. The water should be soft and slightly acid. A temperature of 79-83° F is needed. Spawning is best attempted in an all-glass tank, painstakingly clean and free of infusoria. The act of spawning occurs during the first hours of the morning and lasts for about an hour. 400-600 eggs are laid during the time. After this remove the parents and darken the tank. The fry hatch after about 24 hours and need another 3-4 days to become free-swimming. From this moment on the darkening may be interrupted. The young are very small and weak, grow slowly, and need painstaking care.

Hemigrammus pulcher

Hemigrammus rhodostomus

— **rhodostomus** Ahl: The Rummy-Nosed Tetra.

Of slender, elongated shape, a little compressed laterally. Length about $1\frac{5}{8}''$. Silvery gloss, upper head and snout a vivid red, the caudal fin showing a very pretty pattern. The males are slimmer.

ORIGIN: Lower Amazon region. Breeding this pretty species seems to be a little difficult, and apparently they are not very productive.

Hemigrammus ulreyi

— **ulreyi** (Boulenger): The German Flag Tetra.

SHAPE: As per description of the genus. D 10-11, A 23-26. Length: males up to $1\frac{3}{8}''$, females to $1\frac{3}{4}''$.

COLOR: A transparent greenish-silvery gloss, with a red-white-black band along the sides. The male is slimmer.

RANGE: The Paraguay River and its waters.

CARE AND BREEDING: The care for this species should resemble that of the other *Hemigrammus* species. For some time this fish was confounded with *Hyphessobrycon heterorhabdus*. Never bred in captivity, nor imported in significant numbers.

Hemigrammus unilineatus

— **unilineatus** (Gill): The Feather Fin.

SHAPE: As per description of the genus. D 11, A 23-27. Length up to 2″, the male a littler smaller and slimmer.

COLOR: Simple silver gloss with a dark dash on the caudal peduncle.

CARE AND BREEDING: As per description given for the genus. A fish that swims in schools, loving clear water with 68-77° F, 82° F for spawning. The fish are not exactly sensitive to low temperatures, but become pale and sluggish at them. In procreation, which resembles that of *H. caudovittatus*, they are very productive.

Hemiodontidae: (Half-teeth).

Family of Characin-like fishes of the sub-order of the *Cyprinoidea*, comprising a number of very much appreciated aquarium fishes. The species that are kept in aquaria generally are slim or even very slim, and are mostly small. They are widely distributed over Northern South America. Often the body is only slightly compressed laterally. The mouth is small, and terminal, the head pointed. An adipose fin may exist or not, often even

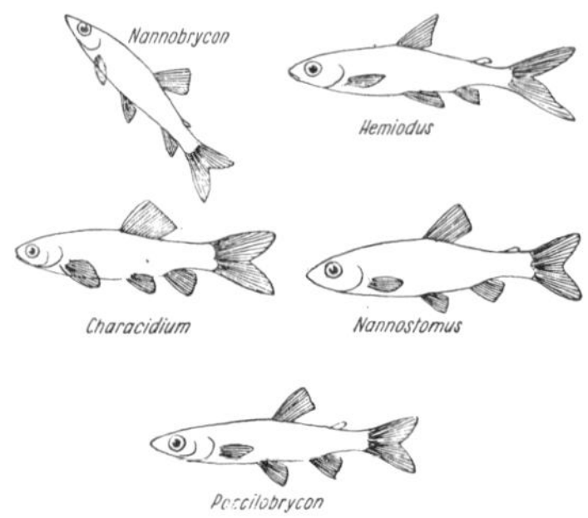

Hemiodontidae, types of the genera

on fish of the same species or of different ages.

Generally the fishes swim with short, sudden movements, through continuous vibrating motions of the vertical fins. These movements may be considered as a characteristic of the family, but only for those species and genera that are spindle-shaped. The manner of swimming often looks peculiarly stiff. Besides this, *Nannobrycon* assumes a sloping position of the body. Many species possess a special night coloring, in which the horizontal stripes are superseded by darker cross bands. They are all peaceable and hardy fishes, which like to live in schools with others of their own species. In non-harmonious communities they easily become shy.

Give them medium-sized tanks, densely planted, with free-swimming space in the middle. A dark bottom enhances their colors. Not very demanding as to nutrition. They eat all kinds of small live foods, substitutionally also dry foods. The *Nannobrycon* species hardly ever pick up food from the bottom. The behavior of these fishes is very charming. The males fight pretty little mock battles. Also the coupling period is full of charm. In part they are egg-scatterers, in part the eggs are hung on firm objects. In all cases the parents are great egg robbers, so that special foresight is necessary to protect the spawn from their attacks. Glass grills on the bottom have proved best for this.

According to HOEDEMANN who, in making systematical divisions, takes into account also the manner of behaving, at present the following genera may be differentiated:

(a) Genera whose manner of living corresponds to the description above: *Poecilobrycon*, *Nannobrycon*, and *Nannostomus*;

(b) Genera with a different behavior, living at the bottom of the water or near it: *Characidium* and *Hemiodus*.

The genera under (a) come from smaller waters or parts of waters, where there are stands of plants, but partly there are currents. It is said that they like especially to stay on swamped shores, where they swim among the flooded grasses against the current. The *Nannobrycon* species are also found in small schools in free spaces of water among the stands of aquatic plants.

Hemiodus: Half-tooth, referring to the teeth, which are found exclusively in the upper jaw.
South American genus of Characin-like fishes, belonging to the family of the *Hemiodontidae*, the members of which are bigger in comparison with the other genera, showing a different manner of living.

— gracilis Guenther:
A little known and rarely imported species coming from the Amazon region, of very elongated and slender shape. Lengths up to 5", Needs densely planted tanks at 77-82° F. Hardy as to foods, but needs occasional helpings of vegetable nutrition.

— semitaeniatus Kner: The Half-Banded Characin.
SHAPE: Quite elongated and compressed laterally. The upper and

Hemiodus semitaeniatus

lower body contours are equally arched. The mouth is slightly subterminal. An adipose fin is present. D 11, A 9-11. Length a little over 8″.

COLOR: Silvery with yellowish and greenish shades. On the middle of the body a round black dot is found from which a black band, widening to the rear, comes out. This goes over onto the lower half of the tail fin, covering this part to the edge.

CARE AND BREEDING: This beautiful, outstanding, and very lively species has proved to be very enduring, but also quite quarrelsome, in the aquarium. They love clear water at 77° F, and plenty of room for swimming. Since the fish are strong eaters, they grow very quickly, especially needing plant food too. Breeding has not been accomplished so far.

Hemirhamphidae: The Half-Beak Pikes.

Family pertaining to the order of the *Synenthognathi*. Small to medium-sized fishes of elongated build, with a more or less rounded cross section, laterally compressed only towards the extremities. The upper jaw is connected with the median jaw, and is motile and shorter than the lower jaw. This is strongly extended and firm. The small teeth sometimes are three-pronged and leave parts of the lower jaw and palate bone free. The vertical fins are dislocated far to the rear. The anal fin of the live-bearing species is somewhat altered in the males. The scales are only loosely inserted. The "beak" is not visible on young specimens. It develops gradually with growth of the fish. Many species show a hook-like, bent, tip of the lower jaw, or else same is provided with a kind of button.

The fresh-water forms feed preferentially on flying food, i.e., on insects that fall on the surface of the water. They are also able to catch flying insects by jumping after them. The lower jaw is slid under the prey, while the previously set upper jaw snaps down like a trap.

Only the manner of living in free nature of the *Dermogenys* species is better known, and permits conclusions on all fresh-water species. The fishes inhabit waters in regions rich in insects, meaning especially swamps, ponds, and very slowly-flowing ditches and rivulets in forest regions. There they appear in schools, swimming along beneath the surface. Most members of the family live in tropical and subtropical seas, and only a few have adapted themselves completely to living in fresh water. Genera, among others: *Hemirhamphodon* and *Dermogenys*.

Hemirhamphodon: The Half-Beak.

Genus of live-bearing Half-Beak Pikes belonging to the family of the *Hemirhamphidae*, with a few species, of which only *H. pogognathus* Bleeker has been imported so far. The species is distributed over the Malayan Peninsula and the greater Sunda Islands, and appears in fresh and brackish waters. Length up to 6″, the female remaining a little smaller. The species is live bearing.

herbivorous fishes: Fishes that need additional plants or plant substances to complete their nutrition are found in numerous fish groups. Nearly all the Carps (*Cyprinids*) eat vegetable food exclusively or additionally, the same occurring with many Characins; but also in many groups of fishes which otherwise are more or less considered predators, for instance, Cichlids, some species temporarily feed on plants. It is known of the *Myleidae* that in part they specialize in very definite tropical fruits. Certain Cichlids, as for instance, the genera *Cichlasoma*, *Etroplus*, and *Pelmatochromis*, are known as occasional vegetable eaters. In such cases not all plants are eaten. Generally they despise water ferns, while other plants, for instance, *Hygrophila*, are preferred and devoured down to the stem. Frequently the algae films are grazed off stones and plants, as for instance, is done by the South American Sucker Catfishes and the Kissing Gouramis (*Helostoma*). The latter in addition to this needs disproportionately small live foods, while the Catfishes are more or less herbivorous. Generalizing one may say that even highly specialized herbivores do not despise the usual kinds of animal foods when they can get them.

hereditary traits: The sum total of all possibilities of development which an organism transmits hereditarily to its progeny.

heredity: The transmission, caused by fecundation or by cellular division, of the characteristics of an organism to its descendants. It may take place either through vegetative sprouting (for instance reproductive tubercles, or shoots in plants, budding in Hydras), through asexual reproductive cells (spores), through simple cellular division (for instance in unicellulars), or through the union of differentiated sexual cells (see GERMINATING CELLS). The sum total of all characters which are transmitted from generation to generation is called the hereditary disposition. The hereditary dispositions, which are typical for a species in its totality as well as for its individuals, are termed the hereditary picture (idiotype). The hereditary picture comprises all possibilities of development of a live being under any conditions of the ambient world. It does not determine the course of its development, but simply represents the manner and way in which it reacts to the influencing conditions of life (reactive norm). A live being can only develop typically, however, if it finds the conditions to which it is adapted. The reactive norm is different for the different species, even under similar conditions of the ambient world, and often it is not the same for single individuals of the same species.

The hereditary picture comprises all dispositions, both of the body design as well as of the functions and of certain manner of behavior, often down to the smallest particulars. From the first instant of begetting on, it establishes a mutual relationship with the ambient world. The product of this mutual interaction is the picture of the appearance (phenotype). The conditions of development may exert so big an influence, that brother or sisters which have developed under different conditions may present different characteristics and features, despite the similar hereditary picture.

Generally the hereditary picture of a species is not completely uniform. To the contrary, it fluctuates within certain limits (range of variation). The total number of individuals of species which populate an undivided area, agreeing to a certain point in the main hereditary characters, but differing distinctly in the secondary ones, is called a population. Even among the descendants of a pair which have grown up under completely similar conditions we find specimens that differ in shape or color, quick or slow-growing ones, ones that are prone to diseases or resistant to them, etc. This is something which also the breeder of aquarium fishes has to include in his calculations. This explains in part which fishes kept in captivity can be changed favorably or disfavorably.

All fishes of natural origin (meaning ones that have not been bred artificially), have to be considered as being of mixed heredity to start with, that is, their begetting links the characters of father and mother, which do not coincide completely. Specimens of pure heredity can only be obtained under continuous selection through inbreeding during breeding experiments (see BREEDING).

Herichthys: Fishes related to the Cichlid genus *Heros*.

A South and Central American genus pertaining to the Cichlid family, which of all American Cichlids ranges farthest North. The genus is closely related to *Cichlasoma*.

— cyanoguttatus Baird & Girard: The Texas Cichlid.

SHAPE: A rather high-backed species. The forehead line rises steeply, while the ventral line runs relatively straight. D XV-XVII/10-12, A V/8-9. Length, in the aquarium, up to about 6″.

COLOR: Dark base with closely spaced pearly-gray to shiny blue dots. During the spawning period the upper body is cream-colored, the belly and breast of the female deep black. Outside the mating time, the SD are minute; the female remains a little smaller than the male.

Herichthys cyanoguttatus

RANGE: Northeastern Mexico, reaching over also into the U.S., especially in the Rio Grande del Norte and its affluents.

CARE AND BREEDING: As described for Cichlids. The species is pugnacious, roots strongly and destroys plants, but is of an indescribable beauty. They are said to be sensitive to old water. Therefore an occasional change of only one third of the water of the tank is advisable. Temperatures of 64-73° F, for breeding 75-82° F, if not in the spawning period, temporary temperatures of 60-64° F are easily withstood. Lowest 54° F.

hermaphrodite: Double-sexed live being. An individual which carries both sexual organs and characteristics. Hermaphroditical developments occur frequently in animals and plants, both as normal and as abnormal conditions.

Herring Fishes: see ISOSPONDYLI.

Herringbone Rivulus, the: see RIVULUS STRIGATUS.

heterandria: With a different male. — *Limia*.

Heterandria: Genus of Tooth Carps belonging to the sub-family of the live bearing Tooth Carps or *Poeciliinae*, with only one known species, which is characterized by a very long, simply built gonopodium.

— formosa Agassiz: The Midget Live Bearer.

SHAPE: Especially the male of this small and slender species belongs among the smallest vertebrates. It is only little compressed laterally.

Heterandria formosa, female

The mouth opening is small and tilted upwards. D 7-8, A 10. Length: males up to $\frac{3}{4}''$, females to $1\frac{3}{8}''$.

COLOR: Yellowish base with a dark brown horizontal band, crossed by some transverse dashes. On the dorsal fin one sees a red spot. SD are the same as in all *Poeciliinae.*

RANGE: Southeast of the U.S.A., from South Carolina to Florida. CARE AND BREEDING: The species is hardy and does well in the smallest containers. They like sunlight, which may cause higher degrees of temperature. It is said that they like a very constant warmth of the water. Lowest 64° F, otherwise 68-73° F, temporarily also more. Dense planting of the tanks is advisable, and the growth of algae is necessary for feeding the fishes. They take all kinds of live and artificial foods, though. In spite of their small size the fish are absolutely not timorous and may prove to be very pugnacious. They are vivacious and like to swim, the males being even a little "jealous" towards each other. Each procreation period lasts for some time. During it one to two young are born daily, a big female yielding a total of about twenty-five. The eggs and young during their period of development are partly fed from the body fluids of the mother in a very primitive manner.

Heteranthera: Genus of aquatic plants belonging to the family of the *Pontederiaceae.*

— zosteraefolia Martius:

GENERALITIES: A very useful, hardy, and quick-growing plant, which may be cultivated both submerged or emerged.

Heteranthera zosteraefolia

SHAPE: The light-green, narrow submerged leaves, and the dark-green emerged ones, are placed alternately on the brittle stem. Shortly before flowering, the submerged plants develop some floating leaves which hold the flower above the surface.

RANGE: This perennial swamp plant is found in swamps and flood regions in Brazil and Bolivia.

CULTIVATION: The submerged form demands unwashed sand as bottom ground. The species likes intense sunlight, but not in excess. Between 64 and 86° F all temperatures are tolerated, but a water warmth of 71° F seems to be the best. No demands are made as to the composition of water. The species may also be cultivated in heated swamp aquaria.

heteroclitus: Dissimilar (in the sexes).

— *Fundulus.*

Heterodonta: Sub-order of clams pertaining to the order of the *Eulamellibranchiata,* class of the Clams or Bivalves, with little developed or missing locking teeth. There are a series of tribes of which only the Zebra Clams or *Dreissenaceae* are described in this book.

heteromorpha: With different body (from that of the other species of *Rasbora ?*)

— *Rasbora.*

Heterophallus: With different gonopodium.

Genus of Tooth Carps pertaining to the sub-family of the live bearing Tooth Carps or *Poeciliinae*. The genus differs from the closely related genus *Gambusia* by minute differences in the construction of the gonopodium.

— rachovi Regan:

SHAPE: A very slender species. D 7, A 10. Length: males $1\frac{3}{16}''$, females $1\frac{3}{4}''$.

COLOR: Metallic greenish gloss, with a length stripe which widens towards the rear and ends in a spot on the caudal peduncle. SD are like those of all *Poeciliinae*.

RANGE: Mexico.

CARE AND BREEDING: A harmless, hardy species. Needs only smaller, but well-planted tanks. Some sunlight is desirable. Temperature around 72° F. All kinds of small foods are taken. The young number 12-15 per litter.

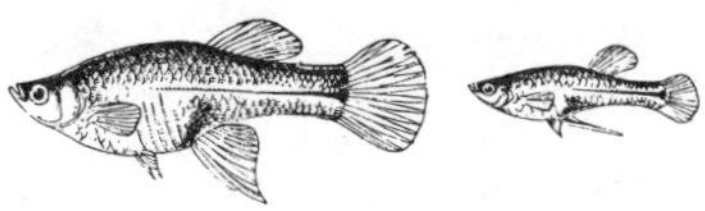

Heterophallus rachovi

Heteropneustes: Which breathe differently.

Genus of Indian Catfishes belonging to the family of the Gill Bag Catfishes or *Clariidae*, with elongated, eel-like body, which is flat at the head but strongly compressed towards the rear. The wide mouth with thick lips and short, pointed teeth on jaws and palate, carries four pairs of barbels. The skin is scaleless and shiny; the eyes are small and insert high up on the body. The fishes possess a breathing sac, which encloses the cauliflower-like gills, and may be filled with water which, in case of need, may be blown out again.

Exclusively twilight and nocturnal fishes, which may become more or less lively in the daytime too, especially when hungry. Being air breathers, they are not sensitive to lack of oxygen.

— fossilis Bloch:

SHAPE: As per description of the genus. D 6-7, A 60-79. The fleshy dorsal fin is only indicated by a fold in the skin. The long anal fin is only slightly separated from the caudal one. Length up to 28″.

COLOR: Dark brown to black with two only rarely existing lighter horizontal stripes. The male is said to be slimmer, the female plumper.

RANGE: In fresh waters in India and Ceylon. The species is frequent everywhere, in spite of living in a quite hidden manner.

CARE AND BREEDING: As per description of the genus. When taken out of the water, the fish sometimes utter a creaking noise. Care is advisable while catching them, as the stings of their pectoral fins may cause painful and hard-to-heal lesions. The species does not need much warmth, 68-73° F being sufficient, but they also withstand higher temperatures.

This Catfish has already been bred in bigger tanks. It is said that the male sticks to the side of the female by suction. The eggs are

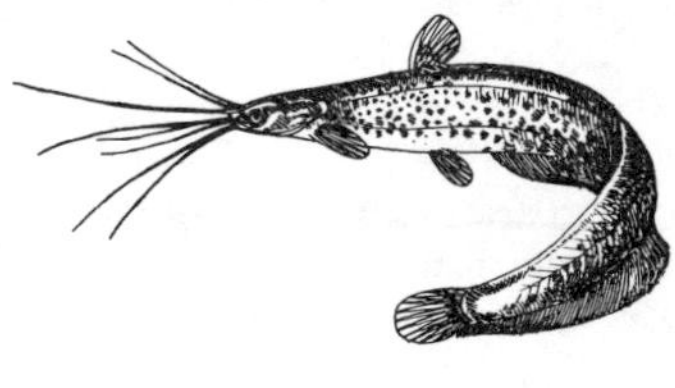

Heteropneustes fossilis

spawned in the sand, where they ball together. Both parents care for their eggs and fry for several weeks.

Heteroptoidea: With differently shaped wings.

Order belonging to the phylum of the insects or *Hexapoda,* the species comprised in which in part suck plant juices, while others suck blood, and whose lower lip is developed into a beak or trunk with several stinging or sucking bristles for this purpose. The construction of the wings is peculiar. The anterior wings form half covers with a fixed upper part and a skin-like tip.

In the first place the aquarist has to pay attention to the sub-order of the Water Tigers or *Hydrocorisae,* to which belong all subaquatic *Heteroptoidae.* Well known are also the Water Striders which run around on the surface, and can be kept in the aquarium with reservations only. These Water Striders which we shall mention here in a few words only, are thin rod-shaped insects, which with the aid of their long legs and of special dispositives are able to keep on the water level due to surface tension. They feed mainly on terrestrial insects that fall into the water. Generally they are found on the surface of quiet waters and in quiet inlets of brooks and rivers.

heterorhabdus: Of different shape.
— *Hyphessobrycon.*

Heterosomata: With unequal body.

Order of Flatfishes belonging to the sub-phylum of the New-Fins or *Neopterygii.* Fishes whose body shape is strongly specialized for living at the bottom of waters. They possess a strongly flattened, unsymmetrical construction of the body, generally with an oval outline. The larvae, built absolutely symmetrically, change with advancing growth so that there appears an upper side with eyes, and a lower, eyeless one. This blind side, which is colorless, reposes on the ground, while the upper one in most cases shows an exceptional capacity to adapt to the color of its surroundings on the bottom. By means of undulatory motions of the fin edges, which run all around the body, the fishes are able to dig in, into the ground, with astonishing rapidity, if the bottom is sufficiently fine. Besides this, in spite of their bizarre shape, they are able to swim relatively well.

Flatfishes are mostly sea dwellers. Only a few species seek fresh water temporarily or permanently. The order comprises five families. Of the family of the Soles (*Pleuronectidae*) a species originating from the East of the U.S.A. has become known, the Fresh-water Sole, *Trinectes maculatus.*

heterotrophy: Alimentation of all animals and non-green plants. Since these cannot assimilate organic substances from inorganic elements, they are forced to take in these nutritional substances either directly in the form of vegetable food, or else indirectly by eating other animals which on their part have eaten plants (the so-called nutritional chains, the first link of which always is a plant).

heterozygotic: Of uneven heredity, due to the confluence of different paternal and maternal hereditary dispositions.

heudeloti: After the name of a French botanist.
— *Tilapia.*

Hexapoda: Insects.

A phylum of invertebrate animals, which quantitatively forms the strongest group of the animal kingdom. It supplies relatively few representatives for the aquarium, though, as most insects are flying or creeping land animals which have only secondarily adapted to life in the water. Head, prothorax and abdomen are generally more or less sharply differentiated. The head comprises the brain and the beginning of the digestive tract. The prothorax is composed of three body rings, which are in part firmly interconnected. The central and lower prothorax bear the wings and must therefore be very firm.

Furthermore the three pairs of legs are connected to it. The prothorax encloses the strong muscles.

The abdomen, consisting of eleven rings, carries the whole intestine. The head bears the antennae and the three pairs of jaws, which, under certain circumstances, may be extraordinarily strong.

Most insects are winged, but leave the egg without wings. Generally there are two pairs of wings, which develop from folds in the skin of the back. Consequently they are no real members. Some insects carry their wings in the same position in repose or flying, others have first to bring them into the flying position. A major preparation for taking off in flight is necessary for the Coleopterans, which have first to prepare their bodies by pumping in air (the so-called act of "counting" of June-bugs). The flying agility and speed of many insects are great. The flying process of the quick-flying insects differs fundamentally from that of birds. Flight is achieved in a manner similar to that of helicopters, but there are also other manners of flying. A number of insects are even unable to fly.

All insects pass through a larval stage. Several changes of skin are necessary before the fully developed animal begins its last cycle of life. Consequently a metamorphosis takes place. It may consist of an ever-increasing perfecting of the wings, as is the case with grass-

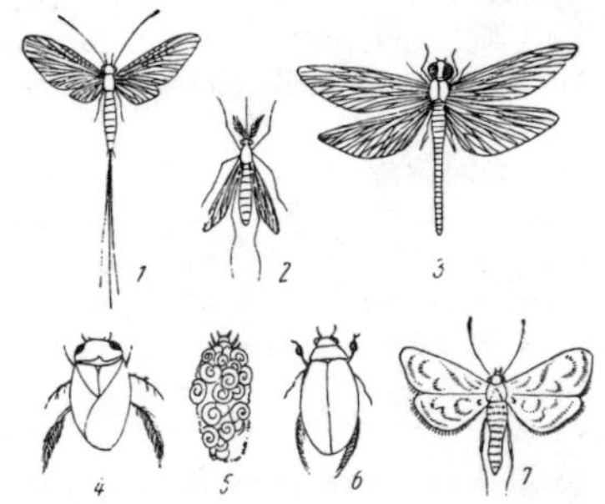

Hexapoda: 1. Ephemerida - 2. Nematocera - 3. Odonata - 4. Heteropteroidea - 5. Trichoptera - 6. Coleoptera - 7. Lepidoptera.

hoppers, for instance. In dragonflies they also develop gradually during the larval stage, but the larvae are adapted to a manner of living different from that of the completed insect. They do not resemble this, the imago, a phenomenon often met in the kingdom of insects. For other insects that undergo a complete metamorphosis, a pupal period intervenes between the larval stage and the imago. Generally the pupa cannot move, and does not take in food. The better-known exceptions to this include the mosquito pupae, which live in the water. During the pupal rest, the body is completely rebuilt, and all organs are developed anew from undifferentiated cells. Wings and eyes come forth completely new, and mostly also the mouth is built in a totally changed shape.

The metamorphosis into the pupa is triggered by cerebral hormones, as larvae with the brain removed never achieve the change.

Insects have an external skeleton of chitin, which is relatively stiff. Growth, and its consequent change of skin, occurs only during the larval period. The completed insect does not grow any more. The intestinal tract may be built in many

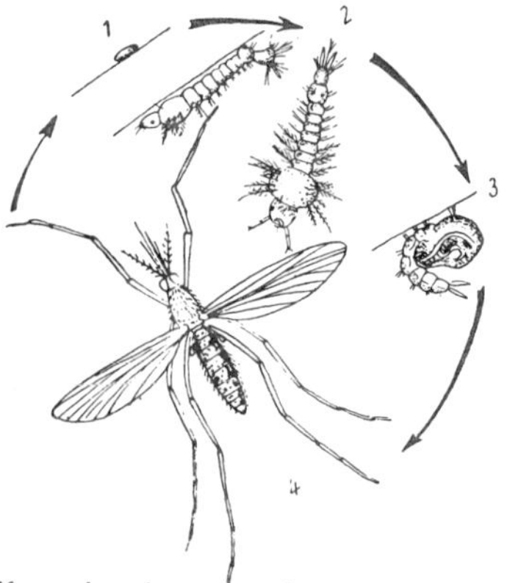

Life cycle of a mosquito - 1. egg - 2. larva - 3. pupa - 4. adult insect.

different ways, according to the manner of feeding. The tube-like heart drives the body fluids through the unclosed system of blood vessels. The blood liquid, which generally is colorless, rarely yellow, green, or red, courses only for short distances through the canals, and empties into the abdominal cavity, where it is again absorbed by the organs and led on. Breathing is done through a system of tracheae. The brain is a small white knob, placed above the gullet. According to the talents of a species, it is more or less complex. Nerve system and sensory organs are generally well developed. The eyes of the completed insects consist of a great number of hexagonal, composite seeing-cells, the so-called facets. In some insect groups they are very keen. Bees, for instance, based on optical impressions, find their way back to the hives over distances of several miles. Still better developed generally is the sense of smell, which enables many insects to present unexplainable phenomena, as for instance when the sexes find each other from distances that go over several miles. Taste, touch, and a sense of vibration too are present. Insects often achieve performances of incredible perfection. Just think of the forms of social organization of the species which set up nations, or of the measures taken to protect off-spring. These acts, though, do not depend on deliberations. Insects act only by instinct and unknowingly. They carry all these abilities as natural dispositions from the egg on, and need neither apprenticeship nor experience. The manners of behavior appear at their given time. The imago behaves differently from the larva. This innate, pre-ordained behavior is called instinct. Many instincts change with metamorphosis or develop only during the pupal stage. Purposeful as the actions of insects may appear to be, and deliberate as they may seem, instinct can only function within its own ambient world, as a unit of the whole which it is. On the whole insects often show a really baffling harmony with the medium in which they live. Just think of the green color of insects living on leaves, of the mimicry of vegetable parts shown in their body shapes, for instance some caterpillars in repose resemble twigs, the outer wings of butterflies bear bark-like patterns, etc. Other insects mask themselves, as for instance, the larvae of the caddis fly. Others still extrude poisonous, pungent, or frightening substances, or may possess a warning color that is especially impressive. The same may apply to stinging or biting species, such as wasps. Other insects, though, that are harmless, seem to imitate the less harmless ones in shape or color (see MIMICRY). For the aquarium only the following groups yield some species which may be of interest as pets, enemies of fishes, or food:

Archiptera: Day-flies (see EPHE-

MERIDA); Dragon-flies (see ODONATA).

Coleoptera: Robber beetles (see ADEPHAGA); Glutton beetles (see POLYPHAGA).

Diptera: Gnats (see NEMATOCERA).

Lepidopteroidea: Caddis flies (see TRICHOPTERA); Butterflies (see LEPIDOPTERA);

Rhynchota: Bugs (see HETEROPTEROIDEA).

hilgendorfi: After the German zoologist Hilgendorf.
— *Alestopetersius.*

hippuroides: Shave-grass-like.
— *Myriophyllum.*

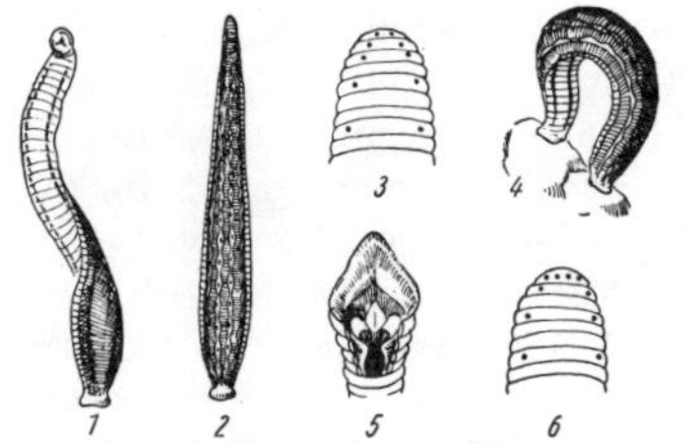

Hirudo medicinalis - 1. and 2. general views - 3. position of eyes - 4. locomotion on solid surfaces - 5. mouth - 6. eye position in a horse leech.

Hirudinea: Leeches.
Order of worms belonging to the class of the *Clitellata,* with a long stretched body which never has bristles. Leeches are soft, and flat on the under side or both on under and upper side. At the front a ventrally disposed sucking cup is found in which the mouth opening is located. A further sucking cup lies at the rear end. Leeches are hermaphroditic. The eggs are extruded in coccoons, sometimes in the soil, on land, into which they dig for spawning. Fertilization generally occurs through self-mating. Leeches change their skins frequently, often nearly daily, by throwing off their upper skins. In part they are blood-suckers, others swallow their prey. The intestine of the blood-sucking species is enlarged by dead-end bags in which major quantities of blood can be preserved for months, being digested little by little. Most species shy from the light, and for some of them sunlight acts lethally. Therefore they are often found beneath stones or in other hiding places. Most species live in fresh water, but may also migrate temporarily to firm land especially in order to lay the coccoons of eggs. Droughts are weathered in moist mud.

Leeches are very good for observation in the home aquarium. The species which lay their eggs on land may be kept in a swamp aquarium. Some species even exert care for their young. Leeches have no place in the fish aquarium.

The order is divided into two sub-orders:

Bristle leeches, or *Acanthobdellae,* and *Archaetobdellae.* These last articulate into three super-families:

(a) Trunk leeches or *Rhynchobdellodea,* to which belongs the Fish leech;

(b) Jaw leeches or *Gnathobdellodea,* with the Medicinal leech; and

(c) Gullet leeches or *Pharyngobdellodea.*

Hirudo medicinalis Linné: Medicinal leech.
A leech, about 6″ long, belonging to the super-family of the jaw leeches or *Gnathobdellodea,* possessing a greenish-black back with lighter longitudinal stripes and a pale-green under-side, spotted with black dots. The mouth opening contains three jaw parts, equipped with many toothlets which act as a saw. A gland in the oesophagus segregates a substance, hirudine, which counter-acts agglutination of the blood while sucking. The body diameter of leeches may swell to three or four times its ordinary size through the intake of blood.

The species inhabits exclusively waters with a muddy bottom and which are abundantly and thickly planted. They can stay out of the water only for short times, at the maximum as long as the skin remains moist.

Their nutrition consists of the blood of vertebrates. Since the species has become rare in free nature at present it is being reared nearly exclusively in breeding farms. They require some years before attacking warm-blooded animals and thus becoming useful to medicine. This happens after about three years, while they become full-grown at the age of five reaching about 20 years altogether. Big leeches suck about 10 grams of blood, digestion of which quantity may last for up to 18 months. They may start sucking again before this time, though, but do not have their full strength and capacity.

After the use of medicinal leeches had fallen into oblivion for a long time as outmoded, today it is again being used more and more.

hispanica: Spanish.
— *Valencia.*

hispida: Brittle, rough.
— *Chara.*

histology: The science of the organic tissues.

history of aquaristics:
The tendency to keep animals from the wilderness in the human home is very old. We therefore can safely assume that very early man has attempted to keep fishes in artificial water containers within the house or the garden, to enjoy their brisk playfulness, or to avoid the disagreeable development of gnats, or else to make observations on the life habits of the animals. The keeping of water plants in garden ponds should be of the same age.

SCHIERIG has collected some indications of this from ancient history. Thus, as early as in the habitations of the old Egyptians one finds special containers for fish, which evidently did not only serve the purpose of keeping edible species. (KELLER: Die Antike Tierwelt, 1913). Also in the home gardens of ancient Rome, as well as in the impluvium of the Roman palaces, such ornamental containers were usual, as has been proved especially through the excavations of Pompeii. These so-called 'piscinae' were populated with fish for the enjoyment of the inhabitants of the home.

Although the Romans had great experience in keeping fish, what they had were fish fattening containers, the vivaria, predecessors of today's aquaria. These were used exclusively to keep and fatten fish for the banquets.

On the other hand, the fish tanks found by the Spaniards at the conquest of Mexico probably were intended for observation purposes. Schierig writes on this: "Tradition has it that in Prince Montezuma's zoological gardens there were artificial containers with fresh and salt water for the breeding and care of fishes and water fowl. It is said that Montezuma's zoological garden had been founded by his ancestors. There is no exact report on these fish containers".

Far back, too, lie the beginnings of keeping fish in artificial containers in the Far East. According to the available reports, the Chinese should have been the first to breed and observe fishes and plants in containers especially built for this purpose, but it is not known whether the Chinese already were aware of the advantage of caring simultaneously for both fishes and plants.

CHEN CHUNG-HSIEN (1955) relates that in the tenth century a Chinese official in Chekiang Province along with other fishes also kept shiny golden-orange colored carp in a pool. A report from the year 1000 mentions goldfish as semi-domestic animals in a temple installation.

By the end of the twelfth century the keeping of such fish had already spread. At that time the emperor Chao Kon kept goldfish in his palace gardens. They also were bred there. After his time the keeping of goldfish in the garden pools of the dominating classes in China became fashionable everywhere. If at first gardens pools that served the purpose, soon it was discovered how to keep and breed the fish in containers. SCHIERIG writes on this: "The first exact notice on this keeping of fish in China originates from official Chinese reports that date back to the year 1369. In that year the Emperor Hung-Wu founded a porcelain factory in King-te-tchen where already there were big ovens for the kilning of ornamental bowls, the so-called 'dragon bowls'. These were the dragon bowls that the Chinese used as containers for fish and aquatic plants, and their use must have been very widely spread in China at that time. Of the Emperor Kia-Tsing, 1522-1566, we know that after commencement of his government he had 300 dragon bowls made. Of the 52 kilns of his factory, at the beginning 32 were used for making dragon bowls. S. W. BUSHELL, who made extensive studies on Chinese culture and the history of Chinese porcelain, calls these dragon bowls 'bowls for goldfish, decorated with a pair of dragons with clouds'. The dragon bowls therefore seem to have served for the keeping and breeding of goldfish already from 14th to the 16th century.

Originally the dragon bowls had the shape of a half-keg. Around the year 1700 appeared also semi-spherical shapes, provided with a flaring-out upper rim, and a shape similar to the goldfish bowls as were formerly usual among us Occidentals. At that time also tub-like containers were made which represent an approximate transition between the dragon bowls and the fish tanks that are in use today. Such shapes, though, were less usual, and only a small number of them have been preserved. In the 17th century the big fish containers in the shape of a half keg represented an important commercial article for the Chinese, as these costly porcelain bowls were used by the European princes, fond of pageantry, in their hothouses.

According to DUERIGEN, the goldfish reached Europe in 1611, probably together with the dragon bowl. In spots, for instance, in Portugal, it had run wild quickly. Around the year 1700 ENGELBERT KAEMPFER, the German discoverer, speaks of the King-Jo, 'a red fish, golden-yellow at the tail', and thus makes it known in larger circles. At the beginning it was a much-sought-after and costly ornamental fish, which only a few opulent ones could afford. Thus the fish that in 1750 the French India Company presented to Mme. Pompadour caused quite a sensation.

The breeding of goldfish is to be derived from its keeping in garden pools and non-transparent containers, as only a fish with striking colors will be noticed in these. About 500 years ago the science of breeding goldfish was brought to Japan from China. From these two countries originate the peculiar varieties, known in the West as veil tails, telescope fish, sky-gazers, egg fish, lion heads, etc. Besides this, these fantastic and partly unnatural shapes cannot be fully appreciated unless kept in the manner usual in China and Japan.

"In Europe it was the Elector of Brandenburg's personal physician, Leonhart Thurneysser zum Thrun (1530-1596), who proved to be the first who kept and observed fishes in a glass container. About 1572 he had the glass works at Grimnitz make a glass sphere, in the middle of which sat a bird, while fish swam around in the outer part. The real purpose of such a combination seems unfathomable. Probably it was more of a plaything than a scientific experiment. It is from nearly a century later only that again we have reports on an aquarium. It was a fisherman from Strassbourg, Leonhart Baldner, who, in a fish book written in 1666, spoke of the possibility of observing captured fish in a glass container, and also reported extensively on the Muhr Weather fish (*Misgurnus fossilis*) and its ability to predict the weather. The next report on aquaria was in the 'Journal de Physique', in 1778, where Abbé Dicquemarre speaks of keeping sea animals and plants in artificial containers for scientific observation. It is not known up to this date whether his idea was put into practice". (SCHIERIG).

Altogether the keeping of animals and plants had an already longish history in science. Initially it had begun with the fact that two or three hundred years ago researchers kept aquatic animals for purposes of observation in any kind of makeshift containers. ROSSMAESSLER, for instance, points out that men like Swammerdam, Leeuwenhoek, Réaumur, Schaeffer, and Trembley have to be named as 'the unknowing inventors of our aquaria'.

During the first times the keeping of aquatic animals, which again and again perished, was subject to great difficulties, as people lacked the fundamental understanding of the symbiosis of animals and plants. Even the creator of the first really effective microscope, ANTHONY VAN LEEUWENHOEK (1723) still used earthenware basins in order to have his observation materials always at hand, and had to bear with the described difficulties. The history of aquaristics is closely related to the scientific struggle for the discovery of oxygen in the 18th century by Priestley and Scheele, furthermore to the interpretation of breathing as a combustion process by Lavoisier and Priestley, who verified this process also in fishes. Spallanzani and a series of further researchers found out through experiments with several aquatic animals that in respiration oxygen is taken in and carbonic acid is eliminated, a process that later on was confirmed by Humboldt and Provençal. Thus now the fact was explained that in the containers used up to that date the animals perished regularly after a certain time, as the carbonic acid expelled in breathing accumulated during a simultaneous consumption of the oxygen. On this the Hollander INGENHOUSS, at the beginning of the 19th century, founded his experiments, based on the conviction that all plants, when under the action of light, take in carbonic acid with which to build their bodies. This was the first step towards the full understanding of the exchange relationship between plant and animal. In the years to follow especially the English continued these experiments in the aquarium. In the year 1841 Dr. S. H. Ward installed a fresh water aquarium with plants and fishes, and reported that the water kept clean and usable for a long time. Considering the situation of aquaristics at the time, Ward's experiments should be considered as blazing new paths, for he was the first one who recognized that, when plants and animals live together, the water keeps clear for a longer time, and that, only with this, conditions are fulfilled for the successful care and breeding of aquatic animals. Of extreme importance to aquaristics also was the proof rendered in 1842 by Dr. Johnston, that growing algae protect sea water from putrefaction for an indefinite time. After the practical experiments of other Englishmen, Warrington, in 1850, gave aquaristics a scientific basis. He reported on the great importance of plants for animal life, and on the urgent need for elimination of organic wastes in putrefaction, as these foul the water and cause the fishes to die.

Warrington also had great success with a salt water aquarium. In a paper he informed that the water had kept completely clear for six weeks and that he had kept some sea anemones in it for over five weeks.

In 1850 P. H. Gosse reports that for several years already he had observed rotatoria in a fresh water aquarium, and that the water always remained clear due to planting the tank with *Vallisneria*, *Myriophyllum*, *Nitella*, and *Chara*. In the field of salt water aquaria Gosse informs in 1852 that of the maritime plants only certain species are fit for planting in the tank, while others decay and foul the water.

"Gosse was the first one, in 1855, to use the word 'aquarium' in his writings" (SCHIERIG).

But also in Germany things did not stand still meanwhile. Also here the aquarium had long ago found admission to the study of the scientist. ROSSMAESSLER states that 'he would have liked to kick himself' when he received word of a writing of Gosse's and thought of the so far unused possibility of spreading the knowledge of Natural Sciences among the people through the aquarium. In the family magazine 'Die Gartenlaube' first appeared some enlightening articles under the title 'Der Ozean auf dem Tische' (The Ocean on the Table), which probably originated under co-operation with Gosse, who is mentioned as adviser only once, though. These works stimulated E. A. Rossmaessler (see this entry) to write his article 'Der See im Glase' (The Lake in the Glass), which too was published in the Gartenlaube in 1856. Considering the effects of this explanatory article, the year 1856 may be considered as the birth year of aquaristics in Germany. In 1857 this was followed by a minute, but basic work of Rossmaessler's under the title 'Das Suesswasseraquarium' (The Fresh Water Aquarium), which reappeared in 1868 in a second printing, edited by Alfred Brehm, but which Rossmaessler did not live to see. In 1875 followed the third printing, and in 1880 the fourth one. The welcome this book found guided the interests of ever-increasing circles to aquaristics. It is therefore only just that Rossmaessler is considered 'the Father of Aquaristics' in Germany.

The fundamental ideas of his writings are true and valid up to this date. According to him the aquarium should serve both for 'instructive fun' and for ornamenting the room. Especially the former aim was much stressed. It already mentions the recommendation to make use of the instructive character of the aquarium in children's education, thus fighting simultaneously against superstition and strangeness to nature.

Of course Rossmaessler's work has to be evaluated in accordance with his times. It was a compilation of the available experience. The number of plants and animals too was still small. Thus he still only describes native plants and lower animals, while he makes nearly no mention of the keeping of fishes. Only in the second printing of 'Das Suesswasseraquarium' is the chapter on fishes substantially enlarged by Brehm.

Through the fact that also salamanders and similar animals are recommended for keeping, the work turns into a libellum against the loathing towards just these beings that prevailed at the time. How insignificant the knowledge of the native water fauna was at the moment is to be seen from the fact that only between 1869 and 1876 Noll brought light into the darkness that covered the manner of reproduction of the Bitterling (*Rhodeus amarus*). In Rossmaessler's era the installation of aquaria was chiefly cultivated for ornamental purposes, while the biological points of view, generally still unknown, were put far back. Predominance obtained for the chalice aquarium, consisting of a big, round glass bowl, which flared out towards the brim. Furthermore the hexagonal box aquarium on a cast-iron frame, and the basin aquarium built of brick and cement with a clay bottom in winter gardens and hot houses. All these tanks had a rock pile in the middle, from which swamp plants, ferns, etc. stuck out over the water surface. Furthermore they mostly were provided with a waterspout.

The works of Rossmaessler were followed in 1868 by a greater opus of Gustav Jaeger, who became famous as the sponsor of the First Aquaristic Show in Vienna, under the title 'Das Leben im Wasser und das Aquarium' (Life in the Water and the Aquarium). Up to the year 1913 it had four printings. In the literature of the time of World War I we find works that have deeply influenced aquaristics through their fundamentality. Here we meet names like Bade, Bruening, Duerigen, Geyer, Zernecke, Stansch, etc. In 1895 Ernst Bade published the first edition of his comprehensive work 'Das Suesswasseraquarium' (The Fresh Water Aquarium), which grew with each printing (of which it had five), and became the standard reference book of German aquaristics. Men like Johannes Paul Arnold—one of the best connoisseurs of ornamental fishes—Dr. Wilhelm Roth, the well-known 'fish doctor', Paul Under, whose masterful photographs of fishes find general recognition even today and have not yet been surpassed, Dr. Wolterstorff, the friend of the salamanders and during long years the editor of the 'Blaetter fuer Aquarien-und Terrarienkunde', are some of the 'old' aquarists of that time.

Meanwhile aquaristics enjoyed growing interest also with the general public. The slowly developing shops and shows had a great part in this. At first, though, they devoted to showing maritime life, in addition to their purely scientific tasks. As yet there were no aquarium fishes worth exhibiting. Thus P. H. Gosse in 1850 staged the first Salt Water Aquarium Show in the Zoological Garden of London, followed two years later by the foundation of a permanent exhibition which gave origin to the London Aquarium. In 1860 a first aquarium exhibition was shown in Vienna. In 1861 a permanent aquarium house was built in Paris. These examples were soon followed by similar foundations in all capital cities. In 1869 the Berlin Aquarium was founded by Alfred Brehm. Among the scientific institutes the oceanic aquarium houses in Naples (founded 1874) and on Heligoland drew special admiration.

Meanwhile a Frenchman had been successful in importing a tropical fish which for the coming development of aquaristics would prove of special significance: the Paradise Fish, *Macropodus opercularis*. In 1869 it was brought from China on board a French man-of-war and handed for breeding to the noted 'pisciculteur' CARBONNIER in Paris. Through their brilliant colors and shape, and the interesting manner of reproduction, the fish caused great wonder and put to shame everything that had been kept in the fresh water aquarium. If so far aquarists had confined their efforts to animals and plants of their home countries, now they turned ever more to the increasing number of imported exotic ornamental fishes. With decreasing intervals now foreign tropicals arrived not only in Europe, but also in other countries. In Germany at first it was American Sunfish, then, in 1892, the Chanchito. By the end of the 19th century these were followed by live-bearing Tooth Carps, which contributed very specially to the development and spreading of aquaristics.

It would be impossible here to enumerate the serial order of all imports. In 1912 a pocket calendar mentions about 180 species imported thus far, while in 1950 the comprehensive index of aquarium fishes imported up to that date, by J. P. Arnold, speaks of no less than 800 species. The exotic fishes and plants now more and more displaced the domestic aquarium inhabitants, the main reason for this is to be found in the fact that the number of small and hardy, but at the same time more colorful and easier to breed, fishes, is much bigger among the tropicals than the corresponding number of cold water fishes. These exotic aquarium fishes have doubtlessly contributed to the quick development of aquaristics in the first place. They have helped to enlarge the biological knowledge of large circles of the population. The different species, known previously to science only, were now also studied in their manner of living, and, above all, in their manner of reproducing. It was unavoidable that the not always easy breeding of fishes should lead to an intensive study of the necessary biological circumstances. Science took over many of those species which, due to their easy care, willingness to propagate, and quick succession of generations, represented proper material for numerous scientific experiments.

It was a natural sequel that the favor found by tropicals, and the ever-increasing demand for them, should also enhance the economic significance of aquaristics. Soon major hatcheries developed. The first of these was founded in 1876 by Paul Matte at Lankwitz, near Berlin. Soon importers began to buy and breed the tropicals brought by sailors from southern ports. If at the beginning imports depended on chance, by and by they began to be effected more and more systematically, to the point that eventually import firms began to outfit their own catching expeditions to tropical lands. These importers have contributed intensively to the knowledge of living conditions in tropical waters, especially so in the last times, as their expeditions are also connected with other scientific tasks. In Germany after World War II especially the firms "Aquarium" in Hamburg, "Tropicarium", in Frankfort, and "Werner", in Munich, have become notable.

During the first times keeping tropical fishes was a costly hobby. New imports and their young reached fantastic prices.

The technique of keeping aquaria developed ever more. The breeding of aquarium fishes, and the need to cover the aquaria, demanded a simple and efficient form of container. Rock piles, castles, plants that protruded over the surface, and waterspouts, began to disappear. The trash in the aquarium was being forced out. Efficient frames were built for voluminous tanks, permitting the use of a minimum area. The tropical origin of the ornamental fishes made necessary that now one should pay full attention to the question of artificial heating. Gadgets to introduce air were built, since they proved necessary for rearing the fry. The interchange of ideas that set in during these years was concerned mainly with technical and practical questions, as well as with a simple description of the newly-introduced fish, plants, and other animals. By gradual work, during decades stone was put upon stone to erect the building of aquaristics. If at first the exchange of ideas was effected by means of letters, with the ever-increasing number of fish fanciers the demand for a technical magazine became louder. The weekly 'Iris', that appeared from 1879 to 1889 gave large space to the discussion of aquaristic questions. The first specialized magazine to appear in Germany, in 1890, was the 'Blaetter fuer Aquarien- und Terrarienkunde' upon which soon followed a whole series of other periodicals, for instance, 'Nerthus', 'Natur und Heim', and especially the 'Wochenschrift fuer Aquarien- und Terrarienkunde', which appeared in 1904. This found its sequel after 1945 in the "DATZ" (Die Aquarien- und Terrarien-zeitschrift). In 1954 this was joined by a second German magazine 'Aquarien und Terrarien'.

In order to aid each other and to exchange experiences, soon the ever-increasing number of aquarium fanciers joined together in aquaristic clubs. The oldest of such foundations was the club 'Aquarium', in Gotha, in the year 1882. In 1884 followed 'Isis', in Munich, and in 1888 the well-known 'Triton' of Berlin. Many of these groups have made a respected name for themselves, not only among amateurs, but also in scientific circles, although the club craze, so characteristic of Germany, may have brought forth very strange blossoms also in this field. Therefore there always were the admonishing voices, who reminded the clubs that their aim was not the development of local club politics, but the mutual help and the discussion of aquaristic problems, as had been the end in view for Rossmaessler. Anyway, the growth of clubs was enormous. A pocket calendar of the year 1912 mentions about one hundred German, and thirty foreign clubs. In 1926 the number of German clubs had already reached 400. Many of these established open-air tanks, built food ponds, devoted themselves to animate youth in the hobby, and gave each other mutual aid through governing federations. Aquaristics had already gained international recognition. In many European and other countries organizations had been created, magazines were edited, and conventions held, to further international exchange. But in many places there were still lacking higher organizations which could have made possible a real co-operation. After many preceding fruitless trials, in 1911 a comprehensive association was founded, but it found difficulties in carrying its point. Only after the two World Wars, the only positive result of which was the ardent desire of all countries for friendly co-operation, things led to an effective federation on a larger scale. In 1954 the WFA (World Federation of Aquarists), a governing international organization, was founded, publishing its own magazine for the exchange of ideas on an international scale. More or less strictly organized groups of aquarium fanciers are today found in nearly all countries of the world. All these organizations have made it their aim to spread aquaristics as a refreshing hobby that educates the people, and to create an international collaboration, as well as to deepen the general knowledge of aquatic biology and to cause world-wide technical and scientific discussion of the related questions.

The technical literature has attained such volume, that it is impossible here to mention simple titles of authors. It is characteristic for the depth that the whole science of aquaristics has reached that, besides the fundamental writings which give practical hints, an ever-increasing number of books appears on the market with a biological evaluation of aquaristics.

The technical development since 1945 is huge. It is based on the experience of a whole century. In general discussion the practical questions are more and more being replaced by the debates on biological problems. The progressing knowledge that every living being forms a unit with its surrounding world has led today's aquarist to pay attention in a much higher degree to the exigencies of life for plants and animals, determining what they both are, and imitating them in his aquarium. Thus it has recently become possible to breed even hard-to-breed fishes, and attempts at growing even the most delicate plants have led to success. But even so, in this field aquaristics still stands at the beginning of its development.

It is the task of both, the various groups and the technical press, to further this scientific development, and to keep up the value of aquaristics as a hobby that refreshes and yields joy and beauty.

Hollandichthys: After the American zoologist, William Jacob Holland.
South American genus belonging to the family of the Characins or Characidae, with only one species.

— multifasciatus (Eigenmann and Norris): The Big Scale Tetra.

SHAPE: Relatively short and high-backed, strongly compressed laterally. The big, supraterminal mouth is equipped with three-pronged teeth. The lateral line is incomplete. D 11, A 28-31. Length up to 5″.

COLOR: Yellowish-brown with 8-9 dark to black horizontal bands and a spot on the shoulder. The fleshy dorsal fin is vividly colored. The ventral outline of the male is a little shallower and the anal fin is bighted in and provided with fine hooklets.

RANGE: Southeastern Brazil.

CARE AND BREEDING: This fish is quite rugged, takes all kinds of food, but is very voracious and a little vicious. It likes to swim but needs hiding places into which to retire occasionally. Temperature 75° F, lowest 59° F. Breeding in the aquarium has not yet been achieved.

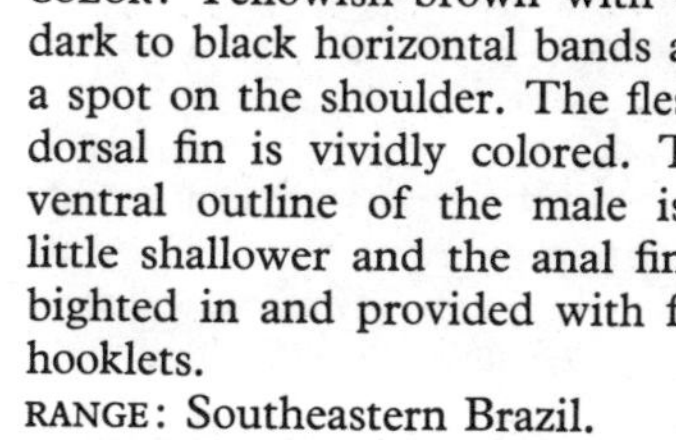

Hollandichthys multifasciatus

holotaenia: With complete band, from end to end.
— *Barbus.*

Homalopteridae: Family pertaining to the sub-order of the Carp-like fishes or *Cyprinoidea.* This family represents a sort of transition from the Carps to the Loaches. All species have sub-terminal mouths, surrounded by barbels. They are bottom fishes that feed both on micro-organisms of the bottom ground and on detritus and algae. The big pectoral fins are jointed horizontally to the body, thus protecting the fishes from sinking into the ground. So far there are no observations on the family in captivity, at least no published ones, despite the fact that just during the last years the fishes have been imported from time to time. Probably they are not much liked by aquarists, for one because they root and dig, on the other hand because they do not show any flashy colors. Doubtlessly, though, they represent an interesting group of fishes which is worth while keeping. Genera, among others: *Homaloptera, Balitora,* and

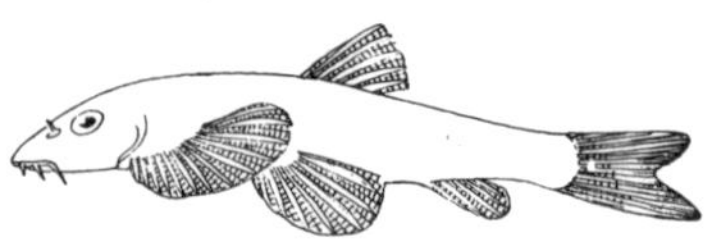

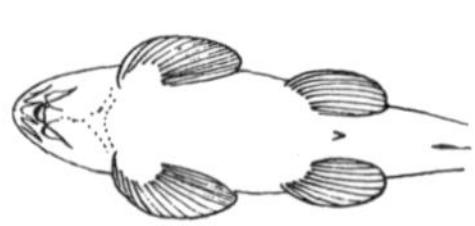

Balitoropsis, type of the genus; same, ventral view; below, Homaloptera, type of the genus.

Hemimyzon.

homanolotus.
— *Pachypanchax.*

homological: Of similar history of development.

homozygotic: Of similar heredity.

Hoplias: The armed one.
Genus of preying Characins belonging to the family of the *Characidae.*

— **malabaricus** Bloch: The Trahira.

SHAPE: Elongated body, only slightly compressed laterally, nearly cylindrical. The mouth opening is very big, and the mouth equipped with especially sharp teeth. The eyes are large and lively. D 13-14, A 10-11. No fleshy dorsal exists. Length up to 20″. (Specimens have been caught in Brazil, in the Araguaia River, measuring up to 48″. Translator's note).

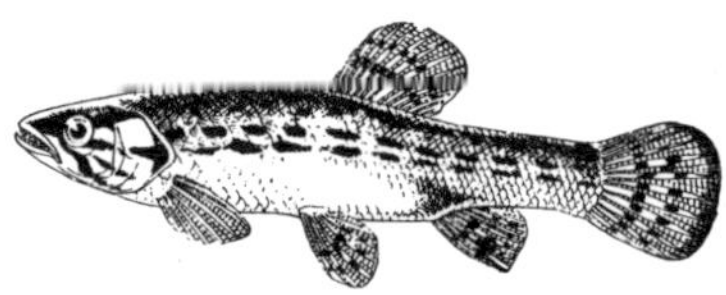

Hoplias malabaricus

COLOR: Olive-brown base with strongly variable dark spots arranged in horizontal stripes, which vanish ever more with increasing age. The male has a more elongated shape.

RANGE: In waters of all kinds that present hiding possibilities, all over South and Central America, from Panama in the North down to the La Plata in the South. Numerous everywhere.

CARE AND BREEDING: The species is a fish of prey which, if carelessly handled, may cause dangerous wounds, even to humans. Especially fit for show aquaria. According to its preying nature, it is especially fond of live fishes, but may be trained to eat meat. Temperatures 73-82° F. Method of procreation is unknown.

Hoplosternum: With armored breast.

South American genus of Catfishes belonging to the family of the Armored Catfishes or *Callichthyidae*, differing from the other genera of the family by their connected armor plates.

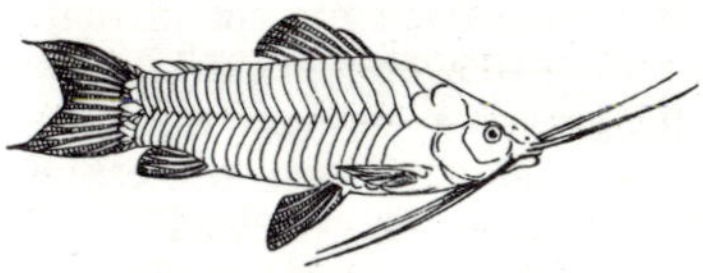

Hoplosternum, type of the genus

— littorale Hancock:

SHAPE: The somewhat compact and sturdy body rises slightly towards the back, while the ventral line is nearly straight. The wide head is flattened down from above. The jaws are toothless. The upper jaw carries two pairs of barbels. The sides of the body and the back are protected by bone plates, those of the back having grown together with the upper lateral plates. The eyes are small. D 9, A 7. The fleshy dorsal fin inserts far back. The upper plates number 25, the lower ones 23.

COLOR: Solid gray-blue to blackish.

RANGE: In clear and still waters of tropical and sub-tropical South America, where there is a muddy bottom.

Hoplosternum littorale

CARE AND BREEDING: No exact knowledge is available on the species, but the care for them should be similar to that given the other Armored Catfishes. According to a report, the fish are said to build a bubble nest.

— thoracatum Cuvier and Valenciennes.

SHAPE: The body is pestle-shaped, a little compact, having nearly the same height from the origin of the dorsal to that of the caudal fin. The head is broad, compressed from the top. Of the two pairs of upper jaw barbels one reaches back beyond the ventral fins. D I/8, A I/6-8. Number of plates: upper 25-26, lower 23-24. Length is not exactly known.

COLOR: Brownish to gray-brown with isolated little dark spots. The first spine of the pectoral fins of the male is stronger and colored a reddish yellow.

RANGE: Northern South America, down to the Amazon region, in shallow waters with muddy bottom.

CARE AND BREEDING: Sufficiently sized tanks are needed to keep them. Temperatures: 68-70° F, temporarily more. Feeding should be done especially with red larvae, enchytrae, and tubifex, but they also take daphnia, and probably vegetable parts too. ARMBRUST speaks of a successful spawning, and mentions as conditions for it a sufficiently roomy tank, low water level (4″), covering with floating plants, and the use of beech leaves to cover the bottom.

At the beginning of the spawning period the males took over certain territories, which they defended approaching the intruder with their barbels (which are usually turned to the front) and trying to hurt him with their pectoral spines. The male built a bubble nest, gathering beech leaves from the bottom, carrying them to the surface, and imbedding them in foam bubbles. The air necessary for this was taken into the mouth and expelled in great quantities through the gills in the form of small bubbles. In each case two to three leaves were incorporated in the nest. The surface of the nest totalled about 20″ x 4″, with a height of about 1¼″. Curiously, only dead leaves, never living ferns, were used. To the contrary, A. could observe that with the building of the bubble nest the ferns begin to die off. They dissolved. A. ventures the supposition that possibly a chemical substance of the bubble secretion could be held responsible for this. During the spawning process the male showed a genital tube about ¾″ long. The female sucked fast to the region of the anus of the male. The act of spawning took place about ¾″ to 1¼″ above the bottom. At the beginning the female sank to the bottom with her folded ventral fin purse, but after 5-10 seconds she swam up to the nest and extruded her eggs there. The male constantly increased the foam nest, even during the spawning. Apparently it also utters a sort of sound when highly excited. The eggs are relatively big, light-yellow-brown in color, and transparent. The big yolk sac is consumed after two days. The male guards eggs and young, but even so it is advisable to remove the parents from the breeding tank. Rear them with chopped tubifex and dry foods.

horae: After a personal name.
— *Botia.*

hormones: Active substances which trigger and direct certain functions of the organism, released into the blood stream and lymph by the glands with internal secretion. They are specific of each species and cannot destroy bones or gastric juices. Place of origin and place of action may lie far apart. Each hormone has one given effect only. Hormones are responsible, among other things, for the development of the so-called secondary sexual characteristics. They are formed as soon as the male and female germinal glands begin to work, in other words, with sexual maturity. Naturally the hereditary factor for the typically male and female characteristics are present in both sexes, but they only begin to show in the general appearance when the germinal glands begin to secrete the corresponding sexual hormones. Also the mating colors of fishes are triggered by hormones. MUNDER called forth the mating colors of male Bitterlings by injecting them with the hormones of other vertebrates, or by adding a hormone preparation to the water. After the hormone is used up, natural colors return. The same experiment may be conducted with female bitterlings, on which it causes extrusion of the oviducts.

WUNDER fixed a clam shell outside an aquarium containing male and female bitterlings. Both sexes reacted immediately by developing the corresponding procreation characteristics (mating colors and warts, and oviducts). Consequently it was the vision of the shell which, acting through the nerve system, excited the germinal cells to produce sexual hormones.

Horn Ferns: see PARKERIACEAE.

Hornwort: see CERATOPHYLLUM DEMERSUM, CERATOPHYLLUM SUBMERSUM.

Hornwort Plants: see CERATOPHYLLACEAE.

Horse Leech, the: see HAEMOPIS SANGUISUGA.

hulstaerti: After a personal name.
— *Barbus.*

Humboldtiana: After the naturalist Alexander von Humboldt.
— *Nymphoides.*

Hummingbird-Lamp-Eye, the: see APLOCHEILICHTHYS MYERSI.

Humpbacked Limia, the: see LIMIA NIGROFASCIATA.

Hunchback Tetra, the: see CHARAX GIBBOSUS.

hybrid: A cross-bred product, coming from parents which diverge noticeably in their hereditary characteristics. Generally hybridization is possible only between strains or sub-species, sometimes also between species which are very closely related to each other or which are not yet firmly established with regard to genetic history. Frequently hybrids are unable to reproduce.

Hydra: see HYDROIDEA.

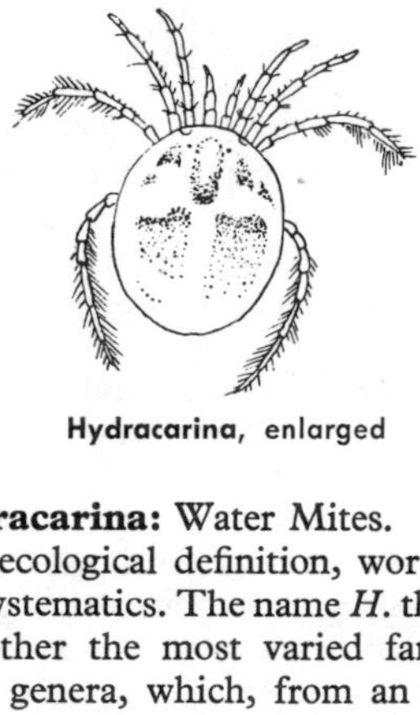

Hydracarina, enlarged

Hydracarina: Water Mites.

An ecological definition, worthless to systematics. The name *H.* throws together the most varied families and genera, which, from an exact and scientific point of view, have no correlationship at all.

A group of mites (see ACARI), with many species, which are generally harmless. They are often introduced in the aquarium together with foods, but many fishes do not eat them. The several species show different colors, ranging from ochre to red. Motion is achieved by lively paddling with their long legs, but should not be confused with the very similar clam crustaceans (see OSTRACODA), which possess only short paddle feet half inside the shell *H.* live preferentially in thickly planted ponds and pools, where they feed on unicellular organisms and microscopic crustaceans. The numerous eggs are laid on the underside of aquatic plants. It should be noted that water mites also live in clams and sponges, as well as in subterranean waters, underground waters, and thermal springs with temperatures up to 120° F.

Hydrilla: Genus of subaquatic plants belonging to the family of the *Hydrocharitaceae.*

— verticillata (Linné fil.) Caspary: The Bottom Nettle.

An *Elodea*-like, perennial plant, ranging over Northeast Europe, South and East Asia, Australia, Indonesia, Mauritius, Madagascar, and East Africa. Found especially in standing and flowing waters with muddy bottoms, where it is rooted to the ground. Specimens coming from colder climates may be kept in unheated tanks. The species differs from the very similar *Elodea canadensis* through its red leaf nervure and the more pronounced teeth on the edge of the leaves. For cultivation see ELODEA.

hydrobiology: The Science of water life and their conditions of living.

Hydrocharyaceae: Water nuts.

Family pertaining to the class of the *Dicotyledoneae.* The *H.* are annual water plants with *Trapa* as their only genus, of the few species of which especially the water nut or water chestnut, *Trapa natans* Linné, is known. It is a decorative plant, rooted to the ground, from where it sends a rosette of leaves and a more or less long stem to the surface. This consists of many diamond-shaped leaves, trouped around an axis, the stem of which is slightly inflated in the middle. The leaves are saw-toothed at the front edge. The flowers are small, the fruits are the well-known water

Trapa natans

nuts, which are equipped with four denticles. The plants may be sown in early spring from seeds that were kept cool and moist in winter. In spring they are laid into an aquarium with sand that has been loosened with a little peat moss. They soon germinate, at 64-68° F. Waternuts are quite rugged plants in the open-air installation, but rather difficult to grow within closed rooms. Since they have become a little rare, they should be protected, and one should avoid collecting them.

Hydrocharis: Water beauty.
Genus of floating plants belonging to the family of the Frogbits or *Hydrocharitaceae*.

— morsus ranae Linné: Frogbit.
GENERALITIES: A nice floating plant, which in summertime thrives as well within the house, but is especially well adapted for open-air installations.
SHAPE: The round water lily-like floating leaves stand in a rosette around a knot on more or less big stems. Superficially considered, the plant resembles a dwarf water-lily. The white flowers grow above the surface.
RANGE: In standing waters in Europe, Asia, Australia, and Northern Africa, especially on the banks of ponds and lakes.

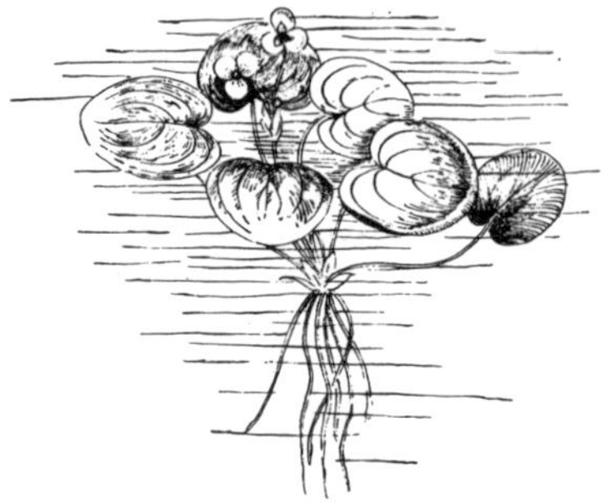

Hydrocharis morsus ranae

CULTIVATION: The plants love a low water level, so that their roots may reach the mud into which they like to penetrate. Within the house they want to be located in a light, not too warm, place. Wild plants should be cleaned carefully after collection, as many aquatic animals, undesirable in the aquarium, deposit their eggs on the underside. Especially the tender leaves are easily attacked by snails, which eat great holes into them. Reproduction takes place in summer by means of shoots, which are connected to the mother plant and often form whole chains. In Autumn the Frogbit retracts, and brings forth winter buds from which in spring the new plants may be grown, if they were watered in a glass with cool water.

The species loves light, especially sunlight, and a water temperature of 64-68° F, if exposed to direct sunshine also higher temperatures.

Hydrocharitaceae: Frogbit Plants.
Very variously built family of aquatic plants belonging to the class of the *Monocotyledoneae.*

Hydrocharitaceae - 1. Elodea - 2. Lagarosiphon - 3. Hydrilla - 4. Hydrocharis - 5. Ottelia - 6. Limnobium - 7. Stratiotes - 8. Vallisneria

Several of the species belong among the steady stock of aquarium plants. The processes of fertilization are very interesting. For this the female flowers generally float on the surface of the water, on long stems, while the male ones grow at the bottom of the plants from where they are released to the surface, being led to the female flowers by winds, etc., thus making possible the fecundation.

Genera, among others: *Elodea, Hydrilla, Lagarosyphon, Vallisneria, Ottelia, Stratiotes, Limnobium*, and *Hydrocharis*.

Hydrocleis: Genus of aquatic plants belonging to the family of the *Butomaceae*.

— nymphoides (Wildenow) Buchenau: The Water Poppy.

GENERALITIES: One of the prettiest water plants with floating leaves, which, under favorable conditions thrives well even in the home aquarium.

SHAPE: The shiny green, heart-shaped leaves possess a more or less long stem. The plant is rooted in the bottom ground and sends a three-foot long shoot frequently to the surface, which is often highly ramified. The yellow flowers, rust-brown on the inside, may attain 2″ in size.

RANGE: Tropical regions of South America, in standing or slow-flowing waters, in which it settles especially the temporarily flooded bays and marginal regions where it forms dense stands.

CULTIVATION: The species is very easy to grow and, under favorable conditions, it may displace all other plants. Therefore WENDT recommends that the only bottom ground it should be given is unwashed sand. No special demands are made as to the composition of water, but it thrives and blooms better in soft water. An essential condition is plenty of light, especially sunlight.

Any temperature between 59 and 86° F is acceptable, but it is advisable to afford the plants a winter rest at 46-50° F. Reproduction in the aquarium takes place exclusively by means of shoots, which develop at the knots of the stems.

Hydrocorisae: Water Bugs.

Sub-order belonging to the order of the *Heteroptoidea*, characterized by an adaptation to life in water, and by their short antennae, located on the underside of the body. Most water bugs breathe by coming to the surface, where they take in atmospheric air. Only a few species have adapted to life at the bottom of the water to a point that permits them to breathe oxygen dissolved in the water. Some species possess thin breathing tubes (snorkels) which they extend over the surface. Others have a thick wad of hair at the extremity of the body, which retains air after having been stuck out of the water while breathing. Often the air reserves collect under the wing covers. The back-swimmers have an air-filled breathing canal on the belly, which explains their peculiar positions for swimming. The water boatmen fill a hollow space in the pectoral

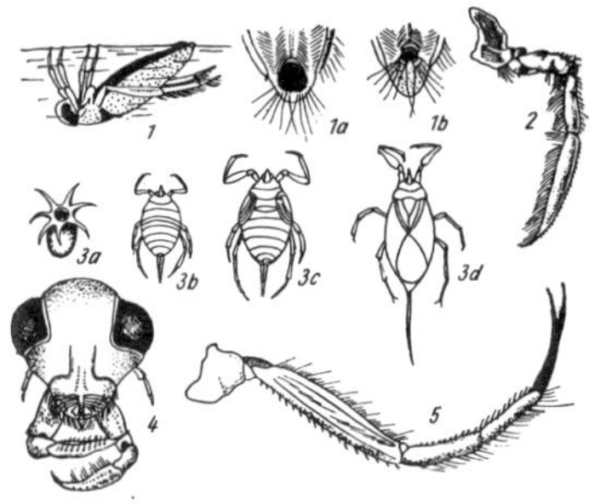

Hydrocorisae - 1. **Notonecta**, breathing - 1a. breathing opening at the end of the body, opened - same, closed - 2. swimming leg - 3a through 3d. developmental stages of the water scorpion **Nepa** - 4. head of **Corixa** - 5. claw leg of **Corixa**.

section with air, which is the reason why in order to breathe they have to leave the water with their fore part.

Some water bugs are very clever swimmers, moving forward with the aid of strong, hairy rowing legs. Others creep around on the ground or among the aquatic plants. Nearly all species are able to fly, but only the water boatmen can pierce the surface directly in order to rise in flight.

Of the German species we shall mention the following: Water boatmen or *Corixidae*, Back-swimmers or *Notonectidae*, Swimming bugs or *Naucoriidae*, and Water scorpions or *Nepidae*.

The Big Water Boatmen *Corixa geoffroyi* is rarely found in standing waters. It has a length of $1\frac{3}{16}''$, its body being elongated, and shiny brown on the upper side. The hind legs are used as oars. For breathing it pierces the water level with its fore part. Air is kept under the wing covers and on the hairy belly. As food, especially algae are to be considered. Micro-organisms are eaten as complementary nutrition only. The male of the Striped water boatman, *Corixa striata*, emits chirruping sounds which are produced by rubbing the front feet over the bill. Other, smaller, *Corixa* species are also able to do this. The sounds probably serve to attract the females.

The back-swimmers, with their most common species, *Notonecta glauca*, have a light back and a dark belly. The long, hairy hind legs act as strong oars. The bugs are predators which chase all species of small life and even fish. The prey is caught, stung, and sucked empty. The genus comprises numerous species which are difficult to differentiate.

The swimmer bugs are often mistaken for water bugs. Well-known is *Naucoris cimicoides*, a bug that reaches lengths of up to $\frac{5}{8}''$, and which also lives as a predator. The fore legs are transformed into strong weapons for attack. The big swimmer bugs also tackle snails, fish fry, and other aquatic animals. The female lays her eggs into the stems of aquatic plants by means of an ovipostor tube.

The Water Scorpion, *Nepa rubra*, and the Water Twig, *Ranatra linearis*, are representatives of the German species of *Scorpion* bugs. The fore legs of *Nepa* form two mighty catching arms, the shape of which has contributed to christen

Hydrocorisae - 1. Corixa **geoffroyi** - 2. egg, enlarged - 3. eggs on **Elodea** leaves - 4. head - female of a backswimmer laying eggs.

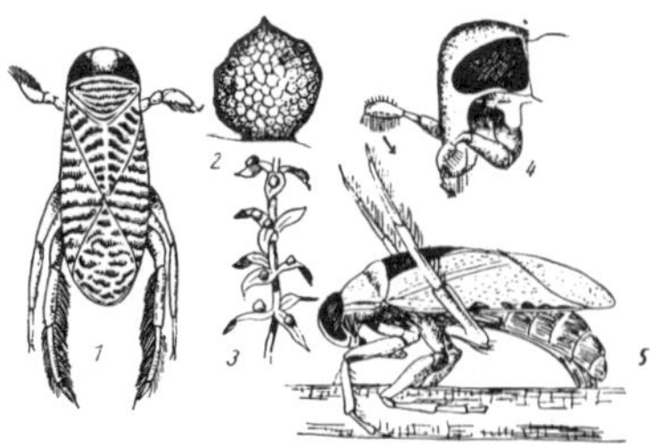

the genus as "scorpion" bugs. In fact they have no connection with the real scorpions, which are related to the spiders or *Arachnidae*. The twig bugs, with their elongated bodies, resemble pieces of wood. This shape probably serves to decoy their prey, to which the slow motion of the genus is a distinct aid. Both kinds of scorpion bugs are efficient predators. Especially the twig bugs are able to conquer even bigger beasts as prey. What they have caught, they scarcely ever release.

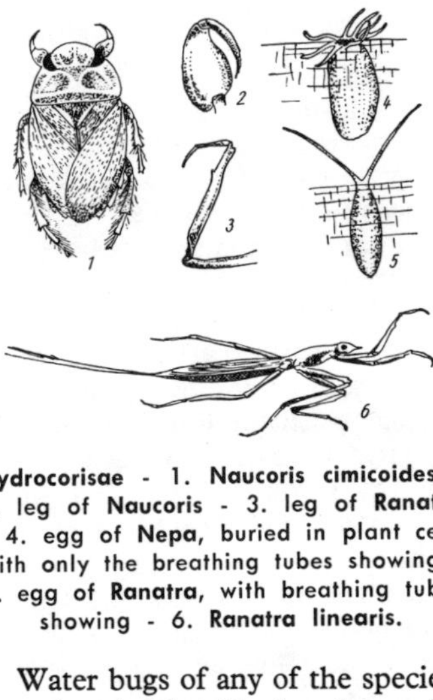

Hydrocorisae - 1. **Naucoris cimicoides** - 2. leg of **Naucoris** - 3. leg of **Ranatra** - 4. egg of **Nepa**, buried in plant cells with only the breathing tubes showing - 5. egg of **Ranatra**, with breathing tubes showing - 6. **Ranatra linearis.**

Water bugs of any of the species mentioned should be kept in separate containers. They have no business at all in decorative aquaria, especially when there are young fry in them. Bigger species of fishes like to eat the smaller species of water bugs.

Hydrodictyaceae: Net algae. Microscopically small to rather big floating green algae, the cells of which unite in colonies. The well-known Water Net, the lattice algae *Hydrodictyon reticulatus*, is well-distributed throughout the inland waters of Europe. Frequently it passes unnoticed, though. The

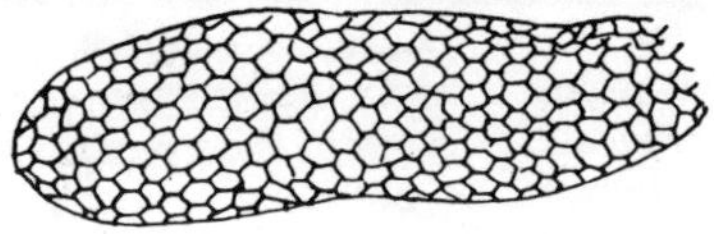

Hydrodictyon; enlarged view below

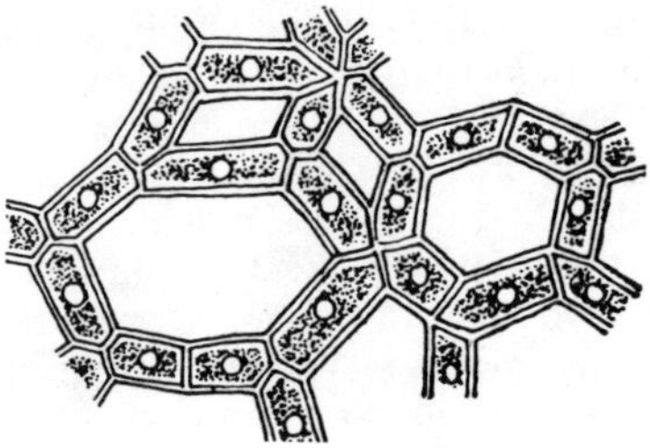

elongated cells are joined together forming a closed, hose-shaped net, which begins at a microscopic size, but may end up with a length of 24″, and a width of 6″. At this time every single mesh has a diameter of ⅜″ or more. The net algae is a work of art of unique beauty.

Hydroidea: Fresh water polyps. Order belonging to the class of the hollow animals or *Coelenterata*, with several genera. The genera *Hydra*, *Chlorohydra*, and *Pelmatohydra* may be considered together in this book.

The body is tubular. Around the mouth opening stands a single wreath of filiform tentacles. The animals anchor to firm foundations to which they stick with their closed extremity, the foot plate, but are able to move. In order to differentiate the several species, the aquarium hobbyist may consider the characteristics of color, size, and number of tentacles. Noteworthy through its very green coloration is the Green Hydra, *Chlorohydra viridissima*, which attains lengths of up to ⅝″ not including the tentacles which in their turn remain a little shorter than the body. This species is found even in the smallest waters. The coloration originates from very simple, unicellular, algae, which live in symbiosis with the polyps, but what the purpose of such symbiosis might be is not very clear. The algae locate in the cells of the entoderm, that is, in the inner layer of the body tube. With sexual reproduction they also follow into the eggs. Notwithstanding this, the polyp may live without its "boarders". The species is widely distributed but hard to detect due to its green color. They are hermaphroditic, egg and sperm cells being developed in the same individual.

A very common species is the brown fresh-water hydra, *Pelmatohydra oligactis* Pallas, which is found mainly in ponds and lakes, It may be of different colors, yellowish, reddish, brownish, or gray. They are very long and may attain 1¼″ without measuring the tentacles. The still microscopically thin catching arms may measure 1″ when extended. The species is heterosexual. The common fresh-water hydra, *Pelmatohydra vulgaris f. attenuata* Pallas, grows to a length of 2″, the tentacles to 2″. The color is brown, in several shades. In the mentioned shape, which is most common, the animals are heterosexual.

Hydras as pets are most interesting for several reasons, even if understandably they are not well-liked in the home aquarium. In the latter they are mainly introduced when feeding daphnia, and are often found to be hard to remove. It is good advice, though, occasionally to observe these animals in a special little glass by means of a magnifier.

The way their body is built has been described under the heading "*Coelenterata.*" The number of catching arms that surround the mouth opening totals 5 to 20, according to species and age. These

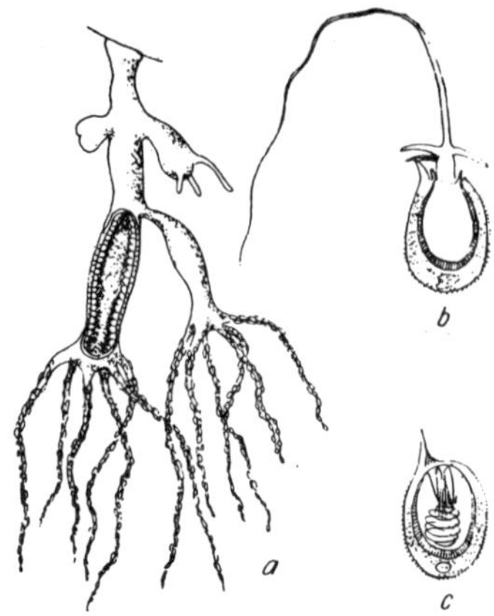

Hydroidea - a. colony b. stinging capsule, opened - c. same, closed.

arms carry the nettle capsules which may be seen as little nodules under a lens.

They are concentrated on the different cells of the arms, but are also found on the other parts of the body. They are artful formations, consisting of undifferentiated cells which penetrate the outer skin of the hydras. The nettle capsule consists of a little bubble, filled with a liquid and closed by a cover out of which protrudes a triggering pin, while the interior harbors a rolled-up, hollow, filament. Upon a touch stimulus, which probably is coupled to a certain chemical stimulus, the cover bursts and the filament jumps out. Parts of the nettle capsule produce wounds on the body of the prey where a venom is injected. Other capsules only hold the prey by wrapping their filaments around its body protuberances. Two other kinds of nettle capsules serve the purpose of locomotion. It is peculiar that "fired off" nettle capsules do not return to their previous location, nor are they replaced. Instead of this, new, undifferentiated cells migrate to their former location in order to form new nettle cells.

Hydras react to disturbances by retracting their tentacles and balling up their bodies into small knots. They migrate after their food, which consists of microcrustaceans and other aquatic micro-organisms, as well as fish alevins in the first stages of development. Similar to the microcrustaceans they too migrate towards the sources of light, thus automatically reaching the regions where food is concentrated most intensely. To do this, they lean over to one side, stick some catching arms with fixing capsules to a foundation, draw up the body, fix it by means of the footplate, extend the catching arms again, and locomote in this way. Doing this, the hydras turn regular somersaults. Greater distances are also covered by putting the footplate up against the surface of the water and thus floating along. All fresh water hydras are very gluttonous. They are able to feed even on animals that are much bigger-sized than the hydras themselves. While they still hold many preys in their arms, others are already being digested inside their bodies. Often the abundant nutrition makes them look swollen up and ball-shaped. Digestion takes place by first dissolving the organisms within the body tube. Smaller particles of food are then sucked in by the cells of the ectoderm, which digest them further. The rest is again expelled through the mouth opening.

Through their gluttony they become a nuisance in the aquarium as they compete for food with the fishes, even if they do not harm them. They can easily tackle very small fry during the first days of life. Bigger young ones may be harmed to a greater or lesser degree.

The manner of reproducing of hydras is very interesting. The most remarkable process is that of budding, in which through tilting out and growing a new hydra develops at some point of the body, on its part too equipped with tentacles and contributing to joint feeding. In this manner, by always developing new buds, and even bud "grandchildren", complete colonies of specimens may develop. This manner of reproduction generally takes place during summer. Sexual reproduction is more rare. There are hermaphroditic and heterosexual species, in many species even male and female specimens. Eggs and sperm cells develop from undifferentiated cells. The eggs may be 1.5 mm in size. The shell is either smooth, or else equipped with prongs and protuberances. A medusa form does not appear.

The fact that hydras are able to regenerate to a wide extent out of undifferentiated cells makes them interesting objects of research. Even the smallest fragments may develop into complete specimens. The most varied species of hydras may be grafted on one another, and so also males and females. Theoretically at least, they may be kept alive indefinitely by artificially impeaching sexual reproduction.

Combating hydras in the aquarium is not always easy. Only a few fishes eat them. *Trichogaster trichopterus*, the Blue Gourami, and its sub-species *T.t. sumatranus* are sure to relish them. Especially younger specimens which receive no other feedings are sure to exterminate these unbidden guests very soon.

Three further prescriptions that serve the purpose are:

For each ten quarts of water take 1 gram ammonium nitrate, dissolve it in a little water and pour it into the tank, raising the temperature by about 7° F. During the 8-10 preceding days feed the hydras richly, stopping the feeding at the time of treatment. Soon you will notice that the hydras first retract their tentacles and then die off. In case of very strong infestations, the measure should be repeated after a few days. Fish fry and plants may safely remain in the tank. Plants feed on nitrate of ammonia.

Another proven means for eradicating hydras consists in hanging rolls of very brightly polished copper wire into the water on the opposing narrow sides of the aquarium. It will be observed that first the hydras lose their catching arms, falling to the bottom after some time. Repeat the measure several times, until no more hydras are seen. It is important that the surface of copper touching the water be the biggest possible.

According to the so-far recorded experiences, these manners of exterminating hydras are innocuous to plants and fishes. It is advisable, though, only to employ them if exterminating the pests by Gouramis should prove impossible.

Hydrophilidae: Water beetles. Family of water beetles belonging to the sub-order of the POLYPHAGA (see these) with a number of species.

The legs often are hairy, and adequate for swimming. Quite a number of species of this family live on land, though, or else on moist shores. The best known representative is *Hydrous piceus* L, which moves with rather uncertain steps, and swims only occasionally, but then quite well. It is a stately beetle with a length of about 2¾″, pitch black, and covered with a shiny film of air on the underside. A sharp carena on the underside protrudes as a prong beyond the hips. Breathing is done at the surface, the antennae taking the air to the hairy underside, where it remains. Food consists mainly of vegetable matter, and animal food is taken only exceptionally. The larva, similar to that of *Dytiscus marginalis*, moves on short legs, ambling over the bottom among plants. It feeds on aquatic insects, worms, snails, etc. *Hydrous piceus* is found especially in densely planted, quiet quarters. It is considered rare, and should be protected.

The eggs are laid among plants, in boat-like cocoons, from which a tube-shaped extension protrudes above the surface of the water. A smaller species with a similar manner of living is *Hydrophilus caraboides* L.

Hydrophilus: The water beetle. See HYDROPHILIDAE.

hydrosulphuric acid (H_2S): A sulphur compound which also develop in badly kept aquaria in the form of a gas smelling of rotten eggs, and which may be highly poisonous. Hydrosulphuric acid originates especially in the bottom soil if this is not sufficiently porous, or from food left-overs after too rich feedings. First of all avoid overfeeding and remove any dying or decaying organisms immediately from the aquarium. In addition to the bad smell, also sulphur bacteria—which cover the inside of the aquarium with a gray white film—may be the signs of a presence of hydrosulphuric acid.

Sulphur in itself is necessary for the vegetable life in the aquarium and is nearly always present in sufficient quantities, since it is contained in all protein compounds, therefore also in the fish food that is daily put into the aquarium. If the tank is well-planted and not too richly stocked with fishes and other animals, if it receives sufficient light and is further aerated on critical days when light is lacking, there will hardly ever rise the danger of developing hydrosulphuric acid in harmful quantities.

Hydrous: The water beetle. See HYDROPHILIDAE.

Hygrophila: Friend of moisture. Genus of swamp plants pertaining to the family of the *Acantheaceae*.

— polysperma (T. Anders): The Indian Water Star.

GENERALITIES: One of the most easy-to-grow aquatic plants, which may be cultivated either submerged or emerged. Possibly the species has not yet been definitely classified.

SHAPE: The pretty, light-green leaves are disposed on very short stems, crossed opposite around the more or less ramified stalk.

RANGE: Southeast Asia, in swamps and shallow waters, on banks and in flood regions.

CULTIVATION: In dense stands or at low water level the plant likes to grow above the water surface. As bottom ground unwashed sand will prove sufficient, but with an admixture of clay the leaves will grow bigger. Reproduction is easily achieved by planting pieces of twigs. Even from parts of the stem or from leaves new plants will result. The species loves light and sun and is eager to grow at any temperature between 64 and 86° F.

Hygrophila polysperma

hymenophysa: With skin blisters. — *Botia*.

Hyphessobrycon: A smaller Brycon (Characin).

South American genus of small, gregarious fishes belonging to the family of the Characins or *Characidae*. The body is more or less elongated, in some species relatively high. The forehead line is often a little indented, throat and the front part of the belly are sometimes a little arched outward. An adipose fin exists. The anal fin is long. The lateral line is incomplete. Difference from the closely related genus *Hemigrammus* is established by the fact that the caudal peduncle of *Hyphessobrycon* is bare of scales.

Lately MYERS, based on comprehensive research, has come to the conclusion that the genus has no reason for existing separately, and that it should again be included in the genus *Hemigrammus*, from which it had been taken in 1909.

Care and breeding prevails in general lines what has already been said for the genus *Hemigrammus*. The fishes like company and feel especially well in tanks that are densely planted on the sides, leaving free swimming space in the middle. They are egg scatterers, the breeding of which generally is easy, but may also be quite difficult for some species.

Spawning takes place after active chasing. Whenever breeding is difficult this difficulty is to be found in the demands of the respective species as to the composition of the water. As a rule rearing the fry is not difficult at all.

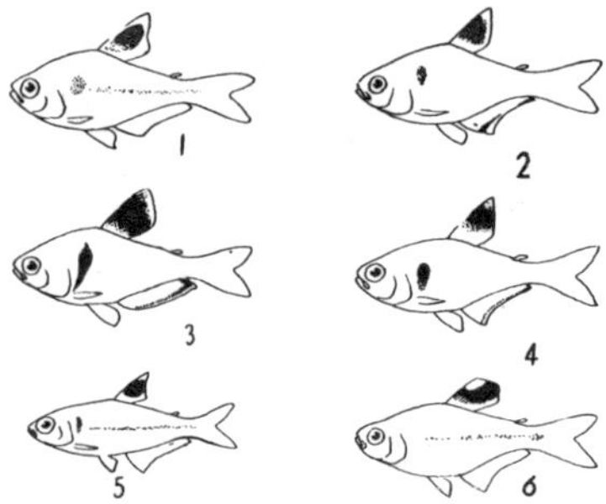

Hyphessobrycon - the callistus group - 1. H. callistus bentosi - 2. H. c. serpae - 3. H. c. callistus - 4. H. c. copelandi - 5. H. c. minor - 6. H. c. rosaceus

— bifasciatus Ellis: The Yellow Tetra.

SHAPE: As per description of genus, relatively stout, strongly compressed laterally. D 11, A 29-32. Length about 1¾″, the males remaining a little smaller.

COLOR: Silvery white with a yellowish to yellow-green shine, younger specimens with reddish fins. The two vertical spots on the shoulder are not always of the same intensity. The male has more lively colors and is slimmer, its anal fin being more strongly indented and provided with small barbs.

Hyphessobrycon bifasciatus

RANGE: In the coastal regions, especially in river mouths and lakes near the seashore of Southeastern Brazil.

CARE AND BREEDING: As per description of the genus, especially similar to that of *Hyphessobrycon flammeus*. The species is gregarious, but not always peaceful. They take all kinds of live and dry foods.

— callistus (Boulenger):

The callistus group has very recently been subjected to an extensive study by HOEDEMAN, which resulted in the conclusion that many species which so far had been considered as distinctly classified in fact are nothing but local forms of *H. callistus callistus*, differing only slightly in shape and certain appearances of color. They are small fishes of slightly elongated figure, with a very long and low anal fin, a reddish coloration, and a shoulder spot that may be more or less visible or vanish totally.

— callistus callistus (Boulenger): The Jewel Tetra.

SHAPE: This species, which is typical of its group, is known to us as *H. serpae*. The real *H. serpae*, though, is no more seen in Europe. D 10-11, A 27-30. Length about 1⅝″.

COLOR: Vivid red, the dorsal fin black with a light base, the anal fin black edged, the shoulder spot appearing clearly and being drawn-out vertically. The male is slimmer and a little more intensely colored. A bred variety, seen in aquaria, has no shoulder spot, is intensely red, and needs higher temperatures. It is presented as *H. minor*. This name is worthless as the real *H. minor* looks quite different. "Minor" in this case is a commercial name.

RANGE: The Paraguay River and other places in the Brazilian state of Matto Grosso.

CARE AND BREEDING: As per description of the genus. They love company, not too small tanks, and a sunny location. Hiding places in well planted corners. 73-77° F, for breeding 78-82° F. Breeding them is not simple. Spawning takes place after lively chasing among fine-feathered plants. After spawning has been achieved, darken the tank a little and remove the parents. Soft water, a little acid and low in infusoria, is a must. The fry hatch after 24-48 hours, and need another three days before becoming free-swimming. Rearing them requires patience and careful feeding, as at the beginning the young are very sensitive.

Hyphessobrycon callistus bentosi

— **callistus bentosi** Durbin: The Unspotted Jewel Tetra.
Sub-species from the lower Amazon. The shoulder spot is absent or only weakly developed. D 11, A 27-30. Very similar to the form of *H. callistus* that has no shoulder spot. Differentiation is possible only at the earliest age, as the fry are red in the sub-species and said to be black in *H. c. callistus*.

— **callistus copelandi** Durbin:
Sub-species from the upper Amazon River, hardly ever imported so far. The shoulder spot vanishes from older specimens. D 11, A 28.

— **callistus minor** Durbin:
The real *minor*, not imported so far. An especially elongated little species, with an only weakly indicated dash-shaped shoulder spot. The shape is narrow and elongated. D 11, A 26-28. So far known only from a small region in British Guiana.

— **callistus rosaceus** Durbin: The Rosy Tetra.
A sub-species similar to *H. ornatus*, which possibly belongs to the *callistus* group too. The connections have not yet been fully explained, though. *H.c. rosaceus* is said to have been imported only once so far, and has then disappeared again. Its

Hyphessobrycon callistus rosaceus

relationship to the *callistus* group is often the subject of doubt.

— **callistus serpae** Durbin: The Red Serpae Tetra.
The basic color is reddish with blue-shimmering fin edges, which often cause the color to change over into violet. The shoulder spot is quite noticeable on younger specimens, but vanishes with age. Central Amazon to Paraguay. D 10-11, A 25-30. The species has not yet been imported. The fish sold as *H. serpae* are *H.c. callistus*.

— **cardinalis:** see CHEIRODON AXELRODI.

— **eos** Durbin: The Dawn Tetra.
A little-imported species from Guiana, about $2\frac{1}{8}''$ long.

— **flammeus** Myers: The Red von Rio.
SHAPE: As per description of the genus. D 10-A 25. Length $1\frac{3}{8}''$ to $1\frac{5}{8}''$.
COLOR: Greenish shiny base with reddish to violet sheen, turning into a strong red towards the extremity of the body. At the front end are 2-3 black shoulder stripes. The fins are reddish to red, the anal of the male having a deep black edge. The female is plumper, sometimes a little bigger.
RANGE: Outskirts of Rio de Janeiro.
CARE AND BREEDING: As per description of the genus. The species

is hardy and enduring, sometimes a little quarrelsome. They love tanks that are not too light and richly planted, but need sufficient room for swimming and exercising. They may even be kept in smaller aquaria. A dark bottom enhances their colors. 68-72° F, for breeding 73-75° F, lowest 64° F. Fish that are kept at too low a temperature get pale.

For breeding use three males to one female. Breeding is easy, but the female sometimes tarries a little. Spawning takes place after intensive chasing. The species is productive, the eggs numbering up to 500 per spawning. Well-fed fish do not go much after eggs and fry. The young hatch after 24 hours and need another three days to swim freely. Rearing them is not difficult.

— **gracilis** Reinhardt: The Glowlight Tetra. See HEMIGRAMMUS ERYTHROZONUS.

— **griemi** Hoedeman: The Red Gold Dot Tetra.

SHAPE: As per description of the genus; D 12-13, A 26-28.

Together with *H. bifasciatus* and *H. flammeus* it belongs to a small group of Characins of similar type, possessing two shoulder spots. Length about 1⅜″.

COLOR: The body is brownish, turning scarlet red when excited. The vertical fins too are scarlet. Front edge and lower border of the anal fin are milk white with inner black border. SD unknown.

RANGE: Imported from the state of Goiás, Brazil. No exact data.

CARE AND BREEDING: Similar to *H. flammeus*.

— **heterorhabdus** (Ulrey): The German Flag Tetra.

SHAPE: As per description of the genus, but especially elongated. D 10, A 20-23. Length up to 1⅜″.

COLOR: A red-white-black longitudinal band on gray-brown-greenish base from the eye to the

Hyphessobrycon heterorhabdus

caudal peduncle. The male is slimmer. Besides this, when seen against light, his swimming bladder is arch-shaped and pointed.

RANGE: The lower Amazon region.

CARE AND BREEDING: As per description of the genus. The species will do also in smaller tanks, which should be well-planted, though, and have a dark background and bottom in order to enhance their colors. Occasional sunlight heightens their well-being. The fish are agile and peaceable. They are somewhat similar to the rare species *Hemigrammus ulrey*. Breeding them is considered difficult. The species is able, though, to withstand a little harder water than, for instance, many tribes of the Neon Tetra. Temperature may be held between 73 and 77° F, being best for breeding at 75° F.

EGGELING points out that breeding is possible throughout the whole year, but bound to certain spawning periods. Of special importance are favorable conditions of lighting. The spawning tank should not be located at too light a spot. A softer water, of 3 to 5° DH is favorable. Otherwise the act of spawning and the rearing of the young are the same as for all other species of the genus. The alevins grow very quickly and may reach full colors after about 6 weeks.

— **innesi** Myers: The Neon Tetra.
SHAPE: As per description of the genus, slender, only slightly compressed laterally. The mouth opening is very small. An adipose fin exists, but is very small too. D 11, A 20-21. Length: scarcely $1\frac{5}{8}$".
COLOR: Luminous green and blue horizontal stripe from the eye to the caudal peduncle. This is colored an intense red. SD are slight, the male being a little slimmer.
RANGE: In dark, flowing, relatively cool jungle waters, but also in the lake-like secondary waters of the upper Amazon, even in Peru.
CARE AND BREEDING: As per description of the genus. The species makes its best impression in schools in not too small tanks with dark bottom and background. They are peaceful and gregarious. The fish like to remain in the middle and lower levels of the water. Generally speaking they like a soft, slightly acid water, but also in this it seems that there are individual differences and tribes that are not so demanding. If no breeding is intended, it will be unnecessary to give any consideration to the softness of the water. The Neon Tetra does not need much warmth; 68-74° F are sufficient, the latter degree of temperature even for breeding. Due to the sensitivity of eggs and fry to infusoria and light, breeding is difficult.

For this one should employ young pairs, which have just reached maturity for spawning. They are best set-up in an all-glass tank without any sand on the bottom. The water may show 2-4 DH and a pH value of about 6.5. After some days one should look whether the water is still crystal clear. Finally put in an adequate pair, which it is best to choose from a community tank, in the evening. The act of spawning of

Hyphessobrycon innesi

such pairs, chosen for their disposition to chase each other already in the community tank, generally already takes place the next morning. Up to the moment of spawning absolutely no food should be given. In all, about 200 eggs are laid. After spawning, remove the parents. The tank must be well darkened, as the slightest entrance of light may endanger success. This is denied by some breeders, though. After five days, when the darkening is relieved, the fry are already free swimming. From this point on they take powder sized live foods. Always feed carefully and moderately in order to avoid the appearance of infusoria. Consequently one has to feed them several times a day. Aeration with fine bubbles is advisable in order to scatter the food throughout the tank. No remainders should be left in the tank, and collecting mulm should be siphoned off cautiously. Water for filling up to level should be of the same composition as that of the container, and boiled besides this. After having withstood the first days of life, the young are quite robust and grow quickly. Colors appear after 6-7 weeks.

With these or similar methods, as first published in detail by Tusche and Nachstedt, the Neon Tetra may be bred successfully even in regions with unfavorable water conditions.

— **loretoensis** Ladiges:
A species originating from the jungle regions of the upper Ama-

zon, rarely imported up to this date. Length up to 1¾″.

— **ornatus** Ahl: The Ornate Tetra.

SHAPE: The species is of relatively high build and looks somewhat sturdy. Otherwise as per description of the genus. D 11, A 26-27. The dorsal fin of the male may end in a point or be flanged. Length about 1½″.

COLOR: Greenish with a crimson glow, which temporarily may be quite intense. The upper half of the dorsal is black, with a porcelain-white edge. The male is slimmer and has more strongly developed fins.

RANGE: From Dutch Guiana to the lower Amazon.

CARE AND BREEDING: As per description of the genus. A peaceful, gregarious species which likes to live in small schools. They like well-planted, a little shadowy tanks with occasional sunlight and moderately soft to very soft water. Temperatures: 73-79° F, for breeding 79-82° F. Breeding is considered difficult. Success depends on mated pairs. A primary condition is absolute cleanliness and water that is free of infusoria. Breeding may be done in already established aquaria as well as in special all-glass tanks.

— **peruvianus** Ladiges:

This so far rarely imported species originates in the jungle regions of the upper Amazon. The body shape resembles that of the Neon Tetra, *H. innesi*, but with its blackish horizontal stripes it is not as beautiful as that species. Lengths up to 2″.

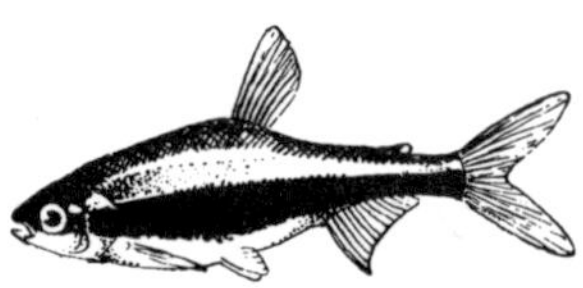

Hyphessobrycon peruvianus

Hyphessobrycon pulchripinnis

— **pulchripinnis** Ahl: The Lemon Tetra.

SHAPE: As per description of the genus. The body is only moderately elongated, the male being a little slimmer than the highbacked female. Lengths up to 1½″.

COLOR: Glassily transparent but with a greenish-gray silvery gloss, temporarily with a pretty yellow glitter. The first rays of the anal fin are edged in vivid yellow and black. The lower half of the iris of the eye is blood red. SD are only minute, the male being slimmer.

RANGE: The surroundings of Belem do Para.

CARE AND BREEDING: As per description of the genus. The species is gregarious, peaceful, and undemanding, but not easy to breed. Breeding is made difficult especially by the fact that not all pairs mate. The moment of full maturity of the spawn too should not be overlooked. It is said that the eggs are not re-absorbed, and that hardening of the spawn may set in. Otherwise, for breeding them, one should act in a manner similar to that described for *Hemigrammus erythrozonus*. Males that chase too vigorously should not be used for breeding.

— **scholzei** Ahl: The Blackbanded Tetra.

A small, vivacious, easy-to-breed species from the Amazon region, which shows no peculiarities in color and behavior. Length up to 2″. Simple silver or brass color,

Hyphessobrycon scholzei

with a black band along the sides, which is cross-shaped on the caudal peduncle.

Hypseleotris: Genus of bottom fishes pertaining to the family of the *Eleotridae* with two still little-known species from the Philippine Islands.

hypselopterus: With tall fins. — *Notropis*.

iberus: From the Iberian Peninsula. — *Aphanius*.

ichthyology: The science of fishes.

Ichthyophonus: see ICHTHYOSPORIDIUM.

Ichthyophthirius, Ichthyophthirius disease:

A widely distributed disease of fishes, caused by a ciliate, *Ichthyophthirius multifiliis* Fouquet (see CILIATA), relatively easy to cure today. It has been stated, though, that lately forms of the disease have appeared which seem quite more complex and which render the up-to-now simple aspect of the disease much more difficult.

It manifests itself by the appearance of small white knots on fins, skin, and eyes. If these knots proliferate, the disease becomes lethal. Contamination takes place through ich-ridden fishes, but the swarming spores may also be introduced into the aquarium with live foods. Especially prone are tropical fishes kept in too cool water. The disease germ is a unicellular organism, up to $\frac{1}{25}''$ in size, the big nucleus of which is bean-shaped to horseshoe-shaped. Its manner of reproduction is remarkable, differing from that of many ciliates in that it rarely takes place by simple cross-division, but that several serialized divisions take place outside the host. Through this many daughter parasites originate. There may be 250 to 1000 free swimming descendants of one animal.

These swarmers are pearshaped, with relatively long ciliae. When they reach a fish, they bore into its epidermis, but generally do not penetrate the dermis, locating between both layers. Here they dig tunnels by means of rotating motions. Often many specimens assemble in such a cave. They prefer especially to attack the regions of the fins and the gills, as in these the skin is especially soft. The destroyed, inflamed epidermis may come off in tatters, and fungi, bacteria, and skin blemishes, if penetrating the wounds, may then cause secondary infections.

The young parasites gradually change their aspect. They grow darker in consequence of the blood and tissue particles taken in as food, and develop the typical big nucleus.

Depending on the ambient temperature, the development to maturity takes 7 to 21 days. Higher degrees of warmth accelerate it. The ripe parasite forms a cyst, which separates from its host and in which division takes place. The developing daughter parasites (swarmers), which at first are quite transparent, are able to burst open the cyst and to leave it after 7 to 8 hours. The swarmers are not able to live a long time without a host. Therefore they are forced to find a fish on which to settle within a short time (about 48 hours, 55 at the maximum, according to SCHAEPERCLAUS).

The disease is widely distributed, especially in aquaria, due to the fact that a heavy population furthers its quick spread. Also in this the experience is true that weakened fishes are especially prone to attack, while healthy and strong specimens may carry one or the other parasite without letting these reach mass reproduction. The disease is curable if detected in time. Things are quite different with a tropical, latent form which has been observed especially lately. We shall revert to it at the end of this entry.

In the cases where it is recognized too late, the usual form of the disease ends lethally. The infection may be introduced by contaminated fishes, as well as plants, stones, and gadgets with cysts sticking to them, and also by live foods among which there may be free-swimming swarmers. Also water that is poured into the aquarium coming from natural sources may contain such swarmers. For this reason such waters should be always heated to about 190° F before using them. Similar to what happens with the *Ichthyosporidium* disease, also to prevent *Ichthyophthirius* a quarantine of a few days of all newly purchased fishes is not sufficient. A few parasites, especially if located in the gills, may easily be overlooked, and only the next generation, which appears with the well-known white nodules in greater quantities, is clearly recognizable. In the tropical aquarium this development takes place earlier. Here two to three weeks should be sufficient, while in cold water tanks a quarantine of four to five weeks has to be considered.

Free-swimming swarmers in the food or among plants, etc., die off after three days.

The parasites within the skin cannot be fought successfully through baths. Measures of treatment and cure have to be directed against the parasites that leave the host. One has to avoid especially that the swarmers after becoming free may again reach a fish as host. The damages to skin, etc. left by the parasite generally are withstood by the fish, if not too extensive. As treatment for fishes especially permanent baths are effective (see CURE OF FISH DISEASES). Conditions are more difficult with the newly appeared, latent, tropical form, which, among others, has also been described by LADIGES. In it the course of the disease in itself could not be made to harmonize with the traditional symptoms even under the most critical observation.

In the commerce of ornamental fishes there are two forms of the disease:

(a) a very thin growth that covers the whole surface of the fish, except the fins;

(b) the well-known growth with cysts measuring $\frac{1}{3}$ to 1 mm., which at first especially attacks the fins.

The first form is especially frequent on imported fishes. Its development generally is tempestuous, and the fishes cannot be saved. Possibly there are two different, even if closely related, germs. It is not out of the question that the tropical form is able to reproduce within the epidermis of the fish and therefore is difficult to hit. LADIGES cites some examples according to which fish healed by quinine treatments still continued spreading the infection without apparently suffering from it themselves.

Ichthyosporidium: *Ichthyophonus.* A disease, widely distributed among aquarium fishes, which up to this date is considered incurable. Its spreading may be explained by the fact that on one hand in the aquarium many fishes are joined

Typical appearance of Ichthyosporidium (Ichthyophonus)

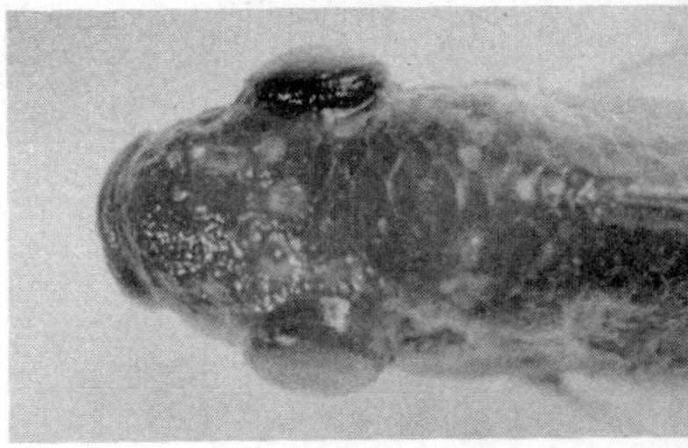

Slightly pop-eyed condition as a result of this disease

Typical appearance of Ichthyosporidium (Ichthyophonus)

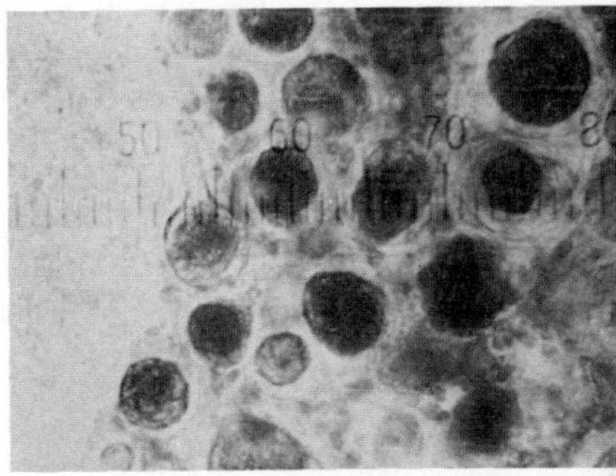

Section of the liver of a fish with a bad case of the disease

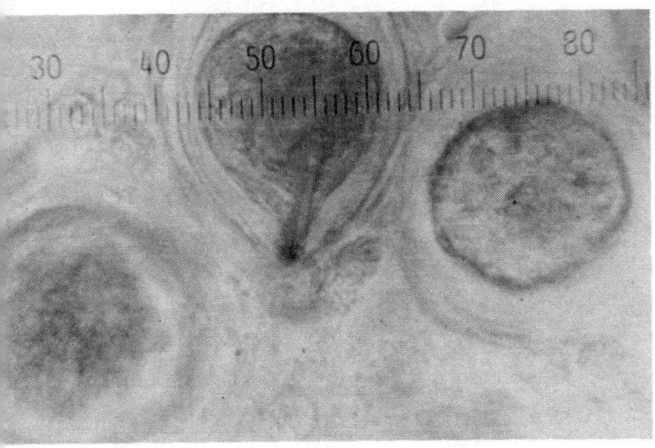

Cysts of Ichthyosporidium, highly magnified

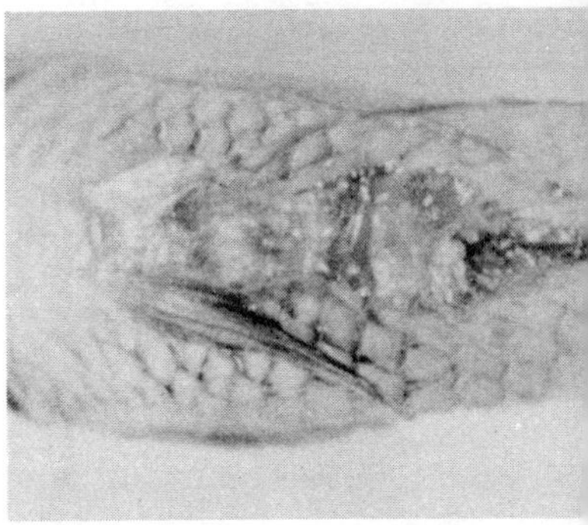

Tumors on the belly of a diseased fish

together in a small space, on the other that errors of care and keeping make them prone to the disease, which may exist in a latent state for a long time, without showing external symptoms. The disease germs are very difficult to eradicate. Normally the incubation period (the time between infection and open eruption) lasts 3-4 weeks, but, if strong and resistant, a fish may encapsule the germs up to the time when, due to some weakening for other reasons, they reach mass reproduction anyway. Generally also there is no mass mortality, one fish after the other being attacked and dying. As reasons for weakening one may consider: exhaustion after spawning, contaminated or otherwise inadequate water, one-sided and faulty feeding, wrong temperatures, lack of oxygen, etc.

The disease is caused by a member of a genus of parasitic fungi (*Ichthyosporidium*), which sponges in the skin, fins, muscles, and in many internal organs. The symptoms are blood spots on the body sores, staggering movements, black spots on the skin, extreme leanness, loss of fins—especially the caudal fin—and scale protrusion. In an advanced stage often the fishes lie on the bottom moving forward joltingly. Frequently they lose their balance and turn around their length axis with the head down. Thereafter they float up to the surface and die.

The germ of the Rotating Disease of Trout (*Ichthyosporidium hoferi*) differs from the *Ichthyosporidium* of aquarium fishes mainly in the manner of reproduction. Division takes place in a cyst, following which the descendant parasites spread in wide channels over the greater surroundings of the mother parasite. For this reason SCHAEPERCLAUS supposes that it may be the case of two different species belonging to the same genus.

The infection is transmitted through newly introduced sick fishes. In most cases the parasites reach the water in the feces coming from infected digestion organs, and are then taken up by the other fishes. Dead specimens should be removed as quickly as possible, as the cysts continue developing for some time even in dead bodies, and the danger of their becoming free-swimming is doubled. Treatments to cure the disease are not known. Therefore, in order to avoid mass contaminations, one has to follow the ensuing rules:

1. Most meticulous care in order to avoid weakening the fishes.
2. Newly purchased or caught fishes should at first be segregated in a separate tank for observation. Avoid especially putting new fishes together with valuable specimens before they have passed the quarantine test. In order to give it more value, quarantine should last at least four weeks. In the case of greater numbers of fishes, it is best to prepare a special all-glass tank, totally bare, without sand and plants, so that it may be easily cleaned and disinfected.
3. If the disease has been detected, one should try to avoid its spreading. Noticeably infected fishes should be destroyed immediately and the infected tank with its population severely quarantined. All accessories and instruments needed for its care should be boiled before using them in other tanks. If the epidemic is of major proportions, it will be best to destroy all plants and fishes, throwing away the sand and disinfecting tank and accessories with a strong solution of potassium permanganate. With adequate care and careful observation, it generally is possible to avoid greater losses of one's fishes. No prevention is known against introducing the disease.

Ide: see IDUS MELANOTUS.

Idus: Genus of school fishes belonging to the family of the Carp-like fishes or *Cyprinidae*. They are fishes of elongated but sturdy body construction, only slightly compressed laterally, a little high-backed and wide-fronted. The mouth is terminal.

— melanotus (Haeckel): The Orfe.
SHAPE: As per description of the genus. D 11, A 12-13. The lateral line is complete.
COLOR: Silvery shiny with a reticulate design. Older specimens have

a dark-green sheen. The dorsal fin is dark, all other fins are red.

RANGE: Widely diffused over East and Central Europe. Orfes are found in rivers or in standing waters that are connected with rivers. They are shore and surface fish.

CARE AND BREEDING: Smaller specimens are well fit for the home aquarium. The brass colored Golden Orfe is especially pretty for the open air pond, having the advantage over goldfish that it remains at the surface. In the home aquarium aeration is needed. Temperatures may come up to 68° F. The species cannot be bred in the aquarium. From March to May it swims up from brackish waters and the sea into the rivers in order to spawn. At this occasion they lay up to 100,000 eggs on stones and plants.

Idus idus: see IDUS MELANOTUS.

Iguanodectes: Which bites like an Iguana, the swamp lizard.

South American genus pertaining to the family of the Characins or *Characidae*, with very slender body, strongly compressed laterally.

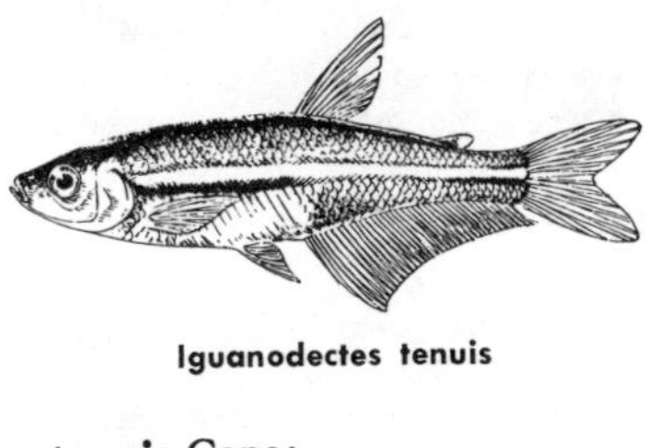

Iguanodectes tenuis

— tenuis Cope:

SHAPE: An exquisitely delicate and slender fish, D 10-11, A 33-38. Length a little above 3½″.

COLOR: Brownish to greenish with a whitish horizontal stripe bordered on the upper edge by a reddish, on the lower edge by a black zone. The front edge of the anal fin of the male is whitish.

RANGE: Guiana, and the central and lower Amazon.

CARE AND BREEDING: This vivacious fish should be cared for in a manner similar to that specified for the different species of *Hemigrammus*. It is completely harmless and may be kept together with even the smallest fishes. It is omnivorous, but also needs vegetable food, therefore sometimes preying on the tips and young shoots of aquatic plants. Temperature 73-82° F.

illumination; lighting of the aquarium: The illumination of the aquarium is of very special importance. It is only sufficient light which makes possible the existence of aquatic plants in aquaria, i.e. their feeding through assimilation of carbon dioxide, and the simultaneous release of oxygen warrants the life of animals, especially fishes. Besides this, sufficient lighting is a vital necessity for most species of fishes, except those which are adapted to nocturnal or twilight life.

Besides the biological value of sufficient lighting, it is only artificial illumination which makes it possible for the working person to enjoy and watch life in the aquarium during free hours of the evening.

In general, natural light is preferable to artificial illumination. This is especially true in those cases where one wants to achieve certain breeding results or biological studies. Natural daylight, especially direct sunlight during some hours per day, cannot be replaced by artificial sources, however excellent they may be. On the other hand it is perfectly possible to make the care for aquaria which serve only as show installations much easier. Furthermore it has to be stated that this latter may be a sufficient substitute where the natural conditions of lighting are unfavorable. In nature illumination is characterized by continuous

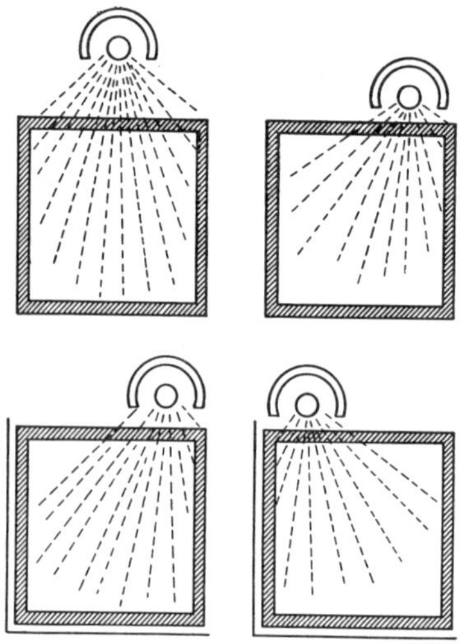

Reflector positions—top, left, too high—top right, correct—bottom left, correct—bottom right, wrong; back lighting does not show reflected fish colors.

change, according to the seasons, hours of the day, cloud covers of the sky, plant shadows, and ice covers due to frost. In part these changes are rhythmically repetitive, differing according to latitude. All this bears deep influence on the live beings in the water. Furthermore light always incides from above. With exception of certain highly specialized waters and water regions (cave waters, wells, jungle waters), the intensity of light is very high. In order to form an idea on this, compare the following figures—according to the Rossmaessler Gesellschaft, Bremen (Rossmaessler Society, Bremen)—

Full sunlight, in midsummer .... 100,000 lux
In the shadow of a tree, during full sunlight .... 10,000 lux
on a glassed-in porch 5,000 lux
Near the window of a room .... 2-3,000 lux
Inside a room, exclusively with artificial lighting .... 20-40 lux

As to the effect of lighting on aquatic plants, see the following entries:
ASSIMILATION, LOCATION OF THE AQUARIUM. In general it has to be said that even minute differences in lighting become noticeable in the extent of the activity of assimilation of the plants. Too prolonged incidence of light is unfavorable, and in part even harmful. In this case, if the tank is overstocked with plants, or even with proliferation of algae, dangerous oversaturations with oxygen (up to 300% of the normal value) may set in. Water in motion eliminates such super saturations, therefore aeration may under certain circumstances be advantageous for too intensely lit aquaria.

Effects of lighting on plant growth—left, too weak; plant is pale and stunted - center, strong infra-red rays; plant grows too long, with yellowish-green leaves - right, strong blue rays; plant remains short, with dark green leaves.

In general the natural conditions of lighting are strongly changed in the aquarium. Daily and seasonal fluctuations often are voided to a great extent by measures taken by the fancier, thus narrowing down the rhythm. Light comes from several sides, only rarely predominantly from above. In scaffoldings it is generally just the natural light from above which is excluded.

The influence of light on the animal organism, including fishes, should not be underestimated, despite the fact that this factor is generally deferred in favor of other ones, such as, for instance, those of the water. The healing, bacteria-killing action of direct sun radiation is well-known, despite the fact that its influence in the aquarium is hard to evaluate, due to the light having passed through several layers of glass. Anyway, it has been observed also in the aquarium that the seasonal and daily rhythm of the sun's radiation may act as a trigger for many vital functions. Seasonally this is the case for many fishes of the Temperate Zones, and also for sub-tropical ones. For these, besides other factors, the amount of sunlight determines the start of the spawning period. Some species of fishes prefer certain hours of the day for the act of spawning. In general all fishes seem to be adapted to certain conditions of lighting, such as, for instance, cave fishes, fishes of the surface, of the central reaches, of the depths, of the bottom, of open, and of densely planted waters.

The majority of all fishes normally swim horizontally, with the back upwards, that is, they move in vertical position with regard to the light. Thus the fishes are optically guided (after RINGWALD). Therefore, whenever possible, the light should incide from above and in front, as the nerve system of the fishes is adapted to this.

Artificial illumination of the aquaria has found increased acceptance during the last years. According to SCHMIDT it should achieve the following: favorable growth of the aquatic plants simultaneously avoiding over-lush development of algae. Good reproduction of the colors and plants and animals, and sufficient illumination of the aquarium. White light (daylight) is a mixture of light rays of different colors. In artificial sources of light the primary color components are generally present in different ratios from those of daylight. Therefore they have very differing influences on the growth of plants. The most beneficial have proved to be those sources of light which, besides the other components, contain a high percentage of red. This is exactly what happens with normal electric light bulbs. Therefore these are very good for occasional additional illumination of smaller tanks, for which one may use bulbs of 15-40 watts, especially since they permit seeing colors quite favorably. Normal electric bulbs, however, have the disadvantage that they transform only about 5% of the energy into light, while the balance is turned into heat. Therefore things get to be rather expensive in the case of permanent lighting or of bigger tanks. A better distribution is found in the rod-shaped light bulbs. Still more favorable, and quite cheaper, are the fluorescent lamps, which are more expensive in the initial outlay, though. They have the advantage of greater production of light. Since this amounts to about three times that of the normal electric bulbs, the result is that we are able to enjoy the quantity of light of a 75 Watt bulb at the price of a 25 Watt one. The installation of the tubes is a little more difficult, since one needs some more accessories (reactor and starter) for them. The tubes are lined inside with a lighting substance, the chemical composition of which determines the color of the light. The useful life of a tube may be of the order of 1500 hours or more, according to make, this figure being liable not to be reached in certain cases. As a rule it is better to use several smaller tubes instead of one big one.

It is difficult to give general data on the necessary intensity of lighting. This depends on the need for light of the plants and animals. In the first place one has to consider that it is easier to light a shallow aquarium down to the bottom than a deep one. Clear, white water absorbs 50% of the light rays which incide from above already at a depth of 12″, while clear, peat-filtered water absorbs 70%, and cloudy water correspondingly more. Watching them carefully, it is easy to find out what the demands of the plants are—thereafter one can easily regulate the intensity of light with artificial lighting. The presence of silicon algae (wrongly: Brown Algae), or of *Diatomeae* on plants and glass panes indicates that the light intensity should be decreased.

RINGWALD gives the following rule of thumb for the output of lamps: for normal bulbs, 2 watts per 16 square inches of bottom area; for fluorescent lamps, 2/3rd watt per 16 square inches of bottom area. According to this, the fluorescent tube is three times more favorable in its production of light. For deep tanks, with a water depth of 12″ and more, as well as for peat-colored water, this norm has to be increased.

It has to be pointed out, however, that the theme 'Illumination of the Aquarium' could hardly be treated exhaustively in theory. One can only give some advice, since conditions in every aquarium may differ. Experimental attempts to establish the most favorable illumination have to be made by the aquarist from case to case, and will nearly always lead to the desired success if expertly conducted.

Decisive for the use of all artificial sources of light is the manner in which they are set up. Basically they should always be placed as near the water surface as possible, and this in a way that the light incides from the front. All plants grow towards the light. If the source of light is placed too far to the rear, the growing tips of the plants (leaf stars) turn towards the light, that is, they more or less turn from the viewer, which impairs their ornamental value. The intensity of light decreases considerably with each inch of distance from the surface. It is always advisable to use good, well-adjusted reflectors, which on one hand shutter off the viewer from the light source, on the other permit making full use of the light in the aquarium. With normal electric bulbs one has to consider that with the great development of heat, there is the danger of bursting the cover glass. In scaffoldings the source of light may simultaneously serve to heat the tanks which stand higher up. Tanks located in complete darkness should receive 10-12 hours daily of artificial lighting, ones that receive additional daylight correspondingly less.

immunity: An acquired specific resistance to one certain disease. It originates from the fact that, after having conquered the disease, the body develops sufficient antibodies to avoid reinfection. The faculty of developing a certain immunity may often be conditioned hereditarily. Immunities may also be called forth artificially by inoculation with dead disease germs.

imports, imported fishes: Fishes of foreign origin, which are caught wild and taken into the aquarium. Fishes of foreign origin, but which have already been bred here, cannot really be considered imports. Thus, for instance, in the South of the U.S.A. and in Guiana certain aquarium fishes are bred in open-air ponds and thereafter exported.

Really imported fishes generally need especially good care and the experience of long years in order to lead them to spawn. They may be most prone to diseases.

inbreeding: Mating of individuals related by blood lines. Aquarists often have very vague ideas about the significance of inbreeding. Especially, it is often blamed for harms coming from another origin. Every breeder of animals of any species knows that for obtaining pure breeding strains not only inbreeding, but even incest breeding is an absolute necessity. Only through these will it be possible to fix desirable breeding qualities in a manner that gives them stability.

To clear this question it is necessary at first to determine that the dispositions of all higher animals, therefore also of fishes, are composed of a male and a female component. If from both sides undesirable characteristics unite to form a pair of dispositions, they become recognizable externally. The danger of inbreeding therefore lies in the encounter of harmful similar dispositions. Of course, in a mating of closely related individuals, such a possibility is great. Such dispositions may be, among others: hereditary bodily or functional defects, as for instance, weakness of instincts, deflections of behavior, dwarf growth, crippling or distortion of certain parts of the body, etc. On the other hand inbreeding may be innocuous if both partners have no harmful hereditary qualities, nor acquire them. It is very difficult, though, to determine this beforehand. Generally one needs a general view over many generations before such qualities may be recognized, and eradicated through selective breeding. It is also self-explanatory that breeders which are mated through inbreeding have to be reared and kept under optimum conditions if one wants to judge whether there are eventual harms caused by inbreeding, for it is obvious that the factors of the surroundings exert great influence on the development of the dispositions of a fish. They act upon shape, size, color, constitution, speed of development, sexual maturing, general aptitudes for life, etc. All these dispositions may be more or less fixed hereditarily, but undergo a very sure development under the influence of the conditions of the surrounding world.

Harms which may really be put at the door of inbreeding are hard to determine. Generally there are other factors which should be held responsible for "signs of degeneration" in ornamental fishes.

The often observed letting-up of fertility in aquarium fishes, which goes as far as complete sterility, may in many cases be caused by inadequate feeding (too fatty foods, containing too much protein and too little bulk contents) or by parasites. Thus, for instance, the so-called Neon Disease, caused by *Plistophora*, may lead to infertility, without the fish showing external signs of infection. Occasionally also cross-breeding may cause sterility in the first or second generation. This is always the case when the crossed partners are too far apart in relationship. This sterility is to be explained by disturbances of the chromosome mechanism.

Very important is the unconscious selection, performed by fanciers among their fishes, but more important still is the omission of any selection at all. An unconscious selection is often caused by the fact that among imports and descendants of imports one looks especially for the willingness to mate in the specimens. This is understandable, but leads of course on one hand to the consequence that many species become easier to breed, while on the other hand all other qualities, even the undesirable ones, are overlooked in favor of the willingness to procreate. The fact that many merchants bring young fishes to the market in the most early stages of development, precludes the possibility of selection right from the beginning. This selection, though, is a primary condition for successful breeding. It is nearly exclusively the lack of this selection, that causes the decline of strains that often occurs in the course of just a few generations. Therefore only the best specimens should be bred and fixed as incontrovertible tribes by further inbreeding. Otherwise we shall always have to continue eliminating hereditary defects. Individuals which show these should be excluded from breeding. If undesirable qualities appear in numbers within one strain, the whole strain should be impeached from reproducing. Especially the diminishing growth of many aquarium fishes is often considered a consequence of inbreeding. In fact one has to consider that in this a whole series of circumstances plays a part. The space factor exerts a considerable influence on the growth of nearly all fishes. This finds its natural reason in the limitation of the liberty to move, as well as in the fact that a fish does not find its needed optimum conditions with a relatively small space, closed off on all sides. Furthermore it has to be considered that the accumulation of uric substances in a small tank may act as a deterrent to growth. It would certainly be possible to lead nearly all species back to their original size through the selection of optimum space conditions during the growing period. Besides this we have to take into account that the small number of imported fishes, from which often our spawns stem, may bring along a narrowing of the width of variation of species from the very beginning. Resuming, we may say that it is not inbreeding in itself, but uncontrolled inbreeding combined with errors in care and keeping, that is to be held accountable for the degeneration of aquarium fishes.

incubation: The time elapsing from infection to manifestation of a disease. The incubation time may last only some hours, but also some weeks. This depends upon the species of the germ and on the resistance of the infected organism.

Indian Laubuca, the: see LAUBUCA LAUBUCA.

Indian River Barb, the: see CYCLOCHEILICHTHYS APOGON.

indica: From India.

— *Nymphoides.*

individual: Single being; referring to the individual.

inequalis: Unequal, uneven.

— *Glandulocauda.*

infection: Penetration of disease germs into the body.

inflammation of the swim bladder: An inflammation of the swim bladder caused by bacteria which often appears as a secondary symptom of infectious dropsy. In these cases the swim bladder is filled with an evil-smelling liquid, the belly is swollen, and the manner of swimming becomes sluggish.

inflorescence: The part of the plant which carries the flowers, developing no foliage leaves, nor growing vegetatively. The different shapes of inflorescences may be seen on the drawing which accompanies this entry.

Infusoria: Name often erroneously applied to all sorts of groups of unicellular organisms, but which really should only be used for the ciliates or CILIATA (see these). Infusoria as feeding material are discussed under the heading of "YOUNG FRY."

inner secretion: Some glands without outlets give their secretion (incretion, hormone) into the blood that flows through them, or directly into the liquid of the abdominal cavity. The activity of these glands is of the maximum importance for numerous body functions. Their inoperativity or irregularity may lead to severe malfunctions. Among others the following functions may be mentioned: The thyroid regulates metabolism. The thymus regulates growth and development of the sexual glands. The pancreas produces digestive fluids and insulin to maintain the sugar level of the blood. The suprarenals influence breathing, heart functions, and circulation. The hypophysis, among other things, regulates the number and function of the pigment cells. The germinating glands produce sexual cells and hormones for the development of secondary sexual characteristics and also to regulate sexual activities.

innesi: After the American printer, William T. Innes.
— *Hyphessobrycon.*

insects: see HEXAPODA.

insignis: Marked, distinguished.
— *Prochilodus.*

instinct: Part of the behavior of animals which as a natural impulse or sensation (leading surely to its aim) permits animals to execute actions necessary for their own preservation, or that of their offspring, without previous experience. Instinct is hereditary. It is significant within the natural surroundings of a species, and may often become nonsensical or unnatural if removed from this ambience. Instincts are bound to species and may differ in minutiae even between closely related species. Therefore they are part of the essential features of a species, similar to all other characteristics. Since generally instincts are severely and absolutely hereditary, they may be included when classifying animals. They exist potentially in all live beings and develop during the span of life according to need and time.

Instincts always appear in the same series of motives and actions. The most different factors may serve as triggers; in fishes, for instance, certain movements, shapes, colors, certain foods, the physical or chemical condition of the water, etc. Each trigger has its sure and innate "plan of reaction." Through the fact that, for instance, in reproduction the plan of reaction is aimed very specifically at the corresponding trigger of the sexual partner, "wrong reactions" (cross-breedings, mis-matings) are largely avoided, respectively impeached from the beginning.

Instincts should not be explained by present conditions only. To the contrary, they were formed together with all other characteristics during the course of development of the tribe.

Every breeder knows that also fishes have a cognate form of the course of instincts. Young fishes, ready to procreate, but reared in solitude, proceed to reproduce in the same way as their parents and exert the same activities necessary for this down to the last detail. Fights, mating, behavior during the act of spawning, care for brood, etc., take place always according to fixed rules, so that one may speak of real protocol. Protocol in the science of behavior is the cycle of behavior which follows fixed rules. The total action is divided into a whole series of single acts, which will originate from one another and overlap. Often one movement or color triggers the next one. The single phases in fishes are often coupled to a certain color. Alevins possess an innate plan of feeding, another one for alarm actions, and, in species that care for their young, an idea of how their parents look, which may be more or less limited. Generally there are certain colors, shapes, or movements of the parents that act as triggers (signals), and the "knowledge" of which is innate in the young. Of what kind these signals are in each case can be determined only through comprehensive experiments for each species. It is to be supposed that the animals act under a strong compulsion which, if repressed for some reason or other, may "dam up". If such damming up becomes too intense, the instinctive act may also be performed at the wrong moment or the wrong place. In this an imaginary threshold is jumped, which normally is opposed to the performance of the instinctive act. In such cases one speaks of the "lowering of the threshold". Thus it may happen, for instance, that fishes which care for their spawn start to care for food balled together in a corner, defending it against other fishes. This may happen whenever they do not find sufficient occasion to perform the care for their spawn normally (idling, or defaulting reaction).

The question in which way instinctive actions may be influenced by individual experience is hard to answer. A hereditary change of instincts naturally is only possible together with a change of the whole aspect of the species. Individual growth of instinctive dispositions, though, may be directed to a certain extent by influence of the surroundings. Also the course of instincts may be influenced by experience. Thus, for instance, the manner of building nests of the Stickleback is fixed hereditarily. The place, though, where such nests are erected, and the materials employed in building them, may well be partially influenced by experience.

insulation and painting of the frame aquarium:
Insulation of frames and metallic bottoms before puttying in the glass panes should receive the maximum attention. It cannot be given sufficient stress, since a faulty insulation may turn out to be the cause of many difficult-to-explain damages and losses of fishes and plants.

Before applying the first coat of primer, perform the following precautionary measures:

(a) Removal of rust and iron particles from new metal parts by means of a spatula or a sanding blower.

(b) Roughening of the surface with rough emery cloth or a wire brush.

(c) Removal of grease and grease stains with a tepid solution of detergent or a thick paste of burnt lime and water. This is applied to frame and bottom, permitted to stand for 10 minutes, washing it off thereafter. To avoid the formation of rust, the metal parts must be dried immediately. Thereafter one may apply a coat of primer with a good vermilion paint.

Vermilion Paint:
1 lb. 7 oz. of varnish of linseed-oil
12½ oz. lead vermilion powder
some drops of drying compound.

Graphite Vermilion:
25 oz. of varnish of linseed-oil
5 oz. vermilion powder
10 oz. finely ground graphite
10 oz. finely ground mica powder
some drops of drying compound.

The primer is applied in two extremely thin coats, each of which must be completely dry before further painting. It is important to work very cleanly without inclusions of strange bodies. Vermilion is a combination of lead and oxygen (lead tetra-oxide), which is poisonous in itself. A linseed oil film is formed, though, which represents an effective sealing-off measure. After this the primer has to be covered with a coat of well-covering protective paint, for which not all kinds of paint may be used. Special paints for aquaria are found in commerce at all times. WAGNER recommends a priming with chlorine-rubber vermilion, and painting with a chlorine-rubber finishing varnish thereafter. Furthermore, finishing varnishes of the kind especially made to insulate water tanks may also be used.

intermedia: In between (between two species).
— *Lebiasina.*

intermediate host: The host of a parasite on which this spends only part of the time of its development, needing another change of hosts and a final host for its conclusion.

intermedius:
— *Echinodorus.*

internodia: Members of plant stems divided by knots.

interruptus: Interrupted.
— *Cheirodon.*
— *Phenacogrammus.*

intestinal diseases of fishes: A number of diseases of the intestinal tract, which may be ascribed to different causes. Infectious Dropsy may lead to inflammation, accumulation of liquids in the intestine, and protraction of the anus. Growths, cysts, and nodules in the intestine generally originate from the attacks of worms and their larvae (see WORM DISEASES). One-sided feeding (however good) with dry food without variegated additional nourishment, especially during the winter months when conditions in the aquarium are unfavorable anyway, is the origin of most intestinal diseases. These may show by noticeable changes in the normal behavior, by paling of the colors, and by the incapacity to reproduce. Similar disturbances may also appear in consequence of one-sided feeding with very nourishing, but bulkless, animal foods, such as White Worms. Furthermore any one-sided feeding, for instance, only daphnia, or only tubifex, or red larvae (*Chironomus*), etc., may have similar results as consequence. Overfeeding the fishes too may be very harmful. Conscientious manufacturers of dry foods try to avoid the disadvantages of too one-sided formulas. An occasional short period of fasting may be favorable, but variegated feeding is always the supreme law.

ions: Wanderers, rovers.
Positively or negatively charged atoms or groups of atoms resulting in solutions of the chemical they represent. According to whether they migrate to the positive (+), or negative (—) pole, when under the action of an electrical current, they are called cations (+), or anions (—). The hydrogen ions condition the so-called natural reaction of water (see CONCENTRATION OF HYDROGEN IONS).

Iridaceae: Sword Lily Plants.
Family of swamp plants belonging to the class of the *Monocotyledonae.* They are perennial herbs or half-shrubs, with a creeping rhizome. The leaves grow up from the ground and are sword-shaped in all species that are of interest for the aquarist. The family is especially distributed throughout the tropics and sub-tropics with many species. One species, the Sword Lily, *Iris pseudacorus* Linné, is also found in the temperate zones. Our Sword Lily is a well-known, easy-to-keep, beautifully flowering plant, cultivated in many artificially bred forms. Being a garden shrub, it is not adequate for the home aquarium, but fits very well into the

open air installation, in which it is nearly indispensable. It is very enduring.

Isidora proteus: see PHYSASTRA PROTEUS.

isidori: After the French explorer Isidore Geoffrey Saint-Hilaire.
— *Marcusenius.*

Isoetaceae: Quiltworts.
Family belonging to the subphylum of the ferns or *Pteridophyta*, with rush-like leaves originating from the ground, and a strongly ramified root stock. The leaves are perforated by air canals. The spores show different shapes, according to sex, and are located separately, in capsules, on the enlarged base of the leaves. The *Isoetaceae* are perennial plants, which range especially over the temperate and sub-tropical zones of the globe. Amongst them forms are found that live submerged, others are amphibian, and some live on dry land.

Isoetes: Remaining alike during the whole year.
Genus of ferns pertaining to the family of the *Isoetaceae* which partially are difficult to distinguish, and therefore are often confused in commerce.

— **echinospora** Durieu: The Porcupine Quiltwort.
A rare species, of small importance for the aquarium, which lives in clear and cool lakes and ponds at considerable depth, and can hardly be cultivated in the home aquarium. It likes a sand bottom containing clay, and soft water at 46-50° F.

— **lacustris** Linné: Common Quiltwort.
A species which is a little easier to cultivate, distributed over Europe, West Siberia, and North America. The thick root stock bears 10-20 dark green leaves, spirally disposed around a common stem of knitting-needlelike shape. There are forms

Isoetes lacustris

with sickle-shaped, arched leaves, as well as with straight ones. The species is relatively enduring in cold water aquaria. It is very brittle, though, and the temperature should not exceed 64° F.

— **maliverniana** Cesati and de Notaris: Malinvernian Quiltwort.
GENERALITIES: The species is a little more enduring than the other ones, and may be cultivated in the tropical aquarium.
SHAPE: As per description of the genus. The lively-green leaves may reach lengths of 40″. They are wavy and wound spirally at the base.
RANGE: In a limited region of incidence in upper Italy, where the species probably was introduced, coming from tropical Asia. Here it lives amphibiously as a swamp plant. When the waters dry out, only the root stock subsists, giving off shoots when new waters collect.
CULTIVATION: The species does especially well at high water levels. It withstands water temperatures of up to 77° F, but it is a little sensitive to attack by algae. Therefore a shaded standing place is advisable. The spore capsules, which are found as slight thickenings at the bottom of the leaves, burst easily, so that often accumu-

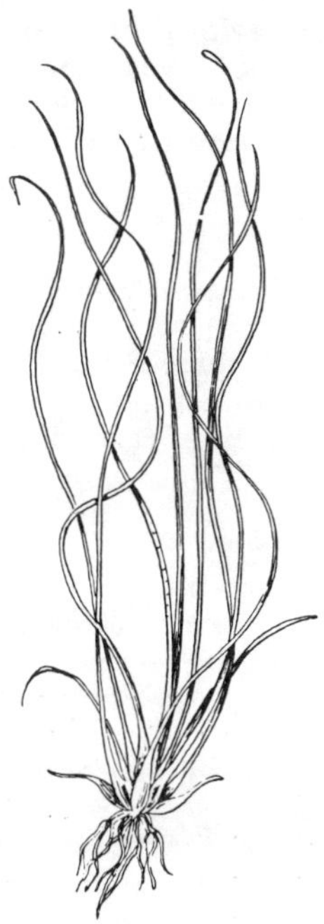

Isoetes malinverniana

lations of young plants around the old ones occur.

— setacea Bosc: Bristly Quiltwort. Enduring, rugged species, of which there is an exclusively submerged form. Formerly it was erroneously marketed as *I. lacustris*. The leaves are pale green and may reach lengths of up to 12″. The species grows slowly, but is well fit for the home aquarium, especially since it withstands higher temperatures. It ranges over Southern France, Portugal, Corsica, Sardinia, and Capri, where it is found in shallow waters that dry out easily.

Isospondyli: Herring Fishes.

Order pertaining to the class of the bone fishes or *Osteichthyes*. For a long time they were classed together with others as the soft-finned ones (*Malocopterygii*), since their fins present only soft rays. The appearance in many cases is ideally fish-shaped. The order comprises many agile swimmers. Many species are of great economical importance, but most families are absolutely unfit for the aquarium. As such we might name, for instance, the real Herrings. Of the Salmonids, which too belong to this order, only a few species can be kept alive in the aquarium, and even then only with special installations. The families most important for the aquarist are the following: the Nile Pikes or *Mormyridae*, the Old-World Knife Fishes or *Notopteridae*, and the Butterfly Fishes or *Pantodontidae*.

isthmensis: Coming from the Isthmus (Costa Rica).

— *Rivulus*.

jacobsoni: After the collector Jacobson.

— *Rasbora*.

jaculatrix: Slingshooter, shooter.

— *Toxotes*.

januarius: From Rio de Janeiro (The Portuguese words "Rio de Janeiro" mean River of January).

— *Phalloptychus*.

January Carp, the: see PHALLOPTYCHUS JANUARIUS.

Japan Barb, the: see BARILIUS NEGLECTUS.

Java Moss: see VESICULARIA DUBYANA.

Javanese Medaka, the: see ORYZIAS JAVANICUS.

javanicus: Coming from Java.

— *Oryzias*.

Jaw Leeches: see GNATHOBDELLAE.

Jaw-less, the: see AGNATHI.

Jenynsia: After Leonard Jenyns-Blomefield.

Genus of live-bearing toothcarps belonging to the sub-family of the *Jenynsiinae* with only a few species, all coming from South America. Formerly known under the synonym *Fitzroya*.

— lineata Jenyns:

SHAPE: As per description of the sub-family. D 8-9, A 8-10. Length: males $1\frac{1}{4}''$ to $1\frac{5}{8}''$, females up to $4\frac{3}{4}''$.

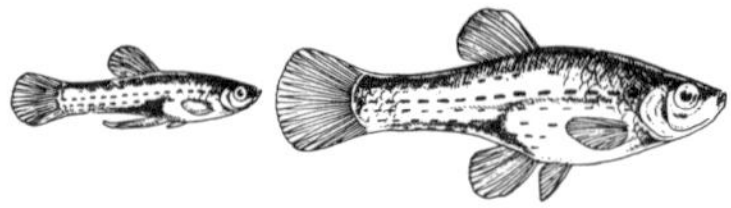

Jenynsia lineata, male behind

COLOR: Olive colored with dot designs on the sides which may be altered according to origin. SD are similar to those of all live bearing Tooth Carps.

RANGE: From Southern Brazil nearly to Patagonia. This fish is the species of Tooth Carps that ranges farthest south of all.

CARE AND BREEDING: A somewhat drab species, that is rarely seen in the aquarium. During youth they are quite peaceable, but become a little pugnacious with increasing age, especially the big females. The fish are absolutely not sensitive to low temperatures, loving warmth, though. They prefer live foods, and take dried ones only in case of extreme need. The 10-100 young may measure up to $\frac{3}{4}''$ at birth, and grow very quickly. Sexual maturity may set in already in the third month of life.

Jenynsiinae: Sub-family of live bearing Tooth Carps belonging to the family of the Tooth Carps or *Cyprinodontidae*. It is represented only by the genus *Jenynsia*, which comprises just a few species. Besides other insignificant anatomical peculiarities, it is the construction of the gonopodium which differentiates the sub-family from the other live bearing Tooth Carps. It is relatively short, and can always be moved to only one side, having thus to correspond to the body construction of the female, as in her the genital opening is dislocated towards one side by a scale. Therefore only pairs of corresponding organs are able to mate.

Jewel Fish, the: see HEMICHROMIS BIMACULATUS.

Jordan, David Starr: American zoologist and notable expert on the American fish fauna. Born 1/19/1851 in Gainsville, N.Y. Pupil of Agassiz. His greatest work is the "Handbook of Vertebrates of the Northern United States," which was published in 1876. In 1896-1900, together with B. W. Evermann, he published the 4-volume work "The Fishes of North and Central America", and in 1905 his well-known "Guide to the Study of Fishes".

Jordanella: After the American zoologist Jordan.
Genus of North American Tooth Carps belonging to the sub-family of the egg laying Tooth Carps or *Cyprinodontinae*, with only one species, which is closely related to the genus *Cyprinodon*. It differs from this only by the longer dorsal fin.

— floridae Goode and Bean: The American Flag Fish.

SHAPE: Short, sturdy, and relatively high-backed, compressed laterally. The snout is short and rounded, the mouth supraterminal, and the jaws are each provided with a row of teeth. D 16-18, A 11-13: The big caudal fin is rounded in a fan-shaped manner. Length 2″ to $2\frac{3}{8}''$, the females often a little bigger.

COLOR: The male is very changeable, and shows special mating colors. It carries a big greenish-luminous dot on olive-brownish base on each scale forming longitudinal rows. The scale edges are partly bordered in vivid red. The fins are colored a beautiful brownish red on yellow-greenish base. The female shows a checkerboard design, with a typical dark spot on the dorsal fin.

RANGE: In smallish and shallow, slowly-flowing and standing waters, from Florida to Yucatan.

CARE AND BREEDING: This hardy species will also live in smaller

Jordanella floridae, male below

tanks. They are omnivorous and especially need vegetable food in the form of algae. The aquaria should be well-stocked with plants and stand in sunny spots. Especial attention should be paid to the temperature. The fish should not be kept too warm. They are very sensitive to too high or too low degrees of warmth, their optimum temperature being around 68° F, for breeding 77° F under the incidence of sunlight. The species is considered rather unsociable toward other fishes. Many specimens may also turn out to be quite shy. *Jordanella floridae* is one of the few species of Tooth Carps which care for their brood. The male digs a kind of hole in the sand, at the foot of plants, which generally, though, is not used. Spawning takes place after stormy chasing, generally in dense stands of plants. At each spawning 5-6 eggs are expelled, totalling a number of 30-70 during a spawning period of 7 days. The male fans the eggs and also cares for the fry which are rarely attacked by the parents. Notwithstanding this, transplanting the young into an algae-covered nursery tank is advisable. They grow up very quickly and may be able to reproduce within three months.

jordani:
— *Anoptichthys.*

jurupari: The devil's fish hook (Indian name).
— *Geophagus.*

Kaempfer, Engelbert: 1651-1716. German physician in the service of the Dutch East India Company, who contributed very much to the knowledge of Japan and East Asia, and who was one of the first Occidentals to report on the breeding of Goldfish in those regions.

Kallopterus: With beautiful fins.
— *Epalzeorhynchus.*

kanumae: After a native name.
— *Mormyrus.*

Keel Belly Barb, the: see OXYGASTER ATPAR.

Kissing Gourami, the: see HELOSTOMA TEMMINCKI.

kitchen salt: Kitchen salt, or sodium chloride (NaCl) plays an important role in maintaining life. It is present in all waters in greater or smaller quantities. Sea water contains an average concentration of 2.7%. The salt content (to which not only kitchen salt contributes) demands that marine life cannot live in fresh water, i.e. water with a weaker salt concentration, and vice-versa. Fishes able to live in both media (euryhaline fishes), and which can pass from one to the other, are capable of compensating the differences in salt concentration through osmosis without causing disturbances in the body economy of water, as happens with fishes that specialize in one medium only (stenohaline fishes).

A solution of kitchen salt in the water often has a healing action by strongly stimulating the epidermis, and thus the whole metabolism. This may mobilize forces to fight the diseases. Furthermore a great number of external parasites cannot withstand the action of salt (see

Cures of Fish Diseases, Medicines). The duration of such baths, though, should not be extreme, as otherwise the fish may become too weakened by increased metabolism during the adjustment of osmosis.

A certain addition of kitchen salt, though, used as a preventive, has been approved for the aquarist. For such additions a percentage of .5% is advisable, meaning 1 lb. of salt per 25 gals. of water.

Often there is no possibility within the household to weigh small quantities of kitchen salt. In such cases the following measurements may serve to give a certain help, without substituting the exact weights, though, which are necessary for preparing healing baths. They are:

one heaped teaspoon—about ½ oz.
one level teaspoon—about ⅜ oz.
one heaped tablespoon—about 1 oz.
one level tablespoon—about ¾ oz.

kneri: After the Austrian ichthyologist Dr. Kner.
— *Bunocephalus.*

Knife Eels: see Electrophoridae.

Knife Fishes, American: see Gymnotidae.

Knife Fishes, Old World: see Notopteridae.

Knife Livebearer, the: see Alfaro cultratus.

knowledge of home waters: The field interests of the aquarist should include exploration of his local bodies of water, their properties, and the fauna and flora that live there. (See Gathering Trips).

koelreuteri: After the Russian naturalist Koelreuter.
— *Periophthalmus.*

krameri: After a personal name.
— *Umbra.*

kribensis:
— *Pelmatochromis.*

Kryptopterus: see Cryptopterus.

Kuhli Loach, the: see Acanthophthalmus semicinctus.

kuhlii: After the German zoologist Kuhl.
— *kuhlii sumatranus* from Sumatra.
— *Acanthophthalmus.*

Labeo: Fringed Lips.
Genus of Carp or Loach-like fishes belonging to the Carp-like or *Cyprinidae*, originating from Asia and Africa. Some of the species grow very big, and are used as food fishes. Characteristic for all species of *Labeo* are the horny tufts around the mouth. It is with the help of these that they rasp off growths. Two pairs of barbels are present, of which one pair is located in front of the nose opening, and is motile. During the rasping-off of food, it serves as a tactile organ. The second pair of barbels is located in the angle of the mouth, and seems to be of secondary importance. Some of the species have only one pair of barbels, or none at all.

Of thc numerous species, so far only two or three have found their way into the fancier's aquarium, due to their beautiful coloration and to reaching only minute sizes. These species come from smaller, clear waters, richly stocked with plants. Too intense light does not suit the fishes as well as twilight. The species of *Labeo* should be kept in schools, as isolated specimens become pugnacious. Anyway, some of the species are a little quarrelsome and one should afford them caves and hiding places. Especially bigger males are often very furious towards weaker females and may chase them to death. The eggs are laid in caves or on stones, and are watched by the male. Successful spawnings have not been described so far. Soft, a little acid water, to which a little tannic acid has been added suits these fishes best. Their well-being makes vegetable food, especially algae, a must. Temperature around 71° F.

Labeo bicolor

Labeo erythrurus

— **bicolor** H. M. Smith: The Red-Tailed Black Shark.

SHAPE: Elongated, looking like a shark. Two pairs of barbels. D 2/13, A 1/6. Length up to 6″.

COLOR: Body and fins are a uniform sooty black, sometimes with a bluish sheen. The tail fin is a fiery red. During youth the vertical fins frequently show white tips.

RANGE: In flowing waters in Thailand.

CARE AND BREEDING: According to BADER the Red-tailed Shark is especially scrappy. Seemingly the behavior of these fish towards one another is strongly influenced by territorial feelings. Even small specimens of about 2″ in length try to oppress one another. After each of the fish has tried to settle a certain territory, very soon active fights for preponderance break out. Parting from respective territories, sharp struggles are fought until one of the fish has secured ascendancy over the others. BADER has been able to observe a veritable order of rank, which had developed after days of fighting. Fish kept alone also attacked other species, thus showing themselves vicious also in this respect.

— **erythrurus** Fowler: The Green Shark.

SHAPE: Elongated, nearly completely round. The fins are relatively big. Two pairs of barbels. Length up to 5″ (?).

COLOR: A longitudinal stripe from the tip of the snout to the edge of the gill cover, on greenish-brown base and a cross band at the origin of the caudal fin. The front pair of barbels is black, the fins being blood-red. The male shows a black seam at the rear edge of the anal fin.

RANGE: Thailand, in the Mekong River.

CARE AND BREEDING: As per description of the genus. There are reports on spawnings of this species. The male cares for the eggs and defends them furiously.

labiosa: Thicklipped.

— *Colisa.*

Lacepede, Bernard-Germain Etienne, Earl of: French naturalist. Born December 26, 1756, died October 6, 1825. After 1795 professor at the Museum of Natural History in Paris, later Minister of State. In 1798-1809 he wrote the five-volume "Histoire des Poissons", i.e., the Natural History of Fishes.

Lace Plants: see APONOGETON.

lacustris: Lake-dwelling.

— *Isoetes.*

ladigesi: After the German ichthyologist Ladiges, discoverer of the species.

— *Telmatherina.*

Laemolyta: Referring to the special construction of the gills.

South American genus of Characins pertaining to the family of the Headstanders of *Anostomidae*. The genus is only slightly differentiated from *Anostomus*.

— **taeniata** Kner: The Banded Headstander.

SHAPE: The elongated body is laterally compressed only near the caudal peduncle, otherwise it is scarcely compressed at all. The mouth is small and supraterminal, the head a little flattened on the top, the body nearly cylindrical. D 12-13, A 10-11. Length up to about 10″.

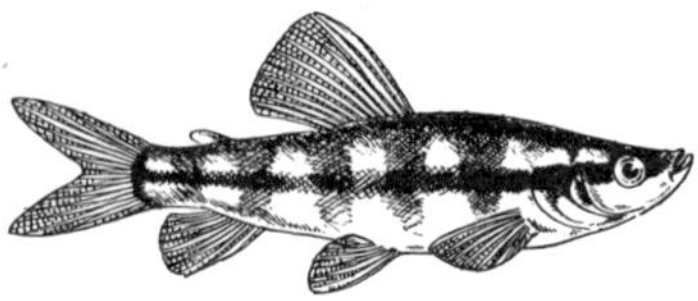

Laemolyta taeniata

COLOR: Brownish to greenish glossy base with a dark longitudinal stripe which is interrupted by some cross-bands.

RANGE: The Amazon region.

CARE AND BREEDING: As described for *Anostomus*. No spawning has been achieved so far.

laevis: Smooth, light, delicate.

— *Phoxinus*.

Lagarosiphon: Referring to the construction of the fruit knot.

Genus of sub-aquatic plants pertaining to the family of the Frogbits or *Hydrocharitaceae*.

— **muscoides** Harvey: Curly Water Pest.

For many years the species has been known commercially as *Elodea crispa*. It is very similar to the Elodeas. The strong, but brittle, main stem bears the light to dark-green, narrow, littlc leaves spiraling around it in mock verticils. They are sharply curled downwards and inwards. The plant does not bloom in the aquarium. Reproduction is similar to that of *Elodea*, by simple division. Each free-floating part of the stem may give origin to a new plant. The species needs much light and sun, but not too high temperatures. 50-77° F will do, about 68° F being best.

ORIGIN: South Africa, in clear waters.

lagoon: Secondary body of water at sea coasts or big lakes and rivers, as a rule consisting of a long-stretched bay, running parallel to the coast or toward the shore, being totally or partly separated from the main water by a generally sandy neck of land. Sea lagoons with fresh water flowing into them, but which simultaneously receive salt water from the ocean, generally harbor a very peculiar biological world, consisting of the fauna and flora of both waters which have undergone a very special development in adaptation to the changed and changing conditions.

lala: After a native, probably slightly deprecating, name.

— *Ambassis*.

lalia: As above.

— *Colisa*.

Lamarck, Jean: 1744-1829. Famous French naturalist who elaborated the first comprehensive theory on the development of the species and pre-supposed a direct influence of the surroundings on the genesis of the species.

lamarckism: The teachings of Lamarck on genetical development exclusively through direct influences of the ambient world. Lamarck's idea was still rather primitive, and was later on substituted by Darwin's theory. Meanwhile Lamarck's idea has, as a whole, again found greater recognition, even if meanwhile it has been essentially improved.

Lamp Eye, the: see APLOCHEILICHTHYS MACROPHTHALMUS.

Lamp Eye Fishes, the: see APLOCHEILICHTHYS.

Lampreys, the: see PETROMYZONIDAE.

lanceolatum: Lance shaped.

— *Alisma.*

lancet fishes: see ACRANIA.

Lancet-Leaved Frog-Bit: see ALISMA LANCEOLATUM.

lancifolia: With lance-shaped leaves.

— *Sagittaria.*

landgrafi: After a personal name.

— *Neolebias.*

landscaped aquarium (aquascaping): A form of aquarium in which the fancier strives to plan his tank according to points of view of geography and landscape. The landscape aquarium may represent an experiment to imitate formally a certain geographical landscape, but it may also fulfill the conditions of such imitations biologically. Of course generally it is hardly possible within the narrow frame of a domestic aquarium to give the idea of a tropical stream, pond, lake shore, etc. even approximately. The landscape aquarium is absolutely justified, though, in shows or public installations, where the scope is to show the fauna and flora of a certain region of the world.

larva: Youth stage of animals which do not develop directly from the egg to the completed individual, but pass through a metamorphosis. The larval form frequently differs widely from the completed animal. In part there may appear organs that are typical of the larva, and disappear again later on. Many lower species of animals present larvae, especially crustaceans and insects. In fishes (see YOUNG FISHES), express larval forms are found, among others, among the Eels, *Polypteridae*, and Lung Fishes (see DIPNEUSTI). Generally also the freshly hatched young, which are not yet completely developed and often are provided with special adhesive organs are called larvae.

latency, latent: Hiddenness, hidden.

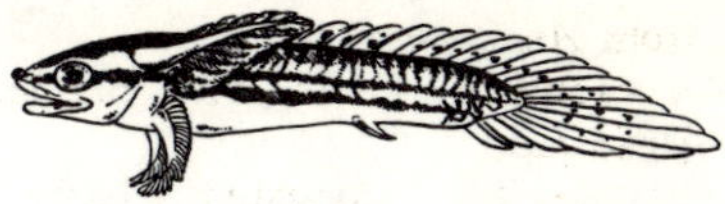

Larva of **Polypterus**, showing external gills

The state of rest for a longer period of any vital process, for instance, the presence of disease germs which do not spread due to having been capsuled, in or due to unfavorable conditions of life.

lateral line, the: see SENSORY ORGANS.

lateristriata: With striped sides.

— *Rasbora.*

lateristriga: With stripes on the sides.

— *Barbus.*

latifolia: With different leaves, of wide variety.

— *Sagittaria.*

latifrons: With wide forehead.

— *Aequidens.*

latipes: With wide foot (referring to the wide anal fin).

— *Oryzias.*

latipinna: With wide fin.

— *Mollienisia.*

Lattice Dwarf Cichlid, the: see NANNACARA TAENIA.

laubuca: After a native name.

— *Laubuca.*

Laubuca: Genus of small school fishes belonging to the family of the Carp-like or *Cyprinidae*, of slender shape, strongly compressed laterally. The lateral line is complete and runs along the lower half of the body. The body may be quite transparent.

— dadyburjori.

— laubuca Hamilton-Buchanan: SHAPE: As per description of the genus, the dorsal contour only a little, the ventral one more strongly arched. The mouth is supraterminal. D 10, A 21. The dorsal fin inserts far back. the pectorals are big and sickle-shaped. Length up to $2\frac{3}{8}$".

Laubuca laubuca

COLOR: Greenish-silvery with a light golden sheen, furthermore a greenish-golden horizontal band and a deep black, gold-edged spot at the tail insertion. The male is slimmer, the female fuller-bodied, especially if viewed from above.
RANGE: In flowing and standing waters, also in rice-paddies all over Southeastern Asia.
CARE AND BREEDING: As described for *Cyprinidae*. The species has only rarely been imported. Imports prove to be rather sensitive, especially to low temperatures. Warmth should not sink below 68° F. Once domesticated, the species is not especially demanding, being peaceful and gregarious, and shows to be especially attractive in larger swarms. Spawning has been accomplished. According to MEYBURG, the spawning occurs during the evening twilight, the male twining lightly around the female. They are egg scatterers.

lazera: After a native name (?). — *Clarias*.

leaf: A part of plants which as a rule fulfills the task of assimilation. In the development of plants the following leaves are differentiated in chronological order: germinating leaves, primary leaves, and secondary leaves. The phases may be very different in their external shape. Sometimes even the secondary leaves may show a great number of diverging shapes. Leaves often stand on a leaf stalk, but this may also be lacking. In such cases we speak of inserting leaves. The surfaces of leaves are covered with nervures, of which the stronger veins—which stand out on the underside—are called leaf ribs. Veins and ribs serve to support the leaf surface and also as conduits of nourishment and of other substances. The upper layer of the skin of leaves shows split openings, through which breathing and assimilation take place.

The amount of assimilation determines the vividness of the green color and the more or less great surface, which often is still enlarged through the fact that the leaves are fine-feathered. The position of the leaves on the stems is different for the different kinds of plants, but often so characteristic for certain species or genera that it represents an aid to systematic classification. Leaves may, for instance, stand opposite on the stems, or disposed in verticils, or else alternately. If they sit directly on the root stock they are called bottom-standing.

The main shapes of leaves found on aquatic plants are shown on the drawing that is part of this entry.

Leaf Feet: see PHYLLOPODA.

Leaf Fish, the: see MONOCIRRHUS POLYACANTHUS.

Lebias: see APHANIUS.

Lebiasina: Liver fish.
South American genus belonging to the family of the Characins or CHARACIDAE (see these). They are fishes of elongated build, little compressed laterally to nearly cylindrical. The scales are very big. The lateral line is incomplete or totally absent. The fins are small, the adipose being generally lacking, but it may appear on one or the

other specimens. The moderately big mouth is supraterminal. Seemingly the swimming bladder serves as an accessory respiratory organ. Up to this date only three species are known.

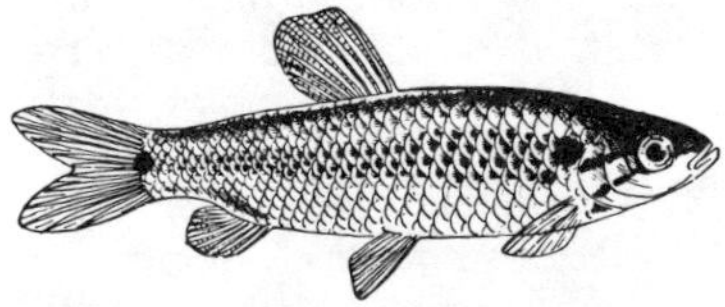

Lebiasina bimaculata

— bimaculata Cuvier and Valenciennes:

SHAPE: As per description of genus. D 9-10, A 10-12. Length up to 8″.

COLOR: Greenish, a luminous green below the dorsal fin, with a violet to reddish, sometimes even yellowish sheen. During the spawning period the fins of the males become a lively poppy-red. Occasionally a dark horizontal band may appear. The male is slimmer and more colorful.

RANGE: In the mountain waters of the Pacific side of the Andes. The species may be quite abundant.

CARE AND BREEDING: This fish is highly appreciated in its home land as an exterminator of malaria mosquito larvae, and is therefore gladly kept in the watering places of the settlements. Due to its accessory respiration, the fish withstands even the most unfavorable circumstances. It is resistant to lack of oxygen in the water, and does not need warmth. In spite of the fact that it feels best at 77° F, it can also bear temperatures as low as 50-54° F. It is a little demanding, though, as to food, and takes only robust live foods. Furthermore the fish are not very peaceful.

The species has only rarely been imported. No spawnings have succeeded so far.

— intermedia Meinken:

A species from the Amazon, very similar to the previous one, which attains up to 6″ in length. Reproduction is unknown.

Lebistes: Small *Lebias*.

Genus of South and Central American Tooth Carps, belonging to the sub-family of the live bearing Tooth Carps or *Poeciliinae*. They are fishes of graceful build, especially the males, which are remarkable for the great diversity in color and shape. The genus, containing many varieties, is spread over Northern South America including the adjacent isles.

— reticulatus Peters: The Guppy.

SHAPE: Small and slender, the male slightly compressed laterally, the female with the front part of the body rounded and a little compressed at the caudal peduncle. The fins of the males are of varied shapes. The gonopodium is only short. Length: males up to 1″, females up to 2″.

COLOR: The male is varicolored, but so changing in the composition of the colors that one fish hardly ever resembles the next one. The colors also spread over the fins. Especially the dorsal and tail fins are beautifully colored, the latter sometimes showing some design even on females. The fins are remarkable for their varied, bannerlike extensions. Especially beautiful in color and rich in shapes are the numerous artificial breeds.

RANGE: Tropical Northern South America, also on Trinidad and Barbados. In these regions the fish live in waters of all kinds as long as they afford the slightest possibility for living. Besides this they have been introduced in several other tropical regions, since they are of great value as exterminators of fever mosquito larvae.

CARE AND BREEDING: As per description of the sub-family. The

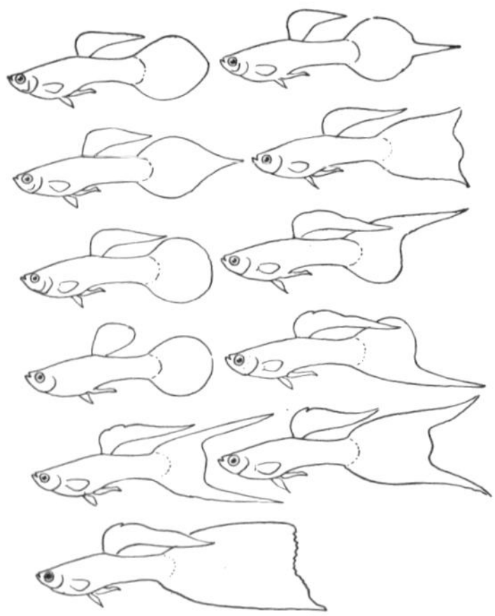

Lebistes reticulatus, male types — left, top to bottom: Cofertail, Speartail, Robson, common Roundtail, Doublesword, Veiltail; right, top to bottom: Pintail, Triangle, Topsword, Bottomsword, Lyretail.

species is peaceful and lively. Especially the males are always showing attention to the females with graceful wooing motions. The fish are not very demanding as to temperature, but one should avoid descents below 64° F, and should not keep them at such a low degree for long times. 71-73° F have shown to be the most favorable temperatures.

In breeding, the species is very productive. Pregnancy lasts 4-6 weeks, after which time 10 to 80 young are born, depending on the size of the female. With adequate food, these grow very quickly. The sexes may be differentiated immediately by a dark spot which the future females carry above the anal fin.

After decades in which only in the rarest cases value was given to selective breeding, and therefore the tribes kept in aquaria developed back in color, shape, and size, lately the fanciers have again begun to pay more attention to the breeding of this species. The Guppy is better for breeding "strains" than any other species, due to its changeability. Not only have there appeared breeders who with great patience and skill have developed remarkably beautiful types, but whole "Guppy clubs" have been founded. These point out rightly that breeding Guppies is apt to arouse understanding for general breeding problems in aquaristics. The specimens exhibited at international competitions are often of remarkable beauty. One has to point out, though, that breeding Guppies requires much time and effort. Below we shall disclose some professional tricks of Guppy breeders:

The Guppy has a natural tendency towards change. Its wild populations are a colorful mosaic of different strains which intermingle frequently at the borders of the different ranges. With such a starting situation the breeder has the best of prospects to breed selectively, from the available material, hereditarily fixed strains which may best correspond to his idea of a standard norm. If he has a firm conception of the breeding aim, subsequent isolation of the desired qualities must some day lead to reaching hereditary firmness of the developed strain.

Such a task is highly exacting on the breeder. He has to make it his only work, if possible. In most cases he will have to acquire the necessary knowledge within the theory of heredity, as breeding Guppies is a genetic problem in the first place. Without theoretical knowledge of internal hereditary processes, no planned and successful breeding of Guppies is possible. (See HEREDITY; BREEDING). Since all fish, the original ones as well as the subsequent generations, have eventually to be separated by sexes, breeding calls for a great number of tanks of different sizes. One cannot do all work in small all-glass containers such as are needed as maternity tanks for pregnant females. To the contrary, growing Guppy fry need plenty of room for their full development. In spite of their great fertility, and the quick succession of generations, the breeding of pure strains demands many years of arduous toil.

Therefore breeding Guppies is nothing for impatient people, and will hardly bring a profitable financial return.

When genetically firm tribes have been attained, the breeder's work is eased up a little, as he now may go on to breeding lines. The fish are bred in communities, always again picking out eventually appearing deviations. Having reached the certainty of possessing genetically firm tribes, such deviations may represent sudden changes in heredity, the so-called mutations, which on their part may become starting points of newly-bred types. As a rule, though, it will be the case of breeding back to previously existing hereditary qualities only.

The single characteristics of Guppies react genetically in very different ways. Partly they are inherited dominantly, that is superseding other qualities, partly recessively, meaning that they are superseded. Furthermore the hereditary transmission of certain characteristics may be tied in with the heredity of sex. Such sexually-tied heredities are found, for instance, in the many characteristics of beauty. In spite of the fact that these show only on the males, they are transmitted exclusively by the females. In the female picture of heredity (genotype) they behave recessively, while they may be dominant in the male.

Below is a table of pairs of characters in their hereditary behavior (according to OSTERTAG).

Dominant	*Recessive*
Wild gray	Gold
Wild Gray	Blonde
Gold	Blonde
Wild gray	Albino
Round tail	Pointed tail
Round tail	Banner tail
Round tail	Veil tail
Round tail	Sword tail
Absence of tail sword	Sword tail
Normal color of tail fin of female	Black spots on tail fin of female
Normal color of tail fin of female	Checkerboard design on tail fin of female
Normal and dwarf growth	Giant growth

It is seen from this, that the most desired qualities behave recessively. Thus they are naturally difficult for the breeder to follow, and make breeding Guppies still more difficult and laborious. In order to make the characters visible, one uses breeding back and inbreeding. Thus there are especially many possibilities of meetings of similar recessive dispositions with pairs of dispositions so that they may become visible in the genotype. Here are some explanations of this:

1. The initial generation with which a breeding (crossing) is begun is called the parental generation—P-generation.

2. Their offspring form the first bastard generation or Filial-generation—F_1-generation.

3. Crossing the F_1-generation with the P-generation, one speaks of breeding back. The resulting generation is called an R-generation.

Starting from the point that both parents of the P-generation had different characteristics, the F_1-generation may behave intermediately (showing a mixture of the qualities), dominantly or recessively.

4. The generations following upon F_1 are marked F_2, F_3, F_4 etc.

In order to enlighten the possibility of the confluence of pairs of dispositions during fertilization, let us mark the dominant characteristics with the capitals A, B, C, etc., and the recessive ones with small letters a, b, c, etc. As is known, when fertilizing the ovum with the spermatozoon, each of the parents contributes with half of the pairs of dispositions after a previous diminution through the reduction of maturity division. After fertilization a complete pair results again from the respective halves. From this result the following possibilities for the three qualities A, B, C only, set forth in the tabulation below:

AA—Aa—aA—aa
BB—Bb—bB—bb
CC—Cc—cC—cc.

In this the pairs Aa, aA, Bb, bB, Cc, and cC are dissimilar in their qualities. They are of divided heredity or heterozygotic. The pairs AA, aa, BB, bb, CC, and cc are similar in their qualities, being of pure heredity or homozygotic.

lebretonis: After the French physician Lebreton.
— *Eleotris.*

Leech Diseases: Infestations with blood-sucking leeches should be quite rare in aquaria, and happen only if these are brought in together with food, on other fishes, rocks, or plants. While sporadic leeches on larger fishes are hardly able to cause mentionable harm, the continuous sucking of several leeches on smaller fishes—if undetected by the hobbyist—may lead to dangerous weakening, skin wounds, and to secondary infections with fungus (*Saprolegnia*) or other parasites. Sometimes the leeches may also be carriers of blood parasites (Sleeping Disease germs).

Anyway, Leech Diseases pose no great problem in our aquaria, as these parasites may easily be removed with some blunt tweezers. If they should be too firmly located, you may first weaken them by bathing the fish for a quarter of an hour in a 2.5% solution of kitchen salt.

Leeches: see HIRUDINEA.

leeri: After the Dutch physician Van Leer.
— *Trichogaster.*

Leeuwenhoek, Anthony van: 1632-1723. Dutch merchant who stepped into the picture as amateur biologist and dedicated his endeavors especially to the construction of optical instruments. He created one of the first effective microscopes with which, among other things, he discovered bacteria and other micro-organisms.

Leiocassis: With smooth head. Genus of Catfishes pertaining to the family of the *Bagridae*, with a few species which range over Southeastern Asia. The body is elongated and covered with a mucous skin, of rounded section, slightly flattened above. The back rises roof-like to the beginning of the dorsal fin. The mouth is semi-subterminal, and provided with two short barbels. Dorsal and pectoral fins have a strong first spine, toothed on the rear side. The adipose fin is rather big, the tail fin deeply indented, and its two lobes sometimes extended.

The species *L. siamensis* Regan seems to reach a length of 8″. It is a fish of dark color with lighter cross bands over the body. It leads a nocturnal life, and is hardly ever seen during daytime, when it hides under roots, etc. from which it hangs upside down.

Food consists of worms, insect larvae, etc.

Its origin is India and Indonesia.

leiurus: With smooth tail.
— *Tetraodon.*

Lemna: Pertaining to pond or swamp.
Genus of floating plants belonging to the family of the duckweeds or *Lemnaceae*, but of small importance for the home aquarium. In this duckweeds are only occasional guests.

— gibba Linné: Humpbacked Duckweed.
A species ranging over the temperate zones of Europe, Asia, and Africa, forming more or less compact mats on the surface of standing waters. The plants, measuring from $\frac{1}{8}''$ to $\frac{3}{16}''$, are rounded, a shiny dark-green on the upper side, strongly arched on the underside, with one root beneath each leaf. The flowers are dull and appear only rarely. Reproduction occurs nearly exclusively through budding, so that often many plants are connected in chains.

— minor Linné: Small Duckweed.
Very similar to the previous species, but smaller and flat on the underside. Ranges over the same regions.

— trisulca Linné: Triangle Duckweed.
A species ranging over Europe, Asia, North America and Australia, deviating in shape from the other duckweeds. The light-green leaves are connected in branch colonies, being triangular, and float on the surface of the water. If it receives sufficient light, this species remains green even in winter.

Lemnaceae: Duckweeds.
Family of perennial aquatic plants pertaining to the class of the *Monocotyledoneae*, which generally floats free on the surface. The body is slightly articulated, always small, and only sparsely provided with roots. The species of one genus have no roots at all. Duckweeds are rarely kept in aquaria. They need

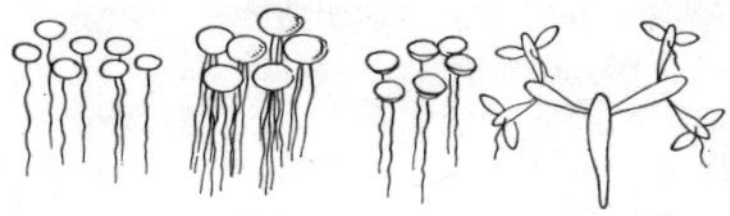

Lemnaceae — left to right: Lemna minor, Spirodella polyrrhiza, Lemna gibba, Lemna trisulca.

light and some sun, and are sensitive against warm waters. Genera: *Lemna, Wolffia, Spirodela.*

Lemon Live-Bearer, the: see MICROPOECILIA BRANNERI.

Lemon Tetra, the: see HYPHESSOBRYCON PULCHRIPINNIS.

Lentiburiaceae: Water Tube Plants.
Family pertaining to the class of the *Dicotyledoneae.* Generally perennial, herb-like, land, swamp or water plants, of which in aquaristics especially the carnivorous species of the genus *Utricularia* are of interest.

Leopard Bush Fish, the: see CTENOPOMA ACUTIROSTRIS.

Leopard Corydoras, the: see CORYDORAS PUNCTATUS JULII.

Leopard Puffer, the: see TETRAODON SCHOUTEDENI.

Leopardus: Leopard-like (in color).
— *Corydoras.*

Lepidocephalus: Scaly head.
Genus of Asiatic Perches belonging to the family of the *Cobitidae* which differs from the very similar *Noemacheilus* species by possessing eight barbels (instead of six, as does *Noemacheilus*). They are provided with spines beneath the eyes. All of them are simple in color, reminding one of the Spotted Weatherfish or *Misgurnus fossilis*, and like to remain hidden in the sand. All species like a soft sand bottom and clear water. They do not withstand the condition of excessive algae growth popularly called "pea soup". Otherwise the genus is hardy and undemanding.

— guntea:
SHAPE: As per description of the genus. The species is a little

plumper than the other members of the genus. Length up to 8″.

COLOR: The basic shade of the body color is a dirty yellow-brown from which dark-brown horizontal bands stand out. The design reminds one of *Misgurnus fossilis* but is not as pretty. The male is slimmer.

RANGE: From Asia Minor to India. The species is divided into some sub-species. It lives mainly in slowly flowing waters.

CARE AND BREEDING: This hardy species feels well at temperatures of about 68° F and in clear water. The bottom should consist of fine gravel, where the fish often dig in. Also hiding-places are sought eagerly. So far there are no reports on successful breedings, in spite of the fact that sometimes the fish spawn in the aquarium. Fine-feathered plants are not advisable for the aquarium where these fish are kept as the mulm they raise sticks to the leaves and makes them look dirty.

— octocirrhus Van Hasselt:

SHAPE: As per description of genus. The species resembles *Cobitis taenia*. Length up to 5″.

COLOR: The design is similar to that of *Cobitis taenia*, but the dots, which flare up steel-blue, are more irregular and only rarely disposed in horizontal rows. A dark spot is found over the middle of the root of the tail fin. The males are slimmer.

RANGE: In flowing and standing waters of Java, Sumatra, and Indo-China.

CARE AND BREEDING: Soft sand bottom, clear, oxygen-rich water, hiding places and temperatures from 60-75° F. The fish are omnivorous. Reproduction unknown.

Lepidoptera: Butterflies.

The order of the butterflies, which is very rich as to species, is found

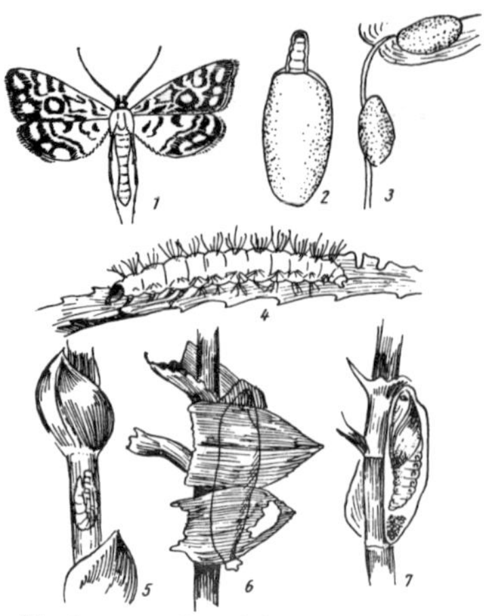

Lepidoptera — 1. adult winged form of **Nymphula** - 2. larval case of a water butterfly, with the fore part of the body showing - 3. cocoons on an aquatic plant - 4. creeping caterpillar of a water butterfly **Paraponyx** - 5. caterpillar imbedded in a water plant stem - 6. cocoon of **Acentropus** - 7. same, opened.

in water only during the larval stage of a few, unimportant species. The caterpillars have more or less adapted to life beneath the surface, either by developing within sturdy pond plants, building shells in the manner of the *Trichoptera*, or else by living free in the water. It happens very rarely that the complete insect lives in the water, but, if so, in a special manner of adaptation parallel to the normal, flying form.

Lepidosiren: Scaly Eel.

South American genus of lung fishes pertaining to the family of the *Lepidosirenidae*, of very elongated build, and with a low fin-edge which encloses the whole rear end of the fish.

— paradoxus Fitzinger: The South American Scaly Eel.

SHAPE: As per description of the genus, the eel-shaped body being of cylindrical shape, covered with numerous very small and thin scales. Paired members exist, but they are only thin and wormlike.

Lepidosiren paradoxus

The jaws are provided with numerous sharp-pointed teeth, which are grown together forming plates and strips. Length up to 50″.
COLOR: Uniformly brownish to greenish gray.
RANGE: In swampy waters of difficult access in Brazil and Paraguay, very specially underneath thick plant stocks.
CARE AND BREEDING: Very interesting for show aquaria. The Lepidosiren lives at the bottom where it moves in a creeping way, but is perfectly able to swim very skillfully. The alimentation consists of sturdy live foods, especially the Mystery Snails of its home country (*Ampullarius*). In captivity it may be trained to eat meat. It is predominantly a nocturnal fish, which loves hiding-places and aquaria with subdued light. 75-82° F.

As soon as conditions in its home water becomes untenable, it buries itself in the mud. During this phase it does not exude a body mucus like its African relative *Protopterus*. Contrarily, the fish form artificial covers of clay pellets which do not rest firmly together, so that the air may permeate them. Thereafter it retires ever deeper into the ground, ever deeper as more intense dryness sets in, gradually also building more covers. The species has not yet been bred in the aquarium.

The eggs are laid in galleries in the mud and are guarded by the male. During this time the male breathes only through the gills and through especially developing breathing organs on the members.

The fry are equipped with adhesive organs and bunched gills which disappear completely after metamorphosis.

Lepidosirenidae: Family of lung fishes pertaining to the order of the *Dipneusti*, with the two genera *Lepidosiren*, and *Protopterus*. Fishes with elongated bodies, partly eel-like, with small scales that are hidden within the skin. The paired fins are mutated into threadlike appendages. The gills are more or less stunted, but in compensation supplemented by accessory respiration through a double lung sac. The larvae are equipped with external gill bushes and with an adhesive gland on the underside of the head.

lepidota: With scaly ears (gill covers).
— *Crenicichla*.

lepidura: With scaly tail.
— *Tilapia*.

Lepidurus apus: Gill foot; see NOTOSTRACA.

Lepisosteidae: Gars.
Family of Ganoids pertaining to the order of the *Ginglymodi*, with bony skeleton, elongated, Pike-like shape, and Alligator-like jaws. The scales are big, diamond-shaped, and covered with s sturdy ganoine film. The fins are developed normally. The strongly extended jaws are equipped with many differently-shaped, strong, and pointed teeth. Probably the swimming bladder serves as an accessory respiratory organ. There is just one genus, the Fresh-water Gar or *Lepisosteus*, from North and Central America.

Lepisosteus: Fresh Water Gar.
Genus pertaining to the family of the Gars or *Lepisosteidae*. The systematical division of the genus is rather difficult, since there are many overlapping local varieties. We must refrain from listing the sub-species in this book.

Lepisosteus, type of the genus

— osseus Linné:
SHAPE: As per description of the family. D 7-9, A 8-9. The small dorsal fin inserts far back. Length up to 60″.
COLOR: Yellowish base with irregular spot designs. SD are unknown.
RANGE: Rivers and lakes of the U.S.A., only in fresh water.
CARE AND BREEDING: This fish of prey, of which only smaller specimens are fit for the home aquarium, but which is especially indicated for show aquaria, is absolutely undemanding as to warmth, and is otherwise quite undemanding. 60-68° F are sufficient. Feed them in the same way as all other fishes of prey. Also this fish takes only live food, preferentially fish.

— platostomus Rafinesque:
Similar species from the Southern U.S.A. and Mexico. Lengths up to 25″. 64-77° F.

— tristoechus Bloch and Schneider:
D 7-8, A 7-8. Length up to 120″. Very similar to all the other species.
ORIGIN: Southern U.S.A., Mexico, and Cuba. 68-75° F.

Lepomis: With scaly gill cover. Genus of North American sunfishes, belonging to the family of the *Centrarchidae*. Very enticing cold water fishes from the U.S.A., with a quite high-backed, laterally compressed body. Head and mouth openings are more or less big, cheeks and gill covers are scaly, the latter frequently provided with a skin extension, the so-called "ear". The dorsal fin divides into a spiny and a soft part, being generally relatively low.

Due to their size the fishes need roomy tanks, but are quite undemanding otherwise. Their enticing behavior, general pretty color, and the interesting manner of reproduction, should afford them more importance than they are enjoying at present. They may be kept at about 59-72° F. In winter the temperature may sink as low as 39° F. At 50° F, though, they begin to become sluggish, but may be kept unrestrictedly in unheated home aquaria. For the bottom choose not-too-rough, well-washed gravel. Plant with cold water plants, especially *Myriophyllum*. The plants may stand densely in the background and on the sides. To this add hiding-places of roots and stones. There must be sufficient space left, though. The fishes like to 'show off'. They are predators, even if not as pronounced ones as other fishes of prey. In case of need some of the species even take dry food. They do not like to have to pick their food from the bottom, though. No demands are made as to the composition of the water, but it must be clear and well-oxygenated.

The spawning period begins about April, at a water temperature of 64° F. Breeding is possible both in the home aquarium and under the open sky. The male woos very furiously, spreading his fins beautifully. He builds a big, shallow pit in the sand, among stones or plants. The female comes to this pit of her own free will when ripe for spawning. Then a couple of mock matings take place under swift gyrations. The real act of spawning is effected with the belly edges turned towards each other while gyrating slowly and waving the fins. In four to five matings, spaced about 10 minutes apart, a total of over 1000 eggs is expelled, falling into the pit and sticking to the sand. Now the female should be taken out. The male exerts the

Lepomis, type of the genus

more or less intensive care for the spawn alone. The fry hatch at about 71° F after about 3 days. After eight days they swim freely, having previously been able to leave the pit, and hanging around it from plants, etc. During this time the water level should be lowered to about 6-8″. The first foods consist of infusoria, rotatoria, and micro-foods. Soon the young will also take bigger-sized powdered food, mashed enchytrae, etc. The fry return occasionally to the nest, which is enlarged and kept clean by the male. During this period the male is very aggressive. The young generally are able to reproduce only in their third year, as they grow slowly, even under good feeding. The male becomes able to fertilize again only after eight weeks.

— **auritus** Linné: The Red-Breasted Bream.

SHAPE: As per description of the genus. D X-XI/11-12, A II/8-10. Length, in its home waters up to 11″, in the aquarium up to about 6″.

COLOR: Greenish to golden-yellow with numerous red and blue dots, of which the first change over into a strong orange color at the belly. The 'ear' is deep black. SD are minute, the male being more intensely colored during the spawning period, the female plumper.

RANGE: In cool, clear waters with sandy bottom in the East of the U.S.A., going south down to Louisiana, but not in the Mississippi Valley. The species is abundant all over its range.

CARE AND BREEDING: As per description of the genus.

— **cyanellus** Rafinesque: The Green Bream.

SHAPE: As per description of the genus. In youth not quite as high-backed as when older. Older specimens are especially short and fat, with the forehead line a little indented. The gill covers are only lightly extended backwards. D X-XI/10-11, A II/8-9. Length, in its home waters up to $6\frac{3}{8}$″, in the aquarium up to $4\frac{3}{4}$″.

COLOR: Not as vividly colored as the other species. Gray-violet with a brassy sheen, during the spawning period with a bluish dot on every scale, beneath this 7 to 8 washed-out cross bands. The 'ear' is only indicated by a black, gold-edged dot on the gill covers. SD are minute, the female being a little plumper during the spawning period.

CARE AND BREEDING: As per description of the genus. The fry grow rather quickly and may be ready to procreate after reaching two years of age.

— **gibbosus** Linné: The Common Sunfish.

SHAPE: As per description of the genus, the mouth relatively small. D X/10-12, A III/10-11. The 'ear' is only short. Length, in its native habitat up to 8″, in the aquarium only 6″.

COLOR: The color appears only after the third year. Blue-green to bluish with numerous red dots and dashes, and an orange-colored belly. Also the fins are beautifully colored. SD are minute, a red dot at the tip of the 'ear' being less intensely colored on the females.

RANGE: Eastern U.S.A., from the region of the Great Lakes to the Delta of the Mississippi. Quite abundant everywhere in clear, well-planted waters with sandy bottom.

Lepomis gibbosus

They have run wild in Bavaria, the Middle Rhine, and in the Oder region of Germany.

CARE AND BREEDING: As per description of the genus. The species needs still less warmth than the previously described ones. Only at 43-41° F do the fish begin to become sluggish. They do not care for their young for as long a period as *L. megalotis*.

— **megalotis** Rafinesque: The Big-eared Bream.

SHAPE: As per description of genus. The 'ear' is especially big. D X/10-12, A IV/8-10. Length, in its native habitat about 8″, in the aquarium up to 5″.

COLOR: Equally a quite colorful species, very similar to the previous one. Outside the spawning period the SD are negligible, during the said time the male becomes a little more colorful, the female plumper.

CARE AND BREEDING: As per description of the genus.

Leporinus: Derived from 'hare' (*Lepus*), probably referring to the shape of the mouth.

South American genus of Characin-like fishes belonging to the family of the Headstanders or *Anostomidae* of elongated and cylindrical build with a pointed head. The small mouth is provided with strong lips which permit grazing off plant growths. An adipose fin exists. The fishes are headstanders which like to dwell among vertical plants. In spite of temporary sluggishness, they may at times become very lively, and do especially well at jumping. The reproduction is unknown, but it is possible that a spawning migration takes place. Of the many species we shall only list the best-known.

— **affinis** Guenther:

A species from Northern South America, which reaches lengths up to 6″. The color is silver-gray with black cross stripes around the body. SD are unknown. Temperatures: 73-82° F. All kinds of bottom foods are taken, worms, larvae, detritus, but also algae growths. The species is completely harmless.

Leporinus fasciatus

— **fasciatus** Bloch:

Very similar to the previous species, ranging over tropical South America from the Orinoco in the North to the La Plata in the South. Length up to 6″. The number of rings around the body increases with age, being five at the beginning and growing up to ten later on. 72-81° F. Surprising ability to jump, up to 7 ft. out of the water.

— **melanopleura** Guenther:

SHAPE: As per description of the genus, relatively elongated. D 12-, A 11. Length up to over 8″.

COLOR: Greenish to reddish gloss with a metallic horizontal stripe.

RANGE: Brazil, South of the Amazon region.

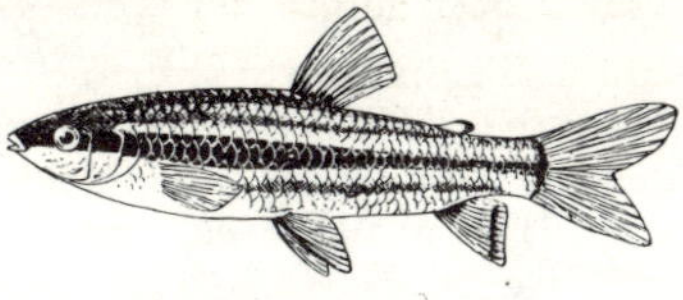

Leporinus melanopleura

CARE AND BREEDING: As per description of the genus. The species is relatively motile and is no pronounced headstander. It likes to stay near the bottom where it searches for food. It also needs vegetable food and takes artificial rations. The fish are peaceful and fit for community tanks.

— striatus Kner:

SHAPE: As per description of genus. D 10-12, A 9-10. Length up to about 10″.

COLOR: Only younger specimens are known, which possess some brown horizontal stripes of changeable intensity on a yellowish-brownish base.

RANGE: Northern tropical South America, East of the Andes.

CARE AND BREEDING: As per description of the genus. A vivacious, friendly, and gregarious species, which, like all *Leporini*, needs rich feeding. It likes warmth, 75-82° F being adequate. During the spawning period the fish are very nervous, and it is possible that in nature they migrate to fixed spawning grounds.

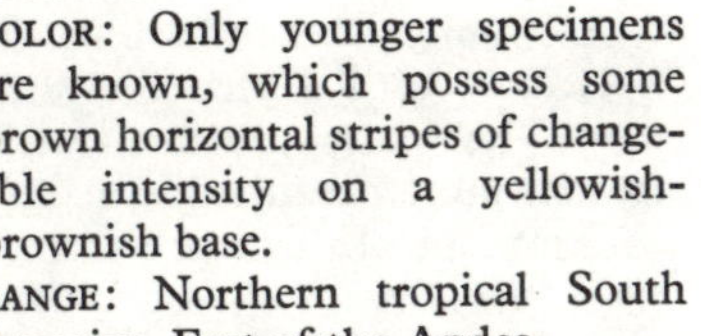

Leporinus striatus

Leptagoniates: Small *Agoniates* (another genus of Characins).
South American genus belonging to the family of the Characins or *Characidae*, of very elongated shape, strongly compressed laterally, and glassy transparency.

— steindachneri Boulenger:

SHAPE: As per description of the genus, with the small mouth opening directed upward. The lateral line is complete and the adipose fin exists. D 10, A 70-75. Length, a little over 4″.

COLOR: Silvery green with a shiny whitish horizontal stripe.

RANGE: The Upper Amazon, also in Peru and Ecuador.

CARE AND BREEDING: The species likes roomy, sunny, not too densely planted tanks with plenty of room for exercising. The fish are nimble swimmers, but occasionally slightly quarrelsome. They take all kinds of foods, as long as it corresponds to their size. Breeding has not yet been achieved.

Leptagoniates steindachneri

Leptodoridae: Glass Crustaceans. Family of predatory small crustaceans belonging to the sub-order of the *Daphnia* or *Cladocera*. Totally transparent animals, which are seen only because of their motion and of their big, darker-colored eyes, when superficially observed. The Glass Crustacean, *Leptodora kindtii*, which grows up to $\frac{3}{8}$″ in length, is one of the biggest German *Cladocera*. The body is elongated, naked, with only a small protected brood space on the back. The pectoral legs are long, articulated, and insert far to the front, near the head. Motion is achieved by rowing with the long, strong antennae. Their prey, mostly daphnia and cyclops, is seen with the big, closely-set eyes, and seized with the preying legs.

Leptolucania: Dwarf *Lucania* (*Lucania* is another genus of Tooth Carps).

North American genus of Tooth Carps pertaining to the sub-family of the egg laying Tooth Carps or *Cyprinodontinae*. It is related to the genus *Fundulus* from which it differs only in small points, such as, for instance, the shorter dorsal fin.

Leptolucania omata, male above

— omata Jordan: The Swamp Killie.

SHAPE: Of elongated and slender build, with big, vivacious eyes and small mouth, provided with small, pointed teeth. D 6-7, A 9-10. Length: males $1\frac{3}{8}''$, females $1\frac{5}{8}''$.

COLOR: Yellow-brown with a blue sheen, the male occasionally with a number of dark cross sttipes on the rear of the body. In all, the male is a little more colorful. Both sexes possess a dark, light-edged dot on the caudal peduncle, the female a second one over the origin of the anal fin.

RANGE: In small waters in the South of the U.S.A.

CARE AND BREEDING: The species is peaceful and gregarious, and is especially lively in company. The jolting manner of swimming, consisting of calm, often-interrupted spurts, is remarkable. No special demands are made as to the size of the tank. Clear water, low level, and a mulmy bottom enhance their well-being. The species is considered as a little in need of warmth. Temperatures around 75° F are advisable, and under direct sunlight they may rise considerably higher. The fish take all kinds of small live foods. Otherwise care and breeding correspond roughly to those of the smaller species of *Aphyosemion*. The eggs are laid on plants and roots near the bottom. They are a little sensitive, but rearing the young is said not to be difficult.

leptos: Lean, thin, narrow.
— *Acentronichthys*.

leptosoma: With frail body.
— *Rasbora*.

leptostachyus:
— *Aponogeton*.

Leucaspius: Shiny white.

Genus of school fishes belonging to the family of the Carplike or *Cyprinidae*, with a very elongated body. The scales are moderately big, and fall off easily. The mouth is supraterminal. The gullet teeth are disposed in two rows. The lateral line is incomplete.

— delineatus (Sieb):

SHAPE: As per description of the genus. D 11, A 14-16. The lateral line pierces only up to 12 scales. The belly outline of the male is often a little indented, so that the fish seems to have been subject to malnutrition. Length up to $3\frac{1}{8}''$.

COLOR: Silvery, the male showing a spawning rash during the spawning period.

RANGE: From the Volga to Eastern France and Belgium, in ditches, puddles, shallow ponds, and lakes, often in schools and small groups.

CARE AND BREEDING: A simply colored, hardy, easy-to-keep, and pretty fish. A skilled swimmer. It needs medium-sized tanks with hiding-places among plants and room for exercising. In a normally stocked aquarium aeration is unnecessary. Remember that fishes from small puddles often are less in need of oxygen than others from bigger waters.

The species is very well adapted for the cold water aquarium due to its liveliness and to its interesting manner of caring for the spawn. The female releases 80-150 eggs in spirals, one after the other, on plant stems, and the male watches over them till the fry hatch. The young hang from a small thread for several days. The male keeps the spawning stem in motion with its snout. Rearing them is as easy as for all Cyprinids.

Leuciscus: Shiny white.

Genus of school fishes belonging to the family of the Carp-like or *Cyprinidae*, of slender build. The gullet teeth stand in a simple row, the central belly region is rounded.

— grislagine Linné:

SHAPE: As per description of the genus. The mouth is subterminal, the snout a little protuberant. D 10, A 11-12. Length up to 10″.

COLOR: Silvery.

RANGE: From the region of the Ob river over Central Europe to the Pyrenees, in flowing waters.

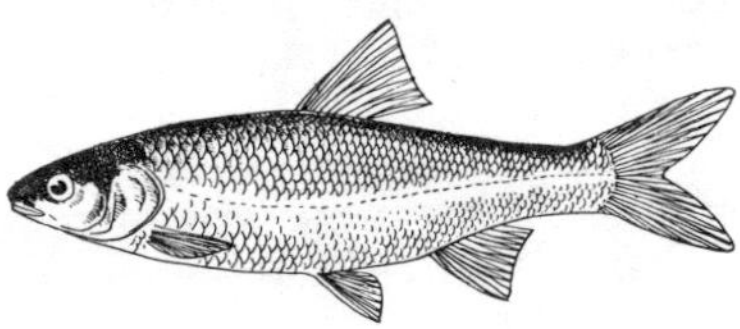

Leuciscus grislagine

CARE AND BREEDING: A rare fish that is a very skilled swimmer, and is found in lakes. It likes a firm, stony bottom, but also keeps willinglynear the surface. Omnivorous. Smaller specimens are easy to keep in the aquarium, in clear, cool water, and with good aeration.

— rutilus Linné: The Red Bream.

SHAPE: As per description of the genus. D 12-14, A 12-14. The lateral line is nearly complete, the small mouth being terminal to supraterminal. Length up to 16″.

COLOR: Silvery, the iris a vivid red, the fins brownish-red.

RANGE: From Siberia to Central France, also in the brackish waters of the Baltic Sea. It likes planted, shallow, and clear waters.

CARE AND BREEDING: Easily kept in the aquarium if afforded clear water and good aeration.

Leuciscus leuciscus: see LEUCISCUS GRISLAGINE.

levis: The rising (from the water). — *Pterodiscus.*

life stages: Clearly defined stages of the development in the individual, usually taking place at the onset of maturity. The juvenile stage indicates individuals of all animal groups which have not yet attained maturity, and do not undergo a distinct metamorphosis. The juvenile forms more or less resemble the adult form, but possess distinct signs which are lost as age increases. Only in a few cases is there a distinct metamorphosis at the beginning of development. Here we have to name for example the larval stage of almost all fishes. This is usually identified by unevenly developed body forms, the result being that the growth of the various body parts is varied, depending on their use. For instance, all juvenile stages possess large heads and poorly developed joints in the first stages of their development. In many cases there is also a protective coloration, shown in young fishes as a glassy transparency or a form-concealing striping, sprinkling, or the like. Very different also are the life requirements and living habits of the two life stages.

The adult life stage usually begins with the onset of sexual maturity, characterized by colorations in conditions of excitement, adult colors, and secondary sex

markings.
lima: File.
— *Sorubim.*
lime: see HARDNESS OF WATER.
limi: Of the mud.
— *Umbra.*
Limia: The origin of the name is not completely clear.
Genus of Tooth Carps belonging to the sub-family of the live bearing Tooth Carps or *Poeciliinae.*

Small fishes, only in part of elongated build, partly also of quite high and compact shape. The different species of *Limia* are peaceful and hardy, but need some warmth. They have to have complementary vegetable food. Breeding is achieved as for all live bearing tooth Carps.

— caudofasciata Regan:
SHAPE: As per description of genus, relatively elongated, but the caudal peduncle of the male is rather high. D 8-10, A 11. Length: males up to 1¾″, females up to 2½″.
COLOR: Olive-brownish with a wide row of dark, glossy little spots along the sides, at the caudal peduncle some vaguely defined cross bands, the belly yellowish to golden-yellow. The male shows an arched stripe on the dorsal fin, the female a dark spot at the base of same.
RANGE: On Jamaica and Haiti, occasionally also on Cuba.

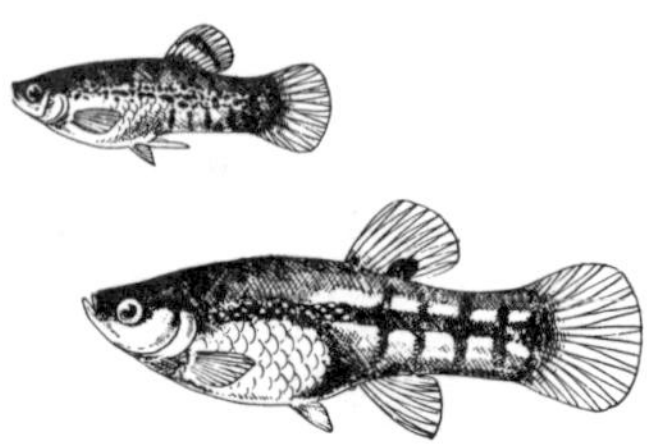

Limia caudofasciata

CARE AND BREEDING: As per description of the genus. A very peaceful and hardy species, which keeps best at 72-77° F, but which is not very sensitive to occasional lower temperatures. The female bears 60 or more young, on which she preys strongly. They need abundant feeding, occasionally also plant food, and grow very quickly, being ready to procreate at the age of 8-9 weeks.

— caudofasciata, var. tricolor: see LIMIA MELANOGASTER.

— heterandria Regan: The Dwarf Limia.
SHAPE: As per description of the genus. A small and slender species. D 8, A 9. Length: males 1¼″, females 1⅝″.
COLOR: On a yellowish base the male carries three narrow cross bands, while the female possesses a faded horizontal stripe. Remarkable is the big pregnancy spot and a dark spot on the dorsal fin of the female. The male has a golden yellow belly and two arched-shaped, dark lines with an orange colored interstice on the dorsal fin.
RANGE: Haiti, where it is probably restricted to a closely-limited region.
CARE AND BREEDING: As per description of the genus and of the previous species. Also *L. heterandria* requires very varied board, and temporary vegetable food. The 20-50 young fry are very sensitive. It seems that they need a sunlit location for their well-being.

— melanogaster Guenther: The Blackbellied Limia.
SHAPE: As per description of the genus. D 8-9, A 8-9. Length: males up to 1¾″, females up to about 2⅜″.
COLOR: Gray-yellowish base with a few dark cross bands at the end of the body. The body covered with a bluish sheen. The male is characterized by a black corner at the

Limia melanogaster

Limia nigrofasciata

caudal peduncle, the black edges of the fins and the orange colored dorsal, while the female has a remarkably big, dark-blue pregnancy spot.

RANGE: Generally in small, flowing waters on Jamaica.

CARE AND BREEDING: As per description of the genus. The male is especially insistent. The pairs chase very quickly through the aquarium, the female trying to hide at the bottom among stones, etc. The twenty to fifty fry may already be able to propagate after about four months. but the males need much longer a time until they develop full colors.

— **nigrofasciata** Regan: The Hunchbacked *Limia*.

SHAPE: As per description of the genus, but the body very high. Especially older males increase so remarkably in height, that, compared with younger specimens, they seem completely altered. D 8-9, A 9. Length: males up to 2″, females up to $2\frac{3}{8}$″.

COLOR: Young fish and males carry many irregular dark cross bands on an olive-colored base. The lower side is yellowish. Older males are glossy greenish, yellow on the belly, breast and belly edge deep black, with the spines of the dorsal fin black too. Many shiny greenish spots are scattered over the bands.

RANGE: In waters of all kinds on Haiti, even in brackish waters. The fish appear in great swarms in their home waters.

CARE AND BREEDING: As per description of the genus. Very especially in need of warmth. Lowest 68° F. They need varied food, especially vegetable food. At 77° F pregnancy lasts for about five to six weeks. The fry measure $\frac{3}{8}$″ to $\frac{1}{2}$″ at birth, and have to be reared with loving care, being very fond of sunlight.

Limia ornata

— **ornata** Regan:
SHAPE: As per description of the genus. D 8-10, A 10. Length: males 1⅜″, females up to about 2⅜″.
COLOR: Yellowish-olive base seeded with numerous black and luminous green dots.
RANGE: Haiti.
CARE AND BREEDING: As per description of the genus. Much in need of warmth too. 77° F and more are advisable. This species too needs additional plant food, especially soft algae. The 5 to 35 young need plenty of warmth and sunlight if they are to thrive. It is reported that the species is sensitive to changes of water or of the tank, and also that generally they are a little shy.

— **vittata** Guichenot:
SHAPE: As per description of the genus, relatively compact, the caudal peduncle especially high. D 9-11, A 10. Length: males up to 2½″, females up to 4″.
COLOR: Greenish-yellow base with a narrow dark horizontal stripe, which is crossed by several cross bands. Under incident light there is a blue sheen. The fins are a pretty orange color with dark designs.
RANGE: In smaller waters on Cuba, both in fresh and brackish water.
CARE AND BREEDING: As per description of genus. This species too loves warmth and sunlight. They are very productive. According to INNES a female in an aquarium in Chicago gave birth to 242 young.

Limia vittata

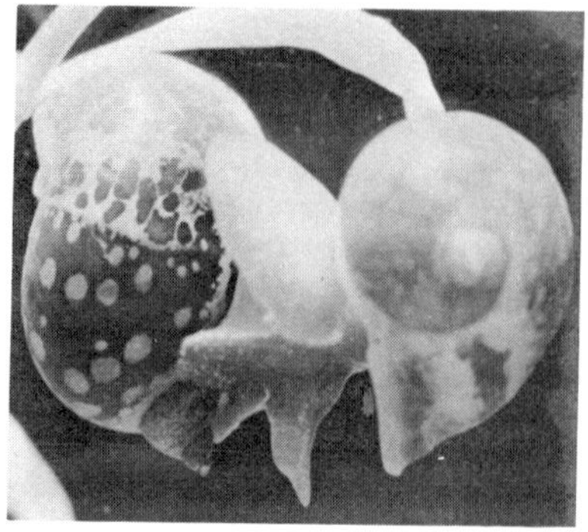

Radix auricularia

Limnaeidae: Mud snails.
Family of fresh water snails belonging to the sub-order of the lung snails or *Pulmonata*, and to the order of the *Basommatophora*. Of very diversified shell construction; even within the same species there are numerous shapes according to living environment. Under certain circumstances each body of water may harbor especially developed shapes. The shell is thin, hornlike, and has a sharp-edged opening. The body is sharply divided from the foot, the antennae are flattened or cylindrical. The shell rises to a conical point. As lung snails the *L.* must from time to time rise to the surface for the intake of air. Reproduction is difficult to systematize as both self-fertilization and alternate insemination occur. The spawn is laid on the underside of aquatic plants, protected by a layer of jelly. The period of development totals about 3 weeks, the young being able to reproduce after a year. The length of the shell of the big species may reach up to 2⅜″.

They are distributed over Europe, Asia, and North America. In the aquarium mud snails are unwelcome guests, unless kept in special jars to study their manner

Limnaea stagnalis

of living. They are vigorous eaters, and attack even sturdy plants. It is rumored that they are exterminators of hydras, but must be considered useless for this as, together with the hydra they also eat the plant on which it sits. The species *Radix peregra* secretes a poison, which, if a bigger number of snails is concentrated, may act lethally on fishes. Furthermore the mud snails may be carriers of parasitic worms. Genera: *Limnaea*, *Galba*, and *Radix*.

The best known mud snail is *Limnaea stagnalis* Linné, the Big Mud Snail, or Pronghorn Snail. It is found in standing and flowing waters, especially in soft, warm waters with plenty of plant growths. If the latter are not available the snails develop stunted shapes. The spawn is eliminated in sausage-shaped bundles measuring up to 2⅜″. Hatching time for the eggs is up to 30 days. The Liver-leech Snail, *Galba truncatula*, is the intermediate host for the larvae of the Liver Leech, which causes liver decay in cattle, sheep, and goats.

Limnobium: Living in the swamp. Genus of floating plants belonging to the family of the Frogbits or *Hydrocharitaceae*.

stoloniferum (Meyer) Grisebach: South American Frogbit.

GENERALITIES: This beautiful, perennial floating plant with its heart-shaped leaves, sponge-like thickened on the underside, is generally known as *Trianea bogotensis*.

SHAPE: The heart-shaped leaves sit on short stems and form a rosette. The roots are long and hairy. Multiplication is achieved through shoots.

RANGE: The species is widely distributed over the tropical regions of South America. There it is found on the surface of standing waters or in the bights of lakes and rivers.

CULTIVATION: Protect the plants in the aquarium against too intense sunlight, as they easily become "burned". They like a well-lit location, where even in winter they decrease little. In warm summers they may also be cultivated under the open sky. Soft water and temperatures between 72 and 82° F are favorable. In order to create a moist-warm atmosphere, the tanks should be covered, but the plants have to be protected against precipitations of water.

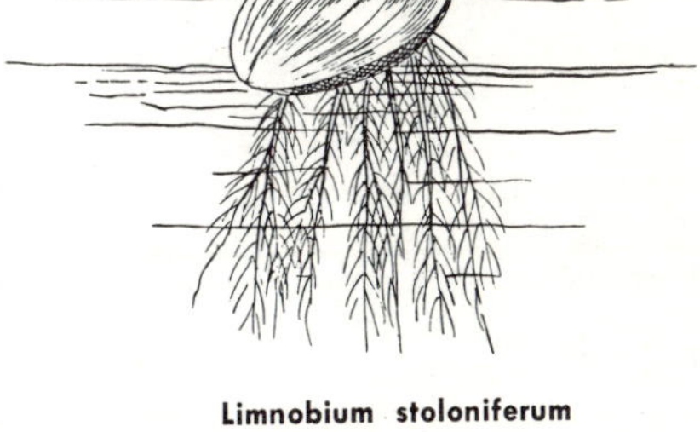

Limnobium stoloniferum

Limnocharis: Monarch of the swamp.

Genus belonging to the family of the *Butomaceae*.

— flava (Linné) Buchanan:

This swamp plant, which grows to relatively big sizes, resembles *Echinodorus*. The yellow flowers stand above the surface in a mock umbrella.

The species with a series of sub-species ranges over Central and South America, one sub-species being said to be found in Siam and Java. It is very useful for tropical swamp aquaria, in which it even blooms if afforded a low water level and moist, warm air. It is unfit for cultivation in open aquaria, as it does not like the dry air of our rooms.

limnology: Science of the inland bodies of water. L. studies the physical and chemical properties of same, as well as their living inhabitants. Limnology and aquaristics have many points in common.

Limnophila: Friend of the swamp. Genus of aquatic plants pertaining to the family of the *Scrophulariaceae*. They are perennial plants, generally cultivated submergedly in the aquarium, which under superficial observation are quite similar to the different species of *Cabomba*. At present about thirty species are known, of which, though, only three are being cultivated in our aquaria. The leaves are either opposite, or else they stand in verticils around the stem. At low water levels and during flowering time differently shaped aerial leaves are developed in the corners of which the small, nearly stemless flowers insert in pairs or in slightly bigger groups. They are white, or delicately purple to rose-colored. The plants may be considered undemanding if one does not take into account that to thrive well they have to have plenty of light. If this is not

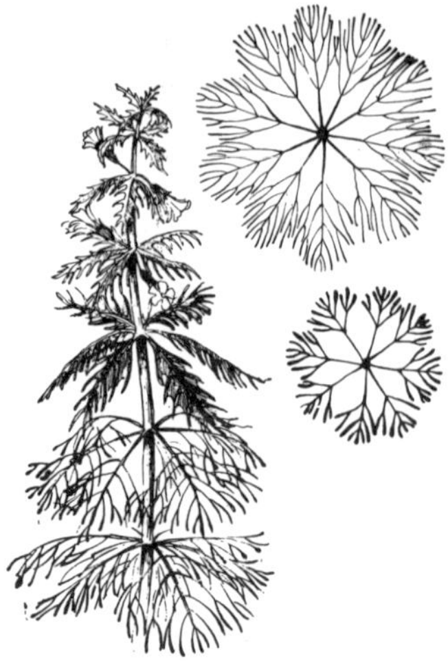

Limnophila, leaf rosettes at right

available, or if one wants to avoid an over-abundant growth of algae, it is more or less possible to help matters with artificial lighting. This is especially the case in winter. For a bottom ground use unwashed sand, which possibly may be mixed with some broken-up clay. Apparently the plants grow better in soft water, but also in waters of medium hardness very favorable results have been achieved. The temperature should not sink below 68° F even in winter, while in summer 77° F and more are most favorable. It is advisable not to aerate the tank, as the mulm stirred up by this settles within the feathered leaves and causes the plants to die. The delicate leaves are willingly taken as food by plant eating fishes, but it has to be pointed out that *L. gratioloides* exudes an actively poisonous secretion which may lead to losses. Wintering of the plants is either done under sufficient artificial lighting in the aquarium itself, or else in small, separate tanks, near windows, for which, according to WENDT, already in late summer tips of stems have to be cut, planted in small pots, and cultivated under moist-warm air as emerged plants. These little pots are put into saucers with sphagnum. For many years the different species of *Limnophila* have been offered as *Ambulia*.

— gratioloides Brown:

GENERALITIES: This species is the most beautiful of all *Limnophilae* cultivated in aquaria, but due to its toxicity it should be handled with a certain caution.

SHAPE: As per description of the genus. The leaves are very finely divided, light green, and stand around the stem in multiple verticils. The emerged leaves are very different in shape. The flowers are white, light purple, or slightly rose-colored. The stems are hairless.

RANGE: Southeast Asia, the Sunda Islands, parts of Australia, and Tropical Africa. There the plants are found in shallow, quiet waters of all kinds, as for instance on the banks of rivers and lakes, in inlets, swamps, and flood regions with changeable water level.

CULTIVATION: As per description of the genus. The plants grow very quickly. Since they are poisonous it is advisable not to do any cutting or trimming in the aquarium, nor to cause them any other lesions. If multiplication is required, cut them, putting the twigs in a saucer with fresh water which is changed from time to time to wash away the venom. Experience shows that the toxicity is strongest in the plants that show the lushest vegetation.

— heterophylla Bentham:

Also this species has submerged leaves that are very finely feathered and stand around the stem in multiple verticils. The aerial leaves are toothed around the edge, and narrowly lanceolate. The flowers are white. The stem is hairless. According to WENDT the plant was frequently offered for sale before World War I (in Germany). After this it disappeared again from the aquaria, and has only lately returned to the market without having been possible to verify the exactitude of the name of the species.

— sessiliflora Blume:

Similar to *L. gratioloides*, but not poisonous. The stem of this species is covered with thin downy hairs, while that of the previous species is smooth.

ORIGIN: India, Japan, Ceylon, the Sunda Island, in the same locations as *L. gratioloides*. Cultivation too is the same for both species.

lineata: Lined, striped.

— *Jenynsia*.

lineatus: Lined, striped.

— *Aplocheilus*.

— *Barbus* (*Puntius*).

— *Esomus*.

Linné, Charles de: 1707-1778. Swedish physician and botanist who founded modern systematics. He introduced the manner of naming live beings with two words that is the present-day binary nomenclature, representing a scientific denomination which permits classing the species in genera. Linné created the first comprehensive and efficient system for classifying plants and animals.

Lipoids: Vitally important chemical compounds, located in the chloroplasts of plants and near the surface of the cell plasma, being soluble in the same manner as the fats. The lipoids play a role in the choice of food substances taken in by cells.

Little Hare, Hareling: see LEUCISCUS GRISLAGINE.

Little Lancet Fish, the: see ACRANIA.

littoral: The shore region of waters. At the sea-shore also the tidal region.

littorale: Shore-dweller.

— *Hoplosternum.*

Live-Bearing Tooth Carps: see POECILIINAE.

Loaches, Gudgeons, Groundlings: see COBITIDAE.

Lobelia: After the English botanist L'Obell.

Genus of swamp plants belonging to the family of the blue-bells or *Campanulaceae.*

— cardinalis Linné: Cardinal Lobelia, Scarlet Lobelia.

GENERALITIES: In its emerged form a well-known ornamental plant, which lately has been cultivated also submergedly and thus has found admittance into the aquarium.

SHAPE: The submerged form strongly resembles the different species of *Ludwigia.* The vigorous stems stand upright, the elongated to rounded-oval leaves, which are somewhat changeable in shape, are placed alternately on more or less long stalks. The leaves have lengths varying from $\frac{3}{4}''$ to $2\frac{3}{8}''$, and widths from $\frac{3}{8}''$ to $\frac{5}{8}''$, ending in a short, blunt tip, but they may also be rounded. The flowers, which generally form scarlet clusters, develop only at low water levels.

Lobelia cardinalis

RANGE: In swampy spots of the temperate regions of the North American continent.

CULTIVATION: Similar to that of the different species of the genus *Ludwigia.* They like to receive an intense illumination, if possible even plenty of sunlight. In order to thrive they need a thick layer of rough-grained sand, abundantly mixed with old clay. Multiplication is only achieved by means of broken-off pieces of the plant, which are set in the sand in order to grow new specimens. Flowers generally develop only if the plants are cultivated under the open sky.

— dortmanna Linne: Water Lobelia.

GENERALITIES: This species is only rarely found in aquaria, as it is not especially rugged.

SHAPE: Over a compact root stock *L. dortmanna* develops a pretty rosette of ribbon-shaped, blunt-tipped submerged leaves. These are fleshy and relatively stiff, the tips generally being a little bent downwards. The leaves, which may number up to twenty-five, reach lengths of up to 4″, and widths of up to 2″. At low water level from the middle of these leaves rises the flower stock on a vigorous stem, growing above the surface. This flower stock bears 3 to 12 purple or white flowers. The plant is perennial and lives exclusively submerged.

RANGE: Europe and North America at the bottom of ponds and lakes, also in moors and swamps, everywhere at very low water levels.

CULTIVATION: *L. d.* grows during the whole year. It is impossible, though, to keep it alive in the aquarium for several years. According to WENDT in the first place it needs light from above. For a bottom, supply not too thin sand, with an admixture of some clay.

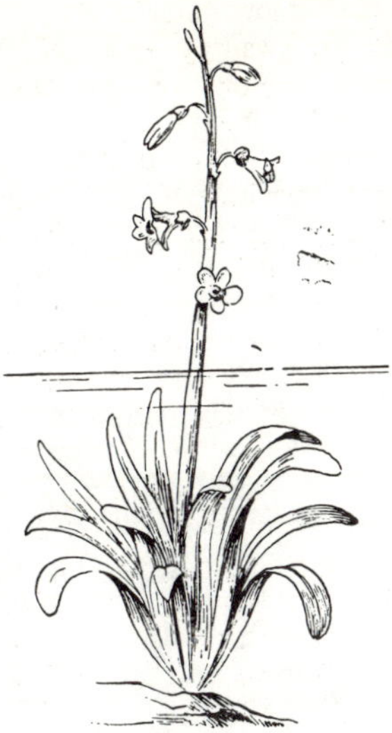

Lobelia dortmanna

Multiplication through seeds is hardly used, as re-planting the lateral shoots is much easier.

locating the aquarium: The location of the aquarium depends on its purpose and on the vital demands of the animals and plants that are kept in it.

Fundamentally an aquarium should always be placed upon a firm, unshakeable base, such as, for instance, a firm table, a support made of angle steel, or, in case of several tanks, a firm trestle of wood or of angle steel. The latter is preferable as its metallic parts do not warp and, being narrower, throw less shadow. When setting up the tanks, pay attention to the fact that the floor beneath it is as firm as possible and does not tremble. Whenever possible, bigger installations should be set up in such a way that they stand directly over the supporting beams of the floor. When setting up jumbo-sized tanks and installations, it may perhaps become necessary to take special steps in order to support the base. Trestles which stand near a wall should be slightly tilted towards same, hooking them firmly to it. As a rule too bright sunlight is not favorable to plants. It aids the development of algae and may cause disagreeable changes in the chemistry of the water or other harm. Therefore it is not advisable, as a rule, to locate aquaria so that they receive southern light (except for fishes that like plenty of sunlight). If it is impossible to keep a certain distance from windows facing the South, the intense sunlight should at least be dampened by curtains or drapes, by covering the lighted sides with white, reddish, or green tissue paper, or else by whitewashing the lighted sides of the aquarium. Furthermore one may also use floating plants in thick layers to fulfill this purpose. So far the most favorable location for aquaria has proved to be near a window facing towards the East, or, if necessary, one facing the West. In such locations the aquarium receives the most desirable sunning, which lasts only for a few hours, while animals and plants that need shadow may be protected by special coverings. At windows facing the North one will have to restrict the stocking of the aquarium to a selection of certain animals and plants, as the loss of light may be considerable, especially in narrow streets.

It is true, however, that many faults of locating the aquarium may today be corrected to a large extent by the use of artificial lighting. For this reason it is possible to keep aquaria successfully even in dark rooms, far from any windows, such as, for instance, a reading nook, without any incidence of daylight.

Whenever possible, set up the aquarium so that the fishes are seen under incident light. Most fishes either possess iridescent colors, which can only be seen if under this kind of light, or else they are strongly translucent. Therefore, if you choose to locate the tank in close proximity to a window, for instance, on a window sill, this will often result in the advantage of intense lighting for the plants, and furthermore fishes that love sunlight will feel especially well, but you will have to give up seeing the real colors. You will have to consider completely different points of view if, for instance, you aim at a certain goal, such as breeding fishes that prefer to spawn under the morning sun, or growing plants that need sunlight in order to bloom and to produce seeds.

All-glass tanks should be placed on a soft base. Frame aquaria should never rest with their whole underside on a flat surface, it being preferable to slip two or three narrow pieces of wood under them in order to make them stand free. This makes surveillance easier and prevents the frame from accompanying all movements of the support.

lohachata: After the native name.
— *Botia.*

Long-Finned Characin, the African: see BRYCONALESTES LONGIPINNIS.

longianalis: With long anal fin.
— *Marcusenius.*

longiloba: With long-lobed leaves.
— *Sagittaria.*

longipinnis: With long fins.
— *Bryconalestes.*
— *Pterolebias.*

longirostra: Long-beaked.
— *Sagittaria.*

longistylus: With long shaft or stem.
— *Echinodorus.*

lönnbergi: After the Swedish ichthyologist Lönnberg.
— *Aphyosemion.*
— *Mastocembelus.*

loretonensis: After the place called Loreto, on the Upper Amazon.
— *Hyphessobrycon.*

Loricaria: Bearer of breast armor. South American genus of Catfishes pertaining to the family of the Armored Catfishes or *Loricariidae.* Fishes of slender shape with big heads and complete armor. The eyes are moderately small; the sides of the head of the males carry bristles. The snout is pointed, the mouth subterminal, the lips protractile and often provided with nodules and fringed edges. The underside of the head is naked. The belly is covered with numerous small bone plates. No adipose fins are present. The caudal peduncle is thin and threadlike.

The genus comprises a whole series of species, of which so far only a few have become aquarium dwellers. They generally are twilight or nocturnal fishes, which hang motionless from rocks or glass panes where they have sucked fast. Only at the beginning of night do they become lively. Some of the species need clear, oxygen-rich, and profusely aerated water. Otherwise hardy, enduring, and undemanding. Food consists of parts of plants, especially algae, live and dead bottom foods, and detritus.

— lanceolata Guenther:
Amored Catfish from the Upper Amazon. Keep at 68-77° F.

— microlepidogaster Regan: The Witch Loricaria.
This species, coming from the State of Rio Grande do Sul, Brazil, is very similar to *L. parva*, but differs from it externally by brighter colors and the lack of the bands from eyes to mouth. Keep at 68-77° F. Breeding as described for *L. parva.*

— parva Boulenger: The Whiptail.
SHAPE: As per description of the

Loricaria parva

genus. D I/7, A I/5. Length up to 5″.

COLOR: Yellow-brownish with indistinct cross bands and spots. SD finally have become known positively after observation during breeding. The males of all species of the genus have whiskery skin excrescences at the sides of the head, which appear especially plainly during the spawning period and which are also found on the pectorals during that time. According to FRANKE the male may also be recognized by its round, pestle-shaped head, while that of the female is more triangular.

RANGE: In swift-flowing, clear waters of Paraguay and the La Plata region.

CARE AND BREEDING: As per description of the genus. Close observations of this species are available, it having been bred with success in captivity. Apparently the males are quite rare. FRANKE gives this as the reason why for such a long time attempts at breeding did not succeed. Both partners clean a rock or something similar as a spawning site. The act of spawning generally takes place at night. During it the male sucks fast behind the pectoral fin of the female. The eggs have a diameter of about 2 mm. Details of the mating could not be verified. The male cares for the eggs until they hatch, after about 7-9 days. During this time it lies closely on the eggs and does not eat. Rearing the relatively big fry is difficult, probably due to lack of appropriate food. Consequently they are rather frail. HAEUSERMANN introduced a spawning of 50-60 eggs, together with the stone onto which it was fastened, into an all-glass tank filled with strongly aerated, acid peat water. The male that was caring for the brood had sucked fast on the eggs and only released them after the stone was taken from the water. After 9-11 days 50-60 Whiptail fry were hanging from the glass. Feeding was done with chopped tubifex. A third of the water was changed daily. After four weeks the young measured $1\frac{1}{8}''$ to $1\frac{5}{8}''$ in length and were already able to eat whole tubifex.

Loricariidae: Armored Catfishes. South American family of Catfishes belonging to the sub-order of the *Siluroidea*, characterized by having the skin totally covered with bony plates. Only the members of one sub-family, the *Argiinae*, so far not represented in our aquaria, are unarmored. The Armored Cats are greatly compressed from above, part of them being wider than high. The armor is of complex structure. They may have an adipose fin or not, it being supported by a strong spike if present. The fishes are mainly plant eaters. Consequently the intestine is very long and rolled up in spirals. The swimming bladder is only small and protected by a bone shell. The mouth is subterminal and transformed into a sucking apparatus, with the aid of which the fishes may both resist currents and go after food. They feed nearly exclusively on plants, as a rule on algae, but also on animal and plant growths. The fishes are mainly inhabitants of swift-flowing, clear waters, but they do not totally avoid stagnant ones. Even in the most violent currents they hold on by means of their sucking discs, to a point that frequently it is impossible to get them off their anchorage without causing them harm. The gill slits are located on the under side of the head.

In mountainous country the Armored Cats are found in heights up to 9000 ft. Genera, among others: *Ancistrus, Farlowella, Loricaria, Otocinclus, Plecostomus,* and *Xenocara.*

loricatus: Armored.

— *Phago.*

lower aquatic animals: In aquaristics a collective name for all species of mono- or multicellular invertebrate animals, the keeping of which in aquaria may be of interest, or which may be related otherwise to aquaristics as live foods or as parasites.

These animals offer a great number of possibilities for observation which the real friend of nature should not miss, especially as in most cases they may be acquired free of cost, and they may always be lodged in auxiliary glasses or jars. Look up the following entries, under which particulars of the different groups are found: *Protozoa,* or Unicellulars; *Sporangiae,* or Sponges; *Coelenterata,* or Hollow Animals; several worm-like animals (see WORMS); *Mollusca,* or Molluscs; *Crustacea,* or Crustaceans; *Chelicerata,* or Spiders; *Hexapoda,* or Insects.

lucas-bahi: Origin of name unknown.

— *Botia.*

lucens: Shiny, luminous.

— *Potamogeton.*

lucidus: Light, luminous.

— *Alburnus.*

Luciocephalidae: Pike-heads. Family belonging to the sub-order of the *Anabantoidea,* which takes a special place within same. For this reason HOEDEMAN proposes to separate the Pike-heads totally from the Climbing Perches and to incorporate them in a special sub-order. The family comprises only one sub-species, of quite elongated, nearly cylindrical shape, with a remarkably big, elongated head and a very long snout. The big, deeply-cleft mouth is equipped with small, cone-shaped teeth. There is no swimming bladder. The accessory respiratory organ is different from that of the Anabantids, as it seems that the Pike-heads have mouth cavity breathing. Excepting the ventral, all other fins are constituted exclusively of soft rays. Only the first hard ray of the ventral is extended.

Luciocephalus: The Pike-Head. Only genus belonging to the family of the *Luciocephalidae,* with only one species.

— **pulcher** Gray: The Pike-Head.

SHAPE: As per description of the family. D 9-12, A 18-19. Length up to 7″.

COLOR: Yellowish base with some dark horizontal bands and stripes.

SD have not yet been firmly determined; they should probably be sought in the differentiated construction of the anal fin.

RANGE: Malaya, Sumatra, Borneo.

CARE AND BREEDING: The Pike-Head is a predatory surface fish which in nature is found both in flowing and standing waters. Prey that swims along is ambushed from hiding places among aquatic plants, being seized in quick rushes. Keeping them is very difficult, obviously because it has been impossible to imitate their natural habitat in the aquarium. The fish need plenty of warmth and are very frail. Reproduction is not yet clearly explained, and spawning them in the aquarium has not yet been achieved. The supposition that they might be live-bearers has not yet been confirmed. It rather seems that they are mouthbreeders, like the species of fighting fishes that live in flowing waters. According to present experience it seems advisable to cause agitation

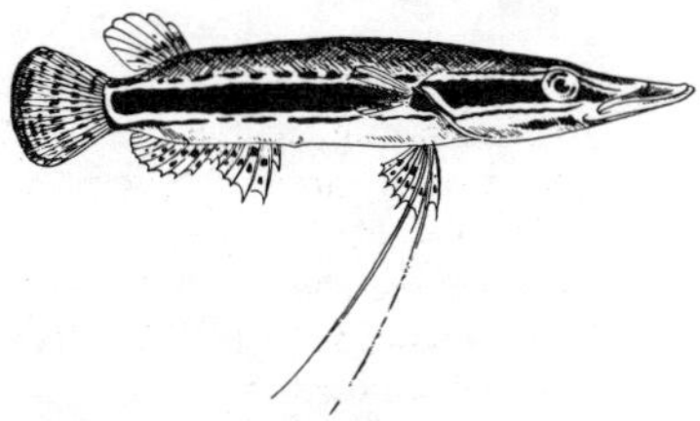

Luciocephalus pulcher

of the water in the tank by strong aeration or filtering, as this possibly contributes to the well-being of the fish. For successful keeping, big aquaria are a must. Even if very hungry the Pike-Head hardly ever eats micro-crustaceans. Five to six full-grown Guppy females are easily devoured at one setting.

Lucioperca: Pike Perch.
Genus of Perches belonging to the family of the real Perches or *Percidae.*

— lucioperca Linné: The Pike Perch.

SHAPE: Elongated body, little compressed laterally. The mouth opening is wide, dentition consisting of small velvet teeth with some pointed predatory teeth and interspersed smaller, pointed teeth. D_1 XIV, D_2 21-22, A 13. Length 25-35″.

COLOR: Gray base with faded cross bands which may disappear completely, and some darker spots and stripes on the fins.

RANGE: Central and Northern Europe. Being a food fish, it has been scattered far beyond its home region. The Pike-Perch prefers deep, murky, standing and flowing waters, especially lakes. A pronounced fresh water fish.

CARE AND BREEDING: Well fit for the cold water aquarium, if smaller specimens are kept, especially because young fish do not need as much oxygen as older ones. Being a predator, it takes live foods only. Keep them well aerated. Breeding them in the home aquarium is impossible. The fish spawn at shallow places near shores where the male digs shallow holes and guards the eggs.

Lucioperca sandra: see LUCIOPERCA LUCIOPERCA.

Luciosoma: With Pike-like body. Genus of Southeast Asiatic school fishes belonging to the family of the Carp-like or *Cyprinidae,* with a big mouth directed upwards. The barbels are short or even stunted to the point of insignificance. Up to the present day four species are known which range over Thailand and Indonesia.

— spilopleura (Bleeker): The Side-Spot Barb.

SHAPE: As per description of the genus. Of very slender build, slightly compressed laterally, the dorsal contour nearly straight. The broad mouth is widely cleft and shows four short barbels. The lateral line is complete. D 9, A 9-11. Length, in its home country, up to a good 25″.

COLOR: Yellow-green scintillating base with a dark shoulder spot which extends to the caudal peduncle in a steel-blue band. This band looks as if it were divided into a row of spots, due to being interrupted by shiny golden dots.

RANGE: Thailand and parts of Indonesia, especially in the waters of the plains.

CARE AND BREEDING: A pronounced surface fish, which lives in schools and chases flying food. It likes to swim and is gregarious, but bigger specimens should not be kept together with small fishes as they prey on them. The species needs plenty of room for swimming. They like sun and warmth. 77-82° F are advisable, lowest 73° F. The young specimens that have been imported so far unfortunately proved to be very frail and hard to keep. Spawning them has not been achieved as yet.

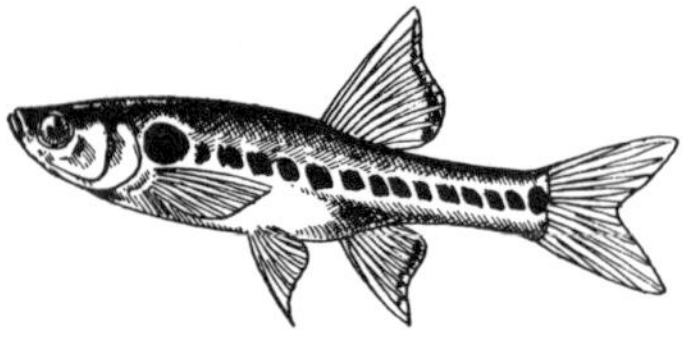

Luciosoma spilopleura

Left, Ludwigia alternifolia - right, Ludwigia palustris

Ludwigia: After a personal name. Genus of swamp plants belonging to the family of the *Oenotheraceae*. All species of *Ludwigia* are especially fit for cold and moderately warm home and swamp aquaria, and very especially for the open air installation. These perennial plants have beautiful leaves, vivid green to brownish green on the upper face, reddish on the lower one. They are alternate or opposite. The small flowers sit in the insertions of the emerged leaves. The plants, which under favorable conditions grow very quickly, may form strong bushes and like to grow above the surface of the water.

— **alternifolia** Linné: Alternate-Leaved Ludwigia.

GENERALITIES: This species, which formerly was often offered commercially as *L. mulertii*, is today only rarely found in aquaria, since it does not stand up well to exclusively submerged cultivation within the house.

SHAPE: The alternate leaves are a lively green, often with a brownish sheen. On the underside they often —but not always—show a reddish tint. The leaves are lancet-shaped and pointed at both ends.

RANGE: Eastern U.S.A., at the shores and margins of waters.

CULTIVATION: This species is especially fit for open-air cultivation, since it resists better if cultivated emerged and needs plenty of fresh air. It likes light and sun, being able to withstand even higher temperatures if under the influence of these.

If they are kept submerged, the water temperature should not rise above 72° F. In winter a rest period at 50-59° F is necessary. No special demands are made as to the composition of the water.

— **natans** Elliot: The Floating Ludwigia.

Also this species has often been sold as *L. mulertii*, being very similar to the previous one, but having opposite leaves. These may show a vivid red on the underside, while the emerged leaves are very shiny on the upper face. This species too likes to grow above the surface of the water. The flowers are yellow.

This plant is better fit for warm aquaria than the previous one. Its home country is in the Southeastern States of the U.S.A., from South Carolina to Florida and down to Mexico.

— **palustris** (Linné): Elliot: Common or Swamp Ludwigia.

GENERALITIES: This species varies strongly in the shape of the leaves and therefore has given origin to several commercial names, having also often been taken for *L. natans*.

SHAPE: The lancet-shaped leaves are light to olive green, not red on the underside and not opposite. The flowers are noted for the absence of the calyx leaves, which makes them a plain-looking green.

RANGE: Europe, Western Asia,

Northern Africa, and the U.S.A.

CULTIVATION: In its vital necessities the plant resembles *L. alternifolia*, but might eventually be considered still more hardy. No special requirements are made as to bottom soil, unwashed sand being sufficient. Reproduction, like in all other species of *Ludwigia*, occurs through the planting of twigs, which are laid in water for a few days until they develop roots. WENDT gives directions for growing them from seeds. According to him, artificial pollination may be used to develop seeds. These are sown in a shallow, covered dish with moist bottom soil, at 64-68° F. When they begin to germinate and the first little leaves appear, the young shoots should be slowly adapted to higher water levels.

Lumbricidae: Earth Worms.

Family of soil-dwelling worms belonging to the order of the *Oligochaeta*, significant in aquaristics as source of food for many species of fishes and other aquatic animals. The short bristles stand in four groups of two each on every sectional ring. They protrude only little beyond the skin, but may be felt distinctly. With their aid the worms are able to hold on to the walls of their tunnels. The tip of the body is formed by the so-called lip, which serves as organ of taste and touch. Earthworms have neither ears nor eyes, but the whole skin is sensitive to light. Through the intake of humus-rich dirt, its elaboration in the intestine, and its final elimination, earthworms do work that is of high importance for the fertility of the soil. The bigger species search for decaying parts of plants, which they drag into their dirt channels. Thus there is a constant interchange between the deeper and higher levels of the soil. Simultaneously the worms achieve an aeration of the ground and faciliate plants in their penetration into the soil. They have many enemies, for instance, man (who persecutes them out of ignorance), birds, moles, and many others. They do not like moisture and try to get out of the way of rain by coming up to the surface as the penetrating waters cause them to suffer from suffocation. Since at this moment they generally are already very tired, they die off in great numbers. Ultra-violet sunrays destroy their blood. The family comprises a series of species which the lay-man finds hard to differentiate.

The Common Earthworm, *Lumbricus terrestris* L., one of the biggest species, is found in gardens, fields, and the soil of woods. Other species too, especially the red Leaf Worms are very good for feeding to fishes.

During cold or dry spells the worms evacuate their intestine and roll up closely within a dirt cave. In this state they are eaten with preference.

The Stinking Earthworm, *Eisenia foetida*, which is found in compost heaps, is inadequate for feeding.

To keep and breed worms one may use containers made of wood, earthenware, or masonry. They should receive a shadowy, but warm location, and should be provided with a tight-fitting lid, but which should permit the entrance of air. Put in a strong layer of good forest soil (do not use compost soil or dirt with admixtures of artificial fertilizer). As food for the worms, which is put on top of the dirt, offer them decaying leaves, leftovers of fruits and vegetables, and especially finely grated carrots. Coffee grounds are said to prevent the development of mildew. Before feeding them to the fishes, worms should be put in a glass jar without any soil, closed off by a piece of muslin. There they empty their intestines and strip off the mucous layer. Then they should be washed and cut into pieces according to need.

Lung Fish, the African: see PROTOPTERUS ANNECTENS.

Lung Fish, the Australian: see NEOCERATODES FORSTERI.

Lung Fishes: see CROSSOPTERYGII.

Lung Snails: see PULMONATA.

lutea: Yellow.

— *Cryptocoryne.*

lutrensis: After a geographical name.

— *Notropis.*

Lymphocystis Disease: A disease caused by virus, rarely observed in the aquarium, which manifests itself through nodules and raspberry-shaped excrescences on skin and fins. The disease may be transmitted from fish to fish. Infected fishes should be taken from the tank and destroyed. No cure is known so far, neither is it known how long the disease germs can live in the aquarium without a host.

lyrata: Lyre-shaped.

— *Cardamine.*

Lyretail, the: see APHYOSEMION AUSTRALE.

Lysimachia: The pacifying one. Genus of swamp plants belonging to the family of the Primroses or *Primulaceae.*

— nummularia Linné: Moneywort.

GENERALITIES: A much-liked aquarium plant, very rugged, undemanding, and extremely decorative.

SHAPE: The rounded, light-green leaves become a little sturdy when cultivated emerged, tender when cultivated submerged, and grow crosswise opposite.

RANGE: Europe, Eastern North America, and Eastern Asia including Japan. The species grows both submerged and emerged on shorelines, moist pastures, temporarily dry ditches, and flood regions.

Lysimachia nummularia

CULTIVATION: Moneywort may be kept completely submerged and may gradually be adapted to higher degrees of temperature. No special demands are made as to the composition of the water and bottom soil. Generally speaking it is easier to grow than the *Ludwigias,* which are hard to keep in warm water aquaria, but to which otherwise it is very similar in its demands. With sufficient light, especially occasional sunlight, it grows eagerly.

maccullochi: After a personal name.

— *Melanotaenia.*

macracantha: Big-spined.

— *Botia.*

macrocephalus: Big-headed.

— *Cryptopterus.*

Macrognathus: Big-jawed. Genus of spiny eels belonging to the family of the *Mastocembelidae.*

macrolepidotus: With big scales.

— *Chalceus.*

— *Gnathonemus.*

macrolepis: With big scales.

— *Mugil.*

Macrones: see SPERATA.

macrophthalmus: Big-eyed.
— *Aplocheilichthys.*

macropoda: With big feet; big-rooted.
— *Elatine.*

Macropods: see MACROPODUS.

Macropodus: Big foot, referring to the fins.
South East Asian genus belonging to the family of the Climbing Perches or *Anabantidae*, which also comprises much-appreciated aquarium fishes. The dorsal fin is often longer than the anal one; the first ray of the ventral is extended. The lateral line is developed back or totally absent. The opercles are toothed.

All in all, the different species are enduring and undemanding. Only the smaller members of the genus may be considered peaceful, while *M. opercularis* has to be said to be pronouncedly bellicose. No special demands are made as to food. Generally live foods are preferred, but occasional dry foods are not scorned. Sunlit, old tanks with plenty of plant growth and algae contribute to their well-being. As to care and breeding, see ANABANTIDAE.

— **chinensis** (Bloch): The Round-Tailed Paradise Fish.
SHAPE: As per description of the genus. The body is elongated, compressed laterally. The small mouth, with its puffy lips, is pointed upwards. D XIV/5-7, A XVIII/9-12. Length up to $2\frac{5}{8}''$.
COLOR: A rather unassuming species. Yellowish-brown base with darker, irregular cross bands. The fins are bluish with weak dots. The male is more intensely colored and the soft parts of the dorsal and anal fins are extended into threads.
RANGE: Eastern China and Korea, in waters of all kinds but especially in bights and bays of rivers and lakes.
CARE AND BREEDING: As per description of the genus. The species was for a long time considered (erroneously) as the "original form" of *M. opercularis* which was supposed to have been bred selectively by the Chinese. The fish are peaceful and absolutely insensitive to low temperatures. 60-73° F are sufficient and it is inadvisable to permit the temperature to rise above 75° F. For breeding join pairs of equal strength, since the male chases rather violently. The water level should be quite low, the best being 2-4″. The species is not very fertile. According to reports received, the building of the bubble nest is a little deficient, but in this there are individual differences. The species is only rarely found in the fish fancier's aquarium.

— **cupanus** (Cuvier and Valenciennes): The Spike-Tailed Paradise Fish.
SHAPE: As per description of the genus. Of elongated build, looking rather sturdy, D XIV-XVII/5-7, A XVI/9-11. Length up to $2\frac{1}{4}''$.
COLOR: Reddish-brown with greenish sheen, under excitement totally dark, often also with indistinct, lighter horizontal stripes. The fins are bluish with reddish dots. The male is characterized by the puffier lips and the tips of the fins which are drawn out into points.
RANGE: In smaller waters of all kinds in India, Thailand, and Ceylon, especially in waters near the seacoast and also in brackish waters.
CARE AND BREEDING: As per description of the genus. The species does not need much warmth, 64-68° F being sufficient, for breeding 77° F. As a rule the bubble nest is small and loose.

— **cupanus dayi** (Koehler): The Brown Spike-Tailed Paradise Fish.
SHAPE: As per description of the genus, but especially elongated

Macropodus cupanus dayi

and supple. D XII-XVII/5-7, A XVI/10-12. Length up to 2⅜″.
COLOR: Brown base with two dark longitudinal bands which may nearly disappear during the spawning period with its totally dark coloration. Breast and belly of the male are reddish to vivid red, the fins are bluish to red with beautiful shiny edges. The central rays of the tail fin are black, less extended on the females, more so on the males.
RANGE: India and Thailand.
CARE AND BREEDING: As per description of the genus, but needing some warmth. Temperatures between 71 and 86° F. Spawnings have been observed both with relatively high and firm bubble nests and without any nest at all. In the latter case the fish are contented with collecting some air bubbles beneath a leaf, or even with spawning in a closed hiding cave. The remainder of the reproduction corresponds to that of the other species of the genus.

Macropodus opercularis

opercularis (Linné): The Paradise Fish.
SHAPE: Elongated but very sturdy, and compressed laterally. D XIII-XVII/6-8, A XVII-XX/11-15. The vertical and the ventral fins are drawn out into threads, especially those of the males. Length up to 3⅛″, the females generally a little smaller.
COLOR: Very variable in color, in a state of excitement a blue-green base with numerous cross bands, the throat and belly of the male velvet black during the mating period. On the opercles, which may be erected when the fish is excited, a blue-green, red-edged spot is found. The fins are bluish to red, with numerous blue dashes and seams. The male is more vivid in color and has pronouncedly puffy lips.
RANGE: From Korea to South China, Vietnam, and Taiwan. There the Paradise Fish is found in shallow, quiet waters, but it does not avoid flowing waters either. It is reported especially to be a dweller of rice paddies.
CARE AND BREEDING: As per description of the genus. The species is still one of the most beautiful and interesting aquarium fishes. In 1869 the Paradise Fish was introduced in Europe by a Frenchman as one of the first exotic species, and soon it was successfully spawned by the well-known fish-breeder Carbonnier. From this tribe stem most of the fish found in our aquaria. The opinion that it is a bred sport produced by the Chinese seems to be untenable. It is true that the noted ichthyologists GUENTHER and BOULENGER have considered the species an artificially bred variety, but KREYNBERG has pointed out years ago that this statement is untenable. K. never saw Paradise Fish kept by Chinese, nor were they offered for sale on the usual fish

markets. On these, Gold Fish and their varieties were found, but never Paradise Fish. Furthermore the species is not reproduced on Chinese objects of art. One may imagine, though, that *Macropodus opercularis concolor*, described hereafter, may be closely related to the present species, or may possibly be only a color sport of same. This question has not been verified so far.

— opercularis concolor Ahl: The Black Paradise Fish.

A sub-species of the previous one, of exquisite beauty. Without cross bands, its body is nearly black during the spawning period. The fins are generally especially drawn out. Origin unknown.

macropterus: With big wings or fins.

— *Centrarchus.*

macrostigma: With big spots.

— *Epiplatys.*

maculata: Spotted.

— *Rasbora.*

maculatus: Spotted.

— *Etroplus.*

— *Phago.*

— *Thoracocharax.*

— *Trinectes.*

— *Xiphophorus* (*Platypoecilus*).

maculosus: Spotted.

— *Tylobranchus.*

maiden birth: see PARTHENOGENESIS.

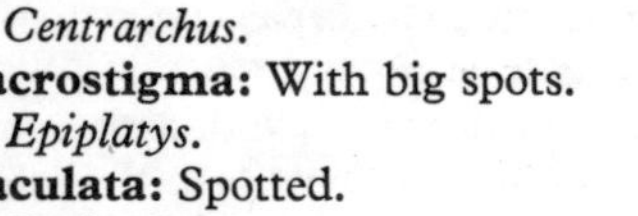

mulm bell

diptube

maintenance and care of the aquarium: The continuous maintenance of the aquarium consists primarily in keeping a certain balance in the "partnership of living in the aquarium" while considering the mutual relationship of interdependence between animals and plants. The more careful you are while feeding, the more you ponder the advisability of doing so before you stock your tank with plants and fishes, but also the more you avoid unnecessary interferences, the less work the maintenance will give you.

This consists in the first place in keeping the front glass plate clean of algae, growths, and dirt, by means of a scraper applied whenever needed. When doing this, don't be a stickler for perfection, as especially on the side from which the light comes, or on the lateral panes, some algae may remain, if they do not proliferate too much. After the resulting mulm has decanted, draw it off from the bottom with a hose, on the tip of which you may stick a mulm bell. The bell serves the purpose of separating the sand from the lighter particles of mulm, thus avoiding its entrance into the hose. The so-called syphons have proved efficient for smaller tanks, and one may also use syphons connected to the aerating system. Also in this one can be clean to an excess. The mulm which remains in the tank, and which rests rather firmly on the bottom if one does not keep too strongly rooting fishes, is food for the plants, and better than many artificial fertilizers. The water that is drawn off while cleaning, should be replaced with fresh water of the same temperature. The water that evaporates is best replaced with distilled water, which one can keep in a glass bottle for this purpose. Filling up with tap water has the disadvantage that with time the hardeners contained in this concentrate to a point where they raise the water hardness within the tank much above the normal level. Generally speaking it is advisable from time to time, say, every 4-6 weeks, to replace part of the water in the tank, drawing off about ¼ of the contents and filling up with fresh water.

majalis: Pertaining to the month of May.
— *Fundulus.*

malabaricus: From the Malabar coast, in India.
— *Danio.*

malabaricus: From Malabar. In this case based on a mistake of the describer, as the fish originates from South America.
— *Hoplias.*

Malacostraca: Higher Crustaceans. Class of crustaceans belonging to the sub-phylum of the *Crustacea*. A group, very rich in shapes, that differentiates from the lower crustaceans by the regular articulation of the body. This consists of a total of 20 segments, of which 13 make up the head and thorax, 6 the abdomen, and one the tail fan. Of importance for the aquarium are the Pill Bugs or *Isopoda*, the Flea Crustaceans or *Amphipoda*, the Ten-Footed Crustaceans or *Decapoda*, and the Crabs or *Brachyura*.

Malapteruridae: Electric Catfishes.
Family of Catfishes belonging to the sub-order of the *Siluroidea*, of awkward shape, with thick heads, big mouths, and puffy lips. A dorsal fin is absent, there being only a bigger adipose fin which inserts more towards the rear. The skin is naked and mucous. The fishes have become remarkable because of their electricity generating organ, which is located symmetrically on both sides within the thick skin that covers the whole body like a coat. Only one genus with one species is known.

Malapterurus: With a soft (adipose) fin above the tail.
Only genus of the Electric Catfishes pertaining to the family of the *Malapteruridae*.

Malapterurus electricus

— electricus Gmelin: The Electric Catfish.
SHAPE: As per description of the family. The very small eyes shine in the dark. The jaws are set with small teeth, disposed in bands. Length up to 20″.
COLOR: Brownish, with dark, somewhat blotted spots, a little lighter towards the caudal peduncle.
RANGE: Tropical West and Central Africa.
CARE AND BREEDING: A voracious predator, which needs vegetable food besides that of animal origin, though. It is quarrelsome, even toward fish of its own species. The reason for the electricity generating organs has not yet been explained. The electric current is hardly needed for purposes of defense, but possibly, similar to what is the case with the South American Electric Eel. *Electrophorus*, to search out prey. Consequently the development of the eyes is imperfect, but the sense of touch is quite well developed. Temperatures from 68 to 79° F. Live foods should not be too lively, as the fish are very clumsy in catching them. Nothing definite is known about reproduction. Native observers state that the Electric Catfish is a mouthbreeder.

malayensis: Coming from Malaya.
— *Esomus.*

malinverniana: After Malinverni, the discoverer of the plant.
— *Isoetes.*

mangrove swamp: One of the most remarkable biotopes. At the place where the tropical rain forest meets the tidal zone of the sea, a peculiar community of plants and animals develops. Certain species of trees stand on aerial roots as if standing on stilts. Their fruits ripen and germinate on the tree itself. They have to fall down during ebb tide and bore into the mud with their tips. The mangrove swamp reaches as far inland as the tides do. It is pronouncedly hostile to mankind, as the air is saturated with moisture and full of swamp gases.

The fauna is made up of tree and water dwellers. The animals have adapted to the constant change of the water level. The water itself may become nearly fresh during the ebb, turning salty during high tide.

Of fishes we find, among others, the Mudskippers (see PERIOPHTHALMUS), which live in schools together with Pilot Fish. Furthermore there live numerous Gobies, and further inland *Psettus* and *Toxotes*. In South American mangrove swamps we find the peculiar Four-eyed Fish (see ANABLEPS).

Many-Hued Mouthbreeder, the: see HAPLOCHROMIS MULTICOLOR.

Many-Spined Fishes, the: see NANDIDAE.

Marble Goby, the: see ELEOTRIS MARMORATA.

Marcusenius: After the Russian explorer Markusen.

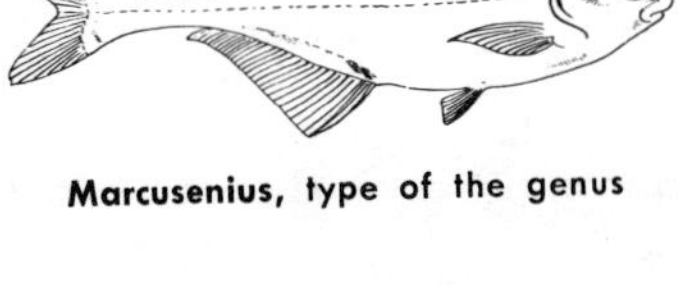

Marcusenius, type of the genus

Genus belonging to the family of the Nile Pikes or *Mormyridae.*

— isidori (Cuvier and Valenciennes):

SHAPE: The body is compact and rounded, the caudal peduncle extraordinarily thin. The strongly curved forehead protrudes over the subterminal mouth. This is equipped with a few two-pronged teeth. D 18-22, A 22-26. Length up to 4″.

COLOR: Brownish, occasionally with blurred darker spots.

RANGE: From the Nile region to the Upper Zambesi, in quiet, densely planted and swampy waters.

CARE AND BREEDING: As per description of the family. A pronounced twilight and nocturnal fish, which likes dense plant thickets with hiding places among roots and layers of mulm. It takes live bottom foods willingly, but besides these also detritus and algae. Temperatures from 73-82° F. Reproduction unknown.

— longianalis Boulenger:

SHAPE: Of a slightly more elongated build than the previous species. D 14-16, A 31-33. The caudal fin is small and deeply forked. Like all Mormyrids, the fish has a weak electricity generating organ. Length up to 5¾″.

RANGE: The lower Niger, Cameroon, in standing and slowly flowing waters with dense plant thickets and muddy bottom.

CARE AND BREEDING: As described for the previous species.

marginatus: With marginal edge.
— *Hemigrammus.*
— *Nannostomus.*

Marisa: Apple Snails.
Genus of tropical giant snails (see ARCHITAENIOGLOSSA).

Markiana: After the American zoologist Mark.
South American genus belonging to the family of the Characins or *Characidae,* with two known spe-

cies. The genus is closely related to the *Moenkhausia* Characins.

— **nigripinnis** (Perugia): The Orange Fin Tetra.

SHAPE: Quite high, in all nearly egg-shaped, strongly compressed laterally. The mouth is supraterminal. D 11, A 44. The upper lobe of the tail fin is a little bit longer than the lower one.

Length a little over 6″.

COLOR: Gray-greenish with darker dots disposed in longitudinal rows. Younger specimens have a black spot on the caudal peduncle. The fins are reddish to orange-colored. The origin of the name '*nigripinnis*' (black-finned) is not clear. It might eventually have derived from the black edge of the anal fin. The fins of the male are more vivid in color.

RANGE: In the La Plata, Paraguay, and Parana rivers, in schools especially in the bights of the rivers.

CARE AND BREEDING: As per description of the family. The species is quite rugged and not exceptionally in need of warmth. Despite the fact that it is a school fish, which likes to live in communities, one should refrain from putting them together with smaller specimens, as the bigger ones attack them. They also like occasionally to eat vegetable foods. Up to this date the species has rarely been imported. Breeding them has succeeded only occasionally. Spawning took place near the bottom, among plants.

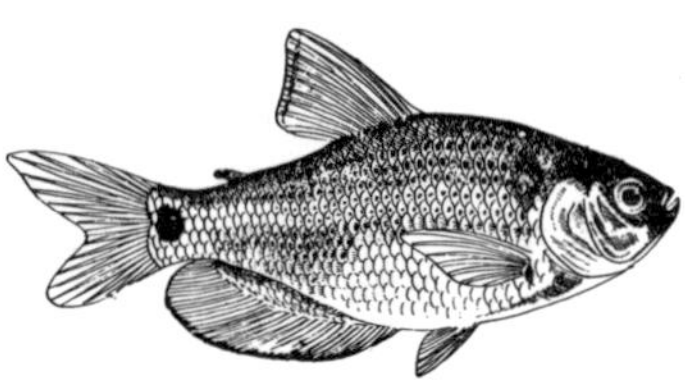

Markiana nigripinnis

marmorata: Mottled, marble-grained.

— *Eleotris.*

marmoratus: Mottled, marble-grained.

— *Symbranchus.*

marnoi: After a personal name.

— *Epiplatys.*

maronii: After the Maroni river, in Guiana.

— *Aequidens.*

Maroni Cichlid, the: see AEQUIDENS MARONII.

Marsilea: Clover Ferns.

Genus of ferns belonging to the family of the pill fruit ferns or *Marsileaceae*. The leaves, which look like four leaf-clover, stand on more or less long stems over the long, creeping, strongly branched root stock. At low water levels they like to emerge above the surface. The plants are in fact swamp dwellers and therefore adapted to an amphibious manner of living. They may develop both submerged and emerged leaves, as well as floating leaves. The spore fruits are located at the insertion of the leaf stems, but in continually submerged plants they usually remain sterile.

Cultivation of the clover ferns is simple. They are hardy and stand up quite well even under relatively unfavorable conditions. Sand with an admixture of some clay is sufficient as bottom soil. For most species it is especially favorable to be kept in swamp aquaria. Reproduction takes place through division of the root stock. Of the many species, the differences between which are only slight, only the two most important ones are described here.

— **drummondii** A. Braun: Drummond's Four Leaf-Clover.

This species is often taken for *M. quadrifolia* in commerce. It comes from Central and Southern Australia, where it is found in muddy, temporarily dry bodies of water. A hardy and perennial plant, which does not want too much warmth, keeping best at 64-72° F. A moderately light, but not too dark location is desirable. No special requirements as to water.

— **quadrifolia** Linné: Common Four Leaf-Clover.

This species is found in small, shallow waters in Europe, as well as in Central and South Asia. It also grows emerged on moist soils, especially if these contain clay. *M. quadrifolia* may be kept colder than the previous species.

Marsileaceae: Pill Fruit Ferns.

Amphibious, perennial ferns, with a thin creeping axis, from which the single leaves strive vertically toward the surface on long stems. At the beginning these are rolled up spirally.

The spores are found in differently shaped spore fruits, which are located at the base of the leaves or the stems. The family usually originates from tropical and subtropical regions. The different species are very similar and can only be differentiated by the expert.

Genera: *Marsilea,* and *Pillularia.*

marthae: After a name.

— *Carnegiella.*

Mastocembelidae: Arrow Beaks, Spiny Eels.

Family belonging to the order of the *Opisthomi,* which is distributed over tropical Africa and Asia with only a few species. They are peculiar fishes of very elongated build. The dorsal and anal fins may grow into a long finny edge which on the fore part of the back develops into many single spines and which connects with the caudal fin at the hind part. The head is pointed, equipped with tube-shaped, motile appendages, which show a certain resemblance to a beak. The nostrils are simple, the eyes are only small, and deeply imbedded in the skin. The opercles have only a small opening at the belly side. The scales are very small; the swimming bladder is closed; ventral fins are absent.

They are predators, living nocturnally, which like to dig into the bottom soil during daytime, developing incredible skill in this. They can also move quite quickly on the bottom. The appendix located on the upper jaw evidently serves as an organ of taste.

The family comprises several genera, of which *Mastocembelus* and *Macrognathus* are the best known.

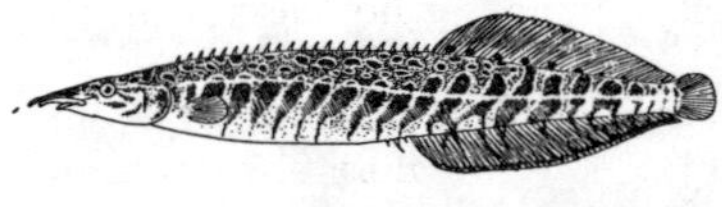

Mastocembelus, type of the genus

Mastocembelus: War beak (Spiny eels, Arrow beaks).

Genus belonging to the family of the *Mastocembelidae.*

— **argus** Guenther: The Peacock-Eye Spiny Eel.

SHAPE: As per description of the genus. D XXXII-XXXIV/60-75, A III/56-75. Length up to 8″.

COLOR: Two or three rows of golden-yellow to yellowish-brown dots contrast with the red-brown base. At the base of the dorsal and anal fins appear crescent-shaped spots.

RANGE: Western and Southern Thailand, in clean waters that show soft bottoms.

CARE AND BREEDING: Since the spiny eels live on the bottom, into which they dig most skilfully, one should offer them soft sand. Contrariwise, soft mulm, which they do not appreciate, should be removed regularly. The fish do not withstand dirty water and are especially sensitive to green water. They are undemanding at temperatures around 72° F, but eat only live foods, especially worms. Reproduction is unknown.

— **loennbergi** Boulenger: Loennberg's Spiny Eel.

SHAPE: Differing from the strongly compressed Asiatic species, this one is nearly round and wormlike slender. D XXVIII-XXXII/100-130. A II/100-130. Length up to 10″.

COLOR: Greenish olive-drab with lighter mottlings and spots. The back is uniformly rust-red to dirty brown, the belly white to yellowish.

RANGE: From West Africa (Sierra Leone and Cameroon) to Lake Chad.

CARE AND BREEDING: As described for *M. argus*.

— **pancalus** Hamilton-Buchanan: The Spotted Spiny Eel.

SHAPE: Elongated, strongly flattened laterally. D XXIV-XXVI/35-42, A III/31-46.

COLOR: Olive- gray green with small lighter to yellowish-white dots and dashes. On the middle of the belly a weak whitish horizontal band.

RANGE: Widely distributed over the whole of Lower India to the mouth of the Ganges. The most common of the species.

CARE AND BREEDING: As described for *M. argus*. This species often leaves the bottom and catches free-swimming foods, as for instance, Daphnia. They are not as sensitive to soiled waters as the other species. It is advisable, though, to be careful with freshly imported specimens, as in most cases one does not know what waters they come from.

The species (?) has already been bred by SCHOENEBECK, that is, reproduction occurred without any interference on the part of the owner. The fish spawned with great regularity in the community tank, searching out the roots of floating plants for this, led by the male. The eggs were laid during the morning hours, the pair pressing closely together and disappearing again immediately thereafter into the bottom soil. In another tank, about ten days after several spiny eels were introduced there, appeared many young arrow beaks measuring about $1\frac{1}{8}''$ to $1\frac{5}{8}''$ and which hugged the glass panes or were floating along in the aeration stream. Feeding the young presented no problem. They reach sexual maturity after one year.

mating: Pairing, copulation. In heterosexual animals the bodily union of two individuals of different sex with a view to fecundation or fertilization. Mating may take place in loose form. We speak of a copulation especially when the semen from the male sexual apparatus is actively transferred to that of the female by means of special organs. Mating and copulation on one hand lead to insemination; fecundation, on the other hand, may be separated in time. In the latter case the semen is stored in a state of perfect preservation within special organs of the female body. Fishes have regular matings. It is the climax of the process of reproduction. The formation of pairs generally is preceded by intense wooing, which in part serves the purpose of accelerating the maturing of the sexual products, partly that of setting in motion the mating in itself. Generally it is the male who is the active partner in wooing, but in some species also the female may play a very active role, as for instance, among some of the Dwarf Cichlids. Also the invitation to start the 'chasing' which precedes the act of spawning may be begun by the female of many school fishes. The formation of pairs may be of different duration or intensity. Species which meet within the school for the act of spawning or only in loose form, unite only for the duration of this act, without a recognizable union of the sexes beyond this period. It is true, though, that even in these groups one finds cases of a certain 'marital fidelity', as for instance, in *Brachydanio rerio*. Species that care for their spawn forming paternal or maternal families, also keep up the union only until the moment when the act of spawning is completed. The now superfluous partner, male or female, is not even tolerated near the spawning site. Also in these cases a more permanent union of the sexes beyond the spawning period probably is rare. Generally it is a fish which is just ripe for spawning that is mated.

Very often, for instance, among Sticklebacks or the Mouthbreeders of the genus *Haplochromis*, the male occupies a certain territory, in the middle of which it builds a nest or cave. The spawn-ripe females approach the nest swimming by in groups, are wooed, and spawn with any male. Then they leave again. In other cases, as for instance among Paradise Fish, the wooing concentrates on one certain female, so that one is under the impression that she is preferred to all others. It is only natural that the pairing off when both partners care for the spawning, meaning in parental families, is more intense and may last longer. In this case the pairs often keep together beyond the mating period itself. The formation of pairs of two individuals should be considered the most frequent, but it is not rare at all that one male mates with several females or vice-versa. Thus one female of the Armored Catfish spawns successfully with several males, while, for instance, several females of the Three-Spined Stickleback complete the number of eggs within the nest of one male. A brood-caring male of *Polycentrus schomburgki* may spawn with a second female the next day or the day thereafter at the same place and possibly over the previous spawn. Another circumstance that points to the often lacking permanence of pairing is for instance also the fact that in many fish species the sexes need a different period of time for maturing the sexual products. Thus male and female fishes may reach maturity for spawning at different moments after the conclusion of a previous act of mating. Therefore they are materially unable to mate with each other again. It is known, for instance, that in some of the Sunfishes the males need a longer resting period, while the females become ripe to spawn again and mate with other males. Examples may also be found in which the opposite happens.

All in all, pairing off with several different partners should be found much more frequently in free nature than in the aquarium, where the fish often is forced into 'monogamy' by the breeder.

The manner of mating is different for the different species of fishes. In the simplest case the pairs swim side by side and scatter eggs and semen freely into the water. It is a fact, though, that during this they often seek a loose mutual contact. Either they juxtapose the belly edges, or else they remain standing on the same spot for a short time, then embrace with the caudal peduncle or the anal fin, or they repel each other with short jerks during which eggs and semen are given forth. This process is the rule among many school fishes. Characins often carry minute hooks on the anal fins of the males, which probably aid in holding fast to the female during the mating. In less frequent cases, for instance, in the

Harlequin, *Rasbora heteromorpha*, the pairs that are willing to spawn segregate and accomplish mating on the underside of a plant leaf. Other species still do it also on plant stems or other firm objects. In such cases we will always find so-called egg hangers.

Embraces with the fins or with the whole body during the act of mating are seen quite frequently. They are the rule for most egg laying Tooth Carps and are found most expressly where there is an aim to concentrate the eggs on a more or less limited spot. More or less close embraces are found, for instance, with the Harlequin, *Badis badis*, and most *Anabantids* (Climbing Perches). Often, though, the simple slipping of the male's anal fin beneath the sexual opening of the female is sufficient to catch or collect the released eggs, to fecundate them, and to let them fall down or to place them in or on a certain spawning medium. Armored Catfishes form a purse out of their ventral fins, into which they slip one or more eggs.

A transference of the male semen into the female sexual organs occurs relatively seldom. Certain Characins (see GLANDULOCAUDINAE) have an internal fertilization which sometimes is even sufficient for several spawnings. There the mating takes place before the act of spawning, but the manner of transferring the spermatozoa has not yet been explained. Fishes that give birth to live fry, for instance, the live bearing Tooth Carps, the Half-Beaks, and others, show a more or less changed anal fin, with the aid of which fecundation is achieved. Generally the sperm is only brought near the sexual opening of the female. The processes are not always very clear. A real copulation among aquarium fishes, though, probably is only found among a very small group of live-bearing Tooth Carps.

mating games: The mating games of fishes are characterized by exactly prescribed motions, which are typical for the species and which generally consist of several serially disposed steps. Among the fishes the simplest form of mating games are found in the egg-scattering swarm fishes, and the most elaborate ones in species that care for their brood. Frequently the mating games are connected with special color phenomena. As a rule it is the male which plays the mating games as a means to woo the female, but in some species, such as, for instance, *Pelmatochromis kribensis*, also the female shows motions that are typical of mating games. The mating games pertain to the behavior of fishes.

matriarchal family: A family form of fishes in which only the female cares for the brood, as for instance happens with *Nannacara anomala*. The closeness of the *M.* is very great. It is interesting to note that in fishes with M. the males generally are much smaller than the females.

May Killie, May Fish, the: see FUNDULUS MAJALIS.

mbu: After the native name.
— *Tetraodon*.

meal worms as fish food: The larvae of the meal bug may constitute an excellent substitute food for many aquarium fishes, especially when they have just changed their skins. It is advisable, though, not to feed them on bran, as is usually done, but on dried green leaves instead of this, for instance on those of birch trees, as many fishes do not eat the larvae due to the mealy contents of their intestine. Bigger fishes, for instance Cichlids, eat the meal worms whole. For all others they should be chopped up.

Medaka, the: see ORYZIAS LATIPES.

Medicinal Leech, the: see HIRUDO MEDICINALIS.

medium: Condition for the existence of all phenomena in nature, as for instance respiratory air for all live beings; in aquaristics water as a carrying and vital substance for the existence of fishes.

As spawning medium one mentions the live or dead substance necessary for laying the eggs, for instance, the bottom soil, algae, rocks, etc.

medusae: In fresh water the free-swimming intermediate generation of fresh-water hydras of the genus *Microhydra.*

meeki: After the American ichthyologist Meek.

— *Cichlasoma.*

megalotis: Big-eared.

— *Lepomis.*

meinkeni: After the German ichthyologist Hermann Meinken.

— *Aphyosemion.*

— *Rasbora.*

Meinken's Aphyosemion: see APHYOSEMION MEINKENI.

Meinken's Rasbora: see RASBORA MEINKENI.

meiosis: Maturity division of the germinating cells, which must precede insemination in order to bring the chromosomes down to the needed half in number and quality.

melanin: Black pigment formed of proteinic substance, found in the chromatophores of the cells.

melanism: Black coloring; see COLOR MISDEVELOPMENTS.

melanistius: With black sail.

— *Corydoras.*

melanogaster: With black belly.

— *Limia.*

Melanoides tuberculata Mueller: The Tower-Lid Snail.

Fresh water snail belonging to the order of the front gills or *Prosobranchia,* with high, pointed shell,

Melanoides tuberculata

closed by a lid of horny substance. The species ranges over Eastern Africa up to Thailand.

During recent years this snail has found more acceptance in the aquarium due to the fact that it feeds especially on algae and detritus, and that it possesses the faculty of digging into the ground, which thus it loosens up. It needs some warmth, though. At temperatures below 68° F it already becomes sluggish and dies below 64° F.

The young are born alive.

melanopleura: With black sides or flanks.

— *Leporinus.*

melanotaenia: Black-banded.

— *Cynolebias* (*Cynopoecilus*).

Melanotaenia: Rainbow Fishes. Genus of Australian school fishes belonging to the family of the *Atherinidae,* which are characterized by a double dorsal fin. The body is elongated and very strongly compressed laterally.

Rainbow fishes are hardy and very easy to keep. They need quite long containers, though, which

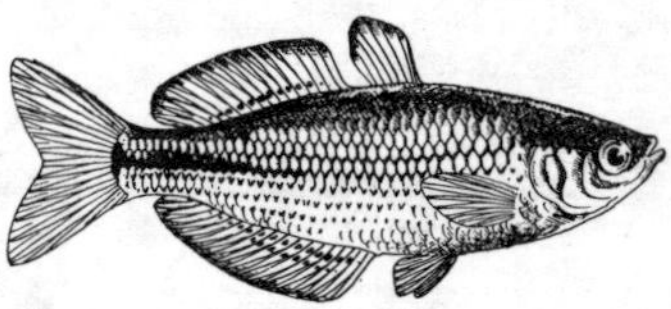

Melanotaenia, type of the genus

afford them plenty of swimming space. *M.* are not especially in need of warmth, but feel better at higher temperatures. All kinds of live and dry foods of corresponding size are taken.

Breeding of all of them takes place in the same manner as is known for the Carp-like fishes or *Cyprinidae*. Contrary to these, though, the spawning period extends over a longer space of time, a few eggs being laid daily. Therefore they are so-called permanent spawners. The eggs hang from threads, singly or in groups of several units, on plants and other firm objects. The parents are not very especially greedy after their spawn, but it is advisable to remove them after 10-12 days, when the first fry begin to hatch. Rearing them is not difficult.

— **maccullochi** Ogilby: The Black-Lined Rainbow.

SHAPE: As per description of the genus. Length up to 2⅜".

COLOR: The hard-to-describe hue of the body, which changes according to the incidence of the light, may be called reddish to blue-green. Between the scales one finds red to blackish-brown dots, disposed in orderly rows. The beautiful fins are brownish to orange-red. The male is slimmer and more vivid in coloring.

RANGE: In flowing waters in Northeast Australia, where they always appear in big schools.

Melanotaenia macculochi

CARE AND BREEDING: As per description of the genus. Temperatures 68-79° F, 73-79° F being most favorable. Lowest 50-54° F. Clear, oxygen-rich, not-too-old water is desirable.

— **nigrans** Richardson: The Australian Rainbow Fish.

A species which is very much like the previous one, reaching a length of 4". Coloring is greenish, the scales being dark-edged, the fins orange-colored, and a red spot being found on the opercles. The male is bigger, slimmer, and more colored. Its dorsal and anal fins are pointed. Home country: Eastern Australia.

CARE AND BREEDING: As per description of the genus. This species is very sensitive to new water.

Melanotaenia nigrans

melanotus: Black-eared.

— *Idus.*

melanura: With black tail.

— *Hasemania.*

melastigma: Black-spotted.

— *Oryzias.*

Merry Widow, the: see PHALLICHTHYS AMATES.

Mesogonistius: With a notch between the hard and soft parts of the dorsal fin.

Genus of North American Perches belonging to the family of the Sunfishes or *Centrarchidae*.

Mesogonistius chaetodon

— **chaetodon** (Baird): The Black-Banded Sunfish.

SHAPE: The body is high, which becomes apparent especially when the fins are erected, oval in outline, and strongly compressed laterally. D X/10-12, A III/12. Length up to 4″.

COLOR: Silvery with more or less distinctly noticeable black cross bands, which are not clearly limited. A shiny spot on the opercle temporarily becomes more evident on the male. During the spawning period the female is considerably more rounded. The male pales completely during the act of spawning.

RANGE: The U.S.A., from Maryland to New Jersey. The species is found in standing or slow-flowing clear waters with sandy bottom.

CARE AND BREEDING: The Black-Banded Sunfish will also live in smaller tanks, but needs some room if it is to have the benefit of its beauty. Especially younger specimens, which rove slowly in schools, look very strikingly pretty in bigger aquaria. The tanks should be well-planted, but still show sufficient free space. It is inadvisable to put them in too-well lit locations, and especially too intense sunlight should be avoided. *M. chaetodon* is gregarious, but its company should consist of calm fishes that fit in with its manner of living. If kept together with lively companions, it easily becomes shy. No special demands are made as to temperature; 59-72° F are sufficient. By no means should the fish be pampered. In winter they should be offered a longish rest at 46-50° F. Temporarily, though, they will also withstand even lower degrees of warmth, and may be kept in unheated aquaria without further danger. Cooly wintered specimens are more resistant. Unfortunately the Black-Banded Sunfish is a little sensitive to sudden fluctuations in temperature and to changes of water or tanks. One should also be careful with the employment of chemicals. Like all Sunfishes, this species too takes only live foods, and will not take dry foods even if very hungry. For breeding, the fish need only low temperatures. Already at 64° F they begin to make preparations for reproduction. The male builds a shallow pit in the sand, preferably at the foot of plants or rocks, defending it against other fishes. The female stays in open water, but approaches the spawning place of its own when ripe for spawning. Actively wooed by the male, it swims to the spawning pit where, after several mock-matings, the eggs are laid while the pair is circling each other. The small, sand-colored eggs stick to grains of sand at the bottom. The male fans and guards the spawn. The fry, which hatch after 3-6 days, still lie in the pit for a few days, but are expelled from there by their father by means of some vehement movements of the fins, hanging from plants and the like thereafter. Soon the fry become free-swimming. They need large amounts of fine food. Feeding on infusoria is not sufficient. If given rich feedings, they grow very quickly, reach full coloring after six weeks, and may be ready to propagate after a year.

metabolism and exchange of energy: The totality of the chemical processes in a live being related to the building up, use, and substitution of components of the live body. Each organism is steadily taking in foods, which inside it are transformed in body substances or which it stores as reserves (starch, fats). This process is called building metabolism or assimilation.

To maintain the vital functions, the body composes these substances of its own, or uses others taken in from outside. This process is called fuel metabolism or dissimilation.

The substances necessary for metabolism are essentially the same for all animals, that is, hydrocarbons, fats, proteins, vitamins, and different minerals. Products of the metabolic decomposition are carbon dioxide, water, and the food derivatives which are expelled as unusable, excrements and urine. The food substances are decomposed (split up) within the digestive tract by enzymes. In nature we differentiate autotrophic, and heterotrophic organisms, with reference to the two main types of metabolism. Autotrophic ones are the green plants which feed on the gases of the air, water, and soil salts with the aid of sunlight (photosynthesis).

Heterotrophic ones are those live beings which feed on oxydable inorganic substances and on organic ones built up by plants. This group includes all animals, the life of which is really made possible by plants. Metabolism firmly links the organisms to the surrounding worlds, which in a certain manner in part flows through them.

metabolism diseases of fishes: Diseases of the metabolic system, with non-parasitic causes. Diseases of the digestive system set in especially after long-lasting one-sided feeding or sudden changes in the manner of feeding. Therefore these are best avoided by variety in feeding in accordance with the preferences of the respective species. (See FEEDING OF FISHES, FOOD, FEEDING). Cures generally are much more difficult.

The most common result of wrong feeding methods is the overfattening of the intestines. It generally appears less in younger specimens, which use up the offered food for growing, but it is a typical characteristic of full-grown older aquarium fishes. Overfattening is one of the most frequent causes of death, and may lead secondarily to other ailments. Confined space, monotonous, and often, too rich fare, high and even temperatures often lead to strong accumulations of fat. This hits especially the ventral cavity with the intestine, the ovaries, kidneys, and the liver. As a rule overfattened fishes do not breed. One of the most frequent infectious diseases which appear as consequences of overfattening is Infectious Dropsy.

Inflammation of the stomach and of the intestine too as a rule result as a sequel of one-sided nutrition. They show up especially often in winter, when one has to make use of makeshift foods, or when one can only offer one-sided foods for long periods, which to boot may even lack sufficient bulk. Often too the fact is neglected that many fishes need additional nourishment with vegetable substances.

metallicus: Metallic, of bronze. — *Girardinus*.

metamorphosis: The change-over into an imago or completed shape, passing through one or more larval stages, as happens, for instance, with insects, but also with higher animals.

Metazoa: Multicellular animals.

Metynnis: With plowshare, referring to the first, often toothed, spine of the dorsal fin.

South American genus of Disc Characins, belonging to the family of the Characins or *Characidae*, of high, nearly perfectly rounded build, strongly compressed laterally. The belly edge is sharp and provided with pointed keeled scales. The adipose fin is well developed, often even relatively long. The anal too is long. In front of the dorsal fin is located a spine which is tilted forward.

— **maculatus** Kner: The Spotted Metynnis.

SHAPE: As per description of the genus. D 17-21, A 37-40. Length up to about 7″.

COLOR: Silvery base shimmering in different colors, with numerous brownish spots.

RANGE: From the Guianas in the North down to the Paraguay River in the South.

Metynnis maculatus

CARE AND BREEDING: The living conditions of this species are not yet quite clear. Young imported specimens, for instance, stand up rather well, and even grow, but die off without apparent cause before reaching sexual maturity. It is supposed that for complete maturation they need a certain plant food which cannot be offered them in the aquarium. Corresponding to their size, they need very spacious tanks with sufficient room for swimming and exercising. The species needs especially much warmth, and may be kept at 68-77° F. In part they are described as very peaceful, others describe them as rather quarrelsome. The fact is that, besides vegetable food, they also eat vigorous live foods, above all small fishes. Spawning them has not yet succeeded.

— **roosevelti** Eigenmann: Roosevelt's Metynnis.

SHAPE: As per description of the genus. D 15-18, A 36-43. Length up to about 6″.

COLOR: Very similar to the previous species. The first rays of the anal fin of the male are extended so that the fin looks more indented, furthermore this fin is blackish on the males, while that of the females is colorless.

RANGE: The Amazon region.

CARE AND BREEDING: This species was bred for the first time by FRANKE. According to his report the fish took nearly exclusively vegetable food. They were kept together with *Pterophyllum*, as they became shy when kept alone. Breeding proved to be difficult. Spawning took place from the middle of the school, while the male embraced the female with the caudal peduncle. The relatively few, big eggs, with a diameter of about 2.5 mm, did not stick to anything but sank down to the bottom. The composition of the water was unimportant. The fry hatched after about four days and needed another five days to become free-swimming. From the first day on they took cyclops nauplii, and a week later smallest cyclops. After four weeks they had reached a length of $2\frac{3}{8}$″ and were even higher than their parents.

— **schreitmülleri** Ahl: The Schreitmueller.

This species, very similar to the preceding one, also comes from the Amazon region. It reaches a length of 5½″ and differs from the previous species by the absence of the spot design. The female has a wider belly, and a narrower, not indented, anal fin.

This species too is not easy to breed. Probably it migrates to certain flood regions during the rainy season in order to spawn there. They were first bred by SCHMIDT. The approximately 2000 eggs were 2 mm. in size. The fry hatched after about three days and became free-swimming after another 3-5 days. After 4 weeks they had reached lengths of about 1⅜″.

mexicanus: Mexican, coming from Mexico.
— *Astyanax.*

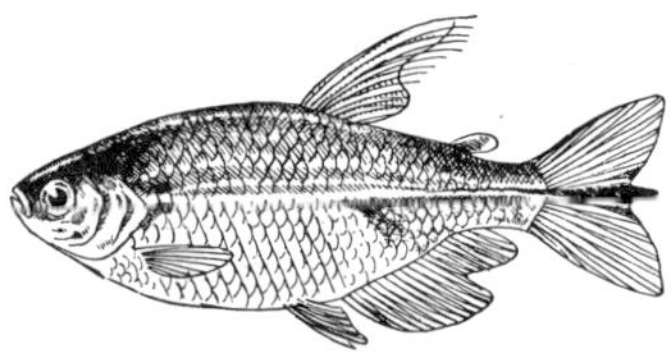

Micralestes - type of the genus

Micralestes: Small *Alestes.*
African genus pertaining to the family of the Characins or *Characidae,* comprising numerous small, but very attractive species of fishes. The body is elongated and strongly compressed laterally. The lateral line is not always complete; an adipose fin is present. The sexes often are differentiated by the extended lobe rays of the anal fin of the males, or by the rays of the dorsal fins which are drawn out into threads. The genus is very rich in species.

— acutidens (Peters): The Pointed-Tooth Tetra.
SHAPE: D 10, A 17-19. Length up to 2½″; otherwise as per description of the genus.

Micralestes acutidens

COLOR: Silver-colored, with a greenish, yellowish, and bluish sheen, and a lead-colored horizontal band. The fins of the males are extended as above, respectively lobate.
RANGE: Tropical Africa, the Nile, the Congo, the Lake Chad system, the Zambesi, and the Limpopo.

CARE AND BREEDING: A very vivacious species loving warmth: 72-82° F. Lowest 68° F. Otherwise hardy, preferring live foods, but occasionally also taking dry ones.

— hilgendorfi (Boulenger): D 10, A 23-26. Length up to 4″, Similar to the previous species.
ORIGIN: The Congo region.

microcephalus: With small head, small-headed.
— *Abramites.*

Microcorydoras: Formerly accepted genus belonging to the family of the Armored Catfishes or *Callichthyidae,* in which the group of the *Corydoras hastatus* was classified.

Microcyprini: Small Carps.
Order belonging to the sub-class of the New Fins or *Neopterygii.* A widely distributed group of fishes which is represented in all parts of the globe except Australia, avoiding the colder regions, though. The order is sub-divided into three families: Tooth Carps or *Cyprinodontidae,* Cave Fishes or *Amblyopsidae,* and *Phallostetidae.*

microdon: Small-toothed.
— *Najas.*

Microgeophagus: An eventually establishable genus belonging to the family of the Cichlids or *Cichlidae,* in which possibly *Apistogramma ramirezi* could be classified.

Microglanis: Small Glanis (Catfish).
Genus of South American Catfishes belonging to the family of the *Pimelodidae.* All of them are small species, which live on the bottom and preferentially eat live foods. They need roomy tanks with hiding places, and 68-77° F. The manner of procreating is unknown, only the act of spawning of *Microglanis parahybae* having been observed. The eggs were laid on a stone.

— parahybae Steindachner:
SHAPE: The compact body, covered only with a rugged skin, is strongly flattened in the front part, especially the big, flat head with three pairs of barbels and the very small eyes. These are covered with a glassy skin and tilted upwards.

D I/6, A 10-14. There is an adipose fin, which is very long-stretched and low. The dorsal and pectoral fins are each provided with a strong spine equipped with saw-like teeth. Length up to 2¾″.
COLOR: Brownish base with blackish bands and spots.
RANGE: In the Parahyba River, in Brazil. (*Translator's Note:* Since I have personally caught *M. parahybae* in the vicinity of Porto Alegre, RS, that is, in the extreme South of Brazil, it is to be supposed that the species is to be found all over the Brazilian territory).
CARE AND BREEDING: This pronouncedly nocturnal and twilight fish lies motionless on the bottom during day-time and only comes forth in the evening. Then it is very lively, though, and searches the tank tirelessly for its food which

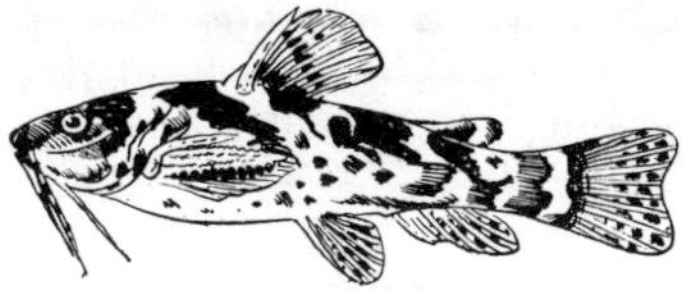

Microglanis parahybae

consists of other small bottom dwellers. It is advisable to offer the fish an aquarium that is located at a not too well lit spot and has hiding places among roots and stones. Not yet bred.

Microhydra: Genus of fresh water hydras belonging to the class of the *Hydrozoa,* of which a few species are known in Germany. *Microhydra germanica* is noted for the fact that in the succeeding generations the species produces a medusa. The hydra has no tentacles, only a few nettle capsules, and forms several branched, minute colonies of ¼ to 2 mm in diameter. Multiplication occurs asexually through division, sexually by developing the medusa from a bud that comes off. This consists of a high-arched, glass-clear bell, the edge of which is provided with a garland of tentacles. It swims by contracting and extending the bell. The medusae lay eggs, from which in turn result hydras. The small medusae of this and other species measuring 1-4 mm, have been found in several regions, and may also suddenly appear in the aquarium.

microlepidogaster: With small scales on the belly.
— *Loricaria.*

microlepis: Small-scaled.
— *Acestrorhynchus.*
— *Mimagoniates.*

Micropoecilia: Small *Poecilia.*
Genus of Tooth Carps belonging to the sub-family of the live-bearing Tooth Carps or *Poeciliinae,* with about five species. They are fishes of rather compact, relatively

short shape, which differ from the closely-related genus *Poecilia* by the different construction of the rather short gonopodium.

— **branneri** (Eigenmann): Branner's Livebearer.

SHAPE: As per description of the genus. D 7-9, A 8. Length, for both sexes, a little above ¾", therefore one of the smallest vertebrates.

COLOR: Brownish to yellowish base with a few unclear cross bands, a gold-edged tail spot, and yellowish fins on the male.

RANGE: The region of the lower Amazon river, especially in waters which are already under the influence of the sea.

CARE AND BREEDING: The species has proved to be a little frail and sensitive, and needs warmth. A constant temperature around 77° F is advisable. They are undemanding as to food, and take all kinds of live foods, soft plant fare, and dry foods. The number of the young is minute, totalling about ten specimens, which are born at the rate of one per day. At birth they are 3/16" to ¼" long, at the beginning very lively and apparently very fit to survive. Unfortunately so far no one has succeeded in rearing the fish to their full size. They never reached a length above ⅜", despite the fact that in their external shape they corresponded totally to the image of the species.

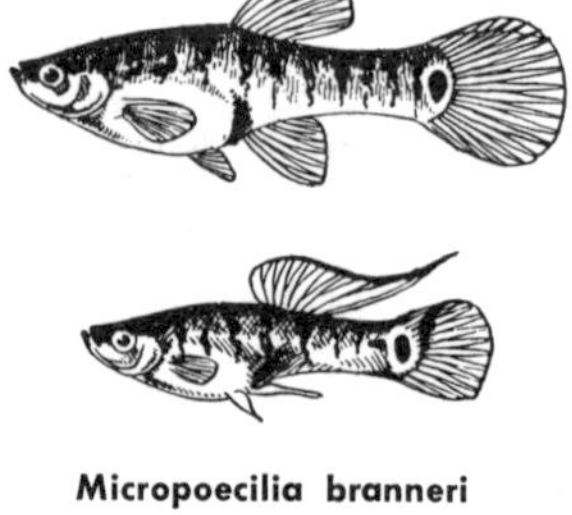

Micropoecilia branneri

Micropoecilia parae

— **parae** (Eigenmann): The Two-Spot Livebearer.

D 6-7, A 8-9, males around ¾", females about 1". Yellowish to greenish, the shoulder spot light-edged. The dorsal fin is dotted brown, the upper edge of the tail fin red with a dark eye-spot.

ORIGIN: The Amazon estuary, but also the coastal regions of Northern South America. Care as for *M. branneri*. Adult imported fish are enduring, but the few fry soon die off.

Micropterus: Genus of North American Perches belonging to the family of the Sunfishes or *Centrarchidae*. Edible fishes that grow rather big, which have also been introduced in Europe and are found there in open waters. *M. dolomieu* Lacepédè (*Grystes nigrivans* Guenther), the black sunfish, and *M. salmoides* (Guenther), the Trout Sunfish, are both pronounced predators which are little fit for keeping in the aquarium.

micropyle: Opening in the membrane of the ovum, through which in fertilization the semen enters and which closes immediately thereafter.

Micro Worms: Very small thread worms belonging to the genus *Turbatrix*, which are bred in cultures. The little worms form an easily bred baby food. It is true, though, that not all species of fishes will eat them. Even under a magnifying glass one notices that the movements of the worms are very intensive, and it is possible that this prevents some fry from eating them. Furthermore they sink relatively quickly to the bottom. Therefore one has to keep feeding controlled amounts, and to pay attention to it. Putting some drops of the micro culture on a piece of blotting paper with a dropper, one lets them dry a little and, laying the side covered with the worms on the surface of the water, they will stay there for a while before sinking to the ground. Fishes that feed from the bottom, for instance Cichlids, Catfishes, certain Barbs, etc., may, of course, easily be reared on micro worms, if attention is given to the necessary variation with other kinds of food.

Breeding them is easy. In a preserve jar, as shallow and wide as possible, one puts the lid of another, smaller jar, so that the free edges are tilted upwards. Then pour milk in the outer, bigger jar, and strew oat flakes in it. The lid in the center remains free. Finally, after this has stood for a few days, the food is seeded with worms from another culture. Now the little worms may be gathered in several ways. Either one collects those that gather at the edge and in the middle of the glass with a soft paint brush, or else one puts a bit of the micro liquid into a glass with water by means of a tea spoon, stirring well, and waiting till the worms have decanted. Then the cloudy water is poured off carefully. Repeat this process a couple of times and you will have only clean, washed micro worms left. If there should still be some coarser particles of oat flakes in the glass, one can sift the whole. After feeding, from time to time, syphon off the worms that have sunk to the bottom, as otherwise they may decay and cause harmful infusoria to rise.

GAERTNER advises that micro worms should be fed under lamp light. For this one fixes a 15-25 watt lamp on the side of the aquarium, near the bottom. The fry migrate towards the light. If the micro worms are introduced in the aquarium at this spot, they will keep floating for a longer time, due to the updraft caused by the warmth of the lamp.

Midget Freshwater Flounder, the: see TRINECTES MACULATUS.

Midget Live Bearer, the: see HETERANDRIA FORMOSA.

Migratory Mussels: see DREISSENACEAE.

Milfoil: see MYRIOPHYLLUM.

Million Fish, the: see LEBISTES RETICULATUS.

Mimagoniates: Imitator to (the genus) *Agoniates*.

South American genus belonging to the family of the Characins or *Characidae*, which, together with other species, belongs to the subfamily of the *Glandulocaudinae*. This group of Characins is characterized by the presence of internal fertilization. The genus differs from the closely related genus *Glandulocauda* only by small divergences in the construction and position of the teeth. An adipose fin is present; the lateral line is incomplete. The species possesses accessory respiration. Their care is similar to that of the other known species of Characins. The fishes are lively, good swimmers, and like to band together in schools. They are undemanding as to food, and will take all kinds of live and dry foods, in addition to vegetable foods. As far as breeding has been achieved, it occurs in a manner similar to that of *Corynopoma*.

— barberi Regan:

SHAPE: As per description of the genus; elongated, strongly compressed laterally, and with a quite sharp belly edge. D 10, A 30-34.

Mimagoniates barberi

Length up to $1\frac{3}{4}''$.

COLOR: Brownish base with a blue length band and blue seams at the edges of the fins. The dorsal of the male is pointed, and the anal a little more indented than that of the female.

RANGE: From Southeastern Brazil down to Argentina, in waters of all kinds, especially in smaller streams. The fish like to keep in swarms in the open water, but flee into plant thickets in case of danger.

CARE AND BREEDING: As per description of the genus. The species has proven a little hard to keep. They are sensitive to fluctuations in temperature, the best range being between 68 and 72° F, for breeding up to 77° F. Higher degrees of warmth are inadvisable. Roomy tanks, in sunny locations and with good aeration are necessary. In these the fish, which are lively and like to swim around, stay near the surface from where they also take their food. Breeding them is not difficult, but the fry are very sensitive and hard to rear. Not a very productive species.

— microlepis (Steindachner): The Blue Tetra.

SHAPE: As per description of the genus; very similar to the previous species. D 10, A 30-34. Length up to $2\frac{3}{4}''$.

COLOR: Silvery with blue sheen, from the middle of the body on a bluish horizontal stripe. The male is more intensely colored, his dorsal and anal fins being a little pointed and the lower lobe of the tail fin slightly arched.

RANGE: Southern Brazil.

CARE AND BREEDING: As per description of the genus. This species is not as sensitive as the previous one. They love sunlight and are best kept at 77° F. From time to time they take in air at the surface, especially during the interesting mating games, when the fish make peculiar movements side by side. It is probable that it is at this moment that they effect insemination, the mechanism of which has not yet been fully explained. While mating, the male embraces the female lightly. After 20-30 hours she scatters her eggs over plants, part falling to the bottom. The female preys strongly on her own spawn. The glass-clear alevins hatch after 26-27 hours. Since the number of eggs is not remarkably great, 75-100 young may be considered a quite good yield from a breeding.

Mimagoniates microlepis

mimicry: Resemblance to other organisms which are protected against enemies by means of venom, stings, or other protective organs which have come forth during the genetical history of development. Through it the respective animal may enjoy the advantages which the imitated live being has. The adaptation of an animal to lifeless

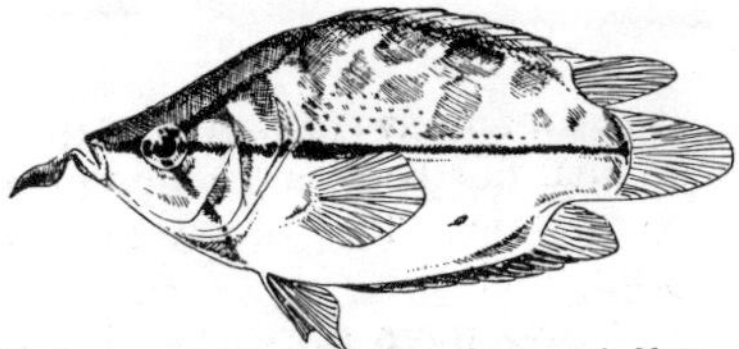

Mimicry — note how the shape of Monocirrhus polyacanthus, plus its manner of gliding through the water, gives it the appearance of a dead leaf.

objects by means of color and shape is called "mimesis". Through this the imitating animal may find protection against enemies, but on the other hand, if it is a predator, it may also escape visual detection by its prey.

Cases of mimicry and mimesis are very frequent among insects. Mimesis is also found, for instance, with the Leaf Fish, *Monocirrhus polyacanthus,* which, being a fish of prey, imitates shape, color, and behavior of dead leaves.

Opinions on the real biological value of mimicry and mimesis are still very much divided since some of the imitators do not share the locations of living with the imitated live beings.

minor: Small.

— *Hyphessobrycon callistus.*

— *Lemna.*

— *Najas.*

Minnow, the: see PHOXINUS LAEVIS.

Misgurnus: Derived from the French popular name of the fish "misgurne".

Genus belonging to the family of the Loaches or *Cobitidae.* Fishes of elongated, eel-like body. The fore part of the body is cylindrical, the tail end strongly compressed laterally. The body is covered with small scales, which are imbedded deep within the skin and may be lacking completely in spots. The fins are relatively small. The mouth is small and sub-terminal. The upper jaw carries two long, the lower one two short pairs of barbels. The fishes have a well-developed intestinal respiration which permits them to remain hidden in the mud for a long time when the waters dry up. Air for breathing is taken in at the surface, with smacking noises, while the used-up air is expelled through the anus. The genus, with a number of species, is distributed over Europe and temperate Asia.

— **fossilis** (Linné): The Weather Fish.

SHAPE: As per description of the genus. It carries spines beneath the eyes, but they are hidden within the thick skin. The frontal nasal pits are extended tube-like. The gill openings form only a narrow slit. D 7-11, A 7-10. Length up to 12″. in the Eastern part of its range sometimes up to 20″.

COLOR: Yellowish-brown base with some beautiful brown horizontal bands. The belly is orange-colored, especially that of the males.

Misgurnus fossilis

RANGE: Central and Eastern Europe to the Volga River, further on a sub-species in East Asia. In stagnant, shallow waters with muddy bottom.

CARE AND BREEDING: In the aquarium the weather fish is absolutely undemanding. It is hardy and endures the worst waters, to which its intestinal breathing enables it especially. Food is taken mainly from the bottom. In dry times it digs into the mud and may remain there for long periods in 'summer sleep'. If put into water, it immediately is able to move again. The fish is sensitive to the electricity of the air or to changes in atmospheric pressures. At these occasions it becomes very restive, which has given rise to its fame as weather forecaster.

The weather fish has already several times been spawned in the aquarium. After an interesting mating game, during which the fish flit around the tank side by side or chasing each other, the spawn is given off singly or in small heaps, on plants near the bottom or on the bottom itself.

misshapings, malformations: Hereditary or acquired changes in construction of the body, which appear also on fishes, especially hereditary distortions of the dorsal spine, shortenings of the facial skull, and stuntings of the fins, as well as hereditary changes in colors (see COLOR MALFORMATIONS). When such phenomena occur among the descendants of fishes, the crippled specimens should be destroyed, and in case of greater percentage of incidences, the whole tribe should be excluded from further breedings, if the malformation remains outside the aim of the breeder.

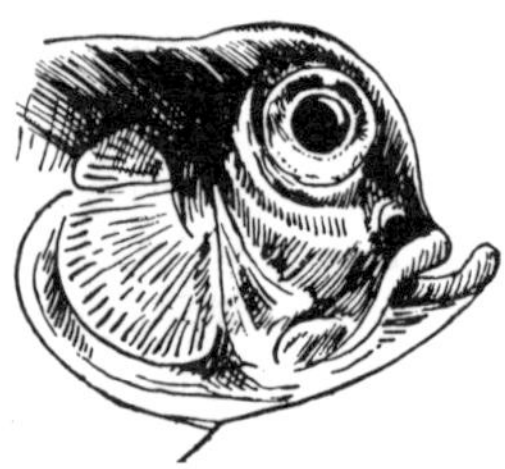

Malformation of the head

mitosis: Division of cells or of nuclei under the development of chromosomes.

miurus: Small-tailed.

— *Tetraodon.*

Mochokidae: Feather-Whiskered Catfishes.

Family pertaining to the sub-order of the Catfishes or *Siluroidea*, the representatives of which have their home countries in Asia and Africa. The family is noted especially for having feathered barbels. The head armor is strong, the remainder of the body unarmored. A further characteristic feature is the big adipose fin, which may extend from the tip of the dorsal to the tail fin.

Nearly all fishes of this family love clean water, plentiful plants, and hiding places. Some of the species are very sensitive to temperature. 75° F should be adequate. The most important genus is *Synodontis.*

modesta: Modest.

— *Botia.*

modification: Re-shaping of an animal or plant species under the influence of conditions of the ambient world.

Moenkhausia: After a personal name.

South American genus belonging to the family of the Characins or *Characidae*, with about forty known species, which are more or less small and strongly divergent externally from each other. The lateral line is complete. The tail fin is in part covered with scales which are smaller than those of the body. An adipose fin is present.

— oligolepis (Guenther): The Glass Tetra.

SHAPE: The diamond to egg shaped body still grows in height with age. In all the fish looks a little awkward. The relatively big mouth opening is tilted obliquely upwards. D 11, A 24-28. Length up to 5″.

COLOR: Silver to brassy sheen, with a deep black spot on the caudal peduncle, which at times is divided. The iris is shiny red. The male is smaller and slimmer.

RANGE: The Amazon region and the Guianas. In smaller waters of the most varied kinds.

Moenkhausia oligolepis

CARE AND BREEDING: This lively fish, which grows relatively big, needs roomy tanks. Only younger specimens are fit for communities as with advancing age they become rather vicious and aggressive, being very voracious. Live foods are preferred, and dry ones taken only occasionally. Temperatures: 68-77° F, for breeding a little higher. Spawning takes place after the manner of most egg-scattering characins, but is not simple. A special 'must' are big tanks. The fry grow very quickly.

— **pittieri** Eigenmann: The Diamond Tetra.

SHAPE: As per description of the genus. The species is of relatively high build. D 11, A 26-29. The fins of the males are strongly developed, especially the dorsal, anal, and ventral fins are elongated with lobes. Length up to $2\frac{3}{8}''$, the males generally a little smaller.

COLOR: Silvery gray with numerous metallic-glistening splinters. The fins are a pretty gray with white edges, which are especially apparent on the males.

RANGE: Lake Valencia and its surroundings, in Venezuela.

CARE AND BREEDING: This very sociable and extraordinarily fast-swimming species needs not-too-small tanks with room for swimming and exercising. They are best kept in communities as otherwise they may become a little shy. During the spawning period the males may sometimes prove a little quarrelsome. Temperatures 72-79° F, occasionally also a little less. No special demands are made as to feeding, but the food should be offered them in rich quantities. The fish look best when in schools of their own species. Then they are of a remarkable beauty, which shows up especially well under incident light. Breeding them is not especially difficult, and takes place in a manner similar to that of most of the other egg-scattering Characins. The fish are set up in pairs, the male chasing very strongly. The eggs number 300-400. The fry keep somewhat hidden, but grow up quickly if given rich feedings.

Moenkhausia pittieri

— **sanctae filomenae** (Steindachner): The Red-Eyed Moenkhausia.

SHAPE: A species of relatively high build, which reminds one strongly of *M. oligolepis*. D 9, A 22-23. The scales are relatively big. The lateral line is incomplete. Length about $2\frac{3}{4}''$, the male remaining a little smaller.

COLOR: Mother-of-pearl with yellowish hue. The dark edging of the scales gives the impression of a reticulate design. At the tip of the caudal peduncle is an outstanding yellow zone, limited by a deep-black band at the rear. The upper part of the big eyes is a shiny blood red. The males are smaller and slimmer than the females.

RANGE: The Paraguay River system.
CARE AND BREEDING: As described for *M. oligolepis*, but this species is said to be more peaceful.

Mogurnda:
Australian genus of fresh water gobies belonging to the family of the Sleeper Gobies or Eleotridae.

— mogurnda Richardson: The Purple Striped Gudgeon.
SHAPE: A robust-looking species, of elongated, nearly cylindrical build. The mouth opening is wide and supraterminal. The dorsal fin is divided into two parts. The ventrals are located in the throat and are not grown together at their origin. Length up to 4″.
COLOR: Olive-brown base with numerous red-brown and greenish spots. Especially the gill covers are ornamented with green, iridescent dots. The pupil of the eye possesses a grayish-green sheen and gives a somewhat 'dead' impression. The females are a little plumper. The genital papilla of the male is pointed, that of the female is broad.
RANGE: The coastal regions of Eastern Australia, both in fresh and brackish waters.

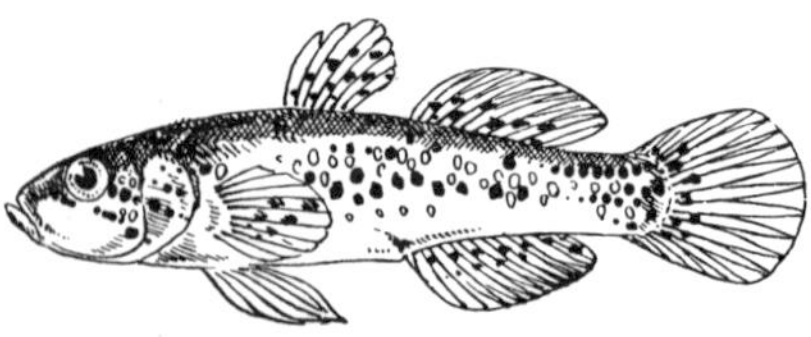

Mogurnda mogurnda

CARE AND BREEDING: A somewhat placid, generally undemanding and rugged species. The fish like to rest on rocks on the ground, leaning on their ventral fins, with only the pectorals in motion to indicate that there is life. They are voracious eaters, which fall ambush-like on their prey and are able to swallow quite considerable bits with their big mouths. They will take exclusively strong live foods. No demands are made as to the composition of the water, but an addition of one teaspoon of salt per 2½ gallons of water is advisable. Outfit the tanks with coarse gravel and hiding places made up of plants, roots and rocks.

Reproduction shows some peculiarities. According to FEIGS the eggs are stuck onto stones. The spawn is closely crowded together and the number of eggs may reach about 400. They have a peculiar, cigar-like shape. Swelling enlarges the egg shell to about 3 mm. in height with 1 mm. in diameter. After three days the embryo with its yolk sac becomes visible within the shell. After another three days it moves freely within the shell, as far as this is possible within the confined space. The head rests in the tip of the egg, while the rear of the body is folded over towards the front. At this time the embryo bursts out of its covering. The yolk sac has already been used up. The hatched fry rest on the ground for some hours, then they begin to swim free. The male watches over the spawn. The caring fish is very sensitive to disturbances. Rearing the fry is very easy as they immediately take normal powdered foods, nauplii of *Artemia* and cyclops, as well as micro and grindal worms.

molecule: The smallest imaginable unit into which a chemical combination may be divided without interfering with its properties.

Mollienisia: Genus of South and Central American Tooth Carps belonging to the sub-family of the live-bearing Tooth Carps or *Poeciliinae*. Some of the species belong among the stateliest fishes of the family, and possess a greatly enlarged dorsal fin. Many species too are prone to black colorings. These forms are offered commercially as Black Mollies.

— **dominicensis** Everman & Clark: A species originating from Haiti, of which the males reach 1½", the females 2⅜". Care corresponds to that of the different species of *Limia*. Similar to these, *M. dominicensis* too loves warmth and needs vegetable food.

— **formosa:**
Mexican natural hybrid between *M. sphenops* and *M. latipinna*, with a peculiar hereditary cycle, where in part only females are produced. The male partners have no influence on the looks of the female hybrids, which again mate with the males of the original species.

— **latipinna** Lesueur: The Sail-fin Mollie.

SHAPE: A robust species that grows very big, of elongated, but evenly high body build, laterally compressed. The head is a little flattened on top. The mouth is supraterminal. The dorsal fin, which on a number of the males is extraordinarily big, has 14 rays. On beautiful specimens the height of the dorsal is greater than that of the body. The species is variable and hard to differentiate from *M. velifera*. According to K. VOGT the visible difference, besides the divergent numbers of rays of the dorsal fins, is based on the fact that the spots at the bottom of same are oval and overlap from one fin ray to the next on *M. latipinna*, while they are round on *M. velifera* and confined to the web between the rays. Length up to 3½".

Mollienisia latipinna

COLOR: The glossy bluish body is covered by a reticulate design interrupted by horizontal stripes. Under incident light each of the scales has a greenish sheen. The female is much simpler in color, as well as plumper. Sex differences are similar to those of all live bearing Tooth Carps.

RANGE: From the Southeast of the U.S.A. to Yucatan, especially in the brackish waters of river mouths.

CARE AND BREEDING: These big Mollies need roomy tanks as otherwise they remain stunted in growth. Imported specimens need an addition of 10-20% sea water or 5% kitchen salt. Aquarium bred fish seem to need the salt addition only if showing signs of unease. In this case they keep shimmying strongly, remaining in one place, with closed fins. The same symptoms are seen too when the temperature sinks too low, as the fish needs much warmth. 75-82° F are most favorable. Lowest temperature 68° F.

Of extreme importance too is food. Being greedy eaters, Mollies need plentiful and variegated food. They eat all kinds of live and dry foods, but cannot dispense with a vegetable addition. This may consist of algae or, if these are not available, of stale lettuce leaves or of quick-cooked and rinsed oat flakes.

If they feel well, the fish are extraordinarily lively. Avoid, though, putting several high-finned males together, as they may tear or destroy one another's dorsals, which do not grow back.

Procreation and breeding offer no special difficulties, not considering the fact that the fry have to be fed very abundantly in order to obtain high-finned specimens among the males. Since this is only noticed after completion of the sexual metamorphosis, and often even considerably later, it may become quite difficult to rear greater numbers of young. Plentiful feeding is a primary condition for a later development of fins. Furthermore the most promising young males have to be kept separate from the first moment of change on, as apparently the development of the high dorsal is hindered by keeping the fry in schools.

— **sphenops** (Cuvier and Valenciennes): The Marbled Mollie.

SHAPE: The species is relatively slender and elongated, only little compressed laterally, especially as far as the females are concerned. The unsightly original form is hardly ever found in aquaria. Sizes are variable.

COLOR: This species presents a whole series of sub-species. In some of these the males stand out through the beautifully colored tail fins, which show an orange-colored, broad edge. Others, on their part, have carmine red fins with black patterns. The best-known are the black mottled or totally black species. The latter are also known as 'Black Mollies'. The black specimens are especially sensitive and in need of warmth.

RANGE: The original form is found in waters of the coastal region from Texas to Venezuela.

CARE AND BREEDING: Peaceful, omnivorous fish, which need vegetable diet like all other species of the genus. The black forms are especially sensitive to fluctuations in warmth, and to low temperatures. The water warmth should never sink below 75° F. Aquaria in which Black Mollies live should never be heated from the bottom, most especially because the fish like to lie down on warm spots and then become prone to diseases. Among

Mollienisia sphenops

the descendants of black pairs one repeatedly finds not purely black young. Sometimes they develop the full color within the course of development, though.

— **velifera** (Regan): The Sail-Fin Mollie.

SHAPE: As described for *M. latipinna*. This species is still bigger than *M. latipinna*, but fish have that been reared in the aquarium do not reach the size of the imported specimens. The possibility that commercially offered specimens may often be crosses between the two species *M. latipinna* and *M. velifera*, is not to be rejected. The dorsal fin has 18 rays.

Mollienisia velifera

COLOR: Glossy blue with reticulate design and greenish-white shiny dots in close rows. Breast and throat become occasionally orange-colored slightly, even on females. Sexual differences are similar to those of *M. latipinna* and of all other live bearing Tooth Carps.

Hyphessobrycon herbertaxelrodi, the so-called "Black Neon Tetra."

Photo by E. Roloff

Centrarchidae (Sunfishes) - **Nandidae** (Nandids) - **Centropomidae** (Glass Perches) - **Scatophagidae** (Scats) - **Toxotidae** (Archer Fishes) - **Percidae** (Perches).

1. **Enneacanthus obesus** - 2. **Monocirrhus polyacanthus**, the Leaf Fish - 3. **Elassoma evergladei**, the Dwarf Sunfish - 4. **Mesogonistius chaetodon**, the Black-Banded Sunfish - 5. **Polycentrus schomburgki**, Schomburgk's Leaf Fish - 6. **Badis badis** - 7. **Lepomis megalotis**, the Long-Eared Sunfish - 8. **Ambassis lala**, the Glass Fish - 9. **Polycentropsis abbreviata**, the African Leaf Fish - 10. **Perca fluviatilis** - 11. **Scatophagus argus**, the Scat - 12. **Toxotes jaculatrix**, the Archer Fish - 13. **Lucioperca lucioperca**.

Cyprinodontinae (Egg-Laying Tooth Carps)

1. **Aphanius sophiae** - 2. **Fundulus chrysotus**, the Golden Ear - 3. **Aphaniops dispar** - 4. **Leptolucania omata** - 5. **Jordanella floridae**, the American Flag Fish - 6. **Cubanichthys cubensis** - 7. **Chriopeops goodei**, the Bluefin - 8. **Aplocheilus lineatus** - 9. **Aplocheilus panchax** - 10. **Epiplatys fasciolatus** - 11. **Aplocheilus blockii** - 12. **Pachypanchax playfairi** - 13. **Epiplatys chaperi**, the Fire-Mouth Panchax - 14. **Epiplatys macrostigma** - 15. **Aphyosemion coeruleum** - 16. **Aphyosemion cognatum** - 17. **Aphyosemion gulare** - 18. **Aphyosemion australe**, the Cape Lopez Lyretail - 19. **Aphyosemion arnoldi** - 20. **Aphyosemion sjoestedti** - 21. **Aphyosemion bivittatum bivittatum** - 22. **Aphyosemion gardneri**.

1. **Macropodus opercularis**, the Paradise Fish - 2. **Sphaerichthys osphromenoides**, the Chocolate Gourami - 3. **Macropodus opercularis concolor**, the Black Paradise Fish - 4. **Macropodus cupanus**, the Spike-Tailed Paradise Fish - 5. **Macropodus cupanus dayi** - 6. **Belontia signata**, the Combtail - 7. **Macropodus chinensis**, the Round-Tailed Paradise Fish - 8. **Betta splendens**, the Siamese Fighting Fish, female of the green strain - 9. **Betta brederi** - 10. **Betta splendens**, wild form - 11. **Betta bellica** - **Betta splendens** male of the white form.

Four male Guppies, **Lebistes reticulatus**, developed by Reinhold Kleiss.

Marigold Platies, a sport developed from **Xiphophorus variatus**

Cyprinodontidae (Tooth Carps) - Poeciliinae (Live-Bearing Tooth Carps)

1. left, **Gambusia punctata**, female - 1. right, male - 2. left, **Gambusia affinis holbrooki**, female - 2. right, male - 3. left, **Belonesox belizanus**, female - 3. right, male - 4. top, **Heterandria formosa**, male - 4. bottom, female - 5. top, **Pseudoxiphophorus bimaculatus**, female - 5. bottom, male - 6. left, **Phallichthys amates**, male - 6. right, female - 7. top, **Phalloceros caudomaculatus**, spotted form, female - 7. center, male - 7. bottom, wild form - 8. left, **Quintana atrizona**, male - 8. right, female - 9. top, **Girardinus metallicus**, female - 9. bottom, male - 10. top, **Poecilistes pleurospilus**, female - 10. bottom, male - 11. top, **Cnesterodon decemmaculatus**, male - 11. bottom, female - 12. left, **Mollienisia sphenops**, black form - 12. center, marbled form, female below - 12. right, orange-tailed form - 12. lower right, red-finned form - 13. **Mollienisia velifera**, male right, female left.

Megalamphodus sweglesi, a recently-introduced Characin.

Photo by E. Roloff

RANGE: In the coastal region of the Mexican Yucatan peninsula, especially in brackish waters, in part also in the sea.

CARE AND BREEDING: As described for *M. latipinna*.

Mollusca: Mollusks.

Phylum of invertebrate animals with soft, little-articulated bodies, which have neither supporting skeleton nor limbs. They are either completely naked, or else the body sits within a protecting shell, the calcium components of which are secreted by the skin. The shell has only little linkage to the body.

The skin is slimy, soft, and often extends into lobate or mantle-like extensions, which may cover the whole body. The shell snails cover their heads with such mantles when they 'retire'. The shells of shell fish or clams originated from bi-lateral mantles. There is a nerve system. The vascular system is partially open, that is, in some places the blood flows directly into the cavities which surround the organs. Most mollusks breathe by means of gills, but some groups show pulmonary respiration.

The beginning of the digestive tract of many groups possesses a motile plate equipped with rasp-like teeth.

Of the two sub-phyla, only the sub-phylum of the *Conchifera*, with the classes of the snails or *Gastropoda*, and the shell fishes or *Bivalvia* contribute to the aquarium dwellers.

monniera: Named after the French botanist Monnier.

— *Bacopa*.

Monocirrhus: With one barbel (on the chin).

South American genus belonging to the family of the Nandids or *Nandidae*, with high body, strongly compressed laterally, wide mouth opening, and extendable jaws. Remarkable for their accommodation to the ambient world (mimesis), through which the fish create the deceptive impression of dead leaves floating in the water. Their manner of living is hidden, nocturnal, and preying.

— polyacanthus Heckel: The Leaf Fish.

SHAPE: As per description of the genus. The forehead line is strongly indented and rises steeply to the insertion of the dorsal fin. From there the back continues with a very insignificant down-tilt to the caudal peduncle, which is very short. The jaws and palate are equipped with small teeth disposed in rows. The lower jaw carries a fleshy extension, which may be erected under excitement, causing the impression of a leaf stem. D XVI-XVII/12-13, A XII-XIII/12-14. Length up to 4″.

COLOR: Brownish, with a thin line along the body, and irregular dark spots. The design varies much from one fish to the next. The tail fin and the soft parts of the dorsal and anal fins are transparent. Sexual differences are only minute, presumably, though, the male is a little smaller and more rounded.

RANGE: Tropical South America, especially in smaller bodies of water, the outer affluents of rivers, in slow-flowing and shady streams in the forests, in swamps, and in pools. There the fish keep near the shores. The species is considered rare, probably because it is hard to catch due to its hidden manner of living.

CARE AND BREEDING: As per description of the genus (see NANDIDAE). The species has rarely been imported so far. They love warmth, 77° F and more should be considered advisable, lowest 72° F. Breeding has been achieved. According to an American report the eggs were stuck on to the glass pane of the aquarium and guarded by the male up to the moment of hatching. The young emerged after four days at 80° F, then hung from a thread for another three days near the spawning site. At the beginning of the free-swimming stage, they already were quite big and immediately took finely sifted daphnia.

Monocotyledoneae: Plants with one germinating leaf.

Class belonging to the sub-phylum of the *Angiospermae*, characterized by the possession of one germinating leaf. The foliage leaves generally have parallel, clearly marked nervures. This class comprises, among others, the following families, which in part are more extensively described under the corresponding entries in this book:

Frog Spoon Worts, or ALISMATACEAE;

Narcissus plants, or AMARYLLIDACEAE;

Water Ear plants, or APONOGETONACEAE;

BUTOMACEAE;

Cyprus grasses, or CYPERACEAE;

Grasses or GRAMINEAE;

Frogbit plants, or HYDROCHARITACEAE;

Water Lentils, or LEMNACEAE;

TYPHACEAE;

SPARGANIACEAE;

NAJADACEAE;

POTAMOGETONACEAE.

Monodactylidae: Family of brackish water fishes belonging to the sub-order of the Perch-like or *Percoidea*, which belong among the typical dwellers of tropical coastal waters. They are characterized by their high body, which is strongly compressed laterally and reminds one a little of *Pterophyllum*. The scales go over far onto the fins. The family comprises only one genus: *Monodactylus*, which is also known as *Psettus*.

The fish demand roomy tanks, as they like very much to swim.

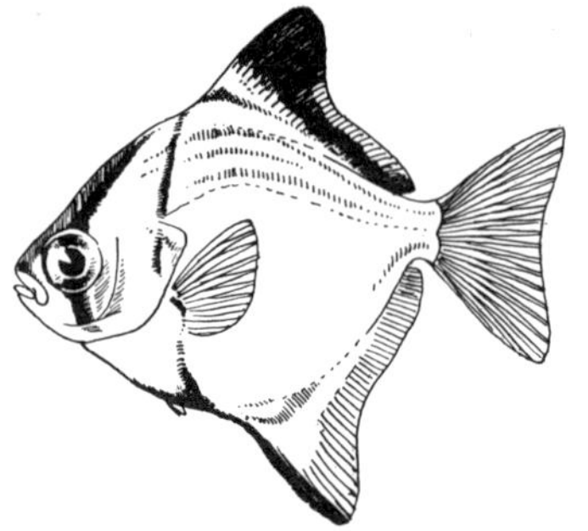

Monodactylus argenteus

Imported specimens are best kept in pure sea water at the beginning, which may then be diluted gradually with fresh water. Specimens, though, that are kept in pure fresh water, have to be put into pure sea water or into strong brackish water from time to time. The species needs warmth, temperatures between 75 and 86° F, lowest 72° F. They take only smaller live foods, always in small quantities only. The fish are a little quarrelsome toward each other, but without any serious consequences of the "disputes." They are sensitive to changes of water as well as lesions during transportation. Nothing is known about their reproduction.

M. argenteus (Linné): Originates in the Red Sea, from the East Coast of Africa down to Australia. The species reaches a length of 8″. Coloring is a pretty silver sheen with yellow fins.

M. falciformes Lacépede comes from the same regions, while the beautiful *M. sebae* Cuvier and Valenciennes, which resembles *Pterophyllum*, comes from the West Coast of Africa.

monoecian: Plants that grow male and female flowers.

Monogenea: Order of leeches with one sucking disc. See TREMATODES.

montevidensis: Coming from Montevideo.

— *Sagittaria*.

montezumae: After the last Aztec potentate Montezuma.
— *Xiphophorus.*

monticola: Mountain dweller.
— *Agnostomus.*

Mormyridae: Nile Pikes.
Family belonging to the order of the Herring fishes or *Isospondyli.* A small group of very peculiar fishes which in part possess a weak electric organ on both sides of the caudal peduncle. The swimming bladder is simple and has an open air passage. The gill covers are covered with a thin skin which leaves only a small breathing cleft open.

The fishes induce one to make comparisons with certain mammals and birds, due to their diversely shaped mouths and to their peculiar body shapes. The extension of the head serves to ferret out food from the mud, for which the small, deeply-imbedded eyes would hardly be of use. The mouth itself is small and equipped only with a few white teeth. Anal and dorsal fins are long and many-rayed.

The Nile Pikes are pure fresh water fishes and are found in the Upper Nile as well as in the whole of tropical Central Africa. They are very shy with regard to light and like to dig in into the mud, coming out only with the beginning of twilight. Due to their quarrelsomeness, even towards members of their own species, they can only be kept in large tanks with sufficient hiding possibilities. In all, they have to be considered primarily as objects of show for public aquaria. It seems that they care for their spawn and build nests. Furthermore it is reported that during the larval stage the fry hang from threads in their nests for 4-5 days.

In 1940 Berg established an order of their own for the family, within the sub-class of the *Neopterygii,* into which he classified the two families *Mormyridae* and *Gymnarchidae,* which differentiate through their respective fins.

Genera, among others: *Marcusenius, Gnathonemus, Mormyrus,* and *Gymnarchus.*

Mormyrus: Genus belonging to the family of the Nile Pikes or *Mormyridae.*

— kanumae Forskal: The Tapir-Trunk Fish.
The body is elongated, only little compressed laterally, the mouth is very small, the lips are very thick and fleshy. The snout is extended like a tapir's trunk. Length up to 20″.

Fish which live nocturnally, coming from the Nile River region, mainly fit for show aquaria. They feed on the smallest live foods, detritus, and algae. Temperature 72-80° F.

morphology: The science of the construction and shape of live beings.

morsus ranae: Frog-bitten.
— *Hydrocharis.*

Mosaic Gourami, the: see Trichogaster leeri.

Mosquito Fish, the: see Gambusia affinis holbrooki.

mosquito larvae: The larvae of the different species of mosquitoes are a nutritious and coveted fish food. In the tropics, during certain periods of the year, they are the main food for many species of fishes. Unfortunately the fact that certain mosquito species sting and suck blood and are partly also transmitters of much-feared fevers has caused biologically valuable ponds and small bodies of water even in our regions—and not only in the Tropics and Sub-Tropics—to be filled up, or to be poured full of coal oil on the surface, or to be poisoned in other ways, killing off all life in them. It has to be pointed out, though, that in the temperate zones mosquitoes generally live in rain barrels, water ditches, and the like, or, like the broods of the meadow gnat, come from inundation zones. The biological harm caused by the senseless fight against them therefore generally is bigger than the apparent gain.

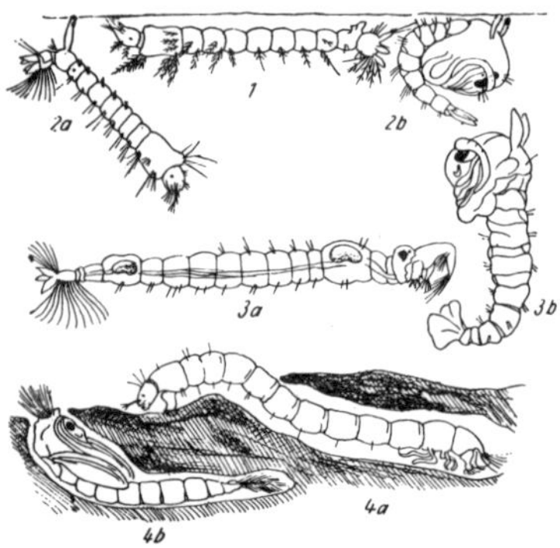

Types of mosquito larvae - 1. **Anopheles** - 2a. **Culex** larva - 2b. pupa - 3a. **Sayomyia** larva - 3b. pupa - 4a. **Chironomus** larva - 4b. pupa.

The mosquito larvae used as fish food are mentioned here in the order of colors commonly used by aquarists. It has to be pointed out, though, that this division, used especially in commerce, has no scientific value at all, as, for instance, the Chironomids, mentioned as 'red mosquito larvae' also present white and green forms.

1. White Mosquito Larvae are the larvae of harmless gnats (*Sayomyia*, formerly called *Corethra*), which are glassily transparent and float horizontally in the water. They are enabled to do this due to two silvery-bright air containers, visible to the naked eye, which are found at the extremities of the body, and which establish the specific weight of this according to the depth of the water by taking in or giving off air. Breathing is not done at the surface, but through the skin directly from the water. The pupae are known by their thick heads and by the vertical position of the body.

White mosquito larvae are found in stagnant waters at any time of the year. In gnat-infested areas they may appear in incredible numbers in small ponds, ditches, etc. To catch them use a net made of a rough fabric, as they are nimble and flee with quick movements of the body when disturbed. They are eagerly eaten by all bigger fishes, but one should take care not to put the larvae in tanks with young fry, as they are predators. They may be kept for long periods of time in larger, well-aerated containers, in cool water, which should be protected against winter frosts, though.

The hatched gnats are easily recognized by the finely articulated antennae of the males. This gnat does not sting.

2. Black Mosquito Larvae are the larvae of stinging mosquitoes of several genera, which are present in rain barrels, ponds, meadow ditches, etc. They are found from late Spring to Autumn, generally in great quantities, in mosquito-infested regions. The eggs are laid in boat-shaped bundles on the surface of the water. The larvae themselves generally hang upside down from the surface, in order to take in air, since their respiratory tubes are located at the end of the body. The motile pupae are easily recognized by their thick heads. In order to breathe, the larvae of *Anopheles*, the feared malaria mosquito, take on an horizontal position. If disturbed, the beasts disappear into the depths turning somersaults, but show up soon again.

Black mosquito larvae are fondly

taken by all fishes, especially so as in the Tropics they often represent their main food. It is advisable, though, not to feed them in bigger quantities than are eaten at a time. Furthermore it is advisable not to store them, considering the plague of mosquitoes they develop in the home.

3. Red Mosquito Larvae are the larvae of Chironomid gnats which live in the mud, and are found in irrigation ditches during the whole year, especially in Winter. Their presence in numbers makes them an important fish food. The fact that they are available also in Winter makes them indispensable for aquaristics.

They are a very nutritious food, which is taken greedily. It has to be observed, though, that one-sided feeding with them may cause the appearance of diseases, which eventually may be explained through the origin of the larvae from sewage ditches. It may happen too, that after some time the fishes decline accepting them. Left-over larvae dig themselves in into the bottom. Therefore one should never feed more than are eaten at a time. With some care red mosquito larvae keep for quite some time. For this one places them in shallow dishes with very little water, which has to be changed daily. The larvae should be rinsed in a thin sieve under a water outlet. They can also be kept for longer periods in damp fabric. They should be kept in cool places, but free of frost. The hatched gnats do not sting.

For further instructions on the nutrition of fishes look up the entries Food, Feeding, and Catching of Food.

Moss Beasts: see BRYOZOA.

Moss Fern: see AZOLLA.

Mosses: see BRYOPHYTA.

Mother-of-Pearl Carp, the: see APHANIUS DISPAR.

Mother-of-Pearl Cichlid, the: see TILAPIA LEPIDURA.

Mother-of-Pearl Dirt-Eater, the: see GEOPHAGUS GYMNOGENIS.

motional sight: Many animals, including numerous fishes, are only able to recognize prey as such if it is in motion. This happens especially with fishes of prey and eaters of micro-animals. Besides this, motional sight probably is also significant for swarm fishes in order to maintain their unity and in order to perceive enemies. According to the behavior of certain species, motion triggers certain reflexes for which we have to consider them as triggers such as, for instance, the snapping reflex, the reaction of flight or of camouflage, etc.

Mountain Grayling, the: see AGONOSTOMUS.

Mourning Cloak Tetra, the: see GYMNOCORYMBUS TERNETZI.

mouth breeders: Comprehensive name for fishes belonging to different families which have the common characteristic of breeding their fry in their mouths. Cases of mouth breeding are found in numerous Catfishes, Climbing Perches, Tooth Carps, Herring fishes, and especially Cichlids. Within this family mainly the members of the genera *Haplochromis*, *Tilapia*, and *Geophagus* care for their fry by mouth breeding.

mouth breeding experiment: Experiments made by PETERS in order to verify the innate behavior of mouth breeding Cichlids. The matter under research was primarily the fact that the fry seek their mother's mouth for protection in case of danger. In some cases, when the female tries to take them in, the young rush towards her from all sides, in other cases, though, they react less strongly and have to be sought out

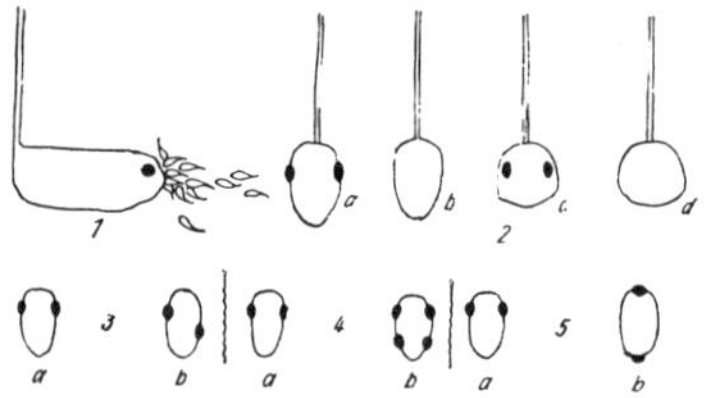

Mouthbreeder experiment, after Peters - 1. dummy, seen from the side - 2. row of dummies, presented separately - a, normal reaction by the fry - b, not as good a reaction - c, slight reaction - d, scarcely any reaction - 3 through 5. dummies presented in pairs, dummy "a" normal and dummy "b" abnormal - pairs 3 and 4 got almost similar reactions between a and b, and with pair 5, a got a distinct preference over b.

by the female. PETERS primarily reaches the conclusion that the behavior of the fry is determined by certain signals of the mother fish. (Experiments with *Haplochromis multicolor*). In order to detect the nature of these signals, a swarm of young fry was put in a glass jar, which in turn was introduced in the tank where the mother was. The female swam towards the young, and these towards her. They thronged in dense masses near her mouth when she tried to snap them up. Thus it was verified that the young are triggered by an optical impression. The fry also reacted to a dead specimen when this was moved around on a wire. In another experiment, with a much bigger Cichlid, *Tilapia natalensis*, it was seen that the young swam actively into the opened mouth of a dead fish, that is, when they were not snapped up.

Experiments with dummies made of putty which, when seen from in front, reminded one of a full-grown *Haplochromis*, and on which the eyes were represented by glass beads, resulted in that the dummy, when moved on a wire, attracted the fry in the same manner as the mother. The young tried to penetrate it. The experiment was repeated with fish that had been taken from the mother's mouth while still in the embryonic stage and had been reared in a glass jar. As soon as these became free-swimming, they were used for the experiment. These fry, which obviously did not know a mother fish and had no experience at all, behaved just like the normally hatched specimens right from the beginning. Thus it is proved that the behavior of fish fry is innate and instinctive.

Thereafter the dummies were given different looks, in order to try out how far the hereditary recognition of the looks of the mother will go. The changes comprised both the shape and the presence, also the absence of eyes. Experimenting with the young that had been reared in a jar it was found that they really make fine distinctions. In this it was determined that besides the shape of the head also the eyes seem to represent an important feature.

In another series of experiments two different dummies respectively, connected by a wire, were presented to the spawn in order to elicit a choice. Also in this the dummy that was more similar to the parent was more or less distinctly preferred. The dissimilar dummies differed from the others by the number and position of the 'eyes'.

In a further experiment, in which young *Tilapia natalensis* had been smuggled among a spawning of *Haplochromis* (still in egg form), it was found that the size of the mother is included in the hereditary notions.

Most interesting too were the experiments in which the own young of two female *Haplochromis* were exchanged for those of the non-mouth breeding Cichlid *Hemichromis bimaculatus*. The mouth breeders cared for the strange young in the same manner as for their own, snapped them up when under stimulus, and kept them in their mouths for longish lapses of time. The fry fled from hasty movements of the caring female (which those of her own species do too) but permitted themselves to be snapped up easily at quieter movements. Repeatedly some young also swam actively into the mouth, and in one case they assembled in a swarm in front of it. PETERS warns against precipitated conclusions, but admits the possibility that the genetic-historical development of mouth-breeding is pre-determined in non-mouth breeding species.

Mud Fish, the: see AMIA CALVA.

Mud Fish, the African: see PHRACTOLAEMUS ANSORGEI.

Mud Skippers: see PERIOPHTHALMINAE.

Mud Snails: see LIMNAEIDAE.

Mugil: The sucker.

Genus belonging to the family of the Sea Graylings, which ranges over the Tropics and Sub-Tropics, the greater number of them living in the oceans, with some species in the brackish water zones and in pure fresh water.

They are lively school fishes, which in part reach considerable size. The oblong body, strongly compressed laterally, is covered with big scales, including the head. No lateral line is found. A special characteristic are the two dorsal fins, which stand far apart, and of which the first is supported by hard, but elastic, rays. The mouth opening is short, the upper lip is fleshy, and the lips are equipped with small skin teeth. The fishes feed on organic detritus and smaller bottom dwellers, which they take in, together with the mud, that is in turn separated by a trap-like apparatus and then expelled again.

Some of the species are fit for the home aquarium, but only with reservations. Attempts at breeding should probably prove to be useless.

Mugiloidea: Sub-order belonging to the order of the Perch-shaped fishes or *Percomorphi*, with two completely separated dorsal fins, the first of which is supported by horny rays. The ventrals insert far forward and are not grown together with the shoulder belt, but are connected with same by a sinewy band. The pectorals insert high. Head and trunk are covered with round or comb scales; a lateral line may exist but may also be lacking. The dentition is developed in various manners, so that teeth may be completely lacking, or may be small and hair-shaped, but may also be big and sharp in some of the groups.

Of the four families of this sub-order we have to mention the *Mugilidae* with the genus *Mugil*, and the Ear Fishes or *Atherinidae*.

mulm syphons, mulm bells: Accessories of variable design which serve the purpose of removing the mulm which collects in aquaria. The oldest and best-known of these gadgets is the syphon with a closed collector bell. It is absolutely sufficient for smaller aquaria. Lately instruments of better construction, so-called mulm aspirators, are being offered. These are connected to the aeration, syphoning off mulm without carrying water along. For major cleaning operation the best is a syphoning hose, onto the end of which one sticks a mud bell in order to avoid that the heavier sand be carried along in greater quantities. The water which is syphoned off is either poured back after decanting the mulm, or else it is replaced by fresh water of the same tempera-

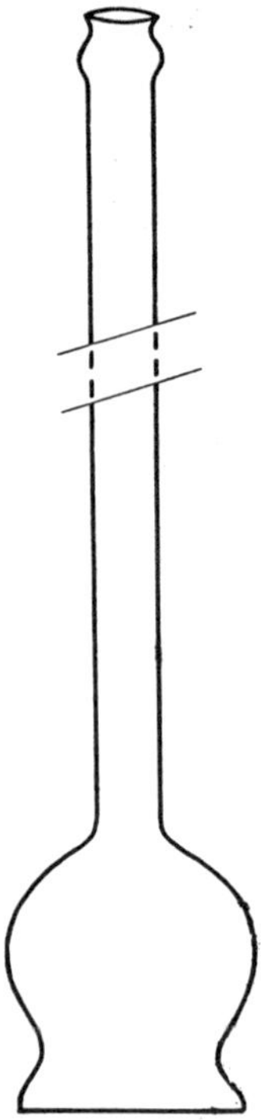

mulm bell

dip tube

ture.

multicolor: Many-hued; varicolored.
— *Aphyosemion bivittatum.*
— *Haplochromis.*

muscle system of fishes: The muscles of the trunk, used for locomotion, take up the main space in a fish's body. They stretch from the occipital bone to the origin of the tail fin, in double rows that are located on both sides of the body axis. The upper, dorsal, part of the rows of muscles is separated from the lower, ventral, part by an horizontal conjunctive tissue. The different parts of the muscles, which on their part too are separated by conjunctive tissue, are inserted into one another like pointed paper bags and are fixed to the spine.

The muscles that move the limbs, that is, the fins, by erecting and dropping them, have developed from parts of the muscles of the trunk. The muscles of the jaw system and of the opercles form an independent group.

muscoides: Moss-like.
— *Lagarosiphon.*

Myleinae: Mill-stone Characins. Especially remarkable sub-family belonging to the family of the Characins or *Characidae*. Fishes of very high build, laterally compressed, which often look peculiarly distorted. The belly edge is more or less sharp, and is provided with toothed, saw-like, rows of scales. The anal fin is long, the adipose well developed, the ventrals very small. Generally with numerous but very small teeth.

Besides animal food, many species temporarily go over to a nearly exclusive vegetable diet. It is said that some of the species specialize on very certain plant foods.

In accordance with their size, all species need roomy tanks in which the fishes have space for swimming and may also move in swarms. The keeping is not simple for all of them. Some species have demonstrated that they may be quite fast-growing in their youth stage, but that later on there may appear difficulties in feeding, and with these stoppages in growth. This may possibly derive from the lack of certain vegetable foods, in search of which the fishes effect migrations in their home waters. Some smaller species, pertaining to the genus *Metynnis*, have proved less problematic, but even these are quite difficult to keep. The *M.* are egg-scatterers which, like most other Characins, spawn from out of the school in open water, or among plants, after stormy chasing. Breeding them is hard, and has not yet been achieved for most species.

The sub-family comprises, among others, the following genera, which are described in this book under the respective entries: METYNNIS, MYLOSOMA, COLOSSOMA, PIARACTUS, and MYLOPLUS.

Myloplus: Genus of disc Characins pertaining to the sub-family of the *Myleinae*, of which so far only a few species have been imported, and which were not able to find their places in our aquaria. In part they are remarkable, beautifully colored fishes, which so far, though, no one has succeeded in breeding. Species pertaining to the genus are *M. schultzei*, *M. arnoldi*, and *M. schomburgki*.

Mylosoma: With mill-stone-like body.

South American genus of disc Characins pertaining to the sub-family of the *Myleinae*, closely related to the genus *Metynnis*, but which, in opposition to these, do not possess a thorny spine. The anal fin is very long, the adipose fin has no rays. No details can be given on the keeping in aquaria of these little-known species.

Myriophyllum: Milfoil.

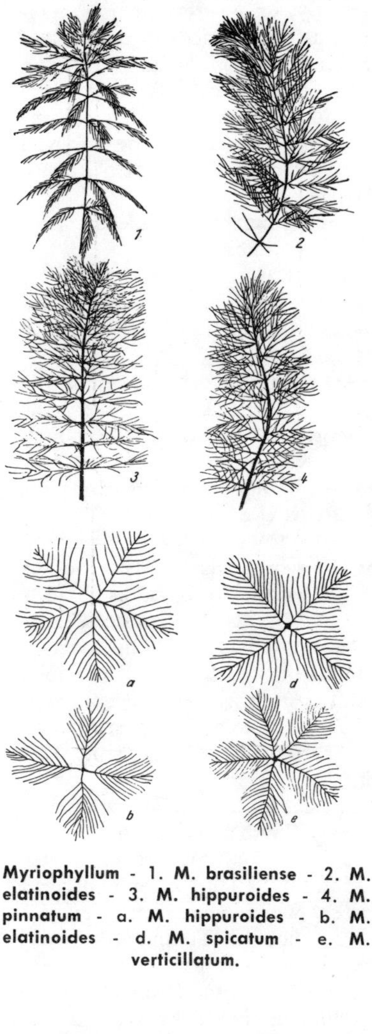

Myriophyllum - 1. M. brasiliense - 2. M. elatinoides - 3. M. hippuroides - 4. M. pinnatum - a. M. hippuroides - b. M. elatinoides - d. M. spicatum - e. M. verticillatum.

Genus of plants belonging to the family of the Sea Berries or *Halorrhagaceae*. It comprises perennial plants, which generally grow submerged or semi-emerged. The vivid green, dark-green, to reddish leaves are thinly feathered. Generally they stand in verticils around the stem, less frequently they are opposite or alternate. During the flowering season, the shoots rise above the water surface in thick stands and form aerial leaves which are somewhat differently shaped. In the insertions of these sit the small, sometimes hermaphroditic flowers. Multiplication, though, mostly occurs through lateral runners. Milfoil is a hardy and decorative aquatic plant, but sometimes only of short duration. As bottom soil unwashed sand, which may contain some clay, will suffice. Most of the species do not pose any special demands as to temperature. To the contrary, if there is a sensitiveness, it is against too high degrees of warmth. This makes them little fit for the tropical aquarium. The plants should not be used in tanks where there are fishes that root strongly, or where one uses aeration, as the whirled-up particles of mulm deposit on the leaves, making them look unseemly and even choking them. Mulm that collects on the bottom should be removed regularly from aquaria planted with *Myriophyllum.*

— **brasiliense** Cambessedes: Brazilian or Chilean Milfoil.

GENERALITIES: Formerly this species was called *M. propserpinacoides.* It may also be used in warmer aquaria.

SHAPE: As per description of the genus. A deep green species, the emerged leaves of which are yellowish to whitish green.

RANGE: South America and the Southern U.S.A.

CULTIVATION: As per description of the genus. Especially good for warm swamp aquaria, as it likes to grow beyond the surface. Temperature: 64-77° F. The location should be well-lit and, if possible, sunny. Also this species degenerates easily in the home aquarium.

— **elationoides** Gaudichaut: Fir-like Milfoil.

A species found in cold fresh-water lakes of South and Central America, adequate for the fresh water aquarium. It loves clear and clean water, which should not be too hard, though. Temperatures 60-68° F or even less. The species likes light, but too strong exposure to the sun should be avoided due to the danger of over-infestation with algae.

— **hippuroides** Muttall: Shave-grass-like Milfoil.

A species coming from clear waters in the U.S.A. and Mexico, and that is being sold as *M. scabratum, M. mexicanum,* or *M. affinis elationoides.* The species prefers hard water and is also fit only for the cold water aquarium.

— **pinnatum** (Walter) Britton: Delicate Milfoil.

Sold commercially as *M. eggelingi, M. tritoni, M. scabratum,* and *M. nitschei.* This species withstands a little more warmth than the others.

SHAPE: The leaves are irregularly opposite and alternate. Real verticils are only rarely found. Due to its tendency to form lateral shoots, the species forms strong bushes.

RANGE: The Eastern U.S.A., Mexico, and Cuba, in clear, not too deep waters.

CULTIVATION: As per description of the genus. Temperatures in summer up to 77° F, in Winter 59-64° F.

— **spicatum** Linné: Ear-Flowered Milfoil.

A species ranging over nearly the whole globe, in clear and peaceful waters. It is also found in brackish waters. Fit only for cold water aquaria. The growth continues also in winter, if the plants are cut back regularly in summer. They form thick bushes. They also withstand hard water.

— **verticillatum** Linné: Verticil-Leaved Milfoil.

A species ranging over Europe, Canada, parts of Africa, and Asia, fit only for cold-water aquaria, and which needs soft water for thriving.

Najadaceae: Nymph Worts.

Plant family pertaining to the class of the single-germinating-leafed plants or *Monocotylodeneae.* They are yearly or perennial plants, coming from fresh, brackish, or salt waters, and ranging over the whole Globe. The stems are richly branched out, and the plants often form dense lawns on the bottom of the water. The leaves sit on the stems. Generally they are from narrow to thread-like, and often the whole plant is very brittle. About 45 species are known, of which only a few can be considered for keeping in the aquarium, these pertain to the genera *Najas* and *Zannichellia.*

Najas: Nymph.

Genus pertaining to the family of the Nymph Worts or *Najadaceae*.

— microdon A. Braun: The Small-Toothed Nymph Wort.

GENERALITIES: The species has often been mistaken for *Elodea callitrichoides*. It is a pretty and ornamental under-water plant for moderately warm to warm aquaria.

SHAPE: The vivid green, generally opposite leaves are finely dented on the edges. Sometimes they even form mock verticils. The single stems may become quite long. The plain-looking flowers insert in the angle of the leaves.

RANGE: Temperate and tropical regions of the American continent, in lawn-like stands at the bottom of the waters.

CULTIVATION: Keeping them is very simple. The plants demand not-too-coarse sand, mixed with some clay, much light, and a temperature of at least 68° F. They are very fast-growing, soon forming dense stands. With sufficient artificial light and warmth they do not recede even in winter. The plants are useful for fishes that hang their eggs in dense plant thickets, but they are a little frail and therefore they should not be used with too lively fishes.

Multiplication occurs through planted twigs which, according to WENDT, have to be stuck in a way that the first two leaf insertions are covered. They then develop roots very quickly. On the other hand sometimes self-seeding may take place in the aquarium. Mistaking them for *Elodea callitrichoides* may kill these plants due to wrong care, as they need warmth.

Najas microdon

— minor Allioni: Minor Nymph Wort.

A smaller, annual species, found in Central and Southern Europe as well as in parts of Asia and Africa, but which is not abundant anywhere. It forms dense lawns in waters with depths up to 15 feet, but is not useful for keeping in the aquarium.

naming: see NOMENCLATURE.

Nandidae: Nander Perches.

Family of small fishes of prey pertaining to the sub-order of the Perch-like fishes or *Percoidea*. The body generally is of high build and strongly compressed laterally. The spiny part of the dorsal and anal fins is very well developed, the soft parts of the same fins as well as of the tail fin being glassily transparent in most species.

They are pronounced predators which take only live foods and lead a more or less nocturnal life. All of them like caves as hiding places from which they ambush their prey. The aquaria should not be located in too well-lit places and should contain shelters made of roots and rocks. All species care for their spawn. The eggs are either hung in caves, on roots, from the underside of big leaves, or beneath floating plants; in one case they are even bedded in a bubble nest and watched by the male. Care for the spawn lasts until the fry become free-swimming. Rearing them with very small live foods is not difficult.

Their range is peculiar. The family comprises only a few genera, with few species, and is found in Asia, Africa, and South America in smaller ranges. It cannot be denied that the presence of the genera points to a possible former connectedness of the continents.

The division of the family into the so-far-known genera is as follows.

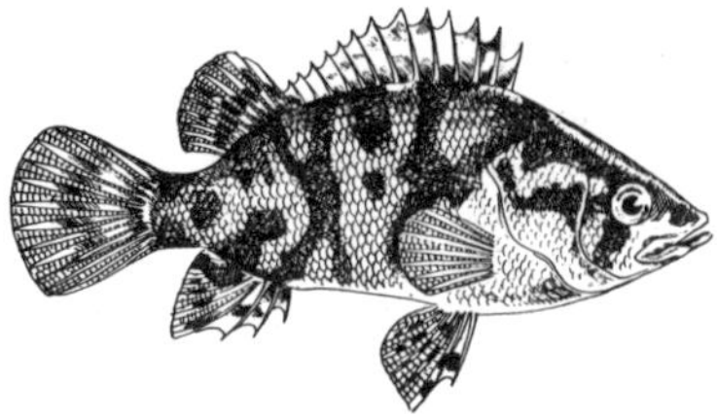

Nandus nandus

brackish waters.

CARE AND BREEDING: As per description of genus. A very voracious fish which only takes vigorous live foods, preferably small fishes. It needs well-planted, not too small aquaria, with plenty of hiding

SUB-FAMILIES	GENERA	RANGE
Nandinae	*Pristolepis*	Southern Asia
	Nandus	Southern Asia
	Badis	Southern Asia
	Afronandus	West Africa
Polycentrinae	*Polycentropsis*	West Africa
	Polycentrus	Northeastern South America
	Monocirrhus	Northeastern South America

Nandus: After the native name.

Genus of Indian Perches pertaining to the family of the Nander Perches or *Nandidae*.

— **nandus** Hamilton-Buchanan: The Multi-Spined Indian Perch.

SHAPE: As per description of genus. The slightly elongated, Perch-like body is strongly compressed laterally. Even the big head is nearly totally covered with scales. The mouth opening is big and may extend far to the front. Palate, jaws, and tongue are covered with numerous small and pointed teeth. D XII-XIV/11-13, A III/7-9. Length up to 6″.

COLOR: Olive-brown base with irregular, darker spots.

RANGE: In quiet waters of Central and Coastal India. The species is not very rare. It is also found in places, clear water, and a temperature of 73-82° F. Breeding has not yet been accomplished.

— **nebulosus** Gray:

A species very similar to the previous one, coming from Malaya and the Sunda Isles. Length up to $5\frac{3}{8}$″. Not yet bred.

Nannacara: Small *Acara* (another genus of Cichlids).

Genus of so-called Dwarf Cichlids pertaining to the family of the Cichlids, of oval-elongated build, moderately compressed laterally. The dorsal fin is very long and starts above the edge of the gill cover. Remarkable is the completely different coloration of the two sexes, especially during the breeding period. The species pertaining to the genus are vivacious and interesting, but rather quarrelsome fishes. They pose no demands at all as to the composition of the water, love warmth, though, and take nearly exclusively live foods. Artificial foods are eaten only occasionally. Reproduction is very interesting, due to the intense care for the brood in the manner of the non-mouthbreeding Cichlids, which is exerted exclusively by the female. This care for the spawn is typical of the so-called 'matriarchal family'. This is already shown by the fact that it is the female which generally takes the more active part. The breeding instinct is extraordinarily strongly developed so that, in these species more than in others, it happens that with the non-fulfillment of the impulse, the repressed instinctive acts are diverted to foreign recipients (Brood care given to food animals, for instance). The female, which is characterized by a striking design, may become very aggressive during the breeding period and does not balk from attacking even much bigger fishes.

Breeding in itself is not difficult, but depends upon finding mated pairs. The mating of pairs, by the way, is sometimes a little hindered by the pugnaciousness of both sexes, but especially of the female. Rearing the fry is not difficult as from the first day of free-swimming on they already take very fine live foods, micro-worms, mashed *enchytrae*, etc.

The genus, of which so far two species have been imported, ranges over Northern South America.

— **anomala** (Regan): The Golden-Eyed Dwarf Cichlid.

SHAPE: As per description of genus. D XVI/8, A III/8. Length up to $2\frac{3}{4}''$, the female generally a little smaller.

COLOR: The male is greenish to brass colored with a dark brown spot on each scale and pretty blue

Nannacara anomala

dorsal fin, the edge of which is bordered with white and red. The female has a design consisting of black stripes, connected by cross stripes and thus forming a checkerboard design. It is not impossible that this color combination in black-yellow-gray could represent a color signal. Throat and belly are often deep black under excitement.

RANGE: In the so-called savannah creeks, the lateral arms of rivers, and other small waters of British Guiana.

CARE AND BREEDING: As per description of genus. Needing a little warmth, 72-82° F.

— **taenia** Regan: The Lattice Dwarf Cichlid.

This species is quite similar to the previous one. D XVI/7, A III/7. Length up to 2″. Like on the previous species, the colors are quite variable. If excited, the male shows a dark length band, generally with four cross bands, on a yellowish base, the throat being black. The female is checkered like that of the previous species. Origin, the Amazon region, in places like those of all South American Dwarf Cichlids.

Nannaethiops: Dwarf African.

African genus of Characin-like fishes related to the family of the African Characins or *Citharinidae*, of moderately elongated body, strongly compressed laterally. The tail fin is in part covered with scales, the upper jaw shows some teeth.

Nannaethiops unitaeniatus

— unitaeniatus Guenther: The African Tetra.

SHAPE: As per description of genus. The terminal mouth is rather narrow and equipped with small, longish, two-pronged teeth. The belly edge is rounded. D 13-16, A 10. Length: males up to $2\frac{3}{8}''$, females a little over $2\frac{3}{4}''$. An adipose fin is present.

COLOR: Brownish with dark longitudinal band which is bordered on the upper edge by a golden to coppery stripe. The caudal peduncle is flushed red. The male has more glowing colors, the female is a little higher-backed, and, especially during the spawning period, quite plump.

RANGE: Tropical Africa, around the Equator, from the White Nile to West Africa.

CARE AND BREEDING: The vivacious, peaceable, and hardy fish looks best in schools of its own kind. If kept in communities with other fishes, it likes to keep apart. Occasionally it may become very shy. Therefore it is advisable to offer it some hiding places by planting the corners of the tank densely. Even smaller aquaria will suffice to keep them in. No special demands are made as to the composition of the water. The fish love sunlight, though, and water temperatures of 72-82° F. With reference to food they are completely unassuming and accept all kinds of prepared and dry foods of appropriate size. Spawning them is not considered difficult. Setting them up for this is best done in pairs taken from the school, the spawn-ripe females being easy to recognize as they may become unshapely thick. The numerous eggs are scattered free, often in plant thickets. According to temperature, the fry hatch after 36-50 hours and become free-swimming after another 3-4 days. Since they are very small, at the beginning they need fine live foods. They often keep out of sight as they like to stay near the bottom. At the age of about 12 months they are already ripe to reproduce.

— tritaeniatus (Boulenger): The Three-Striped African Tetra.

This species is very similar to the previous one, but gives the impression of being sturdier, in spite of the fact that generally they remain smaller. The sides carry three black length stripes. They need even more warmth than *N. unitaeniatus*, whom they otherwise resemble in care and breeding.

Nannobrycon: Small Brycon.

Genus of Characin-like fishes pertaining to the family of the Half-Teeth or *Hemiodontidae*. Up to recently these fishes were included in the genus *Poecilobrycon*, but according to a revision made by HOEDEMAN they represent an independent genus characterized by its vertical slanted body position. The genus *Poecilobrycon* continues for those species which swim horizontally. Whether the opinion of HOEDEMAN, who gathers all known slanted-swimming members of the genus into one species, *P. eques*, is right, remains to be seen. The species pertaining to *N.* are small, awl-shaped fishes, which swim in a slanted position which amounts to around 45° with the head held upright. This stance is not abandoned even during calm motion. Only when fleeing or excited do they assume a normal swimming position for short intervals. During this the fish may become very nimble. The angular position is made possible by the construction of the swimming bladder, which tapers off considerably towards the body extremity, thus giving the front part a strong floating impulse. During slow movements the fish swim by means of vibrating strokes of the soft vertical fins, which insert far back, as well as with the upper lobe of the tail fin. Since during this the body remains completely immobile, it causes the impression of a piece of wood floating in the water. This floating stance has earned the fish the name of "Pencil Fish."

The mouth opening is very small and terminal. The fins insert far back, the lower lobe of the tail fin is a little bigger than the upper one. There is an adipose fin.

The species *N. eques* presents at least two sub-species: *Nannobrycon eques* as prototype, and *N. eques unifasciatus*. Also the species that so far has been known as *Poecilobrycon auratus* Eigenmann might eventually be considered a sub-species of *N. eques*.

— **eques eques** (Steindachner): The Pencil Fish.

SHAPE: As per description of genus. D 9, A 11.

Nannobrycon eques eques

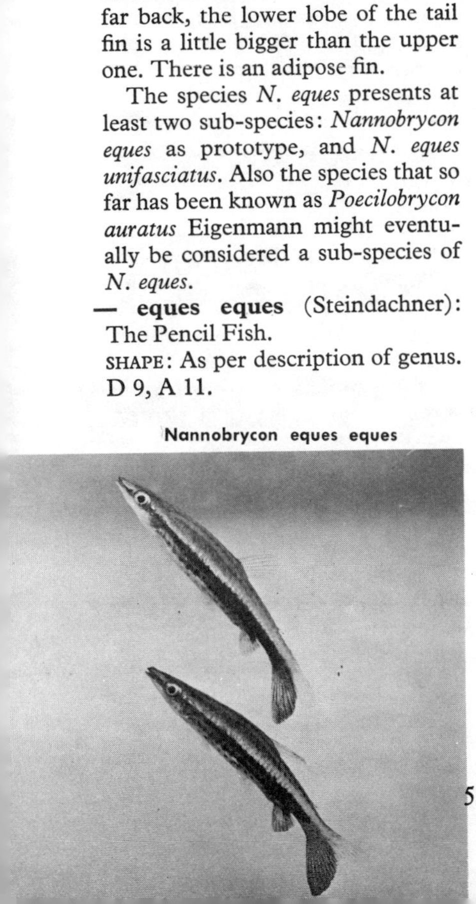

COLOR: Greenish-brown base with a dark longitudinal stripe and above and below this several rows of dots which run together into indistinct stripes. Between the longitudinal stripe and the upper row of dots a golden lustrous zone is found. Like all fishes of this group, the species has a special night coloring in which the longitudinal stripe design is superseded by unclear cross stripes.

RANGE: The Amazon region and Guiana, in smaller flowing waters, on the banks and in lateral arms of rivers which are overgrown with plants, as well as in flood regions. The fish like to dwell on the banks in flooded grass that hangs into the water, among aquatic plants and below the mats formed by floating plants. They like to stand against the weak current in schools.

CARE AND BREEDING: This peaceful, even a little shy, species is best kept in company with fellow members of its own species, or with the closely related *Nannostomus*. The fish eat all kinds of small live foods, as long as it swims free in the water or keeps on the surface. Food that sinks to the bottom is never noticed. For this reason feeding them prepared foods, which otherwise are taken willingly, is difficult as long as the food does not stick to the surface. A very much liked dish is *Enchytrae*. During the intake of food the fish may be very nimble, and in general they are much more motile than their stiff stance leads one to believe. They are, for instance, able to flee lightning-like when you want to catch them.

The Pencil Fish like soft, clear water at about 73-77° F. For breeding the temperature may be heightened up to 82° F. Breeding them is not easy. The fish are set up in pairs in glass-tanks, in which one puts about 10 quarts of soft water. No bottom sand is necessary, and a broad-leaved plant in a jar is introduced. It is advisable to acidify the water a little. A primary condition is the most careful cleanliness of all accessories.

The eggs are hung from the underside of the leaves of aquatic plants, but many of them fall to the bottom. One may try to loosen the remaining ones by carefully shaking the leaves. The parents are undoubtedly eaters of their own eggs, but pay no attention to those that fall to the bottom. As a precautionary measure one may cover the bottom with hazel-nut sized gravel or cover it with a glass grill. In all, the eggs total about 40-60. After spawning, the parents should be removed. The fry hatch after 24 hours and swim free after 5-6 days. During this time it is advisable to darken the tank a little.

As soon as free-swimming is reached, the darkening may be taken off. The alevins are very small and frail. At first they take very small live food (nauplii), and one has to be very careful while feeding. At the beginning growth is very slow, and only after 12 days they reach a length of ¾″.

Nannochromis: Small Chromide (Cichlid).
Genus of small African Chromides pertaining to the family of the Cichlids or *Cichlidae*, closely related to the genus *Pelmatochromis*. The body is very elongated and due to the sunken-in ventral contour of the male, it causes the impression of starvation. The female, to the contrary, is often very plump. The three known species, *N. nudiceps*, *N. dimidiatus*, and *N. squamiceps*, come from the Congo region. In a way they constitute the southernmost advanced post of a group of small Cichlids, which includes especially the genus *Pelmatochromis*, to which the genus *Nannochromis* is closely related. Care and breeding resembles that of the species of *Apistogramma* and *Pelmatochromis*. Temperatures between 72 and 75° F. The female usually exerts the care for the spawn and she is very active. The species has been bred successfully. The fish spawn only if they are first able to dig a cave. For this one should put a sand-filled flower pot or cocoa shell into the aquarium. Hardness of the water and pH value should be lowered. The fry grow rather slowly and the female does not always lead them. Therefore it may occasionally be better to rear the brood in a special nursery tank, removed from the parents.

Nannostominae: Sub-family of Characin-like fishes pertaining to the family of the Half-Teeth or *Hemiodontidae*, which is widely diffused over the Northern half of South America. The sub-family comprises a series of very popular aquarium fishes. They are slender to very slim, small species, often only a little compressed laterally. The head is pointed. The mouth is small and terminal. Intermediate and lower jaw are each set with a row of teeth. The adipose fin may be present or absent, often even on specimens of the same species.

The fish generally swim in short, sudden spurts, by means of vibrating motions of the vertical fins. This causes a peculiarly stiff manner of swimming which in *Nannobrycon* is still allied to a slanted, upward stance of the body. Many species have a special night-coloring in which the longitudinal stripes are blotted out by superimposed darker cross bands.

They are all peaceable and hardy fishes, which like to live in swarms among their own species. In uncongenial company they easily become shy. Offer them medium-sized tanks, densely planted in part, but with sufficient free room for swimming. A dark bottom enhances their colors. No special demands are made as to nutrition, all kinds of small live and prepared foods being taken. Their behavior is very interesting. The males fight charming little mock battles. Also the mating games are very pretty. Part of the species are egg-scatterers, part egg hangers. The parents are intensive egg eaters, and therefore special measures are necessary to protect the spawn from being eaten. Spawning generally has to take place in whole-glass tanks, so that one may keep them perfectly clean thus protecting the sensitive fry against attacks by infusoria. Glass grills on the bottom have rendered good results. According to HOEDEMAN who, when establishing the systematic division also considered the manners of behavior, three genera may be differentiated: *Poecilobryon*, *Nannostomus* and *Nannobrycon*.

Nannostomus: Dwarf mouth.

South American genus of Characin-like fishes pertaining to the family of the Half-Teeth or *Hemiodontidae*, sub-family of the *Nannostominae*. They are small fishes, of slender, awl-shaped build, pointed head, and with small, terminal mouths.

— beckfordi beckfordi Guenther:

SHAPE: As per description of genus and sub-family. The body is especially long-stretched, and only little compressed laterally. D 9-10, A 10-11. Length about $1\frac{3}{4}''$. Aquaristic circles know the species as *N. anomalus*, but it is seldom found in the fancier's aquarium.

COLOR: Yellow-brown with a dark length stripe which does not overlap on to the tail and is followed along the upper edge by a golden band. The belly of the males is a shiny golden yellow. The vertical fins are reddish at the base or in the middle. The males are more intensely colored.

RANGE: The waters of the Amazon, Rio Negro, and British Guiana, in small waters of all kinds, especially in the outer waters of the rivers where dense plant thickets alternate with open water.

Nannostomus beckfordi beckfordi

CARE AND BREEDING: As per description given for the sub-family. Temperature 72-77° F, for breeding up to 86° F. Spawning them demands experience. The species is not considered productive, especially since not all pairs mate. Also these fish are best set up in 6-8 quart glass-tank, filled with soft, slightly acidified water, and containing a bunch of fine-feathered plants as spawning media. The bottom is kept bare, but it is advisable to put the aquarium over a dark base. The males chase intensively, while the 30-60 eggs are laid in the plant thicket. The parents are spawn-eaters. The fry hatch after 40-80 hours, but in some cases the development may also last longer. They are very small, and therefore need the smallest possible food. They grow up quickly, though, and after 8-10 days already take cyclops nauplii, very small micro worms, and later also coarser foods. The change in color takes place after 3-4 months, and after 6-7 months the young are ready to propagate.

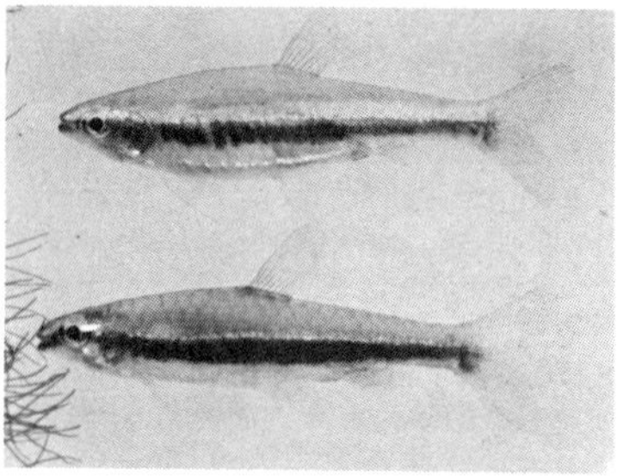

Nannostomus beckfordi aripirangensis

— beckfordi aripirangensis (Meinken):

SHAPE: Similar to the previous species, but a little more compact. The sub-species differs little from the original species except by this characteristic. D 11, A 9-10. Length up to $1\frac{3}{4}''$.

COLOR: Brownish with black longitudinal stripe, which is followed along the upper edge by a narrow golden border, which on its part is bordered with red, the red partly overlapping on to the gold, extending even to the caudal peduncle. The black longitudinal band goes a little distance into the tail fin and is surrounded by a light halo there. The fins are reddish to brick red. The male is more intensely colored; the female plumper.

RANGE: The Amazon region.

CARE AND BREEDING: As described for the previous species.

— bifasciatus Hoedeman:

SHAPE: As per description of genus. The snout is longer than that of *N. beckfordi*. It is doubtful whether this fish may be considered a separate species. It should eventually be joined together with *N. beckfordi* as a sub-species.

COLOR: A black longitudinal stripe stands out over a silvery white basis, being wider than that of the other species of the genus.

RANGE: The Surinam River.

Otherwise all information given for *N. beckfordi* applies also to this fish. During the act of spawning, which takes place at the bottom and among plants, the male plays a more active role than the female.

— marginatus marginatus Eigenmann:

SHAPE: As per description of the sub-family *Nannostominae* and of the genus. Of relatively short and compact build. Very graceful. D 10, A 11-12. Length up to $1\frac{1}{4}''$.

COLOR: With two dark-brown longitudinal stripes which go over on to the tail fin. Between these a broad golden zone. The fins are a pretty brick red at the base and the edge. The male is a little slimmer and also more intensely colored.

RANGE: The Amazon River and the Guianas.

CARE AND BREEDING: As described for the sub-family. Temperature 72-77° F, for breeding a little higher. The species is considered hard to breed. According to TUSCHE-NACHSTEDT setting up is best done in pairs in glass tanks of 8-10 qts. capacity. Special care has to be given to the fact that all materials should be completely clean. The water, which is held to a level of 4″, should not be excessively soft nor acid. The bottom is covered with glass marbles or with a glass grill. As spawning plants put in bundles of peat moss or algae, or, better still a mop of nylon yarn.

Nannostomus marginatus

The fish which are to be spawned, and of which the female should show spawning maturity, are put into the tank in the evening. Under favorable conditions they spawn the next day. During this time one may feed them carefully with rinsed *Enchytraeae*. The act of spawning generally takes place among plants. After spawning, the parents should be removed, and the plants carefully shaken, so that the eggs fall to the bottom. Finally one may cautiously remove the marbles or grill. Thereafter the tank is darkened, and left standing for about five days. After this time the fry, which hatch after about 24 hours, are already free-swimming. They immediately eat live fine food, but grow slowly. Rearing them demands great care.

— marginatus picturatus Hoedeman:

SHAPE: As described for *N. m. marginatus*. They differ from the original form especially by the shorter head, their smaller height, and by having less scales. Length up to 1″.

ORIGIN: Surinam.

All other information coincides with that given for *N. m. marginatus*. Nothing is known about attempts at spawning them.

— trifasciatus Steindachner:

SHAPE: As described for genus and sub-family Nannostominae. D 9-10, A 11. The adipose fin may be lacking but is generally present. Length up to 2″.

COLOR: The most beautiful species of the genus. They show a broad golden band, bordered above and below by a black longitudinal stripe. The fins are in part dotted a pretty brick red. The male is slimmer and shows weak red dots and dashes on the golden band. Furthermore the species differs from *N. marginatus* by its somewhat more elongated build and the red

Nannostomus trifasciatus

dots on the tail fin.

RANGE: British Guiana, the Amazon region, and the Rio Negro.

CARE AND BREEDING: As described for the genus and for *N. beckfordi*.

nanum: Small.

— *Ctenopoma.*

nanus: Small.

— *Hemigrammus.*

Natal Cichlid, the: see TILAPIA MOSSAMBICA.

natalensis: coming from Natal.

— *Tilapia—Tilapia mossambica.*

natans: Swimming, floating.

— *Elisma.*

— *Ludwigia.*

— *Sagittaria.*

— *Salvinia.*

Natantia: Shrimps.

Sub-order of higher crustaceans pertaining to the order of the ten-footed crustaceans or *Decapoda*. Of elongated build, compressed laterally. The body shell is flexible, glassily transparent or prettily colored. The crustaceans swim forward as well as backward with peculiar gliding movements. but in case of danger they can also zoom back lightning-like by means of strokes of the lower part of the body. Most shrimps live in the tropical seas, but quite a number of species live in fresh water. In Europe only a few fresh water forms are found. One of the species bears hair-edged forceps instead of pincers.

In the aquarium shrimps are interesting guests which get along quite well and are lively and companionable. They like a soft bottom with decaying vegetable matter, but take also dead animal foods.

native, or domestic, aquarium: An aquarium used for keeping and observing native animals and plants.

native fishes: Fishes which are indigenous to the area in which the aquarist lives. Mostly they refer to the cold-water species which are native to the temperate zones, where most active aquarists follow the hobby.

nattereri: After the Austrian collector Natterer.

— *Corydoras*.

— *Rooseveltiella*.

Natterer's Piranha: see ROOSEVELTIELLA NATTERERI.

Naucoridae: see HYDROCRISAE, WATER PUNICES.

nauplius, nauplii: Larval stage of lower crustaceans.

nebulosus: With foggy spots.

— *Ameiurus*.

necton: Collective definition for all living things that swim in free water, with active motility of their own and able to overcome the movement of the water itself.

neglectus: Neglected (with regard to systematical classification).

— *Barilius*.

Nemachilus: see NOEMACHILUS.

Nemathelminthes: Tube worms. Tribe pertaining to the series of the *Protostomina*, of which for aquaristics only the Wheel Beasts or *Rotatoria*, the Scratchers or *Acanthocephala*, and, from the class of the Nematodes, the micro worms (see TURBATRIX) are of interest.

Nematocera: Gnats, Mosquitoes. Order of insects pertaining to the sub-tribe of the two-winged ones or *Diptera*. Different from nearly all other insects, they have only one pair of wings, while in the place of the second pair they only have the so-called vibrating stubs, organs the aim of which has not yet fully explained. Metamorphosis is complete and includes larval and pupal stages. The larvae have a set-off head with antennae, pairs of jaws, and generally also eyes. Differing from the greater number of other insects, also the pupae are motile. Most *N.*, but not all of them, have stinging or sucking oral systems. They suck blood, but sometimes no food intake takes place and the oral system is involutioned since the life-span of the insects often is very short and obviates feeding. Mosquitoes, the blood-sucking species of which often become real plagues, are significant for the aquarist by the fact that their larvae represent a coveted fish food (see: MOSQUITO LARVAE). The stinging gnats are represented also (in Germany) by a whole series of genera and species. Of these we mention: the Common Gnat, *Culex pipiens*, the Banded Gnat, *Theobaldia annulata*, and especially the diversified and numerous Meadow Gnats, of the genus *Aedes*, which show up in great numbers.

The Malaria or Fever Mosquitoes are the transmitters of the malaria germ. The repressive measures, which in themselves are necessary, have in many countries led to unbiological methods, which kill off all other live beings in the water together with the mosquitoes. The best biological method of combat in climatically favored regions is the seeding of the waters with larvae-eating fishes, such as certain live-bearing Tooth Carps. The larvae and adult forms of the malaria mosquitoes are easily discerned from the other species by their typical stance.

Neoceratodus: New, still living, *Ceratodus*. *C.*—with horned teeth. Genus pertaining to the family of the *Ceratodontidae*, order of the *Dipneusti*, with only one species. A widely diffused animal group during the Cretacean Era and the Eocene, the members of which are extinct today with the exception of one species. Also *N.* has been more and more restricted by the dry climate of its range in Australia, since, different from all other lung fishes it does not hibernate in mud. Furthermore the sensitive eggs cannot be carried abroad by birds. The fish die when the water dries out, but, due to their pulmonary respiration, they are able to live even in the smallest puddles as long as there is at least a little water. They are appreciated food fishes, which are easy to catch due to their sluggishness. The intake and release of air takes place at the surface, every 30-40 mintues, with a muted noise. Otherwise the fish usually lie on the ground, and only swim a little way farther when disturbed.

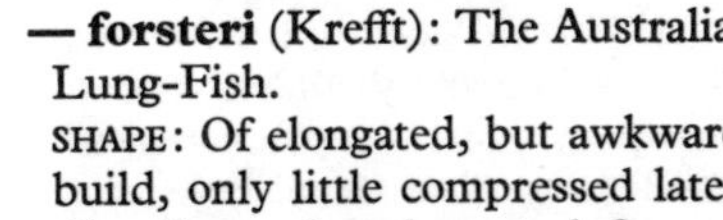

Neoceratodus forsteri

— forsteri (Krefft): The Australian Lung-Fish.

SHAPE: Of elongated, but awkward, build, only little compressed laterally. Pectoral and ventral fins are leaf-shaped and sit on a motile, scaly stalk. The rear of the body is framed by a fin edge formed by the dorsal, anal, and caudal fins. The head is very broad and flattened, the eyes are small and located laterally. Length up to 6 feet.

COLOR: Dark olive-brownish.

RANGE: Queensland, Australia, in the Benett and Mary Rivers.

CARE AND BREEDING: The species can only be kept in big show aquaria, but keeps well at temperatures of 72-83° F. The fish eat nearly exclusively live foods, especially snails and plants, but can also be trained to take meat. The eggs are up to $\frac{1}{4}''$ in size, placed in a jelly cover, and are simply laid on aquatic plants. The spawning period comes in September, which is the end of the Australian dry period. Development takes place without metamorphosis. The fry hatch after 10-12 days. They need several months until fully developed, but have no outer gills nor adhering glands.

Neolebias: New *Lebias*, an erroneous name, due to the fact that originally the fish was taken to be a Tooth Carp.

Genus of Characin-like fishes pertaining to the family of the African Characins or *Citharinidae*, of moderately elongated build, little to strongly compressed laterally, often without adipose fin. The upper jaw is toothless. The different species of *Neolebias* are pretty and peaceful fishes, which remind one vividly of Cyprinids. Since they are a little frail and shy, it is not advisable to keep them together with other lively fishes. They put their best foot forward if kept in pairs or swarms of their own species. Breeding them is not very difficult. Spawning is done in the manner of the egg-scattering Characins, after lively chases, among plants. Since, as a rule, the eggs are expelled singly, and on the other hand their number may be 100-150, the act of spawning lasts for several hours. The fry hatch after 30-40 hours, being very small at first, and need the smallest live foods. It is advisable to set them up for breeding in a whole-glass tank with bare bottom, later on transferring the fry to a nursery tank. If one wants to breed them in a common aquarium, though, which is perfectly possible, the breeders may be permitted to remain there as they hardly eat eggs or young. In this case it will be useful to breed also infusoria in the same tank to a certain extent. The fry stay near the bottom. Rearing them demands care, and 50-60 young may be considered a good yield for any of the species. After overcoming the difficult initial period, the fry grow up relatively quickly and may already be ready to reproduce within 6 to 8 months.

— ansorgei Boulenger:

SHAPE: As per description of genus. The small mouth is terminal D 11, A 8-10. Length up to 1⅜".

COLOR: Green-bluish with a dark length band, which is bordered on the upper edge by a luminous light-green zone. The fins are yellowish to red. The male is slimmer, the female quite plump during the spawning period. During this time the fins of the male are a vivid red, and also the body shows a reddish sheen.

RANGE: Up to this date they have been found only in a narrowly limited region in Equatorial West Africa.

Neolebias ansorgei

CARE AND BREEDING: As per description of genus. The fish are not especially lively, but hardy and quite resistant. In youth they may be a little sensitive to changes of water. As food they prefer live foods of corresponding size and take artificial foods only if none other are available. Temperatures 75-79° F, for breeding up to 86° F. The fry hatch after about 40 hours and are free-swimming after another 4-5 days, being very small. Otherwise as per description of genus.

— landgrafi Ahl: The Red from Cameroon.

This species too ranges over West Africa, from Calabar to Angola. They are small fish which reach a length of about 1⅜". Their color is brownish with a broad and dark longitudinal band, bordered light-green on the upper part. The rear part of the body shows a reddish tinge. The red fins are dark-edged. Otherwise as per description of genus.

— unifasciatus Steindachner:

This species, which, too, homes in West Africa, from Liberia to Gaboon, reaches lengths of up to 1¾", thus being the biggest species of the genus. D 10-11, A 9-10. The total coloration is reddish with a dark brown length band, along which runs a shiny golden zone on the upper part. The fins too are edged reddish to dark. Otherwise as per description of genus.

Neon Disease:

Dangerous disease of the Neon Tetra (*Hyphessobrycon innesi*) and of other frail species of fishes, caused by a microsporidium, *Plistophora hyphessobryconis* Schaeperclaus. The malady, which is lethal, generally manifests itself by the appearance of white or light spots where the muscles show through the skin, as well as by the decaying of fins, destruction of the colors, emaciation, and drawn-in belly. The disease may not show outwardly, though. Thus, for instance, a female Neon Tetra may become sterilized through destruction of her ovaries. Fry may be infected at an early stage, possibly while still hatching. Thus SCHAEPERCLAUS could verify an advanced infection on 8-day old fish, which led to the loss of a whole brood. Infection is caused and transmitted through the expelling of *Plistophora* spores in the excrements of infected fishes, through the falling-off of diseased spots of the musculature, or by the freeing of spores from deceased fishes. Infections of whole broods by attack on the roe within diseased ovaries, too, is imaginable. The development of the disease may be very slow, so that an observation period (quarantine) of newly-bought fishes often does not lead to the detection of the malady. Low temperatures seem to favor its development.

With insufficient care on the part of the breeder the Neon Disease may render the whole breeding stock of the valuable fish worthless. Therefore careful observation of the fishes is of the utmost importance. Cures are hopeless. Infected fish remain transmitters, even after the spores are encysted and have thus become harmless to the host itself for the time being. If even one fish only is infected, the whole population of the aquarium has to be considered as threatened, and, if the incidence increases, all fish in that tank should be destroyed. The aquaria should be disinfected with a 1% solution of chlorine. All bottom soils used for these species of fishes should always be scalded previous to use, in order to prevent a possible infestation.

According to SCHAEPERCLAUS breeders use only fishes that appear perfectly sound in order to create healthy tribes. After spawning, the parents should be killed and tested in order to make sure. The grown-up brood should be kept completely separated from all dubious tribes. At the same time one has to pay much attention to the disinfection of all accessories that are used. Nets have to be disinfected after each use if they are not employed with sound tribes only.

Neon Tetra, the: see HYPHESSOBRYCON INNESI.

Neon Tetra, Red: see CHEIRODON AXELRODI.

Neopterygii: New Fins.
Sub-class pertaining to the class of the Bone Fishes or *Osteichthyes*, which comprises the major part of the still living bony fishes.

Nepidae: see HYDROCORISAE, WATER PUNICES.

nerve system of fishes: Fishes have an elongated, relatively small brain, in which especially those parts are developed which serve to operate the sensory functions. The five sections that are typical of the brains of vertebrates are already developed. Of the twelve nerves that go out from the brain, the following should be mentioned: the paired nerve of smell, which originates in the olfactory lobes of the fore-brain, the seeing nerve, which comes from the vision hills on the intermediate brain, the acoustic nerve, which establishes a connection between the hearing organs and the sensorial organs of the skin, the nerve of taste, and a series of other functional nerves for operating the muscles, the gills, the heart, and the intestine.

The spinal medulla is enclosed by the spinal column. Its main function is to transmit the stimuli coming from the brain. According to the number of vertebrae, the paired nerves branch out from it, forming the unspontaneous, sympathetic nerve system.

neuston: Community of microscopically small organisms living upon, or closely beneath, the water surface. It keeps there due to surface tension. Under favorable circumstances the live organisms which form the Neuston give origin to a 'cream' or fatty film. Also in the aquarium such films may develop.

nevillii: After the discover of the plant, Nevill.
— *Cryptocoryne.*

New Fins, the: see NEOPTERYGII.

new water: As opposed to old water, any water which is free of organic wastes and comes from springs, wells, water mains, or newly-fallen rain water. While old water, which is overcharged with waste products, acts restrainingly on growth and metabolism, new water stimulates these. It is a fact that the vital demands of the species differ, but it is always advisable to change part of the over-aged water of aquaria for additions of new water.

nicaraguensis: Coming from Nicaragua.
— *Gambusia.*

nigri: After the Niger River, in Africa.
— *Xenomystus.*

nigricauda: With black tail.
— *Otocinclus.*

nigripinnis: With black fins.
— *Cynolebias.*
— *Markiana.*
— *Piaractus.*

nigrofasciata: With black stripes, black-banded.
— *Pyrrhulina.*

nigrofasciatum: With black stripes, black-banded.
— *Cichlasoma.*

nigrofasciatus: With black stripes, black-banded.
— *Barbus* (*Puntius*).
— *Limia.*

nigromarginatus: With black margin or edge.
— *Epiplatys.*

Nile Mouthbreeder, the: see TILAPIA NILOTICA.

Nile Pike, the: see POLYPTERUS BICHIR.

nilotica: Coming from the Nile.
— *Tilapia.*

niloticus: Coming from the Nile.
— *Eutropius.*

Nitella: Diminutive of the Latin word 'nitor', i.e., splendor, beauty. Genus of algae pertaining to the family of the Candelabrum Plants or *Characeae.*

Nitella flexilis

— flexilis (Linné): Agardh: Flexible Nitella

SHAPE: The plants are flexible, dirty green to dark-green, and annual or perennial. The 'leaves' stand in verticils around the stem and are divided into two or three points at the tips. The male and female sexual buds sit in the angles of the leaves and appear there in early spring. Fruit bodies appear starting in May.

RANGE: The species ranges over Europe, Asia, and North America, where it forms bushy lawns in smaller waters with muddy bottom.

CULTIVATION: Aquatic nurseries have been cultivating this species for many years, it being useful as a substratum for the spawn of many fishes, as well as to offer hiding places for young fry. In case one uses plants that do not come from nurseries but are gathered wild, it will be advisable to take them from shallow sun-warmed waters, as these adapt more easily to the conditions in the aquarium. They like a well-lit location, but get infested with algae if they receive too much sun-light. When planting them in the aquarium, the thread-like roots should be anchored in the bottom. According to Wendt it is also possible to cultivate the plants from spores.

Besides *Nitella flexilis* there are some other species, differentiation of which is difficult for the amateur, though.

nitrates: In the aquarium salts of nitric acid develop as the final result of the metabolism of proteins, especially through the action of certain bacteria (Nitrification). According to SARTORIUS in free nature one finds 3-15 mg. per liter of water; at 20 mg./ltr. one may already speak of a strong load of waste products, at 50-100 mg./ltr. appear *Diatomaceae* and *Oscillatoriae*. In aquaria with unfavorable conditions one may count on (up to) 30 mg./ltr. of nitrates. Fishes and plants apparently thrive normally. Due to gradual accommodation no poisoning sets in, but one will notice an increasing sluggishness, a diminition of motility, of growth, and of the disposition to spawn. A norm, though, can hardly be established, since every species of fish has its different sensitivity, according to its adaptability.

nitrogen: Chemical symbol N. A gaseous element which, together with oxygen and some other gases, forms the atmospheric air, of which N is the main component. Nitrogen plays an important role also in aquaristics, but only in the form of compounds. The connections are so difficult to grasp for the layman, that in the aquarist's practice the action of nitrogen compounds is only counteracted out of experience. This is the case when the fancier strives for a balanced 'correct' relationship between plant, fish, and a sound world of micro-organisms, in which the latter develops without his interference, in general. Disturbances of this equilibrated relationship show their harmful consequences in that, for instance, an excess of ammonia, or of hydrosulphuric acid may appear. On the other hand, stoppages in plant growth may also result. This is caused by the lack of mineralized decay products.

As is commonly known, fishes and other animals in the aquarium release decomposition products of protein into the water. With the death of organisms, the protein decomposes into amino-acids, from which result ammonia compounds produced as the end products with the help of bacteria.

The same happens when excrements and urine pass into the water through metabolism. Also from these give rise to such compounds as final products. They may be oxidized by bacteria into nitrites (NO_2) and nitrates (NO_3) (nitrification). If any commensurate plant growth is present, the ammonia compounds may also be absorbed directly by the plants and thus be removed from the water.

A very special significance in the circulation of nitrogen in the aquarium is reserved for the bottom soil, since the possibilities of survival of the decay bacteria depends on its 'health', while unfavorable conditions may lead to processes of decay and to the proliferation of harmful bacteria, which on its part may have oxygen-starving as a secondary consequence.

Under certain circumstances ammonia compounds may have poisonous effects on fishes, especially if a simultaneous oxygen-starvation obtains. Also the pH value plays a leading part in this, as alkaline pH values permit the development of increasing proportions of poisonous ammonium hydroxide. There are only few studies available on the noxiousness of accumulated nitrites and nitrates, and these cannot immediately be transferred to the conditions in the fresh water aquarium.

We cannot spare the space to enter into the details of the phenomena in the aquarium here. According to experiments made by KUEHL and MANN, the following are the results: the danger of accumulations of dangerous ammonia compounds is especially great in soft water, since nitrification is linked to certain quantities of calcium. If these are lacking, the process takes place only very slowly. Thus, in very soft water, especially under insufficient lighting, dangers may arise due to stopping plant growths and to decreased assimilation.

Metabolism products (excrement, urine), and dead organisms are decomposed into nitrites and nitrates the more quickly, the more oxygen there is in the water. Under healthy vital conditions plants consume the developed final products very quickly. The plants enjoy healthy conditions when the temperature is correct and there is sufficient light available. Under these conditions the exchange may take place so quickly that the nitrogen compounds do not even have time to appear. For this reason it is possible to have a dangerous concentration of nitrates, such as in the salt water aquarium, where there are no plants.

The circulation of nitrogen in the aquarium is not destroyed by filtering, as the nitrogen compounds, spirits of ammonia, nitrites, and nitrates are not absorbed when in a state of solution. For this reason it is only in the planted aquarium that a sound relationship between producers and consumers of nitrogen is possible.

nobilis: Well-known, distinguished, noble.
— *Ctenops.*

noboli: After the French collector Nobol.
— *Distichodus.*

Nocturnal Characin, the: see PROCHILODUS.

Nodule Disease of Fishes: A disease caused by parasitical protozoa, relatively harmless if the incidence is small, recognizable externally by the appearing of spherical, hemispherical, and grain-of-rice shaped cysts up to 1 mm. in size. The causes are different kinds of sporozoa, especially those of the genus *Myxobolus.* In any case it is advisable to segregate diseased specimens. If a stronger attack should develop at any time, the whole fish population should be destroyed, the aquarium emptied, sand and plants discarded, the tank having to be disinfected during 6 hours with a solution of 10 grs. of chloramine per quart of water.

Noemacheilus (Nemachilus): The Thread-Lipped One.
Genus pertaining to the family of the Gudgeons or *Cobitidae,* which is diffused all over Europe, Northern, Central, and Southern Asia, with a few species which on their part can be divided into many subspecies. The fishes are elongated, cylindrical in the front part, laterally compressed in the rear. The mouth is subterminal and equipped with three pairs of barbels. The intestinal respiration is only moderately developed, and is insufficient to protect against death due to bad condition of the water.

— **barbatulus** (Linné): The Bearded Loach, Groundling, or Gudgeon.
SHAPE: As per description of genus. The fins are relatively well-developed. D 9-12, A 7-11. The lateral line is interrupted on the center of the body. The upper lip is equipped with two pairs of short

barbels, the angle of the mouth with one pair of longer ones. The thorn beneath the eyes is hidden within the skin. The eyes insert high on the head, the anterior nostrils are on the tip of the snout and are tube-shaped. The scales are very small and frail, and may be lacking on many spots of the body. Length 4-5″, some of the Asiatic sub-species up to 8″.

COLOR: Greenish-gray, with brownish, irregular spots, disposed in irregular longitudinal bands. At times the male shows a rash on the inner side of the ventral fins.

RANGE: Nearly all of Europe (excepting the extreme North and South), nearly the whole Soviet Union, North and Central Asia, to Korea. In its whole range the species presents a series of sub-species. They live in clean, clear waters, lakes and swift-flowing brooks, on gravel or stony bottom.

CARE AND BREEDING: Care is not difficult, but the fish need clean, cool water and plenty of oxygen. Therefore good aeration is necessary. They eat all live foods that are found near the bottom, plus organic detritus, etc., which they chew through in search of food. The tanks should be equipped with well-washed gravel, hiding places under rocks, and dense plant thickets.

The spawning period is in April May. The spawn is stuck to stones and plants in shallow spots. SPRANGER succeeded in making spawn-ripe loaches lay their eggs in the aquarium. The fish had jumped up to the cover-plate, remaining there until they stuck on the eggs. Part of these had slid off into the water, and were hanging from the *Fontinalis* moss. These eggs were transferred to a glass-tank, where they hatched after about a week. The size of the fry corresponded to that of newly-born Guppies. At the beginning they were fed infusoria and micro food. Growth was extraordinarily quick. No aeration was given at first, only after the water temperature had risen to 86° F. After 5 weeks the little fish were $\frac{3}{4}$″ long. It is worthy of note that they were reared in a hot-house but never came to the surface to get air, despite the prevailing heat.

— **masyae** H. M. Smith: The Arrow Loach.

SHAPE: As per description of genus, the tail fin deeply forked.

COLOR: On a brownish-olive drab body are 14-20 dark saddle spots and a longitudinal row of dark brown dots. Beneath the middle of the origin of the caudal fin, and at the bottom of the first ray of the dorsal, a black dot is found. With age both fins and barbels become reddish. The male shows a button-like swelling of the forehead.

RANGE: In the flowing waters of Thailand, especially near falls.

CARE AND BREEDING: Clear, oxygen-rich water, and temperatures around 72° F are necessary for their well-being. This species digs itself into the bottom only rarely. They like to swim, and generally catch their live food in open waters. The fish are very sensitive to dirty or green water. So far nothing is known about their reproduction.

Nomaphila stricta (Vahl): The Indian Giant Water Star.

Swamp plant pertaining to the family of the *Acantaceae*, which originally was erroneously considered a species of *Hygrophila*. Imported from Thailand in 1956 by DR. EDUARD SCHMIDT. Probably the plant is widely diffused over Southeast Asia. Similar to *Hygrophila polysperma*, this species lives on the shore and in very shallow waters, in which it easily grows beyond the surface. The plant may be quick-growing. The strong stems hold the opposite, sometimes alternate, three-verticilled, leaves. Depending on living conditions, stems and leaves may be more or less covered with hairs. The leaves are a vivid green, a little lighter on the underside, pointed at the base and at the tip. They are varied in shape and size, but may reach lengths of up to 5″ even in the aquarium.

Cultivation is similar to that of *Hygrophila polysperma*, at 72-77° F, and in not-too-hard water. Extensive observations on cultivation are still lacking.

nomenclature: The conferring of scientific names.

The scientific denominations of animals and plants do not enjoy especially great appreciation among aquarists. They generally are hard to remember for the not scientifically trained fancier, and difficult to pronounce. The frequent and extensive changes in systematics, and consequently in names, make the situation still more difficult. For this reason generally the aquarist is unable to get a clear picture from the scientific names.

With regard to the question whether their use is necessary at all in aquaristics, points that are for, as well as ones that are against these names can be mentioned.

We may say here that the English names may be used within the most limited circles, perhaps even within the English-speaking world, if a uniform agreement can be reached, but even then one could not dispense with the scientific names. The unwillingness to follow the scientific development from this point of view would rob aquaristics of its significance as an auxiliary source for the study of biology. Further to this, aquaristics is an international hobby, and should remain being one.

In international communications, though, only the scientific names are of value and able to guarantee an exact characterization of plants and animals. For the same reason too, science has kept on with the classic languages. The choice of Latin and Ancient Greek for the derivation of words has not only an historical basis, but these dead languages, being neutral, have been approved in international communication. They deter all the little linguistic jealousies beforehand, having become universal languages. For the independent aquarist it is of course possible to keep independent of science, despite the fact that the results of research will prove to be useful also for him, but the same would never hold true for aquaristics. Therefore it is impossible to lose contact with science in the sectors of systematics and nomenclature.

The scientific names obey the rules of the Latin language. Besides this also Ancient Greek plays an important role in the development of names, but as a rule it appears in Latinized form.

The scientific nomenclature takes origin with Linné (Linnaeus), who was the first one to create an effective order of organisms (see SYSTEMATICS), and based it on the binary nomenclature. In this the name is composed of two parts, the first of which indicates the genus, the second one the species. This system was used for the first time correctly for animals, in the 10th edition of the SYSTEMA NATURAE (Linné, 1758). That year is considered as the year of the official introduction of modern systematics and nomenclature. Despite this, though, the tempestuous development of natural science at first did not permit an orderly situation. Only in the year 1905 was an international committee for nomenclature formed, which elaborated firm rules and thus led to a period of greater order in this field.

Meanwhile the meaning of systematics had undergone a deep change. Linné still considered all organisms as unchangeable beings, which owed their origin to an act of creation. With the conclusion, though, that from the beginning one live being has developed from another one, with progressively more complex forms, the primarily purely formal system acquired the sense of mutual relatedness. With this development nomenclature had to be able to express these relationships.

The whole 18th and 19th centuries were full of an industrious scientific activity of collecting. The number of known animals, rose from 4236 in the times of Linné to over one million. During this time numerous fishes were discovered, described, and named. That is how it could happen that species of fishes sometimes received two or more names independently of each other. Thus the so-called synonyms, denominations with similar meaning, arose. Since this situation became untenable with time, the synonyms had to be eliminated in favor of a generally valid denomination, and the further assignment of names had to be submitted to firm rules. In part these rules read as follows:

1. The privilege of the first-given name (priority) has to be observed with painful exactness. Thus the first name given to a species or genus (after 1758) always prevails over all other names given later. This is also the case if a forgotten first description is re-discovered later on.

2. This first, original name, excepting obvious typographical errors, remains forever as it was first published, even if its meaning or its systematical place are inexact.

3. This rule remains in force, even if later-given names should be more apt and should better characterize the features of a species than the original one.

These rules permit a few exceptions. Since, in the fauna or flora no name may be used twice, the name has to be changed if later it is discovered that before the christening another genus had already received this denomination. Differences of opinion in this are subject to the rulings of the international committee. The reasons for applications for certain changes of names, or re-groupings within the system, have to be presented to this committee.

The committee further is empowered to void the rules in certain cases. It may, for instance, protect a name that has been in use for many years and has acquired international popularity against changes in favor of an unknown denomination.

It has been stressed from the beginning that systematics and nomenclature strive after the characterization of a 'natural' system of relatedness.

Unfortunately just Ichthyology is still quite far from reaching this goal, much farther behind than ornithology. This has as a consequence that besides the elimination of the synonyms, many such changes also derive from revisions of the system. Ever new species are being discovered. Genera and families have to be separated. On the other hand, other genera and species have to be classed together. This brings the unfortunate consequence of eternal re-learning for the aquarist (and not only for him!).

It has already been stated that systematics and nomenclature are closely related. Let us consider a scientific name, such as *Betta splendens* Regan. The first word indicates that it pertains to the genus *Betta*. the second one shows the species. The name 'Regan' at the end characterizes the person who first described the species. Sometimes also the date of the first description is added. If a species still has sub-species, the denomination used is one composed of three parts (ternary nomenclature). This happens, for instance, with the Characins of the *Callistus* group. The general denomination for these is *Hyphessobrycon callistus callistus*, the sub-species being called *H. c. bentosi*, *H. c. serpae*, *H. c. rosaceus*, etc. The higher units in systematics are generally characterized by certain endings of the root of the name of the first-described genus. Thus, the genus *Cyprinus* (Carp) lent its name to the family of the *Cyprinidae*. The sub-family is indicated by the final syllable 'inae', *Cyprininae*, and the family by the ending 'idae', for instance, *Cyprinidae*. The next higher group, composed of several families, is the sub-order. It is indicated by the ending 'oidea' (—like), *Cyprinoidea*. For the systematic units that stand above these, for instance the order, the class, etc., no firm rules exist. Likewise there is liberty whenever further sub-divisions have to be introduced between genus and family, family and sub-order, sub-order and order, etc.

The meaning of the scientific name springs from the concepts of the first describer. For this the most different features are used. Sometimes they are those of color, build of the body, certain characteristics of the body, or anything else. The geographic origins and the native names echo in nomenclature. Frequently the names also serve to honor certain personalities of scientific merit. The listing of such motivations could be taken into particular, but this would go far beyond the scope of this book.

Norman, John Roxborouh: 1898-1944. British ichthyologist, pupil and collaborator of C. T. Regan, continued Guenther's 'Catalogue of Fishes'.

North America: Northern part continent of the whole of America, which includes Greenland and the Polar islands, with a surface. Connected with South America by means of the Central American isthmus and the West Indian islands. The central plains, with the Great Lakes in the North and the Mississippi River system, is limited on both sides by mountainous systems which run from North to South. The greatest part of the North American land mass is located within the temperate zone, 1/8 being in the Arctic Zone, and 1/5 in the Tropics. Very few rivers flow into the Pacific Ocean. In the region of the Great Salt Lake, big stretches of land are completely without water outlets. The main aquatic artery is formed by the combined Mississippi and Missouri rivers. The Great Lakes in the North may be considered an internal sea.

Climatically the main regions do not differ strongly from the conditions in Europe and in the corresponding latitudes in Asia. Thus results an extensive accord between fauna and flora of these regions, even if North America shows a great series of animal and plant species which appear on this continent only. Among fishes are especially the Sun Perches (*Centrarchidae*), and the peculiar Alligator Fishes or Gars (*Lepisosteidae*) which are worth mentioning.

Some groups of fishes also lap over from South America, coming through Central America, to the

North America

Northern continent, as, for instance, the egg-laying Tooth Carps, which go quite far to the North, while the live-bearing species are limited to the South. Furthermore we may also find a few species of Characins (*Characidae*), and of Cichlids (*Cichlidae*). To the contrary the Cyprinids (*Cyprinidae*) that are represented in North America have not found their way into South America.

notatus: Dotted.
— *Fundulus.*

Nothobranchius: With false gills. Genus of East African Tooth Carps pertaining to the sub-family of the egg laying Tooth Carps or *Cyprinodontinae*. The construction of the body resembles that of the bigger species of *Aphyosemion*, but is more compact and has a thinner caudal peduncle. The big mouth is strongly equipped with teeth. All species are considered difficult to keep and to breed. Breeding is achieved in a manner similar to that of the species pertaining to the genus *Aphyosemion* which spawn on the bottom. The eggs are laid singly in the bottom soil, and are covered with mud by the motions of the fish. It is advisable to transfer the eggs to breeding dishes, and to let them develop in darkness at constant temperatures of 72-75° F. According to the available experience, a great part of the eggs becomes infested with fungus, which makes a continuous surveillance and elimination imperative. The fry hatch after 5-6 weeks. At the beginning they are small and frail, but they grow rather quickly.

It has been observed that among the aquarium-bred specimens the females often remain considerably smaller in size.

— **guentheri** (Pfeffer):

SHAPE: As per description of genus. D 17-18, A 18-19. Length: males up to 3⅜″, females up to 2¾″.

COLOR: Blue-green body with red dots and a red edge around the scales. The fins are magnificently colored. The female is a simple gray-brown and differs considerably from the male.

RANGE: East Africa, Zanzibar and its hinterland, in fresh and brackish waters.

CARE AND BREEDING: As per description of genus. A fish that is difficult to keep and often very frail, liking roomy, richly planted tanks, with a layer of mulm (peat moss). Like all related tooth Carps, this species should not be kept too warm. The fish are really rather short-lived. At 77° F they are very lively. In accordance with their short span of life, they grow very quickly and are very voracious.

Nothobranchius guentheri

It is not difficult to induce them to spawn. From sexual maturation on they spawn continuously. At each mating, which is effected in the manner of *Aphyosemion coeruleum*, one to a total of about 50-60 eggs are laid at a time.

— **mayeri** Ahl:

SHAPE: As per description of genus. D 16, A 17. Length: males up to 2¾″, females up to 2″.

COLOR: Reddish violet with a wine-red edge around each scale, carmine red little dots on the lower half of the body. The female is much simpler in coloring.

RANGE: East Africa, in the mangrove swamps of the region around Beira.

CARE AND BREEDING: As per description of genus and of the previously described species.

Nothobranchius orthonotus

— **orthonotus** (Peters):

SHAPE: As per description of genus. D 15-16, A 14-15. Length: males up to 2¾″, the females remaining smaller, especially the ones reared in aquaria.

COLOR: Blue-green body with a reddish sheen and numerous wine-red dots which also extend onto the beautifully colored fins. The female is considerably simpler in color.

RANGE: In the mangrove swamps of tropical East Africa.

CARE AND BREEDING: As per description of genus and as indicated for *M. guentheri*.

Nothobranchius rachovi

-- rachovi Ahl:

Another magnificent species, coming from Portuguese East Africa. Length 2¾″, the females smaller and simpler. They like soft and slightly acid, old water.

Notonectidae: see HYDROCRISAE.

Notopteridae: Old World Knife Fishes.

Family of very elongate, strongly laterally compressed, fresh and brackish water fishes, related to the order of the Herring Fishes or *Isospondyli*; which are diffused over Southeast Asia and Tropical Africa. The mouth is big and equipped with small teeth. The anal fin, with the aid of which the peculiarly gliding motion is achieved, is very long and is grown together with the small tail fin. The anal opening is situated far to the front. The scales are small. Nothing is known about the manner of reproducing. The two genera known so far: *Notopterus*, and *Xenomystus*.

Notopterus: With feather (fin) on the back.

Genus of African and South Asian Knife Fishes belonging to the family of the Old World Knife Fishes or *Notopteridae*. It comprises several species which grow rather large. They are elongated fishes, strongly compressed laterally, which possess a small, pennant-like dorsal fin as a special characteristic of the genus. On the belly edge stands a double row of saw-like, connected spines. The swimming bladder is very big. The females lack oviducts, the eggs falling directly into the body cavity before being extruded. The long anal fin, which is connected with the tail fin, causes the peculiarly gliding manner of swimming by its wavy motions. The fish swim backwards as well as forward and are extraordinarily nimble and flexible. They are vicious, quarrelsome, nocturnal predators, which need roomy, richly-planted tanks, placed in not-too-light locations. Feeding is done exclusively on vigorous live foods, aquatic insects and their larvae, snails, and fishes.

Notopterus chitala

During the rainy season the sexually mature specimens migrate to flooded swamps in order to spawn on aquatic plants and the roots of grasses. Thereafter they return to the rivers and channels with their quick-growing brood. They feed on insects and young fishes.

South Asian species are *N. chitala* Hamilton-Buchanan, and *N. notopterus* Pallas. An African species is *N. afer* Guenther. In spite of the external similarity, the *Notopteridae* are not related to the South American Knife Fishes.

— afer Guenther: The African Knife Fish.

SHAPE: As per description of genus. D 6-7, A (including the tail fin) 113-130. The scales are very small. Length up to about 2 ft.

COLOR: Brownish with dark mottlings, growing one-colored with age.

RANGE: Tropical West Africa, from Gambia to the Congo, in quietly-flowing or standing, swampy and densely-planted, warm waters.

Notostraca: Order pertaining to the class of the Leaf-Footed Crustaceans or *Phyllopoda*. The body is flattened from upside down, and covered by a big, vaulted back plate. European species, such as the rare *Triops cancriformis* Bosc, and *Lepidurus apus* L., always appear periodically. They are predators which feed on mud-dwelling animals, and also gnaw on bigger prey with their spine-equipped legs. Both species reach lengths of up to $1\frac{1}{4}''$ including the shell. *Triops* has 60 and *Lepidurus* 41 pairs of swimming feet. The rear of the body is equipped with two long bristles, between which on *Lepidurus* one finds a tongue-shaped, pointed plate on the last body ring, lacking on *Triops*. *Lepidurus* appears between March and May, *Triops* between April and November, in ponds, puddles, and ditches.

The eggs are spawned into the mud, where they continue able to hatch even after drying out. Bigger specimens attack smaller ones. In Germany the males are rare, getting more numerous in warmer regions, both sexes being found in equal proportions in the Tropics. Within the Temperate Zones reproduction generally occurs parthenogenetically.

Notropis: With careened back.

Genus of North American school fishes belonging to the family *Cyprinidae*, of very slender and elongated body, slightly compressed laterally. The vertical fins are relatively big.

— hypselopterus (Guenther): The Banded Shiner.

SHAPE: As per description of genus. D 8, A 11. Length up to 2″.

COLOR: Brownish-green base with a dark longitudinal band on the upper side of which, and parallel to it, runs a red longitudinal band. The fins are in part a pretty red at the base. The female is less vividly colored.

CARE AND BREEDING: These hardy, quick-moving, and peaceful swarm fish should be kept in the manner of all domestic Carps (see CYPRINIDAE). They need long tanks with sufficient room for swimming and exercising. All kinds of live and prepared foods are taken, occasionally also algae and plants. It is advisable not to keep the fish too warm, room temperature without heating being the best. In winter 54-60° F are sufficient, otherwise 64-72° F for breeding 70-74° F. At too high temperatures the fish die easily. The act of spawning takes place in the manner of most egg-scattering Cyprinids, among fine-leaved plants. It seems that not too hard, and slightly acid water is advisable.

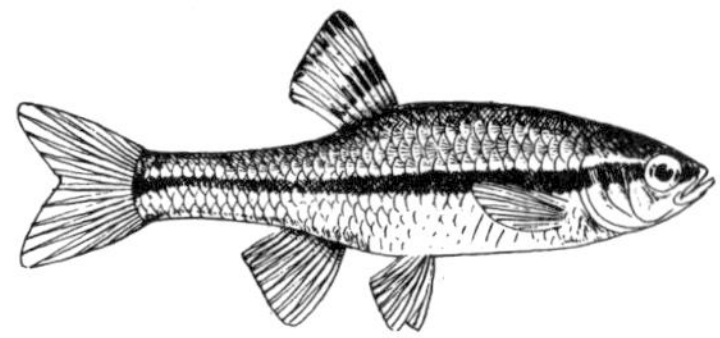

Notropis hypselopterus

— lutrensis (Baird and Girard): The Red-Finned Shiner.

SHAPE: As per description of genus, the head relatively big. D 9, A 8-10. Length up to $3\frac{1}{8}''$.

COLOR: Whitish with reddish, blue, and green hues, the head of the males sometimes a vivid red. The fins are yellowish to red. The female is plumper and simpler in color.

RANGE: Central and Southern U.S.A. to Northern Mexico, in smaller, flowing waters.

CARE AND BREEDING: As described for the preceding species. The fish demand fresh, clear, and strongly aerated water. Frequent changes of part of the water are advisable. During the spawning period, which begins in the middle of May, the male shows a spawning rash.

nummularia: Little coin.

— *Lysimachia*.

nutrition: The intake of nourishment is one of the most important factors in the existence of all living organisms. The major part of the vital functions depends on the continuous influx of nutritional substances, their use as moving forces, or their incorporation into their own body, and the elimination of useless wastes. New body cells are built, dead ones renewed. Motion, the working of the sensory organs, reproduction, etc., incessantly need new nutritional substances, which must be supplied to the body.

The feeding of plants is basically different from that of animals. Life on earth is maintained by energy supplied by the sun. Only green plants, besides red and brown algae and some bacteria, are able to make use of solar energy to transform inorganic substances into organic ones, thus maintaining life and building up their bodies. They are autotrophic, self-feeding, while all other live beings are heterotrophic, that is depending on green plants for their nutrition. They have either to make use of vegetable nutritional substance as herbivores (for which it is unimportant whether it is the case of living plants, or of dead, already decaying ones), or they do this as carnivores, feeding on other animals which on their part have previously eaten plants. The manner of feeding rules the typical differences in body structure and in manner of living between animals and plants. Plants draw their food from the soil (water and dissolved salts) and from the air (carbon dioxide), and build up their body substances as well as their organic nutritional reserves (glucose, protein, fats—see ASSIMILATION) from them. For this the plant has to be provided with the largest possible surface area and, for terrestrial plants, with richly ramified roots, in order to exploit its feeding space to the maximum. This makes it useful for the plant to be (generally) immobilized.

Animals on the other hand (generally) have to hunt for their food, and are adapted to this in their whole body structure. The few groups of animals which, living in waters that abound with food, can afford to lead a temporarily or permanently sessile life, such as sea anemones, sea moss, bryophyta, hydras, etc., show even externally a nearly plant-like structure. Some unicellulars (flagellates) are able to adapt to both autotrophic feeding in the manner of green plants, and to a heterotrophic way like that of animals (see FLAGELLATA).

There are certain differences between the manner of feeding of aquatic plants and animals, and that of the terrestrial live beings, which results from the fact that aquatic organisms are surrounded by water and the salts and gases dissolved therein, the most nutritional substances being more evenly distributed. With regard to the nutrition of aquatic animals it may be stated that the expenditure of strength needed for acquiring food is smaller than that of terrestrial animals in comparison. Even firmly located animals may count upon a laid table nearly regularly. Besides this, dissolved substances penetrate through their skin and their respiratory organs, so that aquatic animals in general are able to go without food for longer periods. In comparison the terrestrial animal is forced to compensate for its rather high need of water, caused by evaporation, by seeking out watering places, and consequently by an additional waste of energy.

nutrition of fishes: Nutrition of the fishes is one of the most important factors in successful care and breeding. As a rule it receives much too little attention, for some very different reasons (see FEEDING, FOOD). In fact, however, nutrition is one of the main factors in breeding, together with water, temperature, size of space, and mating partners. In comparison to the generally one-sided nutrition in aquaristics, it has to be stated that, as a rule, the feeding as done by wild fishes diverges considerably from this norm. The availability of nutritional substances, live or dead, may differ substantially according to geographic location, to the season, the time of day, the weather, the condition of the body of water, etc. The number of fishes which the aquatic space is able to support depends on the quantities of foods available. Therefore these quantities play an important role in the biological equilibrium of a body of water. Further it is mainly the manner of feeding which is the cause of specialization of the fishes in body shape, in the organs which are used for the intake of food, for its division and digestion, and finally in manner of living and behavior. The whole organism is adapted to a certain manner of feeding. Nourishment may also be the cause of restricted or far-reaching migrations of the fishes.

It is difficult to formulate clearly-defined groupings according to the manner of feeding. Many fishes specialize on certain groups of food substances from the worlds of animals or plants, and eat only these, others change their preferred nourishment seasonally or according to age, others still are less discriminating, and eat anything edible. According to their kinds of nourishment we can classify fishes as follows: predators, eaters of micro-organisms, and vegetarians. Besides this fishes may also feed on detritus, which generally also contain algae, unicellulars, and bacteria, as well as decaying organic matters. Many fishes take detritus as occasional food, while others consume it as their main source of nourishment.

As a rule the manners of feeding overlap to a great extent. This is the case especially for those fishes which are able to eat foods of all kinds due to the structure of their alimentary system. Like everywhere else in nature, rigid specializations are relatively rare. Notwithstanding this, the normal habitat of a fish, its body structure (which depends on the habitat) and its main food are interdependent. Thus surface fishes feed mainly on flying insects which they catch by jumping after them or take from the surface; fishes of the open water often are eaters of plankton; those of the plant thickets eat insect larvae, snails, and non-plankton micro-crustaceans, while bottom fishes feed on detritus and animals hidden in the soil. As a rule, the main food changes with the seasons, both regarding quantities as well as kinds. One can always differentiate three groups of nourishment for all fish species: the main food, the occasional food, and the emergency food. Young fry always have special manners of feeding, which on one hand result from their relative size, on the other from the gradual development of their alimentary organs.

The following is a description of the different groups of nutritional animals, plants, and substances. In general these specifications follow the teachings of LADIGES.

A. FOOD ANIMALS:

1. VERTEBRATES, EXCEPT FISHES. This includes many species of small vertebrates which live temporarily or permanently in or at the water, such as rats, mice, shrew-mice, young waterfowl, reptiles, and amphibians with their larvae, of the latter mainly salamanders and frogs. All these are eaten by the larger predatory fishes, additionally also by other fishes and large insect larvae. In our country (Germany)

we mention for this: Muskellunge and Pike, older specimens of trout, very large Eels, and River Catfish. In the tropics the number of such predators is naturally much larger. There we find some species of Characins which feed exclusively on larger vertebrates, for example *Hoplias malabaricus* (*Macrodon traira*), and the well-known *Serrasalminae* or *Piranhas*. Such predatory species are also found in other groups of fishes, but the manner of feeding of these cannot always be clearly defined. It is to be supposed, however, that also large Snake-Head Fish, several kinds of Catfishes, and others attack vertebrates.

2. FISHES. Fishes are not only the main food of a great number of predatory fishes, especially the ones mentioned above, but are also eaten by nearly all other piscine species, at least if the food fishes are small or minute, and if there is a possibility to do so. While in the temperate zones generally only the larger predators may be called fish eaters, in the tropics and sub-tropics we also find smaller species which prey on fishes. Among these we have to mention the Nandids, the Pike-Heads, some Cichlids, Catfishes, and Tooth Carps. It would be wrong, however, to call all fish-eating species predators without further considerations. Pronounced predators in the true sense of the word are characterized by the fact that their mouth and teeth are in some manner developed as trapping organs. The mouth opening is generally very dilatable. The teeth are developed in a way that enables them to hold their prey firmly and to push it down the throat by working in synchronization with one another. Often the snout is extended like a beak. Examples of this are the Pike, the Gars, some of the predatory Characins, and the Pike Top Minnow, *Belonesox*.

The specialization on fishes as principal food often shows also through an elongated and robustly muscular body structure. This permits quick dashes after the prey when something has been recognized as such. Species which also eat larger aquatic insects and the like as their main food besides fishes, Perches or Cichlids, generally do not show this torpedo shape.

The manner in which nourishment is caught helps us to distinguish hunters from ambushers. Ambushing predators commonly stand in plant thickets, or in reed stands, or at the bottom of the water, or even in stone caves, waiting for their prey.

They are often known by their colors, which are mottled or spotted on dirty-colored bases, showing no vivid hues.

Hunting species live more in open water and catch their prey after a more or less long chase.

3. INSECTS. Of special importance for many fishes are air-borne insects, which approach the surface, or fall down on it, forming the so-called 'flying food.' Often the surface fishes specialize on this diet. Other fishes, too, even if they are not pronounced surface-dwellers, eat insects occasionally. This happens especially when, due to the hatching period of many insects, there is an excessive availability of flying food. As surface fishes which specialize on such insects, for instance the tropical Half-Beaks (see DERMOGENYS) possess a remarkable catching device in the structure of their jaws, and the Archer Fish (see TOXOTES) shows an interesting manner of hunting. A large number of surface fishes, many Tooth Carps, Archer Fishes, and Half-Beaks, show luminous spots on the head, which possibly attract insects, either during youth,

or else permanently.

Aquatic insects, water beetles, for instance, are often refused as food, due to their hard chitinous shells, and are for this reason of lesser importance as sources of nourishment. Things are quite different, however, for larvae of aquatic or aerial insects which spend their early development in water, where, being still in a stage of growth, they are soft-shelled. In the tropics such larvae are often the only nourishment available in quantities worth mentioning. Above all are mosquito larvae, free-swimming and bottom-dwelling ones, which represent the main food of many tropical fishes. The larvae of *Culex*, *Anopheles*, and other species, that is 'black' mosquito larvae, appear in huge numbers in tropical waters, and their adult forms represent the main obstacle to human settling in those regions, as mosquitoes often are carriers of dangerous diseases. Since a great number of small fishes specialize on such larvae for their nourishment, they take first rank in the biological fight against the mosquito plague. In the temperate zones we find the larvae of Chironomids, known as blood worms, which are important for feeding our fishes.

4. CRUSTACEANS. In general the higher crustaceans of the temperate zones cannot be considered as a fish food. It seems, however, that in the tropical regions a series of fresh water shrimps and their larvae are eaten by fishes. Of the higher crustaceans which live in the temperate zones of Europe only *Amphipoda* and *Asellus aquaticus* are occasionally eaten by fishes of commensurate size. On the other hand the lower crustaceans—especially the *Phyllopoda* and *Copopoda*—are of great importance as the main nourishment of many species of fishes. It seems that in the tropics, where the water conditions are sometimes unfavorable for the development of the world of small live beings, these micro-crustaceans do not play the same role as in our waters here. Aquarists and importers are ever again reporting on the difficulties they find to provide adequate live foods. LADIGES points out that in numerous nettings he did find *Copepoda*, but never *Cladocera*. Excepting the large predators, nearly all species of fishes willingly eat small crustaceans, especially if these appear in large numbers. The smaller fishes catch them one by one, the larger ones often possess a sifting device in the gills, with which they sift the crustaceans from the water in order to swallow them. Some species do this simply with their gills.

5. MOLLUSCS. Some species of fishes eat snails and small clams. Among our European native species we can mention the Breams and Bleaks as such. Also Eels consume snails after having drawn them from their shells. Some species of tropicals, for instance some Catfishes, Snake-Heads, Cichlids, and Anabantids do the same. Puffers with their hard jaws are specialized in eating snails. Frequently aquarium fishes hurt snails by simply biting off their 'antennae', the lesions being lethal in some cases.

6. WORMS. Certain species of worms play an important role as nourishment. As such we have to mention *Tubifex*, which are available both in the tropics and in the temperate zones, in the first place. Their presence in great numbers often constitutes the nutritional base for many species of fishes. Earthworms, which accidentally fall into the water, too, are willingly eaten by most fishes of commensurate size. Other species of worms, leeches and *Planariae*, are generally

left unmolested and only few fishes eat them.

7. MICRO-ORGANISMS. (Rotatoria and Protozoans).
Organisms which live practically as well as animal growths on all kinds of firm objects, which also consist of micro-organisms, are of great importance as food for baby fishes during their first days of life. Even bigger fishes, Headstanders, Live-bearers, etc., eat micro-organisms together with algae.

B. VEGETABLE FOOD.
Numerous fresh water fishes eat plants as a complement to their food, and some species do this even exclusively. Many fishes take occasional vegetable nourishment, and some kinds of plants frequently enjoy great preference, while others are eaten only in case of need, or totally rejected. Soft growths of algae form an important nourishment for many fishes. Pure vegetarians, however, are not very common. As such are to be mentioned, some of the South American sucker catfishes, which graze off the algae growths from rocks etc., with their specialized mouths. Many Tooth Carps, Cyprinids, Characins, Cichlids, etc. need regular additions of vegetable food. It is reported that certain Characins (*Myleinae*) cannot live without certain fruits which fall into the water, and that they effect major migrations because of them.

C. DETRITUS AND DECAYING ORGANISMS.
A series of fresh water fishes feed on carrion, occasionally even species which cannot specifically be termed as carrion eaters. This may frequently be observed in the aquarium. The fact that lampreys eat carrion willingly has led to the erroneous idea that eels take this as their preferred nourishment. Of course this is absolutely wrong. Other already-decayed substances of animals and vegetable origin, detritus, constitute a quite important source of food for numerous species of fishes. Understandably these are mainly the species which live near, or on, the bottom.

nylon yarn: Nylon threads and fabrics are insoluble in water, soft, very strong, and probably completely harmless. For this reason lately it is being used in aquaristics as filter inlay, as spawning substratum when dyed green, and to make nets.

Nymphaeceae: The Water Lilies. Family of aquatic plants pertaining to the class of the two-germinating-leaved ones or *Dycotyledoneae*, with the genera *Cabomba*, *Nuphar*, *Nymphaea*, and others.

The latter, the so-called Water Lilies, are more or less big aquatic plants, equipped with floating leaves and beautiful flowers, generally fit only for cultivation in hot houses or under the open sky. Some bantam species can also be cultivated in the home aquarium, such as *Nuphar pumilum* (Timm) *Decandolle* from Europe and West Siberia (cold), *Nymphaea Baumii* Rehnelt and Henkel from West Africa (warm), *Nymphaea daubenyana hortorum*, a garden breed (temperately warm), and *Nymphaea tetragona* Georgi from all Temperate Zones of the Globe (cold).

All water lilies need vigorous, deep bottom soil, and plenty of sunlight. The Yellow Water Lily, or Spatterdock, *Nymphaea luteum* (Linné) Smith, puts out very pretty and ornamental emerged leaves from smaller rhizomes, which keep also in heated aquaria for quite some time.

nymphoides: Similar to Water Lily.
— *Hydrocleis*.

Nymphoides: Genus of aquatic plants pertaining to the family of the Gentians or *Gentianaceae*. The

Nymphoides - type of the genus

beautiful, vividly green, floating plants are only poorly suitable for the home aquarium, as they thrive only in well-lit locations. The floating leaves insert on long, peculiar stems, out of which grow the adventitious shoots and the inflorescences. The white flowers, provided with many fringes, are united in bundles of several flowers each.

— **humboldtiana** (Kunth):

RANGE: Tropical South America, in shallow waters with variable level, as well as in the outer waters of rivers, etc.

SHAPE: As per description of genus. The species is also known as *Villarsia humboldtiana* or *Limnanthemum humboldtianum*.

CULTIVATION: This beautiful, rather demanding plant may also be kept under the open sky in warm summers, for which it is more fit than for cultivation in the home aquarium. Under the open sky one should offer them the usual vigorous mixtures of soil, in the aquarium rough sand with a mixture of weathered clay and some peat moss. Multiplication is achieved by planting the adventitious shoots, after these have developed roots, or by seeding. According to WENDT the seeds, originating from artificial pollination, are planted in a dish with wet sand, letting them grow under a glass cover. As soon as the first leaves have developed, they are transplanted, the water level then being raised gradually. Wintering them is not easy. For this one has to put some strong plants into pots filled with clay and peat moss, adapting them gradually to a lower water level. Wintering is effected at 59-65° F, at well-lit locations and in covered jars.

LIGHTING: Much light, if possible direct sunlight.

WATER: They thrive better in soft water, and grow stunted if the hardness is too great.

WARMTH: 68-86° F, even the air having this temperature, 59-65° F for wintering. The plants are a little sensitive to cool spells when kept under the open sky.

— **indica** (Linne) O. Kuntze:

A species very similar to the preceding one, both in looks and in cultivation, coming from India, China, Australia, and the Fiji Islands.

Oarsman: see HYDROCORISAE.

obesus: Obese, plump.

— *Enneacanthus.*

obliqua: Oblique, lopsided.

— *Thayeria.*

occidentalis: Occidental, western.

— *Auchenoglanis.*

ocellaris: With eye spot.

— *Cichla.*

Ocellated Rivulus, the: see RIVULUS OCELLATUS.

ocellatus: With little eyes.

— *Astronotus.*

— *Rivulus.*

Ocellifer: Bearing eyes.

— *Hemigrammus.*

octofasciatum: With eight bands.

— *Cichlasoma.*

Octomitus Disease of Fishes: A disease caused by unicellular flagellates which live as internal parasites. Several of the symptoms are very similar to those of the *Ichthyosporidium* disease. In part the fishes grow abnormally lean, their movements differing from their usual motions. The parasites attack especially the intestine and the gall bladder.

Odonata: Dragonflies.

Order pertaining to the phylum of the insects or *Hexapoda*. Predatory insects which possess a strong biting apparatus and are excellent fliers. Remarkable are the big eyes on the motile head. The legs are tilted forward and are used only for sitting and for catching prey. The rigid wings beat only up and down, the front and rear wings moving independently from each other. Many dragonflies catch their prey on the wing and eat it while flying, others are slower and generally eat while sitting down. Dragonflies pick small insects from leaves, etc. All *Odonata* lay their eggs in the water.

The larvae of dragonflies are well-known to all aquarists. It is very much advisable to keep them in swamp aquaria in order to observe the beautiful metamorphosis they undergo. The larvae finally leave the water climbing up on plant stems. At first they lack wings, which appear as stubs or appendages on the back after some changes of skin. Breathing is done through intestinal or through caudal gills. The intestinal gills consist of tracheae in the thick intestine, the caudal gills are the well-known feather-shaped appendages of the water tigers. The larvae of dragonflies lead a predatory life. They catch their prey by means of the lower lip, which is transformed into an extendable catching mask which they carry folded-up in front of the mouth. Mature larvae leave the water climbing up on plant stems and change their skin. This process, especially the pumping-up of the delicate wings, is worth seeing. Larvae in the aquarium should be fed on micro-crustaceans,

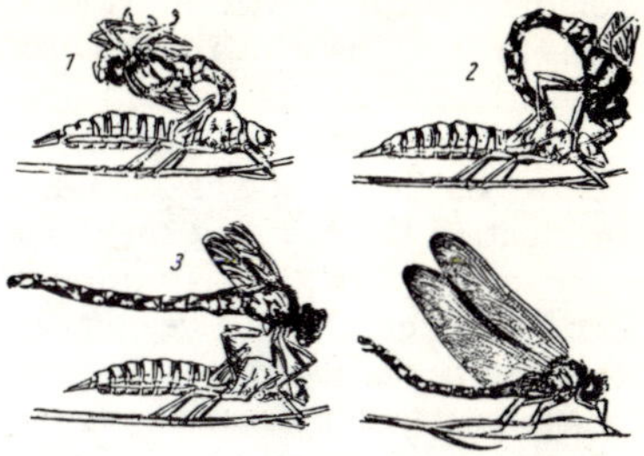

Odonata emerging from pupa 1. the pupa has left the water on a plant stem, and the imago has freed itself from the fore part - 2. the hind part is pulled out - 3 wings begin to spread out.

later on insects of all kinds, tadpoles, etc. Among others, the common dragonfly, *Calopteryx virgo*, is remarkable with its differently colored sexes. The females of dragonflies lay their eggs into the stems of aquatic plants which run beneath the surface, by means of an ovipositor-thorn with which they bore into the plant tissue. They are beautifully colored insects. Also the dragonflies of the family of the *Agrionidae* have an equally pretty shape. Among these we mention especially *Agrion puella*.

The unequal-winged ones are bigger dragonflies. Among these is worth mentioning *Aeschna grandis*, which has a wing span of about 4″.

Dragonflies which often wander in large swarms like grasshoppers are the Four-Spotted Dragonfly, *Libellula quadrimaculata*, and the Flat-Bellied Dragonfly, *Libellula depressa*. It is their larvae which are found most frequently in European waters.

Oenotheraceae: Plant family pertaining to the class of the two-germinating-leaved plants or *Dicotyledoneae* which include, among others, the genus *Ludwigia*.

oily film: In the aquarium a more or less thick and connected film on the surface of the water, which as a rule results from the fact that incoming dust forms a nutritional basis for bacteria which soon cover the surface due to excessive propagation. Oil films may decisively restrict the circulation of gases, not to mention the fact that they look very sloppy. Since rest is a primary condition for their development, they can be destroyed even by weak aeration. If you prefer not to aerate, you may also lift oil films off with sheets of absorbent paper cut to the exact size and shape of the surface and spread over it. This measure, however, has to be repeated periodically.

Old World Knife Fishes: see NOTOPTERIDAE.

Oligochaeta: With few bristles.
Order of worms pertaining to the class of the *Clitellata*, phylum *Annelidae*, characterized by having an annular (ring-shaped) gland, which encircles the body like a belt. During the matings this excretes a mucus which keeps the worms together. No gills, primitive limbs, or antennae are present. The bristles are placed simply in lateral rows, within special skin depressions. The worms are hermaphroditic. The eggs are covered by cocoons. No metamorphosis takes place.

The best-known families are: The Earthworms or *Lumbricidae*, the *Tubificidae*, and the *Enchytraeidae*.

oligolepis: With few scales.
— *Barbus* (*Puntius*).
— *Moenkhausia*.

omata: With eye (spots).
— *Leptolucania*.

One-Spot Barb, the: see BARBUS TERIO.

One-Spot Live Bearer, the: see POECILIA VIVIPARA.

ontogenics: Development of live beings from the egg cell to death.

Onychura: Order pertaining to the class of the leaf-footed crustaceans or *Phyllopoda*. The representatives of this order possess a two-flapped shell, which nearly encloses the body.

Two sub-orders, of which for aquaristics that of the *Cladocera* only is important.

Oodinium pillularis Schaeperclaus: Cause of the *Colisa* Disease. Parasitic flagellates which cause a disease of aquarium fishes that shows externally by the development of yellow-brown, dirty-looking nodules on the skin. In cases of stronger attacks the whole body is covered with a yellow-brown film. The fins get torn. Under a microscope one sees the pear or egg-shaped parasites sitting closely together on skin and fins. After completed growth the parasite falls off, divides 64 times, and finally, with the last division, it forms the motile spores, which are provided with two flagelli and a red eye-spot. These must find a host within 12-24 hours as otherwise they die. Strong attacks are lethal to young fishes. Development is retarded or hindered by low temperatures and darkness. Fishes that are already weakened for some other reason are especially prone. For treatment SCHAEPERCLAUS recommends repeated formalin baths, or long-lasting acriflavine or quinine baths in darkened tanks without bottom soil or plants. Also baths in a 3-5% solution of kitchen salt are said to promise success.

Oogonium: The place where the female sexual cells of lower plants are developed.

opercularis: Pointing to the opercle which is ornamented by a spot.

opercularis concolor:
— *Macropodus*.

Ophiocephaloidea: Snake-Headlike Fishes.
Sub-order of very ancient fishes within the order of the *Percomorphi*. Fishes of elongated build, more or less compressed laterally, sometimes hardly compressed at all. The

Ophiocephalus - type of the genus

head is flattened, provided with a large mouth opening. The nostrils bear tube-shaped extensions. The full-edged scales cover the whole head. The fins are spineless, the vertical ones being very long-stretched. Ventrals may be present or lacking. The swimming bladder is simple. A bony, sack-like extension above the jaws is used as an accessory breathing organ. The presence of this organ was responsible that formerly *O.* were classified together with the Pike-Heads and the Climbing Perches, into the now-voided order of the *Labyrinthici.* With the basis of their position referring to the history of development, as well as based on their body construction, such a classing together is unjustified. On the contrary, the *O.* represent a completely independent group of fishes.

The Snake-Heads range over East and Southeast Asia, India, and Tropical Africa. They generally show a pretty design, but are voracious predators which in part grow very big. For the home aquarium only smaller specimens are fit, but they constitute great attractions in public aquaria. One family (*Ophiocephalidae*), with the genera *Ophiocephalus* and *Channa*, with a series of species, are very popular.

Opisthomi: Order of bone fishes pertaining to the sub-order of the new fins or *Neopterygii.* Fishes of elongated body, with strongly reduced gill slits, without ventral fins. There is only one family, the Spiny Eels or *Mastocembelidae*, which ranges over Africa and Asia with a few species.

opposed: Plant parts, for instance leaves, which are placed opposite each other on the stem.

opposed leaves

optimum conditions: By this one understands the conditions which offer the best possibilities of life between the maximum and minimum range. Optimum conditions do not have to have the same value for the whole course of life. On the contrary, they may be different for the different stages of age, for instance, those of spawn and fry may differ from those for the young that are growing up, and they may be dissimilar for the mating periods and for the rest-periods in-between. Therefore, if one follows a certain aim, as in breeding, one has to pay very exact attention to the demands on the life of the fish species. Furthermore one has to consider that as a rule the optimum conditions are represented by a whole series of complex and different factors. The change of only one of these may bring as consequence changes of the others. Furthermore, one has to consider that under conditions that are located towards the maximum or the minimum points, life is also possible, but that often this does not permit one to reach the desired aim.

Orange Chromide, the: see ETROPLUS MACULATUS.

Orange-Fin Tetra, the: see MARKIANA NIGRIPINNIS.

orbicularis: Round, circular.
— *Ephippicharax.*

organism: A live thing, equipped with organs complimentary to each other.

Ornamental Tet, the: see HYPHESSOBRYCON ORNATUS.

Ornata: Ornamented, ornate.
— *Limia.*

ornatipinnis: With ornate fins.
— *Apistogramma.*

ornatus: Ornate.
— *Epiplatys.*
— *Hyphessobrycon.*

Orontium: From '*aureum*,' golden. Plant genus belonging to the family of the *Araceae.*

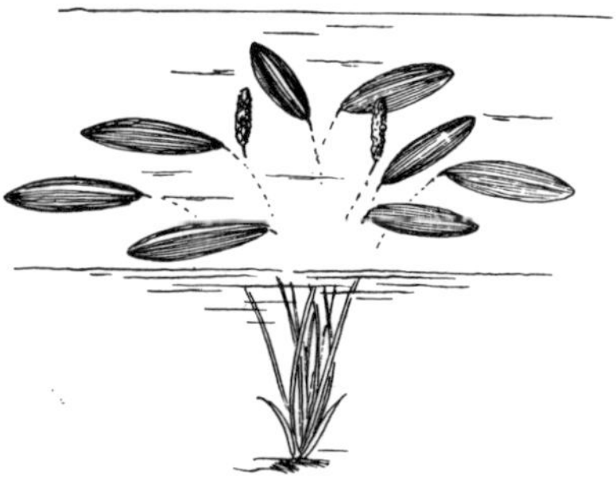

Orontium aquaticum

— aquaticum Linné: Golden Ear.
RANGE: The Southern U.S.A. in still waters of all kinds, also in recesses at shores and in the outer waters of rivers.
SHAPE: This perennial aquatic plant with floating leaves has a root stock that creeps along the bottom. From this the shiny leaves, dark green on the upper face, light green on the lower one, which rise from the bottom, strive towards the surface. The leaves may reach lengths of 10″ and widths of 5″, and are oval or lancette-shaped. The inflorescence protrudes beyond the surface on a long stem.
CULTIVATION: The species is good both for the home aquarium and the open air installation. In the latter it may weather the cold season if protected by a frost cover. The bottom ground should have a height of 4″ and may consist of 2/3 coarse sand and 1/3 aged clay. If cultivated under the open sky in order to achieve especially luxuriant vegetation, one may add a little cow manure. Location, also in the aquarium, should be well-lit and sunny. Under the sky the species recedes in autumn; while in the aquarium it continues growing weakly even in winter. It is advisable, though, to offer the plant a rest period at low temperatures from December to February.
LIGHTING: Very intense, sunlight.
WATER: No special demands.
WARMTH: A cold-water plant; should not be kept too warm.

orthonotus: Straight-backed.
— *Nothobranchius.*

ortmanni: After a personal name.
— *Apistogramma.*

Oryzias: Rice; pertaining to the rice paddy.
Genus of Southeast Asian Tooth Carps belonging to the sub-family of the egg laying Tooth Carps or *Cyprinodontinae.* Small surface fishes of remarkable transparency, with pectorals that insert high and a mouth of which only the lower jaw is articulated. The body is more or less elongated, only slightly compressed laterally. The head and the anterior part of the back are a little flattened. Care and breeding in part present some problems. Considering their size, smaller tanks are sufficient, but some specimens are reported not to be especially peaceable and therefore not very fit for the community tank. No special demands are made as to feeding, all kinds of live foods and occasionally also prepared foods being taken. Spawning takes place

after stormy chasing. The small eggs hang together on threads and are balled together in clumps of 12 to 35, or else they are carried around like grapes until they are brushed off on plants where they remain hanging. The parents are spawn eaters. It is advisable to remove the eggs, putting them into shallow nursery tanks. According to the amount of sunlight and of warmth, both of which favor development very much, the fry hatch within 3-10 days. They should be fed fine dry food or an auxilliary food of egg yolk, mashed *Enchytrae*, etc. It is a fact that at the beginning they feed very well, but, according to experiences undergone in breeding some of the species, a few remain as midgets.

— **celebensis** (M. Weber): The Celebes Medaka.

SHAPE: As per description of genus. D 7-9, A 17-21. Length up to about 2″.

COLOR: Yellowish gray with a light bluish sheen and a narrow dark longitudinal band, which is forked in the tail fin. The fins of the male are bigger, especially the anal fin which is lobately extended.

RANGE: In densely planted, warm, small pools on Celebes Island. Only in fresh water.

— **javanicus** Bleeker: The Javanese Medaka.

SHAPE: As per description of genus, but a little more elongated than the preceding species. D 7, A 21-23. Length up to 1⅝″.

COLOR: Similar in color to the preceding species, the fins of the male being light yellow and a little bigger than those of the females.

RANGE: The Malayan Peninsula, Java.

CARE AND BREEDING: As per description of genus. The fish demands a continuous warmth of 86° F and as much sunlight as possible. For stocking the tanks use fine-leaved plants, which they also use as hiding places since the species is a little vicious. In many cases with this species it has not been possible to make the fry grow beyond a length of about ¾″.

— **latipes** (Schlegel): The Medaka.

SHAPE: As per description of genus. D 6, A 19-20. Length about 1¾″.

COLOR: Very similar in color to *O. celebensis*, but there is a very beautifully golden, artificially bred variety, which has been marketed by tropical breeders. The fins of the male are a little bigger on this species.

RANGE: Japan, in quiet, smaller waters.

Oryzias latipes

CARE AND BREEDING: As per description of genus, but not needing very much warmth. Also, in breeding this species, difficulties have been found after a few generations, either because the fry remain very small, or else because all attempts at breeding fail completely.

— **melastigma** (McClelland): The Black-Spotted Medaka.

D 6, A 20-24. Shape and coloring similar to that of the other species, with several blackish spots on the sides. Males up to 1¾″, the females growing a little bigger.

RANGE: India and Ceylon.

CARE AND BREEDING: Similar to *O. javanicus*. Needs a little warmth, not below 77° F. Also the young of this species remain midget-sized, despite the fact that they develop fully, even showing the sexual differentiation, characterized by the lobate anal fin of the male.

Oscar, the: see ASTRONOTUS OCELLATUS.

osmosis: Adjustment of differences in concentration of solutions of two differently composed liquids through a separating membrane, as through the skin of a fish if this is transposed from fresh to salt water. This makes the dissolving medium, water, run from the side of the weaker concentration to that of the stronger one. The resulting upsetting of the water economy of the body may have ponderous influences on health.

osphromenoides: Similar to the Gourami, *Osphronemus*.

— *Sphaerichthys*.

Osphronemus: The smeller, due to a false interpretation of the labyrinth as an olfactory organ. Genus pertaining to the family of the Climbing Perches or *Anabantidae*.

— goramy Lacépède: The Giant Gourami.

SHAPE: Of oval, relatively compact build, which grows more high-backed with age, compressed laterally. The small mouth with the fleshy lips is supraterminal. D XII-XIII/11-13, A IX-XI/19-21. Length up to 2 ft. possibly able to reproduce when 5-6″ long.

The rays of the ventral fin are grown together and drawn out into long threads. The long anal fin reaches so far back that it seems connected with the tail fin.

COLOR: The fish shows different colors in the different stages of age, being most beautiful in youth when it is reddish-brown with a slight greenish hue, a few darker cross bands, and a black, yellow-edged spot above the end of the anal fin. Later on, only brownish with irregular spots, when old dark-brown. The dorsal and anal fins of the male are pointed.

Probably the original home country of this species was Java. From there it was diffused over all of Southeast Asia as an appreciated food fish. Thus today it is even found in Australia, on Mauritius, and on the Seychelles.

CARE AND BREEDING: Keeping this big fish in the home aquarium is hardly interesting, but it has to be considered an impressive display in bigger public aquaria. It is very voracious and willingly takes also plant foods such as lettuce. Otherwise care and breeding are similar to those of most other Anabantids. The Gourami builds a relatively big bubble nest, which, however, is not too solid.

Ostariophysi: An extensive order belonging to the sub-order of the New Fins or *Neopterygii*. The skeleton is ossified. The modified first four vertebrae establish a linkage between the swimming bladder and the aural labyrinth, the so-called "Weber's Apparatus." The shoulder girdle generally is grown together with the skull.

This order includes the most variedly shaped forms of fishes, so that in systematics it has been subdivided. The systematics used in this book are in accordance with the Zoological Record. The order sub-divides into two sub-orders: the *Cyprinoidea*, and the *Siluroidea*.

Osteichthyes: Bony Fishes.

Class of fishes pertaining to the superclass of the jawed animals or *Gnathostomata*, which includes the greater part of the fishes. The main characteristic is the more or less bony skeleton, which need not always be completely developed. The skin is generally covered with scales. The fins are held up by bony or horny rays. A very ancient group

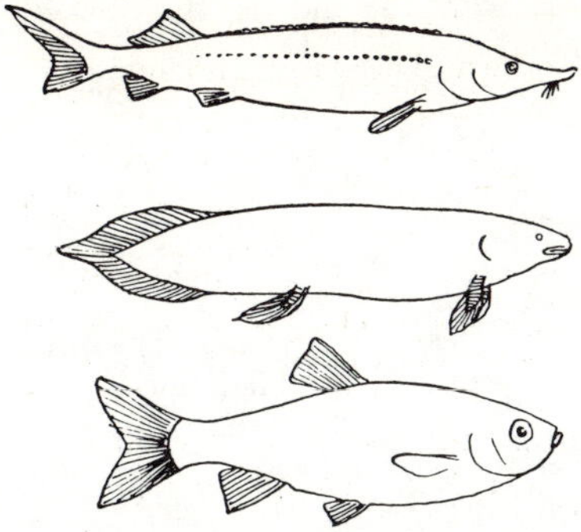

Osteichthyes - Bony fishes - top, **Paleopterygii** - center, **Crossopterygii** - bottom, **Neopterygii.**

of fishes, the predecessors of which were discovered to have existed in the Devionian era, about 330 million years ago. They developed very richly in the ensuing periods of the Earth, despite the fact that many of the lines of development have meanwhile become extinct. For this reason it is impossible to establish uninterrupted relationships between the individual families of *Osteichthyes*, of which single groups have kept up quite ancient characteristics and thus permit interesting conclusions on the past of the bony fishes.

There are three sub-classes: The *Palaeopterygii*, the *Neopterygii*, and the *Crossopterygii*.

Osteoglossidae: Family pertaining to the order of the Herring Fishes or *Isospondyli*, scattered over widely diffused regions with the subfamilies of the *Osteoglossinae* and the *Arapaiminae* in South America, the *Heterodinae* in Equatorial Africa, and the *Scleropaginae* in Borneo, Sumatra, and Northern Australia. All of them are large fresh water fishes, which live predatorily for which reason they are fit only for show installations. The body is covered with hard bone scales. Interesting fishes of which *Osteoglossum bicirrhosum* Vandelli, the Arowana, and *Scleopages formosus* (Schlegel and Mueller) have already been imported several times. Both species are said to be mouthbreeders. Keep them in spacious aquaria at a low water level and with plenty of plants, 77-86° F.

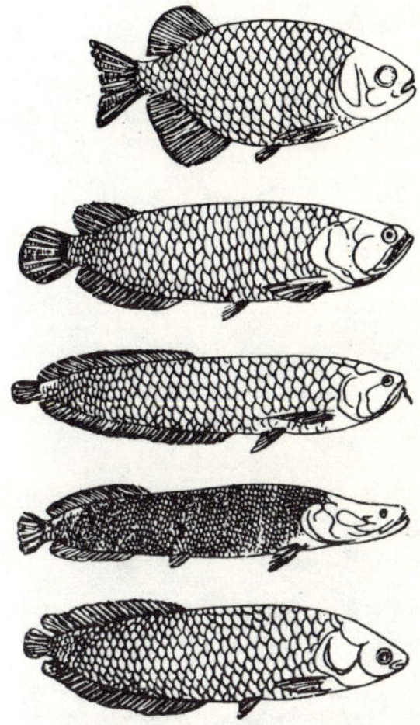

Osteoglossidae, top to bottom: fossil form, **Scleropages, Osteoglossum, Arapaima, Heterotis.**

Ostracoda: Class of micro-crustaceans belonging to the subphylum of the *Crustacea.* The *Ostracoda* are differentiated from all other micro-crustaceans by their body construction. A shell made up of two parts, shut by a strong closing muscle, envelops body and head. The body, divisions of which do not show externally, consists of a head and trunk. The seven pairs of limbs, which protrude from the shell while swimming, and the two pairs of antennae, richly equipped with sensory bristles, are mainly used for locomotion. The fresh water forms have no heart and only one simple eye.

Locomotion is very peculiar. Through alternate up-and-down movements of the two pairs of feelers results a peculiarly rolling manner of swimming which may also be circular if only one pair of feelers is moved.

Reproduction takes place through fertilized and unfertilized eggs. Of some of the species no males are known. From the egg hatches a nauplius which changes its skin eight times until it stops these changes as an adult specimen. Most *Ostracoda* live as shore or bottom forms, in mud or among plants, swimming freely over short distances. They are found especially on dead plants and animals, and also on decaying matter of all kinds.

They are not important as fish food, since as a rule they are not taken due to their hard shell. In breeding tanks no *O.* should be tolerated as they probably attack the spawn and fry that are unable to move. In the warmwater aquarium *O.* have a short life span. In Germany about 70 species are found, which, however, are of no great interest for aquarists.

Otocinclus: Ear-grid, due to the presence of a kind of tympanus. South American genus pertaining to the family of the Armored Catfishes or *Loricariidae*, without adipose fins or swimming bladders. The body is armored, the subterminal mouth built for sucking and holding fast.

— flexilis Cope:

SHAPE: As per description of genus. The bony plates of the body are covered with small spines, the abdomen is protected by an elongated plate. Length up to $2\frac{1}{8}''$.

COLOR: Brownish with irregular darker spots. The male is a little smaller and is slimmer.

RANGE: Rio Grande do Sul (Brazil), especially in clear, swift-flowing secondary waters, where they cling fast with the aid of the sucker mouth.

CARE AND BREEDING: The manner of living of these Catfishes is similar to that of all other Armored Catfishes. They are twilight and nocturnal fish, which need plenty of oxygen as well as shadowy tanks with clear, well-aerated water. Temperatures should not rise too high, 65-72° F being sufficient. The fish are harmless eaters of detritus and algae. PRIOR has succeeded in breeding them, but the act of spawning could not be observed. The fry like to remain in hiding places and show themselves especially in the evening. Other species are *O. nigricauda* Boulenger, also from Rio Grande do Sul, *O. vittatus* Regan, from Southern Brazil, and *O. arnoldi*.

Ottelia: Genus of swamp plants pertaining to the family of the Frog Bits or *Hydrocharitaceae*. *O. alismoides* (Linné) originates from the tropical and sub-tropical regions of Asia, resembling the European Frog-Spoon, but is remarkable for its peculiar leaves.

ovary: The female egg sac. (See SEXUAL ORGANS).

ovary: The female reproductive gland (gonad), which supplies the female reproductive cells (eggs).

Oxygaster: With pointed belly. Genus of Southeastern Asian swarm fishes belonging to the family of *Cyprinidae*, closely related to the genera *Chela* and *Laubuca*.

The body is relatively high, strongly compressed laterally. The dorsal fin inserts far back, the pectorals are well developed. The first ray of the otherwise stunted ventrals is strongly extended. The lateral line is complete, falls down steeply from the upper edge of the gill covers and runs parallel to the lower contour of the body for a short distance. The dorsal line rises roof-like up to the insertion of the dorsal fin. The mouth is supraterminal, lacking barbels. The scales are small. The belly is sharply careened.

— atpar (Hamilton-Buchanan) The Blue Keel Belly.

SHAPE: As per description of genus. D 8, A 22. Length up to 2½".

COLOR: Glassy transparent with silvery sheen, olive-colored towards the back, white on the belly. On the sides a greenish-silvery longitudinal band from the middle of the body to the insertion of the tail fin. Fins yellowish, the iris shiny golden. The male is slimmer.

RANGE: India, Bengal, in standing and flowing waters of all kinds, also in rice paddies.

CARE AND BREEDING: Harmless, lively and a very hardy school fish, which like to stay near the surface without (according to MEYBURG) liking to jump. In accordance with their design, they take their food, which in the aquarium may consist of free-swimming live foods or even of artificial ones, from the surface of the water. Especially fruit-flies and other small insects scattered over the surface are advisable as food. The former failures in keeping *Oxygaster* and the related species seem to originate from a wrong manner of feeding. Temperature 73-77° F, for breeding 79° F. Probably the composition of the water plays a secondary role. In community tanks Keel Bellies should be kept together only with fishes which are especially lively.

MEYBURG achieved breeding them in a 17½ gallon tank, the bottom of which was covered with big pebbles and artificial algae. Temperature 77-99° F, DH 3°, pH 6.7. The fish spawned at twilight under weak artificial illumination. While doing this, the male tried to press the female down from the surface. Then followed a short embrace, which was broken up by the female by means of a violent rotating movement during which the sexual products were released. In each instance 2-30 glass-clear eggs were expelled, which sank quickly to the bottom. The eggs, which have no sticking substance, are rather small, smaller than those of *Brachydanio rerio*. The matings followed in quick succession, so that the spawning was finished after 30 minutes. During this time the parents hardly bothered the eggs. Colors were intense during the mating, the fins, including the ventrals, being carried spread open. According to the prevailing warmth, the fry hatch after 20-24 hours. They may number several hundreds of specimens. The little fish strive to stick to the surface of the water by means of a clinging thread, succeeding in this only after many fruitless attempts. Often they hang from the glass or plant leaves. They are transparent, but after a few hours they take on a darker coloring. Three days after hatching they become free swimming. Feeding them on *Paramaecium* proved unsatisfactory as this moves near the bottom and the fry prefer the surface. For this reason MEYBURG switched to artificial dust food, which was willingly taken. After about a week the smallest nauplii were eaten. During this first period mortality was large, probably due to lack of adequate food.

oxygastroides: Similar to *Oxygaster*.

— *Chela*.

oxygen: A tasteless, odorless, and colorless gas with the chemical symbol O (Oxygenium), which is indispensable for combustion and respiration. Together with carbon dioxide it permits the circulation of gases between animals and plants, which is one of the conditions for living, both in nature and in the aquarium. Despite the fact that the presence of oxygen is a must for life, the oxygen contents of the water must not be too high. To the contrary, there are upper and lower limits. If the percentage of free oxygen dissolved in water falls below the minimum necessary for breathing, breathlessness with the danger of suffocation sets in. This is noted at first by the fact that the fishes go over to emergency breathing at the water surface, trying to catch atmospheric air. Breathing then becomes quicker than normal. This may be seen externally by the accelerated movements of the gill covers. While in this case on one hand the fish is no more able to cover its need for oxygen, on the other hand carbon dioxide accumulates in its body. The consequence is 'carbon dioxide narcosis'.

The fishes' need for oxygen increases with rising temperatures, since these increase metabolism, too. Simultaneously, though, the degree of saturation with oxygen decreases at higher degrees of warmth. Thus sets in a concurrence of two unfavorable factors, which may act very detrimentally, especially if unfavorable biological conditions prevail in the aquarium beforehand, such as may be caused by excessive decaying food or uneaten living food, too dense plant stocks with insufficient lighting, or consumption of oxygen by decay bacteria.

Once the oxygen dissolved in the water is used up under such conditions, it can only slowly be replenished in the aquarium. In such cases aeration will prove useful. It can enrich the water with oxygen again, but cannot remedy the poor biological conditions definitely. Therefore it is always better to carefully balance the living conditions that an aquarium of a certain size affords to a commensurate number of animals and plants. No norm can be established for this. Under all kinds of conditions, however, it is always correct to offer the organisms in an aquarium as much space as possible. In other words this means that aquaria should be as spacious as possible, and that under-stocking with fishes, and a simultaneous limitation of too rich plant growths is the surest protection against losses. Lack of oxygen leads to weakenings of the animal organs. Such weakened fishes become prone to diseases of all kinds, already existing ones becoming worsened and latent infections manifesting themselves.

If the oxygen contents of the water rise above normal, at first the fishes raise their oxygen consumption by moving the gill covers more quickly, breathing normally again after some time. Under intense sunlight the assimilation of plants may produce over-saturations with 200-300% and more of dissolved oxygen, which may cause harm and under certain circumstances even be lethal. At first a state of suffocation sets in, which is indicated by quick motions of the gill covers. After some time these movements cease and a sudden, complete stoppage sets in. Furthermore one may also notice, strong secretions of mucus and blood on the gills and fins. The fishes show excitement, swim up and down along the glass panes, and finally hide, often head-first, on the bottom or among plant thickets, where generally they soon die. Such cases require immediate help. This may consist of a transfer of the fishes to fresh water with the same temperature, or else by expelling the excessive oxygen by means of a vigorous, coarse aeration. Aeration not only serves the purpose of relieving lack of oxygen, but also that of expelling excesses of dissolved gases. Furthermore over-saturation with oxygen may be the cause of the 'Gas Bubble Disease.'

If an aquarium is afflicted with 'green water' during day-light time the water becomes oversaturated with oxygen. The fishes often remain standing motionless at one place and hardly move at all. If the green water does not appear suddenly, giving the fishes time to adapt to it, it will cause no great harm. Things become different, though, when we transfer fishes from normal to green water. There they perish under symptoms of suffocation. While the symptoms described above as consequences of an oxygen over-saturation set in during the day, at night the fishes may suffer from lack of oxygen.

P: Abbreviation for pectoral (fin).

Pachypanchax: Thick Panchax. African genus of Tooth Carps belonging to the genus of the egg laying Tooth Carps or *Cyprinodontinae*, with a body shape that is intermediate between that of the *Aplocheilus* and *Nothobranchius* species. Generally the body is relatively short and compact, only little compressed laterally, the upper parts of head and back being flattened. The snout is wide and rounded, the mouth supraterminal. The insertion of the anal fin is scaly; the dorsal inserts far back.

— homalonotus (Dumeril):

SHAPE: As per description of genus. D 10-11, A 17. Length about $3\frac{1}{8}''$.

COLOR: The body is brown, light greenish to bluish under incident light, the back dark brown. The fins are greenish with a dark edge limiting a lighter zone which is remarkable, especially on the males. Young males especially show such yellow-white seams at the edge of the ventral, anal, and tail fins. They may look intensely yellow while excited. The female is plumper, paler in color, and her fins are rounded.

RANGE: Madagascar, also in brackish waters.

CARE AND BREEDING: A very simple species which only poses some demands as to size of tank. One should consider aquaria of about 20 gal. capacity. The composition of the water has no special significance. It is advisable, though, to offer imports a certain addition of salt or sea water. Later the fish also get used to fresh water. Temperature 75° F, for breeding 80° F. Care is similar to that of *P. playfairi*, but the species is reported to be more peaceable. NIEUWENHUIZEN reports breeding as easy. If only smaller tanks are available for this, it is advisable to keep the sexes separated until they reach maturity for spawning. An addition of one teaspoon of salt per $2\frac{1}{2}$ gal. of water is advisable. The glass-clear eggs, up to 1.5 mm. in size, are preferentially laid among the roots of floating plants or the shoots of fine-feathered aquatic plants. The female is crowded to the spawning place by the male, while he swims in ever tightening circles around his partner. At each mating only one egg is laid, totalling 10 to 20 eggs daily. After a spawning period of about two weeks a rest period begins. It may last up to one week. If well fed, spawning begins anew. The eggs should be collected and deposited in breeding dishes, as the parents prey on them. If the female is chased too intensively, she sometimes gets rid of a greater number of eggs. The eggs develop at a temperature of 75-80° F within 12 to 16 days. According to MEDER the eggs are able to withstand a dry period, provided the soil remains a little moist.

— playfairi (Guenther): Playfair's Panchax.

SHAPE: As per description of genus. D 12-13, A 17-19. Length up to 4″.

COLOR: Greenish with red spots and rows of shiny dots. The female is

Pachypanchax playfairi

considerably paler in color.

RANGE: Tropical East Africa, also Madagascar and the Seychelles, in brackish water in all these places.

CARE AND BREEDING: The species is quarrelsome and very vicious, not only towards members of its own species. They are voracious and need great quantities of live food. Adult specimens also like to eat small fishes. Despite the fact that they have to be considered surface fish, if undisturbed *P. playfairi* also like to stay in the medium and lower layers of the water. They need densely planted tanks with plenty of hiding places among plants. Temperature 73-77° F, a little higher for breeding. An addition of 5-20% of sea water is advisable for imports, eventually also an addition of 0.5% of salt. Domesticated fishes might also profit from a salt addition. The fish spawn in plant thickets, preferring the roots of floating ferns in the manner of the *Aplocheilus* species. The fry hatch after 10-12 days. These like to stay near the bottom and lead a hidden life. Rearing them is not very difficult, especially since they grow very quickly.

Pacu, the: see PIARACTUS NIGRIPINNIS. Brazilian name for *Metynnis* sp.

painting the aquarium: see FRAME AQUARIUM, THE.

paired fins: Collective name for the pectoral and ventral fins.

Palaeopterygii: The Ancient Fins. Sub-class of very ancient, mostly extinct fishes pertaining to the class of the Bone Fishes or *Osteichthyes*. They were widely diffused during Earth's Middle Age, only relatively few species surviving today, which, among others, comprise the two orders *Chondrostei*, and *Cladistia*.

paleatus: Speckled.
— *Corydoras*.

paludarium: see SWAMP AQUARIUM.

paludinosus: Living in swamps.
— *Barbus* (*Puntius*).

palustris: Pertaining to the swamp.
— *Calla*.
— *Ludwigia*.

Panchax: see APLOCHEILUS, EPIPLATYS.

panchax: After the native name.
— *Aplocheilus*.

paniculatus: Bearing panicles.
— *Echinodorus*.

Pantodon: With manifold teeth. Only genus pertaining to the family of the Butterfly-Fishes or *Pantodontidae*, with only one species. Pronounced surface fishes with compact body build of triangular cross section. The back is flattened, the belly slightly pointed, the big mouth opening directed upwards. Especially remarkable are the enlarged pectoral fins, the similarity of these fins to butterfly wings gave the fish its name, as well as the extended, bristle-shaped rays of the ventrals. The butterfly fish is a so-called 'flying fish', the 'flying' however, consists only of long leaps over distances of up to 5 ft., with

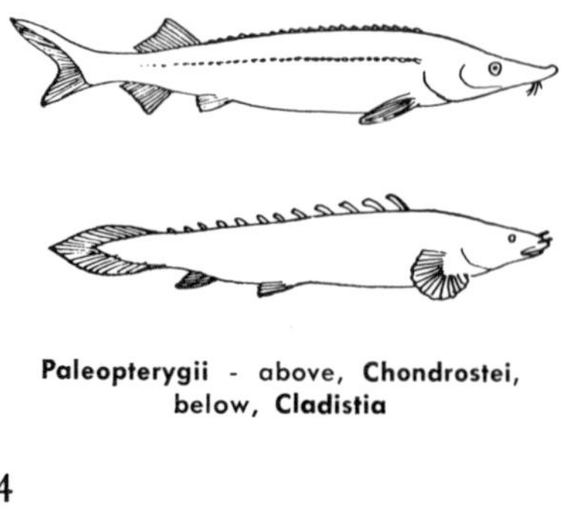

Paleopterygii - above, Chondrostei, below, Cladistia

subsequent gliding off to the water. At present it cannot be stated specifically why the fish execute such leaps. In nature they probably feed only on flying food.

— **buchholzi** (Peters): The Butterfly Fish.

SHAPE: As per description of genus. D 6, A 9-14. Length up to 4″.

COLOR: Shiny silver-gray-green, in part going over into brassy yellow,

Pantodon buchholzi

with darker edges on the scales and dark spots on the sides of the body and on the fins. The anal fin of the female is smooth, while it is deeply indented on the male.

RANGE: Tropical West Africa, the Congo, the Niger, and the upper Zambesi regions. Exclusively in fresh water.

CARE AND BREEDING: The species needs roomy, not too well lit tanks, the surface of which must partially be free, partly covered with floating plants in order to offer the fish the necessary sense of security. The Butterfly Fish is a twilight and nocturnal fish. It stands motionless below the surface during daytime, but may become quite lively in the evening. Considering its ability to jump, the aquarium should naturally be covered. The fish needs warmth, 75-86° F. It takes live foods of all kinds, especially insects, also flour grubs and smaller fishes. Breeding it is difficult and so far has succeeded only in a few cases. After violent chasing and a transitory embrace of the female by the male, during which perhaps internal fertilization takes place, the eggs are set free at the surface, where they remain floating due to their oil contents. For development they need warmth and sunlight. The fry, which hatch after two days at 79° F, at first sink to the bottom and remain there until the yolk sac is consumed. Then they again rise to the surface. The alevins are very difficult to rear, as it is very hard to find them the right growing food. This might perhaps consist of small fry, of aphids, the smallest *Daphnia*, and of *Drosophila* flies, naturally all in their smallest stages.

Pantodontidae: Family belonging to the order of the Herring-shaped fishes or *Isospondyli.* Small fishes with a straight dorsal outline, keel-shaped belly, and a body strongly compressed laterally. The scales are very big. The mouth opening is deeply cleft, and tilted obliquely upwards. The opening of the olfactory pits are extended in the shape of tubes. Especially remarkable are the mighty pectorals, the last ray of which is grown to the body like a wing. The first four rays of each ventral are bristly and strongly extended. Only one genus, with one species, *Pantodon buchholzi*.

Paradise Fish, the: see MACROPODUS OPERCULARIS.

paradoxus: Paradoxical, peculiar.
—*Exodon*.
— *Lepidosiren*.

parae: Coming from Pará, Brazil.
— *Micropeocilia*.

parahybae: After the Parahyba River, in Brazil.
— *Microglanis*.

paralysis of the swimming bladder: Disease of the swimming bladder caused by colds, usually in fishes with accessory respiration, *Anabantids*, and which makes this organ unable to work properly. It develops first of all when the room temperature is too low, thus causing cold air to be taken into the respiratory organs. This also affects the swimming bladder. The fishes move in jumps over the bottom, and can reach the surface, or swim, only with great effort. The swimming bladder frequently becomes strongly reddened. Curing paralysis of the swimming bladder caused by colds may be attempted by transferring the fishes to shallow containers with raised temperature, paying especial attention to the fact that also the room and air temperature has to be sufficiently raised.

Paramecium: Genus of unicellulars pertaining to the phylum of the infusoria or *Ciliata*, class of the genuine infusoria or *Euciliata*, order of the wholly ciliate ones (*Holotricha*), of slipper-shaped body. *Paramecium* has the advantage that, being an excellent baby food for the first days of life, it is completely harmless even in greater quantities, and comparatively easy to breed in cultures. For establishing such cultures one should follow the description given below.

The turnip medium is well-known. For this use 2 or 3 cubes of a turnip cut up into cubes of $\frac{3}{8}$-$\frac{3}{4}$″ per one quart of water. Before putting them to use, the pieces are dried in the sun or in a moderately hot oven. Thus they keep for a long time if stored dry. Such cubes are put into a preserve jar with a capacity of one to three quarts, according to the size of the brood. In order to speed up their decomposition, they may be cut into smaller pieces previously. Now the jar is filled with a mixture of one half tap water and one half pond water. In most cases a seeding with *P.* has already been introduced in the jar with the water. In order to make sure, one may still add a little pond mud.

New cultures may be set up with tap water, being seeded with a few drops from the old one. The same results may be achieved if one adds one or two handfuls of threshed-out rye ears to the 3-qt. jar. It is reported, though, that the yield from turnips is richer than that from rye ears.

SCHABITZ advocates the use of dried dandelions. The cultures should stand in a well-lit place, but not under direct sunlight, as too-intense sunlight retards development. LOHS has observed that the *P.* resulting from turnip cultures were shorter and smaller than the ones from other media. While turnip cultures spoil within a short time, cultures with rye ears kept for months. Naturally they cannot be kept in living rooms, due to the resulting smell.

It is simple to get a clean harvest of the *Paramecia*, which appear in numbers after a few days, by means of a bottle. Take a clear glass bottle (with the longest neck available), and fill it with water from the culture nearly up to the rim. Then shove a swab of cotton, soaked in clean water, into the bottle neck. It must dip into water with its lower part. Then fill up the bottle to the upper edge with clean water. The lower part of the bottle is wrapped up in paper. After some time a number of *P.* work up through the cotton and are in the clean water above it. From there one can easily draw them off with a pipette, or they may be swept into the nursery tank by pulling out the cotton swab, through which a string has been drawn for this purpose. Be careful of equal temperatures, as *P.* are sensitive to changes of warmth. It might pay to put them into a test tube and hang them into the aquarium for some time in order to balance the temperatures. The clean *Paramecia* may also be set up as a permanent culture in a glass tank with aged tap water, being fed on milk. KIESSLING recommends raw cow's milk, and especially sheep's milk. Feeding them should be done very carefully, as too great quantities of milk sour the water and cause the *P.* to die. It is sufficient to dip a teaspoon in milk, rinsing it in the water after letting the excess milk drip off. When the water is clean again, one should feed anew. Such permanent cultures do not give very abundant yields, but they are very useful for seeding turnip cultures and others.

parasites of fishes: Parasites are live organisms that live on or within strange organisms, so-called 'hosts', withdrawing elements from their bodies in order to feed on them. They cause a great number of typical diseases (see DISEASES OF FISHES). Parasites may sponge on or within a fish. According to this they are called external parasites (ectoparasites) and internal parasites (entoparasites), but the separation between both types often is indistinct. Many parasites sponge permanently, that is during their whole life, while others do it periodically, in their youth, or after sexual maturity. Others still seek their host only transitorily in order to feed, living otherwise free. A great number of species are so-called professional parasites, meaning that they have to find a host on which they can live. Otherwise they perish. For periodical parasites this may apply to the period during which they are forced to live parasitically. Others attack only fishes whose resistance has been weakened through other causes. They are the so-called wound or weakness parasites, such as skin discolorers, *Saprolegnia*, and many others. This is explained by the fact that single parasites may live on healthy fishes without causing noticeable harm, and without mass reproduction setting in. The harmful effect of many parasites is caused not only by sapping strength from the body of the host, but also through purely mechanical means (sucking, etc.), and through the development of toxins as by-products of the metabolism of the pests.

Many parasites show great adaptability. They are able to live on quite different hosts, while others specialize on certain species only. Others attack only certain organs. Most parasites fall into the following groups of animals or plants: crustaceans, worms, protozoa, algae, lower fungi, bacteria, and viruses. The highly specialized manner of living of the parasites often produces very peculiar forms of adaptation. We find special organs for adhering, sucking discs and tubes, hook-shaped limbs, as well as cutting and perforating organs. Internal parasites often are also characterized by the ability to live without oxygen. This is complemented by typical changes of the body shape, involution of unnecessary organs, especially digestive ones, and other things. The fertility of many parasites is very great since the probability of finding a host and thus surviving is minute. Very often the process of transferring to the principal host is very complex and needs several intermediate hosts.

parasitic fishes: The small, transparent South American Catfish *Stegophilus insidiosus* sucks blood. It is dangerous to man because it may penetrate the urethra while bathing. Removal can only be effected by surgery, since barbs on the gill covers do not permit pulling it out.

parental family: A form of family in which both parents share the activities of caring for the brood (like *Pterophyllum scalare*). This is the family form which remains together for the longest time.

Parkeriaceae: Water Sprites. Family belonging to the sub-phylum of the Ferns or *Pterophyta* with only one genus and one species. This ranges over nearly all tropical regions of the globe. These ferns have very short stems. Leaf stalks are provided with air chambers and are extremely frail. The ball-shaped sporangia insert singly on the lower side of the leaves of the terrestrial form. The plants grow submerged, semi-submerged, emerged, and as a floating form. Reproduction generally takes place through budding, the buds often appearing in great numbers on the edges of the indentations in the leaves. They are well-liked aquarium plants. Genus: *Ceratopteris*.

parnassifolia: With leaves like those of the Parnassia plant.
— *Caldesia*.

parthenogenesis: Virgin birth. A phenomenon frequent in lower animals, such as micro-crustaceans, by which reproduction always, or periodically, takes place through unfertilized eggs. Parthenogenesis is a result of accommodation to extreme conditions of living which might become dangerous to the existence of a species if the single surviving females were not able to reproduce without fertilization by males. These circumstances generally appear when a scarcity of food endangers the populations. The fertilized eggs which result from matings effected at this time generally are permanent eggs which endure even colds and droughts.

partipentazona: With five incomplete bands.
— *Barbus* (*Puntius*).

parva: Small.
— *Loricaria*.

paternal (father) family: Family form in which only the male exerts the care for the brood, excluding the female both from the building of the nest and the caring for the spawn. The paternal family generally keeps together for periods of time that are shorter than those of the maternal and the parental families.

pauciperforata: Little perforated; referring to the lateral line, which pierces only a few scales.
— *Rasbora*.

paucisquamis: With few scales.
— *Rasbora*.

Peacock Bush Fish, the: see CTENOPOMA OXYRHYNCHUS.

Peacock Cichlid, the: see ASTRONOTUS OCELLATUS.

Peacocks-Eye Sunfish, the: see CENTRARCHUS MACROPTERUS.

Pearl Cichlid, the: see GEOPHAGUS BRASILIENSIS.

Pearl Danio, the: see BRACHYDANIO ALBOLINEATUS.

peat: Brown to brown-black substance of fibrous quality, which originates from the decay of swamp plants with the air sealed off and under pressure (so-called 'incarbonation'). Water takes part in the process. In the formation of peat mainly Peat Mosses (Sphagnum) take part as these form dense mats, often many yards thick, on moors, and the new living mosses grow on the dying layers. The lower, dead strata also contain substances of animal origin besides those coming from plants. The humic acids, which give peat its color as well as the capacity to exchange ions to a certain degree, are also developed. The humic acids acquire special significance through their tanning action. Furthermore peat contains sulphuric acid, and other organic acids, as well as resins, waxes, and hormones.

peat moss filtration: A manner of conditioning water for use in the aquarium which has been well approved, and has led to success in breeding problem species. The peat, which is continuously washed in the filter, releases the substances it contains into the aquarium. The

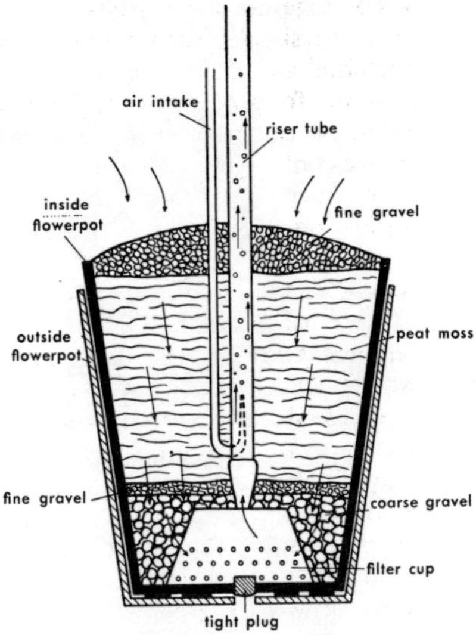

tank should have soft water, the softer it is, the more noticeable the results will be.

At first an acidification takes place, which may lower the supposed neutral point of the water at a hardness of up to 1.5° DH to a pH of 6 to 5.5. Conversely, the acids contained in the peat react with the calcium salts of the somewhat harder water. In this case they cause a de-hardening. In addition to the humic acid, peat contains other acids and reagents such as fatty acids and hormones, which act favorably on plants and animals. According to STERBA humic acid also influences the development of the cellular membrane in the eggs of certain tropical fishes after fertilization. Tanning acts as a precipitator of protein and as an astringent, thus giving secondary combat to bacteria and unicellulars. In aquaristics we should only use high-moor peat, as this contains few mineral components and rivals with the ion compensators in its beneficial action.

As working material, common high-moor balled peat generally suffices, since it is not enriched with fertilizers. The peat should be washed before using, to remove dust particles. Freshly dug peat should be used with caution, as it causes too intense acidification and may contain certain reagents in harmful concentration. MEDER advises one quart of peat, or preferably even less, per 12.5 gallons of water. The necessary quantity is inserted in any aquarium filter, either an inside or an outside one. The filtering element should not be packed too tightly, but should remain permeable. On the other hand it should not contain too many holes, as direct passages of the water will result in insufficient utilization of the peat.

The peat element has to be renewed from time to time. By and by the aquarium water becomes amber colored. When the coloring has progressed to a point that the water, when put into a normal test tube to a height of 4″, looks light amber when viewed from above against a white background, filtration with peat should cease.

Furthermore one has to consider that such colored water absorbs much more light than clean water. According to GEISLER at a depth of 12″ tap water absorbs 49%, peat water 69% of the incidental light rays. In peat water the yellow and red radiations are stronger, the blue and ultraviolet ones weaker. This has to be taken into consideration especially under artificial illumination, as the lamps one uses have to be 50% stronger in this case.

pectinirostris: With a comb-shaped beak.
— *Boleophthalmus.*

pelagial: Living space of the free, open water, simultaneously the collective name of all organisms therein.

Pellegrini, Jacques: French ichthyologist who contributed very much to the diffusion of aquaristics in France. Born in 1873 in Paris. Pellegrini's name is closely intertwined with the development of the Museum of Natural History in Paris. The Trocadero Aquarium owes its foundation to his initiative. At the same time he was one of the first persons who roused the interest of the general public for breeding tropical aquarium fishes.

Pellegrini is the author of many writings and scientific works, most especially on the fish fauna of the tropical regions of Africa, as far as they were under French influence.

pellucida: Transparent.

— *Physailia.*

Pelmatochromis: Referring to the construction of the gill cover.

African genus belonging to the family of the Cichlids or *Cichlidae*, closely related to the genus *Hemichromis*. They are fishes of more or less elongated shape, diverging from the usual Cichlid type, similar to the build of *Apistogramma agassizi*. Several of the species are said to be quite vicious, others, however, are relatively harmless. They love dense plant thickets as hiding places. In part they are mouth breeders. In some cases the female has shown to be the more active partner in mating and caring for the brood, and she is then as a rule the more vividly colored one. The species range over tropical West Africa, in part also in brackish waters.

— annectens Boulenger: The Five-Spotted Cichlid.

SHAPE: The body is moderately high, strongly compressed laterally. D XV/9-10, A III/7-8. Length up to 4″.

COLOR: Strongly variable, generally with blue-green sides which change over into red on the lower part. Four black spots and one spot on

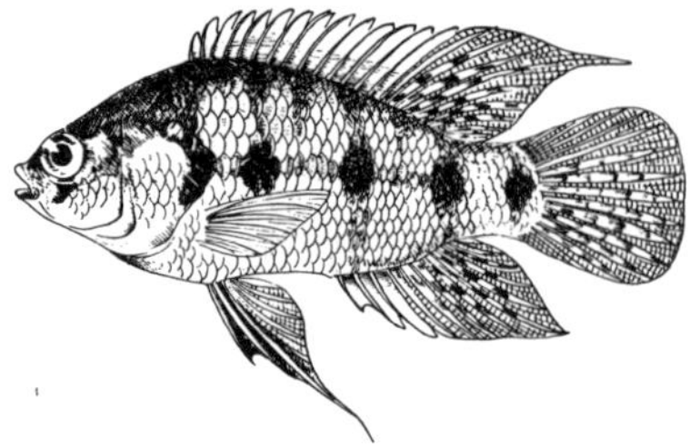

Pelmatochromis annectens

the gill cover. The cheeks are luminously blue, the fins too are beautifully colored. Dorsal and anal fin of the male end in points. The female is not as vividly colored as the male and remains a little smaller. She is reported often to bear a strong white spot on both sides of the body.

RANGE: From the delta of the Niger to Liberia, in coastal waters, also brackish ones, and the tidal zone.

CARE AND BREEDING: As described for *Cichlidae*, and for the genus. They do not harm plants. The fish are very voracious and need vigorous live foods: insect larvae, aquatic insects, etc. Temperature 73-83° F, but not very sensitive to strong fluctuations.

— arnoldi Boulenger: The Dolphin Cichlid.

The body is moderately high, the forehead line steeply rising, especially on older specimens, and indented, similar to that of a dolphin. D XV-XVI/10-11, A III/8-9. Length up to 4″. Not very colorful, yellow-green-silvery with dark spots on the sides. The male has a red belly.

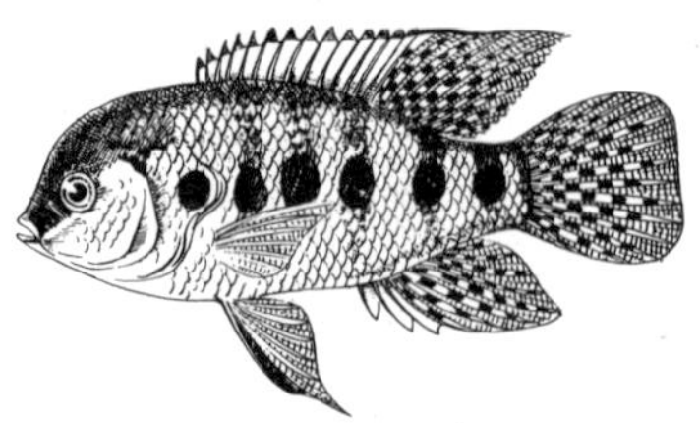

Pelmatochromis arnoldi

ORIGIN: The Lower Niger. Care similar to previous species. Breeding has not yet been achieved.

— **guentheri** (Sauvage): Guenther's Cichlid.

SHAPE: Of moderately high build, strongly compressed laterally. The head, with the large eyes, is big and pointed. The forehead line rises quite steeply to the insertion of the dorsal fin. D XV-XVII/9-12, A II/7-8. Length up to 6½″.

COLOR: Blue-green body with longitudinal and cross stripes and a dark spot on the gill covers. The fins are prettily colored and edged with black on the female.

RANGE: Coastal waters around the Gulf of Guinea within the tidal zone, and which therefore change the salt content intensely.

CARE AND BREEDING: A very beautiful, but vicious species, which eats plants. They need robust live foods and vegetable foods in great quantities. Temperatures 73-77° F, for breeding 77-83° F. According to ARNOLD-AHL the fish are mouthbreeders. The pair helps each other in this and the fry are passed from mouth to mouth.

— **kribensis** (Boulenger): The Purple Cichlid.

SHAPE: Slender, moderately compressed laterally, of cylinder-like shape, which on the male looks a little 'hollow-bellied'. D XVI-XVII/8-9, A III/6-7. Length up to 3⅛″.

COLOR: Very variable, generally yellow-brown with a wide brown longitudinal band and a large purple spot on the side, which often is more luminous on the female. Also the fins are beautifully colored. The female is more intensely colored, the male slenderer with a broader forehead. The dorsal fin shows a broad silvery and golden shining band which on the male runs into the tip of the fin, but ends before this or is interrupted on the females. The tail fin is slightly trapeze-shaped and on the males it shows dark and light spots on the upper half. According to available reports the species may have different colorings and shapes of the caudal fin, depending on geographical origin. We know specimens whose tail fins are rounded, and others where it looks like the "ace of diamonds."

Pelmatochromis kribensis

RANGE: Tropical West Africa.

CARE AND BREEDING: The fish like not-too-small, well-planted tanks, with hiding places and caves made of rocks, roots, coconut shells, flower pots, etc. They are agile and swift swimmers. Live foods are preferred, together with algae. The fish need warmth, 79-86° F. No salt addition is necessary, but they demand not-too-hard water, for breeding 3° DH. The very stormy, but not very interesting game of mating consists in pulling the mouth, quaking, and pressing close together. The pairs spawn only in caves, the bottom of which has to be covered with sand. Both parents care for the spawn. Despite the fact that the female is considered the more active partner, MEDER let the male do the caring alone. Like WAGNER, he too observed that the swarm of fry reacts remarkably to the signals of the caring parents. The young hatch after 3 to 4 days. Rearing them with small live foods is not difficult. Bigger morsels are pre-chewed by the parents.

— **pulcher** Boulenger: The Niger Cichlid.

The body is quite elongated, compressed laterally, the forehead line rising in a curve, similar in shape to the previous species. D XVI/9-11, A III/7-8. Length 4″. Gray-green to carmine-red, with two longitudinal bands and very beautifully colored fins.

ORIGIN: The Lower Niger.

CARE: Similar to that of *P. annectens*. Not yet bred.

— **subocellatus** (Guenther): The Eye-Spot Cichlid.

SHAPE: The body is elongated, moderately compressed laterally, the ventral contour is sometimes more strongly curved than that of the back. D XIV-XIV/8-10, A III/6-8. Length up to 4″, the female slightly smaller.

COLOR: An extremely variable and beautifully colored fish. Especially during the mating period the female is more colorful than the male; the dorsal and anal fins of the male end in points.

RANGE: Tropical West Africa. It is curious to note that the species never was found again after the first imports. Lately HOEDEMAN has presented the opinion that *P. subocellatus* may be the original form of some sub-species, such as *P. kribensis*, *P. pulcher*, etc. These, which so far are being considered separate species, would then have to be called *Pelmatochromis subocellatus kribensis*, etc., but HOEDEMAN is too radical most of the time.

CARE AND BREEDING: As described for *P. annectens*. Also in this species the female is more active than the male. 73-79° F, for breeding 77-81° F. The eggs are reported to hang from threads $\frac{3}{16}$ to $\frac{3}{8}$″ long.

— **taeniatus** Boulenger: The Banded Cichlid.

SHAPE: Similar to *P. kribensis*, which the species resembles. D XVII-XVIII/XVII-XVIII/7-8, A

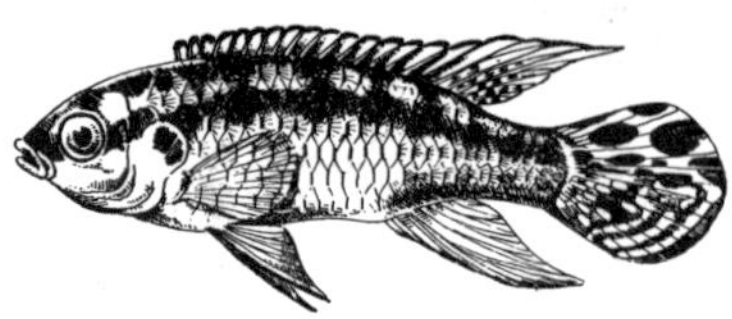

Pelmatachromis taeniatus

III/7. Length up to $3\frac{1}{4}$″, the female is a little smaller.

COLOR: Gray-violet to greenish with two variable longitudinal bands, the belly reddish or yellowish. When excited the female shows a vivid blue, emerald green, or violet coloring. She is more highly colored than the male all in all. The fins, which are pointed on the males, show remarkable sexual differentiations in their design.

RANGE: The lower Niger and its surrounding territory, also in brackish water. Probably this species is nothing but a sub-species of *P. kribensis*.

CARE AND BREEDING: As described for *P. kribensis*.

Penguin, the: see THAYERIA OBLIQUA.

Penny Wort: see LYSIMACHIA NUMMULARIA.

pentazona: With five cross bands. — *Barbus* (*Puntius*).

Peppered Corydoras, the: see CORYDORAS PALEATUS.

Perca: Perch.

Genus belonging to the family of the real Perches or *Percidae*.

— **fluviatilis** Linné: The River Perch.

SHAPE: Of elongated build, which grows higher with advancing age, getting a little pressed-in above the eyes. The terminal mouth is equipped with numerous small brush teeth. The gill cover carries one long thorn and several secondary ones, showing a fine teething at the rear edge. Cheeks and gill covers are nearly totally covered with scales. D_1 XIII-XVII, D_2 I-III/13-15, A 8-9. The two dorsal

Perca fluviatilis

fins are connected by a low skin seam. Length 10-12″.

COLOR: Strongly variable in coloring, according to origin and dwelling places. The most beautiful ones are the Perches that live among plants near the shores, they being greenish to shiny brassy with darker cross bands and reddish to yellowish fins.

RANGE: Diffused over nearly all of Europe and Northern Asia. The River Perch is found in nearly all bodies of water that are clear, mainly in fresh, but also in brackish waters.

CARE AND BREEDING: A fish that lives in schools or swarms, of which smaller specimens only are fit for the aquarium, bigger ones for show aquaria. Being predators, they only take live foods, in huge quantities. According to the size of the fish one should offer them plenty of room, with hiding places, but also sufficient opportunity for swimming and exercising. The best bottom covering is gravel, which should be used together with clean water and abundant aeration. Temperatures, if possible, not above 68° F. Breeding in the aquarium is impossible, as the River Perch only becomes ripe for reproducing after having reached a length of about 7″. The eggs are held together in long wide ribbons by a jelly-like substance, and are brushed off on plants, stones, etc. Rearing the hatching Perch Fry is not difficult. No care for the brood takes place.

Perch-Pike, the: see LUCIOPERCA LUCIOPERCA.

Perch, River, the: see PERCA FLUVIATILIS.

Perch-Shaped Fishes: see PERCOMORPHI.

Perches, True: see PERCIDAE.

Percoidea - top to bottom: Percidae - Monodactylidae - Toxotidae - Nandidae

Percoidea - top to bottom: Cichlidae - Centrarchidae - Centropomidae - Scatophagidae.

Percidae: Genuine Perches.
Family within the order of the Perch-like fishes or *Percoidea*, with two nearly completely separated dorsal fins. The family divides into six genera with many fresh water species, all of which originate from the Northern Hemisphere. The genera are: *Perca*, *Lucioperca*, *Acerina*, and *Aspro*, among others.

Percoidea: Perch-like.
Sub-order belonging to the order of the Perch-shaped fishes or *Percomorphi*, with numerous families, of which for aquaristics one has to mention especially the Sunfishes or *Centrarchidae*, the genuine Perches or *Percidae*, the Leaf Fins or *Monodactylidae*, the Archer Fishes or *Toxotidae*, the Nandids or *Nandidae*, the Cichlids or *Cichlidae*, the *Centromorphidae*, and the Argus Fishes or *Scatophagidae*.

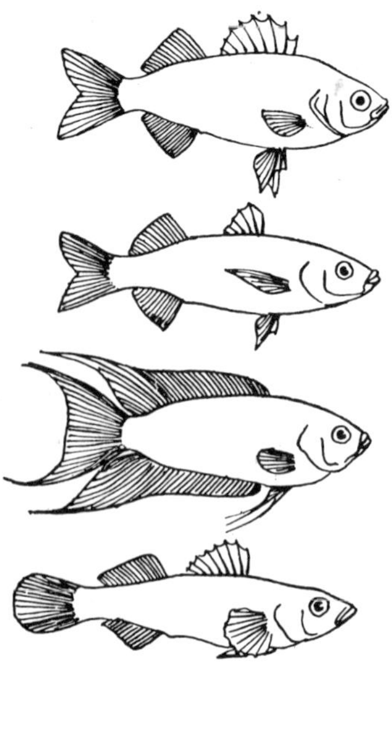

Percomorphi - top to bottom - Percoidea - Mugiloidea - Anabantoidea -Gobioidea.

Percomorphi: Perch-shaped Fishes.
Order of fishes which ranges the whole earth, belonging to the subphylum of the New Fins or *Neopterygii*, also called Perciformes. Fishes with a generally well-developed, partly spiny dorsal fin, and ventrals located on the chest which may be grown together with the shoulder belt.

Of the sub-orders the following are of major importance to aquaristics: 1. *Percoidea*, 2. *Mugiloidea*, 3. *Anabantoidea*, and 4. *Gobioidea*.

perennial: Botanical definition for lasting, enduring.

perennial: Plants that live several years and either do not recede at all, or else the parts that live above the soil may die temporarily, while those below the surface of the soil keep alive. With the onset of favorable vital conditions, new shoots may grow from these.

Periophthalminae: Sub-family pertaining to the family of the Loaches or *Gobiidae*, which are characterized by their ventral fins grown together in the shape of a sucking disc, and through the pectorals provided with strongly muscular insertions which are leg-like and motile. The fishes are able to leave the water and to move on land in jumps by means of these pectorals. The big, protruding eyes are retractile, and may be moved to all sides independent of each other. The family ranges widely over the coastal regions of tropical Asia, Australia, and Africa. Two genera: *Periophthalmus*, and *Boleophthalmus*.

Periophthalmus: Looker-around.
Genus pertaining to the family of the Mud Skippers or *Periophthalminae*, with elongated body of rounded cross section, which is thickened mace-like at the front part. The head is big, the forehead line falls down steeply, the mouth

is subterminal and very wide, the jaws are equipped with small, pointed teeth. The gill clefts are very narrow and permit carrying a certain provision of water even on land, which the fish may fill again by drinking.

Periophthalmus - type of the genus.

The genus inhabits the whole of South Asia down to the Northwest Coast of Australia, crossing over on the other side to the Gulf of Persia and the Red Sea into Africa. The fish are common in the mentioned regions, especially in the mangrove swamps at the mouths of rivers, but also other waters with salty contents of all kinds, but never in fresh waters. They feed exclusively on live foods, which they hunt in water and on land, in which they achieve remarkable leaps. The males are especially quarrelsome towards each other. All Mud Skippers live gregariously in large herds and stand under the guidance of leader fishes. According to their amphibian manner of living, the aquarium should be divided into a dry part and a watery one. Doing this, one should pay attention to the fact that the air temperature within the aquarium should be the same as that of the water. The fishes should be especially protected against drafts, and one should possibly provide for artificial sunlight, such as is given to certain inhabitants of terraria. The dry part of the aquarium should consist of stones and roots, in order to offer possibilities for climbing, of which the fishes make good use. The water level should not surpass 6″ at the deepest spot. The transition to the dry part should be gradual. The water is a mixture of fresh and sea water in equal parts, but the sea water ratio may be greater. One should provide for the possibility of changing the water frequently. Planting the water part is unnecessary.

Temperature 75-82° F. The fish need much warmth. Heating the bottom and irradiation should be preferred. After domestication the fish become very tame and afford the fancier great joy through their peculiarities. Not yet bred. Reproduction unknown. (Species: *P. barbarus* and *P. koelreuteri*).

permanent eggs: Numerous lower animals, such as rotatoria, *Daphnia*, etc. are able to survive unfavorable periods, such as intense cold, or droughts by producing very large, fertilized eggs, which are rich in yolk and are protected by rugged shells. These insure the survival of the species during such periods.

Permutit: see DE-HARDENING OF WATER.

Persian Carp, the: see APHANIUS SOPHIAE.

pertense: Steadfastly stating (its independence within systematics).
— *Apistogramma.*

peruvianus: Coming from Peru.
— *Hyphessobrycon.*

petersii: After the ichthyologist Dr. Peters.
— *Aphyosemion.*
— *Gnathonemus.*

Petersius spilopterus: see ARNOLDICHTHYS SPILOPTERUS.

Petromyzon: Lamprey.
Genus belonging to the family of the *Petromyzonidae*. Interesting for the fact that in them we are able to follow up the development of a new species. The Brook Lamprey, described below, has probably developed in a recent period of earth's history from the River Lamprey, possibly from specimens that were restricted from reaching the sea by

dams and blocking of their way. Similar things occur with other species too in the big lakes of the U.S.A. and of the U.S.S.R. This process, which, according to STERBA, is not yet finished, deserves the greatest interest.

— **fluviatilis** Linné: The River Lamprey.

This species, which reaches lengths of 20″, is found in all coastal waters of Europe. During the spawning period it migrates to the upper reaches of rivers in order to spawn. After the larval period, which lasts for 3-4 years, the fully developed specimens migrate back to the coastal river mouths. During this time their intake of food is enormous. After 1-2 years they reach sexual maturity, and the fish make ready to start the spawning migration. The intestine shrivels and no more food is eaten. The migratory course is often traveled while sucked fast to migrating fishes (Salmons, for instance), or to ships. Shallow spots with gravelly bottoms on the upper courses of rivers and brooks are used as spawning sites. The spawning period runs into April or May, taking place after extensive games of love in "knots" of 10-15 specimens. According to STERBA the building of nests as a common labor of several fishes is an unwarranted rumor and can only be considered a coincidentical observation. The 1200 to 1500 eggs are sticky and adhere to grains of sand, being difficult to see. The larvae dig into the bottom and spend 3-5 years there, sucking water and food through the soil. The larvae mutate into completed specimens within 6-8 weeks. This is the beginning of the migration, with its completely changed manner of living.

River Lampreys are difficult to keep in the aquarium before the migration, easier after it. Then they need big tanks with clear water, flowing if possible, a gravelly bottom, and hiding places. BAHR had milked-off spawn develop, but was unable to keep the larvae alive for more than three weeks. At 54° F and in flowing water the first larvae hatched after 15 days.

— **planeri** Bloch: The Brook Lamprey.

Similar to the previous species, but with lengths of only up to 8″, and the thickness of a lead pencil. It ranges from the Volga westward all over Europe, in fresh water only. The larval period is similar to that of the previous species, but lacks the subsequent migration period. The reproductive period follows immediately upon the metamorphosis. From August to October the fish do not take in any more food, and die shortly after the act of spawning, which occurs in the months between March and June. Thc breeding act is the same as that of the River Lamprey. The building of the above mentioned spawning pits has been observed by PUCHTA, who saw three closely packed swarms of 25-30 specimens each, working in unison in transporting stones the size of hazelnuts and walnuts, and placing them in a circle until a pit 8-10″ long and 3″ deep was formed. The act of spawning could not be observed, but the pits had disappeared the next morning. PUCHTA assumes that this may have been caused by the common labor of the fish, and not by the current.

Petromyzonidae: Lampreys.

Only family of the order of the *Petromyzonoidea,* with an incompletely developed skeleton, pertaining to the class of the Fish-like Round Mouths or *Cyclostomati.* The Eel-shaped body is supported by a flexible chorda, which bears short cartilaginous buckles for conducting the spinal nerves and as points

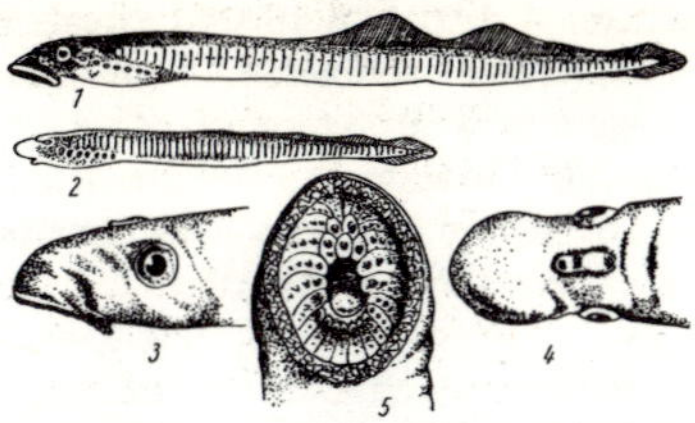

Petromyzonidae - 1. adult - 2. larva, after Plate - 3. head - 4. same, from above - 5. same, from below.

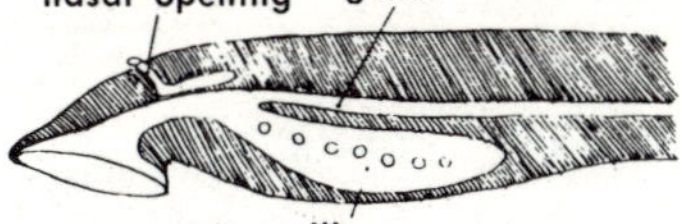

Diagram of the gill openings of a Lamprey, after Sterba.

of support for the musculature. The cartilaginous skull capsule encloses the brain and the organ of balance. The mouth, which is not upheld by jaws, is tilted downwards and is used for sucking fast. On the inside it is equipped with pointed teeth made of a horny substance. The adult specimens, which live as parasites, rasp through the skin of fishes in order to reach the intestines. The big eyes, which are tilted outwards, are covered by the skin of the body. Contrary to the higher vertebrates, the *P.* have only one unpaired olfactory opening. They are gill breathers, the breathing water being inhaled through the mouth or, in specimens that are sucked fast, through the seven punctiform gill clefts from where it is again expelled. These gill holes, together with the real eyes and the nose opening, are considered as eyes, and are responsible for the popular name of the animals, 'Nine-Eyes.' The gill skeleton has a basket-like structure. The intestine runs in a straight line through the ventral cavity, the internal organs leaning on it. The heart, which is divided into auricle and ventricle, is located immediately behind the gills. A tail fin and two, sometimes connected, dorsals are present. The subfamilies and genera differentiate mainly by the number and shape of the teeth.

The *P.* go through a larval stage. After spawning, which probably takes place in fresh water for all species, the worm-shaped larvae develop. They differ so much from the full-grown Lampreys, that formerly they were considered a separate species. The larvae live on micro-organisms of all kinds which they suck into the mouth surrounded by fringed barbels. No teeth are present. The visual apparatus is covered with skin. The small gill openings are located in cavities. The gill intestine goes over directly into the real intestine. Of the approximately eight known genera, only the genus *Petromyzon* is of interest to us.

Lampreys have become quite rare in European waters. They are menaced with extinction by industrial wastes in the waters, this being dangerous especially to the larvae.

Petticoat-Fish, the: see GYMNOCORYMBUS TERNETZI.

pH value: see CONCENTRATION OF HYDROGEN IONS.

Phago: The Eater.

Genus of Characin-like fishes belonging to the family of the African Characins *Citharinidae*. These predatory fishes are elongated and nearly cylindrical in build. Their trunk is covered with thick, ossified scale plates. The ventral region is rounded. The big, beak-shaped mouth is terminal, long, and narrow, the jaws, well-equipped with teeth, give the fishes a pronouncedly pike-like look. The fins are relatively small, the adipose being very small. Four or five species are known.

— **loricatus** Guenther: The Armored Phago.
SHAPE: As per description of genus. D 12, A 11. Length up to 6″.
COLOR: Brownish with bands which are separated by golden-yellow interstices. The fins show darker band designs.
RANGE: The Niger system, in small, standing or slowly-flowing waters.
CARE AND BREEDING: The predator, which takes live foods only, preferably fishes, needs roomy tanks with hiding places among plants, roots, etc. Temperature around 77° F. Not yet bred.

— **maculatus** Ahl: The Spotted Phago.
D 11-12, A 10-11. Length up to 6″. Brownish with dark spots and narrow cross bands.
ORIGIN: The Niger delta, in the same locations as the preceding species. Care too is similar.

Phallichthys: Fish with male sexual organ.
Genus of live bearing Tooth Carps belonging to the sub-family of the *Poeciliinae*.

— **amates** Miller: The Merry Widow.
Probably a local variety of the following species. Length: males 1¼″, females 2″. Gray-green with yellow lower side, and a bluish

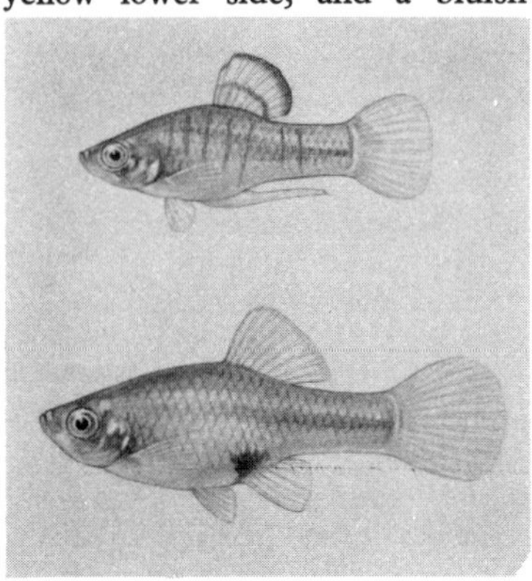

Phallichthys amates

sheen on the flanks. Dorsal fin beautifully yellowish with black edge and white seam.
RANGE: Guatemala.
CARE AND BREEDING: As described for the following species.

Phallichthys pittieri

— **pittieri** (Meek):
SHAPE: The male relatively slim, the female of very high, nearly diamond-shaped build. Strongly compressed laterally, especially in the rear. D 8-10, A 9-10. Length: males up to 1½″, females over 2⅜″.
RANGE: Costa Rica and Panama, in slowly-flowing brooks with clear water.
CARE AND BREEDING: A peaceful species which prefers vegetable foods and eats algae and prepared foods. Temperature 68-77° F. The species is very hardy. With sufficient warmth the pregnancy lasts for 4-6 weeks, the young numbering 10-120. At birth they measure ¼″ and grow very quickly.

Phalloceros: Refers to the antler-like extension of the gonopodium. Genus of Tooth Carps belonging to the sub-family of the live bearing Tooth Carps or *Poeciliinae*.

— **caudomaculatus** (Hensel): The Caudo.
SHAPE: Of quite elongated build, moderately compressed laterally at the front end, strongly so at the caudal peduncle. The head is

rounded and flattened on top. D 8, A 10. Length: males 1″, females up to $2\frac{3}{8}$″.

COLOR: Gray-brown to gray-yellow, with a reticulate design and often with a vertical spot on the caudal peduncle, which is light-edged. A local form from the surroundings of Rio de Janeiro, known as *P. caudomaculatus reticulatus*, is spotted black on both sexes, and a bred form, known as the 'Golden Gambusia' adds a beautiful brassy base to this.

RANGE: The whole Southeast of South America in waters of all kinds, also in the mountains.

CARE AND BREEDING: An extraordinarily strong and hardy species, which thrives under even the most unfavorable conditions. The varieties, however, are much more demanding. While the original form still is lively at 59° F, the tank-raised varieties demand 68-77° F. Nutrition consists of small live and commercial foods, also of vegetables, algae, etc. The original forms yields 20-80 fast-growing fry. The spotted forms sometimes are a little difficult even in this, the litters being less numerous and the young reverting to the original type.

Phalloceros caudomaculatus

Phalloptychus: With folded, collapsible gonopodium.

Genus of live bearing Tooth Carps belonging to the sub-family of the *Poeciliinae*.

— januarius (Hensel): The January Live Bearer.

SHAPE: The elongated body is nearly spindle-shaped and slightly compressed laterally, even at the rear. The gonopodium is very long. D 9, A 10. Length: males 1,″ females up to $1\frac{3}{8}$″.

COLOR: Shiny brownish to bluish, with reticulate design and 8-12 narrow, black cross bands.

RANGE: All of Southeast South America.

CARE AND BREEDING: A species which is easy to keep. 59-68° F are sufficient. They may be frail. A slight addition of salt adds to their well-being. Live foods are preferred. The fish are not very productive. After 5-8 weeks of pregnancy 5-15 young are born, at similar intervals of 1-3 days, similar to what happens with *Heterandria formosa*.

Phanerogamae: Flower plants.

Division of the flora, the main characteristic of which is the development of flowers for reproduction. It comprises the major parts of the plants found in the fresh water aquarium. *Phanerogamae* may be divided into two large groups: the plants with naked seeds or *Gymnospermae*, of which there are none among our aquarium plants, and those with covered seeds or *Angiospermae*.

Pharyngobdellodea: Gullet Leeches.

Super family belonging to the order of the Leeches or *Hirudinea*. Generally small, predatory species, which have no jaws, swim undulatingly, and are often found in great numbers beneath rocks, etc. The food is swallowed. It consists of all aquatic animals that can be caught easily such as tadpoles, insect larvae, etc. The super-family comprises the genus of the Dog or Small Leeches, *Herpobdella*, pertaining to the family of the *Herpobdellidae*. The eggs are laid in cocoons. The leeches are found in standing and flowing waters.

Phenacogaster: With deceptive (peculiarly-scaled) belly.

South American genus of Characins belonging to the family of the Characins or *Characidae*, with about six known species. Small fishes of relatively high shape, strongly compressed laterally. The dorsal fin is high and pointed, the anal long, and the tail fin scaleless. They possess an adipose fin. Above the ventrals are located peculiar scales which give the belly region a square look. The lateral line is incomplete.

— suborbitales Ahl: The Black-Eyed Tetra.

SHAPE: As per description of genus. D 11, A 37. Length up to 3″.

COLOR: Transparent gray-greenish to shining rainbow-hued. Especially remarkable are the big eyes with the black iris. Dorsal and anal fins of the male are a little larger, the first rays of the anal being lobately extended.

RANGE: Southeastern Brazil, especially in small, flowing waters near the coast.

CARE AND BREEDING: The species has rarely been imported and is practically unknown. They are peaceful and omnivorous. Breeding in the aquarium has not yet succeeded.

Phenacogaster suborbitales

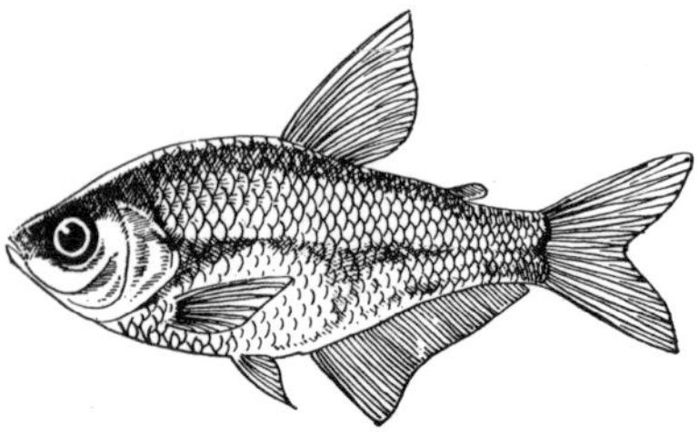

Phenacogrammus: With deceptive lateral line.

African genus belonging to the family of the Characins or *Characidae*.

— interruptus: The Congo Tetra.

SHAPE: Of moderately elongated body, strongly compressed laterally, the outline of the body forms an elongated oval. The eyes are remarkably large. The fins, especially those of the males, are strongly extended, especially the middle part of the tail fin. Length: males up to $3\frac{1}{8}$″, females up to $2\frac{3}{8}$″.

COLOR: A strong silvery shine with delicately colored glossy hues, the fins are gray violet with whitish edges. The tail of the male is lobately extended. The white fins seams are especially remarkable on young males.

RANGE: The Congo system, especially Stanley Pool.

CARE AND BREEDING: A lively school fish which needs much room and causes an especially good impression under incident light. Keep them in the softest possible peat-filtered water for the most favorable results, but the fish also withstand medium hard to hard water. Temperature 73-77° F. The fish eat live and dry foods of all kinds, especially from the surface. After initial difficulties, MEDER was the first who succeeded to breed them. For this they need 75-77° F. The quite big eggs are laid near the bottom among plants. They have no adhesive power. Despite the fact that the parents do not seem to be great egg eaters, it is better to remove them. The eggs may number 400-500. The fry hatch after about six days, become free-swimming after 24-36 hours, and immediately take Cyclops and *Artemia* nauplii.

Phenacogrammus interruptus

Thereafter rearing them is not difficult. Big tanks are a must for breeding.

philander dispersus: *philander*—loving the mate; *dispersus*—dispersed (as to range).

— *Haplochromis.*

Philippine Rasbora: see RASBORA PHILIPPINICA.

philippinica: Coming from the Philippines.

— *Rasbora.*

photosynthesis: see ASSIMILATION. Process by which plants use sunlight to manufacture food.

Phoxinopsis: Similar to the minnow (*Phoxinus*).

South American genus belonging to the family of the Characins or *Characidae.*

— broccae Myers:

SHAPE: This small and graceful species is of relatively compact build. The dorsal outline is slightly arched, and the fish lack an adipose fin. D 9-10, A 16-17. Length a little over 1″.

COLOR: Brownish with reticulate design and dark longitudinal bands, the fins yellowish to reddish. The anal fin of the male is sickle-shaped.

RANGE: In small, flowing waters around Rio de Janeiro.

CARE AND BREEDING: The species is frail and relatively quiet, and also a little perishable. They avoid too intense light, and stay hidden at the bottom. It is advisable to offer them a low water level and a densely planted bottom. The water must be rich in oxygen. No great demands are made as to temperature, 68-75° F being sufficient. According to their whole manner of living, the fish are quiet and reticent in their manner of reproducing. The eggs are scattered freely in plant thickets. The fry hatch after 24-30 hours and need rich supplies of the smallest live foods.

Phoxinus: Genus of European and Asiatic School fishes, belonging to the family of the *Cyprinidae*, with elongated but stout shape, slightly compressed laterally. The snout is blunt, the mouth opening small, dorsal and anal fins are short, the scales are quite small. The gullet teeth are arranged in two rows.

— laevis Agassiz: The Minnow.

SHAPE: As per description of genus. D 10, A 10. The scales are very small. Length up to 5″.

COLOR: Shiny silver with greenish spots which appear especially on the back and the upper half of the body. During the spawning period the male shows a reddish belly, the pectorals being brown. The coloration may be strongly changed in both sexes so that at times hardly any differences will be noted.

RANGE: Northern Europe and Asia, especially in small, clear, flowing waters of the plains and the mountains. The minnow is also found in the so-called trout region and effects migrations.

CARE AND BREEDING: A very beautiful, undemanding, and lively fish, which needs sufficiently roomy tanks if it is to show up well. Gravel bottom and dense planting are a must. A dark bottom enhances the color, since the minnow has the ability to adapt quickly to the coloration of its surroundings. Sunlight is desirable, but the location should not be too intensely lit. Breeding has been achieved in big tanks at low water level. It resembles that of most Carps (see CYPRINIDAE). The Minnow is omnivorous. It is a well-liked subject for scientific research as it was well fit due to its easy keeping in the home aquarium before tropicals were imported in greater numbers.

Phractolaemidae: With protected neck, referring to the design of the gill covers.

Family belonging to the order of the Herring Fishes or *Isospondyli*. African fresh water fishes of elongated shape with a trunk-like, extendable, very small mouth. The big scales are super-imposed like shingles. Above each of the olfactory cavities a short barb is found. Only one genus (*Phractolaemus*), with only one species.

Phractolaemus: Genus pertaining to the family of the *Phractolaemidae*.

— **ansorgei** (Boulenger): The African Mud-Fish.

SHAPE: As per description of family. The body is elongated, with the front part round, slightly compressed laterally towards the rear. D 6, A 6. Length up to 6″.

COLOR: Solid gray-brown. The male is reported to show a spawning rash during the mating period.

RANGE: In a closely limited range in tropical West Africa, only in fresh water, very rare everywhere.

CARE: In well-planted roomy, not-too-well lit aquaria with soft bottom layer. Mudfish are omnivorous, and eat detritus and algae. They need plenty of warmth, 77-82° F. Breeding has not yet been accomplished.

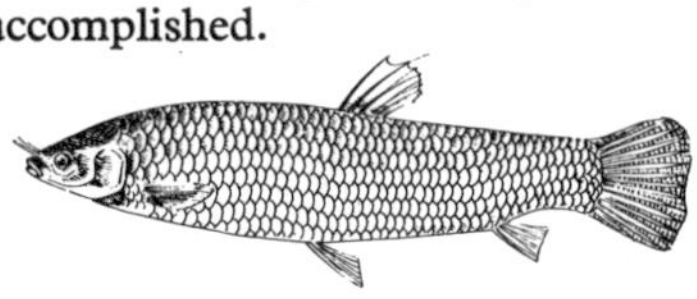

Phractolaemus ansorgei

phutunio: After the native name. — *Barbus* (*Puntius*).

Phyllopoda: Leaf Feet.

Class of small crustaceans belonging to the sub-phylum of the crustaceans or *Crustacea*, generally found in fresh water, the evenly built pectoral feet of which are leaf-shaped and lobate, each carrying a simple small gill sack. The body generally is covered with a shell. As a rule the legs are used to acquire food, and are fixed by the internal pressure of the body fluids. The lateral eyes are paired and quite large. Furthermore there is a single eye on the forehead. Very peculiar is the variable manner of reproduction in which the females show up in great numbers, while the males appear rarely and only at certain times. During the periods of intensive reproduction the former result exclusively from unfertilized eggs, in a so-called "virgin generation" (see PARTHENOGENESIS).

ORDERS: *Notostraca*, and *Onychura*. Of special importance is the order *Cladocera* with the *Daphnia*.

phylogeny: see HISTORY OF DEVELOPMENT.

Physailia: Of the nature of the genus *Ailia*.

African genus of Glass Catfishes belonging to the family of the *Schilbeidae*, of elongated build, strongly compressed laterally, with four whisker threads, and without any dorsal fin.

— **pellucida** Boulenger: The African Glass Catfish.

SHAPE: As per description of genus. The fish are transparent, like glass. The swimming bladder is small; the adipose fin is especially small. A 65-74. Length up to $3\frac{3}{4}$″.

COLOR: Weakly yellowish transparent, slightly reflecting under incident light.

RANGE: From the upper Nile to tropical West Africa.

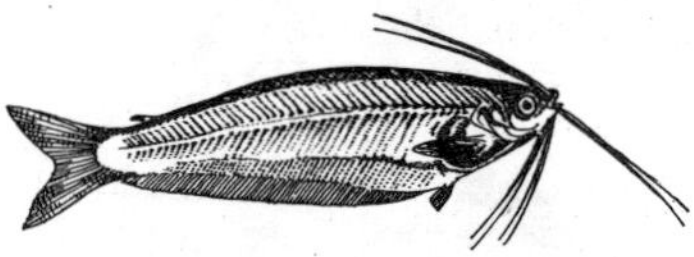

Physailia pellucida

CARE AND BREEDING: This Catfish is a pronounced daylight fish, living in swarms. It is peaceful, harmless, and likes to school at one spot, all specimens facing the same direction. Direct sunlight is undesirable and it is advisable to offer the fish hiding places among dense plant thickets. They are especially fond of live foods. Temperatures 71-77° F and more. Not yet bred in the aquarium.

Physastra (Isidorella) proteus: A small Australian prong-horn snail, reaching lengths of up to $\frac{3}{4}$", of which there is a red form, poor in pigment. Temperatures not below 64° F, the most favorable being 72-79° F. It feeds mainly on algae.

Physidae: Bladder Snails.
Family belonging to the sub-class of the Lung Snails or *Pulmonata*, order of the *Basommatophora*. The shell has only a few spiral turns, of which the last one is very big. The lid has lobate extensions. The antennae are thread-like. All bladder snails are small fresh-water snails, of which *Physa acuta* has become widely diffused among aquarists. They eat meaty foods, as well as the spawn of other snails.

physiology: The science of the functions of organisms and their organs.

phytoplankton: Vegetable plankton.

piaba: After the native name.
— *Cheirodon.*

Piabucus: Two-spotted (from Spanish).
South American genus belonging to the family of the Characins or *Characidae*. Fishes of elongated shape, strongly compressed laterally, on which the sharp-edged ventral outline is more arched than the back. The small, terminal mouth is well-equipped with teeth.

— dentatus (Koelreuter):
SHAPE: As per description of genus. D 10-11, A 42-46. They have an adipose fin. The scales are very small. Length up to 7".
COLOR: Shiny silver with brownish and greenish hues. On the middle of the body a light, shiny, yellow-brown-silvery length band.
CARE AND BREEDING: The species needs roomy tanks with hiding places among plants. Temperature 68-77° F. They need plenty of live food, which is preferably picked up from the bottom. Prepared foods are only eaten in case of need. Breeding has not yet been achieved.

Piaractus: With adipose fin protected by rays.
South American genus of Disc Characins pertaining to the subfamily of the *Myleinae*, characterized by the adipose fin which is nearly totally supported by rays. Two rows of teeth, which stand close together and form a sharp edge in the intermediate jaw. Two or three known species.

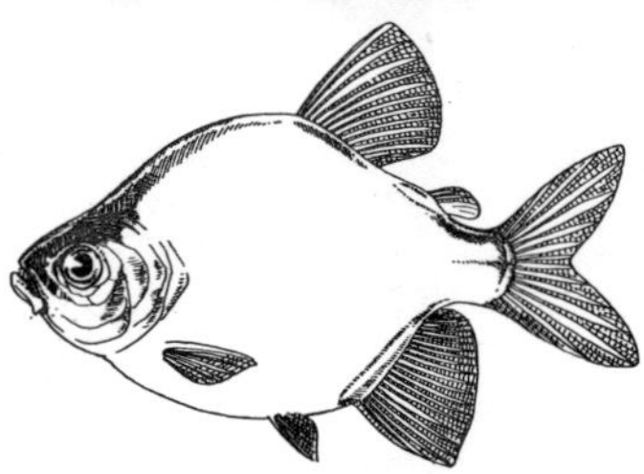

Piaractus - type of the genus

— nigripinnis (Cope): The Pacu.
SHAPE: The body is awkwardly diamond shaped. D 16-17, A 25-27. Length up to over 8".
COLOR: Shiny silvery to greenish with numerous black spots and luminous metallic little dots. Cau-

dal and dorsal fins reddish at the base, the anal of the male brick red and studded with barbs.

RANGE: The Amazon region.

CARE AND BREEDING: As per description of sub-family. The species needs big tanks. It is especially fit for show aquaria. *P. nigripinnis* are peaceable and quiet. but need some warmth, 75° F and more being advantageous.

picta: Painted.

— *Betta.*

Pike, the: see ESOX LUCIUS.

Pike Characin, the: see ACESTRORHYNCHUS.

Pike Cichlids: see CRENICICHLA.

Pike Head, the: see LUCIOCEPHALUS PULCHER.

Pike Heads: see LUCIOCEPHALIDAE.

Pike Top Minnow, the: see BELONESOX BELIZANUS.

Pikes: see ESOCIDAE.

Pill Ferns: see PILLULARIA.

Pilularia: Pill Ferns.

Genus pertaining to the family of the *Marsilaceae*, with several species, coming from Europe, Africa, and America. The manner of living resembles that of the Clover Fern, *Marsilea*. The leaves are awl shaped, and stand up vertically from the creeping main stem. The young shoots are rolled up at the tip. Of little significance for the aquarium.

Pimelodella: Small *Pimelodus*.

South American genus of Catfishes belonging to the family of the *Pimelodidae*.

— **gracilis** (Cuvier and Valenciennes): The Mandi.

SHAPE: Elongated and looking quite graceful, compressed from above at the front and laterally at the rear. The eyes are big, the mouth slightly subterminal. The jaws are studded with bands of very small teeth. Three pairs of barbels, of which those of the upper jaws are quite long. D I/6, A II/9-11. The adipose fin is very big. Length up to 7″.

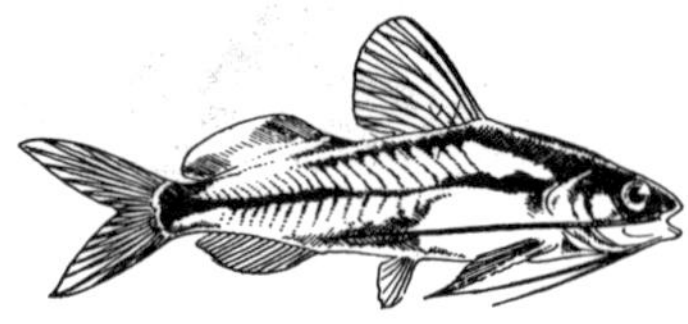

Pimelodella gracilis

COLOR: Gray-green with a blurred longitudinal band, which grows more and more faint with increasing age.

RANGE: From Venezuela to Argentina, in standing and slowly flowing waters of all kinds, only in fresh water.

CARE: A nocturnal bottom fish which is very rugged. Temperature 65-75° F. In not too well lit tanks the fish are very lovely. They are omnivorous, but like to take vigorous live foods which they take from the bottom. Not yet bred.

Pimelodidae: Adipose Fin Catfishes.

Family belonging to the sub-order of the *Siluroidea*, with completely naked skin. The dorsal fin inserts on the front half of the body and is provided with a more or less hard spine, except the two genera where it is lacking. They have an adipose fin which is quite big. The tail fin is short or of insignificant length. There are three pairs of barbels, of which that on the upper jaw may be especially long. The jaws are toothed, the palate is toothed or not. The swim bladder is big and free. The twenty genera are all South American fresh water fishes, such as *Acentronichthys*, *Microglanis*, *Pimelodus*, *Pimelodella*, *Pseudopimelodus*, *Rhamdia*, *Hetapterus*, and *Sorubim*, with numerous species.

Pimelodus: Fatty.

South and Central American genus of Catfishes belonging to the family *Pimelodidae*.

— **clarias** (Bloch): The Pintado.

SHAPE: Of relatively compact build,

Pimelodus clarias

the head flattened, the eyes large, the mouth wide and terminal, with three pairs of barbels, of which those on the upper jaw are very long. The skin is rugged and naked, the lateral line is distinctly visible. D I/6, A 11-12. Dorsal and pectorals are each provided with a strong thorn equipped with a locking articulation, which may cause painful wounds that are hard to heal. The adipose fin is very large. Length up to 12″.

COLOR: Gray-bluish with silvery or golden sheen and with some unclear longitudinal rows of blue-black spots.

RANGE: A widely diffused species, ranging over Central and South America, including the West Indies, being found mainly in the lower parts of rivers.

CARE AND BREEDING: Generally the species leads a nocturnal life, but it may also be relatively lively in daytime. It generally keeps on the bottom from where it also takes its food, consisting mainly of animal substances. Temperature 64-75° F. Not yet bred.

pinnatum: Feathered.
— *Myriophyllum*.

Piranha: see SERRASALMINAE.

piraya: Pirate, robber. Piranha.
— *Pygocentrus*.

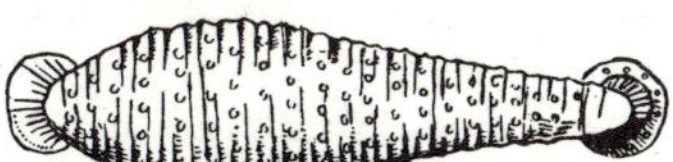

Top: Piscicola geometra. Bottom: Pontobdella muricata

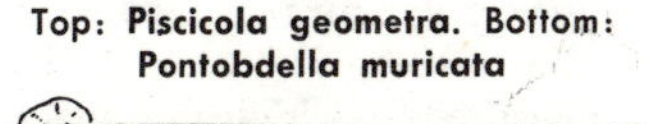

Piscicola geometra Linné: The Common Fish Leech.

Species pertaining to the family of the Fish Leeches (*Ichthyobdellidae*). The Common Fish Leech is found in waters of all kinds, and sucks the blood of Carps and their relatives, Pikes, Perches, etc. Stretched out it measures about 4″, being of rounded build, brown with blackish cross bands. The eggs are laid on aquatic plants, in cocoons that are about $\frac{3}{16}''$ long.

Pistia: The drinking chalice; the drinker.

Genus of floating plants belonging to the family of the *Araceae*.

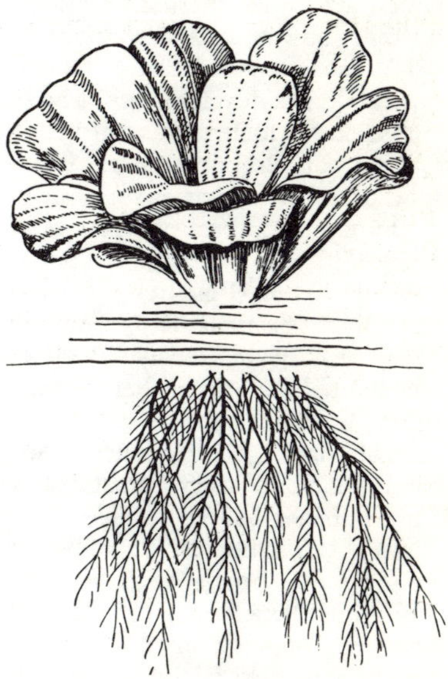

Pistia stratiotes

— stratiotes Linné:

A species dispersed over the tropical and sub-tropical regions of the whole globe, the velvet-like gray-green leaves of which stand in circles as if forming a chalice. The roots are densely feathered whitish to bluish. The minute flowers spring from the leaf insertions. The species does not stand up well in the home aquarium, and generally dies in winter. Winter them as swamp plants in a pot with a mixture of sand and peat moss! The plant demands sufficient moist-warm air, but is sensitive to precipitated water. Reproduction takes place through budding. Very well lit locations, sunlight! 68-82° F and soft water are conditions for thriving.

pittieri: After the American biologist H. Pittier.

— *Moenkhausia.*

— *Phallichthys.*

Planaria: see TURBELLARIA.

plankton: Collective name for all free-floating aquatic organisms, which are either carried or moved by the water and its currents, this being made possible by fatty deposits and the development of body extensions which either protrude far out, or else possess a certain motility of their own.

Quite a number of groups of plankton are known, such as *Limnoplankton* (Plankton of fresh water), *Zooplankton* (Animal Plankton), *Phytoplankton* (Plant or Vegetable Plankton). The plankton of fresh water consists mainly of animal and plant unicellulars, radiolaria, and micro-crustaceans.

Planorbidae: Saucer Snails.

Family belonging to the sub-class of the Lung Snails or *Pulmonata.* Aquarium snails which do not harm the higher plants and therefore may be kept in the community tanks without fear. Especially beautiful are the albino forms, which look more or less red due to the fact that their blood shines through. With these snails one has to be cautious that no freshly-caught wild ones are put together with aquarium fishes, despite the fact that in general the saucer snails are not being considered carriers of disease.

The shells of *P.* generally are compressed laterally to flatness, and evenly wound (Ramshorn Snails). Many species have a very flattened shell. They inhabit standing and slowly-flowing waters with rich growth of plants. Identification of the species is difficult, since all of them may change more or less according to the local conditions of living. Several genera, of which *Planorbis* and *Helisoma* are frequently found in the aquarium.

Planorbis: Ramshorn Snails.

Genus belonging to the family of the Saucer Snails or *Planorbidae* of which the best-known species is *Planorbis* (*Planorbarius*) *corneus* Linné. This species, which is frequent in Central and Northern Germany, is harmless in the aquarium. It too has an albino form. The "cushions" formed by their spawn are long-stretched and elliptical. Like most snails, this species too is sensitive to chemicals. Therefore, when nitrate of ammonia is added to the water to kill hydra, nearly always the snails die too. They are omnivorous, eating detritus of all kinds, dry foods, and algae.

planting the aquarium: The manner in which an aquarium should be stocked with plants depends on the objective at which it is aimed, or else on the points of view that are to prevail in it. Thus the aquarist will proceed according to purely decorative points of view in an Ornamental Aquarium, having, for this reason, a large choice of plants. In the Biotope Aquarium this choice is considerably narrowed down, since the special vital demands of the fishes, which result from the copying of a certain biotope in the aquarium, have to be made to harmonize with those of the fishes. In the Landscape Aquarium, in which one wants to act according to geographical points of view, the choice will still

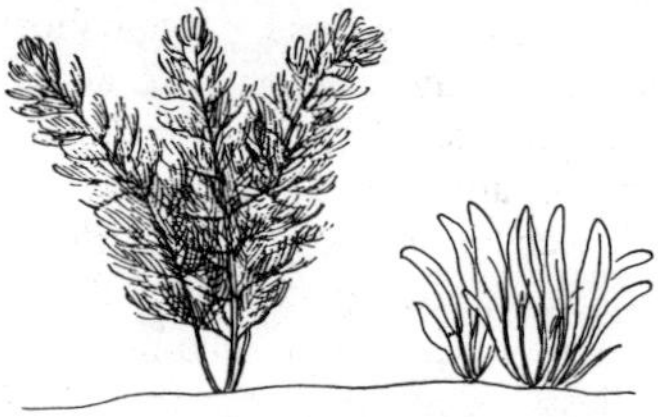

Above, the correct way to plant. Below, the wrong way. Roots should be buried loosely, and crowns should be above the bottom, and not buried.

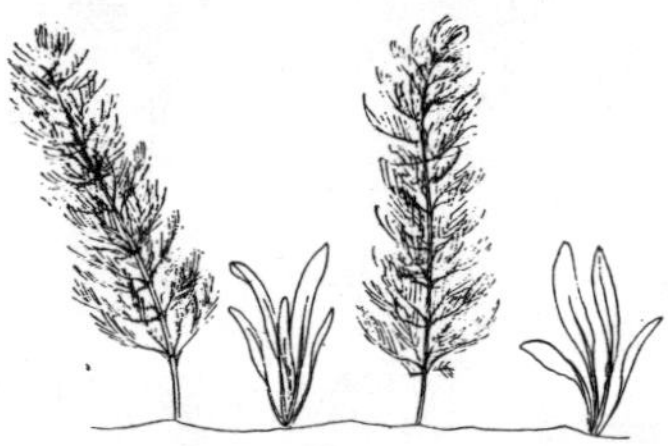

be smaller. In the Breeding Aquarium planting will be subject entirely to the aim of breeding and one will occasionally have to desist totally from using plants. If on the other hand you value the keeping of aquatic plants, the fish population will take second rank to the vital necessities of the plants and will be chosen accordingly. Also the behavior of many species of fishes will be decisive for the planting. If they dig considerably, the plants must only be cultivated in pots or free-floating; if they root, one must give up keeping fine-feathered plants that get dirtied easily. Herbivorous fishes must be kept with rugged plants, which they cannot eat. Fishes that like hiding places should have a plant thicket, and by covering the surface with floating plants one may obtain the half-shade appreciated by many piscine species.

The vital necessities of animals and plants must harmonize. Native animals should be kept together with native plants only, as both need cold water. The needs for warmth have to be respected in the same way as those for illumination, sunlight, degree of water hardness, pH value, etc.

As to the care for aquatic plants in general, see also the entries AQUATIC PLANTS, and CARE FOR THE AQUATIC PLANTS.

Basically, the aquarist should pay the same attention to the care for his plants as he gives to his fishes. For this reason he should not refrain from obtaining the biological and ornamental effects of healthy plants in his tank whenever possible. The balancing action of plants cannot be replaced even by the best possible aeration and filtration, or by any other 'hygienic' measures.

The kinds of plants are, of course, left to the choice of the fancier, considering the bases established above. Fine-feathered, bushy, and small plants should, whenever possible, be planted together in little groups or bushes. Such an arrangement looks better. Big plants such as the Amazon Sword Plant, should stand singly, so that they may be able to spread. Plants which branch out from the stem like Milfoil, Indian Water Star, and others, do not need much distance from each other. Others, which grow runners from the root stock, such as *Cryptocorynes*, and which draw their nourishment more from the soil than from the water, should be kept at a distance of about 16 square inches. In all cases one should always give thought to later growth. For fish species that need room for swimming and exercising only the corners should be densely planted, and the back and side walls set only with single groups of plants. For fish species which like plant thickets and hiding places, the planting should be denser and one may abandon the plants to their natural growth. In such cases, however, one should try to keep some space open so you can see the fish. Big plants should always be planted at a visible spot, so as to give them a chance to be seen. Small plants should be located in a way that does not cut them off from the source of light. Those that need less light may, of course, be planted accordingly.

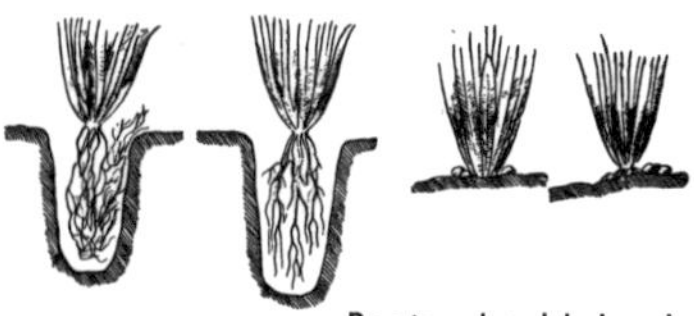

Roots should be buried loosely, and crowns should be above the bottom, and not buried.

A terrace-like disposition of the bottom soil has always proved efficient, and in this also the rear wall may be included in the planting plan, providing projections and plant holes.

Before setting in the plants, pay careful attention to the health of the roots. Black parts should be carefully removed, if they are not in too great number, showing thus that the plant has some root diseases. In such cases the best will be to destroy the affected specimen. The roots should be well cleaned and long roots should be pared and thinned. When planting the plants be careful to have the roots hang down vertically into the setting hole made with your finger or with a piece of wood. By no means should the root tips be bent upwards or hang out over the bottom soil. For many plants one should be able to see the insertion of the roots, the root neck, after closing the hole. The "bottom soil" is pressed fast around the plants before filling up with water. This has the advantage that one can more easily press the plants into the bottom soil, but has the disadvantage that it is hard to evaluate the ornamental value of their location.

If effected after filling up with water, planting is easier ornamentally, since their placement is always visible, but planting is not always feasible without considerable roiling of the water. In such cases, as well as in already established aquaria, one uses pincers, planting scissors, or a planting stick. This, to a large extent, avoids whirling up the soil. Take the previously treated root stock and press it vertically into the ground with the free legs of the pincers or the scissors. As soon as you open the free legs, sand ripples into the root stock and fixes the plant to the bottom. At first, stick the plant deeper into the bottom than it should stand later on, lifting it carefully by the leaves until the point of insertion of the leaves or the root neck is not covered with sand. In this manner it is possible to plant very densely, with the aquarium full of water, without making the rest of the installation

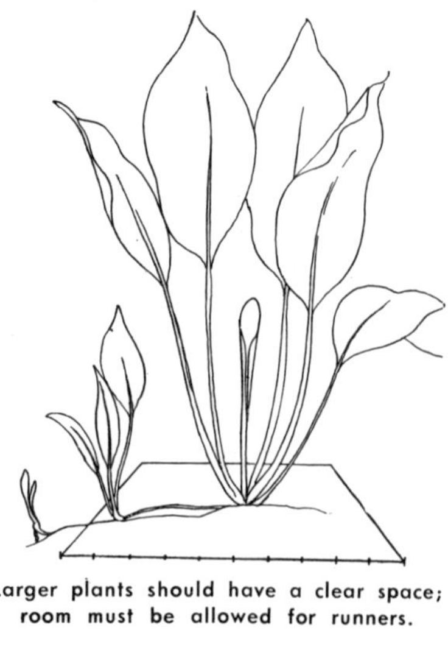

Larger plants should have a clear space; room must be allowed for runners.

suffer any consequences.

If you want to dislocate rooted plants because they are unfavorably located as to light conditions, because they cut off the light from other plants, or even because they are in the way of the fishes, stick your hand into the bottom soil and shove the surrounding gravel to the side, together with the root stock. Frequently this tears off the small roots which sometimes extend far around the plant in the ground, but the plant will soon replace them again.

plants: see AQUATIC PLANTS.

plasm: see PROTOPLASM.

plastic bags: Bags made of transparent polyethylene plastic, which are water and air tight, and which lately are more and more replacing the former metallic cans for the transportation of fishes. The plastic is very strong, and the bags can easily be packed in cartons for shipments over longer distances. Since they can be hermetically sealed, a provision of oxygen may be blown into them from special oxygen tanks. Their use was discovered by AXELROD in 1952.

Plathelminthes: Flat Worms.

Phylum belonging to the Protostomia, with a body that is flattened from above, of different shapes and manners of living. They are lower worms which still lack a real ventral cavity. The organs rest within a conjunctive-like mass between the intestine and the skin. Of interest to aquaristics are the *Turbellaria*, and of the class of the Sucker Worms or *Trematoda*, the genera *Gyrodactylus* and *Dactylogyrus*, which are parasitic on fishes, as well as some of the Tape Worms, which may be permanently or transitorily parasitic in fishes.

Platinum Tetra, the: see GEPHYROCHARAX ATRACAUDATUS.

Platy, the: see XIPHOPHORUS (PLATYPOECILUS) MACULATUS.

Platypoecilus: Flat *Poecilia*.

Genus of live bearing Tooth Carps belonging to the sub-family of the *Poeciliinae*, the individuality of which as a genus has recently been questioned justifiably. The genus was joined to that of the so-called Swordtails or *Xiphophorus* by Myron Gordon and Donn Rosen.

Plecostomus: Welded on by the mouth (referring to the ability of the fish to suck nearly inseparably fast).

Genus belonging to the family of the Armored Catfishes or *Loricariidae*. Moderately-sized fishes of peculiar, compact body shape, of which the front part always is broader than high. They are strongly compressed vertically at the front, and laterally at the caudal peduncle. The back is strongly arched, the belly-side flat. The eyes are small, the snout rounded, the mouth being completely subterminal and forming a sucking apparatus.

— commersoni (Cuvier and Valenciennes): The Sucker Catfish.

SHAPE: As per description of genus. D I/7, A I/4, the dorsal fin is very high, the adipose supported by a hard spine. Length up to 16″.

COLOR: Gray-brown with darker spots.

RANGE: In clear, swift-flowing waters of Brazil and Argentina.

CARE AND BREEDING: These Catfish are pronounced river dwellers which are able to resist even the strongest currents, due to their ability to suck fast. The species leads a nocturnal life and roots strongly. It is advisable to offer them tanks without plants and with hiding places among stones and roots. Too much light should be avoided. The fish are omnivorous and need great quantities of vegetable food. Soaked and rinsed oat flakes may be given as a substitute. The fish often need very much oxygen. Temperature 68-77° F. Not yet bred.

Further species are:

— **punctatus** (Cuvier and Valenciennes).

— **rachovi** Regan:

Both from tropical and subtropical South America, and of similar manner of living.

Plectognathi: Adhering Jaws.

Order belonging to the sub-class of the New Fins or *Neopterygii*. The members of the order are characterized by the fact that instead of teeth on the upper and lower jaw they have tooth plates with which they crack hard-shelled foods, such as snails and clams. The only family of significance for fresh-water aquaristics is that of the Puffers or *Tetraodontidae*.

pleurospilus: Spotted on the sides. — *Poecilistes*.

pleurotaenia: With striped sides. — *Apistogramma*.

pleuston: Collective name for all organisms which float passively at the surface of the water, simultaneously protruding over same with parts of their bodies. In fresh water we have to mention as such only Floating Ferns, Duck Weed, Water Ferns, etc.

Plistophora: see NEON DISEASE.

Plotosus: Swimmer.

Genus of Catfishes belonging to the family of the *Plotosidae*. They are elongated fishes, more or less compressed, of Eel-like agility. The skin is completely naked. The head is flatly compressed, the jaws are well set with teeth. The swimming bladder is big and lies free. The adipose fin is lacking, the anal is very long and grown together with the tail fin. This extends on to the back and simulates a second dorsal. The real dorsal inserts far to the front and is supported by a spine. The members of the genus are mainly found in the sea and the brackish water regions of river mouths in Africa and South Asia, but occasionally they also pass over to pure fresh water.

Plotosus anguillaris

— **anguillaris** (Bloch):

SHAPE: D I/4-5. The dorsal part of the tail fin counts 80-100 rays, A 70-80. Four pairs of barbels. Length up to 12″.

COLOR: Solid brownish.

CARE AND BREEDING: This species dwells mainly in the sea, so that they will need an addition of sea water or of salt. They are pronounced twilight and nocturnal fish, which need a dimly lighted tank. Temperature 72-75° F. According to their size, the fish should be fed vigorous live foods. Difficult to keep in aquaria.

Poecilia: Genus of Tooth Carps belonging to the sub-family of the live bearing Tooth Carps or *Poeciliinae*.

— **vivipara** (Bloch and Schneider): The One-Spot Live Bearer.

SHAPE: Of elongated build, the head slightly flattened on top, slightly compressed laterally in front, but strongly so towards the rear. D 7-9, A 8-10. The gonopodium is short. Length: males up to 1½″, females up to 3″.

COLOR: Yellowish-gray with a dark spot below the insertion of the dorsal fin, the male with a few cross bands on the caudal peduncle. Sex differences otherwise like those of all live bearing Tooth Carps.

RANGE: Northeastern South America in waters of all kinds, even in brackish water. The species is quite common.

Poecilia vivipara, male in front

CARE AND BREEDING: A hardy, peaceful and lively aquarium fish which needs much warmth. The temperature should be kept around 77° F. The fish is considered very productive. Each brood consists of up to 150 fry, which grow very quickly and are ready to reproduce again after 3-4 months if sufficiently well fed.

Poeciliinae: Sub-family of live bearing Tooth Carps, belonging to the family of the Tooth Carps or *Cyprinodontidae*. Small to very small fishes, among which are found the smallest of all vertebrates. The sub-family is limited to the tropical and sub-tropical regions of North, Central, and South America. They are found in all standing and flowing waters that afford the slightest possibility of living. The losses resulting from drying-out of the water, etc. are always compensated for through the tremendous fertility of the fishes. The sub-family contains many species, which tend towards developing variations in shape and color to still enhance the variety of forms. Furthermore, even in nature, a series of species cross-breed easily with each other, so that sometimes the validity of the classification of genera and species is questionable. In all, the systematic classification of this sub-family presents some difficulties.

The small and limited range of the *Poeciliinae* leads to the conclusion that in history of development they are a very young group of fishes, which developed from the egg laying Tooth Carps only after the formation of the present continents had already been completed.

The body is more or less elongated, in some species also more or less compact, and more or less compressed laterally. The whole body, and also parts of the fins, are covered with scales. The external sexual characteristics are especially remarkable, not only by their size and color, but by the anal fin of the males, which is transformed into a mating organ, the 'gonopodium'. The construction of the gonopodium varies according to genus and species, and therefore it is an important characteristic for differentiation and classification.

As a rule the gonopodium is developed out of the 3rd, 4th and 5th rays of the anal fin, while besides this the anal fin, the ventrals, the anus, and the sexual opening are displaced towards the head in this transformation. The gonopodia are complicated organs which are equipped with hooks and other appendages. Besides the gonopodium, frequently more remarkable colors, differences in the construction of the other fins, and the often significant differences in size, differentiate the males from the females. In some cases the females differ so much from the male fish that from the external picture you could only conclude that they belong to different species, while in other cases, however, the sexes are quite similar.

Mating, in species where the female is considerably larger than the male, often meets great obstacles, occurs in a manner in which the male crowds close to the sexual opening of the female with his gonopodium tilted sideways and forward. The sperm is collected together in bundles which glide in, or along the surface of, the gonopodium, and are projected up into the female sexual opening. The female is able to preserve the sperm for a long time, so that the gradually ripening eggs may be fertilized for several subsequent broods. Fertilization and development of the eggs take place within the ovary. Only shortly before birth do the eggs migrate to the oviduct, contrary to what happens with the *Jenynsiinae* and *Goodeinae*, where they develop in the oviduct from the beginning. The duration of pregnancy varies not only with the genus and species, but also with the state of nutrition, temperature, and external conditions. As a rule it lasts 4-6 weeks. Age and size of the mother play a role in this. One or two fry, or up to 100 or more, may be 'born.' The intervals between the births of single young may be considerable, the whole birth process sometimes lasting for several days. The fry are expelled, sometimes two or three at a time, within the egg shell, which they burst with a jolting movement. Then they immediately swim towards the light. They are so developed that immediately after birth they are able to consume the smallest live and dry foods.

All species, with the exception of the Pike Carp, *Belonesox*, which is a predator, are more or less peaceable, but in this we observe certain gradations. Many members of the sub-family are 'beginner's fish' because they are undemanding and will put up with even the smallest tanks due to their minute size. One has to consider, though, that even these only show their full liveliness if they have sufficient room for swimming.

64-68° F are the minimum necessary for their well-being. Some of the species, too, pronouncedly need warmth. The fertilized females, which are characterized both by their plumper bodies and by a dark (pregnancy) spot at the rear of the belly, are set up in aquaria, the illuminated side of which is planted with fine-feathered plants and which has a strong layer of floating plants, such as *Riccia*, *Salvinia*, and perhaps *Utricularia*. The mother preys intensely on her young, and should therefore be removed after having her brood.

As a rule the *Poeciliinae* are omnivores which also accept prepared foods. It has to be noted, though, that one-sided feeding with only such nutrition may harm the digestive organs. In their native habitat the fishes play an important role as exterminators of mosquito larvae, having aided mankind by making vast regions fit for settling, such as the Panama Canal Zone. For this reason some of the species have been transplanted also to South European countries.

Since the *P.* tend towards variations and are in part easy to cross-breed, the breeder who values pure strains must necessarily use only perfectly-shaped and perfectly colored specimens for breeding. Such fish must be kept in pairs, and one should pay attention to the fact that only approved males are mated with approved females. The fry should be carefully and constantly selected during growth.

At the period of sexual maturation the sexes should immediately be separated and kept apart. Only breeder specimens are put together. If they are kept in community tanks, one has to give up the idea of selective breeding.

The best known genera are the following: *Alfaro*, *Belonesox*, *Brachyrhaphis*, *Cnesterodon*, *Gambusia*, *Girardinus*, *Glaridichthys*, *Heterandria*, *Heterophallus*, *Lebistes*, *Limia*, *Micropoecilia*, *Mollienisia*, *Phallichthys*, *Phalloceros*, *Phalloptychus*, *Poecilia*, *Poecilistes*, *Priabella*, *Pseudoxiphophorus*, *Quintana*, and *Xiphophorus*.

Poecilistes: Derived from *Poecilia*.

Genus of Tooth Carps belonging to the sub-family of the live bearing Tooth Carps or *Poeciliinae*.

— pleurospilus (Guenther): Of quite elongated shape, only slightly compressed laterally, nearly spindle-shaped. D 7-8, A 8-10. Length: males nearly $1\frac{1}{4}''$, females a little over 2″. Reddish-olive colored with dark dots along the middle of the body.

ORIGIN: Southern Mexico. A little-known species which probably needs a little warmth.

Poecilistes pleurospilus, male below

Poecilobrycon: Genus of Characin-like fishes of the family of the Half-Teeth or *Hemiodontidae*. After the revision of HOEDEMAN, the so-called 'headstanders' which formerly were included in the genus *Poecilobrycon*, are now placed within the genus *Nannobrycon*, while the small genus *Poecilobrycon* now comprises only three (known) species. Of these so far only *P. harrisoni* Eigenmann, and *P. espei* Meinken have been imported.

Poecilobrycon eques: see NANNOBRYCON EQUES.

Poecilobrycon trifasciatus: see NANNOSTOMUS TRIFASCIATUS.

Poecilobrycon unifasciatus: see NANNOBRYCON EQUES.

Pointed-Head Cichlid, the: see GEOPHAGUS ACUTICEPS.

Pointed-Head Gudgeon, the: see ELEOTRIS BUTIS.

Pointed-Mouth Mollie, the: see MOLLIENISIA SPHENOPS.

poisonings: Poisonings of aquarium fishes are not so rare as one is led to believe. The origin of poisonous substances may be of various causes. Even the natural phenomena of metabolism may generate poisons which cause either acute poisonings, ones that act suddenly, or chronic ones, that are ones that act gradually. Dying organic leftovers may give rise to hydrosulphuric acid, which smells of rotten eggs, and which in great amounts may act lethally. Therefore one should always remove dead fishes, snails, etc., immediately. Excesses of sunlight may cause harmful fluctuations of the pH value towards the alkaline range. Another dangerous phenomenon is the development of ammonium hydroxide which may be generated by green water.

Aquatic animals, too, may generate poisons which act harmfully or even lethally on fishes. Thus the Mud Snail *Radix* (*Limnaea*) *peregra* exudes a quick-acting fish poison, which, when in strong concentration causes unrest, cramps, back-swimming, breathlessness, shimmies, etc. Therefore it is advisable to be cautious when transferring unidentified mud snails (pointed horn snails) to tanks with fishes.

The water may also contain poisons. It is generally known that chlorine is added to tap water in order to exterminate disease germs. Furthermore, SCHAEPERCLAUS reports a case in which a water works, wanting to fight water-bugs in filtration systems and pipes, had added pyrethrum (a contact poison of vegetable origin), which got into the water mains. Also the use of water from natural sources, puddles, ponds, etc., may eventually lead to harm, if these waters were polluted with poisons, such as fertilizers, pest killers, tar, or industrial wastes. Also fallen pine and fir needles in greater quantities, or deposits of *Arbor vitae* (Thuja) in a body of water may add a strong poison to same. Such causes, however, are relatively rare. It is advisable, though, not to use natural waters without inspecting them carefully first.

Another possibility is the admission of poisonous substances from the air through aeration. Thus it is possible to suffer losses of fishes through blowing insect killer sprays, such as is used to kill flies, into the aquarium water. Poisoning symptoms that could stem from similar causes have also been observed in the close vicinity of metal foundries. It is also presumed that aquarium fishes may be poisoned when the tanks stand in rooms where people smoke intensively. Nicotine is an extraordinarily strong-acting fish poison. According to SCHUSTER-WOLDAN 5-10 milligrams of nicotine per quart of water kills small aquarium fishes nearly instantly.

By far the greatest number of poisonings, however, originate from the use of harmful paints and cements, or from badly insulated or uninsulated metallic parts in the aquarium. 'Materials' poisonings frequently are hard to diagnose, and can only be remedied by completely correcting the causes. The use of certain metals for transport cans should be avoided. NAUMANN tested their poisonousness on *Daphnia magna.* The results of this experiment were the following:

Aluminium (poisonous in water with little calcium);
Lead, oxidized (not poisonous);
Iron or steel (strongly poisonous);
Iron or steel, tinned (hardly poisonous);
Iron or steel, nickel-plated chromium-plated (not poisonous);
Iron, enameled white (not poisonous);
Copper (strongly poisonous);
Copper, tinned (weakly poisonous);
Brass (strongly poisonous);
Nickel (poisonous);
Zinc (very strongly poisonous);
Tin (hardly poisonous).

This leads to the conclusion that all metal parts of the frame aquarium, generally consisting of the angle steel frame and the zinc bottom, have to be well protected. It is best to use stainless steel. The poisoning action of common iron or steel is caused by the development of hydroxides which flake off, and which, in soft, slightly acid water that is poor in oxygen, precipitate as a brown film on the alkaline gills or on the alkaline surface of fish eggs, restricting the admission of oxygen, and, secondarily, furthering the insurgence of iron bacteria. An increased poisonous action may also appear (according to BRANDT) when the sulphates of heavy metals combine, such as those of zinc and copper.

SCHAEPERCLAUS advises further that one should not use water from freshly laid pipes or ones that have been out of use for some time, as these often contain astonishingly great amounts of zinc.

Concrete and Eternit (asbestos cement) are poisonous before rinsing. After sufficient washing and weathering (2-3 weeks), however, they lose their toxicity. As a rule be cautious with all paints (see INSULATION AND PAINTING). It is advisable in all cases to paint a sample, such as a piece of tinplate, with the paint you intend to use, and to hang it into a test tank. Celluloid, Trolan, Pollopas, Bakelite, and Vinidur are harmless, according to SCHAEPERCLAUS. Special aquarium cements or putties may develop an eventual toxicity on spots where they are not covered by glass. Therefore one has to use the most seamless cementing possible. Many cements are strongly poisonous. A cement made from linseed oil is poisonous only as long as it is fresh, developing a protective film later on which makes it safe. According to SCHAEPERCLAUS "the testing of commercially made frame aquaria (made in Germany) was extraordinarily disillusioning. Nearly all tanks were strongly poisonous and killed *Daphnia magna* within a few days." The composition of the water has a great influence on the poisonous action of all these substances. Soft, slightly acid waters are generally less favorable than hard ones. Also the sensitivity of fish species, perhaps even that of single individuals or of tribes within the species, toward poisons might be variable.

Poisonings may show the following symptoms: initial strong unrest allied to unusual movements, jumps, and breathlessness, staggering, listing at various angles, lying on the side or on the back, cramps (shimmies), convulsions, changes in color, apathy and death. Chronic poisonings, however, may show symptoms which remind one of other diseases, such as *Ichthyosporidium*. Poisonings can only be cured while still in the initial stages, by changing the water and removal of the causes.

polyacanthus: Many-spined.

— *Monocirrhus*.

Polycentropsis: Looking like *Polycentrus*.

African genus of the family of the Nandids or *Nandidae*, of very high build, strongly compressed laterally. The big head is nearly totally covered with scales, the eyes are large, the mouth opening is very wide and extendable. Jaw bones are equipped with numerous small and pointed teeth.

— **abbreviata** Boulenger: The African Leaf Fish.

SHAPE: As per description of genus, the body nearly round. D XV-XVII/9-11, A IX-XII/8-9. Length up to $3\frac{1}{8}$".

COLOR: Brownish with dark, irregular spots. Sex differences are minute, the belly contour of the female being a little arched outward.

RANGE: Tropical West Africa, in small, slowly-flowing or standing waters, also in brackish ones. There the fish remain near the shores among roots or in similar hiding places. Due to this hidden manner of living they are considered quite rare.

CARE AND FEEDING: Care is similar to that of *Polycentrus*. An addition of a little sea water or salt may be advisable. The species needs much warmth. Temperature 79-86° F, never below 75° F. Breeding them is difficult and has been achieved only rarely so far. The male builds a kind of bubble nest beneath the leaves of floating plants and at low water level. For the act of spawning the female lies on her back, each

Polycentropsis abbreviata

of the singly-extruded eggs being fertilized immediately. They number 30 to 100. The parents may remain in the breeding tank. The fry hatch after 2-3 days, at first hanging from a thread near the nest and then falling down to the bottom where the male has cleaned a place for them. From there they begin to swim freely. The young are very small, but voracious, and they need plenty of infusoria and rotatoria, being very sensitive and frail.

Polycentrus: South American genus of the family of the Nandids or *Nandidae*, with only one species. The body is short and high, compressed laterally. Because of the fact that the soft parts of the fins are translucent, it looks still shorter, as if hacked off. The mouth opening is very big. The jaws are equipped with numerous pointed teeth, and there are bands of teeth on the gullet bone and the palate.

— schomburgki Mueller and Troschel: Schomburgk's Leaf Fish.

SHAPE: As per description of genus. D XVI-XVII/7-8, A XIII-XIV/6-8. Length up to 3½″, the female remaining a little smaller.

COLOR: Very variable, adaptable, dusky brownish to blue-black with a spot design disposed in oblique rows which, however, may disappear completely. During the spawning period the male becomes blue-black. The female is smaller and plumper.

RANGE: Northern South America, in caves on the banks of slowly flowing waters.

CARE AND BREEDING: A nocturnal predator which likes densely planted tanks with hiding places among stones and roots. It likes to keep hidden but is not pronouncedly shy; to the contrary, after getting used to the aquarium it likes to show itself near the front glass. There it frequently remains with

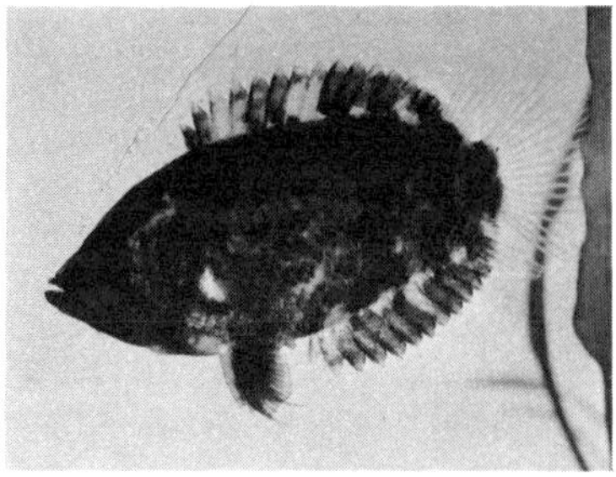

Polycentrus schomburgki

its typical high forehead line, the head bent downwards. A ponderous swimmer which takes only vigorous live foods. The Leaf Fish is a predator, but is rather clumsy in catching foods that swim skilfully. Bigger specimens like to eat small fishes, which generally are caught in the night. The prey are ambushed or cautiously stalked. Temperature 72-79° F, for breeding 82-86° F. The spawning site, a cave or the underside of a big leaf, sometimes also a stone or a glass pane of the aquarium, is cleaned by the male. The act of spawning takes place after peculiar mating play during which the male turns in circles while fluttering his fins. While spawning the female lies on her back. The male cares for the spawn and chases the female away. The parents do not prey on the young, but it is advisable to remove the female immediately after spawning, and the male 2-3 days after the alevins have hatched. At first the fry hang from a mucus thread at the spawning site, later falling to the bottom, and becoming free-swimming after about 8 days. They are very small and need infusoria and rotatoria. The species is very productive.

Polyphaga: Sub-order belonging to the order of the *Coleoptera* or bugs, which includes the family of the *Hydrophilidae*.

Polyphemidae: Predatory *Daphnia*.

Family of vicious micro-crustaceans belonging to the class of the Leaf Feet or *Phyllopoda*. They are interesting animals of peculiar shape. Of interest to aquarists are the Big-Eyed *Daphnia*, *Polyphemus pediculus*, which live in lakes, often in great swarms, near the shores, preying on other micro-crustaceans. It reaches lengths of up to ⅝″, being remarkable for its huge, complex eye, which sees not only differences in light, but also moving prey. They are capable of eating new-born fry.

polyps: see HYDROIDEA.

Polypteridae: Family of bony fishes belonging to the order *Cladistia*. They are elongated, Eel-shaped and have a rounded cross section. The body is covered with strong, diamond-shaped scales, which are lined with a strong film of enamel. The dorsal fin is divided into a series of little fins supported by spines. The swimming bladder is used as an accessory respiratory organ. The *P.* are the only fishes whose swimming bladder ends in the oesophagus like a wind-pipe. In their development they pass through a larval stage.

Very interesting fishes, of which only smaller specimens adapt to the home aquarium, but which otherwise are very fit for show aquaria. The spawning time probably falls into the rainy period, during which large regions are flooded. Probably no care for the spawn is exerted, and the eggs are simply stuck to aquatic plants.

Genera: *Calamoichthys*, and *Polypterus*.

Polypterus: Genus pertaining to the family of the *Polypteridae*, the small dorsal fins of which are provided with two or more articulated rays. They have ventral fins. The genus comprises several species which range over West and Central Africa.

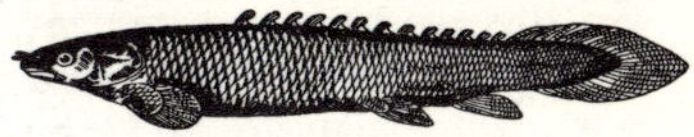

Polypterus bichir

— bichir Geoffrey Saint Hilaire: The Nile Snake-Head.

SHAPE: As per description of genus. Each nostril carries a tentacle. The throat is protected by a bone plate. On the back one sees 8-10 small fins, which go over into the tail fin without interruption. The pectorals are broad and hand-shaped, their insertion being developed foot-like. Length up to 60″.

COLOR: Brownish base with indistinct dark bands and spots which disappear temporarily.

RANGE: Central Africa from the Nile to Lake Chad, especially in bigger streams and rivers.

CARE AND BREEDING: The Nile Snake-Heads are especially adapted for keeping in bigger show installations. They are predators which only eat vigorous live foods, fishes, frogs, the meat of warm-blooded animals, etc. The larvae have external gills in the shape of bunched appendages on the edges of the gill covers.

The fish likes to lie on the bottom, propped up on its pectorals. Despite a temporary sluggishness it is a skilled and swift swimmer. The nose tentacles are used to ferret out food. In their native habitat the Snake-Heads are well-liked food fishes. Temperature 73-82° F. Reproduction unknown.

polyrhiza: Many-rooted.

— *Spirodella*.

Pond Mussels: see UNIONIDAE.

Pond Water Star: see CALLITRICHE STAGNALIS.

pop-eyes: see EXOPHTHALMY.

popular names: Naming animals and plants which are kept in aquaria has always led to differences of opinion among aquarists.

On this we have to comment that to give living organisms names in our own language and thus to circumvent the often difficult-to-memorize scientific designations, is perfectly understandable. As far as our native animals and plants are concerned, in most cases there is already a popular name available which belongs to our linguistic heritage, but unfortunately we have often to see that such names differ according to geographic region and to dialect. Anyway, it should be relatively easy to agree on a generally valid name at least in the technical literature.

For non-native species things are quite different. For these the vernacular names have to be new creations in all cases. This has already been done with some skill for many of them. There are many possibilities for doing this, of which we shall give a few examples below:

1. Analogies with native definitions, which are taken as comparison of the body, head or other features, for example, the 'Pike' Cichlid, the 'Armored' Catfish, the 'Banjo' Catfish, etc.;

2. Borrowing from native languages of the countries of origin (generally used simultaneously as roots for the scientific names), for example 'Danio', or 'Gourami', which are both taken directly from Hindu dialects;

3. Mutilated or abridged uses of scientific names, for instance, 'Mollie', 'Platy', 'Caudo', etc.;

4. Simple translations of scientific names, for example 'the Two-Lined Neotoca', from *Neotoca bilineata*, 'the Ten-Spot' from *Cnesterodon decemmaculatus*, or 'Ortmann's Dwarf Cichlid' from *Apistogramma ortmanni*;

5. Mention of special features in shape or color, such as the Lyre-Tail, the Sword-Tail, the Gold Fish, the Sword Plants, the Silver Dollar, etc.

6. Mention of geographic origins, such as the Egyptian Mouthbreeder, the Cuban Killie, or the Javanese Medaka.

The effort to christen our pets with vernacular designations deserves every praise, as long as it does not tend towards a complete substitution and replacement of scientific names in aquaristics. The latter could not be replaced even by the best English names, since it is they which create international, scientifically unmistakable definitions. It would doubtlessly harm aquaristics if the scientific designations were to take second rank. However, in the exchange between aquarists among themselves, uniform English names deserve our wholehearted support.

population: Totality of individuals of a species or sub-species in a region in which, theoretically or practically, mating is possible without obstacles. The size of the range of a population depends upon the motility of the individuals that belong to the species, as well as of the measurements and connectedness of the living space.

The word 'population' acquired special meaning when science came to the conclusion that a species is composed of a series of forms, races, and sub-species which do not agree completely. According to the modern definition, a species is a circle of populations which, depending on its surroundings, lives in a spatially connected region (or one which was connected spatially within recent times of earth's history). The type of a population, and with it the picture of a species, can only be grasped if one knows all forms which are found within its boundaries.

As long as mating, and with it the exchange of hereditary factors, is possible within the complete population and also within its border regions, no, or only small deviations from the prototype, will appear. If with time, however, and through the most diverse causes, a separation of the branches of a population takes place, the differences increase gradually, and the originally relatively uniform species divides into sub-species, races, and local varieties.

The reason for such separations is to be found in the appearance of so-called "barriers," which may be of a most diversified nature. If, for instance, they are of a geographical nature, through eventual formations of mountain systems, changes may be accompanied by variations in the ecological conditions, after which parts of the population may find especially favorable conditions for development, while others may find especially unfavorable ones.

On the other hand the reasons may be found in the species itself. Thus, a small change in the mating cycle of a branch of a total population may lead to the fact that this branch is now no more able to mate with the balance of the population. HOEDEMAN mentions the following examples for changes in the prototype of a population:

1. Morphological ones: Differences in proportions, color, number of scales, etc.

2. Ecological ones: The inability to adapt in behavior to certain conditions of the changing world.

3. Physiological ones: Changes in sensitivity to temperature, changes in the cycle of reproduction, etc.

Generally one of the factors of change is sufficient to cause dislocations within a population.

Porifera: Sponges.
The simplest class of multicellular invertebrates. The single cells unite into specialized cell groups, but do not yet form real organs, nerves or sensorial cells. In principle a sponge is a fixed pipe, the walls of which are pierced by many pores. Through these pores both oxygen and food (detritus) are sucked in with the water. The water is again expelled through a bigger, collective opening. The pores and this larger opening develop as needed. The food particles within the pipe are caught by the flagellum cells which are located on the inside. They are partially dissolved in the vacuoles within these cells, or else they are eaten by amoeba-like migratory cells. The body of the sponge is supported by an internal skeleton of needles or fibres which consists of calcium, silicic acid, and horn. Reproduction takes place by budding, the new buds remaining connected to each other and forming settlements which blend into a whole. Some of the buds may come off and form new colonies. Sexual reproduction takes place through eggs from which develop ciliate larvae. Only the family *Spongilidae* is of importance within the fresh water aquarium.

porocephala: Porous-headed.
— *Eleotris.*

portalegrensis: Coming from Porto Alegre, state capital of Rio Grande do Sul, Brazil.
— *Aequidens.*

Potamogeton: Neighbor in the river (Spawn Worts).
Genus belonging to the family of the *Potamogetonaceae.* As a rule they are plants that are not very useful in the home aquarium, but very good for the open air pond.

— acutifolius Linné: Pointed-Lead Spawn Wort.
Species equipped only with submerged, narrow, linear, and pointed leaves, which is distributed over Europe, Asia, and Australia. It grows in standing and slowly

Potamogeton acutifolius

flowing waters of the plains. The stems do not grow above the surface.

— **alpinus** Balbis: Alpine Spawn Wort.

A species equipped with submerged and floating leaves, the upper part of which sometimes shows a reddish color. It is found in Europe, Asia, North America, and South Africa. There it thrives not only in the mountains, but also on the plains in standing and slowly flowing waters.

Potamogeton alpinus

— **coloratus** Vahl: Colored Spawn Wort.

Translucent, reedish, lanceolate, submerged leaves, which also may be a little broader. The floating leaves are oval, thin-skinned, and transparent. The submerged form does not bloom. The species is found in Europe, North Africa, Australia, Jamaica, and the Bahamas, where it grows in standing, generally peaty waters of the plains.

— **compressus** Linné: Compressed Spawn Wort.

This species has only submerged leaves, which grow to lengths of up to 8″ and widths of 1½″. The species is easily mistaken for *P. acutifolius*, from which it differs only by the number of flowers. It is found in the same places as *P. acutifolius* and originates from Europe, Siberia, and East Asia.

Potamogeton crispus

— **crispus** Linné: Curly Spawn Wort.

The species has only submerged leaves, which are long and pointed, with wavy and curly edges, often reddish-brown in color. In autumn they develop winter buds. The stems rise above the surface. The plant is distributed over Europe, Asia, Africa, Australia, and North America. It is found in standing and slowly-flowing waters.

This Spawn Wort is very good for open-air pools, since the plant rarely grows algae and always keeps the water crystal clear.

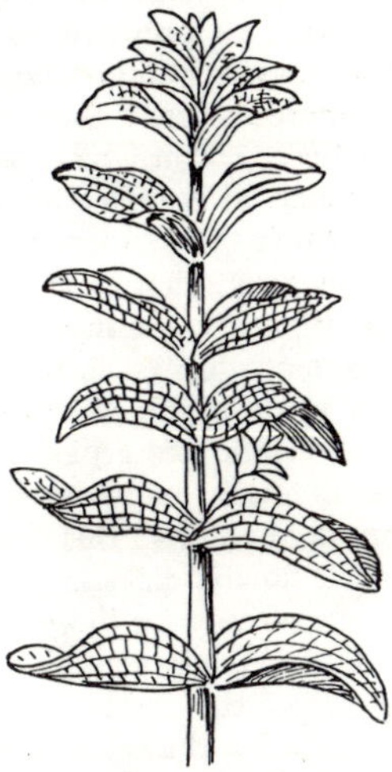

Potamogeton densus

— **densus** Linné: Thick-Leaved Spawn Wort.
Spawnwort with only submerged oblong-lanceolate leaves, slightly bent back, of about $1\frac{1}{2}''$ in length and $\frac{3}{4}''$ in width. *C* species are diffused over Europe, great parts of Asia Minor, Central and Northern Asia, which is found especially in clear, not too swiftly-flowing waters.

— **filiformis** Persoon: Thread-shaped Spawn Wort.
Spawnwort with only submerged, thread-like leaves, up to 2″ long. The species ranges over Europe, Asia, Egypt, and North America, being especially frequent in Northern Germany. It also thrives in brackish water. It prefers flowing waters with rocky or sandy bottom.

— **gayi** A. Bennett:
SHAPE: The exclusively submerged plant has very long, thin stems on which the long, slightly lanceolate, olive-greenish or slightly brownish leaves insert alternately. These have lengths of $1\frac{1}{8}''$ to $2\frac{3}{4}''$, and widths of $\frac{1}{8}''$ to $\frac{3}{16}''$. The stem, which is about $\frac{1}{16}''$ long and carries only a minute number of flowers, hardly rises above the surface.
RANGE: The species ranges over Argentina, Brazil, Chile, and Uruguay.
CULTIVATION: Since the plant is of tropical origin, differing from all other species of *P.*, it keeps relatively well in heated aquaria. It needs soft water and a temperature of 68-77° F. Unwashed sand is a sufficient bottom soil. Near the surface the shoots branch out so densely that in time they form a dense thicket. Such thickets are especially favorable for breeding purposes. Good illumination, however, is needed. Reproduction may occur through pieces of the stems, which grow roots quickly. They also grow shoots along the bottom which send roots down and sprouts up vertically.

— **gramineus** Linné: Grass-Leaved Spawn Wort.
This Spawn Wort, which is equipped with floating and submerged leaves, originates from standing and flowing waters in Europe, Central Asia, Japan, and North America, with a great number of sub-species and cross-breeds.

— **lucens** Linné: Glossy Spawn Wort.
This plant shows only submerged leaves which sit on a long stem and are quite broad. The stem protrudes over the surface. It is found in Europe, Asia, Africa, and Australia, and forms dense strands in the water.

— **natans** Linné: Floating Spawn Wort.
The species develops only floating leaves and is usable for the open

air pool only. It grows in waters of all kinds in Europe, Asia, Africa, North America, and New Zealand.

Potamogetonaceae: Spawn Worts. Family belonging to the class of the single-germinating-leaved plants or *Monocotyloedoneae*, with several genera, which are found all over the whole globe. The family, which has quite a few species, has furthermore developed a whole series of local forms and cross breeds which make classification difficult if not impossible. Generally they are perennial plants with a long rootstock which creeps on or in the bottom and may branch out strongly. Spawn Worts are found in fresh, brackish, and salt water. The leaves are alternate to nearly opposite, submerged or floating. The shapes differ, ranging from oval to narrow lanceolate. Often one sees small secondary leaves near the insertion of the main leaves. Several of the species develop winter buds. The stems often protrude over the surface in the shape of a cob. The fruits generally are similar to stone fruits. Unfortunately the German species of Spawn Wort don't last long in the home aquarium. But they are easy to cultivate in outside pools. Despite manifold experiments (GEYER, WENDT) permanent cultivation in the home aquarium has not yet proved to be possible. The reasons for this are not yet clear. It is possible that the tropical species, or specimens of tropical origin may be more acclimatable. There are no reports at hand on this. So far the few imported plants have not withstood aquarium culture.

Of the genera only *Potamogeton* is worth mentioning here.

Predator Characin, the: see ACESTRORHYNCHUS.

predators: Fishes of Prey.

Fishes which feed on vertebrates, especially on other fishes, and which have bodies specialized for this manner of feeding. Well-known as typical for predatory fishes is the 'torpedo' shape of the Pike, which reappears in the different families of fishes. This shape suggests a lurking manner of living, in which the prey is seized in quick darts from the hiding place. Fishes of prey which chase their food have a body construction which comes nearer that of the other fishes, and on which the fins do not insert as far back as on the Pikes. Most predators swallow their prey head first, and turn it around by releasing it and seizing it again as many times as necessary to put it in the right position. The size of the victims is generally well evaluated, but it may happen that the prey is too big. In this case it is swallowed slowly, digesting it piece by piece, as may be observed in Trout. Only a few predators bite off pieces from the body of their victims, as do the *Serrasalminae* (*Piranhas*) of South America. Smaller fishes of prey often have an oversized, protractable mouth, as the Nandids and the Pike-Heads. The above-mentioned *Serrasalminae* have a special manner of hunting, staging mass attacks on their victims, which sometimes even consist of bigger birds and mammals, from the bodies of which they tear off large pieces with the aid of their strong jaws and razor-sharp teeth.

Predatory Beetles: see ADEPHAGA.

Predatory Daphnia: see LEPTODORIDAE; POLYPHEMIDAE.

Pretty Tetra, the: see HEMIGRAMMUS; PULCHER.

Priabella: Diminutive form of 'priabus', the male organ.

Genus of live bearing Tooth Carps belonging to the family of the *Poeciliinae*.

— bonita (Meek):

SHAPE: Of very elongated build

Priabella bonita, male behind

slightly compressed laterally. D 7-9, A 9-10. Length of both sexes around 2″.

COLOR: Greenish-gray with dark longitudinal stripes, the dorsal and tail fin of the male are dark-edged.

RANGE: Mexico.

CARE AND BREEDING: Undemanding species, which only eats live food, though. The female yields about 30 young per litter.

Priestley, Joseph: 1733-1804. British naturalist who discovered oxygen independently of the Swede SCHEELE.

primary sexual characteristics: All sexual characteristics which are directly related to the sexual function, such as ovaries, testicles, etc. which in fishes generally are located in the interior of the body, so that one cannot readily make use of them for sexing the specimens. For this reason the aquarist generally takes recourse to the secondary sexual characteristics.

Prionobrama: Saw Breams.

South American genus of the family of the Characins or *Characidae*. Closely related to the genus *Aphyocharax*, differing from it only by the longer fins. So far two species are known.

— **filigera** (Cope): The Glass Redfin.

SHAPE: Elongated and slim, strongly compressed laterally. The mouth is supraterminal. D 10-11, A 31-39. They possess an adipose fin. Length around $2\frac{3}{8}$″.

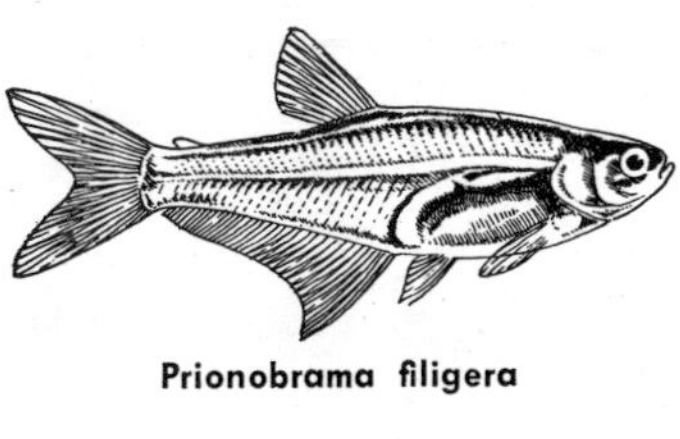

Prionobrama filigera

COLOR: This frail, glassily translucent species is a shiny, greenish-silvery with reddish fins under incident light. The male is marked by a black stripe behind the first white rays of the anal fin, furthermore this fin is a little more arched than that of the female, and the fins of the male are generally redder.

RANGE: The Amazon system.

CARE AND BREEDING: As described for *Aphyocharax*. The Glass Redfins are peaceful school fishes which eat all kinds of dry and live foods. They need much warmth, 75-79° F being advisable, for breeding 79-82° F.

Pristella: Little Saw Fish.

South American genus of the family of the Characins or *Characidae*, with incomplete lateral line. The upper jaw shows saw-like teeth. Two known species.

— **riddlei:** Riddle's Pristella.

SHAPE: Moderately elongated, strongly compressed laterally. D 11, A 20-24. They possess an adipose fin. Length: males up to $1\frac{3}{8}$″, females up to $1\frac{3}{4}$″.

COLOR: Very delicately hued, yellow-brownish-silvery translucent. Especially remarkable are a dark shoulder spot and a dark spot each on the dorsal and anal fins, which both are edged with white and yellow above and below. In the slimmer males the visible internal organs are pointed, in the females round. They have red tails.

RANGE: Northern South America to the lower Amazon, especially in smaller standing or flowing waters of the coastal region, where they often appear in big swarms.

CARE AND BREEDING: A very motile, peaceable species, which likes to swim, is hardy and enduring, and eats only smaller foods. Slightly needing warmth, temperatures 68-79° F. Breeding is not very simple. For this set up two males and one female in a spacious whole-glass tank and cover the bottom with fine-feathered plants. A little sunlight is desirable, but should not be excessive. The act of spawning, like that of most other characins, takes place among fine-feathered plants after stormy chasing. 300-500 eggs are released which are very small and glass-clear. The young hatch after 50-60 hours. Since at first they are very small and sensitive, rearing them with smallest foods is initially a little difficult. Provide for an even temperature.

Pristolepis: With saw-toothed scales.

Genus belonging to the family of the Nandids or *Nandidae*, with one species which grows rather large.

— fasciatus (Bleeker): The Striped, or Tiger, Nander.

SHAPE: Of very high build, strongly compressed laterally, the forehead line rises steeply. The head is covered with scales, the mouth opening relatively small and a little extendable. D XII-XIII/14-16, A III/8. Length over 12″.

RANGE: Fresh waters from Indo-China to Malaya.

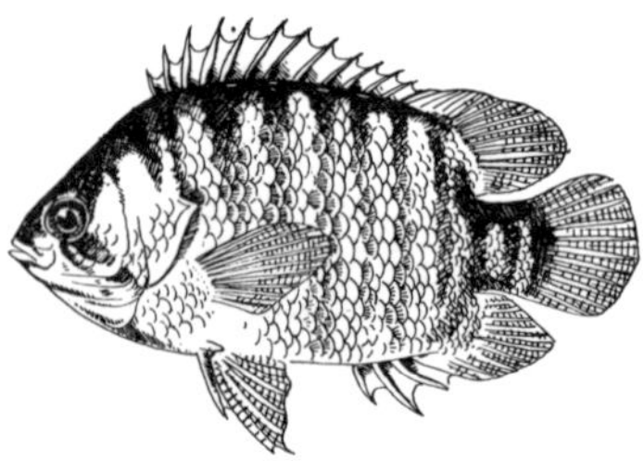

Pristolepis fasciatus

CARE AND BREEDING: A little known species, which is a predator and needs vigorous live foods which correspond to its size. It is especially fit for show aquaria and requires a temperature of 71-75° F.

Prochilodus: South American genus of Characin-like fishes belonging to the family of the Headstanders or *Anostomidae*. Larger fishes with big mouths which may be tilted out as a circular sucking disc. They possess an adipose fin. Fishes which like to jump and root through the bottom with their suckers in search of food. Reproduction is unknown.

— insignis Schomburgk: The Night Tetra.

SHAPE: A large species which reaches lengths of 14″ and comes from the Amazon region and the Guianas.

COLOR: Greenish to reddish shine, with weakly colored longitudinal rows of dots; the tail fin has remarkable stripes.

RANGE: The Amazon region and Guiana.

CARE AND BREEDING: The species loves warmth and a soft bottom in which it can root. It is advisable to put the plants of the aquarium into pots covered with stones. The fish are omnivores which eat all kinds of live and dry foods, as well as algae and other vegetable foods.

— taeniurus Valenciennes: The Striped Night Tetra.

A species from the Amazon similar to the preceding one.

Profundulus: Another *Fundulus*.

Genus of Central American Tooth Carps belonging to the sub-family of the egg laying Tooth Carps or *Cyprinodontinae*. In looks they remind one of the Dog Fishes (*Umbra*).

— punctatus Guenther:

SHAPE: Moderately elongated and of rounded cross section, the head rather broad. D 10-14, A 13-16. Dorsal and anal fin insert far back. Length a little over 4″.

COLOR: Highly variable, according to age, origin, and sex. Greenish body with red spots on the base of each scale, and long cross bands which are very variable. Dorsal and anal fin of the male have a dark edge.

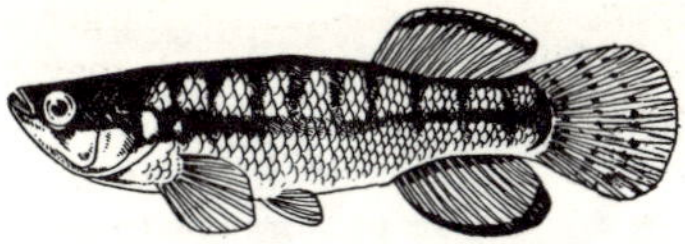

Profundulus punctatus

CARE AND BREEDING: A species that is not difficult to keep and to breed, but which is a little quarrelsome and therefore cannot be kept in company with smaller fishes. The fish needs roomy tanks which are densely planted in spots. They are omnivorous and need very abundant quantities of food. No demands are made as to temperature, 64-72° F being sufficient. The eggs are laid one by one in plant thickets near the surface, after stormy chasing. The alevins, which hatch after 6-10 days, are easy to rear, as they eat powdered dry foods.

Proserpinaca: The one who is creeping forth (from the water).
Genus of swamp plants belonging to the family of the *Halorrhagaceae* related to the genus *Myriophyllum*, and which is cultivated in the same manner.

— **palustris** Linné: American Swamp Water Sprite.
A perennial species provided with creeping root stocks and variably-shaped leaves. The light-green submerged leaves are fine-feathered, the emerged ones, which have saw-toothed edges, are of variable shapes.
RANGE: From Canada to Guatemala and the West Indies.

Prosobranchia: Front Gills.
Sub-class belonging to the class of the Snails or *Gastropoda*. Generally they are sea dwellers, of which only a few families are found in fresh water.

The mouth is snoutlike or provided with a trunk, the foot showing a distinct creeping sole. Many species have a shell lid, and generally one gill consisting of a series of closely-set little leaflets, which is located in front of the heart. The *P.* are heterosexual.

In fresh water we know the family of the Swamp Snails or *Viviparidae*. In tropical waters range the Mystery Snails of the genera *Ampullarius*, and *Marisa*, which occasionally are also kept in the aquarium.

protection of nature: The endeavor to keep up nature in its interrelationship despite human settling, and to protect it against pampering, to protect the extinction of animal and plant species which have become rare, and to maintain the original conditions of whole regions that are remarkable for their beauty and their geological, biological, and cultural features, or to re-create these original conditions and to care for them as a whole. (Protection to natural beauty, protection to natural and cultural monuments, national parks, etc.). The idea of protection to nature can only win through if it finds active co-operation on the part of the population, besides the necessary legislative measures on the part of the government.

The aquarist, as a friend of nature, is especially interested in the maintenance of the aquatic landscape of his native country as well in that of the fauna and flora of its waters. He should consider it his special task to actively oppose all acts that go counter to the idea of protection of nature on the part of individuals or groups (industries, etc.), to advise such people, and to aid the state in its conservation efforts.

proteins: The most important components of protoplasm, and the main vehicles of the vital processes. Live cells are exclusively able to manufacture proteins, these consisting of very complex compounds of oxygen, hydrogen, and carbon, with mixtures of other elements, like sulphur, phosphorus, etc. Compound combinations of the proteins are called *proteids*.

protoplasm: Live cellular matter, carrier of the vital phenomena. A very complex viscous substance, composed of different proteins, fatty substances, salts, and water. Protoplasm maintains life by incorporating different substances from its surroundings into its own body and by eliminating the useless components (metabolism). Lately it has been possible to demonstrate that all phenomena of life are caused by very complex chemical reactions within the protoplasm. Further to metabolism, protoplasm shows a tendency to develop progressively and to multiply and increase its properties.

Protopterus: An indication of the ancient construction of these fishes. Genus belonging to the family of the *Lepidosirenidae*, of slightly compact build, with a low fin edge.

— annectens (Owen):

SHAPE: Of elongated shape and oval cross section. Dorsal, anal, and caudal fin form an uninterrupted seam. The paired limbs are worm-like and have only narrow skin seams. The scales are small and thin. Length up to 26″.

COLOR: Brownish with dark spots.

RANGE: In fresh water swamps of tropical Africa, from Senegal to the Niger, in the region of Lake Chad, also in East Africa to the Zambesi. The waterbeds of the African dry regions carry water only during the rainy season, drying out completely in the interim. After having dug in into the mud with approaching drought, *Protopterus* exudes a mucous substance. This mucus combines with the mud and forms a paper-like but porous cocoon, which prevents the fish from drying out.

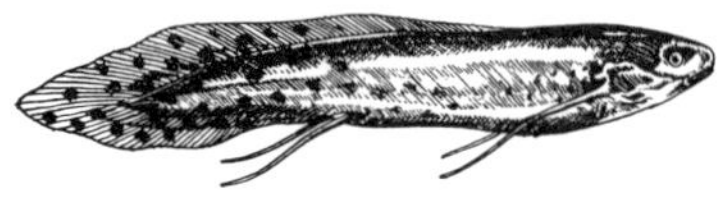

Protopterus annectens

A respiratory connection with the surface is, too, lined with this substance. Through it the fish receives the air necessary for breathing. Naturally during this time metabolism is reduced to the absolute minimum.

CARE AND BREEDING: Proper for show aquaria. Keeping them demands a low water level, soft bottom, and hiding places among plants and roots. *Protopterus* needs much warmth, 77-86° F being advisable. A vicious, quarrelsome predatory fish, it demands vigorous live foods corresponding to its size. The eggs are laid in depressions in the soil and guarded by the male. It has not yet been bred in the aquarium. The larvae have external gills.

Protospondyli: Order belonging to the sub-class of the New Fins or *Neopterygii*. Ancient, mostly extinct fishes, with only one known living family (*Amiidae*), and one species, *Amia calva*. In the middle ages of the earth's history they were a widely distributed group which now permits recognition of a distinct transition from more primiitve forms to the genuine Bony Fishes. The scales and the construction of the tail are very similar to those of the Bony Fishes. The axial skeleton is completely ossified. The swimming bladder is located above the intestine and is connected to the same by a passage. Its walls are of a reticulate structure and are used as an accessory breathing organ.

Protozoa: Sub-division of the fauna which comprises unicellular, seemingly 'primitive' organisms, which partially are border cases between plants and animals. Due to

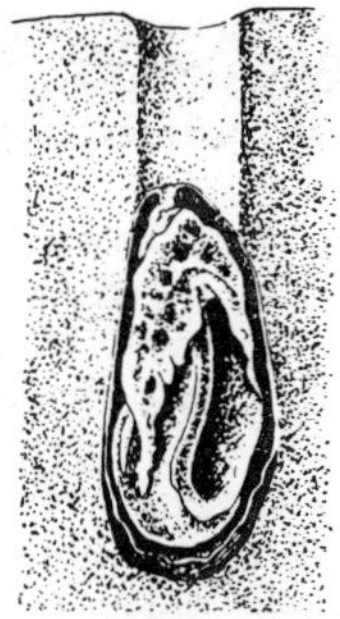

Protopterus in dry season cocoon, after Parker.

their extended period of development, they belong among the oldest forms of life on earth; some of them are highly specialized, and of quite complex construction. The single cell of a protozoan achieves all those things for which the multicellular organism mobilizes a great number of highly specialized cells. Fundamentally the cell of the protozoan differs from the cells of multicellulars in that it is a closed unit which is able to function and to exert all the necessary manifestations of life. Within the cell we recognize one or more nuclei, and many formations called organelles by scientists, which possibly also fulfill sensorial functions. Protozoans are very small, the largest ones being hardly visible to the naked eye. The smallest ones sometimes measure only a few thousandths of a millimeter. As a rule we differentiate a more solid surface layer, the ectoplasm, and the liquid body matter, or endoplasm. Some of the species have solid protective shells, or outer skeletons, made of mineral substances which may be foreign to the body or not. In the endoplasm small bubbles, the vacuoles, effect the metabolism, and are generally developed when they are needed. The carriers of green color, or of other hues, often are unicellular algae which live in symbiosis with the protozoans. Some flagellates show red 'eye' spots, the supposed significance of which are light sensitive organs. For locomotion the protozoans use either mock feet (pseudopodia), which they extend as needed, or rhythmically beating little hairs (cilia, or else walking bristles). In the more highly developed forms the intake of food is effected through a certain spot of the body of the cell, the cellular mouth; less frequently the cells show a cellular anus. Very thin muscle fibres, which are able to contract and to extend, cause the complex movements of the cilia, 'stalks', etc. Certain ciliates eject nettle organelles, the significance of which has not yet been explained, as they could hardly exert a noticeable effect on an attacker.

Reproduction generally takes place through division, after the cell has previously grown to double its size. More rarely there is a multiple division and a development of spores. Sometimes they also produce a 'bud' which is always smaller than its 'mother'. Occasionally processes of fertilization could be supposed to exist, for there are cases either of two individuals fusing together, or else they unite temporarily. The meaning of these processes is not yet totally clear. It is possible that while they take place a new combination of cell parts occurs, which is needed to avoid signs of degeneration. Anyway, these processes serve no immediate function of reproduction as they are never more than the union of two whole individuals.

The number of known species of protozoans is calculated at 10,000-12,000. They are diffused over the whole globe. Generally they are bound to water, or at least to moisture in order to be able to live. Since droughts often are overcome by developing a solid shell (cyst), and the encysted cells in this condition are scattered everywhere by the wind, practically no place on earth is free of them. They are found in waters of all kinds—even in swift-flowing ones—often in such huge quantities that they tinge the water with the color of their bodies.

Experiments with stimuli have shown the presence of a certain 'capacity to learn', which may possibly be caused by simple reflex processes.

In the aquarium one can observe a great number of protozoans, especially if there are algae growths in it and it already has reached a certain age. The presence of a certain number of unicellulars constitutes part of the so-called 'biological balance' in the aquarium, that is, their presence is necessary in order to prevent the proliferation of bacteria, etc. An excessive development of protozoa only takes place if the fancier destroys the state of balance through over-feeding or for other reasons. In such cases a milky clouding appears, which frequently is difficult to eradicate. This condition may be more or less harmless, according to the species of the developing unicellulars. In all cases excessive numbers of them withdraw oxygen from the water. Cloudings caused by excessive protozoans are best fought by putting in *Daphnia* in such quantities that the fishes cannot eat them all. The survivors then make short shrift of the Infusoria. Also a light crimson solution of potassium permanganate may be of help. For information on protozoans in the breeding tank, look up the entries:

PARAMAECIUM.

PHYLA: *Flagellata*, *Rhizopoda*, *Infusoria or Ciliata*, and *Sporozoa*.

protozoan diseases: External and internal diseases of fishes caused by protozoa (flagellates, ciliates, and sporozoa), which are regarded as among the most dangerous maladies. For particulars see the following entries:

COSTIA; OCTOMITUS DISEASE; CHILODONELLA; CYCLOCHAETA; ICHTHYOPHTHIRIUS; NODULE DISEASE; BOILS; PLISTOPHORA; GLUGEA OODINIUM.

providing for the brood: In fishes, a preparatory step with a view to providing for the spawn in a way that the hatching fry may find the most favorable conditions for development that is possible. Providing for the brood varies for the different species and pertains to the hereditary behavior of fishes. Therefore the fish acts unconsciously following an innate compulsion. A simple act of providing for the brood is already recognizable in the migration to certain spawning sites, as happens among Salmonids, Lampreys, some Cyprinids, and some Characins. These migrations may be long or short ones. In the latter case they only lead from one part of the body of water to another one. Quite often the fishes go to shallow inlets, as in them the water may be warmer and simultaneously richer in oxygen. There the hatching fry find abundant edible infusoria, and are protected against many predatory enemies. Of course, this is true in a limited way, only. Instances of providing for the brood are: lodging the eggs in bundles of algae, in the soil, hanging them on plant leaves, roots, and rock, and very especially the placing of the eggs in a clam as done by the Bitterling.

Pseudocorynopoma: False *Corynopoma*.

South American genus of the family of the Characins or *Characi-*

dae, belonging to the sub-family of the *Glandulocaudinae*. Within this it leaves the general scheme in that the species of the genus indulge in internal fertilization. The body is elongated, strongly compressed laterally, with a nearly straight dorsal outline, and a crop-like arched bow. The rather large mouth is supraterminal and well equipped with teeth. The fins are big, and especially those of the male are strongly extended.

— **doriae** Perugia: The Dragon-fin. SHAPE: As per description of genus. D 10-11, A 32-37. Dorsal and anal fins of the male are strongly extended, the tail fin is deeply indented. The pectorals are large. Length up to $3\frac{1}{8}''$, the female remaining a little smaller.

Pseudocorynopoma doriae

COLOR: Shiny silver with gray fins, the male with a black, white, and red dot at the upper and the lower tip of the tail fin. Sex differences are strongly pronounced.

RANGE: Southern Brazil and still farther South to the Plate and Paraguay rivers.

CARE AND BREEDING: A hardy, motile, and peaceful school fish, which is a skilled jumper and an extraordinarily able swimmer. During the spawning period the males are a little quarrelsome. The Dragon-fin may be kept at room temperatures of about 68° F, and up to 77° F under sunlight. Excessive warmth is harmful. It is possible to keep and breed them in open-air pools. Within the house they need spacious, sparsely-planted tanks with space for swimming. *P. doriae* are omnivorous, also eating prepared foods and everything else in huge quantities. Breeding in itself is not difficult, but becomes impossible after some generations. The male chases very peculiarly, with swift movements, quaking and crampedly spreading the fins, often also standing on his head. Setting them up for spawning is done in pairs at 73-77° F. The fish spawn—(this may last for several hours, about 1000 eggs being released)—among fine-feathered plants, in open water. Depending on sunlight and warmth, the fry hatch after 12-24 hours, hanging another three days from firm objects, plants, etc., and needing abundant powdered food immediately thereafter. Rearing them is not difficult. After three months the males can already be identified by the size of their fins.

— **heterandria** Eigenmann: A little-known species from Central Brazil.

Pseudomugil: False *Mugil* (another genus).

Genus belonging to the family of the Ear Fishes or *Atherinidae*. Small fishes of slender shape, with supraterminal mouths, small teeth on upper and lower jaws, large scales, and two separate dorsal fins.

— **signatus** (Guenther): SHAPE: As per description of genus. D_1IV-V, D_2- 7, A I/9-10. The pectorals insert very high, all fins of the males with the first rays strongly extended. Length about $1\frac{3}{4}''$, the female remaining a little smaller.

COLOR: Transparent, silvery to golden, the fins in part a yellowish hue with dark rays.

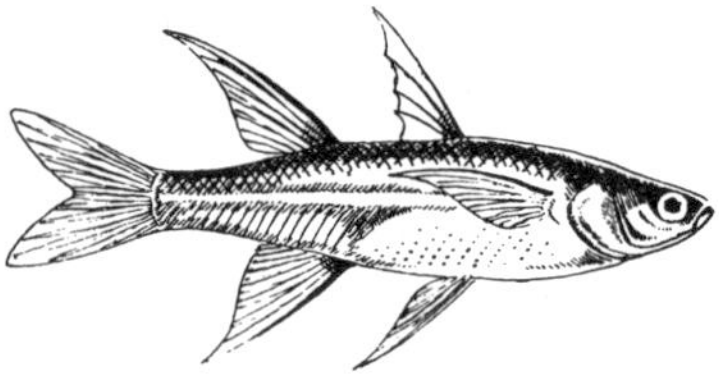

Pseudomugil signifer

RANGE: Northern and eastern Australia.

CARE AND BREEDING: A peaceful school fish, which needs some space for swimming if one wants it to show its most attractive side. It is omnivorous and also eats artificial foods. Slightly sensitive to too low or strongly fluctuating temperatures, 68-77° F being advisable. Breeding has not yet succeeded.

Pseudoxiphophorus: False Sword-tail.

Genus of Tooth Carps of the subfamily of the live bearing Tooth Carps or *Poeciliinae.*

— **bimaculatus** (Heckel): The False Sword-tail.

SHAPE: This variable species has developed a great number of local forms, which differ even in shape and in the number of fin rays. They look quite vigorous and elongated. The caudal peduncle is rather high but the fish is not excessively compressed laterally. The specimens

Pseudoxiphophorus Bimaculatus. Male is lower fish.

from mountainous waters are built higher and broader. The relatively big mouth is equipped with conical, slightly crooked teeth. The simply-built gonopodium is long and pointed, and inserts far to the front. D 11-12, A 12-14. Length: males 1¾″, females up to 3¾″.

COLOR: Shiny gray-green with reticulate design and a spot on the caudal base, the fins partially beautifully colored.

RANGE: Southern Mexico and Central America, in waters of all kinds, both in the coastal plains and in the mountains up to a height of 7500 feet.

CARE AND BREEDING: A rugged and robust carnivorous species which requires especially live foods. The big females are pronouncedly vicious, and fight the males with savage bites. Unfit for community tanks. The species, which needs some warmth, is very productive. Up to 150 fry, which are ⅝″ long, are born, and grow very quickly due to their voraciousness.

Pteridophyta: Ferns.

Sub-division of the phylum of the *Archegoniatae,* among the many families of which only a few are adequate for keeping in the aquarium. In ferns there is an alternation of generations. Plants stemming from sexual reproduction always remain small, and in part they resemble a Fountain Liver Wort or show otherwise divergent shapes. The fertilized egg cells of these plants give origin to an unsexed generation which shows the generally known shapes and has real roots, stems, and leaves. These plants produce spores in an unsexed way from which in turn sexual ferns result.

Families, among others: Quilt Worts or *Isoetaceae*; Horn Worts or *Parkeriaceae*; Pill Worts or *Marsileaceae*; and Floating Ferns or *Salviniaceae.*

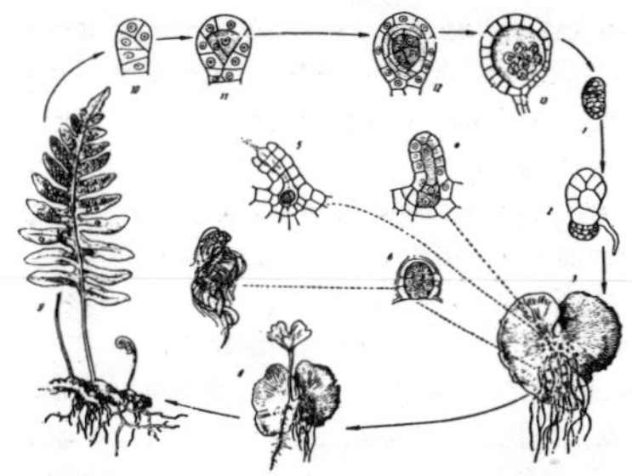

Development of a fern, after Weymar - 1. spore - 2. germinating spore - 3. gamenophyte - 4. closed archegonium - 5. open archegonium - 6. antheridium - 7. spermatozoid - 8. gamenophyte after fertilization with young sporophyte - 9. sporophyte - 10 through 13. development of a sporangium.

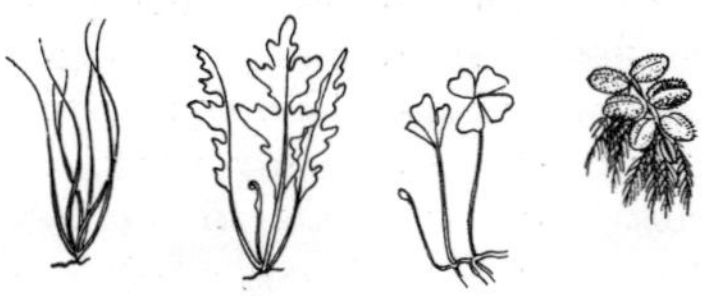

Pteridophyta, left to right - Isoetaceae - Parkeraceae - Marsileaceae - Salviniaceae.

Pterodiscus: Winged Disc.

South American genus of Characin-like fishes belonging to the family of the Hatchet Fishes or *Gasteropelecidae*. A somewhat uncertain genus which perhaps represents no more than a sub-genus of *Gasteropelecus*. It differs from the other genera by lacking teeth of the upper jaw.

— levis Eigenmann:

SHAPE: As per description of family. D 10-11, A 31-35. Length up to $2\frac{3}{8}''$.

COLOR: Shiny silver with a dark longitudinal band and belly edge. The female is broader when seen from above.

RANGE: The region of the lower Amazon.

CARE AND BREEDING: As described for *Gasteropelecus*, but needing still more warmth. The fish likes clear water at 77-80° F. Breeding has not yet succeeded.

Pterolebias: Winged Lebias.

Genus of South American Tooth Carps belonging to the sub-family of the egg laying Tooth Carps or *Cyprinodontidae*. It differs from the closely related genus *Rachovia* by the longer anal fin, and by being more compressed laterally.

— elegans Ladiges:

SHAPE: The body is compressed laterally, especially at the caudal peduncle, the front part of the back being flattened down. D 15, A 22, both ending in points on the males. Length $2\frac{3}{8}''$ to $2\frac{3}{4}''$.

COLOR: Reddish-olive base, on the flanks several cross rows of emerald green dots; a strong emerald green gloss on the gill covers. The fins are mottled emerald green with wine-red designs. The females are considerably simpler in color.

RANGE: The country around Rio de Janeiro, Brazil.

CARE AND BREEDING: No particulars are known so far.

— longipinnis Garman: The Veil Carp.

SHAPE: The body is elongated, less compressed laterally in front, more so towards the rear part, the head flattened from above. D 9-10, A 19-20. All fins are highly developed, especially those of the males. Length, probably 4-5″, the females remaining a little smaller.

COLOR: Greenish-brown to brown-red, with indistinct cross bands and many metallic shiny dots, which also cover the wine-red mottled fins. Home-bred specimens are said to show considerable variations in color as compared to imports. The female is simpler in color. The male has a very big tail fin and its dorsal, anal and ventrals are extended into points.

RANGE: Imported from the surroundings of Santarem, Brazil, probably from periodically flooded regions.

Pterolebias longipinnis

CARE AND BREEDING: In its manner of living the species strongly resembles its closely related genera *Cynolebias* and *Rachovia*. Similar to these it grows quickly, matures rapidly sexually, and has a short span of life. Consequently the fish need abundant and sufficient food, such as mosquito larvae, larvae of other aquatic insects, small earthworms, meal grubs, etc. The opinions on need of warmth still diverge, but possibly the degrees are not as high as is generally presumed. According to KOCH soft, slightly acid water furthers breeding. FOERSCH states that 70-73° F are sufficient. Also temperatures below this are withstood easily. Too high degrees of warmth probably shorten the span of life still more. The fish are rather lively, but are said to be quarrelsome. According to FOERSCH breeding takes place in a manner similar to that of other bottom-spawning Tooth Carps. The bottom of the breeding tank is covered with an about 2″-thick layer of boiled, and squeezed-out peat moss, into which the fish dig for spawning. During this the spawn-ripe female swims in front of the male. The peat moss, with the eggs, is put into jars or dishes and dried slightly but not completely. It seems that the adaptation to waters that are drying up is not as strong as it is the case with *Cynolebias*. After about six weeks the moist peat moss is sprinkled with soft water, and the level is raised slowly over a 3 day period. It is advisable not to shorten the period of development. The fry grow very quickly.

Pterophyllum: Fin-Leaf (Angelfishes).

South American genus of the family of the Cichlids or *Cichlidae*. Laterally strongly compressed fishes of nearly circular construction of the body which looks higher than long due to the extended dorsal and anal fins. The rays of the ventrals are strongly extended and form thread-like, often split, appendages. Very striking, ornamental, and therefore well-liked fishes, which are resistant and relatively hardy. Only a few species are known, of which only the species *P. scalare* has been able to find a place in our aquaria. According to LADIGES the 'species' *P. eimekei* is absolutely uncertain, and probably only a local form, if not a domesticated form of *P. scalare*. The *P.* dwell in standing or slowly-flowing waters with standing or flooded reed-beds, and rock clefts among which they hide. Reproduction occurs after the manner of the other non-mouth-breeding Cichlids. Both parents care for the spawn. The eggs are laid on plant stems, etc.

In conformity with their size they need big and high tanks, with not too low temperatures, not much below 75° F, but preferably quite higher. They eat all kinds of live foods, occasionally also artificial ones. Typical large specimens of the species *P. scalare* at present are kept only occasionally. Generally the aquarium-bred *Pterophyllum* show the characteristics of the '*eimekei*' form or intermediate stages between both.

— **scalare** (Cuvier and Valenciennes): The Angel Fish.

SHAPE: As per description of genus.

Pterophyllum scalare

The forehead contour is more or less strongly indented above the eyes. The form *P. scalare* (*eimekei*) is said to lack this characteristic, and due to its lesser development of dorsal and anal fins it is not as high. D XI-XIII/23-27, A V-VII/24-29, the formula of *P. scalare* (*eimekei*) being D XIII/22-27, A VI/24-25. The upper and lower rays of the tail fin often are extended threadlike, and the longest rays of the dorsal and anal fins often protrude beyond the fin edge. *Scalare:* length up to 6″, height up to 10″. *Eimekei*: length up to 5″, height up to 8″.

COLOR: Shiny silver with more or less distinctly set-off cross bands, which in part continue to the tips of the fins. Lately black, blackish, and other bred forms are being offered commercially, as well as ones showing somewhat extended fins (Black Angels, Lace Angels, Veil-Tail Angels).

RANGE: The region of the central Amazon, especially in the secondary waters, bays, etc. There they generally appear in schools of 10-15 specimens, also in communities with other Cichlids, quite frequent everywhere.

CARE AND BREEDING: A very fetching species which needs sufficiently high tanks. Aquaria that are not too brightly lit and offer hiding places permit the fish to show to their best advantage. Too low degrees of warmth make them prone to diseases, 75-82° F being advisable. They are sensitive to over-aged water and to chemicals.

Breeding depends on mated pairs, which are best found among young fish. Once such pairs have met, spawning them is easy and very productive. The sexes can only be differentiated by the differently-shaped genital papillae, that of the female being blunter, and that of the male more pointed. They spawn on broad plant leaves, plant stems, or on such things as glass panes and tubes, sometimes even on rocks. The fry hatch after about 48 hours and are hung in leaf insertions or from the leaves themselves by the parents. Care and rearing as described for *Cichlidae*.

Puffers, the: see TETRAODONTIDAE.

pulcher: Pretty, beautiful.

— *Hemigrammus*.

— *Luciocephalus*.

— *Pelmatochromis*.

pulchripinnis: Beautiful-finned.

— *Hyphessobrycon*.

Pulmonata: Lung Snails.

Sub-class belonging to the class of the Snails or *Gastropoda*. Generally land snails, represented in the water only by a few groups. Instead of gills they have a texture of venous blood vessels and a respiratory cavity. In youth the organ still works as a gill, developing later into a lung, despite the fact that some species take in water from breathing even then.

With the two orders, *Basommatophora* and *Stylommatophora*, the following families are of interest for aquaristics: Helicoidal Snails or *Helicidae*; Mud Snails or *Limnaeidae*; Bladder Snails or *Physidae*; Saucer Snails or *Planorbidae*; and Coin Snails or *Acylidae* with the genus *Ancylus*.

pumilus: Dwarf-like small.

— *Trichopsis*.

punctata: Spotted, dotted.

— *Gambusia*.

punctatus: Spotted, dotted.

— *Chilodus*.

— *Corydoras*.

— *Plecostomus*.

— *Profundulus*.

Puntius: see BARBUS.

Purple-Striped Gudgeon, the: see MOGURNDA MORGUNDA.

pusillus: Minute, small.

— *Dermogenys*.

putty: see GLAZING.

pygmaea: Pigmy.

— *Umbra*.

Pygmy Catfish, the: see CORYDORAS HASTATUS HASTATUS.

Pygmy Sunfish, the: see ELASSOMA EVERGLADEI.

Pygocentrus: With spine on the rump.

South American genus of meat-eating Disc Characins belonging to the family of Characins or *Characidae*, sub-family of the *Serrasalminae*, with only one species. Closely related to the genus *Rooseveltiella*, from which it differs only by the fact that the adipose fin of older specimens has rays.

— **piraya** (Cuvier): The Piranha.

The Piranha is an awkward-looking fish which shows its predatory nature even externally by its short skull and overdeveloped jaws. The forehead line is steeply arched, the body is strongly compressed laterally. D 17-18, A 31-32. The scales are very small. Length up to above 12″. The color is blue-green with light and dark small dots.

Pygosteus pungitius: see GASTEROSTEUS PUNGITIUS.

Pyrrhulina: The fire-colored one.

South American genus of the family of the Characins or *Characidae*, sub-family of the *Pyrrhulininae*, with about 27 known species. All of them are small, very lively fishes, which are rarely kept in aquaria, despite their beauty and hardiness. All species eat commercial foods besides live ones. To keep them medium-sized tanks with a length of about 20″ will suffice, but they have to be well-stocked with plants so that the female may temporarily withdraw from the violent chasing of the male. Despite the fact that the fishes are considered peaceful, during the spawning period they may become quite nasty and then sometimes a little quarrelsome. In the cases that have become known up to date, spawning took place on broad leaved plants. The male fans the eggs up to the moment of hatching, which causes many of the eggs to come off and fall to the bottom. Therefore it is advisable to remove the male. The fry seem to be of rather slow growth, but rearing them is not exceedingly difficult.

— **brevis** Steindachner: The Dotted-Scale Pyrrhulina.

SHAPE: As per description of sub-family. D 9-10, A 11-12. Length up to $3\frac{3}{8}$″.

COLOR: Bluish to reddish glossy with some rows of red dots along the flanks. The fins are vivid red with black edges, especially those of the males. The female is simpler in color.

RANGE: The regions of the Amazon and the Rio Negro.

CARE AND BREEDING: As per description of genus. The species is not very limber, its manner of swimming being similar to that of the species of *Nannostomus*, which swim in short spurts. They very definitely prefer live foods. The fish like to eat flying food from the surface, which they may even catch by jumping after it. Prepared foods are taken unwillingly only. The species needs some warmth, temperatures between 73 and 86° F. So far no success worthy of mentioning has been achieved in breeding them.

— **nigrofasciata** Meinken: The Red-Dotted Pyrrhulina.

SHAPE: As per description of the sub-family. D 9-10, A 11. Length probably up to 2″.

COLOR: Ochre body color with a dark band and quite beautifully colored fins. The red of the dorsal fin of the male is more vivid, the female being a little smaller and plumper.

RANGE: The origin is not exactly known. The imported specimens come from an unknown location in the Peruvian region of the upper Amazon.

CARE AND BREEDING: As per description of genus. The species is peaceful, gregarious, and not shy. It prefers to stay in the upper levels, in open water. Water warmth between 68 and 77° F. Below 68° F they become a little prone to diseases. The fry, too, stay near the surface. They grow slowly, but recover lost time quickly as soon as they are able to eat coarser foods. After 4 months they have reached a length of about 1¾″.

— **rachoviana** Myers: Rachow's Pyrrhulina.

SHAPE: As per description of genus, relatively compact. D 10, A 11. Length up to 2″, the female remaining a little smaller.

COLOR: Brownish to greenish blue with dark longitudinal band along the upper side of which runs a golden zone. On the sides one sees some rows of small red dots. The female is simpler in color, the fins of the male are bigger and more colored.

RANGE: The lower Parana and the La Plata rivers.

CARE AND BREEDING: As per description of genus. A very vivacious and generally gregarious species, which may become a bit quarrelsome during the spawning period. Temperature 68-73° F, for breeding up to 79° F. During the act of spawning, which lasts about 30 minutes, 50-200 eggs are hung on a leaf of an aquatic plant or something similar, and it is advisable to remove them to a nursery tank.

Pyrrhulina rachoviana

— **vittata** Regan: The Head-Band Pyrrhulina.

SHAPE: As per description of subfamily; rather compact. The fins are well developed, but the upper lobe of the tail fin is not always strongly developed on the males. D 7-8, A 8. Length around 2″.

COLOR: Yellowish-gray, showing a greenish gloss on the sides, with a striking band which begins as a bridle around the lower jaw, continues through the eyes over the gill cover, and ends above the base of the pectoral fins. Another three black spots are found on the caudal peduncle above the insertion of the anal and shortly behind the pectorals. They may turn into bands temporarily. The male shows more intense colors and his fins are more strongly developed.

RANGE: The Amazon region. There is no exact information available, but one may suppose that the fish are found especially in the savannah creeks, that is, in small, flowing waters which are subject to strong sunlight and warmth.

CARE AND BREEDING: As per description of genus. NIEUWENHUIZEN has rendered an exact description of the act of spawning. According

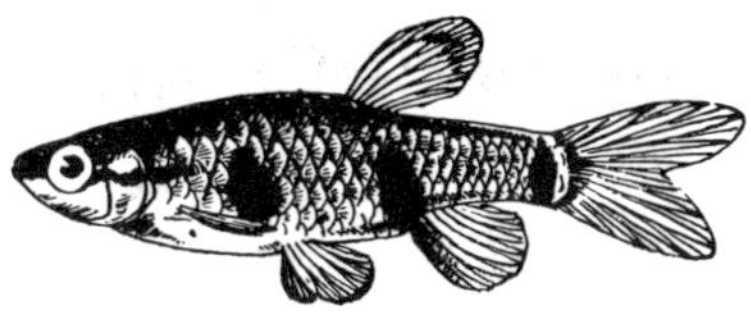

Pyrrhulina vittata

to his report, the male cleaned a spot of about 1¼″ in diameter on the leaf of an aquatic plant, while he did not allow the female near it. Thereafter he looked for her, circled her, and swam back to the cleaned spot while fanning his fins and trembling violently. During this, and also during the act of spawning, the black dot behind the gill cover of the male disappeared completely. After some unsuccessful wooings, the female followed the male and the pair executed a narrow, circular movement on the leaf, while touching each other closely with the rear of the body and while the anal fin of the male rested beneath the sexual aperture of the female. What role was played by this fin was something he could not ascertain.

The eggs may number 200 to 350. They are glassy clear and extraordinarily transparent. The embryos hatch after 24 hours at a temperature of 79° F. Rearing them is relatively easy.

Pyrrhulina filamentosa: see COPEINA ARNOLDI.

Pyrrhulininae: South American sub-family belonging to the family of the Characins or *Characidae*. In part, slightly compact with a robust-looking construction, which is moderately compressed laterally. An adipose fin is either lacking or else it is present during the first stages of youth only to involute later on to fuse with the tail fin. The upper lobe of the widely-indented tail fin generally is bigger than the lower one on full-grown male specimens. Two genera: *Pyrrhulina*, and *Copeina*.

quadrifolia: Four-leaved.
— *Marsilea*.

Quilt Wort: see ISOETES, ISOETACEAE.

quinine: An alkaloid from the bark of the tropical Quina tree. A colorless, bitter-tasting powder, used as a preventive and cure for fever diseases, especially malaria. Used in aquaristics in certain chemical compounds (quinine salts) to fight *Ichthyophthirius* with success.

Quintana: Refers to a peculiarity in the construction of the gonopodium.

— atrizona Hubbs: The Black-Barred Live Bearer.

SHAPE: The species is of relatively high build, rhombic elongated, especially so in the female, and strongly compressed laterally. The frail body is translucent. D 8-9, A 10. Length: males a little above ¾″, females 1⅝″.

Quintana atrizona

COLOR: Translucent yellowish-olive, with a reticulate design and some dark cross bands.

RANGE: Cuba.

CARE AND BREEDING: A hardy species which will content itself with the smallest containers. Desirable, though, is a sunny location and warmth, the best being around 78° F. The fish eat all kinds of live and prepared foods, very preferably also soft algae. They are not especially productive, giving birth to a maximum of 35 young, which may grow very quickly. If well cared for they may be able to reproduce after 3-4 months.

Quiver Flies: see TRICHOPTERA.

Race: Group of members of a species which differ from their fellow members by some characteristic, but are able to interbreed and produce fertile offspring.

rachovi, rachowi: Rachow's.
— *Characidium.*
— *Heterophallus.*
— *Nothobranchius.*
— *Plecostomus.*

Rachovia: After the German ichthyologist Arthur Rachow.
Genus of South American Tooth Carps belonging to the sub-family of the egg-laying Tooth Carps or *Cyprinodontinae*. Fishes of *Rivulus*-like build, but slightly higher in shape and strongly compressed laterally. The genus is related to the genus *Cynolebias*.

— brevis (Regan):
SHAPE: As per description of genus. D 8-9, A 12-14. Length up to 2½″, the female remaining slightly smaller.
COLOR: Greenish-blue with bluish scale edges. The fins blue-green to violet with darker spots and edges, the females simpler in color.
RANGE: The region of the Magdalena River.
CARE AND BREEDING: This so-far rarely imported species is considered a little quarrelsome. It is very lively, but resembles the species in the genus *Rivulus* in its demands on life. The fish are not sensitive to fluctuations in temperature and withstand any degree between 64 and 82° F. Reproduction resembles that of *Cynolebias*. After violent chasing the fish spawn on the bottom where the eggs sink down into the mud, needing 60 days to develop. The fry grow very quickly and are already able to reproduce when 8 weeks old, despite the fact that

Rachovia brevis

they are not yet full-grown.

rachoviana: After Arthur Rachow.
— *Pyrrhulina.*

Rachoviscus: South American genus belonging to the family of the Characins or *Characidae*.

— crassiceps: The Big-Headed *Rachoviscus.*
SHAPE: This a little awkward-looking, relatively high-backed species, diverges strongly from the usual type of Characin. The head is big. There is an adipose fin. The front rays of the anal fin of the male are set with thin hooklets. D 11, A 29. Length up to 2″.
COLOR: Blue-greenish with a long reddish band, which broadens out towards the rear, and with bluish silvery dots scattered over this. The male has bigger fins and is more highly colored.
RANGE: The surroundings of Rio de Janeiro.
CARE AND BREEDING: The species is quite hardy and does well within the aquarium. Furthermore, they do not need much warmth. Breeding is done at a little above 68° F. Live foods are preferred and prepared ones eaten only unwillingly and in case of need. The species is a little vicious. The act of spawning takes place after violent wooing and peculiar quaking movements side by side near the bottom, either in open water or among plants. All attempts at breeding and rearing the young seem not to have succeeded up to now.

Rachow's Darter Characin: see CHARACIDIUM RACHOVII.

Rachow's Pyrrhulina: see PYRRHULINA RACHOVIANA.

radicans: Rooted.

Echinodorus.

rain water: Natural water, especially fit for keeping and breeding aquarium animals and plants, due to relatively small percentages of dissolved mixtures. However rain water is very variable in its composition, depending on the regions through which the clouds have passed before releasing the water, and according to where it precipitates. In this there may occur considerable mixtures of industrial waste gases, which may ruin the value of the water. In general one may say that rain water in densely settled and in industrialized regions is usable only after precipitations which last for several hours. Furthermore one should pay attention to the fact that it should not pick up foreign substances on the way to the collecting containers. For this reason it should, whenever possible, be caught directly, or else channeled over canvas, wood, or similar substances that are safe.

After catching it, rain water should rest for several hours, and it is advisable to filter it through coal or through filter paper before using it, to remove all microscopic organisms.

Rainbow Fishes: see MELANOTAENIA.

Ramirez' Dwarf Cichlid: see APISTOGRAMMA RAMIREZI.

ramirezi: After the Venezuelan collector M. V. Ramirez.
— *Apistogramma.*

Ramshorn Snails: see PLANORBIDAE.

Ranunculaceae: Crow's Foot Plants.

The swamp and aquatic plants of this family generally are unfit for the home aquarium, since they do not last long. In the open air installation, though, they are very beautiful plants. The submerged leaves are finely divided and resemble those of *Cabomba.* The pretty white flowers are hermaphroditic and are held up on the surface by small, rounded floating leaves, arched outward on the edge.

ranunculoides: Crow's-Foot-like.
— *Echinodorus.*

Ranunculus: Crow's Foot.

Genus of the Crow's Foot Plants or *Ranunculaceae.* The species which live in water, of which we shall mention Water Crow's Foot, *Ranunculus aquaticus* Linné; Squarrous Crow's Foot, *R. circinatus* Sibthorp, and the Fan-Like Crow's Foot, *R. flabellaris* Rafinesque, unfortunately are of little use for the home aquarium as they either decay completely within a short time, or else they become very stringy. For cultivation in the open air pond, choose specimens coming from standing waters.

Ranunculus aquaticus

Rasbora: After the native name.

Genus of tropical school fishes belonging to the family of the *Cyprinidae.* They are small to very small fishes, of slender, generally elongated body, more or less compressed laterally. The mouth is terminal to supraterminal, and small. There are no barbels. The lateral line is either short, or else, if it is complete, it runs in an arc along the lower half of the body. The scales are quite large.

About 40 species are known. They resemble the other Cyprinids in care and generally do not present difficulties in breeding. The general rules for care and breeding are repeated here once more: Since nearly all *Rasboras* are very nimble fishes, one should offer them sufficiently big tanks with space for swimming. They always look best in schools of their own species. Feeding them presents no difficulties as they eat live and prepared foods of all kinds.

Many species like to keep near the surface, feeding only on flying foods, which they catch by jumping. Quite a number of species are delicate and transparent and do not cause a striking impression when seen under back lighting that shines through them. For this reason it is advisable to locate the aquaria in a manner that the light reflects on them from the front, as the fishes show their colors only that way. A dark bottom enhances the coloring of some of the species, but many *Rasboras* are brook dwellers and prefer a gravel bottom. A little sunlight is agreeable to nearly all species, and so is not-too-old water that is rich in oxygen.

For breeding use long tanks with a low water level. The bottom should be densely covered with gravel and fine-feathered plants, for which *Nitella*, Water Moss, or green Nylon yarn mops are useful. The falling eggs find protection in this bottom cover against the preying of the parents. Some of the species demand a difficult set-up for spawning. This is pointed out in the following descriptions.

Generally, however, the act of spawning takes place in the manner of that of the *Danios*. Set up several males with one female. Often spawning is done under the morning sun. As a rule rearing the young is not difficult and takes place as described for *Cyprinidae*.

The genus is distributed over the whole of South East Asia, as well as Indonesia and the Philippines. There the *Rasbora* are generally found in flowing or standing, clear waters.

— agilis Ahl:

SHAPE: As per description of genus. The body is elongated and very slim. D 9, A 8. Length around 1¾″.

COLOR: Shiny silvery with yellowish sheen and a dark longitudinal band, bordered by golden yellow on both sides.

The male is slender and more intensely colored.

RANGE: Sumatra.

CARE AND BREEDING: As per description of genus. 72-77° F, for breeding around 79° F. Not yet bred.

— argyrotaenia (Bleeker): The Silver Rasbora.

SHAPE: As per description of genus. D 9, A 8. Length up to 6″.

COLOR: Shiny silvery with yellow bands. The male is slimmer than the female.

RANGE: All over Southeast Asia, in clear, standing or flowing waters, also in brackish water.

CARE AND BREEDING: As per description of genus. The species needs no warmth, 64-71° F being sufficient. Breeding has not yet succeeded.

Rasbora argyrotaenia

— **chrysotaenia** Ahl: The Gold-Striped Rasbora.
SHAPE: As per description of genus, very similar to the species *R. agilis*. D 9, A 8. Length about 1¾″.
COLOR: Shiny greenish with a long golden stripe, bordered by a bluish lower edge. The male is slimmer.
RANGE: Sumatra.
CARE AND BREEDING: As per description of genus. The species is not considered very productive in breeding. The young hatch within 36 hours at 77° F, lie still on the bottom for some days or hang from plants, etc., and swim freely only on the fifth day. The species needs some warmth.

— **daniconius** (Hamilton-Buchanan): The Slender Rasbora.
SHAPE: As per description of genus, especially slender and elongated. The belly edge is rounded, the lateral line is complete. D 9, A 7. Length, in nature 8″, in the aquarium only around 4″.
COLOR: Mother-of-pearl to glossy blue with a blue-black long stripe bordered above and below with gold. The male is slimmer than the female.
RANGE: India and Indo-China, Ceylon, and parts of Indonesia, in flowing and standing waters. Very common everywhere.
CARE AND BREEDING: As per description of genus. Temperature 72-75° F, for breeding 75-79° F.

Rasbora daniconius

Rasbora dorsiocellata

— **dorsiocellata** (Duncker): The Eye-Spot Rasbora.
SHAPE: As per description of genus, slender, the belly edge rounded, D 9, A 8. Length 1½″ to 2″.
COLOR: Silvery with yellowish to bluish sheen and two more or less strongly appearing black longitudinal bands, a deep-black, light-edged spot on the dorsal fin.
RANGE: In flowing and standing waters of all kinds in Malaya and on Sumatra. Not rare anywhere.
CARE AND BREEDING: As per description of genus. Breeding not yet achieved.

Rasbora einthoveni

— **einthoveni** (Bleeker): The Brilliant Rasbora.
SHAPE: The elongated and laterally compressed body may reach lengths up to 3½″. The male is slimmer than the female. D 9, A 8.
COLOR: The back is fawn brown, the belly lighter. In its colors the fish is very similar to *R. daniconius*.
RANGE: Indo-China, and parts of Indonesia, in swarms in waters of

all kinds.

CARE AND BREEDING: As per description of genus. Temperatures 72-75° F, for breeding 77-82° F. It is advisable to grade and separate the young continuously, as the bigger ones prey on their smaller brothers.

— **elegans** Volz: The Yellow Rasbora.

Rasbora elegans

SHAPE: As per description of genus, but looking a little more vigorous than the other species. The belly contour is more strongly arched than the dorsal outline. D 9, A 7. Length, females up to $5\frac{1}{8}''$, the male remaining a little smaller.

COLOR: Silvery with reddish-brown or greenish hues, the scales dark edged, a blue-black spot both on the middle of the body and on the caudal peduncle. The slimmer male shows a yellow anal fin.

RANGE: In flowing and standing waters of Malaya and Indonesia, everywhere in swarms.

CARE AND BREEDING: As per description of genus. Temperature 73-77° F. Not sensitive to great fluctuations.

— **heteromorpha** (Duncker): The Harlequin Rasbora.

SHAPE: As per description of genus, but of relatively high build as compared to the other species, the dorsal contour is more strongly

Rasbora heteromorpha

arched than the belly outline. The belly edge is rounded. The mouth opening is small and tilted obliquely upwards. The lateral line is quite short. D 9, A 8. Length up to around $1\frac{3}{4}''$, the male remaining a little smaller and slimmer.

COLOR: Silvery, often with a vigorous strong purple hue, and a strong blue-black wedge from the middle of the body to the root of the tail. One of the most beautiful tropicals. The male is more vividly colored, shows a red eye, and has the lower tip of the wedge a little extended downward and to the front. The female is plumper, especially if viewed from above, the male being slimmer.

RANGE: Malaya, Southern Thailand, parts of Sumatra, Borneo, and Java. There the Harlequin is found in ditches, ponds, and swamps with moory bottom, which may in part be shaded by marginal plants and overgrown with *Cryptocoryne* and Water Ferns, but which in part also show shorter or longer open stretches. The waters are very soft, some even abnormally so, approaching distilled water. Temperatures generally are very high.

CARE AND BREEDING: Medium-sized tanks with a dark bottom and background, and dense growths of plants on the sides are sufficient to keep this species. The fish look best if they live in swarms in the open water among plants, or else together with *R. maculata*. Generally they do not like the company of other fishes, from which they hold back. Cover the bottom with a layer of boiled and squeezed-out peat moss above the sand.

This fish is very undemanding regarding food, eating all kinds of small live and prepared foods. It needs some warmth, though, even if not as much as is generally presumed by fanciers. Anyway, 71-75° F are adequate for keeping them, 79° F for breeding.

Breeding them is very difficult. For 20 years no one succeeded in achieving it, so that the most diverse suppositions about their reproduction were making the rounds. Probably, however, these difficulties stemmed from inexpert handling on the part of the domestic dealers, as well as from the long route of transportation. Only lately has it been possible to avoid harm to the fish by bringing them in on a short air hop and in greater quantities. Furthermore breeding is a question of the right water, and also of mated pairs. Not all pairs will spawn with each other. For breeding, the fish, which were observed to be mutually attracted to each other while still in the swarm, are put in pairs into a glass tank 10″ long, the bottom of which is covered with a layer of boiled and squeezed-out peat mulm. A bunch of broad-leaved *Cryptocoryne*, planted in a pot filled with peat moss, is set in the middle of the tank. Everything must be meticulously clean. The water must not measure above 2° DH. The pH has to be lowered to 5.5-6.5 by filtering through peat moss or by adding phosphoric acid. It is advantageous to employ very young females, which have just matured sexually, while the males may be older without any harm. The act of spawning takes place under the morning sun, at 79° F or more. The eggs are stuck to the underside of plant leaves, while the male embraces the female with the caudal peduncle. For this the fish lie on their backs. After spawning one should remove the parents. The tank is darkened and remains so for about 6 days. The fry hatch after about 24 hours. After another 5 days, they are already free swimming. Rearing them is done in a manner similar to that used for all other Cyprinids.

— **jacobsoni** Weber and De Beaufort:

SHAPE: As per description of genus. The body is moderately elongated, and a little compressed laterally. D 9, A 8. Length around 2¾″.

COLOR: Brownish with dark-edged scales, and a broad, blue-black long stripe along which runs a strong gold-colored stripe. The male is slimmer.

Rasbora jacobsoni

RANGE: In brooks and standing waters of West Sumatra. The species also rises up to heights of 3000 feet in the mountains.

CARE AND BREEDING: As per description of genus.

— **lateristriata** Bleeker: The Side-Striped Rasbora.

SHAPE: As per description of genus, slender and with rounded belly edge. D 9, A 8. Length up to 4¾″.

COLOR: Brownish to greenish silvery, with dark-edged scales, and a golden to coppery-red longitudinal stripe, which is closed off below by a darker band. The male is slimmer than the female.

RANGE: In standing and flowing waters of Malaya and the Greater Sunda Isles, also in the heights in the mountains.

CARE AND BREEDING: As per description of genus. The species does not need much warmth, 68-72° F being absolutely sufficient.

— **leptosoma** (Bleeker): The Gold-Striped Rasbora.

SHAPE: As per description of genus; very slender. D 9, A 8. Length up to 4″, in the aquarium around 2¾″.

COLOR: Shiny silvery-brownish to silvery-greenish, and with a salmon-colored gold red band, bordered with black on the lower part. The male is slimmer.

RANGE: In brooks and rivers of Indonesia and Sumatra.

CARE AND BREEDING: As per description of genus. Breeding has not yet been achieved.

Rasbora leptosoma

— **maculata** Duncker: The Spotted, or Dwarf, Rasbora.

SHAPE: As per description of genus, but very small and graceful. D 8, A 7, the vertical fins relatively well-developed. Length up to 1″, the female a little bigger.

COLOR: Yellowish base with purple red sheen and black, gold-edged spots, the fins reddish with dots and black spots. The male is slimmer and more vividly colored.

RANGE: Indo-China, Malaya, and Sumatra, instanding and slowly-flowing waters which in part are strongly grown through with plants and have a dark, muddy bottom.

Rasbora maculata

CARE AND BREEDING: Similar to *R. heteromorpha*, with which the species may be put together in communities. Similar to that species they like sunlight and a dark bottom, dense plantings in spots, warmth, and soft water. Temperatures around 73-77° F are sufficient, for breeding 79-82° F. Breeding is similar to *R. heteromorpha*, but demands a still lower water level. The tank may be smaller, and planted with fine-feathered plants in tufts. It is advisable to darken the lower half of the aquarium. The act of spawning takes place under the morning sun. The species is not very productive, and besides this breeding depends strongly on mated pairs. Also in this species mating is done while the male lightly embraces the female.

— **meinkeni** De Beaufort: Meinken's Rasbora.

SHAPE: Of elongated build, lightly compressed laterally. D 9, A 8. Length: males up to 2⅛″, females 2½″.

Rasbora meinkeni

COLOR: Shiny brass with a deep black longitudinal stripe, gold-edged on the upper side. The male is a little more intensely colored.
RANGE: Sumatra.
CARE AND BREEDING: As per description of genus.

— **pauciperforata** Weber and De Beaufort: The Red-Striped Rasbora.
SHAPE: As per description of genus, elongated with very short lateral line. D 9, A 8. Length up to 1¾″.
COLOR: Shiny silver with green sheen and a vigorous red longitudinal stripe, which has a narrow black edge on the lower border. The male is considerably slimmer.
RANGE: In brooks on the Eastern half of Sumatra.
CARE AND BREEDING: As per description of genus. Temperature 70-75° F. Breeding seems not to have succeeded so far.

Rasbora pauciperforata

— **paucisquamis** Ahl: The Big-Scaled Rasbora.
SHAPE: As per description of genus, elongated, with complete lateral line, and compressed laterally. D 9, A 8. Length: females up to 2⅛″, the males remaining a little smaller and slimmer.
COLOR: Shiny brownish to bluish silver. On the rear half of the body the fish carries a dark stripe.
RANGE: Indochina.
CARE AND BREEDING: As per description of genus. Breeding has not yet been achieved so far.

— **philippinica** Guenther: The Philippine *Rasbora*.
SHAPE: As per description of genus; elongated, the ventral contour a little more arched than the dorsal one, the belly edge rounded. The lateral line is complete. D 9, A 8. Length up to 2¾″, the female growing a little larger.
COLOR: Shiny gray-green silver with a darker longitudinal stripe and dark-edged scales. The female is fuller and more vigorous than the male.
RANGE: The Philippine Islands.
CARE AND BREEDING: The species may be wintered in heated rooms of the house without special heating for the tanks.

— **taeniata** Ahl: The Black-Striped Rasbora.
SHAPE: As per description of genus, very slender and graceful. The lateral line is very short. D 9, A 11. Length up to 3⅛″.

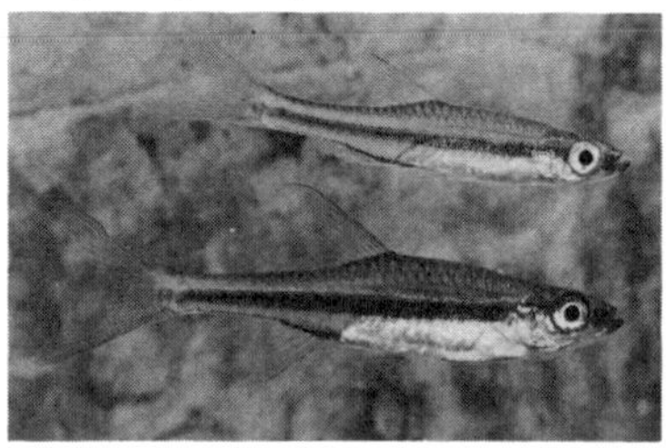

Rasbora taeniata

COLOR: Shiny silver with green and reddish hues and a blue-black longitudinal stripe, bordered with a golden stripe on the upper edge. The male is a little more vividly colored, the female fuller.
RANGE: Sumatra.
CARE AND BREEDING: As per description of genus. The species is not very gregarious, and keep a little apart from other fishes, similar to *R. heteromorpha*.

They need a little more warmth than the other species, 72-75° F is desirable, especially under direct sunlight, which the fish like very much.

— **tornieri** Ahl: The Yellow Rasbora.

SHAPE: As per description of genus, very slender, the lateral line complete. D 9, A 11. Length about 3½″.

COLOR: Very shiny with several dark longitudinal stripes, the interstices between which are luminously golden. The female is a little plumper during the spawning

Rasbora tornieri

season.

RANGE: Sumatra.

CARE AND BREEDING: The species poses no demands at all as to temperatures, 64-72° F being sufficient. Attempts at breeding seem not to have succeeded so far.

— **trilineata** Steindachner: The Scissor-Tailed *Rasbora.*

SHAPE: As per description of genus, very slender, with complete lateral line. D 9, A 8. The tail fin is relatively big and deeply indented. Length not yet exactly known, probably 4¾″ to 6″. The body is very transparent, so that under back-lighting one can easily see the dorsal spine and the swimming bladder.

COLOR: Shiny silvery transparent with a darker stripe and a dark-bordered edge of the lower caudal peduncle. The lobes of the tail fin show a very pretty black and white stripe design which is very striking. The female is noticeably fuller than the male.

RANGE: In standing and flowing waters of Sumatra and Borneo.

Rasbora trilineata

CARE AND BREEDING: As per description of genus. Despite its frailness, the species is quite hardy. They may prove to be temporarily a little shy and are not totally as agile as the other *Rasbora* species. *R. trilineata* is a pronounced school fish, and sometimes the whole swarm stands for long periods in the same spot, flapping their fins. Temperature, 64-77° F.

According to APELT spawning them is not simple, and little productive. It takes place in a manner similar to that of the species of *Danio.* Temperatures may rise up to 82° F.

— **urophthalma** Ahl: The Dotted-Tail Rasbora.

SHAPE: As per description of genus. A graceful and small species. D 9, A 8. Length around 1″, the male a little smaller.

COLOR: Gold-brownish with a dark-blue stripe, gold-red edged on the upper side and ending in a blue-black spot on the base of the tail

Rasbora urophthalma

fin. The male is slimmer, more vividly colored, and has a whitish spot at the base of the dorsal fin.
RANGE: Sumatra.
CARE AND BREEDING: As per description of genus. Small tanks will suffice for keeping them, and may be set-up as for *R. maculata*. The fish should only be kept in schools of their own species as otherwise they easily become shy. Temperature, 70-77° F, for breeding 79-82° F. Spawning probably resembles that of *R. maculata* and *R. heteromorpha*. The eggs are stuck to the underside of leaves of water plants, but are also scattered freely in thickets of *Nitella* and of algae. The act of spawning, during which the fish embrace, is repeated during several successive days. Generally it takes place under the morning sun. The fry hatch after 1-1½ days. This is the time to remove the parents. The very small and transparent fry at first need abundant quantities of *Paramaecium*. The species is not productive.

Rasbora vateriflloris

— vateriflloris Deraniyagala:
SHAPE: As per description of genus, but very similar to *R. heteromorpha* in build. The vertical fins are quite large, the lateral line is very short. D 10, A 8. Length around 1½″.
COLOR: Silvery greenish to mother-of-pearl hued, the lower half of the body and the fins a pretty golden-yellow to orange red. The male is slimmer and more intensely colored.
RANGE: Ceylon.
CARE AND BREEDING: As per description of genus. The species needs much warmth, 75-79° F and more.

Rasborichthys: *Rasbora*-like fish. Genus of tropical swarm fishes belonging to the family of the Carp-like fishes or *Cyprinidae*.

— altior Regan: The Dot-Striped Silverling.
The moderately elongated body is compressed laterally. The dorsal contour is arched. D 9, A 8. Length up to 3⅜″.

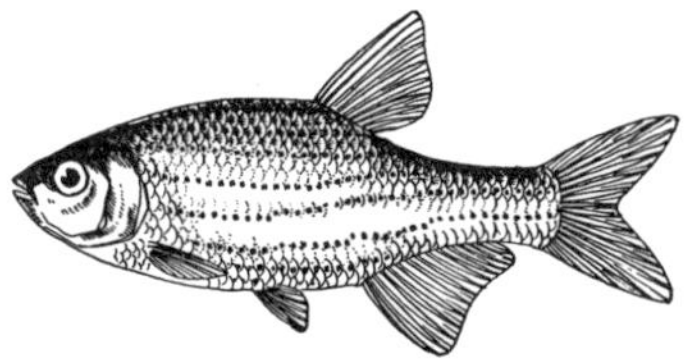

Rasborichthys altior

COLOR: Shiny silver with a blue dot at the bottom of each scale. The male is slimmer than the female.
RANGE: The fish were caught in a brook on Singapore Island.
CARE AND BREEDING: For their well-being the fish need spacious, well-planted tanks with space for swimming and exercising. They are very active, peaceful, and gregarious school fish, which eat all kinds of artificial and live foods. They need much warmth, 72-86° F being suitable. Nothing is known about their reproduction.

recent: That which lives at present.

recessive: Unseen, displaceable; regarding the hereditary factor which is present but is superseded by another, dominant one, and for this reason remains invisible in the general picture.

Red Bream, Red Eye: see LEUCISCUS RUTILUS.

Red-Eyed Moenkhausia, the: see MOENKHAUSIA SANCTAE FILOMENAE.

Red-Finned Glass Perch, the: see AMBASSIS RANGA.

Red From Cameroon, the: see NEOLEBIAS LANDGRAFI.

Red-Lined Rasbora, the: see RASBORA PAUCIPERFORATA.

Red Neon Tetra, the: see CHEIRODON AXELRODI.

Red-Spotted Copeina, the: see COPEINA GUTTATA.

Red 'von Rio': see HYPHESSOBRYCON FLAMMAEUS.

Redling, the: see CHROSOMUS ERYTHROGASTER.

Regan, Charles Tate: 1878-1943. English ichthyologist, pupil of G. A. Boulenger, who arranged the extensive collection of fishes of the British Museum according to modern points of view, and who holds great merits in the field of systematics.

regeneration: The ability of many animals to replace lost or mutilated parts of the body; especially developed in Hydras (see HYDROIDEA).

reitzigi: After the importer, Reitzig, of Berlin, Germany.

— *Apistogramma.*

relay: In aquaristics, a system of contacts which makes it possible to connect or to disconnect one or more heating elements according to need. Relays are generally coupled to thermostats, which either are pre-set to a certain temperature, or else may be adjusted.

reproduction: Reproduction serves the aim of preserving the species, and thus to preserve life beyond the individual. The manners of reproducing in the different groups are differentiated in adaptation to their surroundings. Plants and unicellulars often show asexual reproduction, the new being originating from simple cellular division among unicellulars, or from the development of runners, buddings, etc. in multicellular organisms. Furthermore even unicellular beings may show a kind of sexual propagation by the conjugation of two, probably sexually differentiated cellular organisms, with subsequent division or development of spores. The biological significance of this process is not yet clearly understood.

In higher-developed organisms we come to sexual reproduction through the development of special germ cells. The union of sexually differentiated germ cells transmits the hereditary characters of two individuals of the same species to their progeny. These germ cells, which are sexually different, may either be fertilized within the same individual (hermaphroditically) or in different specimens (heterosexually). The meeting of the sexual cells is made possible by all kinds of measures, both in plants and in animals. In animals the transmission of the male cells (see SPERMATOZOA) to the female cells (see EGG, OVUM) takes place either externally, or else inside the female organism (see MATING, COPULATION). The fusion of the mutual sexual cells is called fertilization or fecundation. In many lower animals, for instance, in microcrustaceans, we also find virgin birth (parthenogenesis), generally in regular alternation with bisexual reproduction, in which the development of the eggs takes place without previous insemination. In general, however, the development of the egg presupposes fertilization.

Since the egg, the developing embryo, and the fry need optimum conditions in order to develop their innate hereditary characters, reproduction is generally conditioned to certain seasons of the year in which these optimal conditions prevail, and the parents often even migrate to certain locations for this. Very frequently the enormous losses of progeny, which result from unfavorable climates or from the attacks of enemies, are compensated by great fertility. These two factors counterbalance each other. Often more complex measures are taken in order to protect the progeny against the dangers of the living world.

In all cases the manner of reproducing represents a phenomenon of adaptation, which has developed in the course of the genetic history. Reproduction only takes place if certain external conditions are satisfied and these may vary for each species. In aquaristics the breeder tries to induce his fishes to reproduce by creating such optimum conditions.

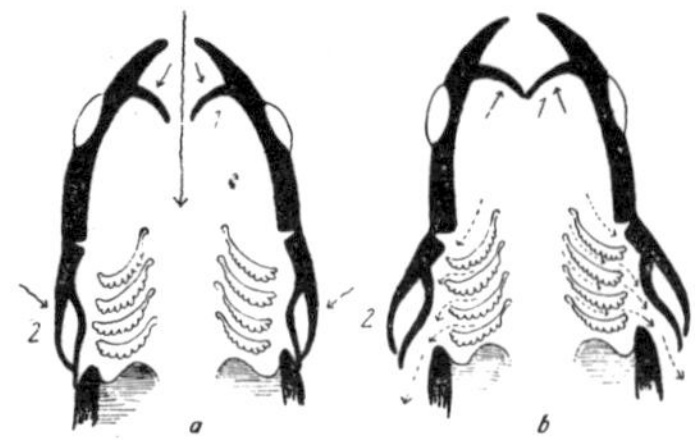

Respiration of a bony fish, after Sterba - A. The oral cavity is distended by muscular action. The resulting suction distends the gum folds, and the opercles (2) press against the body wall. The water streams through the oral opening. B. The oral cavity is compressed, forcing the water out. The gum folds are closed, and the water passes through the gills and the opercular opening.

Reptantia: Scissors Crustaceans. Sub-order belonging to the order of the ten-footed Crustaceans or *Decapoda*. The body is generally flattened, the adbomen is short and may be folded under the thorax as is the case of the crabs. Of significance for aquaristics are the phyla *Astacuar*, with the family of the *Astacidae*, and the Crabs or *Brachyura*.

rerio: After the native name. — *Brachydanio*.

resistance: Hereditary strength to withstand diseases, specialized to specific diseases, or of general nature, generally developed to different degrees individually. Frequently only single individuals, though often also whole tribes are resistant to a certain disease. Due to this fact it is perfectly possible to breed resistant tribes. In order to become effective, though, hereditary resistance has to be aided and developed through favorable living conditions.

respiration, breathing: The slow burning-up of food substances in the body by means of oxygen which must be assimilated from the water or from the atmosphere. Respiration takes place through special organs, in fishes generally inner gills, occasionally, though, through the intestine, parts of the swimming bladder, and other systems. A secondary phenomenon of respiration is the discharge of carbon dioxide gas, which serves as food for plants.

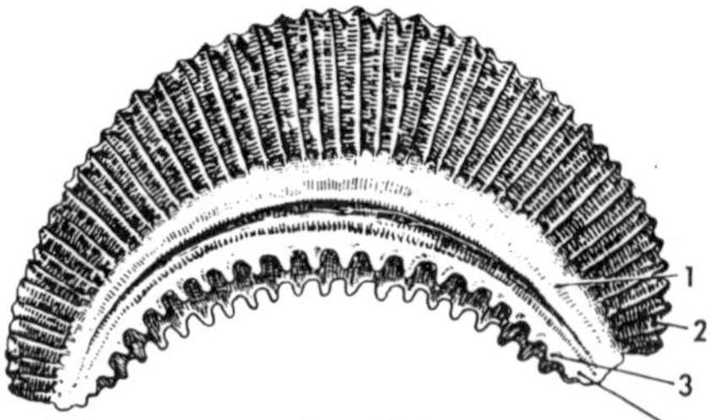

Gill structure - 1. gill bones - 2. gill rakers - 3. lateral lamellae - 4. connective tissue.

respiratory organs of fishes: A great number of fishes breathe by means of gills. These are found at the hind, central to lower, end of the head. Their support is formed by a number of specific bones (gill arches). From the outside the gills are protected by special bones, the movable gill covers (operculi, or opercles). The gills in themselves are formed by skin folds, which are full of blood vessels and sit on the gill arches. On Bony Fishes their number amounts to four pairs, with another pair which carries no gill skin. At the front edge the arches carry rows of differently-sized spines, which form a kind of filter, the gill basket, turned towards the oral cavity. At the rear edge we find delicate paired rows of gill lamelles, thin, strongly blood-flooded extensions of the skin. Breathing takes place by distending the gill cavity in which the gill arches rest. During this distension water is admitted through the mouth, flowing along the gill lamelles while its oxygen is extracted, the water being again expelled through the gill clefts by a contraction of the gill cavity. The larvae of *Axlotls* possess external gills in the form of bushy or feather-shaped appendages on the sides of the head, which develop back later on. One may recognize the respiratory process in fishes even externally by the distension and retraction of the gill covers, both movements together forming one breath. Depending on the temperature and on the oxygen contents of the water, on the speed of metabolism, or on the state of excitement in which a fish finds itself, the rhythm of the respiratory movements becomes quicker or slower. It may fluctuate between 15 and 150 per minute. Excessive acceleration of the movements of the opercles may be a sign of lack of oxygen due to several possible causes. In general the exchange of gases and the metabolism of fishes is not too intensive, for which reason the temperature generally agrees with that of the surrounding water, but may rise several degrees above that of the water under situations of intense excitement or due to very lively movements.

Some fishes are able to breathe atmospheric air, accessorily or nearly exclusively. These use as respiratory organs the mucosa of the mouth or of the intestine, or lung-like, sack-shaped protractions of the gill cavity (as, for instance, happens with the *Clarias* Catfishes), special cavities, connected with the mouth, as for instance, the respiratory labyrinth of the Anabantids, Snake-Heads, etc. The Lung Fish (*Protopterus*) uses its swimming bladder as a lung, the bladder being crossed by separatory walls which are rich in blood vessels. Fishes with much accessory respiration are, as a rule, able to stay out of the water for a more or less long period of time, or else in water that is very poor in oxygen, or even dry up in moist mud. In some cases, such as in Eels, leaving the water is made possible by a narrowing of the gill cleft.

reticulatus: With reticulate, net-like design.
— *Lebistes.*

retina: Tissue at the back of the eyes of vertebrates which contains the light-sensitive visual cells.

retrospiralis: Spiralled backwards.
— *Cryptocoryne.*

Rhinichthys: Fish with nose (that is, with extended snout).
Genus of North American school fishes belonging to the family of *Cyprinidae*, which about twelve known species.

— atratulus atratulus (Hermann): The Black-Nosed Dace.
SHAPE: Slender and only little compressed laterally. The snout protrudes far out, the small, subterminal mouth is equipped with one pair of small barbels. The lateral line is complete. D 7-8, A 7. Length up to $4\frac{3}{4}''$.
COLOR: Strongly variable, according to season and origin. The numerous sub-species and tribes in part show strong differences in coloration. Generally brownish with a blue-black stripe, which is bordered

above with gold, below with white. During the spawning period the lower half of the body is covered with a pretty red sheen. The male is considerably paler in color. In winter the colors of both sexes are the same to a large degree.

RANGE: In clear brooks and rivers of the North American continent, frequent everywhere, and living in small communities.

CARE AND BREEDING: A nimble, vivacious, and peaceful species, requiring large tanks with clear and cool water and vigorous aeration. It winters at temperatures of 39° F. Stock moderately with cold-water plants in order to leave sufficient space for swimming and exercising. For the bottom use well-washed sand, in which the fish like to root. They are omnivorous and hardy.

It is possible to breed them in the aquarium. Spawning takes place in very shallow water, while the pair embraces lightly, only one egg being expelled at a time. One spawning period may protract for months. The fry dwell in shallow water, assorted as to size. The fish may also be bred easily in the open air pond. From time to time one should catch out the fry and remove them to nursery tanks. For methods of rearing them, see CYPRINIDAE.

— **atronasus:** see RHINICHTHYS ATRATULUS ATRATULUS.

rhizoid: Root hair; threads which in certain plants take the place of the real roots.

rhizome: Piece of stem which grows under the ground, generally thickened, developing overground roots and parts of plants. Typical plants with rhizomes are Ferns and Water Lilies.

Rhizopoda: Root Feet.

Phylum of unicellulars or *Protozoa*, characterized by a typical manner of locomotion, to wit, the alternate stretching out and retracting of

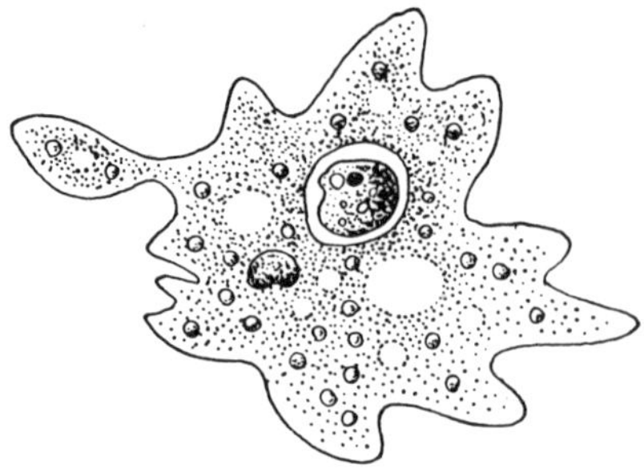

Rhizopoda

'little mock feet' (pseudopodia). The body of some species is protected by shells which are either made of substances from their own bodies, or else from foreign substances. There are no permanent organs for feeding or for locomotion. Reproduction takes place vegetatively, by division, or sexually.

There are several classes, in fresh water especially, such as the *Amoebae* or *Amoebina*, the Shelled *Amoebae* or *Testaceae*, and the Little Sun Beasts or *Heliozoa*.

Rhodeus: The reddish one.

Genus of small Carps belonging to the family of the *Cyprinidae*, remarkable for its manner of reproduction.

— **amarus** Bloch: The Bitterling.

SHAPE: A rather high-backed and laterally strongly compressed fish with an only very short lateral line. D 12-13, A 12. Length up to $2\frac{3}{4}''$.

COLOR: Shiny silver with a luminously green band on the center of the caudal peduncle. During the spawning period the male wears a pretty wedding dress with reddish, violet and bluish shades, and prettily colored fins, with a spawning rash on the snout. The female remains simply silver colored, but develops a 1″ to 2″ long yellowish-crimson colored ovipositor which remains visible for a few days.

RANGE: Central Europe and the

center of the Soviet Union. Largely diffused in all waters that harbor bivalves to receive the eggs.

CARE AND BREEDING: A very interesting, vivacious, and peaceful fish, which likes company. Offer it medium-sized tanks, well-stocked with plants, but also with sufficient open space. Sunlight is desirable. The temperature may rise to 72° F. Since, for breeding, one or more vivalves have to be introduced into the tank, it is advisable to use clean washed sand and to partition off the plants with strips of glass or slate.

For breeding it is best to choose the small Painters Mussel, *Unio pictorum*. Under proper care the spawning period starts in the Spring, from March to May. The eggs, totalling about 40, are introduced into the intake valve of the mussel, and are fertilized by the male who stands above the bivalve. Eggs and fry pass through their stages of development among the gills of the mollusc, the fry at first being kept inside by a swelling behind the head which later is resorbed again. The larvae of the bivalves (glochidia) on their part go through an early phase of development on fishes, digging into their skin.

rhodostomus: Red-mouthed.
— *Hemigrammus*.

rhombeus: Diamond-shaped.
— *Serrasalmo*.

Rhynchobdella: see MACROGNATHUS.

Rhynchobdellodea: Trunk Leeches.
Super-family of the order of the Leeches or *Hirudinea*. Blood-sucking worms, found predominantly on cold-blooded vertebrates. They perforate the skin with a long, protractable trunk. They become pests in breeding tanks because of the fact that they appear in great numbers and thus are apt to cause serious harm to the fishes.

The best-known species is the Common Fish Leech, *Piscicola geometra* Linné.

Riccia: Named after the Italian botanist Ricci.
Genus of water ferns pertaining to the family of the *Ricciaceae*.

— fluitans Linné: Crystal Wort.

GENERALITIES: A very gracile, antler-like floating plant, very useful in the aquarium as a hiding place for young fry.

SHAPE: The thallus is a luminous green, branched out manifoldly in a manner that the closely located single little plants grow together forming thick mats on the surface.

RANGE: A moss that is found all over Europe, Asia, and America, principally in swampy waters. At low water levels the mats may also root in the bottom soil.

CULTIVATION: A very popular aquarium plant which is valuable as a spawning substratum and as an asylum for fry. *Riccia* may also be cultivated at greater depths if jammed between stones. It grows in waters of any degree of hardness, but thrives best in soft water, especially in well-lit, sunny, locations, and at 59-77° F.

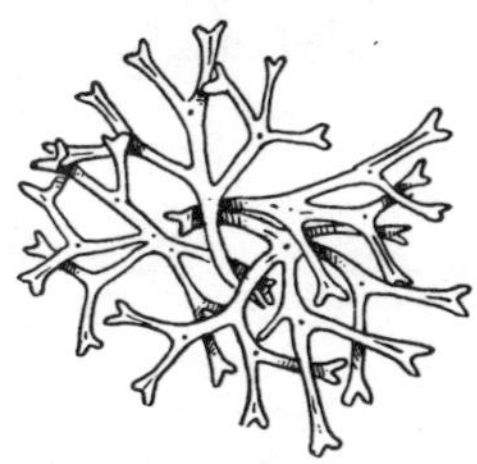

Riccia fluitans

Ricciaceae: Ricci's Liver Mosses.
Family belonging to the phylum of the Mosses or *Bryophyta*, which seems to range over the whole globe. Of the many species, which live on dry land, or in water, only two or three are found in aquaria.

Rice Fish, the: see ORYZIAS LATIPES.

riddlei: After the collector Riddle.
— *Pristella.*

Riddle's Pristella: see PRISTELLA RIDDLEI.

riisei: After the Danish zoologist Riise.
— *Corynopoma.*

Ring-Tailed Pike Cichlid, the: see CRENICICHLA SAXATILIS.

Ring Worms: see ANNELIDES.

riparium: Living on the shore.
— *Amblystegium.*

River Barb, the: see BARBUS FLUVIATILIS.

River Clams: see UNIONIDAE.

River Crayfish, the: see ASTACUS FLUVIATILIS.

— American: see CAMBARUS AFFINIS.

River Lamprey, the: see PETROMYZON FLUVIATILIS.

Rivulus: Brooklet (pertaining to the Rivulet).

Genus of South and Central American Tooth Carps belonging to the sub-family of the egg laying Tooth Carps or *Cyprinodontinae*, of elongated, cylindrical body construction, and slightly flattened back, supraterminal mouth, and with the dorsal fin inserting far towards the rear. They are pronounced surface fishes, which often stand quietly in a hanging position as if waiting. They like to jump or to lie in the sun on the leaves of floating plants. They are able to stick even to vertical surfaces with the aid of their fins. It is reported that in their home waters in mountain brooks, they are able to overcome even stronger rapids by jumping from rock to rock and thus working up in stages. It is also said that during heavy rains they leave the water in order to hunt for land insects.

Generally the fish are not very much liked, due to their quiet manner of living. Nearly all of them need plenty of warmth. They do not make great demands as to feeding, but live foods are visibly preferred. In nature they probably feed mainly on flying food.

Generally the different species of *Rivulus* spawn near the surface, such as on the tips of shoots of fine-leaved aquatic plants, or among the roots of floating ferns. Well-fed breeding specimens rarely prey on their own spawn. The eggs may be gathered and put into breeding plants, or transferred to these together with the plants. The fry hatch after 10-14 days. Rearing them generally is not easy.

— cylindraceus Poey: The Brown *Rivulus.*

SHAPE: As per description of genus. D 10-11, A 13. Length up to $2\frac{1}{8}''$, the female growing a little bigger.

Rivulus cylindraceus

COLOR: Greenish to reddish brown with a dark longitudinal stripe and numerous red dots. Young specimens and females show a light-edged eye-spot on the root of the tail fin, the latter being a little simpler in color.

RANGE: Cuba and Florida.

CARE AND BREEDING: As per description of genus. The species is vivacious and relatively peaceful. They like warmth, 72-79° F being necessary, though the fish withstand lower temperatures but become quite sluggish if subjected to them. In reproduction they are not especially fertile.

Rivulus dorni

— **dorni** Myers: Dorn's *Rivulus.* Shape, care, and breeding as per description of genus. D 8, A 11. The length reaches about 2⅜″. The color is yellow-brown with darker cross bands at the rear of the body and luminous blue-green dots. The female is simpler in color.

ORIGIN: The surroundings of Rio de Janeiro, Brazil.

— **harti** (Boulenger): Hart's *Rivulus*; The Giant *Rivulus.*

SHAPE: As per description of genus. A relatively big species which reaches a length of 4″, the females even a little more. D 8-10, A 15-17.

COLOR: Greenish-brown with blue-green stripes on which rows of red dots are superimposed. The female is more vividly colored and besides this, like the fry, she shows a light-edged eye-spot on the root of the tail.

RANGE: Colombia, Venezuela, and Trinidad.

CARE AND BREEDING: As per description of genus. Despite their size the fish are peaceful and do not even touch the smallest fishes. Unlike the other species of *Rivulus,* they lead a hidden life among plants near the bottom. They need warmth and feel best at temperatures around 77° F.

Rivulus harti

— **isthmensis** Garman: The Dotted *Rivulus.*

SHAPE, CARE AND BREEDING: As per description of genus. Length up to 2¾″. D 9-10, A 11-14. Color greenish to bluish, with yellow lower side and rows of red dots. The female is simpler in color, but, like most species of *Rivulus,* it has an eye-spot near the root of the tail.

ORIGIN: Costa Rica, Panama to Mexico.

Rivulus ocellatus

— **ocellatus** Hensel: The Eye-Spotted *Rivulus.*

SHAPE: As per description of genus. The fish are not quite as slender as the other species. D 8-9, A 11-12. Length up to 2⅜″.

COLOR: Yellowish-greenish with irregular dark-brown cross bands and spots which cover the body and part of the fins. The female is generally a little weaker in color than the male but the eye-spot shows up more intensely.

RANGE: The Brazilian coastal regions, from Santos to Rio de Janeiro.

CARE AND BREEDING: As per description of genus.

— **santensis** (Koehler):

SHAPE: As per description of genus. D 7-8, A 12. Length up to 2⅜″.

COLOR: Green, the lower part yellowish, with rows of dots, and black tinted fins. The female has 1-2 black, white-edged spots on the base of the tail fin.

RANGE: The surroundings of Santos and Rio de Janeiro, Brazil.

CARE AND BREEDING: As per description of genus. The species is said not to need too much warmth, but it becomes very sluggish at temperatures below 70° F. BURGHARD gives an exact description of their breeding. At first he kept the sexes separated. For breeding the male was put in a 2½ gal. glass tank. A nylon mop was used as spawning substratum. The water probably was quite hard. Temperature 73° F. The following day the spawn-ripe females joined the male. The hard-shelled eggs were laid near the surface, probably during the night. They may be picked with one's fingers, or else one transfers the whole nlyon mop with the eggs to a nursery tank and hangs a new mop into the spawning tank. The act of spawning was extended over two whole days. The fry began to hatch after 14 days, but in irregular sequences, so that the last fry showed up six days late. About 10% of the eggs did not hatch, since the young were unable to get out of the egg shell. Sprinkling dry food on the surface was useless. The hatched fry proved to be very hardy. During the first 4½ days they lay on the bottom, and then swam upwards in order to remain near the surface. At first they were fed a preparation of infusoria, then freshly-hatched brine shrimp for a week, later chopped tubifex until they went on gradually to eat minute live foods.

— **strigatus** Regan: The Herring-Bone Rivulus.

SHAPE: As per description of genus. Very graceful. D 8, A 12. Length up to 1⅜″.

COLOR: Blue-green to blue, the lower part orange colored, with rows of red dots and cross bands. The female is more simply colored.

Rivulus strigatus

CARE AND BREEDING: As per description of genus. The species needs much warmth. Temperatures 77-82° F, for breeding up to 90° F. The fish are lively and a little quarrelsome. It is reported that there are mostly males among the offspring.

— **urophthalmus** Guenther: The Golden, or Green, Rivulus.

SHAPE: As per description of genus, rather elongated and slim. D 6-7, A 11-13. Length up to 2⅜″.

COLOR: Brownish with green gloss and red rows of dots along the flanks. There is an orange red color variety of this species which is known as the 'Red *Rivulus*'. The female of the original form has a pronounced tail spot, besides this all females are weaker in color.

RANGE: Eastern South America, from the Guianas in the North to São Paulo in the South, but apparently not in the region of the Rio São Francisco.

CARE AND BREEDING: As per des-

Rivulus urophthalmus

cription of genus. The species is a little vicious and bellicose. The young have to be separated according to size as the bigger specimens attack the smaller ones.

— **xanthonotus** Ahl: The Yellow-Back *Rivulus.*

SHAPE, CARE, AND BREEDING: As per description of genus. D 6, A 11-12. Length up to 2¾″.

COLOR: Yellowish to brown with yellow designs and rows of little red dots. The female is more simply colored and shows an eye-spot at the root of the tail fin.

RANGE: The Amazon region, science lacking exact informations on its origin.

roe-bound, spawn binding: The inability to reabsorb unexpelled eggs, caused by one-sided, too fatty feeding and consequent fattening and degeneration of the ovaries. The supposition that fishes that do not reach the point of spawning must necessarily suffer harm to their health due to being eggbound, is according to SCHAEPERCLAUS, a mistake. Anyway, certain species of fishes are especially prone to being roe-bound, especially the mouthbreeder *Haplochromis multicolor.* Symptoms shown in these cases are: externally, swollen bellies; internally, degeneration of the ovaries. Roe-boundness leads to death.

Roeboides: Hunchback-like.

Central American genus of the family of the Characins or *Characidae.*

— **guatemalensis** (Guenther): The Small-Scaled Glass Tetra.

SHAPE: Elongated and strongly compressed laterally. The back is strongly curved to the insertion of the dorsal fin, and indented above the eyes. The mouth is big, terminal, and equipped with sharp teeth. There is an adipose fin present. D 11, A 47-52. The scales are small. Length up to 6″.

COLOR: Yellowish base with many shiny little dots which become visible under incident light, and a weak greenish-blue stripe. In all, glassily transparent. The fins of the male are a little more intensely colored; during the spawning period he covers his body with a pretty yellowish sheen. The female is plumper.

RANGE: Eastern Central America, from Mexico to Panama, in waters of all kinds, also in brackish ones. The species also goes up into the mountains, and is quite frequent there in flowing waters, being caught as a food fish.

CARE AND BREEDING: A hardy and undemanding fish which likes clear, oxygen-rich water, and sunlight. No special demands are made as to the warmth of the water. It is a fact that it feels better at 77° F, but also lower temperatures down to 59° F are withstood without distress.

The manner of swimming, tilted down and slightly winding, is typical of the species. The fish are voracious, and also a little quarrelsome and envious of each other's food. They demand plenty of live food.

Breeding them has been achieved in big tanks only, but resembled that of most other egg-scattering Characins.

roloffi: After the famous German aquarist E. Roloff, editor of "Tropische Fische."

— *Aphyosemion.*

— *Barbus* (*Capoeta*).

Rooseveltiella: After Theodore Roosevelt.

South American genus of the family of the Characins or *Characidae,* sub-family of the *Serrasalminae,* which differs in the tooth structure from the closely related genus *Serrasalmo.* Only two species are known. This genus comprises the best-known of the so-called Piranhas or Pirayas. They are vigorous, relatively big fishes, not too high in build, the lower edge of the belly of which is studded with saw-like scales. The snout is short, the mouth opening very big, and the jaws especially strongly developed. The teeth are pointed and razor-sharp, in part tilted towards the rear.

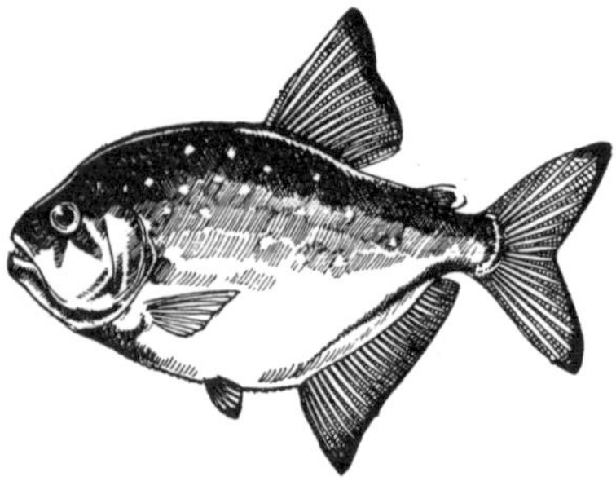

Rooseveltiella nattereri

— **nattereri** (Kner): Natterer's Piranha.

SHAPE: As per description of genus. D 16-18, A 28-32. The scales are very small. Length above 12″.

COLOR: Slate gray with a blackish silver shine and many metallic shimmering dots, the lower part vivid red.

RANGE: All of Eastern South America, from the Guianas in the North to the La Plata in the South, quite frequent everywhere.

Roosevelt's Disc Tetra: see METYNNIS ROOSEVELTI.

rosaceus: Rose-colored, crimson. — *Hyphessobrycon callistus.*

Rose Colored Curimatopsis, the: see CURIMATOPSIS SALADENSIS.

Rossmaessler, Emil Adolph: 1806-1867.

German naturalist and writer who contributed much to the diffusion of the knowledge of the natural sciences through popular books and articles, which he wrote in addition to purely scientific books. Through an article in the magazine 'Die Gartenlaube' under the title 'Der See im Glase' ("The Lake in the Glass", 1856) and through his booklet 'Das Süsswasseraquarium' ("The Freshwater Aquarium") Rossmaessler is considered the 'Father of German Aquaristics'.

Rossmaessler was born on March 3, 1806, the son of an engraver, whom he has to thank for his artistic talent for drawing. At the age of 12 he went to high school in Leipzig, but received only formal education in natural sciences which could hardly satisfy him. Despite this, he soon showed his preference for this knowledge. At the age of 15 he lost his father, and three years later his mother. In 1825 he matriculated at the university in order to study theology, according to the wish of his mother, and with the financial aid of an uncle. He could bring up no interest for these studies, though, and instead of hearing theological lectures he was present at medical and botanical ones, which only increased his desire to dedicate himself totally to the natural sciences. His studies in the field of botany and his visible talent soon procured him influential patrons. Professor Reichenbach got the young naturalist a teaching appointment at the renowned Academy of Forestry in Tharandt, which then was under the direction of Cotta. There he received a professorship in 1830, at the age of 24, not in Botany, but in Zoology. The knowledge necessary for this was painstakingly acquired by him. Despite this, he was soon able to publish his first works on Forestry. One of the first to appear is a work on insects of the forest, followed in 1835 by a self-illustrated compendium on European molluscs. 'Snailology', as R. calls it jokingly, kept him busy during nearly his whole life. Much later he undertook an exploring trip to Spain in its pursuit, financed by English friends.

Emil Adolf Rossmaessler

Rossmaessler was of a pronouncedly independent and progressive mind. He took an active part in the political movements of his time, joined the Liberal Progressive Party, and founded the first Citizens' League in Tharandt. In 1848 he left Tharandt, followed by the ardent votes of the citizenry and of the student body, in order to join Parliament at Frankfurt as a congressman. There he worked as a member of the School Committee, being a vigorous partisan of general schooling for all social levels. In Parliament he was a 'never-vacillating comrade-in-arms of the Left Wing of the House'. After the revolution, he was relieved of his post, had to flee, but was often jailed and persecuted later on. Notwithstanding this, he remained true to his political ideals. It is sublime to follow up how valiantly R. advocated his convictions to the end of his life.

From 1850 on Rossmaessler was busy as an independent naturalistic writer, who saw his task as that of 'bringing science to the people'. In uncounted lecture trips, which led him to the different regions of Germany, he tried to achieve his purpose. Deported several times, he finally turned towards Leipzig, his native city, the striving civic spirit of which finally made it possible for him to settle down. He edited the popular sheet 'Aus der Heimat' (From the Home Country), and published numerous writings and articles on popularized science. As an author Rossmaessler was extraordinarily productive. His popular works, besides which he had also published others of a strictly scientific character, showed special merit through their clearness of presentation and scientific exactitude, allied to simplicity of expression. In the 'Humboldt Clubs' and the 'Societies for the Education of Laborers', Rossmaessler acted untiringly as a lecturer, excellently illustrating his themes with practical maps drawn by himself. This method earned him the derisive nickname of a 'scientific show quack' from his adversaries. Rossmaessler did not let this deter him. Now he stood totally on the side of the simple man of his native city, whom he strived to help by giving him knowledge. To the day of his death he enjoyed great respect in the rising Labor Movement. He was also able to regain recognition in the eyes of science by means of some writings. He is linked to ALFRED BREHM, the well-known author of 'Brehm's Tierleben' by a close co-operation. Jointly they published the book 'Tiere des Waldes' (Animals of the Forest). It is BREHM too, who, after Rossmaessler's death, published a second printing of 'The Fresh Water Aquarium', editing it. Due to a political article, in 1862 Rossmaessler received a jail sentence, which may have hurt the health of the man who anyway was marked by poor health. On April 9, 1867 he succumbed to a disease contracted during a lecturing trip.

Rossmaessler's intents in propagating aquaristics were unmistakably clear. He knew all about the aesthetic and restful effect of his 'lake in the glass', but he himself wanted always that it be considered an ever-living source of educational entertainment. The aquarium was the means by which to carry the light of knowledge into the darkness of illiteracy and superstition.

rostratus: With beak.
— *Echinodorus.*

Rosy Barb, the: see BARBUS (PUNTIUS) CONCHONIUS.

Rosy Tetra, the: see HYPHESSOBRYCON CALLISTUS ROSACEUS.

Rotatoria: Wheel Worms.
Class belonging to the phylum of the Tube Worms or *Nemathelminthes*, which, besides their interesting biological peculiarities, are of special significance for aquaristics as food for young fry. The organisms which the aquarist calls 'pond infusoria' generally are *Rotatoria.*

Rotatoria are not unicellulars, however, as one is led to believe by their minute size, but relatively highly developed multicellular animals, the systematic classification of which is a little uncertain. According to the prevailing concepts, they are placed close to the worms, but one has to keep in mind that this classification is only a formal solution of the problem.

Rotatoria, a rotifer

Rotatoria are cellularly constant, which means that the number of their body cells is a fixed one, though varying according to species, In all about 600 species are known from all over the whole globe. Most of them live in water. Generally they populate fresh water or the brackish water zone. Only a few species are also found in the sea. A number of them live on firm land like beneath mosses, etc. The Wheel Worms of the dry land, as well as some water-dwelling species, withstand dry spells in a state of catalepsy, and may thus be scattered everywhere by the wind, exactly like the permanent eggs of *Rotatoria.* They wake up quickly again when they meet favorable conditions. R. are noted for their great variety. All 600 species are distinctly differentiated from each other, in part even down to small details. All of them are small animals, the largest of them being about 1 mm. long. The popular name Wheel Worm, which resembles the scientific one in meaning, is the result of an error, as formerly, due to insufficient instruments, the crown of cilia around the oral opening was considered a quickly rotating wheel. Even today this impression prevails upon the observer who uses weak magnification.

Altogether R. are very rewarding subjects for observation. There are armored and unarmored species. Especially the latter permit observing the inner processes through their glass-clear covering. It is not difficult to verify under a microscope that these tiny live beings have reached an astonishingly high stage of body development.

The masticating apparatus alone is developed in manifold shapes, the stomach has very remarkable gland clusters, often there is also an intestine present, as well as kidney-like formations. Furthermore one sees ovaries, muscles, brain and nerve fibres, as well as a red 'eye'. They lack special respiratory organs and breathing taking place through the frail body membrane. The colorless blood circulates rhythmically through the body cavity. The trained observer can see the organs in their functions. Many species are lively swimmers, always in motion, and always in search of food. Nutrition consists of unicellulars and algae, which are sent to the mouth opening by 'rotating', that is, by eddying movements of the crown of cilia, in order to be sorted there and chewed by the complex masticating system. The indigestible remainders are expelled by the gullet, only a few species having an intestine and an intestinal opening. Many species are able to fasten to places with the rear end and to move creepingly. Some are able to telescope their long bodies. Others build shells from plants or from their own excrements. The plankton-living forms as a rule have shells and are often equipped with floating spines.

Reproduction generally is achieved through parthenogenesis. In this case only female specimens are found. The eggs ripen without being fertilized often being stuck on the rear of the body in the form of a crown. Development takes place in few days. The hatching young on their part are again only females, who after some days, lay eggs too, thus producing offspring that number billions.

In the fall they spawn smaller eggs, from which hatch males without masticatory tools or feeding organs. With their help arise fertilized, hard-shelled eggs, which are able to withstand frosts and droughts. These permanent eggs are scattered everywhere by the winds and may remain in dry storage for years. It has been proved that they were able to aestivate for 22 years, reviving when put into water.

Roth, Wilhelm: Swiss physician who was the first to acquire merit in the study of diseases of aquarium fishes. Born 1863. In 1912 he wrote 'Die Krankheiten der Aquarienfische und ihre Bekaempfung' (The Diseases of Aquarium Fishes and their Control) a book that was published again in a second edition in 1922, and which for years remained the only publication with a scientific basis in this particular field of aquaristics.

Round-Mouths: see CYCLOSTOMATA.

Round-Tailed Paradise Fish, the: see MACROPODUS CHINENSIS.

Round Worms: see NEMATHELMINTHES, or TUBE WORMS.

Rowing Bugs: see HYDROCORISAE.

Rowing Feet: see COPEPODA.

rubropinnis: Red-finned.
— *Aphyocharax.*

rudimentary organs: Organs that have been stunted in the course of tribal history, the remainders of which are still present today, but have become purposeless.

Rummy-Nosed Tetra, the: see HEMIGRAMMUS RHODOSTOMUS.

runners: Daughter plants which spring from the mother plant, and are not produced by seeds. The runners are connected to the mother plant; later these connections may decay, and the daughter plant leads an independent life. This is a completely asexual

Runner. Parent plant with runner, and a second one budding.

method of reproduction.

rupestris: Rock-dweller.
— *Ambloplites.*

rutilus: Reddish, yellow-red.
— *Leuciscus.*

sachsii: After the German aquarist W. B. Sachs.
— *Barbus* (*Puntius*).

sadanundio:
— *Stigmatogobius.*

Saddle Cichlid, the: see AEQUIDENS TETRAMERUS.

Sagittaria: Arrow Worts.
Genus of swamp and aquatic plants pertaining to the family of the Frog Spoon plants or *Alismataceae,* which in part grow permanently submerged, partly semi-emerged or emerged. The sub-aquatic leaves are narrow to broadly ribbon-shaped. The species are perennial, some of them forming bulbs and winter buds. The inflorescence generally rises above the water surface, but in some cases it remains floating beneath this. Reproduction either through shoots or through seeds. Cultivation is simple. The submerged forms are satisfied with a bottom ground of unwashed sand, with a possible admixture of some old clay. The emerged plants, which are proper either for the swamp aquarium or else for the open air installation, need a richer bottom soil.

Sagittaria eatonii

— eatonii Smith: Eaton's Sag.
GENERALITIES: A submerged *Sagittaria* which forms lawns and which in commerce is erroneously called *S. lorata, pusilla,* or *gracilis.*
SHAPE: This perennial, undemanding, and hardy plant possesses vividly green, narrow ribbon-shaped leaves, which grow to lengths of up to 6″. No floating leaves are developed, only the leaf tips sometimes broaden a little when they reach the surface. The inflorescence grows above the surface, but does not develop in too deep water.
RANGE: The Northeast of the U.S.A., especially in waters with sandy bottom.
CULTIVATION: The plant poses no problems as to the composition of the water, and is besides this able to withstand considerable fluctuations in temperature. It thrives best at 64-72° F. Needs plenty of light, however, especially sunlight, if it is to bloom. The flowers, the petals of which are white, crimson on the underside, sometimes develop fertile seeds if standing in sunny places. If one desires multiplication through seeding, take an all-glass tank with a ¼″ high layer of sand and water of the same depth at a

Nothobranchius guentheri, a popular annual species.

Photo by Dr. W. Foersch

Characidae (Tetras)

1. **Anoptichthys jordani**, the Blind Cave Tetra - 2. **Mimagoniates microlepis** - 3. **Bryconalestes chaperi** - 4. **Iguanodectes tenuis** - 5. **Arnoldichthys spilopterus** - 6. **Astyanax bimaculatus** - 7. **Gephyrocharax valencia**, the Valencia Tetra - 8. **Phenacogrammus interruptus**, the Congo Tetra - 9. **Erythrinus erythrinus** - 10. **Copeina arnoldi**, the Splash Tetra - 11. **Pyrrhulina rachoviana**, Rachow's Pyrrhulina - 12. **Charax gibbosus**, the Humpbacked Tetra - 13. **Corynopoma riisei**, the Swordtailed Characin - 14. **Pyrrhulina brevis** - 15. **Phoxinopsis broccae** - 16. **Pseudocorynopoma doriae**, the Dragonfin Tetra - 17. **Copeina guttata** - 18. **Creagrutus beni** - 19. **Exodon paradoxus** - 20. **Roeboides guatemalensis** - 21. **Thayeria obliqua**, the Penguin - 22. **Crenuchus spilurus** - 23. **Rachoviscus crassiceps**

1. **Aponogeton elongatus** - 2. **Aponogeton distachyus**, blossom - 3. **Aponogeton undulatus** - 4. bud of a blossom - 5. group of blossoms - 6. and 7. individual blossoms, magnified.

Callichthyidae (Armored Catfishes) - **Loricariidae** (Whip-Tail Catfishes) - **Bunocephalidae** (Banjo Catfishes) - **Malapteruridae** (Electric Catfishes) - **Bagridae.**

1. **Corydoras aeneus**, the Bronze Catfish - 2. **Corydoras hastatus hastatus**, the Dwarf Catfish - 3. **Corydoras agassizi** Agassiz - 4. **Corydoras arcuatus**, the Skunk Catfish - 5. **Corydoras melanistius melanistius** - 6. **Corydoras punctatus julii**, the Leopard Catfish - 7. **Corydoras paleatus** - 8. **Plecostomus commersoni** - 9. **Callichthys callichthys**, the Hassar - 10. **Loricaria parva**, the Whip-Tail - 11. **Otocinclus vittatus** - 12. **Bunocephalus kneri**, the Banjo Catfish - 12a. the same, from above - 13. **Malapterurus electricus** - 14. **Leiocassis siamensis.**

Anabantidae (Labyrinth Fishes)

1. **Helostoma temmincki**, the Kissing Gourami - 2. **Ctenopoma oxyrhynchus** - 3. **Trichopsis pumilus** - 4. **Colisa labiosa**, the Thick-Lipped Gourami - 5. **Colisa lalia**, the Dwarf Gourami - 6. **Trichopsis vittatus**, the Croaking Gourami - 7. **Colisa fasciata**, the Giant Gourami - 8. **Trichogaster trichopterus**, the Three-Spot Gourami, Blue variety - 9. **Trichogaster leeri**, the Pearl Gourami - 10. **Trichogaster trichopterus**, the Three-Spot Gourami - 11. **Osphronemus goramy**.

1. **Echinodorus tenellus** - 2. **Echinodorus intermedius** - 3. **Echinodorus brevipedicellatus**, Amazon Sword Plant, narrow-leaved form - 4. **Echinodorus intermedius**, Amazon Sword Plant, long-leaved form.

Characidae (Tetras)

1. **Moenkhausia oligolepis** - 2. **Aphyocharax rubropinnis**, the Bloodfin - 3. **Hasemania melanura** - 4. **Ephippicharax orbicularis**, the Silver Dollar - 5. **Hemigrammus rhodostomus**, the Rummy-nosed Tetra - 6. **Moenkhausia pittieri**, the Diamond Tetra - 7. **Hemigrammus caudovittatus**, the Tetra from Buenos Aires - 8. **Gymnocorymbus ternetzi**, the Black Tetra - 9. **Ctenobrycon spilurus**, the Silver Tetra - 10. **Hemigrammus erythrozonus**, the Glowlight Tetra - 11. **Hemigrammus ocellifer**, the Head and Tail Light Tetra - 12. **Hyphessobrycon innesi**, the Neon Tetra - 13. **Hyphessobrycon pulchripinnis**, the Lemon Tetra - 14. **Hemigrammus pulcher**, the Garnet Tetra - 15. **Hyphessobrycon flammeus**, the Red Tetra - 16. **Hyphessobrycon heterorhabdus**, the Flag Tetra - 17. **Hyphessobrycon callistus callistus** - 18. **Pristella riddlei**, Riddle's Pristella - 19. **Hyphessobrycon ornatus.**

Symphysodon aequifasciata axelrodi, pair with eggs.

Photo by Dr. H. R. Axelrod

temperature of 68-77° F. The seeds are simply sprinkled on the water surface and sink down. Otherwise reproduction takes place through shoots.

Sagittaria filiformis

— **filiformis** Smith: The Thread-like Sag.

GENERALITIES: A submerged Arrow Wort for warm aquaria, which in commerce is erroneously offered as *S. gracilis*, or as *Blyxa echinosperma*.

SHAPE: The submerged leaves are narrow, ribbon-shaped, and form long drawn-out tips. At low water levels oval elongated floating leaves appear, which stand on thin stems. The inflorescences, with the white flowers on their stems, rise only little above the surface. The plants are very graceful.

RANGE: The South of the U.S.A., forming dense lawns at the bottom of waters.

CULTIVATION: The plants like a little more warmth. Multiplication takes place through shoots. Otherwise as per description of genus and of *S. eatonii*.

— **graminea** Michaux: The Grass-like Sag.

GENERALITIES: An Arrow Wort that grows submerged and emerged, especially adequate for the open air. It is often erroneously sold as *S. macrophylla, lancifolia,* or *platyphylla.*

SHAPE: The frail, submerged leaves are ribbon-shaped and attain lengths of up to 8″ with widths of $1\frac{5}{8}$″, growing even longer in very deep waters. The emerged leaves rise above the surface on long stems and are lineal to widely oval. Also the inflorescence grows beyond the surface. The vigorous root stock forms runners at the tip of which develop winter buds when the temperature falls off in autumn.

RANGE: In shallow waters of the U.S.A.

CULTIVATION: The species likes a

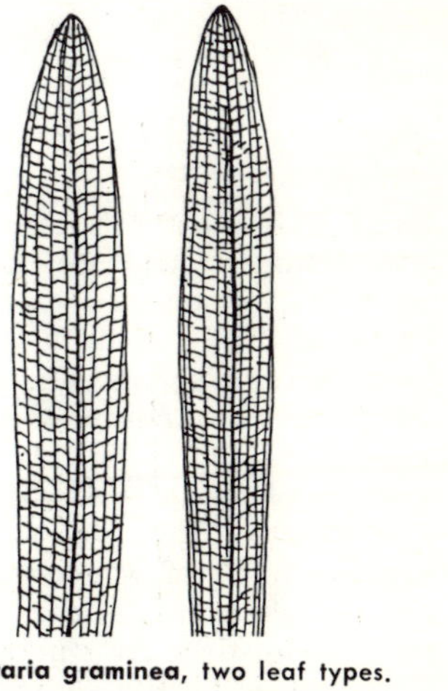

Sagittaria graminea, two leaf types.

rich soil and a well-lit location. It is especially fit for the open air installation.

— **lancifolia** Linné: The Lance-Leaved Sag.

This Arrow Wort too stems from shallow waters of the U.S.A. It is even less adequate for the home aquarium, but very good for the open air installation. The submerged leaves decay very quickly after the narrow to broadly lanceolate aerial leaves appear. The inflorescence is clustery to panicled, the flowers are white.

— **latifolia** Wildenow: The Variable Sag.

GENERALITIES: A very variable species with quite varied vital demands which result from its geographical origin.

SHAPE: Very variable. The different variants cannot be described here. The submerged leaves are ribbon-shaped, the aerial leaves variably arrow-shaped. The inflorescences, which appear only on emerged growths, rise above the surface. The root stock develops runners and bulbs.

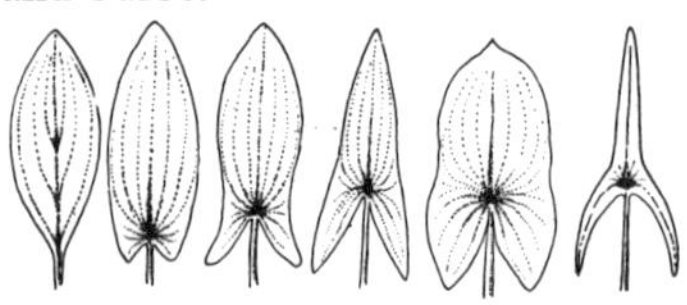

Sagittaria latifolia, types of emerged leaves.

RANGE: U.S.A. and Mexico.

CULTIVATION: The plant may be cultivated in unheated or heated home aquaria, paludaria, or in open-air installations. The plants that stem from northern regions withstand cold winters. The emerged plants in swamp aquaria need plenty of fresh, slightly moist air. The bulbs of winter-resisting open-air plants may remain in the soil, or else they are wintered in glass jars with water or in moist sand.

— **longiloba** Engelmann: The Long-Lobed Sag.

This species resembles the previous one in origin and cultivation. The ornamental aerial leaves are arrow-shaped with very long barbs which are longer than the front part of the leaf.

— **montevidensis** Chamisso and Schlechtendal: The Argentinian Sag.

This vigorous species, which reaches about 2 ft. in height, grows only emerged and is proper for moist-warm paludaria and for the open air. It forms neither runners nor bulbs and its reproduction from seeds is difficult. The aerial leaves are broadly arrow-shaped, the inflorescence may become very tall. Wintering is not complicated. It takes place at 46-50° F as a pot plant in moderately moist soil.

— **natans** Pallas: The Floating Sag.

This Sag is only rarely found in aquaria, since it is very sensitive to warmth. It grows exclusively submerged. The vivid green, blunt-tipped leaves are ribbon-shaped, the floating leaves are lineal to elliptical, and sometimes they show two blunt lobes. The inflorescence remains under water. It ranges over the northern and central parts of the U.S.S.R., Finland, and Sweden.

— **platyphylla** (Engelmann) Smith: The Broad-Leaved Sag.

GENERALITIES: A species that remains submerged even at high water levels, with broad-ribbon-shaped leaves. Generally the submerged forms of other species with similar leaves are offered as *S. platyphylla* in commerce.

SHAPE: This small to medium-sized species possesses 4-10″ long leaves, which are rugged and vivid green. The aerial leaves, which only develop at low water levels or outside the water, are narrowly lanceolate to broadly oval. The inflorescence only develops with an

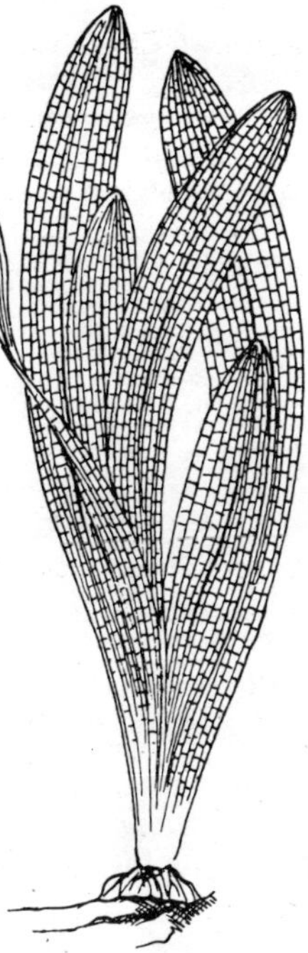

Sagittaria platyphylla

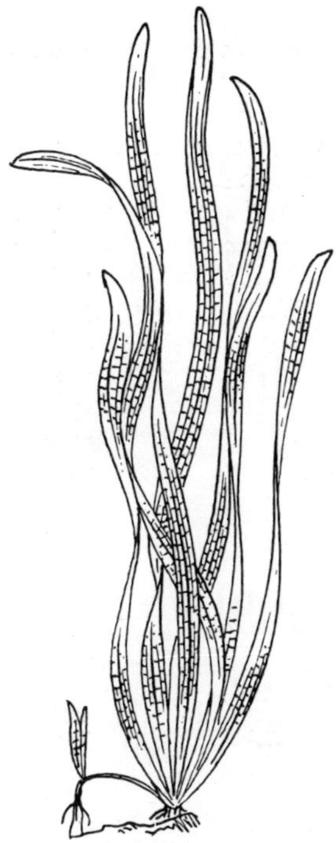

Sagittaria subulata

emerged manner of living. The rhizome is short and compact and produces runners and bulbs.

RANGE: Central and Southern U.S.A., in swamps and at other moist spots.

CULTIVATION: As per description of the genus, otherwise to be cultivated like *S. gramminea*.

— **sagittifolia** Linné: The Common Sag.

The European Sag is not fit for cultivation in the home aquarium, but it is adequate for the swamp aquarium and the open-air installation. The ribbon-shaped submerged leaves, which appear only occasionally, are soon substituted by the variable, arrow-shaped aerial leaves. The species likes a rich bottom that contains clay. In fall it develops winter bulbs, which may be gathered in early Spring and planted in the soil in open-air installations.

— **subulata** (Linné) Buchanan: The Swimming, or Floating Sag.

GENERALITIES: A submerged Arrow Wort which aquarists generally call *S. natans* by mistake. *S. sagittifolia* presents three different forms: *S. s. forma natans*, *forma pusilla*, and *forma gracillima*.

SHAPE: The plant is very similar to *Vallisneria spiralis*, but differs from this by its smaller number of leaf nervures, which are .only three instead of five. The leaves are narrow and ribbon-shaped, the floating leaves, which develop only at low water levels, are lineal or elliptical. The stem of the inflorescence floats beneath the surface of the water, and only the single white flowers float on this. Multiplication takes place through shoots, which sometimes also develop bulbs on their part.

RANGE: The Eastern U.S.A., in shallow spots of standing or run-

Leaf differences between **Vallisneria spiralis**, left, and **Sagittaria subulata**, right. After Wendt.

ning waters.

CULTIVATION: In fact this plant likes light, but it does not need it as much as *Vallisneria spiralis*. It keeps best at 68-73° F, but thrives sufficiently already at 59° F. Temporarily the temperature may sink even lower. An admixture of clay to the unwashed sand makes the plants more vigorous. The dwarf form '*pusilla*' is proper for the smallest tanks.

— teres Watson: The Round-Leaved Sag.

A species which very much resembles *S. eatonii*, and which should be cultivated under the same conditions. It differs from this, among others, by its white flowers.

sagittifolia: Arrow-leaved.

— *Sagittaria.*

Sail Fin Characin, the: see CRENUCHUS SPILURUS.

Sailfin Mollie, Sailfin Mollienisia, the: see MOLLIENISIA VELIFERA.

saladensis: Coming from the Salado River in South America.

— *Curimatopsis.*

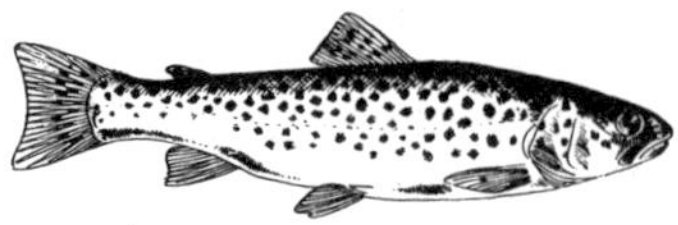

Salmonidae, type of the family.

Salmonids: Salmon Fishes.

Members of the *Salmonidae* family, which belongs to the Herring Fishes or *Isospondyli*. Generally they are medium-sized to big fishes, a special characteristic of which, among others, is the adipose fin, an unsupported continuation of the skin between dorsal and tail fins. Of the numerous species, all of which possess significant utility value as edible fishes, only a few can be kept in the aquarium, and under special precautions (for instance, flowing, cold, and oxygen-rich water). The best-known representatives of the family are Trout and Salmon.

salvini: After the collector O. Salvin.

— *Cichlasoma.*

Salvinia: After the Italian botanist A. M. Salvini.

Genus pertaining to the family of the Floating Ferns or *Salviniaceae*, with oval, very hairy floating leaves which are paired opposite along the common stem and to each of which belong a feathered, root-like subaquatic leaf. The spore capsules insert at the base of this in a ball.

— auriculata Aublet: The Small-Eared Salvinia.

GENERALITIES: A well-liked floating plant for the warm water aquarium.

SHAPE: As per description of the genus. The species is perennial.

RANGE: In tropical South America, on the surface of standing waters, bays and secondary arms of rivers, where the plants often form thick layers.

CULTIVATION: This floating fern likes intense light and a temperature of 64-77° F. It is sensitive to drips of precipitation water, for which reason the covers have to rest in a tilted position. Under favorable conditions it grows exuberantly, the leaves, which may then be slightly folded, pushing up, one over the other. There are some local varieties, and besides this the plants are very variable according to conditions. At too high temperatures with simultaneous insufficiency of light they develop stunted growths with small, round leaves. Multiplication takes place by sprouting. In winter the plants recede a little. A strong layer of *S. auriculata* offers a good cover against too intense sunlight, and simultaneously a spawning medium for some species of fishes which spawn at the surface, as well as a favorable protective zone for fish fry.

— **natans** (Linné) Allioni: The Floating Salvinia.
This species, which ranges over Europe, North Africa, and Asia Minor, is hardly usable for cultivation in the aquarium, since it is only of short duration and recedes in Fall.

sanctae filomenae: After a geographic name.
— *Moenkhausia.*

santensis: Coming from Santos, Brazil.
— *Rivulus.*

Saprolegnia: Fungus, Water Mildew.
Water-dwelling fungi pertaining to the family of the *Saprolegniaceae*, which may belong to the genus *Saprolegnia* as well as to the genus *Achlya*. Generally they attack dead organic substances, live fishes only after a previous weakening by other diseases. Places of incidence are especially open wounds or lesions. Cotton-like coverings appear on the skin, eyes, gills, and fins, on Tooth Carps also on the mouth. Fungus is seen especially on non-fertilized or dead eggs. Also dead fishes, other dead organic substances, leftover food, etc., may be covered with such fungus growths. Therefore *Saprolegnia* are pronounced weakness parasites when they attack live fishes. They permit secondary penetrations of bacteria into the muscles which they permeate with their fungus threads. Thus they are able decisively to make worse an already existant disease.

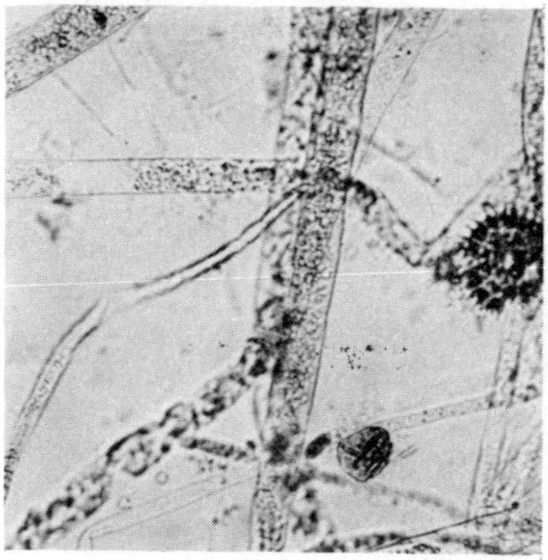

Saprolegnia

If you want to fight the fungus contamination, you will have to destroy the primary causes. Mechanical lesions should be shunned as much as possible, primary skin parasites have to be counteracted as soon as they are detected, and lowerings of temperature have to be avoided for fishes that are sensitive to them. The mildewing of fish eggs, especially in spawnings which hatch in a brood jar, may be prevented by a weak admixture of acriflavine or of methylene blue, as these impeach primary damage done to the eggs by bacteria and unicellulars.

Fungused eggs should be sorted out very carefully with a pipette, and removed, as otherwise the fungi pass on also to the sound eggs.

When transporting fishes one should also add a little acriflavine or methylene blue to the water.

When the first symptoms of a *Saprolegnia* attack appear, one may try to wipe off the parasite with a cotton swab moistened with a solution of permanganate of potassium (1 gram per 1 qt. of water). Possibly also a bath with permanganate of potassium (1 gram per 25 gals of water) lasting 90 minutes, may help. Sometimes also kitchen salt baths (1 oz. per 1 qt. of water) have shown to be efficient, or else painting with a diluted tincture of iodine is said to be a remedy that promises success. Experience shows that raising the temperature to about 86° F may lead to success, if the proliferation is not too intense.

Fighting the fungi is especially difficult if they have attacked the eyes of the fish. Cures of this are reported to have succeeded by paintings with a 2% solution of silver nitrate, which should be repeated several times. After each painting the fish must immediately be put into a 1% solution of common salt, in order to neutralize the silver nitrate and thus to avoid attacking the eye itself.

Saucer Snails: see PLANORBIDAE.

savannah: Grassy plains in the tropics, generally with stands of single trees and/or groups of bushes.

Saw Characins, Saw Tetras: see SERRASALMINAE.

scalare: Stair-like; referring to the step-like rising of the fin rays.

— *Pterophyllum.*

Scale Dot Pyrrhulina, the: see PYRRHULINA BREVIS.

Scardinius: Genus of school fishes belonging to the family of the Carp-like or *Cyprinidae*, of elongated build and strongly compressed laterally. The lateral line is complete. The middle of the belly is sharp-edged, the small mouth terminal, and the mouth cleft steeply tilted upwards.

— erythrophthalmus Linné: The Red-Fin.

SHAPE: As per description of the genus. The dorsal outline is slightly arched and a little indented above the eyes. Between the ventral and anal fins one sees a strong ridge of sharp-edged, bent scales. D 10-12, A 12-15. Length up to 14″.

COLOR: Shiny silver with yellowish to greenish sheen, the iris brass-colored. During the spawning period the male shows a rash on head and neck.

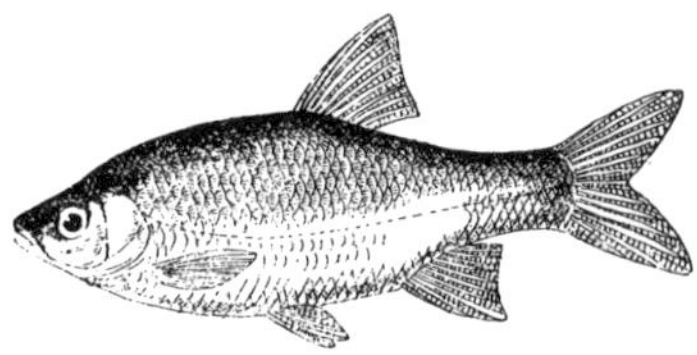

Scardinius erythrophthalmus

RANGE: Europe to Central Asia, in lakes, ponds, and flowing waters, especially in those richly grown with plants and with low water level.

CARE AND BREEDING: A gregarious shore fish which lives mainly on vegetable food. Only smaller specimens are fit for the home aquarium, where they should be kept like all Cyprinids. Very effective in bigger show aquaria. Breeding them in the aquarium is not possible. They are egg-scatterers which lay up to 100,000 eggs among aquatic plants.

Scarlet Lobelia: see LOBELIA CARDINALIS.

Scarlet Tetra, the: see CHEIRODON AXELRODI.

Scatophagidae: Argus Fishes.

Family pertaining to the sub-order of the Perch-like or *Percoidea*, of high body construction, strongly compressed laterally. The spiny and the soft part of the dorsal fin are distinctly differentiated, but connected by a low seam.

They are coastal fishes of East Africa, South East Asia, the Malayan Islands, to China and Australia, found in both the ocean and in brackish waters, and occasionally passing over into pure fresh water. Spawning sites, process of reproduction, and the first stages of youth are unknown.

One genus: *Scatophagus*, with several species.

Scatophagus: Eater of filth. Genus belonging to the family of the Argus Fishes or *Scatophagidae*, of high body build, strongly compressed laterally, which could be called nearly disc-shaped. With increasing age the fishes become ever more hunchbacked, especially the forehead contour being strongly indented. The small mouth is tilted obliquely upwards, the jaws being equipped with small teeth disposed in ribbons. The dorsal fin is divided into two parts which are connected. The Argus Fishes go through a larval stage (*Tholichthys* stage). The smallest known larvae show a length of $\frac{1}{4}''$. Nothing further is known about the biology of their reproduction. In general Argus Fishes may be considered ocean dwellers. From the coast, though, they invade brackish, and even purely fresh waters. They are often also found on coral reefs. *Scatophagus* are omnivorous, feeding mainly on animal and vegetable growths, as well as on organic detritus. Therefore they are found regularly at tropical seaside resorts, on the spot where the drainage waters from the big hotels flow into the sea.

In the aquarium they are vivacious, motile, and relatively peaceful fishes which feel best in company with others. They can also be acclimated to fresh water, especially young specimens. Since they devour even higher plants, their tanks can only be fitted out with rocks or roots. Breeding in the aquarium has not yet succeeded.

— **argus** (Gmelin): The Argus.

SHAPE: As per description of the genus. D_1 X, D_2 I/16-17, A IV/14-16. The scales are especially small. Length up to 12″.

Scatophagus argus

COLOR: They vary very strongly according to origin, age, mood, and composition of the water. In general the fish are greenish to brownish, strongly glossy under incident light, and covered with many round, dark spots. The sexual differences are unknown.

RANGE: One of the most widely distributed tropical fishes, being of the most frequent inhabitants of coastal waters from the Eastern coast of India to Tahiti.

CARE AND BREEDING: As per description of the genus.

— **tetracanthus** (Lacépède):

SHAPE: As per description of the genus. D_1 X, D_2 I/15-16, A IV/14-16. Length up to 16″.

COLOR: Strongly variable bluish to yellowish silver with dark cross bands. The sexual differences are unknown.

RANGE: From Northern Australia and New Guinea to Madagascar and East Africa.

CARE AND BREEDING: As per description of the genus.

Scheele, Charles William: 1742-1786. Swedish chemist who discovered oxygen at nearly the same time as Priestley.

Schilbeidae: Family of Catfishes pertaining to the sub-order of the *Siluroidea*, which, among others, comprises the genera of Glass Catfishes, *Physailia*, and *Cryptopterus*.

Schizophyta: Splitting Plants. Phylum of flowerless plants, which comprises, among others, the *Bacteria* and the Blue Algae or *Cyanophyceae* which are so much disliked in the aquarium. Generally *Schizophyta* are unicellulars, very small plants which live singly or in variably shaped colonies and settlements. Multiplication takes place asexually through division of the body. Some of the species develop permanent spores, which are able to withstand unfavorable times.

scholzei: After a personal name.
— *Hyphessobrycon.*

schomburgki: After a member of the German family of explorers, Schomburgk.
— *Polycentrus.*

school: A form of keeping together of fish communities. One speaks of a school when a number of fishes of the same age swim together.

school and aquaristics: The care for aquaria (and for vivaria in general) has found ever-increasing recognition during the last years. The eminent role of the study of biology, at a time when biological sciences are needed for the basis of human existence, is undisputed. The vivarium, that is, the aquarium, the terrarium, the insectarium, and the cage for small animals, is an excellent means to make schooling interesting and close to nature through observation of the live subject and of the artificially created life community which imitates Nature. It is an effective means to transmit other than dry, bookish learning. For this reason the setting up of vivaria is an object of special attention in the schools of most countries. Numerous school authorities try to give these efforts a firm basis through instructions and through training of the teachers. Civic and youth groups strive to aid the endeavors of the educational authorities and to assist the schools both with advice and in practice. It is obvious that the school vivarium has to serve educational aims, and that for this reason it has to follow other norms than the simple ornamental aquarium. Its observation should lead the child towards live Nature, teach it to recognize its laws, but the aquarium should also, if possible, appeal to one's sense of beauty through having been set up with loving care. The pupil should learn to understand that the essence of Nature rests in the indivisible unity of all phenomena, which should not be upset. Further he should learn to understand the laws of development and the purpose of the organisms created by adaptation.

The knowledge of native Nature will give the pupil an idea of its manifoldness and beauty. With this he should learn to respect life and to love his country. The child itself may collect animals and plants for the school vivarium during excursions and picnics. This will give him an interest in these. He should also care for them himself, naturally under expert guidance. Thus he will gather a live idea of animals and plants, and also of the surroundings in which they live. Thus the love of nature becomes the starting point for all human endeavors to make nature useful to humanity. The child will understand that also the unseemly, despised, and 'ugly' beast may be beautiful or at least interesting. The result will be the knowledge that each live being within Nature's household has a right to existence. Thus the child will reach the point where he no longer torments animals. He will hinder his fellows from doing so if they themselves have not yet grasped the truth that all life deserves the highest respect and must not be destroyed senselessly. From the protection of animals it is only a small step to the protection to Nature in general, as well as to the protection of scenic beauty and landscape, which may thus find an active defender in the child.

The following demands should be met by the school vivarium:

1. It must be set up scientifically, with technically unobjectionable means, and also with all possible regard to esthetic points of view;

2. It must be educational and instructive.

Before proceeding to establish, one should consider the question whether a teacher is available who can survey the set-up, and who can instruct the assisting students. It will be of great advantage if a member of the faculty itself can take over this task, preferably, of course, the teacher of biology. If this should prove impossible, one should try to enlist the aid of a specialized organization, at least until one of the educators has acquired the necessary basis. Also thereafter a mutual aid will always prove advantageous.

Beginners' mistakes should by no means repeat themselves in the school vivarium. Vivaria which suffer from 'lack of knowledge of the caretakers', aquaria with cloudy water, fishes that gasp for air, unkempt interiors, and ever-failing technical installations, go counter to the desired aims. Make-shifts will not help in this case. The best is just good enough for the school vivarium, be it ever so small. It should be clearly understood by the caretaker that he is called upon to make sacrifices of time, and possibly even of money, that the vivaria have to be attended for years, and that the adaptation to the progressive but always repeated plan of teaching demands consideration. He has to think of the unavoidable failures, of technical defects, of diseases, of deficiencies caused by his small scholars or by himself, and he must eventually be prepared to face lack of understanding or even ill will.

Therefore it is advisable at first to practice some restraint, to install only a few tanks preferably, but to set them up unobjectionably, and only to enlarge the installations gradually.

An extremely important question is that of the location. Of course it is difficult to give advice as to this, since generally conditions differ from one place to the next. It should be a basic principle that the children be able to watch the aquaria at all times. This end is not attained if, for instance, they stand in the teachers' rest room and may be viewed only occasionally. Real observations result only from continuous watching of the small events that happen daily, even hourly, in front of the child's eyes. It is advantageous if the aquaria stand in a room which is used alternately by all grades, for instance in the biology lab, where they simultaneously supply live subject matter for teaching. Locations in passages or arcades too may be equally favorable. In this one has to consider, though, whether in winter (especially during vacations or holidays), the school is sufficiently heated to avoid damage done by the cold. Since one will keep mainly native live beings anyway, the most important point will be to observe that the tanks receive no direct freezing temperatures. Tropical aquaria must of course be heated especially, and should possibly be located at a place that insures warmth in any case. Placing the tanks on window sills generally is unfavorable, as there animals and plants are seen against the light, which makes their shapes appear as pale contours only. A better location would be at an angle of 90 degrees to a window, or else against a wall opposite one, if it is not too far distant from the opening. A square angled placement has the advantage that the tanks may be viewed under cross and incident lights, which result in better possibilities of observation. The conditions of illumination and natural light have to be especially well considered. Too much light, especially sunlight, is detrimental, as it causes overwhelming additional work for the caretaker. There is also excessive warmth and over-development of algae which argue against a location at a too brightly lit place for native beings. Southern exposures are never good, but at windows facing east or west one can in most cases avoid too intense sunlight with a clever set-up. Locations with northern exposure may be favorable if sufficient light comes in without being cut off by houses or trees, and one may possibly aid this by artificial additional lighting. Closing off the vivarium corner with an auxiliary wall too may be of advantage, especially if the tanks can be fit into niches in same, if possible in a manner that leaves sufficient space for maintenance. It is a fact, though, that then one must often reckon with many hours of electric lighting during the day.

Two points have to be considered for the location:

1. The caretaker must be able to carry out his work easily and at any moment without obstacles. Gadgets and accessories have to be stored in a special room to which only he himself or especially authorized persons have entrance.

2. By no means should unauthorized persons, especially children, busy themselves with the accessories, electrical installations, aeration, etc. The tanks should be closed off in a way that no one not authorized to do so may reach inside them. It is best to provide all of them with a lid which locks. Finally one has to consider that maintenance involves running expenses which have to be included in the budget planning of the school. An effective installation cannot be built upon the willingness of the caretaker to make sacrifices. One has to think of occasional repairs, completions, foods, but also of fare money, etc. Also the possibility of increasing expenses in electric current and heating have to be taken into account.

For the installation of the aquaria (we cannot spare space here for the discussion of other vivaria), the same general principles are valid which are mentioned in this book under the respective entries. Here we shall only give some special advice: if possible get frame aquaria, and not all-glass ones, as these are more rugged and safer in the long run. The only exceptions are the small tanks for the lower animals of our waters. The frame aquaria should always have a well-insulated bottom, the best for this being a pane of glass. Furthermore the tanks should be equipped with sturdy lids, preferably wooden covers with locks!

As a soil foundation choose only coarse, unwashed sand, covered with a layer of coarse, clear, washed sand, as all other kinds of bottom soil only cause additional work for the caretaker, developing algae, cloudiness, and possible decay. One has to consider that many native plants can only be used for temporary stocking of the aquarium in order to show some special biotope. Many of them degenerate in the aquarium, or they dissolve, and may also retract in winter. Plants that are good for stocking the cold water aquarium, if sufficiently well-lit, are *Elodea canadensis*, *Vallisneria spiralis*, and some of the species of Milfoil. The latter have the disadvantage that easily they get dirtied or overgrown with algae. Hornwort, *Ceratophyllum demersum*, is a lasting plant in summer. Other plants have to be renewed from time to time. For the tropical aquarium there is the usual, larger, choice.

Maintenance should part from the principle that the aquarium should remain as undisturbed as possible. Only the necessary works of caring should be done, and these as sparingly as possible. Above all, the tanks need rest, a rest that should last for several months. Animals and plants that are intended for transitory showing only are preferably kept in auxiliary jars which are easily emptied and refilled at any time. Try to get along with the least possible number of accessories! Filtering and aeration can nearly always be avoided by moderate stocking and careful feeding. When setting up a tropical aquarium, one has to consider that one cannot dispense with a reliable heater (preferably one with automatic thermostatic control, which makes heating independent of surveillance for longer periods). One has to pay attention to the fact, however, that all electrical installations have to be protected against unthinking hands, as they are dangerous, especially to children. Feeding is the source of many failures. Above all, it commonly is done in excess. Special caution should be exerted with prepared foods. Cloudings and water contamination, resulting from wrong feeding, are very hard to remedy. The question of what species of animals should be preferred is answered by the aim of the school aquarium to show our native fauna in the first place. The so-called community tank, with its mixture of different fishes, belongs by no means in a school. One should not permit oneself to be induced to keep in the school tank casually assembled fishes of all kinds which have been 'donated' by well-meaning parents (as a rule because they themselves have become fed up with them). Such a tank is senseless. It shows no biological connection and permits no exploitation in teaching. Generally too the children quickly lose their interest after they have seen their fill of the 'colored fishes' swimming around. To the contrary, one should at first try to re-create a piece of our closest surroundings, for instance, the puddle, the ditch, a corner of a village pond, etc., etc. Materials for this are gathered on a field trip, after having prepared the containers necessary to hold the 'catch'.

In nature the first step is to study a piece of the aquatic landscape carefully, together with the volunteer assistants. Thereafter collecting starts. Aquatic plants, dry reeds, an old, submerged rootstock come along. Lower animals are transferred to the transport jars, predators into individual ones. Back at school the lower animals at first migrate to the small all-glass tanks or preserve jars that have been set up previously, but the fishes go into the garden pond in the school garden. Dragonfly larvae, beetle larvae, fresh water hydras, some water spiders, rower and swimming beetles, snails and clams belong to the yield of the trip, and also a few rarer plants are included, for instance, the beautiful Water Net.

Sticklebacks, Bitterlings, some Loaches and a few Redfins are the first fishes. Later on Minnows, dwarf Catfishes, young Pikes and Perches, Groundlings, perhaps even Bullheads and Crayfish from the nearby brook may follow.

Then it should be tried to shape the planned aquarium after the freshly acquired impressions. Sticklebacks and Bitterlings each get a separate tank in which their reproduction may be watched. After everything is ready, the aquaria are left alone for a few days until everything has tuned up, then the fishes are brought in from the garden pond, or else other specimens are caught on a new trip. Much can be done with these native plant and animal materials without entailing extensive technical expenditure.

Only after having gathered prolonged experience may one also begin to keep and breed exotic tropicals, of course again from the point of view of demonstrating certain biological questions. Also in this case the aquarium should be instructive.

The educational value is enhanced if the aquarium 'speaks for itself' without having to be explained. It is not a bad idea to reach this aim by a flawless description given by the students themselves. This should state all that is seen in the aquarium in simple words, and also what the peculiarities of each animal and plant species are.

school, school fishes: Numerous species of fishes live gregariously and convene in schools. The size and composition of such schools may be quite varied for the different groups of fishes. We find small groups, a little bigger societies which are called 'schools' if they are separated according to ages, and pronounced larger swarms which sometimes, for instance, in the migration of the Minnow (*Phoxinus laevis*), may comprise millions of individuals.

The behavior of fish swarms has not yet been explored in its particulars, except on a very small scale. Frequently swarms of fishes are composed of different sexes and ages. Sometimes it is only in youth that swarms are formed, sometimes specimens that are ripe for spawning leave the swarm in order to pursue reproduction, and reconvene with it later on. The concatenation of the swarm is maintained by factors which are not yet fully known. These trigger the gregarious instinct. Possibly, however, self-training too plays a role. For many swarm fishes the recognition of fellows of the same species and the perception of danger probably occurs through chemical stimuli. Besides this a reaction of the surface nerves to the manner of swimming of fishes of the same kind, as well as an idea of their body characteristics, may be of importance. The principal factor of cohesion may be different for the different species and genera.

Of the many aquarium fishes which are school fishes, many show special colorings which make it possible to keep the school together.

Fishes that come from light-flooded waters, for instance, lakes, open flowing waters, steppe creeks, etc., often show a remarkable silvery sheen: such as, for instance, Bleaks (*Alburnus lucidus*), Redfins (*Scardinius erythrophthalmus*), Silver Dollars (*Ephippicharax orbicularis*) etc. In such waters the sides of the fishes shine from afar, permitting the animals to find each other. Besides this we often find still another eminent characteristic, which consists of a remarkable design. Thus, for instance, *Pristella riddlei* carries black-white signal spots on dorsal and anal fin. Such simple signals would be illusory in dark waters, however, as they would not be visible far enough.

Under such circumstances the colors have to be considerably more intense. For this reason fishes from jungle waters often show luminous spots and dashes, which flash and flare up even under the sparse light which steals through the dense roof of leaves of the jungle trees. The most remarkable example of this is the Neon Tetra, but a great number of other species too show such light signals, be they shiny spots on the iris, on the caudal peduncle, or on other spots of the body. Besides these light signals jungle fishes generally show no special colors.

schottii: After the botanist H. Schott.
— *Sternarchella.*

schraetzer: After the zoologist Schraetzer.
— *Acerina.*

Schreitmueller, Wilhelm: Well-known amateur biologist and aquarist, who wrote many papers and articles and contributed notedly to the diffusion of the knowledge acquired in aquaristics.

Born on January 16, 1870. Architect. Temporarily director of the Aquarium in the Zoological Garden of Frankfurt on the Main. Schreitmueller is the author of the 'Leitfaden zur Pflege und Zucht von Einheimischen und Fremdlaendischen Zierfischen' (Introduction to the Care and Breeding of Native and Foreign Ornamental Fishes). Up to his death he took an active part in the development of aquaristics.

schultzei: After O. Schultze, of Aquarium Hellabrunn.
— *Corydoras.*
— *Myloplus.*

sciadicus: The dark one.
— *Fundulus.*

science of development: see GENETICS.

Scissor-Tailed Rasbora, the: see RASBORA TRILINEATA.

Scissors-Tail, the: see RASBORA TRILINEATA.

Scleroparei: Order of the Armored Cheeks, with the family of the *Cottidae.*

Scorpion Bugs: see HYDROCORISAE.

scratcher diseases: Diseases of the intestinal canal caused by parasitic worms (scratchers, *Acantocephala*), which may be lethal to smaller fishes. The worms, measuring fractions of an inch, dig into the wall of the intestine by means of their clasping organs, causing heavy inflammations, perforations of the intestine, anaemia, and great weakening. Scratchers are introduced in the aquarium together with food, and no transmission from fish to fish takes place. Intermediate hosts are especially *Gammarus pulex*, and *Asellus aquaticus.*

scratchers: see ACANTOCEPHALA.

Scrophulariaceae: Plant family belonging to the class of the Two-Germinating-Leaved ones or *Dicotyledoneae*, of which the genus *Limnophila* is of special significance for aquaristics.

Sea Cow Fishes: see STERNARCHIDAE.

sea water, salt water: Preparing sea water artificially may be necessary even for the fresh water fancier if he keeps certain fishes of the brackish zone. For preparing 25 gals. of artificial sea water, one needs (according to WIEDEMANN):

Sodium Chloride ($NaCl$)	2756 grams
Potassium Chloride (KCl)	67 „
Magnesium Chloride, crystalized, ($MgCl_2 + 6\,H_2O$)	551 „

Magnesium Sulphate, crystallized ($MgSO4 + 7H_2 0$)	692	,,
Sodium Nitrate ($NaNO_2$)	10	,,
Sodium Nitrate ($NaNO_3$)	10	,,
Sodium Bicarbonate ($NaHCO_2$)	25	,,
($NaHCO_3$)	25	,,
Sodium Bromide (NaBr)	10	,,
Potassium Iodide (KI)	0.5	,,
Sodium Phosphate (Na_2HPO4)	5	,,
Strontium Chloride ($SrCl_2$)	1-2	,,

This mixture of salts is dissolved in water. Only after this we add 145 grams of crystallized Calcium Chloride ($CaCl_2 + 6H_2O$), which has previously been dissolved in a little water. If the salt water is to be used undiluted, one has to check its density with a hydrometer (areometer), according to the origin of the pelagic animals. This density is the following:

Mediterranean water	1.027—1.028
North Sea water	1.021—1.023
Baltic Sea water	1.017—1.021

If the mixture is needed as an addition to fresh water, it may be used without further checking in the percentage which corresponds to the demands of the fishes one wants to keep.

secondary sexual characteristics: see SEXUAL DIFFERENTIATION.

secretion: The product of a gland.

securis: Hatchet.

— *Thoracocharax.*

seed cells, sperm cells: see SPERM, SPERMATOZOA.

segments: Body parts or divisions of lower animals, for instance, worms, disposed in rows.

selection, elimination: Selection deserves special merit in the breeding of aquarium fishes and other captive animals, as well as of plants cultivated by humans. It has to substitute for natural selection such as takes place in Nature. Unfortunately the neglect of selection leads to the gradual degeneration of the tribes of fishes kept in our aquaria. Positive measures to increment desirable traits, too, are called selection, negative ones, to destroy undesirable qualities, are eliminations. In aquaristics often a completely unintentional selection takes place, according to the wishes of the breeder. Thus frequently aquarium fishes no longer bear their natural colors after some generations, due to the fact that the most beautiful and most colored specimens are preferred for breeding (see ADAPTATION, INBREEDING, BREEDING).

selection, theory of: see GENETICS.

semicinctus: Half-girdled, half-banded.

— *Acantophthalmus.*

semifasciata: Half-striped.

— *Pyrrhulina.*

semifasciolatus: With half bands.

— *Barbus (Puntius).*

semisubmerged: Half-submerged, speaking of aquatic plants which live half under, half over the water surface.

semitaeniatus: Half-banded.

— *Hemiodus.*

Senegal Cichlid, the: see TILAPIA HEUDELOTI.

Senegal Loach: see ELEOTRIS VITTATA.

sensation of pain in fishes: The sensation of pain in higher animals and in man is limited to the so-called pain spots in the skin, which are the sole causers of pain. Outside of these spots interventions and contacts cause no pain.

Fishes too possess such pain spots. It is difficult to draw conclusions as to the degree of the sensation of pain, as fishes utter no sounds as signs of suffering. Also from movements such conclusions cannot be drawn without objections, as these are also made if one just holds the fish without causing it any pain. Operative interventions, though, have proven that fishes have much less intense sensations of pain than higher vertebrates, which corresponds to their relatively low structure. According to WUNDT deep-going body operations, for instance, may be carried out without the fish making movements of defense, provided that no major nerves are disturbed. Anglers know that fishes start to take the bait immediately again, despite the fact that the hook has just been removed from their mouths. From this one may conclude that the sensation of pain was only minute. Notwithstanding this, it is a known fact that fishes feel pain.

sense of smell of fishes: see SENSORY ORGANS.

sense of taste: see SENSORY ORGANS.

sensory organs and functions of fishes: Their sensory organs are the bridges which connect animals with the surrounding world. In all vertebrates they resemble those also possessed by man. Besides these, though, fishes, which are adapted to life in water, and thus to completely different ambient conditions, have developed some additional sensory organs, which find no comparison in our world of ideas.

Despite this one may keep up the current groupings of sensory organs into those of touch, smell, taste, hearing, and sight.

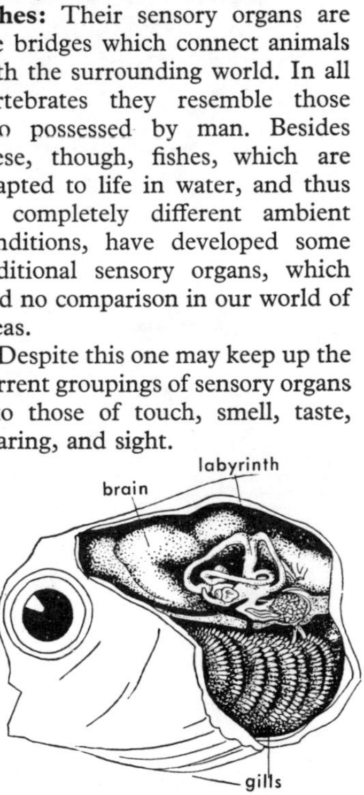

Labyrinth organ of an Ellritze

The sense of touch (tactile sense) puts the fish into a position to feel differences in temperature and pain, to sense contacts, and movements of the water which either result from the current or else through its own or through movements of foreign bodies. The sensation of pain in fishes has already been discussed under the entry Sensations of Pain in Fishes. Besides this, it is a known fact that the epidermis of fishes is sensitive to sudden fluctuations in temperature, to which it is almost never subject in Nature, though. More important, and playing a big role in the life of fishes is the real tactile sense, with the aid of which not only direct contacts may be perceived, but also far-off firm or motile objects, and the slightest movement of the water. All fishes, or at least the greater number of them, live permanently in a more or less dim twilight. As far as cave-dwellers and inhabitants of the deep zones are concerned, some of them are surrounded by nearly complete, or even utter darkness.

For these the tactile sense must play a big role, and indeed the whole surface of their bodies is covered with numerous sensory buds, which as endings of nerve fibers transmit stimuli of contact and concussion with the aid of thin, ciliate, little rods. The sensory buds are concentrated in some places, especially on the head, on and in the mouth, on the barbels and frequently also on certain fins. On many fishes the rodiets lie free on the surface, on others they are hidden in pits or furrows in the epidermis, filled with mucus; many fishes show both kinds. The sensory buds transmit immediate contacts, but many, as was already stated, may also be organs of the so-called tele-tactile sense. Most fishes show additional rows of sensory buds along a certain line of the body, which is located in a narrow channel beneath the skin and the scales, and which is filled with mucus.

In order to permit them to establish a connection with the surrounding world, the scales are pierced at the corresponding places. When closely observed, this region is seen as a thin line, which runs along the flanks of these fishes, either straight or in variably arched curves. Sometimes this lateral line as it is called (*Linea lateralis*, *L. lat.* for short) is only short and pierces only a few scales, and sometimes it may even be lacking totally. Notwithstanding this, also in the latter case we may presume the presence of similar sensory perceptions, only that then the functions of the teletactile sense are exerted by the free sensory buds. For this reason it may happen that in fishes which normally have a lateral line the teletactile sense is preserved even after the destruction of this organ. The lateral line often branches out at the head, that is, it divides into several arms. In any case, fishes are able to sense even the most minute movements of the water may they result from their own motions, from the approach to firm objects or to other animals, or from the movements of others. The sensitivity to currents protects the fishes against collisions even if the eyes are unable to see. Furthermore, according to Wundsch, Bleaks, for instance, eat much larger quantities of mosquito larvae that live in the mud, than of the lazier surface forms of same, due to the fact that their movements stimulate their tactile sense. Perception through the eyes is in this case impossible in the dark depths. Probably the lateral line is also significant for keeping the equilibrium.

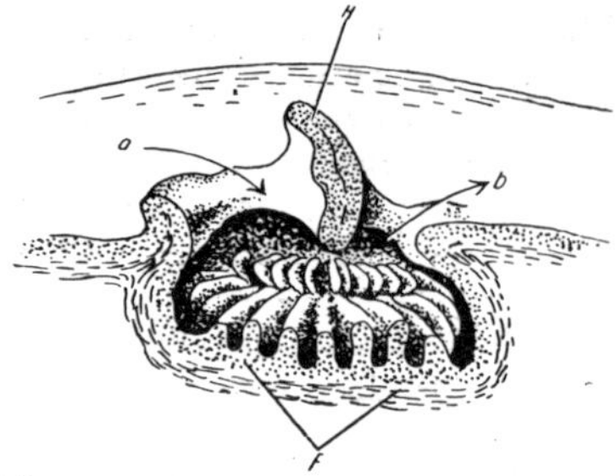

Olfactory pit of an Ellritze. H. Skin protuberance - F. Folds at the base of the olfactory pit - a. front opening b. rear opening (after v. Frisch).

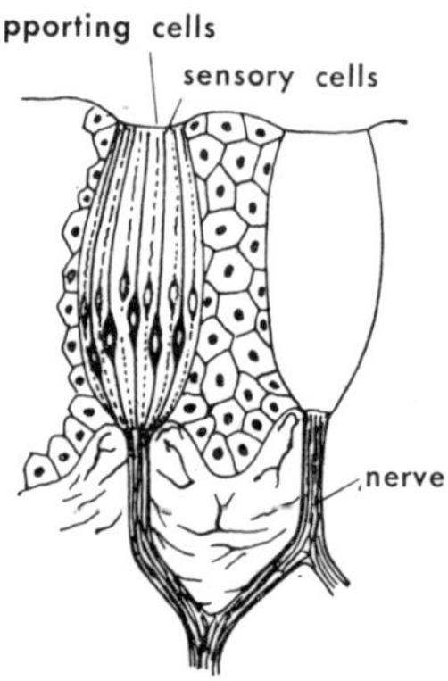

Taste buds from the gum membrane of a Tench (after Butschli).

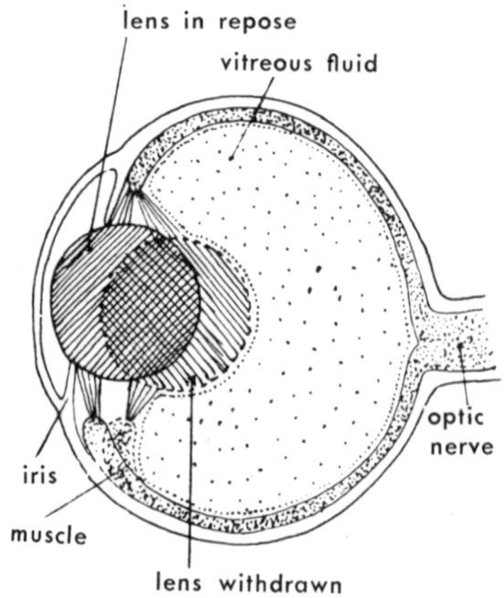

Eye of a bony fish.

The sense of equilibrium has its seat in the static organ, which in a certain way belongs to the fore part of the lateral organs. It is located in the inner ear and consists, among others, of a skin labyrinth with arcades. In the *Ostariophysi* the labyrinth is connected with the swimming bladder by means of a chain of small bonelets, called "Weber's Apparatus". In some other species the linkage is established in a different manner.

The inside of the labyrinth is filled with a liquid. In it are found two or three sensory spots, where the little ear stones or otoliths rest on sensory hairs, on which they exert pressure in case of a change of position. Thus they show the fish its stance in the water and trigger motion reflexes that reestablish the normal position. Also stronger commotions are perceived by the static organ. While the parts that act as organ of equilibrium are well developed, the same cannot be said of the so-called auditory labyrinth which in higher vertebrates, and also in man, perceives sounds. This led to the belief that fishes are deaf, while their sensitivity to sound, which can still be noticed, may derive from the sensitively developed tactile and commotional sense. In attempts at training, however, it has been verified that a great number of fishes (as far as they were tested) react to sounds, while careful attention was given to eliminating other factors which might have led to sensory perceptions. Thus it was possible to train Minnows and Dwarf Catfishes to the sound of whistles and other instruments, and even to cause two Dwarf Cichlids to respond to their names.

This proves that there must be a sensitivity to sound in many fishes, even if not strongly developed, which is in accordance with its minute biological significance. Besides, this many noises are probably perceived as commotions by means of the tactile sense.

The sense of taste has its seat in the so-called 'tumbler' cells. These are tumbler-shaped organs, which are scattered over the whole body of the fish, but are found mainly on the lips, the barbels, the oral cavity, and on some fins, for instance the threadlike fins of many Anabantids. These tumbler cells are surrounded by a protective wall, and protrude from the epidermis. Besides the chemical stimulus of taste, they also react to differences in temperature.

The sense of smell is bound to the paired nasal pits, which are located on the snout, a little above the mouth and to the sides of it. Inside them an olfactory mucosa, disposed in folds, is found. Often the nasal pits are divided into a front and a rear opening by a skin bridge placed over them. The openings may also be extended as tubes (narines). As a rule there is no connection to the oral cavity, that is, the nose pits end blind. They are built in a manner that water flows through them while swimming, and besides this many fishes are able to adjust this flow by means of special muscles.

With regard to taste and smell fishes find themselves in a special position through the fact that they live in water. Man smells the substances that are diffused through the air in the form of gases, and tastes only the four main groups: sweetness, bitterness, saltiness, and sourness. Both sensations, though, combine, and may yield a common perception. Chemical stimuli that are bound to gases naturally cannot affect fishes. Notwithstanding this, fishes can undoubtedly sense smell substances which go even beyond the four abovementioned qualities of taste further to these themselves. The fact in itself that they have nose pits leads to this conclusion.

Again attempts at training have proved that fishes can scent substances that the water current leads to them, and which are tested in the nasal pits. Also from the life in nature it is known that, for instance, school fishes secrete a substance which contributes to keep the swarm together. In Minnows a secretion of wounded members of the swarm triggers a flight reaction (see FRIGHT SUBSTANCES). The four qualities of taste, sweetness, sourness, saltiness, and bitterness are perceived even in solutions that are so weak that they can no more affect our human taste organs. Also in this the pronounced biological need may be responsible for the development of just these two sensory organs. The hunting for food during twilight or in darkness undoubtedly demands an efficient ability to smell. Keeping them in aquaria has also made it known that fishes absolutely do not take all foods without choosing, but that they make noticeable selections according to qualities which appeal to them. It is not without reason that some water bugs protect themselves against being devoured by means of their foetid glands.

The development of the eyes, which serve the sense of sight is good in fishes. It is a fact that certain bottom fishes have quite small eyes, but in general one may say that the eyes of fishes are large and well developed. They are adapted for seeing over short distances, as generally there is no possibility of looking at far places. A fish's eyes are able to put twilight to very good use, due to a series of contrivances. The lens is hard and unchangeable. It protrudes far out, so that light may incide on it from

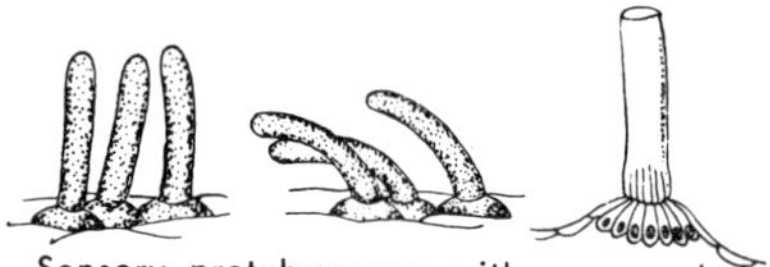

Sensory protuberances with sensory hairs - a and b, of an Ellritze - c, of a Goby. The hairs in b are bent over by a stream of water from the right.

all sides. Therefore the concentration of the rays on the back of the eyes is as intense as possible. In many fishes this back screen shines due to an inlay of luminescent crystals, thus causing complete exploitation of the weak light as if it were a reflector. The accumulation of visual cells, just at the spots where there is the weakest incidence of light guarantees a further heightening of the profiting from the light. The cornea is flat, only little vaulted. The eye is built for seeing from close up, and has to be accommodated to greater distances by means of a special muscle which approaches cornea and retina to each other. After releasing the muscular tension it returns automatically to its normal position. In general one may say that fresh water fishes of the more intensely lit shore regions and of shallow waters enjoy the best developed eyes.

Attempts at training have shown that fishes possess a well-developed capacity for seeing images. During this it has been proved that specimens that were tested learned to differentiate even geometrical

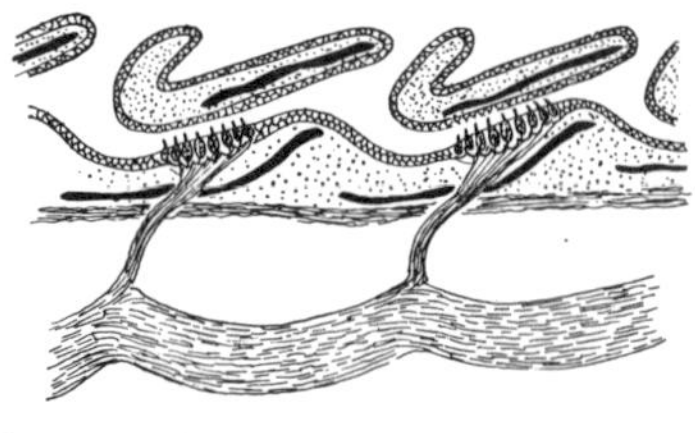

Diagram of a section from the lateral line - the scales form canals where the nerves end in sensory hairs.

figures and letters with minor differences. Also the color sense is quite well developed. Thus the physiological change of colors (see COLORS OF FISHES) having for its aim the accommodation to the surroundings, acts through the eyes and is lost in blinded fishes. In general one may presume that under appropriate conditions fishes see each other in colors, which of course does not mean that the so-called mating colors have also a biological meaning in the choice of partners. The range of the scale of colors reaches even into the spectrum of the ultra-violet rays, which are invisible to the human eye.

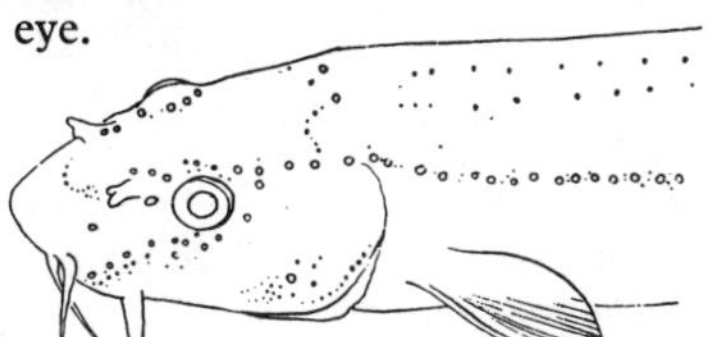

Lateral organs of a Loach. Dots represent sensory protuberances, and circles the pores of the lateral canals.

Summing up, we have to state that we can conclude on the sensory functions of fishes only through their behavior, in which a series of manners of reactions permit cautious comparisons with human behaviors. Others again, as for instance, the tele-tactile sense, are absolutely unlike anything we can imagine, since we do not possess a similar organ. Therefore we must avoid humanizing the manners of behavior of fishes, and also not to imagine that they have feelings that are similar to ours. At least, there is nothing we can say about this. We do not know which 'feelings' move a female fish when seeing a beautifully colored male, and whether there are any such feelings at all, beyond the purely physiological functions. The only trustworthy method, with which one may obtain relatively objective results, is Training.

serpae: Coming from Serpa, a place on the Amazon.
— *Hyphessobrycon callistus.*

Serpae Tetra, the: see HYPHESSOBRYCON CALLISTUS SERPAE.

Serrasalminae: Saw Characins, Saw Tetras.
Sub-family of predatory Disc Characins belonging to the family of the Characins or *Characidae*, of high body build, strongly compressed laterally, the belly edged with saw-like toothed scales. The jaws are equipped each with a row of very strong and extremely sharp teeth. The *Serrasalminae* are very ferocious carnivores, which may become dangerous even to bigger mammals and humans.

They are hardly fit for keeping in the home aquarium, but are excellent subjects for large show installations. Fresh imports often are very frail, probably due to insufficient and inadequate feeding during the transportation. Such weakened specimens are dejected and 'harmless'. The most resistant ones are smaller fishes, which also take food with less difficulty. Domesticated fishes demand care when feeding, as they bite everything that moves. For domestication offer them live fishes at first, and later on meat in whole pieces, which the fishes themselves cut to size by biting off walnut-sized pieces. They often devour each other, even in very big tanks. According to HECK JR. they may be kept in schools, if always well fed. Normally-behaving fishes are then almost never attacked, and the critical moment arrives only when new fishes are put into the Piranha tank. The dazed instant of these is generally considered as the signal to attack by the Piranhas. Generally the *S.* are very nervous.

Temperature 68-77° F. Breeding them in the aquarium should hardly be possible. Reproduction unknown. Genera, among others, *Pygocentrus*, *Rooseveltiella*, and *Serrasalmo*.

Serrasalmo: Saw Characin.
South American genus of Characins belonging to the sub-family of the *Serrasalminae*, with about 12 known species, which differ from the other genera of the family by the kind of teeth with which they are equipped.

— rhombeus Linné: The Spotted Piranha.
A somewhat elongated species, otherwise as per description of the sub-family. D 16-19, A 31-36. Scales very small. The belly edge is equipped with 30-33 tooth scales. Length up to 14″.
COLOR: Dull silver with many irregular gray spots. Sexual differences are unknown.
ORIGIN: Guiana and the Amazon region.

Serrasalmo rhombeus

sessiliflora: With sitting flowers.
— *Limnophila*.

setacea: Bristly.
— *Isoetes*.

setivimensis: After Setiv, the finding place, in North Africa.
— *Barbus* (*Puntius*).

setting up the aquarium: The manner of setting up an aquarium depends on the goal one wants to achieve. A purely ornamental aquarium is set up according to different basic ideas than those that prevail in, for instance, a breeding tank or one used for scientific observations.

Therefore the first thing to do is to establish clearly what you want to achieve and which fishes and plants you want to keep.

If the installation you want to set up is composed of several tanks, try to avoid monotonous uniformity in the decorations. Do not repeat yourself in the use of the decorative means and their placement, and try to create the diversity which finds its motivation in the different origins of fishes and plants. For school fishes of the open water, for instance, use only sand or gravel as a bottom covering, or else larger, rounded stones and rocks taken from the bottom of streams. Fishes of the shore regions, which like caves, should receive rock and root structures, the rocks of which may be a little more sharp-edged.

In addition to plants you may also make use of the following ornaments:

ROCKS are a very effective and natural means with which an aquarium may be installed in a tasteful manner. Slabs of slate, for instance, are especially adequate for setting off rear walls and terraces. The so-called Ancient Rocks (granite, gneiss, basalt, etc.) are preferable to all others, on one hand because they hardly are apt to release hardening substances into the water; on the other because they supply trace elements which may further the life of animals and plants. Calcareous stones, which have a hardening effect, should not be used in connection with fishes which need soft water as a primary condition for their well-being or for breeding. Rocks which contain metals, too, are only rarely usable. Sandstone may also contain hardeners, but it is easy to mold and therefore well-liked. Avoid using rocks with too sharp edges. Dark stones, like dark bottoms, enhance the colors of the fishes.

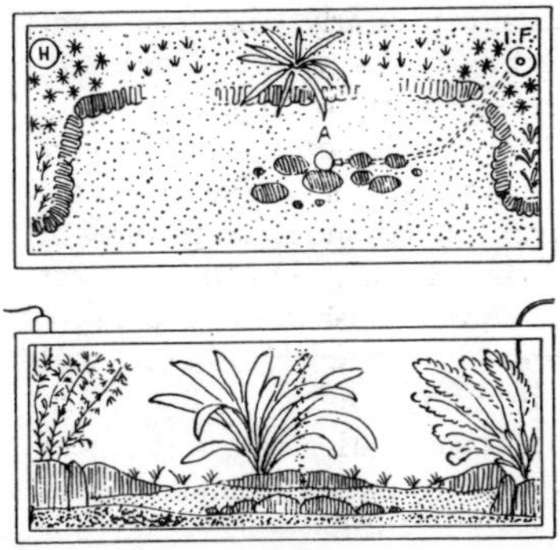

Top and side view of a tank for school fishes

A decoration which enjoys the preference of many hobbyists is petrified wood, which may be cemented together to make rear wall coverings, etc. Any such structures should always be well rinsed and watered before placing them in your aquarium even if they contain only minute quantities of cement. Petrified wood, too, shows some effect on the hardness of water, and should not be used where soft water is desired. According to HARDT and KNACK petrified wood seems also to release nitrates into the water.

Roots of plants, too, are valued as ornaments. Give preference to the roots of alders and willow-trees found under overhanging banks of brooks or ponds. Dead roots are better than live ones, and they should whenever possible have been in water for quite some time. Make sure, also, that they do not show any rotting spots, and boil them for at least one hour before using. Roots have to be weighted down initially with rocks or the like, as they possess a strong buoyancy, which, however, diminishes with time as they grow waterlogged. You can also achieve very beautiful effects with cane stems, ranging from native reeds to bamboo. They may simply be stuck into the bottom soil, where they stand for long periods without rotting. It is advisable previously to dip the tips of these in some waterproof cement. Even so, canes have to be replaced periodically.

Something especially advisable is the use of coconut SHELLS, which not only look ornamental, but are also used as hiding caves by cave-dwelling fishes or fishes which are caring for their broods. Such shells look much more natural than the commonly-used flower pots, and are safer than rock caves, which may cave in if undermined by rooting fishes. Cut the coconuts in half with a small-toothed saw, or cut them to any desired shape or size. They are ready for immediate use after removing the contents, meat and milk. It is safer, though, to rinse them for a few days. Holes of any desired size may be made with a red-hot piece of iron, and the smooth edges may be turned irregular by using nippers. Many kinds of advice have been given for shaping the rear walls of aquaria, something which is especially important if the tank is placed in front of a wall of the house. The simplest solution is to paint the rear pane with some quick-drying paint. You will achieve an interest-

Top and side view of a tank for fishes which like to hide

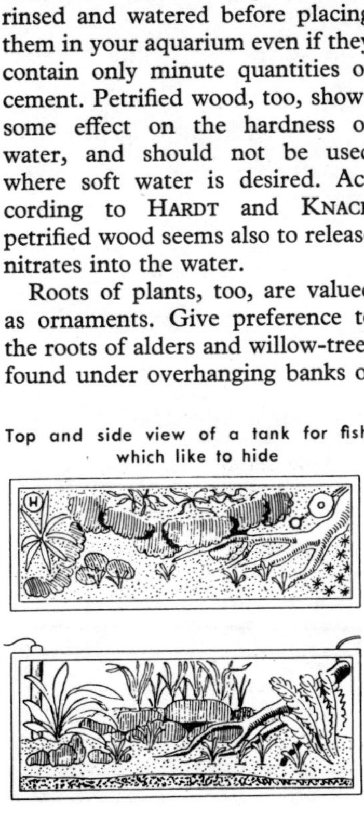

ing effect if you do not put an even coat on it, but if you speckle the rear pane by irregular touches with a paint brush. Quite uncommon and bizarre designs may be created by pressing another glass pane on the still-wet rear pane after painting it. If this is taken way again immediately, the results will look something like ice crystals. It must be said, however, that painted rear walls generally look unnatural. Rear wall decorations placed inside the tank may be cemented together in all kinds of patterns. Be careful, though, not to make them too weighty, nor to leave any open space between them and the rear pane, so that no fish may hide there. Most aquaristic magazines give further periodical hints on this. Well-rinsed peat bricks and slabs, too, have lately been used successfully. They are easy to shape, and may even serve as substrata for plants.

The most effective, and simultaneously the most harmless and space-saving manner of ornamenting rear walls is the background decoration placed behind the aquarium, either on a large wooden board, or else in a big box. With some imagination this will permit you to create the most beautiful and natural effects by using rocks, roots, peat, pieces of cork, cane, etc. Such a background will hardly ever look unnatural and makes the tank appear much wider than it really is. Background decorations may be illuminated by a small light bulb in case of need.

K. THURM recommends using loose peat fibers mixed with a thin glue, which are scattered over a fiber plate with pieces of wood stuck into them. The kind of bottom soil to be used, the ornamental means, such as rocks, roots, etc., the previously prepared water, and the necessary acces-

Rocks in the aquarium. Left-hand picture shows how flat rocks can be piled on their edges to form a background. Right-hand picture shows how narrow, flat rocks can be stacked atop each other for a striated effect.

sories, depend on the aim for which the tank is set up. All this should be very well pondered before you really begin to set up your aquaria. It is always good advice to make a complete plan for this, if possible even a drawing. After you have reached a clear concept of what you want to do, start gathering all accessories, and make sure they are in perfect working order. That you have already chosen the right site (see LOCATING THE AQUARIUM) should be considered self-evident. However, consider still that there have to be possibilities of plugging your accessories into electrical outlets. The spotlessly clean aquarium has already been placed in its location several days previously, and has been filled in order to check whether it will hold water without leaking. Now it should be emptied and smaller leaks plugged with waterproof cement.

A backdrop for the aquarium can be prepared by sketching or painting a screen of the same size as the back and hanging it in place.

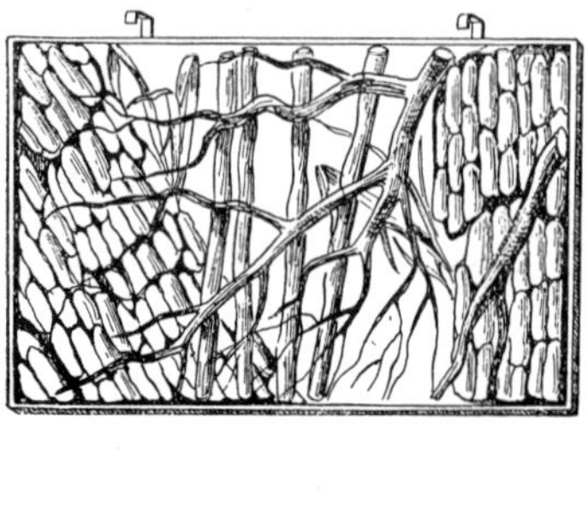

Now put in the planned mixture of bottom soil in a moist state, beginning with the first layer, which contains more plant foods. In tanks intended for strongly-rooting fishes, Cichlids, for instance, you had better first place the rock caves and structures on the bare bottom plate, then put a sufficiently strong layer of clean-washed gravel around them to hold them in place.

After having spread the bottom layer of soil over the whole surface, press it down evenly with a flat piece of wood, and soak up carefully any excess water with a sponge, in order to avoid that it may filter through the cover layer and cloud your water.

Then distribute your rocks on their intended places. Plants in dishes too are imbedded in the soil, leaving $\frac{3}{8}''$ to $\frac{3}{4}''$ of the rims visible, depending on how thick you intend to make the cover layer.

The ancient rule, which says that the bottom soil should slant to one side in order to permit the accumulation of mulm at the deepest spot, is also followed in the present case, without making this an absolute must, though. What is commonly called the 'mud corner' is not absolutely indispensable. If you have set up a terraced structure, which offers the best possibilities for an ornamental disposition of the plants, press the supporting rocks deep into the bottom layer in order to avoid cave-ins.

If you want, you may already install the air ducts for the aerator stone. Bent glass tubing is very good for this, and plastic better still. If you plan to use an underground filter with a filtering bell located in the bottom soil, this too may be set up at this moment. Finally spread the cover layer of clean-washed sand over the whole. Choose finer- or coarser-grained

Aquarium decorations

sand, according to the needs of your animals and plants, or you might even alternate them in spots. After having again soaked up any excess water with a sponge from the cover layer, you may place the remainder of the accessories in the tank. After finishing this task, distribute smaller stones and gravel, which should simultaneously hold down and cover the accessories. During all these steps you have of course paid attention to your previously drawn plan showing the location of your plants. If you are working from a drawing, you will have done this anyway. Now proceed with the planting, but remember that the best is first to fill in the water and then to place the plants.

Filling up with water is done after previously spreading a sheet of packing paper over the whole bottom of the tank, and then to bring in the water from a bucket that is placed above the aquarium with a rubber hose. This will help you to avoid roiling.

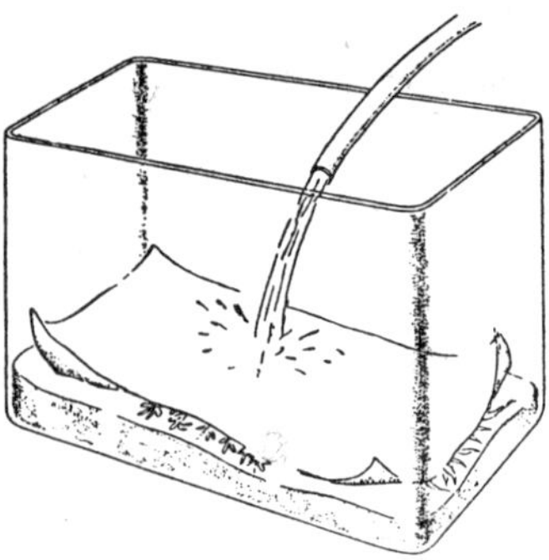

How to fill an aquarium without disturbing plants and gravel

The final step is to cover the tank with a cover glass. Connect the accessories and leave the whole standing for about a week in order to give it time to establish a certain biological equilibrium, and also to give the plants time to strike roots. After this time your aquarium is ready, and you may stock it with fishes and other animals.

severum: Severe.
— *Cichlasoma.*

sexfasciatus: With six stripes.
— *Epiplatys.*

sexual differentiation: As sexual differences we can in the first place consider the primary (direct) characteristics of sex, i.e., the sexual organs of which externally in most cases only the sexual openings are more or less plainly visible. Only in rare cases they are somewhat increased in size and therefore recognizable in their sexually differentiated construction (for instance in many Cichlids), or else they may be transformed into copulation organs.

The aquarist, though, generally only calls on the secondary (or indirect) sexual characteristics for differentiating the sexes, as the primary ones are not visible externally. It is these he thinks of when speaking of sexual differentiation. The sexes of many fishes are more or less distinguishable from a purely external point of view, and sometimes we even find a pronounced dimorphism. In certain cases the difference may only be slight, for instance in Sunfish, *Pterophyllum*, etc. In such cases the breeders usually observe the genital papilla, which protrudes more distinctly shortly before spawning, and is generally slender and pointed in the male, being heavier, and conically blunted in the female. Here and there, as for instance, in *Mesogonistius chaetodon*, there appear transitory differences in color during the act of spawning itself. In most cases the females are recognizable as such during the spawning season due to their greater plumpness, which is noticed especially when looking from above. In difficult cases of slim and transparent fishes, for instance, some of the Characins, *Trichopsis*, and others, one may also pay attention to the body contents, which may be visible due to transparence, and will supply indications as to sexual classification. Often the sexes are of different sizes, in some cases the males being bigger, in others the females. Of course this is a characteristic to which one may only take recourse in the case of full-grown specimens.

Greater intensity of color applies mostly to the male sex. Either both sexes are of basically the same color, which becomes more intense on the males during the procreation period, or else they are completely different. This difference in color and design may go to a point where only an expert can decide that a pair belongs together and to the same species. There arise considerable difficulties for instance in Tooth Carps, where the sexes may differ noticeably in size and shape. Often the color differences appear only during the spawning period

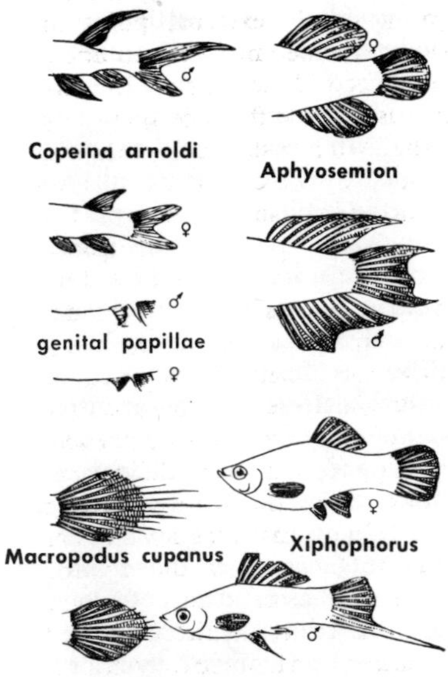

Sex differences

(mating colors). Outside of this period telling the sexes apart may possibly not be very easy. Occasionally both sexes possess the same intense mating colors, and in some cases even the female may be the more highly colored one. This generally happens in those species where the female participates very actively in the spawning business. Simultaneously with the colors, often there appear also noticeable differences in the fins, e.g. swords, high dorsals, threadlike extensions of fin rays, general increase in fin size, etc. (ornamental fins). Also these characteristics belong almost totally to the male sex. Very frequently the males show vertical fins that are pointed at the tips, while those of the females remain rounded (Anabantids, Cichlids, etc.). Occasionally we also find pronounced peculiarities in body shape. In the live bearing Tooth Carps these are explainable by means of the special functions of the female body, but they may appear independently of this, as for instance in the height of older males of *Limia nigrofasciata*. In some groups, e.g. Cyprinids, appears a grainy rash on the head and the front part of the body during the mating season.

sexual mutation: Change of Sex. The fact, observed in fishes, that especially females which already have a normal time of procreation behind them, change into males thereafter.

Sexual mutation has been established as a certainty up to this date in Anabantids and especially in live bearing Tooth Carps (*Poeciliinae*). The process has been the subject of comprehensive investigation, especially in Swordtails (*Xiphophorus helleri*).

According to Breider, the sex of a Swordtail is established at the moment of fertilization. During the embryonic stage the germinal glands are not differentiated, neither to the male, nor to the female side, but it is established hereditarily whether they will develop into testicles or into ovaries. Equally fixed is the eventual moment of sexual differentiation, but it may be accelerated or slowed down by influences of the ambient world. In their earliest stage of youth the fry have an undifferentiated germinal gland. After being born, all of them go through a feminine phase. In due time they begin to develop the hereditarily established sexual organs, the females remaining female, the males changing over definitely. It may happen, though, that individual male fishes at first keep the female organs, so that the change is delayed. This may happen especially often in certain tribes. On the other hand such delays may occur where there are very poor external conditions (for instance lack of space, low temperatures, poor food). Thus, changes may occur only after 3 to 6 months and, under certain extreme circumstances, only shortly before the end of life. In the meantime these 'males' have developed female sexual organs, and may produce perfectly normal young. When the production of the female hormone ceases in fishes that hereditarily are males and which after several litters come to the final stage of life, a late, incomplete change may still happen. These changed 'female' males may be told apart from the normal males by their sturdy shape and size. The process of changing over puts a great strain on the fish. They keep quieter than is normal, retire into hiding places, and the belly line draws in. Many of the late changers die off. If they withstand the process, they soon show a change in behavior. Finally the secondary sexual characters develop, in Swordtails for instance, the sword. In incompletely changed specimens a real change often does not take place. The ovaries remain but shrink up, and no gonopodium is formed.

sexual organs of fishes: Fishes are heterosexual. The sexes (males and females) are more or less differentiated from each other, always by means of primary sexual characteristics, and in many cases also through secondary ones. Fishes possess paired sexual organs. They are located on the two sides of the spine, within the abdominal cavity. In rare cases they may be united into one unpaired sac. In some fishes, for instance the *Salmonidae*, the sexual products are emptied directly into the belly cavity, and are eliminated from there through paired openings (abdominal pores). In the male *Chondrostei* the testicles are attached to the kidneys by means of canals, the semen being emptied through these in the same manner as the urine. The eggs, similar to what happens with the *Salmonidae*, fall directly into the abdominal opening, but are led into the free water by means of a canal that is located along the urinary duct. In most bony fishes the testicles and ovaries change over into the seminal canals, respectively the oviducts, which end together with the urinary duct in a papilla behind the cloaca (genital papilla, genital pores.) In some fishes this papilla is the only visible external sexual characteristic, as for instance in *Pterophyllum*. The paired seminal ducts and oviducts in many bony fishes melt into a single, unpaired canal. The female sexual opening may at times be extended into an ovipositor, as happens notedly with the Bitterling. Viviparous (livebearing) fishes present more or less complex copulatory organs which (in bony fish) are formed from the anal fin. The females of these species often possess special, bag-like tiltings in the oviduct, in which the semen—which often is sufficient for several litters—is kept. Furthermore ovaries or oviducts are enlarged into brood bags in which the eggs go through their development up to the stage where the young become able to swim. Feeding by means of a special food liquid or by feeding strings coming from the body of the mother occurs only in very rare cases.

Sharks: see LABEO.

Sharp-Toothed Tetra, the: see MICRALESTES ACUTIDENS.

Shave-Grasses: see EQUISETACEAE.

Sheepshead Top Minnow, the: see CYPRINODON VARIEGATUS.

shelfordi: After a personal name. — *Acantophthalmus*.

sheljuzhkoi: After a personal name. — *Epiplatys*.

Short-Head Characin, the: see HEMIBRYCON GUPPYI.

Short-Tail Eels, the: see SYMBRANCHII.

shoutedeni: After a personal name.

— *Tetraodon.*

shrimps: see NATANTA.

Siamese Fighting Fish, the: see BETTA.

Siamese Fighting Fish, the: see BETTA SPLENDENS.

Siamese Sucker Loach, the: see GYRINOCHEILUS AYMONIERI.

Side-Dash Rasbora, the: see RASBORA LATERISTRIATA.

Side-Spot Barb, the: see LUCIOSOMA SPILOPLEURA.

Siebold, Karl Theodor Ernst von: 1804-1885. German zoologist who, after extensive research wrote the comprehensive book "Die Suesswasserfische Mitteleuropas" (The Fresh Water Fishes of Central Europe). One of the most competent experts on the world of German and European fishes.

signata: Marked.

— *Belontia.*

signatus: Marked.

— *Pseudomugil.*

silicous earth: Shells of fossil diatoms (silicous algae), which forms large deposits called diatomaceous earth. Due to its resistance and permeability, silicous earth is used in manufacturing aeration stones for aquaria. See AERATION.

Siluridae: Genuine Catfishes.

Family pertaining to the sub-order of the Catfish-like or *Siluroidea*, with completely naked skin. The anal fin is long, the dorsal may be lacking. The family comprises, among others, the native German species, *Siluris glanis.*

Siluroidea: The Catfish-like.

A widely distributed sub-order, rich in species, pertaining to the order of the *Ostariophysi*. The only place on earth where no Catfishes are found are the arctic regions. According to their genetic history they are a quite ancient group of fishes.

The Catfish-like are highly specialized fishes, which differ from the other *Ostariophysi* by having the body completely naked, or else covered with bony plates or bony excrescences, but have in common with them the linkage between the two-compartmented swimming bladder and the ear labyrinth by the so-called Weber's apparatus. Many Catfishes possess an adipose fin, the dorsals and pectorals sometimes showing a heavy first spine. The body is either covered with only a mucous, rugged skin, or else one finds the abovementioned excrescences in the form of armor plates, spines, etc.

All Catfishes are highly interesting inhabitants of the aquarium, which deserve more observation than they generally find. Some of them are pronounced predators, many feed on small aquatic animals and their larvae which hide in the ground, many also on detritus and plants. Most of them lead a hidden, often nocturnal life. Only a few species are day-fishes, which live in loosely connected schools. Generally they feel the need to find security in caves, hiding places, or near firm objects. This should be taken into consideration when setting up the aquarium.

Unfortunately so far breeding has only succeeded in a few cases, since it is often difficult to offer Catfishes natural conditions of life. The sub-order comprises the folfowing families: *Allysidae, Amblycepsidae, Ameiuridae, Amphylidae, Ariide, Auchenipteridae, Bagridae,* Banjo-Fishes or *Bunocephalidae,* Armored Catfishes or *Callichthyidae,* Gill Sac Catfishes or *Clariidae, Diplomyptidae,* Thorn Catfishes or *Doradidae, Helogenidae,* Armored Catfishes or *Loricariidae,* Electric Catfishes or *Malapteruridae, Pagasidae, Pimelodidae, Plotosidae, Pygidiidae,* Glass Catfishes or *Schilbeidae,* Genuine Catfishes or *Siluridae, Sisoridae, Trichomysteridae.*

Silver Bush Fish, the: see CTENOPOMA ARGENTOVENTER.

Silver Dollar, the: see CTENOBRYCON SPILURUS.

Silver Hatchet Fish, the: see THORACOCHARAX SECURIS.

Silver Rasbora, the: see RASBORA ARGYROTAENIA.

Silver Tetra, the: see CTENOBRYCON SPILURUS.

singa: After the native name.
— *Aphyosemion:* see APHYOSEMION SCHOUTEDENI.

single-germinating-leaved plants: see MONOCOTYLEDONEAE.

Six-Banded Panchax, the: see EPIPLATYS SEXFASCIATUS.

sjoestedti: After a personal name.
— *Aphyosemion.*

skeleton of fishes, the: The skeleton of fishes is either cartilaginous or else more or less ossified. Its nature supplies important characteristics of differentiation for the different groups of fishes. Thus, for instance, it is used to differentiate the two great groups of the cartilaginous fishes and the bony fishes. It is true, however, that the transitions between both are a little obscure, and also that in many bony fishes the skeleton may still be cartilaginous in part.

The dorsal spine is the core piece of the skeleton. It is divided into a trunk part and a tail part. In most lower forms the Back String (see CHORDA DORSALIS) is still extensively preserved, but in most fishes it ever more squeezed in during the development of the egg, and finally totally displaced. The tail part of the dorsal column lends the necessary firmness to the tail fin, which is important for locomotion. In the more primitive fishes, it is extended into the upper tip of the tail, being heterocercal (for instance in Sharks and Sturgeons), while in all other fishes it bends upwards at the root of the caudal fin and carries the supporting bones for the fin rays, being homocercal. The symmetry of the tail fin is only apparent.

The dorsal column is composed of a variable number of vertebral bodies. These are connected on the upper side to vaulted pieces which embody the spinal marrow. The vertebral bodies carry extensions also downwards, through which runs the great body artery. Connected with these there is a series of thorny extensions, which rise from the upper vertebral vaults, in the tail part also from the lower ones; furthermore there are the articulated link pieces of the vertebrae, and finally the ribs which enclose the ventral cavity. Special formations are also the so-called spines, which separate the layers of muscles and are ossified separating walls, similar to conjunctive tissues. In principle the axial skeleton is the same for most species of fishes, but in part it is also very much differentiated in single details.

In its front part the dorsal spine is connected with the skull. We shall not describe here the details of the skull of a cartilaginous fish, but shall only make a resumé of single parts of the skull of bony fishes, as in aquaristic literature one often finds references made to them. Not all parts of the skull are totally ossified. To the contrary, in the course of the individual development it is at first built of cartilage. Only later appear bones, which partially deposit over the cartilage, or are formed by the tissue. The head is limited in the upper and lower sides by the occipitals, which may be seen clearly on fishes the head of which is not covered with scales. Many of the bones which in higher animals are grown together, still exist as single bone elements in fishes. Thus, for instance, the lower jaw is still

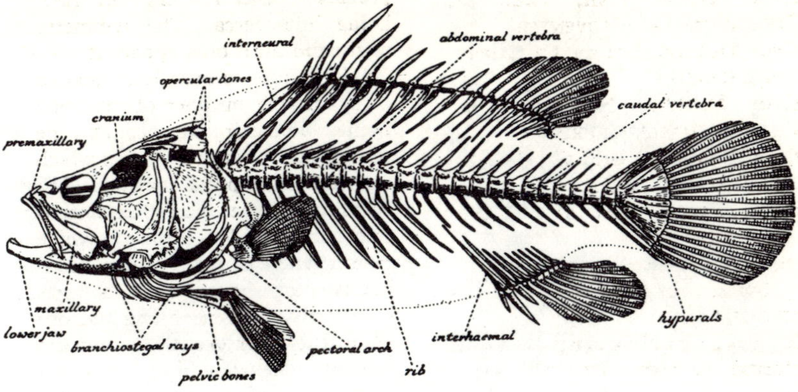

Skeleton of a bony fish

composed of three separate bones, the dental, the articular (which in higher vertebrates has gone over into the ear), and the angular bone (which too goes into the ear). These three bones together compose the mandibular bone. The principal bones of the upper skull are the frontal and the parietal. Both are paired. The lower skull is composed, among others, of the ethmoids, the pterygoids, the sphenoids, the orbitals, and the hyomandibular. To the rear the skull is closed off by the occipitals. The gill opening is closed by the gill cover, which consists of operculum and sub-operculum. The upper jaw is made up of the maxillary and the premaxillary bone, the maxillary often taking over functions other than those of the jaw itself, for instance, that of the base for barbels. The premaxillary acts as the real jaw.

The unpaired fins are deeply imbedded in the muscle tissue on triangular fin carriers, and obtain a certain support from the upper and lower thorny extensions of the dorsal column. The paired pectorals insert on a special shoulder belt, on which, in fishes where they insert on the chest of the throat, also the basal bones of the ventral fins are supported.

skin and skin organs of fishes: The skin of fishes consists of two distinctly differentiated layers: the upper skin or epidermis, and the strong lower skin, or leather skin (cutis).

The epidermis consists of several layers of big and soft cells. Beneath these are many mucus cells to which the fishes owe their slipperiness. It contains only few organs.

Not considering the gland-like luminous cells of certain deep seafishes, though, here we can only mention the nuptial rash of certain Cyprinids, which is formed by the epidermis, as well as some poison glands in which the respective fishes may be connected to fin rays or to spikes on the opercles. In case of wounding, the poison from these may penetrate the wounds and cause prolonged infections, in the case of some tropical species even death for the injured one. The epidermis presents a certain manner of defense against the influences of the ambient water for the cutis, which is rich in organs.

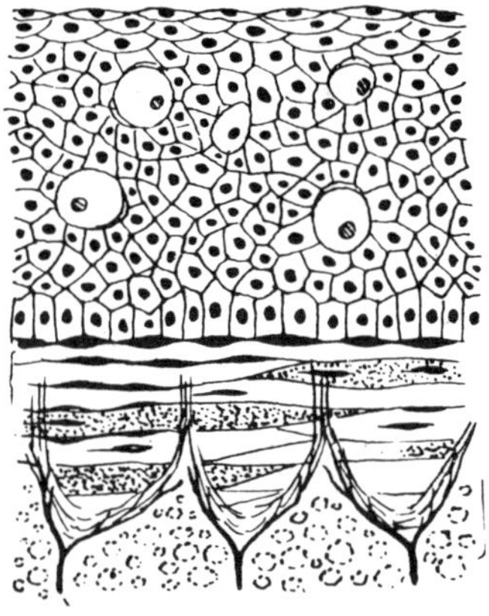

Cross section of a fish's skin

The cutis consists of several layers of conjunctive tissue. It is rich in blood vessels and in nerves. In it are located the organs of the touch-at-distance sense (see SENSORY ORGANS) and the pigmentation cells (see COLORS OF FISHES). The cutis is either naked or else provided with different species of bone formations, for instance skin, teeth, scales, spikes, bony plates, etc. Generally fishes have the scales which are typical for them. These may be formations of different construction. On the Ganoids we find ganoid scales, bony plates, generally diamond-shaped and hard, which are covered with ganoin and possess an enamel-like gloss. The genuine bony fishes show thin and flexible scales, which insert in a scale pocket in the cutis and generally are covered by the epidermis. They are super-imposed in the manner of roof tiles, in length and cross rows,

scales: left, cycloid; right, ctenoid

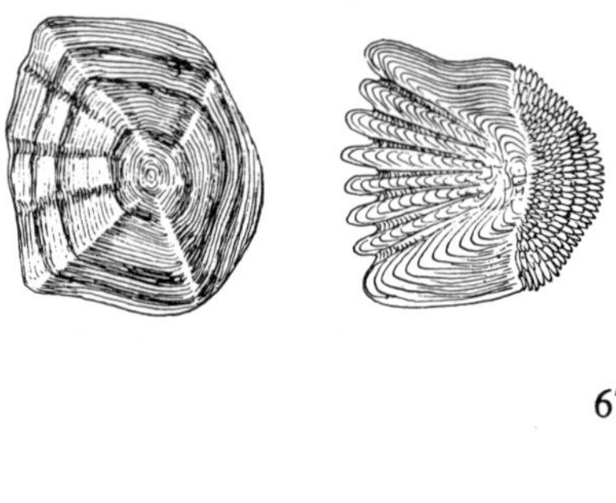

one to two cross rows belonging to each muscle section. The free rim protrudes from the scale pockets. It is either smooth and toothless (cycloid or round scales), or pointed and toothed (ctenoid or comb scales).

Since the scale structure differs enormously in the different groups of fishes, it is taken into consideration when classifying species. For this purpose one uses the scale formula, which is found by counting the longitudinal and the cross rows. Counting the number of scales pierced by the lateral line (or, in case of incompleteness of this organ, by an imaginary line along the middle of the body) one finds the number of cross rows. Starting from there upwards to the insertion of the dorsal fin, and downwards to the root of the ventrals, the total is the number of longitudinal rows. The formula:

$$\text{Sc } 80\text{-}90 \; \frac{8\text{-}10}{17\text{-}20}$$

therefore means that the respective species of fish possesses 80-90 cross rows of scales, 8-10 longitudinal rows on the upper part of the body, and 17-20 on the lower part, totalling 25-30 longitudinal rows of scales. The scales are not changed, but follow along with the growth of the fish. During the growing time ring-shaped layers are deposited on them, which are more separated under favorable conditions, closer together under unfavorable ones. Through these growth rings one may calculate the age of the specimen. In some fish species the scales may be small, degenerated, and deeply imbedded in the skin. In other species they disappear totally.

skin discoloration: Bluish-white discoloration of the epidermis caused by a parasitic animal, accompanied by closing of the fins, scraping and rocking motions, and (secondary) fungus infection. The disease, which in severe cases may lead to death, is contagious and may be caused by several parasites which may co-exist simultaneously. They are:

1. Protozoa: *Trichodina*, *Costia necatrix*, and *Chilodon(ella) cyprinii*.

2. Worms: *Gyrodactilus elegans*, *G. medius*, *G. rarus*, and others, furthermore *Dactylogyrus vastator*, which is mainly a gill parasite. Try to effect treatment whenever possible by instant baths, as longer baths may only be used as a last resort, due to the harm they cause to fishes and plants, in spite of the fact that for convenience's sake they are preferred by fanciers.

Instant baths: (a) Dissolve about ½ oz. kitchen salt in one quart of pure water. Raise the temperature by about 3.5° F. Bathe for approximately 20 minutes.

(b) ¾ to 1⅝ cubic inches of formalin in 2½ gals. of water, carefully mixed and stirred. Raise the temperature a little. Duration of bath: 30-45 minutes.

The baths should be prepared in glass containers, or else in enameled ones. At first always bathe one fish only as a try-out. Fishes that show signs of weakness should be taken out of the bath immediately and put into water of the same temperature.

Prolonged baths: Count 0.6 to 1 gram acriflavine (dissolved in a very small quantity of water) per 25 gallons of water in the installed aquarium. Duration: 2-4 days. After this filter the water until the yellowish-green coloration disappears. One has to take some harm to the plants into account.

After treatment, try to correct errors in the care and keeping of the fishes, as skin discoloration may be the consequence of their weakening through wrong care.

Skull-Less Fishes: see ACRANIA, LANCET FISHES.

sleep of fishes: Numerous species of fishes at night fall into a slumber-like state, on the intensity of which no exact information can be given as no comprehensive observations are available. In all it is dubious whether the state of rest of fishes could be compared to the sleep of higher animals.

Anyway, many fishes fall into a state of decreased activity during daytime, if they are nocturnal fishes, or during the night if they are day fishes. Any aquarist can easily make this observation when at night he suddenly turns on the electric lighting. He will see that most fishes rest in a typical position, generally leaning on plants, the bottom, rocks, or other firm objects. As a rule this state of rest is accompanied by a certain night coloration, which often is quite different from their normal colors. Partially the fishes become very pale, partly very dark, however. Spots and bands may become especially pale, or else they may stand out very intensely. Some groups of fishes, for instance the *Nannostomidae*, possess an especially striking nocturnal color. Such phenomena of coloring may possibly be linked to a typical position of rest or to seeking certain locations.

The states of rest are of different intensities. School fishes of the open water float on one spot, lightly beating their pectorals, but wake up immediately if touched. Other species which live in hiding places or on the bottom need a little more time before becoming active again. Also fry take on typical 'sleeping positions'. Swarms of led young, for instance, those of Cichlids, draw closely together with the beginning of twilight and slowly approach the bottom, where they finally sink to the deepest spot, that is the pit dug by their parents. If the aquarium stays lit, the rest period may be delayed, but after some time even then the swarms take on a rest position. This consists in that the fry crowd closely together and make wagging movements with their tails, while the heads are tilted down.

Slender Rasbora, the: see RASBORA DANICONIUS.

Sleeper Gudgeons: see ELEOTRIDAE.

slipper animalcules: see PARAMECIUM.

Slit Gill Catfishes, the: see SYMBRANCHIDAE.

Small-Scaled Glassfish, the: see ROEBOIDES GUATEMALENSIS.

Small Predator Characin, the: see CRENUCHUS SPILURUS.

Smith, Hugh McCormick: American ichthyologist who wrote comprehensive descriptions of the fish fauna of Thailand after many years of exploring voyages.

Snails: see GASTROPODA.

Snakehead Fishes: see OPHIOCEPHALOIDEA.

Snakehead Loach, the: see ELEOTRIS POROCEPHALA.

Snake-Skinned Gourami, the: see TRICHOGASTER PECTORALIS.

somphongsi: After a geographic name.
— *Tetraodon.*

sophiae: After a place in Iran.
— *Aphanius.*

South and Central America: Central and Southern part of the American Continent, of continental size and sufficiency in itself. For South America this is already seen from its geological development, as North and South America arose as continents in different ages, and their unification through the Central American isthmus took place only later on.

South America comprises an area of about 10.7 million square miles, and the land bridge which connects both continents comprises about 500,000 sq. miles. To this one has to add the area of the West Indian isles, which extend from the Florida peninsula to the mouth of the Orinoco. These isles, the most important of which are the main islands of the Great Antilles, Cuba, Haiti, and Jamaica, as well as Puerto Rico and Trinidad, possess a land area of about 143,000 square miles. Central America measures 1350 miles from the Isthmus of Tehuantepec in the North to the point of insertion in the Gulf of Panama in the South. Mexico, with an area of 1,180,300 square miles, holds an intermediate position between the two part continents as far as animal and plant geography is concerned. It is primarily considered as representing a part of South and Central America in an aquaristic sense.

Mexico with the Californian peninsula in the Northwest and Yucatan in the east, is, excepting a few eastern districts, a strongly mountainous country, some of the highest elevations of which are still active volcanoes (Popocatepetl, 18170 ft.). In the coastal plains, especially in the east, we find mangrove swamps and dunes, behind these savannahs (tree and grass plains), and in the south and southeast, as well as on the eastern slopes of the mountains, tropical jungles, while the western slopes are covered with light forest. The real highlands are characterized by dry plains (cacti, magueys, thorn bushes). The climate in the north and northwest is hot and dry, being tropical in the south, humid and unhealthy on the coast up to a height of about 300 ft. In contrast the highlands are dry, but cool and salubrious.

Central America is a narrow, predominantly mountainous strip of land (its narrowest spot being 30

miles wide), with numerous, partly still active volcanoes. In the lowlands there predominates a humid, tropical climate, on the heights of the mountains, which rise up to about 13,000 ft., a climate with correspondingly decreasing temperatures.

This region, including Mexico, may be considered as one unit. The North Mexican highland with its insufficient rainfalls shows an extensively desert character, with strong daily and seasonal fluctuations of temperature. The coast of South Mexico on its part is rich in swamps, and may experience considerable cooling in winter under the influence of the winds (down to 32° F). Inland larger bodies of water are rare. Due to the mountainous character, the rivers generally have strong gradients and an irregular water level. In Central America itself we find a climatic separation between the Eastern and Western slopes of the mountains. The climate of the Pacific side is influenced by the moist, monsoon-like winds, which cause pronounced rainy seasons in winter, and dry ones in summer. The rainfalls on the Atlantic side depend more on the height of the mountains, which more or less force the northeast trade winds upwards. In the rainy regions one finds tropical jungles (rain forests), in the less rainy districts there are less dense forests or plains with sufficient vegetation. The chain of the Caribbean Islands in general possesses similar climatic conditions. Rivers are found only sparingly. The waters are rather composed of lakes, swamps, ponds, and smaller streams.

The fishes that characterize the whole region are the live bearing Tooth Carps (*Poeciliinae*), together with a number of egg-laying Carps, and a not too great number of Characins and Cichlids. The smaller waters of the Western side and of the islands in general have not favored the development of bigger species of fishes. Only the small, rugged Tooth Carps are well adapted to populate the great number of small and smallest waters and to survive even under the most unfavorable conditions.

South America shows a quite simple division in its construction. With the exception of the extreme south, which for us is meaningless, it possesses only few divided coasts. In the west we find the relatively narrow and high mountainous system of the Andes, which slope off steeply to the Pacific coast. The East shows large and flat alluvial plains which are interspersed by mountains with plateaus of small height. The climate is not uniform. We differentiate: the equatorial lowland climate of the Amazon basin; the tropical oceanic one of the coastal regions; the tropical inland climate of the mountainous lands and plateaus (Venezuela, Guiana, Matto Grosso); the tropical high mountain regions of the Andes with variable temperatures; the dry climates of the West coast; the sub-tropical to temperate continental climate of the La Plata regions; the Argentinian dry provinces; and some other climatic zones which are of no interest for our purposes.

The region of the Amazon Basin is covered with tropical rain forests, and is the biggest jungle territory of the globe. On the slopes of the mountains the rain forest turns into loose, tropical, mountain forest. The mountain country itself is covered with tree and grass plains. In the sub-tropical southern part follow the park countries of the Chaco, and the grassy plains of the Pampas. The Region of the High Mountains, which is cold and dry, shows only sparse plant growth, while the narrow west coast possesses variable vegetational characters. There we find tropical rain forests in the north, desert and dry regions, as well as sub-tropical vegetation in the center, and the Patagonian rain forests in the south.

South America is able to show some mighty river systems. According to the design of the continent, many of them originate in the West or on the plateaus, and flow down to the Atlantic Ocean. The most important of these are: the Amazon River, the Orinoco (1,500 miles), as well as the Rio de la Plata (river region 2 million square miles). Studies and isolated observations are available about part of Guiana and the Amazon region, as well as about other parts of South America, especially from the La Plata region, which were covered by Ladiges and collected in his book 'Fisch in der Landschaft' (Fish in the Landscape). In this Ladiges also points out clearly that the few available studies do not permit one to glimpse a complete picture of South America's fish fauna. Especially reports on finding places do not render conclusions on the complete range of the species of fishes. The number of species is so large, their shapes so confusing, the ecological data in part so contradictory, that it is difficult to form an even-to-some-degree comprehensive picture. Notwithstanding this, the work of Ladiges could never be overvalued as a basis for all further studies. At this point we shall try to reproduce some of the observations of Ladiges in the form of excerpts, without thereby relieving the interested readers of the need to read LADIGES' explanations for themselves.

'A small region of British Guiana was examined, especially parts of two river systems as well as numerous creeks, a few fresh water ponds, and some swamp forests. To this were added the waters of a jungle island lying in the river, the waters of the Botanical Garden of Georgetown, and some ditches and rice paddies. Guiana is defined by the western mountain and plateau country, which turns into rolling hill country toward the East, and finally into a flat, swampy, coastal region. During the whole year abundant rains fall, the temperature is permanently the same, the annual average always remaining around 79° F. The intensity of the rainfalls diverges a little from the plateaus to the coast, as well as according to the seasons. Its maximum occurs in May and June. The great rainy season brings differences of water level of up to 10 feet, and floods. On the coast we find mangrove jungles, and also on the lower reaches of the rivers as far as the influence of the tides goes (in part up to more than 12 miles). Then the coastal regions turn into real jungles. In the interior of the country we find grass and tree plains. Among splendid tropical plants in the Botanical Garden of Georgetown, LADIGES found, among others, Characins of the genus *Pristella*, furthermore two species of Cichlids, among others, *Cichlasoma festivum*, in the very shallow parts of the mud-filled waters, among others, on the leaves of *Nymphaea* that were just covered with a thin layer of water, swarms of Guppy fry.

Some unshaded ditches, about 7 ft. wide, 3 ft. deep, and filled with great quantities of *Elodea*, which in certain spots flowed over into extensive rice paddies, contained Characins of different types and genera, among others, *Copeina*, *Nannostomus*, *Pristella*, *Hyphessobrycon*, and *Hemigrammus*, but also two species of predatory Characins. Besides these also Cichlids, *Polycentrus*, Knife Fish, and *Poeciliinae* were found.

The water was colored a strong reddish-brown.

In brackish coastal ditches there lived *Poecilia vivipara*.

The lower course of a river (the Demerara River), still under tidal influence but without detectable traces of salt, the yellow-gray masses of which flowed sluggishly along, was the subject of further studies.

On the grassy banks, the grass of which grew down into the water, the Headstander *Anostomus anostomus* was found, as well as several members of the family of the *Nannostomidae*, *Pristella riddlei*, *Polycentrus*, and a species of Knife Fish. In the generally shadowed bays with open water, only a little grown with plants on the banks, and in the mouths of bigger creeks he found Disc Characins (*Ephippicharax*), Hatchet Fish (*Gasteropelecus sternicla*), and the Goiter Tetra *Chalcinus elongatus*. On mud banks in the open water he caught *Corydoras punctatus*. Wood-covered river shores with many submerged tree trunks, and creeks showed Cichlids, especially *Geophagus* (mouth-breeding species), and the Tiger Characin, *Hoplias*. Swift-swimming Characins (*Astyanax*, *Hemiodus*, *Moenkhausia*) were found everywhere, and so were certain Catfishes (*Rhamdia*). The inhabitants of the biotope mentioned above were also found in other places, but at the ones mentioned in especially great numbers.

In a tumble-down swimming hole in the woods, with a temperature of 68-72° F, brown water, and a thick layer of wood and leaves on the bottom, *Callichthys callichthys* and species of *Rivulus* were found in addition to frogs. The latter led an amphibian life in the bordering swamp region and fled from the invading fishermen by jumping into the terrestrial plants.

Another river course (Essequibo), which does not come under the influence of the tides, is a plateau river with sand bottom. Its water is clear, slightly brown, swift-flowing, and forms numerous eddies. It possesses both stone and clay banks, as well as shallow sand banks, abandoned arms with Salvinias, floating reeds, and other swamp plants. Therefore it is a water with many biotopes. Also the outbranching secondary waters (creeks) had different characters. There were found some species of Cichlids, especially *Pterophyllum scalare*, as well as some Sucker Catfishes, among strongly fissured rock cliffs, richly grown with algae, standing in the middle of the river. In the shore bays with quiet, clear water, more or less shaded by submerged and emerged shore flora, *Chalceus macrolepidotus*, the Arowana (*Osteoglossum*), and some other species of Characins were found, besides *Cichlasoma festivum*, which was also found among the rock cliffs. In the shallow and shadowless water of the sand bank that faced the river frolicked *Aphyocharax*, in the abandoned arms behind it Nannostomids and Knife Fishes. In the shadowy jungle creeks with low water temperatures and rich deposits of lumber and leaves one saw, among others, the Hatchet Belly *Carnegiella strigata*, the Head-and-Tail-Light *Hemigrammus ocellifer*, and the Leaf Fish *Monocirrhus*, while the plains creeks were populated by Dwarf Cichlids, *Nannacara anomala* and *Apistogramma ortmanni*, as well as Rosy Tets (*Hyphessobrycon callistus rosaceus*) and Splash Tetras (*Copeina arnoldi*).

Ladiges points out especially the presence of *Pterophyllum* among cliffs, into the clefts of which they fled in case of danger. The cliffs were also sought by schools of Characins (*Chalceus*, *Metynnis*), as well as nocturnal species of this group. Also Piranhas are said to appear there occasionally. *Pterophyllum*, and numerous Characins, of which the former showed no cross bands, were found in a shallow, very dirty puddle, in which they had probably remained after the last flood period, thus demonstrating the adaptability of tropical fishes.

The Amazon region is characterized by the continually high temperatures (annual average 77° F), the large quantities of precipitation (96″ as an average), and the only slightly differentiated rainy and dry seasons.

According to Praetorius, the water temperatures fluctuate between 64 and 104° F, the lowest degrees being found in the swift-flowing jungle creeks. The big rivers remain at 82-86° F, on the shallow spots near the shores considerably more.

Aquatic plants in greater quantities are found only in lateral arms and lagoons, their main time of growth falling into the rainy period, about January to March, and coinciding with the spawning period of the fishes. The principal living space for the smaller fishes are the shore regions and the secondary waters. Praetorius found *Pterophyllum* keeping company with *Cichlasoma festivum* in the so-called floating reeds. Unfortunately useful observations on the 'fish country, Amazonia' are utterly sparse.

Southern Brazil is the transition

from the tropics to the milder subtropics and belongs nearly to the temperate zone in its southernmost part. According to geographical altitude and latitude temperatures vary considerably. In the extreme south, and in Northern Argentina there may already appear cold spells. In the winter nights the waters on the plateaus freeze over. Towards the south the seasons begin again to have a meaning. There are periods with summer rains and months that are rain-deficient. In the south there are winter rains and pronounced vernal dry periods. Also here there are mainly Characins, Knife Fishes, Tooth Carps, Catfishes, and Cichlids which represent the fish fauna, as far as it is of interest for the aquarist. Of course they are acclimated to the conditions of the country from which they come. This goes so far that members of the same species, but which come from the south need considerably less warmth than individuals which originate from the tropical or subtropical north. Many of the species are astoundingly resistant with reference to temperature and withstand considerable fluctuations of it. The genus *Cynolebias* shows a special adaptation to the temporarily dry waters of the Argentinian Pampas.

Spanish Carp, the: see APHANIUS IBERUS.

Sparganiaceae: Family belonging to the class of the single-germinating-leaved plants or *Monocotyledoneae.* Perennial swamp plants with long, creeping root stocks from which grow the narrow, lanceolate leaves. The inflorescence is long-stemmed, the fruit-baskets form porcupine-shaped balls. The family ranges over the temperate zones of Europe and Asia, going south to North Africa. The plants are unfit for the home aquarium. Under the open sky they thrive quite well, but are unsightly. Genus: *Sparganium.*

Sparganium ramosum

sparrmanni: After the Swedish zoologist Sparrmann.
— *Tilapia.*

Sparse-Bristled Worms: see OLIGOCHAETA.

spasms: see TIMIDITY.

spawn, act of spawning, spawning period: The totality of the eggs of a fish is called spawn or roe, while when speaking of single units we refer to them as eggs. It is formed within the ovaries of female fishes. The quantity of egg units is relatively great to very great in all fishes. They repose as a long, compact mass, closely compressed, within the bag-shaped cover of the ovaries. Development of spawn sets in when there are conditions favorable to reproduction, these conditions being bound to certain seasons of the year. In consequence of this the reproduction of fishes generally takes place during limited spawning periods. Under the changed conditions of the aquarium, often a confusion of these natural periods takes place. Through a permanence under optimum conditions of living, an overstimulation of the fishes, with harmful consequences, may set in. It is understandable that the development of such big quantities of sexual products as is the rule in both male and female fishes puts an intense strain on them, so that their strength is used up to a high degree. This is reason enough to make rest periods at lower or otherwise adequate temperatures obligatory, even in the aquarium.

As a rule the act of spawning is effected during the mating, i.e., the spawn is fertilized in free water or on a firm basis by the simultaneously emerging spermatozoa. In some cases, though, fertilization also takes place already within the female body, as for instance, is the case with the Characins of the *Glandulocaudinae* family, which show a more or less developed storing of fertilized eggs for future spawnings. In this case the act of spawning is effected in the absence of the male.

Generally it is not the whole provision of ripe spawn that is expelled at once, but the act of spawning is divided into several partial acts, so that it may last for hours as a whole. In other species, for instance, in the egg laying Tooth Carps, the eggs mature gradually within the ovaries. Thus in daily spawnings, which on their part are further divided into parts, only small quantities of eggs are laid, so that the total release of spawn may last from one to several weeks. In such cases we speak of a spawning period or of lasting spawners. See also REPRODUCTION.

spawn substratum: The basis onto which fishes stick spawn, or where they dig such a basis, as for instance, bottom mud, sand, algae, plants, etc.

Spawn Wort: see POTAMOGETON.

Spawn Worts: see POTAMOGETONACEAE.

Spear Leaf: see ANUBIAS.

species: The basic unit of animals or plants in scientific systematics, comprising live beings with relatively uniform and constant characteristics, being of the same descent or the same genetic-historical origin. The members of a species form a reproductive community, i.e., they can produce constantly fertile descendants in their midst, the features of which are hereditarily constant to a wide extent. Members of different species do not hybridize. In cases of exception, the first generation or one of the next ones of the descendants are sterile.

More or less great divergences may occur in the type of the species considered as a whole. These may show both in body features as well as in characteristics of behavior, manner of living, or in the vital needs. Thus, for instance, aquatic plants of the same species in their adaptation to different climatic conditions may be annual in the temperate zones, while they are perennial in the tropics and subtropics. These changes may justify the establishing of sub-species or of geographical races.

Often they may be sub-divided into still smaller groups, such as, for instance, local strains. Species which populate a big region often permit one to see clearly the connectedness of the species when the local strains are neighbors and therefore there are mixed breeds.

Sperata: Indian genus of Catfishes pertaining to the family of the

Bagridae, of elongated build and naked skin. The forehead line rises roof-like to the insertion of the dorsal fin, while the ventral contour is nearly straight. The upper part of the head is flat, the skin on it of a grainy quality. The mouth opening is equipped with four pairs of barbels, of which one pair of upper jaw barbels is so long that it reaches nearly to the tail fin. Dorsal and pectoral fins each carry a strong spike. The adipose fin is especially well developed. The genus is also known as *Macrones* or *Mystus*.

— **tengara** (Hamilton-Buchanan): Probably a local variety of the following species, or identical with same.

— **vittata** (Bloch): The Striped Indian Catfish.

SHAPE: As per description of the genus. D I/7, A 9-12. Length up to $8\frac{3}{8}''$.

COLOR: Golden-yellow base with bluish horizontal stripes. The species possesses several color varieties. Sex differences unknown.

RANGE: In flowing waters of India and Thailand.

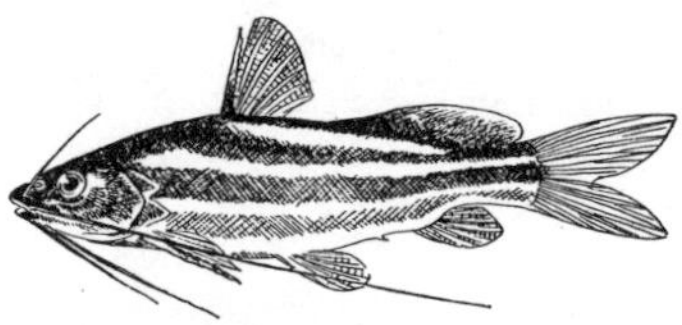

Sperata vittata

CARE AND BREEDING: Striped Catfish are predators, which at first take only live foods, but can also be trained to eat scraped meat and similar substitutes. Toward fishes of their own size they behave quite peaceably. They like not too intensely lit aquaria with sufficient hiding places, where they show themselves also in daytime after having acclimated to the tank. The fish possess a well developed accessory respiration, which enables them to leave the water and to move quite nimbly on land. While doing this they utter noises which are reported to sound like the buzzing of a caught fly.

Temperatures should be held at 72-77° F. Breeding them has not yet succeeded, but the fish spawned in a cement tank in SCHAEME's hatchery many years ago. The big, white eggs were laid among plants, but were all of them attacked by fungus.

sperm: Compound substance, able to fertilize or fecundate, produced by male animals with sexual reproduction, which commonly consists of the semen cells generated by the testicles and are mixed with a generally mucilaginous accompanying liquid.

spermatophores: Little sperm bundles.

Bundles of sperm cells joined together into compact structures by certain secretions, which are found in many arthropods, worms, and lower vertebrates. As such they are either taken to the vicinity of the female sexual opening and absorbed or sucked up by this, or else they are released on the ground, etc., and then hunted up and sucked in by the female. They enable eggs to be fertilized over several reproductive periods, as is the case with the live bearing Tooth Carps and certain Characins.

Sphaerichthys: Fish with round body.

Genus belonging to the family of the Climbing Perches or *Anabantidae*. Small fishes of relatively high build, strongly compressed laterally. In its body shape the species resembles the genuine Gourami, *Osphronemus goramy*. The dorsal fin is relatively long, but the anal fin is still longer. The first ray of the ventral is extended in thread shape.

— **osphromenoides** Canestrini: The Chocolate Gourami.

SHAPE: As per description of the genus. D VII-XI/8-9, A VII-IX/ 19-22. The ventral outline is more arched than the back. The mouth opening is small and tilted upwards. The jaws are equipped with very small teeth. Length up to 2″.

COLOR: Dark brown with narrow, light, irregular cross bands. The male is a little more intensely colored. The dorsal fin is slightly pointed.

According to LADIGES the females carry a sharply limited white horizontal band between the clearly set-off cross bands, which contracts ever more with advancing age and finally disappears leaving only an elongated spot between the first and second complete cross bands. On the males the base of the anal fin becomes occasionally wine red and darker, and the dark edge of this fin is broader than on the female.

RANGE: Malaya, Sumatra, in densely grown, shallow ditches and ponds, but also in slowly flowing streams and ditches.

A breeding pair of Chocolate Gouramis, **Sphaerichthys osphromenoides.**

CARE AND BREEDING: The species is considered quite delicate. Freshly imported specimens prove to be rather prone to diseases, becoming especially often infected with the tropical variety of *Ichthyophthirius* of which LADIGES speaks. After domestication they are said to be quite resistant, however. Anyway, BAHR points out that the care and breeding of these peculiar fish are not especially problematical. They are best kept in well-planted tanks with soft water and dark, peaty bottom. The tank should not be too small, the water level not above 6″. Important is an evenly high temperature of about 84-86° F, the air above the water having to be heated to the same temperature. Therefore we need cover lids that close with a certain precision. Feeding should receive special attention. Probably they eat only live foods, giving preference to black mosquito larvae. It is reported that the danger of overfattening is especially great for the Chocolate Gourami.

Reproduction was completely unknown for a long time, and seems not to be completely understood even today. It is a fact that meanwhile breedings have succeeded, but the reports on them diverge strongly from each other. According to BAHR the male collected air under a floating leaf. The small bubbles, which are not covered with mucus like those of other Anabantids, melted together and then formed a kind of bell with the leaf, which was kept floating by the air. The male showed to be very aggressive in defending the spawning site. The act of spawning took place in the manner of the other Anabantids, with mutual embraces beneath the bell. The eggs floated up into this and were guarded there, as well as the fry which hatched after 24 hours—during six days, that is, until the young left the nest. Rearing the young was done in the manner of all Anabantids. The report of E. SCHMIDT sounds different. According to it the fish are mouth-breeders. The act of spawning took place while embracing closely above the bottom. The eggs which were sliding to the ground were collected by the male and hatched in an enlarged throat sac. The young were released after about a fortnight.

According to the observations of LADIGES (1957) the male built a nest at the surface using parts of plants and some foam bubbles. The fish spawned while loosely embraced and at a distance of 4″ below the nest. The eggs, which sank slowly to the bottom, were taken up in the mouth of the male. A number of eggs, which possibly found no more room in the mouth, were collected by the male and spit up into the nest, where they were left to themselves, since the impulse of caring for the spawn soon gave out in the father.

Therefore we have to say that the conditions are not yet clearly established. We would like to refer to still other Anabantids, for instance, *Macropodus cupanus dayi*, and *Trichopsis pumilus*, for which too there are divergent observations.

Perhaps there are different races and varieties of this species, which differ by their different behavior of caring for the spawn, if the divergences are not caused by the special conditions encountered in captivity.

sphenops: With wedge-shaped face.
— *Mollienisia.*

spicatum: With ears.
— *Myriophyllum.*

Spiders: see CHELICERATA.

Spike-Tail Paradise Fish, the: see MACROPODUS CUPANUS.

— Red: see MACROPODUS CUPANUS DAYI.

spilauchena: With spot on the neck.
— *Aplocheilichthys.*

spilopleura: With spotted sides.
—*Luciosoma.*

spilopterus: With spotted fins.
— *Arnoldichthys.*

spilurus: With spot on the tail.
— *Crenuchus.*
— *Ctenobrycon.*

spinosissimus: Very spiny.
— *Acanthodoras.*

Spiny Catfish, the: see ACANTHODORUS SPINOSISSIMUS.

Spiral Vallisneria, the: see VALLISNERIA SPIRALIS, F. TORTIFOLIA.

spiralis: Wound, turned, spiralled (the female flower stems).
— *Cryptocoryne.*
— *Vallisneria.*

Spirodela: Genus pertaining to the family of the Water Lentils or *Lemnaceae.*

— polyrhiza (Linné): Many-Rooted Water Lentil.
An almost cosmopolitan floating plant with many roots which form tufts.

Splash Tetra, the: see COPEINA ARNOLDI.

splendens: Shiny.
— *Betta.*

splendopleuris: With shiny sides.
— *Aphyosemion bivittatum.*

sponges: see PORIFERA.

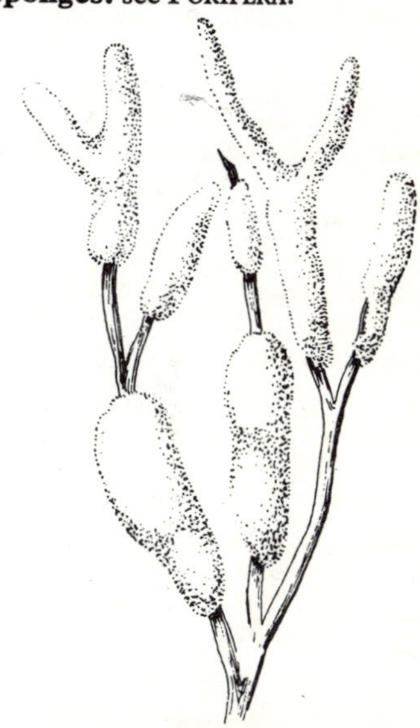

Spongilla

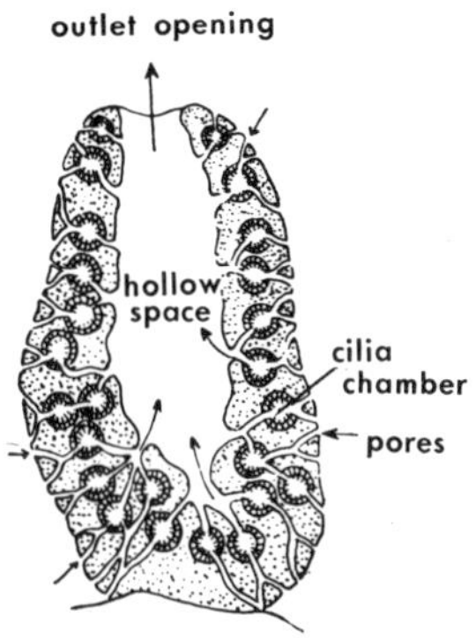

Closeup of a cilia chamber with migratory cells.

Spongillidae: Fresh Water Sponges. Family belonging to the phylum of the sponges or *Porifera,* order of the Horn Sponges or *Cornacuspongia.* Animal colonies without definite shape which are found in lumps as branched structures in fresh water bodies of all kinds, especially in dirty ones. The color is dirty yellow to greenish, the smell disagreeable. The sponges often live symbiotically with green algae. In the aquarium they may occasionally form thick mats on accessories, plants, etc., but they are harmless, except that they hinder the assimilation of the plants which they infest. Sponges are easily scraped off, however.

sporangium: Spore container.

spores: Asexual reproductive cells of lower plants and unicellular animals.

Sporozoa: Spore Animals. Phylum of parasitic unicellulars, belonging to the division of the *Cytomorpha,* of which many species are dangerous disease germs. They comprise, among others, the causers of malaria and of some much-feared fish diseases, as for instance, the Barb Disease.

Spotted Catfish, the: see CORYDORAS MELANISTIUS.

Spotted Cichlid, the: see AEQUIDENS CURVICEPS.

Spotted Danio, the: see BRACHYDANIO NIGROFASCIATUS.

Spotted Gambusia: see GAMBUSIA PUNCTATA.

Spotted Metynnis: see METYNNIS MACULATUS.

Spotted Panchax, the: see PACHYPANCHAX PLAYFAIRI.

spring tasks: see CARE FOR THE AQUARIUM.

stagnalis: Living in water.
— *Callitriche.*

Star Head Top Minnow, the: see FUNDULUS DISPAR.

Star-Spotted Pristella: see PRISTELLA RIDDLEI.

Steatocranus: Fat skull. Genus belonging to the family of the Cichlids or *Cichlidae,* which originates from West Africa, with a few species. One of these species, which was imported in 1956, and which was also bred in the aquarium, has become known in Germany as *S. casuarius* (?). Whether the species that was bred in America, and which bears the name *S. elongatus,* is identical with the previously mentioned one, cannot yet be affirmed. The males of these Cichlids are characterized by the fact that they have a remarkable forehead line, which with age tilts still farther outwards, and which sits on the skull like a cap. Otherwise the species known to us shows no special characteristics. The color is a simple gray to gray-brown. Each scale bears a dark dot, and alternate band design may appear more or less strongly, according to surroundings and mood.

The fishes are no strong rooters. Plants are mostly left unharmed. Also towards each other the species is quite peaceable. Reproduction takes place in the manner of the pit-spawning Cichlids. No special demands are made as to the composition of the water. Temperature 75-80° F; they need some warmth.

Steatogenes elegans (Steindachner): Fat Chin.

South American Knife Fish pertaining to the family of the *Gymnotidae,* without dorsal fin and with whip-like extended tail. A 160-176. Length up to 8″.

COLOR: Ochre colored, with brown cross bands. Sex differences unknown.

Steatogenes elegans

ORIGIN: Guiana and Brazil, especially in the lower Amazon. The species is harmless and due to its small, toothless mouth it can only eat smaller live foods. Not yet bred in the aquarium.

Steel-Blue Gularis, the: see APHYOSEMION GARDNERI.

steindachneri: After the Austrian ichthyologist Steindachner.

— *Leptagoniates.*

sterile: Incapable of reproducing.

Sternachidae: Sea Cow Fishes.

South American family belonging to the sub-order of the Carp-like or *Cyprinoidea,* resembling the family *Gymnotidae* in shape and manner of living. Genera, among others: *Sternarchella.*

Sternarchella schottii (Steindachner):

South American Knife Fish be-

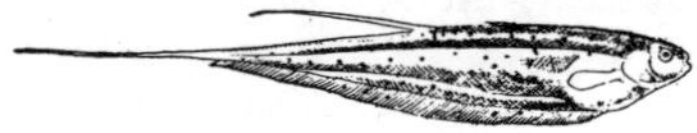

Sternarchella schottii

longing to the family of the *Sternarchidae,* of elongated build, pointed at the rear, and strongly compressed laterally. Instead of a dorsal fin we find a dorsal thread. A tail fin is present, ventrals are lacking, A 174-178. Length up to 11″.

COLOR: Brownish-yellow with darker spots. Sex differences unknown.

ORIGIN: Central Brazil, only in fresh water. Keeping, as per the description given for the family *Gymnotidae,* at 72-82° F. The species is shy and reported to be peaceable.

sternicla: Referring to the arched breast.

— *Gasteropelecus.*

Stickleback, the: see GASTEROSTEUS.

stigma: Spot, mark.

Stigmatogobius: Spotted Loach, Spotted Goby.

Genus belonging to the family of the Sea Loaches or *Gobiidae* which ranges from the Ganges Region to Java, being distributed all over South East Asia and the Australian isles.

— sadanundio (Hamilton): The Knight Goby.

SHAPE: As per description for the genus. A little compact, the fins well developed. D_1 VI, D_2 9-10, A 9-10 (?). Length up to $3\frac{3}{8}$″.

COLOR: Silvery white base with numerous blackish spots on sides and fins. Sex differences unknown.

RANGE: Indonesia, India, Indochina, the Philippines.

CARE AND BREEDING: As described for the species of *Eleotris.* A 10% addition of sea water is advisable. Reproduction unknown.

stimulus: Action of the ambient world upon an organism or upon part of same, which causes an excitation and consequently a reaction.

Stinking Candelabra, the: see CHARA FOETIDA.

stoliczkai: After the collector, Dr. Stoliczka.

— *Barbus* (*Puntius*).

stoloniferum: Bearer of runners, shoots.

— *Limnobium.*

stomach diseases: see INTESTINAL DISEASES.

Stone-Grig, the: see COBITIS TAENIA.

Stone-Perch, the: see AMBLOPLITES RUPESTRIS.

Stone Perch, the: see ACERINA CERNUA.

stones and rocks in the aquarium: see INSTALLATION OF THE AQUARIUM.

stratiotes: Similar to Aquatic Aloes.

— *Pistia.*

Stratiotes: The Soldier.

Genus of emerged and semi-emerged aquatic plants belonging to the family of the Frogbit Plants or *Hydrocharitaceae.*

Stratiotes aloides

— aloides Linné: Crayfish's Claw. A plant that is distributed over Europe and Northern Asia, found in standing waters, in which it grows either submergedly rooted in the soil, semi-emergedly, or floating. The vegetative forms change with the seasons. These 'Aloe-like' plants are fit only for the cold water aquarium. Growing them is best done from winter buds, which are gathered in fall, wintered cooly in a jar, and planted in spring. They need light and sun.

Streamlined Corydoras: see CORYDORAS ARCUATUS.

Streber, the: see ASPRO STREBER.

stress in pronunciation: The stress in Latin or Latinized names causes difficulties, especially to those aquarists who have not had any teaching of the Latin language. Therefore we are giving some basic rules below, which may contribute to make the pronunciation of scientific names easier.

As a rule the last syllable is never stressed in Latin. Exceptions may occur in names taken from native languages, such as for instance, Uaru. We want to point out, however, that, in case of doubt about such formations which may supposedly derive from native languages, the aquarist had better stress them according to the Latin rules.

In Latin one stresses the next-to-last syllable, if it is long, for instance, *fasciata.* If the second last syllable is short, it is the syllable before it that is stressed, for instance, *béllica.* The stress is never displaced still more to the front in Latin. Therefore, when we read a Latin name, we must try to decide whether the second last syllable is long or short in order to know how to place the stress. It is true, however, that this decision is not always simple. Stressing becomes more difficult when the name word is composed of several elements. Even to decide whether a name is a compound word or not might cause difficulties to the layman. The best is perhaps to get advice from a linguist, or else look the matter up in the technical literature. It is especially important in stressing to know whether the name was formed out of two or more Latin names, or whether it is composed of words of Greek origin. In the former case it is subject to the rules of the Latin language, for instance, *trimaculatus*. Otherwise the rules of stress of ancient Greek will apply: the last syllable of the first word is stressed, for instance *Hyphessobrycon*, *Plecostomus*, *Nannostomus*. Greek stressing tends as far towards the beginning of the word as possible.

striatulus: With elongated stripes.
— *Trachicorystes*.

striatus: Striped.
— *Leporinus*.

stricta: Stiff, strict, distended.
— *Nomaphila*.

strigata: Striped.
— *Carnegiella*.

strigatus: Striped.
— *Rivulus*.

strigigena: With stripes on the cheek.
— *Haplochromis*.

Striped Cichlid, the: see AEQUIDENS PORTALEGRENSIS.

Striped Flying Barb, the: see ESOMUS LINEATUS.

Striped Glass Perch, the: see AMBASSIS NANA.

Striped Hatchet Fish, the: see CARNEGIELLA STRIGATA.

Striped Head Characin, the: see PYRRHULINA VITTATA.

Striped Head Thorn Catfish, the: see AMBLYDORAS HANCOCKI.

Striped Knife Fish, the: see GYMNOTUS CARAPO.

Sturgeons: see ACIPENSERIDAE.

submersum: Submerged.
— *Ceratophyllum*.

subocellatus: Provided with eye (spots) in the rear.
— *Pelmatochromis*.

suborbitalis: Referring to the construction of the suborbital bones.
— *Phenacogaster*.

substratum: Basis, feeding ground. The spawning substratum is the base into, or onto, which the spawn of fishes is laid.

Succinea: Amber Snails.
Genus belonging to the family of the spiral snails or *Helicidae*, with only few native (German) species, which are especially suited for the swamp aquarium. They are amphibious snails which may travel immediately from land to water without retracting their antennae. The eyes sit on stems. The shell consists of 3-4 spirals, of which the last is relatively large. The edge of the opening is sharp, the shell being waxen to amber colored. The eggs are laid on the lower parts of terrestrial plants that stand near the edge of the water. If the snails are kept only under water, the tank must be well covered, as otherwise they creep out.

Sucker Catfishes: see LORICARIIDAE, ARMORED CATFISHES.

Sucker Loaches: see GYRINOCHEILIDAE.

sucker worm diseases: In part grave diseases of fishes caused by Sucker Worms (*Trematodes*). Sucker Worms are external parasites that live on the skin or the gills, and are equipped with one or more sucking discs located at the rear of the body, with which they hold fast. Either they undergo their full development on one host, or else there is a simple metamorphosis of free-swimming larvae, which soon settle down again. There is no alternation of generations.

Trematodes may also be internal parasites, generally lacking eyes and equipped with one or two sucking discs. In this case their development is very complex, sexual and asexual reproduction alternating with the succeeding generations. In the change of hosts that takes place, the fish is either an intermediate host, or the final one.

Among others we may mention the causers of skin discoloration, *Gyrodactylus*, and *Dactylogyrus*, furthermore the larvae (cercariae) of Sucker Worms that penetrate fishes and may cause grave damage, for instance, Worm Cataract, and Blood Worm Disease.

sulcatus: Furrowed.

— *Acilius.*

sumatranus: Coming from Sumatra.

— *Acanthophthalmus kuhlii.*

— *Dermogenys.*

— *Barbus (Puntius) tetrazona*

— *Trichogaster trichopterus.*

sun animals: see HELIOZOA.

Sunfish, the Common: see LEPOMIS GIBBOSUS.

— The Big-Eared: see LEPOMIS MEGALOTIS.

— the Green: see LEPOMIS CYANELLUS.

— the Red-Breasted: see LEPOMIS AURITUS.

Sunfishes: see CENTRARCHIDAE.

suratensis: After a geographic name.

— *Etroplus.*

Surinam Pearl Cichlid, the: see GEOPHAGUS SURINAMENSIS.

surinamensis: Coming from Surinam.

— *Geophagus.*

swamp aquarium (paludarium). A type of aquarium which generally is set up as an aquaterrarium, that is, which possesses a distinctly separated land part. Even aquaria with low water levels or with shore constructions from which plants grow above the surface could be considered swamp aquaria. In order to offer such plants sufficient air space, and to generate the generally necessary moist or moist-warm air, the swamp aquarium must either have a water level which does not make use of the full height of the aquarium, or else it must have a glass extension on top of it.

According to the origin of the plants and animals that are kept in it, the paludarium may be set up as a cold or as a warm water aquarium. In order to maintain a tropical paludarium it is necessary not only to heat the water, but also the air space above this. This is best done with the aid of an electric reflector with a correspondingly intense lamp in it, which, besides the warmth also furnishes light, since most emergedly growing swamp plants need an especially great amount of light in order to thrive and especially in order to bloom. Of course all parts that carry current have to conform with the specifications and standards for electric installations in moist rooms.

As a native aquarium, the swamp aquarium is especially well able to show a cross section of a biological community at the water's edge, since many lower animals leave the water for a short time after their metamorphosis.

Swamp Calla: see CALLA PALUSTRIS.

Swamp Friend, the Flowerstemless: see LIMNOPHILA SESSILIFLORA.

— The Gracile: see LIMNOPHILA GRATIOLOIDES.

Swamp Killie, the: see LEPTOLUCANIA OMATA.

Swamp Lid Snails: see VIVIPARUS.

Swamp Love, Yellow: see LIMNOCHARIS FLAVA.

Swamp Screw: see VALLISNERIA.

Swamp Snails: see VIVIPARIDAE.

Swimmer Bugs: see HYDROCORISAE.

swimming bladder: Most fishes possess a swimming bladder, above all those species which move free-swimming. This enables the fish to conform its specific weight to the pressure of the surrounding water, creating a state of fluctuation. The swimming bladder generally is an unpaired sac, often subdivided into several sectors, which, being an extension of the upper wall of the gullet, always are located above the intestine. The inner surface is smooth-walled. In the group of fishes called Physostomes the swimming bladder is connected with the intestine by an air duct. In the Physoclists the swimming bladder remains closed, that is, they lack such an air duct. The gas charge is similar in composition to atmospheric air; it is produced by the 'Red Body', a gas gland. Emptying is either done through the air duct, or else the gas is readsorbed by the so-called oval. The compensation of pressure takes place only slowly, so that in the meantime the fins of the swimming fish have to act as equalizers. In some groups of fishes, which therefore are collectively classed as *Ostariophysi* there exists a linkage between the membrane of the swimming bladder and the ear labyrinth by means of a chain of little bonelets, which is called Weber's Apparatus. This serves the purpose of transmitting changes of pressure which act on the swimming bladder to the balancing organ, and thus to orient the fish to whether it is rising or sinking in the water. The swimming bladder may also act as acoustic cage for the ear, as well as to utter sounds which are produced through pressure on the gas charge or in similar ways. Young fry develop their swimming bladders during the first days of their lives. Therefore they are partly forced first to rise to the surface in order to fill the swimming bladder as soon as they have the ability to swim. In fishes with a closed swimming

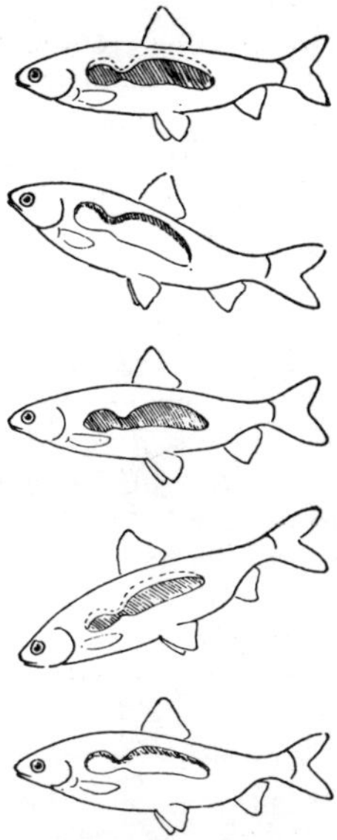

From top to bottom: swim bladder in reduced size; bladder too large; bladder normal for floating fish; swim bladder shrinks as fish dives; swim bladder smaller normally as fish floats in deep water.

bladder, this grows shut only when this has been accomplished. If young fry are hindered from filling their swimming bladders during the first days (too high water level, for instance) the same remains undeveloped and stunted, and the fishes do not become able to swim, remaining so-called 'belly floppers'. In some groups of fishes, above all those that live on the bottom, the swimming bladder may also be involuted or totally lacking.

Swordtail, the: see XIPHOPHORUS.

symbiosis: Joint life of beings of different species for mutual usefulness, for instance, the presence of micro-algae in animal bodies, the union of plants and fungi to form lichens, or the joint life of coral fishes with certain anemones. The aim or usefulness of a symbiosis for both partners is not always clearly recognizable.

Symbranchidae - type of the family

Symbranchidae: Short-Tailed Eels.

Family of Eel-shaped fishes belonging to the order of the *Symbranchii*, with small scales or completely naked skin, in part with well developed gills, in part with rudimentary ones, and with accessory respiration. The family is distributed over South and Central America, West Africa, South and Southeast Asia, Indonesia, and Australia.

They are very interesting and peculiar pets, which need large tanks and hiding places among rocks. For the home aquarium only smaller specimens may be used, otherwise very good for show aquaria. The fish are voracious, vicious, and eat everything they can conquer. Reproduction is unknown. The family is divided into two sub-families, *Symbranchinae* and *Amphipninae*, all of which are inhabitants of fresh and brackish waters.

The *Amphipninae* possess no visible fins. The small, slit-like gill openings can be shut completely, and permit the fishes an amphibic manner of living. Dry periods may be weathered in the mud. Their home is in Asia.

Of the family *Symbranchinae* we shall mention the genus *Symbranchus*, of which the species *S. marmoratus* Bloch has become quite well-known. The fish reach a length of 60″. When they take in atmospheric air, the gill space becomes extended like a sack. Their origin is Northern South America, up to Mexico in the north. The fish are very voracious and predatory. They are best kept alone, as they attack even smaller specimens of their own kind. They do not need much warmth, 68-72° F being sufficient.

Symbranchii: Order within the sub-class of the New Fins or *Neopterygii*. The Eel-like, strongly specialized fishes possess a peculiar body construction. The dorsal spine is rich in vertebral bodies, there are no paired fins, and the remainder are strongly involuted. In the place of the fins there are only skin folds left. The skin is scaleless or covered with very small scales. The gill openings are reduced to only one, which is located on the underside of the body as a narrow slit. They lack a swimming bladder. The relationship to other fishes remains unexplained. One family: the Short-Tailed Eels or *Symbranchidae*.

Symphysodon: With teeth on the linkage of the low branches of the lower jaw, the symphysis.

South American genus pertaining to the family of the Cichlids, of circular, disc-shaped body, strongly compressed laterally. So far only one species with a few local varieties is known.

— discus Heckel: The Discus.

SHAPE: As per description of the genus. Head and mouth opening are relatively small. D VII-IX/26-31, A VI-IX/26-31.

Symphysodon aequifasciata axelrodi, the Discus Fish.

COLOR: Splendidly colored and remarkable fish, of which so far two distinctly differentiated color varieties have become known, of which one is more yellowish, the other more silver-gray. The body shows several vertical, variable, dark-brown cross bands. Forehead and the front part of the back of adult specimens are ornamented with splendid, shiny blue-green bands, which extend also onto the fins. The female is a little fainter in coloring, and more yellowish, being however easy to recognize during the spawning period by the different shape of her genital papilla, which is more cone-shaped and blunt, while that of the male is more pointed. It is reported that the band design of the gray variety, which is said to come from Rio Tapajoz, stands out more vividly.

RANGE: The Central Amazon and its affluents. The species is not rare anywhere, but is hard to catch, since, in case of disturbances, the fish withdraw into thickets of submerged lumber and twigs. They are found especially in bays and lateral arms of the big waters, where there are dense plant growths, and submerged tree trunks and twigs as well as cliffs. Lately there have been commercial offers of fish which are said to come from open air hatcheries in northern South America (?).

CARE AND BREEDING: This very difficult to keep and costly species is not yet fully known in its conditions of life. Mute overhead light enhances the colors; with too intense light the fish become pale. They need large and high tanks with plenty of plants that grow upwards. Soft, slightly acid water, that may have been filtered through peat moss, is advisable for them. In old water they become prone to diseases. For this reason it is advisable to effect a weekly change of about $\frac{1}{5}$-$\frac{1}{4}$ of the entire water contents. The water should show a warmth of 77-80° F or more, lowest 72° F. Feeding them is especially difficult. The fish prefer to starve rather than to eat monotonous or unappealing nourishment. They seem to prefer tubifex worms over all other foods, which probably corresponds to their native eating habits.

The species is very striking and ornamental, and is especially appropriate for show aquaria.

Breeding them is very difficult and has succeeded only in a few cases so far. Partly unconfirmed reports on successful breedings are accumulating lately, and bred fry are found on the market, but it seems that not rarely these originate from open air hatcheries. It is not impossible, though, that with progressing domestication the successes will increase in number. Substantial successes in breeding were lately achieved by SCHMIDT, and WAGNER.

In Germany it was especially WAGNER who effected the first spawning which was not due to chance. According to his report a pair of breeders spawned repeatedly in a 150 gallon tank. After initial bad luck, the broods were regularly reared by the parents. Half the aquarium water was completely de-salted by de-salting compounds; the pH value was fixed at pH 6 by means of phosphoric acid. Temperature constantly 84° F. Furthermore 3 quarts of a decoction of $\frac{3}{8}$ oz. high peat moor moss were poured into the water. After the eggs of the first spawnings were attacked by fungi, finally the first breedings had success. The spawning took place in the manner of *Pterophyllum scalare*, on the leaves of an Amazon Swordplant. The genital papilla of the female protruded strongly; the male showed a somewhat more vigorously developed forehead, and more luminous forehead and neck stripes. The laying of the eggs took place from upwards down, insemination going the same way. According to WINCKLER the eggs have a length of a scant 1.5 mm and a diameter of about 1.25 mm. They are of brownish-yellow color and stick lengthwise to the substratum. The fry hatched after about 50 hours, were sucked free of the egg shells and spit on a cleaned Swordplant leaf by the parents, hanging there from an adhesive thread.

During the nursing phase the parents generally showed a very dark body color and a light clay-yellow head, the latter very specially on the males.

The fry swam in a dense swarm around the parents. In a clearly visible manner they pulled some particles from the parents' skin, and their bellies showed to be filled with a yellow mass which could be seen through the belly wall. In this the whole swarm 'grazed off' one parent at a time. The transition to the other parent took place after a formal relief ceremony, consisting of fin contractions, tilted stand, nudges in the flanks, and swimming side by side. After this the parent that had fed the young up to that moment withdrew to a distance of about 12″, after which the baby fish immediately turned to the fish that was now offering itself. During the night the fry were stuck to the underside of a Swordplant leaf. They were reared on Rotatoria, nauplii of Brine Shrimp, Grindal worms, and Tubifex 'pre-chewed' by the parents. Thus growth was relatively quick. The skin secretion of the parents was still taken as an additional food for a long time.

Synenthognathi: Order of predominantly sea-dwelling fishes belonging to the sub-class of the New Fins or *Neopterygii*, the members of which are characterized by their elongated, often Pike-like, body shape, and by the peculiar, beak shaped snout formations. For aquaristics the family of the Half-Beaks or *Hemirhamphidae* is of interest.

Synnema: Equipped with thread (the meaning is unclear).

Plant genus belonging to the family of the Bear's Foot Plants or *Acanthaceae*, for the time being with one species that may be kept in the aquarium.

— triflorum (Nees) O. Kuntze:

GENERALITIES: A tropical swamp plant imported in 1956 which may also be cultivated submergedly, and which has already found wide recognition due to its willingness to grow and to its ornamental shape. Closely related to *Hygrophila*.

SHAPE: The vertical, vigorous stem may grow to be 10-16″ high. The short peduncled leaves, which may develop the most variable shapes, are light green on the upper face, white green on the lower one. They may reach lengths of 6″. Beginning from the undivided, egg-shaped primary leaves, gradually they develop subsequent leaves with ever more pronounced indentations and teeth, which are of utterly irregular shape. Since they stand crossedly opposite around the stem, the plants form beautiful rosettes, especially when viewed from above. The emerged leaves are a little more uniform in shape, elliptical, slightly pointed, with nearly straight or lightly toothed edges. Stems and leaves are covered with short hairs. The flowers are small, unimposing, and sit in the insertions of the emerged leaves.

RANGE: Southeast Asia (Thailand) in swamps, on the banks of waters, and in rice paddies.

CULTIVATION: Similar to that of *Hygrophila*. The plant likes light, sun, and not too hard waters.

Temperature around 77° F. Vegetative reproduction through shoots which grow from the leaf insertions near the bottom. Parts of stems or leaves, and planted twigs, grow roots very quickly.

Synodontis: African genus of Catfishes belonging to the family of the Feather Whisker Catfishes or *Mochokidae*, of compact build. The body is covered with a rugged, mucous skin. The fins are in part very large, the spine of the dorsal and pectoral fins is provided with a locking articulation and may cause hard-to-heal wounds. The barbels are branched and partly remarkably long. The genus comes from Tropical Africa.

Synodontis alberti

— alberti Schilthuis: The Spotted African Catfish.

A striking Catfish with large fins, the tail fin being deeply forked. The adipose fin is very long. It reaches a length of about 6″. The body is covered with numerous round, dark spots on a lighter base, which also appear on the fins. The barbels of the upper jaw nearly reach the same length as the body. The two pairs of barbels of the lower jaw are shorter, but richly branched.

— nigriventris David: The Congo Back-Swimmer.

This very peculiar, only lately imported species from the Congo region reaches a length of about $2\frac{3}{4}$″. It possesses the peculiar ability to swim on its back for regular periods of time. The fish is adapted to this habit also in its colors, the belly being darker than the back. They are peaceable fish,

Synodontis nigriventris, the Upside-down Catfish.

which become lively predominantly during twilight, and like darkly located aquaria with dense plantings. *S. nigriventris* eat small live foods, but also vegetable fare. Temperatures between 75-79° F. Already bred, but without exact data available so far.

synonym: Scientific name for animals or plants which has been valid and in use for a more or less long time instead of the presently officialized one, and which therefore has become popular. In such cases it is usual to mention also the synonym together with the presently valid name, if this should be necessary to avoid confusions.

synura: Genus of so-called Color Monads, belonging to the phylum of the Whip Animals or *Flagellata* order of the *Chrysomonadinae*, which form colonies up to $\frac{1}{4}$ mm in size, sometimes lending the water a brown color and a disagreeable taste caused by their massed presence. Several dozens of chalice or pear shaped unicellulars sit on a common center with their bases, and tilt outwards two whips each, which serve for locomotion.

systematics: Among aquarists systematics is one of the less-liked subjects, but it is indispensable as an order-bringing basis, which puts all live beings into an externally recognizable relationship. Only systematics makes it possible to compare the single species and whole groups of species according to body shape, functions, and manner of living, as well as to genetic-historical origin. Without this sytematic order it would be impossible to have a comprehensive view of the huge number of the already known organisms on earth. As a shapeless mass of independent beings they would be insurmountable.

Besides this, even from a purely external point of view resemblances strike the superficial observer, which practically demand a grouping in accordance to relationships. Even a layman will admit that, for instance, the Armored Catfishes of the *Corydoras* group must be related to each other. The same goes for the majority of nearly all other fishes. Beyond this, it is understandable that besides these rough accordances the specialist will detect finer connections after more exact observation, and also that he will eventually have to separate species with many external resemblances taking for basis the intimate design of the fins, the teeth, the skeleton, etc.

The scientific study to a greater extent of the live beings of our globe began at the end of the 17th and the beginning of the 18th century. At that time already the need to create an internationally valid order for the purpose of mutual understanding imposed itself imperiously. It is the imperishable credit of LINNE to have created this system on the bases which are valid up to this day. The initial point was given with the 10th edition of his work 'Systema Naturae', which appeared in 1758. Linné linked the systematic order, which meanwhile has suffered many changes, to a special manner of naming the beings, the binary nomenclature. For this he used the Latin tongue. In principle this genial creation is able to cope even with the huge enlargements that Zoology and Botany have undergone with the new discoveries of species in the 18th, 19th, and 20th centuries, which come to millions.

It is understandable that it would be just the new discoveries which would not let the systematic division come to a rest. Animals and plants of the existence of which so far no one has even had an inkling would be all the time upsetting knowledge long deemed certain through the peculiarities of their design. Ever new groupings had to be created. The classification often caused such large difficulties that from time to time it was necessary to decide to rebuild the whole system, above all to make it more comprehensive.

Even today we are at a point where we cannot consider systematical classing as closed. Just remember that, for instance, the vast Amazon region has scarcely been explored ichthyologically. Add to this that now, when the number of new discoveries is no more coming in in such overwhelming numbers, one can start to check the particulars of the system. Through the linking of Systematics to nomenclature, however, it is unavoidable that each re-classing of a group of fishes involves a change in the respective name. This fact may be noticed with regret, but it is unavoidable.

In the course of scientific research it has been proven that all live beings on earth are interrelated in a certain way, insofar as all have branched off from a common stem at an earlier or later period. This made it possible to establish their mutual relationships. This happened with a basis on the available fossils, without regard to all the difficulties surged through this, and disregarding the fact that many branches of the common genealogic tree had meanwhile become extinct, or else based on common characteristics of live organisms. The division into species, genera, sub-families, families, etc. is well known to many aquarists. The great number of species, and the abundance of forms that are difficult to classify, but which are entitled to independent standing in spite of this, made it increasingly necessary to introduce sub-divisions among all these groups. Modern systematics must be ample if it wants to lay claim to be able to face future developments. The sequence of such a classification may then look as follows:

Local variety—race—sub-species —species
sub-genus—genus
Tribe of group or genera
sub-family—family
super-family—sub-order—order
super-order—sub-class—class
super-class—subphylum—phylum
Sub-kingdom—kingdom

At first such a division looks exaggerated. In fact, however, an ample division proves to be more comfortable with time than a narrow one. In the interest of easier handling and of a certain constancy of the work, we have given up a too fine subdivision, and shall use it gradually only at the place where it may be considered right.

taenia: Banded, striped.
— *Cobitis.*
— *Nannacara.*

taeniata: Banded.
— *Laemolyta.*
— *Rasbora.*

taeniatus: Banded, striped.
— *Pelmatochromis.*

taeniurus: With striped tail.
— *Prochilodus.*

T-Barb, the: see BARBUS (PUNTIUS) LATERISTRIGA.

tail rot: Inflammation of the skin, especially of the fins, caused by bacteria, which resembles the fin destruction of other diseases but has different causes. The fins dissolve totally without externally visible cause, frequently with simultaneous *Saprolegnia* (fungus) infection. Most frequently it is the tail fin which is especially attacked. The cause may in part be a hereditary proneness, as often found in the melanistic forms of live-bearing Tooth Carps. Often too, extensive contamination of the water may become the starting point of tail rot. Tests show the presence of bacteria. Cures are difficult. Sometimes the germs disappear after normal water conditions have been re-established. Baths may be tried, but they rarely lead to practical results (1 gram of Acriflavine per 100 qts. of water as a permanent bath for several days). SCHAEPERCLAUS recommends trying the sulphonamides Albucid and Globucid.

Tailor, the: see ALBURNUS BIPUNCTATUS.

Tanichthys: Fish of (the Chinese) Tan.

Genus of East Asian school fishes belonging to the family of the Carp-like or *Cyprinidae*. Small, slender, and vivacious fishes, which remind one vividly of Danios. The genus comprises only one known species, of which perhaps *Aphyocypris* is a sub-species.

— **albonubes** Lin-Shu-Yen: The White Cloud.

SHAPE: As per description of the genus. The small mouth opening is slightly tilted upwards, the lower jaw protrudes a little over the upper one. The dorsal fin is a little shorter than the anal. Length up to $1\frac{5}{8}''$.

COLOR: Olive-greenish with a golden-shiny horizontal band which is bordered below by a brown stripe. The male is slimmer and more vividly colored. The difference between this species and *Aphyocypris pooni* is that the dorsal and anal of *Tanichthys* are of a yellowish color with a red edge, while those of *Aphyocypris* are

The White Cloud, **Tanichthys albonubes**

orange-colored with a yellow edge and a little blue seam.

RANGE: Swift-flowing brooks near Canton, China.

CARE AND BREEDING: An easy-to-keep, vivacious and peaceable fish, appropriate for the community tank. It should not be kept too warm, 64-68° F, for breeding 72° F are entirely sufficient, lowest temperature 50° F. They eat all kinds of small live and prepared foods. It is advisable, though, to keep the fish in bigger schools and to offer the long, not too small aquaria. For breeding too they are quite undemanding. Composition of the water is of no special importance. The process of spawning, hatching of the eggs, and rearing of the fry is similar to that of most egg-scattering Cyprinids. When they are a few weeks old, the young do not lose out to Neon Tetras in intensity of colors. Appropriate also for open air installations.

tanning substances: Water-soluble hydrocarbons with acid reaction, widely distributed in the world of plants. They hinder decomposition and have a harsh taste. Tanning substances are dissolved to a high degree in the so-called acid waters, to which they impart a brownish color. In tropical waters containing many parts of plants in decomposition, the tanning substances cause the so-called 'black waters', to which a series of tropical fishes is adapted. The admixture of tanning substances, which may be obtained from peat or bark of willow, alder, or oak, is of great advantage for the breeding of such species. An acidification of the water may only be reached with pure or nearly pure water.

tape worm diseases of fishes: Tape worms may occur singly in fishes, but also in greater numbers. Especially in case of mass attacks great harm may result, notedly to smaller fishes. The fish may either be the final host, the intermediate host, or both. Externally, infected fishes may show strongly noticeable swellings of the belly or the abdomen. Transmission of the worms may take place through Tubifex, or through Copepods, in which many Tape Worms spend larval stages.

Generally, however, greater numbers of tape worms appear only in the intestines of bigger fishes, so that tape worm diseases are of small importance for the aquarium. The only fish that is more intensely infested is the Stickleback, which is host to tape worms of the genus *Schistocephalus*.

tape worms: see CESTODES.

Tapir-Trunk Fish, the: see MORMYRUS KANUMAE.

Tassel Fins, the: see CROSSOPTERYGII.

taxies: Components of animal behavior. Hereditarily fixed manners, bound to species, of adapting by means of certain motile reactions to space and its stimuli (for instance, currents, contacts, lighting proportions, etc.). Taxies are closely connected with the manner of living, and are intertwined with the other components of behavior. Thus, for instance, the Carp Louse, motivated by stimuli emanating from the bottom, stays always at a certain level above the ground, near the shore at 2-4″. There it has the best chance to find a fish as host.

The fulfillment of the taxies is a necessity of life even for fishes, and has to be respected if they are to enjoy well-being in the aquarium. Many fishes need moving waters, in which the adjustment to the current may be quite variable, other fishes need firm objects on which to rest, etc.

technical accessories: The aquarium is an artificially created underwater landscape. It is a fact that it too is subject to biological laws, but it is largely dependent on its caretaker. Furthermore conditions in the aquarium which are not found in free nature, for instance, restriction of space, shape of same, surface conditions, absence of the stirrings caused by winds and currents, angle of light incidence, etc., imply in that one may well strive after a natural situation, but will never reach it fully. While in free nature animate and inanimate factors balance each other, in the aquarium they are nearly exclusively enhanced or suppressed according to the whim of the aquarist. Therefore it is not infrequent that an unnatural condition is maintained artificially. Furthermore many natural factors have to be imitated artificially in the aquarium. For this we need technical accessories. It is a fact that it is perfectly possible to limit the use of such means to a minimum, but this is not always advisable or desirable. It would be nonsense, for instance, to subject Siamese Fighting Fish to the happenstances of our climate in an unheated aquarium because an electric heater is 'not natural'. Fanciers who are kept busy by their professional activities will find it difficult to survey the heating of the aquarium. In such cases a thermostat may be a great factor of tranquillity for the aquarist, even considering that the controlling mechanism may not be biologically 'right'.

Aeration, and filtration may perfectly well be avoided for long times, if the tank is sparsely stocked with fishes and plants. Notwithstanding this, however, there will always be cases in consequence of which displacements of the 'state of equilibrium' set in, which make it necessary to intervene with technical means and to re-establish normal conditions. It is better, for instance, to correct a clouding of the water by means of filtration, than to clean out the whole tank. Furthermore, considering the circulation of water caused by them, filtration and aeration may be 'more natural' than is generally supposed by the antagonists of such aids.

Therefore it is good to be cautious against losing control in a welter of technical accessories on one hand, but on the other to use them wherever they may prove to be necessary in order to attain the most natural state possible and where they can make the care for the aquarium easier.

Telmatherina: *Atherina* from the swamp.

Genus of small school fishes belonging to the family of the Ear Fishes or *Atherinidae*, which seemingly is limited exclusively to Celebes Island with its four known species. Fishes of elongated build, strongly compressed laterally, with a small mouth that is tilted upwards and equipped with small, pointed teeth. The first of the two dorsal fins is held up by 4-7 flexible spines. The caudal fin is deeply indented, the pectorals insert quite high. The lateral line is complete.

— **ladigesi** Ahl: The Celebes Rainbow Fish.

SHAPE: As per description of the

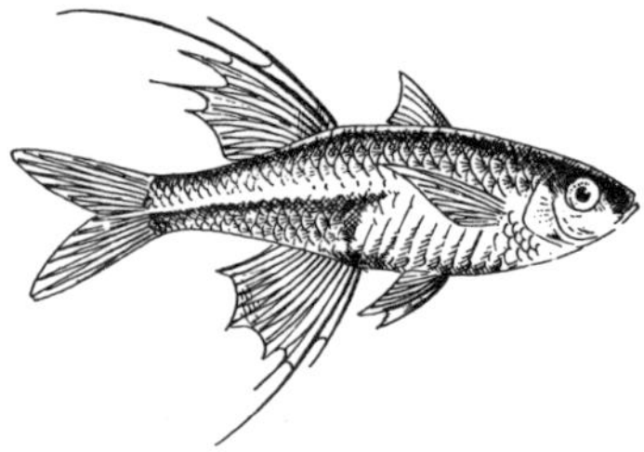

Telmatherina ladigesi

genus. D_1 V, D_2I/7-8, A I/11-12. The first dorsal is very low, the second dorsal and the anal of the male possess single, strongly extended rays, which make the fins look as if they were torn. Length up to 2″, the female remaining a little smaller.

COLOR: Glassily transparent, under incident light yellowish to blue-green silver, back, breast, belly, and part of the fins a beautiful lemon yellow. The extended fin rays are blackish. The male is slimmer and more highly colored. Besides this the males are reported to be already recognizable after they are 10 weeks old by the white dots on the tips of the tail fin lobes and of the pectorals.

ORIGIN: Celebes Island.

CARE AND BREEDING: This extremely vivacious, but peaceable and hardy school fish is at its best in larger schools of its own species. It needs some warmth, 75-82° F being advisable. Considering their vivacity, long tanks are advisable. The water must be clear and rich in oxygen. The degree of hardness may be disregarded, as the fish seems even to prefer harder waters. *T. ladigesi* are omnivorous, eating all kinds of live and prepared foods, only reluctantly from the bottom, however. There are several reports on the fact that they are sensitive to changes of water, transportation, and changes of container. For breeding them use a sufficiently big tank, as well illuminated as possible, and with tufts of fine-feathered plants. The fish give great preference to spawning into mats of Crystal Wort (*Riccia*) below the surface.

The female takes the initiative. When ripe for spawning, she starts chasing the male from the swarm. The eggs are spawned singly, side by side, under violent quivering. Sometimes, too, they are extruded by twos or threes. They are hard and resistant, being about 1 mm. in size, and hang on a little thread from plants. The fish are so-called permanent spawners. One spawning period may last from several days to three weeks. During it, spawnings take place every second day. Apparently the parents do not prey very much on their spawn, but it is advisable every evening to take out the Crystal Wort mats with the eggs, transferring them to all-glass tanks for hatching and rearing, or else daily to skim off the fry which hatch after a few days. At 82° F the alevins hatch within 7-12 days. They immediately eat nauplii of *Cyclops* or of *Diaptomus*, and after one week even those of Brine Shrimp. During the first days one may also feed *Paramecium*. Rearing them demands care and patience, though. Naturally the composition of the water of the nursery tank should be the same as that of the spawning tank. The water level should be held at about 6″. The fry grow very slowly. According to RAUT they are about 1″ long after 3 months, and may be nearly adult after 7-9 months with good feeding.

temmincki: After the Dutch physician Temminck.

— *Helostoma*.

temperature: One of the basic ambient factors which influence the fish. Observing the right temperature of the water is extremely important even if otherwise one could always create conditions in the aquarium that even nearly equal those of free nature. The adaptability of most fishes, however, helps to overcome these faults. It will not always be possible in aquaristics to fulfill the vital demands in all details, as they are very complex for each species of fish.

However, one may differentiate the great groups of the cold water fishes (fishes of the temperate zones), of the fishes with moderate need of warmth (fishes from the sub-tropics), and of the warm water fishes (fishes from the tropics). But also within these groups there are numberless gradations which have occasionally to be observed. In free nature temperature generally is a highly variable factor, despite the fact that there are tropical countries which have minute daily and seasonal variations of temperature. Therefore we find among aquarium fishes those which are adapted to stronger fluctuations of temperature, as well as those which demand even temperatures. Tropical fishes often present smaller demands on temperature than is supposed, if, for instance, they stem from shadowy, swift-flowing jungle waters, or if their spawning periods fall into the cooler rainy season. Fishes follow each fluctuation in warmth with their own body temperature. This compensation takes place very quickly, generally within few minutes. Temperature affects the whole metabolism, which generally increases with higher warmth. This is linked to greater consumption of oxygen, which is seen especially in young fry, decreasing with advancing growth. But also in this we have to count with the special accommodation of each species of fishes. A cold water fish from flowing waters reacts more intensely to an increase in temperature than a fish from a warm pond. The reaction of cold water fishes is generally quite different from that of tropical fishes. The latter have their metabolism and blood circulations braked by decreases of the warmth below a certain limit. But this may also cause lesions in the epidermis, which is sensitive to temperature. The resistance to parasites decreases secondarily, so that diseases, for instance, attacks of fungi (*Saprolegnia*) may set in as a sequel. In general terms, most fishes withstand changes in temperature quite well, if these are not too sudden nor too great.

Tench, the: see TINCA VULGARIS.

tenellus: Very frail.
— *Echinodorus*.

tengara: After the native name.
— *Sperata*.

Ten-Spot, the: see CNESTERODON DECEMMACULATUS.

tenuis: Slender, frail, thin.
— *Iguanodectes*.

teres: With round stem.
— *Sagittaria*.

terio: After the native name.
— *Barbus* (*Puntius*).

ternetzi: After the zoologist Ternetz.
— *Gymoncorymbus*.

Testacea: Shell-Bearing Amoebae. Order belonging to the phylum of the Root Feet or *Rhizopoda* which is characterized by the fact that its members build single-chambered shells from foreign substances or ones of their own, extending only pseudopods from there. The shells are egg or pear-shaped and reach lengths of up to about .02″. They are built by taking up the hard components (grains of sand, etc.), and depositing them on the surface of the cell body. Before the reproductive divisions they incorporate especially abundant materials. After this they build the new, second shell, divide, and immediately

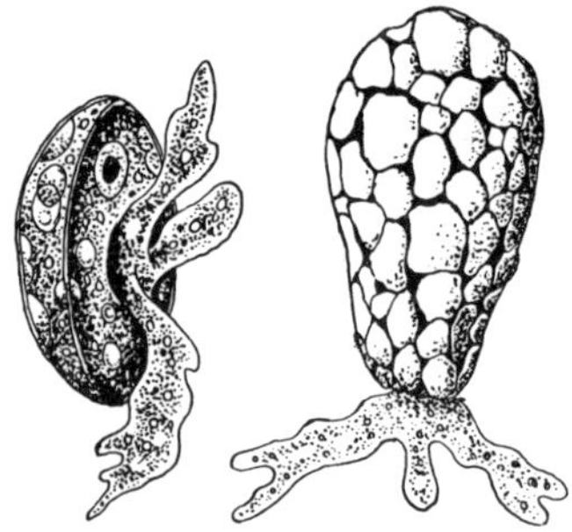

Testacea, Shelled Amoeba.

thereafter the descendant half moves in the new home, while the parent slips back into the old shell. The best known genus is *Difflugia*. The Shell-Bearing Amoebae are without significance for the aquarium, appearing most frequently in filters.

testudineus: Similar to a turtle.
— *Anabas*.

Tetra, the Blue: see MIMAGONIATES BARBERI.

Tetra, the Croaking: see GLANDULOCAUDA INEQUALIS.

Tetra from Buenos Aires, the: see HEMIGRAMMUS CAUDOVITTATUS.

Tetra, the Green: see BRYCONALESTES CHAPERI.

Tetra, the Yellow: see HYPHESSOBRYCON BIFASCIATUS.

tetracanthus: Four-spined.
— *Cichlasoma*.

Tetragonopterus: Squared fin. South American genus belonging to the family of the Characins or *Characidae*. Moderately small fishes of high shape, strongly compressed laterally, and with complete lateral line.

— **chalceus** Aggasiz: The Chatoyant Tetra.

SHAPE: As per description of the genus. D 11, A 28-34. Length up to $4\frac{3}{4}''$.

COLOR: Silvery with shoulder spot and a dark spot on the root of the caudal fin. The male is smaller and slimmer.

RANGE: From Guiana to the Rio S. Francisco, Brazil.

CARE AND BREEDING: A long-lasting species, which does not need much warmth, and easily withstands temperatures down to 59° F. It likes sunlight and plenty of space for swimming. The fish are best kept in company with swift-swimming species of the same size, as they are quarrelsome towards fishes that are smaller. *T. chalceus* eat all kinds of live and artificial foods.

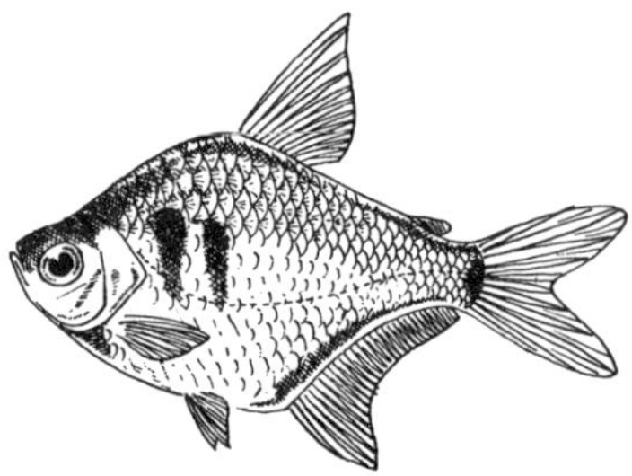

Tetragonopterus chalceus

tetramerus: Foursome, divided into four parts.
— *Aequidens*.

Tetraodon: The four-toothed one. Genus belonging to the family of the Four-Toothed Puffers or *Tetraodontidae*.

— **cutcutia** Hamilton-Buchanan: The Common Puffer.

SHAPE: As per description of the family. D 10-12, A 10. The body is without spines. Length up to 8″.

The Puffer, Tetraodon cutcutia, puffed up.

COLOR: Variable in color. Generally lighter to darker olive-greenish, whitish on the belly with a superimposed reticulate design. During the spawning period the tail of the male is strikingly red-edged. The female is lighter in color and remains a little smaller.
RANGE: The coastal regions of East India and the Malayan Archipelago (?), also in brackish and fresh water.
CARE AND BREEDING: As per description of the family. The fish are quarrelsome despite the fact that there are reports to the contrary on hand. They like to stay near the bottom, hiding behind rocks. Older specimens like to puff up, and even smaller ones are able to do this, but are reported to die easily of the consequences. The male exerts intense care for the spawn.

— **fahaka fahaka** Linné: The Nile Puffer, or Fahak.
SHAPE: As per description of the family. Nearly the whole body is covered with sharp spines. D 12-14, A 10-11. Length up to 18″.
COLOR: Gray to live-drab base with up to 14 horizontal stripes which in youth stand out very clearly, but pale with age. The belly is whitish gray.
RANGE: The river system of the Nile. Two further sub-species:
(a) *T. f. strigosus* Bennet, from the Niger region;
(b) *T. f. rudolfianus* Deraniyagala, from Lake Rudolf. This subspecies is reported to reach lengths of only 2⅜″.
CARE AND BREEDING: As per description of the family. The species is very vicious and unfriendly, at least as far as the genuine Nile Fahak is concerned.

— **fluviatilis** Hamilton-Buchanan: The Green Puffer.
SHAPE: As per description of the family. There may be densely distributed small spines, but they may also lack completely. The nose pit is

Tetraodon fluviatilis

equipped with remarkable appendages. D 15-16, A 13-15. Length up to 7″.
COLOR: Strongly variable in color, generally a greenish base with dark, light-edged, mostly round spots. The underside whitish on young specimens, becoming yellowish to gray later on.
RANGE: In fresh and brackish waters of India and Malaya. The fish do not go over into the sea.
CARE AND BREEDING: As per description of family. According to RANDOW, the species is said not to withstand pure sea water. Small specimens are considered relatively gregarious and peaceable, growing increasingly vicious later on. Spawning is done in brackish water. The eggs are laid on rocks and guarded by the male. RANDOW has succeeded in rearing the young. As food he offered them egg, scraped meat, daphnia, after growing from the infusoria period.

— **leiurus** Bleeker:
SHAPE: As per description of the family. D 14, A 11. The appendages on the nasal pit are tube-shaped, undivided, and possess only one opening. Small spines on the skin. Length up to 5″. A subspecies, *T. l. brevirostris*, differs from the typical form by less dense covering with spines and by the blunter snout.
COLOR: Base, on the upper part brownish-green, on the underside yellowish to silver colored, on this everywhere round to honeycomb-

shaped dark spots. According to GEISER, the female shows lighter spots on a dark base during the act of spawning.

RANGE: In fresh waters of Thailand, Malaya, Java, Sumatra, and Borneo.

CARE AND BREEDING: As per description of the family. The species is pronouncedly quarrelsome, towards its own species as well as towards other fishes. Therefore it is in no way appropriate for keeping in communities. The formerly occasionally presented theory that this fish is peaceable and quiet is due to their being confused with *T. palembangensis*.

GEISER has succeeded in breeding them in greater numbers. Temperature 80-86° F. Hardness of water 12 DH. Feeding, mainly on earthworms. Both parents cleaned a rock in the Cichlid manner, the female showing the above-mentioned colors during this. The 300-500 eggs were released all at once, in a lightning-quick spawning, being immediately fertilized by the male, and the spawn smoothed with the belly by both parents. The care for the spawn, exerted only by the male and consisting of fanning and watching the eggs, lasted to the hatching of the fry. These were then left to themselves. Hatching took 4-5 days at 86° F. Immediately after leaving the egg the fry, which were still carrying a large yolk sac, struggled toward the surface, but kept near the bottom later in the day. Toward the evening they began to become free-swimming. After three days they ate freshly-hatched brine shrimp and *Cyclops* nauplii. GEISER advises siphoning off nine tenths of the water daily, substituting it with fresh water of the same temperature. Already after five days the alevins puffed up to the size of a pea. From the length of $\frac{3}{4}''$ on they showed the behavior of grown specimens.

— **mbu** Boulenger: The Golden-Ringed Puffer.

SHAPE: As per description of family. The nasal appendages are of a remarkable construction. The body is covered with numerous thin spines which may be erected on the belly side. Length up to 30″.

COLOR: Yellowish-white base with darker spot designs. The belly whitish-yellow.

RANGE: Tropical West Africa, the Congo region. Quite common.

CARE AND BREEDING: As per description of family. No detailed reports are available so far.

— **miurus** Boulenger: The Valise Puffer.

SHAPE: A differently built fish. The body is relatively flattened, the eyes are tilted upwards, and so is the elongated mouth opening. The skin is covered with numerous thin spines. D 9-10, A 8-9. Length around $5\frac{1}{2}''$. The head is very big. The tentacles are unimportant.

COLOR: Strongly variable, gray, sand-colored, red, or nearly black on the back, lightly spotted. Belly light colored.

RANGE: The Belgian Congo.

CARE AND BREEDING: This unsociable, probably predatory, fish likes to dig in into the sand, so that only its eyes and snout are visible. It demands good-sized live foods, also fishes.

Tetraodon miurus

— palembangensis Bleeker: The Figure-8 Puffer.
SHAPE: As per description of the family. The nasal appendages are not strongly developed. The skin is covered with well-developed spines. D 10-14, A 11-12. Length, more than 8″.
COLOR: Dark mottled on yellow to green base, the underside whitish-yellow. In part the spots form figure-eights.
RANGE: Southeast Asia, the Malayan Archipelago.
CARE AND BREEDING: As per description of the family. The species bred by GEISER in the Zurich (Switzerland) Aquarium is not *T. palembangensis* as was supposed originally, but *T. leirus brevirostris*.

Tetraodon shoutedeni

— shoutedeni Pellegrin: The Leopard Puffer.
SHAPE: As per description of the family. The body is covered with very small spines. The nasal appendages are very well developed. D 9-10, A 8-9. Length up to 4″.
COLOR: Dark back, especially on the sides rows of dark, rounded spots. Belly yellowish.
RANGE: The Belgian Congo, very common everywhere.
CARE AND BREEDING: As per description of the family. A vivacious, very pleasing fish. Needs additional vegetable food. WERNER observed four spawnings during a month, which followed at intervals of one week. One hatching yielded 200-300 fry, which could not be reared for lack of adequate food.

Tetraodon somphongsi

— somphongsi Klausewitz:
SHAPE: As per description of the family. Nasal tube without tentacles. D 13, A 11. Length unknown.
COLOR: Yellow-brown base with some irregular stripes which generally start from the eyes and run in different directions, part of them saddle-like over the back. The species possesses a strongly developed physiological change of colors. Sex differences unknown.
RANGE: From fresh waters in Thailand.
CARE AND BREEDING: The fish leads a hidden life, especially during daylight, going out after food during the night. According to OSTERMUELLER, they relish especially eating *Gammarus pulex*. The fish are slow eaters which divide their food and chew it up. Furthermore they take tubifex and mosquito larvae, but reject Cyclops and prepared foods. Attacks on the fins of other fishes were observed at night time. In all the fish did not

show themselves to be very sociable, even toward each other, but the threatened ones generally avoided damage by hurried retreats. They show a pronounced territorial sense, and defend their chosen range.

LUELING (1958) publishes interesting details on this, which show that the 'staking of claims' depends on the available space, like that of many other fishes. In a tank with 9 gals. capacity, two specimens guarded one personal territory each. These ranges, each starting from a diagonally opposite corner, had an extension of about 7″ of the water. A third Puffer, which due to insufficient size of the tank could not establish any territorial rights, had to exert frantic efforts not to come too near the center of the other two fishes' homes. The rights of the specimens that lived on their own territories were protected by ramming pushes which were thrust against each other, starting from a 'position of attention' (LUELING). After the fish have stood facing each other with violently vibrating fins and looking fixedly in the eyes of the foe, they try to ram each other, but separate immediately again, the trespassing specimen drawing back from the invaded territory. Sometimes, with stronger excitation, it also came to bluffing. The position of bluffing consists in that the fish stand on their heads while vigorously vibrating their fins, facing each other with their bellies, which during the bluffing phase shows an intense rust-red stripe. Meanwhile the belly is puffed up moderately.

Bluffing very rarely leads to fights. In these, one fish bites fast to the other's back, after which it is carried around in the vertical body stance that derives as a result of this. This phase reminds one of the mating behavior of certain Puffers in which the mating fishes too bite fast on each other.

Tetraodontidae: Puffers.

Family of 'four-toothed' Puffer Fishes belonging to the order of the *Plectognathi* which, instead of the common teeth, possess two broad tooth plates on each jaw. In part these are visible even in closed mouths, giving the impression of a beak.

All members of the family are moderately-sized fishes, of which many species are appropriate also for keeping in fresh water after the necessary accommodation. The body is compact and covered with a hard, leathery skin. The scales are involuted, and are either transformed into spines, or else there are only small nodules on the skin in their place. Head and eyes are large. The hard part of the dorsal fin is involuted, ventrals are totally lacking. The Puffers are able to puff or blow up. The ventral wall is thin and elastic in order to permit this. According to CLARK the stomach is equipped with a strong circular muscle (sphincter) on both ends, which contracts after the entrance of each gulp of water or air, retaining same. When full of air, the fishes swim belly-up on the surface, while the spines, if there are any present, are erected. The releasing of the air is accompanied by a hissing noise. While submerged, they puff up with water, possibly as a means of bluffing during fights and while they are caring for their spawn.

The teeth are used as nutcrackers to crush the shells of mussels and snails, which in free nature represent the main diet of these fishes. In general one needs vigorous live foods for them, but not too lively ones, as all Puffers are indifferent swimmers.

CHLUPATY relates that while

feeding one can distinctly hear the cracking of the firm shells, as well as the creaking friction of the jaws on the glass panes of the tank when the fish swim against these under excitation. Different from most other fishes, the locomotion of the Puffers is achieved by the pectoral fins, which gives their manner of swimming a peculiar stiffness. Many Puffers like to stay in the middle or upper water levels, and only a few move near the bottom. The eyes are relatively big, and are remarkable for their motility, especially as they can be moved to a high degree independently of each other. Puffers are quite vicious and nasty toward each other and are pugnacious also toward other species. Their strong teeth are able to inflict considerable damage. They need roomy tanks with dense planting and hiding caves. In general they are not very sensitive to lower temperatures, but feel well only from 72-79° F on.

Imported fish which do not come from pure fresh water should at first receive an addition of sea water to their tanks, but then one may gradually reduce the percentage of this until the water has reached the point of being fresh again.

For bottom soil use not too coarse sand, for some species, for instance, *Tetraodon miurus* and *Colmesus psittacus*, which like to dig themselves in, only fine-grained bottom soil. The fishes occupy and defend individual caves and hiding places. In general they show a good memory and soon remember feeding places and the image of their caretaker.

Attempts at spawning have remained without results that are worth mentioning. Only lately have they seemed to succeed to a greater extent. *T. cutcutia* was bred many decades ago in a small tank, by SCHAEME. The male cared for the spawn in the manner of the bottom-spawning Cichlids. Rearing the young, however, proved difficult, almost impossible. The species *T. shoutedeni*, kept by WERNER, spawned twice within a space of three weeks, scattering the relatively small eggs all over the tank. One spawning yielded 200 to 300 hatched fry, which already resembled their parents in shape. Lacking their natural food, though, they soon died off. They did not react to the most usual foods. The female frequently took the eggs in her mouth and spit them out again. Whether this represented an act of caring for the spawn is uncertain.

GEISER reports greater successes in breeding *Tetraodon leiurus brevirostris*. According to this report both parents cleaned a rock by fanning it and 'blowing' on it, and spawned in the manner of Cichlids. The eggs were released all at once. The male exerted the care for the spawn alone. The Puffer fry, which hatched after about 4-5 days at 86° F, at first made an endeavor to reach the surface, and only thereafter they collected gradually on the bottom. Growth was relatively quick. They ate Brine Shrimp and Cyclops nauplii from the first day of free-swimming on. GEISER reared about 2000 specimens within one year.

CHLUPATY reports, among others, also on the fact that during the act of spawning the male sucked fast to the belly of the female and was carried around by her in that position.

Genera, among others, *Tetraodon*, *Colomesus*, and *Chonerhinus*.

Tetraodontoidea: Blow Fishes, Puffers.
Sub-order belonging to the order of the *Plectognathi* established by HOEDEMAN and BERG—which comprises the families *Tetraodontidae*,

and *Diodontidae*.

Texas Cichlid, the: see HERICHTHYS CYANOGUTTATUS.

thalictroides: Similar to the Feathered Columbine (*Thalictrum*).
— *Ceratopteris*.

Thallophyta: Phylum pertaining to the plant kingdom, which comprises lower plants which are equipped with nuclei-bearing cells or with nuclear substance, living singly or in colonies. They never possess roots and leaves. The *Thallophyta* include, among others, the *Algae*.

thallus: The body of the lower plants, for instance, of *Algae*, without the common division into roots, stems, leaves, etc.

thayeri: After a personal name.
— *Aequidens*.

Thayeria: Genus of South American fishes belonging to the family of the Characins or *Characidae*, of elongated shape and deeply forked tail fin, the lower lobe of which is longer than the upper one. The fishes are remarkable for their manner of swimming, which is slightly tilted upwards.

— obliqua Eigenmann: The Penguin.

SHAPE: As per description of the genus, elongated, strongly compressed laterally. D 10, A 16-17. Length up to $3\frac{1}{4}''$.

COLOR: Silvery white with black horizontal band which runs into the lower lobe of the tail fin; on both sides of the band a lighter zone. The male is a little smaller and slimmer.

RANGE: The Amazon system.

CARE AND BREEDING: This harmless and active species is especially appropriate for keeping in communities. If kept alone, the fish become a little shy and like to stay hidden among plants. Bigger schools cause a peculiar impression due to their oblique position. The fish are omnivores, but take food

Thayeria obliqua

that has sunk to the bottom only unwillingly and rarely. Temperature, 73-78° F.

Breeding is considered very easy. To set them up for spawning, use a medium-sized tank of about 6 gals. capacity, with fresh, very soft water, at about 82° F.

The 600-800 eggs (?) are laid among plants near the bottom. The fry hatch after 12-15 hours, and become free-swimming after 5 days. However, they are a little sensitive, and are not easy to rear.

— sanctae-mariae Ladiges: The Short-Banded Thayeria.

SHAPE: As per description of the genus. Elongated, strongly compressed laterally. D 12, A 16-17. Length up to $2\frac{3}{8}''$.

COLOR: Brownish olive-colored to silvery-white, with a black horizontal band which begins a little below the dorsal fin and extends into the lower lobe of the caudal. Above and below, the band is limited by a golden-yellow to silver-white zone. The male is slimmer.

RANGE: Brazil, near a village called Santa Maria.

CARE AND BREEDING: See *Th. obliqua*.

thermometers: Floating heat-measuring instruments, especially made for aquaristic purposes, some-

Thayeria sanctae-mariae

times also built in a manner that they may be stuck into the bottom soil by means of a glass foot. It is possible to fix floating thermometers to glass panes by means of a sucking disc made of rubber. When buying them take care that they are exact, which is not always the case. It is advisable to compare them with a recognizedly exact instrument.

thermometer scale: The units used for measuring temperature are the 'degrees'. According to the measuring system used, one has the warmth in degrees centigrade (C), Réaumur (R), or Fahrenheit (F). In the English-speaking world it is usual to measure in 'F'.

thermostats: see HEATING.

Thick-Lipped Gourami, the: see COLISA LABIOSA.

tholloni: After Thollon, the collector.

— *Tilapia.*

thoracatum: Armored.

— *Hoplosternum.*

Thoracocharax: Charax with breast-plate.

South American genus of Characin-like fishes belonging to the family of the Hatchet Bellies or *Gasteropelecidae*, with three known species.

— maculatus Steindachner: The Dotted Hatchet Fish.

SHAPE: As per description of the family. D 10-11, A 35-37. Length up to 3½″.

COLOR: Silvery with metallic shine and many dots disposed in cross bands.

RANGE: Eastern Colombia and Panama.

CARE AND BREEDING: A resistant species, which, like all Hatchet Fishes, likes to catch live foods from the surface. 73-68° F. Cover the tank well! Not yet spawned.

— securis (Filippi): The Silver Hatchet Fish.

SHAPE: As per description of the family. D 13-16, A 38-42. Length around 3″.

RANGE: Tropical South America, East of the Andes, down to the La Plata, not in the regions of the Rio Sao Francisco and of the Orinoco.

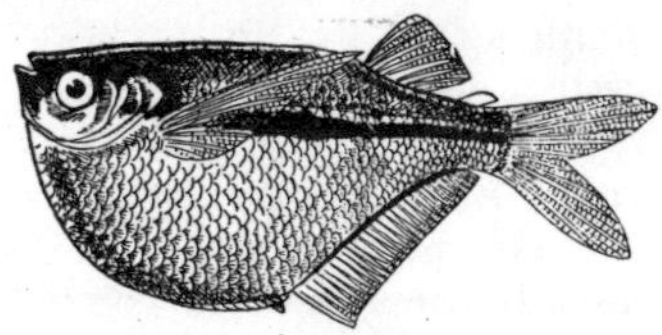

Thoracocharax securis

CARE AND BREEDING: A very frail species that needs much warmth. Even specimens that originate from the South do not withstand temperatures below 68° F.

Thoracostei: Order belonging to the sub-class of the New Fins or *Neopterygii*, with one family that is of importance for aquaristics, the Sticklebacks or *Gasterosteidae*.

Thorn Eyes: see ACANTHOPHTHALMUS.

thought processes of fishes: Fishes possess relatively well developed thought processes, which in science leads to many experiments in training. The Trout, for instance, tends to remain in particular haunts, which it finds again even if removed for quite a distance (experiments made by FRANZ with old Trout, removed for distances up to 3½ miles). Fishes which exercise parental care and build nests find their breeding-site again after being removed for quite a distance. The regular migrations of fishes, as they are of a limited nature, can lead us to believe that fishes possess a well-developed sense of orientation.

Besides, fishes are able to distinctly remember forms, colors, sounds, chemical stimuli, etc. to which they have been trained or have trained themselves to respond.

thread-worm diseases: Diseases caused by thread-worms (Nematodes). Thread-worms appear either mainly as internal parasites, or occasionally also as skin parasites. They undergo a metamorphosis with change of hosts. The youth stages live in mud, or encysted, or else free in fishes. In this case the fish is only an intermediate host. But it may also harbor sexually mature worms as final host. In some cases the fish is both intermediate and final host.

The parasitic larvae initially live free within the skin or the internal organs, but are soon encysted and form relatively large, white cysts on the internal organs. In cases of strong infestation, these may lead to severe inflammations of the infected parts. Besides the native species of Nematodes, also tropical ones have been carried on tropical fishes. Possibly the parasites are also transmitted by tubifex.

There are no proven cures. The only possible protective measure is to avoid using food animals which may be carriers (tubifex, microcrustaceans), but this is hardly feasible for the aquarist who must occasionally depend on these foods totally or at least in part.

Three-lined Pencilfish, the: see NANNOSTOMUS TRIFASCIATUS.

Three-lined Rasbora: see RASBORA TRILINEATA.

Three-spined Stickleback, the: see GASTEROSTEUS ACULEATUS.

Three-spotted Barb: see BARBUS TRISPILUS.

ticto: After the native name.

— *Barbus* (*Puntius*).

Tiger Barb, the: see BARBUS (PUNTIUS) HEXAZONA.

Tilapia: After the native name. Genus of African fishes belonging to the family of the Cichlids or *Cichlidae*, with numerous, hard-to-differentiate species, sub-species, and local varieties, which extend also into Asia Minor, and have been transplanted to India and other Southeast Asiatic countries for economic reasons. Many species of *Tilapia* are mouthbreeders, others care for their spawn in the manner of the bottom-spawning Cichlids.
CARE AND BREEDING: As described for Cichlids. Some of the species are very belligerent and root strongly.

— dolloi Boulenger: The Congo Mouthbreeder.
SHAPE: Of relatively high build, strongly compressed laterally, the forehead a little indented above the eyes. D XV-XVI/9-11, A III/8-9. Length up to 6″.
COLOR: Green with mother-of-pearl sheen and dark-edged scales, which form unconnected horizontal bands. The throat of the male is deep black. The female is similar in color, but a little paler.
RANGE: Tropical Africa, from Spanish Guinea to the Congo region.
CARE AND BREEDING: As per description of the genus. The species is relatively peaceable, and is said not to root too strongly, but needs vegetable food in sufficient quantities. Therefore only hard plants in pots can be used. To cover the need for vegetable food, give them slightly stale lettuce leaves, otherwise live foods as for all Cichlids. The species does not need too much

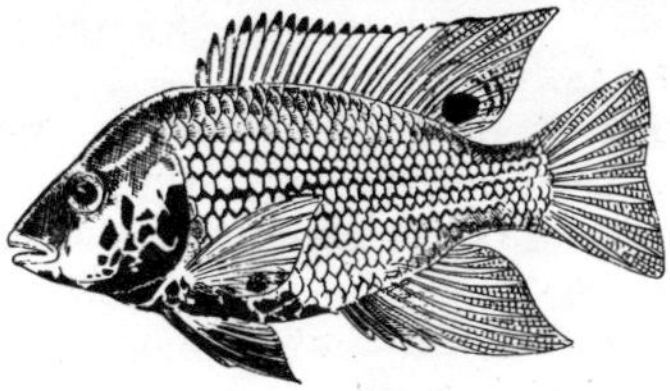

Tilapia galilaea

warmth. 70-73° F are sufficient, for breeding 77° F, lowest 60° F. Due to their size they naturally need roomy tanks. The fish are mouthbreeders and spawn in pits. It is reported that both sexes share the care for the spawn, which lasts for about 4 weeks. At the point of free-swimming the young are already $\frac{1}{8}''$ long.

— **galilaea** (Artedi): The Splendid Mouthbreeder.

SHAPE: The body quite high, strongly compressed laterally, egg-shaped. D XV-XVII/12-14, A III/10-12. Length up to 6″.

COLOR: Silvery-blue base with rows of golden dots and an alternating band design. Sex differences are not exactly known.

RANGE: From Palestine over the Nile River system to tropical West Africa, quite common everywhere, in waters of all kinds, and with many local varieties.

CARE AND BREEDING: As for *T. dolloi*, also omnivorous and needing plenty of plant food. Relatively peaceable in large tanks. Mouthbreeder. In this case, too, both sexes seem to care for the spawn in free nature, but this has not yet been verified.

Tilapia dolloi

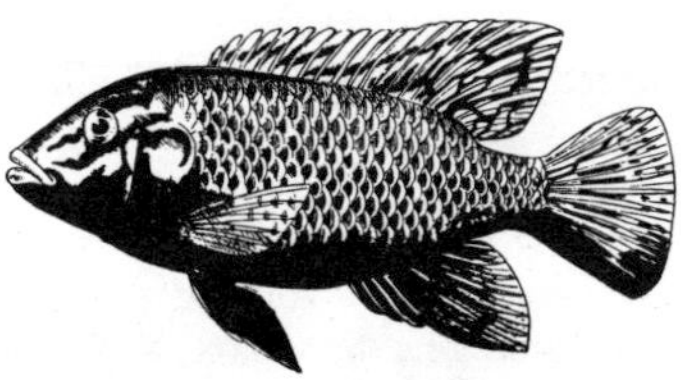

guinasana Trewavas: The Guinas Cichlid.

SHAPE: The body is only moderately high, compressed laterally. D XII-XIV/10-11, A III/8-10. Length up to $5\frac{1}{2}''$, the female remaining a little smaller.

COLOR: This species presents several color sports. In general they are bronze-colored with shiny-metallic scale edges and a deep black throat and belly region. The females differ only little in coloring from the males.

RANGE: Lake Guinas in South West Africa, a very deep, water-filled crater, with steep, rocky shores and clear water.

CARE AND BREEDING: As given for the non-mouthbreeding Cichlids. The species roots little and spares the plants, but needs plant food occasionally. Temperatures 70-75° F and more, lowest temperature 64° F.

— **guineensis** Bleeker: The Guinea Cichlid.

Body quite high, with steeply rising forehead line and slightly vaulted belly contour, strongly compressed laterally. D XV-XVI/11-13, A III/9. Length up to 8″. Olive-greenish with darker spots and beautiful spots on the gill covers.

ORIGIN: The Gold Coast (Ghana) and farther North.

No particulars are known on care and breeding. Probably mouthbreeders.

— **heudeloti** Dumeril: The Senegal Cichlid.

SHAPE: The relatively high body is strongly compressed laterally. The dorsal outline rises steeply, especially on older specimens. D XV-XIII/D XV-XVII/10-14, A III/8-11. Length up to 12″.

COLOR: Highly variable, in general blue-gray to violet, the scales on the sides with silver or gold lustre, the gill covers brass to copper colored. Young specimens possess

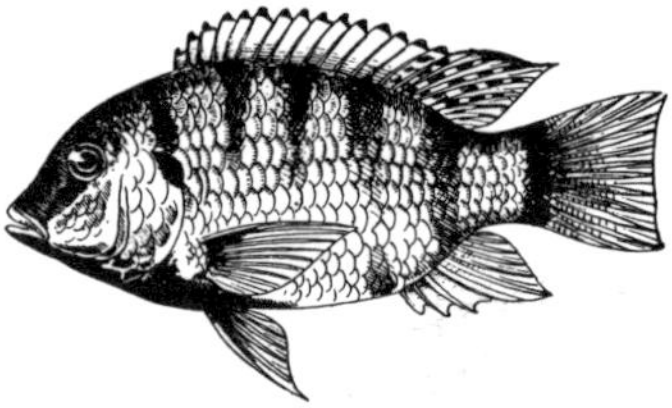

Tilapia heudeloti

blue-black cross bands. During the spawning period throat and breast take on a deep black color, especially on the females. The vertical fins of the males extend into points.

RANGE: The coastal regions of tropical West Africa, from Senegal to the Congo. There the species is found quite frequently both in fresh and brackish waters.

CARE AND BREEDING: As described for *T. dolloi*, but they do not care for the fry for as long as the others. Also for this species the question whether both parents care for the spawn or not has not yet been cleared up. Temperatures 68-73° F, for breeding 77° F, lowest 59° F.

— **lepidura** Boulenger: The Pearl Tilapia.

SHAPE: Relatively high, strongly compressed laterally. D XVI/10-12, A III/8-9. Length up to 8″.

COLOR: Brassy lustre with alternating, faintly-hued cross bands and rows of red dots, the underside red. The female is paler in coloring and the male has pointed dorsal and anal fins.

RANGE: Fresh and brackish waters in Tropical West Africa.

CARE AND BREEDING: As described for *T. dolloi*. A little more warmth, 75° F and higher. Probably a mouthbreeder.

— **mossambica** Peters: The Mozambique Mouthbreeder.

SHAPE: The body is moderately elongated, compressed laterally. The head is a little pointed, the mouth opening big. D XV-XVII/10-12, A III/9-10. Length up to 14″.

COLOR: Very simply colored outside the spawning period; during this time the male blue with red or reddish fins, green shiny dots on these. The sub-species *T.m. natalensis* is coal black with enamel white throat.

RANGE: East Africa from the Nile to Natal in the South, in waters of all kinds, also in the sea, frequent everywhere. Fish that grow a little big and are especially appropriate for the show aquarium. They are vigorous rooters and destroyers of plants. During the spawning period the male becomes quite pugnacious and especially vicious towards the females which are not yet ready to spawn. Therefore one needs a temporary separating pane. Mouthbreeders of which the females care for the brood. Temperatures, 68-77° F, occasionally also less. The time for carrying the fry, which emerge from the mouth after 12-14 days, lasts only a few days. Like all species of *Tilapia*, also this one needs vegetable nutrition to complement the live foods.

— **natalensis** (Weber): The Natal Mouthbreeder.

Formerly a separate species, now included in *T. mossambica*.

— **nilotica** Linné: The Nile Mouthbreeder.

A little-known species that grows very large, ranging over Syria, East and West Africa. Length up to 20″. Mouthbreeders.

— **sparrmanni** Andrew Smith: Sparrmann's Tilapia.

SHAPE: A little-known, but very beautiful species. The body is moderately high, the forehead line rounded, strongly compressed laterally. D XII-XV/9-11, A III/9-10. Length up to 8″.

COLOR: Lustrous greenish with darker cross bands and red dots on each scale. The fins have a broad red edge. Nothing is known about their sex differences.

RANGE: South Africa, from Angola to Natal, in fresh water only. The species is very common everywhere.

CARE AND BREEDING: Care, as per *T. dolloi.* Vigorous plant eaters. Probably mouthbreeders.

Tilapia tholloni

— tholloni (Sauvage):
A pretty, but quarrelsome species which has only rarely been imported and has not yet been able to find its place in the aquarium. It roots strongly, and needs plenty of plant food, so that it is impossible to keep them in planted aquaria. Probably a mouthbreeder.

— zillii (Gervais): Zilli's Tilapia.

SHAPE: Moderately elongated, strongly compressed laterally. D XIV-XVI/10-13, A III/7-10. Length up to 12″, remaining smaller in the aquarium.

COLOR: A very beautiful species, greenish, passing over to reddish on the lower half of the body. The gill cover with luminous blue-green dashes and a remarkable opercular dot. On the insertion of the soft dorsal fin a peacock's eye design. The female is simpler in color, with rounded dorsal and anal. Two white spots at the base to the rear of the dorsal are reported to be characteristic of the female.

Tilapia brevimanis seems to be a sub-species of *T. zillii,* which differs from this species by the

Tilapia zillii

length of the pectorals, which reach beyond the beginning of the anal fin.

RANGE: Africa, North of the Equator, also going over into Asia Minor. There the fish are found in flowing and standing waters of all kinds also in brackish ones and in the watering places of the Sahara.

CARE AND BREEDING: As given for *T. dolloi,* but reported to root strongly. Additional to vigorous live foods, also vegetable food has to be offered. The fish are belligerent and like to jump. Care for the spawn in the manner of the non-mouthbreeding Cichlids.

timidity: Aquarium fishes often show an increased timidity, which appears suddenly without their having shown previous signs of definite nervousness. At the slightest disturbance they race through the aquarium, drive their heads into the sand, corners, or other dark places, where they remain lying in a kind of coma with spread fins. The first coma may end fatally, but generally the fishes recover again. As a rule this increased timidity is caused by contamination of the water. It may be cured by removing the cause, that is by taking out part of the water and replacing it with fresh water of the same temperature.

Often aquarium fishes become timid if they are illuminated only from the sides. Especially Angelfish and other Cichlids may then show the symptoms described above. Light from above will generally help, in extreme cases also a total darkening of the tank for some days.

The timidity of newly imported fishes, or of such that have been transported over longer distances, is generally acquired during transportation and tapers off while they grow used to the new surroundings. Also otherwise calm fishes may become a little more timid after changing over into a new tank, such as happens, for instance, even with the Diamond Perch, *Enneacanthus obesus*.

Tinca: Genus of Carp-like fishes belonging to the family of the *Cyprinidae*, with vigorous body, small scales, and a thick skin rich in mucus cells, which also cover the fins. The mouth is terminal, with two barbels in its corner. The gullet teeth are pestle-shaped.

— vulgaris Cuvier: The Tench.

SHAPE: As per description of the genus. D 4/8-9, A 3-4/6-7. The male has a thickened ray at the front edge of the ventral fins. Length up to 20″.

COLOR: Bronze-greenish, there also being a golden variety with bigger, thin scales.

RANGE: An inhabitant of slow-flowing and standing warmer waters of Europe, especially in shallow, well-planted lakes, rich in spawning places. Reared in hatcheries as an edible fish.

CARE AND BREEDING: Only smaller specimens are appropriate for the home aquarium. Care as described for the Carp (see CYPRINUS).

Tinca vulgaris

titteya: After the native name.
— *Barbus* (*Puntius*).

Tooth Carps: see MICROCYPRINI.

tornieri: After Prof. Tornier, of the Zoological Museum of Berlin, Germany.
— *Rasbora*.

Toxotes: Archer.

Genus belonging to the family of the Archer Fishes or *Toxotidae*. Body shape as per description of the family. LUELING has published comprehensive studies on the genus. According to these, freshly imported specimens are a little sensitive, very frightened, and violent in their movements during the first few weeks. In this regard, however, there are marked individual differences. It is advisable to offer the fishes long tanks with hiding places: lesions on the lower jaw, which they contract due to their frightened behavior, generally heal quickly again. Quite more serious are lacerations and discolorations of the cornea, which may appear when the fish are netted from the tank and collide with the walls of the net. To cure such discolorations LUELING prescribes a bath in Acriflavine in the usual concentration employed against external parasites. Such baths usually show their healing effect after only 48 hours. According to our own experience, slight discolorations caused by netting the fish often disappear by themselves, but caution is always advisable. Archer Fishes like, clear, well-aerated water, low in infusoria, but their need of oxygen is not as great as that of other fishes coming from brackish waters. Domesticated specimens are quite resistant. They may be quite nasty, however, above all toward each other, which should be considered when choosing the aquarium for them, which should offer plenty of hiding places. Vanquished specimens change their color to dirty-gray, to black, especially on the lower half of the body. Generally the intake of food takes place in water, like that of all other fishes, the shooting-down of insects therefore is only an additional manner of feeding. They relish eating daphnia, mosquito larvae, and meal grubs. Especially the latter represent a valuable substitute food in winter, due to their chitinic shell. According to our own experience, soft food animals like tubifex and enchytrae are hardly ever accepted. *Toxotes* give special preference to food taken from the surface, and eat from the bottom only in exceptional cases and after express training to do so. Chopped meal grubs generally float for a while. Daphnia may be kept on the surface if one lets them dry in the net for a few minutes. Spitting after food is done with deadly aim, but the fish also try to catch their prey by jumping after it if its distance from the water surface is not too great. Sated fish do not 'shoot'. According to LUELING they spend a certain energy in doing this, and have first to 'reload' again. Fish which have not spit for some time spend the stored energy in an 'idling reaction', spraying even after food that is already in the water, thus impelling it along before them.

— jaculatrix (Pallas): The Archer Fish.

SHAPE: As per description of the family. D IV/11-12, A III/15-17, the spines of the dorsal fin very strong. Length up to 8″.

COLOR: Shiny white with slightly-slanted, deep-black cross bands, which do not reach the lower edge of the body. Sex differences unknown.

RANGE: Coastal regions from the Red Sea to the Indian Ocean, in the previously mentioned living places.

CARE AND BREEDING: As per description of the family and genus.

Toxotes jaculatrix

Toxotidae: Archer Fishes.

Family belonging to the sub-order of the Perch-like or *Percoidea*, of elongated, Perch-shaped build, more or less strongly compressed laterally. The body is elongatedly diamond-shaped. The head is pointed and flattened, the snout has a very broad mouth opening, but a small oesophagus. The lower jaw is longer than the upper one. Brush-shaped teeth are found on the jaws, the plowshare bone, and on several other bones of the mouth. The eyes are large, vivacious, and expressive, the cornea being vaulted out and very sensitive. The dorsal contour is nearly straight, the ventral one strongly arched. The dorsal fin shows 4-5 strong spines and 15-17 soft rays. The lateral line is complete. Archer Fishes are remarkable for the fact that they shoot down part of their food, which consists of flying insects, with drops of water, if the prey sits on objects outside the water. The shooting-off of the drops is achieved by contracting the muscles of the oesophagus, with the whole body taking aim, especially the lower jaw acting as a launching guide. The drops are thrown with great violence.

Only one genus (*Toxotes*), with five known species, of which the species *T. jaculatrix* and *T. chatareus* are generally found in commerce. The Archer Fishes inhabit the Southeast Asian coastal regions, where they are mainly found in protected sea coves, in mangrove swamps, and in the river mouths. They also migrate far into fresh water.

trace elements: Trace elements are those chemical elements which are dissolved in water only in minute quantities, and which, in traces only, play an important role as catalysts of metabolism. The lack of trace elements may lead to symptoms of starvation, excesses of them to poisonings. In set-up aquaria a lack of trace elements could hardly ever happen, as they are at all times released by the bottom soil and the plants, as well as by the water itself, and are re-introduced into the water with each feeding. Furthermore the quantitative distribution of trace elements in the water is completely uncontrollable in practical aquaristics. The widespread opinion, according to which difficulties in the growth of animals and plants in the aquarium are caused by the scarcity of trace elements is obviously wrong. The elements are needed as traces only, and are always present as such.

Many authors defend the idea that trace elements should be added artificially to the aquarium. We would like to caution our readers against such uncontrollable measures, since the negative consequences generally are bigger than the positive gain.

tracheae: Respiratory organs of arthropods, which form a tube system with breathing openings (*stigmata*), through which the oxygen, instead of passing through lungs or gills, and blood vessels, is taken directly to the spots where it is used. In flying insects (see HEXAPODA) the tracheae frequently are developed into air sacs.

Trachycorystes: The coarsely armored one.
South American Catfish genus belonging to the family of the *Auchenipteridae*. Short, compact fishes with completely unarmored body. The small eyes are strongly displaced towards the sides, the head is flattened from above. An adipose fin is present.

— striatulus (Steindachner):
SHAPE: As per description of the genus. D I/4, A 25-27. The adipose fin is only small; the dorsal placed far to the front, its spine equipped with some rows of dense teeth; the anal fin is quite long. The uptilted mouth opening carries three pairs of barbels. Length up to 10″.
COLOR: Yellow-brown with dark brown spots. The male is known by the thickened first 2-3 rays of the anal fin; furthermore it possesses a tube-shaped uro-genital papilla.
RANGE: South Eastern Brazil.

Trachycorystes striatulus

CARE AND BREEDING: This Catfish is a pronounced twilight and nocturnal fish. It is equipped with intestinal respiration, being very sensitive to changes in atmospheric pressure and storms. It definitely cannot be called choosy as to food, but is very voracious, needing varied, vigorous live foods, above all things also small fishes. It likes to amble along the bottom. Reproduction is unknown, but the construction of the genital opening and the development of the anal fin lead to the conclusion that there are special peculiarities in its propagation.

Trahira, the: see HOPLIAS MALABARICUS.

training: Actions an animal has 'learned' to perform on the basis of certain experiences. If certain stimuli are permitted to act on an

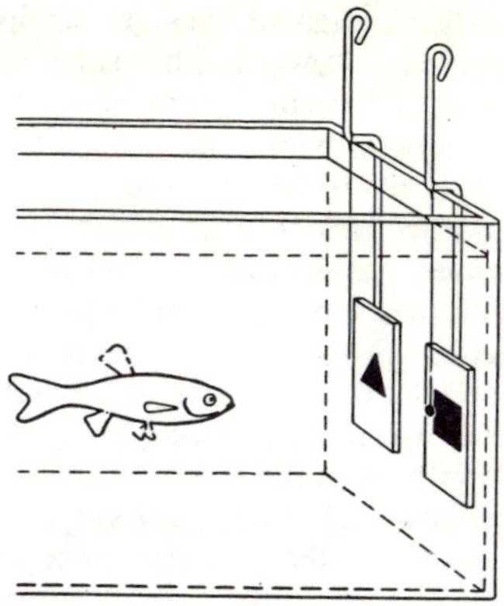

Example of a fish training apparatus

animal through one or more of its sensory organs, this causes an excitation (a metabolic process within the nerve substance) which is transmitted to the nerve center, triggering a certain unconditioned reflex there. Thus, for instance, the sight of food triggers the actions necessary for snapping it up, which are pure reflexes. Such excitations leave certain traces in certain cells of the nerve system (engrams). If other stimuli also are connected with the original one—which may be the mentioned food—for instance, a certain color or shape (signal stimulus), these also leave an engram, which combines with that of the original stimulus. The original stimulus and the signal stimulus together form an association. The animal has learned to react to the signal stimulus (conditioned reflex) and has been trained.

It has been proven that fishes are trainable. This leads to the conclusion that also in Nature they are able to combine experiences with their innate manner of reacting (self-training). This may also happen in the aquarium, for instance, when fishes that were separated by a glass pane for a long time, continue to respect the—in itself invisible—border due to secondary marks (certain plants, and other things. Spatial sense?) even after the separating pane has been removed.

Translucent Bloodfin, the: see PRIONOBRAMA FILIGERA.

Trapa natans: see HYDROCARYACEAE, Water-Nut Plants.

treatment of fish diseases, remedies: Unfortunately a cure of fish diseases in the aquarium is generally only possible in the case of attacks by external parasites, while internal diseases are curable only in the most rare cases. Therefore one has to point out that "a grain of prevention is better than an ounce of cure". (See FISH DISEASES). As a rule the small size of aquarium fishes makes the diagnosis of the malady very difficult. Add to this that specialists able to diagnose the diseases thoroughly by means of the changed behavior of the external aspects are not always easily reached. Recognition of the disease, though, in most cases is a primary condition for the attempt at curing it.

To combat external parasites, medicinal baths have shown best results so far. These may be classed into: instant baths, and prolonged baths. When bathing fishes, it is of the utmost importance to pay the most careful attention to the concentration of the chemicals in order to permit recovery of the fishes after putting them back into pure water. The process of healing begins immediately after killing off the parasites. Instant baths should never be given in metallic containers. If the baths are to be especially short, it is advisable to hang the fish into the bath within a net, in order to be able to take it out immediately in case of need.

INSTANT BATHS:

(a) Kitchen salt baths. Successful in fighting the skin discolorers and gill worms *Gyrodactylus* and *Dactylogyrus*. Dissolve about ½ oz. kitchen salt in one quart of water (solution of about 1-1.5%). Duration of bath 20 minutes. Temperature about 3.5° F higher than normal. This solution is useful also against other skin parasites.

(b) Copper sulphate baths. Not advisable according to SCHAEPERCLAUS. Offer only disadvantages as compared to kitchen salt.

(c) Baths with spirits of ammonia (ammonium chloride) too are not advisable.

(d) Hydrogen peroxide baths too do not offer advantages over kitchen salt (SCHAEPERCLAUS) and are dangerous due to the lack of standardization of commercial solutions.

(e) Baths with Potassium Permanganate may be effective against Carp lice, *Costia, Chilodonella*, and *Trichodina*, but especially against *Saprolegnia*. Instant bath, according to BRUNNER: 1 gram Potassium Permanganate dissolve in 2½ gals. of water. Duration of bath: 5-10 minutes.

PLEHN prescribes as a cure against *Saprolegnia:*

Wipe off the fungi with a pad of cotton soaked in a solution of one gram of potassium permanganate in one quart of water. Thereafter bathe during 90 minutes in a solution of one gram of same in 25 gallons of water. SCHAEPERCLAUS stresses that not too many fishes should be bathed in the same solution in order to reach a uniform action. Therefore set up several containers.

(f) Baths with formalin. Together with the salt bath, this is especially advisable against Skin Discoloration. According to SCHAEPERCLAUS, weak baths are more advisable. ¾ to 1⅝ cubic inches per 2½ gallons of water, carefully stirred, temperature a little higher than normal, duration 45 minutes.

PROLONGED BATHS:

Prolonged baths are especially needed when fighting the *Ichthyophthirius* disease, as only the mother parasites can be killed when they come off the skin, ripe for division. Since it may take weeks until all of them have come off, instant baths are ineffective.

(a) Quinine Bath. Practically all quinine salts are adequate for preparing the baths, but the different salts have differently high quinine contents. The highest percentages are to be found in the following: Quinine hydrochloride with 82%, Acid quinine hydrochloride with 73%, Acid quinine sulphate with 59%, Quinine-Weil with 57%, and Ichtho-Quinine-Weil with 19%. Therefore concentration is to be recalculated in accordance with the quinine contents. SCHAEPERCLAUS prescribes:

Strong bath: 1 gram quinine hydrochloride or quinine sulphate in 12½ gallons of water;

Medium-strength bath: same quantity in 75 quarts of water;

Weak bath: same quantity in 25 gallons.

Sensitive species of fishes, as well as baths without plants or sand bottom, require weak solutions, while strongly planted tanks should be set up with strong solutions. In the latter a diminution of the quinine ratio sets in through adsorption, so that every 3 to 4 days one has to strengthen up the percentage by the addition of 0.5 grams of quinine per 25 gallons of water. Very vague! The best is to bathe the fishes in containers without vegetation, as in already organized aquaria there is always the possibility of harm to the plants and destruction of the important micro-fauna. Prolonged baths also kill monocellular skin discolorers.

(b) Trypaflavine baths: Trypaflavine is a synthetic pigment, the high effectiveness of which was tried out by SCHAEPERCLAUS. Mix 25 gallons of water with 1 gram Trypaflavine (or Rivanol). This is little harmful to the fishes, but one has to count upon eventual harmful influences on the plants. This may largely be avoided by changing the water after the bath. Duration of treatment: 3-21 days.

(c) Methylene-blue bath: Not advisable, as it is less effective than the previous one.

(d) Chloramine bath. Solution: 1 gram in 25 gallons of water. Duration: several days. (For instant baths use 1 gram in 15 quarts. Duration 2-4 hours.) Extremely effective against *Ichthyophthirius* and Skin Discolorations. The drawback consists in that in an organized aquarium the active components are adsorbed too quickly. Therefore one has to keep on adding Chloramine (½ gram per 25 gallons). Repeated warnings have been given against using Chloramine in soft, slightly acid waters. The solution should be prepared in cold water.

Quick immersion baths are hardly to be considered for aquarium fishes.

treatment of water: The fact that certain tropical fishes for their well-being, and especially for breeding, need water that to a certain extent is free of salts of calcium and magnesium, or other salts, and that on the other hand contains admixtures of humic acids, often forces the aquarist to prepare adequate water artificially. In some places it is possible to get appropriate water from springs or other natural waters, or even to draw it from taps. In most cases, however, tap water is too hard, and contains so many salts, that it cannot be considered for keeping, and especially for breeding, certain tropical and sub-tropical fishes and plants. Aquarists have been searching for a long time for ways of removing the water hardness, which seems to be responsible to a great extent for certain failures in the keeping of aquatic plants and the breeding of aquarium fishes. Since 1930 especially the problem of preparing adequate water has been taking up more and more space in the discussions on which are 'the most natural conditions of life' for tropical aquarium fishes, and which are the ways of making them come true.

Aquaristics has three possible ways of removing the hardness from water:

1. Softening it by mixing hard with soft water;

2. Softening it by precipitation of the hardest; and

3. Softening it by removing, respectively exchanging, the salts.

The mixing of hard with soft water has been done for a long time by many aquarists. For this we use the water Nature itself offers us, namely rain water. The eventual failures found in this method do not derive from the rain water itself, but from the admixtures which the same incorporates on its way through the atmosphere and over the different ducts it traverses. Better for this purpose is good distilled water. It has the only disadvantage that in the long run it turns out rather costly, especially if one has to dilute larger quantities of water with high degrees of hardness. In order to substitute the water that evaporates from our tanks, it is advisable always to keep a certain amount of distilled water in a gallon flask available.

The following calculation makes it easy to find the quantities of distilled water that are necessary

A laboratory-type water softener or demineralizer, the Wofatit Filter.

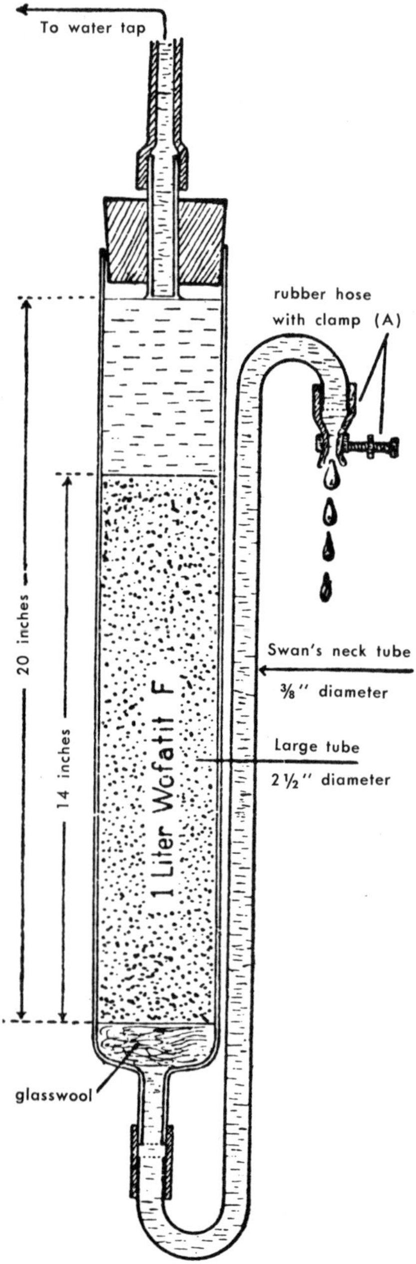

for a water preparation:

(a) $\dfrac{\text{hardness of the initial water}}{\text{desired hardness}} =$ quota of hardness

(b) $\dfrac{\text{desired quantity of water}}{\text{quota of hardness}} =$ quantity of initial water to be used

(c) quota of hardness—1 = mixing factor

(d) mixing factor × quantity of initial water to be used = quantity of distilled water to be used

(e) quantity of distilled water + initial water = total quantity.

Consequently, if one needs 120 qts. of water which instead of a hardness of 24 DH has to show only 4 DH, we have the following calculation:

(a) $\dfrac{24}{4} = 6$

(b) $\dfrac{120}{6} = 20$ qts. of initial water

(c) 6 — 1 = 5 (mixing factor)

(d) 5 × 20 = 100 qts. distilled water

(e) 100 + 20 = 120 qts. total amount, now at 4 DH.

Mixing with distilled water has the advantage that no uncontrollable chemical components are introduced into the water. Even water prepared in this way, however, still cannot compare with natural water, as this contains a number of further components of mineral and organic origin which possibly lack in ours. Before using the water, one should test its pH value.

Softening with chemicals, by precipitating the hardening components is by no means completely advisable. It generally is difficult to carry out, and difficult to control. For this reason we shall not go into details on what methods to use. If you want to experiment with this manner of softening water, you will find instructions in the specialized literature.

Softening by exchange (with Permutit, Wofatit) to the contrary leads to completely useful and usable waters. The hardening components, especially the salts of calcium and of magnesium, are dissolved in the water. If the exchangers are regenerated with kitchen salt (Sodium Chloride) in aqueous solution, they become charged with sodium. If now we send water with hardening components, dissolved calcium bicarbonate, for instance, through the exchanger, this exchanges the calcium for sodium. Instead of calcium bicarbonate, sodium bicarbonate now leaves the exchanging filter. Thus we have obtained a practical softening without desalting. The quantity of salts has remained unchanged, but now the former quantity of calcium bicarbonate has been substituted by the present quantity of sodium bicarbonate. The same refers to all salts of calcium that were contained in the treated water. Since sodium compounds are not hardeners, though, the water has now been softened. The biological action of sodium compounds is not yet known; it seems, however, that sensible displacements take place in the conditions of the water, especially if the initial water had a high degree of hardness. Thus it seems that a disagreeable multiplication of *Diatomeae* (silicous algae), for instance, may take place. Dangerous above all is the rise of the pH value high into the alkaline range conditioned by the exchange. Therefore it is absolutely necessary to test the pH value of such waters. Anyway, waters that have been softened in this manner may safely be used for breeding purposes, since in them generally there is no extended action on animals and plants. WAGNER counsels mixing the softened water with distilled water, in order to reduce the salt contents. A partial or total desalting may also be obtained by using exchangers, though. Both methods are described below. According to FINCK, it is possible to transform the sodium bicarbonate in exchanged water into biologically harmless kitchen salt, by adding exactly measured quantities of 'normal' hydrochloric acid (meaning a solution of 36.5 grams of gaseous hydrochloric acid in 1 liter of water), the resulting quantities of salt being negligible. For this it is necessary at first to check the carbonate hardness (changeable or temporary hardness) in the initial water, which simultaneously shows the measure of alkalinity or capacity to react with acids.

From these data one can calculate the quantity of normal hydrochloric acid to be used.

Simple softening may also be effected in the already installed aquarium with the aid of internal or external filters charged with an exchanger element, if the aquarium water is first cleaned by making it go through a common filter in order to remove dirt. This method, though, is hardly advisable, considering the resulting displacement of the pH value. Softening the water outside the aquarium is more advisable. In softening with WOFATIT (PERMUTIT is used in a similar manner, according to the instructions for use), we proceed as follows: WOFATIT F is a black or reddish-hued artificial resin, which generally is sold in a moist state. Before use, it should generally be soaked in a glass or enamelled dish for 24 hours, and then put into a filter.

LEITHOLD gives the tables below showing the output of one liter of WOFATIT.

It is advisable each time to use up the filtering capacity to the end, storing the water that is not used in a balloon flask. Before re-using the WOFATIT has to be regenerated in the manner described above.

Hardness of tap water in DH	Softened water in ltrs. at 0 DH
5	400
10	200
15	130
20	100
25	80
30	65
35	55
40	50
45	45
50	40

Testing the continued efficiency of the filter may be done after the BOUTRON-BOUDET method (see WATER HARDNESS). If it is exhausted the hardness of the filtered water rises quickly. After use, the filter is stored, with special care being given to the fact that the WOFATIT is kept covered with water. After longer periods without use, the first quarts of water will come out colored brown. This colored water should be discarded. The brown color will disappear after a few moments. If it is handled the right way, alternating use and regeneration, WOFATIT is of infinite duration. The water that is softened to 0° DH is raised to the desired degree of hardness (generally 2-4)) by mixing it with unsoftened water.

(b) Softening and Partial De-Salting with WOFATIT F. WAGNER gives the following instructions on how to do this: Let 3.5 ltr. of a 5% solution of hydrochloric acid run during about an hour through the WOFATIT which has been poured in as described above. Now the filter is ready for use. Discard the first 5 liters of the water that flows now. The water that follows after this is completely softened and partially de-salted. Since it will be too acid, one has to blunt it to the desired pH value by treating it with a solution of sodium bicarbonate. Considering its acidity, one should only prepare it in earthenware or enamelled containers. The filter is exhausted after the water that flows out show traces of hardness in the BOUTRON-BOUDET test.

(c) Softening and De-Salting with WOFATIT S and MD. According to LEITHOLD for this one needs two filters of the kind described above, connecting them in series. One of the filters is filled with one quart of WOFATIT F in the manner described above. Instead of regenerating with kitchen salt, do it with 3 qts. of a 5% hydrochloric acid solution, having it run through for about 25 minutes. Let the filter soak in the remainder of the acid for about half an hour. Then wash it with 3-4 quarts of common water at the same rate of flow. After rinsing, draw 2-3-qts. of water pouring this acid water into the second filter tube and inserting the WOFATIT MD there. Then this WOFATIT is regenerated with 3 qts. of a 7% solution of soda, which in turn also flows through for 25 minutes. This filter too is permitted to soak in the remainder of the liquid for ½ hour.

Now connect both filters by means of a hose. The water that is to be softened and de-salted runs first through the filter with the WOFATIT F, and then through the one with WOFATIT MD. Make a first run of 5-7 qts. in order to rinse out the two filters. After the rinsing is over, the water that comes out from the second filter should not show any murkiness when mixed with a few drops of a 1% silver nitrate solution, only a weak opalescence at the maximum. If a cloudiness in the silver nitrate solution should appear after some time, this is a sign that the WOFA-

TITS are exhausted and must be treated anew in the manner described above.

Also this manner of de-salting the water demands special attention to the pH value which could eventually be corrected with a few drops of hydrochloric acid, if too alkaline, with an admixture of a solution of sodium bicarbonate, if too acid. This water, too, has to be brought to the desired degree of hardness by mixing it with some of the original water. The softening and de-salting with exchangers has shown excellent results in practice, as is demonstrated by the success of WAGNER in breeding *Symphysodon discus*. Also the aquatic plants thrive splendidly in such water, tropical plants, as least, do it much more, than in the hard and salty waters found in the temperate zones.

If you wish to keep the water you have prepared and obtained with such great difficulty softened and de-salted, pay special care to see that the bottom soil is free of hardeners. The most effective is quartz gravel, which is found in commerce in differently grained grades. To make absolutely sure, soak the gravel previously in a 1% solution of hydrochloric acid for a few hours. The gravel is adequate if the solution which covers it still reacts acid. Now wash it with good, soft water. The food stuffs which are necessary for the plants, are replaced again thereafter, by mixing the gravel with some old clay from decaying clay constructions, or burnt clay such as comes from Dutch tile mantelpieces when they are torn down. Fresh clay always contains hardeners. As a rule ocean sand is inadequate, due to the residua of snail and mollusc shells it contains. That no rear wall of mortar or limestone should be used, is self-evident. Also slate may be strongly calcareous. Of rocks, the so-called ancient rocks (basalt, granite, gneiss) are especially well adapted.

According to HOFMANN, the use of a bottom soil free of calcium, and planting it well, may cause a biological de-hardening which may be quite considerable. Moderately hard water—say with a hardness of 10-12 DH—is de-hardened to a very favorable degree even without any artificial means, if one uses such soil with plenty of plant growth. The process of softening extends over a period of several weeks.

Trematodes: Sucker Worms.
Class of parasitic worms belonging to the phylum of the Flat Worms or *Plathelminthes*. Their characteristic are the sucking discs, of which the order *Monogena* has a great number, while the *Digena* generally possess only two of them. Trematodes live both in sea water animals and in fresh water ones, many of them undergoing a change of hosts.

Two orders: *Monogena*, with *Gyrodactylus*; and *Digena*, with the so-called Liver Leech.

Trianea: see LIMNOBIUM.

tribe: In zoology a systematic unit between the sub-family and the genus.

Trichodina: Genus of little hat-shaped ciliates, which, together with other parasites, are in part the causers of skin discolorations of fishes.

Trichogaster: With threads on the belly; referring to the threads of the ventral fins.
Southeast Asiatic genus belonging to the family of the Climbing Perches or *Anabantidae*, which differs from the closely related genus *Colisa* by the shorter dorsal fin and by the fact that the first ray of the ventrals is extended into a thread. This thread represents an additional organ of taste. Head and trunk are relatively high, and the

fish is strongly compressed laterally. The lateral line is interrupted in spots. The small, protractable mouth possesses fleshy lips.

Trichogaster leeri, the Pearl Gourami

— **leeri** (Bleeker): The Pearl, or Mosaic, Gourami.

SHAPE: As per description of the genus, The body is elongated and strongly compressed laterally, the head pointed D V-VII/8-10, A XII-XIV/25-30, all fins well developed, especially on the males. The soft part of the fins partly extended beyond the fin edge. Length above 4″, the female remaining a little smaller.

COLOR: Bluish-violet silvery, with irregular, dark-edged, mother-of-pearl colored dots, which cover the body and part of the fins. A dark band, which is in part interrupted, extends from the mouth to the base of the tail fin. During the spawning period the male is known by the brick-red belly, being also bigger and stronger, and especially by his dorsal fin being strongly developed.

RANGE: Indochina, Malaya, Indonesia, in shallow, warm, and strongly overgrown waters.

CARE AND BREEDING: Keep them in spacious, old, sunlit, and well-planted tanks, covered with floating plants and at a low water level. The species is peaceable even towards smaller fishes, but a little shy and very sensitive to lesions. In general terms one would call them a little delicate, being also very demanding as to temperatures. 75-86° F and more are necessary. The fish eat live foods, occasionally also artificial ones. The food should not be too big-sized, however, since the mouth opening is quite small. Spawning them is not difficult in itself, but depends upon mated pairs. A big and extensive, not too high bubble nest is built, beneath which many males build a cone-shaped sand heap. They are very prolific. Otherwise as described for *Anabantidae.* Able to breed only when nearly full-grown.

Trichogaster microlepis, the Silver Gourami

— **microlepis** (Guenther): The Silver Gourami.

A species recently imported from Thailand which is even slimmer than the preceding one. Length up to 6″. Very small scales lend the otherwise solid-colored fish a very pretty, soft-bluish shiny silver hue. Occasionally they show a weak darker horizontal band. The males are known by their orange-colored fin threads.

CARE AND BREEDING: As described for the preceding species.

— **pectoralis** (Regan): The Snake-Skinned Gourami.

A rare species from Indochina with a horizontal stripe composed of darker spots. Treat them like the two preceding species.

Trichogaster pectoralis, the Snake-skinned Gourami

— trichopterus (Pallas): The Blue, or Three-Spot, Gourami.

SHAPE: The body of the original form is a little higher than that of the blue variety, which in all looks more elongated. D VI-VIII/8-10, A X-XII/33-38. The mouth is small, supraterminal, and moderately protractable, very fleshy-lipped on the male. Length up to 6″.

COLOR: A species which is found in two color varieties, of which the first is more reddish-violet, the second one more shiny blue. When excited both sexes—but more frequently the male—show slanted, irregular cross bands. Besides this the male is easily known by its strongly developed dorsal fin. The Blue Gourami is known as *T.t. sumatranus.*

Trichogaster trichopterus, the Blue or 3-spot Gourami

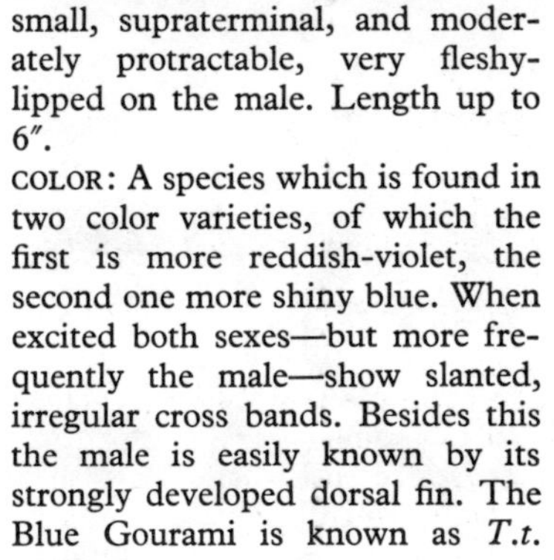

RANGE: India and Indochina, the blue variety on Sumatra.

CARE AND BREEDING: The species needs warmth, but also withstands occasional lower temperatures. 75-82° F are most favorable. Care and breeding as described for the preceding species, but easy to spawn and very fertile. The bubble nest is preferentially built at spots that are free of plants, the nest being spacious and loose.

Trichopsis: Refers to the resemblance to *Trichogaster.*

Southeast Asian genus belonging to the family of the Climbing Perches or *Anabantidae,* of elongated shape and pointed head. The dorsal is short, the anal long. The mouth is small, protractile, and tilted slantedly upwards. The species are remarkable for the fact that under excitement they are able to emit distinctly audible sounds.

— pumilus (Arnold): The Croaking Dwarf Gourami.

SHAPE: As per description of the genus, very small and slender. D III/7, A V/20-22. Length a scant $1\frac{1}{4}$″.

COLOR: Pale yellowish to greenish-gray, with a darker horizontal band composed of spots, sprinkled all over with small, luminous-green splinters which extend also on to the reddish fins. Dorsal and anal fins of the male are a little more pointed, the ovaries of the female showing through yellowish.

RANGE: Vietnam, Malaya, and Sumatra (?).

CARE AND BREEDING: The fish need good care. Above all they need warmth and demand a temperature around 77° F, for breeding 86° F and more. The fish are peaceable omnivores, which above all eat small live foods, but also prepared foods. The sound they emit when excited is like the drone of a toy rattle. It is possible that certain tribes of the species build bubble nests, while according to KOCH and other observers only some air bubbles were collected under a leaf at some distance from the surface. The act of spawning resembles that of the other Anabantids. Differing from many other species, the fry possess adhesive threads on the head, with which they hang from the nest after hatching. The care of the males then consists only in watching the nest. When the sticky thread shrinks, the alevins, which now are free-swimming, leave the nest. Degrees of warmth around 80-86° F speed up development. Up to the moment when they develop the labyrinth, after 4-5 weeks, the water level has to be kept at about 4″. Apparently conditions are the same as for *Macropodus cupanus dayi*, of which some observers report the building of bubble nests, while others speak of spawning in caves, beneath leaves etc.

— **vittatus** (Cuvier and Valenciennes): The Croaking Gourami.
SHAPE: As per description of the genus. Bigger and more vigorous than the preceding species. D II-IV/6-8, A VI-VII/24-28. Length up to $2\frac{3}{8}$″.
COLOR: Yellowish with greenish gloss and some darker length bands, the fins reddish. The male is more vividly colored, his vertical fins extended into threads.
RANGE: In shallow, warm waters of Indochina, Malaya, and Indonesia.
CARE AND BREEDING: An active species which sometimes likes to hide. Very peaceable and needing a little warmth, 72-75° F, for breeding 86° F and more. The fish build a hasty, small, easily-decomposing bubble nest. The fry are minute and need even temperatures in the first days for raising them. Otherwise see *Anabantidae*. A not very productive fish. Breeding them is a little difficult.

Trichoptera: Quiver Flies.
Order pertaining to the sub-order of the Butterfly-like insects or *Lepidopteroidea*. The aquarist generally knows only the larvae of this butterfly-like, unimposing insect. They are elongated, narrow animals, with long antennae, small heads, and protruding eyes, which fold up their wings in roof-shape when sitting. The eggs of Quiver Flies are stuck to aquatic plants and the like under water, in a unified, jelly-covered, generally sausage-shaped spawn.

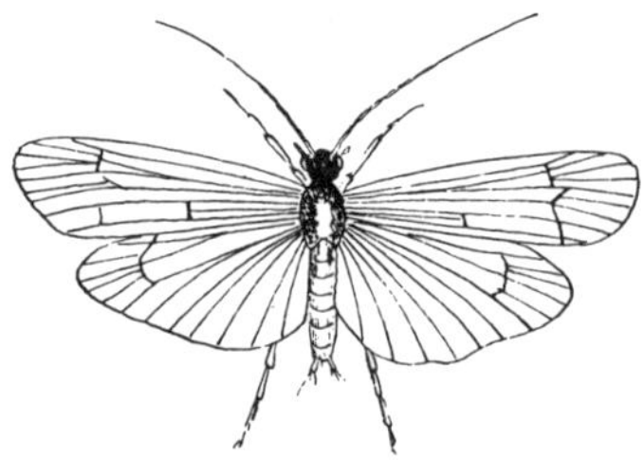

Top: A completely developed Quiver Fly, **Trichoptera**. Center: 6 different types of housings or nests of the Quiver Fly. Below: A larva of the Quiver Fly removed from the nest.

The larvae are elongated, caterpillar-like, and carry long, thin gill threads at the rear end. They build tube-shaped shells out of sand, gravel, pieces of wood, small snail shells, etc. looking out from them only with the head and the front part of the body, and being able to hold on very firmly within the shells by means of extension of the body. The core of the housing consists of a web of spun thread. There are bottom-dwelling forms as well as surface-dwelling ones. The latter build lighter shells out of hollow parts of plants. The larvae are dainty in the choice of their building materials. Their food consists of vegetable substances and smaller animals. Withdrawn from the quiver they become an excellent food for bigger fishes. They may be the spreaders of some kinds of thread worms of fishes. Furthermore not all species build shells, some predatory ones also installing web passages among plants.

trichopterus: Thread-finned.
— *Trichogaster.*

trifasciatus: Triple-striped.
— *Nannostomus.*

triflorum: Three-flowered.
— *Synnema.*

triggers: Phenomena or happenings which in live beings, generally only in animals, cause certain reactions or whole chains of instinctive actions. Triggers may be of many kinds, but it is always specific species that are adapted to very definite triggers. Thus we can say that triggers are specific for the species. Triggers may be chemical stimuli, originating from food bodies, from enemies, or from members of the same species, certain motions and changes of the body of other live beings, certain, generally remarkable colors and signals (mating colors, breeding colors of fishes that care for their brood), the sight of certain organs, sound emissions, etc., etc. The triggers and their reactions are conditioned to each other. A certain trigger is always followed by a specific reaction. We speak of a 'key-to-keyhole' relationship.

trilineata: With three lines.
— *Rasbora.*

Trinectes: Genus of small Flatfishes belonging to the family of the Flounders or *Pleuronectidae*, order of the *Heterosomata*.

— **maculatus** Bloch: The Dwarf Freshwater Flounder.

SHAPE: As per description of the order, elongatedly oval. The left fin seam grows nearly to the mouth opening, the right one to the insertion of the ventrals immediately behind the gill plate. The two eyes are placed closely together on the center of the body and are raised like buttons. Length up to about $2\frac{3}{4}''$.

COLOR: Strongly variable gray-brown to dark-brown base, with numerous irregular darker spots, which change according to the color of the bottom and may also disappear completely. The underside is whitish to yellow. Sex differences unknown.

RANGE: Waters near the coast in the Eastern U.S.A., from Massachusetts (Cape Cod) southward. Found only in pure fresh water.

CARE AND BREEDING: A very interesting fish, despite the fact that its manner of living demands a certain adaptability and understanding on the part of the aquarist. During the day the fish remain buried in the sand or hang sucked fast to the glass sides. Buried Flounders are visible only with great attention and some skill, due to the breathing movements of the gill plate, as well as by their button-like raised eyes. Despite the fact that they lead a predominantly nocturnal life, they get tame so quickly that especially while feeding they become quite lively. The fish are very voracious, naturally preferring to take their food from the bottom, expelling grains of sand etc. through the gill opening. Tubifex, red mosquito larvae, and other live foods that stay on the bottom are eaten with relish, but also free-swimming foods are caught quite skillfully.

Towards other fishes the Flounders are quite harmless. They are very skilled swimmers when disturbed. Reproduction is unknown.

Triops cancriformis: see NOTOSTRACA.

trispilus: Three-spotted.
— *Barbus (Puntius)*.

trisulca: Three-furrowed.
— *Lemna*.

tritaeniatus: Three-striped.
— *Nannaethiops*.

Triangular Clams: see DREISSENACEA.

True Acara, the: see AEQUIDENS THAYERI.

Trunk Barb, the: see EPALZEORHYNCHUS KALLOPTERUS.

Trunk Leeches: see RHYNCHOBDELLODEA.

Trunk Loach, the: see ACANTHOPSIS CHOIRORHYNCHUS.

trunk microcrustaceans: see BOSMINA.

Trunk Puffer, the: see TETRAODON MIURUS.

tube worms: see NEMATHELMINTHES.

Tubifex: The most common (German) species, *T. tubifex* Mueller (the other species are less frequently found) lives in great numbers at the bottom of muddy ditches, ponds, and lakes. Protruding from the mud with the tip of the body, the worms make lively, snaky motions with this tip. They build a tube from body excretions, into which they withdraw lightning-quick in case of danger. The worms

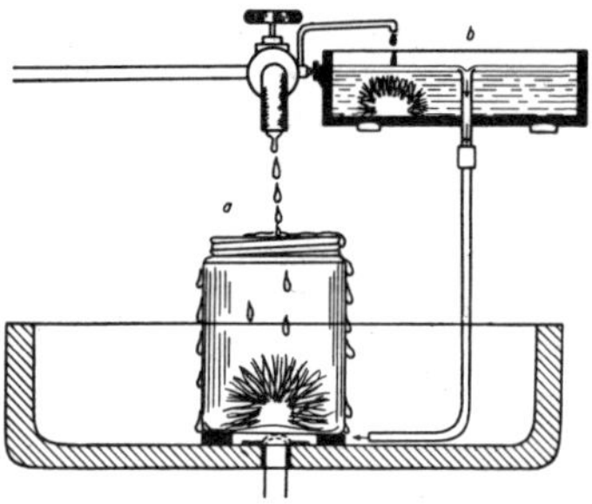

Two types of tubifex storage arrangement under dripping water. (a) is a simple arrangement with water dripping into a jar with about one inch of tubifex on the bottom. (b) is a special little sink with running water and its own outlet.

Floating plastic tubifex ring (European style).

are reddish, $\frac{3}{8}''$ to $2\frac{3}{8}''$ long, and very thin. In greater numbers they give the water bottom a red color. Tubifex are found the year round, even in winter. When using them for food, be careful, as uneaten worms dig in into the bottom and may cause unpleasant and hard-to-remove clouding. Very few fishes have the strength to pull out the worms after they dig in. Generally they tear them off, and the pieces that remain in the soil form foci of decay. *T.* should preferably be fed from a floating feeding sieve. It might also be good to place a shallow glass dish beneath the feeding place, for instance, the lid of a preserve jar.

GATHERING: The mud which contains the tubifex is put on a piece of wire netting, and this hung into the water in a manner that it just touches the surface. The worms try to reach the water and fall through the netting, balling together in clean clusters at the bottom. Keep them just moist on a shallow dish. Very durable also in a container under running water, for instance, in a preserve jar under a slightly open water tap, where too they ball up in lumps.

According to the studies of WAGNER, Tubifex acidify the water (phosphoric acid). This alone is a sufficient reason for cautioning the fancier against overfeeding with Tubifex. Especially in un-buffered waters soon a lowering of the pH value is noticed, which may lead to damage in case of extended action.

Tubificidae: Family of worms pertaining to the order of the Scarce-Bristled ones or *Oligochaeta*, of which especially the genus *Tubifex* is of significance as fish food.

tumors and boils on fishes: We designate as tumors slow-healing wounds that at first are boil-like and closed, but later on open and become attacked secondarily by fungus infection (*Saprolegnia*), and which may be caused by several diseases, e.g. *Ichthyosporidium*, infectious dropsy, etc. In these cases the possibilities of cure are determined by the nature of the diseases. Tumors often appear as irregular, luxuriant, sometimes raspberry-like growths, which frequently have a cancerous character (carcinomas). They are found especially on live bearing Tooth Carps when by superpigmentation (black, and spotted forms) a sickly development of red or black pigment cells is produced. These may then over-develop to a point that they lead to wild, unruly growths on skin and fins, displacing and damaging normal tissues, and finally bursting open. Skin tumors may develop very quickly on hereditarily predisposed fishes, like the melanistic (black) color strains, when the animals get into unfavorable ambient conditions, such as, for instance, water with an abnormally acid pH value.

Similar growths are also observed, for instance, in Fish Pox, the origin of which ailment is as yet unknown. The *Lymphocystis*-disease, during which raspberry-like growths of epidermis cells appear, is caused by a virus.

The study of tumors on fish has proved to be very enlightening for science.

Turbatrix aceti Mueller: Micro Worms.
1-2 mm long little worms which live on bacteria in fermenting vinegar, which belong to the order of the *Rhabditoidea* (Class of the Nematodes or Thread Worms), and to the phylum of the Tube Worms or *Nemathelminthes*. Formerly known as *Anguillula silusiae*.

Turbatrix are an appreciated baby food, which is sold under the name Micro Worms.

Turbellaria: Class pertaining to the phylum of the Flat Worms or *Plathelminthes*, of which the aquarist generally knows the typical genus *Planaria*. They are small, long-stretched, and flat worms, which may be white, yellow, brown, but also black in color. The worms often show especially remarkable, square heads with two or more eyes and sensory pits, which reacting to the most minute chemical stimuli, condition an excellent olfactory perception. The muscles are very strong, the intestine sac-shaped or ramified. *Turbellaria* generally are a nuisance in the aquarium, since they are both competitors for food and predators on eggs and fry to a point that one cannot think of rearing a brood in a tank infested with these worms.

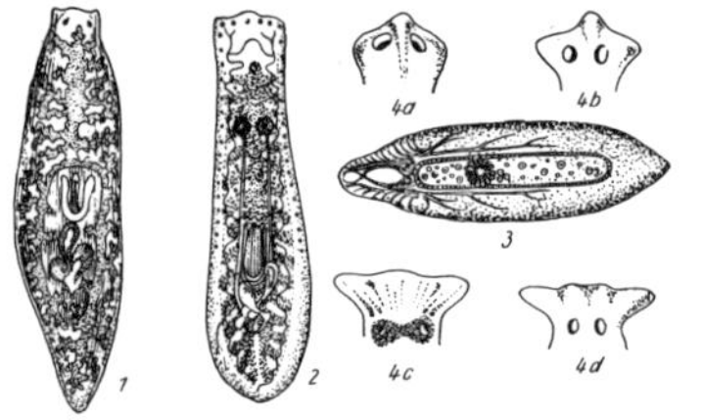

Turbellaria: 1. Type of the genus **Dendrocoelum**; 2. Type of the genus **Planaria**; 3. Type of the genus **Mesostomum**; 4 a., b., c., & d.: Heads of different **Planariae**.

They are nocturnal predators, which keep hidden during the day, feeding exclusively on animal substances. Certain skin glands secrete a weaving substance which condense into nets to catch daphnia, etc. The extendable oesophagus is used to hold the prey, the food generally being showered with venomous little rodlets secreted from the skin of the worms. *T.* grow to ages of up to 5 years, some species being able to encyst and thus even to withstand dry periods. They are hermaphroditic, the eggs being hung up in cysts, which unite several of them.

The best method of fighting them is still with bait. Some chopped meat is put into a thick-meshed bag and hung among plants near the bottom. Their excellent sense of smell leads the worms to the bait during the night, where they collect in the bag and may be taken out carefully and immersed in boiling water together with the bait. This operation should be repeated several times, at intervals of about one week, in order to exterminate all worms, especially those that hatch from eggs in the interim.

Found in the aquarium in several genera, such as, for instance, *Polycelis*, *Dendrocoelum*, and *Planaria*.

Two-Dotted Characin, the: see EXODON PARADOXUS.

Two-Spot Live Bearer, the: see MICROPOECILIA PARAE.

Two-Spotted Barb, the: see BARBUS (PUNTIUS) TICTO.

Two-Spotted Cichlid, the: see CICHLASOMA BIMACULATUM.

Tylobranchus: With calloused spot in the oesophagus.

South American genus of Characin-like fishes, belonging to the family of the Headstanders or *Anostomidae*, of elongated build, only little compressed laterally, and with big head.

The genus very much resembles the closely related genus *Chilodus*, but differs from it by the diverging construction of the anal fin.

The 4th and 5th gill arches are transformed in a way that leads one to think of them as possible organs of accessory respiration.

— maculosus Eigenmann:

SHAPE: As per description of the genus, the small subterminal mouth with thick lips. Gullet bone, and upper and lower jaw are equipped with small teeth. The ventral region is broad and rounded. D 12, A 6-7. Length up to about 6″.

COLOR: Yellowish to whitish, with a black horizontal band and some rows of black dots.

RANGE: Northeastern tropical South America, especially in waters, swamps and ponds near the coast, even in biologically very unfavorable ones.

CARE AND BREEDING: The species cannot be considered a pronounced headstander. It likes densely planted tanks with a soft bottom, through which it likes to root in search of edibles, especially insect larvae, snails, worms, and soft parts of plants. It needs some warmth, and feels best at 75-86° F. Breeding has not yet been achieved.

Typhaceae: Family belonging to the class of the single-germinating-leaved plants or *Monocotyledoneae*. Perennial, vigorous, and generally tall-growing swamp plants, which can only be used for open-air installations, while they are unfit for the home aquarium. From the strong, creeping rootstock spring long, lineal, sometimes a little twisted leaves. The hermaphroditic inflorescences sit jointly on long stems. They form cobs, the male part of the common stand having a smooth surface, while that of the female part is rough and develops a plush-like mass of the small fruits and their flying organs. Only one genus with 9 known species which are distributed over the whole globe (*Typha*).

typicus: Typical, ideal.

— *Phoxinopsis*.

typus: Typical (of the genus).

— *Gymnallabes*.

Uaru: After the Indian name.

South American genus belonging to the family of the Cichlids or *Cichlidae*.

— ampiacanthoides Heckel: The Uaru.

SHAPE: Of very high body build, which still increases in height with age. Very strongly compressed laterally. The forehead contour rises steeply. D XV-XVII/13-16, A VII-X/12-16. Length up to 10″.

COLOR: Varying strongly with the different stages of age. At first totally black, then, in the half-grown phase, with many dark spots, from the length of 4″ on with a broad, wedge-shaped spot on yellowish base. The sex differences are minute, dorsal and anal fin of the male being a little pointed.

RANGE: The Amazon region and Guiana. In dark waters with dense deposits of submerged wood, among which the fish find sanctuary.

CARE AND BREEDING: The species is difficult to keep and to breed. Its demands on life resemble those of *Symphysodon discus*; they are as difficult to feed. Big tanks with many hiding places among rocks and roots, and with muted light, are needed. In part the fish are peaceable and sociable, even if from time to time there are little quarrels. They need warmth, and feel best at temperatures around 86° F. Success in breeding, which takes place like that of all bottom-spawning Cichlids, depends on mated pairs.

ulreyi: After the American zoologist Ulrey.

— *Hemigrammus*.

ulvaceus: Looking like a sea alga (*Ulva*).

— *Aponogeton*.

Umbra: Dog Fish.

Genus belonging to the family of the Dog Fishes or *Umbridae*, one species of which originates from Hungary and Lower Austria, another few species coming from the U.S.A. The Dog Fishes are of elongated, cylindrical build. The small scales also cover the sides of the head. A lateral line is lacking, its place being taken by a thin stripe along the sides, characterized bu its whitish color, in which are located numerous sensory cells. All species possess accessory respiration. Pectoral and ventral fins are moved alternately like the feet of a dog, which gave origin to their name.

— krameri Fitzinger: The European Dog Fish.

SHAPE: As per description of the genus. D 15-16, A 7-8. Length up to 3½″.

COLOR: Brownish with dark stripes disposed in horizontal bands. The sex differences are only minute.

RANGE: In ponds, swamps, and moor waters in the region of Lakes Neusiedler and Platten. There the Dog Fish is found in open spots among reeds. The fish keep near the bottom, and are very shy and

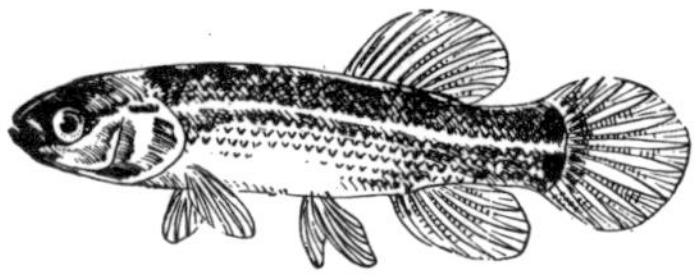

Umbra krameri

hard to catch hiding lightning-quick in the bottom in case of danger.

CARE AND BREEDING: This hardy fish, which may be kept in cold water aquaria like all species from its native country, demands only moderately sized, but richly planted tanks, where it lives hidden among plants. It is tamed relatively quickly, remaining visible near the front pane for long periods during feeding time. The body positions the fish take during rutting are peculiar. The intake of atmospheric air is done in lightning-like spurts to the surface. Dog Fish demand vigorous live foods, and eat prepared foods only exceptionally. Breeding them is possible in spacious aquaria. They work up veritable caves among algae or in dense plant thickets with their bodies, spawning there. After the completed act of spawning these caves are closed and guarded by the male.

The American Dog Fishes, *Umbra limi* Kirtland, and *Umbra pygmaea* de Kay, do not differ considerably from the European species in looks and care.

Umbridae: Dog Fishes.
Family belonging to the order of the Pike Fishes or *Haplomi*. Fishes with a very peculiar geographical distribution, that is with an insular presence around Lakes Neusiedler and Platten in Europe, and in North America. The family differs from the genuine Pikes, among others, by the densely placed velvet teeth, the bigger, full-edged scales, and the fins. Only one genus: *Umbra*.

undulatus: Wavy.
— *Aponogeton*.

Unger, Paul: Well-known German aquarist and amateur photographer, whose photographs of fishes still are the envy of many of today's professionals. Born Dec. 8, 1866 in Berlin, died April 9, 1953. Businessman, later professional photographer. In 1903 co-founder of 'Iris', Frankfort on the Main.

unifasciatus: Single-striped.
— *Neolebias*.

unilineatus: With single line (or stripe).
— *Hemigrammus*.

Unio: Genus of bivalves belonging to the family of the River Mussels or *Uninonaceae*. The family is widely distributed over the temperate zones, and shows numerous forms according to origin. The shells are thick-walled, narrow, elongated, and pointed at the ends. In central Europe science knows three species, with many local varieties, which are: *Unio crassus* Retzius, in quickly flowing waters, *Unio tumidus* Retzius and *Unio pictorum* Linné (The Painters' Mussel), more in quiet waters, *U. tumidus* especially in the plains.

Unionaceae: River Mussels.
Family of mussels pertaining to the order of the *Eulamellibranchiata*, which is very variable according to the vital conditions. The relatively large mussels are separately sexed, sometimes hermaphroditic. The eggs develop within the gill of the mother into larvae (*Glochidia*), which are squirted out together with the breathing water and cling with shell hook and byssus threads to the gills, skin, and fins of fishes, digging in there. They lead a parasitic life until they finish the larval stage. The attacked spots of the fishes show cysts which from outside look very much like *Ichthyophthirius* lesions.

The mussels are very sensitive to

contaminations of the water. Genera, among others: *Unio*, and *Anodonta*.

unitaeniatus: Single-striped.

— *Barbus* (*Puntius*).

— *Nannaethiops*.

urophthalma: With eye-spot on the tail.

— *Rasbora*.

urophthalmus: With eye-spot on the tail.

— *Rivulus*.

usambarae: Coming from Usambara, a region in East Africa.

— *Barbus* (*Puntius*).

Utricularia: With catching bladders (utricles).

Genus of carnivorous aquatic plants belonging to the family of the *Lentiburiaceae*. Perennial, submerged plants with finely divided, often feathery leaves, which bloom with an inflorescence that grows above the surface. They are remarkable for the fact that besides the nutrition that is normal for plants, they also take animal food. The prey—for the small species infusoria, rotatoria, etc., for the bigger ones small crustaceans, small aquatic insects and their larvae, small fishes—is caught and digested with the ingeniously working catching bladders, the so-called utricles. LLOYD found out how these utricles work with the aid of a slow-motion camera. They are closed by a lid, which rests on a counter-stop cocked by tension of the sap. The water pressure closes the bladders tight. When some micro-animal touches certain sensitive bristles near the entrance, the tension is suddenly released, the lid opens, and the water rushes in with great force, sweeping along the prey. Then the plants expel the water, squeezing the prey against the walls of the bladder, and forcing it against the digestive glands. The catch may be huge. Theoretically an *Utricularia* can make one hundred catches a day. 150,000 micro-animals were found in the bladders of one shrub only. Six species are known in Europe. A further number of species is also found in the tropics and subtropics.

— **exoleta** R. Brown: The Dwarf Utricularia.

GENERALITIES: This plant is especially useful as a spawning substratum and asylum for young fry. SHAPE: Stems and leaves are thin, richly ramified and entangled, forming pretty light-green and loose bundles. Each of the leaves may carry up to three utricles, which involute, however, if the water is poor in food.

RANGE: Southeastern Europe, Africa, Australia, and tropical and subtropical Africa, in waters of all kinds, where the plants form dense colonies below the surface and at shallow spots.

Utricularia exoleta

CULTIVATION: The plants need average light, but not too much sun. The temperature should not sink below 64° F. It grows best in soft water. When lacking animal food, the plants grow very long and thin. Reproduction takes place through fragments of the plant, which, when simply put in water, immediately grow new shoots. Harmless to young fry as the utricles are too small for anything but infusoria.

— **vulgaris** Linné: Common Utricularia.

GENERALITIES: The best-known species, which is found in all of Europe and North Africa.

SHAPE: As per description of the genus. The light-green, finely divided leaves stand alternately around a more or less long stem. Depending on the locations, each leaf carries 10-200 utricles which are able to devour even larger plankton animals and fish larvae during the first days of their life.

CULTIVATION: This very beautiful and delicate cold water plant may either be cultivated floating free, or else growing from unwashed sand. Being a carnivorous plant, it is very interesting to keep. Despite the fact that it likes light, it should not be placed in too intensely lit spots, as these carry the danger of algae infestation. Higher temperatures easily lead it to degenerate. Soft, slightly acid water enhances the development.

V: Abbreviation for ventral fin.

vacuoles: "Bubbles" or accumulations of liquids which develop in unicellulars and in which food substances are elaborated. They develop as needed and dissolve again thereafter.

valencia: After Lake Valencia, in Venezuela.

— *Gephyrocharax.*

Valencia: After the Spanish city of Valencia.

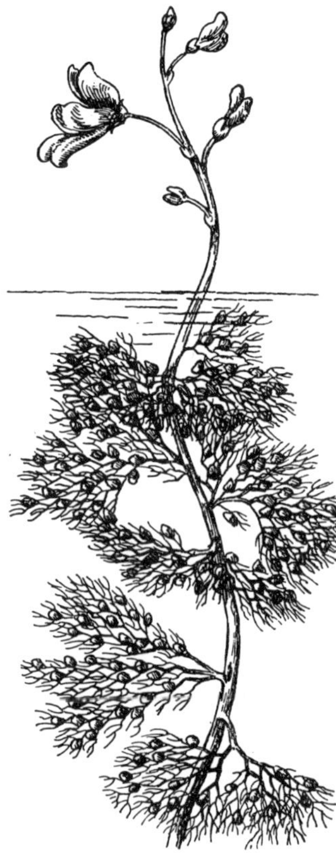

Utricularia vulgaris

European genus of Tooth Carps belonging to the sub-family of the Egg Laying Tooth Carps or *Cyprinodontinae.*

— **hispanica** (Cuvier and Valenciennes): The Spanish Tooth Carp.

SHAPE: Of relatively compact build, short, stout, and only little compressed laterally. The head and the anterior part of the back are flattened. The mouth opening is big and tilted upwards. D 10-11, A 12-14. Dorsal and anal fins insert quite far back. Length, males up to $2\frac{3}{8}$", females up to $3\frac{1}{8}$".

COLOR: Brownish, the male with a deep-black shoulder spot and several cross bands, the female simpler in color with a dark horizontal band. Fins yellowish.

RANGE: Eastern and Southeastern Spain.

CARE AND BREEDING: This resistant and hardy, but rather predatory species demands spacious, well-planted, and sunlit tanks. No exigencies are made as to water temperature. 64-70° F are sufficient, for breeding up to 75° F, lowest 50° F. Since the fish are very voracious offer them plenty of vigorous live foods, additionally also prepared foods. Breeding occurs in the manner of the plant spawning *Aphyosemions*.

The females show themselves to be quite intolerant in this and chase the males away with bites, so that they have to keep hidden until the approaching maturity for spawning makes the female more accessible. Spawning is then done in plant thickets near the surface. The glass-clear eggs, about .1″ in size, are laid singly. At a temperature of 68-75° F. the fry appear after 12-14 days. The parents prey strongly on the spawn. Rearing the young is not difficult.

Valencia Tetra, the: see GEPHYROCHARAX VALENCIA.

Valenciennes, Achille: 1794-1864. French ichthyologist, pupil and collaborator of Cuvier. Together with the latter he published the 'Natural History of Fishes' in French, one of the greatest ichthyological works.

Vallisneria: Eel Grass.

Genus of perennial water plants belonging to the family of the Frog Bits or *Hydrocharitaceae*, which is widely distributed over the tropics, the sub-tropics, and the warmer parts of the temperate zones.

The light-green leaves, which rise from the bottom, are ribbon-shaped. The female flowers grow up to the surface on spirally wound, thin stems. The male flowers sit at the base of the leaves, come off, and float along on the surface to meet the female flowers.

The plants are hardy and need no special care. For bottom soil unrinsed sand suffices, to which one may add some old clay if a stronger reproduction is desired. They need some light, though, as otherwise they grow pale and die.

— gigantea Greabner: The Giant Eel Grass.

GENERALITIES: A very beautiful and stately species, appropriate for big and high tropical aquaria.

SHAPE: As per description of the genus. The leaves may reach lengths of up to 5 ft. and widths of 1⅛″. Shops often offer hybrids of this species with *V. spiralis*. Genuine *V. gigantea* have 7 leaf nervures.

ORIGIN: New Guinea and the Philippines.

CULTIVATION: As per description of the genus. The plants need a stronger soil made up of a 1:1 mixture of sand and clay, to which one may add a little sphagnum in order to loosen it up. Temperatures may range between 77 and 95° F, but should not sink below 64° F.

— spiralis Linné: Common Eel Grass.

GENERALITIES: One of the best-known and most hardy aquatic plants.

SHAPE: As per description of the genus.

RANGE: Distributed over the warmer regions of the temperate zone, the sub-tropics, and the tropics of nearly the whole globe, forming dense lawns in flowing and standing, clear waters.

CULTIVATION: As per description of the genus. Reproduction through abundantly developing runners. If one has plants of the two sexes, one may also grow them from seeds, after artificial pollination by rubbing the male flowers that appear on the surface on the female ones.

Vallisneria showing runner and proper planting depth.

The plants make no special demands as to warmth, but one should avoid letting the temperature sink below 59° F. Apparently soft water is not especially favorable.

— spiralis Linné **forma tortifolia** Wendt: The Screw Vallisneria.
A species which remains smaller, with spirally wound leaves, coming from the South of the U.S.A. The leaf edge is very thinly toothed. Care similar to that of the preceding species, but needing more warmth. Plants that are kept too cold remain small and the spiral turns are less pronounced.

variability: The capacity, more or less inherent to every species, to adapt to different dwelling places and biotopes, within the limits of the general picture of the species and the given situation. This capacity may be closely limited, but also extremely well developed. Furthermore variability also refers to the change of certain characteristics within the same family. (Range of variation, dispersion).

variatus: Varied, changeable.
— *Xiphophorus* (*Platypoecilus*).

Variegated Platy, the: see XIPHOPHORUS (PLATYPOECILUS) VARIATUS.

variegatus: Many-hued, variedly striped.
— *Cyprinodon*.

variety: Sub-species, strain. All individuals of the same species which differ from the original type by certain hereditary, more or less firmly established traits, but which are able to cross-feed unlimitedly with each other among the different strains.

vateriflоris: After the flower of an Indian tree, which the species resembles in color.
— *Rasbora*.

vegetation: The plants that cover Earth in general, also the growth of plants.

vegetative: Manner of reproduction of plants and of certain lower animals in an asexual way through budding.

Veil Carp, the: see PTEROLEBIAS LONGIPINNIS.

velifera: Bearing sail.
— *Mollienisia*.

Venus Fish, the: see APHYOCYPRIS POONI.

Vermes: Worms.
Formerly the definition 'Worms' included all animals which correspond to the current idea of a worm. In modern systematics the former components of this group, which are of different origins, have been classified in several phyla of their own, and in different places within the system. Therefore the definition 'Worm' is no more a systematical unit, but only indicates a body shape. Thus definitions like *Amera*, *Polymera*, and *Oligomera* have become void.

They are presently substituted by the following: Flat Worms, or *Plathelminthes*, Tube Worms or *Nemathelminthes*, and Articulated

Worms or *Annelidae*.

Veronica: Origin of name unknown. Genus of perennial swamp plants belonging to the family of the *Schrophulariaceae* distributed over Europe, Asia, and North Africa with a few species.

— beccabunga Linné:

GENERALITIES: A pretty swamp plant, appropriate above all for the cold swamp aquarium and the open air installation.

SHAPE: The species may appear half-emerged or completely submerged in slightly differing shapes. In the half-emerged state the crossed-opposite and slightly notched leaves are broad-oval, quite robust, and fleshy, while the submerged ones are a little longer, with a whole edge, and a little more frail. The species flowers only in the half-emerged state. The flowers, in numbers of 5-20, form a cluster-shaped inflorescence. The petals are blue, sometimes also white or crimson. Submerged, the plants ramify strongly and grow at the bottom of the waters in dense stands. The stems measure 8-20″.

RANGE: On the shores of smaller waters, as well as in swampy places. The submerged form is generally found in flowing waters only. The species is distributed over Europe, North and West Asia, and North Africa.

CULTIVATION: The species is appropriate for growing in both the domestic aquarium and in the swamp aquarium. In the aquarium it prefers temperatures of 59-64° F, degenerating easily at higher ones. Under favorable conditions, and if it receives sufficient light, it continues growing during the whole year. Coarse sand with an admixture of weathered clay is a sufficient bottom soil. In the swamp aquarium the plants generally recede during winter, but usually thrive again with coming spring.

Veronica beccabunga

At low water levels they grow over the surface and bloom, but need sunlight for this. *V. beccabunga* is especially appropriate for the open-air installation.

Vertebrata: Vertebrates. Sub-phylum belonging to the phylum of the *Chorda* animals or Chordates, the genetic-historically lowest representatives of which are the Jawless ones or *Agnathi*, the higher developed ones being the Jawed Vertebrates or *Gnathostomata*. Vertebrates are characterized by the possession of a more or less developed, cartilaginous or bony, skeleton, the central axis of which is formed by the firm, but movable, dorsal spine, which encloses the dorsal medulla. The skull, which encloses and protects the sensitive brain and a number of sensory organs, is provided with movable feeding instruments (jaws).

vertical fins: Collective name for the unpaired fins; anal, dorsal, and caudal.

verticillata: Verticil-shaped.

— *Hydrilla*.

verticillatum: Verticil-shaped.
— *Myriophyllum.*

Vesicularia: Refers to the bubble-shaped spore cyst.

Genus belonging to the family of the Sleeper Mosses or *Hypnaceae*, of creeping growth, widely ramified with many lateral shoots. The genus is mainly limited to the tropical and sub-tropical regions of Earth.

— dubyana (C. Muell) *brotherus:* Java Moss.

A moss distributed over Indonesia, Malaya, and the Philippines, which generally lives emerged on shore edges, but also at other, dryer places. Java Moss is extraordinarily adaptable, developing numerous growing forms which depend on the local conditions, and may therefore also be cultivated submergedly.

SHAPE: The gracile, richly ramified plant carries densely-standing, tender green, unsymmetrically built, little leaves, when cultivated submergedly. Specimens that are fixed to a spot extend by creeping flatly to all sides, while free-floating ones grow irregularly helter-skelter. The single shoots hardly get bigger than 4″. The numerous rhizomes serve only for holding fast to a base. The spore cysts, which often are produced in great numbers, are brown-red and stand on long stems.

CULTIVATION: This moss was introduced accidentally 25 years ago, but only lately (1957) has it become known in greater circles due to the writings of SAUER. The habitus of the submerged form is strongly dependent on the vital conditions; the species is undemanding, however, with regard to conditions of light and to water compositions. According to SAUER growth was most luxuriant in not too well-lit tanks, and only there the plants developed spore cysts. Since they are sensitive to overinfestation with algae, the relatively small need for light may be of advantage. Nourishment comes exclusively from the water, the rhizoids serve only to keep firmly located. Nearly all materials are appropriate as bottom soil, but the moss seems to grow best on natural rocks. In order to fix them there, put a piece of a stem on the rock, weighted down by a little stone or something similar. Multiplication can be achieved at any moment through cut off twigs. Free growing pieces lie on the bottom. Java Moss represents an especially good spawning substratum. It should be protected as much as possible against the soiling that results from the presence of strongly rooting fishes.

vesiculosa: Covered with small bubbles.
— *Aldrovanda.*

vexillifer: Standard-bearer.
— *Aphyosemion.*

vinegar worms: see TURBATRIX ACETI.

virescens: Greenish.
— *Eigenmannia.*

viridissima: Extremely green.
— *Chlorohydra.*

virulent: Causing diseases; contagious; very poisonous.

vitamins: Active substances which are necessary for the metabolism of animals, acting in smallest amounts, the lack of which may cause severe symptoms of deficiency.

Referring to their influence on aquarium fishes, at present we still have to depend on suppositions. To a certain extent we may also draw conclusions from knowledge acquired in this field in the science of fisheries.

According to MANN, overfattening of the liver (degeneration of the liver), a quite frequent disease among aquarium fishes, is probably traceable to the lack of carotene, which further disturbs the transformation of carotene into Vitamin A, important for growth. Carotene is a preparatory step to Vitamin A. The yellow pigments in the skin are formed of carotene; they may disappear if the supply of this substance is insufficient, respectively re-appear when the substance is supplied again. Carotene is contained in plants (carrots). Fishes generally get it from algae or from prey that eat algae on their part. The intense red coloring of many micro-crustaceans, for instance, which feed on algae, stems from the carotene of these unicellular plants.

Also important for the general well-being of fishes, for their growth, and for the functioning of their digestive organs, is Vitamin B_1, which is found in green plants too. Naturally also many other vitamins are of decisive importance for the thriving of our fishes, but so far nothing certain can be said about them. Anyway, the facts that the suppliers of vitamins and their basic preparatory compounds give shows how important it is to offer aquarium fishes the possibility to eat vegetable foods too.

vittata: Banded.
— *Eleotris.*
— *Limia.*
— *Pyrrhulina.*
— *Sperata.*

vittatus: Banded.
— *Barbus* (*Puntius*).
— *Otocinclus.*
— *Trichopsis.*

vivipara: Viviparous, live-bearing.
— *Poecilia.*

Viviparidae: Swamp Snails.
Family belonging to the sub-class of the Front Gills or *Prosobranchia.* Snails with cone-shaped or spherical shells with a round opening and a generally concentrically striped lid of horny substance. The eyes sit on very short 'horns'. The right-hand antenna of the males is used as a mating organ. All species are live-bearers. The family ranges over all continents, except South America. As a European genus we must mention especially *Viviparus.*

Viviparus: Swamp Lid-Snails.
Genus of snails belonging to the family of the Swamp Snails or *Viviparidae,* with round shells, provided with lids. The snout is long and trunk-like, the right-hand antenna of the male is developed into a sexual organ.

The Swamp Lid-Snails generally remain at the bottom of the aquarium, where they dig in occasionally. Sometimes they also lie with closed lids on the bottom for longer periods. The snails are live-bearers. The young, which are extruded gradually, and which number 30-40, are completely developed at birth, with their shells already showing 3-4 spirals. During the first days of life they are still within a glassily transparent egg shell. It seems that the females die after having had their litters, at least this happens in the aquarium. Otherwise they resist quite well, provided the water is not too warm. Contrary to other aquatic snails, the Swamp Lid-Snails have gills. Therefore they do not come to the surface for breathing. The male is smaller than the female. Viviparus are quite attractive in the aquarium.

The Giant "Mystery" Snail

The genus is distributed over Europe, Asia, and America, with many species. The best-known German one is *V. viviparus* Linné. It is found in standing, richly-planted waters, especially of the plains. The green-brown shell shows three dark bands, and a rounded, clearly set-off point. *V. fasciatus* Mueller lives more in flowing waters and in the mountains.

Volvox: Glittering Sphere.

Genus belonging to the phylum of the whip-bearers or *Flagellata*, class of the Plant Monads or *Phytomonadia*. They are unicellulars which form colonies, usually classified as plants. Beneath a common jelly cover live thousands of individuals, united to a spherical formation that already shows qualities that are peculiar to multicellulars. The whips (flagelli), which are tilted outward, beat all in unison, while the individual cells have already specialized, serving only for locomotion, feeding, or reproduction, respectively. Reproduction is achieved by unsexed division of the settlement, or else through the development of sexual cells (spores). It is in this stage of development that the natural 'death' of a parent animal appears for the first time among unicellulars.

vorax: Voracious.

— *Tilapia.*

vulgaris: Vulgar, common.

— *Tinca.*

— *Utricularia.*

Wagtail Platy: see XIPHOPHORUS (PLATYPOECILUS) MACULATUS.

Walking Fish, the: see ANABAS TESTUDINEUS.

Walking Fishes, the: see ANABANTIDAE.

warm water aquarium: Aquarium that needs constant additional heating and can only dispense with this on a few especially hot summer days. It has been made considerably easier to keep through the design of simple, resistant, and safe heating elements.

As inhabitants we have to consider those fishes and plants which need a nearly perpetual warmth above 68° F for their well-being and breeding.

wasting of plants: Weak growth and pale color of plants, caused mainly by poor amount or composition of light, accompanied usually by too great stretching of the stem parts. In cold-water plants this condition is sometimes also brought on by too much heat.

water: Water, being the vital element of fishes, plants, and all other live beings kept in the aquarium, deserves special study. Water (H_2O) is an oxide of hydrogen. In a pure state it is odorless and tasteless, looking colorless when in thin layers, and blue to deep-blue with increasing depth. It freezes to ice at 32° F, and boils at 212° F.

Water is found in its liquid or solid state everywhere on Earth. In the form of gas it is contained in the atmosphere, chemically bound in many chemicals, fluid in water bodies of all kinds, above or below the surface of the earth, furthermore it is found as the main component of all organisms, and in solid state (ice), among others, in the high mountains and at the Poles. Water shows the tendency always to flow to the lowest point of elevation. Water in interconnected vessels has the tendency to reach the same height of level. Water is a combination of two atoms of hydrogen and one atom of oxygen. It is able to dissolve most substances, and therefore it is not found pure in nature. On its way through the atmosphere, over the surface of the earth, or while penetrating the soil it incorporates many substances. The vaporized water contained in the atmosphere liquefies at lower temperatures into clouds or fog, from which it falls down to earth as rain, dew, snow, or hail. Part of this water evaporates immediately, being reincorporated in the atmosphere; another part, however, penetrates the soil, collects on impermeable layers, and remains there as underground water, resurges from springs, or is brought to the surface by artificial means. A great part of this water, together with its dissolved substances, is assimilated by plant and animal bodies, through which it courses and reacts chemically. The quantity of water held by the plants of the globe, for instance, is huge. In assimilation, part of it, together with carbon dioxide, is transformed into organic substances. Inversely, animals eliminate carbon dioxide and water from the organic substance and return both to the atmosphere by breathing.

The purest water that is found in nature is rain water. It always still contains dissolved atmospheric air, as well as small percentages of ammonia compounds and dust. In industrial regions it is dirtier than in rural ones, being cleanest in the sparsely settled tropics.

The water that penetrates the soil releases part of its oxygen contents, substituting mineral compounds for this. Therefore, the composition of springs and wells depends upon the layers through which their waters pass. Spring water generally contains carbon dioxide, sulphates, and chlorides. In the temperate zones they contain especially salts of calcium and magnesium, which are determinants of its hardness.

Certain exigencies are made as to potable water for sanitary reasons, since it is known how large a role it has played, and is still playing, in the spread of certain diseases (Cholera morbus, dysentery, typhoid). Drinking water must be colorless and odorless, its taste should not be stale, but neither should have predominant flavors of any substances, its temperature should fluctuate as little as possible, and its hardness should not surpass 18° DH. Potable water (tap water) is prepared in a certain manner. First of all it is filtered and chlorinated. Before being used in the aquarium, tap water should be permitted to stand for a while, in order to release the admixture of chlorine and possible inclusions of air.

It is evident that the composition of the water has a deep influence on fishes and plants. This is especially true in that the different species are adapted to different water conditions, some within closer limits, others within broader ones, but which have to be considered by the aquarist if he desires success. (See Ambient World).

Therefore the study of the chemistry of water has become an important part of aquaristics. There are a number of successes to be chalked up, which have considerably changed our knowledge of the biological relationships within the waters of the aquarium. This includes especially the gleaning of knowledge of the dependence of aquatic animals and plants upon the surrounding water and chemical phenomena that take place therein.

water, aged: Water which has been standing for a certain time—at least 3 weeks—for aquarium use; this has for a long time been highly regarded by aquarists. Here it should be made clear that water may not be considered to be aged even if it is kept cool and dark in clean, closed glass containers, which would not be less than the conditions they would get in the aquarium. Such water, which might be useful for breeding, would still have to be considered as fresh water, even if it has stood for a still longer time.

Aged water is much more a water which has been changed by biological and chemical processes in the aquarium. Aquarium water cannot be considered by itself alone, because it is also closely connected with fishes, plants, microscopic life, the bottom, etc. For this reason its characteristics are constantly changing in a manner which is difficult to control. For this reason the water must be given the same consideration as all the other factors in the aquarium. Aquarium water must be cared for. It cannot however be denied that after long use it becomes heavily tainted with waste products, the results of which would probably explain many mishaps with fishes.

All living creatures in the aquarium give off waste substances, which either dissolve immediately or after undergoing a biochemical change. The more fishes which are put into an aquarium, the higher will be the percentage of waste substances which can adversely affect the condition of the water. With the present aids we can only remove a small part of these. The best remedy so far is still a good growth of plants. If it is desired that the aged water in the aquarium does not possess any harmful characteristics, then the cultivation of true aquatic plants, especially those with submerged leaves is recommended. The more plants there are per fish, the more beneficial the characteristics of the water will be. The rule of thumb so often referred to in literature which calls for one fish to every one or two quarts of water does not fulfill these rules. With such a crowding of fishes in such a little space there can be no clean water for any length of time. A healthy condition might be possible if with a good growth of plants one fish the length of a finger to every gallon of water were used.

The small amount of sediment resulting from such an arrangement would be broken down by bacteria and could then be absorbed by the plants as nutrition.

A great influence in the properties of aged water is also wrought by the decorations. Although this influx is often underrated, it often takes only traces of dissolved substances to cause considerable changes in the water's effect on fishes and plants. Of course aged water always contains traces of dissolved elements. Depending on the nature of the decorations and the composition of the bottom, the proportion of such substances could be greater or lighter, which could be the difference between being harmless or dangerous to fish life. In this way the smallest amount of metals in the water could prove poisonous. Limestone and cement should never be put in an aquarium which contains soft, acid water. According to O. Wagner almost all other decorative articles also add characteristics to the water, so that the setting up of an aquarium must be very carefully considered, if unpleasant surprises are to be avoided.

To sum up, it must be considered whether or not most fishes are by nature equipped to withstand great changes in the composition of their water. Only very seldom in Nature does the composition of a body of water remain the same over a period of time. It has been found that many fishes require a certain amount of change in the composition of their water for their welfare.

This is sometimes even a prelude to spawning, acting as a stimulant to their life processes. For this reason the natural spawning periods of many fishes occur at the seasonal changes, when such changes in water properties occur. In the temperate zones this takes place in the Spring months with the melting snows, and in the tropics this would be in the rainy season, or at the time the rain-waters from the tributary systems reach the main stream and affect the water masses there.

In a similar manner very many fishes in the aquarium can be stimulated into spawning by the addition of fresh water, while in the aged water of an aquarium, because of the previously mentioned reasons, diseases or sexual sterility could result. The demands of the fishes in this connection however are very much varied, depending on the individual species. In general it is beneficial from time to time to draw off $\frac{1}{4}$ to $\frac{1}{3}$ of a tank's contents and replace it with fresh water.

water and gas-caused damages to fishes: Health damages caused by the action of water, respectively of substances and gases dissolved in it, may appear quite often among aquarium fishes.
Poisonings with metal salts, chemical components of cements and paints, gases that enter the aquarium from outside, etc. may cause grave diseases. Not unfrequent either are damages caused by a supercharging of the water with metabolism wastes. The state of equilibrium in the circulation of nitrogen is suspended in the aquarium. Much more nitrogen compounds are generated than may be transformed or used up. Such compounds are: urea, nitrates, nitrites, and ammonia. The order in which they are mentioned is that of danger. The fishes become restive, shy, and fall into convulsions easily, eventually succumbing to them. Regular changes of part of the water act as a preventive of this situation. Also the use of tanning substances in the aquarium (roots, leaves, bark, tannic acid) may trigger similar symptoms, if overdosed. After an initially increased unrest, the fishes show complete apathy, and death may follow very quickly. The natural reaction of water (pH value, see CONCENTRATION OF HYDROGEN IONS). Depending on their origin, fishes are adapted to very diverse pH values. While some species withstand pH values within the acidity range (between 5-6) with ease, others by and by show the symptoms of the so-called acidity-disease. If the change in the pH value is slow and gradual, an accommodation may be reached. In some cases, however, it may lead to illness and death. The fishes become sluggish, the fins are closed, or erected shakingly, the skin shows discolorations. The changes are only slight, and death may occur suddenly. Sudden changes to water with completely different pH values may cause sudden death.

Extreme pH values within the alkaline range may bring on the alkalinity disease due to the development of ammonium hydroxyde and of quick-lime. Also an oversaturation with oxygen may lead to typical damages (see OXYGEN).

water bugs: see COLEOPTERA.

water bugs: see HYDROCORYSAE.

water ear: see APONOGETON.

Water Ear, Bernieri's: see APONOGETON BERNIERIANUS.

Water Ear, Crisp: see APONOGETON CRISPUS.

Water Ear, Frail-leaved: see APONOGETON LEPTOSTACHYUS.

Water Ear, Long-leaved: see

APONOGETON ELONGATUS.
Water Ear Plants: see APONOGETONACEAE.
Water Ear, Two-eared: see APONOGETON DISTACHYUS.
Water Ear, Ulva-leaved: see APONOGETON ULVACEUS.
Water Ear, Wavy: see APONOGETON UNDULATUS.
Water Hyacinth: see EICHHORNIA CRASSIPES.
— Blue: see EICHHORNIA AZUREA.
water insects: see HEXAPODA, INSECTS.
Water Key: see HYDROCLEIS.
Water Lentils:
— Humpbacked: see LEMNA GIBBA.
— Many-rooted: see SPIRODELA POLYRHIZA.
— Rootless: see WOLFFIA ARRHIZA.
— Small: see LEMNA MINOR.
— Submerged: see LEMNA TRISULCA.
water lilies: see NYMPHACEAE.
Water Lobelia: see LOBELIA DORTMANNA.
water mites: see HYDRACARINA.
Water Moss: see FONTINALIS ANTIPYRETICA.
water mosses: see FONTINALACEAE.
water nut plants: see HYDROCARYACEAE.
water pest: see ELODEA.
Water Plantain: see ECHINODORUS RADICANS.
Water Scorpion: see HYDROCORYSAE.
Water Spider: see ARGYRONETA AQUATICA.
Water Sprite: see CERATOPTERIS.
Water Star: see CALLITRICHE.
— Indian: see HYGROPHYLA POLYSPERMA.
water star plants: see CALLITRICHACEAE.
Water Tube: see UTRICULARIA.
water tube plants: see LENTIBURIACEAE.
Wavy-leafed Water Chalice: see CRYPTOCORYNE UNDULATA.
Weather Fish, the: see MISGURNUS FOSSILIS.

Weber's apparatus: A bone linkage between the wall of the swimming bladder and the ear labyrinth, formed by the first vertebrae, which characterizes the order of the *Ostariophysi*. It transmits the changes in pressure which act on the swimming bladder to the inner ear, thus helping the fish to keep informed on the water layer in which it is. Possibly this organ also enhances the faculty of hearing.
werneri: After the Austrian zoologist Werner.
— *Barbus* (*Puntius*).
West Indian Grayling, the: see AGONOSTOMUS MONTICOLA.
Whiptail Loricaria, the: see LORICARIA PARVA.
Whirligigs: see GYRINIDAE.
White Cloud, the: see TANICHTYS ALBONUBES.
white worms: see ENCHYTRAEUS.
whole-glass aquarium: The whole-glass aquarium is a tank cast or pressed in one piece. It has a series of disadvantages over the frame aquarium which have forced it more and more into the background, despite its generally cheap price. Above all the walls are never uniformly smooth, so that the contents look distorted. The second disadvantage is that it breaks easily, either due to internal tension, or else through external causes such as scratches, chills etc.

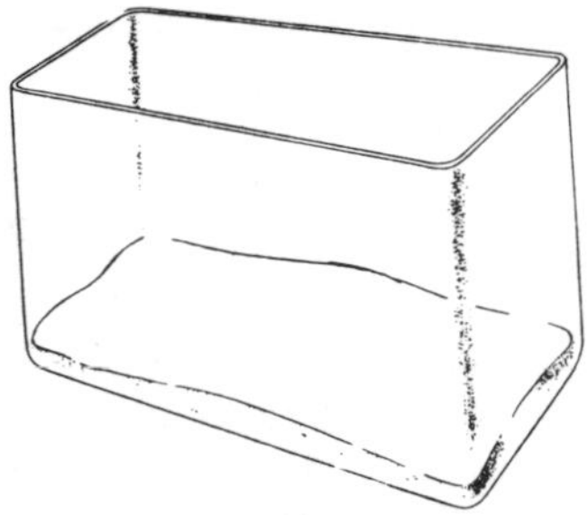

Whole glass aquarium. They are not satisfactory because of the danger of cracking and the distortion of vision.

Notwithstanding this, the smaller-sized whole-glass tank continues being a valuable aid to the fancier. It is very good for transitorily lodging aquatic insects and similar animals which one wants to keep under observation for shorter times. Furthermore it is used for breeding purposes, both to isolate females and to set up sensitive fishes for spawning. It is especially appropriate just for this, due to its being easy to disinfect and to keep clean. Bigger-sized ones are hardly advisable, 10″ side length should be the maximum. Be careful while cleaning. The tanks slip easily from wet hands! Furthermore they split due to scratches resulting from the bottom sand. All whole-glass tanks should be set on supports of paper, corrugated pasteboard, felt, or, in case of bottom-heating, on a piece of tin-plate filled with very fine-grained sand and with the edges bent up to a height of about $\frac{3}{8}$″. In the latter case, however, no guarantee can be given against sudden bursting.

Willow Moss: see FONTINALIS.

Window Cichlid, the: see CICHLASOMA FENESTRATUM.

Wine-red Finned Cichlid, the: see CICHLASOMA CUTTERI.

winter feeding, winter food: The supply of foods in winter depends in part upon the weather conditions, and becomes at times a little difficult due to these. In general, however, the choice of foods is so large today, that, considering the winter restrictions (see WINTERING), sufficient feeding is possible if the cold spell is not too long.

Try to feed as variedly as possible also in winter, a time during which the best intentions often are frustrated by the fact that temporarily certain foods are nearly the only ones available. Fishes which take artificial foods, may be fed with these at least twice weekly. Also in this, one may give them variety by changing the brands and kinds of food. Of the live foods, one has to consider: tubifex, red and white mosquito larvae, *enchytrae*, earthworms, brine shrimp of different sizes, and meal grubs. As an alternative to artificial foods one may also offer lean cooked ham free of tendons.

Below the ice one finds microcrustaceans in variable quantities, especially cyclops, and also water mites and glass larvae. Cultures intended for the supply of enchytrae, earthworms, or meal grubs, have to be set up in September by the latest. For further enlightenment on the basic tenets of feeding, look up the entries NUTRITION and FOOD. An occasional day of fasting does not harm fishes.

wintering of fishes and plants: Nearly all fishes and plants need rest periods, since both in the temperate zones as well as in the subtropics and tropics the seasonal rhythm brings natural climaxes and lowest points in the course of life, to which the live beings are adapted. Despite the fact that, according to the geographical situation, these rest pauses only rarely coincide with our winter months, it is always advisable to employ for such rests our months from November to February with their shortened days (which in modern aquaristics may, of course, be lengthened with artificial illumination) and with the decreased availability of nautral foods. The most important point for all our tropical and sub-tropical pets is not the daily light period which should continue to be 10-12 hours, but the decreased temperature. Naturally the needs in this diverge a little according to the species and its origin, but one may safely consider that a lowering to an average warmth of 72° F with occasional over and under-values is useful to most animals and plants in the aquarium. Cold water fishes and plants (as far as they do not retract totally) also need this pause for resting. For these the temperatures may average 50-57° F, but may also go down to 39° F for short periods.

It is wrong to keep all fishes constantly at summer temperatures, and even more wrong to continue attempts at breeding over the winter. Exceptions are, of course, possible, when the manner of living of a species demands them, as may, for instance, happen with the short-lived bottom-spawning Tooth Carps. It has to be considered only favorable for nearly all organisms in the aquarium—especially with regard to intensions of breeding in spring—to afford animals a rest period with restricted vital activities, and to give plants a stoppage in vegetating.

Wistaria: An erroneous name for *Synnema triflorum*.

Wofatit: see HARDNESS OF WATER; TREATMENT OF WATER.

Wolffia: Genus of Water Lentils, pertaining to the family of the Water Lentil Plants or *Lemnaceae*.

— arrhiza (Linné): The Root-Less Water Lentil.

A species which is distributed over nearly the whole globe. Very small, spherically arched on the underside, and rootless. This recent, very small flowering plant, hardly ever survives in the aquarium.

Wolterstorff, Wilhelm: German naturalist who was closely connected with aquaristics and terraristics.

Born June 16, 1864 in Calbe, Germany, died Jan. 21, 1943. Due to a disease, he lost his hearing in early youth. At the age of 38 he became curator of the Museum of Natural History in Magdeburg, where he made many improvements. The celebrated collection of Batrachians, which unfortunately was destroyed during World War II, was numbered among his additions. For years Wolterstorff was the editor of the 'Blaetter fuer Aquarien und Terrarienkunde', and for three years of the 'Wochenschrift'. Among other things, he introduced Enchytrae as fish food in aquaristics.

Woolly-hand Crab, the: see ERIOCHEIR SINENSIS.

worm cataract of fishes: A severe disease caused by the sucker-worm *Diplostomus volvens* and its larvae, which either consists of the lesions caused by the penetration of the larvae into the fish, or else may lead to complete blindness due to the fact that they settle in the eyes. Smaller fishes may be killed within minutes. Since the intermediate hosts are snails, these should only be put with valuable fishes after a quarantine of at least 6 weeks if they come from wild waters and if there are reasons which make it inadvisable to desist completely from keeping them.

worm diseases of fishes: The number of worms that live parasitically on fishes is large. Consequently, they differ considerably among themselves in shape and manner of living and cause the

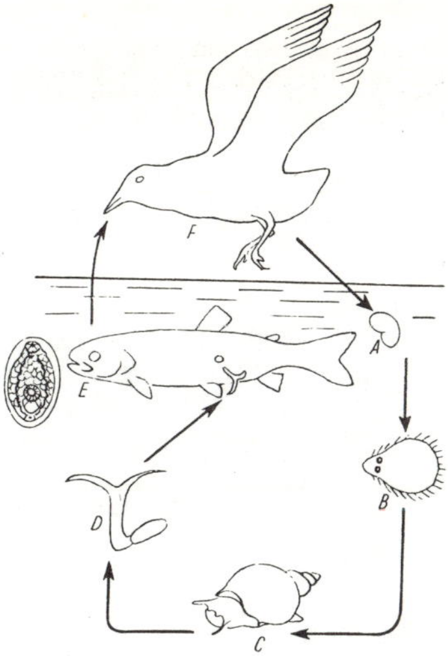

The Life Cycle of a Sucker Worm: (a) egg enters water from bird dropping; (b) free swimming stage of parasite after eggs hatch; (c) parasite uses snail as intermediate host; (d) worm attaches itself to fish and encysts; (f) bird eats fish and starts cycle over.

most diverse disease symptoms. These diseases are shown in the listing below, where the reader will be able to look up the respective entries.

1. LEECH DISEASES. Damages caused by leeches, which are harmless if in small numbers on bigger fishes, but which may become dangerous to smaller aquarium fishes.

2. SCRATCHER DISEASES. Inflammation of the intestine and perforation of its walls caused by parasitic worms with adhering organs, the so-called scratchers.

3. THREAD-WORM DISEASES. Diseases of certain internal organs caused by thread-worms (Nematodes), either coming from their larvae with very harmful consequences, or else from sexually mature worms without significant damage.

4. TAPE-WORM DISEASES. The incidence of tape-worms with the subsequent more or less harmful consequences, in which the fish may be an intermediate or final host.

5. SUCKER-WORM DISEASES. The incidence of external or internal parasitic sucker-worms, which cause several very dangerous diseases of the skin, the gills, the eyes, and the blood.

worms: see VERMES.

xanthorism: Golden coloring. See COLOR MALFORMATIONS.

xanthozona: With golden bands.

— *Brachygobius:* see BRACHYGOBIUS NUNUS.

Xenocara: With uncommon head. Genus belonging to the family of the Armored Catfishes or *Loricariidae,* with broad and flat body, eyes tilted slantingly upwards, and a crown of manifoldly ramified, short tentacles around the snout.

— dolichoptera:

SHAPE: As per description of the genus. D I /8, A I/4. There is an adipose fin. The dorsal fin is very

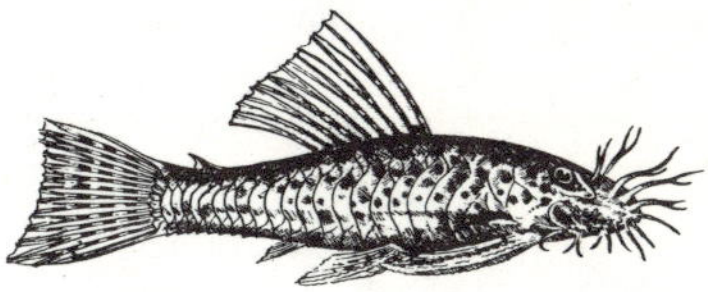

Xenocara dolichoptera

big, the pectorals are equipped with a strong and broad spine. The male possesses larger unarmored spots on the snout, its tentacles being longer and stronger than those of the female. Length up to 6″.

COLOR: Brownish-yellow with darker spots. Sex differences as described above.

RANGE: Clear waters in the Guianas and the Amazon region.

CARE AND BREEDING: A pronounced twilight and nocturnal fish, which keeps hidden all the time if located at a well-lit place. It is harmless and eats all kinds of small foods, also algae, prepared foods and detritus. Keep them at 73-80° F, in oxygen-rich water. Not yet spawned.

Xenomystus: Peculiar and mysterious.

African genus belonging to the family of the Ancient World Knife Fishes or *Notopteridae*. They have no dorsal fin. The endings of the nasal pits are extended into tubes.

— nigri (Guenther): The African Knife Fish.

A species similar to the knife fish *Notopterus*, with very small scales, and 108-130 rays in the anal fin. Length up to 12″.

Xenomystus negri

RANGE: Tropical West and East Africa, exclusively in fresh waters.

CARE AND BREEDING: This Knife Fish is a very skilled swimmer, which, like all similar species, can move forward and backward by means of undulatory movements of the anal fin, with equal agility. Offer it very spacious tanks with dense planting. Sensitive to low temperatures, 73-82° F being necessary for its well-being. Exclusively vigorous live foods are eaten. Reproduction unknown.

Xiphophorus: Sword-bearer.

Genus of Tooth Carps belonging to the sub-family of the live bearing Tooth Carps or *Poeciliinae*, which is widely distributed over Central America. Small, high-backed fishes, the males more or less elongated, the females a little compact. The mouth is supraterminal, the dorsal fin long.

The lower rays of the tail fin of the typical sword-tails may be more or less extended to sword-shaped on the males.

The close relationship between the formerly independent genera *Xiphophorus* and *Platypoecilus*, proven by the unlimited capacity to cross-breed, and bv the existence of many transitory forms, was the reason why both genera were combined in the genus *Xiphophorus*.

— helleri (Heckel): The Sword-Tail.

SHAPE: As per description of the genus. Elongated and slender fishes, the females a little compact, with the body strongly compressed laterally, a little flattened on the upper side of the head and on the front part of the back. The sword extension of the tail fin is especially pronounced. Length, males, without sword, up to $3\frac{1}{8}$″, females up to $4\frac{3}{4}$″.

COLOR: Shiny green with red horizontal stripes of which especially the middle one stands out, and with a green to golden-red sword extension. From the moment of the first mating on the female bears a blue-black pregnancy spot. The species is very variable. A number of very pretty color strains have been grown by means of cross-breeding with sports of the Platy.

RANGE: Mexico, Guatemala, Honduras.

CARE AND BREEDING: As described for all live-bearing Tooth Carps. The males are very skillful swimmers, which swim forwards and

Red Wagtail Swordtail, **Xiphophorus helleri**

backwards with the same speed. They are a little quarrelsome, especially if there are several males belonging to different color strains. Temperature 68-73° F, lowest 64° F. The artificially bred forms may need more warmth. Some of the black-spotted forms have proven to be very delicate. The accumulation of black pigments in the skin may be considered as the initial point of the formation of cancerous growths.

— **maculatus** Guenther: The Platy.

SHAPE: Of compact build, strongly compressed laterally, older specimens—especially females—with the backs growing higher. As a rule the male is considerably more elongated and slender than the female.

COLOR: The original form is yellow-gray with dark spots on the tail root which flow over into each other. The species is very variable in colors, which has led to the selective breeding of a number of color sports which surpass the original form considerably. These have been further improved by cross-breedings with Sword-tails (*Xiphophorus*).

RANGE: Eastern Mexico and Guatemala.

CARE AND BREEDING: As described for all live-bearing Tooth Carps. A very hardy and desirable species. They like warmth but without being sensitive to occasional lower temperatures. 68-79° F are advantageous. Omnivores, which eat all kinds of live and prepared foods. If you want to keep the pretty color sports pure, keep the sexes apart, and mate only those fish which have the desired characteristics.

Xiphophorus (Platypoecilus) maculatus, the Spotted Platy

Xiphophorus montezumae

— **montezumae** (Jordan and Snyder): The Montezuma Sword-Tail.

A South Mexican Sword-tail, only rarely kept in the aquarium, which has not reached great popularity due to its simple colors. It has been the subject of vivid discussions for decades, since it is not clear whether this is not simply a natural cross of the variable members of the genus. The shape is quite plump and compact. The coloring is brownish with a dark length band and a few cross stripes. The sword extension is only short. Length, males up to $1\frac{3}{8}''$, females up to $2\frac{5}{8}''$.

— **variatus** Meek: The Variegated Platy.

SHAPE: A little more elongated than *Xiphophorus maculatus*, and with the caudal peduncle not as high as that of the other species. The females greatly resemble those of *X. helleri*. D 10, A 6-7. Length, males $2\frac{1}{8}''$, females around $2\frac{3}{4}''$.

COLOR: Black-dotted on yellowish, greenish, or bluish base, the throat of the male a vivid orange color, the

Xiphophorus variatus

dorsal fin yellow with black design. Very variable. The female changes its color only after 1½-2 years. The male has completely different colors.

RANGE: Mexico, with many local varieties.

CARE AND BREEDING: A hardy and harmless species which likes some warmth without being excessively sensitive. 68-79° F are adequate. Omnivores which also eat algae and sometimes even higher plants. Therefore they are able to cause considerable damage to the plants when in greater numbers. A very fertile species. The fry are quite large. Rearing them is easy, but the long period of development deters many breeders from breeding varieties of this species. The females should not be set up for breeding immediately after reaching sexual maturity.

Yellow-edged beetle: see DYTISCIDAE.

Yellow Rasbora, the: see RASBORA ELEGANS.

Yellow Tetra: see HYPHESSOBRYCON BIFASCIATUS.

young fry, their rearing and food. The alevin stage commences at the moment of bursting the egg shell, and ends with the beginning of sexual maturity. This span comprises the period of post-embryonic development, and that of the most important and significant growth. Its duration may be very variable. Most aquarium fishes need 9-12 months for it, quick-growing species only up to 3 months, and slowly-growing ones up to 2 years. The conditions of the fry stage are decisive for the development of most hereditary dispositions, which can only be developed totally if the fish grows up under optimum conditions of living. Therefore the aquarist should pay special attention to the rearing of the alevins.

The stage of development in which a young fish begins to burst the egg shell may differ much from one species to the next. As a rule, embryonic development continues for a short time even after leaving the egg. The larval period of the fry lasts 3-10 days, sometimes even longer. During this time the fins and feeding organs are not yet completely developed. The young fishes cannot yet swim and hang from a firm anchorage by means of a sticky secretion, or else they remain under the care of their parents. Alimentation is taken from the remainder of the egg yolk, which still adheres to the alevin in the form of the so-called yolk-sac. Only after overcoming this period does the youngster become able to swim. In some cases, as for instance, happens with some of the egg-laying and live-bearing Tooth Carps, the embryos remain within the egg shell until able to swim. With the advent of the ability to swim, known as "free-swimming", the young fish is forced to fill its swimming bladder. This has been completed only during the larval period, and before its filling it is in all cases connected to the oral cavity, or the intestine. Filling it with air often takes place by gulping air at the surface. For this reason it is advisable to keep the water level as low as possible in order to permit the brood easier access to the surface. Notwithstanding this, the water level is not always a decisive factor, for some fish young also reach this aim by making use of aquatic plants, etc., on which they rest, or else they are impelled to the surface anyway by oil inclusions in the yolk sac.

Naturally young fishes may be especially sensitive to the influences of the ambient world, and in many cases they are not able to withstand well any fluctuations in temperature or changes in the condition of the water. Probably there are also great differences in this, as sometimes they show a remarkable ruggedness. Thus it is known, for instance, that, if one takes some precautionary measures, it is easier to transport the alevins of some species than the corresponding adults. In free nature the fry stage generally falls into the period of the best conditions of living to which a species is adapted. As a first condition the young fish finds available all foods necessary for its development.

Closer observations on the manner of feeding in free nature are still lacking for most species of fishes. Therefore the breeder has rather to take recourse to guesses, comparisons, and try-outs of all available foods. It is understandable that thus feeding within the aquarium may be fundamentally different from that taking place in free nature. The alimentation of young fishes as given by the breeder is generally very one-sided, as he naturally falls back on the food stuffs and food animals which are available at the moment. This circumstance may explain many of the faults of development which cause a "degeneration" of aquarium fishes generally attributed to inbreeding.

To catch dust-fine food, nets made of the finest silk or nylon are best. For the fine kinds of food a net of Triple (XXX) No. 13 type will be sufficient. Most important is the sifting of food, as by the intake of too big specimens, which most fry like to eat, harm may occur. Generally one should feed abundantly. Young fry should swim among food if one wants to obtain satistactory growth. It depends upon the experience of the breeder to find out the adequate quantities. Generally one should feed in the morning and at noon. There are many reasons why no great quantities of food should remain in the tank during night. For very greedy fish one might possibly leave a weak illumination burning even during darkness. Often feeding in a dark room, with a spot of illumination by a flashlight will pay off, as the live food, which generally strives towards the most well-lighted point, will meet the fry within the cone of light.

Dust-fine food usually is difficult to keep. It must be kept in cool, old water. Sparse feeding with blood-stained water may be advisable.

yucatana: Coming from Yucatan. — *Gambusia.*

Zannichellia: After the Italian botanist Zannichelli.

Genus belonging to the family of the Najads or *Najadaceae*, comprising sparsely distributed plants, rarely appropriate for the aquarium, which may also be kept in brackish water. In their habits they resemble the genus *Najas*.

RANGE: The whole globe, in standing and flowing waters, also in brackish regions.

Zebra, the: see BRACHYDANIO RERIO.

zebra mussels: see DREISSENACEAE.

Zebra, or Common, Killie, the: see FUNDULUS HETEROCLITUS.

Zeller, Karl: German aquarist who made a name for himself as breeder and importer. Born August 29, 1872, died March 1, 1949. Was the owner of a well-known fish hatchery in Magdeburg, Germany.

zelleri: After Zeller, the importer.
— *Barbus* (*Puntius*).

Zernecke, E.: German aquarist of the initial period, who contributed considerably to the popularization of aquaristics through his work 'Leitfaden fuer Aquarien- und Terrarienfreunde' (A guide for aquarium and terrarium fanciers), which was published in 1897 by order of the Berlin club 'Triton'. Died August 4, 1949.

zillii: After the French botanist Zilli.
— *Tilapia.*

zingel: After a personal name.
— *Aspro.*

zooplankton: Animal plankton.

zosteraefolia: sea-grass leaved.
— *Heteranthera.*

zygote: The product of the fusion of two sexual cells, and therefore the starting point of a new live being.

FEEDING OF YOUNG FRY: Make it a rule to afford your freshly hatched broods as varied an alimentation as possible, and to employ also other foods—if taken—than the current living animal foods described below. As such one may consider, for instance, good commercial foods, mashed egg yolk, enchytrae strained through cheesecloth, finely chopped tubifex, etc.

Infusoria, which are necessary for rearing many species of fishes during their first days of life, are best gleaned from cultures, as in these one has the possibility from the start to limit the development of only those unicellulars which are desirable as food. Compared to this, catching infusoria from free waters is not advisable, and generally only possible in a limited way with the nets that are generally available. What the fanciers call "pond" infusoria are rotatoria as a rule. In large containers, especially if one does not make a point of breeding in quantities, infusoria may also be bred in the nursery tank.

Another live food for rearing small fry is micro worms, for which one makes cultures of the small vinegar eel *Turbatrix.* Furthermore there are the nauplii of the brine shrimp, *Artemia salina,* and the Grindal worms, belonging to the genus *Enchytraeus.* These latter three feed fishes that have already grown a little.

Especially important are *Rotatoria* and the fry of copepods, as well as certain so-called daphnia and their young.

Micro-worms generally are taken only by rather robust young, especially by those which pick up food that falls to the bottom, for instance, Barbs, Catfishes, Cichlids, etc.

The nauplii of brine shrimp are rather big. In any case, during the first hours after hatching they are so soft-shelled that they can be taken by many of the smallest spawn of fishes.

Grindal worms may be still more divided by removing their body moisture in dry and fine sand. They are also eagerly eaten if crushed and washed.

Rotatoria are very variegated in shape. The sizes are variable, ranging from 1/10 to 2 mm. They are an excellent food, which may be caught in quantities, especially in summer.

Of the *Daphnia* (*Cladocera*) during the first days not even the young are to be considered, as they are all very hard-shelled, and therefore not eaten by the fry at first. About a week after the infusoria period one may start feeding *Bosminae*. The smallest of these may be sifted through No. 9 cheese cloth, which they still penetrate. *Bosminae* differ externally from daphnia in that they move in straight lines and somewhat shakily.

The most important food for young fishes are the nauplii of *Copepoda*, especially of *Cyclops* and *Diaptomus*. *Cyclops* nauplii, which feed by gnawing, though, may become dangerous to alevins if in too great numbers. *Diaptomus* nauplii, on the other hand, which feed by filtration, are harmless. *Cyclops* nauplii hop and jump, while *Diaptomus* nauplii do it alternating between sinking and jumping, or else in spiral-shaped turns. Nauplii are found in all sizes. The smallest ones may be sifted out with No. 12 cheese cloth, while with cheese cloth No. 8 the fully developed specimens come through.

PICTORIAL CATALOGUE

As the aquarist advances in his understanding of the basic aquarium phenomena, he might inquire a bit deeper and want to know not only what causes green water, but how to identify the organisms that he finds when he examines a drop under the microscope.

Often, too, snails' eggs and insect larvae are brought into the aquarium as "extras" on aquarium plants, live foods and in pond water.

The following section is an illustrated catalogue of various kinds of algae, other microorganisms, etc. It is added to the English edition of the "Illustrated Dictionary of Tropical Fishes" with the hope that perhaps it might further your understanding of the wonders and advantages of keeping an aquarium. Not only are aquarium fishes beautiful and interesting, but the water, the plants and the microscopic animals and plants living with your fishes form a new aquarium world that lies open for anyone to see.

Very inexpensive microscopes are now available in every city of the world. May we invite you to obtain one and to examine a few drops of your tank water, or scrape a bit of debris from an old aquarium leaf, or even a bit of slime from your fish. What you see will not only amaze you, but will help you better to understand the miraculous world we live in.

Like fishes, all known plants and animals have names. In the photos that follow, we have tried to give you a popular name along with a scientific name. We hope you enjoy this "fourth dimension" of your aquarium.

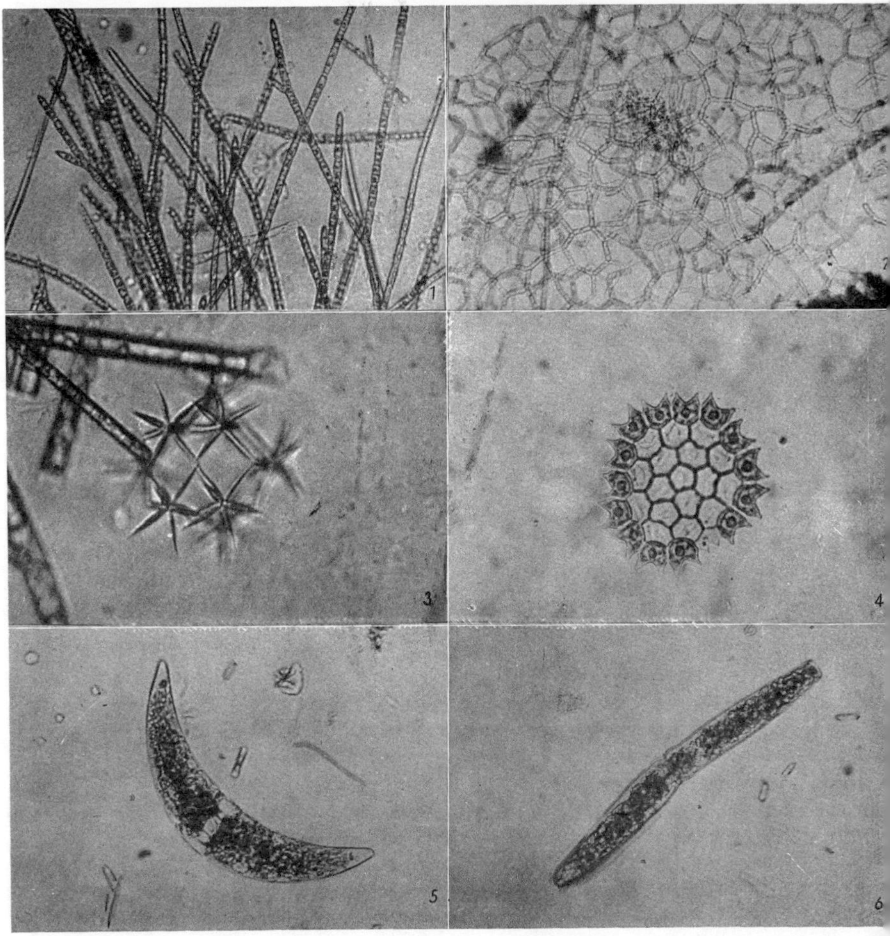

Green algae (Chlorophyaceae) and **Yoke-algae (Conjugatae)** that often appear when **your tanks** turn green. You need a **microscope** to examine them. These photos have been taken with a microscope. 1. This is the green algae **Ulotrichales** which forms on the aquarium plants, rocks, glass sides, etc. 2. Water-net algae of the genus **Hydrodictyon.** 3. Star-shaped algae, forming plankton, **Actinastrum hantzschii.** This is a very beautiful species of algae. 4. Another very beautifully shaped algae is the Purl-edged star algae, **Pediastrum.** It, too, is a plankton. 5. Moon algae is a typical yoke algae of the genus **Closterium.** 6. A very difficult algae to recognize is the yoke algae of the genus **Pleurotaenium.** All microphotographs by Knaack.

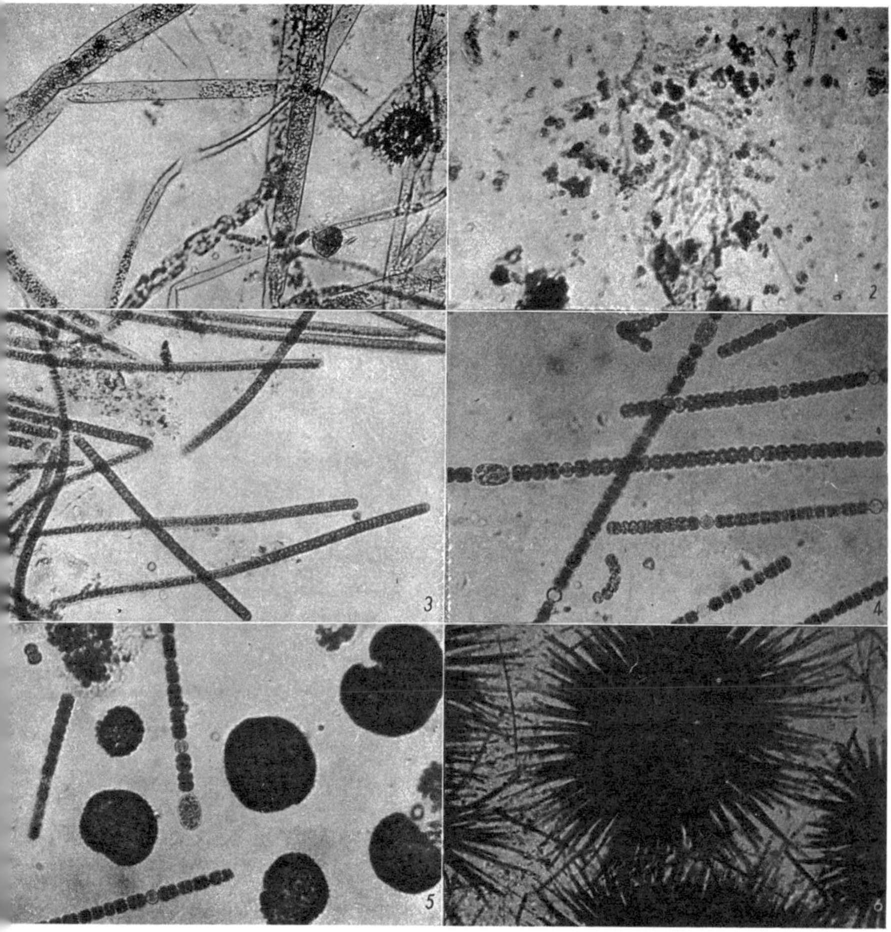

Blue algae (**Cyanophyceae**), small fungi and bacteria. All are enlarged and must be identified under a microscope. 1. Aquatic fungus, **Saprolegnia.** This is the same fungus that attacks dead and dying tissue. 2. A colony of bacteria belonging to the genus **Zoogloea.** 3. Swinging algae of the group **Oscillatoria** which are characteristic of a filthy aquarium. 4. A chain-forming colony of algae of the **Anabaena** group, which when numerous enough can discolor the water. 5. Another water discolorer is the ball colonies of **Coelosphaerium naegelianum.** 6. Jelly-hair algae, **Gloeotrichia echinulata.** All microphotographs are by Knaack.

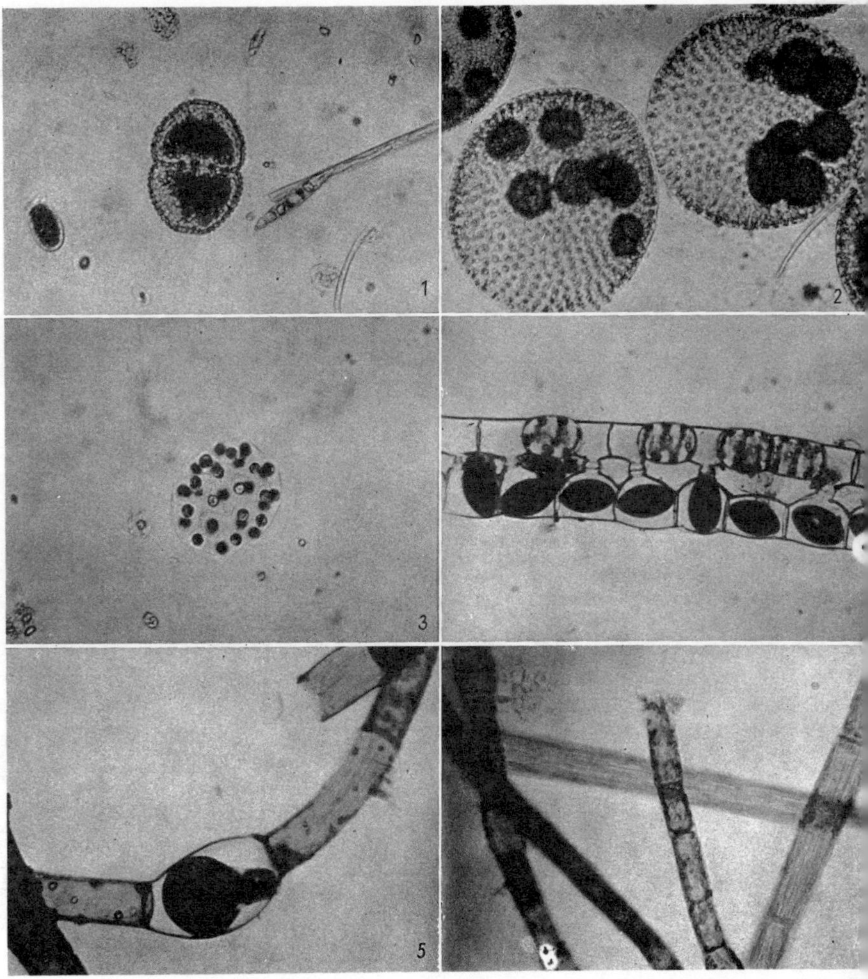

Yoke algae (Conjugatae), Whiplash algae or Flagellates **(Flagellata)** and Green algae **(Chlorophyaceae)**, all magnified - 1. Yoke algae, **Cosmarium** species, found in plankton - 2. Ball-shaped, colony-building Flagellates of the genus **Volvox**, found in plankton - 3. A more weakly magnified photograph showing a colony of **Eudorina** species - 4. Spiral ribbon yoke algae of the genus **Spirogyra**, in conjugation - 5. Thread algae **Oedogenium**, which grows on aquatic plants, rocks and glass, with **egg-cell** - 6. Other Thread algae. Microphotographs 1-3 by Knaack, 4-6 **by Helmert.**

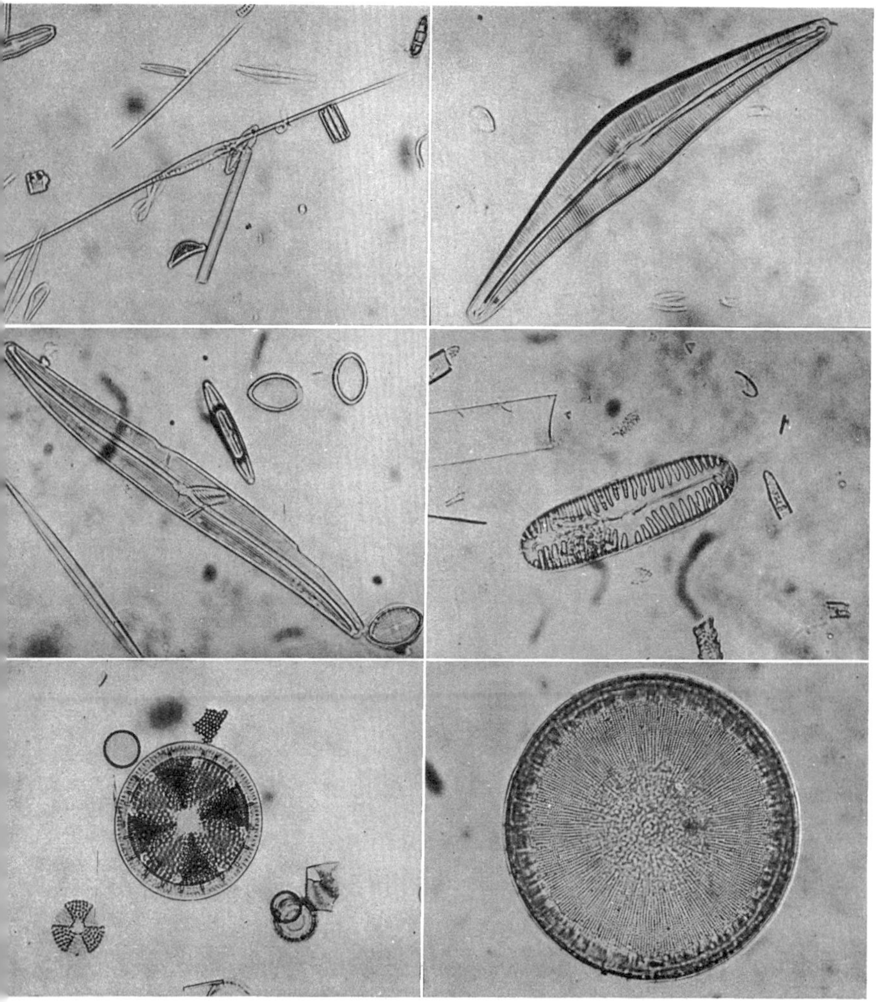

2

4

6

Diatoms are often called "brown algae" by aquarists because of their color. They frequently thrive in an aquarium which is too weakly lighted. All these microphotographs were taken under strong magnification - 1. **Nitschia acicularis,** the Needle diatom, with smaller diatoms - 2. **Cymbella** species - 3. **Gyrosigma acuminatum** - 4. **Pinnularia** species - 5. Diatoms from the ocean - 6. **Coscinodiscus** species. Remains from the shells of diatoms from prehistoric ages often form geological strata many feet thick. All microphotographs by Knaack.

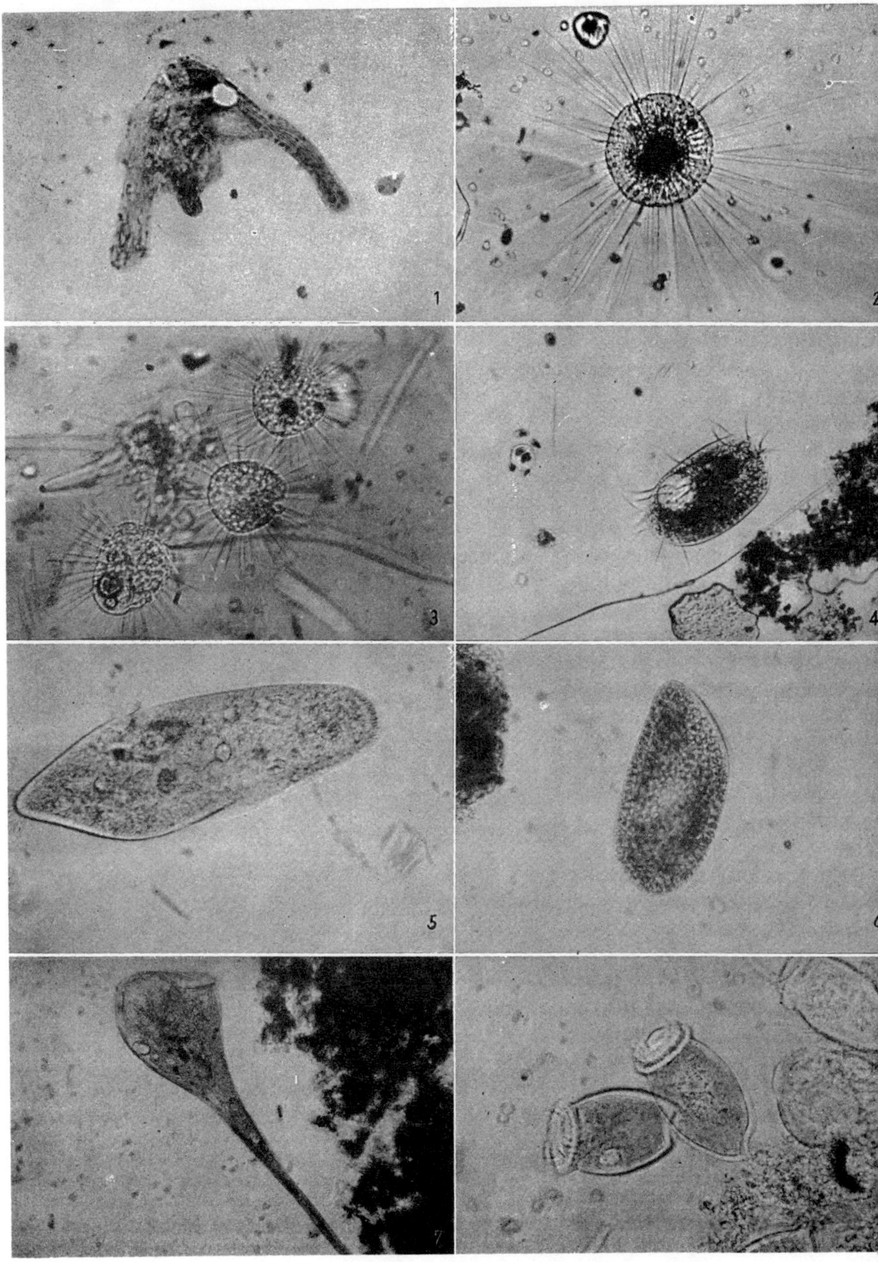

Protozoa, all greatly magnified. The Protozoans make fascinating subjects for microscopic study, besides being easily cultured as food for the smallest fry - 1. **Rhizopoda** in motion - 2. **Heliozoa** - 3. The Heliozoan **Actinosphaerium eichhorni** - 4. Ciliate of the genus **Euplotes** - 5. The Slipper Animalcule **Paramaecium caudatum**, one of the larger **Protozoa** often cultured for fry food - 6. **Paramaecium bursaria**, with stored eggs - Trumpet Animalcules, **Stentor** - 8. Bell Animalcules, **Vorticella**. Microphotographs 1-2 by Helmert, 3-8 by Knaack.

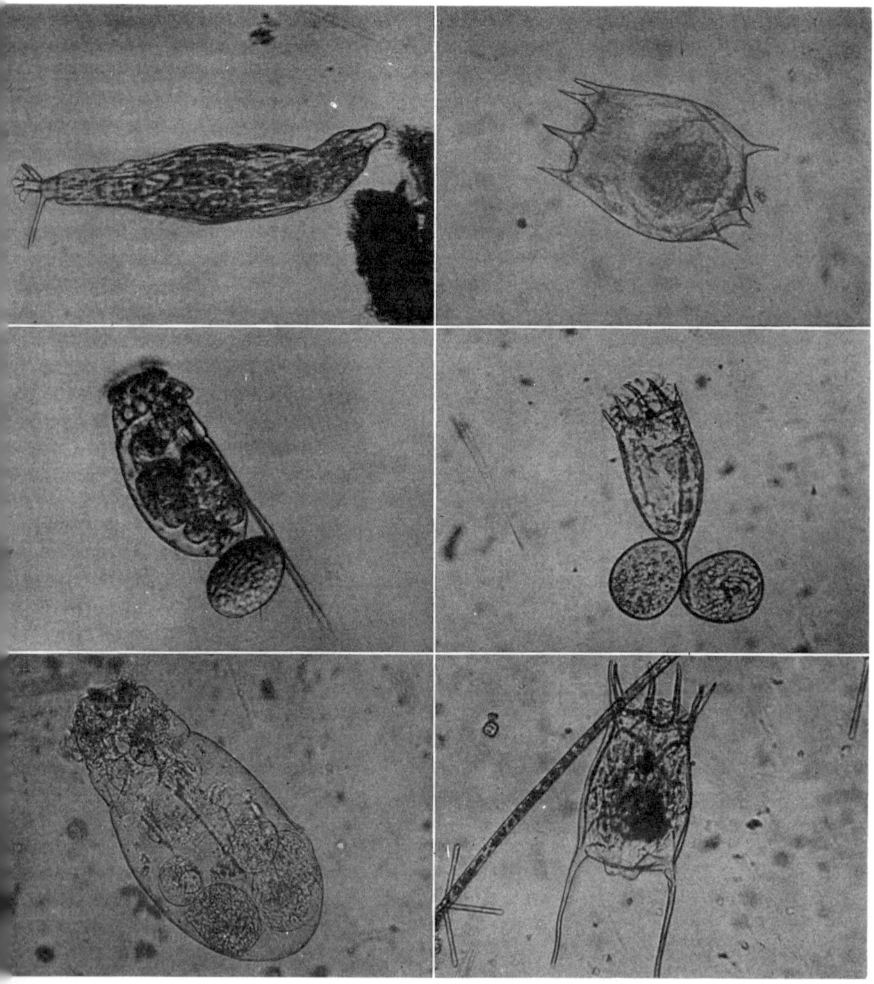

2

4

6

Wheel Animalcules (**Rotatoria**), all greatly magnified. The **Rotatoria** also make valuable microscopic food for tiny fish fry. These creatures are considerably higher in the scale of living things and have a much more complicated body structure than the **Protozoa**. - 1. **Phylodina,** which propels itself on a solid surface like an inchworm. 2. **Brachionus** species. - 3. **Filnia longiseta,** with egg. - 4. **Keratella cochlearis.** - 5. **Asplanchna priodonta.** - 6. **Keratella quadrata.** Microphotographs by Knaack.

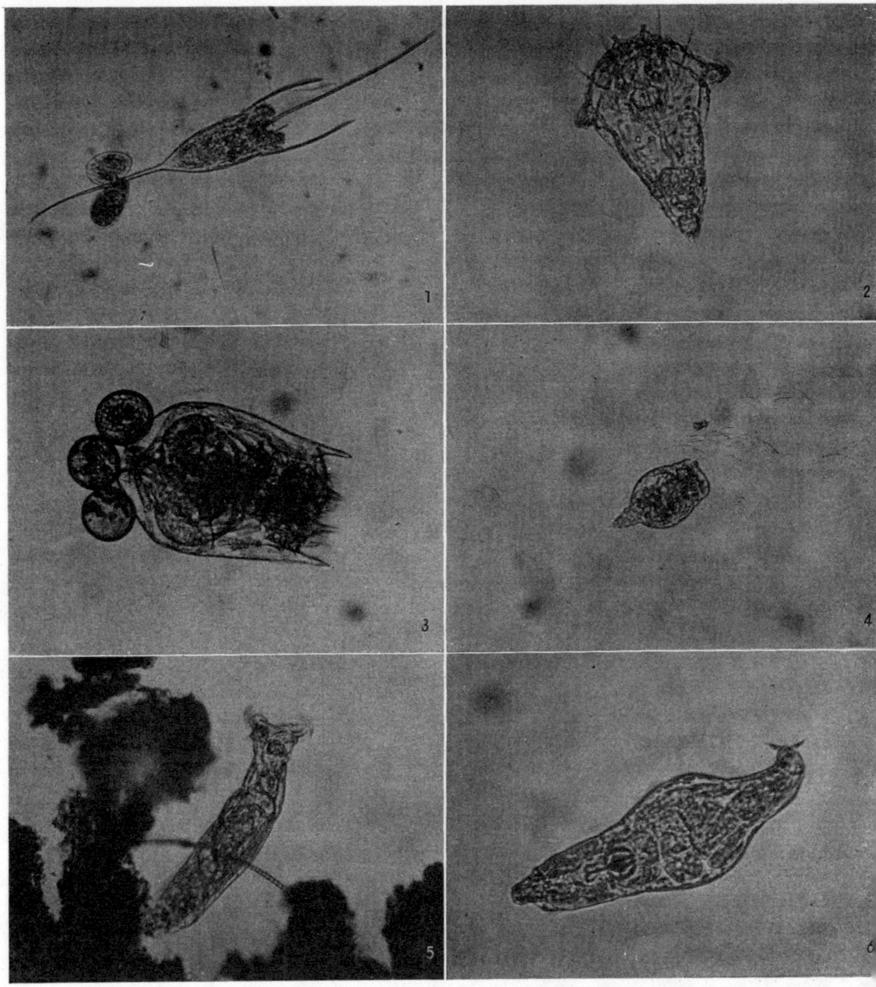

Wheel Animalcules, all greatly enlarged - 1. **Notholca longispina** - 2. **Synchaeta** species - 3. **Brachyonus**, with three thin-shelled male eggs - 4. A male which hatched from one of the eggs - 5. A species of **Rotatoria** which is very numerous in the aquarium, fastened to a mass of detritus and stirring in its food - 6. The same animal, contracted.

Fresh-water Polyps **(Hydroidea)**, Moss Animals **(Bryozoa) and** others, all enlarged 1. Fresh-water Polyp **(Hydra)**, fastened to a glass pane, showing a bud. **Hydra** are dangerous nuisances in the aquarium. They sting grown fishes, and swallow young fry - 2. Moss Animals, **Bryozoa**, form strings of colonies on glass sides and plant leaves. Aside from the fact that they are a bit unsightly, they need otherwise not be discouraged in the aquarium; they help keep the water clear **by** consuming quantities of infusoria, and their tentacles do not deliver a sting which is harmful to a fish - 3. Statoblast of a Moss Animal **Plumatella** - 4. Larva of a Bristle Worm **(Polychaeta)** - 5. A marine Tube **Worm Lonice conchilega** - 6. Another marine worm, **Tomapteris species. Photos** 1-3 by Helmert, 4-6 by Knaack.

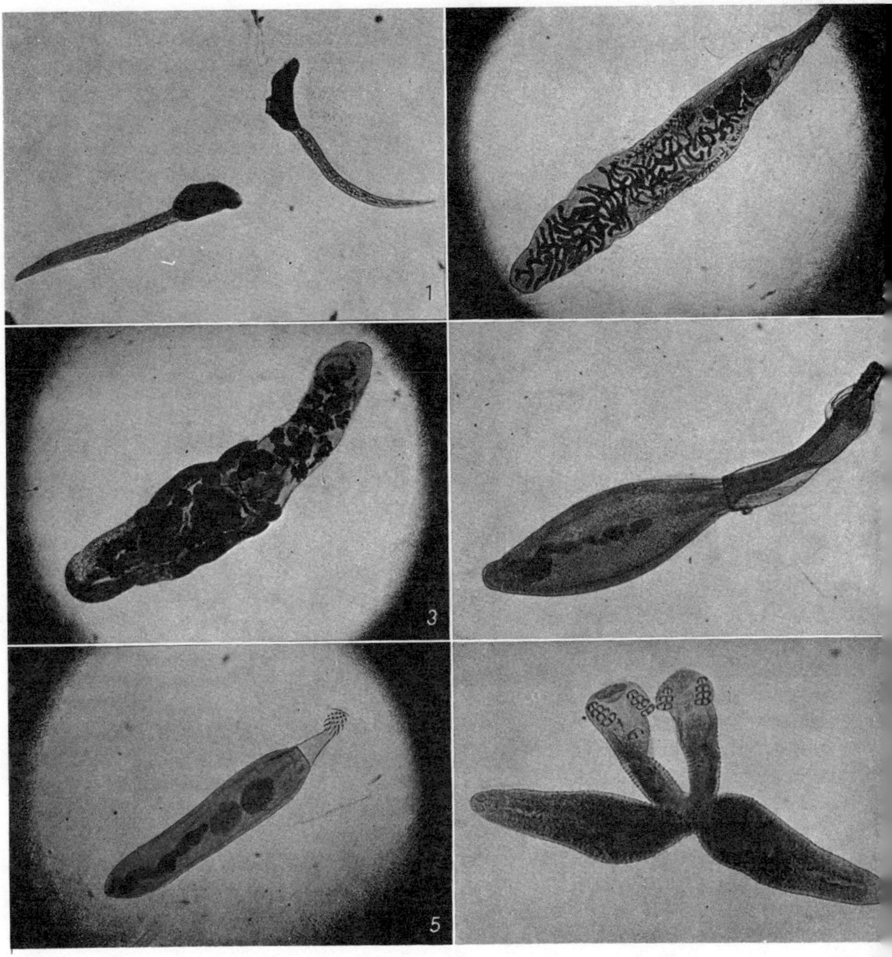

Worms, all enlarged - 1. Carcariae of Sucking-worms **(Trematodes)** of the genus **Dicrocoelium** - 2. Intestinal parasite **Dicrocoelium lanceolatum** - 3. Parasitic worm **Dicrocoelium cygnoides** - 4. Scratcher worm **Echinorhynchus proteus** - 5. Scratcher worm **Echinorhynchus nodulosus**, with extended crown of hooks - 6. **Diplozoon paradoxum**, a worm which leads a parasitic existence by attaching itself to the gills of a fish. These are all worms which are very harmful to fish life, and illustrate the usefulness of a microscope to the aquarist. Without this instrument, it would be impossible to identify such worms and know what is causing many fish ailments. Photos by Knaack.

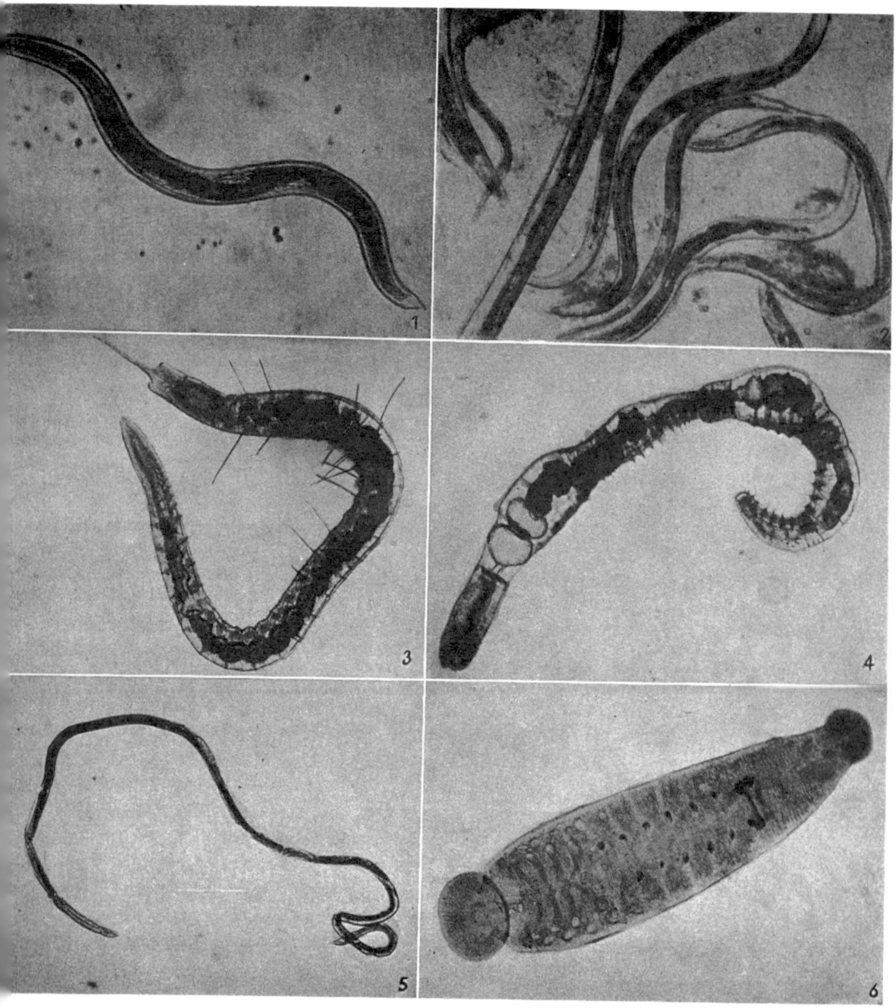

Worms, all enlarged - 1. Typical Threadworm (**Nematodes**) - 2. **Turbatrix** species, from a culture of microworms - 3. Bristle-worm **Stylaria lacustris** - 4. A "chain" of two **Oligochaetae**, one attached to the other - 5. **Gordius**, which lives within Blood Larvae, but is harmless to fish which eat it - 6. Leech **Hemiclepsis marginata**, which attaches itself to frogs and fishes. With the exception of the last, all these are harmless. Photos 1-3-6 by Knaack, 2 by Helmert.

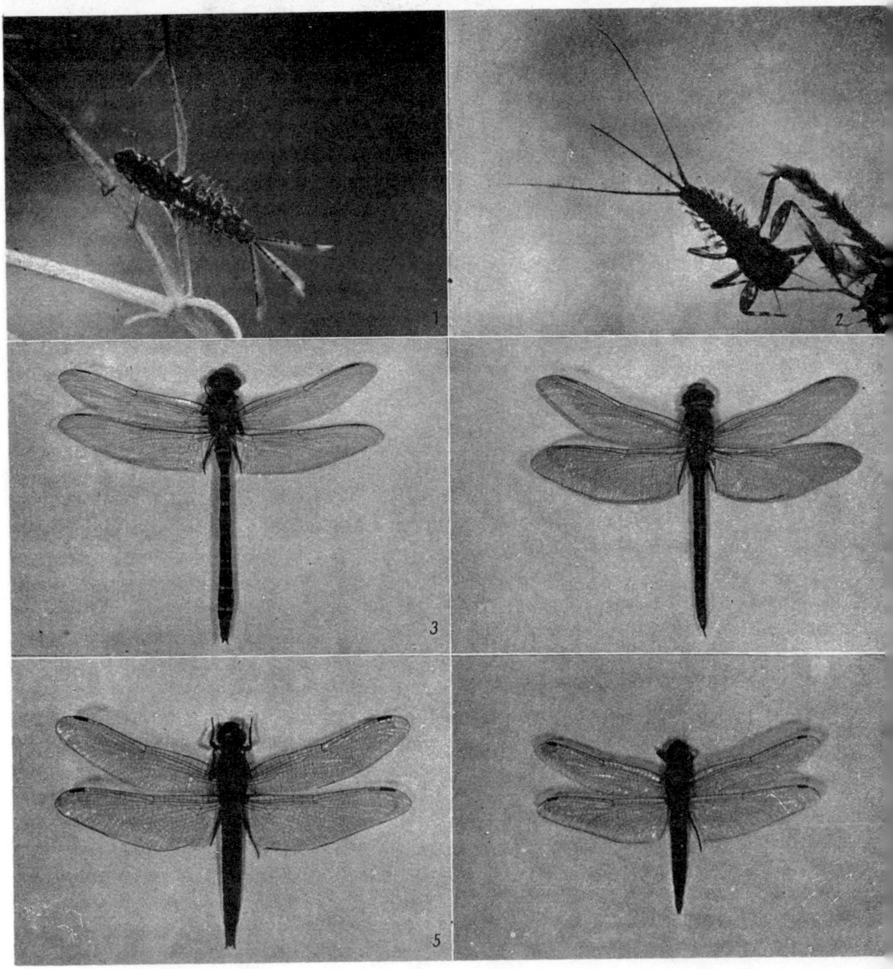

Hexapoda (Insects) - 1. Larva of a Mayfly, **Cloeon, magnified** - 2. Another Mayfly larva, **Heptagena** - 3. Dragonfly **Cordulegaster annulatis,** slightly reduced - 5. **Libellula** species - 6. **Sympetrum** species. Because of their smaller size, the Mayfly larvae do not constitute a great danger to fishes in the aquarium unless they are very young, but the larger Dragonfly larvae are real predators which grasp their prey with their hollow mandibles and suck out their blood. Photos by Knaack.

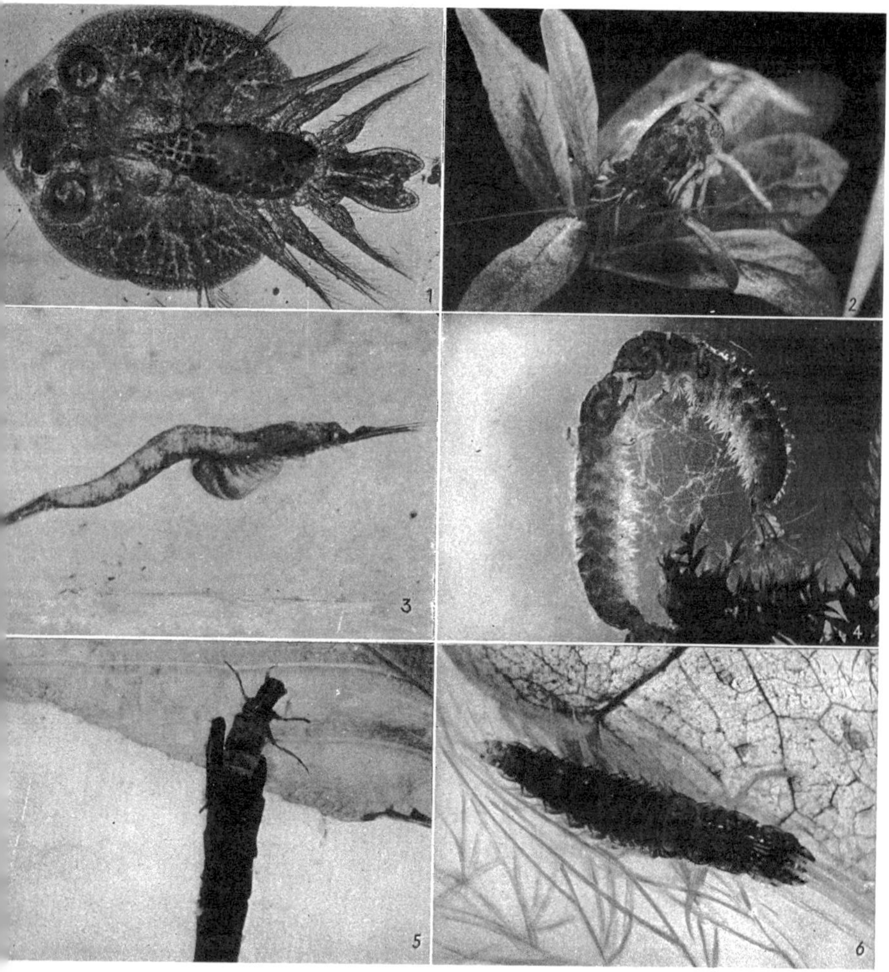

Crustacea and **Hexapoda** (Insects) - 1. Carp Louse **Argulus,** magnified - 2. American Crayfish **Cambarus affinis,** young specimen, slightly enlarged - 3. Fresh-water Shrimp **Mysis,** slightly enlarged. The transparent fins cannot be seen in the photograph - 4. Larvae of the caddis-fly **Hydropsyche** among their spinning threads, enlarged - 5. Caddis-fly larva **Anabolia,** with its case - 6. Larva of **Sialis** species, enlarged. Photos by Knaack.

Crustacea - 1. The common fresh-water shrimp **Gammarus pulex pulex,** slightly magnified - 2. Another fresh-water shrimp **Carniogammarus roesellii,** magnified, in the act of copulation - 3. **Lepidurus apus,** about natural size, top view - 4. Same, from below - 5. The Fairy Shrimp, **Chirocephalus grubei,** female, somewhat enlarged. This shrimp usually swims on its back - 6. Detail of the head of the Carp Louse **Argulus,** showing the eyes and sucking-discs; greatly enlarged. Photos **1-5 by** Knaack, 6 by Helmert.

Hexapoda (Insects) - 1. Dragonfly larva of the sub-order **Zygoptera** - 2. Larva of another sub-order, **Anisoptera**, natural size - 3. Larvae of the common Mosquito, **Culex**, with their breathing-tubes at the surface, enlarged - 4. Larva of **Chironomus**, the so-called "blood larvae", highly magnified - 5. Larva of a "glass larva" **Sayomya**, enlarged - 6. Pupa of the same, enlarged. Mosquito larvae are the most "natural" food for a great number of tropical fresh-water fishes, but have the disadvantage for the hobbyist that if they are not all consumed in the aquarium, they eventually hatch into insects which escape and torment him. Photo 4 by Helmert, others by Knaack.

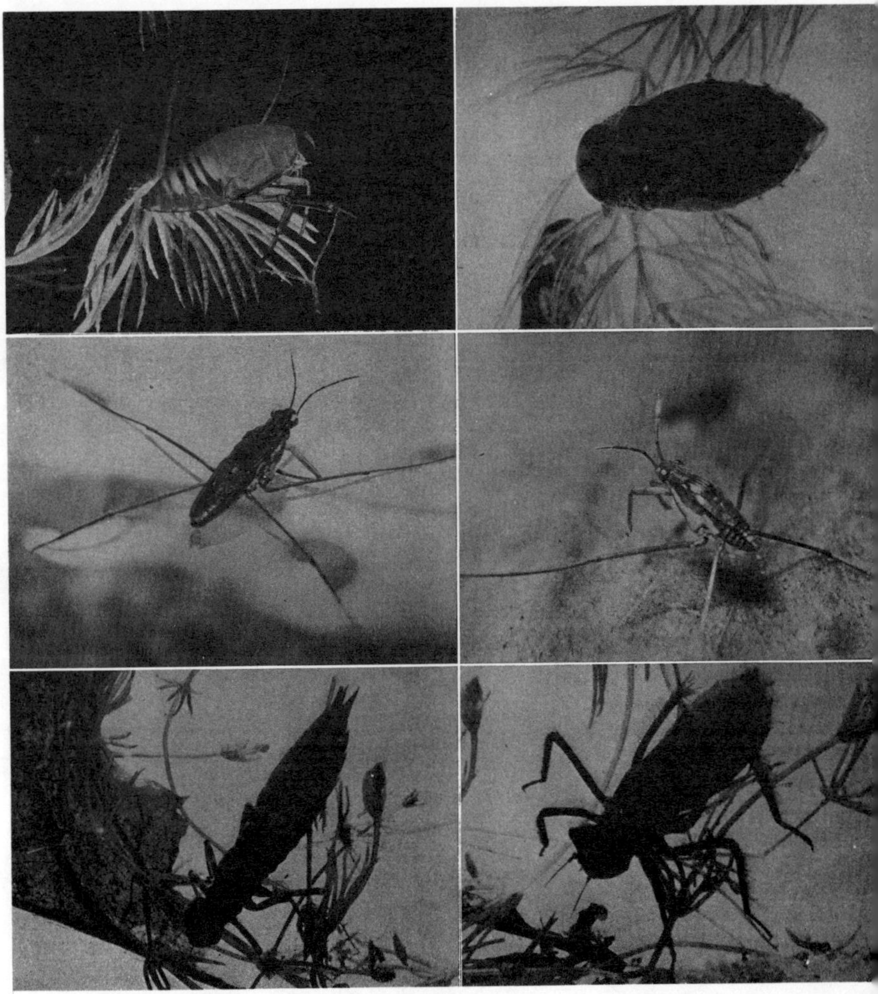

1

3

5

Hexapoda (Insects) - 1. Larva of the Backswimmer **Notonecta glauca**, slightly enlarged. These are usually seen on their backs - 2. Water-beetle **Naucoris cimicoides**, enlarged - 3. Water-strider **Gerris najas** - 4. Larva of the same, both almost natural size - 5. Larva of the Dragonfly **Cordulia** - 6. Larva of the Dragonfly **Brachytron**. These insects are of a predatory nature, and if they turn up in the aquarium, they should be eradicated. This is not always easy, especially with the Dragonfly larvae, who can match their background and are masters at hiding themselves.

2

4

6

Hexapoda (Insects) **1.** The Stick Insect, **Ranatra linearis,** in luring position. A Dragonfly larva approaches - 2. With surprising speed, the larva is captured and held by the forelegs of the Stick Insect - 3. The sting of the Stick Insect has a paralyzing action which takes about a minute to immobilize the prey. After that, the blood is sucked out in a leisurely manner. (Slightly magnified) - 4. The Backswimmer **Notonecta glauca,** slightly magnified - 5. Swimming beetle **Sigara fallenii** - 6. Larva of **Coryxinae,** somewhat enlarged.

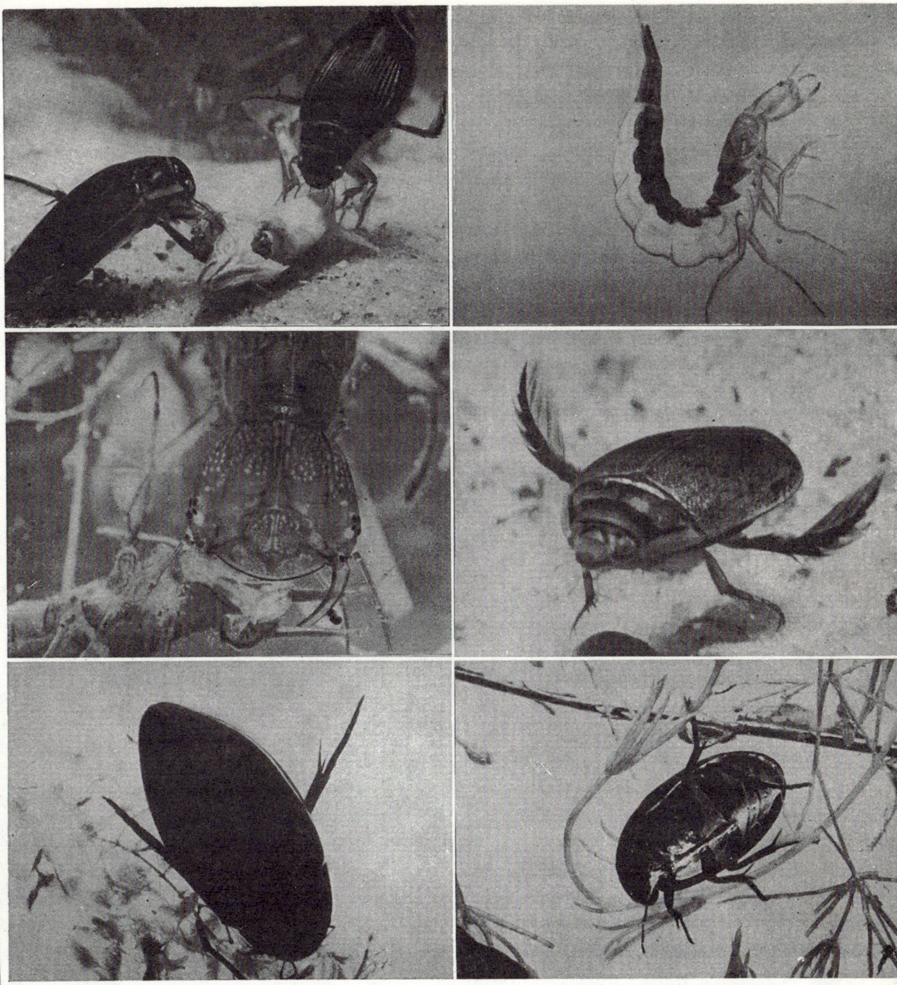

Hexapoda (Insects) - 1. **Dytiscus marginalis**, feeding on a Stickleback. Male is at the left, female is at the right - 2. Larva of **Dytiscus marginalis** - 3. Enlarged view of **Dytiscus marginalis** larva head in the act of sucking the blood of its victim - 4. Furrowed Swimming Beetle **Acilius sulcatus**, slightly enlarged - 5. Giant Water Beetle **Hydrous piceus**, reduced - 6. One of the smaller Water Beetles, **Hydrophilus caraboides**. This view of the underside shows the shining silvery surface. All water beetles can be considered to be predators, and may sometimes be introduced with live foods either in the adult or larval form. Although they may be interesting to observe, avoid putting them in an aquarium which contains fish. Photos by Knaack.

Hexapoda (Insects), all enlarged - 1. Larva of the Brown Swimming Beetle **Colymbetes fuscus** - 2. Larva of the Giant Water Beetle **Hydrous piceus** - 3. Larva of **Hyphydrus ovatus** - 4. Larva of the Furrowed Swimming Beetle **Acilius sulcatus.** **Photos by Knaack.**